NTC's Dictionary of PHRASAL VERBS and OTHER IDIOMATIC VERBAL PHRASES

NTC's Dictionary of PHRASAL VERBS and OTHER IDIOMATIC VERBAL PHRASES

Richard A. Spears

NATIONAL TEXTBOOK COMPANY
4255 West Touhy Avenue
Lincolnwood, Illinois 60646-1975 U.S.A.

Published by National Textbook Company, a division of NTC Publishing Group.

Manufactured in the United States of America.

2 3 4 5 6 7 8 9 AG 9 8 7 6 5 4 3 2 1

CONTENTS

PREFACE

NTC's Dictionary of Phrasal Verbs and Other Idiomatic Verbal Phrases is designed to be an easy-to-use tool for learners of English. The dictionary covers 2,796 verbs in combination with 71 particles—prepositions or adverbs—in 7,634 combinations. There are 13,870 definitions or paraphrases of 12,276 entry heads used in context in 29,967 examples.

This dictionary is concerned with combinations of a verb and one or more adverbs or prepositions that function together as a single unit of meaning. Some people use phrasal verb as a generic term for all such combination; however, verb + particle collocation is more accurate. Many of the phrases that contain these sequences are idiomatic. That is, even if one knows all the words in a phrase and understands all the grammar of the phrase, the meaning may still not be clear. Many sequences that are readily understandable are also included since this book is intended for the new-to-English user as well as for fluent speakers.

TO THE USER

The dictionary is organized in a way that allows the user with no knowledge of grammar to find an expression easily. The user needs to be able to identify (1) the verb in a sentence and (2) the FIRST instance of one of the prepositions or adverbs on the list that appears under **particle** on page xvi. Having identified the verb and the preposition or adverb, the user has only to look up the sequence of verb + particle in the dictionary and select the appropriate entry head.

These sequences, or collocations of verb + particle, fall into a number of grammatical categories including "true" phrasal verbs, prepositional verbs, phrasal-prepositional verbs, or sequences of verb and adverb. (See the section titled "Terms and Symbols," page xv, for definitions and explanations.) Since each of these sequences offers the learner the same types of problems, all of them are included in the same volume. This is, however, primarily a dictionary of form and meaning, and not a dictionary of grammar or categorization. It is intended to satisfy the user's need to know the meaning, usage, and appropriate contexts for each expression. The definitions and examples provide sufficient information to allow a person trained in English grammar to parse the expressions and assign a grammatical description. The dictionary relies on clarity, simplicity, and carefully written examples to lead the user to the meaning and appropriate usage of each expression.

Another important feature for the learner is the indication of human and nonhuman direct objects. Typical standard dictionary entries for phrasal verbs, prepositional verbs, and phrasal-prepositional verbs, as in **put on hold, bail out**, or **see through,** omit all references to direct objects. This dictionary uses the pronouns *someone* and *something* to indicate whether the verb in the phrase calls for an object, where the object should go in the sentence, whether the object can be human, nonhuman, or either one, and if there are different meanings depending on whether the object is human, nonhuman, or either one. All that information is vital to learners of English, although it seems to come perfectly naturally to lifelong English speakers. For example, there is a big difference between *put someone on hold* and *put something on hold*, and between *bail someone out* and *bail something out.* There is also an important difference between *see something through* and *see through something.* These differences would never be evident if the entry heads were listed as **put on hold, bail out,** and **see through**—with no object indicated.

Many phrases containing verb + particle collocations have optional parts. In fact, a phrase may seem hard to understand simply because it is really just a shortened form of an extended, less difficult phrase. This dictionary shows the extended forms of the verb phrases with the frequently omitted parts in parentheses. For example: **bark something (out) (at someone), battle (with someone) (over someone or something), bend over backwards (to do something) (for someone), bicker (with someone) (about someone or something), blow in(to some place) (from some place), brim (over) (with something), build (something) (out) over something, buy something (from someone) (for something).** Ample cross-referencing assures that the selection of the FIRST particle occurring after the verb will lead the user to the correct entry head.

The dictionary does not include most instances of verb + *to* where the *to* is the marker of the infinitive. Thus, *want to do something* would not be an entry under WANT ▸ TO. There are many entries where *be* is treated as the main verb even though it is a linking verb. There are also a number of constructions analogous to **phrasal verbs** (sense 2 in the section "Terms and Symbols," page xvi) where the verb governs adverbs or other function words such as *as* or *onward*.

HOW TO USE THIS DICTIONARY

1. The dictionary uses *index heads* and *entry heads.* An index head is capitalized and consists of a verb followed by a particle separated by an arrowhead (▸), e.g., LAY ▸ OUT, SUCCUMB ▸ TO, or FALL ▸ UNDER. Index heads exist only to help the user move around in the dictionary easily. They have no meaning or structure by themselves.

All the entry heads that contain the two words in the index head are listed in alphabetical order beneath the index head. Under BRING ▸ DOWN will be found **bring someone down, bring someone down to earth, bring something crashing down (around one), bring something down, bring something down on one('s head), bring something down to something, bring the house down.**

To find the entry head you want, you must isolate the verb and its particle from the rest of the sentence. For instance, in the sentence "I backed out of the garage," identify the verb and the first (or only) particle from the list on page xvi, i.e., *back* and *out*. Look under BACK ▸ OUT for the entry head that fits best, i.e., **back out (of something).** Similarly, for "I am afraid that I backed over your bicycle," find **back over someone or something** under BACK ▸ OVER. For "I wish you wouldn't try to badger me into leaving," find **badger someone into something** under BADGER ▸ INTO. For "The pilot had to bail out of the plane," find **bail out (of something)** under BAIL ▸ OUT.

2. An entry head may have one or more alternate forms. The entry head and its alternates are printed in **boldface type,** and the alternate forms are preceded by "AND." Two or more alternate forms are separated by a semicolon (;). For example:

> **bear a grudge against someone** AND **have a grudge against someone; hold a grudge against someone** to carry or sustain resentment or hatred toward someone. □ *I hope you don't bear a grudge against me.* □ *I have no grudge against you.* □ *I hope you hold no grudge against me.*

3. Many of the entry phrases have more than one major sense or meaning. These senses or meanings are numbered with boldface numerals. For example:

back away (from someone or something) AND **back off (from someone or something)** **1.** to move backwards from a person or thing; to withdraw physically from someone or something. □ *You should back away from the fire.* □ *Please back off from the man who is threatening you.* □ *You should back off.* □ *Jane backed away.* **2.** to begin to appear uninterested in someone or something; to withdraw one's interest from someone or something. (Figurative.) □ *The board of directors began to back away from the idea of taking over the other company.* □ *They backed off from the whole idea.*

4. Individual numbered senses may have additional forms that appear in boldface type, in which case the "AND" and the additional form(s) follow the numeral. For example:

break away (from something) AND **break free (from something); break loose (from something)** **1.** [for a piece of something] to come apart or break off from something. □ *A piece of rock broke free from the wall.* □ *A rock broke away from the cliff.* □ *The boards broke loose from the top of the pillar and fell on the porch.* **2.** AND **break oneself away (from something)** [for a person] to leave off doing something, perhaps reluctantly. □ *I broke away from my writing long enough to eat.* □ *I was able to break myself away from my work long enough to eat.* □ *Try to break yourself away from your work for a few minutes, so we can talk.*

5. The boldface entry head (together with any alternates) is usually followed by a definition. Alternate definitions are separated by a semicolon (;). These additional definitions are usually given to show slight differences in meaning or interpretation. Sometimes an alternate definition is given when the vocabulary of the first definition is difficult or idiomatic. For example:

brush over someone or something to deal lightly with an important person or matter; to just barely mention someone or something. □ *I want to hear more. You only brushed over the part I was interested in.* □ *You only brushed over your girlfriend. Tell us about her.*

6. Some entries are followed by instructions to look in a different location. For example:

brush past someone or something See under *BRUSH* ▸ *BY.*

7. A definition may be followed by comments in parentheses. These comments tell about some of the variations of a phrase, explain what it alludes to, give other useful information, or indicate cross-referencing. For example:

bang someone or something around to knock someone or something about; to beat or strike someone or something. (*Someone* includes *oneself.*) □ *Let's bang him around a little and see if that will change his mind.* [T] *Why are you banging around my friend?* □ *Don't bang those pans around.* □ *He banged himself around badly in the car wreck.*

8. When the comments apply to all the numbered senses of an entry, the comments are found before the first numbered sense. For example:

make something up (See also *make up something.*) **1.** to make a bed. □ *We have to make all the beds up and then vacuum all the rooms.* [T] *Did you make up the beds?* [A] *This is a nicely made-up bed. Well done.* **2.** to fabricate something, such as a story or a lie. □ *That's not true. You are just making that up!* [T] *You made up that story!* [A] *I don't want to hear any more made-up tales about ghosts and elves.* **3.** to redo something; to do something that one has failed to do in the past. □ *Can I make the lost time up?* [T] *Can I make up the test that I missed?* [A] *Can I turn in this made-up work for a grade?* [N] *I had to take a make up test.* **4.** to assemble something. □ *They will make up the train in Chicago, and it will leave on time.* [T] *Have they finished making up the pages for the next edition of the magazine?*

9. Some definitions are preceded by additional information in square brackets. This information makes the definition more clear by supplying information about the typical grammatical context in which the phrase is found. For example:

billow out 1. [for something, such as smoke] to burst and flow outward. □ *At the site of the fire, smoke billowed out.* □ *Clouds of ash billowed out of the volcano.* **2.** [for a sheet of cloth] to fill with the wind. (Especially a ship's sail.) □ *The sail billowed out, and we moved forward.* □ *Her skirt billowed out when the wind caught it.*

10. Some entries are cross-referenced to similar idiomatic phrases that are related in form or meaning. For example:

bang one's head against a brick wall to do something stupid and futile. (Idiomatic. See also *beat one's head against the wall* under *BEAT* ▸ *AGAINST.*) □ *You can't do anything about this. You are just banging your head against a brick wall.* □ *I've got to stop banging my head against a brick wall.*

11. Simple examples of the entry head are introduced by a □ and are in *italic type.*

parlay something into something to exploit an asset in such a way as to increase its value to some higher amount. □ *She is trying to parlay her temporary job into a full-time position.* □ *Alice parlayed her inheritance into a small fortune by investing in the stock market.*

12. Examples where the particle and a direct object are transposed are introduced by a [T].

pace something off to mark off a distance by counting the number of even strides taken while walking. □ *The farmer paced a few yards off and pounded a stake into the soil.* [T] *He paced off a few yards.* □ *Walter paced the distance off quickly.*

13. In some sequences of *off of* or *out of*, the *of* is replaced with *from* when the *off* or *out* is moved to precede the direct object. A comment alerts the user to this. Examples showing a *from*-phrase that replaces an *of*-phrase are introduced by [F].

pitch someone or something out ((of) something) to throw someone or something out of something or some place. (The *of*-phrase is paraphrased with a *from*-phrase when the particle is transposed. See the [F] example.) □ *The usher pitched the drunk out of the theater.* [T] *The usher pitched out the annoying person.* [F] *The bartender pitched out the annoying person from the tavern.* □ *The officer arrested the driver because he pitched a can out the car window.*

14. Examples showing the index head as an attributive adjective are introduced by [A].

PLAN ▸ FOR

plan for something **1.** to prepare for something. □ *I need to take some time and plan for my retirement.* □ *We carefully planned for almost every possibility.* [A] *The long-planned-for event was canceled at the last minute.* **2.** to prepare for a certain number [of people or things]. □ *I am planning for twelve. I hope everyone can come.* [A] *The planned-for number of guests was too low.*

15. Examples showing the index head as a noun are introduced by [A].

PLAY ▸ BACK

play something back (to someone) to play a recording to someone. □ *Can you play the speech back to me?* [T] *Please play back the speech to me, so I can hear how I sound.* □ *Let me play it back.* [N] *We listened to the playback for a while, then we left.*

16. Both index heads and an entry heads appear in *slanted type* whenever they are referred to in a definition or cross-reference.

pound something in(to someone) See *hammer something in(to someone)* under *HAMMER ▸ IN(TO).*

17. Some entry heads stand for two or more expressions. Parentheses are used to show which parts of the phrase may or may not be there. For example: **back**

out (of something) stands for **back out** and **back out of something.** Generally, where there are two or more optional prepositional phrases, they can be found in any order in the sentence. Some of these can be quite complicated: **agree (with someone) ((up)on someone or something)** stands for **agree with someone upon someone or something, agree with someone on someone or something, agree upon someone or something, agree on someone or something, agree with someone, agree upon someone or something with someone,** and **agree on someone or something with someone.**

Of course, there must be at least one particle from the list of particles for each entry, so **agree** by itself is not a possibility.

TERMS AND ABBREVIATIONS

□ (a box) marks the beginning of an example.

[A] (a box) containing an A marks the beginning of an example of the use of the *verb + particle collocation* as an attributive adjective.

[F] (a box) containing an F marks the beginning of an example of the use of the *verb + particle collocation* with a *from*-phrase as a replacement for an *of*-phrase.

[N] (a box) containing an N marks the beginning of an example of the use of the *verb + particle collocation* as a noun or nominal.

[T] (a box) containing a T marks the beginning of an example of the use of the *verb + particle collocation* where the particle and a direct object have been transposed.

AND indicates that an *entry head* has variant forms that are the same or similar in meaning as the *entry head.* One or more variant forms are preceded by **AND.**

collocation refers to two or more words that are used together regularly. This dictionary is concerned with *collocations* of verbs and *particles.*

colloquial refers to spoken or informal language style. Sometimes *colloquial* is used to describe an expression, pronunciation, or construction that violates any rule of grammar or style.

compare to means to consult the *entry head* indicated and examine its form or meaning in relation to the *entry head* containing the *compare to* instruction.

elaboration is an expression that is built on, or is an expansion of, another expression.

eligible as an entry refers to *verb + particle collocations* that belong in this dictionary. In some instances, the verb can be used without the *particle* with the same meaning, as with *settle down somewhere,* which means the same with or without the *down.* The dictionary indicates that *down* can be omitted, but the resulting expression is not *eligible as an entry* because there is no *particle.*

entry head is the first word or phrase, in boldface type, of an entry; the word or phrase that the definition explains. (See also *index head.*)

figurative refers to nonliteral expressions. *Stitch something up* is *literal* when it refers to sewing something. It is *figurative* when it refers to finishing something. Most *figurative* expressions are also *idiomatic* to some extent.

formal refers to an expression that is literary in origin or usually reserved for writing.

idiomatic refers to a phrase whose meaning cannot be figured out by studying the meanings of the individual words in the phrase.

index head the capitalized indication of a *verb + particle collocation,* e.g., *GO ▸ UNDER.* (See also *entry head.*)

informal refers to a very casual expression that is most likely to be spoken and not written.

jocular describes an expression that is intended to be humorous.

literal refers to the normal or expected semantic interpretation of a word or sequence of words.

particle can refer to a function word or a grammar word such as an article, conjunction, preposition, negator, determiner, and some directional adverbs. In this dictionary, prepositions and some directional adverbs that are governed by verbs are referred to as *particles.* There are 71 such *particles* used in this dictionary: *aback, aboard, about, above, abreast, abroad, across, after, against, aground, ahead, alike, aloft, along, alongside, among, apart, around, as, aside, askance, astray, at, away, back, before, behind, below, beneath, beside, between, beyond, by, down, for, forth, forward, from, in, inside, into, like, near, next, of, off, on, onto, onward, open, out, outside, over, overboard, past, still, though, through, throughout, to, together, toward, under, until, up, upon, upside-down, upward, with, within, without.*

phrasal-prepositional verb is a *verb + particle collocation* in which a verb governs a *particle* and a prepositional phrase; e.g., *send out for something, put something over on someone, cut down on something, chalk something up to something.*

phrasal verb **1.** is a *verb + particle collocation* in which a verb governs a *particle* that looks like a preposition but functions as an adverb; e.g., *put it down, roll along, stand up, call her up, call up your friend.* The *particle* can occur before or after a direct object. In this dictionary, *entry heads* that are *phrasal verbs* have at least one example with a transposed *particle* (marked Ⓣ). **2.** is a generic term covering *prepositional verb, phrasal-prepositional* verb, the construction described under sense 1, and other *verb + particle collocations* where the *particle* is an adverb or other function word.

prepositional verb is a *verb + particle collocation* in which a verb governs a prepositional phrase; e.g., *blossom into something, apply for something, run over something.*

see means to turn to the *entry head* indicated.

see also means to consult the *entry head* indicated for additional information or to find expressions similar in form or meaning to the *entry head* containing the *see also* instruction.

see under 1. means to go to the *index head* indicated and look for the *entry head* you are seeking *under* the *index head.* **2.** means to go to the *entry head* indicated and look for the phrase you are seeking *within* the entry indicated, usually after AND.

slang refers to highly playful spoken language involving an element of wordplay.

verb + particle collocation a verb and a preposition or adverb that are used together regularly in the same sentence. This is a generic term covering *phrasal verbs, prepositional verbs, phrasal-prepositional verbs,* and other verb + adverb phrases.

NTC's Dictionary of PHRASAL VERBS and OTHER IDIOMATIC VERBAL PHRASES

ABANDON ▸ TO

abandon oneself to something to yield to the comforts or delights of something. ☐ *He abandoned himself to the pleasures of the sauna.* ☐ *The children abandoned themselves to the delights of the warm summer day.*

abandon someone or something to someone or something to leave a person or thing to the care of someone or something; to give up someone or something to someone or something. (Usually with the thought that the abandoned person or thing will not receive the best of care. *Someone* includes *oneself*.) ☐ *They had to abandon the dogs to the storm.* ☐ *We did not want to abandon our buddies to the enemy soldiers.* ☐ *We abandoned the sinking boat to the waters of the lake and tried to swim for shore.* ☐ *He gradually abandoned himself to his attackers.*

ABBREVIATE ▸ TO

abbreviate something to something **1.** to make a set of initials or an acronym out of a word or phrase. ☐ *We will abbreviate this word to something shorter.* ☐ *The phrase was abbreviated to a few letters.* **2.** to make something into a shorter version of itself. ☐ *They abbreviated the second act to just a few songs.* ☐ *The act has been abbreviated to just a few minutes.*

ABDUCT ▸ FROM

abduct someone from someone or something to take away or kidnap a person from someone, or from a particular place, usually in secret. ☐ *The thugs abducted the child from her mother.* ☐ *They abducted the agent from a street corner.*

ABET ▸ IN

abet someone in something to help someone in some deed; to help someone do something illegal. ☐ *Surely you do not expect me to abet you in this crime!* ☐ *Ann was abetted in her crime.*

ABIDE ▸ BY

abide by something to follow a set of rules or instructions; to obey orders or instructions that someone has given. ☐ *Will you please abide by the rules?* ☐ *I promise I will abide by the rules.*

ABIDE ▸ WITH

abide with someone to remain with someone; to stay with someone. (Old and stilted. Primarily heard in the church hymn *Eventide*.) ☐ *You are welcome to abide with me for a while, young man.* ☐ *"Abide with me: fast falls the eventide."*

ABOUND ▸ IN

abound in something to be rich and abundant in something; to have plenty of something. ☐ *The entire area abounds in game and fish.* ☐ *Our garden abounds in carrots, of all things!*

ABOUND ▸ WITH

abound with someone or something to be plentiful with particular objects, persons, or other living beings. ☐ *The forest abounded with bright singing birds.* ☐ *The world abounds in talented people who are too shy to develop their talents.*

ABSCOND ▸ WITH

abscond with someone or something to steal or run away with someone or something; to *make off with someone or something* in secret. □ *The boys absconded with all the dessert.* □ *They absconded with Chuck, whom they held for ransom.*

ABSENT ▸ FROM

absent oneself from someone or something to remain away from or avoid someone or some place. □ *Please don't absent yourself from us for so long!* □ *She absented herself from class too many times.* □ *Fred absented himself from the boring meeting.*

ABSOLVE ▸ FROM

absolve someone from something to prove that an accused person is innocent of something; to demonstrate that someone is innocent of something. (*Someone* includes *oneself*.) □ *The judge absolved Fred from further responsibility.* □ *Bob attempted to absolve himself from the whole business.*

ABSORB ▸ IN

absorb oneself in someone or something [for someone] to become very interested or preoccupied with someone or something. (See also the following entry.) □ *Tom would often absorb himself in his children on weekends.* □ *She will absorb herself in a book this evening.* □ *Sally absorbed herself in her work and got through the week.*

ABSORB ▸ IN(TO)

absorb someone in(to) something [for a group of people or an organization] to include someone in all the activities of the group; to integrate someone into something. (*Absorb in* is colloquial and redundant.) □ *The club absorbed the new members into the organization.* [T] *It's time we absorbed in some new people.* □ *Ann was absorbed into the group quickly.*

absorb something in(to) something [for matter or substance] to draw something into itself. □ *The sponge absorbed all the moisture into its fibers.* □ *The moisture was absorbed into the sponge.*

ABSORB ▸ WITH

absorb something with something to soak up a fluid with something. □ *Henry absorbed the water with a sponge.* □ *The water was absorbed with the sponge.*

ABSTAIN ▸ FROM

abstain from something to avoid an association with or the use of some activity or substance, such as alcohol, drugs, sex, or food. □ *They abstained from alcohol and any other kind of drugs.* □ *I must abstain from too many sweets.*

ABSTRACT ▸ FROM

abstract something from someone or something to steal something from someone or something. □ *The officer was found guilty of abstracting a rather large amount of money from the company.* □ *Karen abstracted some money from her employer.*

abstract something from something to take the important information from a longer document; to extract the essentials or the gist from a piece of complicated writing. □ *Can you abstract a shorter article from all this material?* □ *This short piece was abstracted from a much larger work.*

ABUT ▸ AGAINST

abut (up) against something [for the end or terminus of something] to rest against something firmly. □ *The end of the board abutted against the foundation.* □ *It abuts up against the wall.*

ABUT ▸ ON

abut on something [for something, particularly the edge of a parcel of land] to meet or touch something at its boundary. □ *Our land abuts on the shopping center's parking lot.* □ *The lawn abuts on the wall of the property next door.*

ABUT ▸ UP

abut (up) against something See under *ABUT ▸ AGAINST.*

ACCEDE ▸ TO

accede to someone to agree to someone's wishes or desires. □ *I refuse to accede to you.* □ *You must accede to us.*

accede to something **1.** to agree to the terms or demands that someone has stated. □ *We cannot accede to your demands.* □ *You will accede to them eventually.* **2.** to assume a ruling position; to begin serving one's official duties. □ *She acceded to the office of mayor in January.* □ *Charles will accede to the throne next year.*

ACCEPT ▸ AS

accept someone as something to accept someone as a particular type of person or a person who can serve a particular role. (*Someone* includes *oneself.*) □ *I am pleased to accept you as my friend.* □ *Sally accepted herself as the naughty girl that she is.*

accept something as something **1.** to agree that something will serve in payment of a debt or in return for something. □ *This receipt shows that we have accepted your money as payment on your debt.* □ *This money has been accepted as full payment.* **2.** to resign [oneself] to something that cannot be changed. □ *I must accept what you say as the final decision.* □ *The events of the day have been accepted as a normal turn of events.*

ACCLIMATE ▸ TO

acclimate someone or something to something AND **acclimatize someone or something to something** to cause a person or other living thing to become used to a different climate or environment. (Includes plants and animals. *Someone* includes *oneself.*) □ *We will help acclimate Henry to the new building.* □ *This will help acclimatize Fred to the new situation.* □ *We need to acclimatize the fish to the new water slowly.* □ *It took a while for me to acclimate myself to the new neighborhood.*

ACCLIMATIZE ▸ TO

See the previous entry.

ACCOMMODATE ▸ TO

accommodate oneself to something to adapt oneself to something, such as someone else's needs or a new environment. □ *Please try to accommodate yourself to our routine.* □ *He was unable to accommodate himself to the rules set down by the management team.*

ACCOMMODATE ▸ WITH

accommodate someone with something to provide something special for someone; to manage to do something that provides for someone's needs or desires. (*Someone* includes *oneself.*) □ *We will try to accommodate you with an earlier flight.* □ *I had to accommodate myself with rubber boots borrowed from a neighbor.*

ACCOMPANY ▸ BY

accompanied by something to be provided something extra to go along with something else; to be provided with something to complement something else. □ *Is the dinner accompanied by any wine?* □ *Dinner was accompanied by a fine white wine.*

ACCOMPANY ▸ ON

accompany someone on something **1.** [for someone] to go with someone on a trip, journey, adventure, etc. □ *Would you please accompany me on my journey?* □ *She was not accompanied on her trip.* **2.** [for something] to be brought with someone on a trip, journey, etc. □ *My cameras always accompany me on my travels.* □ *I was not accompanied by my cameras on this trip.* **3.** to complement someone's musical performance by playing on a musical instrument; to provide complementary instrumental music for someone's musical performance. □ *Sally accompanied the singer on the piano.* □ *The singer was not accompanied on the piano.*

ACCOMPANY ▸ WITH

accompany someone with something to use a particular musical instrument to play music that goes along with someone else's musical performance. □ *She accompanied Mary with the piano.* □ *She was accompanied with the piano.*

ACCORD ▸ WITH

accord with something to agree with something; to match up with something; to *jibe with something.* ☐ *Does this accord with what you heard?* ☐ *It accords with my recollection nicely.*

ACCOUNT ▸ FOR

account for someone or something **1.** [for someone] to explain or justify something or someone('s behavior). ☐ *Can you account for your angry response?* ☐ *I simply cannot account for Fred and what he said.* **2.** to know the state of or whereabouts of someone or something. (Usually in reference to some person or thing placed in one's charge.) ☐ *They cannot account for three of the passengers.* ☐ *He cannot account for the money.* [A] *We searched everywhere for the unaccounted-for checks.*

account for something to result in something or cause something; [for something] to serve to explain something. ☐ *Does this account for what has happened?* ☐ *It accounts for everything.*

ACCREDIT ▸ TO

accredit something to someone to assign or attribute a deed to someone; to assign or attribute praise to someone. ☐ *We can accredit this success to Fred and his committee.* ☐ *The arrest was accredited to the rookie cop.*

ACCRUE ▸ TO

accrue to someone or something [for something, usually money, such as interest] to be credited to an account or to a person's account. ☐ *Interest will accrue to your account as long as the account is active.* ☐ *It looks as if no interest accrued to me during the last year.*

ACCUSE ▸ OF

accuse someone of something to charge someone with a crime or a violation of rules or instructions. ☐ *Please don't accuse me of the crime.* ☐ *Mary is accused of the crime.*

ACCUSTOM ▸ TO

accustom someone to someone or something to get someone used to someone or something. (*Someone* includes *oneself.*) ☐ *I think we can accustom Fred to the new rules without difficulty.* ☐ *We will accustom Jimmy to the new babysitter little by little.* ☐ *She was forced to accustom herself to eating at almost midnight.*

ACE ▸ IN(TO)

ace in(to something) to be lucky in getting admitted to something. (Slang.) ☐ *I aced into the history class without trouble.* ☐ *Was it hard to ace in?*

ACE ▸ OUT

ace out (of something) to get out of something through luck; to accomplish something, such as pass a test, through luck; to be very lucky. (Slang.) ☐ *I just aced out of the math test.* ☐ *I hope I ace out too.*

ace someone out to beat someone easily in a contest. ☐ *Our team aced the other team out.* [T] *We aced out the other team.* ☐ *I was aced out again.*

ACHE ▸ FOR

ache for someone AND **hurt for someone** to hurt in sympathy with someone or something. ☐ *Oh, I'm sorry it happened. I just ache for you.* ☐ *Your poor toe! My toe aches for it!*

ache for someone or something AND **hurt for someone or something** to desire someone or something very much. (So much that it "hurts.") ☐ *Jim ached for the sight of Mary, whom he loved deeply.* ☐ *I just ache for her.*

ACKNOWLEDGE ▸ AS

acknowledge someone as something to agree or announce publicly that a person holds a particular office or station, or that a person has particular qualities. (*Someone* includes *oneself.*) ☐ *The crowd acknowledged the mayor as their leader.* ☐ *She found it difficult to acknowledge herself as a failure.*

acknowledge something as something to agree or announce publicly that something is as was said. ☐ *The president acknowledged the statement as the truth.* ☐ *The statement is acknowledged as the truth.*

ACKNOWLEDGE ▸ OF

acknowledge receipt of something to report receiving something, such as a package, letter, or notice. (Idiomatic.) □ *The company acknowledged receipt of the merchandise I returned.* □ *They acknowledged receipt of it yesterday.*

ACQUAINT ▸ WITH

acquaint someone with someone or something to introduce someone to an unfamiliar person or thing; to become familiar with someone or something; to get to know someone or something; to tell someone the facts [about someone or something]. (*Someone* includes *oneself.*) □ *Please acquaint Tom with the way we do things.* □ *Did I ever acquaint you with Karen?* □ *It took a month for Sally to acquaint herself with the facts in the case.*

ACQUIESCE ▸ TO

acquiesce to someone or something to give in to someone or someone's wishes; to agree, perhaps reluctantly, to someone or someone's ideas. □ *We are willing to acquiesce to your demands.* □ *I will never acquiesce to Paul!*

ACQUIT ▸ OF

acquit someone of something to prove and announce someone's innocence of a criminal charge or the blame for some wrongdoing. □ *The investigator acquitted Wally of the charges.* □ *He was acquitted of the crime in a quick trial.*

ACT ▸ AS

act as something to serve in some special capacity, possibly temporarily. □ *Would you mind acting as bartender?* □ *Ann will act as executor if you wish.*

ACT ▸ FOR

act for someone **1.** to represent someone in an official capacity; to represent the interests of someone. □ *I am only acting for the mayor. You should consult the mayor for further information.* □ *Don't worry. I am acting for the owner.* **2.** to take action when the proper person fails to take action. □ *We were forced to act for the board of directors, who refused to do their duty.* □ *I had to act for her since she was out of town.*

ACT ▸ OUT

act something out **1.** to perform in real life a role that one has imagined in a fantasy. □ *When I was onstage, I was really acting an old fantasy out.* [T] *I acted out an old fantasy.* [T] *Todd acted out his dreams, which included all of us.* [A] *Acted-out fantasies or dreams are probably useful, if no one gets hurt.* **2.** to convert one's bad feelings into action rather than words. □ *Don't act your aggressions out on me!* [T] *Don't act out your aggressions on me!* [T] *She acted out her aggression.* [A] *These acted-out feelings tell us what Roger is thinking.* **3.** to demonstrate or communicate something through action rather than words. □ *Act your request out, if you can't say it.* [T] *Act out your request, if you can't say it.* □ *Fred, who had lost his voice, had to act his requests out.*

ACT ▸ UP

act up [for a thing or a person] to behave badly. □ *This car is acting up again.* □ *Andy, stop acting up!*

ACT ▸ (UP)ON

act (up)on something **1.** to take action on a particular problem. (*Upon* is formal and less commonly used than *on.*) □ *You should act upon this problem at once.* □ *I will act on this immediately.* **2.** to take action because of some special information. □ *The police refused to act upon the information they were given.* □ *They will act on your suggestion today.* **3.** to perform on something, usually the stage (in a theater). □ *I acted on the stage at Carnegie Hall once.* □ *Ken has never acted on the stage.*

ADAPT ▸ FOR

adapt something for something to change or alter something for use with something else. □ *Andy adapted the drums for concert use.* □ *Has this radio been adapted for stereo?*

ADAPT ▸ FROM

adapt something from something to derive something from something else; to create by modifying something else. □ *I adapted this musical from a novel.* □ *This planter was adapted from an old cookstove.*

ADAPT ▶ TO

adapt someone or something to someone or something to cause someone or something to fit, adjust to, or get used to someone or something else. (*Someone* includes *oneself.*) □ *Can't you adapt yourself to me?* □ *We adapted our oil furnace to gas.* □ *See if you can adapt your secretary to the firm's hours better.* □ *Is your furnace adapted to gas yet?* □ *Mary was forced to adapt herself to a totally new work schedule.*

adapt to someone or something to adapt or get used to someone or something. □ *Please try to adapt to our routine.* □ *You will have to adapt to me better.*

ADD ▶ IN(TO)

add something in(to something) to introduce something into something. □ *Now, add the eggs into the mixture.* 🅃 *Add in some more eggs.* □ *Are the eggs added in yet?*

ADD ▶ ON(TO)

add (something) on(to something) to extend something by providing more (of something). □ *You added nearly one thousand dollars onto the total.* 🅃 *You added on a thousand dollars to the total!* □ *You added too much on.* 🄽 *I simply refuse to pay for all these add-ons. All I want is a basic car!*

ADD ▶ TO

add fuel to the flames AND **add fuel to the fire** to make things worse. □ *This is bad. You are adding fuel to the flames.* □ *That just adds fuel to the fire!*

add (something) to something to increase the intensity or amount of something by giving more (of something) to it. □ *There is no point in adding to his misery.* □ *You added too much sugar to it.*

ADD ▶ TOGETHER

add something together to sum or total two or more things together. □ *Add these two together and tell me what you get.* □ *He can't add two and two together.* □ *Why haven't these been added together?*

ADD ▶ UP

add something up to sum or total a set of figures. (See also *add up (to something).*) □ *Please add these figures up again.* 🅃 *I didn't add up these figures.*

add up (to something) **1.** [for a set of figures] to equal a total. □ *These figures don't add up to the right total!* □ *The figures just don't add up.* **2.** [for facts or explanations] to make sense. □ *The facts just don't add up to the truth.* □ *This doesn't add up!*

ADDICT ▶ TO

addict someone to something to cause someone to become habituated to something, usually alcohol or another drug. (Also in metaphorical uses. *Someone* includes *oneself.*) □ *The hospital personnel were thought to have addicted John to morphine.* □ *She ended up addicting herself to the substance.*

ADDRESS ▶ AS

address someone as something to speak to one as if one were a specific type of person. □ *Please address the king as Your Majesty.* □ *She is addressed as Madam.*

ADDRESS ▶ TO

address oneself to someone to speak directly to a particular person, rather than someone else. □ *I did not address myself to you!* □ *Sue addressed herself to the clerk, asking for some help with a purchase.*

address oneself to something to turn one's complete attention to something, such as a problem or an issue. (See also *address something to someone.*) □ *Please address yourself to these current, pressing problems.* □ *Let us address ourselves to the pressing problem of the western drought.*

address something to someone **1.** to say something directly to a specific person or group of persons, rather than someone else. (See also *address oneself to someone* and *address oneself to something.*) □ *George addressed his remarks to everyone.* □ *Are you addressing your criticism to me?* **2.** to write someone's name and address on an envelope, package, etc. □ *Gilbert addressed the envelope to Walter.* □ *Is this addressed to me?*

ADHERE ▸ TO

adhere to something 1. to stick to something. □ *The stamp won't adhere to the envelope.* □ *The bandage adhered to her wound.* **2.** to follow or stick to a particular course of action, plan, or set of beliefs. □ *Please try to adhere to the agreed-upon plan.* Ⓐ *These long-adhered-to traditions are an important part of this culture.*

ADJOURN ▸ FOR

adjourn for something to bring a meeting to a temporary close so the participants can participate in some other activity. □ *We must adjourn for the day.* □ *They have adjourned for lunch.*

ADJOURN ▸ TO

adjourn to some place to bring a meeting to a temporary close so the participants can move to another place (where the meeting will be started again). □ *The meeting adjourned to a meeting room on the floor below.* □ *We adjourned to the sitting room.*

ADJUST ▸ TO

adjust (oneself) to someone or something to make changes in one's opinion or attitude toward someone or something, such as a change in one's life or environment. □ *Can't you adjust yourself to all this?* □ *No one can adjust to Sally and her temper.* □ *She couldn't adjust herself to the new attitudes she encountered in college.* □ *These plants will adjust to the low humidity.*

adjust something to something to make something fit something else; to alter something to make it suitable for something else. □ *You need to adjust the temperature to the needs of the plants.* □ *I adjusted the length of the shirt to the school's requirements.*

ADMINISTER ▸ TO

administer something to someone or something to present or apply something to a person or some creature. □ *The vet administered the drug to the cow.* □ *She administered medicine to the suffering patient.* □ *The medicine will be administered to the patient as you directed.*

ADMIRE ▸ FOR

admire someone for something to have a positive feeling toward someone because of something. □ *I really admire you for your courage.* □ *She is admired for her patience.*

ADMIT ▸ INTO

admit someone into some place to allow someone to enter (some place). (*Someone* includes *oneself.*) □ *They refused to admit us into the theater.* □ *She admitted herself into the room, using the key Henry had given her.*

ADMIT ▸ IN(TO)

admit something in(to) something to allow something to be introduced into something else. □ *You cannot admit this document into the body of evidence.* Ⓣ *I will admit in whatever I feel will help my client.* □ *The judge admitted the evidence into the trial.*

ADMIT ▸ TO

See also the previous entry.

admit something to someone to confess something to someone. □ *I found it hard to admit the wrongdoing to my uncle.* □ *Has this been admitted to the proper person?*

admit to something to acknowledge or confess something; to acknowledge or confess to having done something. □ *She did not admit to knowing the man.* □ *Max would not admit to anything.*

ADMONISH ▸ FOR

admonish someone for something to warn or scold someone mildly for doing something. (*Someone* includes *oneself.*) □ *The nurse admonished the patient for not eating her dinner.* □ *Jane admonished herself in a whisper for being late.*

ADOPT ▸ AS

adopt someone as something to choose someone as something. □ *The committee will adopt Jane as its candidate.* □ *Jane was adopted as our candidate.*

adopt something as something to take on something, such as a policy or principle, as one's own. ☐ *I will adopt this policy as my own.* ☐ *The policy was adopted as law.*

ADORE ► FOR

adore someone for something **1.** to be in awe of someone for doing something well. (*Someone* includes *oneself.*) ☐ *Everyone adores Sally for throwing clever parties.* ☐ *He seemed to adore himself for just opening the door for me.* **2.** to be in awe of someone because of a particular trait or feature. (*Someone* includes *oneself.*) ☐ *Robert adores Mary for her smiling eyes.* ☐ *She adored herself for her good figure and pretty face.*

ADORN ► WITH

adorn someone or something with something to decorate or ornament someone or something with something. (*Someone* includes *oneself.*) ☐ *The priestess adorned herself with jewels and a crown.* ☐ *They adorned the room with garlands of flowers.* ☐ *Most of the people I know are reluctant to adorn themselves with furs and jewels.*

ADULTERATE ► WITH

adulterate something with something to dilute or taint something with some other substance. ☐ *They adulterated the wine with some sort of drug.* ☐ *The wine was adulterated with a drug.*

ADVANCE ► ON

See under *ADVANCE ► (UP)ON.*

ADVANCE ► TO

advance something to someone or something (against something) to make an early payment of money promised or owed to a person or organization. ☐ *We advanced the money to Tom against our debt.* ☐ *Tom will advance a week's salary to the clerk.*

ADVANCE ► TO(WARD)

advance to(ward) someone or something to move forward in the direction of someone or something. ☐ *The group advanced toward David.* ☐ *The line of people advanced to the door of the theater.*

ADVANCE ► (UP)ON

advance (up)on someone or something to move toward someone or something. (Typically in military maneuvers or in team sports, such as American football. *Upon* is formal and less commonly used than *on.*) ☐ *The troops advanced on the opposing army.* ☐ *They advanced upon the town.*

ADVERTISE ► FOR

advertise for someone or something to advertise one's intention to purchase something or hire a particular type of person. ☐ *Did you advertise for a butler?* ☐ *We will advertise for the kind of piano we want.*

advertise something for a price to make known by public notice that something is to be sold at a particular price. ☐ *The shop advertised chocolates for four dollars a pound.* ☐ *Is this the one that was advertised for a dollar?*

advertise something for something to make known by public notice, such as broadcast or print notice, that something is available for purchase or rent. ☐ *Did you advertise the car for sale?* ☐ *Was this apartment advertised for rent?*

ADVISE ► ABOUT

advise someone about someone or something to inform someone about someone or something. ☐ *I want to advise you about something that is wrong with your car.* ☐ *I need to advise the committee about Karen.*

ADVISE ► AGAINST

advise someone against someone or something to give someone advice about something or about choosing someone for some purpose. ☐ *I must advise you against trying that again.* ☐ *I advised them against Wally.* [A] *The advised-against activity turned out to be very popular among the students.*

ADVISE ► OF

advise someone of something to inform someone of specific facts or some other information. ☐ *I hope you will advise Larry of his rights.* ☐ *Tom has been advised of the new policy.*

ADVISE ▸ ON

advise someone on someone or something to provide someone with specific advice about someone or something. □ *Would you please advise me on what kind of computer to buy?* □ *We advised them on Fred, who has been acting strangely lately.*

AFFILIATE ▸ TO

affiliate (someone or something) to someone or something AND **affiliate (someone or something) with someone or something** to cause a person or thing to be associated with some other person or thing. (*Someone* includes *oneself.*) □ *We sought to affiliate our chapter to the national organization.* □ *He did not want to affiliate his chapter to the other chapters.* □ *We tried to affiliate John with other people who shared his interests.* □ *I was able to affiliate myself to a group of divers who made frequent trips to the Caribbean.*

AFFILIATE ▸ WITH

affiliate (someone or something) with someone or something See the previous entry.

AFFIX ▸ TO

affix something to someone or something to fasten or attach something to someone or something. □ *Please affix these tags to your luggage.* □ *I affixed a sign to Timmy so the airline people wouldn't let him get lost.*

AFFLICT ▸ WITH

afflict someone with someone to burden someone with an annoying person. (Jocular and figurative. *Someone* includes *oneself.*) □ *Carl afflicted Karen with his little cousin Todd.* □ *I was stupid enough to afflict myself with my young cousin for the weekend.*

afflict someone with something to cause someone to suffer from a disease or disability; to burden someone with trouble. □ *Sam will afflict Ann with a terrible work load.* □ *She is afflicted with a serious disease.*

AGE ▸ OUT

age out (of something) [for an adult] to grow [mentally] out of a behavior problem, such as drug use or criminal acts. (Jargon.) □ *Most of them tend to age out at about 35.* □ *She hasn't aged out yet.*

AGITATE ▸ AGAINST

agitate against someone or something to stir up active dissatisfaction with someone or something. □ *The students were agitating against the new policy.* □ *They started agitating against the dean.*

AGITATE ▸ FOR

agitate for something to stir up active support for something. □ *The committee agitated for a change, but nothing was done.* □ *Walter agitated for recognition frequently.*

AGONIZE ▸ OVER

agonize (oneself) over someone or something to fret or anguish about someone or something. □ *Now, now, don't agonize yourself over the situation. Time cures all.* □ *No need to agonize over Sally. She's okay.* [A] *The much-agonized-over wording offended people anyway.* □ *It was quite foolish to agonize myself over such a small matter.*

AGREE ▸ ABOUT

agree (with someone) (about someone or something) See under *AGREE ▸ WITH.*

AGREE ▸ IN

agree (with something) (in something) See under *AGREE ▸ WITH.*

AGREE ▸ ON

See under *AGREE ▸ (UP)ON.*

AGREE ▸ TO

agree to disagree [for two or more people] to decide only that, after considerable discussion, they concur on nothing except that they disagree about the matter under discussion. (A cliché.) □ *We will agree to disagree. We cannot settle the matter.* □ *We didn't do anything but agree to disagree.*

agree to something to consent to something; to allow something to be done; to approve something. □ *I wish you would agree to my request.* [A] *The agreed-to time was still unsatisfactory for some people.*

AGREE ▸ (UP)ON

agree (up)on someone or something to agree to the choice of someone or something. □ *Couldn't we just agree on John rather than going over the whole list of candidates?* □ *Let's try to agree upon a date.* Ⓐ *I arrived at the agreed-upon time.*

AGREE ▸ WITH

agree with someone [for something] to be acceptable to someone as food. (Idiomatic. Usually negative.) □ *Onions do not agree with me.* □ *Some foods do not agree with people.*

agree (with someone) (about someone or something) AND **agree (with someone) ((up)on someone or something)** [for two or more people] to agree with one another about the facts concerning someone or something. □ *I agree with you about Judy.* □ *He agreed with Sam upon a time for the meeting.* □ *I agree about Tom.* □ *We certainly agree on Tom.*

agree with something **1.** [for something] to look good or go well with something else. □ *This dress does not agree with these shoes, does it?* □ *Your dress agrees with your bag.* **2.** [for something] to be in accord with something else. □ *The texture of the flooring agrees with the straight lines of the wall covering.* □ *Your analysis agrees with mine.*

agree (with something) (in something) [for grammatical features] to match or go together with other grammatical features. □ *The subject and the verb agree in number.* □ *The subject does not agree with the verb.*

AID ▸ IN

aid someone in something **1.** to help someone in some kind of trouble. □ *Will you aid me in this difficulty?* □ *Was he aided in this problem?* **2.** to help someone do something. (*Someone* includes *oneself.*) □ *He aided her in fixing up the back bedroom.* □ *She was unable to aid herself in keeping healthy.*

AIM ▸ AT

aim at something See *aim for someone* under *AIM ▸ FOR.*

aim something at someone or something to point or direct something at someone or something. □ *Wally aimed the hose at Sarah.* □ *He aimed the hose at the base of the bush.*

AIM ▸ FOR

aim for something AND **aim at something** to strive toward a particular goal; to direct oneself or one's energies toward something. □ *You should aim for success.* □ *Aim at getting this done on time.* Ⓐ *We achieved the aimed-for goal.*

aim for the sky to set one's goals very high. □ *I know I have to aim for the sky and hope for the best.* □ *You must aim for the sky.*

AIM ▸ TO

aim to do something to intend to do something; to plan to do something. (Folksy.) □ *Do you aim to help me with this?* □ *I aim to sit right here and smoke.*

AIR ▸ OUT

air out [for something] to remain in the fresh air and become fresher. □ *The pillows are airing out on the balcony.* □ *You don't need to have it dry-cleaned. It needs to air out.*

air something out to allow fresh air to freshen something, such as clothing, a stale-smelling room, etc. □ *Should I air my jacket out?* Ⓣ *Please air out your woolen jacket.* Ⓐ *The aired-out bedding was taken in before the rain.*

ALERT ▸ TO

alert someone to something to make someone aware of trouble or potential trouble. (*Someone* includes *oneself.*) □ *The auditors alerted us to some problems with the accounts.* □ *After she alerted herself to the danger, she kept a close watch on the door.*

ALIENATE ▸ FROM

alienate someone from someone or something to cause someone to feel negative about someone or something.

(*Someone* includes *oneself.*) □ *The teacher alienated the entire class from the subject of calculus.* □ *The television program alienated her from her husband.* □ *Sally alienated herself from her friends mostly out of her own fear of being found out.*

ALIGHT ► FROM

alight from something to get off of something; to get down off something. □ *When she alighted from the bus, a flock of little boys gathered around her and asked for pennies.* □ *Almost three hundred people alighted from the plane.*

ALIGHT ► (UP)ON

alight (up)on someone or something to land on something; [for a bird or other flying creature] to come to rest on something. (*Upon* is formal and less commonly used than *on.*) □ *A small bird alighted on the branch directly over my head.* □ *It alighted upon the branch.*

ALIGN ► WITH

align oneself with someone or something to bring oneself into an alliance with someone or someone's ideas; to associate oneself with someone or someone's cause. □ *She sought to align herself with the older members.* □ *I aligned myself with George on this matter.* □ *They aligned themselves with us so quickly that we didn't altogether trust them.*

align something with something to adjust or straighten something in reference to something else. □ *Try to align this piece with the one next to it.* □ *This one has been aligned with the other one.*

ALLOCATE ► AMONG

See under *ALLOCATE ► TO.*

ALLOCATE ► BETWEEN

allocate something between someone or something See the following entry.

ALLOCATE ► TO

allocate something to someone or something AND **allocate something between someone or something; allocate something among someone or something** to give or assign something to someone or something. (*Between* with two, *among* with three or more.) □ *The committee allocated the cheese to the elderly people in the community.* □ *David allocated the money among all the members.* □ *He allocated the work between Fred and George.* □ *We had to allocate the money between the philanthropy and social committees.*

ALLOT ► TO

allot something to someone or something to give or assign something to someone or something. □ *We will allot a fair amount of money to the hospitals.* □ *I allotted a small portion of the work to Fred.*

ALLOW ► FOR

allow for someone or something to provide for someone or something. □ *Be sure to allow for a large number of sick people.* □ *Please allow for Liz also.*

allow something for someone or something to provide something for someone or something; to provide enough [of something] for someone or something. (Usually with expressions of plenty.) □ *Be sure to allow enough food for the entire group.* □ *I will allow enough room for expansion.*

allow something for something **1.** to allocate a share or a suitable amount of something, such as time, money, space, etc., for something. □ *I allowed only an hour for lunch.* □ *They did not allow enough money for their expenditures this month.* **2.** to give consideration to circumstances or contingencies. □ *We allowed room for expansion when we designed the building.* □ *Allowing a lot for his youth, I forgave him at once.*

ALLOW ► IN

allow someone or something in (something) to permit someone or something to enter something or some place. □ *Will they allow you in the restaurant without a tie?* □ *They won't allow me in.* □ *They don't allow dogs in there.*

ALLOW ► UP

allow someone up (from something) to permit someone to arise or get up. (*Someone* includes *oneself.*) □ *He knocked Peter down and would not al-*

low him up from the ground. ☐ *The doctor won't allow you up!* ☐ *I force myself to sleep. I never allow myself up before noon.*

ALLOY ▸ WITH

alloy something with something **1.** to combine one molten metal into another molten metal. ☐ *Is it possible to alloy copper with nickel?* ☐ *The copper has been alloyed with nickel.* **2.** to combine one quality or attribute with another. (Figurative.) ☐ *She alloyed her courage with a helping of wisdom.* ☐ *Her courage has been alloyed with wisdom.*

ALLUDE ▸ TO

allude to someone or something to refer to someone or something; to make an implication about someone or something. ☐ *I did not mean to allude to someone you disliked so much.* ☐ *I alluded to the accident only once.* 🄰 *The alluded-to remark will not be repeated again!*

ALLY ▸ AGAINST

See *ally (oneself) (with someone) (against someone or something)* under *ALLY ▸ WITH.*

ALLY ▸ TO

ally oneself to someone or something to unite or affiliate with someone or something. ☐ *She sought to ally herself to the older members.* ☐ *Jane allied herself to the teacher almost immediately.*

ALLY ▸ WITH

ally (oneself) (with someone) (against someone or something) to unite with someone in opposition to someone or something. ☐ *The professor allied herself with John against the committee.* ☐ *We allied with the older ones against the younger ones.* ☐ *They allied themselves against the attackers.* ☐ *We allied ourselves against the attackers with the local militia.* ☐ *John allied himself with Fred against all the rest of the boys.*

ALTERNATE ▸ BETWEEN

alternate between someone and someone else or something and something else to choose between two persons or things, alternately. ☐ *The job will alternate between Gil and Ed.* ☐ *The maid will alternate between the first floor and the second floor.*

ALTERNATE ▸ WITH

alternate with someone or something [for someone or something] to serve as a substitute for someone or something. ☐ *I alternated with Fred as the lead in the school play.* ☐ *The red ones will alternate with the green ones.*

alternate with something [for something] to appear repetitively and regularly in a sequence with something else. (For instance, A alternates with B in the sequence ABABAB.) ☐ *In this design the long marks alternate with the circles.* ☐ *The red ones will alternate with the blue ones.*

AMALGAMATE ▸ WITH

amalgamate something with something to unite something with something else; to merge two things. ☐ *We will amalgamate this company with another firm.* ☐ *How long has this company been amalgamated with the other company?*

amalgamate with something to join with something; to merge with something. ☐ *Our group decided to amalgamate with another group.* ☐ *We did not amalgamate after all.*

AMBLE ▸ ALONG

amble along (something) to walk along slowly and casually. ☐ *They ambled along the path.* ☐ *I was just ambling along, minding my own business.*

AMOUNT ▸ TO

amount to something **1.** [for someone or something] to become worthwhile or valuable. ☐ *I hope Charles amounts to something some day.* ☐ *I doubt that this whole business will ever amount to a hill of beans.* **2.** [for something] to be the equivalent of something. ☐ *Why, this amounts to cheating!* ☐ *Your comments amount to treason.* **3.** AND **amount (up) to something** [for a sum of money] to increase (to a large amount). ☐ *Is that everything you want to buy? That amounts to twenty dollars.* ☐ *These charges amount up to a lot.*

amount to the same thing (as something) to be the same (as something); to be the equivalent of something. □ *Whether it's red or blue, it amounts to the same thing.* □ *It all amounts to the same thing.*

AMOUNT ▸ UP

amount (up) to something See under *AMOUNT ▸ TO.*

AMUSE ▸ WITH

amuse someone with someone or something to entertain or interest someone with someone or something. (*Someone* includes *oneself.*) □ *Try to amuse the child with this little toy.* □ *The hostess amused the children with a clever clown.* □ *She was able to amuse herself with the puzzle for a while.*

ANGLE ▸ FOR

angle for something **1.** to fish for something, as with a fishhook and line. □ *Fred was angling for a big bass.* □ *I am angling for whatever I can catch.* **2.** to scheme or plan to get something. (Figurative.) □ *She is just angling for a larger settlement.* □ *Are you angling for a tip?*

ANGLE ▸ OFF

angle off to(ward) something to turn or move toward something at an angle. □ *The road angles off to the right.* □ *This street angles off toward the east.*

ANNEX ▸ TO

annex something to something [for a governmental body of a town or city] to attach a parcel of land onto an existing parcel of land through legal proceedings. □ *The village annexed some adjacent land to itself.* □ *The land has been annexed finally.*

annex to something [for the owner of a parcel of land] to have land attached to an adjacent town or city. □ *We don't want to annex to Adamsville.* □ *They chose to annex to Smithton.*

ANNOUNCE ▸ FOR

announce for someone or something to declare one's political support for someone or something. □ *The senator announced for the Supreme Court nominee.* □ *Our club announced for the youngest candidate.*

ANNOUNCE ▸ TO

announce something to someone to tell something publicly to someone. □ *The president announced it to everyone.* □ *When was this announced to everyone?*

ANOINT ▸ WITH

anoint someone with something to smear or rub oil on a person's head as an honor or blessing; to put a liquid onto oneself. (Mostly in biblical references. *Someone* includes *oneself.*) □ *They anointed the king with oil and praised him greatly.* □ *He anointed himself with a vaporous salve that was meant to help his cold symptoms.*

ANSWER ▸ BACK

answer back (to someone) AND **answer someone back** to talk back (to someone); to argue (with someone). □ *I wish you wouldn't answer back to me that way.* □ *Please don't answer me back like that!* □ *Don't answer back!*

answer someone back See the previous entry.

ANSWER ▸ FOR

answer for someone [for someone] to speak for someone else. □ *I can't answer for Chuck, but I do have my own opinion.* □ *I will answer for him.*

answer for someone or something to explain or justify someone or something; to take responsibility or blame for someone or something. □ *You will have to answer for your children.* □ *I will answer only for my own misdeeds.*

answer (to someone) for something to explain one's actions (to someone). □ *You will have to answer to the general for doing that.* □ *You will have to answer for your mistake.*

ANSWER ▸ TO

answer to someone [in the hierarchy of the workplace] to be under the supervision of someone. □ *You will answer directly to Mr. Wright.* □ *I answer to the boss only.*

answer to someone (about something) to explain or justify (some action) to someone. □ *If you don't do it right, you will have to answer to me.* □ *You will have to answer to me about that!*

answer to the description of someone to fit a particular description. ☐ *Chuck answers to the description of the robber.* ☐ *Max answers to the description of the cat burglar.*

answer to the name (of) something to respond to a particular name. ☐ *I answer to the name Walter.* ☐ *She answers to the name of Claire.*

APOLOGIZE ► FOR

See the following entry.

APOLOGIZE ► TO

apologize (to someone) (for someone) to make an apology to someone for someone else's actions. (*Someone* includes *oneself*.) ☐ *Would you please apologize to Wally for Tom?* ☐ *I apologized for Frank to the hostess.* ☐ *I had to apologize for Frank.* ☐ *I had to apologize to the hostess.* ☐ *He was never able to apologize to himself for his past errors.*

APPEAL ► AGAINST

appeal against something to ask a court of appeals to cancel a ruling made by a lower court. ☐ *My lawyer appealed against the judgment.* ☐ *We will appeal against the ruling.*

APPEAL ► FOR

appeal (to a court) (for something); appeal (to someone or something) (for something) See both under *APPEAL ► TO.*

APPEAL ► TO

appeal (to a court) (for something) to plead to a court of appeals for a favorable ruling. ☐ *She appealed to the court for a retrial.* ☐ *She appealed for an injunction to the circuit court.* ☐ *She appealed for a retrial.*

appeal to someone to please or attract someone. ☐ *This food doesn't appeal to me.* ☐ *The whole idea appeals to me a lot.*

appeal (to someone or something) (for something) to ask someone or a group or plead with someone or a group for something. ☐ *I appeal to you for a little consideration.* ☐ *I appealed to the court for leniency.*

APPEAR ► AS

appear as someone to play the role of someone in the theater, a film, masquerade, etc. ☐ *Molly will appear as Lady Bracknell in* The Importance of Being Earnest. ☐ *I will appear as Miss Prim.*

appear as something to occur in a particular form. ☐ *The tumors appear as shadows on the X ray.* ☐ *The first signs of the disease appear as a fever and a rash.*

APPEAR ► AT

appear at something **1.** to arrive at a particular time. ☐ *I am due to appear at the council at noon.* ☐ *I will appear at the meeting whenever my plane gets in.* **2.** to perform at a particular place. ☐ *She is appearing at the Bijou all month.* ☐ *I will appear at Carnegie Hall soon.*

APPEAR ► BEFORE

appear before someone **1.** to show up in the presence of someone, suddenly. ☐ *The butler appeared before us with no sound or other warning.* ☐ *A frightful specter appeared before me.* **2.** to stand up in front of a particular judge in court. ☐ *You have to appear before Judge Cahill tomorrow.* ☐ *Have you ever appeared before him?*

appear before something to arrive in advance of the appointed time or before some event. ☐ *Please appear a little before you are due.* ☐ *It would be good to appear shortly before the appointed time.*

APPEAR ► FOR

appear for someone to represent or substitute for a person [who is absent]. ☐ *I will appear for you in the council.* ☐ *Who is going to appear for my lawyer, who is ill?*

APPEAR ► IN

appear in court to go to a court of law as a participant. ☐ *She has to appear in court tomorrow.* ☐ *I have to appear in court too.*

appear in something **1.** to be seen in some performance. (Compare to *appear at something*, sense 2.) ☐ *The singer will appear in the opera with the rest of the chorus.* ☐ *I will appear in* Aida. **2.** to be seen wearing something. ☐ *I wouldn't appear in that in public!* ☐ *Would you want to appear in a wrinkled suit?*

APPEAR ▸ UNDER

appear under something [for an actor] to perform under a special name. ☐ *She is appearing under the name of Fifi.* ☐ *I appeared under the stage name Rex Righteous.*

APPEAR ▸ (UP)ON

appear (up)on something to arrive and be seen on something. (*Upon* is formal and less commonly used than *on*.) ☐ *A fly appeared upon the sterile cloths.* ☐ *A small bird appeared on our mailbox.*

APPEND ▸ (ON)TO

append something (on)to something to attach something to something; to hang something onto something. ☐ *Please append these tassels onto your hem.* ☐ *Append this sentence to the last paragraph.*

APPERTAIN ▸ TO

appertain to something [for a responsibility or privilege] to belong to something as a right. ☐ *Do these rights appertain to a third cousin of the deceased?* ☐ *They appertain to no one as they are stated.*

APPLY ▸ FOR

apply (to someone or something) (for something) See under *APPLY ▸ TO.*

APPLY ▸ TO

apply oneself to something to work hard and diligently at something. ☐ *You should apply yourself to your studies.* ☐ *She applied herself to her work and the time passed very rapidly.*

apply something to something 1. to put something onto something. ☐ *Apply the decal to the surface of the glass.* ☐ *A decal has been applied to the glass.* 2. to use something, such as force, effort, etc., on something or in the performance of some task. ☐ *Apply more effort to the job.* ☐ *An even greater effort has been applied to the task.* 3. to use or employ something on something. ☐ *Apply this compress to the wound.* ☐ *A compress was applied to the wound.*

apply to someone or something to affect someone or something; to govern someone or something; to be relevant to someone or something. ☐ *Does this rule apply to me?* ☐ *These policies apply only to very large companies.*

apply (to someone or something) (for something) to ask for something from someone or an organization. ☐ *You must apply to the proper office for permission.* ☐ *I applied to the wrong office for the form.* ☐ *You need to apply to the personnel office.* 🄰 *The applied-for request was finally granted.*

APPLY ▸ WITHIN

apply within (some place) to ask about something inside (some place). (Usually part of a sign or announcement posted outside some place.) ☐ *The sign suggested that I apply within the office.* ☐ *Please apply within.*

APPOINT ▸ TO

appoint someone to something to select or assign someone to serve in a particular role. (Usually focusing on the role of the person or on a group of persons with similar roles. *Someone* includes *oneself*.) ☐ *I am going to appoint you to the position of treasurer.* ☐ *Fred appointed himself to the board of directors, but was sued for doing it.*

APPORTION ▸ AMONG

See the following entry.

APPORTION ▸ OUT

apportion something (out) (among someone) to divide something and distribute it among people. ☐ *He apportioned the cake out among the guests.* 🅃 *He apportioned out the cake among the members.* ☐ *He apportioned the cake among the children.* ☐ *He apportioned the cake out.*

APPRAISE ▸ AT

appraise something at something to study something and place a monetary value on it. ☐ *They appraised the house at twice what it is worth.* ☐ *The gold ring was appraised at a high price.*

APPRENTICE ▸ TO

apprentice someone to someone to assign someone to work as an apprentice to someone. (*Someone* includes *oneself*.) □ *She apprenticed her son to a local printer.* □ *I apprenticed myself to a printer and learned what it means to get really dirty.*

APPRISE ▸ OF

apprise someone of something to inform someone of something. □ *I hope you will apprise me of any change.* □ *Have you been apprised of the new rule?*

APPROACH ▸ ABOUT

approach someone about someone or something to ask someone about someone or something, usually with tact and caution. □ *I will approach Judy about Wally.* □ *She approached Tom about the broken window.*

APPROPRIATE ▸ FOR

appropriate something for someone to take something [from someone else] for oneself; to steal something. (*Someone* includes *oneself*.) □ *George appropriated the car for himself.* □ *Was the car appropriated for George alone?*

appropriate something for something **1.** to allot a certain amount of money for a particular purpose. □ *They will appropriate a fortune for the fair.* □ *A large sum was appropriated for the expenses.* **2.** to take something [from someone else] and use it as something else or for a purpose different from what was intended. □ *Walter appropriated the truck for an ambulance.* □ *A truck has been appropriated for use as an ambulance.*

APPROPRIATE ▸ TO

appropriate something to one's (own) use to take something [from someone] for oneself or one's own use; to steal something through appropriation. □ *She appropriated the money to her own use.* □ *They appropriated the funds to their use.*

APPROVE ▸ OF

approve of someone or something to take a favorable view of someone or something. □ *I don't approve of you.* □ *I don't approve of that kind of thing.* [A] *We finally got an approved-of furnace installed in the basement.*

ARBITRATE ▸ BETWEEN

arbitrate between someone and someone else to mediate between two disagreeing parties; to help two disagreeing parties to resolve their differences. □ *Jane was called upon to arbitrate between the workers and the manager.* □ *I arbitrated between Fred and his stockbroker.*

ARBITRATE ▸ IN

arbitrate in something to serve to mediate or negotiate a settlement in a dispute. □ *She refuses to arbitrate in this dispute.* □ *I will arbitrate in this little disagreement.*

ARCH ▸ OVER

arch (oneself) over to bend or curve over. (*Oneself* includes *itself*.) □ *The tree arched over in the wind.* □ *Arch yourself over gracefully and then straighten up.* □ *Arch over gracefully.* □ *The tree arched itself over in the windstorm.*

arch over someone or something to bend or curve over someone or something; to stand or remain bent or curved over someone or something. □ *The trees arched gracefully over the walkway.* □ *A lovely bower of roses arched over the bride.*

arch something over someone or something to place something above someone or something to form an arch or archway. □ *The cadets arched their swords over the bridal couple.* □ *The willow arched its long flowing branches over the tiny cabin.*

ARGUE ▸ ABOUT

argue about someone or something See *argue (with someone) (over someone or something)* under *ARGUE ▸ WITH.*

ARGUE ▸ AGAINST

argue against someone or something **1.** [for someone] to make a case against someone or something; to oppose the choice of someone or something in an argument. □ *I am preparing myself to argue against the case.* □ *Liz argued against Tom, but we chose him anyway.*

🅐 *The much-argued-against proposition was defeated.* **2.** [for something, such as facts] to support a case against someone or something in an argument; [for something, such as facts] to support a case against the choice of someone or something in an argument. ☐ *I have uncovered something that argues against continuing this discussion.* ☐ *His own remarks argue against the candidate, but he probably will be elected anyway.*

ARGUE ▶ BACK

argue back to argue with or oppose someone; to *answer back (to someone)*; to *talk back (to someone)*. (Usually said of persons who are supposed to take orders without comment.) ☐ *Please don't argue back all the time.* ☐ *I wish you did not argue back so much.*

ARGUE ▶ DOWN

argue someone down to defeat someone in a debate. ☐ *Sally could always argue him down if she had to.* 🅣 *She tries to argue down everyone she meets.*

argue something down **1.** to defeat a proposal or a motion in a meeting through discussion. ☐ *I am prepared to argue the proposal down in court.* 🅣 *She will argue down the proposal in the council meeting.* **2.** to reduce something, such as a bill or a price, by arguing. ☐ *I tried to argue the price down, but it did no good.* 🅣 *Tom could not argue down the bill.*

ARGUE ▶ FOR

argue for someone or something to make a case for someone or something; to speak for someone or something in an argument. ☐ *Are you prepared to argue strongly for this proposal?* ☐ *We will argue for our candidate.* 🅐 *The much-argued-for law was passed in the spring.*

ARGUE ▶ INTO

argue someone into something to convince or persuade someone to do something. (*Someone* includes *oneself.*) ☐ *She was unable to argue the manager into attending.* ☐ *She was unable to argue herself into doing it.*

ARGUE ▶ OUT

argue one's way out (of something) to talk and argue oneself free of a problem. ☐ *You can't argue your way out of this!* ☐ *It's a problem, and there is no way that you can argue your way out.*

argue something out to settle something by discussing all the important points. ☐ *We are going to have to argue this out some other time.* 🅣 *Should we try to argue out every single detail?*

ARGUE ▶ OVER

See the following entry.

ARGUE ▶ WITH

argue (with someone) (over someone or something) AND **argue (with someone) (about someone or something)** to dispute or quarrel (over someone or something) (with someone) ☐ *Are you going to argue with her over something so simple?* ☐ *I wish you wouldn't argue over money with me.* ☐ *We always argue about money.* ☐ *Don't argue with me!*

argue with something to challenge or dispute something; to dispute someone's statement of fact. ☐ *I won't argue with your conclusions.* ☐ *It is not a good idea to argue with the facts.*

ARISE ▶ FROM

arise from something AND **arise out of something** **1.** to get up from something. ☐ *What time did you arise from bed?* ☐ *I arose out of bed at dawn.* **2.** to be due to something; to be caused by something. ☐ *This whole problem arose from your stubbornness.* ☐ *The problem arose out of mismanagement.* **3.** [for something] to drift upward from something. ☐ *The smoke arose from the burning oil wells.* ☐ *The smoke arose out of the base of the wall.* **4.** [for someone] to come from poor or unfortunate circumstances. ☐ *She arose from poverty to great wealth.* ☐ *She arose out of poverty.*

ARISE ▶ OUT

arise out of something See the previous entry.

ARM ▶ AGAINST

arm someone (against someone or something) (with something) to equip someone (with whatever is needed) to fight (against someone or something). (*Someone* includes *oneself*.) □ *They armed themselves against the enemy with guns and ammunition.* □ *We armed them with guns.* □ *We armed them against the attackers.* □ *He armed himself against the threats with a small gun.*

ARM ▸ WITH

See the previous entry.

AROUSE ▸ FROM

arouse someone from something to activate a person out of a state of rest, sleep, or inaction. (*Someone* includes *oneself*.) □ *I could not arouse her from her sleep.* □ *She aroused herself from a deep sleep.*

ARRANGE ▸ FOR

arrange for someone to do something to make plans for someone to do something. □ *I will arrange for Charles to fix it.* [A] *I attended the arranged-for meeting along with the others.*

arrange for something to prepare or plan for something. □ *We will arrange for a celebration.* □ *John arranged for it.*

arrange something for a time to plan something for a particular time. □ *We will arrange a picnic for the afternoon.* [A] *He appeared at the arranged-for time.*

arrange something for someone or something to prepare or plan something for someone or something. □ *They arranged a reception for Frank.* □ *We arranged a dance for the holiday.*

arrange something for something to prepare or adapt music for particular instruments or for a particular musical key. □ *Paul arranged the piece for piano.* □ *This piece was arranged for the piano by Frank's brother.*

ARRANGE ▸ WITH

arrange something with someone or something to prepare or plan something that will include someone or something. □ *We arranged entertainment with clowns and a musician.* □ *I will arrange a fancy dinner with wine and cloth napkins.* □ *Paul arranged a meeting with the opposition.*

ARRIVE ▸ AT

arrive at something 1. to reach a place. □ *When will we arrive at the resort?* □ *We will arrive at home soon.* 2. to reach a conclusion; to make a decision. □ *Have you arrived at a decision yet?* □ *We will arrive at an answer tomorrow.*

arrive (some place) at some time to reach (some place) at a particular time. (Refers to the times that are expressed with *at*. See also *arrive (up)on something* under *ARRIVE ▸ (UP)ON*.) □ *We will arrive at the border at noon.* □ *They arrived at seven.*

ARRIVE ▸ FROM

arrive (some place) from some place to reach or come to a place from another place. (If the first *some place* is missing, the place is either "here" or must be inferred.) □ *They arrived here from New York yesterday.* □ *They arrived from Charleston yesterday.*

ARRIVE ▸ IN

arrive (some place) in something to reach or come to a place; to arrive some place in something 1. to reach a place in a particular vehicle. □ *They arrived here in their car.* □ *We arrived in a bus.* 2. to reach a place in a group. □ *They arrived at the restaurant in a group.* □ *We arrived in a group.*

ARRIVE ▸ (UP)ON

arrive (up)on something to reach [a place] at a particular time. (Usually used with *stroke,* as in the examples. These are the times expressed with *on*. See also *arrive (some place) at some time* under *ARRIVE ▸ AT. Upon* is formal and less commonly used than *on*.) □ *She arrived on the stroke of midnight.* □ *We all arrived upon the stroke of two.*

arrive (up)on the scene (of something) to reach the location of an event in progress. (*Upon* is formal and less commonly used than *on*.) □ *The police arrived on the scene of the crime.* □ *They arrived upon the scene of a frightening accident.* □ *What did they do when they arrived upon the scene?*

ASCERTAIN ▶ FROM

ascertain something from someone to find out or learn with certainty information from someone. ☐ *I need to ascertain some facts from you.* ☐ *A few facts have been ascertained from the interview.*

ASCRIBE ▶ TO

ascribe something to someone or something to attribute something to someone or something; to assert that something has been caused by someone or something. ☐ *Please do not ascribe that attitude to my group.* ☐ *We ascribed the action to Jill and only Jill.*

ASK ▶ ABOUT

ask about See under *ASK ▶ AROUND.*

ask about someone or something to inquire about someone or something. ☐ *I need to ask about Beth. How is she?* ☐ *I want to ask about the status of my proposal.* 🄰 *Our much-asked-about hostess finally put in an appearance.*

ASK ▶ AFTER

ask after someone to inquire about the health and well-being of someone. ☐ *Molly asked after you.* ☐ *I asked after Molly and her family.*

ASK ▶ AROUND

ask around (about someone or something) AND **ask about** to request information (about someone or something) from a number of different sources. ☐ *I don't know the answer. I'll ask around about it.* ☐ *Ask about, will you?* ☐ *Please ask around about her.*

ASK ▶ BACK

ask someone back **1.** [for a host or hostess] to invite someone to come again (to another similar event). ☐ *After the way you behaved, they'll never ask us back.* ☐ *They had been asked back a number of times, but they never came.* **2.** [for someone who has been a guest] to invite a previous host or hostess to come to an event. ☐ *We've had the Smiths to dinner five times. I think it's time they asked us back.* ☐ *I don't care if they ask us back or not.*

ASK ▶ DOWN

ask someone down to invite someone to come to one's home [for a visit]. (Usually said when someone must go to a lower level, travel south, down a hill, or into the country for the visit.] ☐ *Sam asked us down for Friday evening. Shall we go?* ☐ *We have been asked down before.*

ASK ▶ FOR

ask for someone or something to request someone or something. ☐ *The police are at the door asking for Henry.* ☐ *The child asked for a glass of water.* 🄰 *The hostess served her much-asked-for dessert with enormous pleasure.*

ask for something to invite or provoke difficulty or punishment. (Idiomatic. Usually expressed as *it*.) ☐ *You are just asking for a fight.* ☐ *He's asking for it!*

ask for the moon to make outlandish requests or demands [for something, such as money or privilege]. (Idiomatic.) ☐ *She's asking for the moon, and she's not going to get it.* ☐ *Don't ask for the moon. Be reasonable!*

ask someone for something **1.** to request something from someone. ☐ *The diners asked the waiter for a type of wine the restaurant didn't have.* ☐ *A special wine was asked for by a number of patrons.* **2.** AND **ask someone to something** to invite someone to something. ☐ *Janet asked us to a party Friday evening.* ☐ *Janet asked us to dinner.*

ASK ▶ IN(TO)

ask someone in((to) some place) to invite someone inside (some place) ☐ *We asked them into the house.* ☐ *We asked them in.*

ASK ▶ OF

ask something of someone or something to request or demand something from someone, something, or a group. ☐ *I want to ask something of you.* ☐ *We will ask that of the board of directors.* ☐ *You should ask that of your data base.*

ASK ▶ OUT

ask someone out (to something) AND **ask someone out (for something)** **1.** to invite someone to go out (to something or some place) [on a date]. (*To* calls for a place or event. *For* calls for a purpose.) □ *He asked her out to dinner, but she had other plans.* [T] *She couldn't go, so he asked out someone else.* □ *Liz asked Carl out for dinner.* **2.** to invite someone for a visit to a place in the country or some other location remote from the center of things. □ *Tom must be tired of the city. Let's ask him out to our place.* [T] *I don't want to ask out everyone in the whole family again.* □ *Oh, let's ask him out anyway.*

ASK ► OVER

ask someone over to invite someone who lives close by to come to one's home [for a visit]. (Maybe to a house or apartment.] □ *Can we ask Tom over?* □ *He has been asked over a number of times.*

ASK ► TO

ask someone to something See under *ask someone for something* under *ASK ► FOR.*

ASK ► UP

ask someone up to ask someone to come to one's home for a visit. (Usually said when someone must travel north, up a hill, or to an upper-level apartment for the visit.] □ *Let's ask Judy up for the weekend.* □ *She has been asked up before.*

ASPIRE ► TO

aspire to something to seek or aim for something. □ *I aspire to something more important.* □ *I aspire to far greater things.*

ASSAIL ► WITH

assail someone with something **1.** to attack someone with something, such as a weapon or words. □ *The crook assailed the officer with a stream of curses.* □ *The officer was assailed with curses.* **2.** to pester or annoy someone with questions, requests, demands, etc. (*Someone* includes *oneself.*) □ *Don't assail me with all your complaints.* □ *She assailed herself with constant guilty rebukes.*

ASSENT ► TO

assent to something to agree to something. □ *I assent to what you suggest.* □ *She will not assent to our request.*

ASSESS ► AT

assess something at something to estimate or value something at some figure. □ *They assess the value of our house at twice what it would sell for.* □ *The house was assessed at twice its worth.*

ASSIGN ► TO

assign someone or something to someone or something to designate someone or something as belonging to someone or something. (*Someone* includes *oneself.*) □ *They assigned the new car to Roger.* □ *They assigned the new worker to the mail room.* □ *Fred assigned himself to the busiest committee.* □ *I assigned the three new clerks to Mrs. Brown.*

assign something to someone to attribute something to someone; to blame something on someone. □ *We were forced to assign the blame to Robert.* □ *Is the blame assigned to Robert now?*

ASSIMILATE ► (IN)TO

assimilate (in)to something to work into something, such a group or organization. □ *I wanted to assimilate into the organization.* □ *I will assimilate to the club quickly.*

ASSIMILATE ► INTO

assimilate someone or something into something to cause someone or something to be absorbed into something. (People are absorbed into groups. *Someone* includes *oneself.*) □ *We sought to assimilate Arnold into the community.* □ *The manager had to assimilate the new policies into the list of current policies.* □ *They assimilated themselves into the general population.*

ASSIMILATE ► TO

See under *ASSIMILATE ► (IN)TO.*

ASSIMILATE ► WITH

assimilate with someone □ *It's easy for Karen to assimilate with new people.* □ *I want to assimilate rapidly with the other people in my class.*

ASSIST ▶ AT

assist at something to serve as a helper or assistant in some procedure. (Usually refers to a surgical procedure.) □ *Will you assist at surgery this morning?* □ *I would be happy to assist at the procedure.*

ASSIST ▶ IN

assist in something to help with something. □ *May I assist in this?* □ *Please assist in this task.*

assist someone in something to help a particular person working on a task. □ *Please assist Greg in the committee's assignment.* □ *They were assisted in their assignment.*

ASSIST ▶ WITH

assist someone with someone or something to help someone manage someone or something, especially with lifting or physical management. (*Someone* includes *oneself.*) □ *Assist me with Jane, won't you?* □ *Will you assist me with this box?* □ *Sally assisted herself with the math problem. She did it on her own.*

ASSOCIATE ▶ WITH

associate oneself with someone or something to join someone or something as a partner or friend. □ *I wanted to associate myself with a prestigious law firm.* □ *She associated herself with people of low repute.*

associate someone or something with someone or something to link someone or something [in one's mind] to someone or something else. (*Something* and *someone* occur in all possible combinations. *Someone* includes *oneself.*) □ *I always associate Walter with pizza for some reason.* □ *I associate pizza with stringy cheese.* □ *We associate pizza with Jill because she hates the stuff so much.* □ *Fred tended to associate himself with the rich and famous rather than the poor and unknown.*

associate with someone to be friendly with someone; to be acquainted with someone socially in a work setting. □ *We seek to associate with persons like ourselves.* □ *I like to associate with interesting people.*

ASSURE ▶ OF

assure someone of something to guarantee something to someone; to promise someone that something will happen or that a particular state exists. (*Someone* includes *oneself.*) □ *I want to assure you of our good intentions.* □ *Frequently, she had to assure herself of her basic worth.*

ASTOUND ▶ WITH

astound someone with something to shock or amaze someone with something. (*Someone* includes *oneself.*) □ *She astounded us with her skill.* □ *He astounded himself with his sudden burst of vigor.*

ATONE ▶ FOR

atone for something to make amends for an error. □ *You must atone for the bad things you have done.* Ⓐ *Her atoned-for errors were forgiven.*

ATTACH ▶ TO

attach oneself to someone **1.** to become emotionally attached to someone. □ *Fred seems to have attached himself to a much older woman, who has captured his attention.* □ *Somehow, Fred has attached himself emotionally to Susan, and neither of them has any idea of what to do about it.* **2.** to follow after someone; to become a constant companion to someone. □ *Andy's little brother attached himself to Andy and his friends—much to Andy's distress.* □ *John attached himself to his older brother and drove him crazy.*

attach oneself to something **1.** to choose to associate with a particular thing, group, or organization. □ *Todd attached himself to a volleyball team that practices at the school.* □ *The manager attached himself to the luncheon club and became a regular fixture there.* **2.** to connect or secure oneself to something. □ *Tony attached himself to the helm and proceeded to steer the boat.* □ *Susan attached herself to the seat with the belt provided for the purpose.*

attach something to someone or something to connect, affix, or secure something to someone or something. □ *Would you please attach this cord to Fred, so he won't fall out of the boat?* □ *Attach the sensors to Fred, so we can monitor his heart for a while.*

attach to someone [for blame, importance, guilt, fault, etc.] to become fixed onto someone or an organization. □ *A lot of guilt attaches to Henry for his part in the plot.* □ *Most of the blame attaches to Roger.*

attach to something [for something] to be meant to fit onto or into something. □ *This one attaches to this other one right at this point.* □ *This part should have attached to the back of the desk, but it didn't fit.*

ATTEND ▸ TO

attend to someone to listen to someone. (Stilted.) □ *Please attend to your teacher's instruction.* □ *Attend to what is being said.*

attend to someone or something to take care of the needs of someone or something; to respond to a request or demand from someone or something. □ *Please attend to your wounded friend.* □ *Would you attend to this memo?*

ATTEST ▸ TO

attest to something to certify or bear witness to a fact. □ *I cannot attest to what you have reported.* [A] *The attested-to facts do not support the conclusions you have drawn.*

ATTIRE ▸ IN

attire someone in something to dress someone in something. (*Someone* includes *oneself.*) □ *The mother attired her children in new, clean clothes.* □ *She attired herself in her finest garments.*

ATTRACT ▸ TO

attract someone or something to someone or something to draw or pull someone or something to someone or something. □ *The poster attracted a large number of people to the concert.* □ *The shouting attracted a lot of attention to the people who were arguing.*

ATTRIBUTE ▸ TO

attribute something to someone or something to ascribe something to someone or something; to believe that someone or something is the source of something. □ *We attribute our success to your good advice.* □ *I attribute all these ill-mannered memos to Andrew.*

ATTUNE ▸ TO

attune someone or something to someone or something to bring someone or something into accord with someone or something; to adjust someone or something to someone or something else. (Usually metaphorical. Not used for musical tuning. *Someone* includes *oneself.*) □ *You should try to attune yourself to our needs and direction.* □ *Try to attune your comments to your audience better.* □ *Fred was able to attune himself to Mary perfectly, and that is why they get along so well.*

AUCTION ▸ OFF

auction something off to sell something [to the highest bidder] at an auction. □ *He auctioned his home off.* [T] *He auctioned off his home.* [T] *The duke was required to auction off his ancestral home.* [A] *The auctioned-off goods sat in the garage, awaiting their new owners.*

AUDITION ▸ FOR

audition for something to try out for a part in something. (One's singing, speaking, or playing is heard and judged.) □ *I plan to audition for the play.* □ *Liz auditioned for* The Mikado.

audition someone for something to allow someone to try out for a part in a performance; to judge someone's singing, speaking, or playing potentiality for a part in a performance. □ *Will you audition anyone else for the part?* □ *Have you been auditioned for the part?*

AVAIL ▸ OF

avail oneself of something to take advantage of something. □ *Please avail yourself of the opportunity to see this film.* □ *I was not able to avail myself of your help when I needed it.*

AVENGE ▸ AGAINST

avenge oneself (against someone or something) (for something) See under *AVENGE ▸ ON.*

AVENGE ▸ FOR

See the following entry.

AVENGE ▸ ON

avenge oneself (on someone or something) (for something) AND **avenge oneself (against someone or something) (for something)** to get even with someone or something for some hurt or damage. ☐ *They avenged themselves on the entire country for the attack.* ☐ *He avenged himself against the storekeeper for the false arrest.* ☐ *Max avenged himself for the false charge.* ☐ *Tom avenged himself on Bill for Bill's previous attack.*

AVERAGE ▸ OUT

average out to even out ultimately; to be fair over the long term. ☐ *Everything will average out in the end.* ☐ *Yes, it will all average out.*

average out (at something) AND **average out (to something)** to equal something as the average of a set of figures. ☐ *The figures averaged out at what was expected.* ☐ *Will the amounts average out to a manageable sum?* ☐ *Everything will average out.*

AVERAGE ▸ UP

average something up to calculate the average of a set of figures. ☐ *Please average these columns up.* Ⓣ *Please average up these columns.* ☐ *Will you please average these figures up?*

AVERT ▸ FROM

avert something from someone or something to turn or divert something away from someone or something. ☐ *We will attempt to avert attention from the problems.* ☐ *She averted her eyes from Bill when he walked by.*

AWAKE(N) ▸ FROM

awake(n) from something to wake up from something, such as a dream or a deep sleep. ☐ *Tom awakened from a deep sleep with a start.* ☐ *She awoke from her slumbers.*

awake(n) someone from something to cause someone to wake up from something. (*Someone* includes *oneself.*) ☐ *The crowing of the rooster awakened Sally from her slumbers.* ☐ *She awakened herself from a deep sleep when she fell out of bed.*

AWAKE(N) ▸ TO

awake(n) someone to something to make someone alert to something, such as a problem or a need. (*Someone* includes *oneself.*) ☐ *We need to awaken the voters to the need for more taxes.* ☐ *They awakened themselves to their callousness and began to treat other people better.*

awake(n) to something to wake up while experiencing something. ☐ *Mary awoke to the smell of freshly brewed coffee.* ☐ *I love to awaken to music.*

AWARD ▸ FOR

See the following entry.

AWARD ▸ TO

award something (to someone) (for something) AND **award (someone) something (for something)** to give a prize or reward to someone (for something). ☐ *The committee awarded a plaque to Andy for his loyalty.* ☐ *They awarded prizes for thoroughness to two different people.* ☐ *They awarded Andy a prize for running the fastest.*

award something to someone or something [for a judge or other legal body] to decide in favor of a person or group. ☐ *The judge awarded the judgment to the plaintiff.* ☐ *The jury awarded a large sum to the smaller company.*

B

BABY-SIT ▸ FOR

baby-sit for someone 1. AND **baby-sit with someone** to attend and care for a child for a period of time. □ *I'm looking for someone to baby-sit for my cousin.* □ *Will you baby-sit with my cousin?* **2.** to attend and care for a child for someone for a short period of time. □ *Would you mind baby-sitting with Roger for me for a few minutes?* □ *Sure, I will baby-sit for you.*

BABY-SIT ▸ WITH

baby-sit with someone See the previous entry.

BACK ▸ AWAY

back away (from someone or something) AND **back off (from someone or something) 1.** to move backwards from a person or thing; to withdraw physically from someone or something. □ *You should back away from the fire.* □ *Please back off from the man who is threatening you.* □ *You should back off.* □ *Jane backed away.* **2.** to begin to appear uninterested in someone or something; to withdraw one's interest from someone or something. (Figurative.) □ *The board of directors began to back away from the idea of taking over the other company.* □ *They backed off from the whole idea.*

BACK ▸ DOWN

back down (from someone) to withdraw from a confrontation with someone. (Colloquial.) □ *The opposing army finally backed down from our attack.* □ *The protestors backed down.*

back down (from something) to withdraw from a rigid position; to yield a point in an argument. (Figurative.) □ *I hope you will find it in your heart to back down from your position.* □ *The petitioners backed down.*

back down (on something) to lessen or drop an earlier rigid position on something; to yield something in an argument. (Figurative.) □ *She backed down on her demands.* □ *In the end, she backed down.*

back down (something) to go down something backwards, such as a ladder or inclined driveway. □ *Todd backed down the ladder safely.* □ *Looking behind him, he backed down.*

BACK ▸ FOR

back someone for something to support or endorse someone for something, such as a public office. □ *We all back Tom for president.* □ *I am backing the proposal.*

BACK ▸ INTO

back into someone or something to move backwards, bumping into someone or something. (See also *back someone or something into someone or something.*) □ *I'm sorry. I didn't mean to back into you.* □ *I backed into the potted plant.*

back into something to move a car backwards into something, such as a garage or a parking space. □ *Why did you back into the parking space?* □ *Please don't back into the space.*

back someone or something into someone or something 1. to move someone or something backwards into someone or something. (As in pushing or nudging a person or steering a car or other vehicle. *Someone* includes *oneself.*) □ *Don't back your car into anyone.* □ *She backed herself into the lady behind her.* **2.** to guide or direct someone or something backwards into someone or something. (As in giving signals guiding a person's movements or giving guidance signals to a driver.) □ *Using hand signals, the attendant backed all the cars into the parking spaces.* □ *The nurse backed the woman into a little dressing room and told her to get ready.*

BACK ▸ OFF

back off (from someone or something) See *back away (from someone or something)* under *BACK ▸ AWAY.*

back someone or something off (from something) **1.** to move someone or something a short distance from something. (As in pushing or nudging a person or steering a car or other vehicle. *Someone* includes *oneself.*) □ *I backed the car off from the curb a tiny bit.* □ *I backed her off from the manhole cover, which we had to remove.* □ *Tom backed himself off from the fight.* **2.** to guide or direct someone or something a short distance from something. (As in giving signals guiding a person's movements or giving guidance signals to a driver.) □ *Sam backed the driver off from the side of the road a little way.* □ *Using signals, I backed the car off from the crushed bicycle.*

BACK ▸ ONTO

back onto someone or something to go backwards, moving or rolling onto someone or something. □ *The motorcycle backed onto my toe.* □ *Don't back onto anyone!*

back someone or something onto someone or something **1.** to move someone or something backwards onto someone or something. (As in pushing or nudging a person or steering a car or other vehicle.) □ *I backed the car onto the flowers accidentally.* □ *Don't back the car onto my toes!* **2.** to guide or direct someone or something backwards onto someone or something. (As in giving signals guiding a person's movements or giving guidance signals to a driver.) □ *Using hand signals, the mechanic backed the car onto the ramp.* □ *If you are going to guide him in this crowd, don't back him onto anyone's toes!*

BACK ▸ OUT

back out (of something) **1.** [for someone or something] to move out of something backwards. □ *The rabbit tried to back out of its burrow.* □ *The rabbit backed out.* **2.** [for someone] to withdraw from something; [for someone] to *back away (from someone or something).* □ *Are you going to try to back out of our agreement?* □ *You won't back out, will you?*

back someone or something out (of something) **1.** to move someone or something backwards out of something or some place. (As in pushing or nudging a person or steering a car or other vehicle. *Someone* includes *oneself.* The *of*-phrase is paraphrased with a *from*-phrase when the particle is transposed. See the Ⓕ example.) □ *Judy backed the car out of the garage.* Ⓣ *Please back out the car.* Ⓕ *Please back out the car from the garage.* □ *Please back the car out.* □ *She backed herself out of the room.* **2.** to guide or direct someone or something backwards out of something. (As in giving signals guiding a person's movements or giving guidance signals to a driver.) □ *Don backed Fred out of the garage.* □ *Can you help back Fred out?*

BACK ▸ OVER

back over someone or something [for a car or other vehicle] to roll backwards over someone or something. □ *Sandy backed over her brother's bicycle.* □ *She almost backed over her brother.*

BACK ▸ UP

back someone or something up to make someone or something move backwards. (*Someone* includes *oneself.*) □ *Back Bob up a little so the light on him is brighter for the photograph.* □ *Back your car up, please.* □ *With much difficulty, he backed himself up.*

back someone or something up to someone or something **1.** to move someone or something backwards to someone or something. (As in pushing or nudging a person or steering a car or other vehicle. *Someone* includes *oneself*.) □ *She backed the car up to the end of the street.* [T] *She backed up the car to the person at the end of the parking space.* □ *She backed the next guy in line up to the person behind him.* □ *He backed himself up to the wall and just stood there.* **2.** to guide or direct someone or something backwards right to someone or something. (As in giving signals guiding a person's movements or giving guidance signals to a driver.) □ *Using hand signals, Todd backed Mary up to the gas pump.* □ *He then backed his car up to the curb to get it out of the way.*

back someone up to provide someone with help in reserve; to support someone. □ *Don't worry. I will back you up when you need me.* [T] *Will you please back up Nancy over the weekend?* [N] *I am here because I am serving as Tom's backup.*

back something up **1.** to drive a car backwards. □ *Will you back your car up a little?* [T] *I will back up the car.* **2.** to give additional support or evidence about something. □ *My story of the crime will back your story up.* [T] *That backs up my story, all right.* **3.** to obstruct a pathway or channel and cause a slowdown in the flow. □ *The wreck backed the cars up for a long way.* [T] *The wreck backed up the cars.* □ *Some dead rats backed the sewer up.* [A] *The backed-up traffic extended all the way to town.*

back up [for objects] to obstruct and accumulate in a pathway or channel. □ *Something clogged the sewer and it backed up.* [A] *The backed-up sewer wasn't repaired until Tuesday.* [N] *We have a serious backup in the downstairs bathroom.*

back up to someone or something to move backwards to someone or something. (See also *back someone or something up to someone or something*.) □ *The car backed up to the hitchhiker.* □ *The bus backed up to the end of the parking space.*

back up (to something) **1.** to move backwards to something. □ *Back up a little. You are in the way.* □ *Please back up.* **2.** to go back to something said in a conversation. □ *Wait—back up a little. What did you say that phone number was?* □ *Let's back up to what you just said and go over that point again.*

BACKFIRE ▸ ON

backfire on someone [for something, such as a plot] to fail unexpectedly; to fail with an undesired result. □ *Your plot backfired on you.* □ *I was afraid that my scheme would backfire on me.*

BADGER ▸ INTO

badger someone into something to pester someone into doing something. □ *Don't try to badger us into doing it.* □ *We have been badgered into doing it.*

BAIL ▸ OUT

bail out (of something) **1.** to parachute out of an airplane. □ *The pilot bailed out of the plane at the last moment.* □ *At the last moment, he bailed out.* **2.** to escape from or abandon something. □ *I had to bail out of the company because I decided it was failing.* □ *I bailed out before it was too late.*

bail someone or something out (of something) to get someone or something out of trouble or difficulty. □ *I'm really late on this deadline and I need help. Can you bail me out?* [T] *The government will not bail out the failing banks.* □ *No one will bail us out of our difficulties.*

bail someone out (of something) to pay bail or bond money to get a person out of jail. (*Someone* includes *oneself*. The *of*-phrase is paraphrased with a *from*-phrase when the particle is transposed. See the [F] example.) □ *Try to get someone to bail me out of jail.* [T] *Can you bail out your friend?* [F] *Can you bail out your friend from jail?* □ *I don't want to bail him out.* [A] *The bailed-out crook robbed another liquor store that afternoon.* □ *She bailed herself out of jail with her last fifty dollars.*

bail something out to empty a boat of accumulated water. □ *Would you bail* *this boat out?* 🅃 *I will bail out the boat.* 🄰 *I'll take the already-bailed-out boat, thanks.*

bail something out (of something) to take out accumulated water from a boat. (The *of*-phrase is paraphrased with a *from*-phrase when the particle is transposed. See the 🄵 example.) ☐ *Please bail all this water out of the boat.* 🅃 *Yes, bail out the water, please.* 🄵 *Yes, bail out the water from the boat, please.* ☐ *I will bail the water out.*

BALANCE ▸ AGAINST

balance something against something to consider one thing in reference to another; to weigh one possibility against another possibility. ☐ *We will have to balance all the good he did against all the bad.* ☐ *The good will be balanced against the bad in the final reckoning.*

BALANCE ▸ OUT

balance out to equal out; to become even or fair. ☐ *These things all balance out in the end.* ☐ *Don't worry. Things will balance out.*

BALANCE ▸ WITH

balance something with something to offset something with something else; to balance something against something. ☐ *He tends to balance a harsh grading scheme with a strong sense of fair play.* ☐ *Roger balanced the tart soup with a bland first course.* ☐ *They balanced the bad behavior with the good, but still felt there was too much rudeness.*

BALK ▸ AT

balk at something to resist and object to something; to shy away from doing something. ☐ *I hope they don't balk at doing it.* ☐ *They will probably balk at it.*

BALL ▸ UP

ball someone or something up to interfere with someone or something; to mess someone or something up. (Slang. *Someone* includes *oneself.*) ☐ *Who balled this television up?* 🅃 *Someone balled up the television.* ☐ *I hope he doesn't ball me up again.* ☐ *She balled herself up by being late.*

ball something up to roll something up into a ball. ☐ *She balled the clay up and stuck it to the clown's face as a nose.* 🅃 *Why are you balling up the paper?* 🄰 *The balled-up paper wad hit the back of Henry's neck.*

BAN ▸ FROM

ban someone from something **1.** to prohibit someone from doing something. ☐ *We banned everyone from smoking.* ☐ *Everyone has been banned from smoking.* **2.** to prohibit someone from entering something or some place. (The same as *bar someone from some place.*) ☐ *They banned us from the building.* ☐ *The manager banned the children from the theater.*

BAND ▸ TOGETHER

band together (against someone or something) to unite in opposition to someone or something; to unite against someone or something. ☐ *We must band together against the enemy.* ☐ *Everyone banded together.*

BANDAGE ▸ UP

bandage someone or something up to wrap bandages on someone or on someone's wounds. (*Someone* includes *oneself.*) ☐ *We should bandage the wounds up first.* 🅃 *We should bandage up the wounds first.* ☐ *I have to bandage him up before we can move him.* 🄰 *Who is the bandaged-up person over there?* ☐ *She bandaged herself up with the supplies she kept in her backpack.*

BANDY ▸ ABOUT

bandy something about **1.** to spread something, such as someone's good name, around in an unfavorable context; to toss words around in a gossipy fashion. ☐ *Now please don't bandy this matter about to everyone.* 🅃 *There is no need to keep bandying about those rumors.* **2.** to announce something carelessly; to state something casually and inaccurately. ☐ *Stop bandying these matters about so casually.* 🅃 *Why bandy about someone else's business?*

BANDY ▸ WITH

bandy with someone to argue [with someone]; to argue by "playing catch with words." □ *Why are you bandying with me?* □ *She has been bandied with enough. Give her a straight answer.*

BANG ▸ AGAINST

bang against someone or something to knock or strike against someone or something. □ *The shutter banged against the side of the house.* □ *The board banged against me and hurt my shin.*

bang one's head against a brick wall to do something stupid and futile. (Idiomatic. See also *beat one's head against the wall* under *BEAT▸ AGAINST*.) □ *You can't do anything about this. You are just banging your head against a brick wall.* □ *I've got to stop banging my head against a brick wall.*

bang something against someone or something to strike something against someone or something. (Usually refers to striking with something that can make a banging noise.) □ *She banged the spoon against the pan to call everyone to dinner.* □ *He banged the pan against me and made me very angry.*

BANG ▸ AROUND

bang someone or something around to knock someone or something about; to beat or strike someone or something. (*Someone* includes *oneself*.) □ *Let's bang him around a little and see if that will change his mind.* [T] *Why are you banging around my friend?* □ *Don't bang those pans around.* □ *He banged himself around badly in the car wreck.*

BANG ▸ AWAY

bang (away) at something to hit at something repeatedly, causing harm or making noise. □ *Someone is banging away at the door.* □ *Stop banging at the door.*

BANG ▸ IN

bang something in to crush something; to dent or collapse something. □ *Who banged the side of the washing machine in?* [T] *Who banged in the side of the washing machine?* □ *Ted banged in his head on a beam.* [A] *The banged-in door has to be repaired*

BANG ▸ INTO

bang into someone or something to knock or bump into someone or something. □ *Why did you bang into me with your car?* □ *I banged into the door by accident.*

bang something into someone or something to strike someone or something with something. □ *Mark banged his fist into the cushion and swore.* □ *He banged the pole into Liz by accident.*

BANG ▸ ON

bang on someone or something to strike someone or something repeatedly. (Especially to beat on a person or a drum.) □ *Please stop banging on that drum!* □ *Max was banging on Lefty when the cops arrived.*

BANG ▸ OUT

bang something out to play something on the piano, loudly, banging on the keys; to type something on a typewriter by pounding on the keys. (Colloquial.) □ *Let me bang this melody out and see if you can guess who wrote it.* [T] *Please bang out the school song good and loud.* □ *I have to bang out a term paper to turn in tomorrow morning.*

BANG ▸ UP

bang someone up to beat someone up; to assault someone; to damage someone. (*Someone* includes *oneself*.) □ *The crooks banged him up a little bit.* [T] *The crash banged up the passengers in the car.* □ *She banged herself up badly.*

bang something up to crash or wreck something; to damage something. □ *Don't bang my stockpot up!* [T] *Who banged up my stockpot?* [A] *The banged-up old coffeepot serves our needs quite well.*

BANISH ▸ FROM

banish someone or something from some place to ban or evict someone or something from some place. □ *The town council banished motorcycles from all the parks in the town.* □ *The new law banished vagrants from the train station.*

BANK ▸ ON

bank on something to *depend on something;* to be so sure of something that one can trust it as one trusts a bank. (Idiomatic.) □ *I will be there on time. You can bank on it.* □ *I need a promise of your help. I hope I can bank on it.*

BANK ▸ UP

bank something up (against something) **1.** to heap or mound up something so that it presses against something. □ *Walter banked the coals up against the side of the furnace.* 🅃 *He banked up the coals against the side.* □ *Tim banked the coals up.* 🄰 *The banked-up dirt rested against the base of the cliff.* **2.** to heap or mound up something to guard against something. □ *They had to build barriers to hide behind. They banked dirt and rubble up against the oncoming attackers.* 🅃 *Who banked up this dirt against the flood?* □ *The river was rising, so we banked some dirt up.*

BAR ▸ FROM

bar someone from some place to prevent someone from entering some place. (See also *ban someone from something.*) □ *Please don't bar me from the movie theater. I will be quiet from now on.* □ *They were barred from the concert.*

BARE ▸ TO

bare something to someone to reveal or disclose something to someone. □ *I have to know a guy pretty well before I will bare my innermost thoughts to him.* □ *Our involvement was bared to the judge.*

BARF ▸ OUT

barf out to *freak out;* to become deranged, to a greater or lesser degree. (Slang.) □ *Terry barfed out when he heard about the damage Nick had done to his car.* □ *I thought I was going to barf out.*

barf someone out to disgust someone. (Slang. *Someone* includes *oneself.*) □ *You just barf me out!* 🅃 *Roger barfed out everyone at the party.* □ *I barf myself out every time I look in the mirror.*

BARGAIN ▸ FOR

bargain for someone or something See under *BARGAIN ▸ OVER.*

bargain for something to expect or anticipate something; to foresee something. □ *I didn't bargain for this.* 🄰 *The bargained-for price was probably still too high.*

BARGAIN ▸ ON

bargain on something to depend on something; to count on something. □ *I did bargain on Fred's resigning the position.* □ *Is this what we bargained on?*

BARGAIN ▸ OVER

bargain (over someone or something) (with someone) AND **bargain (for someone or something) (with someone)** to negotiate with someone about obtaining someone or something. □ *I refuse to bargain over money with Dan.* □ *We will bargain with the supplier over prices.* □ *You can't bargain over Claire with Jeff as if she were produce!* □ *You can't bargain for people.*

BARGAIN ▸ WITH

See the previous entry.

BARGE ▸ IN

barge in on someone or something to go or come rudely into a place and interrupt people or their activities. □ *Albert barged in on Ted without knocking.* □ *I didn't mean to barge in on your meeting.*

BARGE ▸ INTO

barge into someone or something to bump or crash into someone or something, possibly on purpose. □ *She just barged into me and nearly knocked me over.* □ *Tom barged into the water cooler and hurt his knee.*

BARGE ▸ IN(TO)

barge in(to some place) to go or come rudely into some place. (See also *barge into someone or something.*) □ *He just barged right in without knocking.* □ *Don't barge in like that!*

BARK ▸ AT

bark at someone to speak harshly to someone. □ *Don't bark at me like that!* □ *Ken barked at the children.*

bark at someone or something [for a dog] to make a characteristic sharp sound at someone or something. ☐ *The dog is barking at the traffic again.* ☐ *Their huge dog was barking at me.*

bark something (out) (at someone) See the following entry.

BARK ▶ OUT

bark something (out) (at someone) to say something harshly to someone. ☐ *The sergeant barked the orders out at the recruits.* ☐ *He barked the order at the recruits.* ☐ *He barked the order out.* 🄰 *The barked-out commands frightened them at first.*

BARREL ▶ ALONG

barrel along to move along rapidly. ☐ *The car was barreling along at a fairly rapid clip.* ☐ *Don't barrel along so fast.*

BARREL ▶ IN(TO)

barrel in(to some place) to move into a place rapidly and with great force. ☐ *Tony barreled into the room and interrupted the card game.* ☐ *He just barreled in without knocking.*

BARREL ▶ OUT

barrel out (of some place) to move rapidly out of a place; to burst out of a place. ☐ *The kids barreled out of town as fast as they could go.* ☐ *They heard the police siren and barreled out.*

BARTER ▶ AWAY

barter something away to trade something away; to lose something of value in a trade. ☐ *Don't barter my car away!* 🅃 *Don't barter away anything of such high value.*

BARTER ▶ FOR

barter for something to trade [something] for something else. ☐ *I want to barter for a large amount of cloth.* ☐ *Will you barter for this?*

barter something for something to trade something for something else. ☐ *He sought to barter the car for a large computer.* ☐ *She bartered the piano for a settee.*

BARTER ▶ OFF

barter something off to get rid of something by trading it for something else. ☐ *See if you can barter that old desk off.* 🅃 *She bartered off the desk.*

BARTER ▶ WITH

barter with someone to enter into trading with someone; to bargain with someone. ☐ *Are you willing to barter with me, or is this a cash transaction?*

BASE ▶ (UP)ON

base something (up)on someone or something to ground something, such as one's opinion, decision, or thinking, on someone or something; to found one's ideas or attitude on something. (*Upon* is formal and less commonly used than *on*.) ☐ *I base my opinion on many, many facts.* ☐ *I based my opinion upon my own seasoned judgment.*

BASH ▶ AGAINST

bash something against someone or something to strike something against someone or something. ☐ *He accidentally bashed his head against a beam.* ☐ *She bashed her sore elbow against Ted and hurt them both.*

BASH ▶ AROUND

bash someone or something around to treat someone or something roughly; to beat on someone or something. ☐ *Stop bashing me around, and let's talk.* 🅃 *The robber looked as though he would bash around the clerks.* ☐ *He got mad and bashed around the furniture and then calmed down.*

BASH ▶ IN

bash something in to crush something in. ☐ *Don't bash the door in!* 🅃 *It sounds like someone is bashing in the door.* 🄰 *Do I have to wear this bashed-in hat?*

BASH ▶ UP

bash something up to crash something; to strike something and damage it. ☐ *She bashed the car up badly.* 🅃 *How did she bash up the car?* 🄰 *Please move your bashed-up car away from the front of my house.*

BASK ▶ IN

bask in something to enjoy or revel in something, such as praise, sunshine, fame, etc. ☐ *Alice enjoyed basking in* *her newfound fame.* ☐ *Lily loves basking in praise.*

BAT ▸ AROUND

bat something around **1.** to knock something around with a bat or something similar. ☐ *Terry spent a little time batting a ball around, then he went home.* 🅃 *Let's bat around some balls before we go home.* **2.** to discuss something back and forth. (Figurative.) ☐ *Let's bat this around a little bit tomorrow at our meeting.* 🅃 *Do you want to bat around this matter a little more?*

BATHE ▸ IN

bathe someone or something in something **1.** to cleanse someone or something in something; to coat someone or something all over with some liquid. (In a container of liquid or the liquid itself. *Someone* includes *oneself.*) ☐ *She bathed the baby in warm water.* ☐ *Liz bathed the injured hand in cold water.* ☐ *She bathed herself in the warm springwater and took a long nap under a tree.* **2.** to blanket or spread over someone or something, as with light, vapor, color, etc. ☐ *The candles bathed her in a soft glow.* ☐ *The red of the sunset bathed the trees in an eerie light.*

BATTEN ▸ DOWN

batten something down **1.** to close and seal the cargo hatches on a ship. (Almost always with a ship's *hatches*, as in preparation for a storm at sea.) ☐ *Batten those hatches down before the captain comes by.* 🅃 *Batten down the hatches now!* 🄰 *The poorly battened-down hatches gave way during the storm.* **2.** to close and seal something, such as a window. ☐ *Let's batten these windows down before the storm gets here.* 🅃 *Who is supposed to batten down the windows?*

BATTER ▸ DOWN

batter something down to smash or break down something, such as a wall, door, or (figuratively) any defenses. ☐ *Do they have to batter anything down as part of the construction project?* 🅃 *They battered down the wall as a first step in enlarging the house.*

BATTER ▸ UP

batter someone or something up to damage or harm someone or something. (*Someone* includes *oneself.*) ☐ *Who battered this desk up?* 🅃 *Max threatened to batter up Lefty within an inch of his life.* 🅃 *You really battered up that old car of yours.* 🄰 *What a battered-up old car!* ☐ *You will batter yourself up badly if you fall off this ledge.*

BATTLE ▸ AGAINST

battle against someone or something to wage a fight against someone or something; to attempt to defeat someone or something. ☐ *We are battling against the ancient enemies of ignorance and hatred.* ☐ *I am tired of battling against Karen.*

BATTLE ▸ FOR

battle for something to attempt to win or gain something by fighting or arguing. ☐ *Both of them battled for Kristina's attention.* ☐ *The boys battled for the last piece of cake.*

BATTLE ▸ OVER

See the following entry.

BATTLE ▸ WITH

battle (with someone) (over someone or something) to argue or struggle with someone over someone or something. ☐ *Why do you always have to battle with me over practically nothing?* ☐ *You can't battle over just anything with just anybody!*

BAWL ▸ OUT

bawl someone out to scold someone. ☐ *Then Maggie proceeded to bawl Tony out.* 🅃 *You can't bawl out everyone who was involved. There are too many.*

BAY ▸ AT

bay at something to howl at something. (Usually said of a dog.) ☐ *The dogs were baying at the moon.* ☐ *That animal must be stopped from baying at the moon.*

BE ▸ ABACK

be taken aback to be surprised or disconcerted. (*Taken* is the past participle of *take*, functioning here as an adjective.) ☐ *We were really taken aback by* *her announcement.* □ *No one was more taken aback than I.*

BE ▸ ABOUT

be about to be moving from place to place; to be functioning. (See also *be up and about*.) □ *Is she about yet, or is she still recovering?* □ *Lily is not about yet.*

be about something to be in the process of doing something. □ *You must be about your business, mustn't you?* □ *What are you about now?* □ *I'd better be about my yard work.*

be about to do something to be almost ready to start doing something; to be on the verge of doing something. □ *I am about to leave.* □ *We were about to start eating when the telephone rang.*

BE ▸ ABOVE

be above someone or something to be over someone or something. □ *The plane is now directly above us.* □ *The new painting is above the chair.*

be above something to be too honorable to do something. □ *I thought you were above doing something like what you did.* □ *I am not above a little rough talk.*

BE ▸ AFTER

be after someone or something **1.** to follow someone or something. □ *Tom is after Mary in the line.* □ *Your appointment is after our coffee break.* **2.** to be in pursuit of someone or something. □ *Fred is after Laurie, and he may catch her.* □ *The dog is after a rabbit.*

BE ▸ AGAINST

be against someone or something to be opposed to someone or something. □ *I am against everything you stand for.* □ *Basically, I am against you!*

BE ▸ AROUND

be around someone or something **1.** [for something] to enclose someone or something. □ *The white picket fence is around the house and the yard.* □ *Jimmy was crying loudly. A ring of children was around him, singing "Happy Birthday."* **2.** [for someone or something] to be near someone or something. □ *How long have you been around here?* □ *I don't like people like that to be around me.*

BE ▸ AT

be at a dead end to have reached an impasse; to be able to go no further forward. □ *I can't go on. I'm at a dead end.* □ *We are at a dead end.*

be at an end to have come to a stop; to have reached the end. □ *Things are now at an end.* □ *We are at an end. Goodbye.*

be at loggerheads [for two or more people] to be in contention with each other. □ *They are at loggerheads, as they have been for years.* □ *Sam and I are usually at loggerheads.*

be at loggerheads with someone to be in conflict with someone; to have reached an impasse with someone. □ *Tom is at loggerheads with Bill.* □ *We are at loggerheads with each other.*

be at someone to be argumentative or contentious with someone. □ *She is always at him about something.* □ *I wish you weren't at me all the time.*

be at something to be doing something. (Especially in questions.) □ *What are you at now?* □ *I'm at roof repair.*

be disappointed at someone or something to become sad because of someone or something. (*Disappointed* is the past participle of *disappoint*, functioning here as an adjective.) □ *I am very disappointed at you.* □ *I am really disappointed at what you did.*

be disgusted at someone or something to be sickened at someone or something. (*Disgusted* is the past participle of *disgust*, functioning here as an adjective.) □ *We were disgusted at her carrying-on.* □ *Sam was disgusted at her.*

be revolted at someone or something to be sickened by someone or something. (*Revolted* is the past participle of *revolt*, functioning here as an adjective.) □ *I was revolted at Frank and his behavior.* □ *We were all revolted at the scene of the highway accident.*

BE ▸ AWAY

be away **1.** to be on vacation; to be somewhere else. □ *She is away now. I'll* *have her call you when she gets back.* □ *I was away when you called.* **2.** to be in jail or prison. (Slang.) □ *Lefty's away and will be for a few years.* □ *He is away for a lengthy term.*

BE ▸ BACK

be laid-back to be relaxed and confident. (Informal. *Laid* is the past participle of *lay*, functioning here as an adjective.) □ *The guy is really laid-back. Nothing gets him upset.* □ *Mary is totally laid-back.* □ *The guy is so totally laid-back that nothing fazes him.*

BE ▸ BEFORE

be before someone to be ahead of or in front of someone. □ *Who is before Mary?* □ *I am before all of you.*

be before someone's time to happen before someone was born or old enough to know what was going on. □ *Of course I don't remember it. It was before my time.* □ *All that was before your time.*

BE ▸ BEHIND

be behind bars to be in jail. □ *Very soon, you will be behind bars.* □ *Max should be behind bars.*

be behind (in something) to have failed to do one's work on time; to have failed to keep up with one's work. □ *I can't go out tonight. I'm behind in my work.* □ *I don't like to be behind.*

be behind someone or something **1.** to be to the rear of someone or something. □ *Someone is behind you. Watch out!* □ *Someone is behind the door!* **2.** to support or promote someone or something. □ *I am behind you one hundred percent.* □ *Our committee is behind your proposal.*

be behind the times to be old-fashioned or out of date. □ *You are so old-fashioned! You are too far behind the times.* □ *I am not behind the times.*

BE ▸ BELOW

be below someone to rank below someone. □ *I am below Terri, but my scores are better than Carol's.* □ *I am below everyone in the class.*

be below someone or something to be positioned under or lower than someone or something. □ *The sun is below the horizon.* □ *The swimming hole is below the dam.* □ *Ted and Bill are on the ladder. Ted is below Bill, handing the paint can up to him.*

BE ▸ BENEATH

be beneath contempt to be exceedingly contemptible. □ *What you have done is beneath contempt.* □ *That is beneath contempt.*

be beneath one's dignity [for an act] to be too rude or coarse for someone to do. □ *That kind of thing is beneath my dignity, and I hope yours.* □ *I would have thought something like that to be beneath your dignity.*

be beneath someone [for an act] to be too rude or coarse for someone to do. □ *That kind of thing is beneath Fred. I'm appalled that he did it.* □ *That is beneath you!*

be beneath something to be under or beneath something. □ *What is that beneath the table?* □ *The cat is beneath the piano.*

BE ▸ BESIDE

be beside oneself (with something) to be confused or upset with some emotion in particular. □ *She was beside herself with anger.* □ *She was so angry! She was beside herself.*

be beside the point to be irrelevant; to fail to support the point of information. □ *That is beside the point. Do you have other reasons?* □ *What you said is beside the point.*

BE ▸ BETWEEN

be between someone and someone else or something and something else [for a choice to exist] between a selection of people or a selection of things. □ *The choice is between Fred and Jill.* □ *It's between chocolate cake and cherry pie.*

be divided between something to be separated into different categories. (*Divided* is the past participle of *divide*, functioning here as an adjective.) □ *The applicants for the job seemed to be divided between the overqualified and the* *underqualified.* □ *The dogs were divided evenly between terriers and poodles.*

be torn between someone and someone else or something and something else to be uncertain whether to choose one or the other. (*Torn* is the past participle of *tear*, functioning here as an adjective.) □ *I don't know which to take. I'm torn between Fred and Alice.* □ *I'm torn between red and green.*

BE ▸ BEYOND

be beyond something **1.** to be beyond the help of anything. □ *The poor dog that was hit by a truck is beyond help.* □ *It is beyond the point at which you could help it.* **2.** [for someone] to be in too extreme a state to feel or care. □ *Do what you want. I am beyond caring.* □ *The patient is beyond feeling. It doesn't matter now.*

BE ▸ BY

be possessed by something to be obsessed or driven by something. (*Possessed* is the past participle of *possess*, functioning here as an adjective.) □ *Ned was possessed by a desire to become the best at everything he did.* □ *Jan acts as if she is possessed by the need to be right all the time.*

BE ▸ DOWN

be down **1.** See *be down (from some place)*. **2.** to be depressed or melancholy. □ *Ann's down a little. I think it's just the weather.* □ *I'm always down after a performance.*

be down to be inoperable; to be not working. (Typically and originally said of a computer.) □ *The computer is down again.* □ *My television set was down and I couldn't watch the football game.*

be down and out to be depressed and destitute. □ *The vagrant was down and out, so I gave him a dollar.* □ *I was down and out until I found myself.*

be down at the heels to be worn down; to *be down and out;* to show signs of wear. □ *He is a little down at the heels, but give him a new suit of clothes and he'll look just great.* □ *This jacket is a little down at the heels.*

be down for something to have one's name written down for something. □ *Am I down for an evening appointment?* □ *You are down for Friday.*

be down for the count to be eliminated from something for a period of time, perhaps permanently. (As with a boxer who has been knocked out for the full count of ten.) □ *I can't continue with this course. I'm down for the count.* □ *I'm down for the count. I can't go on.*

be down (from some place) to have come down from some higher place. □ *Billy's down from his tree house.* □ *Is Billy down yet?*

be down on someone or something to be against someone or something. (See also *get down on someone or something.*) □ *You've been down on us all lately.* □ *I'm down on computers lately.*

be down to something to have only a certain thing left. □ *I'm down to my last nickel.* □ *Lily is down to her last dollar.*

be down with something to be sick with some disease. □ *She's down with the flu.* □ *Lily is down with a sore throat.*

BE ▸ FOR

be (all) for someone or something to be (completely) in favor of someone or something; to support someone or something. □ *I'm all for your candidacy.* □ *I'm for Jill in the election.*

be destined for something to be predetermined to achieve or become something. (*Destined* is the past participle of *destine*, functioning here as an adjective.) □ *I know I am destined for something better than this.* □ *We are destined for death in the long run.*

be done for to be finished; to be dead. (*Done* is the past participle of *do*, functioning here as an adjective.) □ *I'm afraid that your cat is done for.* □ *The goldfish looked as if it was either done for or sunning its tummy.*

be headed for something to be destined for something. (*Headed* is the past participle of *head*, functioning here as an adjective.) □ *Harry is headed for real trouble.* □ *She is headed for a breakdown.* □ *They told me I was headed for something really big if I just paid attention to what I said to people.*

be made for someone to have been created to make someone happy; to have been created to please someone or look good on someone in particular. (*Made* is the past participle of *make*, functioning here as an adjective.) □ *You were made for me. I'm glad we got married.* □ *This suit was just made for me!* □ *I was so pleased to find this hat on sale. It seems to be made for me.*

be made for something to have been designed or manufactured for some purpose; to be very suitable for something or some purpose. (*Made* is the past participle of *make*, functioning here as an adjective.) □ *This night was made for love.* □ *This tool was not made for this project.* □ *This wrench is manufactured from the strongest metal. It is made for jobs just like this one.*

be noted for something to be famed for something; to be memorable for something. (*Noted* is the past participle of *note*, functioning here as an adjective.) □ *We were all noted for our polite manners.* □ *The restaurant was noted for its traditional fare.* □ *Tom was noted far and wide for his excellent pies and cakes.* □ *Her course was noted for being extraordinarily hard to get a good grade in.*

be pleased for someone or something to be happy for someone or a group. (*Pleased* is the past participle of *please*, functioning here as an adjective.) □ *I am very pleased for you.* □ *We were all pleased for the committee. The members got all the praise they deserved.* □ *Everyone could see how pleased Sam was for himself and his whole family.*

be pressed for money AND **be pressed for cash, be pushed for cash, be pushed for money** to be needful of money; to be short of money. (*Pressed* is the past participle of *press*, functioning here as an adjective. *Pushed* is the past participle of *push*, functioning here as an adjective.) □ *She is pressed for cash at the present time.* □ *I'm a little pressed for cash at the moment.* □ *We are usually pushed for money at this time of year.* □ *I'm a little pressed for money just now.*

be pressed for time AND **be pushed for time** to be needful of time. (*Pressed* is the past participle of *press*, functioning here as an adjective. *Pushed* is the past participle of *push*, functioning here as an adjective.) □ *If I weren't so pressed for time, I could help you.* □ *I can't talk to you. I'm too pushed for time.* □ *Can't talk to you now. I'm pressed for time.*

be strapped for something to be needing something, usually money. (*Strapped* is the past participle of *strap*, functioning here as an adjective.) □ *I am really strapped for cash. Can you lend me some?* □ *Ted is strapped for money and cannot pay his bills.*

be suited for something to be appropriate for something. (*Suited* is the past participle of *suit*, functioning here as an adjective.) □ *Do you think I am suited for this kind of work?* □ *Mary is well suited for anything dealing with numbers.* □ *Those clothes are not suited for this kind of work.*

BE ▸ FROM

be estranged from someone to be alienated from someone. (*Estranged* is the past participle of *estrange*, functioning here as an adjective.) □ *Toward the end, they were estranged from each other, so a separation was perfectly natural.* □ *She had been estranged from her husband for a number of years.*

be from some place to have originated at some place; to have moved here from some place. □ *I am from Kansas.* □ *Where are you from?*

BE ▸ IN

be all in to be completely tired. □ *I'm all in. I need some rest.* □ *Are you all in yet?*

be disappointed in someone or something to be displeased with someone or something. (*Disappointed* is the past participle of *disappoint*, functioning here as an adjective.) □ *I am very disappointed in you. That was a terrible thing to do.* □ *They were disappointed in the outcome.*

be done in [for someone] to be exhausted. (*Done* is the past participle of *do*, functioning here as an adjective.) □ *I'm really done in!* □ *After all that lifting, Gerald was done in and breathing hard.*

be in to be in attendance; to be available; to be in one's office. □ *Is the doctor in?* □ *Mr. Franklin is not in.*

be in a rut to be in a dull and repetitive routine. □ *I'm so tired of this. I'm really in a rut.* □ *We are all in a rut.*

be in accord (with someone or something) (about someone or something) to agree with someone or something. □ *I am in complete accord with you about the policy changes.* □ *We are in accord about the proposal.* □ *They are in accord with us.*

be in agreement with someone or something to be in conformity with someone or something; to agree with someone or something. □ *We are in total agreement with you.* □ *I am in agreement with your proposal.*

be in at the kill AND **be in on the kill** to be involved at the final moment of something in order to share in the spoils. □ *At the end of the battle, everyone wanted to be in at the kill.* □ *The politicians wanted to be in on the kill.*

be in bloom See the following entry.

be in blossom AND **be in bloom** to be blooming; to be covered with blossoms. □ *All the apple trees are in blossom now.* □ *When are the fruit trees in bloom in this part of the country?*

be in charge of someone or something to supervise someone or something; to be responsible for someone or something. □ *Who is in charge of these children?* □ *I am in charge of all the computers.*

be in contact (with someone or something) to communicate with someone or a group; to share information with someone or a group. □ *I have been in contact with our supplier, who will deliver the part next week.* □ *I am in contact with the Senate committee now.*

be in control of someone or something **1.** to *be in charge of someone or something.* □ *Who is in control of this place?* □ *I am not in control of her. She works for another department.* **2.** to have someone or something mastered or subdued; to have achieved management of someone or something. □ *You should be in control of your dog at all times.* □ *The attendant was instructed to be in control of his patient at all times.*

be in fashion to be in style; to be current and orthodox. □ *Is that kind of thing still in fashion?* □ *It won't be in fashion very long.*

be in focus to be perceived clearly. (Either visual and metaphorical focus.) □ *The picture is not in focus.* □ *Now that things are in focus, I feel better about the world.*

be in for something to be destined for something. (Often punishment.) □ *Now you are in for it!* □ *We are in for a long rainy period.*

be in force [for a rule or law] to be currently valid or in effect. □ *Is this rule in force now?* □ *The constitution is still in force.*

be in hand to be in one's possession. □ *It's in hand. I have it right here.* □ *The papers are in hand. Have no fear.*

be in harmony to be in musical concord or tune. □ *They are not in harmony.* □ *The instruments are in perfect harmony.*

be in harmony with someone or something **1.** to be in musical concord with someone or something. □ *This part is in harmony with the tenor's solo.* □ *The tenor part is not in harmony with the accompaniment.* **2.** to be agreeable or compatible with someone or something. □ *This is in complete harmony with our earlier discussions.* □ *Fred's position is* *quite clear. What you have said is not in harmony with Fred.*

be in jeopardy to be at risk; to be at peril. ☐ *Now everything is in jeopardy.* ☐ *Nothing is in jeopardy.*

be in line to wait in a line of people or traffic. ☐ *I was in line for over an hour.* ☐ *How long were you in line?*

be in line with something to agree with what was anticipated, predicted, or decided on. ☐ *This is completely in line with our predictions.* ☐ *What happened was not in line with what I had expected.*

be in on something to share in something; to be involved in something. ☐ *I want to be in on the planning of the party.* ☐ *I wasn't in on it.*

be in on the ground floor to be involved with something from the very beginning. ☐ *I'm sure you will want to be in on the ground floor.* ☐ *I would like to be in on the ground floor in this deal.*

be in on the kill See *be in at the kill.*

be in over one's head (with someone or something) to be too deeply involved with someone or something. ☐ *They are all in over their heads with this money business.* ☐ *I'm really in over my head.*

be in play **1.** [for a ball, in a game] to be under the effect of the rules of the game. ☐ *The ball is in play again and the activity is furious.* ☐ *The ball is not in play yet.* **2.** [for a company] to be in the process of being taken over by another company. ☐ *The company I bought stock in is now in play.* ☐ *This stock is in play.*

be in power to be in control; to be in charge. ☐ *Who is in power now?* ☐ *No one is in power.*

be in press [for a book] to be in the process of being printed. ☐ *This book is in press. It won't be available for at least two months.* ☐ *This book has been in press for a long time.*

be in season **1.** [for a game animal] to be subject to legal hunting. ☐ *You cannot shoot ducks. They are not in season.* ☐ *Geese are not in season now.* **2.** [for a female animal] to be ready to breed, in estrus, or in heat. ☐ *It's just a nightmare when my dogs are in season.* ☐ *The cat's in season again.*

be in service [for something] to be operating or operable. ☐ *Is this elevator in service?* ☐ *This machine is not in service.*

be in sight **1.** to be within the range of vision; to be visible. ☐ *The goal is in sight.* ☐ *The end of the road is in sight.* **2.** to be known; to be expected. (Figurative.) ☐ *The end of the project is finally in sight.* ☐ *The rain is expected to continue for days. There is no end in sight.*

be in someone's possession to be held by someone; to be owned by someone. ☐ *The book is now in my possession.* ☐ *How long has this object been in your possession?*

be in something **1.** to be within something. ☐ *The cat is in the closet.* ☐ *Lily is in the other room.* **2.** to be in a particular type of business; to deal in a particular product in business. ☐ *Yes, I used to work for the government, but now I am in private industry.* ☐ *Lily is in dancing.*

be in something for someone to have a value for someone; to have a benefit for someone. (Usually a question: **What's in it for me?**) ☐ *What is in this deal for me?* ☐ *There is a lot of money in it for you.*

be in (something) over one's head to be too deeply involved with something. (Compare to *be in over one's head (with someone or something).*) ☐ *This is too much. I am really in over my head.* ☐ *Liz is in this project over her head.*

be in the clear to be safely away from hazard, trouble, or suspicion. ☐ *The police won't arrest you. You are in the clear.* ☐ *I was in the clear when the building collapsed.*

be in the right to be correct; to be morally or legally correct. ☐ *I know I'm in the right.* ☐ *You are not in the right on this point.*

be in the wrong to be wrong; to be morally or legally incorrect. ☐ *I am not in the wrong, you are.* ☐ *No, you are in the wrong.*

be in touch with someone or something **1.** to be sympathetic or sensitive to someone or something; to have contact with someone or something. □ *We talk to each other, but we're not really in touch with each other.* □ *She needs to try more to be in touch with herself and her feelings.* **2.** to be in communication with someone or a group. □ *Are you in touch with your brother, or have you two grown apart?* □ *I am in touch with the person whom you asked about.*

be in tune with someone or something to be in agreement or harmony with someone or something. □ *The violin is in tune with the piano.* □ *The tenor is not in tune with the bass.*

be in use [for some facility or device] to be occupied or busy. □ *Sorry, this room is in use.* □ *How long will it be in use?*

be in vogue to be fashionable; to be faddish. □ *This style of coat is no longer in vogue.* □ *That word isn't in vogue any longer.*

be in with someone to be favored by someone; to experience someone's good will. □ *I'm really in with my Spanish professor.* □ *I am trying to get in with the bank manager so I can get a loan.*

be lost in something to be enveloped in something; engrossed in something. (*Lost* is the past participle of *lose*, functioning here as an adjective.) □ *Ed sat under the tree, lost in reverie.* □ *Excuse me. I didn't hear you. I was lost in my own thoughts.*

be (out) in the open **1.** to be visible in an open space; to be exposed in an open area. □ *The trucks are out in the open where we can see them.* □ *They're in the open.* **2.** [for something] to be public knowledge. □ *Is this matter out in the open, or is it still secret?* □ *Let's get this in the open and discuss it.*

be well in hand to be under control. □ *Is that matter well in hand?* □ *Everything is well in hand. Don't worry.*

BE ► INSIDE

be inside to be indoors; to be within something. □ *I was inside almost all winter.* □ *It is better to be inside when it is freezing.*

BE ► INTO

be into something **1.** to interfere or meddle with something. □ *She is always into other people's business.* □ *I'm sorry I'm into your affairs so much.* **2.** to be interested or involved in something. (Slang.) □ *I'm into model planes right now.* □ *Are you into Chinese food?*

be well into something to be far into something or far along in something. □ *It was well into the morning before she awoke.* □ *The car was well into the tunnel when it broke down.*

BE ► OF

be abreast of something to be up to date on something. □ *Are you abreast of the news, or do you just ignore it all?*

be bereft of someone or something to be left without someone or something. (*Bereft* is the past participle of *bereave*, functioning here as an adjective.) □ *Tom was bereft of all hope.* □ *The child was bereft of his parents.*

be composed of something to be assembled or made out of something. (*Composed* is the past participle of *compose*, functioning here as an adjective.) □ *This cloth is composed of a number of different kinds of fibers.* □ *The committee is composed of people from every department.*

be comprised of someone or something to be made up of someone or something. (*Comprised* is the past participle of *comprise*, functioning here as an adjective.) □ *The committee was comprised of representatives from all areas.* □ *The dessert was comprised of a number of different delicious substances.*

be enamored of someone or something to be inflamed with love for someone or something. (*Enamored* is the past participle of *enamor*, functioning here as an adjective. Both literal and figurative uses. Often an exaggeration.) □ *She is hopelessly enamored of Tom.* □ *Tom is enamored of chocolate ice cream.*

be possessed of something to have

something; to possess something. (*Possessed* is the past participle of *possess*, functioning here as an adjective.) □ *She is possessed of a large amount of money.* □ *Todd wishes he were possessed of a large car and a fine house.*

BE ▸ OFF

be off [for one's plans or predictions] to be incorrect or inexact. □ *My estimate was off a little bit.* □ *Your idea of the plane's arrival time was off, but it did land safely two hours later.*

be off 1. to be not turned on. (As with electric switches or the things they control.) □ *These switches are now off.* □ *Is the fan off?* 2. to have started. (As with runners in a race or any other action.) □ *They're off!* □ *Are the horses off yet?* 3. to be strange or slightly crazy. (Slang.) □ *I'm afraid he's a little off.* □ *I think I am off sometimes.* 4. spoiled. (Especially with milk.) □ *This milk is off. Throw it out.* □ *The milk is off again!*

be off course not to be going in the right direction; not to be following the plan correctly. (Both literal and figurative uses. Originally referred to a ship's course.) □ *The project is off course and won't be finished on time.* □ *I am off course and doing poorly.*

be off on someone or something to be in a rage about someone or something; to be on a tirade about someone or something. □ *Are you off on Sally again? Why can't you leave her alone?* □ *I'm off on my diet again.*

be off (on something) 1. to be incorrect in one's planning or prediction. □ *I was off on my estimates a little bit.* □ *I guess I was off too much.* 2. to have started on something, such as a task or a journey. □ *What time should we be off on our trip?* □ *We should be off by dawn.*

BE ▸ ON

See also under *BE ▸ (UP)ON.*

be bent on something to be determined to do something. (*Bent* is the past participle of *bend*, functioning here as an adjective.) □ *I believe you are bent on destroying the entire country.* □ *I am bent on saving the planet.*

be divided on someone or something [for a number of people] to have differing opinions about someone or something. (*Divided* is the past participle of *divide*, functioning here as an adjective.) □ *Our opinions are divided on what is going to happen.* □ *We were divided on Ann. Some of us wanted to choose her; some did not.*

be lost on someone to be wasted on someone. (Includes humor, effort, etc. *Lost* is the past participle of *lose*, functioning here as an adjective.) □ *My jokes are lost on him. He is too literal.* □ *Our efforts at reform were lost on Mary.*

be on 1. to be turned on. (As with electric switches or the things they control.) □ *Is the motor on?* □ *It's not on now.* 2. [for some agreement or plan] to be confirmed and in effect. (Often with a *for* phrase.) □ *Is everything still on for Friday night?* □ *Yes, the party is on.*

be on course to be going in the right direction; to be following the plan correctly. (Both literal and figurative uses. Originally referred to a ship's course.) □ *Is the project on course?* □ *Nothing I am doing is exactly on course right now.*

be on ice 1. to be stored or preserved on ice or under refrigeration. □ *I have a lot of root beer on ice for the picnic.* □ *All the soda pop is on ice.* 2. [for action on someone or something] to be suspended or left hanging. (Figurative.) □ *I was on ice for over a month while the matter was being debated.* □ *This matter should be on ice for a while.*

be on one's back to be ill in bed. (Also with *flat*.) □ *I've been on my back with the flu for two weeks.* □ *She was flat on her back during her illness.*

be on one's feet 1. to stand up suddenly. (Usually said of an enthusiastic audience.) □ *Suddenly, the entire audience was on its feet.* □ *I was on my feet cheering after the speech was over.* 2. to be able to get up and move around after an illness or surgery. □ *John's on his feet again. He seems to be recovering* *nicely.* □ *He can't wait to get back on his feet after the operation.*

be on (one's) guard (against someone or something) to be alert against someone or something. □ *Try to be on your guard against pickpockets.* □ *I am always on my guard.* □ *Be on guard when you go into the city.*

be on one's honor to be in charge of one's own honest behavior. □ *You are on your honor during the test.* □ *I was on my honor and did not cheat.*

be on one's way ((to) some place) to leave a place for somewhere; to be en route to a place. □ *I have to leave. I am on my way to the bank.* □ *I will be there soon. I'm on my way now.*

be on someone's back to be pestering or harassing someone. (Slang.) □ *You are always on my back about something.* □ *I wish you would not be on my back all the time.*

be on something **1.** to be resting on something. □ *Karen is on that rock over there.* □ *People were on anything that would hold them, resting after the long climb.* **2.** to be taking medication. □ *I am on an antibiotic for my chest cold.* □ *I want you to be on this drug for another week.* **3.** taking an illegal drug or controlled substance and acting strangely. □ *What the matter with that kid? Is he on something?* □ *She acted like as if she were on barbiturates or something.*

be on the back burner [for something] to be on hold or suspended temporarily. □ *The building project is on the back burner for now.* □ *This matter was on the back burner for a long time.*

be on the map to be known or recognized officially. (Not limited to places indicated on maps.) □ *Is this place you are talking about on the map?* □ *No, it's too small to be on the map.*

be on the mark [for someone] to be exactly right; [for something] to be just what is needed. □ *This hot tea is really on the mark!* □ *You are right on the mark.*

be on the move to be moving from place to place; to be busy all the time. □ *Are the cattle on the move now, or are they still grazing?* □ *At last, we are on the move!*

be on the safe side to be cautious and wary; to act conservatively. □ *To be on the safe side, you had better bring some extra money.* □ *I want to be on the safe side.*

be on the scene to be available or present where something is happening or where something has happened. □ *The ambulance was on the scene almost immediately.* □ *I wasn't on the scene when it happened.*

be on the way to be due to arrive soon. □ *We are on the way. We will be there soon.* □ *The package is on the way. We sent it yesterday.*

be on the wrong side of someone to be in someone's disfavor. □ *I don't want to be on the wrong side of the professor.* □ *I am on the wrong side of my brother.*

be on trial **1.** to stand trial before a judge. □ *The criminal was on trial for over three months.* □ *I am not on trial. Don't treat me like that!* **2.** to be tested; to be examined or experimented with. □ *The new strain of wheat is on trial in Kansas at the present time.* □ *The teaching method is on trial in the school system.*

be on with someone [for a date or appointment] to be agreed to and confirmed with someone. □ *Is the Friday date still on with you?* □ *It's on with me.*

be soft on someone to have a crush on someone; to be in love with someone. □ *Ted is soft on Tiffany.* □ *Ted is soft on any girl who will look at him twice.*

be stoked on someone or something to be excited by someone or something. (Slang. *Stoked* is the past participle of *stoke*, functioning here as an adjective.) □ *I am really stoked on that movie.* □ *She was really stoked on Tom.*

be stuck on someone or something **1.** to be attached, as if by glue, to someone or something. (*Stuck* is the past participle of *stick*, functioning here as an adjective.) □ *The gum is stuck on me. How do I get it off?* □ *The gum is stuck on the floor.* **2.** to be in love with someone or something; to be entranced with someone or something. (*Someone* includes *oneself*.) □ *Judy is really stuck on Jeff.* □ *She seems to be stuck on this supplier for some reason.* □ *She is stuck on herself.* **3.** to be confused by something, such as a puzzle or a task. □ *I can't figure Sue out. I'm really stuck on her.* □ *I'm stuck on this question about the tax rates.*

to be soft on someone or something to be too easy on someone or something. □ *You are too soft on Don. He needs more discipline.* □ *Don't be too soft on your dog. Dogs need a certain amount of discipline.*

BE ▸ ONTO

be onto a good thing to have found something useful, promising, or profitable. (See *be onto something*.) □ *This is a great scheme. I know I'm onto a good thing.* □ *I'm onto a good thing. I'm sure I am.*

be onto someone to have figured out what someone is doing; to have figured out that someone is being dishonest. □ *No more cheating. I think they are onto us.* □*I'm onto you!*

be onto something to have found something useful or promising; to be on the verge of discovering something. □ *I think we are really onto something this time.* □ *I am onto a new discovery.*

BE ▸ OUT

be blitzed out to be shocked or disoriented. (*Blitzed* is the past participle of *blitz*, functioning here as an adjective.) □ *Ann was totally blitzed out by the events of the day.* □ *They were totally blitzed out by the news.*

be out at some place to be located at a distant place. □ *Tom's out at the farm and there's no phone there, so you can't talk to him.* □ *Jed is out at the cabin on a hunting trip.*

be out from something to be some distance away from something. □ *I would like to be farther out from the city.* □ *I need to be out from the congestion.*

be out from under someone or something **1.** to be clear of and no longer beneath someone or something. □ *I was glad to be out from under the bed where I had been hiding.* □ *The football player could not get out from under the stack of other players.* **2.** to be free from the control of someone or something. □ *It's good to be out from under the dictator.* □ *I was very glad to be out from under my daily work pressure.*

be out (in blossom) AND **be out (in bloom)** [for a plant or tree] to be blooming; [for flowers] to be open in blooms. □ *All the trees were out in blossom.* □ *The trees won't be out until next week.*

be out in something to be in evidence in some amount, such as large numbers, droves, throngs. □ *The pickpockets are out in droves today. Watch out!* □ *The ants were out in hordes at the picnic.*

be (out) in the open See under *BE ▸ IN.*

be out of action to be not operating temporarily; not functioning normally. □ *The pitcher was out of action for a month because of an injury.* □ *I will be out of action for a while.*

be out of control **1.** to act wildly or violently. □ *Watch out, Sam is out of control.* □ *The machine is out of control.* **2.** [for something, such as a machine] not to respond to direction or instructions. □ *The computer is out of control and making funny-looking characters all over the screen.* □ *My television is out of control and only makes screeching noises.*

be out of fashion to be old-fashioned; to be no longer in style or vogue. □ *This kind of clothing is totally out of fashion.* □ *It is out of fashion now.*

be out of focus to be blurred or fuzzy; to be seen indistinctly. □ *What I saw through the binoculars was sort of out of focus.* □ *The scene was out of focus.*

be out of hand to *be out of control;* to be wild and unruly. □ *Things are com-*

pletely out of hand. Calm down. ☐ *I don't want you to be out of hand.*

be out of keeping (with something) [for some behavior] to fail to fit in with something. ☐ *This kind of thing is completely out of keeping with our standards of behavior.* ☐ *That is quite out of keeping.*

be out of line (with something) to be beyond certain set or assumed limits. ☐ *Your bid on this project is completely out of line with our expectations.* ☐ *You are quite out of line!*

be out of one's depth to be involved in something that is beyond one's capabilities. ☐ *You know, you are really out of your depth in this project.* ☐ *I am sure I am out of my depth.*

be out of one's mind to be silly, insane, or unreasonable. ☐ *You must be out of your mind!* ☐ *I am not out of my mind.*

be out of order **1.** [for something or things] to be out of the proper sequence. ☐ *She noticed that the books on the shelf were out of order.* ☐ *All these cards were alphabetized, and now they're out of order.* **2.** [for something] to be incapable of operating; [for something] to be broken. ☐ *The elevator is out of order again.* ☐ *My stereo is out of order.*

be out of place **1.** not to be in the proper place. ☐ *The book I wanted was out of place, and I almost did not find it.* ☐ *Why is the furniture in this room out of place?* **2.** to be inappropriate. ☐ *That kind of behavior is out of place at a party.* ☐ *Your language is out of place.*

be out of season **1.** [for game] to be unavailable for hunting at a particular time of the year, according to law. ☐ *Ducks are out of season at this time of year.* ☐ *Geese are out of season too.* **2.** [for a foodstuff] to be unavailable at a particular time of the year. ☐ *Sorry, oysters are out of season.* ☐ *Artichokes are out of season.*

be out of service [for something] not to be operating. ☐ *Is this machine out of service?* ☐ *The elevator is out of service.*

be out (of something) **1.** to be gone; to have left some place; to be absent from a place. ☐ *The monkey is out of its cage.* ☐ *Sam is out of the building at present.* ☐ *Sam's out right now.* **2.** to have no more of something. ☐ *Sorry, we are fresh out of cucumbers.* ☐ *Sorry, we're out.*

be out of work to be unemployed; to have lost one's job. ☐ *Todd was out of work for almost a year.* ☐ *Too many people were out of work, and the economy got into trouble.*

be out (on strike) to be away from one's job in a strike or protest. ☐ *The workers are out on strike.* ☐ *We can't do anything while the workers are out.*

be out something to lack something; to have lost or wasted something. ☐ *I'm out ten bucks because of your miscalculation.* ☐ *I'm out the price of a meal.*

be out to something to be away, eating a meal. ☐ *Mary is out to lunch right now.* ☐ *Fred was out to dinner when the phone rang.*

be played out to be too exhausted to continue. (*Played* is the past participle of *play*, functioning here as an adjective.) ☐ *At the end of the race, Donna was played out.* ☐ *After the race, we were played out for the rest of the day.*

be spiffed out to be dressed in one's finest clothes and well groomed. (Informal. *Spiffed* is the past participle of *spiff*, functioning here as an adjective.) ☐ *He got himself all spiffed out for the wedding reception.* ☐ *Man, are you ever spiffed out!*

be well out of something **1.** to be far outside something. ☐ *We were well out of the city when the air-raid sirens went off.* ☐ *I want to be well out of the city, away from the congestion.* **2.** to be better off for not being involved in something. ☐ *I am well out of that class. It was much too hard.* ☐ *I am glad to be well out of this matter.*

BE ▸ OVER

be (all) over (and done with) to be completely finished. □ *When this is all over and done with, we can go home.* □ *It's over! There's nothing more we can do.* □ *That incident is over and done with.* □ *Summer is over now.*

be all over (some place) to be found in every place; to be available in all locations. □ *These little things are all over the place.* □ *There are ants all over!*

BE ▸ PAST

be past something **1.** to have moved on beyond something or some place. □ *You are past the turnoff. Go back.* □ *You are past the point of no return. Don't go back.* **2.** to lack any further positive emotion, such as caring or hoping. □ *I don't care what happens. I am past caring.* □ *We are past hoping. We have given up.*

BE ▸ THROUGH

be shot through with something to be permeated or pervaded with something. (*Shot* is the past participle of *shoot*, functioning here as an adjective.) □ *The crystal vase was shot through with a thousand sparkles made by the sun.* □ *The glass ornaments were shot through with a blaze of color.*

BE ▸ TO

be bound to do something to be certain to do something; to be destined to do something. (*Bound* is the past participle of *bind,* functioning here as an adjective.) □ *Jill's bound to do a good job.* □ *We are bound to tell the truth.*

be disinclined to do something to be unwilling to do something. (*Disinclined* is the past participle of *disincline*, functioning here as an adjective.) □ *I am disinclined to allow you to leave class early.* □ *They were disinclined to allow us to enter the country.*

be doomed to something to be condemned to something; to face something as a future or as a consequence [of something]. (*Doomed* is the past participle of *doom*, functioning here as an adjective.) □ *The project was doomed to failure from the start.* □ *I am doomed to a life of hard work and low pay.*

be hip to someone or something to know about someone or something. (Slang.) □ *I'm hip to your plans, man.* □ *She's hip to you.*

be opposed to something to be in opposition to something. (*Opposed* is the past participle of *oppose*, functioning here as an adjective.) □ *I am strongly opposed to your suggestion.* □ *I am totally opposed to your idea.*

be put to it to be strained or exhausted. (Slang. *Put* is the past participle of *put*, functioning here as an adjective.) □ *Man, I'm really put to it! What a day!* □ *Mary was too put to it to be very helpful for the rest of the day.*

be related to someone to be connected through blood kinship or through marriage to someone. (*Related* is the past participle of *relate*, functioning here as an adjective.) □ *I wonder if he is related to you, because he looks a little like you.* □ *I am not related to anyone here.*

be riveted to the ground to be attached to the ground and unable to move. (*Riveted* is the past participle of *rivet*, functioning here as an adjective.) □ *I was riveted to the ground out of fear.* □ *My feet were riveted to the ground and I could not move an inch.*

be rooted to something to be firmly attached to something. (*Rooted* is the past participle of *root*, functioning here as an adjective.) □ *She is firmly rooted to her homeland and has no intention of emigrating.* □ *The farmer is rooted to the land and will not leave.*

be set to do something to be ready to do something. (*Set* is the past participle of *set*, functioning here as an adjective.) □ *I'm all set to go. Are you ready?* □ *We are set to leave at a moment's notice.*

be slated to do something to be scheduled to do something. (*Slated* is the past participle of *slate*, functioning here as an adjective.) □ *Mary is slated to go to Washington in the fall.* □ *We are slated to leave in November.*

BE ▸ TO(WARD)

be well disposed to(ward) someone or something to be friendly with someone or something; to have a positive or favorable attitude toward someone or something. (*Disposed* is the past participle of *dispose*, functioning here as an adjective.) □ *I am not well disposed toward Walter.* □ *We are quite well disposed to all of them.*

BE ▸ UNDER

be under something to face or endure something such as pressure or a deadline. □ *I have to get back to work. I am under a deadline.* □ *I am under a lot of pressure lately.*

be under the gun (about something) to be under some pressure about something. (Figurative.) □ *The management crowd is under the gun for the mistakes made last year.* □ *We are all under the gun right now.*

BE ▸ UP

be bound up in someone or something to be deeply concerned with someone or something. (*Bound* is the past participle of *bind*, functioning here as an adjective.) □ *She is totally bound up in her children.* □ *She is too bound up in her work.* □ *Jeff is bound up in his problems and can't think straight.*

be bound up with someone or something to be deeply concerned or involved with someone or something. (*Bound* is the past participle of *bind*, functioning here as an adjective.) □ *He's so bound up with his work, he has time for nothing else.* □ *Andrew is bound up with his girlfriend and has time for no one else.*

be cracked up to be something AND **be cracked up as something** to be alleged to be something. (*Cracked* is the past participle of *crack*, functioning here as an adjective. Often negative.) □ *She was cracked up to be a pretty good player.* □ *She was cracked up as a pretty good golfer.* □ *She wasn't what she was cracked up to be.*

be cut up (about someone or something) to be very upset about someone or something. (Slang. *Cut* is the past participle of *cut*, functioning here as an adjective.) □ *Is she still cut up about the lost election?* □ *She is cut up about the defeat.*

be fed up (to some place) (with someone or something) to be disgusted with someone or something. (*Fed* is the past participle of *feed*, functioning here as an adjective. Informal. The prepositional phrases cannot be transposed.) □ *I am fed up to my eyeballs with your complaining.* □ *I am just fed up to here!* □ *We are all fed up with Roger!* [A] *One by one, the members of the fed-up audience walked out.*

be keyed up (about something) AND **be keyed up (over something)** to be excited or anxious. (*Keyed* is the past participle of *key*, functioning here as an adjective.) □ *Why are you so keyed up about nothing?* □ *She is keyed up over her son's health.*

be mixed up with someone else to be involved with another person, possibly romantically. (*Mixed* is the past participle of *mix*, functioning here as an adjective.) □ *I hear that Sam is mixed up with Sally.* □ *Who is Jerry mixed up with now?*

be up 1. [for time] to have run out; [for an allotted period of time] to have ended. □ *Time's up!* □ *Your time is up.* **2.** [for something] to have been launched into the sky. □ *The rocket was up by the scheduled time.* □ *The space shuttle is up.* **3.** [for someone] to be in good spirits. (Slang.) □ *I'm up today. That's better than being depressed.* □ *Is Lily up or down?* **4.** to be awake and out of bed. □ *Aren't you up yet?* □ *I'm not up and won't be for hours.*

be up against something to be in conflict with something; to face something as a barrier. □ *I am up against some serious problems.* □ *Lily is really up against it.*

be up and about to be out of bed and moving about. □ *I'm up and about, but I'm not really well yet.* □ *Lily is not up and about yet.* □ *I've been up and about since 6 A.M.*

be up before someone to stand in front of someone to receive something. (Especially in front of a judge.) □ *Have you* *been up before me before?* □ *I have never been up before any judge.*

be up for reelection to be running for reelection to an office or position. □ *He's up for reelection in the fall.* □ *Lily is up for reelection this fall.*

be up for something **1.** [for someone] to be mentally ready for something. □ *The team is up for the game tonight.* □ *We are all up for the contest.* **2.** [for something] to be available for something, such as auction, grabs, sale, etc. □ *The outcome of the game is up for grabs.* □ *The car is up for sale.*

be up in arms **1.** to be in armed rebellion. □ *The entire population is up in arms.* □ *They are up in arms, ready to fight.* **2.** to be very angry. (Figurative.) □ *Wally was up in arms about the bill for the broken window.* □ *I am really up in arms about what happened.*

be up to date to be modern or contemporary. □ *Is the room up to date, or is it standard?* □ *Your knowledge is not really up to date on this matter.*

be up to someone [for something] to be decided by one person. □ *If it were up to me, I would say yes.* □ *It is up to you!*

be up to something **1.** [for someone] to be plotting something. □ *I think they are up to something.* □ *I am sure that Lily and Max are up to something.* **2.** [for someone] to be well enough or rested enough to do something. □ *I'm not quite up to the party.* □*Are you up to a game of volleyball?*

be up to the minute to be current. □ *This report is up to the minute and fresh from the wire services.* Ⓐ *I would like to find an up-to-the-minute newscast.*

be up with someone to be even with someone; to be caught up with someone. □ *I'm up with the best of them.* □ *Are you up with your colleagues on this one?*

be wrapped up (with someone or something) to be involved with someone or something. (*Wrapped* is the past participle of *wrap*, functioning here as an adjective.) □ *She is all wrapped up with her husband and his problems.* □ *She is just too wrapped up.*

be wrought up to be disturbed or excited. (*Wrought* is an old past participle of *work*, functioning here as an adjective.) □ *She is so wrought up, she can't think.* □ *I am sorry you are so wrought up.*

BE ► (UP)ON

be (up)on someone to be someone's obligation, responsibility. □ *The obligation is upon you to settle this.* □ *The major part of the responsibility is on you.*

BE ► WITH

be big with someone to be famous with or desired by someone. □ *This kind of pizza is supposed to big with people in Chicago.* □ *Rock concerts are big with the kids.*

be disgusted with someone or something to be sickened over someone or something. (*Disgusted* is the past participle of *disgust*, functioning here as an adjective.) □ *I am totally disgusted with Ellen.* □ *We are all disgusted with this mess.*

be dissatisfied with someone or something to be unhappy with someone or something. (*Dissatisfied* is the past participle of *dissatisfy*, functioning here as an adjective.) □ *We are quite dissatisfied with the service provided by the dealer.* □ *I am not dissatisfied with you.*

be even with someone to have equalized the score with someone. (Also without *with someone*, but not eligible as an entry.) □ *After the fight, Wally felt he was even with Albert.* □ *Wally is even with Albert at last.*

be infatuated with someone or something to be in love with someone or something. (*Infatuated* is the past participle of *infatuate*, functioning here as an adjective.) □ *She is infatuated with John.* □ *John is infatuated with chocolate ice cream.*

be infested with something to be contaminated with a swarm or throng of some pest. (*Infested* is the past participle of *infest*, functioning here as an adjective.) ☐ *All the campers are infested with lice.* ☐ *The house is infested with ticks.*

be obsessed with someone or something to be preoccupied with someone or something. (*Obsessed* is the past participle of *obsess*, functioning here as an adjective.) ☐ *Kathy was obsessed with the kitten.* ☐ *Roger was obsessed with Kathy.*

be pleased with someone or something to be happy and satisfied with someone or something. (*Pleased* is the past participle of *please*, functioning here as an adjective.) ☐ *I am quite pleased with you. You did a fine job.* ☐ *We are pleased with your work.*

be seized with something to be affected suddenly by something, such as laughter, coughing, sneezing, fits of rage, etc. (*Seized* is the past participle of *seize*, functioning here as an adjective.) ☐ *Suddenly, I was seized with a fit of coughing.* ☐ *Mary was seized with laughter at the sight of Ted.*

be stricken with something to be afflicted or overwhelmed with something. (*Stricken* is a past participle of *strike*, functioning here as an adjective.) ☐ *Albert was stricken with a strange disease.* ☐ *Fred was stricken with remorse because of his rude remarks.* ☐ *Tom was stricken with the flu after his trip to Russia.*

be taken with someone or something to be highly attracted to someone or something. (*Taken* is the past participle of *take*, functioning here as an adjective.) ☐ *She was really quite taken with the young man who escorted her to the ball.* ☐ *The audience was taken with the stage setting.*

be through with someone or something to be finished with someone or something. ☐ *I'm all through with course requirements. Now I can learn something.* ☐ *Lily is through with Max.*

be with it to be up to date; to be knowledgeable about contemporary matters. ☐ *You're just not with it.* ☐ *I will never be with it!*

be with someone or something to be affecting someone or something. (Usually a question: **What's with someone or something?**) ☐ *What's with this book? Why is it here?* ☐ *What's with Lily? She looks pale.*

be with someone or something for something to be employed by someone or something for a period of time. ☐ *I've been with the company for nearly ten years.* ☐ *Lily has been with Max for years.*

BE ▶ WITHIN

be within one's grasp [for something] to be obtainable; [for a goal] to be almost won. ☐ *Victory is within our grasp, so we must keep playing the game to win.* ☐ *Her goal is within her grasp at last.*

be within one's rights [for one] to act legally in one's own interest. (See the examples.) ☐ *I know I am within my rights when I make this request.* ☐ *You are not within your rights!*

be within range to be inside an area that can be covered by something, such as a gun, camera lens, measuring device, etc. ☐ *The elephant was within range of the lights, so I took lots of pictures.* ☐ *When the ducks were within range of my gun, I sneezed and frightened them away.*

BE ▶ WITHOUT

be lost without someone or something to be unable to function without someone or something. (*Lose* is the past participle of *lost*, functioning here as an adjective.) ☐ *I am just lost without you.* ☐ *The engineer is lost without his pocket computer.*

be without someone or something to lack something or a certain person. ☐ *I hate to be without him.* ☐ *We are without any eggs!*

BEAM ▶ UP

beam someone or something up (to some place) to transport someone or something up to something. (Usually in the context of a "Star Trek" adventure. *Someone* includes *oneself*.) ☐ *The captain asked the first mate to beam him up.*

Ⓣ *Please beam up the crew, Roger.* □ *Beam these samples up to the ship so the doctor can study them.* Ⓐ *The beamed-up crewmen were no worse for the wear.* □ *Scotty was unable to beam himself up to the ship.*

BEAR ▸ AGAINST

bear a grudge against someone AND **have a grudge against someone; hold a grudge against someone** to carry or sustain resentment or hatred toward someone. □ *I hope you don't bear a grudge against me.* □ *I have no grudge against you.* □ *I hope you hold no grudge against me.*

BEAR ▸ DOWN

bear down (on someone or something) to press down on someone or something. □ *Bear down on the pen. You have to make a lot of copies.* □ *Don't bear down too hard.*

BEAR ▸ IN

bear someone or something in mind to remember someone or something; to remain conscious of someone or something. □ *Now, bear what I told you in mind.* Ⓣ *Now, bear in mind what I told you.* □ *I want you to bear me in mind when you are choosing a successor.* □ *Please bear this in mind. Don't let anyone know how much money you have.*

BEAR ▸ OFF

bear off ((of) something) to turn off something. (Informal.) □ *Bear off the main road to the left.* □ *Don't bear off too sharply.*

BEAR ▸ ON

See under *BEAR ▸ (UP)ON.*

BEAR ▸ OUT

bear something out [for facts] to support or confirm a story or explanation. □ *The facts don't bear this out.* Ⓣ *Her story bears out exactly what you said.*

BEAR ▸ TO

bear a resemblance to someone or something to have a degree of similarity to someone or something. □ *This wallet bears a strong resemblance to the one I lost last month.* □ *Do you think that Wally bears any resemblance to Mary?*

BEAR ▸ UP

bear someone or something up to hold someone or something up; to support someone or something. (*Someone* includes *oneself.*) □ *Will this bench bear me up?* Ⓣ *This bench would bear up an elephant.* Ⓣ *The bridge could not bear up the heavy truck.* □ *She bore herself up with the aid of a cane.*

bear someone up to sustain or encourage someone. (*Someone* includes *oneself.*) □ *Your encouragement bore me up through a very hard time.* Ⓣ *I will bear up the widow through the funeral service as well as I can.* □ *He bore himself up with thoughts of a brighter future.*

bear up against something to withstand something. □ *She was unable to bear up against the criticism.* □ *Ken bore up against it well.*

bear up (under something) **1.** to hold up under something; to sustain the weight of something. □ *How is the new beam bearing up under the weight of the floor?* □ *It isn't bearing up. It broke.* **2.** to remain brave under a mental or emotional burden. □ *Jill did not bear up well under problems in her home.* □ *Jill bore up quite well.*

BEAR ▸ (UP)ON

bear (up)on something [for information or facts] to concern something or be relevant to something. (*Upon* is formal and less commonly used than *on.*) □ *How do those facts bear on this matter?* □ *They do not bear upon this matter at all.*

BEAR ▸ WITH

bear with someone or something to be patient with someone or something; to wait upon someone or something. (Especially through difficulties.) □ *Please bear with me for a moment while I try to get this straightened out.* □ *Can you bear with the committee until it reaches a decision?*

BEAT ▸ ABOUT

beat about the bush See under *BEAT ▸ AROUND.*

BEAT ▸ AGAINST

beat against someone or something to strike against someone or something. □ *The wind beat against the sides of the house.* □ *Max beat against Lefty with his fist.*

beat one's head against the wall to act in total frustration. (Figurative.) □ *I felt like beating my head against the wall, I was so frustrated.* □ *No need to beat your head against the wall.*

BEAT ▸ AROUND

beat around the bush AND **beat about the bush** to avoid speaking frankly or to the point; to mince words. (Figurative.) □ *Let's not beat around the bush. Please answer my question.* □ *Stop beating about the bush!*

BEAT ▸ AT

beat at something to strike out at something. □ *He beat at his attacker to no avail.* □ *Lily beat at the snake, but didn't harm it.*

BEAT ▸ BACK

beat someone or something back to drive someone or something back to where it came from. □ *We beat them back to where they were before the war started.* [T] *The army beat back the defenders and saved the town.* □ *They were able to beat the wolves back and make an escape.*

BEAT ▸ DOWN

beat down on someone or something to fall on someone or something. □ *The rain beat down on us for an hour.* □ *The rockslide beat down on the car and totally ruined the body.*

beat someone down to defeat or demoralize someone. (*Someone* includes *oneself.*) □ *The constant bombing finally beat them down.* [T] *The attackers beat down the defenders.* □ *She beat herself down with self-doubt and guilt.*

beat someone down to size to humble someone by beating; to reduce someone's ego by beating. □ *I'll beat him down to size. Then he'll cooperate.* □ *When this experience beats him down to size, he won't be so cocky.*

beat something down **1.** to break something in; to break through something. □ *Don't beat the door down! I'm coming!* [T] *Please don't beat down the door!* **2.** to flatten something. □ *Sam beat the veal down to the thickness of a piece of paper.* [T] *First you have to beat down the meat to a very thin layer.*

BEAT ▸ FOR

beat the drum for someone or something to promote or support someone or something. □ *She is always beating the drum for her own interests.* □ *The publicity specialist beat the drum for Dave, who was running for office.*

BEAT ▸ INTO

beat someone into (doing) something to beat a person until the person agrees to do something or to assume a particular attitude. □ *They had to beat Max into submission.* □ *Max threatened to beat Lefty into robbing the candy store.*

beat someone into something to beat a person until the person turns into a particular physical state, such as a pulp, a mess, etc. (A literal beating with figurative results.) □ *Max threatened to beat Lefty into a pulp if he didn't do as he was asked.* □ *Lefty beat Max into a bloody mess.*

beat something into something to beat or whip something with a utensil, until it changes into something else. □ *Beat the white of the egg into stiff peaks.* □ *Beat the batter into a satiny paste.*

BEAT ▸ IN(TO)

beat something in(to someone or something) to use physical abuse to get someone to learn something; to work very hard to get someone to learn something. (Beating something into someone or someone's head.) □ *Do I have to beat this into your head? Why can't you learn?* [T] *Why do I have to beat in this information?* □ *Can't you learn by yourself? Does someone have to beat it in?*

BEAT ▸ OFF

beat someone or something off to drive someone or something away by beating. □ *They beat the enemy off.* [T] *The* *army beat off the savage attack, saving the town.* 🅃 *I was able to beat off the intruder.*

beat the pants off (of) someone See *beat the hell out of someone* under *BEAT ▸ OUT.*

beat the socks off (of) someone See *beat the hell out of someone* under *BEAT ▸ OUT.*

BEAT ▸ ON

beat on someone or something to pound or hammer on someone or something. □ *She beat on him until he let her go.* □ *Stop beating on that drum!*

BEAT ▸ OUT

beat one's brains out (to do something) to try very hard to do something. (Slang.) □ *If you think I'm going to beat my brains out to do this, you are crazy.* 🅃 *I beat out my brains to do this for you!* □ *I won't beat my brains out again for you!*

beat someone or something out to beat someone or something; to win over someone or something. □ *The other team beat us out readily.* 🅃 *They beat out every other team in the league, too.* □ *I will win! You will not beat me out!*

beat someone's brains out to beat someone very badly. □ *I thought they were going to beat my brains out.* 🅃 *Max tried to beat out Lefty's brains.*

beat the hell out of someone AND **beat the living daylights out of someone; beat the pants off (of) someone; beat the shit out of someone; beat the socks off (of) someone; beat the stuffing out of someone; beat the tar out of someone** to beat or defeat someone very badly. (Caution with *shit. Off of* is colloquial.) □ *Our team beat the hell out of the other side.* □ *We beat the stuffing out of the other side.* □ *Max threatened to beat the socks off of Lefty.*

beat the living daylights out of someone See the previous entry.

beat the shit out of someone See *beat the hell out of someone.*

beat the stuffing out of someone See *beat the hell out of someone.*

beat the tar out of someone See *beat the hell out of someone.*

BEAT ▸ TO

beat someone to something **1.** to get to something before someone else; to claim something before someone else does. □ *You beat me to it.* □ *Ken beat John to the door.* **2.** See *beat someone into something* under *BEAT ▸ INTO.*

beat someone to the draw AND **beat someone to the punch** to make a move more quickly than someone else. □ *You always beat us to the draw when it comes to getting news stories.* □ *We beat the other side to the punch.*

beat someone to the punch See the previous entry.

BEAT ▸ UP

beat someone up to beat someone. □ *The thugs beat him up and left him in the street.* 🅃 *The thug beat up Max.*

beat something up **1.** to whip up something, such as an egg. □ *Beat the egg up and pour it in the skillet.* 🅃 *Beat up another egg and do the same.* **2.** to ruin something; to damage something. □ *The banging of the door has really beat this wall up.* 🅃 *The door handle beat up the wall.* 🄰 *He was driving an old beat-up car.*

beat up on someone to beat someone up. □ *Lefty beat up on Max and made a mess of him.* □ *Don't beat up on me!*

BECKON ▸ TO

beckon to someone to signal someone to come. □ *Wally beckoned to Sally, and she came over to him.* □ *Lily beckoned to Max and he turned his back on her.*

BECOME ▸ OF

become of someone or something to happen to someone or something. □ *Whatever became of Joe and his friends?* □ *I don't know what became of my other plaid sock.*

BED ▸ DOWN

bed down (for something) to lie down to sleep for a period of time. □ *After she had bedded down for the night, the* *telephone rang.* □ *All the chickens bedded down hours ago.*

bed someone or something down (some place) to put someone or something into a bed or on bedding some place. □ *We bedded the kids down on mattresses on the floor.* [T] *We bedded down the horses for the night.*

BEDECK ▸ WITH

bedeck someone or something with something to decorate someone or something with something. (Stilted. *Someone* includes *oneself.*) □ *She bedecked herself with garlands of daisies.* □ *Karen bedecked the room with flowers.* □ *She bedecked herself with fresh blossoms and carried the young deer out into the meadow.*

BEEF ▸ ABOUT

beef about someone or something to complain about someone or something. (Slang.) □ *Stop beefing about Karen.* □ *He is always beefing about his working conditions.*

BEEF ▸ UP

beef something up to strengthen or fortify something. □ *Can we beef the last act up a little bit? It's really weak.* [T] *Try to beef up the defensive plays of the team.* [A] *His beefed-up car made lots of noise.*

BEER ▸ UP

beer up to drink a lot of beer. (Slang.) □ *Those guys are out there beering up like mad.* □ *Stop beering up and go home!* [A] *They are really beered-up!*

BEG ▸ FOR

beg for someone or something to plead to be given someone or something. □ *He missed Jane a lot and was just begging for her.* □ *Jane begged for another helping of ice cream.* [A] *When she finally got her much-begged-for car, she wrecked it almost immediately.*

BEG ▸ FROM

beg something from someone to plead for something from someone. □ *She begged the amount of a telephone call from someone who walked by.* □ *I begged a dollar from a kind lady who went by.*

BEG ▸ OF

beg of someone to beg someone. (Idiomatic. Usually added to a request.) □ *Please help me. I beg of you.* □ *I beg of you to help me.*

beg something of someone to beg someone to do something or grant something. □ *Please help me. I beg it of you.* □ *She begged a favor of Max.*

BEG ▸ OFF

beg off ((on) something) to make excuses for not doing something. □ *I'm going to have to beg off on our date.* □ *I'm sorry, I have to beg off.*

beg something off to decline an invitation politely. □ *She begged the trip to the zoo off.* [T] *We all begged off the dinner invitation.*

BEGIN ▸ BY

begin by doing something to start out by doing something first. □ *We will begin by painting the house.* □ *She began by opening the door.*

BEGIN ▸ WITH

begin with someone or something to start off a sequence with someone or something. □ *Let's begin with a nice clear soup.* □ *I will begin with Liz and take Frank next.*

BEGUILE ▸ INTO

beguile someone into something to charm someone into doing something. □ *You can't beguile me into stealing for you!* □ *I beguiled Tom into driving me to the airport.*

BEGUILE ▸ OUT

beguile someone out of something **1.** to charm someone out of doing something. □ *I will try to beguile them out of doing it.* □ *He beguiled her out of leaving.* **2.** to charm something away from someone. □ *She's trying to beguile the old man out of a substantial amount of his money.* □ *Max beguiled the old lady out of her rings.*

BEGUILE ▸ WITH

beguile someone with something to charm or fascinate someone with something. □ *She beguiled her date with tales of her childhood.* □ *He spent the evening beguiling her with stories of the Old West.*

BEHOOVE ► TO

behoove one to do something [for someone] to be obliged to do something. □ *It behooves you to apologize to her.* □ *It behooves me to save my own skin.*

BELCH ► OUT

belch out to burst, billow, or gush out. □ *Smoke belched out of the chimney.* Ⓐ *The sky was darkened by the belched-out smoke.*

BELCH ► UP

belch something up to billow something upward. □ *The fire belched flames and smoke up.* Ⓣ *The volcano belched up clouds of poison gasses.*

BELIEVE ► IN

believe in someone or something to trust or have faith in someone or something; to accept a fact or what someone says as truth. □ *You must believe in your own abilities.* □ *I believe in myself.*

BELIEVE ► OF

believe something of someone to believe something about someone; to accept a statement about someone as truth. □ *What a terrible thing for Jill to do. I can't believe it of her.* □ *I can believe anything of Max.*

BELLOW ► OUT

bellow something out to cry something out loudly with great force. □ *Don't just say it. Bellow it out!* Ⓣ *Bellow out your name so we know who you are!*

BELLY ► OUT

belly out [for a sheet of fabric, such as a ship's sail] to fill out in the wind. □ *The sails bellied out and the ship began to move.* □ *When the sails bellied out, we began to move forward.*

BELLY ► UP

belly up to something to push or nudge one's way through a crowd to something. (Usually in reference to nudging one's way to a bar.) □ *The cowboy bellied up to the bar and demanded a glass of milk.* □ *Tex strode into the saloon and bellied up to the bar.*

BELONG ► TO

belong to someone or something to be owned by someone or something. □ *This one belongs to me.* □ *This desk belongs to the company. You can't take it home!*

BELONG ► UNDER

belong under someone to be part of someone's assigned responsibility. (Colloquial.) □ *That job belongs under me, not Joe.* □ *No, it belongs under me!*

belong under something to be classified under some general category. □ *This one belongs under the other category.* □ *This file belongs under A.*

BELT ► DOWN

belt someone or something down to secure someone or something down with a belt or strap. (*Someone* includes *oneself.*) □ *Please belt the child's seat down and put the child in it.* Ⓣ *Did you belt down the kids?* □ *We belted the loose parts down so they would not rattle around.* Ⓐ *The belted-down cargo stayed put in the storm.* □ *He belted himself down with the leather strap provided for the purpose.*

belt something down to drink an alcoholic drink rapidly. □ *She belted down a couple of drinks and went out to face her guests.* Ⓣ *How many drinks did Gloria belt down?*

BELT ► OUT

belt something out to yell something out; to sing something loudly. □ *She really knows how to belt a song out.* Ⓣ *She belted out one of the old favorites and everyone cheered.*

BELT ► UP

belt someone up to secure someone with a belt, such as a seat belt. (*Someone* includes *oneself.*) □ *I had to belt her up because the belt was so complicated.* Ⓣ *We belted up the kids securely.* Ⓐ *The belted-up passengers looked very uncomfortable.* □ *The driver asked Tom to belt himself up.*

belt up to secure oneself with a belt, usually a seat belt. (Also a slogan encouraging people to use their seat belts.) □ *Please belt up. Safety first!* Ⓐ *The belted-up child is very safe.*

BEND ▸ BACK

bend back to lean or bend backwards. □ *He bent back to pick up the book, and he fell.* □ *When she bent back, she ripped something.*

bend someone or something back to curve or arch someone or something backward. (*Someone* includes *oneself.*) □ *We bent the child back a little so we could examine the spider bite.* Ⓣ *Ouch! Don't bend back my hand!* □ *Bend the branch back so we can get a better view.* □ *She bent herself back and almost fell over.*

BEND ▸ BEFORE

bend before something to bend under the pressure of something. □ *The trees bent before the wind.* □ *Our roses bent gracefully before the breeze.*

BEND ▸ DOWN

bend down to curve downward; [for someone] to lean down. □ *Please bend down and pick up the little bits of paper you just dropped.* □ *The snow-laden bushes bent down.*

BEND ▸ FORWARD

bend forward to lean forward; to curve forward. □ *The tree bent forward in the wind.* □ *I bent forward to pick up the pencil.*

BEND ▸ IN

bend in to curve or turn inward. □ *The shore bent in about a mile to the west.* □ *The side of the shed bent in under the force of the wind.*

BEND ▸ OUT

bend someone out of shape to make someone angry. (Slang. *Someone* includes *oneself.*) □ *The cheating that was going on really bent Joe out of shape.* □ *Why do you bend yourself out of shape? Chill, man, chill.*

bend something out of shape to distort something by twisting or bending. □ *Jill bent the spring out of shape.* □ *Tom bent the coat hanger out of shape.*

BEND ▸ OVER

bend over [for someone] to bend down at the waist. □ *I bent over and picked up the coin.* □ *When he bent over, something ripped.*

bend over backwards (to do something) (for someone) to work very hard to accomplish something for someone; to *go out of one's way (to do something) (for someone).* (Figurative.) □ *He will bend over backwards to help you.* □ *I bent over backwards for you!* □ *We bent over backwards to finish on time!*

BENEFIT ▸ BY

benefit by something AND **benefit from something** to profit or gain by something. □ *I hope to benefit by the collapse of the banks.* □ *We will all benefit from the new tax laws.*

BENEFIT ▸ FROM

benefit from something See the previous entry.

BENT ▸ ON

See *be bent on something* under *BE ▸ ON.*

BEQUEATH ▸ TO

bequeath something to someone to will something to someone; to leave something to someone. □ *My uncle bequeathed some furniture to me.* □ *I will bequeath this to my grandson.*

BEREAVE ▸ OF

See *be bereft of someone or something* under *BE ▸ OF.*

BEREFT ▸ OF

See *be bereft of someone or something* under *BE ▸ OF.*

BESET ▸ WITH

beset someone with something to surround someone with harassment; to harass someone with something. □ *Please do not beset them with problem after problem.* □ *They beset us with requests for money.*

BESIEGE ▸ WITH

besiege someone with something to attack or overwhelm someone with something. □ *We besieged the enemy with bombs and tanks.* □ *They besieged us with orders for the new book.*

BESMIRCH ▸ WITH

besmirch someone or something with something to dirty or soil someone or someone's reputation with something. (*Someone* includes *oneself.*) □ *Please don't continue to besmirch Alice with that gossip.* □ *You have besmirched my reputation with your comments.* □ *He besmirched himself with vile gossip in order to gain sympathy.*

BESTOW ▸ ON

bestow something on someone to give something to someone; to present something to someone. □ *Her presence bestowed wisdom and grace on her court.* □ *Fine gifts were bestowed on the visiting prince.*

BET ▸ ON

bet on someone or something to wager on someone or something. □ *Are you really going to bet on that horse?* □ *I bet on Paul. He is the fastest runner.*

bet something on someone or something to wager something on someone or something. □ *I bet one thousand dollars on that horse!* □ *Fred bet a few bucks on Ralph in the footrace.*

BET ▸ WITH

bet with someone to make a bet or wager with someone. □ *No, I won't bet with you. That's not my style.* □ *Max will bet with anyone.*

BETROTH ▸ TO

betroth someone to someone to promise someone to someone else in marriage. (*Someone* includes *oneself.*) □ *The king betrothed his daughter to a prince from the kingdom next door.* □ *She betrothed herself to one of the peasant boys from the village.*

BEWARE ▸ OF

beware of someone or something to be cautious and watchful about someone or something. □ *Beware of Ted. He's acting irrational.* □ *You should beware of the dog.*

BIAS ▸ AGAINST

bias someone against someone or something to prejudice someone against someone or something. (*Someone* includes *oneself.*) □ *Please avoid biasing everyone against me.* □ *One bad experience biased all of us against that brand of sausage.* □ *She biased herself against wolves by reading too many horror stories.*

BICKER ▸ ABOUT

bicker (with someone) (about someone or something) See under *BICKER ▸ WITH.*

BICKER ▸ OVER

See the following entry.

BICKER ▸ WITH

bicker (with someone) (about someone or something) AND **bicker (with someone or something) (over someone or something)** to argue with someone about someone or something. □ *Why are you always bickering with her about absolutely nothing?* □ *Don't bicker about money with me all the time.* □ *Please don't bicker with us over these small details.*

BID ▸ DOWN

bid something down to lower the value of something, such as stock, by offering a lower price for it each time it comes up for sale. □ *We bid the price down and then bought all of it.* [T] *I could see that the traders were bidding down the price, but I didn't want to take the risk.*

BID ▸ FOR

bid (something) for something AND **bid (something) on something** to offer an amount of money for something at an auction. □ *I bid a thousand for the painting.* □ *I didn't want to bid for it.* □ *I wouldn't bid a cent on it!* □ *Then don't bid on it!*

BID ▸ ON

bid (something) on something See the previous entry.

BID ▸ TO

bid adieu to someone or something to say good-bye to someone or something. □ *It is time to bid adieu to everyone.* □

I bid adieu to my old tennis shoes and threw them out.

BID ► UP

bid something up to raise the price of something at an auction by offering higher and higher prices; to increase the value of something, such as stock shares, by offering a higher price for it each time it comes up for sale. □ *Who is bidding the price up on that painting?* 🅃 *Someone bid up the price on each painting and then quit.* 🅃 *They bid up the prices of the stock so high that everyone sold it to take the profits.*

BILK ► OUT

bilk someone out of something to get something away from someone by deception. □ *The crooks bilked the old lady out of a fortune.* □ *I was bilked out of a fortune!*

BILL ► FOR

bill someone for something to send someone a bill for something. (*Someone* includes *oneself.*) □ *Just bill me for the balance.* □ *She billed herself for her time and then tried to deduct the bill from her income tax.*

BILLOW ► OUT

billow out **1.** [for something, such as smoke] to burst and flow outward. □ *At the site of the fire, smoke billowed out.* □ *Clouds of ash billowed out of the volcano.* **2.** [for a sheet of cloth] to fill with the wind. (Especially a ship's sail.) □ *The sail billowed out and we moved forward.* □ *Her skirt billowed out when the wind caught it.*

BIND ► DOWN

bind someone or something down to tie or secure someone or something to something. □ *Bind her down so she won't get away.* 🅃 *We will bind down the patient tightly.* □ *They bound the hatch down so it could not be opened.*

BIND ► OVER

bind someone over (to someone or something) to deliver someone to some legal authority. (Law.) □ *They bound the suspect over to the sheriff.* 🅃 *The sheriff will bind over the suspect to the police chief.* □ *When will you bind the prisoner over?*

BIND ► TO

See *be bound to do something* under *BE ► TO.*

BIND ► TOGETHER

bind someone or something together to tie the parts of something together; to tie a number of things or people together. (*Someone* includes *oneself.*) □ *Bind these two parts together.* 🅃 *Can you bind together all three parts?* □ *Bind these two bandits together and lead them to jail.* □ *They bound themselves together, hoping the storm would not carry them all away.*

BIND ► UP

See *be bound up in someone or something* under *BE ► UP.*

bind someone or something up in something AND **bind someone or something up with something** to tie someone or something up in something. □ *They bound her up in leather straps.* 🅃 *I will bind up the larger sticks in strong cord.* □ *We bound the sticks up with cord.*

bind someone or something up (with something) to tie someone or something with string or rope. □ *We bound her up with the drapery cords.* 🅃 *Please bind up both of them with twine.* □ *Could you bind up the newspapers with twine?*

BITCH ► ABOUT

bitch about someone or something to complain about someone or something. (Slang. Use discretion with *bitch.*) □ *You are always bitching about her.* □ *Stop bitching about your job.* 🄰 *The much-bitched-about sergeant was transferred, thank heavens.*

BITCH ► UP

bitch someone or something up to mess someone or something up. (Slang. *Someone* includes *oneself.* Use discretion with *bitch.*) □ *Who bitched this thing up?* 🅃 *I never bitch up anything!* □ *You really bitched me up, you know?* 🄰 *Get this bitched-up mess out of here!* □ *You are always bitching yourself up!*

BITE ▸ BACK

bite back (at someone or something) to fight back at someone; to return someone's anger or attack; to speak back to someone with anger. (Figurative.) ☐ *She is usually tolerant, but she will bite back if pressed.* ☐ *Yes, she will bite back.*

BITE ▸ INTO

bite into someone [for the wind or something similar] to blow sharply against someone, causing a stinging pain. ☐ *The cold wind bit into poor Wally, who only has a jacket.* ☐ *The frigid air bit into my exposed skin.*

bite into something to press one's teeth into something. ☐ *As he bit into the apple, the juices ran down his chin.* ☐ *Lily bit into the sandwich and smiled.*

bite something into something to make marks in something with the teeth or something similar. ☐ *She bit a sample of her dental arch into the material the dentist held in her mouth.* ☐ *She bit her teeth into the gummy stuff carefully.*

BITE ▸ OFF

bite off more than one can chew to take (on) more than one can handle. (As if one had bitten off too much food. The order of the elements of the sentence is idiomatic.) ☐ *I'm afraid I bit off more than I could chew when I accepted that assignment.* ☐ *Lily didn't mean to bite off more than she could chew.*

bite someone's head off to speak sharply and with great anger to someone. (The order of the elements of the sentence is idiomatic.) ☐ *Don't bite my head off! Be patient.* ☐ *I didn't mean to bite your head off.*

bite something off to remove something in a bite. ☐ *Ann bit a piece off and chewed it up.* 🅃 *She bit off a piece.*

BITE ▸ ON

bite on something **1.** to chew on something; to grasp something with the teeth. ☐ *The injured cowboy bit on his wallet while they probed for the bullet.* ☐ *Don't bite on your nails.* **2.** to respond to a lure; to fall for something. ☐ *Do you think the fish will bite on this?* ☐ *No one would bite on that bait. Try another approach.*

BLAB ▸ AROUND

blab something around to gossip something around; to spread some news or secret around. (Slang.) ☐ *It's true, but don't blab it around.* 🅃 *Did you blab around everything I told you?*

BLAB ▸ OUT

blab something out to speak out freely about something that is a secret. (Slang.) ☐ *Don't just blab it out!* 🅃 *Don't blab out the names of the people who were there!*

BLACK ▸ OUT

black out **1.** to pass out; to become unconscious. ☐ *After I fell, I must have blacked out.* ☐ *I think I am going to black out.* **2.** [for lights] to go out. ☐ *Suddenly the lights blacked out.* 🄰 *The blacked-out village was invisible from the air.* 🄽 *There was a short blackout during the storm last night.*

black something out **1.** to cut or turn out the lights or electric power. ☐ *The lightning strike blacked the entire town out.* 🅃 *The manager blacked out the whole building during the emergency to prevent an explosion.* **2.** to prevent the broadcast of a specific television or radio program in a specific area. (Usually refers to a sports event.) ☐ *Will they black the game out around here?* 🅃 *They blacked out the basketball game in this area.* 🄰 *All blacked-out events are seen in other cities.* 🄽 *We couldn't see the game because of the local blackout.*

BLACKMAIL ▸ INTO

blackmail someone into doing something to force a person to do something by threatening to reveal some secret about the person. ☐ *Are you trying to blackmail me into doing what you want?* ☐ *They blackmailed me into doing it.*

BLAME ▸ FOR

blame someone for something to hold someone responsible for something; to name someone as the cause of something. (*Someone* includes *oneself*.) ☐ *Please don't blame Jill for it.* ☐ *She* *blamed herself for everything that went wrong.*

BLAME ▸ ON

blame something on someone to say that something is someone's fault; to place the guilt for something on someone. □ *Don't blame it on me.* □ *I blamed it all on someone else.*

BLANCH ▸ AT

blanch at something to cringe at something; to become pale at the thought of something. □ *Jill blanched at the thought of swimming in that cold water.* □ *Lily blanched at the sight before her.*

BLANCH ▸ WITH

blanch with something to become pale with some emotion, such as anger or fear. □ *He saw the injury and blanched with fear.* □ *Lily blanched with anger as Max walked out.*

BLANK ▸ OUT

blank something out 1. to forget something, perhaps on purpose; to blot something out of memory. □ *I'm sorry, I just blanked your question out.* 🅃 *I blanked out your question. What did you say?* 2. to erase something, as on a computer screen. 🅃 *Who blanked out the information that was on my screen?* □ *Please blank your password out as soon as you type it.*

BLANKET ▸ WITH

blanket someone or something with something to cover someone or something with something. □ *They blanketed the flames with a layer of foam.* □ *The children blanketed Jimmy with leaves and pretended he was lost.*

BLAST ▸ OFF

blast off (for some place) 1. [for a rocket ship] to take off and head toward a destination. □ *The rocket blasted off for the moon.* □ *Will it blast off on time?* 🄽 *The blast-off was the loudest sound I have ever heard.* 2. [for someone] to leave for a destination. (Jocular.) □ *Ann blasted off for the library, so she could study.* □ *I've got to blast off. It's late.*

blast something off something to remove something from something else with a powerful charge, pressure, or force. □ *They blasted the writing off the wall with a stream of sand.* □ *We will have to blast it off the wall.*

BLAZE ▸ AWAY

blaze away (at someone or something) [for gunfire] to fire continually at someone or something. □ *The guns blazed away at the oncoming ducks.* □ *Max blazed away at Lefty.*

BLAZE ▸ DOWN

blaze down (on someone or something) [for the sun or other hot light] to burn down on someone or something. □ *The sun blazed down on the people on the beach.* □ *The stage lights blazed down on the set while the actors rehearsed.*

BLAZE ▸ UP

blaze up 1. [for flames] to expand upward suddenly. □ *The fire blazed up and warmed all of us.* □ *As the fire blazed up, we move away from the fireplace.* 2. [for trouble, especially violent trouble] to erupt suddenly. □ *The battle blazed up again, and the fighting started to become fierce.* □ *As the battle blazed up, the cowards fled into the hills.*

BLAZE ▸ WITH

blaze with something to burn with some quality, such as great heat or sound. □ *The sun blazed with unbelievable heat.* □ *The fire blazed with much crackling.*

BLEACH ▸ OUT

bleach something out to remove the color from something. □ *Wally bleached his jeans out so they looked more stylish.* 🅃 *Can you bleach out this stain?* 🄰 *The bleached-out cushions were replaced with fresh ones.*

BLEED ▸ FOR

bleed for someone to feel the emotional pain that someone else is feeling; to sympathize or empathize with someone. (Figurative.) □ *I just bled for him when I heard his story.* □ *We bled for her as she related her recent experiences.*

BLEED ▸ FROM

bleed from something for blood to emerge from a wound or other source. □ *He was bleeding from a number of wounds.* □ *He bled from his mouth and nose.*

BLEED ▸ TO

bleed to death to die from the loss of blood. □ *If something isn't done, he will bleed to death.* □ *I cut my finger. I hope I don't bleed to death.*

BLEEP ▸ OUT

bleep something out to drown out a sound with another louder sound. □ *The engineer bleeped the rude word out.* 🆃 *She bleeped out the word.* 🅰 *The bleeped-out words were restored in a later editing.*

BLEND ▸ IN

blend in (with someone or something) to mix well with someone or something; to combine with someone or something. □ *Everyone there blended in with our group.* □ *This color doesn't blend in with the upholstery fabric I have chosen.*

BLEND ▸ IN(TO)

blend in(to something) to combine nicely with something; to mix well with something. □ *The oil won't blend into the water very well.* □ *It simply won't blend in.*

blend something in(to something) to mix something evenly into something else. □ *We should blend the strawberry jam into the peanut butter slowly.* 🆃 *You should blend in some more jam.*

BLEND ▸ TOGETHER

blend something together (with something) to mix something evenly with something else. □ *Blend the egg together with the cream.* □ *Blend the ingredients together and pour them into a baking pan.*

BLESS ▸ WITH

bless someone or something with something [for God or fate] to give someone or something a valuable gift. □ *God has blessed us with a bountiful harvest.* □ *Nature blessed the morning with a gentle rain.*

BLIMP ▸ OUT

blimp out to overeat; to eat too much and swell up like a blimp. (Slang.) □ *I blimp out almost every weekend.* □ *If I could stop blimping out, I could lose some weight.*

BLIND ▸ TO

blind someone to something to prevent someone from seeing or understanding something. (Figurative. *Someone* includes *oneself*.) □ *The king blinded his subjects to what was going on by controlling what appeared in the newspapers.* □ *The lies and confusion blinded Jill to what was happening.* □ *She blinded herself to all his faults.*

BLINK ▸ AT

blink at something **1.** to open and close the eyelids quickly, one or more times. □ *I blinked at the bright light and finally had to close my eyes.* □ *Don't blink at the light while I am trying to take your picture.* **2.** to overlook something, such as a mistake. (As if one had blinked one's eyes rather than seeing the error.) □ *I just can't blink at that kind of behavior.* □ *We can't blink at what you did.*

BLINK ▸ BACK

blink back one's tears to fight back tears; to try to keep from crying. □ *She blinked back her tears and went on.* 🆃 *He blinked his tears back.*

BLISS ▸ OUT

bliss out to become disoriented with happiness. (Slang.) □ *She blissed out at the concert, because she loves that kind of music.* 🅰 *Who is this starry-eyed, blissed-out person?*

bliss someone out to disorient someone with happiness. (Slang. *Someone* includes *oneself*.) □ *This kind of weather just blisses me out.* 🆃 *The lovely weather blissed out everyone at the office.* □ *She blissed herself out with thoughts of the future.*

BLITZ ▸ OUT

See *be blitzed out* under *BE ▸ OUT.*

blitz someone out to shock or disorient someone. (Slang.) □ *The accident blitzed her out for a moment.* 🆃 *The* *second act blitzed out the audience and thrilled them to pieces.*

BLOCK ▸ IN

block someone or something in (some place) to place an obstacle that prevents someone or something from getting out of something. (*Someone* includes *oneself.*) □ *I can't get out of my parking space. Someone blocked me in my space.* [T] *Don't block in any of the other cars in the garage.* □ *Don't block me in.* □ *He blocked himself in accidentally.*

BLOCK ▸ OFF

block something off to prevent movement through something by putting up a barrier; to close a passageway. □ *Sam blocked the corridor off with a row of chairs.* [T] *He used some chairs to block off the hallway.* [A] *You cannot go down that blocked-off hallway.*

BLOCK ▸ OUT

block something out 1. to lay something out carefully; to map out the details of something. □ *She blocked it out for us, so we could understand.* [T] *Let me block out this project for you right now.* 2. to obscure a clear view of something. □ *The trees blocked the sun out.* [T] *The bushes blocked out my view of the car that was approaching.*

BLOCK ▸ UP

block someone up to constipate someone. (*Someone* includes *oneself.*) □ *That stuff always blocks me up.* □ *He blocked himself up by eating something he shouldn't.*

block something up to obstruct something; to stop the flow within a channel. (Also without *up*, but not eligible as an entry.) □ *The heaps of debris blocked the channel up.* [T] *It blocked up the channel.*

BLOSSOM ▸ FORTH

blossom forth 1. [for a plant] to burst into flower. □ *All the trees blossomed forth at the same time.* □ *Each spring my tulips blossom forth in all their glory.* 2. to develop or grow quickly. □ *A wonderful idea blossomed forth and caught on quickly.* □ *She suddenly blossomed forth into a young woman.*

BLOSSOM ▸ INTO

blossom into something 1. [for a plant] to develop into full bloom. □ *The bush blossomed into beautiful red roses.* □ *Imagine this brown old bulb blossoming into a lovely flower.* 2. to develop into something. □ *She blossomed into a lovely young lady.* □ *The idea blossomed into a huge real estate development.*

BLOSSOM ▸ OUT

blossom out 1. [for a plant or tree] to become covered with blossoms. □ *The apple tree blossomed out for the last time.* [A] *The greenhouse was filled with blossomed-out plants.* 2. [for a thing or person] to develop fully, physically and intellectually. □ *She blossomed out in her studies and her grades showed it.* □ *In her last year in school, she blossomed out.*

BLOT ▸ OUT

blot someone or something out to forget someone or something by covering up memories or by trying to forget. □ *I try to blot those bad thoughts out.* [T] *I tried to blot out those unhappy thoughts.* □ *I blotted David out and tried to keep him out of my mind.* [A] *Please don't make me bring back those blotted-out memories.*

blot someone out to kill someone. (Slang.) □ *Max sought to blot Lefty out.* [T] *Lefty wanted to blot out Max.*

blot something out to make something invisible by covering it with a spot or smudge. □ *Don't blot the name out on the application form.* [T] *Who blotted out the name on this form?*

BLOW ▸ AWAY

blow away [for something light] to be carried away by the wind. □ *The leaves blew away on the autumn winds.* □ *My papers blew away!*

blow someone away 1. [for something shocking or exciting] to overwhelm a person; to excite a person very much. (Figurative.) □ *The size of the check blew me away.* □ *The noise from the* *concert blew me away.* **2.** to murder someone, usually by gunfire. (Slang.) ☐ *Mr. Big ordered Lefty to blow Max away.* 🅃 *Max tried to blow away Lefty.*

blow someone or something away [for the wind] to carry someone or something away. ☐ *The wind almost blew her away.* 🅃 *The high wind blew away the entire barn.* 🅃 *It nearly blew away all of us.*

BLOW ▸ DOWN

blow someone or something down [for a rush of air] to knock someone or something over. ☐ *The wind blew Chuck down.* 🅃 *It blew down many people.* ☐ *It almost blew the barn down.*

BLOW ▸ IN

See also under *BLOW ▸ IN(TO).*

blow in **1.** See *blow in (from some place).* **2.** See *blow in(to some place) (from some place).* **3.** [for something] to cave in to the pressure of moving air. ☐ *The door blew in in the storm.* ☐ *The window blew in.*

blow in (from some place) [for a wind] to move air in from some place. ☐ *A huge mass of frigid air blew in from Canada.* ☐ *When the cold air blew in, we were dressed in short sleeves.*

BLOW ▸ INTO

blow into something to force air into something. ☐ *He blew into the balloon.* ☐ *I blew into the box, hoping to get some of the little bits of paper out.*

BLOW ▸ IN(TO)

blow in(to some place) (from some place) [for someone] to arrive at a place. (Slang.) ☐ *We blew into town about midnight from Detroit.* ☐ *It was late when we blew in from Detroit.* ☐ *What time did you blow in?* ☐ *I just blew in here from Canada on the train.*

BLOW ▸ OFF

blow off **1.** [for something] to be carried off of something by moving air. ☐ *The leaves of the trees blew off in the strong wind.* ☐ *My papers blew off the table.* **2.** [for a valve or pressure-maintaining device] to be forced off or away by high pressure. (See the examples.) ☐ *The safety valve blew off and all the pressure escaped.* ☐ *The valve blew off, making a loud pop.* **3.** [for someone] to become angry; to lose one's temper; to *blow off (some) steam.* ☐ *I just needed to blow off. Sorry for the outburst.* ☐ *I blew off at her.*

blow off (some) steam to release anger, often through strong language. ☐ *She really needs to blow off some steam.* ☐ *I need to get some exercise and blow off steam.*

blow someone off to ignore or evade someone or someone's wishes. (Slang.) ☐ *Don't blow me off!* 🅃 *She blew off her teacher and didn't even apologize.*

blow someone's doors off [for a truck driver] to speed past another vehicle. (Slang.) ☐ *Wow, he almost blew my doors off!* 🅃 *The truck passed us and blew off our doors!*

blow something off **1.** to evade or skip something important. (Slang.) ☐ *I'm going to blow off classes today.* 🅃 *You blow off classes all the time!* **2.** to fail at something on purpose, especially a test. (Slang.) ☐ *I blew the French test off.* 🅃 *I blew off the French test.* ☐ *Frank blew the exam off and dropped the course.*

blow the lid off ((of) something) to expose something to public view. (Slang.) ☐ *The police inspector blew the lid off the work of the gang of thugs.* ☐ *The investigation blew the lid off.*

BLOW ▸ ON

blow on something to force air across something. ☐ *Jill blew on the hot soup.* ☐ *Blow on the fire to make it burn hotter.*

blow the whistle on someone to call a halt to something that someone is doing. ☐ *The teacher blew the whistle on the plagiarist.* ☐ *The police blew the whistle on the crooks.*

BLOW ▸ OUT

Blow it out your ear! "Go away!"; "Forget it!"; "Never mind!" (Slang.) ☐ *Blow it out your ear, you jerk!* ☐ *Oh, blow it out your ear!*

blow itself out [for a storm or a tantrum] to lose strength and stop; to subside. ☐ *The storm blew itself out.* [A] *This wind is the remnant of a blown-out storm.*

blow someone or something out of the water to destroy utterly someone or something, such as a plan. (Figurative.) ☐ *I will blow him out of the water if he shows up around here.* ☐ *The boss blew the whole idea out of the water.*

blow someone out to kill someone, especially with gunshots. (Slang.) ☐ *Lefty set out to blow Max out once and for all.* ☐ *Lefty wanted to blow Max out too.*

blow someone's brains out to kill someone with a gun. (Slang.) ☐ *He took the gun and blew his own brains out.* ☐ *Careful with that gun, or you'll blow your brains out.* [T] *Max was so upset he wanted to blow out his brains.*

blow something out to extinguish a flame by blowing air on it. ☐ *I blew the candle out.* [T] *I blew out the candle.*

blow something out of (all) proportion to distort something; to exaggerate something. (Idiomatic.) ☐ *The press reports blew the story out of all proportion.* ☐ *They blew the reports out of proportion.*

BLOW ▸ OVER

blow over [for something] to diminish; to subside. (As with a storm or a temper tantrum.) ☐ *Her display of temper finally blew over.* ☐ *The storm will blow over soon, I hope.*

blow someone or something over [for the wind] to move strongly and upset someone or something. ☐ *The wind almost blew us over.* [T] *The wind blew over the shed.* ☐ *It blew the shed over.*

blow someone over to surprise or astound someone. (Figurative.) ☐ *Her announcement just blew me over.* ☐ *The whole event just blew me over.*

BLOW ▸ TO

blow someone or something to something to destroy someone or something by explosion. ☐ *The explosion blew her to bits.* ☐ *The explosion blew the car to pieces.*

blow something to something to destroy an idea or plan by exposing its faults. ☐ *The discovery blew my case to pieces.* ☐ *The opposing lawyer blew my case to smithereens.*

BLOW ▸ UP

blow someone or something up **1.** to destroy someone or something by explosion. (*Someone* includes *oneself.*) ☐ *The terrorists blew the family up as they slept.* [T] *The villains blew up the whole family!* [T] *They blew up the bridge.* [A] *We stopped to look at the blown-up building.* ☐ *He blew himself up with the bomb he was making.* **2.** to exaggerate something [good or bad] about someone or something. (Slang. *Someone* includes *oneself.*) ☐ *I hope no one blows the story up.* [T] *The press always blows up reports of bad behavior.* ☐ *The press blew the story up unnecessarily.* ☐ *She blows herself up whenever she gives an interview.*

blow something up **1.** to inflate something. ☐ *He didn't have enough breath to blow the balloon up.* [T] *They all blew up their own balloons.* **2.** to enlarge a photograph. ☐ *How big can you blow this picture up?* [T] *I will blow up this snapshot and frame it.*

blow up **1.** [for something] to explode. ☐ *The bomb might have blown up if the children had tried to move it.* ☐ *The firecracker blew up.* **2.** [for someone] to have an outburst of anger. ☐ *She got mad and blew up.* [N] *The blowup totally ruined my day.* **3.** to arrive accompanied by the blowing of the wind. (Said of storms.) ☐ *A terrible storm blew up while we were in the movie theater.* ☐ *I was afraid that a rainstorm was blowing up.*

blow up in someone's face [for a plan] to fall apart right while someone is working on it. (Slang.) ☐ *The whole business blew up in my face.* ☐ *I was afraid his plans would blow up in his face.*

BLUFF ▸ INTO

bluff someone into something to mislead or deceive someone into doing something. ☐ *Are you trying to bluff* *me into giving up without a fight?* ☐ *I won't be bluffed into revealing the whereabouts of the emerald.*

BLUFF ▶ OUT

bluff one's way out of something to get out of a difficult situation by deception or cunning. ☐ *You can't bluff your way out of this one.* ☐ *I will try to bluff my way out of this mess.*

bluff someone out of something to get something away from someone through deception. ☐ *We bluffed her out of her share of the pie.* ☐ *I bluffed Liz out of her pie.*

BLURT ▶ OUT

blurt something out (at someone) to say something to someone without thinking. (Usually to say something that should not be said.) ☐ *Why did you blurt that out at everyone?* ☐ *It was a secret. Why did you blurt it out?*

BLUSH ▶ WITH

blush with something [for someone's cheeks] to redden from a particular cause. ☐ *She blushed with shame.* ☐ *You could see that Lily was blushing with anger, even though she tried to conceal it.*

BOARD ▶ OUT

board someone or something out to send someone or some creature away to live, temporarily. (Usually said of a school-age child or a pet.) ☐ *They decided to board Billy out.* 🅃 *They also boarded out the dog.* ☐ *Why did they board them out?*

BOARD ▶ UP

board something up to enclose or seal a building or part of a building with boards. ☐ *We will have to board this house up if we can't sell it.* 🅃 *Should I board up the house while I am gone?* 🄰 *What do you suppose that boarded-up building was?*

BOARD ▶ WITH

board with someone to pay to live with someone temporarily. ☐ *I will board with my aunt when I go to school in Adamsville.* ☐ *I do not wish to board with relatives.*

BOAST ▶ ABOUT

boast about someone or something to brag about someone or something. ☐ *I just have to boast about my grandchildren. Do you mind?* ☐ *Is he boasting about his car again?*

BOAST ▶ OF

boast of someone or something to brag about someone or something. ☐ *She is always boasting of her grandchildren.* ☐ *I don't like to boast of what I did.*

BOB ▶ UP

bob up some place to appear suddenly some place; to pop up some place. ☐ *You tend to bob up where I least expect to find you.* ☐ *Guess who bobbed up on your front steps?*

BODE ▶ FOR

bode somehow for someone or something to foretell or portend fortune or misfortune for someone or something. (Typically with *ill* or *well*.) ☐ *Things do not bode well for the stock market.* ☐ *Things do not bode well for you.*

BOG ▶ DOWN

bog down to become encumbered and slow down; to slow down. (As if one were walking through a bog and getting stuck in the mud.) ☐ *The process bogged down and almost stopped.* ☐ *The whole thing bogged down soon after it started.*

BOGGLE ▶ AT

boggle at something to be amazed at something, particularly something large. ☐ *The audience boggled at the size of the loss.* ☐ *I boggled at what I saw.*

BOIL ▶ AWAY

boil something away **1.** to boil a liquid until it is gone altogether. ☐ *She boiled the water away and crushed the vegetables into a paste.* 🅃 *Boil away some of that water.* **2.** to remove a volatile chemical from a solution by boiling. ☐ *Boil the alcohol away or the sauce will be ruined.* 🅃 *You should boil away some of the alcohol.*

BOIL ▶ DOWN

boil down to something **1.** [for a liquid] to be condensed to something by boiling. □ *Boil this mixture down to about half of what it was.* 🄰 *Pour the boiled-down juices into the pan with the vegetables.* **2.** [for a complex situation] to be reduced to its essentials. □ *It boils down to the question of who is going to win.* □ *It boils down to a very minor matter.*

boil something down **1.** to condense or thicken something, such as a liquid. □ *I have to boil this gravy down for a while before I can serve it.* 🅃 *You boil down the gravy and I'll set the table.* **2.** to reduce a problem to its simple essentials. (Figurative.) □ *If we could boil this problem down to its essentials, we might be able to solve it.* 🅃 *We don't have time to boil down this matter. This is urgent.*

BOIL ▸ OUT

boil something out (of something) to remove something from something by boiling. (The *of*-phrase is paraphrased with a *from*-phrase when the particle is transposed. See the 🄵 example.) □ *I boiled the cleaning fluid out of the cloths.* 🅃 *I boiled out the cleaning fluid.* 🄵 *I boiled out the cleaning fluid from the soiled cloths.* □ *We boiled the oily stuff out.*

BOIL ▸ OVER

boil over [for a liquid] to overflow while being boiled. □ *The pudding boiled over and stuck to the stove.* □ *Don't let the stew boil over!*

boil over (with something) [for someone] to erupt in great anger. □ *The crowd boiled over with anger.* □ *Things got out of hand and the crowd's anger boiled over.*

BOIL ▸ UP

boil something up to cook a batch of food by boiling. (Folksy.) □ *She boiled some beans up for dinner.* 🅃 *She boiled up some beans.*

BOIL ▸ WITH

boil with something to show the heat or intensity of one's anger. □ *You could see that she was just boiling with anger.* □ *Tom was boiling with rage when we got there.*

BOLLIX ▸ UP

bollix something up to ruin something; to mess something up. (Colloquial or slang.) □ *Please don't bollix my stereo up.* 🅃 *Who bollixed up my stereo?*

BOLSTER ▸ UP

bolster someone or something up to prop someone or something up. □ *The carpenter bolstered the shelf up with a nail or two.* 🅃 *He bolstered up the shelf.* 🅃 *We had to bolster up the lady so she wouldn't fall.*

bolster someone up to give someone emotional support and encouragement. □ *We bolstered her up the best we could, but she was still unhappy.* 🅃 *I don't mind bolstering up people who are unhappy.*

BOLT ▸ DOWN

bolt something down **1.** to fasten something down onto something with bolts. □ *Did anyone bolt the washing machine down?* 🅃 *Someone should bolt down this washing machine.* 🄰 *Loosen all those bolted-down brackets.* **2.** to eat something too rapidly. □ *Don't bolt your food down.* 🅃 *She bolted down her dinner and ran out to play.*

BOLT ▸ OUT

bolt out (of some place) to run out of some place. □ *Frank bolted out of the room in a flash.* □ *I bolted out after him.*

BOMB ▸ OUT

bomb out (of something) to flunk out of something, especially school or a job. (Slang.) □ *She was afraid she would bomb out of school.* □ *Her brother bombed out the year before.*

bomb someone out to cause people to flee by bombing their homes and towns. □ *The planes bombed them all out.* 🅃 *They bombed out everyone.* 🄰 *The bombed-out refugees crowded into the makeshift village.*

bomb something out to destroy a place by bombing. □ *I hope they don't bomb our village out.* 🅃 *The planes bombed out the village.* 🄰 *The town had become one bombed-out building after another.*

BOMBARD ▸ WITH

bombard someone or something with something to cast or shoot something at someone or something. ☐ *The boys bombarded the cows with stones and mud.* ☐ *Gerald bombarded his friends with criticism.*

bombard someone with questions to ask someone many questions, one after another. ☐ *The press bombarded the president with questions.* ☐ *The president was bombarded with leading questions.*

BONE ▸ UP

bone up (on something) to study something; to review material for a test. (Slang.) ☐ *I need to bone up on my calculus before the exam.* ☐ *I need more time to bone up before the test.*

BONG ▸ OUT

bong out [for the sound of a bell] to ring forth. (Informal.) ☐ *The chimes bonged out and everyone must have heard them.* ☐ *The bells bonged out all night long.*

bong something out **1.** [for a melody or a chime] to be sounded by a bell. (Colloquial.) ☐ *The bells bonged their familiar melody out.* 🅃 *The doorbell bonged out the melody that signaled the back door.* **2.** [for someone] to play a melody on the piano; to *bang something out.* (Colloquial.) ☐ *Can you bong a well-known tune out so we all can sing?* 🅃 *I can bong out almost any song you know.*

BONK ▸ ASIDE

bonk someone or something aside to knock someone or something aside. (Slang.) ☐ *The huge beast bonked the man aside and kept on going.* 🅃 *Jeff bonked aside the chair as he ran through the room.* ☐ *We bonked aside the people who were in the way and went on by them.*

BOO ▸ OFF

boo someone off (the stage) to jeer and hoot, causing a performer to leave the stage. ☐ *The rude audience booed the performer off the stage.* ☐ *The audience booed the comedian off.*

BOOGIE ▸ DOWN

boogie down (to some place) to go to some place. (Slang.) ☐ *I guess I'll boogie down to the library and study.* ☐ *Let's boogie down and get some pizza.*

BOOK ▸ ON

book someone on something to reserve a place for someone on some travel conveyance. (*Someone* includes *oneself.*) ☐ *They booked us on a direct flight to San Juan.* ☐ *He booked himself on a flight to Manaus.*

BOOK ▸ THROUGH

book someone through (to some place) to make transportation arrangements for someone that involve a number of changes and transfers. (*Someone* includes *oneself.*) ☐ *The travel agent booked me through to Basra.* ☐ *I would be happy to book you through if you would like.* ☐ *She booked herself through to Budapest.*

BOOK ▸ UP

book something up to reserve all the available places. ☐ *The travel agency booked all the good seats up.* 🅃 *Who booked up all these seats?* 🄰 *The booked-up flight was an hour late.*

BOOM ▸ OUT

boom out [for a loud sound] to sound out like thunder. ☐ *His voice boomed out so everyone could hear.* ☐ *An explosion boomed out and frightened us all.*

boom something out [for someone] to roar something out. ☐ *Will someone with a loud voice boom the names out?* 🅃 *The announcer boomed out the names of the players.*

BOOST ▸ UP

boost someone up to give someone a helpful lift up to something. (*Someone* includes *oneself.*) ☐ *She boosted me up so I could get into the window.* 🅃 *They boosted up the child for a better view.* ☐ *Tom boosted himself up so he could reach the cookie jar.*

BOOT ▸ OUT

boot someone or something out to force someone or something, such as a pet, to leave some place. (Figurative.) □ *I booted the cat out and then went to bed.* 🆃 *Why do you have to boot out the cat? Won't the cat just walk out?* □ *The doorman booted the kid out.*

boot someone out (of something) to force someone to leave something or some place. □ *The board booted Greg out of the job.* 🆃 *After a unanimous vote, they booted out all the old guard.*

BOOT ▸ UP

boot something up to start up a computer. □ *She booted her computer up and went to work.* 🆃 *Please go boot up your computer so we can get started.*

boot up to start up one's computer. □ *He turned on the computer and booted up.* □ *Try to boot up again and see what happens.*

BOOZE ▸ UP

booze it up to drink heavily; to drink to get drunk. (Slang.) □ *She wanted to get home and booze it up by herself.* □ *She boozes it up every night.*

booze up to drink heavily. □ *Those guys are always boozing up.* □ *Stop boozing up and go home.*

BORDER ▸ (UP)ON

border (up)on something **1.** [for something] to touch upon a boundary. (*Upon* is formal and less commonly used than *on*.) □ *Our property borders on the lakeshore.* □ *The farm borders upon the railroad right-of-way.* **2.** [for some activity or idea] to be very similar to something else. (Not usually physical objects. *Upon* is formal and less commonly used than *on*.) □ *This notion of yours borders upon mutiny!* □ *It borders on insanity.*

BORE ▸ OFF

bore the pants off (of) someone to bore someone thoroughly. (Figurative. The *of* is redundant and colloquial.) □ *That speech would bore the pants off of anyone.* □ *It bored the pants off me.*

BORE ▸ THROUGH

bore through something to pierce or drill through something. (Literal or figurative uses.) □ *The drill bit could not bore through the steel plate.* □ *Her stare bored right through me.*

BORE ▸ TO

bore someone to death to bore someone thoroughly; to bore someone into a stupor. (Figurative.) □ *You bore me to death.* □ *The concert bored me to death.*

BORROW ▸ FROM

borrow something from someone to request and receive the use of something from someone. □ *Can I borrow a hammer from you?* □ *Sorry, this hammer was borrowed from my father.*

BOSS ▸ AROUND

boss someone around to order someone around. □ *Please don't boss me around so much.* 🆃 *You boss around everybody!*

BOTCH ▸ UP

botch something up to mess something up; to do a bad job of something. □ *You really botched this up.* 🆃 *I did not botch up your project.* 🅰 *Who is responsible for this botched-up mess?*

BOTHER ▸ ABOUT

bother about something to care about something; to take the trouble to deal with something. □ *Please don't bother about this mess. I'll clean it up.* □ *Don't bother about it.*

bother one's (pretty little) head about someone or something to worry about something. (Stereotypically polite Southern talk to a woman.) □ *Now, don't bother your pretty little head about all this.* □ *Don't bother your head about me.*

bother someone about someone or something See the following entry.

BOTHER ▸ WITH ▸

bother someone with someone or something AND **bother someone about someone or something** to annoy someone with someone or something; to worry someone about someone or something. (Either a physical annoyance or a mental annoyance. *Someone* includes *oneself*.) □ *Don't bother me with that!* □ *I wish you wouldn't bother me about Stanley.*

□ *Please don't bother yourself with Tom. I'll take care of him.* □ *Don't bother yourself about the bill. I'll pay it.*

BOTHER ▸ WITH

bother with someone or something to take the time or trouble to deal with someone or something. (Usually negative.) □ *Please don't bother with Jill. She can take care of herself.* □ *Don't bother me with your problems.*

BOTTLE ▸ UP

bottle something up to put some sort of liquid into bottles. □ *She bottled her homemade chili sauce up and put the bottles in a box.* 🅃 *She bottled up a lot of the stuff.*

bottle something up (inside (someone)) [for someone] to keep serious emotions within and not express them. □ *Don't bottle it up inside you.* 🅃 *Don't bottle up all your feelings.* □ *You can't just bottle it up.* 🄰 *She was burdened with many negative, bottled-up feelings.*

BOTTOM ▸ OUT

bottom out finally to reach the lowest or worst point. □ *The prices on the stock market finally bottomed out.* □ *When the market bottoms out, I'll buy some stock.*

BOUNCE ▸ ALONG

bounce along 1. to move along bouncing. (As might be done by a ball.) □ *The ball bounced along and finally came to rest.* □ *The gold ball sort of bounced along until it came to the water.* **2.** [for someone] to move along happily. □ *He was so happy that he just bounced along.* □ *He stopped bouncing along when he saw all the work he had to do.*

BOUNCE ▸ AROUND

bounce something around (with someone) to discuss something with a number of people; to move an idea from person to person like a ball. (Colloquial.) □ *I need to bounce this around with my family.* 🅃 *I need to bounce around something with you.* □ *Let's take some time to bounce this idea around.*

BOUNCE ▸ BACK

bounce back (after something) See under the following entry.

bounce back (from something) 1. [for something] to rebound; [for something] to return bouncing from where it had been. □ *The ball bounced back from the wall.* □ *The ball always bounces back.* **2.** AND **bounce back (after something)** [for someone] to recover after a disability, illness, blow, or defeat. □ *She bounced back from her illness quickly.* □ *She bounced back quickly after her illness.*

bounce something back and forth 1. to bat, toss, or throw something alternately between two people. (Usually with a ball.) □ *The two guys bounced the ball back and forth.* □ *John and Timmy bounced it back and forth.* **2.** to discuss an idea back and forth among a group of people. (Figurative.) □ *Let's bounce these ideas back and forth awhile and see what we come up with.* □ *The idea was bounced back and forth for about an hour.*

BOUNCE ▸ FOR

bounce for something to pay for something as a treat for someone else. (Slang.) □ *Put your money away. I'll bounce for this.* □ *Who will bounce for lunch?*

BOUNCE ▸ OFF

bounce off ((of) something) to rebound from something. (The *of* is colloquial.) □ *The ball bounced off the wall and struck a lamp.* □ *It hit the wall and bounced off.*

bounce something off (of) someone or something to make something rebound off someone or something. (The *of* is colloquial.) □ *She bounced the ball off the wall, turned, and tossed it to Wally.* □ *She bounced the ball off of Harry, into the wastebasket.*

bounce something off (of) someone or something to try an idea or concept out on someone or a group. (Figurative. The *of* is colloquial.) □ *Let me bounce this off of the committee, if I may.* □ *Can I bounce something off you people, while you're here?*

BOUNCE ▸ OUT

bounce out (of something) to rebound out of or away from something. □ *The ball bounced out of the corner into my hands.* □ *The window was open and the ball bounced out.*

BOUNCE ▸ UP

bounce up and down to spring up and down due to natural elasticity or from being jostled or thrown. □ *The ball bounced up and down for an amazingly long time.* □ *I bounced up and down in the back of that truck for almost an hour.*

BOUND ▸ TO

See *be bound to do something* under *BE ▸ TO.*

BOUND ▸ UP

See *be bound up in someone or something* under *BE ▸ UP.*

See *be bound up with someone or something* under *BE ▸ UP.*

BOW ▸ BEFORE

bow before someone or something 1. to bend or curtsy in respect to someone or something. □ *I will not bow before any king or queen.* □ *Henry insisted that I bow before him.* **2.** to submit to someone or something; to surrender to someone or something. □ *Our country will never bow before a dictator's demands.* □ *We will bow before no corrupt politician.*

BOW ▸ DOWN

bow down (to someone or something) 1. to bend or curtsy to someone or something. (Formal or stilted.) □ *Do you expect me to bow down or something when you enter?* □ *He bowed down low to the duchess.* **2.** to submit to someone or something; to yield sovereignty to someone or something. □ *I will not bow down to you, you dictator!* □ *We will never bow down to a foreign prince.*

BOW ▸ OUT

bow out (as something) to retire or resign as something. □ *It's time to bow out as mayor.* □ *I think I will bow out and leave this job to someone else.*

bow out (of some place) to bow as one departs from a place. □ *The servant bowed out of the room.* □ *The servant departed, bowing out as he left.*

bow out (of something) to withdraw from something. □ *I decided to bow out of the organization.* □ *The time had come for me to bow out.*

BOW ▸ TO

bow to someone or something to bend in respect to someone or something. □ *He bowed quickly to the guest and then shook hands.* □ *She faced forward and bowed to the altar.*

bow to someone's demands to yield to someone's demands; to agree to do something that someone has requested. □ *In the end, they had to bow to our demands.* □ *We refused to bow to their demands that we abandon the project.*

BOWL ▸ OVER

bowl someone over 1. to knock someone over. □ *The huge dog ran by and bowled me over.* 🅃 *The wind bowled over all the pedestrians.* **2.** to astound someone. (Figurative.) □ *His statement just bowled me over.* 🅃 *The announcement bowled over everyone.*

BOWL ▸ UP

bowl up to fill a pipe bowl with smokable material. □ *The detective bowled up and struck a match.* □ *Roger bowled up, but forgot to light his pipe.*

BOX ▸ IN

box someone or something in to trap or confine someone or something. (Literal and figurative uses. *Someone* includes *oneself.*) □ *He boxed her in so she could not get away from him.* 🅃 *They tried to box in the animals, but they needed more space.* □ *Don't try to box me in.* 🄰 *She couldn't stand that boxed-in feeling.* □ *He boxed himself in with his ill-planned argument.*

BOX ▸ UP

box someone up to confine someone in a small area. (*Someone* includes *oneself.*) □ *Please don't box me up in that little office.* 🅃 *The boss boxed up Fred in a tiny office.* □ *Why he boxes* *himself up in the little office is beyond me.*

box something up to place something in a box. □ *Please box the books up and put them into the trunk of the car.* 🅃 *Please box up four of these for me.* 🄰 *The boxed-up goods sat on the loading dock, waiting for the truck.*

BRACE ▸ FOR

brace oneself for something to prepare for the shock or force of something. □ *Brace yourself for a shock.* □ *As the boat leaned to the right, I braced myself for whatever might happen next.*

BRACE ▸ UP

brace someone or something up to prop up or add support to someone or something. (*Someone* includes *oneself.*) □ *They braced the tree up for the expected windstorm.* 🅃 *They braced up the tree again after the storm.* □ *Help me brace him up until we get his bed made.* □ *He had to brace himself up with a splint before he could walk.*

brace up to take heart; to be brave. □ *Brace up! Things could be worse.* □ *I told John to brace up because things would probably get worse before they got better.*

BRAG ▸ ABOUT

brag about someone or something to boast about someone or something; to talk proudly about someone or something. □ *He bragged about how selfish he was.* □ *Jill brags a lot about her kids.*

BRAINWASH ▸ WITH

brainwash someone with something to drive specific knowledge or propaganda into someone's brain, by constant repetition and psychological conditioning. (*Someone* includes *oneself.*) □ *The dictator brainwashed his people with lie after lie.* □ *You have brainwashed yourself with your own propaganda.*

BRANCH ▸ OFF

branch off (from something) to separate off from something; to divide away from something. □ *A small stream branched off from the main channel.* □ *An irrigation ditch branched off here and there.*

BRANCH ▸ OUT

branch out to develop many branches, tributaries, or interests. (See the other senses in this group.) □ *I got tired of sales and branched out.* □ *The river branches out near its mouth.*

branch out (from something) **1.** [for a branch] to grow out of a branch or trunk. (Having to do with plants and trees.) □ *A twig branched out of the main limb and grew straight up.* □ *The bush branched out from the base.* **2.** to expand away from something; to diversify away from narrower interests. □ *The speaker branched out from her prepared remarks.* □ *The topic was very broad, and she was free to branch out.*

branch out (into something) to diversify and go into new areas. □ *I have decided to branch out into some new projects.* □ *Business was very good, so I decided to branch out.*

BRASS ▸ OFF

brass someone off to make someone angry. (Slang. Primarily military. As angry as the "brass," or officers, might get about something.) □ *You really brass me off.* 🅃 *The private brassed off the sergeant.*

BRAVE ▸ OUT

brave something out to endure something; to put up with something courageously. □ *I don't know if all the men can brave the attack out.* 🅃 *The soldiers braved out the attack.*

BREAK ▸ AGAINST

break against something [for something] to crash against something. □ *The waves broke against the barrier.* □ *The glass broke against the side of the sink.*

BREAK ▸ AWAY

break away (from someone) AND **break free (from someone); break loose (from someone)** **1.** to get free of the physical hold of someone. □ *I tried to break away from him, but he was holding me too tight.* □ *She broke free from him, at last.* □ *I broke free from the intruder.* □ *I could not break loose from my captors.* □ *At last, I broke free.* **2.** to sever a relationship with another person, especially the parent-child relationship. ☐ *He found it hard to break away from his mother.* ☐ *She was almost thirty before she finally broke free.* ☐ *I found it hard to break loose from my parents.*

break away (from something) AND **break free (from something); break loose (from something)** **1.** [for a piece of something] to come apart or break off from something. ☐ *A piece of rock broke free from the wall.* ☐ *A rock broke away from the cliff.* ☐ *The boards broke loose from the top of the pillar and fell on the porch.* **2.** AND **break oneself away (from something)** [for a person] to leave off doing something, perhaps reluctantly. ☐ *I broke away from my writing long enough to eat.* ☐ *I was able to break myself away from my work long enough to eat.* ☐ *Try to break yourself away from your work for a few minutes, so we can talk.*

break (oneself) away (from something) See the previous entry.

break something away (from something) to break a part or piece of something away from the whole. ☐ *She broke a bit away and popped it into her mouth.* [T] *Todd broke away a piece from the bar of candy.* ☐ *He broke a piece away.*

BREAK ▸ DOWN

break down **1.** [for a mechanical device] to cease working. ☐ *The car broke down in the middle of the expressway.* [A] *Get this broken-down lawn mower out of here!* [N] *This car has had one breakdown after another.* **2.** [for someone] to have an emotional or mental collapse. ☐ *Finally, after many sleepless nights, he broke down totally.* [N] *He suffered from a serious breakdown.*

break down (and do something) to surrender to demands or emotions and do something. ☐ *Max finally broke down and confessed.* ☐ *I knew he would break down.* ☐ *I had to stop and break down and cry. I was so depressed.* ☐ *I was afraid I would break down and cry.*

break someone down to cause a person to submit; to pressure a person to submit to something. ☐ *The police broke her down, and she confessed.* [T] *They found it easy to break down the suspect.*

break something down to destroy a barrier. ☐ *The court broke a number of legal barriers down this week.* [T] *I did not break down your door!*

break something (down) (into something) **1.** to reduce a compound to its components. ☐ *Heat will break this down into sodium and a few gasses.* [T] *Will heat break down this substance into anything useful?* ☐ *We broke it into little pieces.* **2.** to reduce a large figure to its subparts and explain each one. ☐ *She broke the total down into its components.* [T] *Please break down the total into its parts again.* ☐ *I'll break the total down for you.* **3.** to discuss the details of something by examining its subparts. ☐ *Let's break this problem down into its parts and deal with each one separately.* [T] *Breaking down complex problems into their components is almost fun.* ☐ *Let's break this issue down and discuss it.*

BREAK ▸ FOR

break for something **1.** to stop working for something, such as lunch, coffee, etc. ☐ *We should break now for lunch.* ☐ *I want to break for coffee.* **2.** to run suddenly toward something; to increase dramatically one's speed while running. ☐ *At the last moment, the deer broke for the woods.* ☐ *The deer broke for cover at the last minute.*

BREAK ▸ FROM

break free (from someone) See *break away (from someone)* under *BREAK ▸ AWAY.*

break free (from something) See *break away (from something)* under *BREAK ▸ AWAY.*

break loose (from someone) See *break away (from someone)* under *BREAK ▸ AWAY.*

break loose (from something) See *break away (from something)* under *BREAK ▸ AWAY.*

break something free from something to force something to detach from something; to get something out of the hold of something else. □ *I broke the gun free from her grasp.* □ *Someone broke the light fixture free from its mounting.*

break something loose from something to loosen a part of something; to loosen and remove a part of something. □ *The mechanic broke the strap loose from the tail pipe.* □ *The bracket was broken loose from the wall.*

BREAK ▸ IN

See also under *BREAK ▸ IN(TO).*

break in (on someone) **1.** to burst into a place and violate someone's privacy. □ *The police broke in on him at his home and arrested him.* □ *They needed a warrant to break in.* **2.** to interrupt someone's conversation. □ *If you need to talk to me, just break in on me.* □ *Feel free to break in if it's an emergency.*

break in on something to interrupt something; to intrude upon something. □ *I didn't mean to break in on your discussion.* □ *Please don't break in on us just now. This is important.*

break someone in to train someone to do a new job; to supervise someone who is learning to do a new job. (*Someone* includes *oneself.*) □ *Who will break the new employee in?* 🅃 *I have to break in a new typist.* □ *She broke herself in on the new job by practicing at home.*

break something in **1.** to crush or batter something to pieces; to *break something down.* □ *Why are you breaking the door in? Here's the key!* 🅃 *Who broke in the door?* **2.** to use a new device until it runs well and smoothly; to wear shoes, perhaps a little at a time, until they feel comfortable. □ *I can't travel on the highway until I break this car in.* 🅃 *I want to go out this weekend and break in the car.* 🅃 *I hate to break in new shoes.* 🄰 *I want a nice used, broken-in car.* 🄰 *How long is the break-in period on this car?* 🄽 *It was a rough break-in, but finally it was running right.*

BREAK ▸ INTO

break into a gallop [for a horse] to begin to gallop; [for a horse] to speed up to a gallop. □ *My steed broke into a gallop, racing to get home.* □ *Near the stables, the horse broke into a fast gallop.*

break into something to begin to perform or utter suddenly, especially with song, speech, chattering, etc. □ *Suddenly, she broke into song.* □ *As soon as the movie started, the people behind me broke into loud chattering.*

break (out) into tears to begin to cry. □ *Every single child broke out into tears in the movie.* □ *The child broke into tears and started howling.*

break something (down) (into something) See under *BREAK ▸ DOWN.*

break something into something to divide something into smaller pieces. (See also *break something (down) (into something).*) □ *She broke the block of ice into chunks small enough to use in our drinks.* □ *I broke the candy bar into three pieces.*

See *break up (into something)* under *BREAK ▸ UP.*

BREAK ▸ IN(TO)

break in(to something or some place) to force entry into a place criminally; to enter some place forcibly for the purpose of robbery or other illegal acts. □ *The thugs broke into the liquor store.* □ *They broke in and took all the money.* 🄽 *There was a break-in on the next block last week. They took everything!*

BREAK ▸ OF

break someone or something of something to cause someone or something to stop practicing a habit. (*Someone* includes *oneself.*) □ *We worked hard to break the dog of making a mess on the carpet.* □ *I don't think I can break her of the habit.* □ *Tom broke himself of biting his nails.*

BREAK ▸ OFF

break off (from something) [for a piece of something] to become separated from the whole. □ *This broke off from the lamp. What shall I do with it?* □ *This piece broke off.*

break (off) with someone See under *BREAK ▸ WITH.*

break something off ((of) something) to fracture or dislodge a piece off something. (The *of*-phrase is paraphrased with a *from*-phrase when the particle is transposed. See the 🄵 example. The *of* is colloquial.) □ *He broke a piece of the decorative stone off the side of the church.* 🅃 *He didn't mean to break off anything.* 🄵 *He broke off a piece of stone from the wall.* □ *He didn't mean to break it off.*

BREAK ▸ ON

break something on something to strike and break something against something else. □ *She broke the glass on the countertop.* □ *He broke his arm on the steps.*

BREAK ▸ OUT

break out 1. [for widespread fighting] to emerge, erupt, or begin. (See also *break out (with something).*) □ *Fighting broke out again in the streets.* 🄽 *It has been very unpleasant since the outbreak of fighting in the Middle East.* **2.** [for a disease] to erupt and become epidemic. □ *Chicken pox broke out in Tony's school.* 🄽 *There was a terrible outbreak of measles in Bill's class.*

break out in a cold sweat to become frightened or anxious and begin to sweat. □ *I was so frightened, I broke out in a cold sweat.* □ *Larry broke out in a cold sweat when he cut his hand.*

break out in a rash [for the skin] to erupt with a rash. (See also *break out in a cold sweat, break out (with something).*) □ *I knew Dan had the chicken pox, because he broke out in a rash and had a dry cough.* □ *The baby breaks out in a rash all the time.*

break (out) into tears See under *BREAK ▸ INTO.*

break out of something to get out of a confining place or situation; to escape from something or some place. □ *He couldn't break out of a paper bag!* 🄽 *They do everything they can to prevent breakouts at the state prison.*

break out (with something) [for the skin] to erupt with a specific disease such as measles, chicken pox, rubella, etc. □ *Nick and Dan broke out with chicken pox.* □ *They both broke out at the same time.*

break out with something to utter or emit a shout or a cry. □ *The kids broke out with a cheer.* □ *They broke out with laughter every time they saw the lady with the red wig.*

break something out (of something) to remove something from something else by force. (The *of*-phrase is paraphrased with a *from*-phrase when the particle is transposed. See the 🄵 example.) □ *Carefully, she broke the gemstone out of the side of the cliff.* 🄵 *She broke the gemstone out from the cliff carefully.* □ *She broke the gemstone out carefully.*

BREAK ▸ OVER

break over something [for waves] to lift high and tumble over a barrier. □ *The waves broke over the rocks at the shore.* □ *Huge waves broke over the bow of the ship.*

BREAK ▸ THROUGH

break through (something) to force [one's way] through an obstruction. □ *The fire fighters broke through the wall easily.* □ *They broke through with no difficulty.* 🄽 *Dr. Wallace is responsible for a major scientific breakthrough.*

break through (to someone or something) to force [one's way] through an obstruction and reach someone or something on the other side. □ *The miners broke through to their trapped friends.* □ *They broke through easily.*

BREAK ▸ TO

break one's back to do something AND **break one's neck to do something** to go to a great deal of trouble and effort to do something. (Informal.) □ *You surely don't expect me to break my back to do it, do you?* □ *I broke my neck to get this done on time.*

break something to someone to disclose some news or information to someone. (Often said of unpleasant news.) □ *I hate to be the one to break this to you, but there is trouble at home.* □ *We broke the news to Ken gently.*

BREAK ▸ UP

break someone up to cause someone to begin laughing very hard. (*Someone* includes *oneself.*) □ *Everything she says just breaks me up.* 🅃 *The joke broke up the audience.* □ *He broke himself up with the realization of what a silly mistake he had made.*

break something up to put an end to some kind of fighting or arguing. (Figurative.) □ *Okay, you guys, break it up!* □ *Break it up and leave the area!* □ *The teacher broke up the fight in the school yard.*

break something up (into something) to break something into smaller pieces. □ *We broke the crackers up into much smaller pieces.* 🅃 *Please break up the crackers into smaller pieces if you want to feed the ducks.* □ *They broke the crackers up.* 🄰 *She put the pieces of the broken-up vase into a bag.* 🄽 *The breakup of the large company angered the stockholders.*

break up 1. [for something] to fall apart; to be broken to pieces. (Typically said of a ship breaking up on rocks.) □ *In the greatest storm of the century, the ship broke up on the reef.* □ *It broke up and sank.* **2.** [for two people] to end a romance; [for lovers] to separate permanently. □ *Terry and Albert broke up. Did you hear?* 🄽 *It wasn't much of a breakup. They just said good-bye.* **3.** [for married persons] to divorce. □ *After many years of bickering, they finally broke up.* 🄽 *When was the breakup? When did they divorce?* **4.** [for a marriage] to dissolve in divorce. □ *The marriage finally broke up.* 🄽 *It all ended in a rather nasty breakup.* **5.** to begin laughing very hard. □ *The comedian told a particularly good joke, and the audience broke up.* □ *I always break up when I hear her sing. She is so bad!*

break up (into something) AND **break into something** to divide into smaller parts. □ *The glass broke up into a thousand pieces.* □ *It hit the floor and broke up, flinging bits everywhere.*

break up (with someone) to end a romantic relationship with someone. (See also *break (off) with someone.*) □ *Jill broke up with Albert.* □ *I just knew they would break up.* 🄽 *She has been very sad since her breakup with Tom.*

BREAK ▸ WITH

break bread with someone to eat a meal with someone. (Stilted or old-fashioned.) □ *Please come by and break bread with us sometime.* □ *I would like to break bread with you.*

break (off) with someone to end communication with someone; to *break up (with someone);* to end a relationship with someone, especially a romantic relationship, or to create a break between adult members of a family. □ *Terri has broken off with Sam.* □ *We thought she would break with him pretty soon.*

BREATHE ▸ DOWN

breathe down someone's neck 1. [for someone] to hover over someone impatiently, urging completion of something. (Figurative.) □ *Stop breathing down my neck! I'm going as fast as I can.* □ *I wish you would stop breathing down my neck. I can't work any faster.* **2.** [for something] to represent an approaching deadline. (Figurative.) □ *The project deadline is breathing down my neck.* □ *The due date for this paper is breathing down my neck.*

BREATHE ▸ IN

breathe in to inhale; to take air into the lungs. □ *Now, breathe in. Breathe out.* □ *Breathe in; enjoy the summer air.*

breathe something in to take something into the lungs, such as air, medicinal vapors, gas, etc. □ *Breathe the vapor in slowly. It will help your cold.* 🅃 *Breathe in that fresh air!*

BREATHE ▸ INTO

breathe into something to exhale into something; to put one's breath into something. □ *I was told to breathe into a tube that was connected to a machine of some type.* □ *Please breathe into this.*

breathe something into something to revive something; to introduce something new or positive into a situation. (Figurative.) □ *Her attitude breathed* *new life into the company.* □ *The project breathed a new spirit into the firm.*

BREATHE ► OF

breathe something (of something) (to someone) to tell something to someone. (Usually in the negative.) □ *Don't breathe a word of this to anyone!* □ *I won't breathe a word!* □ *I won't breathe a word to anyone!*

BREATHE ► ON

See under *BREATHE ► (UP)ON.*

BREATHE ► OUT

breathe out to exhale. □ *Now, breathe out. Breathe in.* □ *Breathe out slowly.*

breathe something out to exhale something. □ *At last, he breathed his last breath out, and that was the end.* [T] *Breathe out your breath slowly.*

BREATHE ► TO

breathe something (of something) (to someone) See under *BREATHE ► OF.*

BREATHE ► (UP)ON

breathe (up)on someone or something to exhale on someone or something. (*Upon* is formal and less commonly used than *on.*) □ *Please don't breathe upon the food.* □ *Don't breathe on me!*

BREEZE ► ALONG

breeze along to travel along casually, rapidly, and happily; to go through life in a casual and carefree manner. □ *Kristine was just breezing along the road when she ran off onto the shoulder.* □ *We just breezed along the highway, barely paying attention to what we were doing.* □ *Don't just breeze along through life!*

BREEZE ► AWAY

breeze away to leave quickly or abruptly. □ *She said nothing more. She just breezed away.* □ *I breezed away without stopping to say good-bye.*

BREEZE ► IN

breeze in (from some place) See *sweep in (from some place)* under *SWEEP ► IN.*

breeze in(to some place) to enter a place quickly, in a happy and carefree manner. □ *She breezed into the conference room and sat down at the head of the table.* □ *Jerry breezed in and said hello.*

BREEZE ► OFF

breeze off to leave quickly or abruptly. □ *Don't just breeze off! Stay and talk.* □ *Lily breezed off in a huffy manner.*

BREEZE ► OUT

breeze out (of some place) to leave a place quickly. □ *She was here for a moment and then suddenly breezed out.* □ *She breezed out after a few minutes.*

BREEZE ► THROUGH

breeze through (something) **1.** to complete some task rapidly and easily. □ *I breezed through my calculus assignment in no time at all.* □ *It was not hard. I just breezed through.* **2.** to travel through a place rapidly. □ *They breezed through every little town without stopping.* □ *We didn't stop. We just breezed through.*

BREW ► UP

brew something up **1.** to brew something, as in making coffee or tea. □ *Can somebody brew some coffee up?* [T] *Let me brew up a pot of coffee, and then we'll talk.* **2.** to cause something to happen; to foment something. (Figurative.) □ *I could see that they were brewing some kind of trouble up.* [T] *Don't brew up any trouble!*

brew up to build up; [for something] to begin to build and grow. (Typically said of a storm.) □ *A bad storm is brewing up in the west.* □ *Something serious is brewing up in the western sky.*

BRIBE ► INTO

bribe someone into doing something to pay money to get someone to do something. □ *You can't bribe me into doing anything!* □ *Max bribed Lily into leaving early.*

BRICK ► IN

brick someone in to enclose or entrap someone by building a brick wall. □ *The count bricked the visitor in. It was a cruel murder.* [T] *Why did he brick in his visitor?*

BRICK ▸ UP

brick something up to fill up an opening with a brick wall. ☐ *He bricked the doorway up.* Ⓣ *Why did he brick up the opening?* Ⓐ *There was no door, just a bricked-up place where the door had been.*

BRIDGE ▸ OVER

bridge over something to make a bridge or passage over something. ☐ *They bridged over each of the streams as they came to them.* ☐ *I think we can bridge over this little river in a few days if we work hard.*

BRIDLE ▸ AT

bridle at someone or something to show that one is offended by someone or something. ☐ *She bridled at the suggestion that she should go.* ☐ *Tony bridled at Max. Max was going to have to be dealt with.*

BRIEF ▸ ABOUT

brief someone about someone or something AND **brief someone on someone or something** to tell someone the essential details about someone or something. ☐ *We need to brief the president about the latest event.* ☐ *I have to brief Michael on Carl.* ☐ *I will brief Jane on the negotiations.*

BRIEF ▸ ON

brief someone on someone or something See the previous entry.

BRIGHTEN ▸ UP

brighten up to become brighter; to lighten, especially with sunshine. ☐ *The sky is brightening up a little.* ☐ *When the morning sky brightens up just a little, the birds begin to sing.*

BRIM ▸ OVER

brim (over) (with something) to overflow with something. (*Over* does not move.) ☐ *The basket was brimming over with flowers.* ☐ *It was brimming with flowers.* ☐ *It was brimming over.*

BRIM ▸ WITH

See the previous entry.

BRING ▸ ABOUT

bring something about to make something happen. ☐ *I am unable to bring the desired result about.* Ⓣ *He claimed he could bring about a miracle.*

BRING ▸ AGAINST

bring a charge against someone or something to file a complaint against someone or a group; to begin a legal process against someone or a group. (*Charge* can also be *charges* even if only one charge is involved.) ☐ *We brought a charge against the town council.* ☐ *Sam brought charges against Jeff.*

BRING ▸ ALONG

bring someone or something along (to something) to bring someone or something with one to some event. ☐ *I brought my uncle along to the party.* Ⓣ *Please bring along your camera to the show.* ☐ *Please bring your friend along.*

BRING ▸ AROUND

bring someone around (to something) **1.** to help an unconscious person become conscious; to bring a person to consciousness. ☐ *After a moment we were able to bring the victim around to consciousness.* Ⓣ *The smelling salts brought around the victim.* ☐ *The salts brought her around.* ☐ *She was brought around by the smelling salts.* **2.** to convert a person to a particular way of thinking. ☐ *We finally brought her around to our way of thinking.* ☐ *I knew we could bring her around.* ☐ *Ken was brought around to our position.* **3.** to bring a person to visit a place. ☐ *Bring your wife around to our house sometime.* Ⓣ *Bring around your friend to our little gathering.* ☐ *Do bring John around.* ☐ *John was brought around to our place on one of Ken's visits.*

bring something around (to someone or something) **1.** to move something, such as a vehicle, from one side of a building to another. ☐ *Would you kindly have James bring the car around?* Ⓣ *Tony will bring around the car to us.* ☐ *He will bring it around.* ☐ *It was brought around to where the light was better so we could see it.* **2.** to distribute something to someone or a group. (Said by a person who intends to receive what is brought.) ☐ *Please bring the snacks around to us.* Ⓣ *Carl is bringing around* *the snacks to us.* □ *He is bringing the snacks around.* □ *The papers were brought around for us to examine.*

BRING ▸ AWAY

bring something away (from something) **1.** to come away from some event with some important insight or information. □ *I brought some valuable advice away from the lecture.* 🅃 *She brought away some valuable advice from the meeting.* □ *She brought some happy thoughts away.* □ *Was anything of any use brought away from the conference?* **2.** to move something away from something. (A request to move something away from something and toward the requester.) □ *Bring the pitcher of water away from the fireplace.* 🅃 *Bring away the pitcher from the fireplace when you come.* □ *The candle is too near the drapes. Please bring it away.* □ *The chair was brought away from the window.*

BRING ▸ BACK

bring someone back out [for an applauding audience] to succeed in bringing a performer back onto the stage. □ *They brought her back out about seven times, cheering and applauding.* □ *She was brought back out repeatedly for curtain calls.*

bring someone back to reality to force someone to face reality. (*Someone* includes *oneself*.) □ *The rain shower brought her back to reality.* □ *Liz was brought back to reality by a rude shock.* □ *She brought herself back to reality when she jumped into the cold water.*

bring someone or something back **1.** to make someone or some living creature come back to life. (Usually in the negative.) □ *There was nothing that would bring Jimmy's cat back. It was truly dead.* 🅃 *Not even a magician could bring back the cat.* □ *You will never be able to bring Claire back.* □ *She cannot be brought back.* **2.** to make someone or something return. □ *Would you please bring the child back?* 🅃 *Bring back my child!* □ *Please bring back the mustard. We need it now.* □ *The borrowed lawn mower was brought back the next day.*

bring something back to restore an earlier style or practice. □ *Please bring the good old days back.* 🅃 *Bring back good times for all of us.* □ *Those days cannot be brought back.*

bring something back (to someone) to remind someone of something. □ *The funeral brought memories back.* 🅃 *The warm winds brought back the old feeling of loneliness that I had experienced so many times in the tropics.*

BRING ▸ BEFORE

bring someone before someone or something to bring a person to an authority, such as a judge, for criticism or discipline. □ *They brought Terri before the committee for her explanation.* □ *I brought you before me to explain your side of the story.* □ *Wally was brought before the committee.*

bring something before someone or something to bring a matter to the attention of someone or a group. □ *I wanted to bring this matter before you before it got any worse.* □ *I will have to bring this matter before the committee.* □ *Lily was brought before the judge to explain her actions.*

BRING ▸ DOWN

bring someone down **1.** to assist or accompany someone from a higher place to a lower place. □ *Please bring your friends down so I can meet them.* 🅃 *She brought down her cousin, who had been taking a nap upstairs.* □ *Aunt Mattie was brought down for supper.* **2.** to bring someone to a place for a visit. □ *Let's bring Tom and Terri down for a visit this weekend.* 🅃 *We brought down Tom just last month.* □ *They were brought down at our expense for a weekend visit.* **3.** to restore someone to a normal mood or attitude. (After a period of elation or, perhaps, drug use.) □ *The bad news brought me down quickly.* 🅃 *I was afraid that the change of plans would bring down the entire group.*

bring someone down to earth to help someone face reality; to help someone who is euphoric become more realistic. □ *The events helped bring us all down to earth.* □ *I hate to be the one to bring* *you down to earth, but things aren't as good as you think.* □ *They were brought down to earth by the revelation of the truth.* Ⓝ *Yes, I guess I needed a good bringdown. Thanks.*

bring something crashing down (around one) to cause all one's plans to go wrong; to cause someone's basic orientation to collapse. □ *Her actions finally brought everything crashing down around her.* □ *The events brought my whole world crashing down.* □ *My whole world was brought crashing down around me.*

bring something down **1.** to move something from a higher place to a lower place. □ *Bring that box down, please.* Ⓣ *And while you're up there, please bring down the box marked winter clothing.* □ *The box was brought down as requested.* **2.** to lower something, such as prices, profit, taxes, etc. □ *The governor pledged to bring taxes down.* Ⓣ *I hope they bring down taxes.* □ *Taxes were never brought down, in fact, they went up.* **3.** to defeat or overcome something, such as an enemy, a government, etc. □ *The events of the last week will probably bring the government down.* Ⓣ *The scandal will bring down the government, I hope.* □ *The government was brought down by the scandal.*

bring something down on one('s head) to cause the collapse of something or some enterprise onto oneself. (Figurative.) □ *You have brought the whole thing down on your own head.* Ⓣ *You will bring down everything on your head!* □ *He jarred the shelves and the whole business was brought down on his head.*

bring something down to something to make a concept simpler to understand. □ *Why don't you bring all this down to my level?* □ *Everything was brought down to the child's level.*

bring the house down [for a performance or a performer] to excite the audience into making a great clamor of approval. (Figurative.) □ *Karen's act brought the house down.* Ⓣ *She brought down the house.*

BRING ▸ FORTH

bring someone or something forth to present or produce someone or something. □ *Bring the roast pig forth!* Ⓣ *Bring forth the roast pig!* □ *Please bring Mr. Franklin forth.* □ *Bill Franklin was brought forth at the last minute.*

BRING ▸ FORWARD

bring someone or something forward to introduce someone or something; to move someone or something into a more visible position. □ *Please bring him forward so that we can examine him.* □ *Please bring your chair forward so I can see you.* □ *The chair was brought forward as Lily requested.* □ *Bring yourself forward a little.*

BRING ▸ IN

See also under *BRING ▸ IN(TO).*

bring a verdict in [for a jury] to deliver its decision to the court. □ *Do you think they will bring a verdict in today?* Ⓣ *The jury brought in their verdict around midnight.* □ *A verdict was finally brought in by the jury.*

bring someone in (on something) to include someone in some deed or activity. □ *I'm going to have to bring a specialist in on this.* Ⓣ *Please bring in several specialists on this.* □ *Let's bring Dave in before we go any further.* □ *Dave was brought in at the last minute.*

bring something in to earn something —an amount of money; to draw or attract an amount of money. □ *My part-time job brings thirty dollars in every month.* Ⓣ *She brings in a lot of money.* □ *A lot of money was brought in by Lily's parents.* Ⓣ *Their appeal for donations brought in a lot of contributions.*

BRING ▸ INTO

bring someone into the world to deliver a baby; to attend the birth of someone. □ *The doctor who brought me into the world died last week.* □ *I was brought into the world by a kindly old doctor.*

bring someone or something into action to activate someone or something; to cause someone or something to function as intended. □ *The threats brought the police into action.* □ *A kick in the side* *brought the television set into action.* □ *Lily was brought into action by Tom's cries for help.*

bring someone or something into disrepute to dishonor or discredit someone or something. (*Someone* includes *oneself.*) □ *This matter will bring the entire committee into disrepute.* □ *It brings me into disrepute.* □ *Lily was brought into disrepute by evil gossip.* □ *He brought himself into disrepute when he took on the mayor.*

bring someone or something into line (with someone or something) **1.** to make someone or something even with someone or something. □ *I brought the books into line with the others on the shelf.* □ *I brought Jimmy into line with the other scouts.* **2.** to make someone or something conform to someone or something. (Figurative.) □ *We brought Ted into line with the guidelines.* □ *Sam brought his proposal into line with the company standards.* □ *Lily was brought into line by our little talk.* □ *She was not able to bring herself into line with the requirements.* □ *He was brought into line by the other boys.*

bring someone or something into prominence to cause someone or something to become famous or renowned. □ *The accident brought Mike into national prominence.* □ *The current national need for engineers brought our school into prominence.* □ *A terrible scandal brought Lily into prominence.*

bring someone or something into view to cause someone or something to be seen or to be visible. □ *A bright light brought the sleeping cattle into view.* □ *Please bring your child into view.* □ *The distant shore was brought into view by the binoculars.*

bring something into being to cause something to be; to create something. □ *How can I bring my new scheme into being?* □ *The new scheme was brought into being by a lot of hard work.*

bring something into blossom to make a plant or tree bloom. □ *The special plant food brought the rosebush into blossom.* □ *The roses were brought into blossom by the lovely weather.*

bring something into focus **1.** to make something seen through lenses sharply visible. □ *I adjusted the binoculars until I brought the bird sharply into focus.* □ *The flowers were brought into focus by adjusting the controls.* **2.** to make something clearly understandable. (Figurative.) □ *I think we will have a better discussion of the problem if you will say a few words to bring it more sharply into focus.* □ *Please try to bring your major point into focus earlier in the essay.*

bring something into play **1.** to cause something to become a factor in something. □ *Now, this recent development brings some other factors into play.* □ *Something else was brought into play by the strange event.* **2.** [for the shares of a company] to become the subject of a takeover bid. □ *The recent drop in the value of D and D stock brought the company into play.* □ *The company was brought into play by a news story.*

bring something into question to cause something to be doubted; to cause something to be questioned. □ *What you have just told me seems to bring the wisdom of the trip into question.* □ *Your presence here has been brought into question.*

bring something into service to begin to use something; to start something up. □ *They are bringing a much larger boat into service next month.* □ *A newer machine will be brought into service next month.*

BRING ▶ IN(TO)

bring someone or something into contact with someone or something to cause things or people to touch or associate with one another. (*Someone* includes *oneself.*) □ *She hasn't been the same since I brought her into contact with the child who had chicken pox.* □ *Don't bring your hand in contact with the poison ivy.* □ *Don't bring him into contact with Fred.* □ *The poison ivy was brought into contact with your legs, it appears.* □ *She was afraid of bringing* *herself in contact with people who might still be contagious.*

bring someone or something in(to some place) to permit or assist someone or something to enter something or some place. □ *Do you mind if I bring my sister in here with me?* 🅃 *Please bring in your sister.* □ *Bring your sister in.* □ *My sister was brought into the room.*

BRING ▸ OFF

bring someone or something off something to remove someone or something from something or some place. □ *The acid brought the rust off the beam.* □ *We brought Jimmy off the porch so he could see the new kittens in the bushes.* □ *A special solvent brought the old paint off the railing.*

bring something off to cause something to happen; to carry out a plan successfully. (Informal.) □ *Do you think you can bring it off?* 🅃 *She brought off her plan without a hitch!* □ *The plan was brought off without a hitch.*

BRING ▸ ON

See also under *BRING ▸ (UP)ON.*

bring someone on **1.** to bring someone out onto the stage. (See also *bring someone out on something, bring someone up on something.*) □ *Now, for the next act, I'm going to bring a chorus on, and I'm sure you'll love them.* 🅃 *Bring on the clowns!* □ *The clowns were brought on after the elephants.* **2.** to arouse someone sexually. □ *Ted sought to bring Sally on, and she left.* 🅃 *He tried to bring on one of the guests.* □ *Lily was not to be brought on.*

bring something on **1.** to cause something to happen; to cause a situation to occur. □ *What brought this event on?* 🅃 *What brought on the event?* □ *My comments were brought on by something I read last night.* **2.** to cause a case of or an attack of a disease. □ *What brought your coughing fit on?* 🅃 *Something brought it on.* □ *The attack was brought on by allergy.*

bring something on someone to cause something to go wrong for someone. (*Someone* includes *oneself.*) □ *You brought it on yourself. Don't complain.* □ *Max brought this problem on all of us.*

BRING ▸ OUT

bring one out of one's shell to make a person become more open and friendly. □ *We tried to bring Greg out of his shell, but he is very shy.* □ *It's hard to bring Greg out of his shell.*

bring out the best in someone to cause someone to behave in the best manner. □ *This kind of situation doesn't exactly bring out the best in me.* □ *Good weather brings out the best in me.*

bring someone or something out in droves to cause someone or some creature to come out in very large numbers. □ *The announcement of free food brought the students out in droves.* □ *The picnic brought the ants out in droves.* □ *The ants were brought out in droves by all the spilled soda pop and dropped crumbs at the picnic.*

bring someone or something out (of something) to cause someone or something to emerge from something or some place. (The *of*-phrase is paraphrased with a *from*-phrase when the particle is transposed. See the 🄵 example.) □ *The explosion brought the people out of their homes.* 🅃 *It brought out all the people.* 🄵 *The explosion brought out everyone from their homes.* □ *The medication brought Sam out of his depression.* □ *All the people were brought out of their homes by the noise.*

bring someone out on something to make someone come onto the stage from the stage sides or wings. (See also *bring someone on.*) □ *Let's applaud loudly and bring her out on stage again.* □ *Lily was brought out on stage by the applause.*

bring something out to issue something; to publish something; to present something [to the public]. □ *I am bringing a new book out.* 🅃 *I hear you have brought out a new edition of your book.* □ *A new edition has been brought out.*

bring something out (in someone) to cause a particular quality to be displayed by a person, such as virtue, courage, a mean streak, selfishness, etc. □ *You bring the best out in me.* 🅃 *This kind of thing brings out the worst in me.* □ *This brings the worst out.*

bring something out in the open to make something publicly known. □ *We wanted to bring it out into the open sooner, but the politicians refused.* □ *The whole matter was brought out in the open.*

bring something out of mothballs to bring something out of storage and into use; to restore something to active service. (Both literal and figurative uses.) □ *They were going to bring a number of ships out of mothballs, but the war ended before they needed them.* □ *My winter coat was brought out of mothballs just in time.*

bring something out (of someone) to cause something to be said by a person, such as a story, the truth, an answer, etc. □ *We threatened her a little and that brought the truth out of her.* 🅃 *This ought to bring out the truth!* □ *This will bring the truth out.* □ *The truth was brought out by a little persuasion.*

BRING ► OVER

bring someone over from some place to bring someone from a place, from nearby or from across a large body of water. □ *We brought the pianist over from Austria.* 🅃 *They brought over the neighbors from across the street.* □ *A soprano was brought over from Moscow.*

bring someone over ((to) some place) to bring a person for a visit to some place. □ *Why don't you bring her over to our place for a visit?* 🅃 *You should bring over your girlfriend for a visit.* □ *Yes, bring her over.* □ *She could be brought over here.*

bring someone over to something to bring someone for a visit and a meal or other event. □ *Please bring your friend over to dinner sometime.* □ *I hope that your children will be brought over to dinner too.* 🅃 *I want to bring over my husband sometime.*

BRING ► THROUGH

bring someone through something to help someone endure something, such as a disease, an emotional upset, or a stressful period. (*Someone* includes *oneself.*) □ *The doctor brought Tom through the sickness.* □ *Liz was brought through the ordeal by her friends.* □ *She brought herself through the crisis with the help of her strong religious faith.*

BRING ► TO

See *call something to mind* under *CALL ► TO.*

bring one to one's feet AND **bring something to its feet** to make someone or an audience rise up applauding or cheering in approval or in salute to someone or something. (Usually refers to an audience.) □ *The finale brought the audience to its feet.* □ *Liz was brought to her feet by the playing of the national anthem.*

bring one to one's senses to cause someone to return to normal [after being out of control or irrational]. □ *A gentle slap in the face brought him to his senses.* □ *Liz was brought to her senses quickly.*

bring one to oneself to cause one to become rational; to cause one to act normal. □ *A glass of ice water in the face brought her to herself.* □ *I was brought to myself by some smelling salts.*

bring someone or something to a halt to cause someone or something to stop immediately. (*Someone* includes *oneself.*) □ *The explosion brought the lecture to a halt.* □ *I brought the visitor to a halt at the front gate.* □ *Everything was quickly brought to a halt.* □ *They brought themselves to a halt as soon as they heard the command.*

bring someone or something to life to give vigor or vitality to someone or something; to reactivate someone or something. (Figurative.) □ *A little singing and dancing would have brought the play to life.* □ *Some coffee will bring you to life.* □ *The musical was brought to life by the performance of the star.*

bring someone or something to light to present or reveal someone or something to the public. □ *The newspaper story brought the problem to light.* □ *I have brought some interesting facts to light.* □ *The truth was brought to light by the cousin's revelation.*

bring someone or something to someone's attention to make someone aware of someone or something. □ *Thank you for bringing this to my attention.* □ *I am grateful for your bringing her to my attention.* □ *It was brought to Lily's attention first.*

bring someone or something to trial to bring a crime or a criminal into court for a trial. □ *At last, the thugs were brought to trial.* □ *We brought the case to trial a week later.* □ *The case was brought to trial very soon.*

bring someone to to help someone return to consciousness. □ *We worked to bring him to before he went into shock.* □ *He was finally brought to with the smelling salts.*

bring someone to a boil to make someone very angry. (Informal.) □ *This really brought her to a boil. She was fit to be tied.* □ *Lily was really brought to a boil by the news.*

bring someone to account to confront someone with a record of misdeeds and errors. □ *The committee decided to bring Lily to account.* □ *Lily was brought to account by the committee.*

bring someone to do something to cause someone to do something; to encourage someone to do something. (*Someone* includes *oneself.*) □ *What brought you to do this?* □ *I was brought to do this by a guilty conscience.* □ *She finally brought herself to realize how foolish she had been.*

bring someone to heel to cause someone to act in a disciplined fashion; to force someone to act in a more disciplined manner. □ *She tried to bring her husband to heel, but he had a mind of his own.* □ *He was brought to heel by his demanding wife.*

bring something home to someone **1.** to return home with a gift for someone. □ *I brought a box of candy home to the children.* □ *The candy was brought home to Lily by Ken.* **2.** to cause someone to realize something. (Figurative.) □ *My weakness was brought home to me by the heavy work I had been assigned to do.* 🅃 *The accident really brought home to me how frail we really are.*

bring something to a boil to heat liquid to its boiling point; to make something boil. □ *First, you must bring the soup to a boil.* □ *The soup was brought to a boil.*

bring something to a close to end something; to cause something to reach its final point and stop. (*Close* can be replaced with *climax, end.*) □ *I think it is time to bring this matter to a close.* □ *The matter has been brought to a close.*

bring something to a dead end to cause something to reach a point from which it can go no further. □ *The accident brought the project to a dead end.* □ *The study was brought to a dead end by the loss of federal funding.*

bring something to a head to cause a problem to become acute so that it must be attended to; to cause something to reach a crucial point. (Figurative.) □ *The failure of the banks brought many things to a head.* □ *The bad state of the financial system was brought to a head by the many bank failures.*

bring something to a standstill to cause a process or a job to reach a point at which it must stop. □ *The accident brought the work to a standstill.* □ *The strike brought construction to a standstill.*

bring something to a successful conclusion to complete something successfully. □ *They brought the battle to a successful conclusion.* □ *The case was brought to a successful conclusion by the prosecutor.*

bring something to fruition to make something come into being; to achieve a success. □ *Do you think you can bring this plan to fruition?* □ *The plan was brought to fruition by the efforts of everyone.*

bring something to its feet See *bring one to one's feet.*

BRING TO

bring something to mind See *call something to mind* under *CALL ▸ TO.*

BRING ▸ TO

bring something to rest to cause a machine, vehicle, or process to stop. □ *Jill brought the car to rest against the curb.* □ *The car was brought to rest against the curb.*

bring something to someone's aid to bring something with which to help someone. □ *The officer brought medical supplies to our aid.* □ *An ambulance was brought to the injured man's aid.*

bring something to the fore to move something forward; to make something more prominent or noticeable. □ *All the talk about costs brought the question of budgets to the fore.* □ *The question of budget planning was brought to the fore.*

BRING ▸ TOGETHER

bring someone together **1.** to cause people to gather into a group. □ *He brought everyone together in the drawing room.* □ *They were brought together in a large conference room.* **2.** to attempt to get people to agree with one another. □ *I tried to bring them together, but they are too stubborn.* □ *They could not be brought together on a price.*

bring something all together to organize something; to coordinate something or some event. □ *The party was a great success. Lily was the one who brought it all together.* □ *It was a difficult conference to organize, but Sam brought it all together.*

bring something together to assemble things; to gather things together. □ *Thank you for bringing everything together so we can begin work.* □ *Everything was brought together so we could see what there was.* 🅃 *We brought together all the tools that we needed.*

BRING ▸ UNDER

bring someone or something under control to calm someone or something down; to organize and restrain someone or something. (*Someone* includes *oneself.*) □ *Quickly, we brought the fire under control.* □ *It was difficult to bring Andrew under control.* □ *The fire was brought under control.* □ *At last he was able to bring himself under control.*

bring someone or something under one's control to achieve dominion over someone or something. □ *The dictator was at last able to bring the army under his control.* □ *Liz could not bring Teddy under her control.* □ *Walter could not be brought under Lily's control.*

bring someone or something under someone or something to assign someone or something to someone or something; to put someone or something under the management of someone or something. □ *The boss brought the accounting department under the legal department.* □ *I had David brought under me, so I could keep an eye on his day-to-day work.* □ *David was brought under my jurisdiction.*

BRING ▸ UP

bring someone or something up **1.** to cause someone or something to go up with one from a lower place to a higher place. □ *We brought them up and let them view the city from the balcony.* 🅃 *Why did you bring up Tom? Wasn't he comfortable down there?* □ *I brought up some binoculars so you can enjoy the view from up here.* □ *They were brought up from below.* **2.** to mention someone or something. (*Someone* includes *oneself.*) □ *Why did you have to bring that up?* 🅃 *Must you bring up bad memories?* 🅃 *Why did you bring up Walter?* □ *Walter was brought up for discussion.* □ *He brought himself up again and again. What a self-centered person!* **3.** to raise someone or something; to care for someone or something up to adulthood. □ *We brought the dog up from a pup.* 🅃 *We brought up the dog carefully and sold it for a good profit.* □ *I brought Sammy up the best I* *could.* □ *Sammy was brought up with the best child-raising methods.* Ⓝ *They say she has had a good upbringing.*

bring someone or something up to date to modernize someone or something. (*Someone* includes *oneself.*) □ *We brought the room up to date with a little paint and some modern furniture.* □ *I can bring you up to date with a new hairdo.* □ *You will be brought up to date as soon as possible.* □ *Shabby old Tom really needed to bring himself up to date.*

bring someone or something up to something to raise someone or something to a particular standard, level, expectation, etc. (*Someone* includes *oneself.*) □ *What do I have to do to bring Billy up to grade level?* □ *I brought the lab up to state standards in less than a year.* □ *The lab was brought up to standards quickly.* □ *Tom brought himself up to the required level of competence in no time.*

bring someone or something up to speed to cause someone or something to move or operate at a normal or desired speed. (*Someone* includes *oneself.*) □ *Terri did everything she could to bring her workers up to speed, but couldn't.* □ *Can we bring this production line up to speed?* □ *I was brought up to speed through the application of a lot of concentrated effort.* □ *She was unable to bring herself up to speed in time for the contest.*

bring someone up for something **1.** to suggest someone's name for something. (*Someone* includes *oneself.*) □ *I would like to bring Beth up for vice president.* Ⓣ *I will bring up Beth for this office if you don't.* □ *Beth has been brought up for another office already.* □ *Tom always brings himself up for head of the department.* **2.** to put someone's name up for promotion, review, discipline, etc. (*Someone* includes *oneself.*) □ *We brought Tom up for promotion.* Ⓣ *The boss brought up Tom too.* □ *Tom was brought up for something also.* □ *I had to bring myself up for promotion.*

bring someone up on something to make someone come up onto the stage from the audience. (See also *bring someone on.*) □ *The applause brought Wally up on the stage.* □ *Wally was brought up on stage.*

bring someone up on something to provide something while raising a child to adulthood. □ *She brought her children up on fast food.* □ *We were all brought up on television cartoons.* Ⓣ *You shouldn't bring up your children on that kind of entertainment!*

bring someone up sharply AND **bring someone up short** to surprise or shock someone; to make someone face something unpleasant, suddenly. □ *The slap in the face brought me up sharply.* □ *The incident brought me up short.* □ *We were brought up sharply by the revelation.*

bring someone up short See the previous entry.

bring someone up to date (on someone or something) to inform someone of the latest information about something. (*Someone* includes *oneself.*) □ *Let me bring you up to date on what is happening in the village.* □ *Please bring me up to date.* □ *They were brought up to date on the project.* □ *I need some time to bring myself up to date on this project.*

bring something up for something to bring a matter up to be dealt with; to raise an issue that is to be voted on. □ *We will have to bring this up for a vote.* □ *It was brought up for discussion.*

bring up the rear to come along last; to be at the end of a line or procession. □ *She always comes along last, bringing up the rear.* □ *I'll bring up the rear.*

BRING ▸ (UP)ON

bring something (up)on oneself to be the cause of one's own trouble. (*Upon* is formal and less commonly used than *on.*) □ *It's your own fault. You brought it upon yourself.* □ *You brought it all on yourself.*

BRING ▸ WITH

bring something with to carry something along with oneself. (Informal or regional.) □ *Are you going to bring* *your umbrella with?* □ *I brought it with. Don't worry.*

BRING ▸ WITHIN

bring someone or something within range (of someone or something) to cause someone or something to be in someone's or something's [gun] sights. (*Someone* includes *oneself*.) □ *Don't bring the hunters within range of the farmer's gunsights.* □ *The bait brought the geese within range of Jeff and his friends.* □ *The ducks were brought within rage of the hunters.* □ *He foolishly brought himself within range and paid for his foolishness with his life.*

bring something within something to adjust something into a particular range; to adjust a parameter. □ *Let's try to bring your cholesterol within the normal range.* □ *It was brought within the normal range by an expensive drug.*

BRISTLE ▸ AT

bristle at something to show sudden anger or other negative response to something. (As a dog or a cat might raise the hair on its shoulders in anger.) □ *She bristled at the suggestion.* □ *I knew Lily would bristle at the appearance of Max.*

BRISTLE ▸ WITH

bristle with something to demonstrate one's anger or rage with a strong negative response. □ *She was just bristling with anger. I don't know what set her off.* □ *Walter bristled with rage as he entered the police station.*

BROACH ▸ WITH

broach something with someone to mention something to someone; to bring up an idea to someone. □ *I hate to be the one to have to broach this with you, but your trousers are torn.* □ *A delicate matter must be broached with Mr. Rogers.*

BROADEN ▸ OUT

broaden out to become wider; to expand. □ *The river broadened out and became deeper.* □ *The road broadens out here.*

broaden something out to make something wider; to expand something. □ *Now, broaden this part out a little, so it looks like a cloud, not a painted pillow.* [T] *Broaden out the river in your painting so it looks very wide.* □ *The photographic view of the valley can be broadened out by using a different lens.*

BROOD ▸ ABOUT

brood about someone or something AND **brood on someone or something; brood over someone or something** to fret about someone or something. □ *Please don't brood about Albert. He is no good for you.* □ *There's no need to brood on Jeff. He can take care of himself.* □ *I won't brood over this any longer.*

BROOD ▸ ON

brood on someone or something See the previous entry.

BROOD ▸ OVER

brood over someone or something See *brood about someone or something* under *BROOD ▸ ABOUT.*

BROWBEAT ▸ INTO

browbeat someone into something to bully or intimidate someone into something. □ *It won't do any good to try to browbeat me into it.* □ *I was browbeaten into doing it once. I refuse to do it again.*

BROWN ▸ OFF

brown someone off to make someone angry. (Slang.) □ *You really brown me off!* [T] *The private browned off the sergeant.* □ *Harold was really browned off.*

BROWN ▸ OUT

brown out [for the electricity] to decrease in power. (Causing electric lights to dim. Not quite a blackout.) □ *The lights browned out and almost went out altogether.* [N] *There was a brownout every night at midnight on the little island.*

BROWSE ▸ AMONG

browse among something **1.** [for an animal] to wander about among plants and trees, selecting and eating some. □ *The deer were browsing among the goodies in my garden.* □ *The cows were browsing among the plants in the field.* **2.** [for someone] to look at or survey different items of reading material. □ *I browsed among the books on the rack until I found what I wanted.* □ *I browsed among the books for something suitable.*

BROWSE ▸ ON

browse on something [for an animal] to feed on some kind of plant material. □ *The deer browsed on the tender shoots of my garden.* □ *The animal browsed on my carrots.*

BROWSE ▸ OVER

browse over something AND **browse through something** [for someone] to glance through written or printed material. □ *Why don't you browse over this and call me about it in the morning?* □ *I want to browse through this magazine.* □ *When it has been browsed through by everyone, throw it away.*

BROWSE ▸ THROUGH

browse through something See the previous entry.

BRUIT ▸ ABOUT

bruit something about to spread a rumor around; to gossip something around. □ *You really shouldn't bruit that about, you know.* □ *The story was bruited about all over the office.*

BRUSH ▸ AGAINST

brush (up) against someone or something to move past and touch someone or something. □ *I brushed up against the freshly painted wall as I passed.* □ *I guess I brushed against Walter as I walked by.* □ *The houseplant was brushed up against so much that it finally lost all its leaves.*

BRUSH ▸ ASIDE

brush someone or something aside **1.** to push or shove someone or something out of the way. □ *Don't just brush me aside. I almost fell over.* □ *I brushed the branch aside, not realizing it was poison ivy.* □ *The branch was brushed aside casually.* **2.** to cast someone or something away; to rid oneself of someone or something; to ignore or dismiss someone or something. (Figurative.) □ *You must not brush this matter aside.* □ *The clerk brushed the old man aside and moved on to the next person in line.*

BRUSH ▸ AWAY

brush something away (from something) to remove something from something by brushing; to get dirt or crumbs off something by brushing. □ *He brushed a bit of lint away from Tom's collar.* 🅃 *She brushed away the crumbs from the table.* □ *Liz brushed the crumbs away.* □ *The dust was brushed away from his shoes.*

BRUSH ▸ BY

brush by someone or something AND **brush past someone or something** to push quickly past someone or something. □ *She brushed by the little group of people standing there talking.* □ *I brushed by the plant, knocking it over.* □ *You just brushed past me!*

BRUSH ▸ DOWN

brush something down to clean and neaten fur or fabric by brushing. □ *Why don't you brush your coat down? It's very linty.* 🅃 *I brushed down my trousers, and they looked much better.* □ *My coat was brushed down before I left home.*

BRUSH ▸ OFF

brush someone off **1.** to remove something, such as dust or lint, from someone by brushing. □ *The porter brushed Mr. Harris off and was rewarded with a very small tip.* 🅃 *The porter had never brushed off such a miserly man before.* **2.** to reject someone; to dismiss someone. □ *He brushed her off, telling her she had no appointment.* 🅃 *He brushed off Mrs. Franklin, who was only trying to be nice to him.* □ *Mr. Franklin should not be brushed off.* 🄽 *She gave him the brushoff and was glad of it.*

brush something off ((of) someone or something) to remove something from someone or something by brushing. (The *of*-phrase is paraphrased with a *from*-phrase when the particle is transposed. See the 🄵 example.) □ *I brushed a little lint off her collar.* 🅃 *I brushed off the lint that was on her collar.* 🄵 *I brushed off the lint from her* *collar.* □ *Liz brushed it off.* □ *The leaves were brushed off Timmy as he came into the house.*

BRUSH ▸ OVER

brush over someone or something to deal lightly with an important person or matter; to just barely mention someone or something. □ *I want to hear more. You only brushed over the part I was interested in.* □ *You only brushed over your girlfriend. Tell us about her.*

BRUSH ▸ PAST

brush past someone or something See under *BRUSH ▸ BY.*

BRUSH ▸ UP

brush something up to improve one's knowledge of something or one's ability to do something. (See also *brush up (on something).*) □ *I need to brush my French up a little bit.* 🅃 *I need to brush up my French.*

brush (up) against someone or something See under *BRUSH ▸ AGAINST.*

brush up (on something) to improve one's knowledge of something or one's ability to do something. □ *I need to brush up on my German.* □ *My German is weak. I had better brush up.*

BUBBLE ▸ OVER

bubble over **1.** [for boiling or effervescent liquid] to spill or splatter over the edge of its container. □ *The pot bubbled over and put out the cooking fire.* □ *The stew bubbled over.* **2.** [for someone] to be so happy and merry that it spills over onto other people. □ *She was just bubbling over, she was so happy.* □ *Lily bubbled over with joy.*

BUBBLE ▸ UP

bubble up (through something) [for a liquid] to seep up or well up through something, such as from between rocks, through a crack in the floor, or through a hole in the bottom of a boat. □ *The water bubbled up through a crack in the basement floor.* □ *It just kept bubbling up.*

BUCK ▸ FOR

buck for something to try for something; to try to achieve a new status or to get something. (Slang.) □ *Are you bucking for promotion or something?* □ *Ken is bucking for a new job classification.*

BUCK ▸ OFF

buck someone off [for a horse or similar animal] to rear up in an attempt to shake off its rider. □ *The horse tried to buck Sharon off, but she held on tight.* 🅃 *The horse bucked off its rider.*

BUCK ▸ UP

buck up to cheer up. (Slang.) □ *Buck up, chum. Everything will get better.* □ *It's not all that bad. Buck up.*

BUCKLE ▸ DOWN

buckle down (to something) to settle down to work at something; to get serious about doing something. □ *You must buckle down to your studies!* □ *I can't seem to buckle down.*

buckle someone or something down to attach someone or something down with straps that buckle together. (*Someone* includes *oneself.*) □ *They stopped to buckle the load down again.* 🅃 *Did you buckle down the kids?* □ *I buckled the vase down in the seat, as if it were a person.* □ *She buckled herself down with the leather straps provided.*

BUCKLE ▸ IN

buckle someone in to attach someone securely with a vehicle's seat belts. (This includes airplane seat belts. *Someone* includes *oneself.*) □ *Don't forget to buckle the children in.* 🅃 *Did you buckle in the children?* □ *The children are all buckled in.* □ *Please buckle yourself in.*

BUCKLE ▸ UNDER

buckle under **1.** [for something] to collapse. □ *With heavy trucks on it, the bridge buckled under.* □ *The table buckled under.* □ *Her knees buckled under and she collapsed.* **2.** [for someone] to collapse or give in under the burden of heavy demands or great anxiety. (Figurative.) □ *With so much to worry about, she buckled under.* □ *I was afraid she would buckle under.*

buckle under something to collapse under the weight of something. □ *The* *bridge buckled under the weight of the truck and collapsed.* □ *The table finally buckled under.*

BUCKLE ▸ UP

buckle someone or something up to attach someone or something securely with straps that buckle together. (This emphasizes the completeness and secureness of the act. *Someone* includes *oneself.*) □ *Buckle the children up before we leave.* 🅃 *Buckle up your shoes.* 🅃 *I will buckle up Jimmy.* □ *Buckle yourself up, if you please.*

buckle up to buckle one's seat belt, as in a car or plane. □ *Please buckle up!* □ *I wish you would obey the law and buckle up.*

BUD ▸ OUT

bud out [for a flowering plant or tree] to develop buds. □ *How early in the spring do the trees bud out around here?* □ *The trees bud out in early spring.*

BUDDY ▸ UP

buddy up (to someone) to become overly familiar or friendly with someone. □ *Don't try to buddy up to me now. It won't do any good.* □ *He always tries to buddy up, no matter how badly you treat him.*

buddy up (with someone) to join with another person to form a pair that will do something together or share something. □ *I buddied up with Carl, and we shared the canoe.* □ *Carl and I buddied up, and we shared the canoe.* □ *Let's buddy up, okay?* □ *They buddied up with each other.*

BUDGET ▸ FOR

budget something for someone or something to set aside a certain amount of money for someone or something. □ *Did you budget some money for the picnic?* □ *I budgeted a few hundred a month for Andrew.*

BUFF ▸ DOWN

buff something down to polish or smooth something by buffing. □ *I buffed the newly waxed table down with a cloth.* 🅃 *I'm going to go out and buff down the car.*

BUFF ▸ UP

buff something up to polish something to a shine. □ *He buffed his shoes up and went out for the evening.* 🅃 *He buffed up his shoes.*

BUFFET ▸ FROM

buffet someone or something from someone or something to someone or something to shift someone or something back and forth between people, things, or places, as if being tossed around by the waves of the sea. □ *The court buffeted the child from one relative to another.* □ *The office staff buffeted the memo from one desk to another.*

BUG ▸ OFF

bug off to cease bothering [someone]. (Slang.) □ *Bug off! Leave me alone!* □ *I wish you would bug off!*

BUG ▸ OUT

bug out to leave a place; to escape or desert a place. (Slang.) □ *Let's bug out. It's getting dangerous around here.* □ *It's time to bug out.*

BUILD ▸ DOWN

build down to reduce in volume or diminish. (The opposite of *build up.* Said of traffic.) □ *At about six, the going-home traffic begins to build down.* □ *When traffic builds down, I leave for home.*

BUILD ▸ IN(TO)

build someone in(to something) to make a person an integral part of an organization or a plan. □ *We built the mayor's nephew into the organizational structure of the town.* 🅃 *He built in his relatives from the very beginning.* □ *He built them in while he was president.* 🄰 *Todd is sort of a built-in secretary for the company.*

build something in(to something) **1.** to make a piece of furniture or an appliance a part of a building's construction. □ *We will build this chest into the wall about here.* 🅃 *We are going to build in a second chest.* □ *Then we will build another one in.* 🄰 *I would like a room with lots of built-in furniture.* 🄽 *Built-ins save a lot of space in an apartment.*

2. to make a particular quality a basic part of something. □ *We build quality into our cars before we put our name on them.* [T] *We build in quality.* □ *We build quality in.* [A] *This car has a built-in bar.* **3.** to make a special restriction or specification a part of the plan of something. □ *I built the restriction into our agreement.* [T] *I built in the rule.* □ *We built the rule in.*

BUILD ▸ ON

See also under *BUILD ▸ (UP)ON.*

build one's hopes on someone or something to make plans or have aspirations based on someone or something. □ *I have built my hopes on making a success of this business.* □ *I built my hopes on John.*

BUILD ▸ ON(TO)

build on((to) something) to add to something by constructing an extension. □ *Do you plan to build onto this house?* □ *Yes, we are going to build on.*

build something on((to) something) to construct an extension onto a building. □ *We are going to build a garage onto this side of the house.* [T] *We will build on a new garage.* □ *The people next door are not going to build anything on.*

BUILD ▸ OUT

See *build (something) (out) over something* under *BUILD ▸ OVER.*

build out onto something to extend a building onto a particular space. □ *We will build out onto the vacant lot.* □ *We built out onto the old patio.*

build something out of something to construct something from parts or materials. □ *She built a tower out of the blocks.* □ *They will build the tower out of cast concrete.*

BUILD ▸ OVER

build (something) (out) over something to construct something so that it extends over something else, such as water or some architectural feature. □ *We built a deck out over the pond.* [T] *We built out the deck over the pond.* □ *We built over the pond.* □ *We built out over the pond.* □ *We built the deck over the pond.*

BUILD ▸ TO

build something to order to build an individual object according to one special set of specifications. □ *I am having them build it to order—just for us.* □ *The deck will be built to order.*

BUILD ▸ UNDER

build a fire under someone to do something to motivate or stimulate a person to do something. (Figurative.) □ *We tried to build a fire under Terri and get her going, but it had no effect.* □ *I built a fire under Mike, but it did no good.*

BUILD ▸ UP

build someone or something up (from something) to transform someone or something from a lowly start to a better state. (*Someone* includes *oneself.*) □ *I built this business up from nothing.* □ *The publicity agent built this politician up from a small-time party hack.* □ *He built himself up from a 98-pound weakling.*

build someone or something up (into someone or something) to develop or advance someone or something into a particular [good] kind of person or thing. (See also *build someone up, build something up. Someone* includes *oneself.*) □ *The publicity people built her up into a singer whom everyone looked forward to hearing.* [T] *The agent built up the singer into a famous star.* [T] *You have really built up this business.* □ *She built herself up into a widely recognized authority.*

build someone up **1.** to strengthen someone; to make someone healthier or stronger. (*Someone* includes *oneself.*) □ *You need more exercise and better food to build you up again.* [T] *The coach wanted to build up Roger into a stronger player.* □ *I need to do some exercises to build myself up.* **2.** to praise or exalt someone. (*Someone* includes *oneself.*) □ *Claire liked to build Tom up, because she was in love with him.* [T] *Mary also liked to build up Tom.* □ *Don't build yourself up so much.*

build someone up (for something) to prepare someone for something; to lead a person into a proper state of mind to receive some information. (*Someone* includes *oneself*.) □ *We built them up for what was about to happen.* [T] *We had to build up the woman for what we were going to tell her.* □ *They built John up carefully and then told him the bad news.* □ *She built herself up for a wonderful evening.* [N] *After a careful buildup, the manager presented the plans for the project to the board.*

build something up **1.** to add buildings to an area of land or a neighborhood. □ *They are really building this area up. There is no more open space.* [T] *They built up the area over the years.* [A] *I didn't know that this was such a built-up area.* **2.** to develop, accumulate, or increase something, such as wealth, business, goodwill, etc. □ *I built this business up through hard work and hope.* [T] *She built up a good business over the years.* [A] *The built-up value of these securities should make you rich.* **3.** to praise or exalt something; to exaggerate the virtues of something. □ *The master of ceremonies built the act up so much that everyone was disappointed when they saw it.* [T] *He built up the act too much.* [N] *The buildup was exaggerated and ineffective.*

build up to increase; to develop. □ *The storm clouds are building up. Better close the windows.* [N] *There was an enormous buildup of storm clouds, but nothing came of it.*

build up to something **1.** [for a person] to lead up to something or advance to doing or saying something. □ *I can tell you are building up to something. What is it?* [N] *His buildup created greater expectations than he could deliver.* **2.** [for a situation] to develop into something. □ *The argument is building up to something unpleasant.* [N] *The buildup of pressure behind the dam was quite threatening.*

BUILD ▸ (UP)ON

build something (up)on something to construct something on the base of something else. (Both literal and figurative. *Upon* is formal and less commonly used than *on*.) □ *We will build a new house upon the foundation of the old one.* □ *Don't build a house on the side of a hill.*

build (up)on something **1.** to construct something on a particular space. (*Upon* is formal and less commonly used than *on*.) □ *Are you going to build upon this land?* □ *Yes, we will build on it.* **2.** to start with something and add to it. (*Upon* is formal and less commonly used than *on*.) □ *This is good so far. We'll build on it.* □ *We will build upon it.*

BULGE ▸ OUT

bulge out to swell outward; to extend out into a lump or mound. □ *The puppy's tummy bulged out, full of food.* □ *The bag of grass clippings bulged out heavily.*

BULGE ▸ WITH

bulge with something to be swollen with something. □ *The bag was bulging with gifts and candy.* □ *The chipmunk's cheeks bulged with the nuts it had found.*

BULLDOZE ▸ INTO

bulldoze into something to push clumsily into something. (Informal.) □ *Don't just bulldoze into me! Watch where you are going!* □ *Todd bulldozed into the wall, denting it badly.*

BULLDOZE ▸ THROUGH

bulldoze through something to push clumsily and carelessly through something. □ *Don't just bulldoze through your work!* □ *I wish you wouldn't bulldoze through the room.*

BULLY ▸ INTO

bully someone into something to harass or threaten someone into doing something. □ *The coach tried to bully them into agreeing to stay late and practice.* □ *Don't try to bully me into it.*

BUM ▸ AROUND

bum around to waste time; to loaf around doing nothing. (Slang.) □ *All you do is bum around, never getting anything done.* □ *I'm tired of bumming around!*

bum around (with someone) to spend or waste a lot of time with a particular person. (Slang.) □ *He used to bum around with Ted a lot.* □ *You bum around too much.*

BUM ▸ OFF

bum something off (of) someone to beg or borrow something from someone. (Slang. The *of* is colloquial and appropriate in this expression.) □ *Can I bum a cigarette off you?* □ *You can't bum anything off of me that I don't have.*

BUM ▸ OUT

bum out to have a bad time, especially a bad time with drugs. (Slang.) □ *Are you going to bum out again tonight?* □ *Man, is he bummed out!*

bum someone out to discourage someone. (Slang.) □ *This really bums me out.* □ *I am really bummed out about this!*

BUMBLE ▸ THROUGH

bumble through something to get through something clumsily. □ *I guess I will have to bumble through this again.* □ *Lily bumbled through her speech and fled from the stage.*

BUMP ▸ AGAINST

bump (up) against someone or something to strike someone or something accidentally, usually relatively gently. □ *The car bumped up against the curb.* □ *This wall has been bumped against a lot. It needs painting.*

BUMP ▸ ALONG

bump along 1. AND **bump along something** to travel along a rough road. □ *We bumped along on our way to the lake.* □ *We bumped along the road, hanging on to our hats.* 2. [for some plan or situation] to move along awkwardly and unevenly. □ *The whole project bumped along to an uncertain conclusion.* □ *It bumped along for a while and then we all gave it up.*

BUMP ▸ INTO

bump into someone or something 1. to strike someone or something accidentally and gently. □ *Sorry. I didn't mean to bump into you.* □ *I bumped into the piano accidentally.* 2. to happen on someone or something; to meet or find someone or something by chance. □ *Guess who I bumped into on the street today.* □ *I bumped into a real problem at the office today.*

BUMP ▸ OFF

bump someone off to kill someone. (Slang.) □ *Lefty is going to bump Max off, he says.* 🅃 *Max decided to bump off Lefty.*

BUMP ▸ UP

bump someone or something up 1. to raise someone or something to a higher category or level. □ *I wanted to fly first class, but they wouldn't bump me up.* 🅃 *The agent bumped up both of my friends, but not me.* □ *A lot of excitement at work bumped my blood pressure up.* 2. to damage or batter someone or something. (*Someone* includes *oneself.*) □ *The crash and rollover bumped him up a little.* 🅃 *The crash bumped up the driver a little.* 🅃 *It bumped up the car more than a little.* □ *She bumped herself up in the wreck.*

bump (up) against someone or something See under *BUMP ▸ AGAINST.*

BUNCH ▸ UP

bunch someone or something up to pack or cluster things or people together. □ *Bunch them up so you can squeeze them into the sack.* 🅃 *Kelly bunched up the roses and put them in a vase.* □ *Bunch the people up so more will fit in.*

bunch up to pack together or cluster. □ *Spread out. Don't bunch up!* 🄰 *Spread out those bunched-up trumpeters. Each marcher should be an arm's length from the others.*

BUNDLE ▸ IN(TO)

bundle someone in(to something) 1. to put someone, usually a child, into heavy outdoor clothing. (*Someone* includes *oneself.*) □ *Bill bundled Billy into his parka.* □ *He was hard to bundle in because he wouldn't stand still.* □ *Tom bundled himself into his parka and opened the door to go out.* 2. to put someone, usually a child, into bed. □ *She bundled Sarah into bed just in time.*

☐ *June pulled back the sheets and bundled Sarah in.*

BUNDLE ▸ OFF

bundle off to leave in a hurry; to take all one's parcels and leave in a hurry. ☐ *She got ready and bundled off after her bus.* ☐ *Lily bundled off just in time.*

bundle someone off (to some place) to send someone, usually a child, somewhere. ☐ *Robert bundled the children off to school.* 🅃 *They bundled off the kids and got ready to leave themselves.* ☐ *Just in time for the bus, they bundled the kids off.*

bundle something off (to someone or some place) to send something off in a bundle to someone. ☐ *He bundled his laundry off to his mother, who would wash it for him.* 🅃 *Mary bundled off the package to her brother.* ☐ *She put stamps on the package and bundled it off.*

BUNDLE ▸ UP

bundle (oneself) up (against something) to wrap oneself up in protective clothing or bedding as protection against the cold. ☐ *Please bundle yourself up against the frigid wind.* ☐ *Bundle yourself up.* ☐ *Better bundle up.* ☐ *Be sure and bundle yourself up against the cold. It's freezing out there.*

bundle someone up (against something) to wrap someone up in protective clothing or bedding against the cold. ☐ *Wally bundled Billy up against the storm.* 🅃 *You had better bundle up the children against the blizzard.* ☐ *You had better bundle Tom up.*

bundle someone up (in something) to wrap someone up in protective clothing or bedding. (*Someone* includes *oneself.*) ☐ *Bill bundled Billy up in his parka.* 🅃 *Bill bundled up Mary in her parka.* ☐ *He bundled her up.* ☐ *The child bundled himself up into the covers and went to sleep.*

BUNG ▸ IN

bung something in to cram or bang something into something. ☐ *He bunged the cork into the barrel.* 🅃 *With a heavy blow, he bunged in the cork.*

BUNG ▸ UP

bung something up to damage something; to mess something up. (Colloquial.) ☐ *Fred bunged the television set up.* 🅃 *Who bunged up my tape recorder?* 🄰 *Is this bunged-up old pot the only one you have?*

BUNGLE ▸ UP

bungle something up to botch something; to mess something up. (Colloquial.) ☐ *Please don't bungle this job up.* 🅃 *You bungled up the job, and I asked you not to.* 🄰 *How are we going to fix this bungled-up deal?*

BUNK ▸ DOWN

bunk down (for the night) to bed down for the night; to go to bed. (Colloquial.) ☐ *Where are you going to bunk down for the night?* ☐ *I'm tired and ready to bunk down.*

BUNK ▸ TOGETHER

bunk (up) together [for two or more people] to share a bed or a bedroom. ☐ *Shall we bunk together?* ☐ *Shall we bunk up together?*

BUNK ▸ UP

See also under *BUNK ▸ TOGETHER, BUNK ▸ WITH.*

BUNK ▸ WITH

bunk (up) with someone to share a bed or a bedroom with someone. ☐ *Are you going to bunk up with Fred?* ☐ *I'll bunk with Todd.*

BUOY ▸ UP

buoy someone or something up to keep someone or something afloat. (*Someone* includes *oneself.*) ☐ *Use this cushion to buoy yourself up.* 🅃 *The log buoyed up the swimmer until help came.* ☐ *The air trapped in the hull buoyed the boat up.*

buoy someone up to support, encourage, or sustain someone. (*Someone* includes *oneself.*) ☐ *The good news buoyed her up considerably.* 🅃 *Her good humor buoyed up the entire party.* ☐ *She buoyed herself up by keeping in touch with friends.*

BURDEN ▸ WITH

burden someone or something with someone or something to bother or weigh down someone or something with someone or something. (*Someone* includes *oneself*.) □ *Please don't burden us with the bad news at this time.* □ *I don't want to burden the school with a troublesome child.* □ *Please don't burden yourself with this problem. It's my worry.*

burden someone with something to give unpleasant information to someone; to give someone some bad news. □ *I hate to burden you with this, but your cat ran away.* □ *I wish I had not been burdened with all the facts.*

BURGEON ▸ OUT

burgeon out to develop and grow rapidly; to burst forth. □ *The flowers burgeoned out and made life beautiful again.* □ *When the trees have burgeoned out, spring is really here.*

BURN ▸ AT

burn someone at the stake **1.** to execute someone by public burning while tied to a stake. □ *Way back when, they used to burn witches at the stake.* □ *Witches were burned at the stake.* **2.** to chastise someone severely; to punish someone too severely for the nature of the misdoing. (Figurative.) □ *Don't burn her at the stake for spilling the milk!* □ *Donny was almost burned at the stake for nothing at all!*

BURN ▸ AWAY

burn away **1.** [for something] to burn until there is no more of it. □ *All the oil burned away.* □ *The fuel burned away and things are cooling down.* **2.** for something to keep on burning rapidly. □ *The little fire burned away brightly, warming the tiny room.* □ *The candle burned away, giving a tiny bit of light to the huge room.*

burn something away to remove or destroy something by burning. □ *The doctor burned the wart away.* [T] *The doctor burned away the wart.*

BURN ▸ DOWN

burn down **1.** [for a building] to be destroyed by fire. □ *The barn burned down.* □ *There was a fire and the barn was burned down.* **2.** [for a fire] to burn and dwindle away. □ *The flame burned down and then went out.* □ *As the fire burned down, it began to get cold.*

burn something down [for a fire] to destroy a building completely. □ *The fire burned the barn down.* [T] *It burned down the barn.* [A] *The remains of the burned-down house smoldered for a long time.*

BURN ▸ FOR

burn for someone or something to desire someone or something very much. □ *Jim said he was burning for Sally.* □ *I was just burning for another look at her.*

BURN ▸ IN

See also under *BURN ▸ IN(TO).*

burn someone in effigy to burn an image of someone. □ *They burned the president in effigy.* □ *The president of the university was burned in effigy.*

burn something in to run a piece of new electronic equipment for a while to make certain that all the electrical parts will last a long time. □ *Please burn this computer in for a couple of hours before you deliver it.* [T] *The technician burned in the computer.* [N] *Always give your computer a good burn-in during the warranty period.*

BURN ▸ IN(TO)

burn something in(to something) **1.** to engrave, brand, or etch marks or letters into something by the use of great heat. □ *She burned her initials into the handle of the umbrella.* [T] *She burned in her initials.* □ *She burned them in.* [A] *The burned-in letters are easy to read.* **2.** to implant something firmly in someone's head, brain, memory, etc. (Figurative.) □ *She burned the information into her head.* □ *The events of the day burned the memories in.* [A] *No matter what she did, she couldn't shake the burned-in memories of the accident.*

BURN ▸ OFF

burn off [for some excess volatile or flammable substance] to burn away or burn up. □ *A film of oil on the surface of the water was burning off, making dense black smoke.* □ *The alcohol* *burned off and left a delicious flavor in the cherries jubilee.*

burn something off ((of) something) to cause excess volatile or flammable substance to burn until there is no more of it. (The *of*-phrase is paraphrased with a *from*-phrase when the particle is transposed. See the 🄵 example. The *of* is colloquial.) ☐ *We burnt the gasoline off the water's surface.* 🅃 *Why did you burn off the gasoline?* 🄵 *Why did you burn off the gasoline from the surface of the water?* ☐ *I burned the vapors off.*

BURN ▶ OUT

burn (itself) out **1.** [for a flame or fire] to run out of fuel and go out. ☐ *Finally, the fires burned themselves out.* ☐ *The fire finally burned out.* 🄰 *The burned-out fire was cold, indicating that the campers had left a long time ago.* ☐ *The flame burned itself out.* **2.** [for an electrical part] to fail and cease working or make a larger unit cease working. ☐ *The motor finally burned itself out.* ☐ *The motor burned out.* 🄰 *Send the burned-out part back to the factory.* 🄽 *One burnout after another! These cheap motors are not worth it.*

burn (oneself) out to stay at a task so long that one's limit is reached and one is no longer effective. ☐ *I didn't want to burn myself out on the job, so I quit on my own.* ☐ *Finally, I just burned out.* 🄰 *We don't need any burned-out workers around here!* 🄽 *She's turning into a classic burnout.*

burn someone out to wear someone out; to make someone ineffective through overuse. (*Someone* includes *oneself*.) ☐ *Facing all these problems at once will burn Tom out.* 🅃 *The continuous problems burned out the office staff in a few months.* ☐ *She burned herself out as a volunteer in the state prison.* 🄽 *Four years of prison work turned her into a complete burnout.*

burn someone out (of something) to burn down a home(stead) or place of business and drive someone away. (The *of*-phrase is paraphrased with a *from*-phrase when the particle is transposed. See the 🄵 example.) ☐ *The crooks burned the farmer out of his home.* 🅃 *They burned out the farmer.* 🄵 *They burned out the farmers from their homes.* ☐ *The marauders burned them out.* 🄰 *The burned-out farmers had nothing left but the clothes on their backs.*

burn something out **1.** to burn away the inside of something, getting rid of excess deposits. ☐ *The mechanic burned the carbon out of the manifold.* 🅃 *He burned out the carbon.* 🄰 *The burned-out interior of the cask was ready for the whiskey to be put in.* **2.** to wear out an electrical or electronic device through overuse. ☐ *Turn it off. You're going to burn it out!* 🅃 *He burned out the motor.* 🄰 *This is the burned-out part. Throw it away.* 🄽 *We've got another burnout on the light bulb production line.*

BURN ▶ TO

burn someone or something to a crisp to burn someone or something thoroughly. (*Someone* includes *oneself*.) ☐ *The sun burned Jane to a crisp.* ☐ *The fire burned their furniture to a crisp.* ☐ *She fell into the fire and burned herself to a crisp.*

BURN ▶ UP

burn someone up **1.** to destroy someone by fire. ☐ *The barn fire burned Walter up.* 🅃 *The fire burned up both of them.* **2.** to make someone very angry. (Figurative.) ☐ *You really burn me up! I'm very angry at you!* 🅃 *The whole mess burned up everyone.*

burn something up to destroy something by fire. ☐ *Take this and burn it up.* 🅃 *The fire burned up the papers and left no trace.*

burn up to become destroyed or consumed by fire. ☐ *The wood burned up and left only ashes.* ☐ *The deed burned up in the fire.*

BURN ▶ WITH

burn with a low blue flame to be very quietly and intensely angry. ☐ *She was so angry that she was burning with a low blue flame.* ☐ *The boss was burning* *with a low blue flame when I finally got there.*

burn with something 1. [for a fire] to burn with a particular quality. □ *The building burned with great ferocity.* □ *The fired burned with a lot of crackling and popping.* 2. [for someone] to experience intense and consuming feelings of a particular quality. □ *Fred is just burning with envy.* □ *Why is he burning with envy?*

BURST ▸ AT

burst at the seams to be very full and burst, perhaps at the seams. (Both literal and figurative uses.) □ *I am so full! I'm ready to burst at the seams.* □ *The room was so full it was bursting at the seams.*

BURST ▸ FORTH

burst forth to come forth explosively. □ *The words burst forth and frightened everyone.* □ *The blossoms burst forth in the first warm days of the year.*

BURST ▸ IN

burst in ((up)on someone or something) to intrude or come in thoughtlessly and suddenly and interrupt someone or something. (*Upon* is formal and less commonly used than *on*.) □ *I didn't mean to burst in on you.* □ *She feared that someone would burst in upon her.* □ *He just burst in!*

burst in (with something) to interrupt with some comment. □ *Ted burst in with the good news.* □ *He burst in to tell us the news.*

BURST ▸ INTO

burst into flames [for something] to ignite suddenly and burn. □ *The house suddenly burst into flames.* □ *The match burst into flames as it was struck.*

burst into sight to come into view suddenly. □ *The bus finally burst into sight and we knew we weren't stranded.* □ *Suddenly, a tiger burst into sight and caught the hunter off guard.*

burst (out) into something 1. [for plants or trees] to open their flowers seemingly suddenly and simultaneously. □ *The flowers burst out into blossom very early.* □ *They burst into blossom during the first warm day.* 2. [for someone] to begin suddenly doing a particular activity, such as crying, laughing, chattering; or to begin producing the evidence of such activities as laughter, chatter, tears, etc. □ *Suddenly, she burst out into laughter.* □ *The child burst into tears.*

BURST ▸ IN(TO)

burst in(to some place) to intrude or come in thoughtlessly and suddenly. □ *Ted burst into the room and sat down right in the middle of the meeting.* □ *Why did you just burst in?*

BURST ▸ ON

See under *BURST ▸ (UP)ON.*

BURST ▸ OUT

burst out to explode outward; to break open under force. □ *The door burst out and released the trapped people.* □ *When the glass burst out, Gerald was injured.*

burst out doing something to begin to do something suddenly, such as cry, laugh, shout, etc. □ *Suddenly, she burst out singing.* □ *Ted burst out smiling.*

burst (out) into something See under *BURST ▸ INTO.*

burst out (of some place) [for people] to come out of a place rapidly. □ *Everyone burst out of the burning building.* □ *Suddenly, they all burst out.*

burst out of something to explode out of something; to become [suddenly] too big for something, such as clothes, a house, etc. □ *She is bursting out of her dress.* □ *The butterfly burst out of the chrysalis.*

burst out with something to utter something loudly and suddenly. (Compare to *burst in (with something).*) □ *The child burst out with a scream.* □ *Lily burst out with song.*

BURST ▸ THROUGH

burst through something to break through or penetrate something with force. □ *The tank burst through the barrier easily.* □ *The workers burst through the wall after a lot of hard work.*

BURST ► (UP)ON

burst (up)on someone [for an idea] to strike someone suddenly. (*Upon* is formal and less commonly used than *on*.) □ *Then, this really tremendous idea burst upon me.* □ *It burst on me like a bolt of lightning.*

burst (up)on the scene to appear suddenly somewhere; to enter or arrive suddenly some place. (*Upon* is formal and less commonly used than *on*.) □ *The police suddenly burst upon the scene.* □ *They burst on the scene and took over.*

BURST ► WITH

burst with something to have a spurt of a particular feeling, such as joy, pride, excitement, etc. □ *Joe was just bursting with pride because of his triumph.* □ *The children were all bursting with excitement.*

BURY ► AWAY

bury someone or something away (some place) to bury or hide someone or something some place. (*Someone* includes *oneself*.) □ *The dog buried the bone away under a bush.* □ *They buried her uncle away in the cemetery.* □ *They buried him away.* □ *Don't bury yourself away. Get out and have some fun.*

BURY ► IN

bury one's head in the sand to hide from unpleasant facts; to pretend to ignore unpleasant facts. (Figurative.) □ *Joe had a tendency to bury his head in the sand when he faced problems.* □ *When the real crisis loomed, his head was buried in the sand as usual.*

bury oneself in something **1.** to become very busy with something. □ *She buried herself in her work.* □ *He tended to bury himself in his work.* **2.** to hide oneself some place. □ *He buried himself in the back of the little shop and worked quietly.* □ *The lizard buried itself in the sand.*

bury someone or something in something **1.** to inter someone or something in a grave, the ground, a vault, a tomb, etc. □ *They buried the old man in the family vault.* □ *They had to bury the old cat in the backyard.* **2.** to hide or conceal someone or something from view in some place. (Figurative.) □ *The office manager buried Tom in the back room.* □ *Someone buried the manual typewriter in a room full of old junk.*

BURY ► UNDER

bury someone or something under something to hide or conceal someone or something beneath something. □ *Joe buried the money under a stone in the forest.* □ *They buried Aunt Mary under a pine tree.*

BUSH ► OUT

bush out [for something] to develop many small branches or hairs. (Said of a plant, bush, beard, head of hair, etc.) □ *His beard bushed out and really needed trimming.* □ *I hope the hedge bushes out nicely this year.*

BUST ► OUT

bust out (of some place) to break out of some place, especially a prison. (Slang.) □ *Max and Lefty busted out of prison and left the country.* □ *Max and Lefty busted out together.* Ⓝ *Lefty and Max got away with their bust-out, for now anyway.*

bust someone out (of some place) **1.** to help someone escape from prison. (Slang. The *of*-phrase is paraphrased with a *from*-phrase when the particle is transposed. See the Ⓕ example.) □ *Lefty did not manage to bust Max out of prison.* Ⓣ *Lefty wanted to bust out some of his friends.* Ⓕ *Lefty wanted to bust out some of his friends from jail.* □ *Max's old buddy helped bust him out.* Ⓝ *The two punks had some help with the bust-out.* **2.** to flunk someone out of school. (Slang.) □ *The dean finally busted Bill out of school.* □ *The dean busted Bill out.*

BUST ► UP

bust someone up **1.** to cause lovers to separate; to break up a pair of lovers, including married persons. (Slang. See *bust up*.) □ *Mary busted Terri and John up.* Ⓣ *Mary busted up Terri and John.* Ⓝ *Who is responsible for their bust-up—or did they do it themselves?* **2.** to beat someone up; to batter someone.

(Slang.) □ *You want me to bust you up?* 🅃 *Max busted up Lefty pretty badly.*

bust something up **1.** to break or ruin something; to break something into smaller pieces. (Slang.) □ *Who busted this plate up?* 🅃 *Don't bust up plates.* **2.** to ruin a marriage by coming between the married people. □ *He busted their marriage up by starting rumors about Maggie.* 🅃 *He busted up their marriage.*

bust up **1.** [for lovers] to separate or break up. (Slang.) □ *Tom and Alice busted up for good.* □ *They busted up last week.* **2.** [for something] to break up due to natural causes. (Slang.) □ *The rocket busted up in midair.* □ *I saw it bust up.*

BUSTLE ▸ ABOUT

bustle about doing something to go about doing something rapidly and energetically. □ *Greg bustled about all day, doing the chores.* □ *Lily bustled about, getting herself ready.*

bustle about some place to move about some place very busily. □ *They were all bustling about the kitchen, getting the feast ready.* □ *Veronica was bustling about outside, cleaning up the yard.*

BUSTLE ▸ AROUND

bustle around to move about very busily. □ *The people were bustling around, trying to get things ready for the picnic.* □ *I wish you would stop bustling around.*

BUSTLE ▸ OFF

bustle off to leave in haste. □ *Well, I have to bustle off.* □ *I hate to bustle off so soon.*

bustle someone off to help someone leave; to send someone out or away; to *bundle someone off.* □ *The cops bustled the crook off.* 🅃 *They bustled off the crook.*

BUSY ▸ WITH

busy oneself with someone or something to occupy one's time by dealing with someone or something. □ *Tony busied himself with helping Sam.* □ *Mrs. Wilson busied herself with little Jimmy.* □ *She busied herself with her typing and ignored the argument in the next room.*

busy someone with someone or something to keep someone busy dealing with someone or something. (*Someone* includes oneself.) □ *You should busy the children with some activity.* □ *We will busy Randy with cleaning up the garage.* □ *She busied herself with the accounts.*

BUTT ▸ AGAINST

butt (up) against someone or something to press against someone or something firmly. □ *This board is supposed to butt up against the one over there.* □ *The goat butted against Fred, but didn't hurt him.*

BUTT ▸ IN

butt in (on someone or something) to interrupt or intrude on someone or something. □ *I didn't mean to butt in on your conversation.* □ *Please don't butt in.* □ *How can we talk when you keep butting in on us?*

BUTT ▸ INTO

butt into something to intrude upon something; to break into a conversation. □ *Please don't butt into my conversation.* □ *I don't like my conversations being butted into by perfect strangers!*

BUTT ▸ OUT

butt out to exit [as abruptly as one has intruded]. (Slang. The opposite "mate" of *butt in (on someone or something).* Usually a command.) □ *Butt out! Leave me alone!* □ *Please butt out!*

BUTT ▸ UP

butt (up) against someone or something See under *BUTT ▸ AGAINST.*

BUTTER ▸ UP

butter someone up AND **butter up to someone** to flatter someone; to treat someone especially nicely in hopes of special favors. (See also *spread something on thick* under *SPREAD ▸ ON.*) □ *A student tried to butter the teacher up.* 🅃 *She buttered up the teacher again.* □ *She is always buttering up to the teacher.*

BUTTON ▸ DOWN

button something down to fasten something down with buttons. □ *Button your collar down. You look partially dressed.* 🅃 *Please button down your collar.*

BUTTON ▸ UP

button something up to fasten the edges of something with buttons. □ *Button your shirt up, please.* 🅃 *I will button up my shirt.* 🄰 *The buttoned-up shirt looked quite strange on Todd, who usually went about with an open collar.*

button up **1.** to fasten one's buttons. □ *Your jacket's open. You'd better button up. It's cold.* □ *I'll button up in the car.* **2.** to get silent and stay silent. (Slang. See *button up one's lip*.) □ *Hey, button up! That's enough out of you.* □ *I wish you would button up.*

button up one's lip to stop talking. (Idiomatic. The expression *button one's lip* is equally valid, but not an entry.) □ *Please button up your lip!* □ *Will you button up your lip?*

BUTTRESS ▸ UP

buttress something up **1.** to brace something; to provide architectural support for something. □ *We have to buttress up this part of the wall while we work on it* 🅃 *The workers buttressed up the wall.* **2.** to provide extra support, often financial support, for something. (Figurative.) □ *We rounded up some money to buttress the company up through the crisis.* 🅃 *The loan buttressed up the company for a few minutes.*

BUY ▸ AT

buy something at something **1.** to purchase something at a particular place or at a particular type of sale, such as a store, an auction, a clearance sale, etc. □ *I bought this at an auction.* □ *This was bought at an auction.* **2.** to purchase something at a particular price or for a particular level of price. □ *I bought shares in General Motors at forty and a half.* □ *The shares were bought at a good price.*

BUY ▸ BACK

buy something back (from someone) to repurchase something that one has previously sold from the person who bought it. □ *Can I buy it back from you? I have decided I need it.* 🅃 *He bought back his book from George.* □ *I sold it too cheap. I want to buy it back.*

BUY ▸ FOR

See the following entry.

BUY ▸ FROM

buy something (from someone) (for something) to purchase something from someone at a particular price, or for a particular type of payment, such as for cash, for a song, for practically nothing, etc. □ *I bought it from Mark for a reasonable price.* □ *I bought it for a reasonable price from Mark.* □ *I bought it from Mark.* □ *I bought the book for practically nothing.*

BUY ▸ INTO

buy one's way into something to achieve entry or membership in something by paying money. □ *Do you think you can buy your way into this fraternity?* □ *I'm sure I can buy my way into it.*

BUY ▸ IN(TO)

buy in(to something) to purchase shares of something; to buy a part of something the ownership of which is shared with other owners. □ *I bought into a company that makes dog food.* □ *Sounds like a good company. I would like to buy in.*

BUY ▸ OFF

buy someone off to bribe someone to ignore what one is doing wrong. □ *Do you think you can buy her off?* 🅃 *Max tried to buy off the cops.*

BUY ▸ ON

buy something on credit to purchase something, take delivery now, and pay for it later. □ *I bought the car on credit.* □ *I don't buy things on credit.*

BUY ▸ OUT

buy one's way out (of something) to get out of trouble by bribing someone to ignore what one has done wrong. □ *You* *can't buy your way out of this mess, buster!* ☐ *You made this mess and you can't buy your way out!*

buy someone or something out to purchase full ownership of something from someone or a group. ☐ *We liked the company, so we borrowed a lot of money and bought it out.* 🅃 *Carl bought out the owners of the company.* ☐ *He bought the company out.* 🄽 *The company completed the buyout of its competitor with the help of an investment banker.*

buy something out to buy all of a particular item. ☐ *The kids came in and bought all our bubble gum out.* 🅃 *They bought out the bubble gum.*

BUY ▸ UP

buy something up to buy all of something; to buy the entire supply of something. ☐ *He bought the oranges up.* 🅃 *He bought up all the oranges and drove up the price.*

BUZZ ▸ ALONG

buzz along to move or drive along fast. ☐ *The cars were buzzing along at a great rate.* ☐ *Traffic is sure buzzing along.*

BUZZ ▸ FOR

buzz for someone to sound a signal for someone. ☐ *Please buzz for the porter.* ☐ *I buzzed for my secretary and waited for a reply.*

BUZZ ▸ IN(TO)

buzz in(to some place) to come into a place rapidly or unexpectedly. ☐ *The child buzzed into the shop and bought a nickel's worth of candy.* ☐ *I just buzzed in to say hello.*

BUZZ ▸ OFF

buzz off to leave quickly. (Colloquial.) ☐ *I've got to buzz off. Bye.* ☐ *It's time for me to buzz off.* ☐ *Get out of here! Buzz off!*

BUZZ ▸ WITH

buzz with something [for a place] to be busy with something. ☐ *The room buzzed with excitement.* ☐ *The office had better be buzzing with money-making activity when I return.*

C

CADGE ▸ FROM

cadge something from someone to beg or borrow something from someone. (Informal or slang.) ☐ *Go cadge some sugar from the lady next door.* ☐ *Max cadged some money from a man on the street.*

CADGE ▸ OFF

cadge something off someone to beg for something from someone. (Slang.) ☐ *The vagrant cadged a few bucks off the people who walked by.* ☐ *I cadged this jacket off a friendly guy I met.*

CAGE ▸ IN

cage someone or something in to enclose someone or something in a cage or something similar. (Both literal and figurative uses. *Someone* includes *oneself*.) ☐ *Please don't cage me in this tiny room!* [T] *We are going to have to cage in the dogs.* [A] *The caged-in animals looked lonely and depressed.* ☐ *She used her bad temperament to cage herself in.*

CAGE ▸ UP

cage someone or something up (in something) to enclose or confine someone or something in something or someplace. ☐ *They caged the lions up in strong containers for the trip across country.* ☐ *How long did it take to cage up the lions securely?*

CAJOLE ▸ INTO

cajole someone into something to coax or persuade someone to do something. ☐ *They tried to cajole us into helping them.* ☐ *You can't cajole me into doing that!*

CAJOLE ▸ OUT

cajole someone out of something **1.** to coax or persuade someone not to do something. ☐ *Try and cajole her out of going there.* ☐ *I cajoled her out of leaving so soon.* **2.** to coax or persuade someone to give up something or give away something. ☐ *She tried to cajole him out of his inheritance.* ☐ *You can't cajole me out of anything!*

CAKE ▸ WITH

cake someone or something with something to cover someone or something with some sort of substance such as mud, dirt, blood, etc. (*Someone* includes *oneself*.) ☐ *The attendant caked her with hot mud at the beginning of the arthritis treatment.* ☐ *The child caked the front porch with mud.* ☐ *She caked herself with green mud to remove her wrinkles.*

CALCULATE ▸ IN(TO)

calculate something in(to something) to include something in one's figures. ☐ *Did you calculate the cost of the cake into the total?* [T] *Yes, I calculated in all the costs.* ☐ *Did you calculate the heating bill in?*

CALCULATE ▸ ON

calculate on something to think about or plan on something; to reckon on something. (Folksy.) ☐ *Let me calculate on this a little bit.* ☐ *He's busy calculating on a serious problem.*

CALL ▸ ABOUT

call someone about something to call someone on the telephone, seeking information about someone or something. ☐ *I'll call Maggie about Ted and see* *what she knows.* □ *Let me call the manager about this.*

CALL ▸ AROUND

call around (about someone or something) to telephone a number of different people in succession about something. □ *I'll call around about Tom and see if I can find out anything.* □ *I'll call around too.*

CALL ▸ AT

call at some place to visit some place; [for a ship] to put into port at a place. □ *I called at the druggist's for some medicine.* □ *Our ship will call at seven ports.*

CALL ▸ AWAY

call someone away (from something) to ask someone to come away from some place or from doing something. □ *The committee called Kathy away from her office.* [T] *The principal called away the teacher from the classroom.* □ *Why did you call Kathy away?*

CALL ▸ BACK

call back **1.** to call [someone] again on the telephone at a later time. □ *Call back later, please.* □ *I will call back when you are not so busy.* **2.** to return a telephone call received earlier. □ *The note says I am to call back. What did you want?* □ *This is Bill Wilson calling back.*

call someone back **1.** to call someone again on the telephone. □ *Since she is not there, I will call her back in half an hour.* [T] *Carl called back the person who had called earlier.* **2.** to return a telephone call to a person who called earlier. □ *I have to call Judy back now.* □ *I will call him back tomorrow.* **3.** See call *someone or something back.*

call someone or something back to call out that someone or something should come back. □ *As she left, the clerk called her back.* [T] *The clerk called back the customer.* □ *They had to call the order back because it was incomplete.*

call something (back) in See under *CALL ▸ IN.*

CALL ▸ BY

call someone by something to address someone by a particular kind of name. □ *They call me by my maiden name.* □ *Don't call me by my nickname!*

CALL ▸ DOWN

call someone down to criticize or scold someone; to ask someone to behave better; to challenge someone's bad behavior. □ *The teacher called Todd down for being late.* [T] *The teacher called down all the students who were late.*

call something down (on someone) to invoke some sort of punishment from the heavens onto someone. □ *The preacher sounded as though he was calling down the wrath of God on us.* [T] *The prophet called down a plague on the people.* □ *The people were corrupt, so he called a plague down.*

call something down (to someone) to shout something to a person on a lower level. □ *The worker called a warning down to the people below.* [T] *She called down a warning to them.* □ *She called a warning down.*

CALL ▸ FOR

call for someone or something **1.** to shout for or request someone or something. □ *I called for Ted, but he didn't hear me.* □ *I stood on the porch and called for the dog.* **2.** to stop by some place and get someone or something. □ *I must call for Sally at noon.* □ *I will call for the package this afternoon.*

call for something [for a situation] to require something. □ *This situation does not call for this kind of behavior.* [A] *I can supply the called-for ingredients.* [A] *Your uncalled-for behavior has cast a pall on the entire proceedings.*

CALL ▸ FORTH

call someone forth to call to someone to come out or come forward. □ *The troop leader called Wally forth.* [T] *Please call forth Wally again.*

call something forth [for an event] to draw a particular quality or induce a particular behavior. □ *The battle called extraordinary courage forth on the parts* *of the soldiers.* 🅃 *It called forth great courage.*

CALL ▶ FORWARD

call someone forward to call to someone to move forward. □ *The teacher called the student forward to recite.* □ *Don't call me forward. I am not prepared.*

CALL ▶ IN

See also under *CALL ▶ IN(TO).*

call in sick to call one's place of work to say that one is ill and cannot come to work. □ *Four of the accountants called in sick today.* □ *I have to call in sick today.*

call in (to some place) to telephone to some central place, such as one's place of work. □ *I have to call in to the office at noon.* □ *I will call in whenever I have a chance.* 🄰 *The called-in message was delivered anonymously.*

call someone in (for something) **1.** to request that someone come to have a talk. □ *The manager called Karen in for a talk.* 🅃 *The manager called in Gary for questioning.* □ *She called Gary in.* **2.** to request a consultation with a specialist in some field. □ *We will have to call a specialist in for a consultation.* 🅃 *We called in another specialist for an opinion.* □ *We called someone else in.*

call something (back) in to order that something be returned. □ *The car company called many cars back in for repairs.* □ *They called a lot of cars in.* 🅃 *They called in a lot of defective cars.*

CALL ▶ IN(TO)

call someone or something in(to something) to call to a person or a pet to come into something or some place. □ *Would you please call Jeff into the house?* 🅃 *Please call in Jeff.* 🅃 *Please call in the dog.*

call someone or something into something to raise doubts or questions about someone or something. □ *This calls everything you have told me into question.* □ *Are you calling me into question?*

CALL ▶ OFF

call someone or something off ((of) someone or something) to request that someone or something stop bothering or pursuing someone or something. (The *of*-phrase is paraphrased with a *from*-phrase when the particle is transposed. See the 🄵 example. The *of* is colloquial.) □ *Please call your dogs off of my brother.* 🄵 *Call off your dogs from the hunt!* □ *Call your spies off, or else!*

call something off to cancel something. □ *We had to call the picnic off because of rain.* 🅃 *Who called off the picnic?* 🄰 *The called-off picnic is to be rescheduled.*

CALL ▶ ON

See also under *CALL ▶ (UP)ON.*

call on something to draw on something, such as a particular quality or talent. □ *This project calls on all the creative skills you can gather together.* □ *It calls on everything you've got.*

CALL ▶ OUT

call out to shout; to call. □ *Someone called out. Was it you?* □ *Yes, I called out.*

call out to someone to call or shout to someone. □ *She called out to Mike, but he didn't hear her.* □ *Sue called out to her friends.*

call someone or something out to request the services of someone or a group. □ *Things got bad enough that the governor called the militia out.* 🅃 *The governor called out the militia.* 🅃 *The governor called out his hatchet man for the job.*

call someone out to request or demand that someone come out. □ *Ted called Maria out, but she stayed inside.* □ *Todd wouldn't come when I called him out.*

call something out **1.** to draw on something, such as a particular quality or talent. □ *It's times like these that call the best out in us.* 🅃 *These times call out our best.* **2.** to shout out something. □ *Who called the warning out?* 🅃 *You should call out a warning to those behind you on the trail.*

CALL ▶ OVER

call someone over (to some place) to request that someone come to where one is. □ *I will call her over to us, and you can ask her what you want to know.* [T] *Call over the waitress so we can order.* □ *I called Ted over.*

CALL ▶ TO

call a halt to something to demand that something be stopped. □ *We must call a halt to this childish behavior.* □ *The manager called a halt to what was going on.*

call someone to account to ask one to explain and justify one's behavior, policy, performance, etc. □ *The sergeant called the police officer to account.* □ *I called my workers to account.*

call someone to attention to demand that someone assume the formal military stance of attention. □ *Someone called the platoon to attention.* □ *The sergeant called us to attention.*

call someone's attention to something AND **call something to someone's attention** to bring something to someone's notice; to make someone recognize some fact. □ *May I call your attention to the sign on the door?* □ *He called our attention to the notice on the wall.* □ *Did anyone call this letter to your attention?*

call something to mind AND **bring something to mind** to bring something into someone's mind. □ *Your comment calls something unpleasant to mind.* □ *It brings something to mind.* [T] *This calls to mind the time we spent at Niagara Falls.*

call something to order to request that a meeting start. □ *Elaine called the meeting to order on time.* □ *She had to shout to call it to order.*

call something to someone's attention See *call someone's attention to something.*

call to someone to shout to get someone's attention. □ *I called to Fred, but he didn't hear me.* □ *Did you hear me call to you?*

CALL ▶ TOGETHER

call someone together to request that people come together for a meeting. □ *Please call everyone together and we'll discuss this.* □ *I called all the players together.*

CALL ▶ UP

call someone or something up **1.** to request that someone or a group report for active military service. □ *The government called the fourth battalion up for active service.* [T] *They called up another battalion.* [N] *We were not prepared for the call-up.* **2.** to call someone, a group, or a company on the telephone. □ *I will call them up and see what they have to say.* [T] *Please call up the supplier.*

CALL ▶ (UP)ON

call someone (up)on the carpet to request that someone come for a scolding. (Usually to an employer's office. *Upon* is formal and less commonly used than *on*.) □ *The boss will probably call her on the carpet for that mistake.* □ *They called me upon the carpet and gave me what for.*

call (up)on someone **1.** to visit someone. (*Upon* is formal and less commonly used than *on*.) □ *My mother's friends call upon her every Wednesday.* □ *Let's call on Mrs. Franklin this afternoon.* **2.** to choose someone to respond, as in a classroom. □ *The teacher called upon me, but I was not ready to recite.* □ *Please don't call on me. I can't remember a thing.*

call (up)on someone (for something) to choose someone to do or to help with some particular task. (*Upon* is formal and less commonly used than *on*.) □ *Can I call upon you for help?* □ *You can call on me at any time.*

call (up)on someone (to do something) to choose someone to do something. (*Upon* is formal and less commonly used than *on*.) □ *I call upon all of you to make your feelings known to your elected representatives.* □ *I called on George, but he refused.*

CALM ▸ DOWN

calm down to relax; to become less busy or active. ☐ *Now, now, calm down. Take it easy.* ☐ *Please calm down. Nothing bad is going to happen.*

calm someone or something down to cause someone or some creature to be less active, upset, or unsettled. (*Someone* includes *oneself.*) ☐ *Please try to calm yourself down!* 🅃 *Can you calm down your dog?* ☐ *Please calm your horse down.* ☐ *Can you calm yourself down?*

CAMP ▸ OUT

camp out to live out of doors temporarily in a tent or camping vehicle, as on a vacation or special camping trip. ☐ *I love to camp out in the winter.* 🄽 *The children enjoyed the campout even though it was only in their backyard.*

CAMP ▸ UP

camp it up [for performers] to overact or behave in an affected manner. ☐ *The cast began to camp it up in the second act, and the critics walked out.* ☐ *There is no need to camp it up. Play it the way it was written.*

camp something up [for actors] to overact in a performance or to perform something in an affected manner. ☐ *Stop camping it up! This is a play, not a soap opera!* 🅃 *Don't camp up this play!*

CAMPAIGN ▸ AGAINST

campaign against someone or something **1.** to crusade or battle against someone or something. ☐ *Currently, I am campaigning against littering.* ☐ *Sarah is campaigning against crooked politicians.* **2.** to run one's political campaign against someone or something. ☐ *I campaigned against the incumbent and won.* ☐ *John spent a lot of time campaigning against Sarah.*

CAMPAIGN ▸ FOR

campaign for someone or something to support actively someone or someone's candidacy for political office. ☐ *I would be very happy to campaign for you.* ☐ *I want to campaign for the winning candidate.*

CANCEL ▸ OUT

cancel each other out [for the opposite effects of two things] to balance each other. ☐ *The bill for the meal and the payment on the loan cancel each other out.* 🅃 *They canceled out each other.*

cancel out (of something) to withdraw from something. ☐ *I hate to cancel out of the event at the last minute, but this is an emergency.* ☐ *It's too late to cancel out.*

cancel someone out to eliminate someone; to kill someone. (Slang.) ☐ *Max threatened to cancel Lefty out.* 🅃 *Why does he want to cancel out Lefty?*

cancel someone out (of something) to eliminate someone from something. (The *of*-phrase is paraphrased with a *from*-phrase when the particle is transposed. See the 🄵 example.) ☐ *I canceled her out of the pageant because she missed too many rehearsals.* 🅃 *We canceled out all the people who did not show up.* 🄵 *We canceled out the latecomers from the pageant.* ☐ *We had to cancel them out.*

cancel something out to balance the effects of something. ☐ *Sending flowers might cancel the bad feelings out.* 🅃 *The last payment canceled out the debt.*

CAPITALIZE ▸ ON

capitalize on something to build on something; to exploit something to one's own benefit. ☐ *Let's try to capitalize on the strength of the economy and invest for the future.* ☐ *Capitalize on your many assets.*

CAPITULATE ▸ TO

capitulate to someone or something to surrender or submit to someone or something. ☐ *The general finally capitulated and surrendered.* ☐ *I won't capitulate to you.*

CARE ▸ ABOUT

care about someone or something **1.** to hold someone or something dear; to prize someone or something. ☐ *I really care about you.* ☐ *I care about my family.* **2.** to have even minimal regard for someone or something. (Does not imply any of the tender feelings expressed in sense 1. See also the following entry.) ☐ *Don't you care about animals?* ☐ *I care about what happens in Washington.*

care nothing about someone or something to have no regard or respect for someone or something. ☐ *I care nothing about you!* ☐ *She cares nothing about your money!*

CARE ▸ FOR

care for someone to feel tenderly toward someone; to love someone. ☐ *I care for you a great deal, Walter.* ☐ *I care for you too, Alice.*

care for someone or something to take care of someone or something. ☐ *Will you care for my cat while I am away?* ☐ *I would be happy to care for your child.* Ⓐ *Ours are well-cared-for children.* Ⓐ *Your uncared-for hair needs cutting.*

care for something to like the taste of some kind of food or drink. (Usually negative.) ☐ *I don't care for sweet potatoes.* ☐ *I don't care for sweet desserts.*

care nothing for someone or something not to like someone or something. ☐ *She cares nothing for your suggestion.* ☐ *Sarah cares nothing for Jeff.*

CARE ▸ TO

care to do something to want to do something; to be willing to do something. ☐ *I really don't care to see that movie.* ☐ *Would you care to go out for dinner?*

CARP ▸ ABOUT

carp about someone or something to complain about someone or something. (Slang.) ☐ *You are always carping about something.* ☐ *Stop carping about Randy!*

CARP ▸ AT

carp at someone (about someone or something) to complain to someone about someone or something. ☐ *Why are you always carping at me about something?* ☐ *You are always carping at Joan about her brother.* ☐ *Don't carp at me!*

carp at someone or something to criticize someone or something. ☐ *Poor Clara is carping at Bill's carelessness again.* ☐ *Please stop carping at me.*

CARRY ▸ ABOUT

carry someone or something about to carry someone or something with one; to carry someone or something from place to place. ☐ *Do I have to carry these books about all over campus?* ☐ *You are too heavy, sweetie. I don't want to carry you about all day.*

CARRY ▸ ALONG

carry someone along (with someone) [for someone's enthusiasm or power] to affect other people and persuade them. ☐ *The excitement of the play carried everyone along with the actors.* Ⓣ *She carried along the audience with her all the way.* ☐ *She is a very skilled entertainer and can carry the audience along quite well.*

carry someone along (with something) [for something] to transport someone as it moves along. ☐ *The flood carried us along with the debris.* Ⓣ *The rushing water carried along everyone with it.* ☐ *It carried us along at an amazing speed.*

carry something along (with someone) to bring or take something with one, to have something with one and have it handy at all times. ☐ *You should carry this along with you whenever you travel.* Ⓣ *Please carry along this package with you.* ☐ *I'll carry this along with me.*

CARRY ▸ AROUND

carry someone around (with one) **1.** to be the source of transport for someone, usually a child. ☐ *I'm tired of carrying this baby around with me everywhere. Can't I buy a baby carriage?* Ⓣ *I always carry around my child with me.* ☐ *Do I have to carry you around all day?* **2.** to carry the memory or a sense of presence of another person with one. ☐ *I have been carrying my dead grandfather around with me for years.* Ⓣ *She carries around her brother with her in her memories.* ☐ *She should stop carrying him around.*

carry something around (with one) to have something on one's person at all times. ☐ *He carries a gun around with* *him.* 🅃 *Max carries around a gun with him.* ☐ *He always carries a briefcase around.*

CARRY ▸ AWAY

carry someone away [for someone or something] to cause a person to lose control. ☐ *The excitement carried us all away.* 🅃 *The excitement carried away everyone.*

carry someone or something away to take or steal someone or something. ☐ *Someone carried our lawn furniture away.* 🅃 *The kidnappers carried away the child.* ☐ *They carried the child away.*

CARRY ▸ BACK

carry someone back (to some time) to return someone, mentally, to a former time; to remind someone of an earlier time. (*Someone* includes *oneself.*) ☐ *This carries me back to the times of knights and jousting.* ☐ *This magazine article really carries me back.*

carry something back to take something back to where it came from. ☐ *Did you bring this here? If so, carry it back.* ☐ *Carry it back to where it came from.*

CARRY ▸ DOWN

carry something down to take something from a higher to a lower place. ☐ *Would you go up to the attic and carry the trunk down?* 🅃 *Why should I carry down the trunk?*

CARRY ▸ FORWARD

carry something forward to take a figure from one column or category to another. ☐ *Now, carry this figure forward into the tens column.* ☐ *You have to carry this forward. You can't just ignore it.*

CARRY ▸ IN(TO)

carry someone or something in(to some place) to lift and move someone or something to some place. ☐ *Will you carry the baby into the bedroom?* 🅃 *Let me carry in the packages.* ☐ *I'll carry the baby in.*

CARRY ▸ OFF

carry someone or something off to take or steal someone or something. ☐ *The kidnappers carried the child off.* 🅃 *They carried off the child.* ☐ *Someone carried the patio chairs off.*

carry something off **1.** to make something happen; to accomplish something. ☐ *Do you think you can carry the deal off?* 🅃 *Sure, I can carry off the deal.* **2.** to make some sort of deception believable and successful. ☐ *It sounds like a great trick. Can you carry it off?* 🅃 *I can carry off the entire scheme perfectly.*

CARRY ▸ ON

See also under *CARRY ▸ ON(TO).*

carry on (about someone or something) **1.** to talk excitedly or at length about someone or something. ☐ *She was carrying on about the new governor.* ☐ *Jane was carrying on about her job.* ☐ *Stop carrying on, Jane.* **2.** to have an emotional display of distress about someone or something; to behave badly or wildly about someone or something. ☐ *Must you carry on so about virtually nothing?* ☐ *Jane carried on about her husband.* ☐ *Jane is carrying on again.* 🄽 *Now stop all this carrying-on!*

carry on (to something) to continue on to some place or some time. ☐ *Please keep reading. Carry on to the next page.* ☐ *Please continue. Carry on.*

carry on (with someone) to flirt with someone; to have a love affair with someone. ☐ *It looks like Heather is carrying on with James.* ☐ *Heather, stop carrying on!* 🄽 *We've heard a lot about their carrying-on.*

carry on (with something) to continue doing something. (See also *carry something on.*) ☐ *Please carry on with your singing.* ☐ *Oh, do carry on!*

carry something on **1.** to do something over a period of time. ☐ *Do you think you can carry this on for a year?* 🅃 *I will carry on this activity for three years if you want.* **2.** to continue to do something as a tradition. ☐ *We intend to carry this celebration on as long as the family can gather for the holidays.* 🅃

We will carry on this tradition for decades, in fact.

CARRY ▸ ON(TO)

carry something on(to something) to take something onto a vehicle. □ *Do you plan to carry this bag onto the plane?* 🅃 *I'd like to carry on two bags.* □ *Can I carry them on?* 🄰 *How much carry-on luggage am I permitted?* 🄽 *You are allowed only one carryon.*

CARRY ▸ OUT

carry someone or something out to lift up and move someone or something out. □ *Help me carry her out.* 🅃 *Let's carry out the dishes.* □ *I will carry the sleeping child out.*

CARRY ▸ OVER

carry over (to something) **1.** [for a sum or other figure] to be taken to another column of figures. □ *This amount carries over into the next column.* □ *Yes, this number carries over.* **2.** to last or continue until another time. □ *Will this enthusiasm carry over to the following week?* □ *Of course, it will carry over.*

carry someone or something over from something to transport someone or something from somewhere, usually across the sea. □ *The ship carried the travel club over from Spain.* 🅃 *They carried over all my furniture from Paris.* □ *The company offered to carry my family over from London.*

carry someone or something over to something to lift and move someone or something to another place. □ *Please carry this over to the window.* □ *Could you carry Timmy over to his bed, please? He's asleep.*

carry something over until some time to defer something until a particular time. □ *Can we carry this discussion over until later?* 🅃 *We will carry over our discussion until tomorrow.*

CARRY ▸ THROUGH

carry someone or something through something to lift up and move someone or something through something. □ *We will have to carry him through the crowd to the ambulance.* □ *Jane carried the groceries through the doorway.*

carry someone through (something) to sustain someone during something. □ *Can this amount carry you through the week?* □ *Yes, this will carry me through.*

carry through (on something) to carry something out satisfactorily; to complete some act as promised. □ *I hope you will carry through on this project.* □ *Yes, I'll carry through.* 🄽 *You simply have no carry-through! You never finish the job!*

CARRY ▸ WITH

carry someone or something with one to go about with the memory or presence of someone or something with one. □ *I shall carry you with me always.* □ *Jane will always carry that evening with her in her memory.*

carry something with one to have something with one or on one's person. □ *Do you always carry that bag with you?* □ *I always carry a pen with me.*

carry weight with someone to have influence with someone; [for an explanation] to amount to a good argument to use with someone. □ *That carries a lot of weight with the older folks.* □ *What you say carries no weight with me.*

CART ▸ OFF

cart someone or something off to take or haul someone or something away. (When used with *someone* the person is treated like an object.) □ *The police came and carted her off.* 🅃 *Let's cart off these boxes.* □ *They carted the trash off.*

CARVE ▸ FROM

carve something from something to cut something off of or out of something with a knife. □ *He carved a little snowman out of an apple.* □ *Can you carve an elephant from soap?*

CARVE ▸ IN

carve something in stone to fix some idea permanently. (Figurative.) □ *No one has carved this in stone.* □ *After all, it's not carved in stone.*

CARVE ▶ INTO

carve something into something to create a carved object by sculpturing raw material. ☐ *She carved the soap into a little elephant.* ☐ *Ken carved the apple into a tiny snowman.*

CARVE ▶ IN(TO)

carve something in(to something) to cut letters or symbols into something. ☐ *He carved his initials into a tree.* 🅃 *He carved in the letters.* ☐ *He carved them in.* 🄰 *The tree trunk was marred with carved-in letters.*

CARVE ▶ OUT

carve something out to hollow something out by carving; to make something hollow by carving. ☐ *Can he carve a bowl out?* 🅃 *He carved out the bowl of the pipe and then began to sand it.*

carve something out (of something) to remove something from the inside of something else by carving or cutting. ☐ *She carved the insides out of the pumpkin.* 🅃 *She carved out the insides of the pumpkin.* ☐ *John carved the insides out.*

CARVE ▶ UP

carve someone or something up to damage someone or something by careless or purposeful cutting. (*Someone* includes *oneself.*) ☐ *Someone carved the tabletop up. Who did it and why?* 🅃 *Max wanted to carve up Lefty.* ☐ *No one is going to carve me up!* ☐ *He carved himself up pretty badly when his hand slipped on the knife.*

carve something up to divide something up, perhaps carelessly. ☐ *You can't carve the country up!* 🅃 *You can't just carve up one country and give the pieces away.* 🄰 *The carved-up watermelon was shared all around.*

CASE ▶ OUT

case someone or something out to look someone or something over carefully, with a view to additional activity at a later time. (Slang.) ☐ *He came into the room and cased all the girls out.* 🅃 *He cased out the girls.* ☐ *John cased them out.*

CASH ▶ IN

cash in on something to take advantage of something; to earn a profit by exploiting something. ☐ *Everyone was trying to cash in on the current interest in the military.* ☐ *I want to cash in on the idea.*

cash (one's chips) in **1.** to turn in one's gaming tokens or poker chips when one quits playing. ☐ *When you leave the game, you should cash your chips in.* 🅃 *Cash in your chips before you go.* ☐ *I'm going to cash in.* **2.** to quit [anything], as if one were cashing in gaming tokens. ☐ *I guess I'll cash my chips in and go home.* 🅃 *Well, it's time to cash in my chips and go home.* ☐ *I've eaten enough. I'm going to cash in.* **2.** to die. (Slang. Using the same metaphor as sense 2.) ☐ *There's a funeral procession. Who cashed his chips in?* 🅃 *Poor Fred cashed in his chips last week.* ☐ *He took a slug in the gut and cashed in.*

cash something in (for something) to exchange a security for money; to convert a foreign currency to one's own currency; to turn gaming tokens or poker chips in for money. (See *cash (one's chips) in.*) ☐ *I cashed the bonds in for a cashier's check.* 🅃 *I cashed in my bonds for their face value.* ☐ *I cashed the bonds in.* 🄰 *Do they really burn cashed-in bonds?*

CAST ▶ ABOUT

cast about for someone or something See the following entry.

CAST ▶ AROUND

cast around (for someone or something) AND **cast about for someone or something** to seek someone or something in a variety of places; to look here and there for someone or something. ☐ *I will cast around for a used car of the model you requested.* ☐ *I will cast about for someone to help us.* ☐ *I cast around but found no one.*

CAST ▶ AS

cast someone as something **1.** to choose someone to play a particular role in a play, opera, film, etc. (*Someone* includes *oneself.*) ☐ *The director cast her as the young singer.* ☐ *They cast me as a* *villain.* □ *He cast himself as one of the crowd.* **2.** to decide or fantasize that someone is going to follow a particular pattern of behavior in real life. □ *I'm afraid my teachers cast me as a dummy when I was very young.* □ *They cast me as someone who would not succeed.*

CAST ▸ ASIDE

cast someone or something aside to reject or discard someone or something. □ *He simply cast his wife aside, and that was it.* 🅃 *He cast aside his wife and ran off.* □ *Jane cast her coat aside and sat down at the piano.*

CAST ▸ AWAY

cast someone or something away to push or hurl someone or something away. □ *You can't just cast me away!* 🅃 *She cast away the stone she had picked up.* □ *Jane cast the stone away.* 🄰 *They were happy to receive all our castaway clothing.* 🄽 *As soon as I launder these castaways, you can give them out.*

CAST ▸ BACK

cast something back (some place) to throw something back somewhere. □ *I cast the fish back in the water.* □ *Liz cast it back.* 🅃 *Cast back this stone and all the others you took from the pile.*

CAST ▸ BEFORE

cast (one's) pearls before swine to waste something on someone who cannot appreciate it. (A proverb. Pigs would not appreciate pearls.) □ *There is no point in explaining further. You shouldn't cast your pearls before swine.* □ *Don't waste your time on her. You are just casting pearls before swine.*

CAST ▸ DOWN

cast something down **1.** to hurl or throw something down. □ *She cast the glass down, breaking it into a thousand pieces.* 🅃 *She cast down the tray and all that was on it.* **2.** to aim something, usually the eyes, downward. □ *She cast her eyes down as they saw each other again.* 🅃 *He cast down his eyes in shame.* 🄰 *Her downcast eyes were filled with tears.*

CAST ▸ IN

cast (one's lot) in (with someone or something) to join in with someone or a group. □ *He cast his lot in with the others.* 🅃 *She cast in her lot with the others.* □ *She cast in with a questionable crowd.*

CAST ▸ OFF

cast off (from something) [for the crew of a boat or ship] to push away from the dock or pier; to begin the process of undocking a boat or ship. □ *The crew cast off from the dock.* □ *It's time to cast off.*

cast someone or something off to dispose of someone or something; to throw someone or something aside or away. □ *You can't just cast me off like an old coat!* 🅃 *She cast off her husband of three months.* □ *Lee cast off his coat.* 🄰 *She didn't want anyone else's cast-off husband.* 🄽 *What shall I do with this old coat and these other castoffs?*

CAST ▸ ON

cast something on someone or something to place or aim something, such as doubt, aspersions, etc., on someone or something. □ *I never cast a doubt on anything you said!* □ *Jed did not cast aspersions on Fred.*

CAST ▸ OUT

cast someone or something out to throw someone or something out. (Stilted.) □ *You are not going to cast me out on night like this!* 🅃 *Jane cast out the cat and slammed the door.* □ *I cast the offensive child out.*

CAST ▸ UP

cast someone or something up [for the waves] to bring up and deposit someone or something on the shore. □ *The waves cast the body of the sailor up, and it was found on the shore.* 🅃 *The waves cast up the body of a sailor.* □ *The action of the waves cast a lot of driftwood up.*

CATAPULT ▸ INTO

catapult someone or something into something to thrust or force someone or something into something, such as fame, glory, the limelight, front-page news, etc. (Figurative.) □ *The success catapulted her into the limelight.* □ *The scandal catapulted the contractual arrangements into public scrutiny.*

CATCH ▸ AT

catch someone at something to discover someone doing something. ☐ *We caught her at her evil deeds.* ☐ *Don't let me catch you at that again!*

CATCH ▸ FOR

catch hell for something to get a severe scolding for doing something. (Use discretion with *hell*.) ☐ *I knew I would catch hell for doing it, but I did it anyway.* ☐ *You will catch hell for that!*

CATCH ▸ FROM

catch something from someone to get a disease from someone. ☐ *I hope my children catch the chicken pox from your children. Better to have it while you are young.* ☐ *I don't want to catch a cold from you.*

CATCH ▸ IN

catch someone in the act (of doing something) to discover someone doing a [bad] deed at the very moment when the deed is being done. ☐ *I caught her in the act of stealing the coat.* ☐ *Yes, I caught her in the act.*

catch someone or something in something to trap someone or something in something. ☐ *We caught David in the snare by accident.* ☐ *The battle caught the unfortunate horse in the cross fire.* ☐ *The disputants caught us in the middle.*

CATCH ▸ OF

catch (a)hold of someone or something to grasp or seize someone or something. ☐ *See if you can catch hold of the rope as it swings back and forth.* ☐ *I couldn't catch ahold of her.*

catch sight of someone or something to see someone or something for just a short time; to glimpse someone or something. ☐ *I was not able to catch sight of her.* ☐ *We caught sight of the last train, speeding away down the track.*

CATCH ▸ OFF

catch one off one's guard to find someone unprepared; to approach someone who is temporarily unwary. ☐ *I can't answer. You caught me off guard.* ☐ *I caught her off guard and she couldn't answer.*

catch someone off balance to approach someone who is in an unstable position, or unprepared for the encounter; to frighten someone who is in an unstable position. ☐ *You caught me off balance when you approached from behind.* ☐ *I caught her off balance and she nearly fell.*

CATCH ▸ ON

catch on (to someone or something) to figure out someone or something. ☐ *I finally caught on to what she was talking about.* ☐ *It takes a while for me to catch on.*

catch on (with someone) [for something] to become popular with someone. ☐ *I hope our new product catches on with children.* ☐ *I'm sure it will catch on.*

catch something on something to snag something on something. ☐ *I caught the pocket of my trousers on the drawer pull and almost ripped it off.* ☐ *He caught the sleeve of his uniform on a rough place.*

CATCH ▸ OUT

catch someone out to discover the truth about someone's deception. ☐ *The investigator tried to catch me out, but I stuck to my story.* ☐ *You can't catch me out that easily.*

CATCH ▸ UP

catch someone up in something [for excitement or interest] to extend to and engross someone. ☐ *The happenings caught everyone up in the excitement.* ☐ *The accident caught us all up in the resultant confusion.*

catch someone up (on someone or something) to tell someone the news of someone or something. (*Someone* includes *oneself*.) ☐ *Oh, please catch me up on what your family is doing.* ☐ *Yes, do catch us up!* ☐ *I have to take some time to catch myself up on the news.*

catch someone up short to surprise someone; to find someone unprepared. ☐ *Your sudden arrival caught me up short.* ☐ *The demands the visitors placed on me caught me up short.*

catch something up in something to ensnare and capture something in something. □ *We caught a large number of fish up in the net.* [T] *We caught up many fish in the net.*

catch up (on someone or something) to learn the news of someone or something. □ *I need a little time to catch up on the news.* □ *We all need to catch up on Tony.* □ *I need some time to catch up.*

catch up (on something) to bring one's efforts with something up to date; to do the work that one should have done. □ *I need a quiet time so I can catch up on my work.* □ *I have to catch up and become more productive.* [N] *I am so behind! I have to play catch-up when I should be doing something new.*

catch up (to someone or something) to get even with or equal to someone or something. (Almost the same as *catch up (with someone or something).*) □ *I finally caught up to Fred, who was way ahead of me in the race.* □ *Jane caught up to the bus that had almost left her behind.* □ *Don't worry, I'll catch up.*

catch up (with someone or something) to increase the rate of movement or growth to become even with or equal to someone or something. (Almost the same as *catch up (to someone or something).*) □ *Martin is finally catching up with his taller brother.* □ *This puppy will never catch up with the others.* □ *The competing companies will never catch up with this one.* □ *I'm smaller than the others. Will I ever catch up?*

CATCH ► WITH

catch one with one's pants down to discover someone in the act of doing something. (Figurative, although literal uses are possible.) □ *The whole council was using tax money as their own. Some citizens caught the council members with their pants down and they intend to press charges.* □ *We caught them with their pants down.*

catch someone with something **1.** to discover or apprehend someone with something—usually something stolen or illicit. □ *They caught Elizabeth with the stolen money.* □ *Don't let them catch you with the money!* **2.** to apprehend someone with the aid of something. □ *We caught the speeder with radar.* □ *The cops caught Lefty with the help of an informer.*

CATER ► TO

cater to someone or something **1.** to provide for or care for someone or something. □ *I believe that we can cater to you in this matter.* □ *Our company caters to larger firms that do not wish to maintain a service department.* **2.** to provide special or favorable treatment for someone or something. □ *I'm sorry, but I cannot cater to you and not to the others.* □ *We do not have the time to cater to special requests.*

CAUTION ► ABOUT

caution someone about someone or something AND **caution someone against someone or something** to warn someone against someone or something. □ *Haven't I cautioned you about that before?* □ *Hasn't someone cautioned you about Daniel?* □ *Let me caution you against going.*

CAUTION ► AGAINST

caution someone against someone or something See the previous entry.

CAVE ► IN

cave in [for a roof or ceiling] to collapse. □ *The roof of the mine caved in when no one was there.* [N] *There was a serious cave-in over in the old mine. No one was hurt.*

cave in (on someone or something) [for a roof or ceiling] to collapse on someone or something. □ *The roof caved in on the miners.* □ *The roof caved in.* [N] *No one was injured in the cave-in.*

cave in (to someone or something) to give in to someone or something. □ *Finally, the manager caved in to the customer's demands.* □ *I refuse to cave in.*

CAVIL ► AT

cavil at someone to find fault with someone; to complain about someone constantly. □ *Will you never cease caviling at all of us?* □ *There is no need to cavil at me day and night!*

CEDE ▸ TO

cede something to someone to grant a parcel of land to someone. ☐ *We refuse to cede that land to you.* ☐ *They ceded the land to the city for a park.*

CELEBRATE ▸ FOR

celebrate someone for something to honor someone for having done something. ☐ *The people celebrated the astronaut for a successful journey.* ☐ *She was celebrated widely for her discovery.*

CEMENT ▸ ON(TO)

cement something on((to) something) to fasten something onto something with glue or cement. ☐ *Cement this handle back onto the cup.* 🅃 *Now, cement on the other handle.* ☐ *I will cement it on for you.*

CEMENT ▸ TOGETHER

cement something together to fasten something together with glue or cement. ☐ *Use this stuff to cement the vase together.* ☐ *Will you cement these parts together?*

CENSURE ▸ FOR

censure someone for something to criticize someone formally for having done something. ☐ *Please don't censure us for doing our duty.* ☐ *The legislature proposed to censure one of its members.*

CENTER ▸ AROUND

center around someone or something to make someone or something the central point in something; to be based on someone or something. ☐ *All of this centers around your ability to control the rising water.* ☐ *The outcome centers around the weather next week.*

CENTER ▸ ON

center on someone or something to focus on someone or something. ☐ *Let us center on the basic problem and try to solve it.* ☐ *I want to center on Liz and her contributions to the firm.*

center something on someone or something to base something on someone or something. ☐ *Let us center the discussion on Walter.* ☐ *We centered our whole meeting on the conservation question.*

CHAFE ▸ AT

chafe at something to be irritated or annoyed at something. ☐ *Jane chafed at the criticism for a long time afterward.* ☐ *Jerry chafed for a while at what Ken had said.*

CHAIN ▸ DOWN

chain someone or something down to fasten someone or something down with chains. ☐ *They chained the bicycle rack down so no one could steal it.* ☐ *They chained the raving maniac down and called the police.* 🅃 *You should chain down your patio chairs.* ☐ *The sheriff threatened to chain Max down.*

CHAIN ▸ TO

chain something to something to connect things together with chains. ☐ *We chained all the bicycles to one another so no one could steal them.* ☐ *We will have to chain the lawn furniture to a tree if we leave it out while we are on vacation.*

CHAIN ▸ UP

chain someone up to bind someone in chains. ☐ *We will have to chain him up until the police get here.* 🅃 *Chain up the criminal.*

chain something up 1. to restrict an animal's movements by attaching it to something with chains. ☐ *You are going to have to chain that dog up.* 🅃 *Please chain up your dog.* 🄰 *A chained-up dog guarded the entrance to the club.* **2.** to lock or secure a door or gate with chains. ☐ *Please chain the gate up again when you come through.* 🅃 *Yes, chain up the gate.*

CHALK ▸ OUT

chalk something out 1. to draw a picture of something in chalk, especially to illustrate a plan of some type. ☐ *The coach chalked the play out so the players could understand what they were to do.* 🅃 *She chalked out the play.* **2.** to explain something carefully to someone, as if one were talking about a chalk drawing. (Often figurative.) ☐ *Here, let me chalk it out for you. Listen carefully.* 🅃 *She chalked out the details of the plan.*

CHALK ▸ UP

chalk something up **1.** to write something on a chalkboard. ☐ *Let me chalk this formula up so you all can see it.* 🅃 *I'll chalk up the formula.* **2.** to add a mark or point to one's score. ☐ *Chalk another goal up.* 🅃 *Chalk up another basket for the other side.*

chalk something up against someone to blame someone for something; to register something against someone. ☐ *I will have to chalk another fault up against Fred.* 🅃 *She chalked up a mark against Dave.*

chalk something up to something to account for something with something else; to blame something on something. ☐ *You can chalk her mistake up to ignorance.* ☐ *Chalk Ted's success up to preparedness.* 🅃 *I will chalk up this defeat to his youth.*

CHALLENGE ▸ ON

challenge someone on something to dispute someone's statement, remarks, or position. ☐ *They challenged him on his statement.* ☐ *I think Fred is wrong, but I won't challenge him on his estimate.*

CHALLENGE ▸ TO

challenge someone to something to dare someone to do something; to invite someone to compete at something. ☐ *I challenge you to a round of golf.* ☐ *Jerry challenged us to debate the issues.*

CHAMP ▸ AT

champ at the bit to be very eager. (Like a horse chewing on its bit, anxious to get going.) ☐ *Everyone was champing at the bit to get going.* ☐ *Juan wanted to go and was champing at the bit.*

CHANCE ▸ (UP)ON

chance (up)on someone or something to find someone or something by accident; to happen on someone or something. (*Upon* is formal and less commonly used than *on*.) ☐ *I chanced upon a nice little restaurant on my walk today. The prices looked good too.* ☐ *I chanced on an old friend of yours in town today.*

CHANGE ▸ BACK

change back (from something) to return to the original form, state, or selection, from some other form, state, or selection. ☐ *We are going to change back from our most recent change.* ☐ *We didn't like our new supplier, so we changed back.*

change back ((in)to someone or something) to return to the original form. ☐ *The problem, which had been nearly impossible, changed back to a minor matter within a week.* ☐ *Then Superman changed back into mild-mannered Clark Kent.* ☐ *He changed back to Kent.* ☐ *He popped out of sight and changed back.*

change something back to cause something to return to the original form. ☐ *Whoever changed the television channel should change it back.* 🅃 *Change back the channel!*

CHANGE ▸ INTO

change into someone or something to alter one's or its state to another state. ☐ *The wizard changed into a lovely maiden.* ☐ *As the moon rose, our meek, ineffectual Wally Wilson changed into a bloodthirsty werewolf.*

change someone or something into someone or something to make someone or something change form or state. (*Someone* includes *oneself*.) ☐ *The magician claimed he could change Wally Wilson into Paul Newman.* ☐ *Paul Newman changed the magician into a baby grand piano.* ☐ *He suddenly changed himself into a smiling friend rather than the gruff old man we had first seen.*

CHANGE ▸ OFF

change off [for people] to alternate in doing something. ☐ *Tom and I changed off so neither of us had to work at it all the time.* ☐ *Let's change off periodically.*

CHANGE ▸ OUT

change out of something to take off a set of clothing and put on another. ☐ *I have to change out of these wet clothes.* ☐ *You should change out of your casual* *clothes and put on something more formal for dinner.*

CHANGE ▸ OVER

change over (from someone or something) (to someone or something) to convert from something to something else; to convert from someone to someone else. ☐ *We decided to change over from oil to gas.* ☐ *We changed over to gas from oil.* ☐ *We changed over from Ted to Alice.* 🄽 *The changeover was accomplished with no difficulty.*

CHANGE ▸ TO

change to something to convert to something; to give up one and choose another. ☐ *We will change to standard time in the fall.* ☐ *I decided to change to gas for heating and cooking.*

CHANGE ▸ WITH

change places with someone to trade or exchange situations or locations with someone. ☐ *He has a big car, but I wouldn't change places with him for the world.* ☐ *Juan decided to change places with Ken.*

change something with someone to trade or exchange something with someone. ☐ *I changed coats with Fred and fooled a few people.* ☐ *Will you change seats with me?*

CHANNEL ▸ INTO

channel something into something **1.** to divert water or other liquid through a channel into something. ☐ *The farmer channeled the irrigation water into the field.* ☐ *Juan channeled the water into the potato field.* **2.** to divert something, such as energy, money, effort, into something. ☐ *The government channeled a great deal of money into rebuilding the inner part of the city.* ☐ *I can't channel any more of our work force into this project.*

CHANNEL ▸ OFF

channel something off **1.** to drain off water or some other liquid through a channel. ☐ *The front yard is flooded, and we will have to channel the water off.* 🅃 *Let's channel off the water before it gets too deep.* **2.** to drain off or waste energy, money, effort, etc. ☐ *The war channeled the resources off.* 🅃 *The war channeled off most of the resources of the country.*

CHARGE ▸ AGAINST

charge something against something to debit the cost of something against something. ☐ *Can I charge this item against the entertainment account?* ☐ *Don't even try to charge it against your income tax.*

CHARGE ▸ AT

charge at someone or something to bolt forward to attack someone or something. ☐ *The elephant charged at the hunter.* ☐ *I was afraid that the water buffalo was going to charge the Jeep.*

CHARGE ▸ DOWN

charge down on someone or something [for an animal or vehicle] to race or bolt against someone or something. ☐ *The angry elephant charged down on the hunters.* ☐ *The speeding truck charged down on the small shed.*

CHARGE ▸ FOR

charge (something) for someone to demand an amount of money to pay for someone's ticket, fare, admission, treatment, etc. ☐ *Tickets are expensive. They charged nearly four dollars for the baby.* ☐ *I didn't realize they charged for babies.*

charge (something) for something to demand an amount of money in payment for something. ☐ *You are charging too much for this.* ☐ *You really shouldn't charge for it at all.*

CHARGE ▸ IN(TO)

charge in(to some place) to bolt or run wildly into a place. ☐ *The people charged into the store on the day of the sale.* ☐ *They all charged in like thirsty camels.*

CHARGE ▸ OFF

charge off to bolt or run away. ☐ *He got angry and charged off.* ☐ *Juan charged off to talk to the boss.*

charge something off as something to consider something a financial loss and deduct the loss from federal taxes; to assign something to the tax loss category in accounting. (Compare to *write something off (on something).*) □ *I will have to charge this off as a loss.* □ *Try to charge it off as a business expense.*

CHARGE ▸ ON

charge something on something **1.** to put the cost of something on a credit card or credit account. □ *I would like to charge this purchase on my credit card.* □ *What card do you want to charge it on?* **2.** to demand the payment of interest or a penalty on something; to demand a certain percentage of interest on something. □ *They charged an enormous amount of interest on the loan.* □ *The bank charged a penalty on the late payment.* □ *The bank charged nearly 12 percent interest on our loan.*

CHARGE ▸ OUT

charge out of some place to bolt or stomp out of some place. □ *Carol charged out of the house, trying to catch Sally before she got on the bus.* □ *Juan got mad and charged out of the office.*

CHARGE ▸ TO

charge something (up) to someone or something to place the cost of something on the account of someone or a group. □ *I will have to charge this up to your account.* □ *Do you have to charge this to my account?* □ *Is this order charged to anyone yet?*

CHARGE ▸ UP

charge someone up to excite someone; to make a person enthusiastic about something. (*Someone* includes *oneself.*) □ *The excitement of the day charged them up so they could not sleep.* [T] *The speaker charged up the crowd.* □ *He reread the report, hoping to charge himself up enough to make some sensible comments.*

charge something up **1.** to apply an electrical charge to a battery. □ *How long will it take to charge this battery up?* [T] *It takes an hour to charge up your battery.* **2.** to load or fill something, such as a fire extinguisher. □ *We had to send the extinguishers back to the factory, where they charged them up.* [T] *How much does it cost to charge up an extinguisher?* **3.** to reinvigorate something. □ *What can we do to charge this play up?* [T] *A murder in the first act would charge up the play.*

charge something (up) to someone or something See under *CHARGE ▸ TO.*

CHARGE ▸ WITH

charge someone or something with something to make someone or a group pay the cost of something. □ *I will have to charge Bill with the cost of repairs.* □ *The manager will charge the account with about forty dollars.*

charge someone with something **1.** to place criminal charges against someone. □ *The police charged Max with robbery.* □ *Am I charged with speeding? I was hardly moving!* **2.** to order someone to do a particular task. □ *The president charged him with organizing the meeting.* □ *We charged her with locating a suitable hall.*

CHARM ▸ WITH

charm someone with something to enchant or fascinate someone with something. □ *He charmed her with stories of his house on the beach.* □ *She charmed him with her polite manner.*

CHART ▸ OUT

chart something out (for someone or something) to lay out a plan or course for someone or something. □ *The first mate charted the course out for the skipper.* [T] *The first mate charted out the course for us.* □ *Shall I chart it out?* [T] *I will chart out the course for our journey.*

CHASE ▸ AFTER

chase after someone or something to pursue or hunt for someone or something. □ *She is always chasing after men.* □ *Jane is chasing after a goal that can never be hers.*

CHASE ▸ AROUND

chase around after someone or something to look here and there for something; to seek someone or something in many different places. □ *I don't want to have to spend a whole day chasing around after exotic foodstuffs for this* *recipe of yours.* ☐ *I chased around after Roger and never found him.*

chase someone or something around to follow someone or something around in pursuit. (There is an implication that the person or thing pursued is attempting to elude whatever is in pursuit.) ☐ *The dog chased us around in play.* 🅃 *It chased around all the children.* ☐ *The children chased the dog around.* ☐ *The dog chased the cars around.*

CHASE ▸ AWAY

chase someone or something (away) from some place See under *CHASE ▸ FROM.*

CHASE ▸ DOWN

chase someone or something down to track down and seize someone or something. ☐ *Larry set out to chase Betsy down.* 🅃 *The police chased down the suspect.* ☐ *They chased her down.*

CHASE ▸ FROM

chase someone or something (away) from some place AND **chase someone or something out of some place** to drive someone or something away from or out of a place. ☐ *The crowd chased the thief from the building.* ☐ *We chased the people out of the building.* ☐ *The dog thought it had chased the cars away from its house.*

CHASE ▸ IN

chase someone or something in(to some place) to drive someone or some creature into a place. ☐ *They chased all the buffalo into the corral.* 🅃 *The cowboys chased in the buffalo.* ☐ *They chased the chickens into the chicken house.*

CHASE ▸ OUT

chase someone or something out of some place See under *CHASE ▸ FROM.*

CHASE ▸ UP

chase someone or something up to seek someone or something out; to look high and low for someone or something. ☐ *I will chase Tom up for you.* 🅃 *I will try to chase up a buyer for your car.* 🅃 *See if you can chase up a taxi.*

chase someone or something up something to drive someone or an animal up something, such as a tree, a hill, a cliff, etc. ☐ *The ranchers chased the mountain lion up a tree.* ☐ *The panther chased the hunter up the side of the barn.*

CHAT ▸ ABOUT

chat about someone or something to talk idly about someone or something. ☐ *We need to chat about Molly.* ☐ *I want to chat about your expenditures a little.*

CHATTER ▸ ABOUT

chatter about someone or something to talk idly and rapidly about someone or something. ☐ *All the guests were chattering about something or other.* ☐ *People are chattering about you and Claire. Do you want to know what they are saying?*

CHATTER ▸ AT

See the following entry.

CHATTER ▸ AWAY

chatter (away) (at someone or something) **1.** to talk incessantly to or at someone or something. ☐ *The parrot was chattering away at its reflection in the mirror.* ☐ *The kids were chattering away.* ☐ *Stop chattering at me!* **2.** [for a small animal, such as a squirrel] to scold someone or something. ☐ *The little squirrel chattered away at the crow.* ☐ *The crow came close and the squirrel chattered away again.*

CHATTER ▸ FROM

chatter from something [for one's teeth] to shake together uncontrollably because of the cold, a cold wind, the dampness, a fever, etc. ☐ *My teeth were chattering from the extreme cold.* ☐ *It was a terrible illness. My teeth chattered from the chills that followed the fever.*

CHEAT ▸ AT

cheat at something to use deception while competing [against someone]. ☐ *They say she cheats at cards.* ☐ *Juan is likely to cheat at getting the contracts.*

CHEAT ▶ ON

cheat on someone [for one member of a couple] to be unfaithful or have a love affair. □ *Terry was found cheating on Amy.* □ *Amy was also cheating on Terry.*

CHEAT ▶ OUT

cheat someone out of something to get something from someone by deception. (*Someone* includes *oneself.*) □ *Are you trying to cheat me out of what is rightfully mine?* □ *She cheated herself out of an invitation because she lied about her affiliation.*

CHECK ▶ BACK

check back (on someone or something) to look into the state of someone or something again at a later time. □ *I'll have to check back on you later.* □ *I'll check back later.*

check back (with someone) to inquire of someone again at a later time. □ *Please check back with me later.* □ *Okay. I'll check back.*

CHECK ▶ IN

check in (at something) to go to a place and record one's arrival. □ *When you get there, check in at the front office.* □ *All right. I'll check in when I arrive.*

check in on someone or something to go into a place and look in on someone or something there. □ *I think I will go check in on Timmy.* □ *Let me check in on how things are going in the kitchen.*

check in (with someone) to go to someone and indicate that one has arrived some place. □ *Please check in with your manager.* □ *I have to go check in.*

check someone in to record the arrival of someone. (*Someone* includes *oneself.*) □ *Ask the guard to check you in when you get there.* 🅃 *Tell the guard to check in the visitors as they arrive.* □ *She checked herself in and went on to the dressing room.*

check something in **1.** to record that someone has returned something. □ *I asked the librarian to check the book in for me.* 🅃 *Did the librarian check in the book?* 🄰 *The checked-in books just sat there untouched.* **2.** to take something to a place, return it, and make sure that its return has been recorded. □ *I checked the book in on time.* 🅃 *Did you really check in the book on time?* **3.** to examine a shipment or an order received and make certain that everything ordered was received. □ *I checked the order in and sent a report to the manager.* 🅃 *Tim checked in the order from the supplier to make sure that everything was there.*

CHECK ▶ INTO

check into something **1.** to investigate a matter. □ *I asked the manager to check into it.* □ *Something is wrong, and I will check into it.* **2.** to sign oneself into a place to stay, such as a hotel, hospital, motel, etc. □ *She checked herself into a private hospital for some kind of treatment.* □ *They checked into the first motel they came to on the highway.*

CHECK ▶ OFF

check someone or something off to mark or cross out the name of a person or thing on a list. (*Someone* includes *oneself.*) □ *I am glad to see that you were able to come. I will check you off.* 🅃 *I checked off the recent arrivals.* □ *I checked the items off.* □ *Mary checked herself off and proceeded to start the day's work.*

CHECK ▶ ON

check on someone or something to look into the legitimacy or condition of someone or something. □ *Sarah will check on the matter and report to us.* □ *I will check on Jeff.* □ *While you're upstairs, would you check on the baby?*

CHECK ▶ OUT

check out [for someone or something] to prove to be correctly represented. □ *Everything you told me checks out.* □ *Your story checks out, Max.*

check out (from something) to do the paperwork necessary to leave a place and leave. (Virtually the same as *check out (of something).*) □ *I will check out from the office and come right to where you are.* □ *I'll be there as soon as I check out.* 🄰 *There was no one at the checkout desk.* 🄽 *Checkout is at noon.*

check out (of something) to do the paperwork necessary to leave a place, such as a hotel. ☐ *I will check out of the hotel at about noon.* ☐ *I check out at noon.*

check someone or something out to evaluate someone or something. (*Someone* includes *oneself.*) ☐ *It sounds good. I'll check it out.* 🆃 *I'll check out everyone else.* ☐ *The doctor will check you out.* ☐ *She checked herself out, but found no broken bones.*

check someone or something out of something to do the paperwork necessary to remove someone or something from something or some place. (*Someone* includes *oneself.*) ☐ *I will have the manager check you out of the hotel and send you the bill.* ☐ *The clerk checked the projector out of the learning center.* 🅰 *The checked-out books are put on this shelf to keep them separate from the others.* ☐ *Todd checked himself out of the hospital and went back to his job.*

CHECK ▸ OVER

check someone or something over to examine someone or something closely. (*Someone* includes *oneself.*) ☐ *You should have the doctor check you over before you go back to work.* 🆃 *The doctor checked over the children who had shown the worst symptoms.* ☐ *The mechanic checked the car over.* ☐ *After checking herself over, Sally picked up her parcels, got up, and continued to walk down the street.*

CHECK ▸ THROUGH

check someone through (something) to allow one to pass through something after checking one's papers, tickets, passes, etc. ☐ *The guard checked us through the gate, and we went about our business.* ☐ *We checked them through.*

check something through (to some place) to have one's luggage sent directly to one's final destination. ☐ *Please check these bags through to Madrid.* ☐ *I will check your bags through.*

check through something to examine something or a collection of things. (Usually refers to papers or written work, can also refer to the things referred to in the paperwork.) ☐ *Check through this and look for typographical errors.* ☐ *I'll check through it for you.*

CHECK ▸ UP

check up (on someone or something) to determine the state of someone or something. ☐ *Please don't check up on me. I can be trusted.* ☐ *I see no need to check up.* 🅽 *The mechanic says the car needs a good checkup.*

CHECK ▸ WITH

check with someone (about something) to ask someone about something. ☐ *You should check with the concierge about the bus to the airport.* ☐ *Please check with your agent.*

CHEER ▸ FOR

cheer for someone or something to give a shout of encouragement for someone or something. ☐ *Everyone cheered for the team.* ☐ *I cheered for Jane.*

CHEER ▸ ON

cheer someone or something on to encourage someone or something to continue to do well, as in a race. ☐ *We cheered them on, and they won.* 🆃 *We cheered on the team.* ☐ *Sam cheered Jane on.*

CHEER ▸ UP

cheer someone up to make a sad person happy. (*Someone* includes *oneself.*) ☐ *Let's try to cheer Karen up.* 🆃 *Yes, let's cheer up Karen.* ☐ *Usually I can cheer myself up on days like this, but not today.*

cheer up [for a sad person] to become happy. ☐ *After a while, she began to cheer up.* ☐ *Cheer up! Things could be worse.*

CHEESE ▸ OFF

cheese someone off to make someone angry. (Slang.) ☐ *You sure know how to cheese Laurel off.* 🆃 *Bobby cheesed off every person in the club.*

CHEW ▸ AT

chew (away) at something to gnaw or chew something for a period of time. ☐ *The puppy chewed away at the leather belt all night.* ☐ *The little animal chewed at the belt until it was ruined.*

CHEW ▸ AWAY

chew (away) at something See the previous entry.

chew something away to gnaw something off; to gnaw at something until it's all gone. □ *You can see what's left of it. Most of it has been chewed away by some animal.* 🅃 *Some animal chewed away the top of my shoe!*

CHEW ▸ OFF

chew something off ((of) something) to bite or gnaw something off something. (The *of*-phrase is paraphrased with a *from*-phrase when the particle is transposed. See the 🄵 example. The *of* is colloquial.) □ *The puppy chewed the heel off of my shoe.* 🄵 *It chewed off the heel from my shoe.* □ *The puppy chewed the heel off.*

CHEW ▸ ON

chew on someone or something to gnaw someone or something. □ *The dog was chewing on my shoe.* □ *It started chewing on me and I kicked it.*

CHEW ▸ OUT

chew someone out to scold or berate someone. (Slang.) □ *I expect he will want to chew me out.* 🅃 *The sergeant chewed out the recruit.* 🄽 *The boss gave them all a good chewing-out.*

CHEW ▸ OVER

chew something over to discuss something. (Slang.) □ *Let's sit down and chew this over.* 🅃 *We'll chew over the whole business right now.*

CHEW ▸ UP

chew someone or something up to damage or ruin someone or something by pinching, grinding, biting, etc. □ *The machine chewed Jason up a little.* 🅃 *The lawn mower chewed up the flowers.* □ *Stay away from the mower or it will chew you up.*

chew something up to grind food with the teeth until it can be swallowed. □ *You had better chew that stuff up well.* 🅃 *Please chew up your food well.*

CHICKEN ▸ OUT

chicken out (of something) to withdraw from something, usually out of cowardice. (Informal or slang.) □ *Please don't chicken out of this now.* □ *I chickened out at the last minute.*

chicken out on someone to decide not to do something for or with someone. □ *Come on, don't chicken out on me now!* □ *Ken chickened out on us and won't be going with us.*

CHIDE ▸ FOR

chide someone for something to tease or scold someone for doing something. □ *Please don't chide us for doing what we did.* □ *Maria chided Gerald for being late.*

CHILL ▸ OUT

chill out to calm down; to relax. (Slang.) □ *Why don't you guys chill out for a while?* □ *Chill out! Don't waste your energy getting angry.*

CHIME ▸ IN

chime in (with something) to add a comment to the discussion. □ *Little Billy chimed in with a suggestion.* □ *He chimed in too late.*

CHIP ▸ AT

chip (away) at something to break off tiny pieces of something little by little. □ *The mason chipped away at the bricks.* □ *He chipped at the block of marble gently.*

CHIP ▸ AWAY

chip away [for something] to break off or break away in small chips. □ *The edges of the marble step chipped away over the years.* □ *Some of the stone figures had chipped away so badly that we couldn't see what they were.*

chip (away) at something See under *CHIP ▸ AT.*

chip something away (from something) to break off tiny pieces of something. □ *All the player's cleats chipped the marble steps away.* 🅃 *Someone chipped away little bits of the marble from the step.*

CHIP ▸ IN

chip in (on something) (for someone) to contribute money toward something for someone. □ *Would you please chip in on the present for Richard?* □ *Will* *you chip in for Randy?* □ *I would like to chip in on the gift.* □ *I won't chip in.*

chip in (with something) (on something) (for someone) AND **chip in (with something) (for something) (for someone); chip something in (on something) (for someone)** to contribute money for a gift for someone. □ *Would you like to chip in with a little cash on a gift for Carol?* □ *I will chip in a little with you on a gift for Carol.* □ *Would you chip in with a few bucks for a gift for Carol?* □ *Would you chip a few bucks in on a gift for Carol?* □ *Would you chip in a few bucks on a gift for Carol?* □ *I will chip in with you.* □ *I will chip in on a gift.* □ *I will chip in for Carol.*

CHIPPY ▶ AROUND

chippy around to be sexually promiscuous. (Slang.) □ *They say she chippies around a lot.* □ *Wally doesn't chippy around at all.*

CHISEL ▶ IN

chisel in (on someone or something) to use deception to share something belonging to someone or a group. (Slang.) □ *I won't chisel in on your deal.* □ *You had better not chisel in!*

CHISEL ▶ OUT

chisel someone out of something AND **chisel something out of someone** to get something away from someone by cheating. □ *Are you trying to chisel me out of what's mine?* □ *Max tried to chisel me out of my money.*

chisel something out of someone See the previous entry.

CHOKE ▶ BACK

choke something back to fight hard to keep something from coming out of one's mouth, such as sobs, tears, angry words, vomit, etc. □ *I tried to choke the unpleasant words back, but I could not.* 🅃 *She choked back her grief, but it came forth nonetheless.* □ *I could hardly choke my tears back.*

CHOKE ▶ DOWN

choke something down to work hard to swallow something, usually because it tastes bad. □ *The medicine was terrible, but I managed to choke it down.* 🅃 *She choked down the horrible medicine.*

CHOKE ▶ OFF

choke someone off to prevent someone from continuing conversing. □ *The opposition choked the speakers' debate off before they finished.* 🅃 *Why did they want to choke off the speakers?*

choke something off **1.** to strangle or crush a living creature's windpipe. □ *The tight collar on the cat tended to choke its airstream off.* 🅃 *The collar choked off its airstream.* **2.** to put an end to debate or discussion; to stop the flow of words from any source. □ *Are they going to choke the debate off?* 🅃 *The chairman tried to choke off debate but failed.*

CHOKE ▶ ON

choke on something to begin to gag and cough on something stuck in the throat. □ *The dog choked on the meat.* □ *The restaurant patron began to choke on a fishbone.*

CHOKE ▶ OUT

choke something out of someone to force a person to tell something, usually by threatening to kill the person. □ *Max tried to choke the information out of him, but Lefty fought his way free.* □ *If you don't tell me the answer I want, I will choke it out of you.*

CHOKE ▶ TO

choke someone to death to strangle a person until life ceases. □ *The intruder looked as though he was going to choke me to death, but he was just going to rip off my necklace.* □ *Max tried to choke Lefty to death.*

CHOKE ▶ UP

choke someone up to cause someone to feel like sobbing. □ *Sad stories like that always choke me up.* □ *Your complaints choke me up considerably.*

choke something up **1.** to clog something up; to fill up and block something. □ *Branches and leaves choked the sewer up.* 🅃 *Rust choked up the pipes.* **2.** to cough or choke until something that has blocked one's windpipe is brought up. □ *The old man was unable to choke up the* *candy that was stuck in his windpipe.* 🅃 *He choked up the chunk of meat and could breathe again.*

choke something (up) with something See under *CHOKE ▸ WITH.*

choke up 1. to feel like sobbing. □ *I choked up when I heard the news.* □ *He was beginning to choke up as he talked.* **2.** to become frightened or saddened so that one cannot speak. □ *I choked up when I heard the news.* □ *I was choking up, and I knew I would not be able to go on.* □ *Henry was so choked up he couldn't speak.*

choke up (about someone or something) to become very emotional about someone or something. □ *I choke up about Tom every time I think about his illness.* □ *I choked up at the thought.*

choke up (with something) to become very emotional with sighs, sobs, and tears. □ *She choked up with tears and had to leave the room.* □ *She choked up and had to borrow a hankie.*

CHOKE ▸ WITH

choke something (up) with something to clog something up with something. □ *The long growing season choked the river up with weeds.* 🅃 *The bright sun choked up the river with a growth of water hyacinths.* □ *The hyacinths choked the river with greenery.*

CHOOSE ▸ AMONG

choose among someone or something to make a choice of a person or thing from a variety of possibilities. □ *We will choose among the names on the list you gave us.* □ *I need to choose among the car models available.*

CHOOSE ▸ AS

choose someone as something to select someone to be something. (*Someone* includes *oneself.*) □ *We will choose her as our representative.* □ *I chose Sam as my assistant.* □ *She chose herself as representative to the council.*

CHOOSE ▸ BETWEEN

choose between people or things to choose one from a selection of two persons or things in any combination. (*Someone* includes *oneself.*) □ *You are going to have to choose between your wife and your job.* □ *I can't choose between chocolate and vanilla.* □ *Can you choose between Ted and Alice?* □ *I am unable to choose between myself and one of the others.*

CHOOSE ▸ FOR

choose someone or something for something to select someone or something for a particular purpose, office, title, etc. (*Someone* includes *oneself.*) □ *I chose red for the club color.* □ *I will choose Alice for prom queen.* □ *She chose herself for the presidency.*

choose something for someone to select something for someone, perhaps as a gift. □ *I will probably choose flowers for your mother.* □ *I will choose a red car for your brother.*

CHOOSE ▸ FROM

choose from someone or something to make a selection of a person or thing from groups of persons or things. □ *You will have to choose from these people only.* □ *Ron chose from the items in the catalog.*

CHOOSE ▸ UP

choose up sides to select opposing sides for a debate, fight, or game. □ *Let's choose up sides and play basketball.* □ *The children chose up sides and began the game.*

CHOP ▸ BACK

chop something back to prune vegetation; to reduce the size of plants by cutting. □ *Why don't you chop those bushes back while you have the shears out?* 🅃 *Chop back the bushes, please.*

CHOP ▸ DOWN

chop someone or something down to destroy something, such as a plan or an idea; to destroy a person's plan, idea, or argument. (Figurative.) □ *The committee chopped the idea down in its early stages.* 🅃 *They chopped down a great idea.* 🅃 *Why chop down George? He had a good idea.* □ *The committee chopped George down, and he just gave up.*

chop something down to fell a tree or a pole; to fell a person by cutting with a sword or something similar. □ *George chopped the tree down for some unknown reason.* [T] *He chopped down the cherry tree.* [A] *The chopped-down trees were burned and the wood was wasted.* □ *The knight chopped the peasant down and then rode off.* [T] *The knight chopped down the peasant.*

CHOP ▶ IN(TO)

chop someone or something (up) (in(to) something) See under *CHOP ▶ UP.*

CHOP ▶ OFF

chop someone off to stop someone in the middle of a sentence or speech; to *cut someone off (short).* □ *I'm not finished. Don't chop me off!* [T] *The moderator chopped off the speaker.*

chop something off to cut something off, perhaps with an axe. □ *Chop this branch off, please.* [T] *I'll chop off the branch.*

chop something off ((of) something) to cut something off something, perhaps with an axe. (The *of*-phrase is paraphrased with a *from*-phrase when the particle is transposed. See the [F] example. The *of* is colloquial.) □ *We chopped the dead branches off the tree.* [T] *You should chop off the other branch.* [F] *You should chop off the other branch from the tree.* [A] *The chopped-off branches were trimmed and used for firewood.*

CHOP ▶ UP

chop someone or something (up) (in(to) something) to cut someone or something up into something smaller, perhaps with an axe or a cleaver. □ *The murderous butcher chopped up his victim into bits.* [T] *I chopped up the onion into little pieces.* □ *I chopped it into pieces.* □ *Max threatened to chop Lefty up.* □ *He threatened to chop him into one-inch cubes!* [A] *Place the chopped-up meat in the skillet and brown it.*

CHORTLE ▶ ABOUT

chortle about someone or something AND **chortle over someone or something** to chuckle or giggle about someone or something funny. □ *I was chortling about Elaine's silly puppy for a long time.* □ *Elaine chortled about me and my dislike for cats.* □ *I couldn't help chortling over her.*

CHORTLE ▶ OVER

chortle over someone or something See the previous entry.

CHORTLE ▶ WITH

chortle with something to chuckle or giggle because one is gleeful, happy, mirthful, etc. □ *Tom chortled with glee at Sarah's misfortune.* □ *Fred chortled with a wicked little laugh when Ken slipped on the ice.*

CHOW ▶ DOWN

chow down to eat a meal. (Slang.) □ *What time do you chow down around here?* □ *We chow down from sunrise to sunset.*

chow something down to eat something. (Slang.) □ *Here, chow this doughnut down.* [T] *She chowed down two doughnuts.*

CHUCK ▶ AWAY

chuck someone or something away to push or shove someone or something out of the way. □ *She chucked the children away and ran to lock the door to protect them.* [T] *He chucked away his clothes in a drawer.* □ *The rock star approached, and the guard chucked the teenagers away.*

chuck something away to throw something away. (Colloquial.) □ *Would you please just chuck this away?* □ *I don't want to chuck away any paper that's been used on only one side.*

CHUCK ▶ DOWN

chuck something down to eat something; to gobble food. (Slang.) □ *Don't just chuck your food down. Enjoy it!* [T] *I'll be with you as soon as I chuck down this hamburger.*

CHUCK ▶ IN(TO)

chuck something in(to something) to pack something into something. □ *She chucked her clothes into the suitcase and left.* [T] *Just chuck in all your clothes and let's go.* □ *Chuck them in.*

CHUCK ▸ OUT

chuck someone out (of something) to throw someone out of something or some place. (The *of*-phrase is paraphrased with a *from*-phrase when the particle is transposed. See the F example.) □ *The bouncer chucked the drunks out of the tavern.* T *He chucks out about three drunks a night.* F *Jeff chucks out a couple of bums a night from the tavern.* □ *Sam chucked Jeff out.*

CHUCK ▸ OVER

chuck something over something to throw something over something. □ *Here, chuck this over the wall, and let's go.* □ *If you chuck another soda pop can over the fence, I will file a complaint.*

CHUCK ▸ UNDER

chuck someone under something to pat or tap someone under something, usually the chin. □ *He said hello to little Mary and chucked her under the chin.* □ *Please don't chuck me under the chin! I am not a child, you know!*

CHUCK ▸ UP

chuck something up to vomit something up. □ *Don't give cake to the dog. It will just chuck it up again.* T *The dog chucked up the cake.*

CHUCKLE ▸ ABOUT

chuckle about someone or something AND **chuckle over someone or something** to giggle about someone or something. □ *I had to chuckle about Wally and his broken-down old car.* □ *We all chuckled about the entire incident.* □ *We chuckled over how angry Jed was.*

CHUCKLE ▸ OVER

chuckle over someone or something See the previous entry.

CHUCKLE ▸ WITH

chuckle with something to giggle because one is gleeful or happy. □ *He chuckled with unsurpressed mirth at the antics of the strangely dressed people.* □ *Sally chuckled with glee at the thought of Ken slipping on the ice.*

CHUG ▸ ALONG

chug along [for a train engine] to labor along slowly. (Steam locomotives made the sound "chug, chug.") □ *The train chugged along to the top of the hill.* □ *Our little engine chugged along at an even pace, moving toward New Delhi.*

CHUM ▸ UP

chum up to someone to become friendly with someone. □ *Todd chummed up to Martin.* □ *I don't want to have to chum up to anyone I don't want to work with.*

chum up with someone to become buddies with someone. □ *He seems to have chummed up with Fred.* □ *Juan quickly chummed up with all the guys in his class.*

CHURN ▸ OUT

churn something out to produce something in large numbers, perhaps carelessly. □ *We churn toys out by the thousand.* T *This factory can churn out these parts day and night.*

CHURN ▸ UP

churn something up to stir up a liquid; to mix up material suspended in water. □ *The oars of our boat churned the shallow water up, leaving little clouds of sediment in our wake.* T *The oars churned up the mud.*

CIRCLE ▸ AROUND

circle (around) (over) someone or something [for a plane or a bird] to fly around above someone, something, or some place. □ *The plane circled around over us for a few minutes and then went on.* □ *It circled over all of us.* □ *It circled around over the field.* □ *The buzzards circled around for a while and then flew off elsewhere.*

circle around someone or something to form a circle around someone or something. □ *The people circled around the piano and joined in singing.* □ *Everyone circled around the birthday girl.*

CIRCLE ▸ OVER

circle (around) (over) someone or something See under *CIRCLE ▸ AROUND.*

CIRCULATE ▸ AMONG

circulate among someone or something to move at random within a gathering of people or things. □ *Karen circulated among the guests, serving drinks.* □ *The guests circulated among the flower beds in the garden.*

CIRCULATE ▸ THROUGH

circulate something through something to route something through something; to make something travel through something. □ *Walter circulated the memo from the boss through the department.* □ *I would like for you to circulate this through the members of the club.* □ *This pump circulates the hot water through the heating pipes.*

circulate through something 1. [for a fluid in a closed system of pipes or tubes] to flow through the various pathways of pipes and tubes. □ *Cold water circulates through the entire building and keeps it cool.* □ *Blood circulates through the veins and arteries, carrying food to, and nutrients away from, all parts of the body.* 2. to travel through something; to make the rounds through something. □ *Rumors circulated through the department about Tom's retirement.* □ *Please circulate through the room and hand out these papers to each person over thirty.*

CITE ▸ FOR

cite someone for something 1. to honor someone for doing something; to give someone a citation of honor for doing something good. □ *The town council cited her for bravery.* □ *They cited Maria for her courageous act.* 2. to arrest or arraign someone for breaking a law; to issue a legal citation to someone for breaking a law. □ *The officer cited her for not cutting her grass.* □ *An officer cited the driver for driving too fast.*

CLAIM ▸ FOR

claim something for someone or something to declare that something is the property of someone or a group, such as a nation. (Often said of a piece of land.) □ *The small country claimed the mountainous area for itself.* □ *Roger claimed all the rocky road ice cream for himself.*

claim something for something to make a claim for money in payment for damages. □ *David claimed one thousand dollars for the damaged car.* □ *She claimed a lot of money for the amount of harm she experienced.*

CLAM ▸ UP

clam up to become silent. (Informal. Closing one's mouth in the way that a clam closes up.) □ *Everyone clammed up and would say nothing.* □ *Why don't you clam up for a while?*

CLAMBER ▸ INTO

clamber into something to climb into something. □ *All the campers clambered into the bus.* □ *They clambered into the bus and the bus pulled off.*

CLAMBER ▸ ON(TO)

clamber on(to something) to climb onto something clumsily. □ *The kids clambered onto the tractor and tried to start it.* □ *The tractor stopped and the kids clambered on.*

CLAMBER ▸ UP

clamber up something to climb up something clumsily. □ *The wall climbers clambered up the wall quickly.* □ *Tricia clambered up the hill until she got out of breath and had to go back.*

CLAMOR ▸ AGAINST

clamor against someone or something to raise a great outcry against someone or something. □ *The crowd clamored against the mayor.* □ *The citizens clamored against the new taxes.*

CLAMOR ▸ FOR

clamor for someone or something to raise a great outcry for someone or something. □ *Everyone was clamoring for Mark. They just loved him.* □ *The children were clamoring for ice cream.*

CLAMP ▸ DOWN

clamp down (on someone or something) to restrain or limit someone or someone's actions. □ *The police clamped down on the gang.* □ *They had to clamp down to keep the streets safe.*

CLAMP ▸ ON

clamp something on((to) something) to press or squeeze something onto something else. ☐ *Clamp this board onto the table.* ☐ *Sharon clamped it on.*

CLAP ▶ IN(TO)

clap someone in(to) something to shove or push someone into something. (Colloquial.) ☐ *Be good or the sheriff will clap you into jail.* ☐ *The cops clapped Max into jail.*

CLAP ▶ ON(TO)

clap something on(to) something to slap or pound something onto something else. ☐ *The police came and clapped a sign onto the car saying it was abandoned.* ☐ *Do not clap any signs on my fence.*

CLAP ▶ OUT

clap something out to clap the rhythmic beat of something in order to learn it. (Music.) ☐ *All right, now. Let's clap the rhythm out.* 🅃 *We'll clap out the rhythm.*

CLAP ▶ TOGETHER

clap something together to slap two things, usually hands, together so that they make a noise. ☐ *The boys clapped their hands together as loudly as they could whenever a goal was scored.* ☐ *One of the orchestra members clapped two blocks of wood together periodically, making a very loud noise.*

CLASH ▶ AGAINST

clash against something **1.** to wage a battle or attack against someone or something. ☐ *The troops clashed against the enemy.* ☐ *We clashed against the opposite side for over three days.* **2.** to look bad against something of a different color. ☐ *This color clashes against the red of my coat.* ☐ *The red clashes against the purple background.*

CLASH ▶ OVER

See the following entry.

CLASH ▶ WITH

clash (with someone) (over someone or something) to fight or argue with someone about someone or something. ☐ *The customer clashed with the pharmacist over the price of the medicine.* ☐ *I clashed over Sally with the school principal.*

clash with something [for the color of something] to conflict with or mismatch another color. ☐ *This red clashes with the purple of the drapes.* ☐ *This red does not clash with purple. It looks gorgeous.*

CLASP ▶ TO

clasp someone or something to something to hold on to and press someone or something against one's body, chest, breast, bosom, the pain, the ache, etc. ☐ *He clasped a wad of cloth to the bleeding wound.* ☐ *She clasped the child to her breast and hugged him.*

CLASS ▶ WITH

class someone or something with someone or something to group something with something similar; to group someone with someone similar. (*Someone* includes *oneself*.) ☐ *Please don't class this car with anything you've ever driven before.* ☐ *Don't class me with the furniture!* ☐ *She classed herself with Mary and some of the other all-time greats.*

CLATTER ▶ AROUND

clatter around to move around among things, making noise. ☐ *Stop clattering around! It's late.* ☐ *I wish you would not clatter around.*

CLAW ▶ OFF

claw something off ((of) someone or something) to rip or tear something off from someone or something. (The *of*-phrase is paraphrased with a *from*-phrase when the particle is transposed. See the 🄵 example.) ☐ *We saw a guy clawing his burning clothes off himself.* 🅃 *He clawed off his burning clothes.* 🄵 *He clawed off the burning clothes from his body.* ☐ *He clawed them off.*

CLAW ▶ TO

claw one's way to the top to climb to the most prestigious level ruthlessly. ☐ *He was the type of hard-hitting guy who claws his way to the top.* ☐ *She clawed her way to the top, fighting at every step.*

CLEAN ▶ DOWN

clean someone or something down to clean someone or something by brushing or with flowing water. (*Someone* includes *oneself*.) ☐ *He was covered with* *mud and we used the garden hose to clean him down.* 🅃 *Please clean down the sidewalk.* □ *He was so dirty I just wanted to clean him down!* □ *He cleaned himself down with water from the hose.*

CLEAN ▸ OFF

clean something off to take something off something; to remove something such as dirt or dirty dishes. □ *Please clean the table off and put the dishes in the kitchen.* 🅃 *I'll clean off the table.* 🄰 *The cleaned-off table served as our conference table.*

clean something off ((of) something) to remove something from something. (The *of*-phrase is paraphrased with a *from*-phrase when the particle is transposed. See the 🄵 example.) □ *Judy cleaned the writing off the wall.* 🅃 *I'm glad she cleaned off the writing.* 🄵 *I'm glad she cleaned off the writing from the wall.* □ *Sam cleaned it off.*

CLEAN ▸ OUT

clean someone or something out (of something) to remove people or things from something or some place. (The *of*-phrase is paraphrased with a *from*-phrase when the particle is transposed. See the 🄵 example.) □ *Someone should clean those bums out of political office.* 🅃 *Yes! Clean out those bums.* 🄵 *Clean out the bums from office!* □ *Clean the dust out of the cupboards.* □ *Clean them out!* □ *The anxious customers cleaned the delicatessen out of salami.* 🄰 *Put the cleaned-out pumpkin on a stable counter before you cut it.* 🄽 *This whole place needs a good clean-out.*

clean someone out **1.** to act as a laxative on someone; to clear out someone's bowels. (*Someone* includes *oneself*.) □ *This stuff will really clean you out.* 🅃 *The bad food cleaned out the campers.* □ *She used some sort of medicine to clean herself out.* **2.** to take all of someone's money; to empty someone's pockets, purse, or wallet of money. (Colloquial.) □ *The bill for that meal really cleaned me out.* 🅃 *The enormous bill cleaned out the customer.* □ *I'm totally cleaned out. Not a cent left.*

clean something out to remove dirt or unwanted things from the inside of something. □ *Someone has to clean the garage out.* 🅃 *I'll clean out the garage.* 🄽 *Please give this vat a good cleaning-out.*

CLEAN ▸ UP

clean one's act up to start behaving better. □ *You had better clean your act up and be a better citizen.* 🅃 *Clean up your act!*

clean someone or something up to get someone or something clean. (*Someone* includes *oneself*.) □ *Please go into the bathroom and clean yourself up.* 🅃 *I'll clean up the kids a little bit before we leave for dinner.* □ *Can you clean this place up a little?* 🄰 *The cleaned-up act was still too rude for many people.* □ *Oh, go clean yourself up. You're a mess.* 🄽 *Why don't you give the attic a good cleaning-up before it gets too hot today?* 🄽 *The teacher assigned two students for the cleanup.*

clean up (on someone or something) to make a large profit from someone or some business activity. □ *We are really going to clean up on this product.* □ *We will clean up on Tom. He is buying everything we have.* □ *We are really going to clean up.*

clean up the floor with someone to beat someone up. (Slang.) □ *If you don't shut up, I'll clean up the floor with you.* 🅃 *You won't clean the floor up with me!*

CLEAR ▸ AWAY

clear something away to take something away. □ *Please clear the tea things away.* 🅃 *Would you clear away the dishes?*

CLEAR ▸ FOR

clear something for publication to approve the wording of something so it can be published. □ *The government refused to clear the story for publication.* □ *I want to clear this for publication as soon as possible.*

CLEAR ▸ FROM

clear something from some place to take something away from a place. □

Please clear all these papers from the desk. □ *Would you clear the dishes from the table?*

CLEAR ▸ OF

clear someone of something to show that a person is innocent; to exonerate someone of a crime. (*Someone* includes *oneself*.) □ *An investigation cleared me of the charges.* □ *They were unable to clear themselves of the charges.*

CLEAR ▸ OFF

clear off ((of) some place) to depart; to get off someone's property. (The *of* is colloquial.) □ *Clear off my property!* □ *Clear off, do you hear?*

clear something off ((of) something) to take something off something. (The *of*-phrase is paraphrased with a *from*-phrase when the particle is transposed. See the 🄵 example. The *of* is colloquial.) □ *Please clear the dishes off the table.* 🅃 *I'll clear off the dishes.* 🄵 *I'll clear off the dishes from the table.* □ *Please clear them off.*

CLEAR ▸ OUT

clear out (of some place) to get out of some place. □ *Will you all clear out of here?* □ *Please clear out!*

clear someone or something out (of some place) to make someone or something leave a place. (The *of*-phrase is paraphrased with a *from*-phrase when the particle is transposed. See the 🄵 example.) □ *Please clear all the people out of here.* 🅃 *Clear out the people quickly, please.* 🄵 *Clear out the people from this place.* □ *Would you clear the boxes out of this room?* □ *Please clear them out.*

CLEAR ▸ UP

clear something up **1.** to clarify something; to take away the confusion about something. □ *Let me take a few minutes to clear things up.* 🅃 *I would like to clear up this confusion for you.* **2.** to cure a disease. □ *I think I can clear this up with a salve.* 🅃 *Will this salve clear up the rash?*

clear up **1.** [for something] to become more understandable. □ *At about the middle of the very confusing lecture, things began to clear up.* □ *I was having trouble, but things are beginning to clear up.* **2.** [for a disease] to improve or become cured. □ *His cold cleared up after a couple of weeks.* □ *I'm sure your rash will clear up soon.* **3.** [for the sky] to become more clear. □ *Suddenly, the sky cleared up.* □ *When the sky cleared up, the breeze began to blow.*

CLEAR ▸ WITH

clear something with someone to get someone's approval for something. □ *You will have to clear this with the main office.* □ *I will clear this with the comptroller.*

CLEAVE ▸ TO

cleave to someone to be sexually faithful, usually to one's husband. (Stilted and biblical. As in the traditional marriage ceremony, "And cleave only unto him.") □ *She promised to cleave only to him for the rest of her life.* □ *They will cleave only to each other for their entire lives.*

CLICK ▸ WITH

click with someone **1.** to be understood or comprehended by someone suddenly. □ *His explanation clicked with Maggie at once.* □ *The instructions don't click with me at all.* **2.** [for something new] to catch on with someone; to become popular with someone very quickly. □ *The new product clicked with consumers and was an instant success.* □ *I hope this greeting card clicks with the person I am sending it to.*

CLIMB ▸ DOWN

climb down (from something) to dismount something; to come down from something. □ *The child climbed down from the roof.* □ *Please climb down!*

CLIMB ▸ ON

climb on the bandwagon to join the supporters of a popular cause. □ *I do not intend to climb on the bandwagon.* □ *In the end, I climbed on the bandwagon with everyone else.*

CLIMB ▸ ON(TO)

climb on(to) something to ascend to or mount something. □ *I climbed onto the side of the truck.* □ *Tommy climbed on the truck.*

CLIMB ▸ OUT

climb out (of something) to get, crawl, or move out of something. □ *He climbed out of the wreckage and examined himself carefully for injuries.* □ *He climbed out very carefully.*

CLIMB ▸ UP

climb up something to ascend something; to scale something. (Also without *up*, but not eligible as an entry.) □ *The hikers took two hours to climb up the hill.* □ *The adventurer tried to climb up the side of the building.*

CLING ▸ TO

cling to someone or something **1.** to hold on tight to someone or something. □ *The child clung tightly to his mother.* □ *As she drifted in the sea, she clung to a floating log.* **2.** to hold onto the thought or memory of someone or something; to have a strong emotional attachment to or dependence on someone or something. □ *Her parents clung to the old ways.* □ *Harold clung to the memory of his grandmother.*

CLING ▸ TOGETHER

cling together [for two or more creatures] to hold on tightly to each other. □ *The two children clung together throughout the ordeal.* □ *The baby baboon and its mother clung together and could not be separated.*

CLIP ▸ FROM

clip something from something to cut something out of or away from something; to cut something off of something. □ *I clipped the picture from the magazine.* □ *I clipped the straggly hairs from his head.*

CLIP ▸ ON(TO)

clip something on((to) someone or something) to attach something to someone or something with a clip. □ *I clipped a little name tag onto him before I put him on the plane.* 🅃 *I clipped on a name tag.* □ *Liz clipped it on.*

CLIP ▸ OUT

clip something out (of something) to remove something from something by clipping or cutting. (The *of*-phrase is paraphrased with a *from*-phrase when the particle is transposed. See the 🄵 example.) □ *Please clip the article out of the magazine.* 🅃 *Could you clip out the article?* 🄵 *I will clip out the article from the magazine.* □ *Sam clipped it out.*

CLOAK ▸ IN

cloak someone or something in secrecy to hide or conceal someone or something in secrecy. (*Someone* includes *oneself.*) □ *Patrick cloaked his activities in secrecy.* □ *The agents cloaked the spy in secrecy, making her identity a mystery.* □ *She cloaked herself in secrecy and was viewed as a recluse.*

cloak something in something to disguise something in something; to conceal the true nature of something with something. □ *They cloaked the whole project in secrecy.* □ *She cloaked her true intentions in a sympathetic manner.*

CLOCK ▸ AT

clock someone or something at something to measure the speed of someone or something to be a certain figure. □ *I clocked the runner at a record speed for the race.* □ *Karen clocked the horse at three minutes flat.*

CLOCK ▸ IN

clock in to record one's time of arrival, usually by punching a time clock. □ *What time did she clock in?* □ *She forgot to clock in today.*

clock someone in to observe and record someone's time of arrival. (*Someone* includes *oneself.*) □ *The manager says he clocked you in at noon. That's a bit late, isn't it?* 🅃 *Does she clock in everyone?* □ *Henry clocked himself in and went straight to work.*

CLOCK ▸ OUT

clock out to record one's time of departure, usually by punching a time clock. □ *I will clock out just before I go home.* □ *Juan clocked out before the official closing time.*

clock someone out to observe and record someone's time of departure. (*Someone* includes *oneself.*) □ *The manager clocked him out at about midnight.* 🅃 *Does the manager clock out* *everyone?* □ *Jane clocked herself out and went home.*

CLOCK ▸ UP

clock something up **1.** to record the accumulated hours, miles, etc., of some device or machine. (The recording is usually done by a meter of some type such as a speedometer, an elapsed time meter, etc. □ *She must have clocked two hundred flying hours up in six months.* [T] *She clocked up a lot of hours.* **2.** to reach a goal that is worthy of being recorded. (Typically sports journalism. Compare to *chalk something up.*) □ *Patrick clocked a fantastic number of points up this year.* [T] *He sure clocked up a lot of goals.*

CLOG ▸ UP

clog someone up [for some kind of food] to constipate someone. □ *This stuff clogs me up. I can't eat it.* [T] *This food clogs up people who eat it.*

clog something up [for something] to obstruct a channel or conduit. □ *The leaves clogged the gutters up.* [T] *They clogged up the gutter.* [A] *The clogged-up pipes had to be cleaned out.*

clog up [for a channel or conduit] to become blocked. □ *The canal clogged up with leaves and mud.* [A] *No water would flow through the clogged-up sewer.* [N] *There is a serious clog-up in our sewer line.*

CLOG ▸ WITH

clog something with something to block or obstruct a channel or conduit with something. □ *The neighbors clogged the creek with their grass clippings.* □ *Please don't clog the drain with garbage.*

CLOSE ▸ AROUND

close around someone or something to move to surround someone or something. □ *The clouds closed around the mountaintops.* □ *The children closed around the birthday boy.*

CLOSE ▸ DOWN

close down [for someone] to close a business, office, shop, etc., permanently or temporarily. □ *This shop will have to close down if they raise taxes.* □ *I am afraid that you will have to close down for a while because of the gas leak.*

close someone or something down to force someone or someone's business, office, shop, etc., to close permanently or temporarily. □ *The police closed the bookstore down.* [T] *They closed down the shop.* □ *The recession closed down Tom, whose shop could just barely make it in good times.*

CLOSE ▸ IN

close in around someone or something to move to surround someone or something. □ *The police closed in around the thieves.* □ *We closed in around the escaped ducks.*

close in for the kill **1.** to move in on someone or something for the purpose of killing. □ *The wolves closed in for the kill.* □ *When the lions closed in for the kill, the zebras began to stampede.* **2.** to get ready to do the final and climactic part of something. (Figurative.) □ *The woman closed in for the kill and he knew he was soon to be engaged.* □ *The car dealer closed in for the kill with contract in hand.*

close in (on someone or something) to move in on someone or something. □ *The cops were closing in on the thugs.* □ *They closed in quietly.*

close someone or something in (something) to contain someone or something in something or some place; to seal someone or something inside something. (*Someone* includes *oneself.*) □ *Please don't close me in here!* □ *Don't close the bird in such a small cage.* □ *Don't close me in!* [T] *The thick shrubbery closed in the tiny yard too much.* □ *They closed themselves in by building that horrible fence.* [A] *Please stay out of the closed-in area.*

CLOSE ▸ OFF

close something off to prevent entrance into something; to *block something off.* □ *Please don't close this passageway off.* [T] *They closed off the passageway anyway.* [A] *They were putting together a new exhibit in the closed-off hall.*

CLOSE ▸ ON

close on something to complete the sale and transfer of property, especially real estate. □ *We closed on the new house on April 16.* □ *We were able to close on our old house on June 2.*

close something on someone or something 1. to shut something so someone or something cannot get through. □ *I closed the door on Wally and he was kept out of the room.* □ *Please close the door on all that noise so we can converse without any disturbance.* 2. to put an end to something; to prevent further action, discussion, negotiation, etc., on someone or something. □ *I closed the door on the argument.* □ *Have you completely closed the door on further negotiation?*

close the books on someone or something to declare that a matter concerning someone or something is finished. □ *It's time to close the books on Fred. He's had enough time.* □ *We will close the books on this account once and for all.*

CLOSE ▸ OUT

close someone out of something to prevent someone from getting into something, such as a class, a room, a privilege, etc. □ *They closed me out of the class I wanted.* Ⓐ *The closed-out students complained to the dean.* Ⓝ *You can't get into this class. It's a closeout.*

close something out 1. to sell off a particular kind of merchandise with the intention of not selling it in the future. □ *These are not selling. Let's close them out.* Ⓣ *They closed out the merchandise that wouldn't sell.* Ⓐ *They had nothing on sale in that store except closed-out merchandise.* Ⓝ *This item is on closeout. We will not carry it again.* 2. to prevent further registration in something. □ *We are going to have to close this class out.* Ⓣ *The registrar closed out the class.* Ⓐ *The closed-out classes were reopened for a brief time.*

CLOSE ▸ TO

close one's eyes to something AND **shut one's eyes to something** to ignore something; to pretend that something is not happening. (Figurative.) □ *You must not close your eyes to this matter.* □ *Maria simply shut her eyes to the whole affair.*

close something to someone to prevent someone or some type of person from participating in or attending something. □ *We closed membership to everyone else.* □ *They had to close the registration to nonresidents.*

close the door to something 1. to refuse to admit something through a door. □ *The manager closed the door to our group.* □ *He let us in but closed the door to our bicycles.* 2. to refuse to deal with something. (Figurative.) □ *The council closed the door to further discussion of solutions.* □ *Juan closed the door to debate.*

CLOSE ▸ UP

close someone or something up 1. to close someone or someone's business, office, shop, etc., temporarily or permanently. □ *Tom's restaurant nearly went out of business when the health department closed him up.* Ⓣ *The health department closed up the restaurant.* □ *Dave's shop was failing. The bank closed him up.* 2. to close someone or something completely. (Said of a person being stitched up at the end of a surgical procedure.) □ *Fred, would you close her up for me?* Ⓣ *Fred closed up the patient.* □ *I closed up the box and put it on the shelf.*

close up [for an opening] to close completely. □ *The door closed up and would not open again.* □ *The shop closed up and did not open until the next day.*

close up shop to close one's business or shop, permanently or temporarily. (Idiomatic.) □ *It's dark outside. Time to close up shop.* □ *Let's close up shop and go home.*

CLOSE ▸ WITH

close with someone or something to end a performance with a particular act or event. □ *The show is almost over and we will close with Sarah Miles, who will announce her own song title.* □ *The evening closed with a magic act.*

CLOSET ▸ WITH

closet someone with someone to put someone into a private room with someone else, for the purposes of conducting business. (*Someone* includes *oneself*.) ☐ *The council closeted the lawyer with the complaining witness so they could discuss things.* ☐ *She closeted herself with the president and finally, once and for all, had her say.*

CLOTHE ▸ IN

clothe someone in something to dress someone in something. (*Someone* includes *oneself*.) ☐ *She clothed her children in the finest garments.* ☐ *He clothed himself in his finest for the wedding.*

CLOUD ▸ OVER

cloud over **1.** [for the sky] to fill with clouds; [for the sun] to be obscured by clouds. ☐ *It was beginning to cloud over, so we went inside.* ☐ *The sky clouded over and it began to get chilly.* **2.** [for something once clear] to become opaque; to become clouded. ☐ *My vision seemed to cloud over, and I could see very little.* ☐ *The mirror clouded over as the steam rose from the hot water in the sink.*

CLOUD ▸ UP

cloud up [for the sky] to fill with clouds. ☐ *By midmorning, the sky had clouded up.* ☐ *I hope it doesn't cloud up today.*

CLOWN ▸ AROUND

clown around (with someone) to join with someone in acting silly; [for two or more people] to act silly together. (See also the following entry.) ☐ *The boys were clowning around with each other.* ☐ *The kids are having fun clowning around.*

CLOWN ▸ WITH

clown (around) with someone or something to play around and act silly with someone or something as the object of one's clowning. (See also the previous entry.) ☐ *Stop clowning around with me!* ☐ *Stop clowning with the audience!*

CLUE ▸ IN

clue someone in (on something) to inform someone about something. ☐ *Would you please clue me in on what you are talking about?* 🅃 *I will clue in everyone on this matter if you want.* ☐ *Please clue me in.*

CLUNK ▸ DOWN

clunk down [for something] to drop or fall, making the sound "clunk." ☐ *A large piece of metal clunked down right in front of me.* ☐ *A tree branch clunked down on the roof and damaged a few shingles.*

clunk something down to drop or place something on something so that it makes a clunking noise. ☐ *He clunked the engine part down on the table.* 🅃 *He clunked down the part on the table.*

CLUSTER ▸ AROUND

cluster around someone or something [for a group of people or things] to bunch together, surrounding someone or something. ☐ *The birds clustered around the chimney top to keep warm.* ☐ *The kids clustered around the police officer.*

cluster someone or something around someone or something to bunch people or things together around someone or something. (*Someone* includes *oneself*.) ☐ *She clustered the cups around the punch bowl.* ☐ *Liz clustered the children around the storyteller.* ☐ *Karen clustered the children around the fire.* ☐ *They clustered themselves around the injured child.*

CLUSTER ▸ TOGETHER

cluster together to bunch or group together. ☐ *All of the bats clustered together on the roof of the cave.* ☐ *The children clustered together in small groups here and there on the playground.*

CLUTCH ▸ AT

clutch at someone or something to grasp at or grab for someone or something. ☐ *He clutched at the roots of the trees along the bank, but the flood swept him away.* ☐ *Karen clutched at* *me, but lost her grip.* □ *He clutched at the railing for support.*

CLUTCH ▶ TO

clutch someone or something to something to grasp and hold someone or something to something. □ *She clutched the baby to her bosom.* □ *Lee clutched the ice pack to his head.*

CLUTCH ▶ UP

clutch up to become momentarily paralyzed with fright or anxiety. (Slang.) □ *She clutched up at the last minute and couldn't go on stage.* □ *Juan became frightened and clutched up.*

CLUTTER ▶ UP

clutter something up to mess something up; to fill something or some place up with too many things. □ *Heaps of newspapers cluttered the room up and made it a fire hazard.* 🅃 *Who cluttered up this house?*

COACH ▶ FOR

coach someone for something to train or drill someone in preparation for doing something. □ *Elliott coached his roommate every night for the contest.* □ *Juan coached Alice for the play.*

COALESCE ▶ INTO

coalesce into something [for two or more things] to blend or fuse and become one thing. □ *The colors coalesced into a gray blur.* □ *In the distance, the various people coalesced into a blur.*

COAST ▶ ALONG

coast along to roll or move along with little or no effort. □ *We just coasted along on the flat prairie.* □ *We coasted along until we came to the bottom of the hill.*

COAT ▶ WITH

coat someone or something with something to put a layer of something on someone or something. (*Someone* includes *oneself.*) □ *Her manager coated her with grease before she began the channel swim.* □ *The cook coated the chicken with batter and dropped it into the hot fat.* □ *She coated herself with suntan lotion, hoping to avoid a sunburn.*

COAX ▶ INTO

coax someone or something into something **1.** to urge or persuade someone or some creature to go into something. (See also under *COAX ▶ TO.*) □ *We coaxed the bear into the trap with fresh meat.* □ *The teacher coaxed the child into the kindergarten classroom.* **2.** to urge or persuade someone or some creature into doing something. □ *We coaxed her into singing for us.* □ *Janet coaxed the dog into sitting up and begging.*

COAX ▶ OUT

coax someone or something out of something **1.** to urge or persuade someone or some creature to give something up. □ *He almost wouldn't sell it, but I coaxed him out of it.* □ *I coaxed the cat out of the canary it was holding in its mouth.* **2.** to urge or persuade someone or some creature to come out of something. □ *She coaxed the puppy out of the carton.* □ *Janet coaxed the child out of the closet with a promise of a piece of cake.*

COAX ▶ TO

coax someone to do something to urge someone to do something. (See also under *COAX ▶ INTO.*) □ *The kids coaxed her to let them go swimming.* □ *Can I coax you to try some of this pie?*

COBBLE ▶ UP

cobble something up to make something or put something together hastily or carelessly. □ *Who cobbled this thing up? Take it apart and start over.* 🅃 *The kids cobbled up their model planes.*

COERCE ▶ INTO

coerce someone or something into something to force or compel someone or some creature to do something. □ *I could not coerce her into doing it.* □ *You cannot coerce a cat into anything.*

COEXIST ▶ WITH

coexist with someone or something to exist agreeably with or at the same time as someone or something. □ *I decided that I would have to coexist with your policies.* □ *It is hard for cats to coexist with dogs.*

COGITATE ▸ ON

cogitate on something to think about something. (Folksy.) □ *Cogitate on this idea for a while.* □ *I will have to cogitate on this for a few days. I'll get back to you.*

COHABIT ▸ WITH

cohabit with someone **1.** [for an unmarried person] to live with an unmarried person. □ *You might say that she cohabited with him for a period of time.* □ *They were cohabiting with one another.* **2.** to copulate with someone. (Euphemistic.) □ *She had been cohabiting with him, and she admitted it in court.* □ *Did you cohabit with her more than once?*

COIL ▸ AROUND

coil (itself) around someone or something [for something or some creature] to wrap itself around someone or something. □ *The monkey's tail coiled itself around the branch.* □ *The huge python coiled around poor Roger.* □ *The snake coiled itself around the terrified mouse.*

COIL ▸ UP

coil (itself) up [for something] to wrap or roll itself into a coil. □ *The snake coiled itself up, trying to hide.* □ *It coiled up, ready to strike.* □ *The spring coiled itself up when it broke loose.* [N] *I almost stepped on the coiled-up snake.*

coil (itself) up into something [for something] to wrap or twist itself into a particular shape. □ *The frightened snaked coiled itself up into a knot.* □ *The spring coiled up into its original shape.* □ *The worm coiled itself up into a tight knot.*

coil something up to roll or twist something into a coil. □ *Maria coiled the strip of stamps up and put them in the little dispenser.* [T] *Please coil up the rope.* [A] *He produced a coiled-up length of wire that couldn't be straightened.*

COINCIDE ▸ WITH

coincide with something to agree with or match something; [for something] to happen at the same time as something else. □ *This pattern coincides with the pattern we see in the carpet.* □ *My birthday sometimes coincides with Thanksgiving Day.*

COLLABORATE ▸ WITH

collaborate with someone or something to work together on something with someone or a group. □ *I will collaborate with Amy on this one.* □ *I was forced to collaborate with a totally uninformed committee.*

COLLAPSE ▸ INTO

collapse into something **1.** to fall down into something. □ *She was so tired, she collapsed into the chair.* □ *Juan collapsed into a chair and fell fast asleep.* **2.** [for someone] to fall into a particular kind of despair. □ *The poor man collapsed into a deep depression.* □ *Scott collapsed into his own personal brand of grieving.*

COLLAPSE ▸ UNDER

collapse under someone or something to cave in under the weight of someone or something. □ *The framework collapsed under the weight of the spectators.* □ *The bridge collapsed under the heavy traffic.*

COLLATE ▸ WITH

collate something with something to compare or match something with something. □ *Try to collate these figures with that other list.* □ *I can't collate these notations with the entries they go with.*

COLLECT ▸ AROUND

collect around someone or something to gather around someone or something; to accumulate around someone or something. □ *The guests collected around the table that held the birthday cake.* □ *The children collected around the birthday boy.*

COLLECT ▸ FOR

collect (money) for someone or something to solicit money for the benefit of someone or something. □ *I would like to collect some money for Fred, who is in the hospital.* □ *I am collecting for the church building fund.*

collect (money) for something to solicit money that is owed. □ *I'm collecting* *money for payment on your loan.* ☐ *Someone is here collecting for the newspaper delivery.*

COLLECT ▶ FROM

collect something from someone **1.** to gather up something from someone; to gather money from someone. ☐ *I'm here to collect used clothing from you.* ☐ *The paper boy is here to collect money from us.* ☐ *She is out collecting money from the neighbors.* **2.** to take a medical specimen from a person. ☐ *I am here to collect a urine specimen from the patient.* ☐ *The phlebotomist collected the specimen from Todd and left the room.*

collect something from someone to gather something from someone. ☐ *We collected almost two thousand dollars from the students.* ☐ *The cabin attendants collected all the headsets from the passengers.*

COLLECT ▶ ON

collect on something to take or receive payment on a debt or promise. ☐ *I have come to collect on your debt.* ☐ *I will have someone else collect on this bill.*

COLLECT ▶ UP

collect something up to gather something up. ☐ *Collect your things up, and let's go.* 🅃 *I collected up my things and left.*

COLLIDE ▶ WITH

collide with someone or something to crash with or bump into someone or something. ☐ *The bus collided with a truck.* ☐ *Maria collided with Alice, but neither was hurt.*

COLLUDE ▶ WITH

collude with someone or something to plot or conspire with someone or a group. ☐ *Did you collude with the sheriff in this matter?* ☐ *The president colluded with the board of directors in this matter.*

COLOR ▶ IN

color something in to paint or draw color on a pattern or outline. ☐ *Here is a sketch. Please color it in.* 🅃 *Color in the sketch, please.*

COMB ▶ FOR

comb something for someone or something to look all over or all through something for a particular person or thing. ☐ *The police combed the entire neighborhood for the criminals.* ☐ *I combed the entire house for the missing paper.*

COMB ▶ OUT

comb something out to comb something and make it straight or neat. ☐ *She combed her hair out.* 🅃 *She combed out her hair every morning.*

comb something out (of something) to remove knots and snarls from something by combing. (The *of*-phrase is paraphrased with a *from*-phrase when the particle is transposed. See the 🄵 example.) ☐ *I had to comb the gum out of her hair.* 🅃 *I had to comb out the gum.* 🄵 *I had to comb out the gum from my hair.* ☐ *Maria combed it out.*

COMB ▶ THROUGH

comb through something to look through something, examining it thoroughly. ☐ *I combed through all my belongings, looking for the lost papers.* ☐ *The vet combed through the dog's coat, looking for insect pests.*

COMBINE ▶ AGAINST

combine something against someone or something to join something together in opposition to someone or something. ☐ *We will combine forces against the enemy.* ☐ *We combined our various talents against the opposite team.*

COMBINE ▶ WITH

combine something with something to mix something with something else. ☐ *I want to combine the red flowers with the pink ones for a bouquet.* ☐ *First, combine the eggs with the sugar.*

COME ▶ ABOARD

come aboard to get onto a boat or ship. ☐ *Please come aboard. We are shoving off now.* ☐ *Please ask everyone to come aboard.*

COME ▶ ABOUT

come about [for a boat] to change its angle against the wind; [for a boat] to change tack. □ *The boat will have to come about. The wind shifted.* □ *We came about and went back.*

come clean (with someone) (about something) See under *COME ▸ WITH.*

COME ▸ ACROSS

come across as someone (to someone) to be perceived as a particular type of person by other people. □ *You come across as a reasonable kind of guy to most people.* □ *He comes across as a really strange person.*

come across like someone or something (to someone) to appear or seem like someone or something to other people. □ *You always come across like a madman to people.* □ *She comes across like the Queen of the Nile to most people who meet her.*

come across someone or something to find someone or something by accident; to happen on someone or something. □ *I came across this book at the library.* □ *Lynn came across Kelly by accident.*

come across (with something) to deliver what is expected of one. (Colloquial.) □ *You had better come across with what you owe me.* □ *You owe me money, and I wish you would come across.*

COME ▸ AFTER

come after someone or something to pursue someone or something; to chase after someone or something; to chase someone or something down. □ *Hurry up! Let's get going before they come after us.* □ *The cat ran as fast as possible because a lot of dogs were coming after it.*

COME ▸ ALONG

come along (with someone) to come with or go with someone. □ *Please come along with me.* □ *Come along, let's go.*

COME ▸ APART

come apart to break apart; to break up. □ *The missile came apart in midair.* □ *I was afraid our car would come apart on that rough road.*

come apart at the seams **1.** to split open at a seam; to break apart from being overfilled. (Both literal and figurative uses.) □ *The house is about to come apart at the seams. There are so many people there.* □ *This old coat is coming apart at the seams.* **2.** to break down completely; to fall apart emotionally or mentally. (Figurative.) □ *My whole sense of being came apart at the seams.* □ *Her mental processes simply came apart at the seams.*

COME ▸ AROUND

come around **1.** to agree in the end; to agree finally. □ *I knew you would come around in the end.* □ *Finally, she came around and agreed to our terms.* **2.** to return to consciousness. □ *After we threw cold water in his face, he came around.* □ *Ken came around almost immediately after he had fainted.*

come around (to doing something) to agree to do something eventually, after a long wait. □ *Finally, she came around to painting the kitchen.* □ *She hesitated for a long time, but eventually Lynn came around.*

come around (to something or some place) to come to some place for a visit. □ *You must come around to our place for a while.* □ *Do come around sometime.*

come around (to visit) AND **come around (for a visit)** to pay a casual visit to someone. □ *Why don't you come around to visit next week?* □ *Why don't you come around for a visit next week?* □ *Please come around sometime.*

COME ▸ AT

come at someone or something **1.** to make a threatening move toward someone or something. □ *The gorilla came at the naturalist, but it was just a bluff.* □ *Walter came at the cake as if he were going to snatch the whole thing.* **2.** to attack someone or something. □ *The elephant came at us and almost wounded Scott.* □ *The cat came at the mouse and pounced on it.*

COME ▸ AWAY

come away empty-handed to come back without anything. □ *I'm afraid I didn't get what I wanted. I came away empty-handed.* □ *I do not intend to come away empty-handed.*

come away (from someone or something) to move away from someone or something. □ *Please come away from the fire. You will get burned if you don't.* □ *Come away from that filthy person!* □ *Come away!*

come away with someone to go away or travel away with someone. □ *Come away with me and we will get married.* □ *Come away with me and we'll find a nice place to eat.*

COME ▸ BACK

come back to return to an advantageous or favorable state or condition. □ *Walter practiced his singing every day, hoping to come back in a wave of glory.* □ *When will the good old days come back?* Ⓝ *The old actress made a great comeback.*

come back (from some place) to return from a place. □ *When will you come back from Detroit?* □ *Please come back soon.*

come back to someone [for a memory] to return to someone's consciousness. □ *Everything you said suddenly came back to me.* □ *All the old memories came back to me and made me feel very sad.*

come back (to someone or something) to return to someone or something. □ *Please come back to me. I'm lonely.* □ *Come back to your home!* □ *Please come back!*

COME ▸ BEFORE

come before someone or something **1.** [for one] to present oneself in the presence of someone or a group. □ *Thank you for coming before this committee with your testimony.* □ *The judge said I would have to come before her again next month.* **2.** [for an issue] to be raised before someone, a board, committee, etc.; [for an issue] to appear on the agenda of someone or a deliberative body. □ *The matter of the broken windows came before the school board at last.* □ *The question came before the business manager.* **3.** [of persons or things in an order or a line] to be in front of or in advance of someone or something. □ *This one comes before that one.* □ *She comes before me.*

COME ▸ BETWEEN

come between someone and someone else **1.** to be in between two people. □ *That's my place, there. I come between Maria and Lynn.* □ *In the line of contestants, I come between Bob and Bill.* **2.** to interfere in someone else's romance; to break up a pair of lovers. □ *Don't come between Terri and Jeff.* □ *I don't want to come between Terry and Heather, but there is this attraction, you see.*

come between something and something else to have a position between one thing and another. □ *April comes between March and May.* □ *This volume comes between numbers fourteen and sixteen.*

COME ▸ BY

come by (some place) to stop some place for a visit. □ *Can you come by our place for a few minutes on the way home?* □ *Please come by sometime.*

come by something to find something; to get something. □ *I hope you came by this money honestly.* □ *I come by all my ideas from my own experience.*

COME ▸ DOWN

come down (from something) **1.** to come to a lower point from a higher one. □ *Come down from there this instant!* □ *Come down, do you hear?* **2.** to move from a higher status to a lower one. □ *He has come down from his original position. Now he is just a clerk.* □ *He has come down quite a bit.* Ⓝ *Walter experienced quite a comedown.*

come down (hard) (on someone or something) to scold or punish someone or a group severely. □ *The teacher came down hard on the cheaters.* □ *The manager came down hard.* □ *The judge really came down on the petty crooks.* □

The critics came down much too hard on the performance.

come down in the world [for someone] to move to a lower class or status. □ *From the clothes that he wore, I could see that he had really come down in the world.* Ⓝ *Her new job turned out to be quite a comedown.*

come down to earth to become realistic. □ *Please try to come down to earth and face reality.* □ *You are going to have to come down to earth and learn to live within your means.*

come down to some place to come to some place in the south or in a lower altitude for a visit. □ *Come down to our place in Florida this winter if you want.* □ *I hope Tom can come down to our place in the country for a while.*

come down to something to be reduced to something; to get to the fundamentals of something. □ *It comes down to this: I just eat too much.* □ *It all comes down to whatever you think is right.*

come down with something to catch a disease. □ *Dan came down with chicken pox.* □ *I don't want to come down with the flu again.*

COME ▸ FOR

come for someone to arrive to get someone. □ *I have come for Amy. Is she ready?* □ *The mothers came for their children at about five o'clock.*

COME ▸ FORTH

come forth to come out; to move forward and appear. □ *Please come forth and meet your cousins.* □ *All the stage crew came forth and received some applause.*

COME ▸ FORWARD

come forward **1.** to move oneself forward. □ *Come forward and stand by me.* □ *Please come forward and meet your Great-aunt Clara.* **2.** to present oneself to offer evidence in court voluntarily. (Idiomatic.) □ *Why did you not come forward earlier in the trial?* □ *I was afraid to come forward during the trial.*

come forward with something to bring something, such as information, to someone's attention. □ *Colleen came forward with a new idea.* □ *I hope you each can come forward with something useful.*

COME ▸ FROM

come from behind to advance from a rear position; to advance from a losing position. (Refers to being behind in a score or in a race.) □ *Our team came from behind to win the game.* □ *The horse I bet on came from behind and almost placed second.*

come from far and wide to arrive from everywhere; to arrive from many directions and great distances. □ *People came from far and wide.* □ *The deer came from far and wide to lick the salt block we had put out.*

come from someone or something to arrive from someone or something; [for something] to have originated with someone or something. □ *Did this letter come from Alice?* □ *A notice came from the Internal Revenue Service.*

come home from some place to arrive home from another place. □ *The soldiers came home from the war.* □ *When will you come home from the office?*

come (up) from behind to advance in competition; to improve one's position relative to the positions of other things or people. □ *The horse was working hard to come up from behind.* □ *Lee was losing in the election, but he began to come from behind in the last week.*

COME ▸ IN

See also under *COME ▸ IN(TO).*

come in **1.** to enter. (Often a command or polite request.) □ *Please come in.* □ *If you will come in and have a seat, I will tell Betty that you are here.* **2.** to arrive; [for a shipment of something] to arrive. □ *New models come in almost every week.* □ *When do you expect a new batch to come in?* □ *The tomatoes will come in at the end of July.* □ *The election results came in early in the evening.* **3.** [for a broadcast] to be received satisfactorily. □ *Can you hear me? How am I coming in?* □ *You are coming in all right.*

come in a body [for a number of people] to arrive at a place in a group. □ *All the guests came in a body and there was quite a crowd for a while.* □ *They came in a body and left one by one.*

come in for something to be eligible for something; to be due something. □ *You are going to come in for a nice reward.* □ *Your report came in for a lot of criticism at the last board meeting.*

come in handy [for something] to be useful. (Idiomatic.) □ *This will come in handy some day.* □ *I think that this gadget will come in handy in the kitchen.*

come in on something to join into some activity or business deal. □ *Can I come in on this deal?* □ *I want to come in on this with you.*

come in out of the rain **1.** to seek shelter from the rain. □ *Come in out of the rain!* □ *Tell all the children to come in out of the rain. It will be over soon.* **2.** to wake up to reality; to *come down to earth*. (Slang.) □ *Hey, man! Come in out of the rain! Use your head!* □ *He's too dumb to come in out of the rain.*

come in somehow to finish in a certain position or rank. □ *Fred came in fourth in the race.* □ *He was afraid he would come in last.*

come in useful to be useful. □ *This will come in useful some day.* □ *Your report has come in useful a number of times.*

come in with someone to enter a place in the company of someone. □ *I came in with those people over there.* □ *Whom did you come in with?*

come into conflict [for things or people] to conflict or to be at odds with one another. □ *The various policies came into conflict at the last moment.* □ *Bill and Bob came into conflict over almost everything.*

COME ▸ INTO

come into being to begin existence. □ *This idea came into being during the last decade.* □ *When did this organization come into being?*

come into bloom AND **come into blossom** **1.** [for a flower] to bloom. □ *This rose comes into bloom later in the summer.* □ *When do they normally come into blossom?* **2.** [for a plant, bush, or tree] to begin to have many blossoms. □ *When do these bushes come into bloom?* □ *They come into blossom in June.*

come into blossom See the previous entry.

come into conflict with someone [for someone] to begin to conflict with someone else. □ *John came into conflict with José and his ideas.* □ *This was one of those days when I came into conflict with everyone.*

come into effect to become valid, effective, or operable. □ *When did these rules come into effect?* □ *They came into effect while you were on vacation.*

come into existence to begin existence; to begin to be. □ *This country came into existence in the early part of the fifteenth century.* □ *When did this little town come into existence?*

come into fashion to become stylish or fashionable. □ *Do you think that a design like this will ever come into fashion?* □ *That kind of dance will never come into fashion.*

come into one's or its own to become independent; to be recognized as independent and capable. □ *Finally, the Adamsville symphony orchestra came into its own.* □ *Maria is coming into her own as a concert pianist.*

come into play to become an important factor in something; to go into force. □ *When does this factor come into play?* □ *Everything will come into play at the last moment when we all get together.*

come into power to begin to reign; to ascend to power. □ *The king came into power in the middle of this century.* □ *When did the current queen come into power?*

come into prominence to become notable; to become renowned. □ *She first came into prominence during the late forties, when she starred in a few mov-*

ies. □ *Wally came into prominence when he won the state championship.*

come into season **1.** [for a game animal] to be subject to legal hunting. □ *When do ducks come into season around here?* □ *Deer came into season just yesterday.* **2.** See *come in(to) heat* under *COME ► IN(TO).*

come into service to begin to be used; to begin to operate and function as designed. □ *When did this elevator come into service?* □ *I think that this machine came into service during World War II.*

come into sight AND **come into view** to become visible; to move closer so as to be seen. □ *The tall buildings of the city came into sight first.* □ *A large herd of elephants came into view in the distance.*

come into (some) money to get some money unexpectedly, usually by inheritance. □ *She came into a lot of money when she turned twenty.* □ *I hope I can come into some money some day.* □ *I will never come into money, so I will have to earn it.*

come into someone's possession to become someone's property; to be given to someone. □ *When did this piece of property come into your possession?* □ *A very interesting document has come into my possession.*

come into the world to be born. □ *I came into this world nearly seventy years ago.* □ *Little Timmy came into the world on a cold and snowy night.*

come into view See *come into sight.*

COME ► IN(TO)

come in(to) contact with someone or something **1.** to touch someone or something, probably accidentally. □ *How many people have come into contact with the sick man?* □ *He came in contact with almost no one.* **2.** to meet up with and learn about someone or something. □ *Have you ever come into contact with trigonometry before?* □ *I have never come in contact with anything so difficult.*

come in(to) heat AND **come in(to) season** [for a female animal] to enter into the breeding season. □ *This animal will come into heat in the spring.* □ *When did your dog come in season?*

come out in(to) the open AND **come (out) into the open** **1.** [for someone or something] to move from a concealed position to an open area. □ *Sooner or later, she will have to come out in the open.* □ *The deer finally came into the open.* **2.** [for someone who has been hiding] to appear in public. □ *The thief came out into the open and was recognized by one of the witnesses to the crime.* □ *The agents finally came into the open.*

come out in(to) the open (with something) to make something known publicly. □ *The auditors came out into the open with the story of the bankruptcy.* □ *After much fuss about its secret dealings, the city council came out in the open.*

COME ► OF

come of age to reach a mature age. □ *When you come of age, you will understand.* □ *She doesn't come of age for a few more years.* [N] *Coming-of-age is a great celebration in many cultures.*

come of something to result from something. □ *I don't think that much will come of this.* □ *Nothing at all will come of it.*

come short of something to do something almost; to fail to reach something completely. □ *The workers came short of finishing the job on time.* □ *We came short of our goal.*

COME ► OFF

come off to happen as planned; to come to fruition; to succeed. (Colloquial.) □ *When is this party going to come off?* □ *Did the concert come off okay?*

come off ((of) something) [for something] to become detached from something else. (The *of* is colloquial.) □ *This piece came off of the top, not the bottom.* □ *There is a broken place here. I think something came off.*

come off (of) something **1.** [for something] to detach from, fall off, or drop off something. (The *of* is colloquial.) □

The paint came off the west side of the house because of the hot sun. ☐ *A wheel came off Timmy's tricycle.* **2.** to get down off something; to get off something. (The *of* is colloquial.) ☐ *Come off that fence!* ☐ *Please come off of that horse!* **3.** [for someone] to become more modest or humble; [for someone] to stop being foolish or pretentious. ☐ *Come off that arrogant attitude!* ☐ *Come off it!*

come off second best to be second to someone or something; to get the poorer end of a bargain. ☐ *As usual, he came off second best with a little less prize money than the winner.* ☐ *I don't want to come off second best again.* ☐ *In the end, he came off second best since his share was almost worthless.*

COME ▸ ON

See also under *COME ▸ (UP)ON; COME ▸ ON(TO).*

come on 1. to hurry along after someone. (Usually a command.) ☐ *Come on! We'll be late.* ☐ *Don't linger behind. Come on!* **2.** [for electricity or some other device] to start operating. ☐ *After a while, the lights came on again.* ☐ *I hope the heat comes on soon.* **3.** to walk out and appear on stage. ☐ *You are to come on when you hear your cue.* ☐ *Juan did not come on when he was supposed to.* **4.** [for a pain] to begin hurting; [for a disease] to attack someone. ☐ *The pain began to come on again, and Sally had to lie down.* ☐ *As a fainting spell came on, Gerald headed for a chair.* **5.** to yield; to agree. (Usually a command.) ☐ *Come on! Do it!* ☐ *Come on, now! Be a sport!* **6.** [for a program] to be broadcast on radio or television. ☐ *When does the news come on?* ☐ *The news didn't come on until an hour later.*

come on as something to appear to be something; to project one's image as something. ☐ *The senator comes on as a liberal, but we all know better.* ☐ *He comes on as a happy guy, but he is miserable.*

come on (duty) to begin to work at one's scheduled time. ☐ *When did you come on duty tonight?* ☐ *What time does she come on?*

come on in, the water's fine 1. to get into the water and swim. (Idiomatic. Usually a polite command.) ☐ *As Todd swam along, he said to Rachel, "Come on in. The water's fine."* ☐ *Come on in. The water's fine, and you'll love it.* **2.** to begin to do anything. (Figurative. A catch phrase encouraging someone to do something.) ☐ *You will like skiing. Come on in, the water's fine.* ☐ *I think you would like working here, and I'm happy to offer you the job. Come on in, the water's fine.*

come on in((to) something) to enter something or some place. (Usually a friendly request.) ☐ *Come on into the house and have a cold drink.* ☐ *Please, come on in.*

come on somehow to advance in some fashion, manner, rate, or degree. ☐ *Darkness comes on early these days.* ☐ *The illness comes on by degrees.*

come on strong to be very bold or impertinent when meeting new people. ☐ *That guy came on too strong and frightened the poor girl.* ☐ *Do you have to come on so strong? You are frightening.*

come on the scene 1. to arrive at a place. ☐ *When we came on the scene, the ambulances were already there.* ☐ *The police came on the scene and began directing traffic.* **2.** to become part of a situation. ☐ *She thought she was in love with Harry until Bob came on the scene.*

come on (to someone) to attempt to interest someone romantically or sexually. (Colloquial.) ☐ *He was trying to come on to me, but I found him yucky.* ☐ *He started to come on, but I left.* Ⓝ *Her come-on was almost irresistible.*

come (right) on top of something [for something] to happen immediately after something else. ☐ *The accident expenses came right on top of the costs of her illness.* ☐ *The bad news came on top of some other problems we were having.*

COME ▸ ON(TO)

come on((to) someone or something) to find someone or something by accident; to happen onto someone or something. □ *When I was out on my walk, I came on a little shop that sells leather goods.* □ *I came on an old friend of yours downtown today.*

COME ▸ OUT

come out **1.** to exit; to leave the inside of a place. □ *Please come out. We have to leave.* □ *When do you think they will all come out?* **2.** to result; to succeed; to happen. □ *I hope everything comes out okay.* □ *It will come out okay. Don't worry.* [N] *What was the outcome of the conference?* **3.** to come before the public; to be published; to be made public. □ *A new magazine has just come out.* □ *When will your next book come out?* **4.** to become visible or evident. □ *His pride came out in his refusal to accept help.* □ *The real reason finally came out, and it was not flattering.* **5.** [for a young woman] to make a social debut. □ *She came out at a large party.* □ *Does your daughter plan to come out this year?* [A] *Her mother gave her a large coming-out party.* [N] *Her coming-out was covered in all the newspapers.* **6.** to reveal one's homosexuality. □ *Herbie finally came out when he was forty-five.* □ *His mother was a little annoyed when he came out.*

come out against someone or something to announce or reveal that one is opposed to someone or something. □ *Our leaders came out against Mr. Wallace.* □ *Maria came out against Chuck.*

come out ahead to end up with the advantage; to end up with a profit. □ *Don't worry. You will come out ahead in the end.* □ *I have never come out ahead on one of these deals.*

come out ahead of someone to end up with more profit, benefit, or advantage than someone else. □ *I came out ahead of Dave in the contest.* □ *It was a tricky deal, and no one came out ahead of anyone else.*

come out at someone or something to emerge and attack someone or something. □ *The dogs came out at us, but we got away.* □ *Betsy's bulldog came out at my bike as I rode by.*

come out at something AND **come out to something** to result in a certain amount, as the result of mathematical computation. □ *The total charges came out at far more than we expected.* □ *The final bill came out to only half what we had expected.*

come out badly [for efforts at something] to have a bad result. □ *I'm sorry that everything came out badly.* □ *I hope it doesn't come out badly.*

come out for someone or something to announce or reveal that one supports someone or something. □ *The lawyers all came out for the judge's ruling.* □ *Roger came out for Lynn, who was running for mayor.*

come out in favor of someone or something to announce or reveal that one is in favor of someone or something. □ *I thought the mayor would come out in favor of more public housing.* □ *Lynn came out in favor of Roger.*

come out in something **1.** to come outside wearing something in particular. □ *You shouldn't come out in that skimpy jacket.* □ *I didn't mean to come out in my pajamas. I just wanted to get the newspaper.* **2.** to break out with a rash. □ *She came out in a horrible rash.* □ *The baby has come out in a rash again.*

come out in the wash [for a problem] to become solved; [for a problem] to fade away during the normal course of events. (Colloquial. Figurative in this sense.) □ *Don't worry. It will all come out in the wash.* □ *In the end it was all settled. It all came out in the wash.*

come (out) into the open See under *COME ▸ IN(TO).*

come out of nowhere to appear suddenly without warning. □ *The storm came out of nowhere.* □ *Max came out of nowhere and attacked Lefty.*

come out of one's ears [for someone or something] to be very abundant. (Figurative.) □ *I've got paper clips coming out of my ears.* □ *We are very busy at the factory. We have orders coming out of our ears.*

come out of one's shell to become more sociable and open with people. ☐ *He needs to come out of his shell and make some friends.* ☐ *She was unable to come out of her shell and socialize.*

come out of someone or something to emerge from someone or something. ☐ *Did that horribly long thorn come out of me?* ☐ *The lion came out of its den.*

come out of something AND **come out from something** to exit from something. ☐ *When will they come out of there?* ☐ *The people came out from the houses and celebrated.*

come out of something to result from something. ☐ *Did anything come out of the meeting?* ☐ *Nothing at all came out of our discussions.*

come out of the blue to appear or be revealed suddenly; to emerge suddenly. (As if something appeared out of a clear blue sky.) ☐ *Suddenly, this plane came out of the blue and roared over our heads.* ☐ *A really good idea suddenly came out of the blue.*

come out on something [for someone] to succeed with something; [for someone] to do well or poorly on a business venture. ☐ *How did you come out on the Adams project?* ☐ *How did you come out on that business venture?*

come out on top to end up being the winner. (Figurative.) ☐ *I knew that if I were virtuous, I would come out on top.* ☐ *Harry came out on top as I knew he would.*

come out to be to end up being a certain way. ☐ *I do not know what this sculpture will come out to be.* ☐ *When I start writing a poem, I never know what it will come out to be.*

come out to something See *come out at something.*

come out well to end up well. ☐ *I hope things come out well.* ☐ *Everything will come out well in the end.*

come out with something **1.** to publish something. ☐ *When are you going to come out with a new edition?* ☐ *The publisher decided not to come out with the book.* **2.** to express or utter something. ☐ *He came out with a strong dissenting opinion.* ☐ *It was over an hour before the president came out with an explanation.*

come out with something to say or shout something. ☐ *My nephew comes out with the cleverest remarks.* ☐ *Who came out with that rude remark?*

COME ▸ OVER

come over to come for a visit. ☐ *Why don't you come over next week?* ☐ *I would love to come over.*

come over someone [for something] to affect a person, perhaps suddenly. ☐ *I just don't know what came over me.* ☐ *Something came over her just as she entered the room.*

come over someone or something to move over and above someone or something. ☐ *A cloud came over us and rained like fury.* ☐ *A storm came over the city and did what it had to.*

come over (to our side) to join up with our side; to become one of our group, party, etc. ☐ *Seven of the other team came over to our side.* ☐ *I hope that Lynn comes over.*

come over to something to change to something; to convert to something. (Similar to *come over to our side.*) ☐ *We are going to come over to gas next year.* ☐ *Why don't you come over to a diesel-powered car?*

COME ▸ THROUGH

come through to be approved; to be sanctioned. ☐ *The mortgage came through.* ☐ *If the loan comes through, the car is yours.*

come through (for someone or something) to produce or perform as promised for someone or a group. ☐ *You knew I would come through for you, didn't you?* ☐ *The team came through for the college again.* ☐ *I knew they would come through.*

come through (something) **1.** to survive something. ☐ *We were never sure we would come through the ordeal.* ☐ *I knew I would come through all right.* **2.** to pass through something. ☐ *Please* *chain the gate up again when you come through.* □ *Please come through now.*

come through (with something) to produce or deliver something as promised. □ *Finally, Bob came through with the money he had promised.* □ *I knew he would come through.*

COME ▸ TO

come close (to someone or something) **1.** to approach very near to someone or something. □ *Come close to me and keep me warm.* □ *I didn't touch it, but I came close to it.* □ *I really came close that time.* **2.** to approximate someone or something in a specific quality. □ *When it comes to kindness, you don't even come close to Jane.* □ *You don't come close to the former owners in caring for your property.* □ *The book came close to the movie in popularity.*

come home to someone [for a fact] to be recognized suddenly by someone. □ *Suddenly, it came home to me that you thought I was Ronald.* □ *The importance of the events of the day finally came home to me.*

come home to someone or something to arrive home and find someone or something there. □ *I like to come home to a happy house.* □ *I look forward to coming home to you.*

come to to become conscious; to return to consciousness. □ *After just a few seconds, she came to.* □ *He came to just after fainting.*

come to a bad end to end up badly; to die in a bad or unpleasant way. □ *I always knew he would come to a bad end.* □ *Poor Max will probably come to a bad end.*

come to a boil **1.** [for a liquid] to reach the boiling point. □ *The soup came to a boil and the chef reduced the flame.* □ *How long will it take for this stuff to come to a boil?* **2.** [for a problem or situation] to reach a critical or crucial stage. (Figurative.) □ *Finally, things really came to a boil.* □ *Everything came to a boil after Mary announced her engagement.* **3.** [for someone] to get very angry. (Figurative.) □ *You could see Alice was coming to a boil.* □ *Fred was coming to a boil and clearly he was going to lose his temper.*

come to a climax to reach the end; to come to the end. □ *The party came to a climax when two people fell into the pool.* □ *Everything came to a climax when the police arrived with a search warrant.*

come to a conclusion **1.** [for a process] to reach the end and be finished. □ *At last, the process of buying a house came to a conclusion.* □ *I was afraid that the opera would never come to a conclusion.* **2.** to reach a decision. □ *We talked for a long time but never came to any conclusion.* □ *Can we come to a conclusion today, or do we have to meet again?*

come to a dead end **1.** to reach a point where one can go no farther. □ *We went down the road until we came to a dead end.* □ *The road comes to a dead end about a mile farther.* **2.** to have run out of possible ideas, solutions, energy, etc. □ *I've come to a dead end. I'm fresh out of ideas.* □ *The committee came to a dead end on the matter and tabled the whole business.*

come to a halt to stop; to slow down and stop. □ *Slowly, the train came to a halt.* □ *After the bus came to a halt, more people got on.*

come to a head [for a problem] to reach a critical or crucial stage. (Figurative.) □ *Things were getting worse all month. Finally everything came to a head when Walter broke the dean's window.* □ *At the end of the week, everything came to a head and Sam was fired.*

come to a standstill [for something] to slow down and finally stop. (Usually refers to something that is progressing, such as work, traffic, negotiations.) □ *At siesta time, things come to a standstill.* □ *At the height of rush hour, everything comes to a standstill.*

come to a turning point to reach a time when things may change; to reach a point at which a change of course is possible or desirable. (Originally nautical. Now figurative.) □ *Things came to a turning point when Bob could no longer afford the payments on his car.* □ *I* *think we have come to a turning point and there ought to be some improvement henceforth.*

come to an impasse to reach a deadlock, stalemate, obstruction, etc., in a situation. (Not normally used to refer to a blocked roadway.) □ *The negotiations have come to an impasse.* □ *The committee has come to an impasse in its deliberations.*

come to an untimely end [for one] to die before one's time. □ *The young athlete came to an untimely end.* □ *You would have thought that Max would have come to an untimely end by now.*

come to attention to assume a formal military posture, standing very straight. □ *Almost immediately, the soldiers came to attention.* □ *Everyone came to attention.*

come to blows (over someone or something) AND **come to blows (about someone or something)** to reach the point of fighting about someone or something. □ *Let's not come to blows over this matter.* □ *We may yet come to blows about Walter.* □ *Let's not come to blows.*

come to fruition to happen; to occur as suspected or intended. □ *When will all of these good things come to fruition?* □ *Our hard work and the end we planned for will soon come to fruition.*

come to grief to experience something unpleasant or damaging. □ *In the end, he came to grief because he did not follow instructions.* □ *Lefty came to grief because he did not see Max around the corner.*

come to grips with someone or something to begin to deal with someone or something in a sensible way. (Figurative.) □ *We must all come to grips with this tragedy.* □ *I cannot come to grips with Ed and his problems.*

come to harm to experience something bad; to get damaged or harmed. (Idiomatic.) □ *I sincerely hope that you do not come to harm.* □ *I hope no one comes to harm.*

come to life to become vigorous or lively. □ *About midnight, the party really came to life.* □ *The actors didn't come to life until the middle of the second act.*

come to light [for something] to become known or to be discovered. □ *Many surprises have come to light since then.* □ *Nothing new has come to light since we talked last.*

come to mind to be remembered. □ *Nothing comes to mind at the moment. Ask me again next week.* □ *Something important has just come to mind. Can we talk sometime today?*

come to much **1.** to amount to a large amount of money. (Usually negative.) □ *The bill did not come to much.* □ *Considering what we had, it didn't come to much.* **2.** to count for much; to be important or meaningful. (Usually negative.) □ *No one thought he would come to much.* □ *All that discussion did not come to much.*

come to naught to come to nothing; to end up as nothing. □ *After all my hard work, everything came to naught.* □ *All our efforts came to naught.*

come to no good to end up badly; to come to a bad end. □ *The tough kid came to no good in the end.* □ *Max will come to no good some day if he hasn't already.*

come to nothing to end up as nothing. □ *But in the end, it all came to nothing.* □ *All our efforts came to nothing.*

come to one's feet to stand up. □ *The audience came to its feet, cheering.* □ *Fred came to his feet to greet Roger.*

come to one's senses to begin thinking sensibly. □ *I'm glad he finally came to his senses and went on to college.* □ *I wish you would come to your senses and get a job.*

come to oneself to begin acting and thinking like one's normal self. □ *I began to come to myself and realize what I had done.* □ *Please come to yourself and stop acting so strangely.*

come to pass to happen; to take place. □ *And when do you think all these* *good things will come to pass?* □ *Do you think it will really come to pass?*

come to rest to stop; to slow down and stop. □ *The ball rolled and rolled and finally came to rest.* □ *Where did the ball come to rest?*

come to someone's assistance to arrive and help someone. □ *A kindly truck driver came to our assistance, and we were moving again almost at once.* □ *I hope someone will come to my assistance soon.*

come to someone's attention AND **come to someone's notice** to be told to, revealed to, or discovered by someone. □ *It has come to my attention that you are not following the rules.* □ *Your comments have just come to my notice.*

come to someone's notice See the previous entry.

come to someone's or something's rescue to rescue or save someone or something. □ *The paramedics came to our rescue at once.* □ *A big donor came to the college's rescue.*

come to something to be a question of something. □ *When it comes to chess, she's the best player in the club.* □ *He is impossible when it comes to budgeting.*

come to something to end up being important or significant. □ *Do you think this work will come to anything?* □ *I don't think this will come to what we were promised.*

come to something with something to bring a particular quality to a task or job. □ *She comes to the job with a number of good qualities.* □ *Ann comes to this position with a lot of experience.*

come to terms (about someone or something) AND **come to terms (on someone or something)** [for two or more people] to reach an accord on someone or something. □ *Ed and Alice came to terms about money.* □ *They did not come to terms about Wally.* □ *They did not come to terms on the price.* □ *Finally, they came to terms.*

come to terms with someone or something [for one or more persons] to deal with someone or something or reach an agreement on someone or something. □ *Finally, she began to come to terms with her problems.* □ *Todd eventually came to terms with his teenage son.* □ *They eventually came to terms with each other.*

come to terms (with someone or something) (about someone or something) AND **come to terms (with someone or something) (on someone or something)** to reach an accord with someone or something on someone or something. □ *Ed came to terms with Alice about money.* □ *They did not come to terms with the merchant on the price.* □ *They could not come to terms on Timmy with the school principal.* □ *Did they ever come to terms?*

come to the fore to become prominent or noticeable. □ *The importance of the announcement came to the fore when we thought about it for a while.* □ *A fine young candidate came to the fore in the last days of the political convention.*

come to the point to arrive at the major point of an argument or discussion. □ *Please come to the point.* □ *I am just now coming to the point.*

come to the same thing to amount to the same thing. (Folksy.) □ *No matter whether you call it a war or a police action, it comes to the same thing.* □ *It all comes to the same thing whether you do it or I do it.*

come to this to result in this situation. □ *Who would believe it would come to this?* □ *I was afraid it would come to this.*

COME ▶ TOGETHER

come together to arrive and join or touch together. □ *The ends of the boards just came together. They were almost too short.* □ *We came together in the park, just as we had agreed.*

come together (on something) to discuss and agree on something. □ *I hope we can come together on a price.* □ *I'm sure we can come together.*

come together (to something) to attend something together; to go to an event together. □ *Alice and I are going to come* *together.* ☐ *We will come to the party together.*

COME ▸ UNDER

come under something to be classed in the category of something. ☐ *This request comes under the category of a plain nuisance.* ☐ *Your proposal comes under the heading of new business and is out of order.*

COME ▸ UP

come up 1. to come from a lower place to a higher one. ☐ *You can come up now. They are gone.* ☐ *Come up and enjoy the view from the tallest rooftop in the county.* **2.** to come near; to approach. ☐ *He came up and began to talk to us.* ☐ *A heron came up while we were fishing, but it just ignored us.* **3.** to come to someone's attention. ☐ *The question of what time to be there never came up.* ☐ *The matter came up, but it was never dealt with.*

come up against someone or something to reach an obstacle in the form of someone or something. ☐ *I have come up against something I cannot handle.* ☐ *I have never come up against anyone like him before.*

come up for air 1. to lift one's head out of the water to breathe. ☐ *After staying under water for almost two minutes, Jason had to come up for air.* ☐ *How long will it be before he has to come up for air?* **2.** to stop what one is doing for a rest. (Figurative.) ☐ *Whenever you come up for air, I have a question for you.* ☐ *I want you to go to the store for me when you come up for air.* **3.** to stop kissing for a moment and breathe. (Figurative and colloquial.) ☐ *Don't those kids ever come up for air?* ☐ *When are you two going to come up for air?*

come up for auction to be placed on public sale, available to the person willing to pay the highest price. ☐ *This piece of property will come up for auction next week.* ☐ *When the Wilson farm comes up for auction, I'll make a bid for it.*

come up for something to be eligible for something; to be in line or sequence for something. ☐ *She comes up for reelection in April.* ☐ *How soon does your driver's license come up for renewal?*

come (up) from behind See under *COME ▸ FROM.*

come up in the world to advance in life; to rise to a position of wealth and power. ☐ *Well, I see you are coming up in the world.* ☐ *Tom has come up in the world a lot since I last saw him.*

come up smelling like roses AND **come up smelling like a rose** to end up blameless. (Colloquial.) ☐ *You seem to want to cause a lot of damage and still come up smelling like roses.* ☐ *In the end, she came up smelling like a rose.*

come up something [for a tossed coin] to turn out to be either heads or tails. ☐ *We tossed a coin, and it came up heads.* ☐ *The coin came up tails.*

come up through the ranks to rise to a position of leadership by working up through the sequence of lower ranks or positions. ☐ *He came up through the ranks. He did not start out as president.* ☐ *The general came up through the ranks. There is no other way to become a general.*

come up to something to meet or be equal to something. ☐ *Does this ice cream come up to your standards?* ☐ *Ann's lecture did not come up to her typical performance.*

come up with someone or something to find and deliver someone or something; to identify and locate someone or something. ☐ *I hope I can come up with something for her birthday present before next week.* ☐ *I'm sure I can come up with someone to fill your needs.* ☐ *I don't have any ideas now, but I'll try to come up with something by Monday.*

COME ▸ (UP)ON

come (up)on someone or something to find or happen on someone or something. (*Upon* is formal and less commonly used than *on*.) ☐ *I came upon Walter while I was in the bookstore.* ☐ *I came on this little store near Maple Street that has everything we need.*

COME ▸ WITH

come clean (with someone) (about something) to be honest with somebody about something. (Slang.) ☐ *I want you to come clean with me about this girl you have been seeing. What's going on?* ☐ *You had better come clean about it.* ☐ *Sam will come clean with me. I know he will.*

come with (someone or something) to depart in the company of someone or something; to travel with someone or a group. (Colloquial and regional without the object.) ☐ *Come with me. We'll go to my place.* ☐ *Are you going to come with the tour?* ☐ *Are you going to come with?*

COME ▸ WITHIN

come within an ace of something to come very close to [doing] something. (Colloquial.) ☐ *I came within an ace of leaving school. I'm glad you talked me out of it.* ☐ *Donna came within an ace of having an accident.*

come within an inch of someone or something AND **come within a hair('s breadth) of someone or something** to come very close to someone or something. ☐ *The bullet came within an inch of Heather.* ☐ *The car came within a hair of the bus.* ☐ *Sam came within a hair's breadth of striking his head on the beam.*

come within something **1.** to be in the category of something; to be under the domain of someone or something. ☐ *This comes within the domain of the treasurer.* ☐ *This matter doesn't come within my area of expertise.* **2.** to be inside a stated range, such as price, time, weight, range, etc. ☐ *This comes within my price range. I'll take it.* ☐ *If the turkey comes within my weight requirements, I'll buy it.*

COMMENCE ▸ WITH

commence with someone or something to start a procedure affecting a number of people or things by choosing a particular person or thing first. ☐ *Each meeting commences with a reading of the minutes of the last meeting.* ☐ *The doctor commenced with Lynn and took everyone else in the order in which they had arrived.*

COMMEND ▸ FOR

commend someone for something to praise someone for doing something. ☐ *I must commend you for your efforts.* ☐ *The committee commended Ralph for his good work.*

COMMEND ▸ TO

commend someone to someone or something to recommend or speak well of someone to someone or a group. ☐ *I commend Walter to your organization. He would make a good member.* ☐ *We commended your organization to Walter, who may wish to become a member.*

COMMENT ▸ ABOUT

comment about someone or something AND **comment (up)on someone or something** to make a remark about someone or something. ☐ *Please don't comment about what happened.* ☐ *There is no need to comment upon this event.* ☐ *Please don't comment on Liz. She is sorry.*

COMMENT ▸ (UP)ON

comment (up)on someone or something See the previous entry.

COMMISERATE ▸ WITH

commiserate with someone to share one's misery with another person who is also miserable. ☐ *I stopped by Bruce's house to commiserate with him.* ☐ *Let us have lunch sometime and commiserate with each other.*

COMMIT ▸ FOR

commit someone or something for something to promise someone or something for a particular purpose or time. (*Someone* includes *oneself*.) ☐ *I can't commit myself for Friday night.* ☐ *We are unable to commit any more funds for your project.*

COMMIT ▸ ON

commit oneself on something to agree to something; to promise or pledge to do something. ☐ *I'm sorry, but I can't commit myself on this matter.* ☐ *I just cannot commit myself on that at this time.*

COMMIT ► TO

commit oneself to someone or something to devote oneself to someone or something; to be faithful to someone or something. □ *He committed himself to his wife.* □ *She settled down and committed herself to her job.* □ *She decided to commit herself to George for as long as she lived.*

commit oneself to something 1. to agree to something; to promise or pledge to do something. □ *Yes, I will commit myself to the repair of the door frame.* □ *Will you commit yourself to finishing on time?* 2. to promise to support and assist something. □ *I can't commit myself to your cause at the present time. Maybe next month when I am less busy.* □ *She committed herself to being there on time.* □ *I hope you will commit yourself to this project.*

commit someone or something to something to pledge or assign someone or something to something. (See the previous two entries for reflexive uses.) □ *The boss committed Ralph to the task.* □ *I cannot commit any more money to your project.*

commit something to memory to memorize something. □ *Do we have to commit this to memory?* □ *The dress rehearsal of the play is tomorrow night. Please make sure you have committed all your lines to memory by that time.*

COMMUNE ► WITH

commune with someone or something to experience wordless communication with someone or something. □ *She went on long walks to commune with nature.* □ *He enjoyed going off on a retreat to commune with the monks.*

COMMUNICATE ► TO

communicate something to someone to say or write something to someone; to tell someone something. □ *Will you please communicate my regards to her?* □ *I intend to communicate your request to the front office this morning.*

COMMUNICATE ► WITH

communicate with someone 1. to correspond or talk with a person. □ *I have to communicate with Wally first.* □ *As soon as I have communicated with Fred, I can give you an answer.* 2. to really make oneself understood with a person. □ *I just don't seem to communicate with Sam, no matter what I do.* □ *We just can't seem to communicate with each other.*

COMMUTE ► BETWEEN

commute between places to travel between the place where one works and the place where one lives. □ *I have to commute between Chicago and Detroit every week.* □ *Mary has commuted between New York and Los Angeles for years.*

COMMUTE ► FROM

commute from some place to travel to work from some place. □ *I commute from way out in the country.* □ *Betty commutes from only a few miles away and will be here very soon.*

COMMUTE ► INTO

commute something into something to change something into something. □ *No one, as it turns out, can commute lead into gold.* □ *I had hoped to commute this argument into a sensible discussion, but it is hopeless.*

COMPARE ► TO

compare someone or something to someone or something to liken people or things to other people or things; to say that some people or things have the same qualities as other people or things. (See the comment at *compare someone or something with someone or something. Someone* includes *oneself.*) □ *I can only compare him to a cuddly teddy bear.* □ *Please don't compare the circus bear to my Uncle Harry.* □ *I would compare Roger to Sam in that they are both bald.* □ *He compared himself to one of the knights of the round table.*

COMPARE ► WITH

compare someone or something with someone or something to consider the sameness or difference of sets of things or people. (For many people this phrase is identical in meaning to *compare someone or something to someone or something. Someone* includes *oneself.*) □

Let's compare the virtues of savings accounts with investing in bonds. ☐ *When I compare Roger with Tom, I find very few similarities.* ☐ *Comparing Roger with an inert mass of protoplasm yields many similarities.* ☐ *Please compare Tom with Bill on this characteristic.*

COMPARTMENTALIZE ▶ INTO

compartmentalize something into something to segment or divide something into smaller things; to assign the parts of something into categories. ☐ *We will have to compartmentalize this large area into a number of smaller offices.* ☐ *His brain seemed to be compartmentalized into a number of different centers.*

COMPEL ▶ TO

compel someone to do something to force someone to do something; to drive someone to so something. (*Someone* includes *oneself.*) ☐ *You can't compel me to do that.* ☐ *She compelled herself to try, even though she was ill.*

COMPENSATE ▶ FOR

compensate for something to counterbalance or counteract something; to make up for something. ☐ *Your present kindness will not compensate for your previous rudeness.* ☐ *I think that this money will compensate for your trouble.*

compensate someone for something to pay someone [back] money for something. ☐ *Don't worry. I will compensate you for your loss.* ☐ *Let us compensate you for your expenses.*

COMPETE ▶ AGAINST

compete against someone to contend against someone; to play against someone in a game or contest; to vie against someone. ☐ *I don't see how I can compete against all of them.* ☐ *She refused to compete against her own brothers.*

compete against something to fight or struggle against something. ☐ *It was hard to be heard. I was competing against a wedding reception in the next room.* ☐ *I do not wish to compete against the audience when I lecture.*

COMPETE ▶ FOR

compete for someone or something to contend against or contest [someone] for someone or something; to struggle for someone or something [against a competitor]. ☐ *They are competing for a lovely prize.* ☐ *Ed and Roger are competing for Alice.*

COMPETE ▶ IN

compete in something to enter into a competition. ☐ *I do not want to compete in that contest.* ☐ *Ann looked forward to competing in the race.*

COMPETE ▶ WITH

compete with someone or something to contend against someone, something, or a group; to play in a competition against someone, something, or a group. ☐ *I can't compete with all this noise.* ☐ *Please stop competing with me.*

COMPILE ▶ FROM

compile something from something to make up something from something; to collect and consolidate something from something. ☐ *She compiled a book of poetry from verses written by her friends.* ☐ *Lynn compiled a picture book from family photographs going back almost a century.*

COMPLAIN ▶ ABOUT

complain about someone or something to protest someone or something; to grouch about someone or something. ☐ *Oh, stop complaining about everything.* ☐ *You are always complaining about me.* 🄰 *The constantly complained-about food was, in fact, almost inedible.*

COMPLAIN ▶ OF

complain of something to moan and suffer from a disease; to report the symptoms of a disease or health condition. ☐ *Todd complained endlessly of the pain.* ☐ *Kenneth complained of a headache and general weakness.* ☐ *The patient was complaining of a headache.*

COMPLAIN ▶ TO

complain to someone to grouch or protest to someone. ☐ *Don't complain to me.* ☐ *I will complain to the manager.*

COMPLIMENT ▶ ON

compliment someone on something to say something nice to someone about something connected to that person. ☐

I was pleased with Alice's work and complimented her on it. ☐ *They complimented me on my new tie.*

COMPLY ▸ WITH

comply with something to conform to something; to obey guidelines or regulations; to agree to something. ☐ *I hope you decide to comply with our rules.* ☐ *I cannot comply with the conditions you have set down.* ☐ *I am happy to comply with your request.*

COMPORT ▸ WITH

comport oneself with something to behave in a certain manner. ☐ *I hope you are able to comport yourself with better behavior next time.* ☐ *The old man was able to comport himself with dignity.*

COMPOSE ▸ OF

See *be composed of something* under *BE ▸ OF.*

COMPOUND ▸ WITH

compound something with something to unite some substance with another; to mix something with something else. ☐ *The pharmacist compounded the medicine with a sugar syrup for the child.* ☐ *Can this unpleasant medicine be compounded with something to make it palatable?*

COMPRESS ▸ INTO

compress something into something **1.** to squeeze or press something into something, such as a mold or container. ☐ *We compressed the tomatoes into the jar.* ☐ *I cannot compress any more clothing into the suitcase.* **2.** to form something into a shape by applying pressure. ☐ *He compressed the mass of paper into a tight ball.* ☐ *The clay was compressed into the shape of a brick upon the application of pressure to the mold.*

COMPRISE ▸ OF

See *be comprised of someone or something* under *BE ▸ OF.*

COMPROMISE ▸ ON

compromise (on someone or something) (with someone) to reach a middle ground with someone on a matter concerning someone or something; to make concessions to someone on some point concerning someone or something. ☐ *I intend to compromise on this matter with them.* ☐ *Are you going to compromise with me on this issue?* ☐ *I will not compromise on this.* ☐ *I am happy to compromise with you.*

COMPROMISE ▸ WITH

See the previous entry.

COMPUTE ▸ AT

compute something at something to calculate the total of something to be a certain figure. ☐ *I compute the total at nearly three thousand dollars.* ☐ *The tax people computed the penalty at an enormous amount.* ☐ *She computed the interest at 6 percent.*

CON ▸ INTO

con someone into something to deceive someone into something. (Slang. *Someone* includes *oneself.*) ☐ *The crooks conned her into buying a new furnace even when her old one was fine.* ☐ *You are just conning yourself into believing your plan will work.*

CON ▸ OUT

con someone out of something to get something away from someone by trickery. ☐ *Are you trying to con me out of the money?* ☐ *Max conned the merchant out of a lot of money.*

CONCEAL ▸ FROM

conceal someone or something from someone or something to hide someone or something from someone or something. (*Someone* includes *oneself.*) ☐ *Are you trying to conceal something from me?* ☐ *I cannot conceal Roger from the police.* ☐ *We could not conceal the present from Roger.* ☐ *I tried to conceal Ed from Roger, but he saw him anyway.* ☐ *Tom concealed himself from view.*

CONCEDE ▸ TO

concede something to someone or something to yield something to someone or a group; to grant something to someone or something. ☐ *At midnight, Ronald conceded the election to his opponent.* ☐ *Our party finally conceded the election to the opposing party.*

concede to someone or something to yield to someone or a group; to give in to someone or a group. □ *In the end we conceded to the demands of the group.* □ *I will not concede to you.* □ *Our party finally conceded to the opposing party.*

CONCEIVE ► OF

conceive of someone or something to think of or invent the notion of someone or something. □ *Who on earth ever conceived of doing this?* □ *He is unbelievable. I would not be able to conceive of him if he did not already exist.*

conceive of someone or something as someone or something to think of someone as being someone else; to think of something as being something else. □ *I can't conceive of you as a pilot.* □ *I can conceive of this little church as a very interesting dwelling.*

CONCENTRATE ► AT

concentrate at some place to gather thickly at a place. □ *The mosquitoes concentrated at the door, which was sort of a fast-food restaurant for them when the people came out.* □ *All the thirsty children concentrated at the water fountain.*

concentrate someone or something at something to cause people or things to gather at a place; to cause people or things to convene or converge at a place. □ *You shouldn't concentrate all the guards at one entrance.* □ *The general concentrated all the big guns at the entrance to the valley.*

CONCENTRATE ► ON

concentrate something on someone or something to focus something on someone or something; to center on someone or something. □ *Let's try to concentrate our efforts on finishing this job today.* □ *She concentrated her attention on Lynn.*

CONCENTRATE ► (UP)ON

concentrate (up)on someone or something to focus one's thinking on someone or something; to think intensely about someone or something. (*Upon* is formal and less commonly used than *on*.) □ *Please concentrate upon Jeff. He is the one we should discuss.* □ *Try to concentrate on your work more.*

CONCERN ► ABOUT

concern oneself about someone or something AND **concern oneself over someone or something** to turn one's thoughts and consideration to someone or something. (*Someone* includes *oneself*.) □ *Please do not concern yourself about me.* □ *I hope you will concern yourself over your work a little more.* □ *Please don't concern yourself about me. I'll do okay.*

CONCERN ► IN

concern someone in something to bring someone into some matter; to engage someone in something; to occupy someone with something. □ *Don't concern Dave with this. He doesn't know anything about fish.* □ *The wrong committee was concerned in this from the very beginning.*

CONCERN ► OVER

concern oneself over someone or something See *concern oneself about someone or something* under *CONCERN ► ABOUT*.

CONCERN ► WITH

concern someone with someone or something to busy someone with someone or something; to worry someone with thoughts of someone or something. (Compare to *concern someone about someone or something. Someone* includes *oneself*.) □ *I hope Jennifer does not concern herself with this matter.* □ *Try to concern him with something other than his work.* □ *I concern myself with too many details.*

CONCUR ► IN

concur in something to agree about something; to agree that something needs to be done. □ *I am very glad that we concur in this matter.* □ *We do not seem to concur in the matter of salary.*

CONCUR ► ON

concur on someone or something [for two or more people] to agree on someone or something. □ *We concur on Randy.* □ *Do we concur on this matter?*

concur (on someone or something) (with someone) to agree with someone about someone or something. ☐ *I certainly do concur on this matter with all of you.* ☐ *I concur with you on Tom.* ☐ *We concurred with the committee on you.* ☐ *We concurred on the plans with the council.*

CONCUR ▸ WITH

See the previous entry.

CONDEMN ▸ AS

condemn someone as something to blame or judge someone as being something bad. ☐ *The team condemned Larry as a traitor.* ☐ *Max was condemned as a common thief.*

CONDEMN ▸ FOR

condemn someone for something to blame or judge someone for something or having done something. (*Someone* includes *oneself.*) ☐ *I really can't condemn her for doing it. I would have done it too.* ☐ *Don't condemn yourself for the accident. It was no one's fault.*

CONDEMN ▸ TO

condemn someone to something to sentence someone to something; to punish someone with a particular punishment. (*Someone* includes *oneself.*) ☐ *I don't want to condemn you to a life of unpleasantness.* ☐ *By confessing, he condemned himself to many years in prison.*

CONDENSE ▸ (IN)TO

condense something (in)to something to compress or reduce something to something; to shrink or abridge something into a smaller version. ☐ *Condense this into half its size.* ☐ *You should condense this novel to a short story.*

CONDESCEND ▸ TO

condescend to do something to degrade or humble oneself in doing something. ☐ *I will not condescend to respond to that remark.* ☐ *"Will you condescend to join us for dinner?" teased Bob.*

condescend to someone to talk down to someone; to treat one as if one were below oneself; to patronize someone. ☐ *Please do not condescend to me.* ☐ *There is no need to condescend to the children. They are just small, not stupid.*

CONDITION ▸ TO

condition someone or something to something **1.** to train or adapt someone or an animal to do something. (*Someone* includes *oneself.*) ☐ *You should try to condition your children to sleep later.* ☐ *I conditioned the cat to behave rationally.* ☐ *Over the years, he had conditioned himself to run for hours at a stretch.* **2.** to train or adapt someone or an animal to something. (*Someone* includes *oneself.*) ☐ *Will you be able to condition the dog to a higher altitude?* ☐ *We could never condition the cat to the finer points of domestication.* ☐ *I conditioned myself to the extreme cold.*

CONDUCT ▸ AWAY

conduct someone away (from someone or something) to lead someone away from someone or something. ☐ *The usher conducted the gentleman away from the front of the auditorium.* ☐ *Can you conduct Fred away from the area?* ☐ *Please conduct him away.*

CONDUCT ▸ INTO

conduct someone in(to something) to lead someone into something or some place. ☐ *The usher conducted the gentleman into the hall.* ☐ *Please conduct him in.*

CONDUCT ▸ OUT

conduct someone out (of something) to lead someone out of something or some place. (The *of*-phrase is paraphrased with a *from*-phrase when the particle is transposed. See the Ⓕ example.) ☐ *The usher conducted the gentleman out of the hall.* ☐ *He led out the guests from the hall.* ☐ *Please conduct them out.* ☐ *Please conduct the guests out.*

CONFEDERATE ▸ WITH

confederate with someone or something to organize, join, or unite with someone or a group. ☐ *A number of states confederated with one another and formed a loose association.* ☐ *I confederated* *with the neighbors and we filed a joint complaint.*

CONFER ▸ ABOUT

confer (with someone) (about someone or something) See under *CONFER ▸ ON.*

CONFER ▸ ON

confer on someone or something AND **confer about someone or something** [for two or more people] to discuss someone or something. □ *Let's confer on Liz.* □ *We need to confer about this.*

confer (on someone or something) (with someone) AND **confer (with someone) (about someone or something)** to discuss someone or something. (See also under *CONFER ▸ (UP)ON.*) □ *Let us confer on this matter with the headmaster.* □ *I want to confer with you on this matter.* □ *I need to confer with you about Walter.*

CONFER ▸ (UP)ON

confer something (up)on someone to grant something, such as an academic degree, to someone, usually in a ceremony. (*Upon* is formal and less commonly used than *on.*) □ *The university conferred an honorary degree upon her.* □ *They conferred a degree on the chemist.*

CONFER ▸ WITH

confer (on someone or something) (with someone) See under *CONFER ▸ ON.*

CONFESS ▸ TO

confess something to someone to admit something to someone; to admit having done something to someone. □ *Tom confessed his involvement to the boss.* □ *Max confessed stealing the watch to the police.*

confess to something to admit having done something. □ *He will not confess to the crime.* □ *In the end, Max confessed to it.*

CONFIDE ▸ IN

confide in someone to speak freely or trustingly to someone. □ *I hope you feel that you can confide in me.* □ *Ann did not feel like confiding in anyone.*

CONFIDE ▸ TO

confide something to someone to disclose secret or private information to someone; to entrust secret or private information to someone. □ *I confided my feelings to my uncle, who had no advice for me.* □ *You can confide it to me.*

CONFINE ▸ TO

confine someone or something to something to limit someone or something to a particular place; to imprison someone or some creature in a particular place. (*Someone* includes *oneself.*) □ *Would you please confine the dog to the basement?* □ *The principal confined the children to their classrooms for the day.* □ *She confined herself to the small room for over a year because of her fear of crowds.*

confine something to someone or something to limit something or the doing of something to a particular place. □ *Please try to confine your comments to John.* □ *Can we confine this discussion to the agenda?*

CONFINE ▸ WITHIN

confine something within something to contain someone or some creature within something. □ *We were unable to confine the deer within the yard.* □ *Could you confine all your car-repair mess within the garage?*

CONFIRM ▸ IN

confirm someone in something to perform a religious rite that ties one more closely to one's religion. □ *They confirmed her in the church this morning.* □ *She was confirmed in the church at an early age.*

CONFISCATE ▸ FROM

confiscate something from someone or something to seize or impound something from someone or a group. □ *The police confiscated all the handguns in town from the citizens.* □ *The dean confiscated the beer from the dormitory.*

CONFLICT ▸ WITH

conflict with something to clash with something. (Does not refer to fighting.) □ *This date conflicts with my hair appointment.* □ *As far as I can tell, the* *date you suggest does not conflict with anything.*

CONFORM ▸ TO

conform something to something to make something fit or suit something else. □ *Max conformed his story to what Lefty had told the police instead of to the truth.* □ *I will have to conform this piece of wood to the piece that it must butt up against.*

conform to something to agree with guidelines or regulations; to behave within guidelines or regulations. □ *I hope that your policies will conform to our guidelines.* □ *Will this part conform to your regulations?*

CONFORM ▸ WITH

conform with something to match or agree with a model, plan, or set of specifications. (Compare to *conform to something.*) □ *Does this part conform with the specifications?* □ *This one conforms quite well.*

CONFRONT ▸ WITH

confront someone with something to face someone with incriminating evidence, charges of wrongdoing, or criticism. □ *The angry husband confronted his wife with the evidence of her financial irresponsibility.* □ *The police confronted Bill Wilson with the witness's statement.*

CONFUSE ▸ ABOUT

confuse someone about something to cause someone to be puzzled or bewildered about something. □ *She confused me about the time of the concert.* □ *I wish you wouldn't confuse me about those things.*

CONFUSE ▸ WITH

confuse someone or something with something to use something to confuse someone or some creature. □ *You have confused me with your clever talk.* □ *Don't confuse me with facts.* □ *You confused the dog with your orders.*

confuse someone with someone else or something with something else to mix someone up with someone else; to mix something up with something else. □ *I'm afraid you have confused me with my brother.* □ *Don't confuse the old ones with the new ones.*

CONGRATULATE ▸ (UP)ON

congratulate someone (up)on something to compliment or wish happiness to someone because of something. (*Upon* is formal and less commonly used than *on*.) □ *I want to congratulate you on your recent success.* □ *I congratulate you on your new job!*

CONJECTURE ▸ ON

conjecture on something to speculate on or guess about something. □ *I will not even conjecture on the outcome.* □ *Dave conjectured on what might happen.*

CONJURE ▸ UP

conjure someone or something up **1.** to make someone or something appear, seemingly by the use of magic. □ *The magician conjured seven white doves up.* 🅃 *Then the magician conjured up a horse.* 🅃 *Can one magician conjure up another magician?* **2.** to manage to locate someone or something. (When the task is so difficult that it might take magic to accomplish it.) □ *I think I can conjure a pencil up for you.* 🅃 *Do you think you can conjure up a large coffee urn in the next half hour?* 🅃 *Do you think you could conjure up the waiter? I want my check.* **3.** to manage to think up or imagine someone or something in one's mind. (Folksy.) □ *Can you conjure a vision of Sarah up?* 🅃 *All I could do was to conjure up thoughts of starving children.* □ *I couldn't even conjure a picture of my own mother up.*

CONK ▸ OFF

conk off to fall asleep. (Slang.) □ *I conked off about midnight.* □ *I was so tired that I nearly conked off.*

CONK ▸ OUT

conk out to fall asleep. (Slang.) □ *I was so tired that I conked out on the way home.* □ *I want to go home and conk out.*

CONNECT ▸ TO

connect someone or something (up) to someone or something AND **connect someone or something (up) with some-**

one or something 1. to link, in one's mind, someone or something to a person, event, or object. (*Someone* includes *oneself*. Colloquial or informal with *up*.) □ *Jeff connected Maggie up to the electrocardiograph.* □ *Eric connected the machine to the wall plug.* □ *The telephone operator connected Eric up to Susan.* □ *I connected myself up to a person with similar interests.* 2. to argue that someone or something is linked to a criminal or a criminal act. □ *I think I can connect Max up to the bank robbery.* □ *I can connect Eric to the crime.* □ *The police connected the earring to Susan.*

connect something (up) (to something) to attach something to something else physically. (Colloquial or informal with *up*.) □ *Connect this wire up to that little terminal.* 🅃 *Please connect up this wire to the junction.* □ *I connected it up.* □ *I connected it to the wall plug.* □ *I will connect up the wire to the terminal.*

connect (up) to something to attach to something; to attach something to some electrical device. □ *When we finish the house, we will connect up to the utilities.* □ *We have to connect to the outside telephone lines ourselves.*

CONNECT ▸ UP

See the entries under *CONNECT ▸ TO* and *CONNECT ▸ WITH.*

CONNECT ▸ WITH

connect someone or something (up) with someone or something See *connect someone or something (up) to someone or something* under *CONNECT ▸ TO.*

connect (up) with someone or something 1. to form an association with someone or a group. (The *up* is colloquial.) □ *Let's connect up with some other people and form an organization through which we can express our views.* □ *We need to connect with the elements in society that can help us with our problems.* 2. to meet with someone or a group; (The *up* is colloquial.) to communicate with someone or a group, especially over the telephone. (Informal.) □ *I tried to connect up with Bob over the phone, but I could never reach him.* □ *We could not connect with the council to discuss these matters.*

connect with something 1. [for something] to touch or strike something, as with a baseball and bat. (Colloquial.) □ *The bat connected with the ball and drove it into left field.* □ *When the bat connected with the ball, it made a terrific noise.* 2. to attach or join (on)to something. □ *This wire connects with the black wire on the left side.* □ *What does this wire connect with?*

CONNIVE ▸ AT

connive (at something) (with someone) to scheme at something (with someone); to plot something (with someone). □ *Are you conniving at something with Ronald?* □ *Are you and Ronald conniving with Tom at something I shouldn't know about?* □ *Stop conniving with people!*

CONNIVE ▸ WITH

See the previous entry.

CONSCRIPT ▸ INTO

conscript someone into something to force someone into military service; to draft someone. □ *The war-torn country was even conscripting children into the army.* □ *Fred was conscripted into the army.*

CONSECRATE ▸ TO

consecrate someone or something to God to pledge someone to the service of God; to dedicate something to the glory or service of God. □ *I now consecrate my life to the service of the Lord.* □ *They consecrated the new church building to the glory of God.*

CONSENT ▸ TO

consent to something to agree to permit something to happen. □ *I will not consent to your marriage.* □ *There is no need for you to consent to anything.*

CONSIDER ▸ AS

consider someone as something to think of a person as a particular type of person. (*Someone* includes *oneself*. Also without *as*, but not eligible as an entry.) □ *I don't consider you as a possible* *candidate.* □ *I consider myself as a perfect candidate.*

CONSIDER ► FOR

consider someone for something to think about offering someone a job, office, or other responsibility. □ *Would you consider David for the job?* □ *I could not possibly consider you for the position.*

CONSIGN ► TO

consign something to someone or something 1. to entrust something to someone, something, or some place. □ *We consigned all the available merchandise to our regular customers.* □ *What shipping company should we consign these boxes to?* 2. to assign something for shipment to a place. □ *Bill consigned this batch to Denver.* □ *The clerk consigned the box to the back room.*

CONSIST ► OF

consist of someone or something to include people or things; to be made up of people or things. □ *This bread consists of flour, water, sugar, oil, and yeast.* □ *The council consists of all the elected officials.*

CONSOLE ► ON

console someone on something to comfort someone about something. □ *I want to console you on your recent loss.* □ *They consoled Fred on the continuing difficulties he was having.*

CONSOLE ► WITH

console someone with something to use something to comfort someone. (*Someone* includes *oneself.*) □ *We consoled her with a bunch of flowers.* □ *He sat down and consoled himself with a beer or two.*

CONSORT ► WITH

consort with someone to associate with someone. □ *It is said that she consorts with thieves.* □ *No one worth anything would consort with Max.*

CONSPIRE ► AGAINST

See the following entry.

CONSPIRE ► WITH

conspire (with someone) (against someone or something) to join with someone in a plot against someone or something else. □ *The brothers conspired with the coach against the school board.* □ *Ed conspired with Sam against Roger.* □ *Ed conspired with Sam against the plan.* □ *Ed and Roger conspired against the plan.* □ *Ed conspired with Sam.*

CONSTRAIN ► FROM

constrain someone from doing something to prevent someone from doing something; to hold someone back from doing something. □ *I hope this doesn't constrain you from trying out for the play.* □ *His handicap did not constrain him from finishing the race.*

CONSTRUCT ► FROM

construct something from something AND **construct something out of something** to build something, using something. □ *Do you want to construct the house from wood?* □ *Shall we construct the building out of stone?*

CONSTRUCT ► OUT

construct something out of something See the previous entry.

CONSTRUE ► AS

construe something as something to interpret something to mean something. □ *Please do not construe this as criticism.* □ *We mistakenly construed her comments as positive.*

CONSULT ► ABOUT

consult (with) someone (about someone or something) to ask someone about someone or something. □ *Please consult with me about all your plans.* □ *You should consult the architect about your needs.* □ *Please consult with me first.*

CONSULT ► WITH

See the previous entry.

CONTAMINATE ► WITH

contaminate someone or something with something to get someone or something dirty with something; to pollute someone or something with something. (*Someone* includes *oneself.*) □ *She contaminated the patient with her dirty hands.* □ *Don't contaminate our water* *with chemicals.* ☐ *After he was prepped for surgery, he accidentally contaminated himself with the soiled cloth.*

CONTEND ▸ AGAINST

contend against someone or something to fight or compete against someone or something. ☐ *Do we have to contend against all this criticism?* ☐ *Ed refuses to have to contend against Eric.*

CONTEND ▸ FOR

contend (with someone) (for something) to fight someone for something; to compete with someone to win something. ☐ *I don't want to have to contend with Sally for the job.* ☐ *I don't want to have to contend for the job with Ed.* ☐ *I don't want to have to contend for the job.* ☐ *I refuse to contend with you even a moment longer.*

CONTEND ▸ WITH

contend with something to put up with something; to struggle with the problems caused by someone or something. ☐ *I cannot contend with your temper anymore.* ☐ *I wish we did not have to contend with this changeable weather.*

CONTENT ▸ WITH

content oneself with someone or something to be satisfied with someone or something. ☐ *You are going to have to content yourself with less.* ☐ *Can he content himself with just one woman?* ☐ *You will just have to learn to content yourself with fewer trips to the Caribbean.*

CONTINUE ▸ BY

continue by doing something to keep going by starting to do something. ☐ *You are doing very well in this piano lesson. Please continue by playing the other sonata.* ☐ *After the interruption, Wally continued by explaining his position on the trade negotiations.*

CONTINUE ▸ WITH

continue with something to keep going with whatever was being done before. ☐ *Oh, please continue with your discussion.* ☐ *Do you mind if I continue with my knitting as we talk?*

CONTRACT ▸ FOR

contract (with someone) (for something) See under *CONTRACT ▸ WITH.*

CONTRACT ▸ OUT

contract something out to make an agreement with someone to do a specific amount of work. (Rather than doing it oneself or in one's own place of business.) ☐ *I will contract this out and have it done by experts.* 🅃 *I contracted out this kind of job the last time.*

CONTRACT ▸ WITH

contract (with someone) (for something) to make an agreement with someone to produce or supply something, or do something. ☐ *I will have to contract with an expert for that part of the project.* ☐ *We contracted with John for a new kitchen.* ☐ *Did you contract for plumbing work with Eric?*

CONTRAST ▸ TO

contrast someone or something to someone or something See the following entry.

CONTRAST ▸ WITH

contrast someone or something with someone or something AND **contrast someone or something to someone or something** to examine people or things in a way that will show their differences. ☐ *Contrast Sally with Sam, for instance, to see real differences.* ☐ *It is easy to contrast Eric to a statue. He is always in motion.* ☐ *Contrast the busy geometry of a French garden to an English meadow.*

contrast with someone or something to be different from someone or something. ☐ *Bill's attitude really contrasts with the attitude of his twin brother, Bob.* ☐ *This color really contrasts with that one.*

contrast with something [for a color] to show a marked difference to another color; [for a color] to complement another color. ☐ *The black one contrasts nicely with the white one.* ☐ *Does red contrast with green?*

CONTRIBUTE ▸ FOR

contribute something (to someone) (for someone or something) to donate something to someone for the benefit of someone or something. □ *I hope you will contribute at least a dollar to Ed for Tom's birthday present.* □ *Will you contribute a dollar for Tom to Mary when she comes around?* □ *Please contribute a few bucks to Eric.* □ *Can you contribute a dollar for the gift?*

CONTRIBUTE ▸ TO

See also the previous entry.

contribute to something 1. to donate something to some cause. □ *Please contribute to the fund for the needy.* □ *Will you contribute to the cause?* 2. to add to or exacerbate something. □ *The dry weather contributed to the failure of the crops.* □ *Your lateness contributed to the shortness of the evening.*

CONVALESCE ▸ FROM

convalesce from something to get well from a disease, operation, or injury. □ *I spent three weeks in bed convalescing from the flu.* □ *Donna needed some time to convalesce from her surgery.*

CONVERGE ▸ (UP)ON

converge (up)on someone or something 1. to meet on someone or something; to grow together so as to focus on someone or something. (*Upon* is formal and less commonly used than *on*.) □ *Our interests converged on the matter of the failing economy.* □ *Our discussions converged on Eric.* 2. to gather near or around someone or something. (*Upon* is formal and less commonly used than *on*.) □ *Everyone converged on the wounded sailor.* □ *The shoppers converged on the store as it opened for business.*

CONVERSE ▸ ABOUT

converse (with someone) (about someone or something) to talk about someone or something. □ *Please converse with Ted about that.* □ *I need to converse about last night with you.* □ *The principal needs to converse with you.* □ *We need to converse about Sally.*

CONVERSE ▸ WITH

See the previous entry.

CONVERT ▸ FROM

See both entries under *CONVERT ▸ (IN)TO.*

CONVERT ▸ (IN)TO

convert (from something) ((in)to something) to change from one thing into another. □ *We converted from oil to natural gas.* □ *We converted to gas from oil.* □ *I had hoped he would convert from an impatient youth into a relaxed gentleman. He did not.*

convert someone or something (from something) ((in)to something) to change someone or something from something into something else. □ *Can we convert you from a meat eater into a vegetarian?* □ *Would you be willing to convert your oil furnace to a gas one?* □ *I would like to convert to gas.* □ *Does it cost a lot to convert from oil?*

CONVERT ▸ TO

See both entries under *CONVERT ▸ (IN)TO.*

CONVEY ▸ FROM

See the following entry.

CONVEY ▸ TO

convey something (from someone or something) (to someone or something) to carry or transport something from someone or something to someone, something, or some place. □ *I conveyed the box from the table to John.* □ *Please convey every good wish from those of us in the Midwest to those on the East Coast.* □ *Would you convey my blessings to the lovely couple?* □ *The Eston Trucking Company conveys all kinds of goods to the southern part of the country.*

CONVICT ▸ OF

convict someone of something to pronounce someone guilty of something. □ *In the end, they convicted her of theft.* □ *The police wanted to convict Max of the crime.*

CONVINCE ▸ OF

convince someone of something to persuade someone that something is true. (*Someone* includes *oneself*.) □ *You will never convince me of that.* □ *I will* *probably convince myself of the need to find a better job.*

CONVULSE ▸ WITH

convulse someone with something to cause someone to quake or jerk because of pain or emotion. ☐ *The comedian convulsed the audience with laughter.* ☐ *The audience was convulsed with laughter.*

COOK ▸ OUT

cook (something) out to cook food out of doors. ☐ *I will cook this out. It's too hot in the kitchen to cook there.* 🅃 *Shall we cook out chicken tonight?* ☐ *Yes, let's cook out.* 🄽 *Mary's father planned a cookout for her birthday.*

COOK ▸ UP

cook something up **1.** to prepare a batch of some kind of food by cooking. (Folksy.) ☐ *Fred cooked a batch of beans up for the ranch hands.* 🅃 *He cooked up some food for dinner.* **2.** to devise or concoct something. (Figurative.) ☐ *Fred cooked up a scheme that was supposed to earn him a lot of money.* ☐ *I don't have a plan right now, but I think I can cook something up in a few days.*

cook something up (with someone) to arrange or plan to do something with someone. (The *something* is usually the word *something*. Figurative. See *cook something up*.) ☐ *I tried to cook something up with Karen for Tuesday.* 🅃 *I want to cook up something with John.* ☐ *Let's see if we can cook something up.* 🄰 *The hastily cooked-up plans fell through.*

COOL ▸ DOWN

cool down AND **cool off** **1.** to become cooler. ☐ *After the sun set, things began to cool down a bit.* ☐ *The evening began to cool off.* **2.** [for someone] to become less angry. ☐ *They were very angry at first, but then they cooled down.* ☐ *Cool off, you guys!*

cool someone down AND **cool someone off** to make someone less angry. (*Someone* includes *oneself*.) ☐ *Things are less threatening now. That ought to cool him down.* ☐ *Time cooled them off a little.* ☐ *She meditated for a while to cool herself down.*

cool someone or something down AND **cool someone or something off** to make someone or something less hot. (*Someone* includes *oneself*.) ☐ *Use ice to cool him down and reduce his fever.* ☐ *The refrigerator cooled the pudding off in a hurry.* ☐ *Here, have a cold drink. Cool yourself down.* 🅃 *The ice cooled down the feverish child.* 🅃 *We need to cool off the pudding in a hurry.*

COOL ▸ OFF

See the entries under *COOL ▸ DOWN.*

COOP ▸ UP

coop someone or something up to confine someone or something in a small place. (*Someone* includes *oneself*.) ☐ *Don't coop me up. I can't stand small places.* 🅃 *You had better not coop up these kids all day.* 🅃 *We had to coop up the dogs for a while.* 🄰 *These cooped-up kids have to get out where they can run and play.* ☐ *I can't coop myself up in a little room like this for two weeks.*

COOPERATE ▸ ON

See the following entry.

COOPERATE ▸ WITH

cooperate (with someone) (on something) to work together in harmony with someone on something. ☐ *Please cooperate with me on this project.* ☐ *Can you cooperate on this with me?* ☐ *I hope we can cooperate on this.* ☐ *I would like to cooperate with you.*

CO-OPT ▸ INTO

co-opt someone into something to convince one's opponent to adopt one's position or philosophy. ☐ *They tried to co-opt the students into rioting.* ☐ *There is no point in trying to co-opt them into it. They are too clever.*

COORDINATE ▸ WITH

coordinate something with something **1.** to make something harmonize with something else. ☐ *I want to coordinate my hat with my shoes.* ☐ *Is this tie coordinated with my jacket?* **2.** to synchronize something with something else. ☐ *Let us coordinate our actions in this* *matter.* □ *I think we should coordinate our departure times with that of Fred.*

COP ▸ FROM

cop something from someone or something to steal or swipe something from someone or something. (Slang.) □ *Some thug copped my watch from me.* □ *Max copped food from a number of stores.*

COP ▸ OUT

cop out (of something) AND **cop out (on something)** 1. to withdraw from doing something. (Slang.) □ *Are you copping out of this job?* □ *No, I'm not copping out!* □ *I'm not copping out on this.* Ⓝ *Your excuse is just a cop-out!* 2. to break one's promise about doing something. (Slang.) □ *You said you would and now you are copping out of it.* □ *I'm not copping out. I just can't find the time.* Ⓝ *This guy is a liar! He specializes in cop-outs.*

cop out (on someone) to break one's promise to someone. (Slang.) □ *Come on! Don't cop out on me!* □ *You promised me you would do it! Don't cop out now!*

COPE ▸ WITH

cope with someone or something to endure someone or something; to manage to deal with someone or something. □ *I don't think I can cope with any more trouble.* □ *I can't cope with Mike anymore.*

COPULATE ▸ WITH

copulate with someone or something to have sexual intercourse with someone or something. □ *After the dog has copulated with the bitch, they should be separated.* □ *He said he wanted to copulate with whom?*

COPY ▸ DOWN

See the following entry.

COPY ▸ FROM

copy something (down) (from someone or something) to copy onto paper what someone says; to copy onto paper what one reads. □ *Please copy this down from Tony.* Ⓣ *Ted copied down the directions from the invitation.* □ *Jane copied the menu down from the waitress.* □ *She copied it down.* □ *She copied it from a book.*

COPY ▸ OUT

copy something out to copy something by hand. □ *I have to copy this out again. I lost the first copy.* Ⓣ *Please copy out this article for me.*

copy something out of something to copy something onto paper from a book or document. □ *Did you copy this out of a book?* □ *I did not copy this paper or any part of it out of anything.*

CORDON ▸ OFF

cordon something off to mark off an area where people should not go with a rope, tape, ribbon, etc. □ *The police cordoned the scene of the crime off, and we could not even get close.* Ⓣ *They cordoned off the area.* Ⓐ *I thought I told you to stay out of the cordoned-off area!*

CORK ▸ UP

cork something up 1. to close and seal a bottle with a cork. □ *I think we should cork this up and save it for later.* Ⓣ *Cork up the bottle for later.* 2. to stop up one's mouth and be quiet. (Slang.) □ *Cork it up and listen!* Ⓣ *Cork up your mouth!*

CORRELATE ▸ WITH

correlate something with something to match or equate something with something else. □ *Can you correlate her comment with what she said yesterday?* □ *This does not correlate with our earlier assumptions.*

correlate with something to match or equate with something. □ *This does not correlate with your earlier story.* □ *What she said yesterday does not correlate with what she is saying today.*

CORRESPOND ▸ ABOUT

correspond (with someone) (about someone or something) See under *CORRESPOND ▸ WITH.*

CORRESPOND ▸ TO

correspond to something to match up with something; to harmonize with something. □ *This one corresponds to the one over there.* □ *An X in this box* *corresponds to another X in the box on the other side of the application form.*

CORRESPOND ▶ WITH

correspond (with someone) (about someone or something) to write letters back and forth with someone about someone or something. ☐ *I will have to correspond with the manager about that.* ☐ *I corresponded about this with my brother.* ☐ *I corresponded with my brother for over a year.* ☐ *We corresponded about Fred.*

COST ▶ OUT

cost something out to figure out the costs of some complex purchase of goods or services. ☐ *Give me a minute to cost this out, and I will have an estimate for you.* 🅃 *Do you have time to cost out these specifications?*

COTTON ▶ (ON)TO

cotton (on)to someone or something to begin to like or agree to someone or something quickly; to take to someone or something. ☐ *She began to cotton to Fred, despite his country ways.* ☐ *She cottoned onto June's way of thinking*

COTTON ▶ UP

cotton up to someone to make friends with someone; to be overly friendly with someone; to flatter or fawn on someone in hopes of favorable treatment. ☐ *James set out to cotton up to the parents of his friends.* ☐ *Just watch her cotton up to the teacher!*

COUCH ▶ IN

couch something in something to express something in carefully chosen or deceptive words. ☐ *He tended to couch his explanations in arcane vocabulary.* ☐ *She couched her words in an overly polite manner.*

COUGH ▶ OFF

cough something off to cough and cough until something falls off one's body, usually one's head. (Informal.) ☐ *I had the flu. I nearly coughed my head off.* ☐ *I thought Gerald was going to cough his head off.*

COUGH ▶ OUT

cough something out **1.** to say something while coughing. ☐ *He coughed the words out, but no one could understand him.* 🅃 *He coughed out the name of his assailant.* **2.** to say something unwillingly, concealing the utterance in a cough. ☐ *Finally, he coughed the instructions out, and we pretended we understood them.* 🅃 *He coughed out the instructions, or at least he claimed to have given them.*

COUGH ▶ UP

cough something up **1.** to get something out of the body by coughing. ☐ *She coughed some matter up and took some more medicine.* 🅃 *She coughed up stuff all night.* **2.** to vomit something. ☐ *The dog coughed the rabbit up.* 🅃 *The dog coughed up the food it had eaten.* **3.** to produce or present something, such as an amount of money. (Slang.) ☐ *You will cough the money up, won't you?* 🅃 *You had better cough up what you owe me, if you know what's good for you.*

COUNSEL ▶ ABOUT

counsel someone about something to give advice to someone about something. ☐ *Who can counsel me about the proper books to buy?* ☐ *Will you counsel George about how it is done?*

COUNSEL ▶ AGAINST

counsel someone against something to advise someone against doing something. ☐ *The lawyer counseled her against suing the government.* ☐ *I was counseled against going there alone.*

COUNT ▶ AGAINST

count against someone [for something] to be held against someone; [for something] to weigh against someone. ☐ *I hope this mistake doesn't count against me.* ☐ *Don't worry, it won't count against you at all.*

count something against someone to hold something against someone. ☐ *I'm afraid we must count this against you.* ☐ *Don't count that last strike against the batter.*

COUNT ▸ AMONG

count someone among something to consider someone as a particular type of person or part of a particular group. (*Someone* includes *oneself*.) □ *I count her among my closest friends.* □ *Rachel counted herself among the luckiest people alive.*

COUNT ▸ AS

count someone or something as something to consider someone to be a particular type of person. (*Someone* includes *oneself*.) □ *I count Todd as one of the possible candidates.* □ *I count this one as one of the best.* □ *Do you count yourself as a pessimist?*

count something as something to treat or think of something as if it were something else. □ *I count this as a win.* □ *Did you count that one as a fair ball?*

COUNT ▸ DOWN

count down to count backwards to an event that will start when zero is reached. □ *The project manager was counting down—getting ready for the launch of the rocket.* Ⓝ *They had to halt the countdown to correct a minor problem.* □ *I can still hear the captain counting down: "Five, four, three, two, one, zero, blastoff!"*

COUNT ▸ FOR

count for something 1. to be valid for something; to be worth something. □ *Doesn't all my work count for anything?* □ *You count for a lot as far as I'm concerned.* **2.** to be considered as something. □ *Does this count for the reward?* □ *This one does not count for anything.*

COUNT ▸ FROM

count from something (up) to something to say or list the numbers from one number to some other number. □ *Now, count from 100 up to 300 by threes.* □ *Timmy can count from 1 to 40.*

COUNT ▸ IN

count someone in (for something) AND **count someone in (on something)** to include someone as part of something. (Informal. *Someone* includes *oneself*.) □ *Please count me in for the party.* □ *Do count me in on it.* □ *Yes, count me in.* □ *Should I count myself in?*

count someone in on something See the previous entry.

count something in to include something in a count of something. □ *Did you count the tall ones in?* Ⓣ *Did you count in the tall ones in the corner?*

COUNT ▸ OFF

count off [for a series of people, one by one] to say aloud the next number in a fixed sequence. □ *The soldiers counted off by threes.* □ *The sergeant told them to count off.*

count someone or something off to count people or things, to see if they are all there. □ *Let's count them off to see who's missing.* Ⓣ *Count off each person, one by one.* □ *I counted each one off.*

COUNT ▸ ON

See under *COUNT ▸ (UP)ON.*

COUNT ▸ OUT

count someone out to declare someone "out" in baseball. □ *The umpire counted the player out.* Ⓣ *He counted out three of them during the first inning.*

count someone out (for something) to exclude someone from something. (*Someone* includes *oneself*.) □ *We are going to count you out for the party unless you pay in advance.* □ *Please don't count me out yet!* □ *I must count myself out for the nomination.*

count something out to disregard something; to eliminate a possibility. □ *We'll have to count out the possibility of his being elected.* □ *Never count it out. It can always happen.*

count something out to give out things, counting them, one by one. □ *She counted the cookies out, one by one.* Ⓣ *She counted out the cookies to each child.*

COUNT ▸ UP

count someone or something up to count things or people to see how many there are. □ *Let's count them up and see how many we have.* □ *I counted all the guests up, and there are too many to* *seat.* ☐ *Please count up all these books and tell me how many there are.*

count up to something **1.** to say or list the numbers from zero on up to a certain number. ☐ *Can you count up to a million?* ☐ *I can count up to any number you name, and I will do it if you will stay around to listen.* **2.** to equal a specified total; to add up to something. ☐ *That counts up to a lot.* ☐ *The money we earned today counts up to just enough to pay for the electricity we used today.*

COUNT ▸ (UP)ON

count (up)on someone or something to rely on someone or something. (*Upon* is formal and less commonly used than *on.*) ☐ *Can I count upon you to do the job?* ☐ *You can count on me.* ☐ *Can I count on the court to rule fairly?*

COUNT ▸ WITH

count with someone to be important to someone. ☐ *This cooperation really counts with me.* ☐ *All my efforts do not count with her.*

COUNTER ▸ WITH

counter someone or something with something to refute someone or something with something. ☐ *She countered our evidence with an eyewitness.* ☐ *I countered Nancy with a better argument.*

counter with something to say something in refutation of something; to strike back with something. ☐ *Aren't you going to counter with an argument?* ☐ *He countered with a punch in the jaw.*

COUPLE ▸ (ON)TO

couple something (on)to something AND **couple something on(to something)** to attach something to something. ☐ *Couple this connector to that one.* ☐ *Couple this onto it.* ☐ *Couple the green one onto the red one.* ☐ *Couple this on.*

COUPLE ▸ TO

See the previous entry.

COUPLE ▸ TOGETHER

couple something together to attach two parts of something together. ☐ *Couple these two cars together and put them on track seven.* ☐ *You have to couple the ends of the two hoses together before you turn on the water.*

COUPLE ▸ UP

couple someone and someone else or something and something else up to pair people up; to pair things up. ☐ *The camp director coupled Sam and Tom up.* ☐ *The yardmaster coupled all the cars up.*

couple up (with someone) [for one person] to join another person. ☐ *I decided to couple up with Larry.* ☐ *Larry and I coupled up with each other.* ☐ *Larry and I coupled up.* ☐ *By midnight, they all had coupled up and were dancing.*

COUPLE ▸ WITH

couple someone with someone AND **couple something with something** to join one person with another to make a pair; to join one thing with another to make a pair. ☐ *I coupled Todd with Amy for the dinner party.* ☐ *We coupled the money issue with the election issue for our discussions.*

couple with someone to have sexual intercourse with someone. ☐ *Did you say she coupled with him?* ☐ *They coupled with each other.*

couple with something to attach or join to something. ☐ *This railroad car will couple with the caboose.* ☐ *These cars did not couple with the others properly, and there was almost an accident.*

COURSE ▸ THROUGH

course through something to run, race, or flow rapidly through something. ☐ *I believe, sometimes, that ice water courses through your veins.* ☐ *No, perfectly red blood courses through them.*

COVER ▸ AGAINST

cover someone or something against something **1.** to cover someone or something as protection against something. (*Someone* includes *oneself.*) ☐ *You should cover your nose against the cold.* ☐ *I covered little Jimmy against the night's drafts.* ☐ *I covered myself against the bitter cold.* **2.** [for an insurer] to provide insurance on someone or something against some peril. ☐ *The in-*

surance policy covered us against losses. □ *This policy covers your car against theft.*

COVER ▸ FOR

cover for someone to act on someone's behalf while someone is elsewhere. □ *I will cover for you while you are away.* □ *Please cover for me.*

cover someone or something for something [for an insurer] to provide protection to someone or something for a particular price. □ *One company will cover the car for about a thousand dollars.* □ *This policy covers you for a few dollars a week.*

cover (up) for someone to conceal someone's wrongdoing by lying or working in someone's place. □ *Are you covering up for the person who committed the crime?* □ *I wouldn't cover for anyone.* 🄽 *It was a clumsy cover-up, and it failed miserably.*

COVER ▸ IN

cover someone in something to place something over someone or something to serve as clothing or concealment. □ *They covered her in green cloth leaves, and that was her costume.* □ *The designer had covered her in swags of pink satin.*

COVER ▸ UP

cover someone or something up to place something on someone or something for protection or concealment. (*Someone* includes *oneself.*) □ *Cover the pie up, so Terry won't see it.* 🅃 *Cover up the money, so they won't know we were gambling.* 🅃 *Cover up Jimmy so he doesn't get cold.* □ *Tom—hiding in the leaves—covered himself up so no one could see any part of him.*

cover something up to conceal a wrongdoing; to conceal evidence. □ *They tried to cover the crime up, but the broken lock gave them away.* 🅃 *She could not cover up her misdeeds.*

cover (up) for someone See under *COVER ▸ FOR.*

COW ▸ INTO

cow someone into something to intimidate someone into doing something through the use of guilt or shame. □ *You can't cow me into doing it. Those tricks don't work on me.* □ *You can cow Wally into almost anything.*

COWER ▸ AWAY

cower away from someone or something to shrink away from someone or something in fear. (Also without *away,* but not eligible as an entry.) □ *The coyote cowered away from the fire.* □ *The dog cowered away from the threats of the worker.* □ *After their argument, both Roger and Dave cowered away from the people who had gathered to watch them.*

COWER ▸ DOWN

cower down from something to crouch down, displaying an emotion, such as fear. □ *They cowered down from sheer terror.* □ *I would cower down from fright in a similar situation.*

COWER ▸ FROM

cower from something to draw back from the fear of something. (See also under *COWER ▸ DOWN.*) □ *The wolves cowered from the flames.* □ *Some excited hyenas cowered from the lions as they passed by.*

COZY ▸ UP

cozy up (to someone) **1.** to snuggle up to someone as if to get warm. □ *The children cozied up to their mother.* □ *They cozied up to each other.* □ *They cozied up to keep warm.* **2.** to try to get in good with someone; to try to increase one's influence with someone by being extra nice and friendly. □ *The salesman tried to cozy up to the customer.* □ *I hate salesmen who cozy up.* □ *Roger got in trouble for trying to cozy up to the boss.*

CRACK ▸ DOWN

crack down (on someone or something) to put limits on someone or something; to become strict about enforcing rules about someone or something. □ *The police cracked down on the kids.* □ *They cracked down once last year too.* 🄽 *The police crackdown on gambling had no effect on the bingo parlor.*

CRACK ▸ OPEN

crack open [for something brittle] to break or split open. □ *The egg cracked open and a chick worked its way out.* □ *The side of the mountain cracked open and molten lava flowed out.*

crack something open to break or split something open. □ *I will crack the egg open and put it in the skillet.* 🅃 *Roger cracked open four eggs accidentally.*

CRACK ▸ UP

See *be cracked up to be something* under *BE ▸ UP.*

crack someone or something up to damage someone or something. (*Someone* includes *oneself.*) □ *Who cracked my car up?* 🅃 *Who cracked up my car? Who was driving?* □ *The accident cracked him up a little.* □ *She cracked herself up pretty badly in the accident.*

crack someone up to make someone laugh very hard; to make someone break out laughing. (Informal or slang.) □ *You and your jokes really crack me up.* 🅃 *She really knows how to crack up an audience.*

crack up 1. to have a crash; to have a wreck. □ *The car ran off the road and cracked up.* 🄽 *There is a serious crack-up on the expressway. Try to avoid it.* **2.** to break out laughing. □ *The audience cracked up at the actor's incompetence.* □ *We all cracked up at the silly situation the clown had gotten into.* **3.** to go crazy. (Slang. See also under *NUT ▸ UP.*) □ *Things were so hectic, I thought I was going to crack up.* □ *Some students actually crack up near the end of the semester.*

CRAM ▸ FOR

cram for something to study very hard for something. □ *I have to go cram for a test now.* □ *If you would study during the school term, you would not have to cram.*

CRAM ▸ IN(TO)

cram someone or something in(to something) to stuff or crush someone or something into something. (*Someone* includes *oneself.*) □ *Can you really cram seven kids into that car?* 🅃 *Then she crammed in one more.* □ *He crammed his clothes in and closed the drawer.* □ *She crammed herself into the tiny car and drove away.*

CRAM ▸ WITH

cram someone or something with someone or something to fill someone or something by stuffing with someone or something. (*Someone* includes *oneself.*) □ *You won't be happy till you cram all of us with cake and ice cream.* □ *They crammed the car with teenagers.* □ *He crammed his drawer with his socks.* □ *Tom crammed himself with doughnuts and coffee.*

CRANK ▸ OUT

crank something out to produce something rapidly and perhaps carelessly. (Slang.) □ *The factory really cranks those radios out.* 🅃 *This assembly line cranks out radios all day long.*

CRANK ▸ UP

crank someone or something up to get someone or something started. (As if winding up a mechanism or turning the crank of an early automobile. *Someone* includes *oneself.*) □ *Please crank the motor up, and let's go.* 🅃 *Crank up the motor, and let's go.* □ *See if you can crank your brother up and get him going on time today.* □ *Some mornings, I can't crank myself up enough to get to work on time.*

CRAP ▸ OUT

crap out to die. (Slang.) □ *Max almost crapped out from the beating he took.* □ *The dog just crapped out. What shall we do?*

crap out (of something) to lose on a roll of the dice in a dice game called craps and leave the game and the other players. □ *Wally crapped out of the game early in the evening.* □ *He crapped out early.*

crap out (of something) (on someone) 1. to withdraw from doing something with someone because of fear or cowardice. (Slang.) □ *Are you going to crap out of this game on me?* □ *Don't crap out on me!* □ *Please don't crap out of the game.* □ *Oh, he crapped out!* **2.** to quit doing something with someone or withdraw because of exhaustion. (Slang.) □ *Don't crap out of this on me! Pull yourself together!* □ *Don't crap out on me!* □ *Please don't crap out of this project.* □ *He crapped out again!*

CRASH ▶ AROUND

crash around to move around, knocking things over and making a lot of noise. □ *Stop crashing around. I'm trying to sleep.* □ *The people upstairs were crashing around and I couldn't get any sleep.*

CRASH ▶ DOWN

crash down (around someone or something) AND **crash down (about someone or something); crash in (on someone or something)** [for something] to collapse on someone or something. (Both literal and figurative uses.) □ *Her whole life crashed down around her.* □ *The walls crashed down around the people hiding in the room.* □ *Everything he was familiar with crashed down about him.* □ *Her life crashed in on her.* □ *The branches of the tree crashed down on the house.* □ *The old barn crashed down.*

CRASH ▶ INTO

crash into someone or something to bump or ram into someone or something. □ *The student crashed into the teacher.* □ *The car crashed into a bus.*

CRASH ▶ OUT

crash out (of some place) to break out of some place, such as a prison. □ *Max and Lefty crashed out of the state prison last week, but they were captured.* □ *They crashed out at midnight.*

CRASH ▶ THROUGH

crash through something to break through something. □ *The cows crashed right through the fence.* □ *Don't crash through the door. I'll open it as soon as I get it unlocked.*

CRASH ▶ TO

crash to something to fall down to something and make a crashing sound. □ *The tray of dishes crashed to the floor.* □ *Everything crashed to the floor and was broken.*

CRASH ▶ TOGETHER

crash something together to bring things together with great force, making a loud noise. □ *Fred crashed the cymbals together and the sound could have wakened the dead.* □ *Don't crash those pans together. It drives me crazy.*

crash together to ram or push together with great force. □ *The two cars crashed together, making a loud noise.* □ *The ships crashed together, opening a gaping hole in the side of one of them.*

CRASH ▶ WITH

crash with someone to spend the night at someone's place. (Slang.) □ *I don't need a hotel room. I can crash with Tom.* □ *There is no room for you to crash with me.*

CRAVE ▶ FOR

crave for something to desire something strongly. (Also without *for*, but not eligible as an entry.) □ *I really crave for some chocolate.* □ *What do you crave for?*

CRAWL ▶ ACROSS

crawl across something [for someone] to travel across something on hands and knees; [for an insect or something similar] to walk across something. □ *You will have to crawl across the open area to get to safety.* □ *The caterpillar crawled across the leaf and stopped for dinner at the end.*

CRAWL ▶ ALONG

crawl along something [for someone] to travel the length of something on hands and knees; [for an insect or something similar] to walk the length of something. □ *She crawled along the catwalk, fearing to look down.* □ *A beetle crawled along the pencil and fell off the end.*

CRAWL ▶ BACK

crawl back to someone to go back to someone humbly. □ *I knew you would come crawling back to me!* □ *I wouldn't crawl back to him for all the tea in China.*

CRAWL ▸ IN(TO)

crawl in(to something) **1.** to dress in some kind of clothing. □ *I crawled into my pants and threw on a shirt.* □ *He finally found his pants and crawled in.* **2.** to get into bed. □ *At about ten o'clock, she crawled into bed.* □ *She pulled back the covers and crawled in.* **3.** to creep into something. □ *The cat crawled into the room and meowed.* □ *The cat crawled in and tried to look innocent.*

CRAWL ▸ OUT

crawl out to get out by crawling. □ *The bears finally woke up and crawled out.* □ *In the cave, I injured my leg and I had to crawl out.*

crawl out from under someone or something **1.** to crawl from beneath someone or something. □ *A few people were able to crawl out from under the wreckage.* □ *Tom crawled out from under the other players after he was tackled with the football.* **2.** to get free of the control or domination of someone or something or from the demands of a responsibility. □ *I hope you are not trying to crawl out from under your responsibilities.* □ *I really want to crawl out from under the mess I'm in at work.*

crawl out of something to get out of something by crawling. □ *The injured man crawled out of the overturned car.* □ *Donna crawled out of the cave.*

CRAWL ▸ OVER

crawl over something to cross over something, by crawling. □ *We crawled over the pile of boxes.* □ *Timmy crawled over the carpet and stood up at the coffee table.*

CRAWL ▸ WITH

crawl with someone or something [for a place] to be thick with crawling creatures, in the manner of ants. (Idiomatic. Usually *crawling with.*) □ *The place was crawling with tourists.* □ *The picnic grounds were crawling with ants.*

CREASE ▸ UP

crease something up to get creases or folds into something that is supposed to be flat; to wrinkle one's clothing. (Also without *up*, but not eligible as an entry. The entry is parallel to *messed up.*) □ *You will crease your jacket up if you don't sit up straight.* 🅃 *I was sitting so long that I creased up my pants.*

CREDIT ▸ FOR

credit someone or something for something to give someone or something the praise deserved for doing something. □ *We must credit Sarah for her efforts on our behalf.* □ *We have to credit the storm for saving the crops.*

CREDIT ▸ TO

credit something to someone or something **1.** to give someone or something well-deserved praise. □ *The entire organization credited much praise to Jeff.* □ *We had to credit much of our success to the weather.* **2.** to record a sum owed to the account of someone or something. □ *I will credit this payment to your account.* □ *I am afraid that I accidentally credited your payment to George.*

CREDIT ▸ WITH

credit someone or something with something **1.** to give someone or something well-deserved praise for doing something or having something. (*Someone* includes *oneself.*) □ *We have to credit Jeff with saving us a lot of money.* □ *We will credit the weather with part of the success of the picnic.* □ *I can hardly credit myself with having made this event a success.* **2.** to record a payment made to the account of someone or something. (*Someone* includes *oneself.*) □ *I will credit you with this payment as you request.* □ *The boss told her to credit herself with another one hundred dollars.* □ *Your account has been credited with this payment.*

CREEP ▸ ACROSS

creep across something **1.** to travel across something slowly and carefully; to sneak across something. □ *The scouts crept slowly across the rope bridge.* □ *The cat crept across the floor, stalking some poor unseen creature.* **2.** [for light, fog, etc.] to move slowly across a place or an area. □ *A heavy fog crept across the coastal areas.* □ *The spotlight crept across the stage from one* *side to the other, as if looking for the performer.*

CREEP ▸ ALONG

creep along something to travel along something slowly and carefully; to sneak along something. □ *Creep along the side of the building until you reach the door.* □ *The cat crept along the kitchen counter, just demanding to be scolded.*

CREEP ▸ AWAY

creep away to travel away slowly and carefully; to sneak away. □ *The boys were completely ashamed and crept away.* □ *The cat crept away quietly.*

CREEP ▸ BY

creep by [for time] to pass slowly. □ *The minutes crept by as I awaited Mrs. Barron's telephone call.* □ *I know the days will creep by until we finally move into the new house.*

CREEP ▸ INTO

creep into something to go into something or a place slowly and carefully; to sneak into something or a place. □ *The cat crept into the bedroom.* □ *Max planned to creep into Aunt Em's house and take her silverware.*

CREEP ▸ OUT

creep out from under something to move from beneath something slowly and carefully; to sneak from beneath something. □ *The mouse crept out from under the chair and just sat there.* □ *What rock did you creep out from under?*

creep out of something to go out of something or a place slowly and carefully; to sneak out of something or a place. □ *A little mouse crept out of the cupboard.* □ *The fox crept out of the henhouse, carrying a chicken.*

CREEP ▸ OVER

creep over someone or something **1.** to move carefully or slowly over someone or something. □ *The shadows crept over the picnic and made everyone realize what time it was.* □ *Dusk crept over us.* **2.** [for something, such as an insect] to walk or crawl over someone or something. □ *A huge ant crept over me, and I just lay there.* □ *A beetle crept over the cabbage leaf.*

CREEP ▸ UNDER

creep under something to move slowly and carefully underneath something; to sneak underneath something. □ *The dog crept under the table to escape punishment.* □ *The chipmunk crept under a pile of leaves and watched what we were doing.*

CREEP ▸ UP

creep up to move gradually and slowly upward. □ *We could see them creeping up in the dim light of dawn.* □ *Dusk crept up and swallowed us in darkness.*

creep up on someone or something to sneak up on someone or something. □ *Please don't creep up on me like that. You scared me to death.* □ *The cat crept up on the mouse.*

CRIB ▸ FROM

crib something from someone or something to cheat by copying something from someone or something. □ *Did you crib this essay from Jennifer?* □ *It appears that you cribbed this directly from the textbook.*

CRINGE ▸ AWAY

cringe away from someone or something to pull back or away from someone or something. □ *The child cringed away from the teacher.* □ *Why did you cringe away from the dentist chair?*

CRINGE ▸ BACK

cringe back (from someone or something) to draw away from someone or something in avoidance. □ *The cat cringed back from the fire.* □ *The child cringed back from the huge dog.* □ *Seeing the fire, the cat cringed back.*

CRINGE ▸ BEFORE

cringe before someone or something to cower or recoil in the presence of someone or something. □ *Jeff cringed before the wrath of the policeman.* □ *He cringed before the altar.*

CRINGE ▸ FROM

cringe from something to shrink back from something threatening. □ *The child cringed from the teacher's angry* *glare.* □ *The poor old dog cringed from the shouts of its angry master.*

CRINKLE ▸ UP

crinkle up to wrinkle up. □ *Her nose crinkled up when she laughed.* [A] *Put all the crinkled-up cellophane in the box.*

CRITICIZE ▸ FOR

criticize someone for something to reprimand or censure someone for something. □ *I hope you don't criticize me too severely for my part in this matter.* □ *Maria criticized Ken for not being there on time.*

CROCK ▸ UP

crock someone or something up to damage or harm someone or something. (Slang.) □ *I really crocked my car up last night.* [T] *I crocked up my car.* □ *The accident crocked me up a bit.* [A] *I don't want your old crocked-up car parked around here!*

CROP ▸ OUT

crop out to appear on the surface; [for something] to reveal itself in the open; to begin to show above the surface. □ *A layer of rock cropped out at the edges of the desert.* □ *A little anger began to crop out.* [N] *An outcrop of sandstone was visible near the riverbank.*

crop someone or something out [for a photographer] to cut or trim out someone or something from a photograph in the process of making the photograph smaller. □ *The photographer cropped Mr. Jones out of the picture.* [T] *This is a bad view. See if you can crop out the ugly fence at the side of the house.*

CROP ▸ UP

crop up to appear without warning; to happen suddenly; [for something] to begin to reveal itself in the open. □ *A new crisis has cropped up.* □ *Some new problems cropped up at the last minute.*

CROSS ▸ FROM

cross from some place to some place to move across something from one point to another. □ *We crossed from one side of the hall to the other, looking for a seat.* □ *I have to cross from Illinois to Missouri over a rickety old bridge.*

CROSS ▸ OFF

cross someone or something off ((of) something) to eliminate someone's name from a list or record. (*Someone* includes *oneself*. The *of* is colloquial.) □ *We will have to cross her off our list.* [T] *We crossed off Sarah.* □ *I crossed the sweater off of the list and gave it away.* □ *Looking at the length of the list, Alice was willing to cross herself off.*

CROSS ▸ OUT

cross someone or something out to draw a line through the name of someone or something on a list or record. (*Someone* includes *oneself*.) □ *You can cross me out. I'm not going.* [T] *Please cross out Sarah.* □ *I crossed the sweater out. It was an error.* □ *Alice crossed herself out without any argument.*

CROSS ▸ OVER

cross over 1. to cross something such as a river or a street. □ *This is a very wide river. Where do we cross over?* □ *Let's cross over here where it's shallow.* **2.** to change sides, from one to another. □ *Some players from the other team crossed over and joined ours after the tournament.* [N] *The spy made a secret crossover and fooled everyone.* **3.** to die. (Folksy and euphemistic.) □ *Uncle Herman crossed over long before Aunt Pearl.* □ *He said he was ready to cross over.*

cross over into some place to go from one country into another, by crossing a border, river, mountain range, etc. □ *The refugees crossed over into Switzerland.* □ *We crossed over into Missouri at dawn.*

cross over something to go some place by crossing a border, river, mountain range, etc. □ *Do we want to cross over the river at this point?* □ *How do we cross over the highway?*

CROSS ▸ UP

cross someone up to spoil someone's plans. □ *You had better not cross me up again!* [T] *I hear that you crossed up Sarah.*

CROSS ▸ WITH

cross something with something **1.** to go across something, using a particular type of vehicle. □ *The explorers crossed the river with their Jeep.* □ *We can't cross this stream with the canoes. It's too fast.* **2.** to interbreed something with something else. □ *I crossed this smaller chicken with the stronger one.* □ *It is possible to cross a horse with a donkey.*

cross swords with someone to become the adversary of someone. □ *I sure don't want to cross swords with Ellen.* □ *Gloria was looking forward to crossing swords with Sally.*

CROUCH ▸ AROUND

crouch around [for people or other creatures] to stoop or squat within an area. □ *Everyone crouched around, hoping the bomb would fall somewhere else.* □ *The baboons crouched around, grooming one another.*

CROUCH ▸ DOWN

crouch down to stoop or huddle down. □ *Crouch down here, next to me.* □ *Suddenly, Tex crouched down and reached for his pistol.*

CROW ▸ ABOUT

crow about something AND **crow over something** **1.** [for a rooster] to cry out or squawk about something. □ *The rooster was crowing about something—you never know what.* □ *The rooster was crowing over some issue that was important only to itself.* **2.** [for someone] to brag about something. □ *Stop crowing about your successes!* □ *She is crowing over her new life.*

CROW ▸ OVER

crow over someone or something See *crow about something.*

CROWD ▸ AROUND

crowd around someone or something to flock or swarm around someone or something. □ *The children crowded around the department store Santa, eager for their chance at talking to him.* □ *Everyone crowded around the radio to listen.*

CROWD ▸ IN

See also under *CROWD ▸ IN(TO).*

crowd in (on someone or something) to press or crush around someone or something. □ *Please don't crowd in on the guest of honor.* □ *Can you keep them back from me? I don't like it when they crowd in.* □ *The people crowded in on us and frightened us a little bit.* □ *Don't crowd in on the display case. It is an antique.*

CROWD ▸ IN(TO)

crowd in(to some place) to push or squeeze into some place. □ *Please don't try to crowd into this place.* □ *Too many people are trying to crowd in.*

crowd someone or something in(to something) to push or squeeze someone or something into a place or a container. (*Someone* includes *oneself.*) □ *They tried to crowd a dozen people into that tiny room.* 🅃 *Then they crowded in one more.* □ *Don't try to crowd too many in.* □ *They all tried to crowd themselves into the same room.*

CROWD ▸ OUT

crowd someone or something out (of something) to push or force someone or another creature out of something. (The *of*-phrase is paraphrased with a *from*-phrase when the particle is transposed. See the 🄵 example.) □ *Don't crowd your brother out of line!* 🅃 *Don't crowd out my favorite plants with all your rosebushes!* 🄵 *Don't crowd out anybody from this place!* □ *I don't want to crowd anything else out.*

CROWD ▸ THROUGH

crowd through (something) [for a number of people] to push through something. □ *The little group of revelers crowded through the door.* □ *They all tried to crowd through.*

CROWD ▸ TOGETHER

crowd someone or something together to push or squeeze people or things together. (*Someone* includes *oneself.*) □ *See if you can crowd them together and get more in the row.* □ *I am afraid that I crowded the plants together too much.*

☐ *Look at how they crowd themselves together.*

crowd together to pack tightly together. ☐ *The tenants crowded together in the lobby.* ☐ *All the kittens crowded together to keep warm.*

CROWD ▸ WITH

crowd something with someone or something to pack too many people or things into something. ☐ *The ushers crowded the room with visitors.* ☐ *Aunt Victoria had crowded the room with the busy trappings of a bygone era.*

CROWN ▸ WITH

crown someone with something **1.** to place a crown made of something on someone's head. ☐ *They crowned the prince with the heavily jeweled royal crown.* ☐ *The queen was crowned with the coronation crown.* **2.** to strike someone on the head with something. (Slang. *Someone* includes *oneself.*) ☐ *She crowned him with a skillet.* ☐ *Roger crowned Sam with a bottle.* ☐ *The carpenter crowned himself with a board he knocked loose.*

crown something with something to place something on the very top of something. ☐ *She crowned the stack of pork chops with a cooked apple.* ☐ *The chef crowned the cake with swags of golden icing.*

CRUISE ▸ AROUND

cruise around in something to drive or ride around in something. ☐ *Would you like to cruise around in a car like that?* ☐ *They really liked cruising around in the motorboat.*

CRUMB ▸ UP

crumb something up to mess something up; to make something crummy. (Slang.) ☐ *Who crumbed my room up?* 🅃 *Who crumbed up my room?*

CRUMBLE ▸ AWAY

crumble away to break away in little pieces. ☐ *The cathedral was crumbling away because of the acidic rain.* ☐ *One of my teeth is just crumbling away.*

CRUMBLE ▸ INTO

crumble into something to break apart and fall down into bits and pieces. ☐ *The base of the pillar suddenly crumbled into dust.* ☐ *The bones of the mummy crumbled into dust as the body was lifted from the box.*

crumble something (up) (into something) to crunch up or break up something into pieces. ☐ *Now, crumble the dried bread up into crumbs.* 🅃 *Crumble up the bread into crumbs.* ☐ *Ed crumbled the soil up to make planting easier.*

CRUMBLE ▸ UP

See the previous entry.

crumble up to break up into little pieces. ☐ *The cake, which was very dry, crumbled up when I tried to cut it.* ☐ *The ancient newspaper crumbled up when I turned the page.*

CRUMPLE ▸ UP

crumple someone or something up to fold up or crush someone or something. ☐ *Walter crumpled the paper up.* 🅃 *He crumpled up the paper.* ☐ *The accident crumpled the poor dog up, but it recovered.*

crumple up to fold up; to shrivel up. ☐ *She was so frightened that she just crumpled up.* ☐ *Fran crumpled up in a dead faint.*

CRUNCH ▸ DOWN

crunch something down to press or crush something down, breaking it with a crunching noise. ☐ *Sally crunched the flowerpot down, breaking it.* 🅃 *She crunched down the vase accidentally.*

CRUNCH ▸ UP

crunch someone or something up to break someone or something up into pieces. (Also without *up,* but not eligible as an entry.) ☐ *That machine will crunch you up. Stay away from it!* 🅃 *A number of blows with the hammer crunched up the rocks into pebbles.* ☐ *Try to crunch the larger chunks up.*

CRUSADE ▸ AGAINST

crusade against someone or something to campaign or demonstrate against someone or something. ☐ *You are al-*

ways crusading against one cause or another. □ *Ed started crusading against Eric and the latter threatened suit.*

CRUSADE ▸ FOR

crusade for someone or something to campaign or demonstrate for someone or something. □ *I can hardly crusade for the defeat of a friend.* □ *Ed went on a crusade for Eric, hoping to get him elected.*

CRUSH ▸ AGAINST

crush (up) against someone or something to press hard against someone or something. □ *The crowd crushed up against the people standing in line.* □ *The eager theatergoers crushed against the lobby doors.*

CRUSH ▸ DOWN

crush someone or something down 1. to press or force someone or something down. (Also without *down*, but not eligible as an entry.) □ *Crush the leaves down so you can put more into the basket.* 🅃 *Crush down the leaves and fill the basket higher.* □ *The weight of the stone crushed Giles Corey down.* 🄰 *Just pull out all the crushed-down seedlings.* **2.** to suppress someone or something. (Colloquial with *down;* standard without *down.*) □ *The dictator crushed the opposition down ruthlessly.* 🅃 *He crushed down this revolt.* □ *The army crushed the peasants down ruthlessly.*

CRUSH ▸ IN

crush something in to force something inward; to break something in. □ *The beam nearly crushed Jason's head in.* 🅃 *He tried to crush in the door.*

CRUSH ▸ (IN)TO

crush something (in)to something to grind or break something into bits and pieces. □ *He crushed the fennel seeds into a powder.* □ *The roller crushes the rocks to bits.*

CRUSH ▸ OUT

crush something out to put out a fire or flame by crushing. □ *She crushed her cigarette out and put the butt into the sink.* 🅃 *Please crush out your cigarette.*

crush something out of someone or something to press or squeeze something from someone or something. □ *He crushed the juice out of the grapes.* □ *He thought that the weight of the lumber would crush the life out of him.*

CRUSH ▸ TO

See also under *CRUSH ▸ (IN)TO.*

crush someone or something to something to press or squeeze someone or something into a particular state, such as death, a pulp, nothing, etc. □ *The anaconda crushed the tapir to death.* □ *Donna crushed the bananas to a pulp and put them into the cake batter.*

CRUSH ▸ UP

crush something up to reduce the mass of something by crushing. □ *Crush this up and put it in the sauce.* 🅃 *Crush up a clove of garlic and put it in the sauce.*

crush something up (into something) 1. to press something with great force until it is reduced to something smaller. □ *The chef crushed the almonds up into a powder and sprinkled them on the dessert.* 🅃 *Please crush up the almonds into a powder.* □ *I will crush them up.* **2.** to break something up into small pieces. □ *The machine crushed the glass up into chunks and sent them on to be recycled.* 🅃 *It crushed up all the glass into tiny bits.* □ *The machine crushed it up.*

crush (up) against someone or something See under *CRUSH ▸ AGAINST.*

CRY ▸ FOR

cry for someone or something 1. to weep for the absence or loss of someone or something. □ *No need to cry for me. Take care of yourself.* □ *She cried for her lost cat.* **2.** to shout a demand for someone or something. □ *She cried for help, but no one heard her.* □ *Tony cried for Walter, but he did not hear.* **3.** to cry or bawl, signaling the need or want for someone or something. (As done by a baby.) □ *The baby cried for a bottle.* □ *Little Jimmy was crying for his mother.*

CRY ▸ OUT

cry one's eyes out to cry very hard. (Figurative.) □ *She was so sad. I thought she would cry her eyes out.* □ *I almost cried my eyes out.*

cry out against someone or something to shout in anger against someone or something. □ *The crowd cried out against the police.* □ *She cried out against Eric, who had insulted her grossly.*

cry out for someone or something **1.** to shout praise or encouragement for someone or something. □ *Everyone in the street cried out for the mayor to make an appearance.* 🄽 *Their outcry could be heard throughout the building.* **2.** to shout out demands for someone or something. □ *The children cried out for ice cream.* □ *The mob was crying out for Roger, whom they saw as the villain in the whole affair.*

cry out (in something) to scream or shout in pain, joy, anger, etc. □ *The child cried out in pain.* □ *On seeing his father, the overjoyed little boy cried out.* 🄽 *The audience made a joyous outcry when the star appeared.*

cry (something) out (to someone or something) to yell something to someone or some creature. □ *She cried a warning out to the others.* 🅃 *Sally cried out a warning to the people behind her.* □ *The trainer cried a command out to the runaway horse.*

CRY ▸ OVER

cry over someone or something to weep because of someone or something. (See also the following entry.) □ *There's no need to cry over it. Things will work out.* □ *She is still crying over her lost love.*

cry over spilled milk **1.** [for a child] to cry because of spilled milk. (Almost always negative. In this case, the phrase is used to comfort the child.) □ *Now, don't cry over spilled milk.* □ *There is no need to cry over spilled milk.* **2.** to be unhappy about what cannot be undone. (Figurative.) □ *He is always crying over spilled milk. He cannot accept reality.* □ *It can't be helped. Don't cry over spilled milk.*

CRY ▸ TO

cry oneself to sleep to weep until sleep overtakes one. □ *The baby cried herself to sleep.* □ *The baby finally cried herself to sleep.*

CUDDLE ▸ UP

cuddle up (to someone or something) to nestle or snuggle close to someone or something to get warm or to be intimate. □ *She cuddled up to him and went to sleep.* □ *Let's cuddle up to the warm wall, near the fireplace.*

cuddle up (with someone) to snuggle close to someone. □ *Tommy cuddled up with his mother.* □ *Let's cuddle up and get warm.* □ *They cuddled up with each other.*

cuddle up (with something) to snuggle into a chair or bed with a book. □ *I want to go home and cuddle up with a good book.* □ *I need a book so I can go home and cuddle up.*

CUE ▸ IN

cue someone in to give a signal or cue to someone at the right time, usually in a performance of some kind. □ *Be sure to cue me in when you want me to talk.* 🅃 *Cue in the lighting technician at the right time.*

CULL ▸ FROM

cull someone or something (out) (from something) AND **cull someone or something out (of something)** to eliminate someone or something from a group. □ *We will cull the older pigeons out from the flock.* 🅃 *They culled out the slower runners from the team.* □ *The coach culled the slower runners from the team.* □ *They culled them out.* □ *We culled the bad pigeons out of the flock.*

CULL ▸ OUT

See the previous entry.

CULMINATE ▸ IN

culminate in something to climax in something; to end with something. □ *The contest culminated in a victory for the best band.* □ *The play-offs culminated in a big win for the Chicago team.*

CUP ▸ TOGETHER

cup something together to put one's cupped hands together. □ *He cupped his hands together and scooped up the water.* □ *You have to cup your hands together if you want a drink.*

CURE ▸ OF

cure someone of something to rid someone of a disease, ailment, bad habit, or obsession. (*Someone* includes *oneself.*) □ *I hope that cures you of asking too many questions.* □ *Will you please try to cure yourself of your constant interrupting?*

cure something of something to eliminate the cause of a malfunction in a machine or a device. □ *I think I have cured the stapler of jamming all the time.* □ *I can't seem to cure the committee of procrastination.*

CURL ▸ UP

curl something up to roll something up into a coil. □ *She curled the edges of the paper up while she spoke.* 🅃 *Why did she curl up the paper?* 🄰 *Put the curled-up papers under some books, so they will flatten out.*

curl up and die to withdraw and die. (Figurative.) □ *I was so embarrassed, I just wanted to curl up and die.* □ *Poor Alice almost curled up and died.*

curl up (in(to) something) **1.** to roll into a coil. □ *The snake curled up into a neat coil.* □ *It curled up so we couldn't get at it.* 🄰 *The curled-up snake suddenly came to life.* **2.** to roll into a coil in a resting place, such as a chair or a bed. □ *Colleen curled up in the chair and took a nap.* □ *She curled up and took a nap.*

curl up with someone or something to snuggle up to someone or something. □ *She curled up with her husband and fell asleep.* □ *Elaine curled up with the family dog to keep warm.*

CURRY ▸ WITH

curry favor with someone to beg for favor from someone; to flatter and cater to someone. □ *She is always trying to curry favor with the teacher.* □ *Don't try to curry favor with me.*

CURSE ▸ AT

curse at someone or something to *swear at someone or something;* to cast curse words or curses at someone or something. □ *He cursed at the jammed toaster and pounded his fist on the counter in anger.* □ *Please don't curse at me.*

CURSE ▸ FOR

curse someone for something to damn someone for doing something; to invoke evil upon someone for doing something. (*Someone* includes *oneself.*) □ *She cursed her mother for ever having borne her.* □ *Over and over, she cursed herself for ever having come there.*

CURSE ▸ WITH

curse someone or something with something **1.** to damn someone or something with something, especially a verbal curse. □ *She cursed him with the fervent wish that he rot in hell.* □ *She cursed the day he was born with an unprintable oath.* **2.** to afflict or oppress someone or something with something. □ *His upbringing cursed him with a strong sense of guilt.* □ *The incident cursed the town with a dismal reputation for years.*

CURTAIN ▸ OFF

curtain something off to separate something or some place with a drape, screen, or curtain. □ *We will curtain this part of the room off and you can sleep there.* 🅃 *We will curtain off part of the room.* 🄰 *Please stay out of the curtained-off area.*

CURTSY ▸ TO

curtsy to someone [for a woman] to dip or bow in deference to someone. (The mate of to *bow.*) □ *Of course, I curtsied to the queen! Do you think I'm an anarchist?* □ *The little girls curtsied after they did their dance number.*

CURVE ▸ TO

curve to something to bend or bow toward something, some direction, or some place. □ *The road curved to the left.* □ *One of her toes curves to the right.*

CUSS ▶ OUT

cuss someone out to scold someone severely. (Folksy.) ☐ *Stop cussing me out! I didn't do anything wrong.* 🅃 *Don't cuss out the guests!*

CUT ▶ ACROSS

cut across (something) to travel across a particular area; to take a shortcut across a particular area. ☐ *Please don't cut across the neighbor's yard anymore.* ☐ *Walk around; don't cut across.*

CUT ▶ ALONG

cut along something to make a cut following a line or guide. ☐ *Please cut along the dotted line.* ☐ *My hand is too shaky to cut along the line neatly.*

CUT ▶ AROUND

cut around something to move rapidly around something, such as a corner, pole, beam, etc. ☐ *The cat cut around a corner and escaped from the dog.* ☐ *The speeding car cut around the light pole and almost hit it.*

CUT ▶ AT

cut at someone or something **1.** to thrust a knife or something similar at someone or some creature. ☐ *The hoodlum cut at me, but I dodged the blade.* ☐ *He cut at the dog, but it had no effect on the vicious animal.* **2.** to cut slowly and laboriously on someone or something. ☐ *He cut at the chair leg carefully, trying not to remove too much.* ☐ *The doctor cut at the ligaments, removing the diseased parts carefully.*

CUT ▶ AWAY

cut something away (from something) to separate something from something by cutting. ☐ *The doctor cut the wart away from the patient's foot.* 🅃 *She cut away the wart.* ☐ *Eric cut the bushes away from the front door.* ☐ *He cut the old surface roots away so no one would trip.*

CUT ▶ BACK

cut back (on something) to reduce the use, amount, or cost of something. ☐ *You are all going to have to cut back on water usage.* ☐ *You simply must cut back.* 🄽 *We are going to have to introduce a number of budgetary cutbacks.*

cut back to someone or something [for a film or television camera] to return to a picture of someone or something. ☐ *Suddenly, the camera cut back to the actor, who—unprepared—just stood there.* ☐ *The scene cut back to the veranda overlooking the bay.*

cut something back to prune plants; to reduce the size of plants, bushes, etc. ☐ *Let's cut these bushes back. They're getting in the way.* 🅃 *Don't cut back my roses!* ☐ *They have been cut back already.*

CUT ▶ DOWN

cut down (on something) to reduce the amount of something or of doing something; to use or buy less of something. ☐ *You will have to cut down on your use of water.* ☐ *They told us to cut down.* ☐ *The doctor told him to cut down on his drinking.* ☐ *It was hard for him to cut down.*

cut someone down to kill someone with a weapon, such as a sword, or with gunfire, etc. ☐ *The bandits cut the bystanders down and fled.* 🅃 *The gunman cut down an innocent pedestrian.*

cut someone down to size to make someone more humble. ☐ *I am going to cut that kid down to size once and for all.* ☐ *Max needs to be cut down to size.*

cut something down **1.** to chop something down; to saw or cut at something until it is felled. ☐ *Stop cutting the trees down!* 🅃 *Don't cut down that tree!* 🄰 *The cut-down trees were burned and wasted.* **2.** to destroy someone's argument; to destroy someone's position or standing. ☐ *The lawyer cut the testimony down quickly.* 🅃 *The lawyer cut down the witness's story.* **3.** to reduce the price of something. (Also without *down*, but not eligible as an entry.) ☐ *They cut the prices down to sell the goods off quickly.* 🅃 *I wish they would cut down the prices in this store.*

cut something down to something to reduce something to a manageable size. ☐ *We cut the program down to size and it was very enjoyable.* ☐ *It was better when we cut it down to a manageable* *size.* 🅃 *We cut down the program to a half hour.*

CUT ▸ FROM

cut (oneself) loose from someone or something to get out from under the domination of someone or something. □ *At last, she cut herself loose from her mother.* □ *She had to cut loose from home.* □ *Everyone wished that Todd would cut himself loose from his mother.*

cut someone or something loose from something to sever the connection between people or things, in any combination. □ *Wally cut the child loose from the tree where his playmates had tied him up.* □ *I cut the cord loose from the anchor by mistake.*

cut something from something to remove something from something by cutting. □ *She carefully cut the blossoms from the bush.* □ *A few blossoms were cut from the bush.*

CUT ▸ IN

cut in ahead of someone or something to move quickly and carelessly into line ahead of someone, as in a line of people or in traffic. □ *A red car cut in ahead of me and nearly caused me to run off the road.* □ *Careful! Don't cut in ahead of that car!*

cut in (on someone) **1.** [for someone] to ask to replace one member of a dancing couple. □ *Excuse me, may I cut in?* □ *Please don't cut in.* **2.** [for someone] to interrupt someone who is talking. □ *While Gloria was telling us her story, Tom kept cutting in on her.* □ *I'm talking. Please don't cut in!*

cut in (on something) **1.** to interrupt something, especially some sort of electronic transmission. □ *I didn't mean to cut in on your announcement.* □ *Who cut in on my telephone call?* **2.** to join in something even when not invited. □ *Can I cut in on this little party?* □ *Yes, do cut in.*

cut in (with something) to interrupt [someone] with a comment; to speak abruptly, interrupting what someone else is saying. □ *Jimmy cut in with a particularly witty remark.* □ *Must you always cut in while others are talking?*

cut someone in (on something) to permit someone to participate in something; to share something with someone. (Slang. *Someone* includes *oneself.*) □ *We don't want to have to cut her in on the money.* □ *Can you cut me in?* □ *What makes you think you can cut yourself in on our deal?*

CUT ▸ INTO

cut something into something to slice or chop something into very small pieces, bits, etc. □ *We cut the meat into one-inch cubes for the stew.* □ *Eric cut the ribbon into two-foot lengths.*

CUT ▸ IN(TO)

cut in(to something) to slice something; to gouge something. □ *We sliced into the watermelon and found it to be spoiled.* □ *It was a beautiful apple, but when she cut in, she found out that she had been cheated.*

cut something in(to something) to mix something into something else. (Colloquial.) □ *Carefully cut the butter into the flour mixture.* 🅃 *Now, cut in some more butter.* □ *Cut some more butter in.*

CUT ▸ OFF

cut off to turn off of a road, path, highway, etc. □ *This is the place where you are supposed to cut off.* 🄽 *When you come to a cutoff on the left, continue on for about mile.*

cut one's nose off to spite one's face to do something spiteful [against someone or something] and end up harming oneself. (Figurative.) □ *Don't cut your nose off to spite your face. Admit that you were wrong!* 🅃 *She has a tendency to cut off her nose to spite her face.*

cut someone off at the pass to thwart someone's efforts; to impede someone's plan or efforts. (Slang.) □ *They are ahead now, but we'll cut them off at the pass.* 🅃 *Try to cut off the bandits at the pass!*

cut someone off (short) to interrupt someone; to prevent someone from continuing to speak. (See also *chop some-*

one off.) ☐ *In the middle of her sentence, the teacher cut her off short.* ☐ *Please don't cut me off like that.*

cut someone or something off from something to isolate someone or something from some place or something. ☐ *They cut the cattle off from the wheat field.* ☐ *The road construction cut Jane off from her office.* 🅃 *The tanks cut off the troops from their camp.*

cut someone's water off to squelch someone; to thwart someone. (Slang.) ☐ *Well, I guess that cuts your water off!* 🅃 *It sure cuts off my water.*

cut something off **1.** to shorten something. ☐ *Cut this board off a bit, would you?* 🅃 *Cut off this board a little, please.* **2.** to turn something off, such as power, electricity, water, the engine, etc. ☐ *Would you please cut that engine off?* 🅃 *Cut off the engine, Chuck.* 🄽 *What time is the electricity cutoff? I want to have some candles ready.*

cut something off to shorten something by cutting away part of it. ☐ *Please cut these jeans off for me.* ☐ *I would be happy to cut off the jeans.* 🄽 *She always wears cutoffs in the summer.*

CUT ▸ ON

cut one's eyeteeth on something to grow up experiencing something; to have had the experience of dealing with something [successfully] at a very early age. (Idiomatic.) ☐ *Of course, I like fishing. I cut my eyeteeth on fishing.* ☐ *Fred cut his eyeteeth on writing detective novels.*

cut oneself on something to slice one's flesh with something accidentally. ☐ *Careful, you will cut yourself on that knife.* ☐ *Careful! Don't cut yourself on that broken glass.*

cut something on something **1.** to slice something on or against something, accidentally. ☐ *I cut my finger on the knife.* ☐ *Maria cut her foot on the broken glass.* **2.** to slice something that is lying on something else. ☐ *I cut the tomatoes on the cutting board your mother gave us.* ☐ *Fred cut the meat on the counter.*

CUT ▸ OUT

cut out to depart; to leave in a hurry. (Slang.) ☐ *Good-bye. I have to cut out.* ☐ *It's time I was cutting out. See you!*

cut out for some place to leave quickly for some place. (Colloquial.) ☐ *The kids all cut out for home.* ☐ *When they heard the dinner bell, the Wilson kids cut out for home.*

cut out for someone or something to run hurriedly toward someone or something. (Slang.) ☐ *At the last minute, he cut out for the gate, which was closing very fast.* ☐ *The child cut out for his mother, who had come to get him at school.*

cut out to be something [for someone] to be destined to be something or a particular type of person. ☐ *I don't think I was cut out to do this.* ☐ *We weren't cut out to be laborers.*

cut someone or something out to eliminate someone or something. ☐ *Now, cut that out!* ☐ *We have to cut Chuck out. There are too many better men on the team.*

cut something out to stop doing something. (Colloquial. Usually a command. Typically: **Cut that out!**) ☐ *Cut that noise out!* 🅃 *Cut out that noise!* ☐ *Now, cut that out!*

cut something out (of something) AND **cut something out (from something)** to cut a pattern or shape from cloth, paper, sheet metal, etc.; to remove something from something by cutting; to excise something from something. (When both *out* and *of* are used, no direct object can intervene.) ☐ *Sam cut a pig out from the paper.* ☐ *I cut the picture out of a magazine.* 🅃 *I cut out the shape of the moon from the paper.* ☐ *Cut the pictures out and pin them up.* ☐ *The doctor cut the tumor out.* 🅃 *She cut out the tumor.* 🄰 *The cutout pieces were stacked on the counter.* 🄽 *After you have finished making the cutouts, put them all in a box.*

cut the ground out from under someone to destroy one's foundation of operation; to thwart someone's efforts. (Colloquial.) ☐ *The clever move by the* *opposition party cut the ground out from under the prime minister.* 🅃 *The parliamentary move cut out the ground from under Scott.*

CUT ▸ THROUGH

cut through something **1.** to penetrate something by cutting; to slice through something. ☐ *The worker cut through the steel door with a torch.* ☐ *Walter cut through the rind of the watermelon.* **2.** to eliminate or neutralize something complicated, such as red tape, bureaucracy, difficulties, etc. (Figurative.) ☐ *I will try to cut through all the red tape for you.* ☐ *I am sure someone can help us cut through all this red tape.*

CUT ▸ TO

See also under *CUT ▸ (IN)TO.*

cut someone or something to something **1.** to chop or slice up someone or something, especially to bits or pieces. (*Someone* includes *oneself.*) ☐ *The chef cut the carrots to pieces.* ☐ *The lawn mower will cut you to bits if you get under it.* ☐ *Careful with that knife, or you'll cut yourself to pieces.* **2.** to destroy an argument; to destroy someone's argument. ☐ *The lawyer heard her argument and cut her to bits.* ☐ *She cut the argument to pieces.*

cut someone to the quick AND **cut someone to the bone** **1.** to injure someone severely emotionally. ☐ *Your heartless comments cut me to the quick.* ☐ *Her remarks cut him to the bone.* **2.** to slice the flesh of someone or some animal clear through to the bone. (*Someone* includes *oneself.*) ☐ *With the very sharp knife, David cut the beast to the quick in one blow.* ☐ *He cut his finger to the bone with the sharp knife.* ☐ *Todd cut himself to the quick with the machete.*

cut to someone or something to shift the radio, movie, or television audience's attention abruptly to someone or something new. ☐ *Suddenly, the engineer cut to the announcer.* ☐ *The technical director cut to a remote unit that was covering an accident.* ☐ *The camera cut to scenes of Atlanta burning.*

CUT ▸ UP

See *be cut up (about someone or something)* under *BE ▸ UP.*

cut someone or something up (into something) to slice or chop someone or something into smaller pieces. ☐ *Sam cut the carrots up into tiny cubes.* 🅃 *He cut up the carrots into long slender strips.* ☐ *The lawn mower will cut you up into hamburger if you are not careful!* 🄰 *Drop the cut-up meat into a hot skillet and brown it.*

cut someone up **1.** to gash or carve on someone by cutting. ☐ *The thugs cut him up badly, just for talking back.* 🅃 *They cut up their victim into pieces.* **2.** to cause someone severe emotional distress. (Slang.) ☐ *That rebuke really cut me up.* ☐ *Your criticism cut him up pretty badly.* 🅃 *The critic really cut up the performer.*

cut the pie up to divide something up. (Colloquial.) ☐ *It all depends on how you cut the pie up.* 🅃 *How should I cut up the pie?*

cut up to act silly; to have a carefree time. ☐ *Now, stop cutting up and get serious.* 🄽 *He's always joking. He's a real cutup.*

CUT ▸ WITH

cut loose with something to yell something out very loudly. (Folksy.) ☐ *Suddenly, the cowboy cut loose with a loud yell.* ☐ *Tex cut loose with a stream of curses that would make a tomato blush.*

cut someone or something with something to slice someone or something with something. (*Someone* includes *oneself.*) ☐ *Don't cut yourself with that knife.* ☐ *He cut the bread with a dull knife and ruined it.*

cut something with something to dilute something with something else. ☐ *They cut the liquor with cold water.* ☐ *Please cut this with some soda. It's too sweet, otherwise.*

D

DAB ▸ AT

dab at something to touch or pat something. ☐ *The painter dabbed at the canvas, making little changes here and there.* ☐ *Don't just dab at the wall, spread the paint on!*

DAB ▸ OFF

dab something off ((of) something) to pat or wipe something off something. (The *of* is colloquial.) ☐ *Please dab the butter off your chin.* 🅃 *Please dab off the butter.* ☐ *Dab the moisture off of them.* ☐ *Yes, dab it off.*

DAB ▸ ON

dab something on((to) something) to pat or paint carefully something onto something else. ☐ *Dab some medicine onto the scratch.* 🅃 *Dab on some medicine.* ☐ *Just dab some on.*

DABBLE ▸ AT

dabble at something to play at doing something; to do something halfheartedly. ☐ *Don't just dabble at history. Settle down and do it right.* ☐ *She dabbles at painting.*

DABBLE ▸ IN

dabble in something to be involved in something in a casual manner. ☐ *She dabbled in local politics for a while.* ☐ *I want to dabble in something new for a while.*

DALLY ▸ OVER

dally over something to waste time doing something. ☐ *Don't dally over your food. Eat your dinner.* ☐ *I wish you wouldn't dally over your food.*

DALLY ▸ WITH

dally with someone to flirt with someone; to waste time with someone of the opposite sex. ☐ *Sam is dallying with that Johnson girl again.* ☐ *Stop dallying with her and get back to your studies!* ☐ *You'll never get your work done if you keep dallying with Mary.*

DAM ▸ UP

dam something up to erect a barrier in a river, stream, brook, etc. ☐ *We are going to have to dam this stream up to make a pond for the cattle.* 🅃 *Let's dam up this stream.* ☐ *Why is this river dammed up?* 🄰 *We got our drinking water from a dammed-up stream.*

DAMN ▸ WITH

damn someone with something **1.** to curse someone with words. ☐ *She damned him with curse after curse.* ☐ *Maria damned Joe with the worst curses she could think of.* **2.** to denounce or defeat someone in a particular way. (*Someone* includes *oneself.*) ☐ *She damned him with her insincere words of praise.* ☐ *She damned herself with the evidence she had hoped would save her.*

DAMP ▸ DOWN

damp something down **1.** to make something damp. ☐ *Damp the clothes down before you iron them.* 🅃 *Please damp down the clothes first.* **2.** to reduce the intensity of a flame, usually by cutting down on the air supply, as with a damper. ☐ *Please damp the air supply down.* 🅃 *Damp down the air supply or you are going to end up with a raging inferno.*

DAMP ▶ OFF

damp off [for seedlings] to die from too much water. □ *All the new plants damped off, and we had to buy some from the nursery.* □ *The little seedlings damped off and were gone.*

DANCE ▶ AT

dance at something to celebrate in honor of someone at something, usually a wedding. (Figurative.) □ *I will dance at your wedding—if you invite me, of course.* □ *If you think I will dance at your wedding, you had better be nicer to me!*

DANCE ▶ ON

dance on air to be very happy; to be euphoric. (Figurative.) □ *I was so happy, I could have danced on air.* □ *She was just dancing on air, she was so happy.*

DANCE ▶ TO

dance to another tune to change one's manner; to reverse one's behavior, usually from cocky to contrite. (Figurative.) □ *When you realize what will happen to you if you continue to act this way, you will dance to another tune.* □ *You will be dancing to another tune when you hear what I have to say.*

dance to something to respond to music or rhythm with dancing. □ *I can't dance to that!* □ *That music is horrible. No one can dance to that.*

DANCE ▶ WITH

dance with someone to perform social dancing with another person. □ *Do you think you would like to dance with Wally?* □ *Would you please dance with me?*

DANGLE ▶ BEFORE

dangle something before someone AND **dangle something in front of someone** to lure someone with something. (Both literal and figurative uses.) □ *He dangled the bait before Wally, hoping to get him to agree to the meeting.* □ *He dangled the money in front of Eric, hoping to make him change his mind.*

DANGLE ▶ FROM

dangle from something to hang from something. □ *A number of colorful glass balls dangled from the branches of the tree.* □ *Some loose threads dangled from the bottom of his jacket.*

dangle something from something to hang something loosely from something else. □ *She dangled a few small bells from the bottom of her skirt during the holidays.* □ *I dangled a bit of fish from the window so I could see how high the cat would jump.*

DANGLE ▶ IN

dangle something in front of someone See under *DANGLE ▶ BEFORE.*

DART ▶ ABOUT

dart about to move about quickly. □ *The little fish were darting about everywhere.* □ *People were darting about, to and fro, during the noon rush hour.*

DART ▶ ACROSS

dart across something to run quickly over something. □ *A small animal darted across the road in front of the car.* □ *I tried to dart across the street, but the traffic was too heavy.*

DART ▶ AT

dart a glance at someone or something to shoot a quick look at someone or something. □ *She darted a glance at him and looked quickly away.* □ *He darted a glance at the door and looked even more uncomfortable.*

DART ▶ FROM

See the following entry.

DART ▶ OUT

dart out (of something) (at someone or something) AND **dart (out) (from something) (at someone or something)** to shoot quickly out of something toward someone or something. □ *The ferret darted out of its burrow at the children.* □ *The snake darted out at the frog.* □ *The mouse darted out of its hole.* □ *The snake darted out from its hole at the frog.* □ *Something darted out over there.* □ *The snake darted from its hole.*

DASH ▶ ACROSS

dash across something to run quickly across some area. □ *John dashed across the spaces between the houses and ran in* *the door.* ☐ *The dog dashed across the yard and confronted the meter reader.*

DASH ▶ AGAINST

dash someone or something against someone or something to throw or fling someone or something at or against someone or something. (*Someone* includes *oneself.*) ☐ *Sam dashed the bottle against the floor, shattering it.* ☐ *Alice dashed the box against Ed, throwing him off balance.* ☐ *Max dashed Lefty against Bruno.* ☐ *Henry dashed himself against the wall, hoping that the oncoming car would miss him.*

DASH ▶ AWAY

dash away to run away; to leave in a hurry. ☐ *I must dash away. See you tomorrow.* ☐ *Juan had to dash away.*

DASH ▶ OFF

dash off [for someone] to leave in a hurry. ☐ *I have to dash off. Good-bye.* ☐ *Ken dashed off and left me behind to deal with the angry customer.*

dash something off 1. to make or do something quickly. ☐ *I will dash this off now and try to take more time with the rest of them.* 🅃 *I will see if I can dash off a cherry pie before dinner.* **2.** to write a note or letter quickly and send it off. ☐ *I have to dash this note off, then I will be with you.* 🅃 *I'll dash off a note to her.*

DASH ▶ ON

dash cold water on something to be discouraging about something; to be pessimistic about something. (Figurative. Also literal uses.) ☐ *I hate to dash cold water on your plans, but I can't go to the opera on Thursday.* ☐ *He sure dashed cold water on the project.*

DASH ▶ OUT

dash out (for something) [for someone] to leave a place in a hurry to get something. ☐ *Harry dashed out for some cigarettes.* ☐ *Excuse me. I just have to dash out.*

DASH ▶ OVER

dash over (for something) [for someone] to come to one's dwelling quickly for something such as a brief visit. ☐ *I just dashed over for a cup of sugar. Can you spare it?* ☐ *I needed some sugar, so I just dashed over.*

DASH ▶ TO

dash something to something to break something into small pieces. ☐ *She dashed the glass to pieces on the floor—she was so mad.* ☐ *The potter dashed the imperfect pot to pieces.*

DATE ▶ BACK

date back (to someone or something) to have origins that extend back to the time of someone or something. ☐ *This part of the palace dates back to Catherine the Great.* ☐ *This is old! It really must date back.* ☐ *Carl had an old rifle that dates back to the Civil War.*

DATE ▶ FROM

date from something to have an existence that extends from a particular time. ☐ *This building dates from the beginning of the last century.* ☐ *These books date from the 1920s.*

DAUB ▶ ON

daub something on ((to) something) to smear or paint something onto something else. ☐ *The painter daubed a bit of yellow onto the canvas.* 🅃 *Daub on a bit of yellow here.* ☐ *She daubed the medicine on.*

DAUB ▶ WITH

daub something with something to smear or paint something with something sticky, such as paint, grease, makeup, etc. ☐ *The mechanic daubed the part with grease and put it back where it came from.* ☐ *The end of the chair leg was daubed with glue and set into place.*

DAWDLE ▶ ABOUT

dawdle about to waste time in a place; to waste time talking idly. ☐ *Don't dawdle about. Get moving.* ☐ *Tim has been dawdling about all morning.*

DAWDLE ▶ ALONG

dawdle along to move along slowly and casually. ☐ *The boys dawdled along on their way to school.* ☐ *We were just dawdling along, talking about life. We didn't know we were late.*

DAWDLE ▸ AWAY

dawdle something away to waste a particular amount of time; to let a period of time slip away, wasted. ☐ *You didn't finish your work because you dawdled most of your time away.* 🅃 *You dawdle away too much time.*

DAWDLE ▸ OVER

dawdle over something to waste time when one should be doing a particular task; to loaf while eating or drinking something. ☐ *Don't dawdle over your hamburger. The plane leaves in fifteen minutes.* ☐ *Don't dawdle over it. Get it done.*

DAWN ▸ (UP)ON

dawn (up)on someone [for a fact] to become apparent to someone; [for something] to be realized by someone. (*Upon* is formal and less commonly used than *on*.) ☐ *Then it dawned upon me that I was actually going to have the job.* ☐ *It never dawned on me that that might be the case.*

DAYDREAM ▸ ABOUT

daydream about someone or something to have fantasies about someone or something. ☐ *Poor Alice is always daydreaming about Albert.* ☐ *Albert is dreaming about running away to Tahiti.*

DEADEN ▸ WITH

deaden something with something to dull or anesthetize pain with something. ☐ *The doctor deadened the area with something before she began to stitch.* ☐ *I will deaden the pain with a local anesthetic.*

DEAL ▸ IN

deal in something to trade in something; to buy or sell something. ☐ *I don't deal in shoddy merchandise.* ☐ *Max deals in stolen goods and other contraband.*

DEAL ▸ IN(TO)

deal someone in(to something) **1.** to pass out cards to someone, making that person a player in a card game. ☐ *Can you deal me into this hand?* 🅃 *Deal in anyone who wants to play.* ☐ *Deal me in!* **2.** to permit someone to take part in something. (Informal.) ☐ *Let's deal him into this project.* 🅃 *Yes, deal in this guy.* ☐ *Should we deal her in?*

DEAL ▸ OUT

deal someone out (of something) **1.** to skip someone when dealing a hand of cards. ☐ *Please deal me out of the next hand. I have to go make a telephone call.* ☐ *They dealt her out because she would not pay attention to the game.* **2.** to remove someone from participation in something. (Informal. The *of*-phrase is paraphrased with a *from*-phrase when the particle is transposed. See the 🄵 example.) ☐ *They dealt me out at the last minute.* 🅃 *They dealt out Fred, too.* 🄵 *They dealt out Fred from the game, too.* ☐ *Wally dealt him out.*

deal something out to pass something out piece by piece, giving everyone equal shares. ☐ *The manager dealt the proposals out, giving each person an equal number to read.* 🅃 *I'll deal out some more proposals.*

DEAL ▸ WITH

deal with someone or something to manage someone or something. ☐ *This is not a big problem. I think I can deal with it.* ☐ *I am sure I can deal with Jill.*

DEBATE ▸ ABOUT

debate (with someone) (about something) See under *DEBATE ▸ WITH.*

DEBATE ▸ ON

debate on something to hold a long and disciplined discussion on a particular subject. (Also without *on,* but not eligible as an entry.) ☐ *We can debate on this all night if you think we will settle anything in the end.* ☐ *Are they still debating on the question?*

DEBATE ▸ OVER

debate over someone or something to discuss or argue about the disposition of someone or something. ☐ *We will debate over Tom and what to do about him tomorrow.* ☐ *I refuse to debate over this matter.* 🄰 *The much-debated-over matter was settled in court.*

DEBATE ▸ WITH

debate (with someone) (about something) **1.** to enter into a long and disciplined discussion on a particular subject with someone. □ *Our team debated with the other team about the chances for world peace.* □ *I debate with Randy in the next round.* □ *We will debate about health care.* **2.** to argue with someone about something. (*Someone* includes *oneself*.) □ *I do not intend to debate with you about that matter.* □ *I will not continue debating with you.* □ *Tom did not agree to debate about it.* □ *I debated with myself about going.*

DEBIT ▸ AGAINST

debit something against someone or something to record a charge for something against someone's account or against a particular category of an account. □ *I will have to debit this against your account.* □ *The clerk debited the charge against you.*

DEBIT ▸ TO

debit something to someone or something to make a charge for something to someone or something. □ *To whose account can we debit this charge?* □ *Let's debit it to Jane.*

DEBIT ▸ WITH

debit something with something to charge something for something. □ *They debited Fred's account with the whole bill.* □ *The bank debited my checking account with the cost of the new checks.*

DECEIVE ▸ INTO

deceive someone into something to trick someone into doing something. □ *She deceived me into giving her my car keys.* □ *You can't deceive me into doing what you want me to do.*

DECEIVE ▸ OUT

deceive someone out of something to get something from someone by trickery. □ *She deceived me out of a lot of money.* □ *Max tried to deceive me out of what was rightly mine.*

DECEIVE ▸ WITH

deceive someone with something to cheat someone with something or with deceptive words. (*Someone* includes *oneself*.) □ *You cannot deceive me with your fancy talk.* □ *You are just deceiving yourself with fancy talk.*

DECIDE ▸ AGAINST

decide against someone or something to rule against someone or something; to make a judgment against someone or something. □ *We decided against Tom and chose Larry instead.* □ *Jane decided against the supplier.*

DECIDE ▸ AMONG

decide among someone and someone else or something and something else to choose from three or more people; to choose from three or more things. □ *I couldn't decide among all the choices on the menu.* □ *I will decide among Fred, Tom, and Alice.*

DECIDE ▸ BETWEEN

decide between someone and someone else or something and something else to choose one from two people; to choose one from two things. □ *I could not decide between Tom and Wally.* □ *We could not decide between them.*

DECIDE ▸ FOR

decide for someone or something to rule in favor of someone or something; to make a judgment for someone or something. □ *The jury decided for the plaintiff.* □ *The judge decided for me.*

DECIDE ▸ IN

decide in favor of someone or something to make a decision to choose someone or something. □ *I hope you decide in favor of chocolate chip ice cream.* □ *We decided in favor of Andrew because he made the best case.*

DECIDE ▸ ON

See the following entry.

DECIDE ▸ (UP)ON

decide (up)on someone or something to choose someone or something; to make a judgment about some aspect of someone or something. (*Upon* is formal and less commonly used than *on*.) □ *Will you please hurry up and decide upon someone?* □ *I decided on chocolate.*

DECK ▸ OUT

deck someone or something out (in something) AND **deck someone or something out (with something)** to decorate someone or something with something. (*Someone* includes *oneself*.) □ *Sally decked all her children out for the holiday party.* 🅃 *She decked out her children in Halloween costumes.* □ *Tom decked the room out with garlands of flowers.* □ *He decked the hall out.* □ *She is all decked out for the party.* 🄰 *All the decked-out people of the town were walking to their various churches.* □ *She decked herself out in her finest clothes.*

DECK ▸ WITH

deck something with something to decorate something with something. (Especially in the carol "Deck the halls with boughs of holly.") □ *We put out some decorations, but we certainly were not going to deck the halls with a lot of stuff.* □ *Our living room is all decked with colorful paper ornaments for the holiday season.*

DECLARE ▸ AGAINST

declare oneself against someone or something to state one's opposition to someone or something publicly. □ *I must declare myself against the amendment.* □ *June declared herself against Karen.* □ *The politician declared himself against whatever the voters were already against.*

declare war against someone or something AND **declare war on someone or something** 1. to announce that one will fight a war with someone or some country. □ *A group of countries declared war against the aggressor.* □ *The general declared a personal war on the dictator.* 2. to announce a serious campaign against a type of person or a serious problem. □ *The president declared war against crime and criminals.* □ *The pressure group declared war on waste.*

DECLARE ▸ FOR

declare (oneself) for someone or something to state one's support of someone or something. □ *Susan declared herself for Mary's candidacy.* □ *I have not yet declared for any particular policy.* □ *Todd declared himself for the candidacy of Mary Brown for mayor.*

DECLARE ▸ ON

declare war on someone or something See *declare war against someone or something* under *DECLARE ▸ AGAINST.*

DECORATE ▸ FOR

decorate someone for something to award someone a medal or ribbon for doing something important or brave. □ *The town decorated her for her heroic act.* □ *She was decorated for her heroism.*

DECORATE ▸ WITH

decorate something with something to adorn or ornament something with something. □ *I will decorate the cake with roses made of sugar.* □ *Can I decorate your car with streamers for the parade?*

DEDICATE ▸ TO

dedicate someone or something to someone or something 1. to reserve someone or something for the use of someone or something. □ *The manager dedicated four members of the typing pool to the exclusive use of the legal department.* □ *The boss dedicated the expensive laser printer to the exclusive use of the new employee.* □ *The committee dedicated a corner in the library to books on agriculture.* 2. to pledge someone or something to someone, something, a deity, or religious purposes. (*Someone* includes *oneself*.) □ *The elders dedicated the building to the glory of God.* □ *The senators had dedicated the temple to Venus.* □ *He dedicated himself to the prosecution of justice.*

DEDUCE ▸ FROM

deduce something from something to infer or conclude something from a set of facts. □ *Can I deduce a bit of anger from your remarks?* □ *I deduce nothing from everything I have heard today.*

DEDUCT ▸ FROM

deduct something from something to subtract an amount from another amount. □ *Are you going to deduct this* *from your income taxes?* □ *Mr. Wilson deducted the discount from the bill.*

DEED ▸ OVER
See the following entry.

DEED ▸ TO
deed something (over) to someone to grant something, such as land, to someone; to transfer legal title to something to someone. □ *Grudgingly, he deeded the land over to Walter.* □ *He deeded the property to his niece.*

DEFACE ▸ WITH
deface something with something to mutilate or vandalize something with something. □ *Someone defaced the wall with spray paint.* □ *Please don't deface the facilities.*

DEFAULT ▸ ON
default on something to fail to act in some way regarding something, such as fail to make a payment, thereby losing right to the thing in question. □ *You are not going to default on your loan, are you?* □ *She defaulted on the last payment and lost the car.*

DEFECT ▸ FROM
defect from something to run away from something; to forsake something. □ *Thousands of soldiers defected from the army.* □ *Roger would never think of defecting from the armed services.*

DEFECT ▸ TO
defect to something to forsake one group and take up with another. □ *Will he defect to the other side?* □ *David defected to a small East European country.*

DEFEND ▸ AGAINST
defend someone or something against someone or something **1.** to advocate the cause of someone or something against someone or something else. (*Someone* includes *oneself*.) □ *The lawyer defended her against the plaintiff.* □ *She defended the company against the suit.* □ *They defended themselves against the charges.* **2.** to stand against an attack; to provide a defense against attack. (*Someone* includes *oneself*.) □ *Don't worry, I will defend you against any muggers.* □ *We defended ourselves against the attack.* □ *The army defended the town against the enemy soldiers.* □ *They defended themselves against the attacking army.*

DEFEND ▸ WITH
defend someone with something to repel danger from someone with something. (*Someone* includes *oneself*.) □ *Here, defend yourself with this club.* □ *Mary defended herself with karate.*

DEFER ▸ TO
defer to someone or something (on something) to yield to someone or something on some question or point. □ *I will defer to Mary on that question.* □ *She would not defer to the committee on anything.* □ *On this matter, I defer to you.*

DEFINE ▸ AS
define something as something to label something as being something. □ *I define that kind of behavior as just plain rude!* □ *We have to define that comment as careless and unthinking.*

DEFLECT ▸ AWAY
See the following entry.

DEFLECT ▸ FROM
deflect something (away) from someone or something to divert someone or something away from someone or something; to cause someone or something to veer away from someone or something. □ *The secretary deflected the reporter's questions from the candidate.* □ *He deflected the oncoming tackle from his pathway.* □ *Walter's car deflected the force of the crash.* □ *The shield deflected the spears away from the warrior.* □ *The special lenses deflected the harmful rays from the user's eyes.*

DEFRAUD ▸ OF
defraud someone (out) of something to cheat someone out of something. □ *The crooks defrauded the town out of a fortune.* □ *The clerk defrauded the employer of a great deal of money.*

DEFRAUD ▸ OUT
See the previous entry.

DEGENERATE ▸ INTO

degenerate into something to decay into something; to break down into something. □ *The rally degenerated into a riot.* □ *I was afraid that the party would degenerate into a rock concert.*

DEIGN ▸ TO

deign to do something to lower oneself to do something. □ *She will never deign to join in with us.* □ *I expect that he will not deign to have dinner with us.*

DELEGATE ▸ TO

delegate someone to something to appoint someone to something; to appoint someone to be something. □ *I will delegate Jane to be our representative.* □ *Donna was delegated to attend the conference.*

delegate something to someone to assign a task to someone; to appoint someone to do a specific task. □ *I will have to delegate this job to Sam, who knows how to do these things.* □ *The job was delegated to Sally.*

DELETE ▸ FROM

delete something from something to remove something from something; to cross something out from something. □ *Will you please delete this line from the contract?* □ *The line was deleted from the contract.*

DELIBERATE ▸ ABOUT

deliberate about someone or something to think about someone or something. □ *How long do you intend to deliberate about Carol?* □ *We will deliberate about this matter as long as it takes to do it right.*

DELIBERATE ▸ ON

deliberate on someone or something to consider what to do about someone or something; to weigh the alternatives concerning someone or something. □ *Let's deliberate on this for a while.* □ *Tomorrow we will deliberate on Karen and Sue.*

DELIBERATE ▸ OVER

deliberate over someone or something to discuss and argue about someone or something. □ *We will deliberate over this question tomorrow.* □ *We have been deliberating over Karen long enough.*

DELIGHT ▸ BY

delight someone by something (See also *delight someone with something.*) to please someone with something; to please someone by doing something. □ *You delighted me by your pleasant attitude.* □ *I was delighted by your proposal.*

DELIGHT ▸ IN

delight in someone or something to take great pleasure in someone or something. (Formal or stilted.) □ *I delight in your interest in my work.* □ *We all delight in James. What a fine boy!*

DELIGHT ▸ WITH

delight someone with something to please someone with something, such as a gift. □ *We delighted Alice with a gift of money.* □ *She was delighted with the gift.*

DELIVER ▸ FROM

deliver someone from someone or something to save or rescue someone from someone or something. □ *The hero delivered the children from a fiery death.* □ *Thank you for delivering me from a very boring meeting by calling me to the telephone.*

DELIVER ▸ OF

deliver someone of something to free someone from some burden or problem; to liberate someone from some confinement. (*Someone* includes *oneself.*) □ *He was looking for someone to deliver him of his burdensome responsibility.* □ *He was delivered of his burden.*

DELIVER ▸ OVER

deliver someone or something (over) (to someone or something) to transfer someone or something to someone or something; to yield over someone or something to someone or something. □ *When will you deliver the deed over to me?* 🅃 *I will deliver over the deed when I have your check.* □ *When will they deliver the hostages over to the commission?*

DELIVER ▸ TO
See the previous entry.

DELIVER ▸ UP
deliver something up (to someone) to render or yield something to someone. □ *Will you please deliver the documents up to Jane?* 🅃 *Will you please deliver up the documents to Jane?* □ *Would you deliver them up soon?*

DELUDE ▸ INTO
delude someone into something to fool someone into thinking something. (*Someone* includes *oneself.*) □ *You can't delude me into believing you.* □ *Todd deluded himself into believing he was back at home.*

DELUDE ▸ WITH
delude someone with something to fool or trick someone with something. (*Someone* includes *oneself.*) □ *She deluded us with her clever talk.* □ *Don't delude yourself with false hopes.*

DELUGE ▸ WITH
deluge someone or something with something to overwhelm someone or something with something; to "flood" someone or something with something. (Literal and figurative uses.) □ *The people on the dock deluged us with questions.* □ *The force of the waves deluged the town with water.*

DELVE ▸ INTO
delve into something to examine or study something carefully; to enter into the examination or study of something. □ *He delved into the solution of the problem facing him.* □ *I am just now delving into a study of the Trojan Wars.*

DEMAND ▸ FROM
demand something from someone or something to command that something be received from someone or a group. (See also the following entry.) □ *The muggers demanded money from everyone.* □ *The petitioners demanded a response from the board of directors.*

DEMAND ▸ OF
demand something of someone or something to command that something be received from someone or a group; to demand that someone or a group do something. □ *He demanded a lot of money of Bill.* □ *She demanded too much of her automobile.* □ *She will demand a lot of work of you.*

DEMONSTRATE ▸ AGAINST
demonstrate against someone or something to make a public show against someone or something. □ *The citizens demonstrated against the new policies.* □ *A number of protestors demonstrated against the mayor.*

DEMONSTRATE ▸ FOR
demonstrate for someone or something to make a public show in favor of someone or something. □ *We will all demonstrate for Walter's candidacy.* □ *A number of protestors demonstrated for the mayor.*

DEMONSTRATE ▸ TO
demonstrate something to someone to show someone how something works. □ *Would you please demonstrate this radio to me? I may want to buy it.* □ *The new products were demonstrated to the board of directors in advance.*

DEMOTE ▸ FROM
demote someone (from something) (to something) to lower someone's rank from one rank to another. □ *The manager demoted Bill from cashier to clerk.* □ *The army demoted her from lieutenant to sergeant.*

DEMOTE ▸ TO
See the previous entry.

DEMUR ▸ AT
demur at something to dispute something; to challenge something. □ *I fear I must demur at your suggestion that I am aloof and condescending.* □ *Alice demurred at the suggestion.*

DENOUNCE ▸ AS
denounce someone as something to brand someone as something; to call someone something bad publicly. □ *The mayor denounced her opponent as a crook.* □ *Anne was denounced as a crook.*

DENOUNCE ► FOR

denounce someone for something to criticize someone publicly for doing something. □ *The candidate denounced the governor for raising taxes.* □ *Donna denounced the mayor for incompetence.*

DENT ► UP

dent something up to mar or make depressions in something. □ *I don't want to dent my car up. It's still new.* 🅃 *He dented up my car!* □ *Wow, is this dented up!* 🄰 *She pulled a dented-up top hat out of the trunk and laughed.*

DENUDE ► OF

denude someone or something of something to strip something from someone or something. □ *The prison guards denuded the new prisoner of his garments.* □ *The wind denuded the trees of their leaves.*

DENY ► TO

deny someone or something to someone to prevent someone from having someone or something. □ *Would you deny her children to her after all these long months?* □ *I would not deny food to a starving man.*

DEPART ► FOR

depart for some place to leave for some place. □ *When shall we depart for the airport?* □ *When do we depart for St. Petersburg?*

DEPART ► FROM

depart from some place to leave from some place or something; to set out from some place or something. □ *When will you depart from here?* □ *We departed from Moscow on time.*

DEPEND ► (UP)ON

depend (up)on someone or something to rely upon someone or something. (*Upon* is formal and less commonly used than *on*.) □ *Can I depend on you to do this right?* □ *You can depend upon me.* □ *Can I depend on this old car to get me there?*

DEPICT ► AS

depict someone as something to show someone as something; to make someone appear to be something. (*Someone* includes *oneself*.) □ *It does no good to depict him as a hero.* □ *The artist depicted himself as a much younger man than he really was.*

DEPLETE ► OF

deplete something of something to use up all of a certain thing that something has. □ *They will deplete the soil of its nutrients by planting the same thing over and over.* □ *The soil was depleted of its nutrients.*

DEPORT ► FROM

deport someone (from some place) (to some place) to expel or exile someone from one place to another. □ *The government deported Jane from this country to her homeland.* □ *They deported Tom to Brazil from this country.*

DEPORT ► TO

See the previous entry.

DEPOSIT ► IN(TO)

deposit something in(to) something to put something into something. □ *Please deposit your chewing gum into the wastebasket.* □ *You should deposit your money in the bank.*

DEPRIVE ► OF

deprive someone of something to take something away from someone. (*Someone* includes *oneself*.) □ *If you don't behave, I will deprive you of your driving rights.* □ *They deprived themselves of a good time by pouting.*

DEPUTIZE ► AS

deputize someone as something to assign someone the limited power to act in some capacity. □ *The sheriff deputized Chuck as an aid during the uprising.* □ *Chuck was deputized as an officer of the law.*

DERIVE ► FROM

derive from something to come from something; to evolve from something. (Usually in reference to a word and its etymological history.) □ *This word derives from an ancient Celtic word.* □ *What does the English word* skirt *derive from?*

derive something from someone or something to draw or abstract something from someone or something. ☐ *She derives a lot of spiritual support from her religion.* ☐ *She derives her patience from her mother.*

derive something from something to show how something is descended from something else. ☐ *Is it possible to derive this word from Greek?* ☐ *Is this word derived from Latin?*

DESCEND ▸ FROM

descend from someone [for a living creature] to come from a particular set of ancestors. ☐ *I descended from a large family of Dutch traders.* ☐ *Wally is descended from an early pioneer family.*

descend from something to come down from something. ☐ *The bird descended from the top of the tree to a lower branch.* ☐ *Take care when you descend from the ladder.*

DESCEND ▸ INTO

descend into something to go down into something. ☐ *The butler descended into the cellar for another bottle of wine.* ☐ *Fred descended into the canyon on an organized tour.*

DESCEND ▸ ON

See under *DESCEND ▸ (UP)ON.*

DESCEND ▸ TO

descend to something **1.** to go down to something. ☐ *I must descend to the lower level to greet the guests.* ☐ *Gerald descended to the front door to see who was there.* **2.** to condescend to do something; to stoop to doing something; to lower oneself to do something bad. (Figurative.) ☐ *I refuse to descend to the performance of such menial duties.* ☐ *I will not descend to doing that kind of thing.*

DESCEND ▸ (UP)ON

descend (up)on someone or something to arrive or come to someone or something in great numbers. (Figurative. Compare to raindrops or falling snowflakes. *Upon* is formal and less commonly used than *on*.) ☐ *The petitioners descended upon the mayor's office in droves.* ☐ *Complaints descended on the mayor by the thousand.*

DESCRIBE ▸ AS

describe someone or something as something to describe a person or a thing as something or as being in some state. (*Someone* includes *oneself*.) ☐ *Would you describe her as a woman of average height?* ☐ *We described the building as a collection of contemporary architectural clichés.* ☐ *Would you describe yourself as nervous?*

DESCRIBE ▸ TO

describe someone or something to someone to characterize or portray a particular person or thing to someone. (*Someone* includes *oneself*.) ☐ *Will you describe her to me, please?* ☐ *I need you to describe the lost suitcase to me.* ☐ *Please describe yourself to me so I will know you.*

DESENSITIZE ▸ TO

desensitize someone to something to make someone less sensitive to something. ☐ *The doctor wanted to desensitize the allergic child to pollen.* ☐ *I took injections to desensitize me to house dust.*

DESERT ▸ FOR

desert someone or something for someone or something to leave someone for someone else; to leave something or some place for some other thing or place. ☐ *She deserted her husband for another man.* ☐ *The soldier deserted his post for a pickup game of basketball.* ☐ *Lefty "Fingers" Moran deserted his devoted wife for a nightclub chanteuse.*

DESERT ▸ TO

desert someone or something to someone or something to abandon someone or something to someone or something; to let someone or something have something or something. ☐ *Who deserted this child to her horrible fate?* ☐ *Scott deserted his picnic luncheon to the ants.* ☐ *Sam deserted his claim to the horde of grubby prospectors.*

DESERVE ▸ FROM

deserve better from someone or something to merit better treatment from someone. ☐ *We deserve better from* *someone who is supposed to be our friend.* ☐ *I deserve better from Bill.*

DESIGN ▸ FOR

design something for someone to conceive of something for someone; to draw up plans of something for someone. ☐ *Ann designed a new kitchen for us.* ☐ *Would you design a book cover for me?*

design something for something to conceive of something that is to be part of something else; to draw up plans for something that is to be part of something else. ☐ *The engineers designed a cure for the rattling problem.* ☐ *Bob, the computer programmer, designed a fix for the bug in the program.* ☐ *She designed a system of shelving for the library.*

DESIGNATE ▸ AS

designate someone or something as something to choose or name someone or something as something. (*Someone* includes *oneself.*) ☐ *Alice will designate Andrew as our representative.* ☐ *The town council designated our street as being in greatest need of repair.* ☐ *She designated herself as the person to talk to.*

DESIST ▸ FROM

desist from something to stop doing something. ☐ *You must desist from further attempts to contact your wife.* ☐ *I wish you would desist from calling me Willie.*

DESPAIR ▸ OF

despair of something to give up all hope of something. ☐ *Do not despair of his returning.* ☐ *I despair of ever seeing her again.*

DESPISE ▸ FOR

despise someone for something to hate someone for something or for doing something. (*Someone* includes *oneself.*) ☐ *I just despise him for running away!* ☐ *She despised herself for her actions.*

DESPOIL ▸ OF

despoil something of something to make something, such as a town, tomb, or building, lose value by stealing from it; to rob something of something. ☐ *The vandals despoiled the castle of much of its furnishings.* ☐ *The land was despoiled of its fertility by overplanting.*

DESTINE ▸ FOR

See *be destined for something* under *BE ▸ FOR.*

destine someone for something to determine that someone should receive or achieve something in the future. ☐ *Her many talents destined her for a distinguished career.* ☐ *Larry's intelligence destined him for big things.*

DETACH ▸ FROM

detach someone or something from someone or something to separate or disconnect someone or something from someone or something. ☐ *The high command detached Wallace from his platoon.* ☐ *The technician detached the sensors from Harry's chest.*

DETAIL ▸ FOR

detail someone for something to choose someone to do a particular task. (Originally military.) ☐ *Sam detailed Private Bailey for guard duty.* ☐ *Donna was detailed to investigate the matter.*

DETAIL ▸ TO

detail someone to someone or something to assign someone to someone or a group. (Military.) ☐ *I will detail Private Bailey to that job.* ☐ *The general detailed a lieutenant to the platoon that was going to the front.*

DETECT ▸ IN

detect something in something to recognize or identify something in something. ☐ *Can you detect the anger in her voice?* ☐ *I detect a bit of sarcasm in your comments.*

DETER ▸ FROM

deter someone or something from something to prevent or discourage someone or a group from doing something. ☐ *We can't seem to deter them from doing it.* ☐ *They were not deterred from their foolish ways.*

DETRACT ▸ FROM

detract from someone or something to lessen or diminish someone or something. ☐ *The large pieces of furniture detracted from the lovely design in the* *carpet.* ☐ *The furniture detracted from the simplicity of the room.* ☐ *Alice's beauty did not detract from her clever, but plainer, sister.*

DEVELOP ► FROM

develop (from someone or something) (into someone or something) to grow or evolve out of someone or something into someone or something else. ☐ *Her interest in music developed from a child-like curiosity to a full-fledged professional career.* ☐ *The flower developed from a little knot of a bulb.* ☐ *The bulb developed into a beautiful flower.* ☐ *She developed from a gangly girl into a lovely woman.*

DEVELOP ► INTO

See the previous entry.

DEVIATE ► FROM

deviate from something **1.** to wander away from something, such as a path, road, etc. ☐ *Please do not deviate from the path. You will crush the wildflowers.* ☐ *I will not deviate one inch from the route you have prescribed.* **2.** to vary from the normal procedure. ☐ *Please do not deviate from the prescribed procedure.* ☐ *They did not deviate from her instructions.*

DEVIL ► FOR

devil someone or something for something to bother or harass someone or some creature for something. ☐ *The child kept deviling her mother for an ice cream cone.* ☐ *The stockholders kept deviling the president for an explanation of his enormous salary.* ☐ *The kittens continued to devil the mother cat for their dinner.*

DEVOLVE ► (UP)ON

devolve (up)on someone or something [for something, such as a task] to be passed on to someone or a group. (*Upon* is formal and less commonly used than *on.*) ☐ *This job, I am afraid, devolves upon you and you alone.* ☐ *The task of repairing the damage devolved on Diane.*

DEVOTE ► TO

devote oneself to someone or something to dedicate or give oneself over to someone or something. ☐ *Do you agree to devote yourself to this task?* ☐ *She devoted herself to Roger.* ☐ *She devoted herself to the preparation of the meal.*

devote someone or something to someone or something to dedicate someone or something to the use or benefit of someone or something. (*Someone* includes *oneself.*) ☐ *I will devote a few of my people to your project.* ☐ *Sarah devoted all of her time to Roger.* ☐ *He devoted himself to repairing the damage he had caused.*

DICKER ► FOR

dicker (with someone) (for something) AND **dicker (with someone) (over something)** to bargain with someone for something; to haggle with someone for something. ☐ *I don't want to stand here dickering with you for a cheap trinket.* ☐ *We dickered with each other over the price.* ☐ *I don't want to waste time dickering with them.*

DICKER ► OVER

See the previous entry.

DICKER ► WITH

dicker (with someone) (for something) See under *DICKER ► FOR.*

DICTATE ► TO

dictate (something) to someone **1.** to speak out words to someone who writes them down; to speak words into a recording device to be written down later by someone. ☐ *Walter dictated a letter to his secretary.* ☐ *Please come in so I can dictate to you.* **2.** to lay out or spell out the exact terms of something to someone. ☐ *You can't dictate the rules to us.* ☐ *Please don't dictate to me.*

dictate to someone to give orders to someone in an authoritative manner. ☐ *Don't dictate to me! I am not your subject.* ☐ *I really don't like being dictated to.*

DIDDLE ► OUT

diddle someone out of something to cheat someone into giving up something. (Slang.) ☐ *The boys diddled the old man out of a few bucks.* ☐ *He was diddled out of his last dime.*

diddle something out of someone to get something from someone by deception. ☐ *We diddled about forty bucks out of the old lady who runs the candy shop.* ☐ *They diddled Larry's last dime out of him.*

DIDDLE ▸ WITH

diddle with something to fiddle or mess with something. (Slang.) ☐ *Come on! Don't diddle with it!* ☐ *Stop diddling with the stereo controls.*

DIE ▸ AWAY

die away to fade away. ☐ *The sound of the waterfall finally died away.* ☐ *When the applause died away, the tenor sang an encore.*

DIE ▸ BACK

die back [for vegetation] to die part way back to the roots. ☐ *The hedge died back in the winter and had to be replaced in the spring.* ☐ *This kind of grass dies back every year.*

DIE ▸ BY

die by something to perish by a particular cause or device. (Often refers to execution as a death sentence.) ☐ *He died by electrocution.* ☐ *She was condemned to die by hanging.*

DIE ▸ DOWN

die down to fade to almost nothing; to decrease gradually. ☐ *The fire died down and went out.* ☐ *As the applause died down, a child came on stage with an armload of roses for the singer.*

DIE ▸ FOR

die for someone or something **1.** to perish for the benefit or glory of someone or something. ☐ *He said he was willing to die for his country.* ☐ *She would die for her child if necessary.* **2.** to experience great physical or emotional desire for someone or something. (Figurative.) ☐ *He was just dying for Jane, but she would have nothing to do with him.* ☐ *Freddie was dying for a glass of water—he was so thirsty.*

DIE ▸ FROM

die from something See under *DIE ▸ OF.*

DIE ▸ IN

die in one's boots AND **die with one's boots on** to perish while still active and working. ☐ *When I go, I'll die in my boots!* ☐ *I can't retire. I will have to die with my boots on.*

die in something to perish in a particular calamity or accident. ☐ *They both died in an accident.* ☐ *Wally did not want to die in the war.*

DIE ▸ OF

die of something AND **die from something** **1.** to perish from an injury or a particular disease. ☐ *The puppy died of some strange dog disease.* ☐ *What did it die from?* **2.** to experience a strongly felt need. (Figurative.) ☐ *I was just dying of curiosity!* ☐ *I almost died from curiosity.*

DIE ▸ OFF

die off [for a living thing] to perish one by one until there are no more. ☐ *Most of the larger lizards died off eons ago.* ☐ *It would be really bad if all the owls died off.* ☐ *The cucumber blossoms all died off.*

DIE ▸ ON

die on someone to perish while in someone's care. ☐ *"Don't die on me!" cried the emergency room nurse.* ☐ *We don't like for patients to die on us.*

DIE ▸ OUT

die out **1.** [for a species or family] to perish totally because of the failure to produce offspring. ☐ *I am the last one in the family, so I guess it will die out.* ☐ *The owls might die out if you ruin their nesting area.* **2.** [for an idea, practice, style, etc.] to fade away through time. ☐ *That way of doing things died out a long time ago.* ☐ *It died out like the horse and buggy.*

DIE ▸ TO

die to do something to be very eager to do something. ☐ *I am just dying to go to the Amazon basin.* ☐ *We were dying to go there and visit.*

DIE ▸ WITH

die with one's boots on See under *DIE ▸ IN.*

die with something to be anxious in a particular way or with a particular quality. (Figurative.) □ *He was dying with curiosity about the telephone call.* □ *Tom was dying with the need to know what was going on.*

DIFFER ► ABOUT

differ about something AND **differ on something** [for people] to disagree about something. □ *Nick and Tony differ about a number of things.* □ *I'm afraid that you and I differ on this matter.*

DIFFER ► FROM

differ (from someone) (on something) to hold an opinion about something that is different from someone else's. □ *I'm afraid I differ with you on that point.* □ *You and I differ on that.* □ *When it comes to spending money, I seem to differ from Walter.*

differ from something [for something] to be different from something else. □ *No, this one differs from the one you saw because it has a bigger handle.* □ *How does this one differ from that one?*

DIFFER ► IN

differ in something [for people or things] to be different in a specific way or in specific ways. □ *They differ only in the color of their eyes and the size of their shoes.* □ *They differ in size and shape.*

DIFFER ► ON

See *differ (from someone) (on something)* under *DIFFER ► FROM* and *differ with someone (on something)* under *DIFFER ► WITH.*

DIFFER ► WITH

differ with someone (about something) AND **differ with someone (on something)** **1.** [for someone] to disagree with someone about something. □ *I must differ with you about that.* □ *We differ with you.* □ *I don't differ with you on that point.* **2.** [for someone] to argue with someone about something. □ *Tom was differing with Terry rather loudly about which one of them was going to carry the flag.* □ *Let's stop differing with each other on these simple things!*

DIFFERENTIATE ► BETWEEN

differentiate between someone or something and someone or something else **1.** to recognize the difference between people or things in any combination. (Usually refers to two entities.) □ *In your painting, I cannot differentiate between the costume of the figure in front and the flowers in the background.* □ *Can't you differentiate between Billy and his brother?* □ *I can't differentiate between a donkey and a burro.* **2.** to establish or create the difference between people or things. □ *Why don't you do something to differentiate between Billy and his brother?* □ *I will try to differentiate between the figure in the foreground and the flowers in the background.*

DIFFERENTIATE ► FROM

differentiate someone or something from someone or something else **1.** to recognize the difference between people and things; to tell the difference between people and things. □ *How do you differentiate this one from that one?* □ *Can you differentiate Bill from Bob?* **2.** to make people and things different. □ *I will differentiate this one from that one by painting this one red.* □ *The twins' mother used different-colored clothing to differentiate Bill from Bob.*

DIFFUSE ► THROUGH

diffuse something through something to distribute or scatter something through something else. □ *The chemical process diffused the purple color through the liquid.* □ *Let us try to diffuse the medication through the bloodstream as rapidly as possible.*

diffuse through something to spread or scatter through something. □ *The gas diffused through the office with the help of the ventilating system.* □ *The dye diffused through the water rapidly.*

DIG ► AT

dig at someone or something **1.** to poke or jab at someone or something. □ *Don't dig at me all the time. My side is getting sore where you jabbed me.* □ *Stop digging at the wall! Look what you've done!* **2.** to make a cutting remark about someone or something.

(Figurative.) □ *She is always digging at him.* □ *Fred was digging at the company he works for.*

DIG ▸ DOWN

dig down 1. to excavate deeply. □ *They are really having to dig down to reach bedrock.* □ *We are not to the buried cable yet. We will have to dig down some more.* 2. to be generous; to dig deep into one's pockets and come up with as much money as possible to donate to something. □ *Please dig down. We need every penny you can spare.* □ *Dig down deep. Give all you can.*

DIG ▸ FOR

dig for something 1. to excavate to find something that is buried. □ *They are digging along the river bank for a special kind of clay.* □ *I want to dig for gold in Alaska.* 2. to go to great pains to uncover information of some kind. (Figurative.) □ *The police were digging for some important information while they questioned Lefty "Fingers" Moran.* □ *There is no point in digging further for the name of the inventor. I have it right here.*

DIG ▸ IN

See also under *DIG ▸ IN(TO).*

dig one's heels in to become very stubborn; to be obstinate and unyielding. (Almost always used figuratively.) □ *She dug her heels in and would tell us no more.* 🅃 *She just dug in her heels!* □ *The dog dug in her heels and refused to move.*

dig someone or something in something to poke someone or something in something, such as the ribs, the side, the cheek, etc. □ *He dug Wally in the ribs as he finished telling the joke.* □ *Jed dug the cow in its side with a stick, trying to make it move into the barn.*

DIG ▸ INTO

dig something in(to something) to stab or jab something into something. □ *Dig your fork into that heavenly cake!* 🅃 *He dug in his fork.* □ *Jed dug his fork in and took a huge bite.*

DIG ▸ IN(TO)

dig in(to something) 1. to use a shovel to penetrate a mass of something. □ *He dug into the soft soil and made a hole for the roots of the bush.* □ *He grabbed a shovel and dug in where he thought the tree ought to go.* 2. to begin to process something; to go to work on something. □ *I have to dig into all these applications today and process at least half of them.* □ *Jed got out the stack of applications and dug in.* 3. to begin to eat food. (Slang.) □ *We dug in to the huge pile of fried chicken.* □ *I stuck the corner of my napkin in my collar and dug in.*

DIG ▸ OUT

dig out (of something) to channel or excavate one's way out of something. □ *The miner had to dig out of the cave-in.* □ *They were too exhausted to dig out.*

dig someone or something out (of something) to excavate in order to get someone or something out of something; to dig about in order to get someone or something out of something. (*Someone* includes *oneself*. Also figurative uses. See the examples. The *of*-phrase is paraphrased with a *from*-phrase when the particle is transposed. See the 🄵 example.) □ *Let's dig the bones out of the sand and send them to the museum.* 🅃 *She dug out the bones.* □ *Jimmy found Tim and dug him out of the pile of leaves in which he had been hiding.* □ *The dog dug itself out of the rubble of the fallen building.* 🄵 *I dug out my old tennis racket from the closet.*

DIG ▸ UP

dig some dirt up (on someone or something) to find out some gossip about someone or something. (Figurative.) □ *I'll get even with her by digging some dirt up on her family.* 🅃 *I dug up some dirt on her.* □ *Isn't it just like her to go to all that trouble to dig up some dirt?*

dig someone or something up to locate someone or something. (Colloquial.) □ *I hope I can dig someone up by Friday night.* 🅃 *Can you dig up a substitute?* □ *I think I can dig a date up by Friday night.*

dig up to listen carefully. (Slang.) ☐ *Dig up, you guys! Listen!* ☐ *All right! Dig up! This is important.*

DIGRESS ▸ FROM

digress from something [for a speaker or writer] to stray from the subject. (Also without *from something,* but not eligible as an entry.) ☐ *I am going to digress from my prepared text.* ☐ *You will pardon me if I digress from my point a little.*

DILATE ▸ ON

dilate on something to speak or write in great detail on some subject. (Compare to *open up about someone or something.*) ☐ *I am sure you do not wish me to dilate further on this matter.* ☐ *Please do not dilate on this matter further.*

DILLY-DALLY ▸ AROUND

See the following entry.

DILLY-DALLY ▸ WITH

dilly-dally (around) with someone or something to waste time frivolously with someone or something. ☐ *Stop dilly-dallying around with your friends.* ☐ *Don't dilly-dally with me!* ☐ *He is always dilly-dallying around with his work.* ☐ *Jack spends a lot of time dilly-dallying around with Claire.* ☐ *He liked to dilly-dally with the girls.*

DIM ▸ DOWN

dim down [for the lights] to go dim. ☐ *The lights dimmed down for a few seconds.* ☐ *Open the stage curtain when the houselights dim down.*

dim something down to make lights dim; to use a dimmer to lower the lights. ☐ *Why don't you dim the lights down and put on some music?* 🅃 *Let me dim down the lights and put on some music.*

DIM ▸ OUT

dim out [for a light] to grow dim and go out altogether. ☐ *The lights dimmed out twice during the storm.* ☐ *I was afraid that the lights would dim out completely.* 🄽 *We found the candles as soon as the dimout began.*

DIM ▸ UP

dim something up to use a dimmer to make the lights brighter. (Theatrical. A dimmer is a rheostat, variable transformer, or something similar. The expression, a seeming contradiction, is the opposite of *dim something down.*) ☐ *As the curtain rose, the electrician dimmed the lights up on a beautiful scene.* 🅃 *You dimmed up the lights too fast.*

DIN ▸ IN(TO)

din something in(to someone) to repeat something over and over to someone. (Figurative. As if one could "hammer" words into someone.) ☐ *The teacher dinned it into her constantly, but it did no good.* 🅃 *He dinned in the same message over and over.* ☐ *He needed to learn Spanish, so he bought a tape recorder and dinned it in day and night.*

DINE ▸ AT

dine at some place to eat at a place. ☐ *We really like to dine at the small cafe on the corner.* ☐ *I hope we can dine at a fine restaurant for our anniversary.*

DINE ▸ IN

dine in to eat at home rather than at a restaurant. ☐ *I think we will dine in tonight.* ☐ *I am tired of dining in. Let's go out.*

DINE ▸ OFF

dine off something to make a meal of something; to make many meals of something. (Formal.) ☐ *Do you think we can dine off the leg of lamb for more than one meal?* ☐ *I hope we dine off the turkey only one more time.*

DINE ▸ ON

dine on something to eat something. ☐ *We are dining on roast beef tonight.* ☐ *What will we be dining on tonight?*

DINE ▸ OUT

dine out to eat away from home. ☐ *I love to dine out so I don't have to cook.* ☐ *We both want to dine out tonight.*

DIP ▸ IN(TO)

dip in((to) something) **1.** to reach into a liquid. ☐ *I dipped into the dishwater, looking for the missing spoon.* ☐ *I* *dipped in and there it was.* **2.** to reach into a substance, usually to remove some of the substance. □ *I dipped into the sour cream with a potato chip and brought out an enormous glob.* □ *He grabbed the jar of peanut butter and dipped in.* **3.** to take out part of something one has been saving. (Figurative.) □ *I had to dip in to my savings in order to pay for my vacation.* □ *I went to the bank and dipped in. There wasn't much left.* **4.** to lower into a liquid; to sink into a liquid. □ *The oars dipped into the water and came out again.* □ *The lower branches sagged down to the water and dipped in.*

dip something in((to) something) to put something into a substance in order to take some of it. □ *Tom dipped some of the bread into the cheese sauce.* 🅃 *Dip in the bread again and get some more cheese on it.* □ *I dipped the soap in to get it wet enough to work up a lather.*

DIP ▸ TO

dip to something to decline to a lower level quickly or briefly. □ *The temperature dipped into the lower twenties overnight.* □ *The stock market dipped to a very low level during the day Friday.*

DIRECT ▸ AGAINST

direct something against someone or something to aim a remark or a weapon at someone or something. (Very close to *direct something at someone or something.*) □ *We directed the guns against the occupied village.* □ *Ted said he had directed his remark against Judy.*

DIRECT ▸ AT

direct something at someone or something to aim something at someone or something. (Very close to *direct something against someone or something.*) □ *Are you directing your remarks at me?* □ *Please direct the hose at the bushes.*

DIRECT ▸ TO

See also under *DIRECT ▸ TO(WARD).*

direct someone's attention to someone or something to focus someone's regard or concern on someone or something; to cause someone to notice someone or something. □ *May I direct your attention to the young man in the purple costume?* □ *The announcer directed our attention to the magician who was coming on stage.*

direct something to someone to address, designate, or send something to someone. □ *Shall I direct the inquiries to you?* □ *Please direct all the mail to the secretary when it is delivered.*

DIRECT ▸ TO(WARD)

direct something to(ward) someone or something to send, throw, push, or aim something to someone or something. □ *Tom directed the ball toward Harry.* □ *Should I direct this inquiry to Alice?* □ *Please direct it to the front office.*

DIRTY ▸ UP

dirty something up to get something dirty. □ *Those pants are brand-new! Don't dirty them up!* 🅃 *Don't dirty up your brand-new pants!*

DISABUSE ▸ OF

disabuse someone of something to rid someone of an incorrect idea. (*Someone* includes *oneself.*) □ *Please allow me to disabuse you of that assumption.* □ *Please disabuse yourself of the notion that you are perfect.*

DISAGREE ▸ ABOUT

disagree (with someone) (about someone or something) See under *DISAGREE ▸ WITH.*

DISAGREE ▸ ON

disagree on someone or something [for people] to hold opposing views about someone or something. □ *We both disagree on Tom and whether he can do the job.* □ *We will always disagree on politics.*

DISAGREE ▸ WITH

disagree with someone [for food or drink] to upset someone's stomach. □ *Milk always disagrees with me.* □ *Onions disagree with my husband, so he never eats them.*

disagree (with someone) (about someone or something) to hold views about someone or something that are opposed to someone else's views. □ *I take it you disagree with me about Tom.* [T] *Don't disagree about Tom with me.* □ *I disagree about this with almost everyone.* □ *I disagree with you.*

DISAPPEAR ▸ FROM

disappear from something to vanish from something or some place, especially from sight, view, or the face of the earth; to have been taken away from something. □ *Jack disappeared from the face of the earth.* □ *The car pulled away and disappeared from sight down the road.* □ *The ship disappeared from view.*

DISAPPOINT ▸ AT

See *be disappointed at someone or something* under *BE ▸ AT.*

DISAPPOINT ▸ IN

See *be disappointed in someone or something* under *BE ▸ IN.*

DISAPPOINT ▸ WITH

disappoint someone with someone or something to displease someone with someone or something. (*Someone* includes *oneself.*) □ *I hope I haven't disappointed you with the size of the donation.* □ *She chose Tom and disappointed us all with him.* □ *I disappointed myself with my performance.*

DISAPPROVE ▸ OF

disapprove of someone or something to object to someone or something. □ *I disapprove of her choice for maid of honor.* □ *Do you disapprove of me?*

DISBAR ▸ FROM

disbar someone from something to take the right to practice law away from a lawyer. □ *The state board disbarred Todd from practicing law in his own state.* □ *Sally was also disbarred from practicing law.*

DISCERN ▸ BETWEEN

discern between someone or something and someone or something to detect the difference between people and things. □ *I cannot discern between the dark trees and the dark sky behind them.* □ *I cannot discern between the person and the background.*

DISCERN ▸ FROM

discern someone or something from something to detect the difference between someone or something and something. □ *I can hardly discern Tom from the busy background in this picture.* □ *I can't discern anything from that cluttered scene.*

discern something from someone or something to learn or determine something from someone or something. □ *We discerned a lot from Tom.* □ *We discerned a lot from our discussions with Tom.*

DISCHARGE ▸ FROM

discharge someone from something **1.** to fire someone from a job. □ *The manager discharged Walter from his position with the bank.* □ *Walter was discharged from his job.* **2.** to permit a person to leave a place, such as a hospital or the armed service. □ *They discharged her from the hospital today.* □ *She was well enough to be discharged from the hospital.*

discharge something from something to fire a bullet or a round from a gun. □ *I discharged two bullets from the gun accidentally.* □ *Randy discharged about twenty rounds from his automatic rifle.*

discharge something (from something) (into something) to let something out of something into something else. □ *She discharged some nitrogen from the tank into the laboratory by accident.* □ *The technician discharged oxygen from the tank into the atmosphere.* □ *We discharged water from the aquarium.*

DISCHARGE ▸ INTO

See *discharge something (from something) (into something)* under *DISCHARGE ▸ FROM.*

DISCIPLINE ▸ FOR

discipline someone for something to punish or chastise someone for doing something. □ *I will have to discipline you for that.* □ *Mary was disciplined for taking part in the fiasco.*

DISCLOSE ▸ TO

disclose something to someone to tell or reveal something to someone. □

Tony refused to disclose the location of the papers to me. □ *Please disclose the names to me at once.*

DISCONNECT ► FROM

disconnect someone or something from someone or something to break the connection between things or people. (*Someone* includes *oneself.*) □ *The telephone operator disconnected Larry from his caller.* □ *Ted disconnected Larry from Tom.* □ *Sam disconnected the telephone from the network.* □ *He disconnected himself from Maggie and hung up the phone.*

DISCOURAGE ► FROM

discourage someone from something to dissuade someone from doing something. □ *I hope I can discourage Tom from leaving.* □ *I do not want to discourage you from further experimentation.*

DISCOURSE ► (UP)ON

discourse (up)on someone or something to lecture about someone or something. (*Upon* is formal and less commonly used than *on.*) □ *I would like to discourse upon this matter awhile.* □ *The committee chose to discourse on Tom and his latest fiasco rather than deal with the budgetary problems it faces.*

DISCRIMINATE ► AGAINST

discriminate against someone or something to single out a type of person or thing for special negative treatment or denial of equal treatment; to act in a prejudicial manner against someone or something. □ *This law discriminates against short people.* □ *You discriminate against wheelchairs.*

DISCRIMINATE ► BETWEEN

discriminate between someone and someone else or something and something else to distinguish between people or between things. □ *I find it hard these days to discriminate between my friends and my enemies.* □ *Can you discriminate between this shade of pink and that one?*

DISCUSS ► WITH

discuss someone or something with someone to talk about someone or something with someone. □ *I need to discuss Mickey with you.* □ *We need to discuss compensation with the boss.*

DISEMBARK ► FROM

disembark from something to get off of a ship or a plane. □ *We disembark from the ship in Manaus.* □ *At what time do we expect to disembark from the plane?*

DISENGAGE ► FROM

disengage (oneself) from someone or something to detach oneself from someone or something; to untangle oneself from someone or something. □ *I wanted to disengage myself from the person I was talking to and go home.* □ *We disengaged from the argument.* □ *She disengaged herself from the talkative lady and went about her business.*

disengage something from something to detach something from something. □ *Sally disengaged the locking mechanism from the cupboard door and peeked in.* □ *The coupling was disengaged from the boxcar, and the car separated and rolled away.*

DISENTANGLE ► FROM

disentangle someone or something from someone or something to untangle someone or something from someone or something. (*Someone* includes *oneself.*) □ *I helped disentangle Tony from the coils of ropes he had stumbled into.* □ *They worked feverishly to disentangle the dolphin from the net.* □ *He disentangled himself from the net.*

DISGUISE ► AS

disguise someone or something as someone or something to dress or make someone up to appear to be someone or something. (*Someone* includes *oneself.*) □ *We disguised the child as a witch.* □ *We disguised Gerald as a pumpkin.* □ *She sought to disguise the pumpkin as squash.* □ *She disguised herself as a duchess and fooled the palace guard.*

DISGUISE ► IN

disguise someone in something to conceal someone's identity in a costume or makeup. (*Someone* includes *oneself.*) □ *We disguised her in men's clothing and* *got her across the border.* □ *She disguised herself in a clown suit.*

DISGUST ▸ AT

See *be disgusted at someone or something* under *BE ▸ AT.*

DISGUST ▸ WITH

See *be disgusted with someone or something* under *BE ▸ WITH.*

DISH ▸ ON

dish on someone to gossip about or slander someone. (Slang.) □ *Stop dishing on her. She never hurt you!* □ *They spent an hour dishing on Wally.*

DISH ▸ OUT

dish something out (to someone) 1. AND **dish something up (for someone)** to place food into dishes for someone. □ *Please dish the lasagna out to everyone.* 🅃 *Todd dished out the lasagna to everyone.* □ *He dished it out.* □ *He dished some up for everyone.* □ *He dished some up.* **2.** to give out criticism or punishment to someone. □ *He really knows how to dish the punishment out, doesn't he?* □ *He can really dish it out, but can he take it?* 🅃 *The boys dished out too much criticism of the meal. They were sent from the room.*

DISH ▸ UP

dish something up (for someone) See the previous entry.

DISINCLINE ▸ TO

See *be disinclined to do something* under *BE ▸ TO.*

DISLODGE ▸ FROM

dislodge someone or something from someone or something to loosen and remove someone or something from someone or something. □ *We were unable to dislodge her from office.* □ *Gene was able to dislodge the bone from his throat.*

DISMISS ▸ AS

dismiss something as something to put something out of one's mind or ignore something as something. (The second *something* can be a noun or an adjective.) □ *I dismissed the whole idea as foolishness.* □ *It was not possible to dismiss the whole matter as a one-time happening.* □ *Molly dismissed the whole event as accidental.*

DISMISS ▸ FOR

See the following entry.

DISMISS ▸ FROM

dismiss someone (from something) (for something) to discharge someone from employment for some reason; to fire someone from a job for some cause. □ *We will have to dismiss him from employment for bad behavior.* □ *She was dismissed from the bank for making many errors in one month.*

DISMOUNT ▸ FROM

dismount from something to get down from something, such as a horse, bicycle, etc. □ *She dismounted from her horse and fled into the house.* □ *Please dismount from the bicycle and wheel it into the shed.*

DISPATCH ▸ FROM

dispatch someone from some place to send someone from some place. □ *I dispatched a messenger from here over an hour ago.* □ *A telegram will be dispatched from my office first thing in the morning.*

DISPATCH ▸ TO

dispatch someone or something to someone or something to send someone or something to someone, something, or some place. □ *I will dispatch a new copy of the damaged book to you immediately.* □ *I dispatched a messenger to the office.* □ *Gene will dispatch a messenger to you.*

DISPENSE ▸ FROM

dispense something (to someone) (from something) to distribute something to someone from something or some place. □ *The nurse dispensed aspirin to everyone from a large bottle.* □ *The nurse dispensed aspirin from a large bottle to anyone who asked for it.*

DISPENSE ▸ TO

See the previous entry.

DISPENSE ▸ WITH

dispense with someone or something to get rid of someone or something; to brush someone or something aside. □ *I* *think we will dispense with Tom for the rest of the day.* □ *We will have to dispense with the expensive gifts this year.*

DISPLAY ► TO

display something to someone to show something to someone. □ *The peacock displayed his tail feathers to the other birds.* □ *Would you please display the artwork to the committee?*

DISPOSE ► OF

dispose of someone to kill someone. (Slang.) □ *Max suggested that he would dispose of Lefty if Lefty continued to be a pest.* □ *The boss ordered Max to dispose of Lefty.*

dispose of someone or something to get rid of someone or something. □ *How can I dispose of this bothersome customer?* □ *Where shall I dispose of this waste paper?*

DISPOSE ► TO(WARD)

See *be well disposed to(ward) someone or something* under *BE ► TO(WARD).*

DISPOSSESS ► OF

dispossess someone of something to separate someone from a possession. □ *Do you intend to dispossess us of our home?* □ *They were dispossessed of the only possession they had.*

DISPUTE ► WITH

dispute something with someone to argue with someone about something, such as an amount of money. □ *The customer disputed the amount of the check with the waiter.* □ *Please don't feel like you have to dispute every bill with the supplier.*

dispute with someone over something to argue with someone about something. □ *I advise you not to dispute with the boss over every little thing.* □ *Tim is disputing with Sam over the whole business.*

DISQUALIFY ► FOR

disqualify someone or something for something AND **disqualify someone or something from something** to invalidate someone's or something's claim to something. □ *Does this disqualify me for the team?* □ *This disqualifies our team, doesn't it?* □ *Does it disqualify us from competition?*

DISQUALIFY ► FROM

disqualify someone or something from something See the previous entry.

DISSATISFY ► WITH

See *be dissatisfied with someone or something* under *BE ► WITH.*

DISSENT ► FROM

dissent from something to disagree with something. □ *We have chosen to dissent from the decision the rest of you made.* □ *Fred dissented from almost everything that everyone else agreed on.*

DISSOCIATE ► FROM

dissociate oneself from someone or something to break one's connection with someone or something. □ *They decided to dissociate themselves from our organization.* □ *I was forced to dissociate myself from her.* □ *We advised her to dissociate herself from the gang.*

dissociate oneself from someone or something to separate oneself from someone or something. □ *I am obliged to dissociate myself from Tom and his friends.* □ *Harry could not dissociate himself from the plan.* □ *I must dissociate myself from that remark.*

DISSOLVE ► IN

dissolve in something to break down into a liquid state in something. □ *Salt will dissolve in warm water.* □ *This material will not dissolve in oil.*

dissolve something in something to cause something to break down into a liquid state in something. □ *First, dissolve the salt in some warm water.* □ *Dissolve this medicine in water.*

DISSOLVE ► (IN)TO

dissolve (in)to something [for a film or television picture] to fade away into some other picture. (Figurative.) □ *The scene dissolved into a shot of the interior of the castle.* □ *At this point in the script, dissolve to a face shot of Walter.*

DISSOLVE ► INTO

dissolve into something **1.** [for a substance] to liquefy when placed in a liquid. □ *The gelatin dissolved into the* *hot water.* □ *Please dissolve the salt into the water.* **2.** [for someone] to begin suddenly to display laughter, tears, giggles, gales of laughter, etc. (Figurative.) □ *The children dissolved into tears.* □ *I tried to make the audience dissolve into laughter.*

dissolve something into something to cause a film or television picture to fade away into some other picture. □ *The director dissolved the picture into the next scene.* □ *At this point, the picture should be dissolved into a side shot of the exterior.*

DISSUADE ▸ FROM

dissuade someone from something to discourage someone from (doing) something. □ *I hope to dissuade her from getting married until she graduates.* □ *I could not dissuade him from his plan.*

DISTANCE ▸ FROM

distance oneself from someone or something **1.** to separate oneself physically from someone or something. □ *She wanted to distance herself from the fighting in the corridor.* □ *I distanced myself from her from then on.* **2.** to separate oneself ideologically from someone or something. □ *She felt that he would want to distance himself from her radical politics.* □ *He had to distance himself from those policies if he wanted to be reelected.* □ *I will be better when I can distance myself from the accident.* □ *You must distance yourself from the scandal if you want to be accepted.*

DISTILL ▸ FROM

distill something from something to get a volatile product from something by heating. □ *They distilled the lighter components from the raw oil.* □ *The alcohol was distilled from the fermenting grain.*

DISTINGUISH ▸ AMONG

distinguish oneself among someone to make oneself stand out from other people because of one's achievements. □ *I hope someday to distinguish myself among my peers.* □ *He distinguished himself among his classmates.*

DISTINGUISH ▸ BETWEEN

distinguish between someone or something and someone or something **1.** to perceive the difference between different people and things, in any combination. □ *Can't you distinguish between Tom and your real enemies?* □ *He can't distinguish between a good runner and that shed over there!* **2.** to create or emphasize the difference between people and things, in any combination. □ *Try to distinguish between the figure in the foreground and the flowers in the background in your painting.* □ *I used red to distinguish between the new part and the old.*

DISTINGUISH ▸ FROM

distinguish someone and something from someone and something **1.** to tell the difference between different people and things, in any combination. □ *I cannot distinguish Billy from Bobby.* □ *She could not distinguish between basil and oregano.* **2.** to delineate or emphasize the boundary between people and things, in any combination. □ *I cannot distinguish Tom's head from the sky in the background.* □ *We could not distinguish the leaves of the bushes from the leaves of the trees, no matter how carefully I drew them.*

DISTRACT ▸ FROM

distract someone from something to turn someone's attention from something. □ *I hate to distract you from your work, but I have some important news.* □ *You haven't distracted me from anything.*

DISTRIBUTE ▸ AMONG

distribute something among someone to give out shares of something to three or more people. □ *We must distribute the money among the various charities.* □ *The food was distributed among the people who showed up.*

DISTRIBUTE ▸ AROUND

distribute something (all) around to give shares of something to people. □ *I distributed many gifts all around to everyone.* □ *We distributed the drinks around.*

DISTRIBUTE ▸ BETWEEN
distribute something between someone to give out shares of something to two people. ☐ *He distributed the remaining cake between Dave and Don.* ☐ *Please distribute the magazines between the two boys.*

DISTRIBUTE ▸ OVER
distribute something over something to spread something over something or over an area. ☐ *Distribute the icing over the entire cake.* ☐ *Walter distributed the sand over the icy spots.*

DISTRIBUTE ▸ TO
distribute something to someone to give out something to someone. ☐ *Can you distribute this clothing to the needy people who live around here?* ☐ *I will distribute the ice cream to the party guests.*

DIVE ▸ IN(TO)
dive in(to something) **1.** to plunge into something; to jump into something headier. ☐ *Don't dive into that water! It's too shallow.* ☐ *Donna dived into the pool.* ☐ *David walked to the edge of the pool and dived in.* **2.** to plunge into some business or activity. (Figurative.) ☐ *I can't wait to dive into the next project.* ☐ *Clara dives into her work eagerly every morning.*

DIVE ▸ OFF
dive off (of) something to jump off something headfirst. (The *of* is colloquial.) ☐ *Rachel dived off of it.* ☐ *She dived off the high diving board.*

DIVERGE ▸ FROM
diverge from something to move in a different direction from something. ☐ *Her line of thinking diverged from generally accepted thought on this point.* ☐ *The driveway diverges from the main road without any indication of the fact that it is a driveway.*

DIVERGE ▸ TO
diverge to something to turn to a particular direction. ☐ *A narrow road diverged to the left.* ☐ *A narrower channel diverged to the left of the island.*

DIVERT ▸ FROM
divert someone or something from someone or something to turn someone or something aside or away from someone or something. ☐ *We could not divert his attention from his mother.* ☐ *I could not divert the woman from her interest in the book.*

DIVERT ▸ INTO
divert something into something to channel something into something. ☐ *We will have to divert the runoff water into the culvert.* ☐ *Let's divert this stream into the ditch.*

DIVERT ▸ ONTO
divert something onto something to channel something onto something. ☐ *Temporarily, they diverted the southbound traffic onto the side streets.* ☐ *Jed diverted the little stream onto the field.*

DIVERT ▸ TO
divert someone or something to someone or something to channel or redirect someone or something to someone or something. ☐ *The farmers diverted the stream to a different channel.* ☐ *The guards diverted the museum visitors to the great hall.* ☐ *A barrier diverted the passengers to the customs inspector.*

DIVEST ▸ OF
divest someone or something of something to take something away from someone or something. (*Someone* includes *oneself*.) ☐ *The judge divested the company of its foreign holding.* ☐ *The court divested her of her stocks.* ☐ *She divested herself of her coat and hat.*

DIVIDE ▸ AGAINST
divide someone against someone or something to cause people to separate into two groups, one of which opposes someone or something. ☐ *The issue divided the children against their parents.* ☐ *The argument divided the president against the board of directors.*

DIVIDE ▸ AMONG
See under *DIVIDE ▸ UP.*

DIVIDE ▶ BETWEEN

See *be divided between something* under *BE ▶ BETWEEN.*

See also under *DIVIDE ▶ UP.*

divide something between people or things to give equal shares of something to specific people or groups. (In a strict sense, only between two entities. Colloquially, between two or more.) ☐ *I will have to divide the toys between the two children.* ☐ *The board divided the year's profits between the president and the board itself.* ☐ *He divided the tasks between the day crew and the night crew.*

DIVIDE ▶ BY

divide by something to perform mathematical division by a particular number. ☐ *Can you divide by sixteens?* ☐ *Add this figure to the next column and divide by twenty.*

divide something by something to perform mathematical division on something, using a particular number. ☐ *Now, divide this sum by the figure in column seven.* ☐ *Can you divide 1,400 by 59?*

DIVIDE ▶ FROM

divide something (off) (from something) **1.** to separate something from something else. ☐ *Let's divide the chickens off from the ducks and put the chickens in the shed.* 🅃 *We divided off the chickens from the ducks.* **2.** to separate something from something else, using a partition. ☐ *We divided the sleeping area off from the rest of the room.* 🅃 *A curtain was used to divide off a sleeping area.* 🅃 *Don divided off the sleeping area.*

DIVIDE ▶ INTO

divide something into something **1.** AND **divide something in something** to separate something into parts. ☐ *I will divide it into two parts.* ☐ *I will divide the cake in half.* ☐ *If you divide the pie in fourths, the pieces will be too big.* **2.** to do mathematical division so that the divisor goes into the number that is to be divided. ☐ *Divide seven into forty-nine and what do you get?* ☐ *If seven is divided into forty-nine, what do you get?*

DIVIDE ▶ OFF

divide something (off) (from something) See under *DIVIDE ▶ FROM.*

DIVIDE ▶ ON

See *be divided on someone or something* under *BE ▶ ON.*

DIVIDE ▶ UP

divide something (up) (between someone or something) AND **divide something (up) (among someone or something)** to give something out in shares to people or groups. (More colloquial with *up*. *Between* with two; *among* with more.) ☐ *Please divide this up between the visitors.* ☐ *Please divide this up among the visitors.* 🅃 *Please divide up this pie between the children.* 🅃 *Please divide up this pie among the children.* ☐ *Do we need to divide this up so carefully?*

DIVIDE ▶ WITH

divide something with someone to share something with someone. ☐ *I will divide one with you.* ☐ *They refused to divide it with us.*

DIVORCE ▶ FROM

divorce oneself from something to separate oneself from something, such as an idea, policy, philosophy, etc. ☐ *She was not able to divorce herself from the obsession that had grasped her.* ☐ *You should divorce yourself from those limiting ideas.*

DIVULGE ▶ TO

divulge something to someone to reveal something to someone. ☐ *Promise that you will not divulge any of this to anyone.* ☐ *She refused to divulge their names to us.*

DIVVY ▶ UP

divvy something up (between someone) AND **divvy something up (among someone)** to divide something up between two people or among three or more people. ☐ *Would you like to divvy this money up?* 🅃 *Please divvy up this money between you.* ☐ *Can you divvy this up among the members of the gang?* ☐ *I want to watch you divvy it up.*

DO ▸ ABOUT

do something about someone or something to manage or deal with someone or something. □ *Can you please do something about Bob? He is too noisy.* □ *We were not able to do anything about the excessive rent increase.*

DO ▸ AS

do as something to serve as something; to be usable as something. □ *This spoon will do as a small shovel.* □ *This jacket will not do as formal wear.*

DO ▸ AWAY

do away with oneself to commit suicide. □ *The doctor was afraid that Betty would do away with herself.* □ *I wouldn't think of doing away with myself.*

do away with someone or something 1. to get rid of someone or something. □ *I think they are going to do away with a number of people in the accounting department.* □ *Let's do away with this old porch swing.* **2.** to kill someone or some creature. □ *Are you trying to do away with my cat?* □ *Lefty really wanted to do away with Max.*

DO ▸ BY

do somehow by someone to treat someone in a particular manner; to benefit someone to some degree. (Idiomatic.) □ *I think she did quite nicely by you. She was very generous.* □ *They did fine by me.*

do something by hand to do something with human hands rather than machines. □ *I did this by hand. Don't you see the little imperfections?* □ *Do we have to do this work by hand?*

DO ▸ FOR

do for someone 1. to provide for someone; to serve someone. (Folksy. Often a question: **What can I do for you?**) □ *Do you expect me to stay home and do for you for the rest of my life?* □ *I can't do for all of them!* **2.** to suffice for someone; to be sufficient for someone. □ *Will this amount of sweet potatoes do for you?* □ *Yes, this will do for me fine.* **3.** See *be done for* under *BE ▸ FOR.*

do for something to serve as something; to substitute as something. □ *I think that this stone will do nicely for a doorstop.* □ *This stick will just not do for a stirring spoon.*

do somehow for someone to benefit or harm someone in some degree. (Colloquial.) □ *This one does fine for me. I don't need a different one.* □ *This does okay for me. I'm satisfied.*

DO ▸ IN

See *be done in* under *BE ▸ IN.*

do someone or something in 1. to wear someone or some creature out. (*Someone* includes *oneself.*) □ *All this walking will do me in.* T *The walking did in most of the hikers.* □ *The climbing did them in.* A *The totally done-in runner panted heavily.* □ *I did myself in running the race.* **2.** to destroy or ruin someone or something. □ *Who did my car in?* T *Who did in my car?* □ *He lost all his money on the horses and did himself in.* **3.** to kill someone or some creature. (*Someone* includes *oneself.*) □ *Max tried to do Lefty in.* T *Max tried to do in Lefty.* □ *The speeding car did my cat in.* □ *Be careful or you'll do yourself in!*

DO ▸ OUT

do someone out of something to swindle something away from someone; to defraud someone of a right or of property. (Slang. *Someone* includes *oneself.*) □ *Are you trying to do me out of what's mine?* □ *Max tried to do her out of everything she had.* □ *I did myself out of a week's vacation by quitting when I did.*

DO ▸ OVER

do someone or something over to remodel or redecorate something; to redo someone's appearance. □ *I am going to have to do this room over. It is beginning to look drab.* T *Yes, you should do over this room.* □ *There's no need to do it over.* □ *The beauty consultant did Janet over, and now she looks like a model.* A *I just love your done-over dining room!*

do something over to repeat something; to do something again. □ *I am afraid that you are going to have to do* *this over again.* □ *Would you do this one over, please?*

DO ▸ TO

do justice to someone or something to do well for someone or something; to grant someone or something all due esteem and honor. □ *This small sofa does not do justice to this magnificent room.* □ *Although the gown is beautiful, it does not do justice to the radiance of your smile.*

DO ▸ UP

do someone or something up to make someone or something attractive; to decorate or ornament someone or something. (*Someone* includes *oneself.*) □ *Sally did Jane up for the party.* [T] *She did up Jane nicely.* [T] *Would you do up this present for Jane? It's her birthday.* □ *She did herself up just beautifully.*

do something up **1.** to fasten, zip, hook, or button some item of clothing. □ *Would you do my buttons up in back?* [T] *Please do up my buttons.* **2.** to wrap up something, such as a package, gift, etc. □ *I have to do this present up before the party guests get here.* [T] *Do up the presents quickly. They are coming up the walk.* [A] *What a nicely done-up package!* **3.** to arrange, fix, repair, cook, clean, etc., something. □ *I have to do the kitchen up before the guests get here.* [T] *Do up the kitchen now, please.*

do something up somehow to do something thoroughly in a particular manner. (Especially *brown*, which is part of an idiom.) □ *Fine job, John. You really did it up brown.* □ *They did this package up nicely.* [T] *She did up the report nicely.*

DO ▸ WITH

do business with someone to trade or bargain with someone; to conduct commerce with someone. □ *You sound reasonable. I think I can do business with you.* □ *I am sure we can do business with one another.*

do something with someone or something **1.** to use someone or something in some way. □ *Can you do something with this bracket, or shall I throw it away?* □ *We can't do anything with the new secretary. Find us another.* **2.** to improve or refresh someone or something. □ *I would like to do something with this room. It is so drab.* □ *I can't do anything with this child! Keep him at home.* **3.** to manage as well as possible with someone or something; to *make do with someone or something.* □ *We will just have to do whatever we can with what we have.* □ *We will do what we can with this employee until you find a better one.*

do with someone or something to do as well as possible with someone or something; to *make do with someone or something.* □ *I will just have to do with the car I now have.* □ *Can she do with just one chair for a while?*

DO ▸ WITHOUT

do without (someone or something) to manage or get along without someone or something that is needed. □ *I guess I will have to do without dinner.* □ *Yes, you'll do without.*

DOCK ▸ AT

dock (something) at some place to bring a boat or ship to a dock. □ *Let's dock our boat at the left side of the pier.* □ *We docked at the marina overnight.*

DOCK ▸ FOR

dock someone or something for something to subtract money from someone or someone's account for payment of a debt or as punishment; to withhold money from someone's pay in payment of a debt or as punishment. □ *I will have to dock you for any breakage you cause.* □ *I was docked for being absent for half a day.*

DOCK ▸ FROM

dock something from something to withhold money from an amount due to someone. □ *I will have to dock this from your paycheck.* □ *The boss docked ten dollars from my monthly pay.*

DOCTOR ▸ UP

doctor someone up to give someone medical treatment. (Folksy. *Someone* includes *oneself.*) □ *Give me a minute to doctor Fred up, and then we can con-*

tinue our walk. 🅃 *I'll doctor up Fred with a Band-Aid; you can go on ahead.* 🄰 *The hastily doctored-up man staggered into the emergency room.* □ *I'll just doctor myself up a little and then go on to the hospital.*

DODDER ▸ ALONG

dodder along to walk along unsteadily, as in old age. □ *Both of the elderly ladies doddered along very slowly.* □ *We dodder along because we can't go any faster.*

DODGE ▸ BEHIND

dodge behind something to duck behind something; to move quickly and evasively behind something. □ *She dodged behind a tree to hide from Mark.* □ *The turkey dodged behind a tree to elude the hunter.*

DOLE ▸ OUT

dole something out (to someone) to distribute something to someone. □ *The cook doled the oatmeal out to each camper who held out a bowl.* 🅃 *Please dole out the candy bars, one to a customer.* □ *She doled it out fairly.*

DOLL ▸ UP

doll someone up to dress someone up in fancy clothes. (*Someone* includes *oneself.*) □ *She dolled her children up for church each Sunday.* 🅃 *She dolls up all her kids once a week.* 🄰 *The nicely dolled-up children were paraded before the assembled grandparents.* □ *I just love it when you doll yourself up like that.*

DONE ▸ FOR

See *be done for* under *BE ▸ FOR.*

DOOM ▸ TO

See *be doomed to something* under *BE ▸ TO.*

doom someone or something to something to destine someone or something to something unpleasant. (*Someone* includes *oneself.*) □ *The judgment doomed her to a life in prison.* □ *Your insistence on including that rigid clause doomed the contract to failure.* □ *They doomed themselves to low wages for the rest of their lives.*

DOPE ▸ OUT

dope something out **1.** to figure something out. (Slang.) □ *He spent a lot of time trying to dope the assignment out so he could understand it.* 🅃 *It's hard to dope out a reading assignment after midnight.* **2.** to explain something carefully. (Slang.) □ *He doped it all out to them very carefully so that no one would be confused.* 🅃 *He doped out the information slowly and patiently.*

DOPE ▸ UP

dope someone or something up to give drugs to someone or some creature. (Either legal or illegal drugs. *Someone* includes *oneself.*) □ *Her parents doped her up with medicine so she would sleep through the night.* 🅃 *It's dangerous to dope up a child night after night.* □ *The jockey doped the horse up.* 🄰 *The doped-up patient just moaned.* □ *She had the flu, so she doped herself up and went to bed.*

DOSE ▸ WITH

dose someone or something with something to give medicine to someone or some creature. □ *You should dose the child with a little nonaspirin painkiller.* □ *She dosed the horse with a mild tranquilizer.*

DOSS ▸ DOWN

doss down (for some time) to lie down to sleep for a period of time. (Slang.) □ *Chuck dossed down for a few hours before the evening performance.* □ *It's midnight: time to doss down.*

DOT ▸ WITH

dot something with something to put little bits or dots of something on something. □ *She dotted her face with red marks to make it look as if she had measles.* □ *The chef dotted the cake with blobs of buttery icing.*

DOTE ▸ (UP)ON

dote (up)on someone or something to adore someone or something. (*Upon* is formal and less commonly used than *on.*) □ *His aunt simply dotes upon him.* □ *Mary dotes on vanilla ice cream.*

DOUBLE ▸ AS

double as someone or something [for someone] to serve in two capacities. □ *The chaplain will have to double as a nurse in the wards.* □ *This table doubles as a desk during busy times.*

DOUBLE ▸ BACK

double back (on someone) to follow one's own pathway back toward a pursuer. □ *The deer doubled back on us, and we lost its trail.* □ *The horse doubled back, eluding the dogs.*

double back (on something) to follow one's own pathway back toward where one started. □ *I doubled back on my own trail.* □ *The horse doubled back.*

DOUBLE ▸ IN

double in brass (as something) to serve also as something. (Originally said of a musician who could play the brass instruments as well as other instruments.) □ *Wally doubled in brass as a clerk.* □ *Louis doubled in brass as a brass player.*

DOUBLE ▸ OVER

double over to bend in the middle. □ *Suddenly, he doubled over and collapsed.* □ *The people in the audience doubled over with laughter.*

double someone over to cause someone to bend in the middle. □ *The blow to the back of the head doubled Steve over.* □ *The wind almost doubled Debbie over.*

double something over to fold something over. □ *Double the paper over twice, then press it flat.* □ *Double the cloth over a few times before you pack it away.*

DOUBLE ▸ UP

double up (on someone or something) [for people] to deal with someone or something in pairs. □ *We are going to have to double up in this job.* □ *We will double up and get it done.*

double up (with someone) to share something with someone. □ *We don't have enough. You will have to double up with Sam.* □ *Let's double up and use the book together.* □ *We'll double up with each other.*

double up (with something) to bend in the middle with something such as laughter, howls, pain, etc. (Sometime figurative or an exaggeration.) □ *The man doubled up with laughter when he heard why we were there.* □ *He laughed so hard that he doubled up.*

DOUSE ▸ WITH

douse someone or something with something to splash or drench someone with something. □ *She doused her brother with a bucket of cold water.* □ *They had to keep dousing the porpoise with cold water to keep it healthy.*

DOVETAIL ▸ INTO

dovetail something into something to fit something neatly into something; to make something interlock nicely with something else. (Both literal and figurative uses.) □ *The carpenter dovetailed the new drawer front into the old drawer sides.* □ *She dovetailed her story into mine perfectly and the police let us go.*

DOVETAIL ▸ WITH

dovetail with something to fit neatly into something; to interlock nicely with something. (Both literal and figurative uses.) □ *This part dovetails with this part and makes a firm fit.* □ *The side of the drawer dovetails with the front of the drawer.* □ *Your story doesn't dovetail with mine very well.*

DOWNGRADE ▸ TO

downgrade someone or something to something to decrease the status of someone or something to something. □ *In effect, this downgrades your project to unimportant.* □ *I didn't mean to downgrade you to the assistant status.*

DOZE ▸ OFF

doze off (to sleep) to slip away into sleep. □ *I dozed off to sleep during the second act of the opera.* □ *I was so comfortable that I just dozed off.*

DRAFT ▸ FOR

draft someone for something to select someone for something or to do something. □ *We drafted a bunch of the boys for moving tables.* □ *The committee drafted some of the members for kitchen work.*

DRAFT ▸ INTO

draft someone into something **1.** to conscript someone into the armed services. □ *The draft board drafted Scott into the army.* □ *Todd was drafted into the army.* **2.** to convince someone to participate in something. □ *She drafted some of the boys into helping her move tables.* □ *They were drafted into helping.*

DRAG ▸ AT

drag at something to suck on something, such as a cigarette, pipe, cigar, etc. □ *He dragged at a nasty cigar stuck in his pasty face.* □ *She dragged at the cigarette once, then stubbed it out.*

DRAG ▸ AWAY

drag something away (from something) to pull something away from something or some place. □ *He dragged the sofa away from the wall so he could clean behind it.* 🅃 *He had to drag away the sofa in order to plug in the lamp.* □ *We worked together to drag it away.*

DRAG ▸ BEHIND

drag behind to follow along behind someone. □ *His little brother came along, dragging behind.* □ *Stop dragging along behind!*

drag something behind one to pull something that is behind one. □ *The child dragged the wooden toy behind him.* □ *What is that you are dragging behind you?*

DRAG ▸ DOWN

drag someone or something down **1.** to pull someone or something to a lower level. (*Someone* includes *oneself.*) □ *The lions dragged the antelope down and made dinner out of it.* 🅃 *They dragged down the antelope.* □ *The weight of the scuba equipment dragged the diver down.* □ *He dragged himself down to where he was safe from the gunfire.* **2.** to debase someone or something; to corrupt someone or something. □ *The bad acting dragged the level of the performance down.* 🅃 *The bad acting dragged down the level of the performance.* □ *Don't let your colleagues drag you down.* □ *Don't drag me down with the rest of you.*

DRAG ▸ IN

drag someone in on something to force someone to join something or participate in something. □ *Don't drag me in on this.* □ *Let's try to drag some of the others in on this.*

DRAG ▸ IN(TO)

drag someone or something in(to something) **1.** to haul or pull someone or something into something or some place. (*Someone* includes *oneself.*) □ *The child's mother dragged him into store after store, looking for new shoes.* 🅃 *She dragged in the child to get some shoes.* □ *Despite his broken leg, he dragged himself into the shelter.* **2.** to involve someone or a group in something. □ *Please don't drag me into your argument.* □ *Don't drag the committee into this argument.* □ *It is a mess, and please don't drag me into it.*

DRAG ▸ OFF

drag someone or something off ((of) someone or something) to pull someone or something off someone or something. (The *of*-phrase is paraphrased with a *from*-phrase when the particle is transposed. See the 🄵 example. The *of* is colloquial.) □ *The police officers dragged the boys off of the top of the wall.* 🅃 *The cops dragged off the boys and took them home.* 🄵 *The police dragged off the protesters from the dance floor.* □ *We dragged the fallen tree off.*

drag someone or something off (to someone or something) to haul someone or something away to someone, something, or some place. □ *The cops dragged her off to jail.* 🅃 *They dragged off the criminal to the judge.* □ *We dragged him off.*

DRAG ▸ ON

See also under *DRAG ▸ ON(TO).*

drag on to go on slowly for a very long time; to last a very long time. □ *The lecture dragged on and on.* □ *Why do these things have to drag on so?*

drag on something to pull or suck on something such as a cigarette, pipe, cigar, etc. ☐ *He dragged again on his pipe, which was beginning to sound like a bubble pipe and smell like a garbage incinerator.* ☐ *She kept dragging on a funny little cigarette.*

drag one's feet on something to progress slowly or stall in the doing of something. ☐ *Why is she taking so long? I think she is just dragging her feet on this matter.* ☐ *I didn't mean to drag my feet on this matter.*

DRAG ▸ ON(TO)

drag someone or something on((to) something) to pull or lead someone or something to a particular place, such as a stage, platform, dance floor, etc. ☐ *The master of ceremonies dragged her onto the stage for another bow.* 🅃 *Then he dragged on the next performer.* ☐ *Fran dragged Andrew on and tried to make him sing.*

DRAG ▸ OUT

drag out to last for a long time. ☐ *The lecture dragged out for nearly an hour.* ☐ *How much longer do you think this thing will drag out?*

drag something out to make something last for a long time. ☐ *Why does the chairman have to drag the meeting out so long?* 🅃 *Don't drag out the meetings so long!*

drag something out of someone to force someone to reveal something; to pull an answer or information out of someone laboriously. ☐ *Why don't you just tell me? Do I have to drag it out of you?* 🅃 *We had to drag out the information, but she finally told us.*

DRAG ▸ OVER

drag someone or something over to someone or something to pull or haul someone or something to someone or something. (*Someone* includes *oneself.*) ☐ *He dragged the chair over to the window so he could sit and watch the children.* 🅃 *Drag over a chair to the table and sit down.* ☐ *Drag a chair over here.* ☐ *He dragged himself over to the window and signaled for help.*

DRAG ▸ THROUGH

drag someone or something through something **1.** to pull someone or something through something. (*Someone* includes *oneself.*) ☐ *I dragged my brother through the opening into the room.* ☐ *We dragged the sofa through the window because we couldn't get it through the door.* ☐ *She had to drag herself through the mud to get to solid ground.* **2.** to debase someone or something. (*Someone* includes *oneself*. Usually with *mud.*) ☐ *Do you have to drag me through the mud? Can't I have a few secrets?* ☐ *I don't want you to drag me through all this.* ☐ *She dragged herself through the mud in her autobiography.*

DRAG ▸ UP

drag someone up to force someone to come up or to come and stand nearby. (*Someone* includes *oneself.*) ☐ *He wouldn't come on his own, so I dragged him up.* 🅃 *You will have to drag him up. He is too tired to walk by himself.* ☐ *I had to drag myself up to bed.*

drag something up to pull something close, such as a chair, stool, etc. (Colloquial.) ☐ *Please drag a chair up and sit down.* 🅃 *Drag up a chair and sit for a while.*

DRAGOON ▸ INTO

dragoon someone into something to force someone into doing something. ☐ *We dragooned the boys into helping us.* ☐ *She was trying to dragoon some of the men into setting up the banquet tables.*

DRAIN ▸ AWAY

drain away [for something] to flow away. ☐ *All the water drained away and the fish lay dead on the bottom of the pond.* ☐ *When the water drained away, we found three snapping turtles in the bottom of the pond.*

drain something away (from something) to channel some liquid away from something. ☐ *Drain all of the standing water away from the foundation of the house.* 🅃 *Drain away the water from the foundation.* ☐ *Please drain it away.*

DRAIN ▸ FROM

drain from something to flow out of something. ☐ *All the dirty oil drained from the engine.* ☐ *The milk drained from the jug and covered the bottom of the refrigerator.*

drain something from someone or something to cause something to flow out of someone or something. ☐ *The farmers drained the water from the flooded fields.* ☐ *The doctor drained the fluids from Roger after his operation.*

DRAIN ▸ OF

drain someone or something of something **1.** to empty something out of someone or something. ☐ *He drained the glass of the remaining beer.* ☐ *The doctor drained John of the remaining fluids.* **2.** to exhaust someone or something of something, such as energy, motivation, etc. ☐ *This day has drained me of all my motivation.* ☐ *The first performance drained the cast of all its energy.*

DRAIN ▸ OFF

drain something off (from something) to cause or permit something to flow out of something. ☐ *Drain some of the fat off the gravy before you serve it.* 🅃 *Please drain off the fat!* ☐ *Oh, yes! Drain it off, please!*

drain something off (of something) to cause or permit something to flow from the surface or top of something. (The *of*-phrase is paraphrased with a *from*-phrase when the particle is transposed. See the 🄵 example.) ☐ *Drain some of the broth off the chicken.* 🅃 *Drain off the broth.* 🄵 *Drain off the broth from the chicken.* ☐ *Drain the fat off.*

DRAIN ▸ OUT

drain out to flow out or empty. ☐ *All the milk drained out of the container onto the bottom of the refrigerator.* ☐ *All the oil drained out of the crankcase.*

drain something out to cause something to flow out. ☐ *Drain all this water out.* 🅃 *Please drain out the water.*

drain something out of something to cause something to flow from something; to empty all of some liquid out of something. (The *of*-phrase is paraphrased with a *from*-phrase when the particle is transposed. See the 🄵 example.) ☐ *She drained the last drop out of the bottle.* 🅃 *She drained out the last drop.* 🄵 *She drained out the last drop from the bottle.*

DRAPE ▸ AROUND

drape something around someone or something to wrap or hang something around someone or something. (*Someone* includes *oneself*.) ☐ *She draped the shawl around her shoulders and felt a little warmer.* ☐ *Mother draped a towel around Timmy and went into the next room for his pajamas.* ☐ *Vera draped the blanket around herself.*

DRAPE ▸ IN

drape someone or something in something to wrap someone or something in something. (*Someone* includes *oneself*.) ☐ *They draped her in golden silks, but she still looked like a country girl.* ☐ *They draped the statue in polka-dot cloth for the party.* ☐ *She draped herself in the fur coat and giggled.*

DRAPE ▸ OVER

drape oneself over something to sprawl on a piece of furniture. ☐ *He draped himself over the armchair and dropped off to sleep.* ☐ *He came in and draped himself over Mrs. Bracknell's grandmother's antique chair.*

drape over (something) [for cloth] to cover something and hang down. ☐ *The robe draped over her knees, but she was still cold.* ☐ *The cloth draped over and reached down to the floor.* ☐ *Make sure that the tablecloth drapes over all the way around.*

DRAPE ▸ WITH

drape someone or something with something to hang something on someone or something. (*Someone* includes *oneself*.) ☐ *They draped each guest with a makeshift toga.* ☐ *They draped the statue with a brightly colored loincloth.* ☐ *She draped herself with beautiful silks and yards of pearls.*

DRAW ▶ AGAINST

draw against something to withdraw money from something in advance. ☐ *I can draw against my allowance—at least a small amount.* ☐ *You cannot draw against your salary.*

DRAW ▶ AHEAD

draw ahead (of someone or something) to pull or move ahead of someone or something in motion. ☐ *I drew ahead of the car in front of me.* ☐ *The horse I was racing against drew ahead.*

DRAW ▶ ALONGSIDE

draw (up) alongside ((of) someone or something) See under *DRAW ▶ UP.*

DRAW ▶ APART

draw apart from someone or something to pull away from someone or a group. ☐ *Don't draw apart from the rest of us.* ☐ *Walter drew apart from the group.*

draw something apart to pull something open or apart. ☐ *She drew the curtains apart and looked out the window.* 🅃 *She drew apart the curtains a little bit.*

DRAW ▶ ASIDE

draw (oneself) aside [for someone] to move aside. ☐ *I drew myself aside so the children could pass.* ☐ *He drew himself aside so Maggie could pass.* ☐ *She drew aside so the children could pass.*

draw someone aside to pull or steer someone aside. ☐ *The teacher drew Bob aside to have a word with him.* ☐ *He drew the student aside to make a private comment.*

DRAW ▶ AT

draw the line at something to restrict oneself from doing something as extreme as some specific deed. ☐ *I draw the line at cheating on my taxes.* ☐ *Max does not draw the line at anything.*

DRAW ▶ AWAY

draw away (from someone or something) to pull back or away from someone or something. ☐ *Please don't draw away from me. I won't bite.* ☐ *She drew away.*

draw something away (from someone or something) **1.** to capture attention or praise due to someone or something. ☐ *Her sterling performance drew attention away from the big star in one of the other roles.* 🅃 *She drew away too much attention.* ☐ *Don't draw the applause away from Susan.* **2.** to lure or attract something away from an attack on someone or something; to attract gunfire aimed at someone or something. ☐ *She sought to draw the gunfire away from the others.* 🅃 *She tried to draw away the gunfire.* ☐ *She drew it away.*

DRAW ▶ BACK

draw back to pull back; to respond to being pulled back. ☐ *The main drape drew back, revealing a beautifully set stage.* ☐ *The cat drew back as the snake hissed at it.*

draw back (from someone or something) to pull back from someone or something; to recoil from someone or something. ☐ *The timid puppy drew back from my hand.* ☐ *She drew back from me, shocked.*

DRAW ▶ BETWEEN

draw a line between something and something else to distinguish between something and something else. ☐ *I draw a line between thinking about stealing and actually doing it.* ☐ *I cannot draw a line between the two. They are both wrong.*

DRAW ▶ DOWN

draw something down to pull something down. ☐ *She drew the shades down to cut off the bright sunlight.* 🅃 *She drew down the shades.*

DRAW ▶ FOR

draw for something to choose lots for something, without looking; to draw a token for something from a set of tokens concealed in something. (The tokens can be slips of paper, one of which is marked as the winner, or straws, one of which is longer or shorter than the others.) ☐ *Let's draw for it. The winner gets it.* ☐ *Everyone wants it. We will draw for it.*

draw straws for something to decide who gets something by choosing a token from an unseen set of tokens, originally straws of different lengths. (The tokens can be slips of paper, one of which is marked as the winner, or straws, one of which is longer or shorter than the others.) ☐ *We drew straws for the privilege of going first.* ☐ *Let's draw straws for it.*

DRAW ▸ FORTH

draw something forth to pull something forward or where it can be seen. ☐ *Carl drew a booklet forth and began to show it to the people sitting on either side of him.* 🅃 *She drew forth her dagger and threatened the bandit.*

DRAW ▸ FROM

draw from something to sketch from a particular source, such as memory, real life, a photograph, etc. ☐ *He is a very good artist. He can draw from a photograph or a painting.* ☐ *I will try to draw from memory.*

draw something from something **1.** See *draw someone or something out (of something)* under *DRAW ▸ OUT.* **2.** to sketch something from a particular source, such as memory, real life, a photograph, etc. ☐ *She drew a beautiful scene from her memory.* ☐ *Ann drew the scene from the photograph.*

DRAW ▸ IN(TO)

draw someone or something in(to something) **1.** to pull someone or something into something; to attract someone or something in. ☐ *She drew the child into the shoe store and plunked her down.* 🅃 *Liz opened the door and drew in the child.* ☐ *The advertisement drew a lot of people in.* **2.** to sketch a picture, adding someone or something into the picture. (*Someone* includes *oneself.*) ☐ *She drew a little dog into the lower corner of the picture.* ☐ *I drew the man in.* ☐ *She drew herself into the scene.* **3.** to involve someone or something in something. ☐ *Don't draw me into this argument.* ☐ *This is not the time to draw that argument into the discussion.*

DRAW ▸ NEAR

draw near [for a particular time] to approach. ☐ *The time to depart is drawing near.* ☐ *As the time drew near, Ann became more and more nervous.*

draw near (to someone or something) to come near to someone or something. ☐ *Draw near to me, and let me look at you.* ☐ *Draw near to the table and look at this.*

DRAW ▸ OFF

draw something off (from something) to remove a portion of a liquid from something; to cause something to flow from something. ☐ *The steward drew some wine off from the cask.* 🅃 *He drew off some wine.* ☐ *We drew some more off.*

DRAW ▸ ON

draw a bead on someone or something **1.** to locate someone or something in the sights of a gun. ☐ *Max drew a bead on Lefty and pulled the trigger.* ☐ *The hunter drew a bead on the deer.* **2.** to prepare to deal with or obtain someone or something. (Figurative.) ☐ *You could see she was drawing a bead on Ted's job.* ☐ *She drew a bead on Ted.*

draw on someone or something to use someone or something in some beneficial way. ☐ *I may have to draw on your advice in order to complete this project.* ☐ *If there is some way you can draw on me to your advantage, let me know.*

DRAW ▸ OUT

draw someone or something out (of something) **1.** to lure someone or some creature out of something or some place. (The *of*-phrase is paraphrased with a *from*-phrase when the particle is transposed. See the 🄵 example.) ☐ *I thought the smell of breakfast would draw him out of his reverie.* 🅃 *The good smells drew out the rest of the family.* 🄵 *The good smells drew out the boys from their rooms.* 🄵 *The magician drew out a rabbit from the hat.* ☐ *The warm sunlight drew the snake out of its lair.* **2.** to pull someone or something out of something or some place. (The *of*-phrase is paraphrased with a *from*-phrase when the particle is transposed. See the 🄵 example.) ☐ *We drew him out of the slot in the wall where he lay hiding.* 🅃 *We drew out the concealed microphone.* 🄵 *We drew out the concealed microphone* *from a crack in the baseboard.* ☐ *Tom drew the stowaway out of the locker.*

draw someone out to seek a response from someone. ☐ *He was a very shy child. We tried to draw him out, but he just blushed.* T *We were unable to draw out the elderly man.*

draw someone out (on someone or something) AND **draw someone out (about someone or something)** to find out someone's private thoughts about someone or something. ☐ *I tried to draw him out on this matter, but he would not say any more.* T *I tried to draw out the speaker, but she was very careful about what she said.* T *Fred wanted to draw out information about the company's plans, but the controller had nothing to say.* ☐ *We were not able to draw her out as hard as we tried.*

draw something out **1.** to extend something in time. ☐ *Do we have to draw this thing out? Let's get it over with.* T *Stop drawing out the proceedings.* A *I am tired of these long, drawn-out meetings!* **2.** to lengthen something. ☐ *She drew the bubble gum out and made a long pink string.* T *Look at her drawing out that gum. What a mess!* A *She placed the drawn-out taffy on the counter and cut it into chunks.*

draw something out (of someone) to get some kind of information from someone. (The *of*-phrase is paraphrased with a *from*-phrase when the particle is transposed. See the F example.) ☐ *He kept his mouth closed and we couldn't draw anything out of him.* T *We were able to draw out the information we wanted.* F *We were able to draw out the information from the agents.*

DRAW ▶ OVER

draw something over someone or something to cover someone or something with something. ☐ *She drew the cover over the sleeping form.* ☐ *Polly drew some plastic over her work and left for the day.*

DRAW ▶ TO

draw someone's attention to someone or something to attract someone to center on someone or something. ☐ *Now, I would like to draw your attention to Fred, the gentleman we have all heard so much about.* ☐ *Could I draw your attention to the statue standing at the entrance?*

draw something to to close something, such as curtains, drapes, etc. ☐ *She drew the drapes to and turned on the lights.* ☐ *Please draw the door to as you leave.*

draw something to a close to make something come to an end. ☐ *It is time we drew this evening to a close.* ☐ *Ann drew the meeting to a close with a few words of encouragement.*

draw to a close to come to an end. ☐ *The school year is drawing to a close.* ☐ *As this project draws to a close, you should make sure that everything we promised has been done.*

DRAW ▶ TOGETHER

draw people or things together to pull people together; to pull things together. ☐ *She drew her toys together in preparation for leaving.* T *She drew together all the people she wanted to talk to.* ☐ *Please draw them all together.* ☐ *They drew themselves together to keep warm.*

draw someone together to make people seek one another for emotional support. ☐ *The accident drew them all together.* ☐ *Do you think the meeting will draw us together better?*

DRAW ▶ TO(WARD)

draw someone or something to(ward) someone or something to pull someone or something to someone or something. ☐ *She drew him toward her and kissed him.* ☐ *Todd drew the child toward the light.* ☐ *Kelly tried to draw the chair to the window.*

DRAW ▶ UP

draw oneself up (to something) to stand up straight and reach a certain height. ☐ *Walter drew himself up to his six-foot height and walked away.* ☐ *She drew herself up and walked away.* ☐ *Tom drew himself up to his full height.*

draw something up **1.** to pull something close by, such as a chair, stool, etc. ☐ *Draw a chair up and sit down.* T *She* *drew up a chair and sat down.* **2.** to draft a document; to prepare a document. □ *Who will draw a contract up?* 🅃 *I will draw up a contract for the work.* 🄰 *The poorly drawn-up papers were rejected by the court.*

draw up to pull up; to shrink up. □ *When they got wet, his trunks drew up and became very tight.* □ *This cheap underwear has a tendency to draw up.*

draw (up) alongside ((of) someone or something) to move up even with someone or something in motion. □ *The police officer drew up alongside us and ordered us to pull over.* □ *A car drew up alongside of us.* □ *Draw up alongside that car.*

DREAM ▸ ABOUT

dream about someone or something AND **dream of someone or something** to have mental pictures about someone or something, especially in one's sleep. □ *I dreamed about you all night last night.* □ *I dreamed of a huge chocolate cake.* 🄰 *How would you like to go on an often-dreamed-about vacation?* 🄰 *The trickster promised her undreamed-of riches.*

DREAM ▸ AWAY

dream something away to waste away a period of time having fantasies. □ *I just want to sit in the sun and dream the day away.* 🅃 *Don't dream away your life!*

DREAM ▸ OF

dream of doing something to have a fantasy of doing something. □ *I dream of owning a house like that.* □ *Clara dreamed of sailing off into the sunset with Roger.*

dream of someone or something See under *DREAM ▸ ABOUT.*

DREAM ▸ UP

dream something up to invent something; to fabricate something. (The *something* can be the word *something*.) □ *I don't know what to do, but I'll dream something up.* 🅃 *Please dream up a solution for this problem.*

DREDGE ▸ UP

dredge someone or something up **1.** to scoop something up from underwater. □ *The workers dredged the lifeless body up from the cold black water.* 🅃 *They dredged up the lifeless body.* □ *They were amazed to dredge up an equally surprised scuba diver.* **2.** to seek and find someone or something. (Figurative.) □ *I will see if I can dredge a date up for Friday.* 🅃 *Can you dredge up a date for me?* □ *I don't have a wrench here, but I'll see if I can dredge one up.*

DRENCH ▸ IN

drench someone or something in something AND **drench someone or something with something** to soak someone or something in something. (*Someone* includes *oneself*.) □ *A sudden downpour drenched them in warm rain.* □ *The rain drenched them with the warm droplets that one always finds in this part of the world.* □ *He spilled his drink and drenched himself in cola.*

DRENCH ▸ WITH

drench someone or something with something See the previous entry.

DRESS ▸ AS

dress (up) as someone or something to dress in the manner of someone or something. □ *I am going to dress up as a ghost for Halloween.* □ *Larry will dress up as the pumpkin from Cinderella.* □ *Sam will dress as himself.*

DRESS ▸ DOWN

dress someone down to scold someone. □ *His mother dressed him down but good.* 🅃 *I hate to have to get mad and dress down some helpless kid.*

DRESS ▸ FOR

dress for someone to clothe oneself to please someone. □ *I don't dress for you! Don't tell me how to dress!* □ *Sally says she dresses for her friends, but she really dresses for herself.*

dress for something to clothe oneself suitably for some occasion or activity, or for success. □ *Finally, I learned to dress for success.* □ *I can wear my tuxedo if you want me to dress for dinner.*

DRESS ▸ IN

dress someone or something (up) (in something) See under *DRESS ▸ UP.*

DRESS ▸ UP

dress (oneself) up to dress in fancy dress. □ *They dressed themselves up in their finest.* □ *Please dress up for the dance.* □ *I just love to dress myself up for a party.*

dress someone or something up to make someone or something appear fancier than is actually so. (*Someone* includes *oneself.*) □ *The publicity specialist dressed the actress up a lot.* 🅃 *They dressed up the actress so much that no one recognized her in person.* □ *They dressed up the hall so it looked like a ballroom.* 🄰 *Look at all these nicely dressed-up people!* □ *Go dress yourself up for the party.*

dress someone or something (up) (in something) to clothe, decorate, or ornament someone or something in something. (*Someone* includes *oneself.*) □ *She dressed her dolls up in special clothing.* 🅃 *She dressed up her dolls in tiny outfits.* 🅃 *She dressed up all of them.* □ *Roger dressed his nephew up for the service.* □ *Dress yourself up in your finest.*

dress someone (up) (as someone or something) to dress someone to look like or impersonate someone or something. (*Someone* includes *oneself.*) □ *She dressed her little girl up as a witch for Halloween.* 🅃 *She dressed up her little girl as a fairy.* □ *Martha dressed June up.* □ *I dressed myself up as Santa Claus.* □ *Please dress yourself up as a clown for the contest.*

dress (up) as someone or something See under *DRESS ▸ AS.*

DRIFT ▸ ALONG

drift along to float along; to be carried along. □ *The boat just drifted along lazily with the current.* □ *The project drifted along until we received the direction we needed.*

DRIFT ▸ APART

drift apart (from someone or something) [for two or more people or things] to be carried along in different ways; to separate slowly from someone or something. □ *He drifted apart from his friends.* □ *The boats drifted apart from one another.* □ *As the years went by, they drifted apart.* □ *The boats drifted apart in the current.*

DRIFT ▸ AWAY

drift away (from someone or something) to move away slowly from someone or something stationary. □ *The boat drifted away from the shore.* □ *As it drifted away, the people on the island became hysterical.*

DRIFT ▸ BACK

drift back (to someone or something) to move back to someone or something slowly, on the surface of water. (Considerable metaphorical use.) □ *The canoe drifted back to shore.* □ *Finally he drifted back to her and they made up.*

DRIFT ▸ IN

drift in(to something) to move slowly and gradually into something. □ *The people drifted slowly into the hall.* □ *The boats drifted into the masses of pondweed.*

DRIFT ▸ OFF

drift off to move slowly away. □ *The boat slowly drifted off and was gone.* □ *The clouds drifted off and were soon gone.*

drift off to sleep to fall asleep gradually. □ *At last, he drifted off to sleep.* □ *During that boring lecture, I drifted off to sleep a number of times.*

DRIFT ▸ OUT

drift out to move out of a place slowly. □ *After there was no more food, the people drifted out, one by one.* □ *The boat drifted out and almost got away.*

DRIFT ▸ TO(WARD)

drift to(ward) someone or something to move slowly and gradually toward someone or something. □ *The clouds drifted toward us, and we could see that a storm was coming.* □ *As the clouds drifted to us, we could feel the humidity increase.*

DRIFT ▶ WITH

drift with something to float along with something; to be carried along at the same rate as something. (Literal and figurative uses.) □ *He paddled the canoe into the center of the stream and let it drift with the current.* □ *He is not very decisive and is as likely as not to drift with the tide of sentiment.*

DRILL ▶ DOWN

drill down to something to bore downward to something or some distance. □ *We drilled down to a layer of water-bearing sand, hoping to make a well.* □ *They had to drill down to bedrock to make a base for the piers that hold the building up.*

DRILL ▶ IN

drill someone in something to give someone practice in something. □ *Now, I am going to drill you in irregular verbs.* □ *The teacher drilled the students in the use of the passive.*

DRILL ▶ INTO

drill into something to bore into or penetrate something. □ *The worker drilled into the wall in three places.* □ *Please don't drill into the wall here, where it shows.*

DRILL ▶ IN(TO)

drill something in(to someone or something) to force knowledge into someone or something. □ *Learn this stuff! Drill it into your brain.* 🅃 *Drill in this information so you know it by heart!* □ *Yes, I will drill it in.*

DRINK ▶ DOWN

drink something down to drink something; to consume all of something by drinking it. (Also without *down,* but not eligible as an entry.) □ *Here, drink this down, and see if it makes you feel better.* 🅃 *Drink down this medicine.*

DRINK ▶ IN

drink something in to absorb something; to take in information, sights, a story, etc. □ *Terry and Amy drove up the top of the hill to drink the sights in.* 🅃 *They drank in the beautiful view.*

DRINK ▶ TO

drink to someone or something to toast someone or something; to take an alcoholic drink in honor of someone or something. □ *I'll drink to that!* □ *Let us drink to our guest of honor, Wallace J. Wilson!*

DRINK ▶ UNDER

drink someone under the table to be able to drink more alcohol than someone else. (The loser of this contest will collapse under the table before the winner has finished drinking.) □ *I bet I can drink you under the table.* □ *Max drank Lefty under the table.*

DRINK ▶ UP

drink something up to drink all of something. □ *Who drank all the root beer up?* 🅃 *I drank up the root beer.*

drink up to drink something; to drink all of something. □ *Drink up, and let's get going.* □ *Let's drink up and be on our way.*

DRIP ▶ INTO

drip into something [for a liquid] to fall into something drop by drop. □ *The water dripped into the bowl we had put under the leak.* □ *Is the water still dripping into the sink?*

drip something in(to something) to make something fall into something drop by drop. □ *Alice dripped a little candle wax into the base of the candlestick.* 🅃 *Don't pour it all into the jar. Drip in a little at a time.* □ *Don't just drip it in. Pour it all in at once.*

DRIP ▶ WITH

drip with something **1.** to be heavy or overloaded with something to the point of overflowing. □ *The foliage dripped with the heavy morning dew.* □ *Her clothing dripped with seawater as she climbed back onto the deck.* **2.** [for someone's speech] to show certain states of mind or attitudes. □ *Her voice dripped with sarcasm.* □ *The old lady's voice dripped with sweetness and affection.* □ *His words dripped with dejection.*

DRIVE ▸ AROUND

drive someone around something to transport a person in a vehicle on a tour of something or some place. (*Someone* includes *oneself*.) □ *Fred will drive you around the park.* □ *He spent an hour driving himself around town.*

drive someone around the bend to drive someone crazy; to make someone very frustrated. (Idiomatic. *Someone* includes *oneself*.) □ *You are going to drive me around the bend!* □ *Finally, she drove herself around the bend.*

drive something around something **1.** to steer or propel something around something. □ *Wally drove the small car around the post easily.* □ *Please drive your truck around the corner carefully.* **2.** to propel a vehicle through different parts of a place. □ *He drove his new car around town, hoping everyone would see it.* □ *We drove the car around the parade route twice so everyone could get a good look at it.* **3.** to force or herd creatures around something. □ *We drove the cattle around the garden, trying to keep them from trampling the vegetables.* □ *It is not possible to drive cattle around something they want to go through.*

DRIVE ▸ AT

drive at something to be making a point; to be hinting at something; to work up to making a point. □ *What are you driving at? What's the point?* □ *I could tell Mary was driving at something, but I didn't know what it was.*

DRIVE ▸ AWAY

drive away to leave some place driving a vehicle. □ *They got in the car and drove away.* □ *They drove away and left us here.*

drive someone or something (away) (from some place) to repel someone or some creature from some place. □ *We drove the monkeys away from the pineapples.* 🆃 *We drove away the monkeys from the fruit.* □ *Get out there and drive those deer out of my flowers!* □ *The gang's activity drove a lot of people away from the neighborhood.* □ *His drinking drove away his family and his friends.*

DRIVE ▸ BACK

drive back to propel a vehicle back to where it started. □ *Mary drove back and parked the car where it had been when she started.* □ *You drive us there and I'll drive back.*

drive someone back on something to force someone to tap reserves of something. □ *The hard times drove them back on their life savings.* □ *The challenges of the meeting drove her back on all her personal resources.*

drive someone back to someone to force someone to return to someone, such as a spouse, lover, parent, etc. □ *Her bad experience with her new friend drove her back to her husband.* □ *Being homeless was no fun, and soon Wally was driven back to his parents.*

drive someone or something back to force someone or something away; to force someone or something to retreat. □ *The infantry drove the attackers back into the desert.* 🆃 *They drove back the invading army.* □ *We drove them back.*

DRIVE ▸ BETWEEN

drive a wedge (in) between someone and someone else to cause people to oppose one another or turn against one another. (Figurative.) □ *The argument drove a wedge between Mike and his father.* 🆃 *It drove in a wedge between Mike and his father.*

drive between something and something to run a vehicle between things or places. □ *I can't drive between work and home in less than thirty minutes.* □ *The cab driver drove between the airport and downtown over twelve times in one day.*

DRIVE ▸ DOWN

drive down (to some place) to run a vehicle to a relatively lower place or to a place in the south. □ *We are going to drive down to Houston for the weekend.* □ *We were going to fly, but it will be nice to drive down.*

drive someone down (to some place) to transport someone to a relatively lower place or to a place in the south. (*Some-*

one includes *oneself*.) □ *We have to drive Andrew down to school in the fall.* □ *She drove herself down to the hospital.* □ *Would you drive Sally down when you come this weekend?*

drive something down to force the price of something down. □ *The lack of buyers drove the price down.* 🅃 *The lack of buyers drove down the price.*

drive something down (to some place) to transport a vehicle to a place by driving it there. □ *I will drive the car down to the college and leave it there for you.* 🅃 *I'll drive down the car and meet you.* □ *Do I have to drive the car down? Can't you fly up here and get it?*

DRIVE ▸ FROM

drive someone or something (away) (from some place) See under *DRIVE ▸ AWAY.*

DRIVE ▸ IN

See also under *DRIVE ▸ IN(TO).*

drive a wedge (in) between someone and someone else See under *DRIVE ▸ BETWEEN.*

DRIVE ▸ INTO

drive someone into a corner **1.** to force someone into the place where two walls intersect. □ *They drove him into a corner and captured him there.* □ *When he is driven into a corner, he will fight.* **2.** to force someone into a position or state where there are few choices and no escape. (Figurative.) □ *You have driven me into a corner, so I guess I have to give in.* □ *Todd was driven into a corner.*

drive something into the ground to dwell on a point far too long. (Figurative.) □ *I've heard enough about that. You are driving it into the ground.* □ *Donna has a tendency to drive a good story into the ground.*

DRIVE ▸ IN(TO)

drive in(to something) to enter something or some place by driving. □ *She drove right into the garage and stopped the car before she realized that she was not at her own house.* □ *She drove in and looked around.*

drive something in(to something) **1.** to steer or guide a vehicle into something. □ *Liz drove the car into the garage.* 🅃 *Liz drove it in.* □ *She drove in the car.* □ *He drove the truck right into the abutment.* **2.** to pound or hammer something into something. (See also *drive something into the ground.*) □ *Using a heavy mallet, he drove the stake into the hard earth.* □ *The stake was driven into the soil.* 🅃 *With a mighty hammer blow, she drove in the nail.* □ *Walter drove the stake in.*

DRIVE ▸ OFF

drive off to leave somewhere, driving a vehicle. □ *She got in her car and drove off.* □ *Please don't drive off and leave me!*

drive someone or something off to repel or chase away someone or something. □ *The campers drove the cows off before the animals trampled the tents.* 🅃 *They drove off the cows.* □ *They drove them off.*

DRIVE ▸ ON

drive on to continue driving; to continue with one's journey. □ *We drove on for a little while.* □ *The traffic jam is breaking up, so we can drive on.*

drive someone on (to something) to make someone move onward toward some kind of success. (*Someone* includes *oneself*.) □ *She said her parents drove her on to her great success.* 🅃 *They drove on their daughter to great things.* □ *The thought of earning a large salary drove him on.* □ *He drove himself on, even when he was exhausted.*

DRIVE ▸ OUT

drive one out of one's mind to make someone go crazy; to frustrate someone. □ *You are driving me out of my mind.* □ *Henry was driven out of his mind by all the negative comments.*

drive out (to some place) to propel a vehicle to a place that is away from the center of things. □ *We drove out to a little place in the country for a picnic.* □ *Why don't you drive out this weekend? We would love to have you here.*

drive someone or something out (of something) to force or chase someone or some creature out of something or some place. (The *of*-phrase is paraphrased with a *from*-phrase when the particle is transposed. See the Ⓕ example.) □ *We drove them all out of the country.* Ⓣ *We drove out the troublesome kids.* Ⓕ *We drove out the troublesome kids from the theater.* □ *They had to drive the raccoons out.*

DRIVE ▸ OVER

drive over (to some place) to motor to some place that is neither close by nor far away. □ *Let's drive over to Larry's place.* □ *Yes, let's drive over. It's too far to walk.*

DRIVE ▸ THROUGH

drive through (something) to motor from one side of something to the other; to pass through something while driving. □ *We drove through some nice little towns on the way here.* □ *We didn't stop. We just drove through.* Ⓐ *We were lined up at the only drive-through window at the bank.*

DRIVE ▸ TO

drive someone to despair to depress someone; to frustrate someone. □ *Sometimes you drive me to despair!* □ *The recent problems drove her to despair.*

drive someone to distraction to confuse or perplex someone. □ *Can't you see you're driving her to distraction?* □ *This mess is driving me to distraction.*

drive someone to drink [for someone or something] to cause someone to turn to alcohol as an escape from frustration. □ *That's enough to drive you to drink.* □ *She was driven to drink by her approach to her problems.*

drive someone to something to force someone to do something. (*Someone* includes *oneself*.) □ *She drove him to leaving her.* □ *She drove herself to stay awake.*

drive someone to the wall AND **force someone to the wall** to force someone into a defenseless position. □ *We drove them to the wall with our successful arguments.* □ *Stand on your own two feet. Don't let them force you to the wall.*

drive something home to someone to make something clearly understood to someone. (Figurative.) □ *I hope this really drives the importance of safety home to you.* □ *The events of the day really drive the importance of being prepared home to me.* Ⓣ *The accident drove home the importance of wearing seatbelts to everyone concerned.*

DRIVE ▸ UP

drive someone up the wall to frustrate or irritate someone. □ *You are driving me up the wall with your constant questions.* □ *All this mess is driving me up the wall.*

drive someone up (to some place) to transport someone to a place on a higher level or to a place in the north. □ *Ralph drove Sally up to the cabin.* □ *He was going to drive her up last week, but could not.*

drive something up AND **force something up** to force the price of something upwards. □ *Someone is buying a lot of this stuff and driving the price up.* Ⓣ *They are driving up the price.* □ *They forced up the price by cornering the market on these goods.*

drive up (to some place) to arrive some place in a vehicle. □ *She drove up to the door and stopped.* □ *Sally drove up and honked.* Ⓐ *Our car was tenth in line at the drive-up window.*

drive up to something to motor up close to something; to pull a car up to something. □ *The car drove up to the curb and stopped.* □ *If you want to order fried chicken here, you drive up to the window and place your order.*

DRIZZLE ▸ DOWN

drizzle down (on someone or something) to rain on someone or something. □ *The light rain drizzled down on the garden.* □ *The rain drizzled down and soaked us because we had no umbrella.* □ *A light rain drizzled down all day.*

DRONE ▸ ON

drone on to continue to make low-pitched noise or to speak in a dull and boring voice. ☐ *The professor droned on for what seemed like hours.* ☐ *Why does he drone on so? Is he asleep too?*

drone on (about someone or something) to lecture or narrate in a low-pitched, dull, and boring manner. ☐ *The dull old professor droned on about Byron—or was it Keats?* ☐ *It was Shelley and, yes, he did drone on.*

DRONE ▸ OUT

drone something out to make a loud and low-pitched noise; to utter human speech in a low-pitched and monotonous manner. ☐ *The announcer droned the winning numbers out.* 🅃 *She droned out the winning numbers.*

DROOL ▸ OVER

drool (all) over someone or something **1.** to drip saliva on someone or something. ☐ *You're drooling all over my plate!* ☐ *The dog drooled all over my hand.* **2.** to envy or desire someone or something. (Figurative. As if one were very hungry.) ☐ *The boys stood there, drooling over the fancy sports car.* ☐ *Wally Wilson spent many hours drooling over photographs of Marilyn.*

DROP ▸ ACROSS

drop across someone or something [for something long or wide] to fall on and lay on someone or something. ☐ *A snake dropped across the hood of the tourist bus as it passed under a tree.* ☐ *As I lay sleeping, a ceiling panel dropped across me and woke me up.*

drop something across something **1.** to let something fall in such a way that a rift is bridged; to let something fall in such a way that a pathway is blocked. ☐ *The helpers dropped a tree across the ravine as a bridge.* ☐ *Let's drop a little rug across the threshold.* ☐ *They dropped a huge boulder across the road so no one could pass.*

DROP ▸ AROUND

drop around (for something) to come for a casual visit that includes something such as tea, dinner, a drink, etc. ☐ *Drop around for a drink sometime.* ☐ *Yes, please drop around.*

drop around (sometime) to come for a casual visit at some future time. ☐ *Why don't you all drop around sometime for a visit?* ☐ *You must drop around sometime.*

DROP ▸ AWAY

drop away **1.** to fall off; to fall away. ☐ *The leaves were still dropping away from the trees in November.* ☐ *The dead branches dropped away from the tree.* **2.** to reduce in number over time. ☐ *His friends gradually dropped away.* ☐ *As the other contenders dropped away, Mary's chances improved.*

DROP ▸ BACK

drop back **1.** to fall back to an original position. ☐ *His arm raised up, and then dropped back.* ☐ *The lid dropped back to its original position as soon as we let go of it.* **2.** to go slowly and lose one's position in a march or procession. ☐ *He dropped back a bit and evened up the spacing in the line of marchers.* ☐ *He got tired and dropped back a little.*

DROP ▸ BEHIND

drop behind (in something) to fail to keep up with a schedule. ☐ *I don't want to drop behind in my work.* ☐ *She is dropping behind and needs someone to help her.*

drop behind (someone or something) **1.** to reduce speed and end up after someone or a group, at the back of a moving line. ☐ *I dropped behind the rest of the people, because I can't walk that fast.* ☐ *I dropped behind the speeding pack of cars and drove a little slower.* **2.** to fail to keep up with the schedule being followed by someone or a group. ☐ *My production output dropped behind what it should have been.* ☐ *I stayed later at work to keep from dropping behind.*

DROP ▸ BELOW

drop below someone or something to fall to a point lower than someone or something. ☐ *The gunman dropped below the cowboy's hiding place and got* *ready to take a shot.* □ *The temperature dropped below the freezing point.*

DROP ▸ BY

drop by (some place) AND **go by (some place)** to stop for a casual visit. (*Go by* means to stop at, not to pass by, in this expression.) □ *I hope you can drop by our house sometime.* □ *We really want you to drop by.* □ *We went by the house, but there was no one home.*

drop by the wayside AND **fall by the wayside** **1.** to leave a march or procession to rest beside the pathway. (The origin of the figurative usage in sense 2.) □ *A few of the marchers dropped by the wayside in the intense heat.* □ *Our work on the new procedures fell by the wayside.* **2.** to fail to keep up with others. (Figurative.) □ *Many of the students will drop by the wayside and never finish.* □ *Those who fall by the wayside will find it hard to catch up.*

DROP ▸ DOWN

drop down **1.** [for someone] to fall down or stoop down. □ *Suddenly, Ted dropped down, trying not to be seen by someone in a passing car.* □ *I dropped down as soon as I heard the loud sounds.* **2.** [for something] to fall from above. □ *The tiles on the ceiling dropped down, one by one, over the years.* □ *The raindrops dropped down and gave the thirsty plants a drink.*

drop down (on someone or something) to fall on someone or something. □ *The leaves dropped down on the newly mowed lawn.* □ *A bug on the ceiling dropped down on Wally.* □ *The wind blew a mighty puff and a thousand leaves dropped down.*

drop someone or something down to let someone or something fall. □ *He dropped his pants down, revealing the swimming trunks beneath.* [T] *The rescuer dropped down the baby to the doctor a few feet below.* □ *Sam went to the well and dropped a rock down.*

DROP ▸ FROM

drop someone or something from something **1.** to release someone or something from some higher point. □ *The eagle dropped the cat from a great height and snuffed out all nine lives in a few seconds.* □ *Max threatened to drop Lefty "Fingers" Moran from the top of the Empire State Building.* **2.** to exclude someone or something from something. (Figurative.) □ *We had to drop Sally from out guest list.* □ *The professor was forced to drop the failing students from the course.*

DROP ▸ IN

See also under *DROP ▸ IN(TO).*

drop in to come for a casual visit. □ *Please drop in when you get a chance.* □ *I hope you don't mind if I drop in for a while.*

drop in (on someone) to come for an unexpected, casual visit. □ *Guess who dropped in on us last night?* □ *I never thought Wally Wilson would drop in without calling first.*

drop in one's tracks **1.** to collapse from exhaustion. □ *I was so tired, I dropped in my tracks.* □ *Kelly almost dropped in her tracks from overwork.* **2.** to die instantly. □ *Finally, one day, he worked so hard that he dropped in his tracks.* □ *I know that someday I will just drop in my tracks.*

drop in (to say hello) to come for a brief, friendly visit. □ *We just dropped in to say hello. How are you all?* □ *We just wanted to drop in and see you.*

DROP ▸ IN(TO)

drop someone or something in(to something) to let someone or something fall into something. □ *He dropped a quarter into the slot and waited for something to happen.* [T] *He dropped in a quarter.* □ *Johnny Green dropped a cat into a well.* □ *He went to the well and dropped a cat in.*

DROP ▸ OFF

drop off **1.** [for someone or something] to fall off something. □ *The leaves finally dropped off about the middle of November.* □ *When do the leaves normally drop off in Vermont?* **2.** [for a part of something] to break away and fall off. □ *The car's bumper just dropped off—honest.* □ *I lifted boxes until I* *thought my arms would drop off.* **3.** to decline. (Figurative.) □ *Attendance at the meetings dropped off after Martin became president.* □ *Spending dropped off as the recession became worse.*

drop off (to sleep) to fall asleep. □ *She dropped off to sleep after she ate.* □ *After a few minutes of sitting, Grandfather dropped off.*

drop someone or something off ((at) some place) **1.** to let someone or a group out of a vehicle at a particular place; to deliver someone or something some place. □ *Let's drop these shirts off at the cleaners.* [T] *Let's drop off Tom and Jerry at the hamburger joint.* [T] *Please drop off my shirts too.* □ *I'd be happy to drop them off.* [N] *For what time should we plan the drop-off?* **2.** to give someone or a group a ride to some place. □ *Can I drop you off somewhere in town?* [T] *I dropped off the kids at the party.* □ *I can't drop you off there because I'm not going there.*

drop someone or something off (of something) to let someone or something fall from something; to make someone or something fall from something. (The *of*-phrase is paraphrased with a *from*-phrase when the particle is transposed. See the [F] example.) □ *They dropped the feather off the top of the building.* [T] *Jake dropped off a feather and it fell to the ground.* [F] *Jake dropped off a feather from the top of the building.* □ *Max took Lefty to the top of the building and threatened to drop him off.*

DROP ► ON

drop someone or something on someone or something to release something so it falls on someone or something. □ *Poor Alice dropped an iron on her toe.* □ *I accidentally dropped the baby on the floor.* □ *The crane dropped the worker on one of the bystanders. It was a terrible accident.*

drop something on someone to give someone some bad news. (Figurative.) □ *Sally dropped some really bad news on Walter.* □ *I'm sorry I had to drop it on you like that.*

DROP ► OUT

drop out (of something) **1.** [for someone] to resign from or cease being a member of something; [for someone] to leave school. □ *Sally dropped out of school for some unknown reason.* □ *But why did she drop out?* [N] *The mall was filled with dropouts and the homeless.* **2.** to fall out of something. □ *One by one, the divers dropped out of the plane.* □ *The marshmallows dropped out of the bag.* **3.** [for the bottom of something] to break loose and drop. (Both literal and figurative.) □ *The bottom dropped out of the box, spilling everything everywhere.* □ *The bottom dropped out, and we lost a lot of money.*

drop someone or something out (of something) to let someone or something fall out of something. □ *She dropped the paper out of the window.* □ *Max threatened to drop Lefty out of the open door of the plane.* □ *The litterbug opened the window, and he dropped the paper out.*

DROP ► OVER

drop over to come for a casual visit. □ *We would love for you to drop over.* □ *I would really like to drop over soon.*

DROP ► UP

drop up (some place) to come for a visit to a place that is relatively higher or in the north. □ *Drop up and see us sometime.* □ *Please drop up when you can.*

DROWN ► IN

drown in something **1.** to be asphyxiated in some liquid. □ *Wouldn't you hate to drown in that nasty, smelly water?* □ *I am not choosy about what I don't want to drown in.* **2.** to experience an overabundance of something. (Figurative.) □ *We are just drowning in cabbage this year. Our garden is full of it.* □ *They were drowning in bills, not money to pay them with.*

drown someone or something in something **1.** to cause someone or some creature to die of asphyxiation in a liquid. (*Someone* includes *oneself.*) □ *He accidentally drowned the cat in the bathtub.* □ *Max wanted to drown Lefty in* *the East River.* □ *She drowned herself in the lake.* **2.** to inundate someone or something with something. (Figurative. *Someone* includes *oneself.*) □ *I will drown you in money and fine clothes.* □ *Lefty drowned the nightclub singer in fancy jewels and furs.* □ *There are so many apricots this year. I practically drowned myself in apricots.*

DROWN ▸ OUT

drown someone or something out **1.** [for a flood] to drive someone or some creature away from home. □ *The high waters almost drowned the farmers out last year.* [T] *The water drowned out the fields.* □ *The flood almost drowned us out.* **2.** to make more noise than someone or something. □ *The noise of the passing train drowned our conversation out.* [T] *The noise of the passing train drowned out our conversation.* □ *The train drowned us out.*

DRUM ▸ IN(TO)

drum something in(to someone) AND **drum something in(to someone's head)** to teach someone something intensely. (As if one were pounding knowledge into someone's head.) □ *Her mother had drummed good manners into her.* [T] *She drummed in good manners day after day.* □ *The teacher drummed the multiplication tables into Tom's head.* □ *The teacher drummed them in.*

DRUM ▸ ON

drum on something to tap, thump, or beat on something in rhythm. □ *Who is drumming on the table?* □ *Please stop drumming on the wall.*

DRUM ▸ OUT

drum someone out of something to force someone to leave a position or an organization. □ *The citizen's group drummed the mayor out of office.* [T] *They drummed out the crooked politicians.*

drum something out to beat a rhythm, loudly and clearly, as if teaching it to someone. □ *Drum the rhythm out before you try to sing this song.* [T] *Drum out the rhythm first.*

DRUM ▸ UP

drum some business up to create business or trade in some item. □ *I'll go out and drum some business up.* [T] *Please go out and drum up some business.*

DRY ▸ OFF

dry someone or something off to remove the moisture from someone or something. (*Someone* includes *oneself.*) □ *Please dry your feet off before coming in.* [T] *Dry off your feet before you come in here!* □ *Todd dried the baby off and dressed him.* [A] *Please put these on the dried-off counter.* □ *I have to dry myself off before I catch cold.*

DRY ▸ OUT

dry out **1.** to become dry. □ *The clothes finally dried out in the wet weather.* [A] *I don't care for dried-out herbs.* **2.** to allow alcohol and the effects of drunkenness to dissipate from one's body. □ *He required about three days to dry out completely.* □ *He dried out in three days.*

dry someone out to cause someone to dissipate the effects of alcohol or drunkenness. □ *Put him in the hospital and dry him out!* [T] *We have to dry out those two drunks and get them into court by ten o'clock.* [A] *See if those recently dried-out winos need any help.*

dry something out to make something become dry. □ *Dry this out and put it on immediately.* [T] *Dry out your jacket in the clothes dryer.* [A] *There was nothing left but a few heaps of dried-out leaves.*

DRY ▸ UP

dry something up **1.** to cause moisture to dry away to nothing. □ *Dry this spill up with the hair dryer.* [T] *Will the hair dryer dry up this mess?* [A] *The dried-up seepage left some stains on the carpet.* **2.** to cure a skin rash by the use of medicine that dries. □ *Let's use some of this to try to dry that rash up.* [T] *This medicine will dry up your rash in a few days.* [A] *A few dried-up pox remained.*

dry up **1.** [for something] to dry away to nothing. □ *Finally, the water on the roads dried up, and we were able to con-*

tinue. □ *When will the fields dry up so we can plant?* **2.** [for someone] to be quiet or go away. (Slang.) □ *Dry up, you jerk!* □ *I wish you would dry up!*

DUB ▸ IN

dub something in to mix a new sound recording into an old one. □ *The actor messed up his lines, but they dubbed the correct words in later.* 🅃 *They dubbed in his lines.* 🄰 *You can tell there is a lot of dubbed-in dialog in the movie.*

DUB ▸ OVER

dub over something to record a replacement sound over another sound in a recording. □ *They had dubbed over all the dialog in the movie.* □ *It doesn't matter if you say a word wrong on the tape. We can dub over it.*

DUCK ▸ DOWN

duck down to stoop down quickly, as if to avoid being hit. □ *He ducked down when he heard the gunshot.* □ *Duck down and get out of the way.*

DUCK ▸ OUT

duck out (of some place) to sneak out of some place. □ *She ducked out of the theater during the intermission.* □ *When no one was looking, she ducked out.*

duck out of something to evade something; to escape doing something. □ *Are you trying to duck out of your responsibility?* □ *Fred tried to duck out of going to the dance.*

DUDE ▸ UP

dude (oneself) up to dress up well; to dress in fancy or stylish clothing. (Slang.) □ *I have to go dude myself up for the party.* □ *I'm not going to dude up tonight.* □ *Why don't you dude yourself up so we can go out tonight?*

DUKE ▸ OUT

duke someone out to punch someone; to knock someone out. (Slang.) □ *Ted duked Sam out.* 🅃 *Ted duked out Tony and Nick.*

DUMMY ▸ UP

dummy up to become silent; to refuse to talk. (Slang.) □ *Whenever I ask her about it, she dummies up.* □ *Max dummied up when they questioned him.*

DUMP ▸ ON

dump on someone or something to criticize or insult someone or something. (Slang. *Dump* can also mean "defecate." Use with discretion.) □ *She dumped on him about it.* □ *Stop dumping on me all the time.*

dump something on someone to pour out one's troubles to someone. (Colloquial.) □ *She dumped all her grief on her friend, Sally.* □ *I wish you wouldn't dump all your problems on me.*

DUMP ▸ OVER

dump all over someone to criticize someone severely; to castigate someone. (Slang.) □ *Why do you have to dump all over me? I didn't do anything wrong.* □ *Don't dump all over your friends!*

DUN ▸ FOR

dun someone for something to harass someone to pay a bill or deliver something. □ *If you don't pay the bill, they will dun you for it day and night.* □ *My job is to dun people for payment of their bills.*

DUNK ▸ IN(TO)

dunk someone or something in(to something) to submerge someone or something in something, fully or partially. (*Someone* includes *oneself.*) □ *They dunked him into the pool as a way of celebrating.* 🅃 *Liz pulled the cup of coffee toward herself and dunked in her doughnut.* □ *She dunked herself into the cold water for just a minute.*

DUST ▸ OFF

dust someone off to punch or beat someone. (Slang.) □ *We dusted them off one by one.* 🅃 *We had to dust off all those big guys.*

dust someone or something off to wipe or brush the dust off someone or something. (*Someone* includes *oneself.*) □ *Dust this vase off and put it on the shelf.* 🅃 *Please dust off this vase.* □ *Tom dusted Fred off and offered him a chair.* □ *He got up and dusted himself off.*

DUST ▶ OUT

dust something out to brush the dust out of something. □ *Dust this cabinet out and put the china back in.* 🅃 *Please dust out this cabinet.*

DWELL ▶ IN

dwell in someone or something to live in someone or something; to reside in someone or something. (Germs, parasites, spirits, demons, etc., dwell in persons. Persons and other living creatures dwell in things.) □ *This little bacterium dwells in people.* □ *I always wanted to dwell in a great Gothic castle for a month or two.*

DWELL ▶ (UP)ON

dwell (up)on someone or something to remain on the [important] subject of someone or something for a long time. (*Upon* is formal and less commonly used than *on*.) □ *I can't dwell upon this subject anymore.* □ *There is no need to dwell on Sarah further.*

dwell (up)on something to live on something, such as the planet Earth. (*Upon* is more formal than *on*.) □ *This is the largest turtle that dwells upon the earth.* □ *Many creatures dwell on this earth.*

DWINDLE ▶ AWAY

dwindle (away) (to something) See under *DWINDLE ▶ TO.*

DWINDLE ▶ DOWN

dwindle (down) (to something) See the following entry.

DWINDLE ▶ TO

dwindle (away) (to something) AND **dwindle (down) (to something)** to shrink, contract, or diminish to something. □ *The noise dwindled away to nothing.* □ *It just dwindled away.* □ *It dwindled to virtually nothing.*

E

EARMARK ▸ FOR

earmark something for someone or something to reserve someone for someone or something. ☐ *Tom earmarked the best of the steaks for his own guests.* ☐ *I have earmarked this chair for the family room.*

EASE ▸ ALONG

ease someone or something along to help someone or something to move along, very carefully. (*Someone* includes *oneself.*) ☐ *Just ease the piano along little by little.* ☐ *She eased the shy child along.* ☐ *Fred eased himself along, panting at every step.*

EASE ▸ AWAY

ease away (from someone or something) to pull away from someone or something slowly and carefully. ☐ *The great ship eased away from the pier.* ☐ *The ship eased away slowly.*

EASE ▸ BACK

ease back on something to move something back slowly and carefully. (Usually refers to a throttle or some other control on an airplane or other vehicle.) ☐ *Ann eased back on the throttle and slowed down.* ☐ *Please ease back on the volume control a little. You will deafen us.*

EASE ▸ DOWN

ease someone or something down (from something) to let someone or something downward from something gently. (*Someone* includes *oneself.*) ☐ *The rescuers eased the injured hiker down from the mountain.* 🅃 *They eased down the hiker carefully.* ☐ *We eased her down.* ☐ *She eased herself down and stood at the bottom of the ladder, looking up where she had been.*

EASE ▸ OF

ease someone of something to relieve someone of something, such as pain, a burden, etc. ☐ *The doctor eased Ralph of his pain.* ☐ *Can I ease you of your burden?*

EASE ▸ OFF

ease off [for something] to diminish. ☐ *The rain began to ease off.* ☐ *The storm seems to have eased off a little.*

ease off (from someone or something) to move away from someone or something, slowly and carefully. ☐ *Ease off carefully from the deer, so you don't frighten it.* ☐ *Ease off quietly.*

ease off (on someone or something) to let up doing something to someone or something; to diminish one's pressure or demands on someone or something. ☐ *Ease off on him. He's only a kid!* ☐ *Ease off! He's just a kid!*

EASE ▸ ON

ease on out (of something) **1.** to continue moving out of something, slowly and carefully. ☐ *I was able to ease on out of the parking space, but only with difficulty.* ☐ *I looked both ways and eased on out.* **2.** to leave something, such as an office or position, quietly and without much embarrassment. (See also under *EASE ▸ OUT.*) ☐ *The bum finally eased on out of office without much public notice.* ☐ *He eased on out while the press was concerned with some other crisis.*

ease someone on out (of something) **1.** to help someone continue to get out of something. (*Someone* includes *oneself.*) □ *We helped ease her on out of the car.* □ *With care, we eased her on out.* □ *After taking a look around, Tom eased himself on out of the opening.* **2.** to help someone decide to leave something, such as an office or position, quietly and without much embarrassment. (*Someone* includes *oneself.*) □ *The scandal eased her on out of office in a way that an election might not have.* □ *The scandal eased her on out.* □ *After encouragement from the board, he eased himself on out of the job.*

EASE ▸ OUT

ease out (of something) to move out of something, slowly and carefully; to retreat from something. □ *I eased out of the parking space with no trouble.* □ *I looked both ways and eased out.*

ease someone out (of something) **1.** to get someone out of something carefully. (*Someone* includes *oneself.*) □ *The paramedics eased the injured man out of the wreckage.* □ *Please ease me out carefully.* □ *The bystanders eased the injured child out of the wrecked car.* □ *I eased myself out of the chair and walked away.* **2.** to get someone out of an office or position quietly and without much embarrassment. (*Someone* includes *oneself.*) □ *We eased the sheriff out of office without a fight.* □ *We eased him out just before the election.* □ *He eased himself out of office, and no one was suspicious.*

EASE ▸ UP

ease up (on someone or something) to treat someone or something more gently. (See also *ease off on someone or something.*) □ *Ease up on the guy! He can only do so much.* □ *Ease up on the gas! You want to kill us all?* □ *Please ease up! I'm tired.*

EAT ▸ AT

eat (away) at someone [for a problem] to trouble someone constantly. (Figurative.) □ *The nasty situation at work began to eat away at me.* □ *Nagging worries ate at me day and night.*

eat (away) at something **1.** to eat something eagerly and rapidly. □ *They ate away at the turkey until it was all gone.* □ *We just ate at it little by little.* **2.** to erode something. □ *The acid ate away at the metal floor.* □ *Fingers have a mild acid that eats at the metal of the doorhandle.*

EAT ▸ AWAY

See also the two previous entries.

eat something away to erode something; to consume something bit by bit. □ *The acid ate the finish away.* [T] *It ate away the finish.*

EAT ▸ IN

eat in to eat a meal at home. □ *I really don't want to eat in tonight.* □ *Let's eat in. I'm tired.*

EAT ▸ IN(TO)

eat in(to something) to erode into something; to etch something. □ *The acidic water ate into the rocks on the shore.* □ *The acid ate in and weakened the structure.*

EAT ▸ OFF

eat something off ((of) something) to erode something off a larger part. (The *of*-phrase is paraphrased with a *from*-phrase when the particle is transposed. See the [F] example. The *of* is colloquial.) □ *The acidic rain ate the finish off the steeple.* [T] *The acid ate off the finish.* [F] *The acid ate off the finish from the car's bumper.* □ *It ate the chrome off.*

EAT ▸ ON

eat high on the hog to eat very well; to live well and eat good food. (Folksy.) □ *We used to eat pretty high on the hog, but lately we're lucky to have more than one meal a day.* □ *We can afford to eat high on the hog these days.*

EAT ▸ OUT

eat one's heart out (about someone or something) **1.** to grieve about someone or something. □ *Don't eat your heart out about Tom. You've lost him forever.* □ *No sense eating your heart out.* **2.** to suffer from envy of someone or something. □ *She ate her heart out about*

Sally's new car. □ *Get your own car. Don't eat your heart out.*

eat out to eat a meal away from home. □ *I just love to eat out every now and then.* □ *Let's eat out tonight. I'm tired.*

eat out of someone's hand to do exactly as someone says; to grovel to someone. □ *I've got her eating out of my hand. She'll do anything I ask.* □ *He will be eating out of your hand before you are finished with him.*

eat someone out to scold someone severely. (Colloquial. Originally military.) □ *The teacher ate the student out and scared him to death.* 🆃 *Mr. Wilson really ate out the secretary.*

eat someone out of house and home to eat everything that someone has in the house. (Figurative. *Someone* includes *oneself.*) □ *That dog is eating us out of house and home.* □ *Poor Sally ate herself out of house and home day after day.*

eat something out **1.** to eat a meal or a particular food away from home. □ *We eat fish out but we don't cook it at home.* □ *We almost never eat breakfast out.* **2.** [for something or some creature] to consume the inside of something. □ *The ants ate the inside of the pumpkin out.* 🆃 *The ants ate out the pumpkin.*

eat (something) out of something to eat food directly from a container, such as a bag, box, can, etc. □ *You shouldn't eat out of the can.* □ *Maria was eating potato chips right out of the bag.*

EAT ► THROUGH

eat through something to erode all the way through something. □ *The acid ate through the countertop and ruined everything in the drawers below.* □ *The vinegar ate through the top of the pickle jar.*

EAT ► UP

eat someone up **1.** to consume a person. (Figurative.) □ *The whole idea of going to the South Pole was just eating her up.* □ *Juan's obsession almost ate him up.* **2.** [for insects] to bite a person all over. (Figurative.) □ *These mosquitoes are just eating me up!* □ *Don't let the bugs eat you up.* **3.** [for someone] to overwhelm and devastate someone. (Figurative.) □ *The guy is a devil! He just eats people up!* □ *Fred will just eat you up. He is a vicious administrator.*

eat something up **1.** to devour all of some food or some creature. □ *They ate the turkey up and no one had to eat leftovers.* 🆃 *Please eat up the turkey.* **2.** [for someone] to believe something completely. □ *Your story was really good. Everybody just ate it up.* 🆃 *They will eat up almost any lie.*

eat up to eat everything; to eat eagerly. (Usually a command to begin eating. Compare to *drink up.*) □ *Come on, let's eat up and get going.* □ *Eat up, you guys, and get back to work!*

EAVESDROP ► ON

eavesdrop on someone to listen in on people having a private conversation. □ *I saw her eavesdropping on them.* □ *Please don't eavesdrop on me.*

eavesdrop on something to listen in on a private conversation. □ *She was eavesdropping on their conversation.* □ *Maria was eavesdropping on the telephone call.*

EBB ► AWAY

ebb away to recede; to subside; to flow back. □ *His life ebbed away little by little.* □ *As the sunlight ebbed away, the sky took on a grayish color.*

ECHO ► BACK

echo back to something [for something] to recall something similar in the past. □ *This idea echoes back to the end of the last century, when people thought this way.* 🅰 *Her echoed-back words kept him awake all night.*

ECHO ► WITH

echo with something **1.** [for a large space] to resound with the echoing sounds of a loud noise. □ *The cathedral echoed with the sounds of the organ.* □ *The valley echoed with the sound of horses' hoofs.* **2.** [for something] to have reminders of something. (Literary and very limited.) □ *My thoughts echoed with the sounds of spring.* □ *The room echoed with happier days.*

ECONOMIZE ▸ ON

economize on something to save money by cutting the cost of something. □ *We will have to economize on our food budget.* □ *We can only economize on a few things.*

EDGE ▸ ACROSS

edge (one's way) across (something) to make one's way across something carefully. □ *The hikers edged their way across the narrow ledge.* □ *Now, edge your way across and don't look down.* □ *They edged across very carefully.*

EDGE ▸ AROUND

edge (one's way) around something to make one's way around something carefully. □ *I edged my way around the table, trying not to disturb anyone.* □ *Sam edged around the perimeter of the room.*

EDGE ▸ AWAY

edge away (from someone or something) to move cautiously away from someone or something. □ *We edged away from the dirty man in the ragged clothes.* □ *As others saw the gun, they edged away.*

EDGE ▸ BY

edge by (someone or something) to move carefully past someone or something. □ *Try to edge by the portly gentleman carefully. He is very grumpy about being bumped.* □ *Edge by as carefully as you can.*

EDGE ▸ OUT

edge someone out (of something) to pressure someone gradually to leave something; to put gradual pressure on someone to retire from a job. □ *We grasped the child's hand and edged her out of the stable without frightening the horses.* □ *Edge him out before the lion wakes up.*

edge something out (of something) to move something out of something very carefully, bit by bit. □ *Sam edged the control rod out of the reactor, using the remote control device.* □ *Mary edged the car out of the parking place.*

EDGE ▸ WITH

edge something with something to put an edging of something onto something. □ *The tailor edged the hem with lace, making the skirt appear longer.* □ *The hem was edged with lace.*

EDIT ▸ OUT

edit something out (of something) to strike out words or sentences from something that is going to be published; to cut out textual material in the editing process. (The *of*-phrase is paraphrased with a *from*-phrase when the particle is transposed. See the F example.) □ *She edited the bad words out of the essay.* T *Frank edited out the bad words.* F *She edited out the bad words from the story.* □ *Sam edited the swearwords out.*

EDUCATE ▸ FOR

educate someone for something to train someone through education for something or to do something. (*Someone* includes *oneself.*) □ *I wasn't educated for doing this kind of thing.* □ *He had spent many years educating himself for just this kind of job.*

EDUCATE ▸ IN

educate someone in something to train someone about something; to school someone in something. (*Someone* includes *oneself.*) □ *Her parents educated her in the ways of the old country.* □ *She had educated herself in the ways of big business.*

EGG ▸ ON

egg someone on to incite someone to do something; to encourage someone to do something. □ *I want Richard to stop making up those horrible puns. Please don't egg him on.* □ *She does not need any encouragement. Don't egg her on.*

EJECT ▸ FROM

eject someone from some place to use force to make someone leave a place; to throw someone out of some place. □ *The management ejected Sam from the theater.* □ *He was ejected from the theater.*

EKE ▸ OUT

eke something out to extend something; to add to something. □ *He* *worked at two jobs in order to eke his salary out.* 🅃 *He managed to eke out a living.*

ELABORATE ▶ ON

elaborate on someone or something to give additional details about someone or something. □ *Would you care to elaborate on that?* □ *I want to know more about Kelly. Could you elaborate on her?*

ELBOW ▶ ASIDE

elbow someone aside to push someone aside with one's arm. □ *She elbowed the other woman aside and there was almost a fight.* 🅃 *The rude woman elbowed aside all the other people.*

ELBOW ▶ THROUGH

elbow (one's way) through something to push or drive oneself through something, such as a crowd, perhaps using one's elbows or arms to move people out of the way. □ *She elbowed her way through the crowd.* □ *Jerry elbowed through the people gathered at the door.*

ELECT ▶ AS

elect someone as something to select someone to be something by ballot. (Also without *as*, but not eligible as an entry.) □ *We elected her as our representative.* □ *She was elected as our president.*

ELECT ▶ TO

elect someone to something to select someone to be a member of something by ballot; to select someone to be an officer in something by ballot. □ *We elected you to office, so do your job.* □ *Tom was elected to the congress.*

ELEVATE ▶ TO

elevate someone or something to something to raise the status of someone to something; to promote someone to something higher, such as a job, a better status, etc. (*Someone* includes *oneself.*) □ *The success elevated her to a new rank and higher pay.* □ *The boss's attention elevated the policy question to the highest priority.* □ *She sought to elevate herself to some sort of social goddess.*

ELICIT ▶ FROM

elicit something from someone to obtain information from someone. □ *I hoped to elicit a statement from the mayor, but I could not reach her.* □ *Larry was not able to elicit anything from Jane.*

ELIMINATE ▶ FROM

eliminate someone or something from something to remove someone or something from something. (*Someone* includes *oneself.*) □ *We had to eliminate Jeff from the list.* □ *The cook eliminated veal from the menu.* □ *She sought to eliminate herself from consideration.*

ELOPE ▶ WITH

elope with someone to sneak away and marry someone. □ *Sally eloped with Tom, and everyone was relieved.* □ *I don't want to elope with Juan. I want a church wedding.*

EMANATE ▶ FROM

emanate from someone or something to arise from or come out of someone or something. □ *A strange smell emanated from the basement.* □ *Some kind of eerie light emanated from the eyes of the statue.*

EMANCIPATE ▶ FROM

emancipate someone from someone or something to free someone from someone or something. (*Someone* includes *oneself.*) □ *The president emancipated the slaves from their bondage.* □ *The planter emancipated Fred from slavery long before the law was written.* □ *She sought to emancipate herself from the drudgery of typing by learning to operate a computer.*

EMBARK ▶ FOR

embark for some place to leave for some place, usually in a ship or an airplane. □ *We are embarking for Liverpool tomorrow morning.* □ *Maria is embarking for London in just a few minutes.*

EMBARK ▶ ON

embark on something to begin something, typically a journey; to begin a project. □ *They embarked on their* *journey from San Juan.* □ *When will you embark on your new project?*

EMBARRASS ▸ ABOUT

embarrass someone about someone or something to make someone feel bad or ashamed about someone or something. □ *Please don't embarrass me about my mistake again.* □ *There is no need to embarrass her about her unfortunate sister.*

EMBARRASS ▸ INTO

embarrass someone into doing something to shame someone into doing something. □ *They tried to embarrass me into doing it, but I resisted.* □ *Juan tried to embarrass Fred into going home early.*

EMBARRASS ▸ WITH

embarrass someone with something to use something to make someone feel bad or ashamed. □ *Please don't embarrass me with that old story again.* □ *Maria embarrassed Henry with a reminder of what had happened.*

EMBED ▸ IN

embed someone or something in something to insert someone or something in something. (*Someone* includes *oneself.*) □ *They embedded Max in concrete before they threw him in the river.* □ *Laura embedded jewels and sequins in the candles and turned them into clever gifts.* □ *Because of her struggling, she embedded herself firmly in the fresh concrete.*

embed something in something to stick something into something. □ *The mugger only embedded his knife in the cloth of the victim's coat.* □ *A ring was embedded in the bread dough by accident.*

EMBELLISH ▸ WITH

embellish something with something **1.** to ornament something with something. □ *He embellished the painting with too many little decorations.* □ *The room has been embellished with too many baroque sconces.* **2.** to add to a story with detail. □ *The storyteller embellished the tale with the names of people in the audience.* □ *I always try to embellish my tales with a little local color.* **3.** to add untrue things to a story. □ *He tends to embellish the truth with a few imaginative details.* □ *There is no need to embellish this story with anything untrue.*

EMBEZZLE ▸ FROM

embezzle something from someone or something to steal something from someone or a group. □ *They caught her embezzling funds from the bank.* □ *Jerry's business partner embezzled a large sum from Jerry.*

EMBLAZON ▸ ON(TO)

emblazon something on(to) something **1.** to decorate something with something. □ *The workers emblazoned wild decorations on the door.* □ *They emblazoned their name on the side of the building.* **2.** to put some writing or symbols that proclaim something onto something. □ *The knight emblazoned his name onto his shield.* 🅃 *The craftsman emblazoned the knight's name on his shield.*

EMBLAZON ▸ WITH

emblazon something with something to decorate something with writing or symbols that proclaim something. □ *They emblazoned the wall with pictures of past triumphs.* □ *His shield was emblazoned with the family crest.*

EMBODY ▸ IN

embody something in something to actualize something in something; to make something represent something else in actuality. □ *I tried to embody both good and evil in my painting.* □ *A strong sense of knowing is embodied in her writing.*

EMBROIL ▸ IN

embroil someone in something to entangle someone in something; to get someone involved in something. (*Someone* includes *oneself.*) □ *Please do not embroil me in your squabbles.* □ *I wish I could keep from embroiling myself in this kind of mess.*

EMERGE ▸ AS

See the following entry.

EMERGE ▸ FROM

emerge (from something) (as something) to come out of something as something. □ *He emerged from his isolation as a changed man.* □ *The caterpillar would emerge as a butterfly in a short time.* □ *A new man emerged from prison.*

EMIGRATE ▸ FROM

emigrate (from some place) (to some place) to move away from a foreign land to a new land. □ *My family emigrated from England to this country over two centuries ago.* □ *They emigrated to this country from England.*

EMIGRATE ▸ TO

See the previous entry.

EMIT ▸ FROM

emit something (from something) (into something) to discharge something from something into something else. □ *The snake emitted poison from its fangs into the cup the man held.* □ *It emitted venom into the cup from its fangs.* □ *The snake emitted venom from its fangs.*

EMIT ▸ INTO

See the previous entry.

EMPATHIZE ▸ WITH

empathize with someone to have an understanding about the way someone feels; to feel emotional pain with someone. □ *I can really empathize with what you must be going through. I've been through the same thing.* □ *I empathize with people who have the same problems that I have.*

EMPLOY ▸ AS

employ someone as something to pay someone to work in some capacity. □ *I employed Fred as a personal secretary for about three months.* □ *Can you employ me as a stock clerk?*

EMPLOY ▸ FOR

employ someone for something to hire someone for a particular purpose. □ *I employ him for special chores around the factory.* □ *Kelly employed Walter for emergency repairs on the night shift.*

EMPLOY ▸ IN

employ someone in something to pay someone to work in a particular type of work. □ *I employ Tom in machine maintenance.* □ *Laura is employed in accounting.*

EMPOWER ▸ TO

empower someone to do something to authorize someone to do something; to grant someone the power to do something. (*Someone* includes *oneself.*) □ *I will empower you to collect the dues of the members.* □ *The prime minister empowered himself to oversee tax collection.*

EMPTY ▸ INTO

empty into something [for a river, stream, or man-made conduit] to pour its contents into something. □ *The Amazon River empties into the Atlantic Ocean.* □ *The drainage pipe empties into the river.*

EMPTY ▸ IN(TO)

empty something in(to something) to pour something into something else. □ *Now, empty the can of soup into the pan.* 🅃 *Open the can and empty in the contents.* □ *Open it and empty it in.*

EMPTY ▸ OUT

empty someone out to cause someone to empty the bowels, stomach, or bladder. (*Someone* includes *oneself.*) □ *This medication will empty you out.* 🅃 *This stuff could empty out an army!* □ *He used a powerful physic to empty himself out.*

empty something out to remove or pour all of the contents from something. □ *Please empty this drawer out and clean it.* 🅃 *She emptied out the aquarium and cleaned it well.*

ENABLE ▸ TO

enable someone to do something to make it possible for someone to do something. □ *This money will enable me to open my own business.* □ *My uncle enabled me to open my own candy shop.*

ENAMOR ▸ OF

See *be enamored of someone or something* under *BE ▸ OF.*

ENCASE ▸ IN

encase someone or something in something to contain someone or something in something. (*Someone* includes *oneself*.) ☐ *We encased her broken leg in a splint and raced to the hospital.* ☐ *Sammy encased the butterfly in a glass display box.* ☐ *The strange frog encased itself in a casket of mud.* ☐ *The diver encased himself in the experimental hard suit.*

ENCHANT ▸ WITH

enchant someone with something 1. to bewitch someone or something with a magic spell. ☐ *The wizard enchanted them with a sleep spell that kept them quiet during dinner.* ☐ *The children were enchanted with a spell that made them forget.* 2. to fascinate someone or some creature with some object. ☐ *She enchanted the children with the little drawings she made of them.* ☐ *We were enchanted with her drawings.*

ENCLOSE ▸ (WITH)IN

enclose someone or something (with)in something to contain someone, something, or some space inside of something. (*Someone* includes *oneself*.) ☐ *We enclosed the people in a safe area while the accident was being cleaned up.* ☐ *The farmer enclosed the pig within a new pen.* ☐ *Tom enclosed himself in the carton and made noises like a puppy.*

ENCOMPASS ▸ (WITH)IN

encompass someone or something (with)in something to surround or include someone or something within the domain or span of something. ☐ *We encompassed the group within our administrative area.* ☐ *They could not encompass our family in their limited scheme.*

ENCOURAGE ▸ IN

encourage someone in something to give support to someone about something in particular. ☐ *We want to encourage her in her musical career.* ☐ *Ted encouraged me in my efforts to become a baseball player.*

ENCOURAGE ▸ TO

encourage someone to do something to inspire or stimulate someone to do something; to give someone the courage to do something. (*Someone* includes *oneself*.) ☐ *We encouraged her to develop her musical talents.* ☐ *He encouraged himself to eat by muttering about how good hospital food really is.*

ENCROACH ▸ (UP)ON

encroach (up)on someone or something to infringe or trespass on someone or something; to move into the space belonging to someone or something. (*Upon* is formal and less commonly used than *on*.) ☐ *I did not mean to encroach upon your property.* ☐ *I need lots of space. Don't encroach on me.*

ENCUMBER ▸ WITH

encumber someone or something with someone or something to burden someone or something with someone or something. (*Someone* includes *oneself*.) ☐ *Please do not try to encumber me with your debts.* ☐ *She encumbered the marriage with a number of children from a previous marriage.* ☐ *She encumbered herself with the weight of both children and her purse.*

END ▸ IN

end in something [for something, such as a play, film, opera, etc.] to end in a particular way. ☐ *The opera ended in a lengthy duet before the death of the heroine.* ☐ *The party ended in a champagne toast.*

END ▸ UP

end something up to terminate something; to bring something to an end. ☐ *He ended his vacation up by going to the beach.* 🆃 *She ended up her speech with a poem.*

end up to come to an end. ☐ *When will all this end up?* ☐ *I think that the party will have to end up about midnight.*

end up at something to be at something or some place at the end. ☐ *The plane ended up at Denver airport because of a storm in Colorado Springs.* ☐ *We ended up at home for the evening because the car broke down.*

end up by doing something to do something at the end of something. ☐ *I ended up by leaving quite angry and frustrated.* ☐ *Ann ended up by leaving early.*

end up doing something to have to do something one has tried to get out of doing. ☐ *I refused to do it, but I ended up doing it anyway.* ☐ *Juan didn't want to end up going home alone.*

end up somehow to come to the end of something in a particular way. ☐ *I really didn't want to end up this way.* ☐ *I ended up broke when my vacation was over.*

end up something to become something at the end of everything. ☐ *I always knew I would end up a doctor.* ☐ *If I don't get a job, I will end up a beggar.*

end up with someone or something to finish with the possession of someone or something or in the company of someone or something. ☐ *Careful or you will end up with Johnny for the weekend.* ☐ *Do you want to end up with the bill?* ☐ *I thought my date was with Sally, but I ended up with her twin sister.*

END ▸ WITH

end with something to make something the final element, just before the end. ☐ *We will end with the singing of the school song.* ☐ *The concert ended with a vigorous march.*

ENDEAR ▸ TO

endear someone to someone or something to cause someone to be cherished by someone else or a group. (*Someone* includes *oneself.*) ☐ *Her good humor endears her to all of us.* ☐ *Sally endears herself to everyone because she is so funny.* ☐ *She failed to endear herself to her husband's parents.*

ENDEAVOR ▸ TO

endeavor to do something to try to do something. ☐ *Whenever I endeavor to console her, she breaks down again.* ☐ *Maria endeavored to comfort Henry.*

ENDOW ▸ WITH

endow someone or something with something 1. to give something to someone or something. ☐ *We endowed her with the courage she needed to do the job.* ☐ *Gerald endowed the proceedings with a distinctive atmosphere.* 2. to provide someone or something with a large sum of money that will provide income. ☐ *I will endow a professor with some of my fortune.* ☐ *The family endowed a chair in the humanities at the university.*

ENFOLD ▸ IN

enfold someone in something to wrap or contain someone in something. (*Someone* includes *oneself.*) ☐ *He enfolded the tiny baby in a soft blanket.* ☐ *Sarah enfolded herself in the silk sheets and giggled with glee.*

ENFORCE ▸ ON

enforce something on someone to make a law effective with regard to someone. ☐ *I can't enforce this on her if I don't enforce it on you.* ☐ *This law can't be enforced on anyone.*

ENGAGE ▸ AS

engage someone as something to hire someone to serve as something. ☐ *Yes, I engaged her as a secretary just last month.* ☐ *Will you engage me as a general troubleshooter?*

ENGAGE ▸ IN

engage in small talk to take part in casual conversation; to participate in idle chatter. ☐ *We all just stood around engaging in small talk.* ☐ *There is nothing worse than hours engaged in pointless small talk.*

engage someone or something in something 1. to make someone or a group busy doing something. ☐ *She knew how to engage the boys in useful activity.* ☐ *The den mother engaged the Cubs in a woodworking project.* 2. to draw someone or something into something. ☐ *The enemy sought to engage our troops in battle but failed.* ☐ *I tried to engage Gerald in conversation.*

ENGAGE ▸ TO

engage someone to someone to betroth someone to someone. (*Someone* includes *oneself.*) ☐ *Her parents engaged her to the man she ended up marrying.*

☐ *She engaged herself to some guy she met at a singles bar.*

ENGORGE ▸ ON

engorge (itself) on someone or something [for some creature] to drink its fill of blood. ☐ *The vampire bat engorged itself on a number of creatures last night.* ☐ *Mosquitoes engorge on human victims.*

ENGORGE ▸ WITH

engorge (itself) with something [for some creature] to fill up with blood. ☐ *The horde or mosquitoes engorged itself with my blood all night long.* ☐ *When the vampire had engorged itself with enough blood, it flew back to its cave.*

ENGRAVE ▸ INTO

engrave something into something to cut symbols into something. ☐ *She engraves a lovely design into the soap that she puts out for guests.* ☐ *Todd engraved his initials into the bark of the tree.*

ENGRAVE ▸ ON(TO)

engrave something on(to) something to cut symbols into the surface of something. ☐ *She engraved her initials onto the side of the tree.* ☐ *Ted engraved her name on the bracelet.*

ENGRAVE ▸ (UP)ON

engrave something (up)on something **1.** to cut letters or a design into the surface of something; to *engrave something on(to) something.* ☐ *He asked them to engrave his initials upon the back of his watch.* ☐ *He engraved his name on the desk top.* **2.** to imprint something firmly on someone's mind. ☐ *I engraved the combination to the safe upon my brain.* ☐ *The teacher engraved the definition of a noun on my consciousness.*

ENGRAVE ▸ WITH

engrave something with something **1.** to carve something, such as letters, into something. ☐ *He engraved the soft pewter with an old motto.* ☐ *Can you engrave my watch with a date?* **2.** to carve on something, using some tool or device. ☐ *The worker engraved the watch with a sharp stylus.* ☐ *Can I engrave this bracelet with this tool? Is it sharp enough?*

ENGROSS ▸ IN

engross someone in something to occupy someone's time or thinking with something. ☐ *You can't expect me to engross Tom in my work.* ☐ *We were all engrossed in what the speaker had to say.*

ENGULF ▸ IN

engulf someone or something in something to swallow up someone or something in something. ☐ *The fog engulfed the small town in its thickness.* ☐ *It engulfed us in anonymity.*

ENJOIN ▸ FROM

enjoin someone or something from something to order someone or something not to do something. ☐ *The judge enjoined her from further action in this matter.* ☐ *The company was enjoined from further dumping of waste.*

ENJOIN ▸ TO

enjoin someone to do something to order someone to do something. ☐ *We sought to enjoin her to remain in office.* ☐ *Sally wants to enjoin the committee to finish its work on time.*

ENLARGE ▸ (UP)ON

enlarge (up)on something to add details to a report about something. ☐ *Would you care to enlarge upon your remarks?* ☐ *I enlarged on my original comments.*

ENLIGHTEN ▸ ABOUT

enlighten someone about someone or something AND **enlighten someone on someone or something** to tell someone the facts about someone or something. (*Someone* includes *oneself.*) ☐ *Please enlighten me about this trip you are planning.* ☐ *Would you enlighten me on the current state of things?* ☐ *Enlighten me about Sarah.* ☐ *She enlightened herself about automobile engines.*

ENLIGHTEN ▸ ON

enlighten someone on someone or something See the previous entry.

ENLIST ▸ FOR

enlist (oneself) for something to sign up for something; to enroll for something. □ *I enlisted myself for service in the army.* □ *Sam wouldn't enlist for service.* □ *Todd enlisted himself for the army last week.*

enlist someone for something to enroll someone for something; to seek help for something from someone. □ *I enlisted all of them for the understudy parts.* □ *Can I enlist you for the committee?* □ *We enlisted the boys for ushers and traffic managers.*

ENLIST ▸ IN

enlist (oneself) in something to join something; to join the armed services. □ *She decided not to enlist herself in the air force.* □ *Bill enlisted in the army.* □ *Sally enlisted in the navy so she could see the world.*

enlist someone in something to recruit someone into something; to recruit someone into the armed services. □ *They tried to enlist me in the army, but I decided against it.* □ *David enlisted his brother in an organization that gave assistance to peasants in South America.*

ENMESH ▸ IN

enmesh someone or something in something **1.** to entangle someone or a group in something. (*Someone* includes *oneself.*) □ *Don't enmesh yourself in these ropes and chains.* □ *I didn't mean to enmesh you in this net. I should have kept it out of the way.* □ *Jane enmeshed herself in the net that had been set out to dry.* **2.** to get someone or a group involved in some problem. (*Someone* includes *oneself.*) □ *They enmeshed us in their problems even though we tried to avoid it.* □ *We enmeshed the entire committee in the lawsuit.* □ *Why do I always enmesh myself in someone else's business?*

ENRICH ▸ WITH

enrich someone or something with something to improve or enhance someone or something with something. □ *You might want to enrich this soup with a little milk or cream.* □ *The teacher enriched her students with field trips and films.*

ENROLL ▸ FOR

enroll (someone) for something to sign someone up for something; to allow someone to join something. (*Someone* includes *oneself.*) □ *I intend to enroll myself for physics next year.* □ *Todd enrolled himself for a refresher course in shorthand.*

ENROLL ▸ IN

enroll (someone) in something to sign someone up to be in something. (*Someone* includes *oneself.*) □ *They enrolled me in calculus against my wishes.* □ *I want to enroll myself in the history class offered at the latest hour.*

ENSCONCE ▸ IN

ensconce oneself in something to establish oneself in something; to settle oneself into something; to place oneself firmly into something. □ *He ensconced himself in the most comfortable chair.* □ *Sally ensconced herself in the huge throne and pretended she was a queen.*

ENSHRINE ▸ IN

enshrine someone or something in something **1.** to honor someone or something by placement in a shrine. □ *You just want to enshrine me in a fancy car!* □ *Bill enshrined his grandfather's watch in a glass dome.* **2.** to keep the memory of someone or something in a special place in one's heart or mind. □ *He has enshrined her in his heart.* □ *Bob enshrined Jill's memory in his heart.*

ENSNARE ▸ IN

ensnare someone or something in something to capture someone or something in something. (Both literal and figurative uses. *Someone* includes *oneself.*) □ *She sought to ensnare him in his own framework of lies.* □ *Dave ensnared the rabbit in his trap.* □ *Henry ensnared himself in the trap they had laid for deer.*

ENSUE ▸ FROM

ensue from something to result from someone or something. □ *What ensued from the change in policy was not antici-*

pated at all. ☐ *A very serious problem ensued from the events of the day.*

ENTANGLE ▸ IN

entangle someone or something in something **1.** to catch or tangle up someone, a group, or some creature in something. (*Someone* includes *oneself.*) ☐ *Careful! Don't entangle your foot in the anchor chain.* ☐ *Somehow I entangled the dog in the fishing net.* ☐ *Todd entangled himself in the net.* **2.** to get someone or a group involved in something. (*Someone* includes *oneself.*) ☐ *She was trying to entangle us in her latest cause.* ☐ *They entangled us in their lawsuit.* ☐ *Don't entangle yourself in my problems!*

ENTANGLE ▸ WITH

entangle someone or something with something to get someone or something tangled up with something. (*Someone* includes *oneself.*) ☐ *He sought to entangle the pursuing mugger in a mass of ropes and boards.* ☐ *Sam entangled the rabid dog in the rope and got away.* ☐ *He entangled himself with the ropes on the deck.*

ENTER ▸ BY

enter (something) by something AND **enter (something) through something** to enter something or some place by way of a certain entrance. ☐ *We entered the building by the west door.* ☐ *You should enter through the revolving door only.* ☐ *Please enter by the front door.* ☐ *Can you enter through the other door?*

ENTER ▸ IN

enter in something to enroll as a participant in something, such as a contest, competition, etc. ☐ *She was not ready to enter in the competition.* ☐ *I can't enter in that contest. I'm not prepared.*

ENTER ▸ INTO

enter into something **1.** to get into something. ☐ *She entered into the house and immediately went to work.* ☐ *As the people entered into the cathedral, they became quiet.* **2.** to join in something. ☐ *I couldn't get him to enter into the spirit of the party.* ☐ *She just loves to enter into things and have a good time with people.*

ENTER ▸ IN(TO)

enter someone or something in((to) something) to enroll someone or something in something; to make someone or something a competitor in something. (*Someone* includes *oneself.*) ☐ *I will enter you into the contest whether you like it or not.* ☐ *Ed entered his favorite horse in the race.* ☐ *She entered herself into the contest.*

ENTER ▸ ON

See under *ENTER ▸ (UP)ON.*

ENTER ▸ THROUGH

enter (something) through something
See *ENTER ▸ BY.*

ENTER ▸ (UP)ON

enter (up)on something **1.** to come in at a particular point as marked by something. ☐ *We entered the theater upon the most delicate point of the story.* ☐ *We entered on the tail end of a live scene.* **2.** to begin something. ☐ *Todd entered upon a new phase of his life.* ☐ *He entered on the management of a new project.*

ENTERTAIN ▸ WITH

entertain someone with something to provide something for amusement or refreshment to someone. (*Someone* includes *oneself.*) ☐ *Will you try to entertain the children with a game or two, please?* ☐ *She entertained herself with the puzzle.*

ENTHRALL ▸ WITH

enthrall someone with something to charm or captivate someone with something. ☐ *They enthralled us with the beauty of their singing.* ☐ *The children enthralled us with their rustic dances.*

ENTICE ▸ AWAY

entice someone or something away (from someone or something) to lure someone or something away from someone or something. ☐ *I could not entice him away from the football game on television.* 🅃 *I enticed away the guys from the game.* ☐ *Food enticed them away.*

ENTICE ▸ INTO

entice someone or something into something 1. to lure someone or something into something. ☐ *Can I entice you into the house for some cold lemonade?* ☐ *We were able to entice the squirrel into the box with nuts.* 2. to lure someone or something into doing something. ☐ *We finally enticed him into running for office.* ☐ *Donna enticed the cat into coming down from the tree.*

ENTICE ▸ WITH

entice someone or something with something to lure someone or some creature with something. ☐ *We tried to entice him with a description of the cake, but he was not interested in coming.* ☐ *If the cat won't come in, try enticing it with a bit of fish.*

ENTITLE ▸ TO

entitle someone to do something [for something] to qualify someone to do something. ☐ *This ticket entitles you to go in and take a seat.* ☐ *Does this paper entitle me to get a discount?*

entitle someone to something [for something] to qualify someone to receive something. ☐ *Does this ticket entitle me to a seat in the balcony?* ☐ *Will this paper entitle me to a discount?*

ENTOMB ▸ IN

entomb someone or something in something 1. to place someone or something in a tomb. (*Someone* includes *oneself*.) ☐ *In the opera, they entombed Aida and her lover in a dusty place where they sang themselves to death.* ☐ *They accidentally entombed the queen's jewels in the vault with her.* ☐ *She entombed herself in her final resting place and waited for death.* 2. to imprison someone or some creature in a tomblike enclosure. ☐ *Please don't entomb me in that huge, cold office.* ☐ *Unknowingly, when they closed the door, they had entombed a tiny mouse within.*

ENTRAP ▸ IN(TO)

entrap someone (in(to) something) (with something) to use something to deceive someone into involvement in something. ☐ *The investigators entrapped Max into breaking the law with promises to buy the goods he stole.* ☐ *They entrapped him with their promises.* ☐ *They entrapped Max into breaking the law.*

ENTRAP ▸ WITH

See the previous entry.

ENTREAT ▸ TO

entreat someone to do something to beg someone to do something. ☐ *They entreated us to come back at any time.* ☐ *I entreat you to think it over again.*

ENTRUST ▸ TO

entrust someone or something to someone to place someone or something into the protection of someone. ☐ *Can I entrust Johnny to you while I shop?* ☐ *I entrusted my share of the money to Fred until I returned to town.*

ENTRUST ▸ WITH

entrust someone with someone or something to trust someone to provide protection and care for someone or something. (*Someone* includes *oneself*.) ☐ *Can I entrust you with Johnny while I go in and vote?* ☐ *I entrusted Fred with my share of the money until I returned.* ☐ *I would not even entrust myself with the care of this priceless vase!*

ENTWINE ▸ AROUND

entwine around someone or something to weave or wind around someone or something. ☐ *The snake entwined around the limb of the tree.* ☐ *The huge python entwined around the horrified farmer.*

entwine something around someone or something to weave or wind something around someone or something. ☐ *They entwined their arms around each other.* ☐ *Jack entwined the garland of flowers around Jill.*

ENUNCIATE ▸ TO

enunciate something to someone to state something to someone quite distinctly. ☐ *Now, enunciate it to everyone, because they probably did not understand you the first time.* ☐ *I will enunciate it to you one more time, slowly.*

ENVELOP ► IN

envelop someone or something in someone or something to wrap someone or something in someone or something. (*Someone* includes *oneself*.) □ *The fog enveloped us in its grasp.* □ *Mountains of fog rolled in and enveloped the house in its smothering grasp.* □ *He enveloped himself in his cloak and melted into the background.*

ENVISAGE ► AS

envisage someone or something as someone or something to imagine or visualize someone or something as someone or something. (*Someone* includes *oneself*.) □ *I envisaged you as a more graceful person than you are.* □ *We envisaged the living room as sort of a gathering place for the entire family.* □ *She envisaged herself as the annointed savior of the entire planet Earth.*

ENVISION ► AS

envision someone as someone else or something as something else to imagine or fantasize someone as someone else; to imagine or fantasize something as something else. (*Someone* includes *oneself*.) □ *I envision her as the next Sarah Bernhardt.* □ *We envisioned this as larger than it turned out to be.* □ *I was unable to envision myself as an office worker.*

ENVY ► FOR

envy someone for someone or something to regard one with jealousy or resentment because of someone or something one has. □ *I envy you for your lovely car.* □ *We all envy you for your beautiful children.*

EQUAL ► IN

equal someone or something in something to be even or identical with someone or something in something. □ *John equals Bill in strength and size, I think.* □ *This cake equals that one in texture but not in richness.*

EQUATE ► TO

equate someone to someone else or something to something else to claim that someone is in some manner the same as someone else; to claim that something is in some manner the same as something else. □ *I would equate Tom to Wally when it comes to native ability.* □ *You cannot equate my car to that jalopy you drive!*

EQUATE ► WITH

equate someone or something with someone or something to compare people and things, in any combination. □ *I tend to equate Tom with trouble.* □ *I equate the Johnsons with a long boring evening.*

EQUIP ► FOR

equip someone or something (with something) (for something) to outfit someone or something with something for something; to provide equipment for someone or something for some purpose. (*Someone* includes *oneself*.) □ *We equipped everyone with a spade for digging.* □ *They equipped the rescuers with equipment for any conceivable occurrence.* □ *She equipped herself with what she needed for the trip.*

EQUIP ► WITH

equip someone or something (with something) (for something) See under *EQUIP ► FOR*.

equip something with something to add a piece of equipment to something. □ *We will equip our truck with a plow blade and plow snow this winter.* □ *This car is equipped with air-conditioning.*

ERASE ► FROM

erase something from something to delete or wipe something from something. □ *Please erase the writing from the blackboard.* □ *I will erase the incorrectly spelled word from my paper.*

erase something from something to remove something from something. (Figurative.) □ *Erase that smile from your face!* □ *I hope you will erase that thought from your mind.*

ERUPT ► FROM

erupt from something to burst out of something or some place. □ *A billow of smoke erupted from the chimney.* □ *A mass of ashes and gasses erupted from the volcano.*

ERUPT ▸ INTO

erupt into something to become a serious problem suddenly; to blow up into something. (Figurative.) □ *The argument erupted into a terrible fight.* □ *They were afraid the fight would erupt into a riot.*

ESCALATE ▸ INTO

escalate into something to intensify into something; to increase gradually into something. □ *This argument is going to escalate into something serious very soon.* □ *These cases of the flu could escalate into a real epidemic.*

escalate something into something to cause something to intensify. □ *He escalated the argument into a vicious fight.* □ *The dictator tried to escalate the disagreement into a cause for war.*

ESCAPE ▸ FROM

escape (from someone or something) (to some place) to get away from someone, something, or some place to another place. □ *Max escaped from prison to a hideout in Alabama.* □ *He escaped to Alabama from one of the worst-run prisons in the land.*

ESCAPE ▸ TO

See the previous entry.

ESCORT ▸ FROM

escort someone or something from something to accompany or lead someone or something away from something or some place. □ *A police officer escorted them from the auditorium.* □ *A band of honorary pallbearers escorted the coffin from the chapel.*

ESCORT ▸ TO

escort someone or something to something to accompany or lead someone or something to something or some place. □ *We escorted the women to their seats.* □ *Claude escorted Harry to the exit and bade him farewell.*

ESTABLISH ▸ AS

establish someone or something as someone or something **1.** to validate or confirm someone or something as someone or something. (*Someone* includes *oneself.*) □ *After some effort, we established him as a good trial lawyer.* □ *As soon as we establish her as a viable candidate, we will launch the publicity campaign.* □ *She established herself as an authority on rare books.* **2.** to determine that someone or something is actually as represented. (*Someone* includes *oneself.*) □ *I established the man at the door as a representative of the gas company.* □ *I was able to establish myself as the person I said I was, and they let me in.*

ESTABLISH ▸ IN

establish someone or something in something to set someone or something up in something or some place; to install someone or something in something or some place. (*Someone* includes *oneself.*) □ *We established a hot dog stand in the park.* □ *My uncle established me in the candy business.* □ *We tried to establish ourselves in business, but we failed.*

ESTIMATE ▸ AT

estimate something at something to reckon the cost of something at a particular amount. □ *I estimate the cost at about one hundred dollars.* □ *The cost of repairing the car was estimated at over four thousand dollars!*

ESTRANGE ▸ FROM

See *be estranged from someone* under *BE ▸ FROM.*

ETCH ▸ IN(TO)

etch something in((to) something) to erode a design or message into something with acid. □ *They etched their family crest into their good crystal.* 🆃 *He etched in his initials.*

EVACUATE ▸ FROM

evacuate someone (from something) (to something) to remove someone from something or some place to another thing or place. □ *They had to evacuate everyone from the subway station to a nearby building.* □ *The rescuers evacuated the people from the flames.* □ *They evacuated the passengers to the closest platform, where the medics were waiting.*

EVACUATE ▸ TO
See the previous entry.

EVALUATE ▸ AS
evaluate someone as something to judge someone's performance as something. (*Someone* includes *oneself*.) □ *I will have to evaluate you as a new student.* □ *We must evaluate ourselves as teachers and leaders.*

EVEN ▸ OFF
even something off to make something even or smooth. □ *Please even this surface off before you paint it.* 🅃 *You need to even off this surface.*

EVEN ▸ OUT
even something out to make something even or level. □ *Please even the road out.* 🅃 *They evened out the surface of the road.*

EVEN ▸ UP
even something up to make something even, square, level, equal, balanced, etc. □ *I'll even the table up.* 🅃 *See if you can even up the legs of this table. It wobbles.*

EVICT ▸ FROM
evict someone from some place to force someone to move out of something or some place. □ *They evicted the squatters from the building.* □ *They were evicted from their home.*

EVOLVE ▸ FROM
evolve (from something) (into something) AND **evolve (out of something) (into something)** to develop from something to something else; to develop from a more primitive form to the present form. □ *This creature evolved from a smaller, horselike creature into what we know as a horse.* □ *The horse evolved out of this little thing into the horse of today.* □ *My horse evolved out of this little animal?*

EVOLVE ▸ INTO
See the previous entry.

EVOLVE ▸ OUT
evolve (out of something) (into something) See under *EVOLVE ▸ FROM.*

EXACT ▸ FROM
exact something from someone to demand something from someone; to take something from someone. □ *The bill collector sought to exact payment from them for a debt that had been paid off long ago.* □ *You cannot exact a single cent from me.*

EXAMINE ▸ FOR
examine someone or something for something to inspect someone or something for the presence of something. (*Someone* includes *oneself*.) □ *I examined the child for signs of abuse.* □ *You had better examine this dog for ticks.* □ *Don't forget to examine yourself for ticks after you return from the hike.*

EXAMINE ▸ IN
examine someone in something to give someone an examination in a particular subject. □ *The committee examined her in her knowledge of history.* □ *I was examined in math.*

EXAMINE ▸ ON
examine someone on something to give someone an examination covering certain material. □ *I will have to examine you on this chapter myself.* □ *The committee examined Larry on his knowledge of photography.*

EXCEED ▸ BY
exceed someone or something by something to surpass someone or something by some amount. □ *Wally exceeded his quota by two hundred.* □ *He exceeded Larry by a large amount.*

EXCEED ▸ IN
exceed someone or something in something to surpass someone or something in something. □ *Tom exceeds only Walter in just plain stupidness.* □ *Walter exceeded the Rock of Gibraltar in hardheadedness.*

EXCEL ▸ AT
excel at something to do something in a superior fashion. □ *She really excels at running.* □ *Wally does not excel at anything.*

EXCEL ► IN

excel in something to be superior in something. □ *Sally excelled in athletic ability.* □ *Frank always hoped he would excel in math.*

EXCERPT ► FROM

excerpt something from something to select a part of something from the whole. □ *We excerpted a few short scenes from the play and performed them for the class.* □ *A few paragraphs had been excerpted as an example.*

EXCHANGE ► FOR

exchange something for something to trade something for something else. □ *I will exchange this one for a larger size.* □ *Can this be exchanged for something more suitable?*

EXCHANGE ► WITH

exchange something with someone to trade something with someone. □ *I exchange Christmas presents with him, but I never see him otherwise.* □ *Let's exchange coats with each other.*

EXCITE ► ABOUT

excite someone about something to stimulate someone about something. □ *I thought the stories would excite her about going, but they did not.* □ *She was excited about the trip to Moscow.*

EXCITE ► IN

excite something in someone to arouse something in someone; to arouse someone with something. □ *The movie excited a lot of hatred in the general population.* □ *The smell of jasmine in the warm air excited a romantic streak in me.*

EXCLUDE ► FROM

exclude someone or something from something to leave someone or something out of something; to leave someone or something off a list. (*Someone* includes *oneself.*) □ *Did you mean to exclude me from the party?* □ *I excluded chocolate cake from the shopping list.* □ *I exclude myself from consideration for the nomination.*

EXCUSE ► FOR

excuse someone for something to pardon someone for something or for (doing) something. (*Someone* includes *oneself.*) □ *Please excuse me for this mess. I've not been able to clean the house.* □ *I can't excuse myself for not doing it.*

EXCUSE ► FROM

excuse someone from something to permit a person not to do something; *to exempt someone from something.* (*Someone* includes *oneself.*) □ *Please excuse me from attending the meeting.* □ *I must excuse myself from the discussion.*

EXEMPLIFY ► BY

exemplify something by something to use something to explain or illustrate something. □ *He exemplifies wisdom by his decisions.* □ *Roger exemplifies virtue by the way he treats his employees.*

EXEMPT ► FROM

exempt someone from something to release someone from the obligation to do something; to allow a person not to be affected by a rule or law. (*Someone* includes *oneself.*) □ *I cannot exempt anyone from this rule.* □ *The members of Congress exempted themselves from the wage freeze.*

EXERCISE ► IN

exercise someone or something in something to give someone or some creature practice in doing something; to drill someone or some creature at something. (*Someone* includes *oneself.*) □ *Please exercise the dog in obedience routines.* □ *I hope you will exercise me in my Spanish irregular verbs.* □ *I exercised myself in the martial arts.*

EXERCISE ► OVER

exercise something over someone to hold power, influence, control, etc., over someone. □ *See if you can exercise some control over your appetite.* □ *I wish I could exercise some influence over the committee.*

EXHORT ► TO

exhort someone to do something to urge or pressure someone to do something. □ *She exhorted us to do better, but we only did worse.* □ *The boss exhorted the workers to work harder.*

EXILE ▸ FROM
exile someone (from something) (to something) to force someone to leave something or some place and go to something or some place. □ *The government exiled him from his hometown to an island off the coast of South America.* □ *They exiled Gerald to another country.*

EXILE ▸ TO
See the previous entry.

EXIT ▸ FROM
exit (from something) (to something) to go out of something or some place to another. □ *The children exited from the school to the parking lot when the fire alarm rang.* □ *We exited to the main street from the parking lot.*

EXIT ▸ TO
See the previous entry.

EXONERATE ▸ FROM
exonerate someone from something to vindicate someone from something such as a crime, accusation, charge, etc. (*Someone* includes *oneself*.) □ *The trial did not succeed in exonerating Sam from the charges of vagrancy.* □ *I want an opportunity to exonerate myself from the charges.*

EXORCISE ▸ FROM
exorcise something from someone AND **exorcise something out of someone** to remove or cast out evil from someone. □ *We saw a movie about a priest who exorcised a demon from a young girl.* □ *He exorcised all the evil out of her.*

EXORCISE ▸ OUT
exorcise something out of someone See the previous entry.

EXPAND ▸ INTO
expand into something to grow into something; to enlarge into something. □ *The little problem expanded into a big one in no time at all.* □ *In no time at all, the vegetable garden had expanded into a small farm.*

expand something into something to enlarge something into something; to make something grow into something. □ *She expanded her business into a national company.* □ *I would like to do something to expand this room into a more usable space.*

EXPAND ▸ (UP)ON
expand (up)on something to add detail to a report about something. □ *Would you please expand upon that last remark?* □ *May I expand on your remarks?*

EXPATIATE ▸ ON
expatiate on someone or something to say or write many words about someone or something. □ *She expatiated endlessly on the evils of tobacco.* □ *I have heard you expatiate on Harry quite enough, thank you.*

EXPECT ▸ FOR
expect someone or something for something to anticipate someone or a group to attend something. □ *I expect you for dinner on Thursday.* □ *We expected all of the board of directors for the meeting.*

EXPECT ▸ FROM
expect something from someone or something AND **expect something out of someone or something** **1.** to anticipate receiving something from someone or a group. □ *I expect a letter from you at least once a week while you are gone.* □ *We expect at least a postcard out of you.* **2.** AND **expect something (out) of someone or something** to demand something from someone or something. □ *I expect more effort from you. Get to work.* □ *We all expect a lot of you.* □ *The boss expects a lot out of you.* **3.** AND **expect something (out) of someone or something** to anticipate a certain kind of behavior from someone or something. □ *We expected better from you. I'm very disappointed in your behavior.* □ *We really expected better behavior of you.*

EXPECT ▸ OF
expect something (out) of someone or something See under the previous entry.

EXPECT ▸ OUT

expect something out of someone or something See under *EXPECT ▸ FROM.*

EXPEL ▸ FROM

expel someone from something to force someone to leave something or some place; to eject someone from something or some place. □ *The two men expelled the fighters from the tavern.* □ *Ken was expelled from the building.*

expel something from something to force something out of something. □ *The machine expelled cup after cup from its opening.* □ *The volcano expelled huge globs of molten lava.*

EXPEND ▸ FOR

expend something for something to pay a certain amount for something. □ *I expended an enormous amount for skin creams.* □ *How much money did you expend for this gaudy tie?*

EXPEND ▸ IN

expend something in something to use or consume something in some activity. □ *You expend too much energy in talking.* □ *Harry expended a lot of time in the preparation of his speech.*

EXPEND ▸ ON

expend something on someone or something to use something on someone or something. □ *Don't expend too much energy on him. He isn't worth it.* □ *There is no point in expending any more money on this car.*

EXPERIMENT ▸ IN

experiment in something to conduct research or experiments about something. □ *The research group is experimenting in the field of biomechanics.* □ *We want to experiment in thermodynamics.*

EXPERIMENT ▸ (UP)ON

experiment (up)on someone or something to use someone or something as the subject of an experiment. (*Upon* is formal and less commonly used than *on.*) □ *Do you think we should experiment upon people?* □ *The researchers were experimenting on a new drug that might cure rabies.*

EXPERIMENT ▸ WITH

experiment with someone or something to try different experiments on someone or something; to use different people or things as key variables in an experiment. □ *They are supposed to be experimenting with new drugs.* □ *We no longer experiment with animals.*

EXPLAIN ▸ AWAY

explain something away to explain something so that it is no longer a problem. □ *You can try to explain it away if you want, but that won't solve the problem.* 🅃 *You can't just explain away all your problems.*

EXPLAIN ▸ TO

explain someone or something to someone to give information or instruction about someone or something to someone. (*Someone* includes *oneself.*) □ *Please explain it to me.* □ *Can you explain Andrew to me?*

EXPLODE ▸ WITH

explode with something **1.** to burst out saying something; to be about to burst with eagerness to say something. (Figurative.) □ *The children exploded with their protests.* □ *Hanna was exploding with questions.* □ *I was about to explode with a comment, but I waited for my turn.* **2.** to produce a sudden abundance of something. (Figurative.) □ *The fields exploded with an enormous crop of field mice.* □ *The flowers exploded with blossoms.* **3.** to make a loud noise upon exploding or releasing energy. □ *The bomb exploded with a thunderous roar.* □ *When the joke was finished, the audience exploded with laughter.*

EXPORT ▸ TO

export something to some place to sell something abroad to a particular country. □ *They are now exporting their products to Hungary.* □ *We are exporting all our product line to Eastern Europe.*

export something to someone or something to sell something abroad to someone or some country. □ *The company exported alcohol to Brazil.* □ *We only export books to our agents abroad.*

EXPOSE ▸ TO

expose someone or something to someone or something **1.** to show someone or something to someone or something. (*Someone* includes *oneself*.) □ *You should not expose the children to Mr. Brown.* □ *Do not expose the film to the light.* □ *She exposed herself to the scrutiny of the cameras.* **2.** to open someone or some creature to the dangers of a disease or someone with a disease. □ *Try to expose your children to chicken pox while they are young. It's horrible when you are an adult.* □ *He accidentally exposed his sheep to an infected animal.* □ *I want to bring Timmy over and expose him to your little Sally while she has chicken pox.*

expose something or oneself to someone or something to disclose someone's or something's secrets to someone or a group. (To *expose oneself* also has sexual connotations, referring to the sexual organs, especially of the male.) □ *He exposed his inner thoughts to everyone there.* □ *She refused to expose herself to the ears of the curious and ceased talking.* □ *He exposed himself to the public when he revealed his involvement in the arms sale.*

EXPOSTULATE ▸ ABOUT

expostulate about someone or something AND **expostulate on someone or something** to comment or argue intensely about someone or something. □ *He always seems to be expostulating on something. He never just talks.* □ *Sam is expostulating on Bill again.* □ *What are you expostulating about now?*

EXPOSTULATE ▸ ON

See the previous entry.

EXPOUND ▸ ON

See under *EXPOUND ▸ (UP)ON.*

EXPOUND ▸ TO

See the following entry.

EXPOUND ▸ (UP)ON

expound ((up)on someone or something) (to someone) to speak at length about someone or something to someone. (*Upon* is formal and less commonly used than *on*.) □ *Let me expound upon Tom to you for a while. I think you would like to meet him.* □ *Please do not expound on Bill anymore.* □ *There is no need to expound to me.*

EXPRESS ▸ ON

express oneself (to someone) (on something) to say what one thinks about something. □ *I will express myself to Karen on that matter at another time.* □ *She expressed herself on Karen to the entire group.* □ *I need to express myself to you on this matter.*

EXPRESS ▸ TO

See the previous entry.

EXPROPRIATE ▸ FOR

See the following entry.

EXPROPRIATE ▸ FROM

expropriate something (from someone or something) (for someone or something) to seize something from someone or something for someone or something. □ *The government expropriated the land from the peasants for an airfield.* □ *They expropriated land for a highway.* □ *They expropriated land from the farmers.*

EXPUNGE ▸ FROM

expunge something from something to erase something from something. □ *The judge ordered the clerk to expunge the comment from the record.* □ *Please expunge the lawyer's remark from the transcript.*

EXPURGATE ▸ FROM

expurgate something from something to cleanse something by removing something. (Often refers to editing objectionable material from written or broadcast material. □ *They expurgated the best parts from the novel.* □ *We will expurgate the offensive matter from the article.*

EXTEND ▸ ACROSS

extend across something to spread across something. ☐ *The shadows extended across the whole land.* ☐ *The fog extended across the low-lying land.*

EXTEND ▸ FROM

extend (from something) (to something) to spread from one point to another point. ☐ *The cloud of smoke extended from one end of town to the other.* ☐ *It extended to the end of the road from our front gate.*

EXTEND ▸ OVER

extend over someone or something to spread over someone or something. ☐ *The smoke extended over Tom and his friends, who were having a picnic.* ☐ *The cloud extended over the entire valley.*

EXTEND ▸ TO

extend credit to someone to permit someone to purchase something on credit. ☐ *I cannot extend credit to you.* ☐ *Will you extend credit to my older brother?*

extend (from something) (to something) See under *EXTEND ▸ FROM.*

extend something to someone **1.** to grant something to someone; to offer something to someone. ☐ *Todd extended an offer of one million dollars for the land.* ☐ *I extended the offer to everyone there.* **2.** to reach out with something to someone. ☐ *He extended his hand to her in greeting.* ☐ *Ken extended the tray full of goodies to Roger.*

extend something to something **1.** to lengthen something to reach something. ☐ *We extended the telescope to its full length.* ☐ *Extend your arm to the wall and see how straight you can make it.* **2.** to push a stated deadline further into the future. ☐ *I will extend the deadline to Friday.* ☐ *We cannot extend the due date any more.*

extend to someone or something to reach all the way to someone or something. ☐ *This policy extends to you also.* ☐ *The road extends to Los Angeles.*

EXTOLL ▸ AS

extoll someone or something as something to praise someone or something as something. ☐ *We extolled her as a heroine.* ☐ *The speaker extolled the medicine as a cure-all.*

EXTORT ▸ FROM

extort something from someone to steal something from someone; to force someone to give something by making threats. ☐ *The crook was trying to extort a lot of money from the widow.* ☐ *The authorities caught Max trying to extort a great deal of money from the bank.*

EXTRACT ▸ FROM

extract something from someone or something to remove something from someone or something; to make someone or a group give something. ☐ *We extracted the juice from the oranges.* ☐ *They extracted the truth from her.* ☐ *The bill collector extracted the payment from the debtor.*

EXTRADITE ▸ FROM

extradite someone from some place to have someone sent from some place to face criminal prosecution. ☐ *The state's attorney sought to extradite Max from Missouri.* ☐ *Max was extradited from Indiana.*

EXTRAPOLATE ▸ FROM

extrapolate something from something to reason out the answer from the known facts. ☐ *I cannot extrapolate what he meant from these notes.* ☐ *Can you extrapolate the answer from this article?*

EXTRICATE ▸ FROM

extricate someone or something from someone or something to disentangle someone or something from someone or something; to free someone or something from someone or something. (*Someone* includes *oneself.*) ☐ *I tried to extricate myself from her, but she made it hard for me to get away politely.* ☐ *I managed to extricate the ring from the vacuum cleaner bag.* ☐ *I could not extricate myself from her. She just talked* *and talked.* □ *I was not able to extricate myself from the clutches of the mob.*

EXULT ► AT

exult at something AND **exult over something** to rejoice because of something; to rejoice about something. □ *We exulted at the end of the hostilities.* □ *The citizens exulted over the elections.*

EXULT ► IN

exult in something to take great pleasure in something; to enjoy something immensely. □ *I exult in the beauty of a spring day.* □ *We exulted in the glory of summer.*

EXULT ► OVER

exult over someone or something See under *EXULT ► AT.*

F

FACE ► AWAY

face away (from someone or something) to turn away from someone or something. ☐ *Please face away from me while I change clothes.* ☐ *I'll face away. You go right ahead.*

FACE ► DOWN

face someone down to make a face-to-face stand with someone who eventually backs down. ☐ *Chuck succeeded in facing Tom down.* 🅃 *Facing down Tom wasn't difficult for Chuck.*

face something down to turn something face downward. ☐ *Ted drew a card and faced it down.* ☐ *Face your cards down when you leave the card table.*

FACE ► FORWARD

face (oneself) forward to turn oneself to the front. (Also with many other directions—*backward, to the right, to the left,* etc.) ☐ *Would you face yourself forward for the photograph?* ☐ *Please face forward.* ☐ *Ask him to face himself forward.*

face someone or something forward to turn someone or something to the front. (Also with many other directions—*backward, to the right, to the left,* etc.) ☐ *Please face your brother forward now.* ☐ *Face the book forward so we can read the title.*

FACE ► INTO

face (someone or something) into something to turn someone or something directly toward something. (*Someone* includes *oneself.*) ☐ *Face the sail into the wind.* ☐ *Please face into the camera.* ☐ *Ask him to face himself into the sunset for the next picture.*

FACE ► OFF

face off **1.** to begin a hockey game with two players facing one another. ☐ *They faced off and the match was on.* 🄽 *The players prepared for the faceoff.* **2.** to prepare for a confrontation. (From sense 1.) ☐ *The opposing candidates faced off and the debate began.* ☐ *They faced off and I knew there was going to be a fight.* 🄽 *The political face-off between the President and the Congress took a new turn this morning.*

FACE ► ON(TO)

face on(to) something [for something] to have a view out onto something. ☐ *The house faced onto the sea and provided a beautiful view of the incoming ships.* ☐ *Our office building does not face onto the street.* ☐ *We asked for a room that faces on the main square.*

FACE ► UP

face up (to someone or something) to confront with courage someone or something representing a threat or unpleasantness. ☐ *You are simply going to have to face up to Fred.* ☐ *You must face up to the authorities if you have done something wrong.* ☐ *You will simply have to face up.*

FACE ► WITH

face someone with something to present evidence of something to someone. ☐ *When I faced him with the evidence, he confessed immediately.* ☐ *The police faced Max with the witness's story.*

face something with something to install something on the surface of something. □ *We faced the kitchen walls with yellow tile.* □ *The wall was faced with tile.*

FADE ▶ AWAY

fade away to diminish to nothing or almost nothing. □ *The sound slowly faded away.* □ *As the light faded away, we had to resort to candles.*

fade away into something to diminish into something. □ *The light faded away into nothing.* □ *The sound of the drums faded away into the distance.*

FADE ▶ BACK

fade back (into something) to move back into a particular area. (Football.) □ *He faded back to receive the pass.* □ *Quickly and unnoticed, he faded back.*

FADE ▶ DOWN

fade down [for sound] to diminish. □ *The roar of the train faded down as it passed and fled into the night.* □ *As the thunder faded down, the sun began to break through the clouds.*

fade something down to turn down a sound. □ *The radio engineer faded the music down and the announcer's voice began.* [T] *She faded down the music.*

FADE ▶ FROM

fade from something [for something] to leave something gradually, such as one's consciousness, memory, view, etc. □ *The image faded from her memory at last.* □ *The scene faded from view as the stage lights dimmed.*

FADE ▶ IN

fade something in to bring a picture, sound, or both into prominence. (Broadcasting.) □ *The technician faded the picture in and the program began.* [T] *Fade in the picture a little faster next time.*

FADE ▶ INTO

fade into something to diminish or change into something. □ *The light of dusk faded into blackness.* □ *In the corner of the painting, the deep reds faded into lavender.*

FADE ▶ OUT

fade out to diminish and go away altogether. □ *The light in the distance faded out as the sun began to rise.* □ *The light faded out as the candles burned themselves out, one by one.* [N] *The fade-out at the end of the play left a feeling of uncertainty. We didn't know if it was the end or if the power had failed.*

fade something out to diminish something altogether. (Broadcasting.) □ *At the end, you should fade the music out completely.* [T] *Fade out the music earlier.*

FADE ▶ UP

fade something up to increase the sound gradually. (Broadcasting.) □ *The director faded the music up and then down again before the announcer spoke.* [T] *Fade up the music when the announcer stops talking.*

FAG ▶ OUT

fag someone out to tire someone out. (Informal or slang.) □ *All that work really fagged me out.* □ *All the campers here fagged out when they got home.*

FAIL ▶ IN

fail in something to have not earned passing or satisfactory grades in some school subject. □ *George is failing in geometry.* □ *I hope I do not fail in math.*

FAIL ▶ ON

fail someone on something to give someone an unsatisfactory grade on an assignment or test. □ *She failed us all on the math assignment.* □ *The teacher failed half the class on the assignment.*

FAINT ▶ AWAY

faint dead away to faint and be unconscious. □ *I almost fainted dead away.* □ *David will faint dead away when he reads this.*

FAINT ▶ FROM

faint from something to faint because of something. □ *I nearly fainted from fear!* □ *Three people along the parade route fainted from the heat.*

FAIR ▶ OUT

fair something out to distribute something fairly. (Folksy.) □ *She faired the* *meager stew out the best she could.* 🅃 *Walter faired out the pie.*

FAKE ▸ OFF

fake off (to someone) to pass the football to someone in a sly manner. (Football.) □ *Wally faked off to the guy to his right.* □ *No one saw Wally fake off.* 🄽 *The crowd cheered at the masterful fakeoff.*

FAKE ▸ OUT

fake someone out to deceive someone; to fool someone. (Slang. *Someone* includes *oneself*.) □ *You really faked me out. I never would have guessed it was you.* 🅃 *The student tried to fake out the teacher.* □ *He faked himself out when he tried to beat the odds.* 🄽 *The governor's entire term was one big fakeout.*

fake someone out of something to get something from someone by deception. (Slang.) □ *He faked Tom out of his football tickets.* □ *She faked me out of a lot of money.*

FALL ▸ APART

fall apart to break into pieces; to disassemble. (Both literal and figurative uses.) □ *The whole thing fell apart.* □ *Gerald's whole life began falling apart.*

fall apart at the seams **1.** [for something] to break apart where its parts are joined. □ *The dress fell apart at the seams.* □ *I wouldn't have thought that a coat that cost that much money would just fall apart at the seams.* **2.** [for someone] to break down mentally; [for something] to *fall apart*. (Figurative.) □ *Poor Ralph simply fell apart at the seams.* □ *All of our plans simply fell apart at the seams.*

FALL ▸ AT

fall (down) at something to prostrate oneself before or at the feet of someone or something. □ *She fell down at the feet of the horrid man who held her child.* □ *She fell at his feet.*

FALL ▸ AWAY

fall away (from someone or something) **1.** [for something] to drop away from someone or something. □ *The paint is falling away from the sides of the house.* □ *Over the years, all the paint fell away.* **2.** [for someone] to move back or retreat from someone or something. (Literal and figurative uses.) □ *The soldiers fell away from the line of battle.* □ *One by one, they fell away.* □ *The candidate's supporters fell away from her when they heard about the scandal.*

fall away toward something to slant downward toward something. □ *The yard fell away toward the shore of the lake.* □ *The broad expanse of prairie land fell away toward the river bottom land, and beyond that, the river itself.*

FALL ▸ BACK

fall back to move back from something; to retreat from something. □ *The gang members fell back and I took that opportunity to get away.* □ *The troops fell back to regroup.* 🄽 *After the first fallback, they surged ahead again.*

fall back on(to) someone or something **1.** to fall backwards onto someone or something. □ *She stumbled and fell back onto the lady behind her.* □ *She fell back on the couch.* **2.** to begin to use someone or something held in reserve. (Figurative.) □ *We fell back on our savings to get us through the hard times.* □ *We had to fall back on our emergency generator.*

FALL ▸ BEHIND

fall behind (in something) AND **fall behind (on something); fall behind (with something); get behind (in something); get behind (on something); get behind (with something)** to lag behind schedule in some kind of work or some other scheduled activity. □ *You are falling behind in your car payments.* □ *I tried not to get behind on them.* □ *Please don't fall behind with your payments.* □ *I won't fall behind again.*

fall behind (someone or something) to lag behind someone or something. □ *You have fallen behind everyone else in class.* □ *Our production fell behind that of the other production line.*

FALL ▸ BELOW

fall below something to drop to a lower level than something. □ *The temperature has fallen below freezing again.* □

When the audience fell below two hundred a night, they closed the play.

FALL ▸ BENEATH

fall beneath something to drop under something. □ *The thimble fell beneath the sofa.* □ *The gift that Bob had purchased for Maggie fell beneath the wheels of a truck.*

FALL ▸ BETWEEN

fall between something and something else to drop between things. □ *My loose change fell between the cushions of the sofa.* □ *I hope that my candy doesn't fall between the table and the wall. I would never be able to move the table to get it.*

FALL ▸ BY

fall by something to drop in value by a certain amount. □ *The gas stocks fell by nearly 10 percent today.* □ *If the stock market falls by four hundred points, I'm going to jump off a cliff.*

fall by the wayside See under *DROP ▸ BY.*

FALL ▸ DOWN

fall down to drop or topple. □ *The baby fell down.* □ *Walk carefully on this ice or you will fall down.*

fall (down) at some place See under *FALL ▸ AT.*

fall down on someone or something to fall and drop onto someone or something. □ *Bits of the ceiling paint fell down on us and into our food.* □ *The leaves fell down on the lawn.*

fall down on the job to fail to do an efficient job. □ *Henry has been falling down on the job.* □ *All of the workers tend to fall down on the job on Friday.*

fall (down) to something See under *FALL ▸ TO.*

FALL ▸ FOR

fall for someone to fall in love with someone. (Also with the added cliché, *in a big way.*) □ *I fell for her in a big way. She's gorgeous!* □ *Ted fell for Alice and they decided to get married.*

fall for something to believe something without reservation. (Also with the added cliché, *in a big way.*) □ *Surely, you don't expect me to fall for that!* □ *She fell for the story in a big way!*

FALL ▸ FROM

fall from grace **1.** to sin and get on the wrong side of God. (A Christian concept.) □ *It was either fall from grace or starve from lack of money. That's how thieves are made.* □ *Given the choice between falling from grace and starving, few people choose to starve.* **2.** to do something wrong and get in trouble with someone other than God. □ *I hear that Ted lost the Wilson contract and has fallen from grace with the boss.* □ *The accounting department has fallen from grace and more of the employees may be replaced by a computer.*

fall from power to go out of power; to go out of office. □ *The dictator fell from power after the riots.* □ *Every ruler will fall from power sooner or later.*

fall from someone or something to fall off of someone or something. □ *The books fell from the top shelf in the earthquake.* □ *The clothing fell from the model and the artists began to sketch.*

FALL ▸ IN

See also under *FALL ▸ IN(TO).*

fall in to get into line and stand at attention. (Military. Often a command.) □ *The commander ordered that the troops fall in.* □ *If you don't fall in now, you'll all have to do a hundred push-ups.*

fall in (for something) to assemble for a particular activity. □ *Will you please fall in for mail call?* □ *If you don't fall in, you don't get your mail.*

fall in love [for two people] to become enamored of each other. □ *They fell in love.* □ *When they fell in love, they thought it would last forever.*

fall in love (with someone or something) to become enamored of someone or something. □ *I simply fell in love with the dress. I had to have it.* □ *I fell in love with her.*

fall in on someone or something to cave in on someone or something; to collapse on someone or something. □ *The* *roof of the cave fell in on the workers.* ☐ *The ceiling fell in on the diners.* ☐ *I was afraid that the ceiling would fall in on the grand piano.*

fall in with someone or something to become involved with someone or a group. ☐ *I'm afraid that he fell in with the wrong kind of friends.* ☐ *John fell in with Max, who had served time in prison.*

fall in with something to concur with something; to harmonize with something. ☐ *We had to fall in with her wishes.* ☐ *The statement falls in exactly with my view.*

FALL ▶ INTO

fall into a trap **1.** to get caught in a trap. ☐ *The tiger fell into a trap and leapt out again immediately.* ☐ *The boys tried to get a squirrel to fall into a trap, but squirrels are too clever.* **2.** to be deceived or misled; to get tricked into something. ☐ *I think I have fallen into a trap and you are the one who tricked me into it.* ☐ *She fell into a trap and ended up paying far more than she should have.*

fall into decay to degenerate; to rot. ☐ *The house was very old and had fallen into decay.* ☐ *The small town fell into decay, and people moved out.*

fall into disfavor to lose one's influence; to be preferred less and less. ☐ *This style of government fell into disfavor some years ago.* ☐ *Poor Lee fell into disfavor and lost all his special privileges.*

fall into disgrace to become without honor. ☐ *The mayor fell into disgrace because of his financial dealings.* ☐ *We fell into disgrace because of our financial dealings.*

fall into disuse to be used less and less. ☐ *The pump had fallen into disuse and the joints had rusted solid.* ☐ *Since my books had fallen into disuse, I sold them to a used-book dealer.*

fall into someone's trap to become entrapped by someone; to be caught by someone's maneuvering. ☐ *I think that Terry has fallen into my trap. I have tricked him at last.* ☐ *You fell into the trap they set for you.*

fall into the wrong hands to become associated with the wrong person; to become the possession of the wrong person. (Figurative.) ☐ *I don't want these plans to fall into the wrong hands.* ☐ *This could be dangerous if it fell into the wrong hands.*

FALL ▶ IN(TO)

fall in(to) line (with someone or something) **1.** to get into a line with other people or a group. ☐ *I fell in line with the others and waited my turn.* ☐ *Please fall in line and stay there.* **2.** to behave in a manner similar to someone or something. (Figurative.) ☐ *You are expected to fall into line with the other people.* ☐ *We want you to fall in line.*

fall in(to) place to move into place; to fit into the correct place. (Both literal and figurative.) ☐ *At last, things began to fall into place, and life became livable again.* ☐ *In the end, everything fell in place.*

fall in(to something) to drop into something. ☐ *The rabbit fell into the hole and was trapped.* ☐ *It went right up to the hole and fell in.*

fall in(to step) to get into the same marching pattern as everyone else as regards which foot moves forward. (Everyone should be moving the same foot forward at the same time.) ☐ *I just can't seem to fall into step. I am very uncoordinated.* ☐ *Fall in! March with the others!*

FALL ▶ OF

fall short of something to be inadequate in some way. ☐ *This plan falls short of solving our problems.* ☐ *Your comments fell short of explaining everything.*

FALL ▶ OFF

fall off to decline. ☐ *At dawn, the horrible insect noises of the night began to fall off.* ☐ *As business began to fall off, so did my income.* N *There was a terrible falloff in our business last spring.*

fall off (of) a log to do something very easy. (Idiomatic. Usually included in the phrase **as easy as falling off (of) a log**. The *of* is colloquial, but almost always included in the expressions.) ☐ *Taking the test was as easy as falling off a log.* ☐ *Baking an apple pie is as easy as falling off a log.*

fall off ((of) something) to drop off something. (The *of* is colloquial.) ☐ *A button fell off my shirt.* ☐ *I fell off the log.* ☐ *The twigs fell off of him as he stood up.*

fall off the wagon to start drinking alcohol after a period of abstinence. ☐ *I hear that Bill fell off the wagon again.* ☐ *He did what he could to avoid falling off the wagon again.*

FALL ▸ ON

See also under *FALL ▸ (UP)ON.*

See also under *FALL ▸ ON(TO).*

fall (flat) on one's face **1.** to fall down, face first. ☐ *Bobby fell flat on his face and skinned his nose.* ☐ *Down he went—he fell on his face.* **2.** to fail miserably, usually in a performance. (Figurative.) ☐ *She was terrible in the play. She fell flat on her face.* ☐ *The whole play fell on its face.*

fall on deaf ears [for a request] to go unheard or to be ignored. ☐ *Her pleading fell on deaf ears.* ☐ *All of his demands fell on deaf ears.*

fall on hard times to experience difficult times. ☐ *Since the war, her family had fallen on hard times.* ☐ *We fell on hard times during the recession.*

fall on one's knees AND **fall to one's knees** to kneel down, usually in respect. ☐ *The people fell on their knees and prayed in gratitude for their salvation from the flood.* ☐ *They fell to their knees in awe.*

FALL ▸ ON(TO)

fall on(to) someone or something to collapse toward or onto someone or something. ☐ *The fence fell onto the car, denting it severely.* ☐ *The branch fell on David.*

FALL ▸ OUT

fall out to happen; to occur. ☐ *As things fell out, we were too late.* ☐ *Things fell out the way they had to. We cannot influence fate.*

fall out of bed **1.** to roll out of one's bed onto the floor. ☐ *I fell out of bed and broke my arm.* ☐ *Billy fell out of bed and started to cry.* **2.** [for a measurement] to drop very low very fast. (Slang.) ☐ *The major stock averages fell out of bed today as the market suffered its second severe crash in two months.* ☐ *The temperature fell out of bed last night.*

fall out of favor (with someone) to lose someone's favor or approval. ☐ *This style of house has fallen out of favor with most people lately.* ☐ *Saving money has fallen out of favor.*

fall out of love (with someone) to stop being in love with someone. ☐ *She claimed she had fallen out of love with him.* ☐ *He also had fallen out of love.*

fall out of something to topple out of something; to fall from the bottom of something. ☐ *Mary fell out of the tree and hurt herself.* ☐ *Don't fall out of that tree!* ☐ *The bottom fell out of the stock market today, leaving investors wondering what to do with their money.*

fall out with someone (about someone or something) AND **fall out with someone (over someone or something)** to have a disagreement with someone about someone or something; to have a quarrel with someone. ☐ *Tony fell out with Nick about the video game.* ☐ *They fell out with each other over the game.* ☐ *It's a shame to fall out with your brother.*

FALL ▸ OUTSIDE

fall outside something to be beyond someone's power, responsibility, or jurisdiction. ☐ *This matter falls outside my bailiwick.* ☐ *Her offense fell outside of the manager's jurisdiction.*

FALL ▸ OVER

fall (all) over oneself (to do something) to rush eagerly and awkwardly to do something. (Figurative.) ☐ *The boys fell all over themselves to open the door for Sarah.* ☐ *Larry fell over himself trying to help Sarah on with her coat.*

fall over to topple over and fall down. ☐ *The fence fell over and dented the car.* ☐ *I felt faint and almost fell over.*

fall over backwards (to do something) to go to great extremes to do something; to endure all sorts of trouble to do something. ☐ *She fell over backwards to make everyone comfortable.* ☐ *Just do your best. There is no need to fall over backwards.*

fall over someone or something to stumble over someone or something. ☐ *Sam came into the house and fell over a kitchen chair.* ☐ *Walter fell over Roger, who was napping on the floor.*

FALL ▸ OVERBOARD

fall overboard to fall from a boat or a ship into the water. ☐ *Someone fell overboard and they had to stop the boat and go back.* ☐ *The lady's sunglasses fell overboard.*

FALL ▸ THROUGH

fall through [for something, such as plans] to fail. ☐ *Our party for next Saturday fell through.* ☐ *I hope our plans don't fall through.*

fall through something to fall and break through something. ☐ *One of the skaters fell through the thin ice.* ☐ *A number of hailstones fell through the roof of the greenhouse.*

FALL ▸ TO

fall (down) to something to fall or drop to something below. ☐ *The coconut fell down to the people below.* ☐ *It fell to the people shaking the tree.*

fall to to begin doing something. ☐ *She asked for help, and everyone fell to.* ☐ *Fall to, you guys!*

fall to one's knees See *fall on one's knees* under *FALL ▸ ON.*

fall to pieces **1.** to break into pieces. ☐ *The road was so rough the car almost fell to pieces.* ☐ *I was afraid that my bicycle would fall to pieces before I got there.* **2.** to become emotionally upset. (Figurative.) ☐ *I was so nervous, I fell to pieces and couldn't give my speech.* ☐ *Roger fell to pieces and couldn't attend the sales meeting.*

fall to someone or something to become the responsibility of someone or a group. ☐ *It falls to you to go and tell Mrs. Wilson that you broke her window.* ☐ *The responsibility falls to the board of directors.*

FALL ▸ TOWARD

fall toward something to drop or fall in the direction of something. ☐ *She fell toward the curb rather than toward the traffic.* ☐ *The tree fell toward the garage rather than toward the house.*

FALL ▸ UNDER

fall under someone or something to drop down and end up beneath someone or something. ☐ *The old man fell under the wheels of the truck, but he suffered only minor injuries.* ☐ *The child tripped and fell under Mrs. Rogers, who almost did not see her.*

fall under someone's spell **1.** to come under the magical control of a magician or similar person. ☐ *The damsel fell under Merlin's spell and sat there speechless.* ☐ *As the children fell under the witch's spell, they went to sleep.* **2.** to be fascinated by someone; to be enchanted by someone. ☐ *She was so beautiful. I fell under her spell at once.* ☐ *Wally fell under Donna's spell and became helpless in her presence.*

FALL ▸ (UP)ON

fall (up)on someone or something **1.** to collapse on top of someone or something. (*Upon* is formal and less commonly used than *on.*) ☐ *The bridge fell upon a boat passing beneath it.* ☐ *A small branch fell on Jerry.* **2.** [for something] to become the responsibility of someone or a group. ☐ *It falls upon you to have the window repaired. After all, you broke it.* ☐ *The job of fixing the window falls on you.*

fall (up)on someone (to do something) to become someone's responsibility to do something. ☐ *It falls upon you to explain this matter to her.* ☐ *It falls on you to fix the window.*

FALL ▸ WITHIN

fall within something to belong to a specific category or classification. ☐

This falls within the realm of the medical profession. There's no more I can do for you. ☐ *Does this fall within your area?*

FALTER ▸ IN

falter in something to hesitate in doing something; to exhibit a lack of something, such as faith, loyalty, perseverance, etc. ☐ *He did not falter in his effort to see the project through to the end.* ☐ *I promised not to falter in my loyalty.*

FAMILIARIZE ▸ WITH

familiarize someone with something to help someone get to know or understand someone or something. (*Someone* includes *oneself*.) ☐ *I hope you will take the time to familiarize yourself with the instructions before you set out to operate this device.* ☐ *Let me take a moment to familiarize myself with the facts of the case.*

FAN ▸ OUT

fan out to spread out over a wide area. ☐ *The searchers fanned out, looking for the lost spectacles.* ☐ *Let's fan out and search a wider area.*

fan out (from some place) to spread outward from a particular area. ☐ *The paths seem to fan out from the wide trail that starts at the house.* ☐ *The trails fanned out and soon we were all separated.*

fan something out to spread something out so that all parts can be seen better. (As one opens a wood and paper fan.) ☐ *Todd fanned the cards out so we could see which ones he held.* 🅃 *He fanned out the cards.*

FANCY ▸ AS

fancy someone as someone or something to imagine that someone were someone else or some type of person. (*Someone* includes *oneself*.) ☐ *Can you fancy her as a zookeeper?* ☐ *I can fancy him as a tall dark stranger.* ☐ *I really don't fancy myself as a farmer.*

FARM ▸ OUT

farm someone out **1.** [for someone in control] to send someone to work for someone else. ☐ *I have farmed out my electrician for a week, so your work will have to wait.* 🅃 *We farmed out the office staff.* **2.** to send a child away to be cared for by someone; to send a child to boarding school. ☐ *We farmed the kids out to my sister for the summer.* 🅃 *We farmed out the kids.*

farm something out **1.** to deplete the fertility of land by farming too intensely. ☐ *They farmed their land out through careless land management.* 🅃 *They farmed out their land.* **2.** to make money by renting out land or buildings. ☐ *I farmed the pasture out.* 🅃 *I farmed out the west pasture to Bill Franklin, who will graze his cattle there.* **3.** to send work to someone to be done away from one's normal place of business; to subcontract work. ☐ *We farmed the sewing out.* 🅃 *We always farm out the actual sewing together of the dresses.*

FASHION ▸ INTO

fashion something into something to make, form, or convert something into something else. ☐ *He fashioned the newspaper into a temporary rain hat.* ☐ *Sarah fashioned the clay into a little bowl.*

FASHION ▸ ON

fashion something on something to model something on something else; to pattern something after something else. ☐ *She fashioned her dress on something she had seen in a history book.* ☐ *Donna fashioned the plan on the one Robert had used.*

FASHION ▸ OUT

fashion something out of something to make something from something; to convert something into something else. ☐ *He tried to fashion a dog out of balloons.* ☐ *Elaine was expert at fashioning a bow out of chocolate.*

FASTEN ▸ DOWN

fasten something down (to something) to attach something down to something else. ☐ *Fasten this board down to the top of the workbench.* 🅃 *Please fasten down the board.* ☐ *I'll fasten it down.* 🄰 *She couldn't budge the fastened-down bracket.*

FASTEN ► ON

See under *FASTEN ► (UP)ON.*

FASTEN ► (ON)TO

fasten someone or something (on)to someone or something to attach people or things together. (In any combination. *Someone* includes *oneself.*) □ *Sylvia fastened the notice onto the wall near the door.* □ *He fastened himself onto the side of the boat with a length of rope.* □ *I fastened a note onto Jimmy, so his kindergarten teacher would read it and remind him to wear his gloves home.*

FASTEN ► TO

See the previous entry.

FASTEN ► UP

fasten something up to close something up, using buttons, a zipper, snaps, hooks, a clasp, or other things meant to hold something closed. □ *Please fasten this up for me. I can't reach the zipper.* 🅃 *Please fasten up my buttons in back.*

FASTEN ► (UP)ON

fasten (up)on someone or something 1. to take firm hold of someone or something. □ *She fastened upon me and would not let me go until she finished speaking.* □ *I don't like people who fasten on you.* **2.** to fix one's attention on someone or something. □ *He fastened upon the picture for a brief moment and then turned away.* □ *The baby fastened on the television screen and watched it for many minutes.*

FAST-TALK ► INTO

fast-talk someone into something to use deceitful talk to get someone to do something. □ *You can't fast-talk me into giving you money. How dumb do you think I am?* □ *Max tried to fast-talk Lefty into robbing a bank with him.*

FAST-TALK ► OUT

fast-talk someone out of something to use deceitful talk to get someone not to do something or to give something up. □ *Don't try to fast-talk me out of it.* □ *Max tried to fast-talk Lefty out of his share of the money.*

FATHER ► ON

father something on someone to regard someone as the author or originator of something. □ *Do not attempt to father that stupid idea on me!* □ *We fathered the whole plan on the president. And we learned later she had nothing to do with it.*

FATTEN ► UP

fatten someone or something up (with something) to use something to make someone or some creature fat. (*Someone* includes *oneself.*) □ *We will fatten the calf up with corn.* 🅃 *I don't know why they keep fattening up their children with so much food.* □ *They keep fattening them up.* 🄰 *How much is one of those nice, fattened-up chickens?* □ *I fattened myself up with lots of good food.*

fatten up on something 1. to get fat by eating something. □ *The cattle fattened up on the succulent grass.* □ *The bears have to fatten up on food before they hibernate for the winter.* **2.** to become prosperous due to something. (Figurative.) □ *The corporations fattened up on easy profits and low taxes.* □ *The directors of the company fattened up even during the recession when the workers were laid off.*

FAULT ► FOR

fault someone for something to blame or criticize someone for something. (*Someone* includes *oneself.*) □ *I can't fault you for that. I would have done the same thing.* □ *He tended to fault himself for the failure of the project.*

FAVOR ► WITH

favor someone with something to present something to or honor someone with something. (Usually stilted.) □ *Perhaps Miss Wilson will favor us with a song.* □ *I know that Walter will favor us with another piece on the piano.*

FAWN ► OVER

fawn (all) over someone to flatter someone excessively; to *curry favor with* someone. □ *Please stop fawning all over the guests. You are embarrassing* *me.* ☐ *She always fawns over us when we visit.*

FAWN ▸ (UP)ON

fawn (up)on someone to praise and flatter someone. ☐ *Aunt Mabel fawned on the new baby till the poor child was rescued by her mother.* ☐ *Please don't fawn on me. It's yucky!*

FEAR ▸ FOR

fear for someone or something to be afraid for the safety of someone or something; to worry about someone or something. ☐ *I fear for Tom. He has gone to a very dangerous place.* ☐ *I don't want to go there. I fear for my car.*

FEAST ▸ (UP)ON

feast one's eyes (up)on someone or something to enjoy the sight of someone or something. (*Upon* is formal and less commonly used than *on*.) ☐ *Just feast your eyes on that beautiful beach.* ☐ *Jane feasted her eyes on Roger for a while and then went on with her studying.*

feast (up)on something to eat a great deal of something; to eat a feast built around something in particular. ☐ *We will feast upon turkey for weeks.* ☐ *We feasted on the fish Harry had caught.*

FEATURE ▸ AS

feature someone as something **1.** to imagine someone to be something or a particular type of person. ☐ *I really can't feature you as a ship's captain.* ☐ *Alice had always featured Fred as a fairly even-tempered person.* **2.** to give special prominence to someone in a particular part in a play, film, opera, etc. ☐ *They featured Laura as the lead singer in the group.* ☐ *The management refused to feature Roger in the film.*

FEATURE ▸ IN

feature someone in something **1.** to imagine someone wearing something. ☐ *I can't feature you in that ridiculous dress.* ☐ *Can you feature Fran in that hat?* **2.** to imagine someone being in something or some place. ☐ *I can't feature you in Paris. You are too rural to enjoy a place like Paris.* ☐ *Can you feature David in New York City?*

FED ▸ UP

See *be fed up (to some place) (with someone or something)* under *BE ▸ UP.*

FEED ▸ BACK

feed something back into something to return something back to where it came. ☐ *I tried to feed the stamps back into the machine, but, of course, they wouldn't go.* ☐ *The machine made too many brackets, but you can't feed them back into it.* [N] *Your feedback has provided us with much valuable information.*

feed something back to someone to give or hand something back to someone. ☐ *We fed the rope back to those in line behind us.* [T] *Feed back the papers to the clerk.*

FEED ▸ INTO

feed something into something to put something into something; to push a supply of something into something. ☐ *I fed all the coins into the telephone and waited to be connected.* ☐ *I will feed every coin I have into the phone and see what it does for me.* ☐ *Did you feed the data into the computer?*

FEED ▸ OFF

feed off (of) something to eat something in particular customarily. (The *of* is colloquial.) ☐ *This creature feeds off fallen fruit.* ☐ *Mosquitoes feed off of me!*

FEED ▸ ON

See under *FEED ▸ (UP)ON.*

FEED ▸ TO

See also under *FEED ▸ (IN)TO.*

feed something to someone to tell someone lies. (Figurative.) ☐ *Don't try to feed that nonsense to me! I know it isn't so.* ☐ *Please don't feed any of those lies to Mark.*

feed something to someone or something to give someone or some creature food. ☐ *Don't feed pizza to the baby.* ☐ *I fed the leftover turkey to the dog.*

FEED ▸ UP

See *be fed up (to some place) (with someone or something)* under *BE ▸ UP.*

FEED ▸ (UP)ON

feed (up)on someone or something to eat someone or something. (*Upon* is formal and less commonly used than *on*.) □ *They say that some Bengal tigers feed upon people.* □ *They feed on anything that moves.*

FEED ▸ WITH

feed someone or something with something 1. to feed something to someone, a group, or some creature. □ *The camp cook fed them with hot dogs and beans.* □ *We fed the dogs with the leftovers.* 2. to use a tool or utensil to feed someone, a group, or some creature. (*Someone* includes *oneself*.) □ *He fed the baby with a spoon.* □ *We fed the entire group with paper plates.* □ *She fed herself with a spoon, because there was no fork.*

FEEL ▸ ABOUT

See *feel (around) (for someone or something)* under *FEEL ▸ AROUND.*

feel somehow about someone or something to have ideas, opinions, or reaction regarding someone or something. □ *I feel good about him.* □ *Do you feel good about the vote?* □ *How do you feel about Sally?*

FEEL ▸ AROUND

feel (around) (for someone or something) AND **feel (about) (for someone or something)** to try to find someone or something by feel [rather than sight]. □ *He felt around for the soap in the bathtub.* □ *She felt for the dog at the foot of the bed, but it wasn't there.* □ *Gerald felt about for a pencil.* □ *I felt about for Jane in the dark.*

FEEL ▸ FOR

feel (around) (for someone or something) See under *FEEL ▸ AROUND.*

feel for someone to feel the emotional pain that someone else is feeling; to empathize or sympathize with someone. □ *I really feel for you. I'm so sorry it turned out this way.* □ *Fred felt for Dave, but there was nothing he could do for him.*

FEEL ▸ LIKE

feel like someone or something to have the feel of someone or something; to seem to be someone or something according to feel. □ *Whoever this is feels like Tom. Sort of soft and pudgy.* □ *This thing feels like a rubber hose, not a hot dog.*

feel like something to desire something; to find it acceptable to do or have something. (Colloquial.) □ *I feel like a nice big glass of iced tea.* □ *Do you feel like a swim?*

FEEL ▸ OUT

feel out of place to feel uncomfortable in a certain place or situation. □ *I feel very much out of place in such a glorious, grand ballroom.* □ *We really feel quite out of place at this party.*

feel out of something to feel alienated from something. □ *I feel out of things lately. Are people ignoring me?* □ *I feel a little out of it at this party, but I will try to join in the fun.*

feel someone out (about someone or something) to find out what someone thinks about someone or something. □ *I will feel him out about what he thinks about going to Florida.* 🅃 *Let me feel out the boss about this matter.* □ *I felt the boss out. The answer will be no, so don't ask.*

FEEL ▸ TO

feel equal to someone to sense that one is equal to someone else. □ *I certainly feel equal to Randy. He's nothing special.* □ *I don't think that Bill feels equal to Bob, even though they are twins.*

FEEL ▸ UP

feel someone up to feel someone sexually. (Use discretion with topic.) □ *I heard him say he really wanted to feel her up.* 🅃 *He wanted to feel up the girl.*

feel up to something to feel like doing something; to feel well enough to do something. □ *I'm sorry, but I don't feel up to going out.* □ *Do you feel up to playing a game of cards?*

FEEL ▸ WITH

feel something with something to touch and explore something with something. □ *I felt the soft little creature with my hand.* □ *Don't feel that thing with your bare hands.*

FENCE ▸ IN

fence something in to enclose some creature or something within a fence or barrier. ☐ *We fenced the yard in to keep the dogs at home.* Ⓣ *We had to fence in the dog.* ☐ *We fenced the garden in.*

FENCE ▸ OFF

fence someone or something off (from something) to separate someone or something from something with a fence or barrier. (*Someone* includes *oneself.*) ☐ *We fenced the children's play area off from the rest of the yard.* Ⓣ *Dave fenced off the play area.* ☐ *We fenced off the children from the rest of the yard.* Ⓐ *Please stay out of the fenced-off area.* ☐ *He fenced himself off from the rest of the crowd.*

FENCE ▸ OUT

fence someone or something out to keep someone or something out with a fence or barrier. ☐ *We decided that living in the woods was satisfactory only if we fenced the wildlife out.* Ⓣ *We had to fence out the deer.* ☐ *We hoped we had fenced prowlers out with the tall electric fence.*

FENCE ▸ WITH

fence with someone **1.** to practice the sport of fencing with someone. ☐ *The two guys fenced with each other for over an hour.* ☐ *Do you want to fence with me, just for practice?* **2.** to argue with someone; to battle someone with words. (Figurative.) ☐ *Don't fence with me! Do what I tell you.* ☐ *I wish you wouldn't fence with me when I tell you to do something.*

FEND ▸ FOR

fend for someone to provide for someone; to take care of someone; to defend someone. (*Someone* includes *oneself.*) ☐ *At the age of twelve, I was made an orphan and had to fend for myself.* ☐ *He is now old enough to fend for himself.*

FEND ▸ OFF

fend someone or something off to hold someone or something off; to fight someone or something off. ☐ *We knew we could fend them off only a little while longer.* Ⓣ *They could not fend off the attackers.* ☐ *Max fended Lefty off.*

FERRET ▸ OUT

ferret something out (from something) to seek something out from something. (As if someone were using a trained ferret to locate and retrieve something from a small place.) ☐ *We will have to ferret the mouse out from behind the stove.* Ⓣ *We can ferret out the mouse with the aid of the cat.* Ⓣ *I cannot ferret out a tiny animal.*

FERRY ▸ ACROSS

ferry someone or something across (something) to transport someone or something across a river on a ferryboat. ☐ *Can we get someone to ferry us across the lake to the island?* ☐ *Will someone please ferry this car across?* Ⓣ *After they ferried across all the cars, they closed the ferryboat down for the night.*

FERRY ▸ AROUND

ferry someone around to transport people here and there in small batches. ☐ *I really don't want to spend all my days ferrying children around.* ☐ *I am tired of ferrying children around. Do they ever grow up?* Ⓣ *I spent the entire afternoon ferrying around a bunch of kids.*

FESS ▸ UP

fess up (to something) to confess to having done something. (Folksy.) ☐ *I tried to get the boy to fess up to doing it, but he wouldn't do it.* ☐ *Come on, fess up.*

FESTOON ▸ WITH

festoon someone or something with something to drape or garland someone or something with something. (*Someone* includes *oneself.*) ☐ *Karen festooned her daughter with flowers for the party.* ☐ *The kids festooned the gymnasium with crepe paper and garlands of plastic flowers.* ☐ *She festooned herself with the garlands of flowers.*

FETCH ▸ IN

fetch something in to bring or pull something in. □ *Would you please fetch some more firewood in?* 🅃 *Can you fetch in the paper?*

FETCH ▸ OUT

fetch something out (of something) to pull something out of something. (The *of*-phrase is paraphrased with a *from*-phrase when the particle is transposed. See the 🄵 example.) □ *Could you fetch me another hot dog out of the pot?* 🅃 *I'll fetch out a hot dog for you.* 🄵 *He will fetch out a wiener from the pot.* □ *Let me fetch one out for you.*

FETCH ▸ UP

fetch up some place to reach a place; to end up at a place. □ *We fetched up at Sam's house at about midnight.* □ *The car fetched up at the cabin and everyone got out.*

FEUD ▸ ABOUT

feud (with someone) (about someone or something) See under *FEUD ▸ WITH.*

FEUD ▸ OVER

feud (with someone) (over someone or something) See the following entry.

FEUD ▸ WITH

feud (with someone) (over someone or something) AND **feud (with someone) (about someone or something)** to fight with someone over someone or something; to have an ongoing battle with someone about someone or something. □ *Some of the neighbors are feuding with each other over the parking places on the street.* □ *Don't feud over her with me!* □ *They are feuding about land.*

FIDDLE ▸ AROUND

fiddle around (with someone or something) to play around with someone or something. □ *I will fiddle around with this for a while and maybe I can fix it.* □ *I wish you would stop fiddling around and hire someone to fix it.*

FIDDLE ▸ AWAY

fiddle something away to waste something. (Informal.) □ *She fiddled the afternoon away.* 🅃 *Don't fiddle away the afternoon. Get to work.*

FIDDLE ▸ WITH

fiddle with someone or something to tinker or play with someone or something. □ *Please don't fiddle with the stereo controls.* □ *Leave your brother alone. Don't fiddle with him. He's cranky.*

FIDGET ▸ AROUND

fidget around to wiggle and twitch nervously. □ *The child sat there, fidgeting around for over ten minutes.* □ *Please don't fidget around so.*

FIDGET ▸ WITH

fidget with something to play with something nervously. □ *Please don't fidget with your zipper.* □ *Carl is always fidgeting with his left ear.*

FIGHT ▸ ABOUT

fight about someone or something to have a battle or argue about someone or something. □ *Why do we always have to fight about money?* □ *Let's not fight about Ed.*

fight ((with) someone or something) (about someone or something) See under *FIGHT ▸ WITH.*

FIGHT ▸ AGAINST

fight against someone or something to battle against someone or something. □ *The boxer refused to fight against the challenger, who was much stronger.* □ *He fought against the disease to the very end.*

fight against time to race against the clock; to have to do something by a certain time. □ *The surgeons fought against time and saved the patient in the end.* 🄽 *It will be a fight against time to get there before the plane leaves.*

FIGHT ▸ AMONG

fight among someone [for people] to fight among themselves. □ *When we became insulted and left, they started fighting among themselves.* □ *When the bully left, the boys continued to fight among themselves.*

FIGHT ▸ BACK

fight back (at someone or something) to defend oneself against someone or something; to retaliate against someone or something. ☐ *You are going to have to fight back at them. You can't expect us to defend you.* ☐ *It's hard for me to fight back.*

fight (one's way) back to something to struggle to return to something or some place. ☐ *She fought her way back to the head of the line.* ☐ *Jan fought back to good health.*

FIGHT ▸ DOWN

fight someone or something down to fight against and defeat someone or something. ☐ *We fought the opposition down and got our bill through the committee.* 🅃 *We had to fight down Fred, who wanted something entirely different.*

fight something down **1.** to struggle to hold something back; to struggle to keep from being overwhelmed by something. ☐ *She fought her anger down, and managed to stay till the end.* 🅃 *She fought down the urge.* **2.** to struggle to swallow something; to fight to get something down one's throat. ☐ *It tasted terrible, but I managed to fight it down.* 🅃 *She fought down the medicine.*

FIGHT ▸ FOR

fight for someone or something to go to battle for the benefit of someone or something; to go to battle in the name of someone or something. ☐ *They all went off to fight for their country.* ☐ *The soldiers fought for the queen and the survival of the empire.* ☐ *I guess I will have to learn to fight for my rights.*

FIGHT ▸ OFF

fight someone or something off to repel an attack from someone or something. ☐ *We fought the mosquitoes off, but they returned almost immediately.* 🅃 *She fought off the mosquitoes all evening.* ☐ *Jed fought the attacker off.*

FIGHT ▸ ON

fight on to continue to fight. ☐ *The boys fought on until one of them was down.* ☐ *They fought on until they were exhausted.*

FIGHT ▸ OUT

fight one's way out of something to struggle to get out of something or some place. ☐ *He fought his way out of the crowded room and out through the door.* ☐ *He couldn't fight his way out of a paper bag.*

fight something out to settle something by fighting. ☐ *Do we have to fight this out? Can't we use reason?* 🅃 *I prefer to fight out this matter.*

FIGHT ▸ OVER

fight over someone or something to fight a battle that decides who gets someone or something. ☐ *Well, let's not fight over Tom. You can have him. I can make a better team without him.* ☐ *The children were fighting over who would get the largest piece of cake.*

fight (with someone or something) (over someone or something) See under *FIGHT ▸ WITH.*

FIGHT ▸ THROUGH

fight (one's way) through something **1.** to struggle to get through something; to struggle to penetrate something. ☐ *I'll have to fight my way through all this crepe paper in order to reach the punch bowl.* ☐ *The room was filled with trash, and I had to fight through it to get to the other door.* **2.** to struggle to work through all of something. ☐ *I have to fight my way through this stack of papers by noon.* ☐ *I am tired of fighting through red tape.*

fight something through (something) to force something through some sort of procedure or process; to *railroad something through (something).* ☐ *The governor fought the bill through the legislature successfully.* 🅃 *She fought through the bill successfully.* ☐ *Our committee fought it through.*

FIGHT ▸ TO

fight to the death to engage in a battle that isn't finished until one side is dead. ☐ *The two men looked as though they were going to fight to the death.* 🄽 *It looked like a fight to the death, for sure.*

FIGHT ► WITH

fight someone or something with something to attack or battle someone or something with something. □ *We can't fight the enemy with clubs and pitchforks!* □ *I fought him with my bare fists.*

fight ((with) someone or something) (over someone or something) AND **fight ((with) someone or something) (about someone or something)** to do battle or argue with someone or something about someone or something. □ *The terrier fought with the collie over the piece of meat.* □ *I don't want to fight you over Harry.* □ *Let's not fight about Randy.* □ *Jerry wanted to fight with Sam.*

FIGURE ► AS

figure someone as something □ *I figured her as a reliable worker.* □ *We figured them all as good credit risks.*

FIGURE ► IN

figure in something to be involved or implicated in something. □ *The men figured in the robbery.* □ *Roger figured in the plans for the new court house.*

figure someone or something in (on something) to plan on having someone or something included in something. □ *Please figure another ten people in on the picnic.* [T] *I will figure in those people.* □ *I will figure them in.*

FIGURE ► IN(TO)

figure someone or something in((to) something) to reckon someone or something into the total. (*Someone* includes *oneself*.) □ *I will figure the electric bill into the total.* [T] *We can figure in one more person.* □ *Did you figure David in?* □ *Did you figure yourself into the final total?*

FIGURE ► ON

figure on someone or something to count on someone or something; to assume something about someone or something. □ *I am figuring on twelve people for dinner next Friday.* □ *We are figuring on you and your wife for dinner next weekend.* □ *I didn't figure on so many chairs in this room.*

figure on something to plan on something; to count on doing something. □ *We figured on going down to the country next weekend.* □ *Did you figure on doing the repair work yourself?*

FIGURE ► OUT

figure someone or something out to comprehend someone or something; to understand someone or something better. (*Someone* includes *oneself*.) □ *I just can't figure you out.* [T] *I can't figure out quiet people readily.* □ *It will take a while for me to figure the instructions out.* □ *Well, I can't figure myself out. I don't know how you could either.*

FIGURE ► UP

figure something up to add up the amount of something. □ *Please figure the bill up. We have to go now.* [T] *I will figure up the bill right away.* □ *I will figure up how many yards of material I need.*

FILCH ► FROM

filch something from someone to grab or steal something from someone. (Now slang.) □ *The young boy filched a candy bar from the store.* □ *Who filched my wallet from me?*

FILE ► AGAINST

file something against someone to lodge a criminal charge against someone. □ *Sally filed a charge of assault against Max.* □ *The old man filed charges against the attacker.*

FILE ► AWAY

file something away to put something away, usually in a file folder or file cabinet. □ *She filed the letter away for future reference.* □ *Please file this away. You will need it some day.*

file something away (from something) AND **file something off ((of) something)** to remove something from something else by filing. (The *of* is colloquial.) □ *The dentist filed the sharp place away from the tooth.* [T] *The dentist filed away the sharp place from the tooth.* □ *The dentist filed the point off.* □ *She filed it off.* □ *Betty filed it away.*

FILE ▸ DOWN

file something down to level off a protrusion by filing. □ *File this edge down so no one gets cut on it.* [T] *Please file down this edge.*

FILE ▸ FOR

file for something to submit an application or document for something. □ *The company filed for bankruptcy.* □ *Let's file for reorganization.*

file something for something to submit an application or document for something. □ *I filed an application for a scholarship. I hope I get it.* □ *Did you file the application forms for admission to college?*

FILE ▸ IN(TO)

file in((to) something) [for a line of people] to move into something or some place. □ *The people filed into the hall quietly.* □ *Everyone filed in quietly.*

FILE ▸ OFF

file something off ((of) something) See *file something away (from something)* under *FILE ▸ AWAY.*

FILE ▸ OUT

file out (of something) [for a line of people] to move out of something or some place. □ *The people filed quietly out of the theater.* □ *They filed out at the end.*

FILE ▸ PAST

file past (someone or something) [for a line or procession] to move past someone or something. □ *The people filed past the coffin, looking sadly at the still figure inside.* □ *As they filed past, some wept openly.*

FILE ▸ WITH

file something with someone or something to submit an application or a document to someone or a group. □ *You must file this copy with the state office.* □ *I will file this with my boss.*

FILL ▸ IN

fill in [for an indentation, hole, etc.] to become full. □ *The scar filled in after a few months.* □ *Will this hole in the ground fill in by itself, or should I put some dirt in?*

fill in (for someone or something) to substitute for someone or something; to take the place of someone or something. □ *I will have to fill in for Wally until he gets back.* □ *I don't mind filling in.* [N] *Tom was a fill-in for Sue, who was ill.*

fill someone in (on someone or something) to tell someone the details about someone or something. □ *Please fill me in on what happened last night.* [T] *Please fill in the committee on the details.* □ *Please fill me in!*

fill something in **1.** to add material to an indentation, hole, etc. to make it full. □ *You had better fill the crack in with something before you paint the wall.* [T] *You should fill in the cracks first.* [A] *They were unable to find the filled-in hole.* **2.** to write in the blank spaces on a paper; to write on a form. □ *Please fill this form in.* [T] *I will fill in the form for you.*

FILL ▸ OUT

fill out to become full; to gain weight. □ *About a month after her debilitating illness, Maggie began to fill out again.* □ *The fruit on the trees began to fill out and we knew it was going to ripen soon.*

fill something out to complete a form by writing in the blank spaces. □ *Please fill this form out and send it back to us in the mail.* [T] *I will fill out the form as you asked.*

FILL ▸ TO

fill something to something to add material to something up to a certain point. □ *Fill the barrel up to here and no higher.* □ *Please fill the glass to the top.*

FILL ▸ UP

fill someone or something (up) (with something) to put as much as possible into someone or something. (*Someone* includes *oneself*. The *up* is colloquial. The *up* and *with something* cannot be transposed.) □ *We filled him up with chili and crackers.* [T] *We will fill up the basket with leaves.* □ *I will fill the basket with flowers.* □ *She filled it up.* □ *All that chili and crackers filled them up.* □ *He kept filling himself up with all that propaganda.*

fill up **1.** to become full. ☐ *The creek filled up after the heavy rain yesterday.* ☐ *The rain barrel began to fill up during the storm.* **2.** to fill one's gas tank. (Informal.) ☐ *I've got to stop and fill up. I'm running low.* ☐ *We will fill up at the next little town.*

FILL ▸ WITH

fill someone or something (up) (with something) See under *FILL ▸ UP.*

fill someone's head with something to put some kind of ideas into someone's head. ☐ *Who's been filling your head with ideas like that?* ☐ *Mary has been filling my head with ideas about how to get rich.*

FILM ▸ OVER

film over [for something] to develop a film on its surface. ☐ *The windows had filmed over because of all the cigarette smoke.* ☐ *Her eyes filmed over with the cold.*

FILTER ▸ IN(TO)

filter in(to some place) **1.** to leak or seep into some place. ☐ *The smoke filtered into his room and made him wake up.* ☐ *It filtered in and burned our eyes.* **2.** [for people] to come into a place, a few at a time, over a period of time. ☐ *One by one, the guests filtered into the room.* ☐ *They filtered in and started on the snacks.*

FILTER ▸ OUT

filter something out (of something) to remove something from a fluid by running it through a filter. (The *of*-phrase is paraphrased with a *from*-phrase when the particle is transposed. See the [F] example.) ☐ *We filtered the odors out of the water and made it fit to drink.* [T] *I'm glad you filtered out the odor.* [F] *I'm glad you filtered out the odor from the water.* ☐ *The new filter filtered the odor out very well.*

FILTER ▸ THROUGH

filter through (something) to pass or seep through something. ☐ *The water filtered through the coffee grounds and dripped into the pot.* ☐ *The clear water filtered through and left the junk behind.*

FIND ▸ AGAINST

find against someone or something [for a jury or a judge] to announce a decision against one side of a case. ☐ *The jury found against the defendant, who was a horrible witness.* ☐ *The court found against the corporation and levied a fine.*

FIND ▸ AROUND

find one's way around (something) to discover a way to move around something or some place. ☐ *Can you find your way around or shall I have someone take you?* ☐ *Don't worry. I can find my way around.*

FIND ▸ FOR

find for someone or something [for a jury or a judge] to announce a decision in favor of one side of a case. ☐ *The judge found for Mrs. Franklin, and that made everyone quite happy.* ☐ *The court found for the law firm and admonished the disgruntled client.*

FIND ▸ IN

find it in something to do something AND **find it in oneself to do something** to discover the goodness within oneself that will move one to do something. ☐ *Do you think you could find it in your heart to forgive me?* ☐ *Could you find it in yourself to give poor Oliver another chance?*

find someone in to learn or discover that one is at home; to learn or discover that one is in one's office. ☐ *I expected to find you in at this time of night.* ☐ *Did you really expect to find me in on a Friday night?*

FIND ▸ OUT

find out (something) (about someone or something) (from someone or something) to learn something about someone or something from someone or something. ☐ *What did you find out about Terry from Mr. Franklin?* [T] *I didn't find anything out about Roger from the newspaper stories.* ☐ *I found out what I wanted to know about pancakes from the encyclopedia.* ☐ *What did you find out about Bill?* ☐ *I don't know if she's going. I didn't find out.*

find someone out 1. to discover that someone is not at home. ☐ *We arrived to find them out.* ☐ *Sam found Frank out when he arrived to collect the debt.* 2. to discover something surprising or shocking about someone. ☐ *I don't want them to find me out.* ☐ *We found her out despite her deviousness.*

find something out the hard way to learn something by [bad] experience; to learn something only with difficulty. ☐ *I'm very sorry you had to find it out the hard way.* 🅃 *I found out the truth the hard way.*

FIND ▸ WITH

find fault with someone or something to blame or criticize someone or something. ☐ *Please don't find fault with me all the time.* ☐ *Sharon has found fault with the installation of the water cooler.*

find favor with someone to win the praise of someone. ☐ *The maid found favor with the family and was given a large salary increase.* ☐ *Mary found favor with her employer because of her good ideas.*

FINE ▸ FOR

fine someone for something to demand a monetary penalty from someone for having done something. ☐ *The judge fined her for speeding.* ☐ *The agency fined our company for having the wrong kind of floor in the rest rooms.*

FINGER ▸ AS

finger someone as someone to identify someone as a certain person. (Slang. As if one were pointing a finger at someone.) ☐ *Max fingered Lefty as the gunman.* ☐ *Lefty fingered Max as the one who did it.*

FINISH ▸ BY

finish (something) by doing something to bring something to a conclusion by doing something. ☐ *She finished the lecture by naming her sources.* ☐ *Sharon finished by reading a poem.*

FINISH ▸ OFF

finish someone or something off 1. to complete some activity being performed on someone or something. ☐ *Let's finish this one off and go home.* 🅃 *Yes, let's finish off this one.* ☐ *Nancy is cutting Elaine's hair. When she finishes her off, she will be ready to leave.* 2. to kill someone or some creature. (Slang.) ☐ *They had to finish the wounded bear off with a revolver.* 🅃 *The hunter finished off the bear.* ☐ *Max really wanted to finish Lefty off once and for all.*

finish something off to eat or drink up all of something; to eat or drink up the last portion of something. ☐ *Let's finish the turkey off.* 🅃 *You finish off the turkey. I've had enough.* 🅃 *Let's finish off this pot of coffee and I'll make some more.*

finish (something) off with something to bring something to a conclusion with something. ☐ *She finished the dinner off with fancy cheeses and fruit.* 🅃 *She finished off the dinner with pie.* ☐ *Gerald finished the concert off with a piece he had written.*

FINISH ▸ UP

finish someone or something up to finish doing something to someone or something. ☐ *The hairdresser had to work fast in order to finish Mrs. Wilson up by quitting time.* 🅃 *She finished up Fred in a short time.* ☐ *I will finish this typing up in a few minutes.*

finish up to complete the doing of something. ☐ *When do you think you will finish up?* ☐ *I will finish up next week sometime.*

FINISH ▸ WITH

finish with something to complete something; to become done with something. ☐ *I will finish with this soon, and you can have it.* ☐ *When will this be finished with?*

FINK ▸ ON

fink on someone to inform the authorities on someone. (Slang.) ☐ *You're not going to fink on me, are you?* ☐ *Chuck finked on all of us.*

FINK ▸ OUT

fink out (on someone) to choose not to do something with someone. (Slang.) ☐ *Come on, you guys, don't fink out on me!* ☐ *Please don't fink out!*

FIRE ▶ AT

fire at someone or something to shoot at someone or something. ☐ *Max fired at Lefty.* ☐ *The cowboy fired at the rattlesnake.*

fire something at someone or something to shoot a gun or a similar weapon at someone or something. ☐ *Max fired his gun at Lefty.* ☐ *Someone fired a gun at my car!*

FIRE ▶ AWAY

fire away (at someone or something) to shoot at someone or something continually. ☐ *The cops began to fire away at the target.* ☐ *Lefty fired away at Max.* ☐ *They aimed at the target and fired away.*

FIRE ▶ BACK

fire back (at someone or something) to shoot back at someone or something. ☐ *The gunman fired back at the police.* ☐ *The police fired back.*

fire (something) back at someone or something to shoot a gun back at someone or something. ☐ *We fired about ten rounds back at them.* ☐ *The soldiers in the fort did not fire back at the attackers.*

fire something back to someone or something to send something back to someone or a group immediately. (Colloquial. To send something very fast, as if it were being fired from a gun.) ☐ *Look this over and fire it back to me immediately.* ☐ *Fire this back to the printer as soon as you have proofed it.*

FIRE ▶ INTO

fire something into someone or something to shoot something into someone or something. ☐ *She fired the gun into a special box that stopped the bullet. She would then examine it under a special microscope.* ☐ *Max fired two shots into Lefty, but even that did not stop him.* ☐ *The soldiers fired their rifles into the crowd.*

FIRE ▶ OFF

fire something off (to someone) to send something to someone immediately, by a very rapid means. (To send something to someone very fast, as if it were being fired from a gun.) ☐ *Fire a letter off to Fred, ordering him to return home at once.* 🅃 *I fired off a letter to Fred as you asked.* ☐ *I finished the letter and fired it off.*

FIRE ▶ ON

See under *FIRE ▶ (UP)ON.*

FIRE ▶ OVER

fire over something to shoot over something, usually people's heads. ☐ *We fired over their heads to warn them to stay away.* ☐ *Wally fired over the target.*

FIRE ▶ UP

fire someone up (with something) to use something to get someone excited. (*Someone* includes *oneself.*) ☐ *We fired the boys up with the desire to win.* 🅃 *The coach had fired up the players.* ☐ *She fired herself up and completed the job alone.* ☐ *His lecture fired them up.* ☐ *They were all fired up about the game.* 🄰 *We had a really fired up team for the last game.*

fire something up to start an engine. ☐ *Fire the old thing up and let's get going.* 🅃 *Fire up the engine, and let's go.*

fire up to light a cigarette, cigar, or pipe. (Slang.) ☐ *One by one, the guests went outside and fired up.* ☐ *I have to get out of here and fire up.*

FIRE ▶ (UP)ON

fire (up)on someone or something to shoot at someone or something; to shoot in the direction of someone or something. (*Upon* is formal and less commonly used than *on.*) ☐ *The troops fired upon the advancing army.* ☐ *The cops fired on Max.*

FIRE ▶ WITH

fire someone with something [for someone's words] to fill someone with anger, enthusiasm, hope, expectations, etc. ☐ *The speech fired the audience with enthusiasm for change.* ☐ *We were fired with eagerness to carry on.*

FIRM ▶ UP

firm something up **1.** to make something more stable or firm. ☐ *We need to firm this table up. It is very wobbly.* 🅃

You need to learn to firm up your meringues better. **2.** to make a monetary offer for something more appealing and attractive. ☐ *You will have to firm the offer up with cash today, if you really want the house.* 🅃 *Please firm up this offer if you still want the house.* 🄰 *Your firmed-up offer is still unacceptable.*

firm something up to put something into final form; to bring something closer to settlement. (Figurative.) ☐ *They firmed up the contract last week,* ☐ *She is getting ready to firm up her offer on the house.*

firm up **1.** to become more stable or viable; to recover from or stop a decline. (Figurative.) ☐ *The economy will probably firm up soon.* ☐ *I hope that cattle prices firm up next spring.* **2.** to develop better muscle tone; to become less flabby. ☐ *I need to do some exercises so I can firm up.* ☐ *You really ought to firm up.*

FISH ▸ FOR

fish for something **1.** to try to catch a particular kind of fish. ☐ *We are fishing for cod today, but we'll take whatever we get.* ☐ *We will fish for perch from the riverbank.* **2.** to seek some kind of information. (Figurative.) ☐ *You could tell the lawyer was fishing for something from the vague way she asked the questions.* ☐ *The telephone caller was fishing for too much information, so I hung up.*

FISH ▸ OUT

fish someone or something out (of something) to pull someone or something out of something or some place. (The *of*-phrase is paraphrased with a *from*-phrase when the particle is transposed. See the 🄵 example.) ☐ *She is down at the riverbank, fishing driftwood out of the water.* 🅃 *She fished out a lot of wood.* 🄵 *She fished out an olive from the jar.* ☐ *We need more wood. Please fish it all out.*

FISH ▸ UP

fish something up (out of something) to pull or hoist something out of something. ☐ *The old shopkeeper fished a huge pickle up out of the barrel.* 🅃 *He fished up a huge pickle.* 🅃 *Please fish up another one.*

FIT ▸ AROUND

fit around something to wrap around something. ☐ *This part fits around the top and keeps the water out.* ☐ *Will this wrench fit around the bolt?*

FIT ▸ FOR

fit someone for something to measure someone for something. ☐ *I have to fit him for his tuxedo. I'll take his measurements and leave.* ☐ *She was fitted for her gown in only one afternoon.*

fit someone for something to prepare someone for something; to make someone suitable for some purpose or activity. ☐ *His education did not fit him for working with children.* ☐ *Her temperament does not fit her for this kind of work.*

fit someone or something (up) (with something) (for something) See under *FIT ▸ UP.*

FIT ▸ IN

fit in (somehow) (with something) to match up or harmonize with something in some fashion. ☐ *This fits in well with my plans.* ☐ *This fits in very poorly with what I had planned.*

FIT ▸ IN(TO)

fit in((to) something) [for something] to be a suitable size to go into something. ☐ *This peg does not fit into this hole.* ☐ *It simply doesn't fit in.*

fit someone or something in((to) something) to manage to place someone or something into something. ☐ *I think I can fit you into my schedule.* 🅃 *I have fit in three people already today.* ☐ *The shelf is tight, but I think I can fit one more book in.*

FIT ▸ ON(TO)

fit something on((to) something) to manage to place something onto something. ☐ *See if you can fit this lid onto that jar over there.* ☐ *Sorry, I can't fit it on.*

FIT ▸ OUT

fit someone or something out (for something) to equip someone or something for something; to outfit someone or something for something. (*Someone* includes *oneself*.) □ *We are going to fit our boat out so we can live on it during a long cruise.* 🅃 *We fit out the children in funny costumes for Halloween.* □ *We fit them all out and sent them off to their costume party.* □ *Let's fit ourselves out for the expedition.* 🄽 *She gave her dad a new fishing outfit for his birthday.*

FIT ▶ TO

fit something to something to make something suit something else. □ *Please try to fit your remarks to the audience.* □ *Can you fit the main course to the needs of all the people who are coming to dinner?*

FIT ▶ TOGETHER

fit something together to put the parts of something together. □ *First you have to fit the pieces together to see if they are all there.* □ *I think I can fit the parts of the model airplane together.* 🅃 *Do you think you can fit together all the parts of the puzzle?*

fit together [for things] to conform in shape to one another. □ *All the pieces of the puzzle fit together. They really do.* □ *This thing doesn't fit together.*

FIT ▶ UP

fit someone or something (up) (with something) (for something) to provide someone or something with something for a particular purpose. (*Someone* includes *oneself*.) □ *We fit the couple up with fins, masks, and snorkels for skin diving.* 🅃 *The clerk fitted up the couple with diving gear for their vacation.* □ *She fit them with tanks and weights.* □ *She fit them up for diving.* □ *Tom fit himself up with a new fishing rod for the trip.*

FIT ▶ WITH

fit someone or something (up) (with something) (for something) See under *FIT ▶ UP.*

fit with something to harmonize with something; to go well with something. □ *Do you think that your behavior fits with the occasion?* □ *This coat doesn't fit with these slacks.*

FIX ▶ FOR

fix something for something to prepare something for a meal. □ *I will fix some chili for lunch.* □ *Will you fix something good for dinner tonight?*

FIX ▶ ON

See under *FIX ▶ (UP)ON.*

FIX ▶ ON(TO)

fix something on(to) something to attach something onto something. □ *We fixed a notice onto the broken door so people wouldn't use it.* □ *Please fix a label on this package.*

FIX ▶ OVER

fix something over to redo something; to redecorate something. □ *I want to fix this room over next spring.* 🅃 *I really want to fix over this room.*

FIX ▶ UP

fix someone or something up to rehabilitate someone or something. □ *The doctor said he could fix me up with a few pills.* 🅃 *The doctor fixed up the hunter and sent him home.* □ *I fixed the car up so it was safe to travel in.* □ *Is the car fixed up yet?* 🄰 *They returned the fixed-up race car to the race almost immediately.*

fix someone up (with someone) **1.** to find a date for someone. □ *I will fix you up with a date for Friday night.* 🅃 *I fixed up my cousin with a date.* □ *I will fix you up with my cousin.* **2.** to provide someone with a sexual partner. (Colloquial.) □ *The bellboy tried to fix Wally up with a woman.* 🅃 *He tried to fix up Wally with a friend.* □ *He fixed Wally up.*

fix someone up (with something) to supply someone with something. □ *I will fix you up with some alcohol and Band-Aids.* 🅃 *The clerk fixed up the lady with what she needed.* □ *Larry wanted some film and the clerk fixed him up with the best.*

FIX ▶ (UP)ON

fix (up)on someone or something to become preoccupied with someone or something. (*Upon* is formal and less commonly used than *on*.) □ *She seems* *to have fixed upon becoming a pilot.* □ *James is quite fixed on Janet.*

FIX ► WITH

fix something with someone 1. to get someone's agreement or permission for something. □ *Don't worry, I'll fix it with your boss.* □ *Can you fix things with my brother? He doesn't want me to do this.* 2. to apologize or make amends to someone for something. □ *She is upset at you, but you can fix it with her, I'm sure.* □ *I will fix it with her. Don't worry.*

FIZZ ► UP

fizz up [for a liquid] to sparkle and bubble with many tiny bubbles; [for a liquid] to effervesce. □ *The cola drink fizzed up and spilled over.* □ *As she poured the soda pop, it fizzed up over the glass.*

FIZZLE ► OUT

fizzle out 1. [for a liquid] to lose its effervescence. □ *This seltzer has fizzled out. I need a fresh glass of it.* [A] *I don't want any fizzled-out soda pop.* 2. [for an item in a fireworks display] to fail to operate properly, often producing only a hiss. □ *That last rocket fizzled out. Set off another one.* □ *A lot of the fireworks fizzled out because it was raining.* 3. to fade or sputter gradually to nothing. □ *Finally, the engine fizzled out and we came to a halt.* □ *The party began to fizzle out about midnight.* □ *The last clerk I hired fizzled out after the first week.*

FLACK ► OUT

flack out AND **flake out** to collapse with exhaustion; to lie down because of exhaustion. (Slang.) □ *All the hikers flacked out when they got there.* □ *After a few hours, the hikers all flaked out.* [A] *Oh, man, I'm totally flacked out!*

FLAG ► DOWN

flag someone or something down to show a signal or wave, indicating that someone should stop. □ *Please go out and flag a taxi down. I'll be right out.* [T] *She went to flag down a taxi.* □ *The hitchhiker tried to flag us down.*

FLAKE ► AWAY

flake away (from something) [for bits of something] to break away from the whole gradually or from natural causes. □ *Bits of stone flaked away from the surface of the statue year after year.* □ *The bits flaked away under the feet of the students.*

FLAKE ► DOWN

flake down to go to bed and go to sleep. (Slang.) □ *I've got to go home and flake down for a while.* □ *Tom is flaked down for the night.*

FLAKE ► OFF

flake off ((of) something) [for bits of something] to break away from the whole, perhaps under pressure or because of damage. (The *of*-phrase is paraphrased with a *from*-phrase. The *of* is colloquial.)) □ *Little bits of marble began to flake off the marble steps.* □ *Bits flaked off from the whole.* □ *The stone began to flake off after the earthquake.*

flake something off (of something) to make bits or flakes break off from the whole. (The *of*-phrase is paraphrased with a *from*-phrase when the particle is transposed. See the [F] example.) □ *The sculptor flaked bits of stone off the block, but you could not yet see what the block was going to become.* [T] *She flaked off a little more.* [F] *She flaked off a little more from the side of the statue's foot.* □ *The sculptor flaked a little more off near the chin.*

FLAKE ► OUT

flake out See under *FLACK ► OUT.*

FLAME ► UP

flame up 1. [for something] to catch fire and burst into flames. □ *The trees flamed up one by one in the forest fire.* □ *Suddenly the car flamed up and exploded.* 2. [for a fire] to expand and send out larger flames. □ *The raging fire flamed up and jumped to even more trees.* □ *As Bob opened the door and came in, the fire flamed up and brightened the room.*

FLAME ► WITH

flame with something [for someone's eyes] to blaze with anger, resentment, lust, vengeance, etc. □ *His eyes flamed with resentment when he heard Sally's good news.* □ *Her eyes flamed with hatred.*

FLANK ▶ (UP)ON

flank (up)on someone or something to be at the side of someone or something. (*Upon* is formal and less commonly used than *on*.) □ *The Victorian mansion flanked on the tall, modern apartment building.* □ *It flanked on a broad expanse of fir trees.*

FLAP ▶ AROUND

flap around [for a sheet of something] to blow, flop, or slap around, perhaps in the wind. □ *The sails flapped around, making a lot of noise.* □ *The awning flapped around during the night.*

FLARE ▶ OUT

flare out to spread out; to widen. (Said especially of one opening of a cylinder.) □ *The end of the pipe flared out to a larger diameter.* □ *The top of the vase flared out, and was decorated with little blobs of colored glass.*

flare something out to spread something out; to make something wider. (Said especially of one end of a cylinder.) □ *Can you flare the end of this pipe out a little?* 🅃 *Flare out the end of this pipe.*

FLARE ▶ UP

flare up **1.** [for something] to ignite and burn. □ *The flames flared up at last—four matches having been used.* 🄽 *There was a sudden flare-up in the forest after the lightning strike.* **2.** [for a fire] to expand rapidly. □ *After burning quietly for a while, the fire suddenly flared up and made the room very bright.* 🄽 *The smoldering campfire produced a sudden flare-up that frightened the campers.* **3.** [for a disease] to get worse suddenly. □ *My arthritis flares up during the damp weather.* 🄽 *I'm sorry I missed the meeting. I had a flare-up of my cold.* **4.** [for a dispute] to break out or escalate into a battle. □ *A war flared up in the Middle East.* □ *We can't send the whole army every time a dispute flares up.*

flare up (at someone or something) to lose one's temper at someone or something. □ *I could tell by the way he flared up at me that he was not happy with what I had done.* □ *I didn't mean to flare up.* 🄽 *I can't bear another one of his flare-ups!*

FLASH ▶ ACROSS

flash across something **1.** [for something bright] to move quickly across something. □ *The telephone number flashed across the television screen too fast for me to copy it down.* □ *The spotlight flashed across the audience, blinding me as it went by.* **2.** [for an idea or image] to move quickly through one's mind. (Figurative.) □ *A solution to the problem suddenly flashed across my mind.* □ *Thoughts of food flashed across my mind, and I began to be very hungry.*

FLASH ▶ AROUND

flash something around to display something so everyone can see it. (Usually something one would hold in one's hand.) □ *Don't flash your money around on the streets.* 🅃 *She flashed around the pictures of her grandchildren every chance she got.*

FLASH ▶ AT

flash something at someone or something **1.** to shine a light quickly on someone or something. □ *Larry flashed a light at Frank to verify his identity.* □ *We flashed the light at each doorway, looking for the address we had been sent to.* **2.** to show something, such as a badge, to someone or a group quickly. □ *The cop flashed his badge at the suspect.* □ *The security officer came in and flashed his badge at the board of directors.*

FLASH ▶ BACK

flash back (on someone or something) to provide a glimpse of someone or something in the past. (In films, literature, and television.) □ *The next scene flashed back on Fred's murder.* □ *The story then flashed back, giving us information out of the past.* 🄽 *The movie was nothing but one flashback after another.*

flash back (to someone or something) to return briefly to a view of someone or something. (In films, literature, and television.) ☐ *The story suddenly flashed back to Tom when he was a child.* ☐ *The story flashed back to Tom's childhood.* ☐ *The scene suddenly flashed back, and that confused the audience a lot.* [N] *We saw a portrayal of the murder in a cleverly staged flashback.*

FLASH ▸ INTO

flash into one's mind [for an idea or image] to enter one's mind for an instant. ☐ *A brilliant idea flashed into her mind, and she wrote it down.* ☐ *When the idea flashed into my mind, I closed my eyes and tried to forget it.*

flash into view to move quickly into view. ☐ *Suddenly, a doe and her fawn flashed into view.* ☐ *A bright parrot flashed into view and squawked raucously.*

FLASH ▸ OFF

flash off [for a light] to go off suddenly. (See also *flash on*.) ☐ *The light flashed off and it was dark for a few minutes.* ☐ *When the lights flashed off, I was setting my watch.*

FLASH ▸ ON

flash on [for a light] to turn on suddenly. ☐ *The light flashed on and woke us up.* ☐ *When the light flashed on, I had just been getting to sleep.*

flash on someone or something [for a light] to shine on someone or something suddenly or in bursts. ☐ *The neon light flashed on John's face, making him look quite strange.* ☐ *The light flashed on the window shade, startling the occupants of the room.*

FLASH ▸ OUT

flash out [for a light] to shine out of something suddenly or in bursts. ☐ *The light flashed out, signaling us to stay away from the rocks.* ☐ *Under the door, we saw a light flashing out. Someone was watching television in that room.*

FLASH ▸ THROUGH

flash through something [for an idea or image] to move quickly through one's mind. ☐ *Suddenly, a great idea flashed through my mind.* ☐ *The same idea flashed through all of our minds at once.*

FLASH ▸ UP

flash something up (some place) to shine a light upwards toward something. ☐ *Flash your light up into the tree.* [T] *She flashed up her light at the cat in the tree.* ☐ *Gloria flashed the light up.*

FLASH ▸ WITH

flash with something [for someone's eyes] to communicate something. ☐ *Her green eyes flashed with anger.* ☐ *Ellen's eyes flashed with recognition when she saw me.*

FLATTEN ▸ OUT

flatten someone or something out to make someone or something flat. ☐ *If you fall under the steamroller, it will flatten you out.* [T] *Flatten out that dough a little more.* ☐ *Please flatten it out.* [A] *He stood there holding the flattened-out suitcase, staring at the departing truck.*

FLAVOR ▸ WITH

flavor something with something to season a food with something. ☐ *He flavors his gravy with a little sage.* ☐ *Can you flavor the soup with a little less pepper next time?*

FLECK ▸ WITH

fleck something with something to put little specks of something on something. ☐ *They flecked the little figures with some kind of powder that made them sparkle.* ☐ *His hair was flecked with gray.*

FLEE ▸ FROM

flee from someone or something to run away from someone or something. ☐ *The child fled from the old man.* ☐ *The children fled from the wrath of the old man.*

FLEE ▸ TO

flee to something to escape to something or some place. ☐ *We fled to our little place on the coast. They never found us.* ☐ *The little mouse fled to its hole in the wall when the cat came around.*

FLESH ▶ OUT

flesh out to become more fleshy. ☐ *She began to flesh out at the age of thirteen.* ☐ *After his illness, Tom fleshed out and regained his strength.*

flesh something out (with something) to make the frame or skeleton of something complete; to add detail to the basic framework of something. ☐ *I will flesh this out with more dialogue and music here and there. Then we'll have a fine play.* 🅃 *We will flesh out the outline with more details later.* ☐ *Give me the outline and I will flesh it out.*

FLEX ▶ OUT

flex something out of shape to bend something out of its normal shape. ☐ *Don't flex all the hangers out of shape. We need a few in the closet.* ☐ *Who flexed the gate out of shape?*

FLICK ▶ OFF

flick something off to turn something off, using a toggle switch. ☐ *Mary flicked the light off and went out of the room.* ☐ *Please flick the light off as you go out the door.* 🅃 *Please flick off the light.*

flick something off ((of) someone or something) to brush or knock a speck of something off of someone or something. (The *of*-phrase is paraphrased with a *from*-phrase when the particle is transposed. See the 🄵 example. The *of* is colloquial.) ☐ *She flicked a speck of lint off his collar.* 🅃 *She flicked off the lint.* 🄵 *She flicked off the lint from his collar.* ☐ *Harriet flicked it off.*

FLICK ▶ ON

flick something on to turn something on, using a toggle switch. ☐ *Mary came into the room and flicked the light on.* ☐ *Please flick the light on as you go out the door.* 🅃 *Please flick on the light.*

FLICK ▶ OUT

flick out 1. [for the ends of a flame] to reach out as the flame burns. ☐ *The flames flicked out and threatened the cold fingers that were too close.* ☐ *The flames flicked out of the device used to heat the soup.* **2.** [for the tongue of a reptile] to come out suddenly. ☐ *The snake's tongue flicked out regularly.* ☐ *The lizard's tongue flicked out and attracted the bird that grabbed the poor creature and ate it.*

flick something out [for a reptile] to push out its tongue quickly. ☐ *The lizard flicked its tongue out repeatedly.* 🅃 *The lizard kept flicking out its tongue at regular intervals.*

FLICK ▶ THROUGH

flick through something to turn quickly through the pages of something. ☐ *Colleen flicked through the magazine, looking only at the advertisements.* ☐ *I have only had time to flick through the manuscript, but it looks okay.*

FLICK ▶ WITH

flick something with something to touch, stroke, or flip at something with something. ☐ *She flicked her finger at the fly that had lighted nearby.* ☐ *Tom flicked the vase with his sleeve and knocked it over.*

FLICKER ▶ OUT

flicker out [for a flame] to dwindle, little by little, until it goes out. ☐ *The candle flickered out, leaving us in total darkness.* ☐ *When the last flame flickered out, the room began to get cold.*

FLINCH ▶ FROM

flinch from someone or something to move back suddenly from someone or something; to *shrink (back) (from someone or something)* suddenly. ☐ *She struck at him and he flinched from her.* ☐ *At the last minute the center fielder flinched from the ball.*

FLING ▶ AROUND

fling someone or something around to sling or throw someone or something around. (*Someone* includes *oneself.*) ☐ *Don't fling your wet clothing around. You are messing up the whole room.* 🅃 *Don't fling around all your clothes.* ☐ *Bill wanted to take Bob by the collar and fling him around a bit, but he kept his temper under control.* ☐ *Don't fling yourself around like that. You'll bump into something and hurt yourself.*

FLING ▸ ASIDE

fling someone or something aside to toss or sling someone or something aside or out of the way. ☐ *She flung the covers aside and leaped out of bed.* 🅃 *She flung the covers aside.* ☐ *Claire flung Walter aside and ran out the door.*

FLING ▸ AT

fling oneself at someone to force oneself on someone; to yield oneself to someone romantically and aggressively. ☐ *What could I do? She flung herself at me!* ☐ *Tom had a bad habit of flinging himself at every girl he met.*

fling something at someone or something to throw something at someone or something. ☐ *Don't fling that towel at me!* ☐ *Don't just fling that paper at the wastebasket, hoping it will get there!*

FLING ▸ AWAY

fling someone or something away to throw or sling someone or something away or out of the way. ☐ *You can't just fling me away! I am your eldest son!* 🅃 *You can't just fling away the things you don't want!* ☐ *Get rid of this. Fling it away!*

FLING ▸ BACK

fling one's head back to throw one's head back. ☐ *She flung her head back and laughed heartily.* 🅃 *She flung back her head and laughed.*

fling someone or something back **1.** to sling or throw someone or something backwards. ☐ *I had to fling the child back, away from the fire.* 🅃 *I flung back the door and ran out.* ☐ *Walt grabbed at the door and flung it back.* **2.** to return someone or something by slinging or throwing. ☐ *She took the little fish and flung it back into the water.* 🅃 *Did you fling back the ball to Roger?* ☐ *Lefty pushed the hostage to Max and Max flung him back.* ☐ *Fling this back.*

FLING ▸ DOWN

fling someone or something down to throw or push someone or something down. (*Someone* includes *oneself.*) ☐ *He flung the book down in great anger.* 🅃 *He flung down the book.* ☐ *Max flung Lefty down in a fit of jealous rage.* ☐ *She flung herself down, just missing getting hit by the sword.*

FLING ▸ IN(TO)

fling something in((to) something) to throw something into something. ☐ *I will fling this thing in the trash. It is junk!* 🅃 *Liz opened the laundry chute and flung in her clothes.* ☐ *She flung them in.*

FLING ▸ OFF

fling something off (of oneself) **1.** to yank something off of oneself hastily. (The *of*-phrase is paraphrased with a *from*-phrase when the particle is transposed. See the 🄵 example.) ☐ *She flung the blanket off herself.* 🅃 *She flung off the blanket.* 🄵 *She flung off the covers from most of her body.* ☐ *Sarah flung the blankets off.* **2.** to pull or take off an article of clothing. (The *of*-phrase is paraphrased with a *from*-phrase when the particle is transposed. See the 🄵 example.) ☐ *Larry flung his jacket off and went straight to the kitchen.* 🅃 *He flung off his jacket.* 🄵 *They will fling off the stones from the top of the cliff.* ☐ *Todd flung his jacket off.*

fling something off ((of) something) to yank or pull something off something. (The *of*-phrase is paraphrased with a *from*-phrase when the particle is transposed. See the 🄵 example.) ☐ *He flung the bedspread off the bed and dived in.* 🅃 *He flung off the covers and dived into bed.* 🄵 *He flung off the covers from the bed.* ☐ *Dave flung the blankets off.*

FLING ▸ ON

fling something on (oneself) to put an article of clothing onto oneself hastily. ☐ *She got up and flung on her robe.* ☐ *She flung her robe on and went to answer the door.*

FLING ▸ OUT

fling someone or something out (of) something to sling or throw someone or something out of something or some place. (*Someone* includes *oneself.*) ☐ *In anger, she flung the cat out of the window.* 🅃 *She flung out the cat and closed* *the window.* ☐ *Max opened the door and flung Lefty out.* ☐ *In total despair, he flung himself out of the window.*

FLING ▸ UP

fling something up in someone's face to bring a problem up and confront someone with it. (Figurative.) ☐ *Don't fling it up in my face! It's not my fault!* 🅃 *I don't like anyone to fling up my past in my face.*

fling something up (in something) to throw one's arms or hands up in an expression of some emotion, such as despair, horror, disgust, resignation. ☐ *She flung her hands up in despair.* 🅃 *She flung up her hands in despair.* ☐ *Despairing, she flung her hands up.*

FLIP ▸ AROUND

flip around to turn end for end, all the way around, quickly. ☐ *The alligator flipped around and hissed at us.* ☐ *The kitten flipped around and pounced on my hand.*

FLIP ▸ OFF

flip someone off AND **flip someone out** to give someone the finger, a rude sign. (The *digitus impudicus.*) ☐ *The youth flipped the police officer off. Not a good idea.* ☐ *He flipped off the cop.* ☐ *You better not flip a cop out!*

FLIP ▸ OUT

flip out to lose control of oneself. (Slang.) ☐ *After a sleepless night, Wally simply flipped out.* ☐ *I felt like I was going to flip out.*

flip someone out See *FLIP ▸ OFF.*

FLIP ▸ OVER

flip over to turn over quickly. ☐ *The fish flipped over and flipped back over again.* ☐ *The cat flipped over and ran away.*

flip over someone or something to become very excited about someone or something; to lose control because of someone or something. (Slang.) ☐ *I flipped over her the first time I ever saw her.* ☐ *The guests really flipped over the Beef Wellington!*

flip someone or something over to turn someone or something over quickly. (*Someone* includes *oneself.*) ☐ *We flipped the fish over and removed the scales from its other side.* 🅃 *I flipped over the fish.* ☐ *Billy flipped Bobby over and started hitting him on the other side.* ☐ *Mary flipped herself over, grabbed the gun, and shot the crook in the gizzard.*

FLIP ▸ THROUGH

flip through something to go quickly through the leaves of a book, etc., page by page. ☐ *She flipped through the book, looking at the pictures.* ☐ *Don't just flip through it. Read it.*

FLIRT ▸ WITH

flirt with someone to tease or trifle with someone romantically. ☐ *Are you flirting with me?* ☐ *Everyone knows that married men don't flirt with anyone.*

FLIT ▸ ABOUT

flit about to move about quickly; to dart about. ☐ *A large number of hummingbirds were flitting about.* ☐ *Butterflies and moths flitted about among the trees and flowers.*

FLIT ▸ FROM

flit from someone to someone or something to something to move quickly from person to person or thing to thing. ☐ *The butterfly flitted from flower to flower.* ☐ *Tom flitted quickly from person to person, handing out snacks and beverages.* ☐ *The singer flitted from table to table, working the crowd for tips.*

FLOAT ▸ AROUND

float around to float from here to there freely. ☐ *All sorts of paper and trash were floating around on the surface of the pond.* ☐ *Water hyacinths floated around, making a very tropical scene.*

FLOAT ▸ INTO

float into something to move slowly into something, as a ship in the water. ☐ *She floated into the room, looking like Cinderella before midnight.* ☐ *Tom and Gloria floated into the theater like a king and queen. They must have rehearsed it.*

FLOAT ► ON

See under *FLOAT ► (UP)ON.*

float on air [for someone] to feel free and euphoric. □ *I was so happy, I was floating on air.* □ *Mary was floating on air after her interview.*

FLOAT ► THROUGH

float through something **1.** to move slowly through something. □ *The boats floated through the water slowly and gracefully.* □ *As the clouds floated through the sky, they cast blotchy shadows on the ground.* **2.** [for someone] to move aimlessly through something. (As if semiconscious.) □ *She has no ambition. She's just floating through life.* □ *He floated through his work that day. It is probably done all wrong.*

FLOAT ► (UP)ON

float (up)on something to drift as if on the surface of something; to drift along through the air. (*Upon* is formal and less commonly used than *on*.) □ *The little tufts of dandelion seeds floated upon the breeze.* □ *The fluff floated on the breeze.*

FLOCK ► AFTER

flock after someone or something to follow someone or something in a group. □ *The children flocked after the man playing the flute.* □ *They flocked after the sheep that were being led to pasture.*

FLOCK ► AROUND

flock around someone or something to crowd around someone or something. □ *All the children will flock around the magician to see how the tricks are performed.* □ *The guests flocked around the birthday cake.*

FLOCK ► IN

flock in to arrive in great numbers. □ *The people just flocked in to hear the famous rock star.* □ *The audience flocked in and jostled one another for the seats.*

FLOCK ► IN(TO)

flock in((to) some place) to move into some place in crowds. □ *People were flocking into the store where everything was on sale.* □ *They flocked in in droves.*

FLOCK ► TO

flock to someone or something to come to someone or something in great numbers. □ *Many people flocked to the doctor who offered a special treatment.* □ *The kids flocked to the movie theater on Saturday afternoon.*

FLOCK ► TOGETHER

flock together to gather together in great numbers. (Typically said of birds and sheep.) □ *A large number of blackbirds flocked together, making a lot of noise.* □ *Do sheep really flock together in a storm?*

FLOG ► TO

flog someone to death to beat someone to death. □ *In the movie, the captain ordered the first mate to flog the sailor to death.* □ *Donald was almost flogged to death.*

flog something to death to dwell on something so much that it no longer has any interest. □ *Stop talking about this! You've flogged it to death.* □ *Walter almost flogged the whole matter to death before we stopped him.*

FLOOD ► IN(TO)

flood in(to something) to pour into something. (Both literally, with water, and figuratively.) □ *The people flooded into the hall.* □ *We opened the door and the people flooded in.* □ *The water flooded in under the door.*

FLOOD ► OUT

flood out (of something) to pour out of something or some place. (Both literal and figurative uses.) □ *The people flooded out of the theater, totally disgusted with the performance.* □ *The water flooded out of the break in the dam.* □ *Jimmy tipped over the jug of milk and the contents flooded out.*

flood someone or something out (of something) [for too much water] to force someone or something to leave something or some place. (The *of*-phrase is paraphrased with a *from*-phrase when the particle is transposed. See the [F] example.) □ *The high waters flooded* *them out of their home.* 🅃 *The high waters flooded out a lot of people.* 🄵 *The high waters flooded out a lot of people from their homes.* □ *The water flooded many farms out.* 🄰 *The flooded-out families are to gather in the school auditorium.*

FLOOD ▶ WITH

flood someone or something with something to inundate someone or something with something. (Usually figurative.) □ *We flooded them with praise and carried them on our shoulders.* □ *The rains flooded the fields with standing water.*

FLOP ▶ AROUND

flop around **1.** [for something] to turn around awkwardly; [for a fish out of water] to squirm and flap. □ *The hose flopped around, throwing water first this way and then that, knocking down plants as it flopped.* □ *A number of fish flopped around in the bottom of the boat.*

FLOP ▶ AS

flop as something to be a failure as something. (Colloquial.) □ *He flopped as an actor.* □ *I don't want to flop as a public speaker.*

FLOP ▶ DOWN

flop down to sit down heavily or awkwardly. □ *Be graceful. Don't just flop down!* □ *When I reached the chair, all I could do was flop down.*

flop something down (on(to) something) to drop or slap something down on something. □ *She flopped the liver down on the cutting board.* 🅃 *She flopped down the raw meat.* □ *Frank flopped the papers down and walked out.*

FLOP ▶ INTO

flop into something to fall or drop into something, such as bed, a chair, a bathtub, etc. □ *Maggie flopped into the chair and slipped off her shoes.* □ *Tom flopped into bed and fell fast asleep.*

FLOP ▶ OVER

flop someone or something over to turn someone or something over, awkwardly or carelessly. □ *They flopped the unconscious man over, searching every pocket.* 🅃 *They flopped over the injured man.* □ *The medics flopped him over, looking for any injuries.*

FLOUNCE ▶ IN(TO)

flounce in(to some place) to move into a place with exaggerated or jerky motions. □ *A couple of teenagers flounced into the store and started examining the most expensive merchandise.* □ *They flounced in and caught the eye of the security guard.*

FLOUNCE ▶ OUT

flounce out (of some place) to bounce or bound out of some place. □ *She turned up her nose and flounced out of the shop.* □ *She flounced out in anger.*

FLOUNDER ▶ AROUND

flounder around to struggle or wallow around. □ *The whole company is just floundering around and getting nowhere.* □ *The horse floundered around, trying to get across the soggy pasture.*

FLOUNDER ▶ THROUGH

flounder through something **1.** to struggle through something, such as a mire, swamp, etc. □ *The Jeep floundered through the swamp without getting stuck.* □ *The horse floundered through the muddy field.* **2.** to struggle awkwardly through a difficult situation. (Figurative.) □ *We floundered through the performance. I don't know how we did it, but we did it.* □ *I don't know how we did it. We just floundered through it, I guess.*

FLOW ▶ ACROSS

flow across something to stream or glide across something. □ *A mass of cold air flowed across the city and froze us all.* □ *The floodwaters flowed across the fields and ruined the spring planting.*

FLOW ▶ ALONG

flow along to move along evenly, as a liquid flows. □ *At the base of the dam, the river began to flow along at a slower pace.* □ *The project flowed along quite nicely.*

FLOW ▶ AWAY

flow away to course or move away. ☐ *The floodwaters flowed away as fast as they had come.* ☐ *All the spilled water flowed away.*

FLOW ▶ FROM

flow from something to run out from something. ☐ *The blood flowed from the wound and cleaned it well.* ☐ *The oil flowed from the cracked engine and made a mess on the floor.*

flow (from something) (to something) to course from one thing to another. ☐ *This water flows all the way from Minnesota to the Gulf of Mexico.* ☐ *It flows to the river from this very drain.*

FLOW ▶ IN(TO)

flow in(to something) to course into something; to pour into something. (Both literal and figurative.) ☐ *The strength flowed into my body, and I felt alive again.* ☐ *The water flowed in when I opened the door on the flood.*

FLOW ▶ OUT

flow out (of something) **1.** to course out of something. ☐ *The apple juice flowed out of the press as we turned the crank.* ☐ *It stopped flowing out when we had crushed the apples totally.* **2.** to issue forth from something. ☐ *The people flowed out of the stadium exits.* ☐ *At the end of the game, the people flowed out in a steady stream.*

FLOW ▶ OVER

flow over someone [for some kind of feeling] to envelop someone. (Figurative.) ☐ *A sense of peace flowed over her.* ☐ *All sorts of good feelings flowed over the crowd as they listened to the speaker.*

flow over someone or something to course over someone or something. ☐ *The water flowed over the land, covering everything.* ☐ *She slipped and fell into the icy creek and the water flowed over her, freezing her almost to death.*

FLOW ▶ TO

flow (from something) (to something) See under *FLOW ▶ FROM.*

FLOW ▶ WITH

flow with something to have some liquid coursing on the surface or within someone or something. ☐ *The sewers were flowing with the floodwaters.* ☐ *Her veins must flow with ice water. She is so cold.*

FLUB ▶ UP

flub something up to mess something up; to ruin something. (Slang.) ☐ *I saw you play in the tournament last Friday. You really flubbed it up, if you don't mind me saying so.* 🅃 *You really flubbed up the tournament.*

flub up to make an error. (Slang.) ☐ *I flubbed up again!* 🄽 *What a stupid flub-up! I'm sorry I did it!*

FLUCTUATE ▶ BETWEEN

fluctuate between someone and someone to waver between choosing one person and another. ☐ *I am fluctuating between Sam and Tony as my choice.* ☐ *The manager fluctuated between Mary and Sarah.*

fluctuate between something and something to move between one thing and another. ☐ *Things seemed to fluctuate between the very good and the very bad.* ☐ *The weather fluctuates between too hot and too cold.*

FLUCTUATE ▶ WITH

fluctuate with something to vary in accord with something. ☐ *The tides fluctuate with the phase of the moon.* ☐ *Frank's blood pressure fluctuates with his mood.*

FLUFF ▶ OUT

fluff something out [for a bird] to move its feathers outward. ☐ *The parrot said good night, fluffed its feathers out, and went to sleep.* 🅃 *The bird fluffed out its feathers.*

FLUFF ▶ UP

fluff something up to make something soft appear fuller or higher. ☐ *Fluff up your pillow before you go to bed.* 🅃 *She fluffed up her pillow before retiring.* 🄰 *A fluffed-up pillow always seems cooler in the summer.*

FLUNK ▸ OUT

flunk out (of something) to fail and have to leave school or a course in school. □ *Please try not to flunk out of college this time!* □ *I hope I don't flunk out.*

flunk someone out to give one a grade that forces one to leave school or a course. □ *The math professor flunked me out. He expects too much.* 🅃 *She flunked out half the class!*

FLUSH ▸ AWAY

flush something away to wash something unwanted away. □ *Flush all this away and be done with it.* 🅃 *Fred flushed away all the leaves on the sidewalk.*

FLUSH ▸ FROM

flush someone or something (out) (from something) AND **flush someone or something (out) (of something)** to cause someone or something to leave a hiding place. (Originally from hunting.) □ *The police flushed the gunman out from his hiding place.* 🅃 *They flushed out the crooks.* □ *The cops flushed Max "The Gross" Googan and Lefty "Fingers" Moran out of their hideout.*

FLUSH ▸ OF

flush someone or something (out) (of something) See the previous entry.

FLUSH ▸ OUT

flush someone or something (out) (from something) See under *FLUSH ▸ FROM.*

flush something out to clean something out with a flow of liquid. □ *Flush the fuel line out to clean it.* 🅃 *Please flush out the fuel line and clean it.*

FLUSH ▸ WITH

flush with something [for one's face] to communicate something, such as anger, embarrassment, rage, etc. □ *He faced the woman he had dreamed about all his life. His face flushed with recognition and his heart pounded.* □ *Ellen's face flushed with embarrassment.*

FLUTTER ▸ ABOUT

flutter about AND **flutter around** **1.** to fly about with quick, flapping motions of the wings. □ *The moths fluttered about aimlessly.* □ *A few birds fluttered around.* **2.** to move about quickly and busily. □ *Aunt Margaret fluttered about, picking up after everyone.* □ *Stop fluttering around and sit down!*

flutter about something AND **flutter around something** **1.** to fly around something or some place. □ *The moths were fluttering about the light bulb.* □ *The butterflies fluttered around the bright flowers.* **2.** to keep moving busily within a particular place. □ *The maid fluttered about the house, dusting and arranging.* □ *She fluttered around the house from room to room.*

FLUTTER ▸ AROUND

flutter around something See the previous two entries.

FLUTTER ▸ DOWN

flutter down [for flying or falling things] to flap or float downward. □ *The butterflies fluttered down onto the flowers.* □ *The leaves fluttered down from the trees when the breeze blew.*

FLUTTER ▸ OVER

flutter over someone or something to fly or flap above someone or something. (Also said of a person being fussy about someone or something.) □ *The little moths fluttered over us while we were in the garden.* □ *The birds flutter over the fountain, eager for a bath.*

FLY ▸ ACROSS

fly across something [for a bird or a plane] to wing across something. □ *A bird flew across the open area in the forest.* □ *A large jet flew across the clear blue sky.*

FLY ▸ APART

fly apart to break apart, throwing pieces around. □ *Don't run the engine too fast or it will fly apart!* □ *Mary's bicycle wheel flew apart during the race.*

FLY ▸ AROUND

fly around to soar or float aloft randomly. □ *There were insects flying around everywhere.* □ *Planes flew around all day and all night, making it hard to sleep.*

fly around someone or something to soar or float in the air near someone or something. ☐ *We saw seven helicopters flying around the stadium.* ☐ *A bunch of mosquitoes flew around me.*

FLY ▸ AT

fly at someone or something to attack someone or something suddenly and violently. (Both literal and figurative uses.) ☐ *The angry bird flew at its attacker.* ☐ *She flew at him, threatening to scratch his eyes out.*

FLY ▸ AWAY

fly away to take flight and depart. ☐ *The owl hooted one last hoot and flew away.* ☐ *All the birds flew away when the cat came around.*

FLY ▸ BY

fly by **1.** to soar past. ☐ *Three jet fighters flew by.* ☐ *A huge hawk flew by, frightening all the smaller birds.* **2.** [for time] to go quickly. (Figurative.) ☐ *The hours just flew by, because we were having fun.* ☐ *Time flew by so fast that it was dark before we knew it.*

FLY ▸ FROM

fly from someone or something (to something) to escape from something or some place to a place of safety. ☐ *The family had to fly from their pursuers to a place of safety in the country.* ☐ *They flew from the people chasing them.*

fly from something (to something) to go from something or some place to some other place by air. ☐ *We had to fly from Miami to Raleigh to get a flight to Chicago.* ☐ *We were able to fly from Miami at the last minute.*

FLY ▸ IN

See also under *FLY ▸ IN(TO).*

fly in the face of someone or something AND **fly in the teeth of someone or something** to challenge someone or something; to go against someone or something. ☐ *This idea flies in the face of everything we know about matter and energy.* ☐ *You had better not fly in the face of the committee.* ☐ *The whole idea flew in the teeth of the bylaws of the organization.*

fly in the teeth of someone or something See the previous entry.

FLY ▸ INTO

fly into a rage to become enraged suddenly. ☐ *When he heard the report, he flew into a rage.* ☐ *We were afraid that she would fly into a rage.*

fly into something **1.** to go to something or some place by air. ☐ *When are you going to fly into the airport?* ☐ *We will fly into Detroit tomorrow.* **2.** to crash into something while flying. ☐ *The plane flew into the tall building.* ☐ *Birds sometimes fly into tall buildings.* **3.** to pass into something, such as fog, clouds, wind, etc., while flying. ☐ *We flew into some clouds, but the flight was not rough.* ☐ *The plane flew into some fog as it was landing.*

FLY ▸ IN(TO)

fly in(to something) to arrive in an airplane at something or some place. ☐ *I flew into Denver on time.* ☐ *When did you fly in?*

fly someone or something in(to some place) (from some place) to transport someone or something to some place from some place. (*Someone* includes *oneself*.) ☐ *We flew the documents into Adamsville from Springfield.* 🅃 *We flew in the documents to Chicago from Springfield.* ☐ *We had to fly the visitors in from Detroit.* ☐ *We flew them in.* ☐ *He flew himself into West Lafayette from Orlando.*

FLY ▸ OFF

fly off **1.** to take to flight quickly. ☐ *The stork flew off before we got a good look at it.* ☐ *The little birds flew off and things were quiet again.* **2.** to leave in a hurry. (Figurative.) ☐ *Well, it's late. I must fly off.* ☐ *She flew off a while ago.*

fly off (at) the handle to lose one's temper. (Informal.) ☐ *Todd flies off at the handle very easily.* ☐ *There is no need to fly off the handle.*

fly off with someone or something **1.** to depart with someone or something by air. ☐ *The eagle flew off with the kitten.* ☐ *The pilot flew off with the copilot.* **2.** to leave in a hurry with someone or something. (Figurative.) □ *She flew off with her packages before she got her change.* □ *Dave flew off with his brother because they had to meet a train.*

FLY ▸ OUT

fly out (of something) **1.** to leave a place by air. □ *We are going to fly out of Manaus on a charter.* □ *We flew out on time.* **2.** to leave a place quickly. (Figurative.) □ *We flew out of there as fast as we could.* □ *She opened the door and flew out.*

fly someone or something out (of something) to transport someone or something out of something by air. (*Someone* includes *oneself*. The *of*-phrase is paraphrased with a *from*-phrase when the particle is transposed. See the F example.) □ *They flew the tourists out of the troubled area on chartered flights.* T *They flew out the tourists the minute the trouble started.* F *They flew out the tourists from the little country.* □ *The government flew them out.* □ *He flew himself out of there as soon as he could get his plane refueled.*

FLY ▸ OVER

fly over someone or something to soar or glide over someone or something. □ *We saw an eagle fly over us.* □ *The plane flew over the desert.*

FLY ▸ PAST

fly past someone or something to soar or glide past someone or something. □ *The stone flew past Mike's left ear, and he ducked.* □ *The plane flew past the cloud bank.*

FLY ▸ TO

fly to someone or something to go to someone or something quickly and eagerly; to flee to someone or something. □ *She flew to his arms as he got off the boat.* □ *Harry flew to Gloria and hugged her tight.* □ *Tom flew to his cabin in the woods to escape the pressures of his job.*

fly to something to go to something or some place by air. □ *After Miami, we fly to Chicago.* □ *Let's fly to Paris for lunch.*

FLY ▸ UP

fly up to something to go by air to a place at a higher elevation or to a place in the north. □ *We will fly up to St. Paul for the holidays.* □ *I want to fly up to Alberta, Canada, for the summer.*

FOAM ▸ AT

foam at the mouth **1.** to create froth or foam around the mouth, as with some diseases. □ *The poor dog was foaming at the mouth and looked quite dangerous.* □ *What does it mean when a cow foams at the mouth?* **2.** to be extraordinarily angry. (Figurative.) □ *She was so angry, she was almost foaming at the mouth.* □ *Walter was foaming at the mouth with rage.*

FOAM ▸ UP

foam up [for something, such as soap or milk] to make foam or lather. □ *Milk will foam up when it is boiled.* □ *The boiling soup foamed up and slopped over the pot.*

FOB ▸ OFF

fob someone or something off (on(to) someone) to get rid of someone or something by transferring someone or something to someone. □ *Don't try to fob your girlfriend off on me!* T *She fobbed off her brother onto her friend.* □ *I took him to my grandmother's house and fobbed him off.*

FOB ▸ ON(TO)

See the previous entry.

FOCUS ▸ ON

focus on someone or something **1.** to make a camera lens pass a sharp image of someone or something. □ *I focused on the flower and pressed the shutter release.* □ *I focused on Fred and snapped just as he moved.* **2.** to dwell on the subject of someone or something. □ *Let's focus on the question of the electric bill, if you don't mind.* □ *Let us focus on Fred and discuss his progress.*

focus something on someone or something **1.** to aim a lens at someone or something and adjust the lens for clarity. □ *I focused the binoculars on the bird and stood there in awe at its beauty.* □ *He focused the camera on Jane and* *snapped the shutter.* **2.** to direct attention onto someone or something. (Figurative.) □ *Could we please focus the discussion on the matter at hand for a few moments?* □ *Let's focus our attention on Tom and discuss his achievements so far.*

FOG ▶ OVER

fog over [for something made of glass] to become covered over with water vapor. □ *The windshield fogged over because I forgot to turn on the defroster.* □ *The mirror fogged over and I couldn't see to shave.* Ⓐ *I couldn't see anything in the fogged-up mirror.*

FOG ▶ UP

fog something up to make something made of glass become covered with a film of water. □ *The moisture fogged the windshield up and we had to stop to clean it off.* Ⓣ *The moisture fogged up the glass.*

fog up [for something made of glass] to become partially or completely obscured by a film of water. □ *The glass fogged up and we couldn't see out.* Ⓐ *She couldn't see through the fogged-up window.*

FOIST ▶ OFF

foist someone or something off (on someone or something) to cast someone or something unwanted off on someone or a group. □ *Please don't try to foist cheap merchandise off on me.* Ⓣ *Don't foist off your brother on me!* □ *You can't foist that stuff off! It's worthless! People won't buy it!*

FOLD ▶ AWAY

fold something away to fold something up and put it away. □ *Please fold the maps away.* Ⓣ *Please fold away the maps neatly.* Ⓐ *We spent the night on an uncomfortable foldaway bed.*

FOLD ▶ BACK

fold back [for a sheet of something] to bend back. □ *The cloth folded back, revealing the faded upholstery below.* □ *The top page folded back, revealing a neatly typed manuscript.*

fold something back to bend a sheet or flap of something back. □ *She very carefully folded the page back to mark her place in the book.* Ⓣ *She folded back the page to mark her place in the book.* □ *The surgeon folded the flap of skin back, revealing the torn ligament.* Ⓣ *He folded back his shirt cuffs carefully.*

FOLD ▶ IN(TO)

fold something in(to something) to blend something, such as eggs, into batter. □ *Carefully, the chef folded the eggs into the other ingredients.* Ⓣ *The chef folded in the eggs.* □ *Now fold the egg whites in carefully.*

fold something into something to make an object by folding something, such as paper or cloth. □ *He folded the paper into a little bird.* □ *Wally can fold a sheet of paper into an airplane that flies.*

FOLD ▶ OVER

fold something over to double something over; to make a fold in something. □ *I folded the paper over twice to make something I could fan myself with.* □ *Fold the cloth over a few times before you put it away.*

FOLD ▶ UP

fold something up to double something over into its original folded position. □ *Please fold the paper up when you are finished.* Ⓣ *Please fold up the paper.*

fold up 1. [for something] to close by folding. □ *The table just folded up with no warning, trapping my leg.* Ⓐ *The folded-up card table fell over and made a great noise.* □ *I would like to find a map that would fold up by itself.* **2.** [for a business] to cease operating. □ *Our shop finally folded up because of the recession.* □ *Tom's little candy shop folded up.* **3.** [for someone] to faint. □ *She folded up when she heard the news.* □ *I was so weak that I was afraid I was going to fold up.*

FOLLOW ▶ ABOUT

follow someone or something about AND **follow someone or something around** to go the same route as someone or something all the time; to trail someone or something. □ *Why are you* *always following me about?* □ *Stop following me around.* □ *One car is following another car around. What's going on?*

FOLLOW ▸ AROUND

follow someone or something around See the previous entry.

FOLLOW ▸ IN

follow in someone's footsteps AND **follow in someone's tracks** to imitate someone's way of life; to take after someone, usually a relative, especially in the choice of occupation. □ *I admire what you have done, and I intend to follow in your footsteps.* □ *I will follow in your tracks.*

follow in someone's tracks See the previous entry.

FOLLOW ▸ ON

follow on (after someone or something) **1.** to depart and arrive after someone or something. □ *I can't leave now. I will have to follow on after the others.* □ *I follow on later.* **2.** to die at a date later than someone or a group. □ *She followed on after her husband a few years later.* □ *He went in June and she followed on in August.*

FOLLOW ▸ OUT

follow someone or something out to go out right after someone or something. □ *I followed her out and asked her if I could take her home.* □ *The dog followed Billy out and went to school with him.*

FOLLOW ▸ THROUGH

follow through (on something) to supervise something to its completion; to oversee something to make sure it gets done properly. □ *I want someone to follow through on this project.* □ *It isn't enough to start a project; you've got to follow through.*

follow through (with something) AND **follow something through** to complete an activity, doing what was promised. □ *I wish you would follow through with the project we talked about.* □ *You never follow through!* □ *When you start a project, you should be prepared to follow it through.* 🄽 *The supervisor provided the necessary follow-through, and the project was completed on time.*

FOLLOW ▸ UP

follow someone up AND **follow up (on someone)** to check on the work that someone has done. □ *I have to follow Sally up and make sure she did everything right.* 🅃 *I follow up Sally, checking on her.* □ *I'll follow up on her.* □ *Someone has to follow up.* 🄽 *The supervisor gives every project a follow-up to see how well things were done.* 🄰 *They would not provide the patient with follow-up care.*

follow something up AND **follow up (on something)** **1.** to check something out. □ *Would you please follow this lead up? It might be important.* 🅃 *Please follow up this lead.* □ *I'll follow up on it.* □ *Yes, please follow up.* **2.** to make sure that something was done the way it was intended. □ *Please follow this up. I want it done right.* 🅃 *Please follow up this business.* □ *I'll follow up on it.* □ *I'll follow up.*

follow up (on someone) See *follow someone up.*

follow up (on something) See *follow something up.*

FOOL ▸ AROUND

fool around to waste time doing something unnecessary or doing something amateurishly. □ *Stop fooling around.* □ *I wish you didn't spend so much time fooling around.*

fool (around) with someone or something See under *FOOL ▸ WITH.*

FOOL ▸ INTO

fool someone into something to deceive someone or oneself into doing something. □ *You'll never fool me into believing you.* □ *We fooled the boss into giving us all the day off.*

FOOL ▸ WITH

fool (around) with someone or something **1.** to waste time in the company of someone or a group. □ *Stop fooling around with those guys. They're up to no good most of the time.* □ *Better not fool around with the army. Go get a good job if you can.* **2.** AND **fool with**

someone or something to tamper with someone or something. □ *You had better not fool around with my little sister.* □ *Don't fool with that thing!* **3.** AND **fool with someone or something** to challenge or threaten someone or something. □ *You had better not fool around with me, if you know what's good for you.* □ *Don't fool with the police force!*

FORAGE ▸ AROUND

See the following entry.

FORAGE ▸ FOR

forage (around) for something to search for something, especially something to eat. □ *I will go to the kitchen and forage around for some cereal or something.* □ *The deer got into the garden and were foraging for a good meal.*

FORCE ▸ DOWN

force someone or something down to press or push someone or something downward. □ *I forced him down and slipped the handcuffs on him.* 🅃 *The cop forced down the thug and handcuffed him.* □ *I forced the dog down and held it there.*

force something down to force oneself to swallow something. □ *I can't stand sweet potatoes, but I manage to force them down just to keep from making a scene.* 🅃 *She forced down the sweet potatoes.*

force something down someone's throat to force someone to accept something. (Both figurative and literal uses.) □ *Don't try to force it down my throat! I don't want it!* □ *You can't force that nonsense down my throat!*

FORCE ▸ FROM

force someone or something from something to drive someone or some creature away from something. □ *We forced the cattle from the yard, putting them back into the pasture.* □ *I forced Tom from the room and locked the door.*

FORCE ▸ IN(TO)

force someone or something in(to something) **1.** to make someone or something go into something. □ *Please don't force me into that little room!* 🅃 *They forced in many people to the small room.* □ *They forced them all in.* **2.** to make someone or something fit into something. □ *Don't try to force the plug into the socket.* 🅃 *Don't force in the plug.* □ *After all that, he forced it in.* □ *Sam forced his buddy into the cabinet, and left him well hidden there.*

FORCE ▸ OFF

force someone or something off (of) something **1.** to get someone, something, or some creature off something. (The *of*-phrase is paraphrased with a *from*-phrase when the particle is transposed. See the 🄵 example. The *of* is colloquial.) □ *I had to force the cat off the sofa. She is so stubborn.* 🅃 *I had to force off the cat. She is so stubborn.* 🄵 *I forced off the cat from her favorite resting place.* □ *I had to force her off.* **2.** to make someone or a group resign from a board, committee, panel, etc. (The *of*-phrase is paraphrased with a *from*-phrase when the particle is transposed. See the 🄵 example. The *of* is colloquial.) □ *They forced her off the board before she could change any of their policies.* 🅃 *They forced off the dissenters.* 🄵 *They forced off the troublesome members from the board.*

force someone or something (off) on someone See the following entry.

FORCE ▸ ON

force someone or something (off) on someone to make someone take someone or something. □ *I didn't want it, but she forced it off on me.* □ *She forced her nephew on me and went out shopping.*

FORCE ▸ OUT

force someone or something out (of something) to drive someone or something out of something or some place. □ *The citizen's group forced the governor out of office.* 🅃 *They forced out the governor.* □ *We forced him out.*

FORCE ▸ THROUGH

force someone or something through something to push someone or something through an opening. □ *First, you must force the others through the opening and then go through yourself.* □ *We* *forced the sofa through the door and scarred up the doorjamb.*

force something through something to press or drive something through resistance. ☐ *They forced the bill through the legislature.* ☐ *We were not able to force the matter through the board of directors.*

FORCE ► TO

force someone to the wall See *drive someone to the wall* under *DRIVE ► TO.*

FORCE ► UP

force something up See *drive something up* under *DRIVE ► UP.*

FORECLOSE ► ON

foreclose on something to take the property on which a mortgage is held; to satisfy a loan by taking ownership of the property put up for security on the loan. ☐ *If you don't pay, we will be forced to foreclose on your house.* ☐ *The bank foreclosed on our property.*

FOREWARN ► ABOUT

forewarn someone about something AND **forewarn someone of something** to warn someone about someone or something. ☐ *They forewarned us of your strange behavior.* ☐ *Didn't we forewarn you about Max's problem?*

FOREWARN ► OF

forewarn someone of something See the previous entry.

FORGET ► ABOUT

forget about someone or something **1.** to put someone or something out of one's mind. ☐ *Don't forget about me!* ☐ *You ought to forget about all that.* **2.** to fail to remember something at the appropriate time. ☐ *She forgot about paying the electric bill until the lights were turned off.* ☐ *She forgot about the children and they were left standing on the corner.*

FORGIVE ► FOR

forgive someone for something to pardon someone for something. (*Someone* includes *oneself.*) ☐ *Please forgive me for being late.* ☐ *He never forgave himself for harming her.*

FORK ► OUT

fork money out for something to pay money out for something. (Slang.) ☐ *Do you think I'm going to fork twenty dollars out for that little book?* 🆃 *I won't fork out any money for something like that.*

fork something out (to someone) **1.** to serve food to someone, using a fork. (Folksy.) ☐ *The cook forked the fried chicken out to everyone quite generously.* 🆃 *He forked out the chicken to everyone.* ☐ *He brought up a big dish of fried chicken and forked it out.* **2.** to give out something to someone. (Slang.) ☐ *We forked the coupons out to everyone who asked for them.* 🆃 *We forked out the coupons.* ☐ *We forked the coupons out.*

FORK ► OVER

fork something over (to someone) to give something to someone. (Slang. Usually refers to money.) ☐ *Come on! Fork the money over to me!* 🆃 *Fork over the money!* ☐ *Fork it over!*

FORK ► UP

fork something up to serve something up with a fork. ☐ *The cook forked up the pork chops, one to a person.* 🆃 *Could you fork up another pork chop for me, please?*

FORM ► FROM

form from something [for something] to develop from something; [for something] to assume a shape, using something else as raw material. ☐ *Suddenly, an idea began to form from the things that you had said.* ☐ *It seemed that a figure was forming from the mists arising from the swamps.*

form something from something AND **form something out of something** to shape something from something. ☐ *He formed a tiny elephant from the clay.* ☐ *Wally formed a mound out of the sand.*

FORM ► INTO

form someone or something into something to shape someone or something into something. (Both literal and figurative.) ☐ *We formed the people into a* *line.* □ *Kathy formed the clay into a small elephant.*

form (up) into something [for a group of people] to assume the shape of something. □ *The boys formed up into a jagged line.* □ *We'll form into a line.*

FORM ▸ OUT

form something out of something See *form something from something* under *FORM ▸ FROM.*

FORM ▸ UP

form (up) into something See under *FORM ▸ INTO.*

FORTIFY ▸ AGAINST

fortify someone or something (against something) (with something) to strengthen someone or some creature against something with something. (*Someone* includes *oneself.*) □ *I'll need a cup of hot chocolate to fortify me against the storm.* □ *We have to fortify the dogs against the cold with extra food.* □ *We'll fortify them with seal meat.* □ *Before a party, she would fortify herself with a shot of liquor.*

FORTIFY ▸ WITH

See the previous entry.

FORWARD ▸ FROM

forward something (from some place) (to someone or some place) to send something onward to someone from the place it was originally received. □ *We forwarded the letter from Chicago to Springfield.* □ *Kelly forwarded the letter to her brother.* □ *Can I forward a package from this office?*

FORWARD ▸ TO

See the previous entry.

FOUL ▸ OUT

foul out (of something) [for a basketball player] to be forced out a game because of having too many fouls. □ *The center fouled out in the first fifteen minutes.* □ *Two other players fouled out soon after.*

FOUL ▸ UP

foul someone or something up to *mess someone or something up. (Someone* includes *oneself.*) □ *Who fouled this typewriter up?* [T] *Who fouled up this machine?* □ *Someone fouled me up!* □ *These accounts are completely fouled up.* [A] *How can I correct this fouled-up mess?* □ *You sure fouled yourself up in the last game.*

foul up to *mess up.* (Colloquial.) □ *Somebody fouled up real bad!* [N] *Who is responsible for this foul-up?*

FOUND ▸ (UP)ON

found something (up)on something to establish something on some kind of basis or justification. (*Upon* is formal and less commonly used than *on.*) □ *The owners founded this company upon prompt service.* □ *We founded our business on practically no money.*

FRAME ▸ IN

frame something in something 1. to place a frame of something around something. □ *Let us frame the photograph in a wood frame rather than a metal one.* □ *Alice chose to frame the painting in a simple, unmatted frame.* **2.** to express something in a particular way. □ *He framed his comments in very simple language.* □ *I hope you frame your remarks more clearly next time.*

FRAME ▸ OUT

frame something out to build the basic wood structure of a building, such as a house. □ *The carpenters, working fast, framed the whole house out in a day.* [T] *They framed out the house.*

FRAME ▸ UP

frame someone up to make someone take the blame for a crime; to make someone appear guilty of a crime. (Slang.) □ *They framed Max up, but he doesn't know it yet.* [T] *They framed up Max.* [N] *I didn't do it! It's a frame-up!*

FRATERNIZE ▸ WITH

fraternize with someone or something to associate with someone or a group; to consort with someone or a group. □ *They were instructed not to fraternize with the enemy.* □ *Don't fraternize with Lefty "Fingers" Moran.*

FREAK ▸ OUT

freak out (on something) to lose control of one's mind because of something, usually a drug. (Slang.) □ *She freaked out on the stuff she was smoking.* □ *She took some stuff and freaked out immediately.* 🄰 *She is totally freaked-out.* 🄰 *A bunch of freaked-out kids crowded around the fancy car.*

freak out (over someone or something) AND **freak out (at someone or something)** to lose control of one's mind because of someone or something that has happened. □ *I absolutely freaked out over the whole business!* □ *Don't freak out at me!* □ *He's always freaking out.* 🄽 *The kid's a freak-out.*

freak someone out to make one lose one's mind. (Slang.) □ *This movie just freaked me out!* 🅃 *The accident freaked out everybody.* 🄽 *The concert was a real freak-out.*

FREE ▸ FROM

free someone or something from someone or something to release or unburden someone or something from someone or something. (*Someone* includes *oneself*.) □ *We freed the raccoon from the trap.* □ *Max tried to free himself from the police officer.* □ *The dog tried to free itself from the dogcatcher.* □ *As hard as he tried, he couldn't free himself from the guilt.*

FREEZE ▸ IN

freeze someone or something in something to preserve the image of someone or something in a particular situation. (In one's memory or through photography.) □ *I tried to freeze her in my memory so I would have her with me always.* □ *I froze the scene in my memory.* □ *I was able to freeze the event in a picture.*

FREEZE ▸ INTO

freeze something into something **1.** to use cold to solidify something into a different state, usually water into ice. □ *The extreme cold froze the water of the river into solid ice.* □ *The cold snap froze the water in the puddles into hard sheets of ice.* **2.** to use cold to solidify something into a particular shape. □ *We froze the ice cream into the shape of a penguin.* □ *This ice tray will freeze water into little round balls of ice.*

FREEZE ▸ (ON)TO

freeze (on)to something [for something] to touch something very cold and freeze hard and fast to it. □ *My hand froze to the railing.* □ *The branch froze onto the side of the house.*

FREEZE ▸ OUT

freeze someone out (of something) **1.** to isolate someone from something or a group. (*Someone* includes *oneself*. The *of*-phrase is paraphrased with a *from*-phrase when the particle is transposed. See the 🄵 example.) □ *After his impossible behavior they froze him out of all social events.* 🅃 *The group froze out a number of people from the organization.* □ *We froze them out because they had insulted us.* □ *By her actions, she froze herself out of most social relationships.* **2.** to make it so cold in a place that someone has to leave. □ *Are you trying to freeze us out of here? Turn up the heat!* 🅃 *They nearly froze out everyone.* □ *Don't freeze us out!* 🄽 *Close the window! Who is responsible for this freeze-out?*

FREEZE ▸ OVER

freeze over [for a body of water] to get cold and form a layer of ice on top. □ *The pond froze over, so we went skating.* 🄰 *The frozen-over pond was not really ready for skating.*

FREEZE ▸ TO

See also *FREEZE ▸ (ON)TO.*

freeze someone or something to death to make someone or something cold enough to die. (Both literal and figurative uses.) □ *This weather is going to freeze us all to death.* □ *I was afraid that the cold snap would freeze the dog to death.*

FREEZE ▸ UP

freeze up **1.** [for something] to freeze and stop functioning. □ *The joint froze up and wouldn't move anymore.* 🄰 *How do I thaw my frozen-up water pipes?* **2.** [for someone] to become frightened and anxious, and be unable to continue with something. □ *I froze up and couldn't* *say anything more.* [A] *How can we help the frozen-up dancers?*

FRESHEN ▶ UP

freshen someone or something up to revive or restore the appearance or vitality of someone or something. (*Someone* includes *oneself*.) □ *What can we do to freshen this room up?* [T] *A cold shower freshened up the runner.* □ *Let me take a moment to freshen myself up before we go into the dining room.*

FRET ▶ ABOUT

fret about someone or something AND **fret over someone or something** to worry about someone or something. □ *Please don't fret about it.* □ *There is no need to fret over Larry.*

FRET ▶ OVER

fret over someone or something See the previous entry.

FRIGHTEN ▶ AWAY

frighten someone or something away AND **frighten someone or something off** to scare someone or something off. □ *The noise frightened the burglar away.* [T] *Something frightened away the prowlers.* □ *The high prices frightened the shoppers off.* □ *You frightened the deer off!*

FRIGHTEN ▶ INTO

frighten someone or something into something **1.** to scare someone into doing something. □ *You can't frighten me into leaving!* □ *Let's try to frighten the coyotes into running away.* **2.** to scare someone or something into entering something or some place. □ *The trouble in the neighborhood frightened most of the residents into their houses.* □ *We frightened the little mouse back into its hole.* **3.** to scare someone or something into a particular state. □ *They frightened me into a quivering mass.* □ *The mouse was frightened into a state of confusion.*

FRIGHTEN ▶ OFF

frighten someone or something off See under *FRIGHTEN ▶ AWAY.*

FRIGHTEN ▶ OUT

frighten someone or something out of something **1.** to scare someone or some creature into leaving something or some place. □ *We scared the squirrel out of the garage.* □ *I frightened the prowler out of the yard.* **2.** to scare someone or some creature into giving something up, such as one's wits, its wits, a year's growth, its mind, one's mind, etc. □ *Oh, you frightened me out of a year's growth!* □ *You frightened that dim-witted raccoon out of its mind.*

frighten the (living) daylights out of someone AND **frighten the wits out of someone** to scare someone severely. □ *Gad! You frightened the living daylights out of me!* □ *You frightened the wits out of your mother!* □ *Don't blow that trumpet at this time of night. You'll frighten the daylights out of everyone in the neighborhood.*

FRIGHTEN ▶ TO

frighten someone to death to scare someone into dying. (Figurative.) □ *That kind of talk frightens me to death.* □ *The door slammed and frightened me to death.*

FRITTER ▶ AWAY

fritter something away to waste something little by little. □ *Don't fritter all your money away!* [T] *Don't fritter away all your time.*

fritter something away (on someone or something) to waste something, such as money, on someone or something, foolishly. □ *Did you fritter good money away on that thing?* [T] *You frittered away one hundred dollars on that piece of junk?* □ *Don't fritter your time away!*

FRIVOL ▶ AWAY

frivol something away to waste something frivolously. (Informal or slang.) □ *Are you going to frivol the whole day away?* [T] *She frivoled away the whole day.*

FRONT ▶ FOR

front for someone or something to serve as the public contact or public "face" for someone or something.

(Slang.) □ *Her publicity agent fronted for her most of the time.* □ *Max fronted for a gang of thieves.*

FRONT ▸ ON

front on something [for a building or a piece of land] to face out on something. □ *The property fronts on a lovely boulevard that has very little traffic.* □ *Our house fronts on a lake.*

FROST ▸ OVER

frost over to become covered with frost. □ *The windows had all frosted over in the night.* □ *The car windows frosted over.* Ⓐ *We couldn't see through the frosted-over windows.*

FROTH ▸ UP

froth something up to whip something up until it is frothy. □ *Froth the milk up before you add it to the sauce.* Ⓣ *Froth up the milk before you pour it in.*

froth up [for something] to build up a froth when whipped or boiled. □ *The mixture began to froth up as Dan beat it.* □ *The milk frothed up as it began to boil.*

FROWN ▸ AT

frown at someone or something to scowl at someone or something. □ *Please don't frown at me. I didn't do anything.* □ *Frank frowned at the dog and gave it a kick.*

FROWN ▸ ON

frown on someone or something to disapprove of someone or something; to show displeasure or disapproval of someone or something. □ *The Internal Revenue Service frowns on tax cheaters.* □ *Aunt Clara always seemed to frown on my cousin for some reason.*

FRY ▸ UP

fry something up to cook something by frying. (Folksy.) □ *Let's fry some chicken up for dinner.* Ⓣ *We fried up some chicken.*

FUEL ▸ UP

fuel something up to put fuel into something. □ *I have to fuel this car up before I go any farther.* Ⓣ *I need to fuel up the car.*

fuel up to fill one's tank with fuel. □ *Let's stop here and fuel up.* □ *I need to fuel up at the next little town.*

FULMINATE ▸ AGAINST

fulminate against someone or something to denounce someone or something. □ *The workers were fulminating against their employer.* □ *They are fulminating against the president of the union.*

FUMBLE ▸ FOR

fumble for something to grab awkwardly at something. □ *He fumbled for his wallet, hoping Wally would pay the bill.* □ *Tex was shot while fumbling for his gun.*

FUME ▸ ABOUT

fume about someone or something AND **fume over someone or something** to be very angry about something; to keep one's anger at someone or something to oneself. □ *She was just fuming over her broken vase.* □ *She was still fuming about Larry the next morning.* □ *Are you still fuming over Larry?*

FUME ▸ AT

fume at someone to rage at someone. □ *She was really fuming at Sam, who had broken her table leg.* □ *She is still fuming at him over that.*

FUME ▸ OVER

fume over someone or something See under *FUME ▸ ABOUT.*

FURNISH ▸ FOR

furnish something for someone or something AND **furnish someone or something with something** to provide something for someone or a group. □ *I would be happy to furnish dinner for the visitors.* □ *I furnished the board of directors with the information.*

furnish something for something to provide something to be used as something. □ *Could you furnish the salad for our picnic?* □ *We can't furnish enough money for the whole party.*

FURNISH ▸ WITH

furnish someone or something with something See *furnish something for someone or something* under *FURNISH ▸ FOR.*

FUSE ▸ WITH

fuse something with something to bond something together with something. ☐ *You have to fuse the upper layer to the lower layer with heat.* ☐ *He used heat and pressure to fuse the rubber patch to the bottom of the rubber raft.*

fuse with something to bond with something. ☐ *The metal has fused with the glass coating on the tank.* ☐ *I didn't know that metal could fuse with glass.*

FUSS ▸ ABOUT

fuss about AND **fuss around** to go about fussing and complaining; to move about in a busy manner. ☐ *Don't fuss about so much. Things will take care of themselves.* ☐ *Now, stop fussing around and sit down.*

fuss about someone or something to complain about someone or something. ☐ *What are you fussing about now?* ☐ *Are you still fussing about Tony?*

FUSS ▸ AROUND

fuss around See under *FUSS ▸ ABOUT.*

fuss (around) with someone or something See under *FUSS ▸ WITH.*

FUSS ▸ AT

fuss at someone or something to complain at someone. ☐ *Stop fussing at me!* ☐ *The squirrel is fussing at the dog.* ☐ *There is no point in fussing at the toaster!*

FUSS ▸ OVER

fuss over someone or something to go to a lot of bother about someone or something. ☐ *My aunt always fusses over me and my sister.* ☐ *You spend a lot of time fussing over your hair.*

FUSS ▸ WITH

fuss (around) with someone or something to keep bothering with someone or something; to *fiddle with someone or something.* ☐ *Don't fuss around with it. We'll have to get a new one.* ☐ *Don't fuss with your children. They will get along just fine without all that attention.*

FUTZ ▸ AROUND

futz around to waste time. (Slang.) ☐ *Stop futzing around and get the job done.* ☐ *I wish you would stop futzing around!*

FUTZ ▸ UP

futz something up to mess something up. (Slang.) ☐ *Who futzed the computer up?* 🅃 *Who futzed up the computer?*

G

GAG ► ON

gag on something to choke on something; to retch on something. ☐ *The dog is gagging on whatever you gave her.* ☐ *This fish is good, but I hope I don't gag on a bone.*

GAIN ► BY

gain by something to increase or advance by a specified rate or amount. ☐ *He is gaining by leaps and bounds.* ☐ *The horse gained by a length near the end of the race and almost came in first.*

gain something by doing something to achieve some benefit by doing something. ☐ *What did he gain by dropping out of school?* ☐ *I will gain some degree of security by investing in U.S. Treasury Bonds.*

GAIN ► FROM

gain from something to benefit from something. ☐ *I hope you gain from this experience.* ☐ *What do you think I will gain from this?*

gain something from something to earn or achieve something from something. ☐ *I hope you gain something worthwhile from all this.* ☐ *I know I will gain some valuable experience from this job.*

GAIN ► IN

gain in something to advance in a particular quality. ☐ *Todd grew in stature and gained in wisdom.* ☐ *Mary gained in experience as the weeks went on.*

GAIN ► ON

gain on someone or something to begin to catch up or move ahead of someone or something. ☐ *We were gaining on them when they suddenly sped up.* ☐ *Our horse was gaining on the horse in front.*

GAIN ► OVER

gain dominion over someone or something to achieve total authority over someone or something. ☐ *The dictator sought to gain dominion over the entire country.* ☐ *Harry was not happy until he had gained dominion over the people who worked for him.*

GALLIVANT ► AROUND

gallivant around to travel around aimlessly. ☐ *Why don't you stop gallivanting around and come home for a while?* ☐ *Mary is off gallivanting around with her boyfriend.*

GALLOP ► THROUGH

gallop through something **1.** [for a horse] to pass through something at a gallop. ☐ *Her horse galloped through the garden and dumped her in the cabbages.* ☐ *A few horses galloped through the meadow.* **2.** to go through something quickly. (Figurative.) ☐ *Mike galloped through his song and left the stage in a hurry.* ☐ *Don't just gallop through your homework!*

GALUMPH ► AROUND

galumph around to go around looking for someone or something or transporting someone or something; to move around, exhausted and dragging. (Colloquial.) ☐ *I am so tired of galumphing around, dropping off and picking up kids.* ☐ *I have to stop galumphing around day after day.*

GALVANIZE ▶ INTO

galvanize someone into action to stimulate someone into some activity. ☐ *The explosion galvanized Martha into action.* ☐ *We were galvanized into action by the storm.*

GAMBLE ▶ AWAY

gamble something away to lose all of something, gambling. ☐ *He gambled all his money away.* 🅃 *He gambled away all his money.*

GAMBLE ▶ ON

gamble on someone or something **1.** to make a wager on something concerning someone or something. ☐ *I wouldn't gamble on it happening.* ☐ *Don't gamble on Betty. You'll be sorry.* **2.** to run a risk by choosing or depending on someone or something. ☐ *I wouldn't gamble on Ted's being able to come. I don't think he can.* ☐ *Don't gamble on Ted. I'm almost sure he won't come.*

GANG ▶ UP

gang up (against someone or something) to organize against someone or something. ☐ *We may have to gang up against the opposition to make our point.* ☐ *Yes, we will have to gang up.*

gang up (on someone or something) [for a group] to make an assault on someone or something. ☐ *They ganged up on us!* ☐ *We can't do it alone. We will have to gang up.*

GAPE ▶ AT

gape at someone or something to stare at someone or something in wonder. ☐ *Don't just stand there, gaping at me. Come in.* ☐ *Stop gaping at the storm clouds and get in here.*

GARB ▶ IN

garb someone in something to dress someone in something. (*Someone* includes *oneself.*) ☐ *He hoped that someday he wouldn't have to garb his children in rags.* ☐ *She garbed herself in her finest clothes and got ready to meet her husband's family.*

GARBAGE ▶ DOWN

garbage something down to gobble food down. (Slang.) ☐ *Don't just garbage your food down! Enjoy it!* 🅃 *He always garbages down his pizza.*

GARNER ▶ IN

garner something in AND **garner something up** to take something in and store it; to harvest something in and store it. (Originally referred to grain stored in a granary.) ☐ *Will they garner the crop in on time this year?* 🅃 *They had garnered in the entire crop by late October.* ☐ *They garnered the crop up.* ☐ *They garnered in their possessions and left.*

GARNER ▶ UP

garner something up See the previous entry.

GARNISH ▶ WITH

garnish something with something to embellish or decorate something, such as food, with something. ☐ *For the final presentation, I will garnish the dish with a sprig of parsley.* ☐ *The roast was garnished with slices of apple.*

GAS ▶ UP

gas something up to put gasoline into a vehicle. ☐ *I have to gas this car up soon.* 🅃 *I will stop and gas up the car at the next little town.*

gas up to supply oneself with gasoline, usually by putting it in a vehicle. ☐ *We have to stop and gas up the next chance we get.* ☐ *We need to gas up very soon.*

GASP ▶ AT

gasp at someone or something to inhale sharply in surprise or shock at someone or something. ☐ *I gasped at the sight that lay before me.* ☐ *I saw how weary Denise looked and I gasped at her.*

GASP ▶ FOR

gasp for air to fight for a breath of air. (After one has been deprived of air.) ☐ *Walter popped to the surface of the water and gasped for air.* ☐ *The injured dog appeared to be gasping for air.*

gasp for breath to labor for one's breath. (Usually because of physical exertion.) ☐ *She ran and ran until she was gasping for breath.* ☐ *The fish swam around the surface, gasping for breath.*

GASP ▸ OUT

gasp something out to utter something, gasping. ☐ *She gasped the words out haltingly.* ⓣ *Dan was just able to gasp out the instructions before he passed out.*

GATHER ▸ AROUND

gather around someone or something to collect around someone or something. ☐ *Let's all gather around her and hear her out.* ☐ *Please gather around the table for dinner.*

gather someone or something around (oneself) to collect people or things around oneself; to draw someone or something to oneself. ☐ *He gathered a lot of arty people around himself.* ☐ *She liked to gather exotic plants around herself.*

GATHER ▸ FROM

gather something from someone to collect something from someone. ☐ *I will gather the papers from Wally, and you go get those that Ted is working on.* ☐ *Would you gather the pictures from everyone? We have to leave now and take them with us.*

gather something from someone or something to learn something from someone or something; to infer something from someone or someone's remarks. (The *something* is often a clause shifted to another position in the sentence.) ☐ *I gather from your brother that you do not approve of her.* ☐ *We gathered that from your remarks.*

gather something from something to collect something from something. ☐ *Kristine gathered the honey from the beehives.* ☐ *I gathered my money from the cashier.*

GATHER ▸ IN

gather something in **1.** to collect something and bring it in; to harvest something. ☐ *We gathered the pumpkins in just before Halloween.* ⓣ *We gathered in the pumpkins just in time.* **2.** to fold or bunch cloth together when sewing or fitting clothing. ☐ *Try gathering it in on each side to make it seem smaller.* ⓣ *I will have to gather this skirt in.*

GATHER ▸ IN(TO)

gather someone in(to something) to assemble or bring people into something or some place. ☐ *The hostess gathered the children into the house just as the storm hit.* ⓣ *She gathered in the children.* ☐ *Harry gathered them in before the storm.*

GATHER ▸ TO

gather someone or something to oneself to draw someone or something to oneself. ☐ *The hen gathered her chicks to herself.* ☐ *Harry gathered the poker chips to himself.*

GATHER ▸ TOGETHER

gather someone or something together to assemble people or things together in one place. (*Someone* includes *oneself.*) ☐ *Gather everyone together in the drawing room for a meeting.* ⓣ *Please gather together all the suspects so that they can be questioned again.* ☐ *Would you gather all your papers together and put them away?* ☐ *They gathered themselves together to discuss the matter.*

gather together to assemble together. ☐ *We will gather together on the main deck for a meeting.* ☐ *Let's all gather together this evening and sing.*

GATHER ▸ UP

gather something up to collect something; to pick something up. ☐ *Let's gather our things up and go.* ⓣ *Please gather up your things.*

GAWK ▸ AT

gawk at someone or something to stare at someone or something, obviously and awkwardly. ☐ *Why are you standing there, gawking at me?* ☐ *The tourists stood at the foot of the mountain and gawked at the top.*

GAZE ▸ AROUND

gaze around (at someone or something) to look all around at someone or something. ☐ *The manager gazed around at each of us, and finally spoke.* ☐ *Tourists gazed around at the scenery for a while and got back in the bus.* ☐ *We just stood there, gazing around.*

gaze around (some place) to look around at one's surroundings. ☐ *Laura* *entered the room and gazed around the place.* ☐ *She came in and gazed around.*

GAZE ▸ AT

gaze at someone or something to stare at someone or something. ☐ *I stood for an hour, gazing at the sea.* ☐ *She gazed at me for a moment and then smiled.*

GAZE ▸ ON

gaze on someone or something to look at someone or something; to survey someone or something. (Stilted.) ☐ *She gazed sullenly on the ruin that had been her home.* ☐ *The teacher gazed on the student and frightened her.*

GAZE ▸ OUT

gaze out on something to look out on something, such as a lovely view, from inside a building. ☐ *She gazed out on the flowering trees and knew that life would go on.* ☐ *Henry sat for hours, gazing out on the lake.*

GEAR ▸ TO

gear something to someone or something to match something to the needs of someone or something. ☐ *I will try to gear this course to freshmen.* ☐ *My professor does not gear the course to me.*

GEAR ▸ UP

gear someone or something up (for someone or something) to prepare someone or something for someone or something. (*Someone* includes *oneself.*) ☐ *We will have to gear the workers up for higher levels of production.* 🅃 *We have to gear up the workers for the arrival of the new manager.* ☐ *We geared ourselves up for Frank, who was coming to lecture to us.* ☐ *They spent all morning gearing themselves up for the event.*

GENERALIZE ▸ ABOUT

generalize about someone or something AND **generalize on someone or something** to interpret someone or something in very general terms. ☐ *Sometimes it isn't wise to generalize about a complicated matter.* ☐ *She is very complex and it is difficult to generalize on her.*

GENERALIZE ▸ FROM

generalize from something to assume a general pattern in something from specific observances of something. ☐ *You can hardly generalize from only two instances.* ☐ *You can't generalize anything from that!*

GENERALIZE ▸ ON

generalize on someone or something See under *GENERALIZE ▸ ABOUT.*

GET ▸ ABOARD

get aboard something to get onto a ship or an airplane. ☐ *What time should we get aboard the ship?* ☐ *Everyone can get aboard at noon.*

GET ▸ ABOUT

get about AND **get around** to move around freely. ☐ *I can hardly get about anymore.* ☐ *It's hard for Aunt Mattie to get around.*

GET ▸ ACROSS

get across (something) to manage to cross something. ☐ *We finally got across the river where it was very shallow.* ☐ *Where the water was low, it was easy to get across.*

get someone or something across (something) to transport someone or something across something. (*Someone* includes *oneself.*) ☐ *We have to get everyone across the bridge before the volcano erupts again.* ☐ *Let's get the truck across also.* ☐ *I had to work hard to get myself across the bridge without a rest stop.*

get something across (to someone) to make someone understand something. (Especially if the details are difficult to understand or if the person being explained to understands poorly.) ☐ *I hope I can get this across to you once and for all.* ☐ *Try as I may, I just can't get this across.* ☐ *She doesn't pay any attention and I don't think I am getting it across.*

GET ▸ AFTER

get after someone **1.** to bother someone about doing something. ☐ *I will get after Fred about his behavior.* ☐ *Please don't get after me all the time.* **2.** to begin to chase someone. ☐ *The other boys* *got after him and almost caught him.* ☐ *Henry got after Bill and almost caught up with him.*

GET ▸ AHEAD

get ahead (in something) to advance in one's employment. ☐ *I work day and night, but I can't seem to get ahead in my job.* ☐ *I don't know what I have to do to get ahead.*

get ahead in something to progress in something. ☐ *He worked very hard to get ahead in school.* ☐ *I want to get ahead in life.*

get ahead of someone or something to move ahead of someone or something. ☐ *I managed to get ahead of everyone else in our party and get tickets for everyone.* ☐ *Try to get ahead of the truck in front of us.*

get ahead of something to manage to keep up with one's work; to take care of all one's responsibilities, especially financial ones. (See also *stay ahead of something* under *STAY▸ AHEAD.*) ☐ *By the end of the week, I usually can get ahead of my duties, but not by much.* ☐ *Jerry can't seem to get ahead of his work.*

get ahead of the game to progress in the world; to overcome various barriers to success. (Colloquial.) ☐ *It is very difficult to get ahead of the game financially.* ☐ *I worked very hard to get ahead of the game.*

GET ▸ ALONG

get along **1.** [for people or other creatures] to be amiable with one another. ☐ *Those two just don't get along.* ☐ *They seem to get along just fine.* **2.** to leave; to be on one's way. ☐ *I've got to get along. It's getting late.* ☐ *It's time for me to get along. See you later.*

get along in years to get old. ☐ *Old Mr. Martin is getting along in years.* ☐ *Fred said he was getting along in years, and that's why his joints ached.*

get along on something to manage to survive with just something. ☐ *I think we can get along on what I earn.* ☐ *I can't get along on what they pay me.*

get along with someone **1.** to be friends with someone. ☐ *Please try to get along with your brother.* ☐ *I try to get along with everyone.* **2.** to go on; to depart; to go and "take oneself along." (Folksy. Only with *you.*) ☐ *Get along with you, now. Get going!* ☐ *Get along with you, Sally!*

get along with someone or something to manage with someone or something; to manage with only something. ☐ *I can't get along with only one assistant.* ☐ *Mary said she could not get along with the old computer.*

get along without someone or something to manage without someone or something. ☐ *I don't think I can get along without you.* ☐ *Laura can't get along without her dictionary.*

GET ▸ AROUND

get around See under *GET ▸ ABOUT.*

get around someone or something **1.** to cluster around someone or something. ☐ *Tell everyone to get around the cat so she won't run away.* ☐ *Let's get around Mary and sing "Happy Birthday" to her.* **2.** to manage to go around someone or something. ☐ *We couldn't get around the fallen tree, so we turned back.* ☐ *Mary couldn't get around the people standing in the hallway.* **3.** to avoid or elude an authority or regulation that constitutes a barrier; to circumvent someone or something in order to get one's way. ☐ *We knew she would oppose us, so we got around her and got it approved by someone else.* ☐ *I know I can find a way to get around the rule.* ☐ *The kids really know how to get around their grandmother. She gives them anything they ask for.*

get around to someone or something to be able to deal with someone or something eventually. ☐ *I will get around to you in a moment. Please be patient.* ☐ *The mechanic will get around to your car when possible.*

get someone around the table to collect people together for discussion or bargaining. ☐ *We have to get everyone around the table on this matter.* ☐ *If I* *can get them around the table, I'm sure I can make them agree.*

GET ▶ AT

get at someone or something **1.** to manage to lay hands on someone or something; to get someone or something. □ *Just wait till I get at Charlie J. Wilson!* □ *I want to get at that chocolate cake.* **2.** to manage to attack someone or something. □ *The dog was chained up, so it couldn't get at us.* □ *The army was unable to get at the munitions storage area.*

get at something to arrive at a point of discussion; to work toward stating a point of discussion or an accusation. □ *What are you trying to get at?* □ *We were trying to get at the basis of the problem.*

get mad at someone or something to become angry at someone or something. □ *Don't get mad at me!* □ *There is no point in getting mad at the car that hit you.*

GET ▶ AWAY

get away to move away. (Often a command.) □ *Get away! Don't bother me!* □ *I tried to get away, but he wouldn't let me.*

get away from it all to go somewhere in order to avoid what one is leaving behind. (Idiomatic.) □ *I need a few days off to get away from it all.* □ *Everyone needs to get away from it all every now and then.*

get away (from someone or something) **1.** to go away from someone or something. □ *Please get away from me!* □ *Get away from that cake!* **2.** to escape from someone, something, or some place. □ *Max did get away from the police but not away from Lefty.* □ *Mary couldn't get away from the telephone all morning.* N *The guest made his getaway before the hostess even noticed he was there.*

get away with murder to do something very bad and not get punished for it. (Figurative.) □ *That guy always gets away with murder—just because he's cute.* □ *Why does Wally think that you are getting away with murder?*

get away with someone or something to escape, taking someone or something with one. □ *The kidnapper got away with little Brian.* □ *The burglars got away with a lot of cash and some diamonds.*

get away with something AND **get by with something** to do something and not get punished for it. (See an elaboration at *let someone get by with something* under *LET ▶ BY.*) □ *You can't get away with that!* □ *Larry got by with the lie.*

get someone or something away from someone or something to take someone or something away from someone or something, in any combination. (*Someone* includes *oneself.*) □ *Please get that cigar away from me!* □ *See if you can get Timmy away from the horse.* □ *I couldn't get myself away from the dessert table.*

GET ▶ BACK

get back (at someone) to get revenge on someone. □ *I will get back at her someday, somehow.* □ *I'll get back, don't worry.*

get back in(to) circulation **1.** to resume one's social contacts; to continue to make new friends and develop a social life. □ *After her illness, Kristine looked forward to getting back into circulation.* □ *I want to get back in circulation and have some fun.* **2.** to become available for dating. □ *Now that Fred and Amy are through, Amy is getting back into circulation.* □ *Now that you're divorced, when are you going to get back into circulation?*

get back in(to) (the) harness to return to one's job. □ *I don't look forward to getting back into the harness next Monday.* □ *When my vacation is over, I have to get back into harness the very next day.* □ *I'm not looking forward to getting back in harness.*

get back on one's feet **1.** to recover from an illness and leave one's sickbed. (Both literal and figurative.) □ *I will go back to work as soon as I get back on my* *feet.* □ *I want to get back on my feet as soon as possible.* **2.** to recover from anything, especially financial problems. (Figurative.) □ *I can't afford to buy a car until I get a job and get back on my feet.* □ *I'll get back on my feet and start living normally.*

get back (some place) to manage to return to some place. □ *I can't wait till we get back home.* □ *When will we get back? Is it much farther?*

get back to someone or something to return to dealing with someone or something. □ *I will have to get back to you. I can't deal with this matter now.* □ *I want to get back to my work.*

get someone or something back to receive someone or something back; to recover someone who had been taken away; to recover something that had been taken away. □ *Beth finally got her car back.* 🅃 *She got back her car.* □ *The frightened parents got their child back and the kidnappers were put in jail.*

GET ▸ BEHIND

get behind (in something) AND **get behind (on something); get behind (with something)** See *fall behind (in something)* under *FALL ▸ BEHIND.*

get behind someone or something to back or support someone or something; to put oneself into a position to "push" or promote someone or something. □ *Let's all get behind Andrew for president!* □ *I want all of you to get behind the committee and support their efforts.*

GET ▸ BETWEEN

get between someone or something and someone or something to position oneself between people and things, in any combination. □ *She got between Dan and his career.* □ *The dog got between the archer and the target.*

GET ▸ BEYOND

get beyond someone or something 1. to move to the other side of something. □ *When we get beyond this bad road, I'll have to check the tires.* □ *I have to get beyond the large gentleman standing in the hall.* **2.** to finish with someone or something; to solve problems relating to someone or something. □ *Things will be better when we get beyond this financial crisis.* □ *When the country gets beyond President Adams, things will have to get better.*

GET ▸ BY

get by (on something) to survive with only something; to survive by relying on something. □ *I can't get by on that much money.* □ *That is a very small amount of money to live on. No one could get by.*

get by (someone or something) to move past someone or something. □ *I need to get by this intersection, and then I will stop and look at the tires.* □ *Please let me get by.*

get by with something See under *GET ▸ AWAY.*

get by without someone or something to survive without someone or something. □ *I can't get by without you.* □ *We can probably get by without two cars.*

get someone or something by (someone or something) 1. to get someone or something to permit someone or something to pass. □ *Do you think I can get my cousin by the border guards?* □ *I don't think I can get this sausage by the customs desk.* **2.** to get someone or something to approve someone or something. (The first *someone* includes *oneself.*) □ *You will never get this joke by the censors!* □ *I could hardly get myself by the rigorous examination of the committee.*

GET ▸ DOWN

get down (from something) to get off something; to climb down from something. □ *Please get down from there this instant!* □ *Get down before you fall!*

get (down) off one's high horse See under *GET ▸ OFF.*

get down (on all fours) to stoop down and get on hands and knees. (Idiomatic.) □ *He got down on all fours and played with the children.* □ *Mary got down and walked around like a dog.*

get down on someone or something to turn against someone or something. ☐ *I don't know why the teacher got down on Chuck.* ☐ *Everyone sure got down on fast food.*

get down (on something) to concentrate on something. (Slang.) ☐ *Come on, man! Let's get down.* ☐ *Let's get down on this studying business, what do you say?*

get down to brass tacks to begin to talk seriously about the important details of something. (Cliché. Figurative.) ☐ *Enough of this small talk. Let's get down to brass tacks.* ☐ *Let's stop talking and get down to brass tacks.*

get down to cases to begin to deal with specific issues. ☐ *It's time to get down to cases and stop dealing with generalities.* ☐ *I don't have a lot of time, so let's get down to cases.*

get down to something to reach the point of dealing with something; to begin to work on something seriously. (Especially with *business, brass tacks, work, cases.*) ☐ *Now, let's get down to business.* ☐ *It's time to get down to brass tacks.*

get (down) to work (on someone or something) See under *GET ▸ TO.*

get someone down to make someone depressed or sad. ☐ *Now, now, don't let this matter get you down.* ☐ *All of this is beginning to get me down.*

get someone or something down (from something) to bring someone or something down from a higher place. (*Someone* includes *oneself.*) ☐ *See if you can get my cat down from the tree.* 🅃 *Please get down the sugar from the top shelf.* ☐ *Would you help me get Timmy down from the tree?* ☐ *Somehow, he got himself down from the garage roof.*

get someone or something down something to manage to put or force something downward. ☐ *We finally got her down the stairs, but it was struggle.* ☐ *Don had to push and push to get his laundry down the chute.*

get something down in black and white to record some important information in writing. (Refers to the black of ink and the white of paper.) ☐ *Be sure to get it down in black and white.* ☐ *I'm glad we have agreed on a price. I want to get it down in black and white.*

get something down (on paper) to write some information down on paper; to capture some information in writing. ☐ *This is important. Please get it down on paper.* ☐ *Please speak slowly. I want to get this down.*

GET ▸ FOR

get something for someone to obtain something for the use or benefit of someone. ☐ *I will get a new book for you. Sorry I messed the old one up.* ☐ *Would you get a glass of water for me?*

get something for something 1. to obtain a part or attachment for an object. ☐ *I need to get a part for the vacuum cleaner.* ☐ *Would you please get a bulb for my flashlight?* **2.** to receive an amount of money in exchange for something; to sell something for a specific price. ☐ *I got nearly two thousand dollars for my car.* ☐ *How much did they get for their house?* **3.** to get something for a certain amount of money. ☐ *I got my car for only $1500.* ☐ *She got her dinner for a song.*

GET ▸ FROM

get blood from a stone AND **get blood from a turnip** to do something impossible. (A proverb. Usually negative.) ☐ *After all, you can't get blood from a stone.* ☐ *Do you think you can get blood from a turnip?*

get free from someone or something See *get free of someone or something* under *GET ▸ OF.*

get someone or something free from someone or something to liberate someone or something from someone or something. (*Someone* includes *oneself.*) ☐ *We finally got cousin George free from the talkative old man.* ☐ *We managed to get the board we needed free from the heap.* ☐ *As soon as I get myself free from Miss Prism, I will join you.*

get something from someone or something 1. to receive something from someone or something. □ *I got this belt from my aunt for my birthday.* □ *I got a letter from the bank about the loan we applied for.* 2. to contract a disease from someone or something. □ *I got chicken pox from my son.* □ *I probably got my cold from walking in the rain.*

get there from here to travel to a place from this place. (Usually negative. Often in jest.) □ *Sorry, you just can't get there from here.* □ *I am beginning to believe that you just can't get there from here.*

GET ▸ IN

See also under *GET ▸ IN(TO).*

get a word in (edgewise) to manage to speak when someone else is doing all the talking. □ *People were talking so much, I couldn't get a word in edgewise.* □ *I couldn't get a word in, so I stopped trying.*

get in bad (with someone) to get into trouble with someone; to get into someone's disfavor. □ *I hope I don't get in bad with your husband.* □ *I'll be quiet around the boss. I don't want to get in bad.*

get in (good) with someone to get into someone's favor. (Informal.) □ *I hope I can get in good with the teacher. I need an A in the course.* □ *Mary is always trying to get in with the people who are in charge.*

get in on something 1. to become involved in something. □ *I wanted to get in on the meeting, but I wasn't invited.* □ *Do you want to get in on this matter?* 2. to receive a share of something. □ *I want to get in on the new European business that is supposed to develop.* □ *We will all want to get in on the scheme.*

get in on the ground floor to join something at its beginning. (Figurative.) □ *If you are starting a new project, I want to get in on the ground floor.* □ *Invest now so you can get in on the ground floor.*

get in over one's head to get too deeply involved in something. □ *I'm afraid she got in over her head.* □ *I didn't want to get in over my head.*

get in someone's hair [for someone] to become an annoyance to someone. (Figurative.) □ *You can watch what I am doing, but don't get in my hair.* □ *I wish you wouldn't get in my hair when I'm trying to do something.*

get in someone's way to interfere with someone's purposes or movement. □ *Please don't get in my way.* □ *That dog of yours is always getting in my way.*

get in something with someone to enter something or some place that already contains someone. □ *I got in the car with Fred, and we drove off.* □ *Mary got into the taxi with the strange man and slammed the door.*

get in touch (with someone) 1. to reach someone by letter or telephone. □ *I tried to get in touch with her, but she never answered her phone.* □ *I just couldn't seem to get in touch.* 2. to become more intimate with someone or oneself. □ *I need to get in touch with myself and the way I really feel about things.* □ *I tried talking to him, but I just can't seem to get in touch.*

get it in the neck to receive trouble or punishment. (Slang.) □ *You are going to get it in the neck if you are not home on time.* □ *I got it in the neck for being late.*

get something in order to arrange something properly. □ *Please get your desk in order.* □ *I wish you would get things in order.* □ *Please get these files in order.*

GET ▸ INSIDE

get inside something 1. to go inside of something or some place. □ *Get inside the house and wait for me.* □ *Get inside the car so you won't get wet.* 2. to learn about the inner workings of something or some organization. □ *I can't wait to get inside that company and see what makes it tick.* □ *Someone needs to get into the front office and straighten things out.*

GET ▸ INTO

get into a mess 1. to get some part of one into a sloppy or messy substance. □ *Look at your shoes! You really got into a mess.* □ *Please don't get into a mess in the park.* 2. to get into difficulty; to get into trouble. (Informal.) □ *Now you have really gotten into a mess.* □ *I got into a real mess at work.*

get into a rut to get into a type of boring habitual behavior. (Figurative.) □ *My life has gotten into a rut.* □ *I try not to get into a rut.*

get into an argument (with someone) (about someone or something) to enter a quarrel with someone about someone or something. □ *I don't want to get into an argument with you about Dan.* □ *Mary got into an argument about money with Fred.* □ *I really don't want to get into an argument.*

get into an argument (with someone) (over someone or something) to enter a quarrel with someone about who will end up with someone or something. □ *You take the big one. I don't want to get into an argument with you over it.* □ *Mary got into an argument over the best player with the captain of the other team.*

get into full swing [for things] to begin happening at the maximum rate; [for business or activity] to reach its peak. □ *It's best to get all the preliminaries out of the way before things get into full swing.* □ *I hope things get into full swing soon.*

get into high gear to begin operating at maximum speed or efficiency. (Alludes to the gears of a vehicle.) □ *Business will improve when the summer season gets into high gear.* □ *Things usually get into high gear shortly after the beginning of the school year.* □ *He never gets into high gear until after his third cup of coffee.*

get into hot water (with someone) (about someone or something) to get into trouble. (Slang or informal. Idiomatic.) □ *You are going to get into hot water with Rebecca about that.* □ *Amy got into hot water about Todd with Rebecca.*

get into one's stride 1. [for a runner] to reach a comfortable and efficient pace. □ *I got into my stride right away, and that helped win the race.* □ *She never got into her stride, and that's why she lost.* 2. to reach one's most efficient and productive rate of doing something. (Figurative.) □ *When I get into my stride, I'll be more efficient.* □ *Amy will be more efficient when she gets into her stride.*

get into someone to bother someone; to affect someone. (Usually a question: **What's gotten into someone?**) □ *I just don't know what's gotten into her.* □ *I don't know what got into me.*

get into something 1. to tamper with something; to open something and bother the contents. □ *Who got into my desk?* □ *Someone has been getting into my work after the office closes.* 2. to put oneself into clothing. □ *As soon as I get into this coat, I will help you load the car.* □ *Let me get into my boots, and then I'll be with you.* 3. to enter something or some place. □ *I got into the theater just before the rain started.* □ *Let's get into the car and go.* 4. to become involved in something; to develop an interest in something. (Slang.) □ *I can really get into sailing, I think.* □ *No matter how hard I try, I can't get into basketball.*

get something into a mess to cause something to become messy or untidy; to cause something to become unmanageable. □ *When he made the spaghetti sauce, he got the kitchen into a real mess.* □ *You have got these accounts into a mess!*

get something into someone's (thick) head AND **get something through someone's thick skull** to manage to get an understanding of something into someone's brain. □ *I want you out of here! Can't you get that into your thick head?* □ *Will you please get these instructions through your thick skull?*

get something into something to manage to put something into something. □ *I got the notice into tomorrow's newspa-*

per. ☐ *I will get the ribbon into the typewriter right away.*

GET ▶ IN(TO)

get in(to) the act to participate in something. (Colloquial.) ☐ *Everybody wants to get into the act! There is not room here for everyone.* ☐ *I want to get in the act.*

get in(to) the swing of things to join in with people and their activities; to become more social and up to date. (Idiomatic.) ☐ *Come on, get into the swing of things! Don't be so stuffy.* ☐ *Mary found it hard to get in the swing of things.*

get one's hooks in(to someone or something) to obtain a strong and possessive hold on someone or something. ☐ *She just can't wait to get her hooks into him.* 🅃 *He finally got in his hooks and guarded her jealously.* ☐ *He finally got his hooks in.*

get someone in(to something) to manage to get someone enrolled into something; to manage to get someone accepted into something. (*Someone* includes *oneself*.) ☐ *Somehow, we managed to get Jody into a fine private school.* ☐ *We got her in at last!* ☐ *Well, I managed to get myself into the class I wanted.*

get someone or something in(to something) to manage to fit someone or something into something. (*Someone* includes *oneself*.) ☐ *I will try to get you into the beginning of the line.* ☐ *The key is bent, but I think I can get it in.* ☐ *I am sure I cannot get myself into my tuxedo. It's too tight.*

get something in(to someone or something) to make something enter someone or something. ☐ *Get that morphine into her before she goes into shock.* ☐ *Get this stuff into the refrigerator before it spoils.*

GET ▶ OF

get a load of someone or something to get a good look at someone or something. (Slang.) ☐ *Wow! Get a load of that car!* ☐ *Get a load of Mary!*

get abreast of someone or something to learn the news about someone or something. ☐ *I need to get abreast of what's going on in Egypt.* ☐ *The press corps has to get abreast of the president.*

get (a)hold of someone or something **1.** to grasp someone or something. ☐ *I got hold of him and dragged him back from the edge just in time.* ☐ *I got hold of his hand and held on tight.* **2.** to locate someone or something. ☐ *I got hold of a replacement part in Peoria. They are shipping it to us today.* ☐ *Try to get hold of a plumber, would you?* **3.** to reach someone or a group on the telephone. ☐ *I got hold of her just as she was going out the door.* ☐ *I was able to get hold of the factory and cancel the order.*

get free of someone or something **1.** to rid oneself of the burden of someone or something. ☐ *Can't I get free of this problem?* ☐ *I can't seem to get free of Randy.* **2.** AND **get free from someone or something** to liberate oneself from someone or something. ☐ *I tried to get free of Mr. Franklin, but he kept talking and wouldn't let me interrupt.* ☐ *Is there any way that somebody can get free of Tom?* ☐ *I couldn't get free of the nail that had snagged my sleeve.*

get the best of someone to win against someone; to top someone. ☐ *I don't want him to get the best of me.* ☐ *She always tries to get the best of other people.*

get the hang of something to learn how something is done. ☐ *Pretty soon, you'll get the hang of it.* ☐ *I hope he gets the hang of how to do it soon.*

get the worst of something to get the poorest share of something; to suffer the most from something. ☐ *I knew I would get the worst of the deal because I was absent when the goods were divided up.* ☐ *I'm sorry that you got the worst of it.* ☐ *The little town on the border got the worst of the attack.*

get wind of something to hear of something. ☐ *I got wind of the news about Albert.* ☐ *When did you get wind of it?*

GET ▸ OFF

get a load off one's mind to tell someone a lot of things that have been bothering one; to unbosom oneself. ☐ *Can I talk to you? I've got to get a load off my mind.* ☐ *I really have to get a load off my mind.*

get (down) off one's high horse to become humble; to be less haughty. (Idiomatic.) ☐ *It's about time that you got down off your high horse.* ☐ *Would you get off your high horse and talk to me?*

get it off with someone to have sexual intercourse with someone. (Slang.) ☐ *She said she wanted to get it off with him.* ☐ *She said all he wanted was to get it off with just anybody.*

get off easy AND **get off lightly** to receive little or no punishment for doing something wrong. ☐ *She really got off easy, considering what she did.* ☐ *You got off lightly in court. She is a hard judge.*

Get off it! **1.** "Stop acting so arrogant!" ☐ *Get off it, you jerk!* ☐ *Get off it! That's too much!* **2.** "You're lying!" ☐ *Get off it, you liar!* ☐ *Get off it! That can't be true.*

get off ((of) someone or something) to get down from someone or something. (The *of* is colloquial.) ☐ *Please get off of me. I can't play piggyback anymore.* ☐ *Get off the sofa!*

get off ((of) something) to stop discussing the topic that one is supposed to be discussing [and start discussing something else]; to stray from the topic at hand. (The *of* is colloquial.) ☐ *I wish you wouldn't get off the subject so much.* ☐ *This writer gets off his topic all the time.*

get off ((of) work) AND **get off (from work)** **1.** to leave one's work at the end of the day. (The *of* is colloquial.) ☐ *What time do you get off from work?* ☐ *I get off work about five o'clock.* ☐ *She gets off from work later than I do.* **2.** to be absent from one's work with permission. ☐ *I think I can get off of work so I can go to the doctor.* ☐ *Sorry, I can't join you. Things are busy at the office, and I can't get off.*

get off (on something) **1.** to begin a journey. ☐ *They got off on their trip early.* ☐ *When do you hope to get off in the morning?* **2.** to get high on some kind of drug. (Slang.) ☐ *Max likes to get off on marijuana.* ☐ *He is always trying to get off.* **3.** to get excited by something. (Slang.) ☐ *She gets off on baby lambs.* ☐ *One look at lambs frolicking in the meadow, and she gets off.*

get off on the right foot (with someone or something) AND **get off to a good start (with someone or something)** to start out correctly; to begin something carefully and cautiously. ☐ *This time, I want to get off on the right foot with him.* ☐ *I tried to get off to a good start with my new job.* ☐ *Kathy made every effort to get off on the right foot.*

get off on the wrong foot (with someone or something) AND **get off to a bad start (with someone or something)** to start out incorrectly; to begin something, making foolish errors from the start. ☐ *I don't want to get off on the wrong foot with my new in-laws.* ☐ *Kelly tried to prevent getting off on the wrong foot with the new manager.* ☐ *I certainly don't want to get off to a bad start.*

get off one's ass AND **get off one's rear; get off one's butt** to get up and get busy; to stop loafing and get to work. (Caution with *ass*. *Butt* is also offensive to some people. Slang.) ☐ *Get off your ass and get busy!* ☐ *It's time you got off your butt and started to work.*

get off someone's back AND **get off someone's case** to stop harassing someone. (Slang.) ☐ *Leave me alone! Get off my back!* ☐ *I wish you would get off my case.*

get off someone's case See the previous entry.

get off someone's tail **1.** to stop following someone closely, usually in an automobile. ☐ *Get off my tail! Keep your distance!* ☐ *I wish that car behind me would get off my tail.* **2.** to stop bothering someone; to stop monitoring someone's actions. ☐ *Get off my tail! I can manage without you.* ☐ *Who needs your help? Get off my tail!*

get off something to climb down from something. ☐ *Please get off the stairs. You know you can't play on the stairs.* ☐ *I wish that the children would get off that wall before they fall off.*

get off the dime to start moving; to get out of a stopped position. (Slang.) ☐ *Why don't you get off the dime and complete some of these projects that you started?* ☐ *As soon as the board of directors gets off the dime on this proposal, we will have some action.*

get off the hook to be relieved of a responsibility. (Idiomatic.) ☐ *I'm glad I don't have to go to the meeting. I was quite happy to get off the hook.* ☐ *I wanted to get off the hook on that issue, but I'm stuck with it.*

get off to a bad start See *get off on the wrong foot.*

get off to a good start See *get off on the right foot.*

get off to sleep to manage to get to sleep finally. ☐ *About midnight everyone finally got off to sleep.* ☐ *I wasn't able to get off to sleep until dawn.*

get off to something to leave for something. ☐ *I've got to get off to my violin lesson.* ☐ *We have to get off to the hospital immediately!*

get off with someone to move aside with someone to discuss something. ☐ *I got off with Charles and we discussed the contract.* ☐ *We got off with the client and explained the offer a little better.*

get off with something to receive only a light punishment for something. ☐ *Let's hope John gets off with a light sentence.* ☐ *Max got off with only a few years in prison.*

get some weight off one's feet to sit down. (Colloquial.) ☐ *Come in and get some weight off your feet.* ☐ *I need to sit down and get some weight off my feet.*

get someone off to get someone cleared of a criminal charge. ☐ *Ted's lawyer got him off, although we all knew he was guilty.* ☐ *I hope someone can get her off. She is innocent no matter how it looks.*

get someone off the hook to get someone freed from a responsibility. (*Someone* includes *oneself.*) ☐ *I think I can get you off the hook for next Friday.* ☐ *What do I need to do to get myself off the hook?*

get someone or something off (of) someone or something to remove someone or something from someone, oneself, or something. (*Someone* includes *oneself.*) ☐ *Come in and get those wet clothes off yourself.* ☐ *Get him off of me!* ☐ *Get that guy off my clean sofa!* ☐ *You get yourself off that ladder right now!*

get something off one's chest to unburden oneself; to confess something; to criticize or make a personal complaint to someone. ☐ *You will feel better if you get it off your chest.* ☐ *I have to get this off my chest. I'm tired of your rudeness to me!*

get something off the ground **1.** to get something into the air. ☐ *I'll announce the weather to the passengers as soon as we get the plane off the ground.* ☐ *I hope they get this plane off the ground soon.* **2.** to get something started. (Figurative.) ☐ *When we get this event off the ground we can relax.* ☐ *It is my job to get the celebration plans off the ground.*

get something off (to someone or something) to send something to someone or something. ☐ *I have to get a letter off to Aunt Mary.* 🅃 *Did you get off all your packages?* ☐ *I have to get this parcel off to the main office.*

Where do (you think) you get off? "What do you think you are doing?"; "Who do you think you are?" (Slang.) ☐ *How rude! Where do you think you get off?* ☐ *Where do you get off, talking to me like that?*

GET ▸ ON

See also under *GET ▸ ON(TO).*

get a grip on oneself to get oneself under control. ☐ *Calm down, man! Get a grip on yourself!* ☐ *I encouraged him to get a grip on himself.*

get a grip on something **1.** AND **get a hold on something** to get a good grasp on something. ☐ *Try to get a grip on the* *ropes and pull yourself up.* □ *You should get a hold on the knob and turn it firmly.* **2.** to learn something thoroughly. □ *I need to get a grip on the basics of accounting.* □ *Try to get a hold on all the facts first.*

get a hold on something See the previous entry.

get a move on to hurry up. (Usually a command.) □ *Get a move on! We are going to be late!* □ *Get a move on, Polly!*

get it on **1.** to begin something. (Slang.) □ *Come on, man! Let's get it on! What are you waiting for?* □ *Get it on! We have to get going.* **2.** to have sexual intercourse. (Slang.) □ *She said he said he had to get it on.* □ *They are always sneaking off somewhere to get it on.*

get on to get along; to thrive. □ *Well, how are you two getting on?* □ *We are getting on okay.*

get on in years to grow older; to be aged. □ *Aunt Mattie is getting on in years.* □ *They were both getting on in years.*

get on one's horse to prepare to leave. (Slang. Usually with no horse present.) □ *It's time to get on my horse and get out of here.* □ *I've got to get on my horse and go.*

get on someone's case to begin to pick on someone; to begin to try to solve someone's problems. (Slang.) □ *Are you going to get on my case too?* □ *Please stop getting on my case all the time.*

get on someone's nerves to annoy someone. □ *You are beginning to get on my nerves.* □ *That radio is getting on my nerves.*

get on someone's wrong side See *get on the wrong side of someone.*

get on the bandwagon AND **hop on the bandwagon** to adopt the popular opinion; to begin to do what everyone else is doing. (Informal.) □ *Larry is not the kind to get on the bandwagon right away.* □ *Some people will hop on the bandwagon no matter what the cause is.*

get on the good side of someone AND **get on someone's good side** to gain favor with someone. □ *I tried to get on the good side of the teacher, but that teacher has no good side.* □ *First of all, don't try to get on the boss's good side.*

get on the stick to get busy; to become alert and efficient. (Slang.) □ *Get on the stick, you twit!* □ *You people had better get on the stick and do your jobs.*

get on the wrong side of someone AND **get on someone's wrong side** to get out of favor with someone. □ *Don't get on the wrong side of her.* □ *I do what I can not to get on the wrong side of people.*

get on to someone to catch on to what someone is doing; to see through someone's deception. □ *By the time we got on to the con artists, they were out of town.* □ *The sheriff was on to Jed, and Jed wanted to get out of town fast.*

get on with someone to get along with someone. □ *How does Colleen get on with Tracy?* □ *I hear that Mary gets on with Henry quite well.*

get on with something to continue doing something. □ *Let's get on with the game!* □ *We need to get on with our lives.*

get on without someone or something to survive and carry on without someone or something. □ *I think we can get on without bread for a day or two.* □ *Can you get on without your secretary for a while?*

get one on one's feet AND **put one on one's feet** to get someone back to normal, financially, medically, mentally, etc. □ *When I get Tom on his feet, he will buy a new car.* □ *We will put him on his feet and help him along.* □ *When I get myself on my feet, things will be better.*

get one's hands on someone or something See under *put one's hands on someone or something* under *PUT ▸ ON.*

get something on to put on an article of clothing. □ *Go get your boots on, and we'll go out for a long walk.* 🅃 *Get on your coat and hat so we can leave.*

get something on its feet AND **put something on its feet** to get something organized and functioning; to get something started up and functioning. □ *Trying to get this company on its feet is harder than I thought.* □ *What will it take to put this company on its feet again?*

get something on someone or something to find out bad things about someone or something; to find damning evidence against someone or a group. □ *I've gotten something on Albert that would really shock you.* □ *The state prosecutor has gotten something on the city council.* □ *She is trying to get something on her husband so she can divorce him.*

get started on something to begin doing something; to take the first steps to do something. □ *When do we get started on this project?* □ *I want to get started on this right away.*

get the drop on someone to draw a gun faster than someone else. (Gangster and cowboy slang.) □ *The cop got the drop on Max.* □ *Jed tried to get the drop on the sheriff, but he failed badly.*

get the edge on someone to be slightly ahead of someone; to have a slight advantage over someone. □ *I know I can get my story filed first and I really want to get the edge on my competitors.* □ *Mary was always trying to get the edge on Chuck.*

get the goods on someone to find conclusive and damning evidence against someone. (Slang.) □ *The state prosecutor got the goods on Max and threw him in jail.* □ *The sheriff had been trying to get the goods on Jed for a long time.*

get the jump on someone to do something before someone else does; to do something before one's competitor does. (Slang.) □ *Each reporter is trying to get the jump on the others with the story about the earthquake.* □ *Kelly finally got the jump on Sam.*

get the lowdown on someone or something to find out the story about someone or something. (Slang.) □ *I want to get the lowdown on what happened at the club last night.* □ *He got the lowdown on Tom.*

get the upper hand on someone to get into a position that dominates someone; to achieve dominion over someone. (Informal.) □ *Mr. Franklin has to get the upper hand on everyone he deals with.* □ *There is no point in trying to get the upper hand on the boss.*

GET ▸ ON(TO)

get on(to) someone (about something) to remind someone about something. □ *I'll have to get onto Sarah about the deadline.* □ *I'll get on Gerald right away.*

get on(to) something **1.** to get aboard something; to climb on something. □ *Get onto the wagon and join the rest of us.* □ *Get on the bus quickly.* **2.** to pick up a telephone receiver to talk to someone. □ *I'll get onto the extension and talk with Fred.* □ *I'll get on the phone and call Fran right away.*

get someone on(to) someone or something to assign someone to attend to someone or something. □ *Get someone onto the injured man in the hall right now.* □ *Get someone on the telephone switchboard at once!*

GET ▸ OUT

get a kick out of someone or something to get pleasure or a thrill from someone or something. (Informal.) □ *I really get a kick out of her stories.* □ *We all get a kick out of Heidi.*

get a rise out of someone to provoke a response from someone. □ *I thought that remark would get a rise out of you.* □ *It did not get a rise out of Chuck. It only made him mad.*

get out [for something] to become publicly known. □ *We don't want the secret to get out.* □ *The word soon got out that he had a prison record.*

get out from under someone or something **1.** to move from beneath someone or something. □ *Will you please get out from under my bed?* □ *The dog got out from under her just before she sat down.* **2.** to get away from the control of someone or something. □ *Finally, she got out from under her mother.* □ *He *was never able to get out from under the boss and perform on his own.*

get out of a mess to get out of trouble; to get out of some unpleasant involvement. (Also with *this, that,* etc.) □ *Please help me get out of this mess.* □ *What do I have to do to get out of this mess?*

get out of one's face to stop bothering or intimidating someone. (Slang.) □ *Look, get out of my face, or I'll poke you in yours!* □ *Get out of my face, you creep!*

get out of someone's sight to go away immediately. (Said in anger.) □ *Get out of my sight!* □ *Please get out of my sight forever!*

get out of someone's way AND **get out of the way** to move out of the path or route. □ *Will you please get out of the way?* □ *The dog got out of the way just before I stepped on it.*

get out (of something) **1.** to escape from something. □ *I've got to get out of here.* □ *Max wanted to get out of jail, but didn't know how.* □ *He doubted that he would get out alive.* **2.** to get free of the responsibility of doing something. □ *Are you trying to get out of this job?* □ *You agreed to do it, and you can't get out of it!*

get out (of something) to depart from something or some place. □ *I've got to get out of here!* □ *Go on, get out!*

get out of the wrong side of the bed AND **get up on the wrong side of the bed** to have done something that puts one in a bad mood. (Figurative.) □ *Wow! She really got out of the wrong side of the bed this morning.* □ *I'm afraid that I got up on the wrong side of the bed this morning.*

get out while the getting's good to escape while escape is still possible. (Colloquial and idiomatic.) □ *Come on. Let's get out while the getting's good.* □ *I decided to get out while the getting was good.*

get out with it to manage to get something said. (Colloquial.) □ *Stop stuttering around! Get out with it!* □ *Get out with it! I don't have all day!*

get out with something to escape with something intact, such as one's life, one's head, one's wallet, etc. □ *That's a rough place to visit. I just barely got out of there with my wallet and watch!* □ *We were lucky to get out of the flooded areas with our lives.*

get some kind of mileage out of something to get [sufficient] use or service from something. (Both literal and figurative senses. *Some kind of* typically includes *more, better, good,* etc.) □ *I wish I could get better mileage out of this car.* □ *He knows how to get a lot of mileage out of a pair of shoes.*

get someone or something out of one's head AND **get someone or something out of one's mind** to remove thoughts or images of someone or something from someone's thinking. □ *Forget her! Get her out of your head.* □ *I can't seem to get this melody out of my head.* □ *As hard as she tried, Mary couldn't get Ken out of her mind.*

get someone or something out of one's sight to remove someone or something from one's presence. (Often said in anger.) □ *Get that child out of my sight!* □ *Please get that cake out of my sight.*

get someone or something out of someone or something to release or extricate someone or something from someone, something, or some place. (*Someone* includes *oneself.*) □ *See if you can get the cat out of this cabinet.* □ *I can't get the nail out of the board.* □ *We have to operate and get those bullets out of this guy.* □ *Sally could not get herself out of the mess she was in.*

get someone or something out of the way to remove someone or something out of the path or route. □ *Get your big feet out of my way!* □ *Please get your child out of the way!*

get someone out of a jam to get someone out of trouble. (Slang. *Someone* includes *oneself*. Other forms, such as *this* and *that,* can replace *a*.) □ *Thanks for getting my brother out of that jam.* □

How am I going to get myself out of this jam?

get something out **1.** to remove or extricate something. □ *Please help me get this splinter out.* 🅃 *Would you help me get out this splinter?* □ *The tooth was gotten out without much difficulty.* **2.** to manage to get something said. □ *He tried to say it before he died, but he couldn't get it out.* □ *I had my mouth full and couldn't get the words out.*

get something out in the open to reveal something publicly. □ *Let's get this out in the open where everyone can know what's been going on.* □ *I want to get this whole matter out in the open.*

get something out of one's system **1.** to eliminate something harmful from the body, usually through defecation or perhaps by vomiting. □ *When you get all that out of your system, you'll feel better.* □ *I need to get this illness out of my system.* **2.** to do something that one has been afraid to do for a very long time. □ *I went ahead and ate the whole pie and got that craving out of my system.* □ *I feel better now that I have gotten it out of my system.* **3.** to do so much of something that one does not want or need to do it anymore. □ *I got riding roller coasters out of my system when I was young.* □ *He has to get some of this rebelliousness out of his system.* □ *I got all my sadness out of my system.*

get something out of someone to cause or force someone to give specific information. □ *We will get the truth out of her yet.* □ *The detective couldn't get anything out of the suspect.* □ *They got a confession out of him by beating him.*

get something out of someone or something to remove something from someone or something. □ *He probably will be okay when they get the tumor out of him.* □ *Please get that dog out of the living room.*

get something out of the way to get something completed; to finish something and not have it to worry about any longer. □ *Let's get the housecleaning out of the way before we go to the beach.* □ *I hope we can get this matter out of the way and get along to more important things.*

get the most out of someone or something to achieve the greatest output of work, effort, production, etc., out of someone or something. □ *I do what I can to get the most out of life.* □ *I try to get the most out of my employees.*

GET ▶ OUTSIDE

get outside of something to exit something or some place; to manage to get outside of something. □ *I got outside of the building just before the explosion.* □ *Let's get outside of this place where the air is fresher.*

GET ▶ OVER

get an advantage over someone to get into a position superior to someone; to get the upper hand on someone. □ *I want to get an advantage over him before I ask him to help me.* □ *If I can get an advantage over Roger, I can win.*

get over someone or something **1.** to move or climb over someone or something. □ *Fred was slumped ahead of me in the trench. I managed to get over him and moved on toward the big gun at the other end.* □ *I couldn't get over the huge rock in the path, so I went around it.* **2.** to recover from difficulties regarding someone or something. □ *I almost never got over the shock.* □ *Sharon finally got over Tom. He had been such a pest.*

get over something to recover from a disease. □ *It took a long time to get over the flu.* □ *I though I would never get over the mumps.*

get over (to some place) **1.** to go to some place. □ *I have to get over to Molly's place and pick up some papers.* □ *Go ahead and start without me. I'll get over as soon as I can.* **2.** to cross over something to get somewhere. □ *I want to get over to the other side.* □ *I can't find a way to get over!*

get over (with) [for something] to conclude; to come to an end. □ *I hope this thing gets over with pretty soon.* □ *When will the lecture get over?*

get someone over a barrel to have one in an awkward position, so that one is likely to capitulate. □ *I'm afraid he's got you over a barrel.* □ *I want to get him over a barrel to get even.*

get something over (to someone) **1.** to deliver something to someone. □ *Get these papers over to Mr. Wilson's office right away.* □ *He needs it now, so try to get it over as soon as you can.* **2.** to make someone understand something; to succeed in explaining something to someone. □ *I finally got it over to him.* □ *He tries to understand what I'm talking about, but I can't get it over.*

get something over (with) AND **get something over and done with** to bring something to a conclusion. □ *I'll be glad when we get this over with.* □ *I want to get this over and done with as soon as possible.*

GET ▸ PAST

get past (someone or something) **1.** to move around or ahead of someone or something that is in the way. □ *We have to get past the cart that is blocking the hallway.* □ *We just couldn't get past.* **2.** to pass ahead of someone or something that is moving. □ *I want to get past this truck, then we can get into the right lane.* □ *When we get past, I'll stop and let you drive.*

get something past someone or something **1.** to move something around or ahead of someone or something that is in the way. □ *Let's get the piano past the bump in the floor, then we'll figure out how to move it farther.* □ *See if you can get the trunk past Mary, who is blocking the way.* **2.** to get someone or a group to approve something; to work something through a bureaucracy. □ *Do you think we can get this past the censors?* □ *I will never get this past Mr. Franklin.*

GET ▸ THROUGH

get someone or something through (to someone or something) to manage to get someone or something transported or connected to someone or something. (*Someone* includes *oneself.*) □ *I hope I can get her through to her hometown in Italy.* □ *Do you think I can get this parcel through to Istanbul?* □ *You'll never get that through.* □ *Is there any way I can get myself through to Budapest on tonight's train?*

get someone through (something) **1.** to manage to help someone get through some kind of barrier. (*Someone* includes *oneself.*) □ *I will do what I can to get you through the front office. From then on, it's up to you.* □ *The first stage is difficult. I can help you get through, but not beyond that.* □ *I cannot get myself through that wall of humanity.* **2.** to help someone survive some ordeal. (*Someone* includes *oneself.*) □ *The doctors got her through her ordeal.* □ *We will get you through. Don't worry.* □ *We helped him get himself through the initiation.*

get someone through to someone or something to manage to get something to someone or some place. □ *Can I get a message through to Rome?* □ *I hope Bob can get word through to his cousin.*

get something through someone's thick skull See under *GET ▸ INTO.*

get through (something) **1.** to complete something; to manage to finish something. □ *I can't wait till I get through school.* □ *I'll get through in five years instead of four.* **2.** to penetrate something. □ *We couldn't get through the hard concrete with a drill, so we will have to blast.* □ *The hardest drill bit we have couldn't get through.*

get through to someone or something **1.** to make contact, usually on the telephone, with someone or a group. □ *I could not get through to her until the end of the day.* □ *Harry couldn't get through to his office.* **2.** to manage to get one's message, feelings, desires, etc., understood by someone or a group. □ *I am really angry! Am I getting through to you?* □ *Nancy really wanted to get through to the bank and they just seemed to ignore her.*

get through with someone or something **1.** to finish with someone or something. □ *I can't wait to get through with this lecture.* □ *Every student was anxious to get through with the professor.* **2.** to manage to transport someone or something through difficulties or barriers. □ *Customs was a mess, but we got through with all our baggage in only twenty minutes.* □ *I got through with my aged father without any trouble.*

GET ▸ TO

get access to someone or something to have permission to approach someone or something; to have the right to use someone or something. □ *I finally managed to get access to Brian so I could question him.* □ *I need to get access to a special book in the library.*

get close to someone to become friendly or intimate with someone. □ *She really won't let anyone get close to her.* □ *It is difficult to get close to Wally.*

get close to someone or something **1.** to come near to someone or something. □ *Don't get close to me. I have a cold.* □ *If you get close to the fire, you may get burned.* **2.** to approximate someone or something in some quality or measure. □ *This brand of frozen fish does not even get close to that brand in flavor and freshness.* □ *Tom doesn't even get close to Nancy when it comes to artistic ability.*

get (down) to work (on someone or something) to begin to deal with someone or something; to start working seriously with someone or something. □ *We are meeting to discuss what to do about Tom. Let's get down to work on him.* □ *Please get to work on the revisions.* □ *Let's get to work.*

get hip to someone or something to learn about someone or something; to adapt to someone or something. (Slang.) □ *The boss began to get hip to Mary.* □ *She finally began to get hip to what was going on.*

get home to someone or something to manage to return home to someone or something there. □ *The infantryman wants to get home to his wife.* □ *I like to get home to a nice warm house.*

get something home to someone or something to carry something home [quickly] to someone or something. □ *I have to get this pizza home to my parents before it gets cold.* □ *Please get this ice cream home to the refrigerator.*

get something to someone to have something delivered or transported to someone. □ *Will you please get this to Joe Wilson today?* □ *I'll try to get it to you by the end of the day.*

get to first base (with someone or something) to make some sort of progress with someone or something. (Informal.) □ *I couldn't get to first base with the proposal for the project.* □ *We talked and talked, but I didn't even get to first base.*

get to someone to bother someone. (Informal.) □ *This kind of rudeness really gets to me.* □ *Is this unpleasantness beginning to get to you?* □ *She really gets to me sometimes.*

get to someone or something to manage to reach someone or something. (Either physically or with a message.) □ *I got to her on the telephone and told her what to do.* □ *I simply couldn't get to the office before it closed.*

get to the bottom of something to get to the basis of a problem or issue. □ *Let's get to the bottom of this problem once and for all.* □ *The boss told us to get to the bottom of the problem at once.*

get to the point (of something) to arrive at the purpose of something. □ *Please get to the point of all this.* □ *Will you kindly get to the point?*

get to the top (of something) **1.** to get to the highest point of something. □ *We finally got to the top of the mountain and planted the flag.* □ *We had tried twice before to get to the top.* **2.** to work up to the highest status in something. □ *She got to the top of her field in a very short time.* □ *It takes hard work to get to the top.*

get used to someone or something to become accustomed to someone or something. □ *Sharon can't get used to Harry.* □ *I don't think I will ever get used to this postmodern architecture.*

get wise to someone or something to figure out what is going on with someone or a group; to figure out what dishonesty someone or a group is practicing. □ *The teacher finally got wise to the boys in the back row.* □ *I think you should get wise to the city council.*

GET ▶ TOGETHER

get it (all) together to organize oneself, physically or mentally. (Slang.) □ *I hope I can get it all together soon and start living like a normal person.* □ *Someday, I'll manage to get it together.*

get one's act together to organize oneself; to get oneself onto a schedule. (Slang.) □ *I've got to get my act together and start getting my work done.* □ *Why don't you get your act together and get a job?*

get one's head together to organize oneself mentally. (Slang.) □ *I've got to get my head together and get going.* □ *I need to take some time off and get my head together.*

get one's stuff together to assemble one's possessions. (Slang.) □ *I've got to get my stuff together and get going.* □ *Will you all please get your stuff together so we can get going?*

get someone or something together to gather people or things together. □ *Let's see if we can get both sides together and discuss this.* □ *I want to get Tom and Sharon together for a conference.*

get something together (for something) to arrange a party or other gathering for a certain time. □ *I'll try to get a meeting together for Friday afternoon.* □ *I'm sure we can get something together.*

get together **1.** [for people] to meet together or come together. □ *Let's get together for a meeting next Friday.* □ *When can we get together?* Ⓝ *Are you coming to my little get-together tomorrow night?* **2.** [for a couple] to have a date. □ *Can we get together next Friday evening?* □ *Let's get together sometime.*

get together (with someone) (about someone or something) to meet with someone about someone or something. □ *I want to get together with you two about this problem.* □ *I will get together about the new members with the rest of the committee.*

get together (with someone) (on someone or something) **1.** to meet with someone about someone or something. □ *I would like to get together with you on this Wilson matter. What would be a good time for you?* □ *Let's get together on Fred.* □ *Let's get together with Tom and Sharon.* **2.** to agree with someone about someone or something. □ *I would like to get together with you on this, but we are still nowhere near agreement.* □ *I want to get together on price with the suppliers.*

GET ▶ UNDER

get someone or something under control to restrain someone or something; to get someone or something functioning in an orderly fashion. (*Someone* includes *oneself*.) □ *Please try to get your friend under control.* □ *Can you get your dog under control?* □ *Please try to get yourself under control!*

get someone or something under something to manage to move someone or something beneath something. □ *Get this box under the table where it won't be seen.* □ *See if you can get the children under the table during the storm.*

get someone under one's thumb to get control over someone; to gain dominion over someone. □ *She couldn't wait to get him under her thumb.* □ *I don't want to get you under my thumb. I just want you to stop doing things that are harmful to you.*

get something under one's belt **1.** to eat some food; to get food into one's stomach. □ *I need to get something solid under my belt. I've had it with soup.* □ *I want to get a nice juicy steak under my belt.* **2.** to have achieved something; to score something. (Figurative.) □ *Minnie has over four hundred wins under his belt.* □ *This fighter pilot has over 150 kills under his belt.* **3.** to learn how to do something. (Figurative.) □ *Finally, she got good painting techniques under her* *belt.* ☐ *When I get the right procedures under my belt, I will be more efficient.*

get under someone's skin to irritate someone. (Slang.) ☐ *You are beginning to get under my skin.* ☐ *All the loud music and smoke finally began to get under his skin.*

get under something to get beneath something. ☐ *The cat came in and got under the sofa where she couldn't be seen.* ☐ *Why don't you get under the table where Billy won't find you?*

GET ▸ UP

get enough nerve up (to do something) AND **get the nerve up (to do something)** to work up enough courage to do something. (Also with other nouns: *courage, guts, pluck, spunk,* etc.) ☐ *I hope I can get enough nerve up to ask her for her autograph.* 🅃 *I wanted to do it, but I couldn't get up enough nerve.* 🅃 *I thought he would never get up the courage to ask me for a date.*

get (oneself) up to arise from bed; to rise to one's feet. ☐ *I've got to get myself up and get going.* ☐ *Come on! Get up!* ☐ *Get yourself up and get going.*

get (oneself) up-to-date to modernize oneself. ☐ *Buy some new clothes and get yourself up-to-date.* ☐ *You should try to get up-to-date.* ☐ *Please do what you can to get yourself up-to-date.*

get someone or something up against something to stand or line someone or something up against something. (*Someone* includes *oneself.*) ☐ *Let's get these sandbags up against the door quickly!* ☐ *Get a few people up against the door and tell them to hold it closed.* ☐ *Get yourself up against that wall!*

get someone up to wake someone up; to get someone out of bed. (*Someone* includes *oneself.*) ☐ *I've got to get John up, or he will be late for work.* ☐ *Can you get yourself up, or should I call you?*

get someone up (for something) to get someone into peak condition for something; to prepare someone for something. ☐ *I hope we can get Walter up for the race.* ☐ *Sharon was not quite prepared for the race, and the trainer did everything possible to get her up.*

get someone's back up to get someone or oneself angry; [for someone] to become stubborn or recalcitrant. (Refers to the way a cat puts its back up when it is threatening.) ☐ *I knew she would get her back up if I tried to tell her what to do.* ☐ *Please don't get your back up.*

get someone's blood up to get someone or oneself angry. (Figurative.) ☐ *That kind of language really gets my blood up.* ☐ *That will really get his blood up!*

get someone's dander up to get someone or oneself angry. (Figurative.) ☐ *You make me so mad! I really get my dander up when I have to deal with you.* ☐ *That kind of thing really gets his dander up.*

get something sewed up to finish something; to get something secured. ☐ *As soon as I get the Wilson contract sewed up, we can discuss Mr. Franklin's project.* ☐ *I will get this all sewed up soon.*

get something up to organize, plan, and assemble something. ☐ *Let's get a team up and enter the tournament.* 🅃 *I think we can get up a team quite easily.* 🅃 *She got a party up on very short notice.*

get something wrapped up to get something completely finished. ☐ *We'll get this contract wrapped up in no time at all.* ☐ *I hope we can get this wrapped up soon.*

get up a thirst to do something that will make one thirsty. (Colloquial.) ☐ *Jogging makes me get up a thirst.* ☐ *Doing this kind of work always gets up a thirst with me.*

get up against someone or something to press close against someone or something. ☐ *I got up against the wall, out of the way.* ☐ *The child got up against his father to stay warm.*

get up an appetite to do something to make one very hungry. ☐ *He can't seem to get up an appetite these days.* ☐ *Whenever I jog, I really get up an appetite.*

get up from something to go to a standing position from a lower position.

☐ *She got up from the chair and walked to the door.* ☐ *I don't want to get up from this hammock unless I just have to.*

get up in the world to become famous and wealthy. ☐ *By the looks of that new car, I see you are getting up in the world.* ☐ *Mary is getting up in the world.*

get up off (of) something to rise up and get off something. (The *of* is colloquial.) ☐ *Please get up off the sofa. I have to turn the cushions over.* ☐ *Get up off of me!*

get up on one's hind legs to get angry and assertive. (Figurative.) ☐ *She got up on her hind legs and told them all to go to blazes.* ☐ *She has a tendency to get up on her hind legs and tell people off.*

get up on the wrong side of the bed See *get out of the wrong side of the bed* under *GET ▸ OUT.*

get up something to manage to climb something. ☐ *I was so tired I couldn't get up the stairs.* ☐ *The entire group was able to get up the side of the mountain.*

get up steam to begin to be stronger and more powerful. (Figurative. As a steam locomotive builds enough pressure to start to move.) ☐ *The movement to cut taxes is getting up steam.* ☐ *Our little organization just couldn't get up enough steam to become effective.*

get up to something **1.** to climb up to something. ☐ *We finally got up to the top.* ☐ *How long will it take to get up to the top of the building?* **2.** to arrive as far as something. ☐ *We got up to the halfway point and stopped.* ☐ *Will we ever get up to the second floor?*

get up with something **1.** to move up even with something. ☐ *When I get up with Fred, I can expend a little less energy.* ☐ *I want to get up with that truck and see if I know the driver.* **2.** to arise from bed with something, such as a fever, a headache, a cold, a sore throat, etc. ☐ *I got up with a headache this morning.* ☐ *Quite often, I get up with a sore throat.*

get worked up (about someone or something) AND **get worked up (over someone or something)** to get excited or angry about someone or something. ☐ *I hate to get worked up about this kind of thing.* ☐ *Now, now. Don't get worked up over Sam.* ☐ *There's no need to get worked up.*

GET ▸ WITH

get even with someone to get revenge on someone; to pay someone back for something. ☐ *I will get even with you yet!* ☐ *She intends to get even with me.*

get involved with someone or something to become associated with someone or something. ☐ *I don't want to get involved with those people.* ☐ *Heidi got involved with the city zoo as a volunteer.*

get smart with someone to begin acting fresh with someone; to be impertinent with someone. (Informal.) ☐ *Don't get smart with me!* ☐ *I wish you wouldn't get smart with me.*

get someone with child to cause a woman to conceive. (Biblical. Stilted or euphemistic. *Someone* includes *oneself.*) ☐ *The first thing he did after he got married was to get his wife with child.* ☐ *She deliberately set out to get herself with child, as they say.*

get something going with someone to start a romance or affair with someone. (Informal.) ☐ *Todd got something going with Amy, and they both look pretty happy.* ☐ *I want to get something going with Chuck.*

get with something to modernize; to act up-to-date. (Slang.) ☐ *Get with it, you nerd!* ☐ *I wish you guys would get with it and win this ball game.*

GET ▸ WITHIN

get within something to get inside of something, such as a container, a room, range of gunfire, boundaries, etc. ☐ *You won't be able to hear what they are saying until you get within range of the P.A. system.* ☐ *As soon as I got within earshot of the music, I decided that I really didn't belong there.*

GIGGLE ▸ AT

giggle at someone or something to snicker or chuckle at someone or something. □ *Are you giggling at me?* □ *Fran giggled at the antics of the clown.*

GIVE ▸ AWAY

give someone away (to someone) **1.** [for the bride's father] to give the bride away to the groom. □ *Mr. Franklin gave Amy away to Terry just as he had done in the rehearsal.* □ *He was reluctant to give his daughter away.* **2.** to reveal something secret about someone to someone else. (*Someone* includes *oneself.*) □ *Please don't give me away. I don't want anyone to know my plans.* □ *Alice did everything she could to keep from giving herself away.* 🄽 *You guessed it! What was the giveaway?*

give something away (to someone) **1.** to donate to, or bestow something upon, someone. □ *I gave the old clothing away to Tom.* 🅃 *I gave away my coat to Tom.* □ *Don't just give it away!* 🄽 *I don't think I want any giveaways, thank you.* **2.** to tell a secret to someone. □ *Please don't give the surprise away to anyone.* 🅃 *Don't give away my secret.* □ *I had planned a surprise party but Donna gave it away.* **3.** to reveal the answer to a question, riddle, or problem to someone. □ *Don't give the answer away to them!* 🅃 *Don't give away the answer!* □ *Carla would have figured it out, but the audience gave it away.*

GIVE ▸ BACK

give someone or something back (to someone or something) to return someone or something to someone or something. □ *Please give it back to me.* □ *You took Gloria away from me. You had better give her back.* □ *She gave the pencil back to the carpenter.*

give something back (to someone) (with interest) **1.** to return money to someone with an additional amount for interest. □ *You are going to have to give that money back to me with interest.* □ *Please give it back!* **2.** to return something to someone in excess of what was received. □ *We will give back all your kindness to you with interest.* □ *We will give it all back with interest.*

GIVE ▸ FOR

give cause for something to serve as a just cause for something; to warrant something. □ *Your comments give cause for further investigation.* □ *I didn't give cause for you to do anything.*

give someone credit (for something) AND **give credit to someone (for something)** **1.** to praise someone for doing something. (*Someone* includes *oneself.*) □ *I think you have to give Brian credit for finding the money.* □ *You have to give credit to Brian. He works so hard.* □ *We must all give credit to Sharon.* □ *I guess I don't give myself enough credit for what I can do.* **2.** to praise someone for having a particular quality. □ *We give her a lot of credit for her ability to get people to work out their differences.* □ *We will give credit to Sharon for her good humor.* **3.** to grant a credit to someone's account as an adjustment for some other transaction. □ *I will give you credit for the returned merchandise.* □ *We gave credit to Brian for the check he sent us.*

give something for something **1.** to exchange something for something. □ *I will give two ducks for a hen.* □ *Jed gave two pigs for an old motorcycle.* □ *I'll give you two dollars for one of those cakes.* **2.** to give back what one was given. □ *Don't hit me! I will give blow for blow.* □ *I will give you two punches for every one you land on me.*

GIVE ▸ FORTH

give forth with something AND **give out with something** to say or shout something. □ *The kids in the street gave forth with cries of excitement.* □ *Walter gave out with a loud whoop when he heard the good news.*

GIVE ▸ IN

give in to cave in; to push in. □ *The rotting door gave in when we pushed, and we went inside.* □ *The wall gave in where I kicked it.*

give in (to someone or something) to give up to someone or something; to capitulate to someone or something. □ *Why do I always have to give in to you?* □ *I'm the one who always gives in.*

GIVE ▸ OF

give an account of someone or something (to someone) AND **give someone an account of someone or something** to tell a narrative about someone or something to someone. (The first *someone* includes *oneself.*) ☐ *You are going to have to give an account of yourself to your parole officer.* ☐ *Please give an account of your day to my secretary.* ☐ *Give me an account of every minute.*

give evidence of something to show signs of something; to give proof of something. ☐ *You are going to have to give evidence of your good faith in this matter. A nominal deposit would be fine.* ☐ *She gave evidence of being prepared to go to trial, so we settled the case.*

give of oneself to give one's time and effort without stint. ☐ *She always gives of herself when she is needed.* ☐ *I don't mind giving of myself, if it's for a good cause.*

GIVE ▸ OFF

give off something to release something, such as smoke, a noise, an odor, fragrance, etc. ☐ *The little animal gave off a foul smell.* ☐ *The flower gave off its heavy perfume at dusk.*

GIVE ▸ ON

give someone a pat on the back to congratulate or praise someone. (*Someone* includes *oneself.*) ☐ *Let's all give Andrew a pat on the back.* ☐ *She gave herself a pat on the back for her patience.*

GIVE ▸ OUT

give out 1. to wear out and stop; to quit operating. ☐ *My old bicycle finally gave out.* ☐ *I think that your shoes are about ready to give out.* **2.** to be depleted. ☐ *The paper napkins gave out and we had to use paper towels.* ☐ *The eggs gave out and we had to eat pancakes for breakfast for the rest of the camping trip.*

give out with something See under *GIVE ▸ FORTH.*

give something out 1. to distribute something; to pass something out. ☐ *The teacher gave the test papers out.* 🅃 *The teacher gave out the papers.* **2.** to make something known to the public. ☐ *When will you give the announcement out?* 🅃 *The president gave out the news that the hostages had been released.*

GIVE ▸ OVER

give oneself over to someone or something 1. to surrender to someone or something. ☐ *He went to the station and gave himself over to the police.* ☐ *Max gave himself over to the officer.* **2.** to devote oneself to someone or something. ☐ *Laurie gave herself over to her work and soon forgot her pain.* ☐ *David gave himself over to the religious order.* ☐ *She had long ago given herself over to morning walks and evening meditation.*

give something over (to someone or something) to hand something over to someone or something. ☐ *Please give the money over to Sherri, who handles the accounts.* ☐ *She is waiting at the front office. Just go there and give it over.*

GIVE ▸ TO

give (an) ear to someone to listen to someone; to pay special attention to what someone says. ☐ *Sally wants you to give an ear to her before you leave.* ☐ *Please give ear to me.*

give (an) ear to something to listen carefully to what is being said. ☐ *Please give an ear to what she is saying.* ☐ *Give ear to what I have to say.*

give birth to someone or something to have a child; [for an animal] to bring forth young. ☐ *She gave birth to a baby girl.* ☐ *The cat gave birth to a large number of adorable kittens.*

give birth to something to bring forth a new idea, an invention, a nation, etc. (Figurative.) ☐ *The company gave birth to a new technology.* ☐ *The basic idea of participatory democracy gave birth to a new nation.*

give chase to someone or something to chase someone or something. ☐ *The police gave chase to the crooks for a few blocks.* ☐ *The dogs gave chase to the cyclists.*

give credence to someone or something to believe someone or something. ☐ *How can you give credence to a person like Henry?* ☐ *I can't give any credence to Donald.*

give credit to someone (for something) See *give someone credit for something* under *GIVE ▸ FOR.*

give currency to something to utter something around; to spread something that is likely to be untrue. ☐ *I can't give any currency to anything Ralph Jones says.* ☐ *We give no currency to those stories.* ☐ *His actions gave currency to the rumor that he was about to leave.*

give rise to something to cause something; to instigate something. ☐ *The attack gave rise to endless arguments.* ☐ *Her comments gave rise to further speculation as to the source of her money.*

give something to someone to bestow something, such as a gift, on someone. ☐ *Please give this to Sally Wilson.* ☐ *Who gave this book to me? I want to thank whoever it was.*

give teeth to something AND **put teeth in(to) something** to make something powerful; to give something a real effect. (Figurative.) ☐ *The severe penalty really gives teeth to the law.* ☐ *Strong enforcement puts teeth in the regulation.*

give the lie to something to show that something is a lie. ☐ *The evidence gives the lie to your testimony.* ☐ *Your own admission of your part in the conspiracy gives the lie to your earlier testimony.*

give voice to something to utter something; to say something that one has worried about. ☐ *Finally, she gave voice to her concerns.* ☐ *Tom gave voice to his basic concern.*

give way to someone or something to yield to someone or something; to give preference to someone or something. ☐ *The cars gave way to the pedestrians.* ☐ *The motorboats have to give way to the sailboats.*

give weight to something to attach importance to something. ☐ *I give a lot of weight to your opinion.* ☐ *Kelly gave no weight at all to the comments by Betty.*

GIVE ▸ UNDER

give something under something to give something because of something, such as a promise, threat of something, an oath, etc. ☐ *He gave the money under threat of exposure. I think that is blackmail.* ☐ *You will have to give the same testimony under oath. Is that all right?*

GIVE ▸ UP

give oneself up to someone or something 1. to surrender to someone or something. ☐ *Walter gave himself up to Agent Bond.* ☐ *Fran gave herself up to the disease.* ☐ *Walter gave himself up to the police.* 2. to devote oneself to someone or something; to *give oneself over to someone or something.* ☐ *She gave herself up to her children and their care.* ☐ *Fran gave herself up to tennis.* ☐ *Jane refused to give herself up to weightlifting, which is a full-time hobby.*

give someone a leg up 1. to provide a knee as a support for someone to place a foot on to get higher, as in mounting a horse, or climbing over something. ☐ *I gave her a leg up, and soon she was on her horse.* ☐ *Can I give you a leg up?* 2. to give someone a helping hand; to give someone a boost. ☐ *Please give me a leg up with this heavy carton.* ☐ *I needed for someone to give me a leg up. I was too tired to do it all myself.*

give someone or something up (for lost) to abandon someone or something as being lost; to quit looking for someone or something that is lost. ☐ *We had given the cat up for lost when she suddenly appeared.* 🅃 *We gave up the cat for lost.* ☐ *We gave her up for lost.* ☐ *We looked and looked but had to give him up.*

give someone or something up (to someone) to hand someone or something over to someone or something; to relinquish claims on someone or something in favor of someone else. ☐ *We had to give the money we found up to the police.* 🅃 *We gave up the money to the police.* ☐ *Mary still wanted it, but she had to give it up.*

give someone up for dead **1.** to give up hope for someone who is dying; to abandon a dying person as already dead. □ *The cowboys gave up their comrade for dead and rode off.* [T] *We gave up the poor old man for dead and went to telephone the police.* **2.** to abandon hope for someone's appearance. □ *We were delighted to see you. We had almost given you up for dead.* [T] *After an hour, they gave up their guest for dead.*

give something up **1.** to forsake something; to stop using or eating something. □ *I gave coffee up because of the caffeine.* [T] *They advised me to give up sugar in all forms.* **2.** to quit doing something. (Informal.) □ *Oh, give it up! You're not getting anywhere.* [T] *You should give up smoking.*

give up to quit; to quit trying. □ *I give up! I won't press this further.* □ *Are you going to give up or keep fighting?*

give up (all) hope to stop hoping for something. □ *Don't give up hope. There's always a chance.* □ *We had given up all hope when a miracle happened.*

give up (on someone or something) to give up trying to do something with someone or something, such as being friendly, giving advice, managing, etc. □ *I gave up on jogging. My knees went bad.* □ *Gloria tried to be friendly with Kelly, but finally gave up.*

give up the fight AND **give up the struggle** **1.** to quit fighting; to stop trying to do something. □ *Don't give up the fight. Keep trying.* □ *Mary refused to give up the struggle.* **2.** to give up and die. □ *At the end of months of pain, she gave up the fight.* □ *In the end, even after the operation, he gave up the struggle.*

give up the ghost to die. (Euphemistic or jocular.) □ *At about noon, she gave up the ghost.* □ *You looked so peaceful, sleeping there. For a while, I was afraid you had given up the ghost.*

GIVE ▸ WITH

give with something to give something to someone. (Slang.) □ *Come on! Give with the money!* □ *You had better give with the information if you know what's good for you.*

GLANCE ▸ AROUND

glance around (some place) to look quickly around some place. □ *He glanced around the room, looking for his friend.* □ *Mary glanced around, looking for her friend.*

GLANCE ▸ AT

glance at someone or something to look quickly at someone or something. □ *Sharon glanced at Todd to see if he looked as if he was ready to go.* □ *I glanced at my watch and realized how long all this had taken.*

GLANCE ▸ BACK

glance back (at someone) **1.** to look quickly again at someone. □ *He glanced back at Mary, so he could remember her smile.* □ *She saw him briefly, but never even glanced back.* **2.** to look quickly at someone who is behind you. □ *Dan glanced back at the man chasing him and ran on even faster.* □ *He glanced back and ran faster.*

GLANCE ▸ DOWN

glance down (at something) to look quickly downward at something. □ *Sherri glanced down at her watch and then pressed on the accelerator.* □ *She glanced down and hurried off.*

GLANCE ▸ OFF

glance off ((of) someone or something) to bounce off someone or something. (The *of* is colloquial.) □ *The bullet glanced off the huge boulder.* □ *The baseball glanced off of Tom and left a bruise on his side where it had touched.* □ *The stone glanced off the window glass without breaking it.*

GLANCE ▸ OVER

glance over someone or something to examine someone or something very quickly. □ *I only glanced over the papers. They look okay to me.* □ *The doctor glanced over the injured woman and called for an ambulance.*

GLANCE ▸ THROUGH

glance through something to look quickly at the contents of something. □

I glanced through the manuscript, and I don't think it is ready yet. ☐ *Would you glance through this when you have a moment?*

GLARE ▸ AT

glare at someone or something to scowl at someone or something. ☐ *Don't glare at me!* ☐ *I glared at the cat and thought mean thoughts.*

GLARE ▸ DOWN

glare down on someone or something **1.** [for someone] to scowl down at someone or something. ☐ *The judge glared down on the accused.* ☐ *I glared down on the cat, which ignored me, as usual.* **2.** [for the sun] to burn down brightly on someone or something. ☐ *The sun glared down on the beach and the steaming bodies that were unfortunate enough to be born pale.* ☐ *The bright sun glared down on the desert rocks.*

GLASS ▸ IN

glass something in to enclose something, such as a porch, in glass. ☐ *I want to glass this porch in, so we can use it in the winter.* 🅃 *We glassed in our porch last year.*

GLAZE ▸ OVER

glaze over [for something] to be covered over with a coat of something cloudy or ice. ☐ *The roads glazed over and became very dangerous.* ☐ *The street is glazed over badly.* ☐ *Todd's eyes glazed over when he thought of his narrow escape.*

GLEAM ▸ WITH

gleam with something to sparkle or shine with something. ☐ *The crystal goblets gleamed with the sparkling candlelight.* ☐ *The glass gleamed with a bright reflection.*

GLEAN ▸ FROM

glean something from someone See under the following entry.

glean something from something **1.** to gather the leftovers of something from something; to gather the ears of grain left in a field after a harvest. ☐ *The poor people gleaned their entire living from what was left in the fields.* ☐ *We will have to go out and glean something from the fields.* **2.** AND **glean something from someone** to figure something out from bits of gossip. ☐ *I was able to glean some important news from Tommy.* ☐ *Tell me the news you gleaned from the people in town.* ☐ *From what I can glean from the newspapers, things are going all right.*

GLIDE ▸ ACROSS

glide across something to float or slide across something. ☐ *The skaters glided across the frozen expanse of the river.* ☐ *The small plane glided across the sky.*

GLIDE ▸ AWAY

glide away (from someone or something) to slide or float away from someone or something. ☐ *The skaters glided away from the center of the rink.* ☐ *The canoes glided away from the judge who had started off the canoe race.*

GLIDE ▸ OFF

glide off to slide or float away. (Can be figurative.) ☐ *The clouds glided off and the sun became very hot.* ☐ *Marsha glided off as silently as she arrived.*

GLINT ▸ WITH

glint with something to sparkle or glint with something. ☐ *Her bright eyes glinted with the sunlight.* ☐ *The crystal goblet glinted with the orange firelight.*

GLISTEN ▸ WITH

glisten with something to sparkle or shimmer with something. ☐ *The trees glistened with a thin coating of sleet.* ☐ *Fran's eyes glistened with a few tears.*

GLITTER ▸ WITH

glitter with something **1.** to sparkle with something. ☐ *Her earrings glittered with many tiny diamonds.* ☐ *The tree glittered with tiny ice crystals.* **2.** [for eyes] to shine with strong emotion. ☐ *Her eyes glittered with anger.* ☐ *The eyes of the great beast glittered with ravenous hunger.*

GLOAT ▸ OVER

gloat over something to rejoice smugly over something; to be glad that something unfortunate has happened to someone else. ☐ *He gloated over his* *good luck in a way that made all of us angry.* ☐ *Please don't gloat over my misfortune.*

GLORY ▸ IN

glory in something to take great pleasure in something; to revel in something. ☐ *He just glories in all the attention he is getting.* ☐ *Gloria tends to glory in doing things just exactly right.*

GLOSS ▸ OVER

gloss over something to cover up, minimize, or play down something bad. ☐ *Don't gloss over your own role in this fiasco!* 🅃 *I don't want to gloss this matter over, but it really isn't very important, is it?* 🄰 *These glossed-over matters will have to be dealt with properly at some time.*

GLOW ▸ WITH

glow with something **1.** [for something] to put out light, usually because of high heat. ☐ *The embers glowed with the remains of the fire.* ☐ *The last of the coals still glowed with fire.* **2.** [for someone's face, eyes, etc.] to display some quality, such as pride, pleasure, rage, health. ☐ *Her healthy face glowed with pride.* ☐ *Tom's eyes glowed with eager expectation.* ☐ *Her eyes glowed with a towering rage.*

GLOWER ▸ AT

glower at someone or something to scowl intently at someone or something. ☐ *The judge glowered at the witness until order was restored.* ☐ *Fred glowered at the painting of his uncle, hating the subject of the picture.*

GLUE ▸ DOWN

glue something down to fix something down onto something with cement. ☐ *Glue the edge of the rug down before someone trips over it.* 🅃 *You should glue down the rug.* 🄰 *The glued-down quarter fooled a lot of people.*

GLUE ▸ ON(TO)

glue something on((to) something) AND **glue something to something** to attach something to something else with cement. ☐ *Please glue the binding onto this book. Someone pulled it off.* 🅃 *Please glue on the binding.* ☐ *Could you glue the leg back on this chair?*

GLUE ▸ TOGETHER

glue something together to attach the pieces of something together with glue. ☐ *She glued the pieces of the model plane together.* 🅃 *She glued together all the loose pieces.*

GLUT ▸ WITH

glut someone or something with something to overfill someone or something with something. (*Someone* includes *oneself.*) ☐ *She gluts her children with food—there's no wonder they are fat.* ☐ *Don't glut the cat with too much fish!* ☐ *Sally would glut herself with doughnuts, given the chance.*

GNAW ▸ AT

gnaw (away) at someone to worry someone; to create constant anxiety in someone. ☐ *The thought of catching some horrible disease gnawed away at her.* ☐ *A lot of guilt gnawed at him day and night.*

gnaw (away) at someone or something to chew at someone or something. ☐ *I hear a mouse gnawing away at the wall.* ☐ *The mosquitoes are gnawing at me something awful.*

GNAW ▸ AWAY

See the two previous entries.

GNAW ▸ ON

gnaw on something to chew on something. (Usually said of an animal.) ☐ *The puppy has been gnawing on my slippers!* ☐ *This slipper has been gnawed on!*

GO ▸ ABOUT

go about AND **go around** **1.** [for a rumor] to go from person to person. ☐ *What is this story about you that I hear going about?* ☐ *There was a nasty rumor about Gerald going around.* **2.** [for a disease] to spread. ☐ *There is a lot of this flu going about these days.* ☐ *There is a bad cough going around.*

go about one's business to mind one's own business and to continue with one's own activities. ☐ *Please go about your business. Pay no attention to us.* ☐ *I* *had nothing to do with it. I was just going about my business when it happened.*

go about something to approach the doing of something in a particular way. □ *How should I go about researching this topic?* □ *Would you tell me how to go about it?*

go about with someone or something AND **go around with someone or something** to go around in the company of someone or something. □ *I always go about with my friends.* □ *Fran has been going around with James.*

go overboard about someone or something to exceed what is necessary regarding someone or something. □ *No need to go overboard about the visit of the president of the board. A small reception would be quite appropriate.* □ *I wish you wouldn't go overboard about Mary.*

GO ▶ ABOVE

go above and beyond one's duty AND **go above and beyond the call of duty** to exceed what is required of one. (Idiomatic.) □ *Doing what you ask goes above and beyond my duty.* □ *My job requires me to go above and beyond the call of duty almost every day.*

go above someone See *go over someone('s head)* under *GO ▶ OVER.*

go above someone or something to travel over someone or something. □ *The model airplane went above us at the last minute.* □ *Fortunately, the bird went above the house at the last instant.*

GO ▶ ACROSS

go across (something) to cross something, such as water, a bridge, land, the ocean, etc. □ *We went across the ocean in just three hours.* □ *How long did it take you to go across?*

go across something to someone or something to cross something to someone, something, or some place on the other side. □ *We went across the bridge to the island.* □ *We came upon a little foot bridge and went across to the other side.* □ *Timmy went across the bridge to his mother.*

GO ▶ AFTER

go after someone or something **1.** to pursue someone or something. □ *The dogs went after the burglar.* □ *I went after the gang that took my wallet.* **2.** to charge or attack someone or some creature. □ *The bear went after the hunters and scared them to death.* □ *Then the bear went after the hunting dogs and killed two.* **3.** to investigate someone or something for possible criminal prosecution. □ *The prosecutor went after Max first, knowing that Max was generally no good.* □ *The police detectives went after the whole gang.* **4.** to follow someone or something; to come in sequence after someone or something. □ *Mary went first and I went after her.* □ *The ones beginning with N go after those beginning with M.*

GO ▶ AGAINST

go against someone or something to disfavor someone or something; to turn against someone or something; to oppose someone or something. □ *When did the trial go against us?* □ *The weather went against the cruise on the second day out.*

go against the grain **1.** to rub or cut across the alignment of the grain of a piece of wood. □ *You sawed it wrong. You went against the grain when you should have cut the length of the grain.* □ *You went against the grain and made a mess of your sanding.* **2.** [for something] to run counter to one's feelings or ideas. (Figurative.) □ *The idea of actually taking something that is not mine goes against the grain.* □ *Your proposal goes against the grain.*

GO ▶ AHEAD

go ahead of someone or something to get in front of and proceed someone or something. □ *Please let me go ahead of you.* □ *The car carrying the parade marshall went ahead of the others.*

go ahead with something **1.** to continue with something; to continue with plans to do something. □ *Can we go ahead with our party plans?* □ *Let's go ahead with it.* 🄽 *The board of directors gave the go-ahead for the project.* **2.** to carry something ahead. ☐ *Please go ahead with the baggage. I will meet you at the ticket counter.* ☐ *Will you please go ahead with the cake? I will bring the ice cream in a minute.*

GO ▸ ALONG

go along **1.** to continue; to progress. ☐ *Things are going along quite nicely.* ☐ *I hope everything is going along well.* **2.** to accompany [someone]. ☐ *Can I go along?* ☐ *If you're going to the party, can I go along?*

go along (with someone) for the ride **1.** to accompany someone just to be taking a ride. ☐ *Why don't you go along with us for the ride?* ☐ *I am going to the store. Do you want to come along for the ride?* **2.** to accompany someone. (Figurative.) ☐ *I'll just go along for the ride. I don't want to play golf with you.* ☐ *He wasn't invited to the party. He just went along for the ride.*

go along with someone or something **1.** to agree with someone or agree to something. ☐ *I will go along with you on that matter.* ☐ *I will go along with Sharon's decision, of course.* **2.** to consent on the choice of someone or something. ☐ *I go along with Jane. She would be a good treasurer.* ☐ *Sharon will probably go along with chocolate. Everyone likes chocolate!*

GO ▸ AROUND

go around See also under *GO ▸ ABOUT.*

go around to serve a need; to serve all who have a need. ☐ *There's not enough coffee to go around.* ☐ *Will there be enough chocolates to go around?*

go around doing something to move around doing something. ☐ *She keeps going around telling lies about me.* ☐ *Please stop going around knocking things over.* ☐ *She goes around helping whomever she can.*

go around in circles **1.** to move on a circular path. ☐ *The model plane went around in circles until it ran out of fuel.* ☐ *The oxen went around in circles, pulling along a beam that was connected to the millstone.* **2.** to act in a confused and disoriented manner. (Figurative.) ☐ *I've been going around in circles all day.* ☐ *The children have been going around in circles, waiting for you to arrive.*

go around someone to avoid dealing with someone. (Figurative.) ☐ *I try to go around Steve. He can be very difficult.* ☐ *We will want to go around the boss. He will say no if asked.*

go around (someone or something) to pass around someone or something. ☐ *I went around the garbage can, but Steve bumped right into it.* ☐ *The other pedestrians went around Steve, who sat at the base of the pole, dazed.*

go around the bend **1.** to follow a turn in the road or pathway. ☐ *The car went around the bend.* ☐ *I saw the train go around the bend in the distance.* **2.** to go crazy. (Figurative.) ☐ *Poor Sam went around the bend last week.* ☐ *I was afraid I was going around the bend.*

go around with someone or something See *go about with someone or something* under *GO ▸ ABOUT.*

GO ▸ AS

go as someone or something to pretend to be someone or a type of person. ☐ *There's a costume party this weekend. I'm going as Santa Claus.* ☐ *My husband and I are going as bananas.*

GO ▸ ASTRAY

go astray **1.** to wander off the road or path. ☐ *Stick to the path and try not to go astray.* ☐ *I couldn't see the trail and I almost went astray.* **2.** [for something] to get lost or misplaced. ☐ *My glasses have gone astray again.* ☐ *Mary's book went astray or maybe it was stolen.* **3.** to turn bad or wander from the way of goodness; to make an error. ☐ *I'm afraid your son has gone astray and gotten into a bit of trouble.* ☐ *I went astray with the computer program at this point.*

GO ▸ AT

go at one another tooth and nail to fight one another like animals. (Figurative. *One another* can be *each other.*) ☐ *The man and his wife went at one another tooth and nail.* ☐ *The children* *would go at one another tooth and nail almost every evening.*

go at someone or something to attack or charge someone or something. ☐ *The bear went at the hunter and then retreated.* ☐ *She went at him and hit him.* ☐ *The alligator suddenly swam forward and went at the boat, thrilling the tourists within.*

GO ▸ AWAY

go away to leave. (Often a command.) ☐ *Go away and leave me alone.* ☐ *Please go away!*

go away for something **1.** to leave for a period of time. ☐ *I have to go away for a week or two.* ☐ *Sharon went away for a few days.* **2.** to leave in order to get something and bring it back. ☐ *Excuse me. I have to go away for a soft drink.* ☐ *He went away for a pizza. He'll be right back.*

go away with someone or something **1.** to leave in the company of someone or something. ☐ *I saw him go away with Margie.* ☐ *She went away with the others.* **2.** to take someone, some creature, or a group away with one. ☐ *He went away with the baby in his arms.* ☐ *He went away with the package.*

GO ▸ BACK

go back to return to the place of origin. ☐ *That's where I came from, and I'll never go back.* ☐ *I don't want to go back.*

go back on something to reverse one's position on something, especially one's word or a promise. ☐ *You went back on what you promised! Can't I trust you?* ☐ *I don't want to go back on my word, but there has been an emergency.* ☐ *I hope she doesn't go back on her word.*

go back to someone or something to return to someone, something, or some place. ☐ *She went back to her husband after a few months.* ☐ *Sharon had to go back to her office for a few minutes.*

go back to square one to return to the starting point. (Figurative. Refers to the squares of a board game.) ☐ *It's back to square one. We have to start over.* ☐ *It looks like it's back to square one for you.*

go back to the drawing board to return to the planning stage, so that a failed project can be planned again. (Figurative.) ☐ *These plans have to go back to the drawing board.* ☐ *I thought these problems went back to the drawing board once already.*

go back to the salt mines to return to one's work. (Refers to slave labor working in salt mines. Often in the expression, **Back to the salt mines.** Idiomatic.) ☐ *It's late. I have to go back to the salt mines.* ☐ *What time do you have to go back to the salt mines Monday morning?*

GO ▸ BEFORE

go before someone or something **1.** to precede someone or something. ☐ *Do you wish to go before me?* ☐ *I will go before the other waiters and clear the aisles.* **2.** to appear before someone or something. ☐ *Sharon went before a magistrate and laid out her complaint.* ☐ *Then Mary went before the entire board of directors.*

go (on) before (someone) **1.** to precede someone. ☐ *Please go on before me. I will follow.* ☐ *She went on before.* **2.** to die before someone. (Euphemism.) ☐ *Uncle Herman went on before Aunt Margaret by a few years.* ☐ *He went before her, although we had all thought it would be the other way around.*

GO ▸ BEHIND

go behind someone's back **1.** to move behind someone; to locate oneself at someone's back. ☐ *The mugger went behind my back and put a gun to my spine.* ☐ *Bob went behind my back and pushed me through the opening.* **2.** to do something that is kept a secret from someone. (Figurative.) ☐ *I hate to go behind her back, but she makes so much trouble about things like this.* ☐ *Please don't try to go behind my back again!*

GO ▸ BELOW

go below to go beneath the main deck of a ship. (Nautical.) ☐ *I will have to go below and fiddle with the engine.* ☐ *The* *captain went below to escape the worst of the storm.*

GO ▸ BETWEEN

go between someone or something and someone or something to get in between people or things, in any combination. □ *The dog went between Mr. Franklin and the wall.* □ *The arrow went between Jed and Tex, injuring neither of them.*

GO ▸ BEYOND

go beyond someone or something to pass ahead of someone or something. □ *I went beyond the place where I should have turned off.* □ *Fred went beyond me a half block before he remembered who I was. Then he came back and said hello.*

go beyond something 1. to do more of something than the expected amount; to go further with something than was required. □ *You clearly went beyond what was required of you.* □ *Sharon went beyond the basic requirements.* **2.** to go past something or some place. □ *We went beyond the town and lost our way.* □ *They went beyond the turnoff.*

GO ▸ BY

go by (some place) See *drop by (some place)* under *DROP ▸ BY.*

go by (someone or something) to pass by someone or something. □ *We went by Alice without even noticing her.* □ *We went by the store without stopping.* □ *We went by because we were in a hurry.*

go by the name of something to be known by a specific name. □ *She goes by the name of Gladys George.* □ *I used to go by the name of George.*

GO ▸ DOWN

go down 1. to sink below a normal or expected level or height. □ *The plane went down in flames.* □ *The ship went down with all hands aboard.* **2.** to descend to a lower measurement. □ *Her fever went down.* □ *The price of the stock went down yesterday.* **3.** to be swallowed. □ *The medicine went down without any trouble at all.* □ *The food simply would not go down. The puppy was going to starve.* **4.** to fall or drop down, as when struck or injured. □ *Sam went down when he was struck on the chin.* □ *The deer went down when it was hit with the arrow.*

go down in defeat AND **go down to defeat** to submit to defeat. □ *The team went down in defeat again.* □ *She fears going down in defeat.* □ *The team went down to defeat in every game this season.*

go down in flames to fail spectacularly. (Figurative slang. Also literal, nonslang uses.) □ *The whole project went down in flames.* □ *Todd went down in flames in his efforts to win the heart of Marsha.*

go down (in history) (as someone or something) to be recorded for history as a significant person or event. □ *You will go down in history as the most stubborn woman who ever lived.* □ *She will go down as a very famous woman.* □ *George went down in history as a great compromiser.*

go down on one's knees to kneel down. □ *The people went down on their knees and prayed.* □ *Larry went down on his knees and asked for forgiveness.*

go down something to descend something; to fall down something. □ *She went down the ladder very carefully.* □ *I did not want to go down those steep stairs.*

go down the chute AND **go down the drain; go down the tube(s)** to fail; to be thrown away or wasted. (Slang.) □ *Everything we have accomplished has gone down the chute.* □ *The whole project went down the drain.* □ *I hate to see all my hard work go down the tubes!*

go down the drain See *go down the chute.*

go down the line to go from person to person or thing to thing in a line of people or things. □ *She went down the line, asking everyone for a dollar for a cup of coffee.* □ *Sam went down the line, passing out tickets.*

go down the tube(s) See *go down the chute.*

go down to defeat See *go down in defeat.*

go down to someone or something to travel to someone, something, or some place that is downtown, at a lower level, or in the south. □ *We went down to Amy's aunt in Memphis.* □ *Fran went down to Tiffany's place on the first floor.*

go down to something [for something] to decline or diminish to some level. □ *His temperature has gone down to normal.* □ *Will the temperature go down to freezing tonight?*

go down with something to be stricken with a disease. □ *Beth went down with the flu.* □ *She went down with a high fever.*

GO ▶ FOR

go for broke to risk all one's money; to risk everything. (Slang.) □ *I went for broke and bet everything on the horses.* □ *I decided to go for broke and make a bet.*

go for nothing **1.** [for something] to be done for no purpose. □ *All our work went for nothing.* □ *Our efforts at helping out went for nothing.* **2.** [for something] to be sold for a very low price. □ *This merchandise can go for nothing.* □ *I don't want this good stuff to just go for nothing.*

go for someone or something **1.** to go out for someone or something; to go fetch someone or something. □ *I am going for bread—do we need anything else from the store?* □ *Roger went for his aunt, who had arrived at the station.* **2.** to find someone or something interesting or desirable. □ *I really go for chocolate in any form.* □ *Tom really goes for Gloria in a big way.*

go for something to make the effort to do or get something. □ *Go for it!* □ *Keep trying to win. Go for the gold.*

go overboard for someone or something to do far more than is necessary for the benefit of someone or something. □ *Don't go overboard for us, please.* □ *There is no need to go overboard for the party Friday night.*

GO ▶ FORWARD

go forward with something to continue with something; to do something that is planned. □ *We will go forward with our plans.* □ *Let's go forward with the plan.*

GO ▶ FROM

go from bad to worse to progress from a bad situation to one that is worse. □ *Things went from bad to worse in a matter of days.* □ *I'm afraid that things are going from bad to worse.*

go from one extreme to the other to change from one thing to its opposite. (Idiomatic.) □ *Can't you get things in balance? You go from one extreme to another.* □ *Nothing is smooth here. Things go from one extreme to another.*

GO ▶ IN

go around in circles See under *GO ▶ AROUND.*

go in and out of something to pass in and out of something or some place. □ *The nervous little mouse kept going in and out of its hole.* □ *The cat kept going in and out of the back door.*

go in for something to enjoy doing something; to be fond of something. □ *Laurie goes in for skating and skiing.* □ *We don't go in for that kind of thing.*

go in one ear and out the other [for information or instruction] to fail to be understood by someone. (Informal.) □ *Everything I said went in one ear and out the other.* □ *Her comments went in one ear and out the other.*

go in someone's favor [for something] to change to someone's benefit. (Refers to very changeable things like game scores, wind direction, or chance in general.) □ *Things appear to be going in our favor—finally.* □ *The game was going in our favor during the first half.*

go in the right direction **1.** to head in the right direction. □ *Are you sure we are going in the right direction?* □ *We were supposed to turn back there. We are not going in the right direction.* **2.** to be progressing sensibly. □ *Well, everything seems to be going in the right direction—for now anyway.* □ *Do you* *feel that this project is going in the right direction?*

go in with someone (on something) to join efforts with someone on a project; to pool financial resources with someone to buy something. □ *I would be happy to go in with you on the charity ball. I'll find a hall.* □ *Yes, we can pool our money. I'll go in with you.* □ *Let's go in with Sally on a gift for Walter.*

GO ▸ INTO

go into a huddle **1.** [for team members] to get into a small circle and plan what they are going to do next. □ *They went into a huddle to plan their strategy.* □ *The players will go into a huddle and decide what to do.* **2.** [for people] to group together to talk and decide what to do. (Both literal and figurative uses.) □ *We went into a huddle to plan our sales strategy.* □ *We need to go into a huddle and come up with a good plan.*

go into action to begin doing something; to start to operate at full speed or efficiency. □ *The team really went into action after the first ten minutes.* □ *We went into action when we heard the alarm.* □ *They all went into action at dawn.*

go into one's act to begin one's act or performance; to begin to behave in a way typical to oneself. □ *The curtain opened and Steve went into his act.* □ *I go into my act whenever I hear my music.* □ *I went into my act and everyone thought I was back to normal.*

go into one's song and dance to begin to tell the same old story or give the same old explanation. □ *Please don't go into your song and dance about being the best in the world.* □ *I did not get an answer. He just went into his old song and dance about not having enough money.*

go into orbit **1.** [for a rocket, satellite, etc.] to rotate around a heavenly body in a fixed path. □ *The satellite went into orbit just as planned.* □ *When did the moon go into orbit?* **2.** [for someone] to get very excited. (Figurative slang.) □ *She was so upset, she went into orbit.* □ *Todd went into orbit when he heard the price.*

go into service to start operating. □ *When will the new elevator go into service?* □ *It has already gone into service.*

go into something **1.** to enter some line of business or a profession. □ *He went into accounting when he got out of college.* □ *I want to prepare to go into law enforcement.* **2.** to examine or study something; to discuss and explain something. □ *I need to go into this more.* □ *When we have time, we need to go into this question more thoroughly.* □ *The teacher went into the assignment in great detail.*

go into (the) service to enter one of the military services. □ *She went into the service when she got out of high school.* □ *I chose not to go into the service.* □ *When did your husband go into service?*

GO ▸ IN(TO)

go in((to)something) to enter something; to penetrate something. □ *The needle went into the vein smoothly and painlessly.* □ *It went in with no trouble.*

GO ▸ NEAR

go near (to) someone or something to approach someone or something. □ *Don't go near Sue. She's got chicken pox.* □ *Now, don't go near the water!*

GO ▸ OFF

go off **1.** [for an explosive device] to explode. □ *The fireworks all went off as scheduled.* □ *The bomb went off and did a lot of damage.* **2.** [for a sound-creating device] to make its noise. □ *The alarm went off at six o'clock.* □ *The siren goes off at noon every day.* **3.** [for an event] to happen or take place. □ *The party went off as planned.* □ *Did your medical examination go off as well as you had hoped?*

go off (by oneself) to go into seclusion; to isolate oneself. □ *She went off by herself where no one could find her.* □ *I have to go off and think about this.*

go off half-cocked to do something without sufficient preparation or thought. (Idiomatic.) □ *Please don't go off half-cocked. Listen to the rest of the re-*

port. □ *Sam has a tendency to go off half-cocked.*

go off into something to go away to something; to depart and go into something. □ *He went off into the army.* □ *Do you expect me just to go off into the world and make a living?*

go off on a tangent to pursue an irrelevant course while neglecting everything else. □ *Don't go off on a tangent. Stick to your job.* □ *Just as we started talking, Henry went off on a tangent about the high cost of living.*

go off the deep end to get overly involved in something; to overdo something. □ *Now, don't go off the deep end. Be sensible.* □ *He has a habit of going off the deep end about almost everything.*

go off with someone to go away with someone. □ *Tom just now went off with Maggie.* □ *I think that Maria went off with Fred somewhere.*

GO ▶ ON

go easy on someone or something to be gentle on someone or something; not to be too critical of someone or something; to take it easy on someone or something. □ *Go easy on Sherri. She's my friend.* □ *Try to go easy on the report. They did the best they could.*

go easy on something not to use too much of something. (Colloquial.) □ *Go easy on the catsup. There isn't very much left.* □ *I hope you will go easy on the water. There's a water shortage.*

go on 1. to continue. □ *Please go on.* □ *Can I go on now?* 2. to hush up; to stop acting silly. (Always a command. No tenses.) □ *Go on! You're crazy!* □ *Oh, go on! You don't know what you are talking about.* 3. to happen. □ *What went on here last night?* □ *The teacher asked what was going on.*

go on (and on) about someone or something to talk endlessly about someone or something. □ *She just went on and on about her new car.* □ *Albert went on about the book for a long time.*

go on at someone to rave at someone. □ *He must have gone on at her for over an hour—screaming and waving his arms.* □ *I wish you would stop going on at me.*

go (on) before (someone) See under *GO ▶ BEFORE.*

go on doing something See *go on with something.*

go on for an age AND **go on for ages** to continue for a very long time. □ *The symphony seemed to go on for an age.* □ *It seemed to go on for ages.*

go on for something to continue for a period of time. □ *The lecture went on for what seemed like days.* □ *She went on for an hour without pausing for questions.*

go on something 1. to begin something, such as a diet, rampage, drunk, etc. □ *I went on a diet for the second time this month.* □ *Fred went on a rampage and broke a window.* 2. to start acting on some information. □ *We can't go on this! We need more information before we can act on this matter!* □ *Can you please give us more information to go on?*

go on the block [for something] to go up for auction; [for something] to be placed on the auction block. □ *Our farm went on the block last week. Got a good price.* □ *When this painting goes on the block, I hope I get a lot for it.*

go on to something to advance to something or to doing something. □ *After a few years she went on to even greater heights.* □ *Larry went on to found his own company.*

go on tour [for a performing group] to go from place to place, performing. □ *Our play went on tour across the state.* □ *If we make the play a success, we will go on tour.*

go on with something AND **go on doing something** to continue with something. □ *I can't go on with this. I have to rest.* □ *You simply cannot go on doing this!*

go on (with you) to go away. (Always a command. No tenses.) □ *It's time you left. Go on with you!* □ *Go on. Get yourself home.*

GO ▸ OUT

go all out (for someone or something) to do everything possible for someone or something. ☐ *We went all out for George. We haven't seen him for weeks.* ☐ *We went all out and it was not appreciated at all.*

go out 1. to leave one's house. ☐ *Call me later. I'm going out now.* ☐ *Sally told her father that she was going out.* 2. to become extinguished. ☐ *The fire finally went out.* ☐ *The lights went out and left us in the dark.*

go out for someone or something to leave in order to bring back someone or something. ☐ *Albert just went out for a newspaper.* ☐ *Fran went out for Bob, who was on the back porch, smoking a cigarette.*

go out (for something) to try out for a sports team. ☐ *Walter went out for football in his junior year.* ☐ *Did you ever go out for any sports?*

go out for something to go outside to do something, such as smoke, or get something, such as fresh air. ☐ *Jeremy went out for a breath of fresh air.* ☐ *Let's go out for a drink.*

go out in search of someone or something to leave to find someone or something. ☐ *I went out in search of someone to help me.* ☐ *Mary went out in search of Gloria.*

go out like a light to pass out totally and quickly. (Informal.) ☐ *Max hit Lefty on the head, and he went out like a light.* ☐ *Henry fell and went out like a light.*

go out of bounds [for a player or the ball] to go outside the boundaries of the playing area. ☐ *The ball went out of bounds just at the end of the game.* ☐ *The whistle blew when Juan went out of bounds.*

go out of business to stop doing commerce or business. ☐ *The new shop will probably go out of business if things don't get better.* ☐ *I have to work hard to keep from going out of business.*

go out (of fashion) [for something] to stop being stylish. ☐ *That style went out of fashion a long time ago.* ☐ *I hope that this suit doesn't go out of fashion soon.* ☐ *That kind of hat went out years ago.*

go out of focus 1. [for the image seen in a camera] to become blurred. ☐ *I stepped back and the scene went out of focus, and I had to adjust the camera.* ☐ *I jarred the camera and the view went out of focus.* 2. [for something] to become blurred or hard to perceive. ☐ *My vision went out of focus, and then I passed out.* ☐ *I needed new glasses because everything was always going out of focus.*

go out of one's head AND **go out of one's mind** 1. to go crazy. ☐ *If I have to stay around here much longer, I'll go out of my head.* ☐ *I nearly went out of my mind, just sitting there doing nothing.* 2. to lose control of oneself. (Figurative.) ☐ *Whenever he drinks he almost goes out of his head.* ☐ *He read the letter and went out of his mind.*

go out of one's mind See *go out of one's head.*

go out of one's way (to do something) (for someone) to deviate from one's route to do something for someone; to put out extra effort to do something for someone. ☐ *I think I can go out of my way a little to drop this off for you.* ☐ *Please don't go out of your way to do it.* ☐ *I went out of my way to make that appointment for you!* ☐ *I won't go out of my way for you.*

go out of play [for a ball] to roll away out of the playing area so that the game stops. ☐ *The ball went out of play and the whistle was blown.* ☐ *When the ball went out of play, the referee blew the whistle.*

go out of service [for something] to stop working; [for something] to have been turned off so it cannot be used. ☐ *This elevator went out of service last week.* ☐ *How long has it been since this thing went out of service?*

go out of sight 1. [for something] to move so far away that it is no longer visible. ☐ *The rocket went out of sight before we could focus our cameras on it.*

☐ *As their car went out of sight, we remembered what they had forgotten.* **2.** [for the cost of something] to become extraordinarily high. (Figurative slang.) ☐ *The cost of gasoline is going out of sight.* ☐ *Food is going out of sight these days.*

go out (of something) to leave something or some place. ☐ *I went out of there feeling sorry for myself.* ☐ *I went out with a smile on my face.*

go out of something [for someone or something] to leave from something or some place. ☐ *She went out of the house for the last time and did not even look back once.* ☐ *Let's go out of the driveway carefully, watching for approaching cars.*

go out on a limb to put oneself into a dangerous position to do something; to risk something. (Figurative.) ☐ *I don't want to go out on a limb, but I think we can afford to do it.* ☐ *If I had to go out on a limb, I would say that it will be a month before your merchandise will be delivered.*

go out (on strike) to strike; to participate in a work stoppage. ☐ *The teachers are about to go out on strike.* ☐ *All the workers went out on strike.*

go out to someone [for one's sympathy, heart, etc.] to be aimed toward someone. ☐ *All of my sympathy went out to her. I knew just how she felt.* ☐ *My thanks go out to you all.*

go out to someone or something to go outside to someone, something, or some place. ☐ *Andrew went out to the car waiting in the drive.* ☐ *Janet went out to the man sitting on the front step and asked what he wanted.*

go out with someone to go on a date with someone; to date someone on a regular basis. ☐ *Will you go out with me next Saturday?* ☐ *Do you want to go out with Alice and Ted tomorrow night?* ☐ *Mary's parents are upset because she's going out with someone they don't approve of.*

go out with something to go out of fashion at the same time as something else went out of fashion. (Idiomatic.) ☐ *That style went out with the bustle.* ☐ *Your thinking went out with the horse and buggy.*

GO ▸ OVER

go ape over someone or something to get very excited over someone or something. (Slang.) ☐ *The kids went ape over the rapper.* ☐ *Betty went ape over one of the new pop singers.*

go over (somehow) [for someone or something] to be accepted or well received. ☐ *The party went over very well.* ☐ *The party really went over.*

go over someone or something to examine someone or something. ☐ *The doctor will go over you very carefully, I'm sure.* ☐ *I went over the papers and found nothing wrong.* 🄽 *The doctor gave the old man a good going-over.*

go over someone('s head) AND **go above someone** to go to an authority higher than someone. ☐ *I don't want to have to go over your head, but I will if necessary.* ☐ *I had to go over Fran to get it done.* ☐ *My boss wouldn't listen to my complaint, so I went above her.*

go over something to review something. ☐ *Susan went over the vocabulary before the French test.* ☐ *You should go over your notes between classes.*

go over the hill to escape from the military; to desert. (Slang.) ☐ *The guys who went over the hill got caught a day later.* ☐ *Max tried to go over the hill when he was in the military.*

go over the wall to escape from prison. (Slang.) ☐ *Max tried to go over the wall, but they caught him.* ☐ *Lefty went over the wall and was free for a week.*

go over to some place to travel to some place; to cross water to get to some place. ☐ *We went over to Cedar Point and spent the day having fun.* ☐ *John went over to the other side of the stadium for the rest of the tournament.*

GO ▸ OVERBOARD

go overboard (on someone or something) to lavish something on someone, a group, or something. ☐ *There is no need to go overboard on this group of* *people.* □ *Please don't go overboard on the party.* □ *No need to go overboard.*

GO ▸ PAST

go past someone or something to pass by someone or something. □ *You went right past Tom. Did you mean to?* □ *Did I go past it?* □ *Her performance goes past anything we have seen on this stage before.*

GO ▸ THROUGH

go (right) through someone AND **go through someone like a dose of salts** [for something] to be excreted very soon after being eaten; [for something] to go immediately through the alimentary canal of a person. (Use with discretion.) □ *No, thanks. This stuff just goes right through me.* □ *The coffee went through me like a dose of salts.*

go through to be approved; to pass examination; to be ratified. □ *I hope the amendment goes through.* □ *The proposal failed to go through.*

go through someone to work through someone; to use someone as an intermediary. □ *I can't give you the permission you seek. You will have to go through our main office.* □ *I have to go through the treasurer for all expenditures.*

go through someone like a dose of salts See *go (right) through someone.*

go through someone or something [for something sharp] to penetrate someone or something. □ *The sword went through the knight cleanly and quickly.* □ *The nail went through all three boards.*

go through something **1.** to search through something. □ *She went through his pants pockets, looking for his wallet.* □ *He spent quite a while going through his desk, looking for the papers.* **2.** to use up all of something rapidly. □ *We have gone through all the aspirin again!* □ *How can you go through your allowance so fast?* **3.** [for something] to pass through an opening. □ *The piano wouldn't go through the door.* □ *Do you think that such a big truck can go through the tunnel under the river?* **4.** to pass through various stages or processes. □ *The pickles went through a number of processes before they were packed.* □ *Johnny is going through a phase where he wants everything his way.* **5.** to work through something, such as an explanation or story. □ *I went through my story again, carefully and in great detail.* □ *I would like to go through it again, so I can be sure to understand it.* **6.** to experience or endure something. □ *You can't believe what I've gone through.* □ *Mary has gone through a lot lately.* **7.** to rehearse something; to practice something for performance. □ *They went through the second act a number of times.* □ *We need to go through the whole play a few more times.*

go through the changes to experience the changes and difficulties of life. □ *He's really been going through the changes lately.* □ *Timmy isn't going through the changes fast enough for me.*

go through the mill to experience difficulties; to advance by doing difficult things. (Usually with *have.*) □ *You look as if you've really gone through the mill.* □ *I know I am getting to that age when I'll really have to go through the mill.*

go through the motions to appear to be doing something; to do something perfunctorily but ineffectually. □ *You don't seem to be doing your job—just going through the motions, I'd say.* □ *She is just going through the motions. She can't seem to keep her mind on things.*

go through (the proper) channels to use the proper procedure, working through the correct people and offices to get something done; to cooperate with a bureaucracy. □ *I'm sorry. I can't help you. You'll have to go through the proper channels.* □ *I didn't get what I wanted because I didn't go through the proper channels.*

go through the roof **1.** to become very angry. (Colloquial.) □ *She saw what had happened and went through the roof.* □ *My father went through the roof when he saw what I did to the car.* **2.** [for prices] to become very high. □

These days, prices are going through the roof. □ *The cost of coffee is going through the roof.*

go through with something to complete something the outcome of which was in doubt; to do something in spite of problems and drawbacks. □ *I have to go through with it, no matter what.* □ *I just couldn't go through with it.*

GO ▸ TO

go to to go to hell. (Colloquial and euphemistic. Often a command.) □ *Oh, go to!* □ *Go to, you creep!*

go to bat against someone to aid someone against someone else. (Figurative.) □ *I would be happy to go to bat against Dan.* □ *We refused to go to bat against one of our friends.*

go to bat (for someone) to do something in support of someone. (Figurative.) □ *I knew that you would go to bat for me.* □ *I'm behind you all the way. I'm ready to go to bat anytime.*

go to bed to get into bed to sleep. □ *I went to bed about midnight.* □ *It's time for me to go to bed.*

go to bed (with someone) to have sexual intercourse with someone. (Not necessarily in bed.) □ *Someone said that Terry went to bed with Amy.* □ *She and Frank went to bed.*

go to bed with the chickens to go to bed at sundown—at the same time that chickens go to sleep. (Colloquial or folksy.) □ *They say that farmers go to bed with the chickens.* □ *We always go to bed with the chickens and get up early too.*

go to blazes to go to hell. (Euphemistic. Often a command.) □ *As far as I'm concerned, you all can go to blazes.* □ *Go to blazes, you creep!*

go to extremes (to do something) to be excessive in one's efforts to do something. □ *Dear Jane will go to extremes to make us all comfortable.* □ *Let's not go to extremes!*

go to hell to go to hell and suffer the agonies therein. (Often a command. Caution with *hell*.) □ *Oh, go to hell!* □ *Go to hell, you creep!*

go to it to start something actively; to do something with vigor. (Colloquial.) □ *Time to play ball. Go to it!* □ *Let's go to it, you guys!*

go to pieces **1.** [for something] to fall apart into many pieces. □ *The vase—which had been repaired many times—just went to pieces, there on the piano.* □ *When the window was hit by the ball, it went to pieces.* **2.** [for something] to become nonfunctional. (Figurative.) □ *His plan went to pieces.* □ *All her hopes and ideas went to pieces in that one meeting.* **3.** [for someone] to have a mental collapse. (Figurative.) □ *Poor Jane went to pieces after her divorce.* □ *Fred went to pieces during the trial.*

go to pot to degrade; to decline in value, status, utility, etc. (Slang.) □ *Everyone says the neighborhood is going to pot, and they want us to leave.* □ *This lawn is going to pot. We need to work on it.*

go to press [for a publication] to be sent to the printing presses. □ *The book went to press last week. We expect finished books by the first of the month.* □ *The book you want to order hasn't even gone to press yet.*

go to press (with something) [for someone] to cause something to be printed. □ *The columnist went to press with the rumor without checking any of her usual sources.* □ *We are going to press with a series of books on textiles.*

go to rack and ruin AND **go to wrack and ruin** to fall apart and be worthless; to go into a dilapidated state. □ *The whole project went to rack and ruin just because of you!* □ *Everything went to wrack and ruin!*

go to sea to become a sailor. □ *I went to sea at an early age.* □ *When I get older, I'm going to go to sea too.*

go to seed **1.** [for a plant] to produce seed; [for a plant] to spend its energy going to seed. □ *The lettuce went to seed and we couldn't eat it.* □ *Plants like that ought not to be allowed to go to seed.* **2.** [for a lawn or a plant] to produce seeds because it has not had proper care. □ *You've got to mow the grass. It's* *going to seed.* □ *Don't let the lawn go to seed. It looks so—seedy!* **3.** [for something] to decline in looks, status, or utility due to lack of care. (The same as *run to seed.*) □ *This old coat is going to seed. Have to get a new one.* □ *The front of the house is going to seed. Let's get it painted.*

go to someone (about someone or something) to discuss one's problems with someone or something with someone else. □ *I went to the boss about the new secretary.* □ *This is a real problem. I'll have to go to the manager.*

go to someone or something to travel to or toward someone or something. □ *We went to her as soon as she called saying she needed us.* □ *Are you going to the bank?*

go to someone's head **1.** [for something, such as fame or success] to make someone conceited. □ *Don't let all this praise go to your head.* □ *Too much success will go to her head.* **2.** [for alcohol] to affect someone's brain. □ *That last glass of champagne went right to her head.* □ *Any kind of liquor goes to my head.*

go to the bathroom **1.** to move or travel to the bathroom. □ *I'm going to the bathroom. Where do you think I am going?* □ *Please go to the bathroom and pick up the towel you used.* **2.** to urinate or defecate. (Euphemism.) □ *I have to go to the bathroom.* □ *We had to stop the car so Sam could go to the bathroom.*

go to the bother (of doing something) See *go to the trouble (of doing something).*

go to the bother (to do something) See *go to the trouble (to do something)*

go to the dogs to fall apart; to become ruined. □ *When everything seems to be going to the dogs, it's time for vacation.* □ *The whole meeting went to the dogs.*

go to the heart of the matter to get to the central point of a matter. □ *Now, the next speaker ought to go to the heart of the matter.* □ *I hope that her comments will go to the heart of the matter.*

go to the polls to go to a place to vote; to vote. □ *What day do we go to the polls?* □ *Our community goes to the polls in November.*

go to the trouble (of doing something) AND **go to the bother (of doing something)** to endure difficulties in doing something. □ *Please don't go to the trouble of cooking a big dinner.* □ *I don't need a big meal. There's no need to go to the bother.*

go to the trouble (to do something) AND **go to the bother (to do something)** to make the effort to do something. (*The* can be replaced with a variety of modifiers: *a lot of, a whole lot of, any, all the,* etc.) □ *Sally went to a lot of trouble to plan this party, so we really must attend.* □ *If she went to the trouble to do it, you ought to at least thank her.* □ *There's no need of going to all the bother to fix a large meal.*

go to the wall (on something) to hold out to the very last on some issue. □ *I will go to the wall on this point.* □ *This is a very important matter and I will go to the wall if necessary.*

go to town to move very rapidly; to do something with great vigor. (Informal.) □ *The team is really going to town.* □ *They weren't very good last year, but they're really going to town this year.*

go to trial [for a case] to go into court to be tried. □ *When will this case go to trial?* □ *We go to trial next Monday.*

go to war (over someone or something) to wage a war over someone or something. (Literal and figurative.) □ *We aren't going to go to war over this, are we?* □ *Do you want to go to war over Sarah? Is she that important to you?* □ *Calm down and behave yourself. You act as if you want to go to war.*

go to waste [for something] to be wasted or unused. □ *I hope all this pizza doesn't go to waste.* □ *I don't want any of the usable material to go to waste.*

go to work on someone to beat someone; to pressure someone in some way to do something. □ *Max went to work on Lefty, who gave in immediately.* □ *The* *police went to work on Paul, who told them what they wanted to know.*

go to work (on someone or something) to begin working on someone or something. ☐ *The masons went to work on repairing the wall.* ☐ *The surgeons went to work on the patient.* ☐ *Come on! Let's go to work!*

go to wrack and ruin See *go to rack and ruin.*

GO ▸ TOGETHER

go together **1.** [for things] to fit together; to belong together. ☐ *This sweater and these slacks go together perfectly.* ☐ *Your socks don't go together!* **2.** [for people] to date one another regularly. ☐ *They have been going together for two months.* ☐ *I don't think we should go together anymore.*

GO ▸ TO(WARDS)

go toward someone or something to move toward someone or something. ☐ *The child went toward the open door.* ☐ *The dog went toward the cat and the cat ran away.*

GO ▸ UNDER

go under **1.** to sink beneath the surface of the water. ☐ *After capsizing, the ship went under very slowly.* ☐ *I was afraid that our canoe would go under in the rapidly moving water.* **2.** [for something] to fail. (Figurative.) ☐ *The company went under exactly one year after it opened.* ☐ *We tried to keep it from going under.* **3.** to become unconscious from anesthesia. ☐ *After a few minutes, she went under and the surgeon began to work.* ☐ *Tom went under and the operation began.*

go under someone or something **1.** to pass beneath someone or something. ☐ *The boats went under us as we stood on the bridge.* ☐ *The boat went under the bridge.* **2.** to belong beneath someone or something. ☐ *That box goes under the bed.* ☐ *Max, the assassin, was told that the bomb went under the prime minister.*

go under the knife to submit to surgery; to have surgery done on oneself. (Colloquial.) ☐ *She goes under the knife tomorrow for her gall bladder.* ☐ *Frank lives in constant fear of having to go under the knife.*

go under the name of something [for someone or something] to be known under a particular name. ☐ *Now she goes under the name of Suzanne.* ☐ *The man you just met goes under the name of Walter Sampson.*

go under the wrecking ball to be wrecked or torn down. ☐ *That lovely old building finally went under the wrecking ball.* ☐ *I hate to see good architecture go under the wrecking ball.*

GO ▸ UP

go belly-up to fail; to die. (Slang. As with a dead fish.) ☐ *The business went belly-up after one year of operations.* ☐ *We did everything we could to keep the company from going belly-up.*

go up [for something] to go higher. ☐ *Gasoline prices are still going up.* ☐ *Prices keep going up and up, no matter what.*

go up against someone to compete with someone; to face someone in competition. ☐ *She is going up against Rodney in the spelling bee.* ☐ *The champ went up against the challenger in a match last Friday.*

go up in flames AND **go up in smoke** **1.** to burn up completely. ☐ *The entire forest went up in flames!* ☐ *The expensive house went up in smoke.* **2.** [for value or investment] to be lost suddenly and totally, as in a fire. (Usually figurative.) ☐ *Everything we own has gone up in flames.* ☐ *The entire investment went up in smoke.*

go up in smoke See *go up in flames.*

go up in the world to advance oneself in the world in terms of fame or wealth. ☐ *You will go up in the world. I can tell.* ☐ *Gerald went up in the world very fast for such a young man.*

go up something to climb up something. ☐ *The monkey went up the tree in no time.* ☐ *How fast can you go up this rope?*

go up the wall to exhibit great frustration, as if climbing up the wall in frustration. (Figurative.) ☐ *I was so upset, I* *almost went up the wall.* ☐ *We went up the wall waiting for you.*

go up to someone or something to approach someone or something. ☐ *The temperature will go up to near one hundred today.* ☐ *I went up to her and asked her for a match.*

GO ▶ WITH

go badly with someone or something [for something] to proceed badly for someone or something. ☐ *I hope that things are not still going badly with you.* ☐ *Things are going very badly with the project.*

go well with someone or something [for something] to proceed nicely for someone or something. ☐ *I hope things are going well with you.* ☐ *Things are going very well with the project.*

go with someone to date someone steadily. ☐ *Mary has been going with Jack for over two years.* ☐ *How long have you been going with her?*

go with (someone or something) to depart in the company of someone or a group. (Colloquial when the object of the preposition is omitted.) ☐ *Jim's not here. He went with the last busload.* ☐ *I'm leaving now. Do you want to go with?*

go with the flow to move along with the things or people around one. (Slang.) ☐ *I never fight the trend. I just go with the flow.* ☐ *I can't go with the flow. I am an independent thinker.*

go with the tide to move along with whatever forces touch one. ☐ *I just go with the tide. I never fight fate.* ☐ *She just goes with the tide, never giving a thought to thinking for herself.*

GO ▶ WITHOUT

go without saying to be understood and known without having to be said. ☐ *It goes without saying that you have not been a great help around here.* ☐ *That goes without saying.*

go without (someone) to manage without a particular type of person. ☐ *I can't go without a doctor much longer.* ☐ *I need a doctor now. I simply can't go without.*

go without (something) to manage without something. ☐ *We can go without food for only so long.* ☐ *I simply can't go without.*

GOAD ▶ INTO

goad someone into something to urge or coerce someone into doing something. ☐ *Don't try to goad me into it. I just won't do it!* ☐ *We goaded Mary into going with us.*

GOAD ▶ ON

goad someone on to urge someone onward, possibly with jeers or challenges; to urge someone to continue. ☐ *The cheering crowd goaded the team on to victory.* ☐ *I goaded Jed on to taking the risk.*

GOBBLE ▶ DOWN

gobble something down to eat something very fast, swallowing large chunks. ☐ *The dog gobbled the meat down in seconds.* ☐ *Don't gobble your food down.* 🆃 *The cat gobbled down the sardines.*

GOBBLE ▶ UP

gobble someone or something up to eat someone or something completely and rapidly. ☐ *The wolf said that he was going to gobble Red Ridinghood up.* 🆃 *The wolf wanted to gobble up the little girl.* ☐ *The dog gobbled the meat up.*

gobble something up to use up, buy up, or occupy all of something. ☐ *The shoppers gobbled all the sale merchandise up in a few hours.* 🆃 *They gobbled up everything.*

GOGGLE ▶ AT

goggle at someone or something to stare at someone or something with bulging eyes. ☐ *Don't stand there goggling at me!* ☐ *The child stood there and goggled at the newborn lamb.*

GOOF ▶ AROUND

goof around to act silly. (Slang.) ☐ *The kids were all goofing around, waiting for the bus.* ☐ *Stop goofing around!*

GOOF ▶ OFF

goof off to waste time. ☐ *Stop goofing off and get your work done.* ☐ *You are always goofing off when I need you.* 🅽

Gerald is just a goof-off and won't help out.

GOOF ▸ UP

goof someone or something up to mess someone or something up; to ruin someone's plans; to make something nonfunctional. (*Someone* includes *oneself.*) □ *Who goofed this machine up?* Ⓣ *Who goofed up the machine?* □ *You really goofed me up!* Ⓐ *Take that goofed-up television set away and bring us a new one.* □ *I was afraid I would goof myself up, but everything came out all right.*

goof up (on something) to make an error with something; to blunder while doing something. (Slang.) □ *Please don't goof up on this job.* □ *If you goof up one more time, you're finished.*

GOOSE ▸ UP

goose someone or something up to cause someone or something to function more rapidly, powerfully, responsively, etc. (Slang.) □ *She goosed the engine up and sped off.* Ⓣ *She goosed up the engine and sped off.* □ *Somebody needs to goose Frank up and get him working better.*

GORE ▸ TO

gore someone or something to death [for a horned animal] to kill someone or some creature with its horns. □ *The bull nearly gored the matador to death.* □ *The deer tried to gore the panther to death.*

GORGE ▸ ON

gorge oneself on something AND **gorge oneself with something** to eat something to the point of fullness. □ *Don't gorge yourself on the snacks. Dinner is in ten minutes.* □ *You have gorged yourself with cheese! No wonder you're not hungry.* □ *Claire gorged herself on the doughnuts that Fred bought.*

GORGE ▸ WITH

gorge oneself with something See the previous entry.

gorge someone or something with something to fill someone or something with something. (*Someone* includes *oneself.*) □ *She gorged the dog with canned food.* □ *Why does she gorge her daughter with snacks and stuff?* □ *The puppy gorged itself with all the hamburger Paul had set out to thaw.*

GOSSIP ▸ ABOUT

gossip about someone or something to talk maliciously about someone or something. □ *Who are you gossiping about now?* □ *They are gossiping about what happened last weekend.*

GOUGE ▸ OUT

gouge something out (of someone) to cheat someone out of something. (Compare to *chisel something out of someone.*) □ *They gouged the money out of the old man.* □ *The crooks gouged the life savings out of the old lady.*

gouge something out (of something) to scoop or chisel something out of something. (The *of*-phrase is paraphrased with a *from*-phrase when the particle is transposed. See the Ⓕ example.) □ *Tom gouged a horrible furrow out of the wood of the piano bench.* Ⓣ *He gouged out a horrible scratch.* Ⓕ *He gouged out a huge chunk of wood from the board.* □ *Who gouged this scratch out?*

GRAB ▸ AT

grab at someone or something to grasp at someone or something; to try to seize someone or something. □ *He grabbed at me, but I got away unscathed.* □ *I grabbed at the rope, but missed.*

GRAB ▸ AWAY

grab someone or something away (from someone or something) to snatch someone or something away from someone or something. □ *Teddy's mother grabbed the dirty candy away from him before he got it in his mouth.* □ *I grabbed the meat away from the dog.* □ *Sam saw the knife and grabbed it away.*

GRAB ▸ FOR

grab for someone or something to clutch at someone or something. □ *She grabbed for the handle, but missed.* □ *The teacher grabbed for the little boy and held him.*

GRAB ▸ ON(TO)

grab on(to someone or something) to grasp someone or something; to hold on to someone or something. ☐ *Here, grab onto this rope!* ☐ *Grab on and hold tight.*

GRACE ▸ WITH

grace something with something to adorn something or some place with something, especially a person's presence. ☐ *The lovely lady graced our home with her presence.* ☐ *The stage was graced with flowers and a few palm trees.*

GRADE ▸ DOWN

grade someone down on something to give someone a low ranking, rating, or score on some performance. ☐ *I had to grade you down on your essay because of your spelling.* ☐ *Please don't grade me down for a minor mistake.*

grade someone or something down to lower the ranking, rating, or score on someone or something. ☐ *I had to grade you down because your paper was late.* 🅃 *I graded down the paper because it was late.*

GRADUATE ▸ FROM

graduate from something to earn and receive a degree from an educational institution. ☐ *I graduated from a large midwestern university.* ☐ *Bill intends to graduate in the spring.*

GRADUATE ▸ IN

graduate (in something) (with something) to earn a degree in some subject with honors, etc. ☐ *I graduated in math with highest honors.* ☐ *Sharon graduated with honors in medicine.*

GRADUATE ▸ WITH

See the previous entry.

GRAFT ▸ ON

graft something on(to something) to splice a living part onto another living part. ☐ *The gardener grafted a red rose onto the roots of another species.* 🅃 *The gardener grafted on a red rose.* ☐ *Sharon took some strong roots and grafted an experimental variety of rose on.* ☐ *The surgeon grafted skin from Sam's hip onto his shoulder.*

GRANT ▸ TO

grant something to someone to give or award something to someone. ☐ *The foundation granted a large sum of money to Jane for her research.* ☐ *They granted an award to Kelly.*

GRAPH ▸ OUT

graph something out to draw a graph of something. ☐ *Please take this data and graph it out.* 🅃 *Graph out this data, please.*

GRAPPLE ▸ FOR

grapple (with someone) (for something) to fight or scuffle with someone to grab something. ☐ *The cop grappled with the thief for the gun.* ☐ *He grappled for the gun with Max.* ☐ *The cop grappled for a few seconds with Max.*

GRAPPLE ▸ WITH

grapple (with someone) (for something) See under *GRAPPLE ▸ FOR.*

grapple with something to deal with a problem; to get a "good hold" on a problem. (Figurative.) ☐ *I have enough to grapple with now. No more problems, please.* ☐ *I cannot grapple with any additional problems.*

GRASP ▸ AT

grasp at someone or something to try to seize someone or something. ☐ *He grasped at the bar and held on tight.* ☐ *The beggar grasped at the pedestrian and lost his grip.*

grasp at straws to do something that is futile; to propose something that is hopeless. ☐ *You don't have a solution. You are just grasping at straws.* ☐ *We are just grasping at straws. There is nothing we can do.*

GRASP ▸ BY

grasp someone or something by something to hold onto someone or something by something. ☐ *He grasped his friend by the hand and pulled him to safety.* ☐ *Sharon grasped the dog by its collar and held on tight.*

GRATE ▸ ON

grate on someone to annoy someone; to rub someone the wrong way. □ *Your attitude really grates on me.* □ *Everything you say grates on me.*

grate on something **1.** to rub, scrape, or abrade something. □ *The tree branch is grating on the side of the house.* □ *The bottom of the door is grating on the threshold. Please fix it.* **2.** to irritate or wear on someone's nerves. □ *That sound is grating on my nerves.* □ *That woman grates on my nerves.*

GRAVITATE ▸ TO(WARD)

gravitate to(ward) someone or something to move slowly toward someone or something, as if being pulled by gravity. □ *People tend to gravitate toward the kitchen at parties.* □ *Unless you watch them, they will gravitate toward rude behavior.* □ *Everyone gravitated toward the hostess toward the end of the party.*

GRAZE ▸ AGAINST

graze against someone or something to brush or scrape against someone or something. □ *The car grazed against the side of the truck.* □ *I grazed against an old man as I was jogging this morning.*

GRAZE ▸ ON

graze on something **1.** [for animals] to browse or forage in a particular location. □ *The cattle are grazing on the neighbor's land.* □ *I wish they wouldn't graze on other people's land.* **2.** [for animals] to browse or forage, eating something in particular. □ *The deer are grazing on my carrots!* □ *The cows were grazing on the meadow grasses for weeks.*

GREET ▸ WITH

greet someone or something with something to welcome someone or something with something; to accost someone or something with something upon arrival. □ *I greeted her with a large bouquet of roses.* □ *The sun greeted the day with bright rays of light.* □ *Tom greeted the visitor with a warm handshake.*

GRIEVE ▸ FOR

grieve for someone or something to mourn for someone or something. □ *Don't grieve for me. I'm okay.* □ *She grieved for her lost chances.*

GRIEVE ▸ OVER

grieve over someone or something to lament and pine for someone or something. □ *Now, don't grieve over a lost cat.* □ *There is no reason to continue grieving over him.*

GRIN ▸ AT

grin at someone or something **1.** to smile a beaming smile at someone or something. □ *The entire class grinned at the camera.* □ *I grinned at her and she turned away quickly.* **2.** to smile a beaming smile at the thought of, or mental picture of, someone or something. □ *He grinned at the thought of his coming home to his family.* □ *He thought of her trying to open the surprise package he had sent, and he grinned at her and her efforts.*

GRIN ▸ FROM

grin from ear to ear to smile a very wide, beaming smile. □ *She was grinning from ear to ear as she accepted the prize.* □ *We knew Timmy was happy because he was grinning from ear to ear.*

GRIND ▸ AWAY

grind away (at someone) to needle, criticize, and nag someone continually. □ *Why are you always grinding away at me?* □ *Leave me alone. Stop grinding away!*

grind away (at something) to crush something into particles continually. □ *The machine ground away at the rocks, making tons of gravel.* □ *It ground away, making a terrible noise in the process.*

grind something away to remove something by grinding. □ *Grind the bumps away and make a smooth wall.* 🅃 *Please grind away the bumps.*

GRIND ▸ DOWN

grind someone down to wear someone down by constant requests; to wear someone down by constant nagging. □ *If you think you can grind me down by* *bothering me all the time, you are wrong.* 🅃 *The constant nagging ground down the employees at last.*

grind something down to make something smooth or even by grinding. □ *Grind this down to make it smooth.* 🅃 *Please grind down this rough spot.*

GRIND ▸ INTO

grind something into something to pulverize something into powder, grit, particles, etc. □ *The machine ground the rocks into gravel.* □ *The mill ground the grain into flour.*

GRIND ▸ IN(TO)

grind something in(to something) to crush or rub something into something. □ *People's feet ground the cigarette ashes into the carpet.* 🅃 *Their feet ground in the ashes.* □ *Please don't grind the dirt in!* 🄰 *The carpet was ruined by the ground-in dirt.*

GRIND ▸ ON

grind on [for something] to drag on endlessly. □ *The hours ground on without anything happening. I was so tired of waiting.* □ *The lecture ground on, minute after minute.*

GRIND ▸ OUT

grind something out 1. to produce something by grinding. □ *Working hard, he ground the powder out, a cup at a time.* 🅃 *He ground out the powder, a cup at a time.* **2.** to produce something in a mechanical or perfunctory manner. □ *The factory just keeps grinding these toys out, day after day.* 🅃 *The factory grinds out toys all day long.*

GRIND ▸ TO

grind something to something to keep grinding something until it is something. □ *I ground the fennel seeds to a powder and threw them in the simmering sauce.* □ *The wheels of the cars, trucks, and buses had ground the football to a broken mass.*

grind to a halt to slow down and stop. □ *Every day about noon, traffic in town grinds to a halt.* □ *The bus ground to a halt at the corner and someone got off.*

GRIND ▸ TOGETHER

grind something together to rub things together. □ *Stop grinding your teeth together.* □ *The stones ground together as we drove over them.*

GRIND ▸ UP

grind something up to pulverize or crush something by crushing, rubbing, or abrasion. □ *Please grind the fennel seeds up.* 🅃 *Grind up the fennel seeds and sprinkle them on the top.* 🄰 *Put a little bit of ground-up nutmeg on top of the eggnog.*

GRIPE ▸ ABOUT

gripe (to someone or something) (about someone or something) See under *GRIPE ▸ TO.*

GRIPE ▸ AT

gripe at someone to complain to someone. □ *Stop griping at me!* □ *There is no need to gripe at your little brother.*

GRIPE ▸ TO

gripe (to someone or something) (about someone or something) to make specific complaints to someone about someone or something. □ *Don't gripe to me about what she said to you!* □ *There is no need to gripe about the job to everyone.*

GROAN ▸ ABOUT

groan about someone or something to complain about someone or something. □ *What are you groaning about?* □ *She is groaning about her work.*

GROAN ▸ OUT

groan something out to say something with a groan. □ *He groaned the name out.* 🅃 *He groaned out the name of his assailant before he passed out.*

GROAN ▸ UNDER

groan under something 1. to groan while bearing a heavy burden. □ *He groaned under the weight of the trunk.* □ *The rafters groaned under the heavy weight of the pianos.* **2.** to suffer under a burden. □ *For years, the people had groaned under the cruel ruler.* □ *We groaned under the rule of Rudolph just as we had groaned under Maurice.*

GROAN ▸ WITH

groan with something to groan because of something, such as pain. ☐ *She groaned with pain, but no one helped her.* ☐ *I think the old man was groaning with boredom more than anything else.*

GROOM ▸ AS

groom someone as something to prepare someone for a job or position. ☐ *He was grooming his son as his successor.* ☐ *They groomed Charles as the next treasurer.*

GROOM ▸ FOR

groom someone for something to prepare someone for something; to prepare someone to be someone. ☐ *The boss is grooming his son for the presidency of the company.* ☐ *They are grooming the vice president for the top position.*

GROOVE ▸ ON

groove on someone or something to show great interest in someone or something. (Slang.) ☐ *I really groove on that slow rock.* ☐ *Nancy really grooves on Bob Dylan.*

GROPE ▸ ABOUT

grope (about) (for someone or something) AND **grope (around) (for someone or something)** to feel around blindly for someone or something. ☐ *In the darkness, he groped about for his glasses.* ☐ *Fran groped for the light switch and found it.* ☐ *Timmy groped around for his mother, who lay sleeping in the darkened room.*

GROPE ▸ AFTER

grope after someone or something to reach for a departing or fleeing person or thing awkwardly or ineffectually. ☐ *The feeble hand groped after the departing form.* ☐ *I groped after the cat as it ran under the bed.*

GROPE ▸ AROUND

grope (around) (for someone or something) See under *GROPE ▸ ABOUT.*

GROPE ▸ AT

grope at someone or something to reach for someone or something blindly. ☐ *She groped feebly at the form she could hardly see.* ☐ *Sharon groped at Frank as he ran out to get the doctor.*

GROPE ▸ FOR

grope (about) (for someone or something) See under *GROPE ▸ ABOUT.*

GROSS ▸ OUT

gross someone out to disgust someone. (Slang. *Someone* includes *oneself.*) ☐ *The movie grossed us all out.* 🅃 *It grossed out everyone.* 🄰 *About thirty grossed-out kids left the movie before it was over.* ☐ *He grossed himself out by looking at the pictures of the crash.*

GROUND ▸ IN

ground someone in something to instruct someone in an area of knowledge. ☐ *We grounded all our children in the basics of home cooking.* ☐ *We were all grounded in basic cooking by the time we were six.*

GROUND ▸ ON

ground something on something to build a firm basis for something on something else. ☐ *He grounded his thinking on his detailed research.* ☐ *His thinking was grounded on years of reading.*

GROUP ▸ AROUND

group someone or something around someone or something to gather people or things around people or things. (*Someone* includes *oneself.*) ☐ *The photographer grouped the wedding party around the bride for the picture.* ☐ *The photographer then grouped them around the cake.* ☐ *They grouped themselves around the table where the snacks were located.*

GROUP ▸ TOGETHER

group someone or something together to gather people or things together. ☐ *Try to group all the smokers together at one table.* ☐ *Steve grouped all the dictionaries together.*

GROUP ▸ UNDER

group something under something to classify something under some category. ☐ *They have now grouped the fungi under their own families.* ☐ *We should group all the older ones under a separate category.*

GROUSE ▸ ABOUT

grouse about someone or something to complain about someone or something. (Colloquial.) ☐ *What are you grousing about now?* ☐ *I am grousing about you!*

GROUSE ▸ AT

grouse at someone or something to criticize someone or some creature directly to the person or creature. ☐ *Stop grousing at me!* ☐ *Sharon is grousing at the cat again.*

GROVEL ▸ ABOUT

grovel (about) in something See under *GROVEL ▸ IN.*

GROVEL ▸ BEFORE

grovel before someone or something to prostrate oneself before someone or something. ☐ *The prisoner groveled before his accusers.* ☐ *The member of the cult groveled before the altar.*

GROVEL ▸ IN

grovel (about) in something to wallow around in the dirt, etc., while prostrating oneself. ☐ *The poor fellow groveled about in the mud, trying to keep from being beaten.* ☐ *Why are you there, groveling in the dust?*

GROVEL ▸ TO

grovel to someone to kneel in deference to someone; to kowtow to someone. ☐ *You don't have to grovel to me!* ☐ *I refuse to grovel to anyone.*

GROW ▸ APART

grow apart (from someone or something) **1.** [for things] to separate as they grow. ☐ *These trees tend to grow apart from each other as they get bigger.* ☐ *They need to grow apart so they won't be too crowded.* **2.** [for people] to separate from one another gradually. ☐ *Over the years, they grew apart from each other.* ☐ *Ted and Sharon grew apart and saw less and less of each other.*

GROW ▸ AWAY

grow away from someone [for someone] to become less intimate with someone; [for someone] to become independent of someone gradually. ☐ *She has grown away from her husband over the years.* ☐ *We expect our children to grow away from us.*

grow away from something [for something] to move away from something as it grows. ☐ *The tree grew away from the house—thank heavens.* ☐ *See if you can train the vine to grow away from the fence.*

GROW ▸ BACK

grow back [for something that has come off] to grow back again. (Includes parts of plants, lizards' tails, teeth in some creatures, finger- and toenails, etc.) ☐ *The lizard's tail grew back in a few months.* ☐ *The leaves will grow back in a month or so.*

GROW ▸ DOWN

grow down (into something) [for roots] to sink and dig downward as they grow. ☐ *The young roots grew down into the rich soil.* ☐ *The roots grew down and drew up the precious water.*

GROW ▸ FROM

grow from something to develop and grow from a seed, bulb, corm, etc. ☐ *This huge tree grew from a little seed.* ☐ *What kind of plant grows from this bulb?*

grow something from something to propagate a plant from a seed, bulb, corm, etc. ☐ *I grew these tomatoes from seeds.* ☐ *Can you grow a mango tree from a seed?*

GROW ▸ IN

grow in something **1.** [for someone] to increase in some quality, such as wisdom, strength, stature, etc. ☐ *As I got older, I was supposed to grow in wisdom and other good things.* ☐ *Sam grew in strength as he got over the disease.* **2.** [for a plant] to develop or flourish in something or some place. ☐ *These plants grow in rich soil with moderate moisture.* ☐ *They will grow well in this soil.*

GROW ▸ INTO

grow into something **1.** [for a child] to develop into a particular type of person. ☐ *The child grew into a tall, powerful athlete.* ☐ *I hope I have grown into a fine person.* **2.** [for a plant] to develop into a mature specimen of its species. □ *This twig will grow into an oak tree.* □ *I hope this seedling grows into a fine mango tree.* **3.** [for a situation or a problem] to develop into something more serious. □ *I hope this matter doesn't grow into something worse.* □ *This business is growing into a real crisis.* **4.** [for a plant, tumor, toenail] to penetrate into something as it grows. □ *The roots of the tree grew into our sewer line.* □ *Try to keep the tree roots from growing into the foundation.* Ⓐ *Sally is suffering from an ingrown toenail.*

grow into something to grow enough to fit something. □ *The shirt is a little large, but Timmy will grow into it.* □ *My shoes are too big, but I will grow into them.*

GROW ▶ ON

grow on someone **1.** [for a fungus, tumor, parasite, etc.] to live and grow on someone's skin. □ *I've got this stuff growing on me and I want to get rid of it.* □ *Is that a rash or is something growing on you?* **2.** [for something] to become familiar to and desired by someone; [for something] to become habitual for someone. (Figurative.) □ *This kind of music grows on you after a while.* □ *Kenneth sort of grows on you after a while.*

GROW ▶ OUT

grow out [for something that has been cut back] to regrow. □ *Don't worry, your hair will grow out again.* □ *Will the grass grow out again, do you think?*

grow out of something **1.** to develop and grow outward from something. □ *Soft green shoots grew out of the trunk of the tree.* □ *A bush grew out of the gutter and hung down the front of the house.* **2.** [for a problem] to develop from something less serious. □ *This whole matter grew out of your failure to let the cat out last night.* □ *A big argument has grown out of a tiny disagreement!* **3.** to age out of something; to outgrow something. □ *Finally, Ted grew out of his bedwetting.* □ *Hasn't that problem been outgrown yet?*

grow out of something to grow so much that some article of clothing does not fit. □ *Timmy's getting so tall that he's grown out of all his clothes.* □ *He grew out of his suit, and he's only worn it three times.* Ⓐ *I give his outgrown clothes to charity.*

GROW ▶ OVER

grow over something [for vegetation] to cover over something as it grows. □ *The vines grew over the shed and almost hid it from view.* Ⓐ *They will have to clear the grown-over pathways before they can expect people to go there.*

GROW ▶ TOGETHER

grow together [for things] to join together as they grow and develop. □ *Two of these trees grew together when they were much smaller.* □ *The broken ends of the bone grew together far more rapidly than Chuck had thought.*

GROW ▶ UP

grow up to become mature; to become adult. □ *All the children have grown up and the parents are left with a lot of debts.* Ⓐ *I expect you to act like grown-up people.* Ⓝ *Now, we are all grown-ups, aren't we?*

grow up into someone or something to mature into a type of person or a person who does a particular job. □ *She grew up into a fine young lady.* □ *I want to grow up into a strong and healthy person.*

GROWL ▶ AT

growl at someone or something to snarl at someone or something. □ *Don't growl at me like that.* □ *The dog growled at the cat.*

GROWL ▶ OUT

growl something out to say something, growling or snarling. □ *Jane growled a few words out.* Ⓣ *She growled out a few words and the gates opened for us.*

GRUB ▶ AROUND

grub around (for someone or something) to search around for someone or something. (Slang.) □ *I went to the attic and grubbed around for my old uniform.* □ *The guys went out and* *grubbed around for another soccer player.*

grub around (in something) to wear old or "grubby" clothes around. (Colloquial.) ☐ *I was grubbing around in my jeans when Alice showed up.* ☐ *I was wearing my jeans and just sort of grubbing around when she came.*

GRUMBLE ▶ ABOUT

grumble about someone or something to complain about someone or something. ☐ *What are you grumbling about now?* ☐ *The students were grumbling about the teacher.*

GRUMBLE ▶ AT

grumble at someone to complain to someone. ☐ *Go grumble at someone else. I'm tired of listening.* ☐ *Stop grumbling at me!*

GRUNT ▶ OUT

grunt something out to say something with a snort or grunt. ☐ *Jane grunted a command out to someone.* 🅃 *She grunted out a curt command and the gate opened.*

GUARANTEE ▶ AGAINST

guarantee against something to certify that something bad will not happen. ☐ *No one can guarantee against that happening.* ☐ *I can't guarantee against something going wrong.*

guarantee something against something (for something) to certify that something will not fail, break, or wear out, usually for a period of time. ☐ *We guarantee this radio against flaws for one year.* ☐ *I have to buy insurance to guarantee my car against defects.*

GUARD ▶ AGAINST

guard against something to take care to prevent something. ☐ *You must guard against that yourself.* ☐ *I will guard against theft.*

GUARD ▶ FROM

guard someone or something from someone or something to protect someone or something from someone or something. ☐ *The assistant manager will guard your valuables from thieves.* ☐ *She guarded the kitten from the angry dog.* ☐ *Ted guarded Gretchen from Max.*

GUESS ▶ AT

guess at something to estimate something; to give an opinion about what something might be. ☐ *I hate to just guess at it, but if you insist: ten feet long.* ☐ *Go ahead, guess at it.*

GUFFAW ▶ AT

guffaw at someone or something to laugh at someone or something very hard and raucously. ☐ *The audience guffawed at the clown's antics.* ☐ *The old man guffawed at the clown.*

GUIDE ▶ ACROSS

guide someone or something across (something) to lead or escort someone or something across something. ☐ *I had to guide him across the desert.* ☐ *The bridge was very narrow and Jill got out to guide the truck across.* ☐ *We had to guide it across.*

GUIDE ▶ AROUND

guide someone around (something) to lead or escort someone on a tour of something or some place. ☐ *Please let me guide you around the plant, so you can see how we do things here.* ☐ *I would be happy to guide you around.*

guide someone around something to lead someone to one side or the other of something. ☐ *I guided the blind man around the excavation so he would not fall in.* ☐ *Let me guide you around the post.*

GUIDE ▶ AWAY

guide someone away (from someone or something) to lead or escort someone away from someone, something, or some place. (Usually said of someone who requires help or guidance.) ☐ *An usher guided the children away from the grave.* ☐ *Please guide your grandmother away.*

guide something away from someone or something **1.** to lead something away from someone or something. ☐ *I guided the lawn mower away from the children.* ☐ *Please stand there and guide the cars away from the plantings along the driveway.* **2.** to channel or route something away from someone or something. ☐ *The farmer guided the creek water away from the main channel through a narrow ditch.* ☐ *We had to guide the sheep away from the road.*

GULP ▶ BACK

gulp something back to force or hold back tears, sobs, etc. ☐ *He gulped his sobs back and clutched at his wound.* 🅃 *He gulped back his sobs.*

GULP ▶ DOWN

gulp something down to drink all of something, usually quickly. ☐ *He gulped his coffee down and left.* 🅃 *He gulped down his coffee.*

GUM ▶ UP

gum something up to mess something up; to make something move slowly or inefficiently, as if it were a machine with sticky gears. ☐ *You really gummed the works up.* 🅃 *He gummed up the works by his carelessness.* 🄰 *Send the gummed-up motor back to the manufacturer.*

GUN ▶ DOWN

gun someone or something down to shoot someone or some creature. ☐ *Max tried to gun Lefty down.* 🅃 *Max tried to gun down Lefty.*

GUN ▶ FOR

gun for someone **1.** to seek one out to shoot one. (Slang.) ☐ *They say that Max is gunning for Lefty.* ☐ *Jed is gunning for the sheriff.* **2.** to seek someone out in anger. (Figurative slang.) ☐ *The boss is gunning for you.* ☐ *I think that Walter is gunning for me.*

GUSH ▶ FORTH

See the following entry.

GUSH ▶ FROM

gush (forth) (from someone or something) AND **gush (forth) (out of someone or something); gush (out) (from someone or something)** to spout out of someone or something. (Can be words, water, blood, vomit, etc. The optional elements cannot be transposed.) ☐ *The blood gushed forth from his wound.* ☐ *Curses gushed forth from Sharon.* ☐ *Water gushed forth out of the broken pipe.* ☐ *The words gushed out from her mouth.* ☐ *The curses gushed from her mouth in torrents.*

GUSH ▶ OUT

gush (forth) (out of someone or something) See the previous entry.

GUSH ▶ OVER

gush over someone or something **1.** [for liquid] to flood over someone or something. ☐ *The floodwaters gushed over the farmland.* ☐ *The hot soup gushed over the cook as the huge pot tipped over.* **2.** [for someone] to heap praise, flattery, and compliments on someone or something. (Informal.) ☐ *Aunt Mattie always gushed over us children so much that we dreaded her coming.* ☐ *All the guests gushed over my beet salad.*

GUSH ▶ WITH

gush with something [for something] to flow with something. ☐ *The stream gushed with the sudden runoff of the storm.* ☐ *The faucet gushed with brownish water, so I turned it off.*

GUSSY ▶ UP

gussy someone or something up to dress someone or something up; to make someone or something fancy. (Folksy. *Someone* includes *oneself*.) ☐ *She gussied the kids up for the wedding.* 🅃 *See if you can gussy up this room a little before folks get here.* ☐ *She spent hours gussying herself up for the dance.*

GUZZLE ▶ DOWN

guzzle something down to drink something rapidly and eagerly. ☐ *He guzzled the beer down and called for another.* 🅃 *He guzzled down the beer and called for another.*

GYP ▶ OUT

gyp someone out of something to cheat something away from someone. (Slang.) ☐ *That guy tried to gyp me out of my prize money!* ☐ *He gypped me out of a lot of money!*

H

HABITUATE ► TO

habituate someone to someone or something to accustom someone to someone or something. (*Someone* includes *oneself.*) □ *Soon she will habituate the baby to the new feeding schedule.* □ *The office staff worked hard to habituate the new employee to the schedule.* □ *She did everything she could to habituate herself to the new routine.*

HACK ► APART

hack someone or something apart **1.** to chop up someone or something. □ *The murderer hacked the victim apart.* [T] *He hacked apart the victim.* □ *The butcher hacked the chicken apart.* **2.** to criticize someone or something severely. (Informal. *Someone* includes *oneself.*) □ *She just hacked him apart for his poor showing in the play.* [T] *The critic hacked apart all the actors in the play.* □ *The critic hacked the play apart.* □ *He could not discuss his performance without hacking himself apart.*

HACK ► AROUND

hack around to waste time. (Slang.) □ *I'm just hacking around and killing time.* □ *Stop hacking around and get to work.*

HACK ► AT

hack (away) at someone or something to chop at someone or something, continuously. □ *The brutal murderer hacked away at his victim.* □ *The woodchopper hacked at the tree and finally got it down.*

HACK ► AWAY

See the previous entry.

HACK ► DOWN

hack something down to chop someone or something down. □ *Who hacked this cherry tree down?* [T] *Who hacked down this cherry tree?*

HACK ► OFF

hack someone off to make someone angry. □ *You really hack me off!* [T] *Jack had hacked off just about everybody by the time he had been there a day.*

hack something off to chop something off. □ *I need to get up that tree and hack that big branch off before it bangs on the house.* [T] *Please hack off that big branch.*

HACK ► OUT

hack something out (of something) **1.** to cut or chop something out of something. (The *of*-phrase is paraphrased with a *from*-phrase when the particle is transposed. See the [F] example.) □ *Jill hacked the bone out of the roast.* [T] *She hacked out the big bone.* [F] *She hacked out the big bone from the leg of lamb.* □ *Sally hacked it out.* **2.** to fashion something by carving or chiseling from something. (Informal. The *of*-phrase is paraphrased with a *from*-phrase when the particle is transposed. See the [F] example.) □ *He hacked a rabbit out of the chunk of wood.* [T] *In no time, the carver had hacked out a rabbit.* [F] *In no time, the carver had hacked out a rabbit from the chunk of wood.* □ *Using more speed than skill, he hacked it out.*

HACK ► THROUGH

to cut one's way through something. □ *We had to hack our way through the* *jungle.* □ *The surveyors hacked a pathway through the undergrowth.*

HACK ▸ TO

hack something to something to cut something up into something, such as pieces, bits, smithereens. □ *The editor hacked my story to smithereens.* □ *Don't hack the turkey to pieces!*

HACK ▸ UP

hack something up 1. to chop something up into pieces. □ *Hack all this old furniture up and we'll burn it in the fireplace.* 🅃 *Hack up this stuff and we'll burn it.* **2.** to damage or mangle something. □ *Who hacked my windowsill up?* 🅃 *Who hacked up my windowsill?*

HAGGLE ▸ ABOUT

haggle about something to bargain or negotiate about something. □ *They are always willing to haggle about the price, so don't take the first price you're given.* □ *I wish you wouldn't try to haggle about everything when we shop.*

HAGGLE ▸ OVER

haggle (with someone) (over someone or something) to argue with someone over someone or something. □ *I don't want to haggle with you over Tom and whose team he's going to be on.* □ *Let's not haggle over the price.* □ *There is no point in haggling with her.*

HAGGLE ▸ WITH

See the previous entry.

HAIL ▸ AS

hail someone as something to praise someone for being something. □ *The active members hailed him as fraternity brother of the year.* □ *Sally was hailed as an effective leader.*

HAIL ▸ FROM

hail from some place to come from some place; to originate in some place. □ *He hails from a small town in the Midwest.* □ *Where do you hail from?*

HAM ▸ UP

ham something up to perform in something in an exaggerated and exhibitionist manner. □ *Stop hamming it up! This is a serious drama.* 🅃 *She really hammed up her part in the play.*

HAMMER ▸ AT

hammer (away) at someone to interrogate someone; to ask questions endlessly of someone. □ *The cops kept hammering away at Max until he told them everything they wanted to know.* □ *They hammered at Max for hours.*

hammer (away) at something 1. to pound at or on something, such as a door. □ *Who is hammering away at the door?* □ *The police are hammering at the door.* **2.** to dwell overly long on a point or a question. □ *Stop hammering away at the same thing over and over.* □ *The agents asked question after question. They would not stop hammering at the issue.*

HAMMER ▸ AWAY

See both entries under *HAMMER ▸ AT.*

HAMMER ▸ DOWN

hammer something down to pound something down even with the surrounding area. □ *Hammer all the nails down so that none of them will catch on someone's shoe.* 🅃 *Hammer down all these nails!*

HAMMER ▸ IN(TO)

hammer something in(to someone) AND **pound something in(to someone)** to teach something to someone intensively, as if one were driving the information in by force. (Figurative.) □ *Her parents had hammered good manners into her head since she was a child.* 🅃 *They hammered in good manners every day.* □ *They pounded proper behavior into the children.* □ *The teacher held a review session on the material and really pounded the stuff in.*

hammer something in(to something) AND **pound something in(to something)** to drive something into something as with a hammer. □ *Todd hammered the spike into the beam.* 🅃 *He hammered in the spike.* □ *He hammered it in with two hard blows.* □ *The carpenter pounded the nail into the board.* 🅃 *The carpenter pounded in the nail.*

HAMMER ▸ ON

hammer on someone or something to pound on someone or something. □

The cop hammered on the poor man over and over. □ *Sharon hammered on the door for a long time.*

HAMMER ▸ ON(TO)

hammer something on(to something) to pound something onto something. □ *I hammered the lid onto the paint can.* 🆃 *She hammered on the lid very tightly.* □ *She used a mallet to hammer it on.*

HAMMER ▸ OUT

hammer something out **1.** to hammer a dent away; to make a dent even with the surrounding area. □ *I'm going to have to have someone hammer this dent in my fender out.* 🆃 *It will take a while to hammer out the dent.* **2.** to expand something by hammering it thinner. □ *He hammered the gold out into a very thin sheet.* 🆃 *He hammered out the gold into thin sheets.* **3.** to arrive at an agreement through argument and negotiation. □ *The two parties could not hammer a contract out.* 🆃 *At last, we were able to hammer out an agreement.*

HAND ▸ AROUND

hand something around to pass something around. □ *Hand this around and let everyone look at it.* 🆃 *Hand around these pictures so everyone gets to see them.*

HAND ▸ BACK

hand something back (to someone) to return something to someone by hand. □ *Would you please hand this paper back to Scott?* 🆃 *Hand back this book to Fred, if you please.* 🆃 *Sharon handed back the key and thanked the custodian.*

HAND ▸ DOWN

hand someone down something to pass something to a person on a lower level. □ *Hand this wrench down to the man under the sink.* 🆃 *Please hand down this wrench.*

hand something down [for a court] to issue a ruling. □ *The appeals court handed down a negative opinion.* □ *The court has not yet handed down a ruling.*

hand something down from someone to someone to pass something down through many generations. □ *I hope we can make it a tradition to hand this down from generation to generation.* 🆃 *I will hand down this watch from generation to generation.* □ *It is a family tradition to hand this book down from mother to daughter.*

hand something down (to someone) to pass on something to a younger person, often a younger relative. □ *I will hand this down to my grandson also.* 🆃 *I will hand down this dress to my niece.* □ *When I am finished with this, I will hand it down.*

HAND ▸ IN

hand something in (to someone) See under *PASS ▸ IN.*

HAND ▸ OFF

hand something off (to someone) to pass a football directly to another player. (Football.) □ *Roger handed the ball off to Jeff.* 🆃 *He handed off the ball.* □ *Tim handed it off.*

HAND ▸ ON

hand something on (to someone or something) **1.** to pass something on to someone or a group. □ *Please hand this on to Walter after you've read it.* □ *Please read this and hand it on.* **2.** to bequeath something to someone or a group. □ *I want to hand this land on to my children.* 🆃 *The family will hand on the business to a foundation.*

HAND ▸ OUT

hand something out (to someone) to give something out to someone. □ *The judge was known for handing heavy fines out.* 🆃 *She handed out large fines.* 🆃 *Sally handed out food to the poor.* 🅽 *Some people are always looking for a handout.*

hand something out (to someone) to pass something, usually papers, out to people. □ *The teacher handed the tests out to the students.* 🆃 *Please hand out these papers.* □ *Hand them out, if you would.* 🅽 *The teacher came prepared with a number of handouts.*

HAND ▸ OVER

hand someone or something over (to someone or something) to deliver someone or something to someone or a group; to relinquish someone or something to someone or a group. □ *The kidnappers handed the child over to the go-between.* 🅃 *All right, hand over the hostage.* □ *The police officer demanded that the gunman hand over the gun.*

HAND ▸ TO

hand it to someone to give someone credit [for something]. (Usually with some expression of obligation, such as *must, got to, have to* etc.) □ *You've really got to hand it to Jane. She has done a fine job.* □ *We have to hand it to Fred. He was great.*

hand something to someone to give something to someone by hand. □ *The clerk handed her a message when she stopped at the desk.* □ *This message was just handed to me.*

HAND ▸ UP

hand something up to someone to pass something to someone who is on a higher level. □ *Please hand this cup of coffee up to Carl.* 🅃 *Please hand up this coffee to Carl.*

HANG ▸ AROUND

hang around (some place) to loiter some place; to be in a place or in an area, doing nothing in particular. □ *Why are you hanging around my office?* □ *It's comfortable here. I think I'll hang around here for a while.* □ *Stop hanging around and get a job.*

hang around with someone to spend time doing nothing in particular with someone. □ *You spend most of your day hanging around with your friends.* □ *I like to hang around with people I know.*

HANG ▸ BACK

hang back (from someone or something) to lag back behind someone or something; to stay back from someone or something, perhaps in avoidance. □ *Why are you hanging back from the rest of the group?* □ *Come on! Don't hang back!*

HANG ▸ BEHIND

hang behind (someone or something) to stay behind someone or something. □ *Don't hang behind us, please. Come on up here and walk with us.* □ *Fred is hanging behind and may get lost at the next turn.*

HANG ▸ BY

hang by a thread [for one's life] to just barely continue. (Figurative.) □ *Her life hung by a thread until the respirator could be made to work again.* □ *The miners' lives hung by a thread while the rescuers worked toward them.*

hang by something **1.** to be suspended at the end of something, such as a rope, chain, string, etc. □ *The bag is only hanging by a string.* □ *The food hung by a rope from a tree to protect it from the bears that wandered into camp now and then.* **2.** to dangle, suspended by some body part, such as thumbs, legs, etc. □ *I was hanging by my legs on the exercise bar when the rain started.* □ *I can hang by my middle fingers!*

hang someone by the neck to kill someone by tying a noose around the neck and dropping the victim in order to break the neck or strangle the victim. (*Someone* includes *oneself.*) □ *The executioner hanged him by the neck until he died.* □ *He hanged himself by the neck.*

HANG ▸ DOWN

hang down to hang; to droop. □ *The sides of his mouth hung down in a permanent frown.* □ *I don't care for the way these drapes hang down.*

hang down (from someone or something) to be suspended from someone or something. □ *A length of rope hung down from Jane, and I grabbed it.* □ *Grasping vines hung down from the towering trees.* □ *Thousands of vines hung down.*

HANG ▸ FOR

hang someone for something **1.** to execute someone by hanging for doing something. □ *The state prosecutor will try to hang you for this crime.* □ *The sheriff wanted to hang Jed for shooting John's horse.* **2.** to extract an overly severe punishment for some deed. (An exaggeration.) □ *They are trying to hang me for a parking ticket.* □ *You can't hang me just for coming in late!*

HANG ▸ FROM

hang from something to be suspended from something. ☐ *Colorful decorations hung from the branches of the tree.* ☐ *What is that hanging from the side of the building?*

hang someone or something from something to suspend someone or something from something. ☐ *The captain wanted to hang him from the highest yardarm, but had to settle for throwing him to the sharks.* ☐ *I hung a colorful decoration from the windowsill.*

HANG ▸ IN

hang in the balance to be determined; to wait until something happens to cause a decision to be reached. ☐ *Her life hung in the balance while the doctors decided what to do.* ☐ *The decision will hang in the balance until the boss gets back from vacation.*

hang in there to endure something patiently; to keep trying. (Slang.) ☐ *Just hang in there. Things will get better.* ☐ *Hang in there. You will win one yet.*

HANG ▸ OFF

hang off to wait quietly to one side. ☐ *The boys hung off a little, waiting to see what would happen next.* ☐ *Hang off awhile and don't do anything.*

HANG ▸ ON

See also under *HANG ▸ ON(TO).*

hang a few on to take a few alcoholic drinks. (Idiomatic.) ☐ *Jeff went out last night to hang a few on, but he overdid it.* ☐ *Jerry hangs a few on every evening.*

hang on **1.** to wait awhile. ☐ *Hang on a minute. I need to talk to you.* ☐ *Hang on. Let me catch up with you.* ☐ *Please hang on. I'll call her to the phone.* **2.** to survive for awhile. (Figurative.) ☐ *I think we can hang on without electricity for a little while longer.* ☐ *We can't hang on much longer.* **3.** to linger or persist. ☐ *This cold has been hanging on for a month.* ☐ *This is the kind of flu that hangs on for weeks.*

hang on someone's coattails to achieve success by attaching oneself to a successful person. ☐ *Now that I am moderately famous, everyone who ignored me for a decade is trying to hang on my coattails.* ☐ *He is just hanging on her coattails.*

hang on someone's every word to listen closely or with awe to what someone says. (Figurative.) ☐ *I am hanging on your every word. Please go on.* ☐ *The audience hung on her every word throughout the speech.*

hang on (to someone or something) AND **hold on (to someone or something)** **1.** to grasp someone or something. ☐ *She hung on to her husband to keep warm.* ☐ *She sat there and hung on, trying to keep warm.* ☐ *Jane hung on to Jeff to keep from slipping on the ice.* **2.** to keep someone or something. ☐ *Please hang on to Tom. I need to talk to him.* ☐ *If you have Ted there, hang on. I need to talk to him.* ☐ *Hang on to your money. You will need it later.*

Hang on to your hat! AND **Hold on to your hat!** "Get ready for what's coming!"; "Here comes a big shock!" (Informal.) ☐ *There is a rough road ahead. Hang on to your hat!* ☐ *Here we go! Hold on to your hat!*

hang one on See *tie one on* under *TIE ▸ ON.*

hang something on someone to blame something on someone; to frame someone for something. (Slang.) ☐ *Don't try to hang the blame on me!* ☐ *The sheriff tried to hang the bank robbery on Jed.*

hang something on someone or something to drape or hook something on someone or something. ☐ *Hang this sign on Walter and see how he looks.* ☐ *Please hang this sign on the front door.*

HANG ▸ OUT

hang out (of something) to hang as if flowing out of something. ☐ *Your shirttail is hanging out of your pants.* ☐ *My shirttail was hanging out.*

hang out (some place) to spend time in a place, habitually. (Colloquial.) ☐ *Is this where you guys hang out all the time?* ☐ *The boys spend too much time hanging out.* Ⓝ *They are in their hangout.*

hang out (with someone or something) to associate with someone or a group on a regular basis. ☐ *She hangs out with Alice too much.* ☐ *I wish you would stop hanging out with that crowd of boys.* ☐ *Kids hang out too much these days.*

hang something out (of something) to suspend something outside of something while it is attached to the inside of something. ☐ *He hung the rope out of the window so he could escape the burning building.* ☐ *She ran to the window and hung the rope out.*

HANG ▸ OVER

hang over someone or something **1.** to be suspended over someone or something. ☐ *A fancy crystal chandelier hung over us.* ☐ *An ornate ceiling fan hung over the table.* **2.** [for some pervading quality] to seem to hover over someone or something. ☐ *An aura of gloom hung over Joe.* ☐ *A dismal pall hung over the gathering.*

hang over someone('s head) [for something unpleasant] to worry someone. ☐ *I have a horrible exam hanging over my head.* ☐ *I hate to have things hanging over me.*

hang something over someone or something to suspend something over someone or something. ☐ *Sally hung the colorful mobile over the baby.* ☐ *Please hang these garlands over the party table.*

HANG ▸ TOGETHER

hang together **1.** [for something or a group of people] to hold together; to remain intact. ☐ *I hope our bridge group hangs together until we are old and gray.* ☐ *I don't think that this car will hang together for another minute.* **2.** [for a story] to flow from element to element and make sense. ☐ *This story simply does not hang together.* ☐ *Your novel hangs together quite nicely.* **3.** [for people] to spend time together. ☐ *We hung together for a few hours and then went our separate ways.* ☐ *The boys hung together throughout the evening.*

HANG ▸ UP

hang something up **1.** to return the telephone receiver to its cradle. ☐ *Please hang this up when I pick up the other phone.* 🅃 *Please hang up the phone.* **2.** to quit something. (Slang. Usually with *it*.) ☐ *I've had it with this job. It's time to hang it up.* ☐ *Just hang it up. Don't bother with it.*

hang up **1.** [for a machine or a computer] to grind to a halt; to stop because of some internal complication. ☐ *Our computer hung up right in the middle of the job.* ☐ *I was afraid that my computer would hang up permanently.* **2.** to replace the telephone receiver after a call. ☐ *I said good-bye and hung up.* ☐ *Please hang up and place your call again.*

hang up (on someone or something) **1.** AND **hang up (in someone's ear)** to end a telephone call by returning the receiver to the cradle while the other party is still talking. ☐ *She hung up on me!* ☐ *Tim hung up in my ear!* ☐ *I had to hang up on all that rude talk.* **2.** to give up on someone or something; to quit dealing with someone or something. (Figurative slang.) ☐ *Finally, I had to hang up on Jeff. I can't depend on him for anything.* ☐ *We hung up on them because we knew we couldn't make a deal.*

HANG ▸ WITH

hang someone or something with something to suspend someone or something with something, such as a rope, chain, thread, etc. (The past tense *hanged* is usually used only with the hanging of people.) ☐ *The executioners hanged the criminal with a rope and later with a chain.* ☐ *They hung the picture with a golden cord.*

hang with someone or something to remain with someone or a group. (Slang.) ☐ *Hang with us for a while and we'll wait and see who else shows up.* ☐ *I decided to hang with the company to see how things would work out for me.*

HANKER ▸ AFTER

hanker after someone or something AND **hanker for someone or something** to want someone or something; to long for someone or something. (Folksy and cowboys.) ☐ *I hanker after a nice big beefsteak for dinner.* ☐ *Tom sure could* *play that guitar. I really hanker after Tom and his guitar.*

HANKER ▸ FOR
hanker for someone or something See the previous entry.

HAPPEN ▸ ON
See under *HAPPEN ▸ (UP)ON.*

HAPPEN ▸ TO
happen to someone or something to befall someone or something; to occur to someone or something. ☐ *What is going to happen to me?* ☐ *Something awful happened to your car.*

HAPPEN ▸ (UP)ON
happen (up)on someone or something to find someone or something, as if by accident. ☐ *I just happened upon a strange little man in the street who offered to sell me a watch.* ☐ *Andrew happened on a book that interested him, so he bought it.*

HARBOR ▸ AGAINST
harbor something against someone or something to have and retain bad feeling of some kind toward someone or something. ☐ *I harbor no ill will against you.* ☐ *Alice does not harbor any bad feeling against the company that let her go.*

HARDEN ▸ OFF
harden something off to accustom a young plant to normal weather so it can be moved from a protected environment to the out-of-doors. ☐ *We put the plants by the open window to harden them off.* 🆃 *We hardened off the plants.*

HARDEN ▸ TO
harden oneself to something to make oneself callous toward something unpleasant. ☐ *You will have to learn to harden yourself to tragedies like this. They happen every day in a hospital.* ☐ *She had learned to harden herself to the kinds of poverty she had to work in.*

HARDEN ▸ UP
harden something up to make something hard or strong. ☐ *Put the meat in the freezer awhile to harden it up before you try to slice it thin.* 🆃 *Harden up the ice cream a little in the freezer.*

HARK ▸ BACK
hark back to someone or something to be reminiscent of someone or something in the past. ☐ *That hairdo harks back to Veronica Lake.* ☐ *These shoes hark back to the last century.*

HARMONIZE ▸ WITH
harmonize with someone or something to blend with someone or something musically. ☐ *Please try to harmonize with the rest of the singers!* ☐ *Will you harmonize with the piano, please?*

HARNESS ▸ TO
harness someone or something to something to attach someone, something, or some creature to something with a harness. (*Someone* includes *oneself.*) ☐ *The instructor harnessed me to the little sailplane, and I really began to get nervous.* ☐ *Andrew harnessed the horses to the little wagon.* ☐ *She harnessed herself to the plow, always willing to help.*

HARNESS ▸ UP
harness something up to put a harness on some creature, such as a horse. ☐ *You had better harness the horses up so we can go.* 🆃 *Please harness up the mare for me.*

HARP ▸ ON
harp on someone or something to dwell on someone or something. ☐ *I wish you would quit harping on Jeff all the time. He couldn't be all that bad.* ☐ *Stop harping on my mistakes and work on your own.*

HASH ▸ OVER
hash something over (with someone) to discuss something with someone. ☐ *I need to hash this matter over with you.* 🆃 *I've hashed over this business enough.* ☐ *We need to get together with Rachel and hash this over.*

HASH ▸ UP
hash something up **1.** to chop something up. ☐ *Now, hash the onion and garlic up and put it in the skillet.* 🆃 *Now, hash up the onion and brown it.* **2.** to mess something up. ☐ *Somebody hashed my manuscript up!* 🆃 *Somebody hashed up my manuscript!*

HASSLE ▸ ABOUT

hassle someone about something AND **hassle someone with something** to harass someone about something. □ *Come on! Don't hassle me about the deadline!* □ *Stop hassling me with all the little details.*

HASSLE ▸ WITH

hassle someone with something See the previous entry.

HATCH ▸ OUT

hatch something out to aid in releasing some creature from an egg. □ *They hatched lots of ducks out at the hatchery.* 🆃 *The farmer hatched out hundreds of chicks each month.*

HAUL ▸ BEFORE

haul someone (up) before someone or something to bring someone into the presence of someone or something, usually some officer of the law. (Informal.) □ *The officer hauled the suspect up before the judge.* 🆃 *She hauled up the suspect before the judge.* □ *Elaine hauled Fred before the board of examiners.*

HAUL ▸ DOWN

haul something down to pull something down from a higher level. □ *Terry hauled the sail down and put it away.* 🆃 *Please haul down the mainsail.*

HAUL ▸ FROM

haul something (from some place) (to some place) See under *HAUL ▸ TO.*

HAUL ▸ IN

haul someone in [for an officer of the law] to take someone to the police station. □ *The officer hauled the boys in and booked every one of them.* 🆃 *He hauled in the young boys.*

HAUL ▸ OFF

haul off and do something **1.** to draw back and do something, such as strike a person. (Folksy.) □ *She hauled off and slapped him hard.* □ *Max hauled off and poked Lefty in the nose.* **2.** to do something without a great deal of preparation. (Folksy.) □ *The old man hauled off and bought himself a house.* □ *Someday, I'm going to haul off and buy me a new car.*

HAUL ▸ OVER

haul someone or something over to something to drag someone or something over something. □ *She hauled the boy over to the mess he made and forced him to clean it up.* □ *Ken hauled the logs over to the fireplace and laid the fire.*

haul someone over the coals to scold someone severely; to give someone a lot of trouble and criticism. □ *The boss hauled us all over the coals for our failures.* □ *They hauled us over the coals for not finishing on time.*

HAUL ▸ TO

haul something (from some place) (to some place) to drag something from one place to another. □ *I don't want to have to haul this thing from home to office and back again.* □ *I hauled my suitcase to the airport from my hotel.*

HAUL ▸ UP

haul someone (up) before someone or something See under *HAUL ▸ BEFORE.*

haul something up (from something) to drag or pull something up from below. □ *Jeff hauled the bucket up from the bottom of the well.* 🆃 *He hauled up the bucket.* □ *Please haul the bucket up.*

haul up (some place) to arrive some place; to end up some place. □ *After dark, we hauled up at a nice little motel where we spent the night.* □ *It was after midnight when we finally hauled up.*

HAVE ▸ ABOUT

have a thing about someone or something **1.** to have a special fear or dislike of someone or something. □ *Kelly has a thing about Tim. She simply hates him.* □ *I have a thing about snakes.* **2.** to have a craving for someone or something. □ *I have a thing about Maggie. I guess I'm in love.* □ *Elaine has a thing about strawberry ice cream. She can't get enough of it.*

have doubts about someone or something to have questions or suspicions about someone or something. □ *I have doubts about Alice and whether she can* *do it.* ☐ *We have no doubts about the usefulness of this project.*

have feelings about someone or something to have preferences or notions about someone or something. (Usually in the negative.) ☐ *I don't have any feelings about Jeff. You can choose him if you want.* ☐ *I have no feelings about this matter. Do what you want.*

have one's wits about one to be alert; to have the full resources of one's mind available to one. ☐ *I'm sorry I did that. I'm afraid I didn't have my wits about me.* ☐ *You should have your wits about you when you attempt something so complicated.*

have someone or something about AND **have someone or something around** to have someone or something nearby habitually. ☐ *I really don't want to have all those people about all the time.* ☐ *It's good to have a fire extinguisher around.*

have something about someone or something to have some type of thought, premonition, idea, notion, etc., about someone or something. ☐ *I have an idea about Tom and what he can do to help.* ☐ *Joel has no notion about how to do this.*

HAVE ▸ AGAINST

have a grudge against someone See under *BEAR ▸ AGAINST.*

have something against someone or something to have a reason to dislike someone or something. (Note the replacements for *something* in the negative in the examples.) ☐ *Do you have something against me?* ☐ *I have nothing against chocolate ice cream.* ☐ *We don't have anything against you.*

HAVE ▸ AROUND

have someone around (for something) to have someone come for a visit, tea, dinner, etc. ☐ *We really should have the Wilsons around for an evening of bridge.* ☐ *Yes, let's have them around.*

have someone or something around See *have someone or something about* under *HAVE ▸ ABOUT.*

HAVE ▸ AT

have a crack at something AND **have a go at something** to take a try at doing something. (Slang.) ☐ *John wants to try it. Let him have a crack at it.* ☐ *Let him have a go at doing it.*

have at someone to go at someone; to attack someone. ☐ *The boys had at the gang members and gave them a beating.* ☐ *I just knew John was going to have at Fred.*

have at something to begin to do something to something; to "attack" something. (Colloquial. Usually with *it*.) ☐ *Here's your dinner. Have at it!* ☐ *The contract is ready for you to sign. Have at it.*

HAVE ▸ BACK

have back at someone to get even with someone; to give back to someone what one was given. ☐ *I am going to have back at Jill for gossiping about me.* ☐ *Frank said he was going to have back at all of us.*

have someone back to invite someone for a return visit. ☐ *We would love to have you back sometime.* ☐ *We want to have you back the next time you are in town.*

HAVE ▸ BY

have someone by someone or something to position someone next to someone or something; to ask someone to move next to someone or something. ☐ *I'll have Mr. Franklin by Mrs. Wilson on this side of the table.* ☐ *The hostess decided to have Andrew by the door.*

have someone by something to hold onto someone by something. ☐ *She had me by the shoulder and I couldn't get away.* ☐ *Timmy had Billy by the collar and was punching him on the shoulder.*

HAVE ▸ DOWN

have someone down to have someone for a visit to a place that is on a lower level or in the south. ☐ *Why don't we have Roger down for the weekend?* ☐ *They had us down to their place in Florida.*

have someone or something down to have brought someone or something to the ground, as in a struggle. ☐ *Max had Bruno down, and was sitting on his chest to keep him down.* ☐ *The dogs had the bear down, but the bear was fighting hard.*

HAVE ▸ FOR

have a flair for something to have a talent for doing something; to have a special ability in some area. ☐ *Alice has quite a flair for designing.* ☐ *I have a flair for fixing clocks.*

have a gift for something to have a natural talent for doing something. ☐ *Tony has a gift for writing short stories.* ☐ *Sharon has a gift for dealing with animals.*

have a nose for something to have the ability to sense or find something, such as news, trouble, gossip, etc. ☐ *She really has a nose for news. She's a good reporter.* ☐ *Fred has a nose for gossip.*

have a soft spot (in one's heart) for someone or something to have a fondness for someone, something, or some creature. ☐ *I have a soft spot in my heart for Jeff. I'll always be his friend.* ☐ *Elaine has a soft spot for kittens.*

have (a) use for someone or something **1.** to have need for someone or something. (Often negative. Note the use of *any* and *no*.) ☐ *I have no use for Josh and his big fancy car.* ☐ *See if you have use for this hammer.* ☐ *Do you have any use for this?* ☐ *I have no use for that.* **2.** to like someone or something. (Often negative. Note the use of *any* and *no*.) ☐ *I don't have any use for sweet potatoes.* ☐ *I have no use for Harry.*

have something for a meal to serve or eat something at a particular meal, such as breakfast, lunch, dinner, supper, etc. ☐ *We had eggs for breakfast.* ☐ *What did you have for dinner?*

have something for someone to have a gift for someone; to have something in reserve for someone. ☐ *I have some cake for you in the kitchen if you need it.* ☐ *Do you have any more for Oliver?* ☐ *We have a present for you. Here. I hope you like it.*

have something for something to have a remedy for a problem, disease, etc.; to possess something used for some purpose. ☐ *I have something for tight jar lids. It will open them immediately.* ☐ *I have some medicine for that disease.*

have the stomach for something **1.** to be able to tolerate certain foods. ☐ *Do you have the stomach for spinach and those other greens?* ☐ *We just don't have the stomach for onions anymore.* **2.** to have the courage or resolution to do something. ☐ *I don't have the stomach for watching those horror movies.* ☐ *Ken doesn't have the stomach for fighting.*

have time for someone or something to have the time to deal with someone or something. (Often negative.) ☐ *I'm sorry, I don't have time for you today.* ☐ *I don't think I have time for a game of chess.* ☐ *I have time for one short game.*

HAVE ▸ IN

have a hand in something AND **have a part in something** to play a part in something; to help with something. ☐ *I would like to have a hand in the planning process.* ☐ *I will not let Jane have a part in this project.*

have a place in something to have a role in some plan or some activity. ☐ *Do I have a place in the negotiations?* ☐ *Mary did not have a place in any of this.*

have a soft spot (in one's heart) for someone or something See under *HAVE ▸ FOR.*

have a stake in something to have something at risk in something; to have a financial or other interest in something. ☐ *I have a stake in that company. I want it to make a profit.* ☐ *I don't have a stake in it, so I don't care.*

have a voice in something AND **have a say in something** to have some control over what happens in some process; to have the right to speak about the way a plan is being made. ☐ *I want to have a voice in the way it is done.* ☐ *Rachel is supposed to have a say in this too.*

have confidence in someone to trust someone; to know that someone will be true. □ *I have confidence in you, and I know you will do well.* □ *Randy tends not to have confidence in anyone.*

have faith in someone to believe someone; to trust someone to do or be what is claimed. □ *I have faith in you. I know you will try your best.* □ *We have faith in you and know you can do it.*

have it in for someone to be mad at someone; to wish to harm someone. □ *Jane seems to have it in for Jerry. I don't know why.* □ *Max has it in for Lefty.*

have it in one to do something to have the motivation or inspiration to do something. □ *She just doesn't have it in her to go back home.* □ *I wanted to help out, but I just didn't have it in me.*

have one foot in the grave to be almost dead. (Figurative.) □ *I was so sick, I felt as if I had one foot in the grave.* □ *Poor old Uncle Herman has one foot in the grave.*

have one's hand in something to exercise control over something; to play an identifiable role in doing something. □ *She always has to have her hand in everything.* □ *I want to have my hand in the arrangement.*

have someone in to call or invite someone into one's home. □ *I'll have the plumber in to fix that leak.* □ *We had friends in for bridge last night.*

have someone in one's spell AND **have someone under one's spell** to have enchanted or captivated the attention of someone. □ *She has him in her spell.* □ *Ken has Karen under his spell.*

have someone or something in mind to be thinking of someone or something as candidates for something. (*Someone* includes *oneself*.) □ *Did you have anyone in mind for the job?* □ *I have something in mind for the living-room carpeting.* □ *He probably had himself in mind when he spoke about the need for new blood.*

have someone or something (well) in hand to have someone or something under control. □ *I have the child well in hand now. She won't cause you any more trouble.* □ *We have everything in hand. Don't worry.*

have something in hand to have something in one's hand, ready to be used. □ *I have the hammer in hand. Just point me toward a nail and I'll pound it.* □ *She had a pen in hand and was ready to sign the contract.*

HAVE ▶ OF

have the best of both worlds to have the good of two opposing things. (Idiomatic.) □ *I have the best of both worlds—high salary and low cost of living.* □ *Sometimes you can't get everything you want. You can't always have the best of both worlds.*

have the best of someone or something to defeat someone or something. □ *I'm afraid you have the best of me.* □ *We had the best of the opposite team by the end of the first half.*

have the patience of someone to have patience equal to that of someone. (The *someone* is often *Job* or *a saint*.) □ *Steve has the patience of Job.* □ *Dear Martha has the patience of a saint.*

have the worst of something to receive the worst part of something. □ *We will have the worst of the busy times tomorrow during the annual sale.* □ *I have had the worst of it already. It's easy from now on.*

HAVE ▶ ON

have a crush on someone to have a temporary and intense love for someone. □ *Billy has a crush on his first-grade teacher.* □ *Sam has a crush on Lily.*

have an effect on someone or something to cause a result in someone or something. □ *The storm had a bad effect on the baby, who cried all night.* □ *Will this have an effect on my taxes?*

have an impact on someone or something to leave an impression on someone or something. □ *The sharp change in interest rates had an impact on the housing market.* □ *Your story really had an impact on me.*

have designs on someone or something to have plans to use or acquire someone or something; to have plans to manipulate someone or something for one's own purposes. ☐ *Steve has designs on Mary.* ☐ *I have designs on that corner office.*

have one eye on someone or something to monitor someone or something. ☐ *I have to have one eye on you at all times or you will get into trouble.* ☐ *I have one eye on the gas gauge of my car whenever I am driving.*

have one's eye on someone or something to have a wish to acquire someone or something; to have been looking at someone or something with thoughts of acquisition. ☐ *I have my eye on that piece of property. I'm going to buy it some day.* ☐ *Karen has had her eye on Dave for some time now.*

have pity on someone or something to feel sorry for someone or some creature; to be compassionate toward someone or some creature. ☐ *Please! Have pity on us. Let us come in!* ☐ *Elaine had pity on the kitten and gave it a home.*

have some bearing on something to have relevance to something. (Note the use of *no* and *any* in the negative.) ☐ *I know something that has some bearing on the issue you are discussing.* ☐ *This has no bearing on anything that will happen today.* ☐ *This doesn't have any bearing on all that.*

have someone or something on one's hands to have the burden of someone or something; to have someone or something unneeded. ☐ *I've had my grandchildren on my hands for a few days. They have so much energy!* ☐ *I have a lot of home-grown tomatoes on my hands. Do you want some?*

have someone or something on one's mind to have thoughts about someone or something constantly; to have an idea about someone or something. ☐ *I guess I love Jeff. I have him on my mind all the time.* ☐ *I have food on my mind all the time.*

have someone or something on the brain to be obsessed with someone or something. (Slang.) ☐ *Karen has Ken on the brain.* ☐ *That guy has food on the brain!*

have something on to be wearing something. ☐ *You certainly have a lovely dress on.* 🅃 *You have on a lovely dress.*

have something on one('s person) to carry something about with one. ☐ *Do you have any money on your person?* ☐ *I don't have any business cards on me.*

have something on someone or something to have evidence against someone or something. ☐ *I have something on Jeff, so I think he will cooperate.* ☐ *The prosecutor has some evidence on the company and will probably take it to court.*

have the edge on someone to have the advantage over someone; to have the upper hand on someone. ☐ *I have the edge on Randy in that I always get into the office first.* ☐ *Wally has the edge on Don in the race for promotion.*

have (too much) time on one's hands to have extra time; to have time to spare. ☐ *Your problem is that you have too much time on your hands.* ☐ *I don't have time on my hands. I am busy all the time.*

HAVE ▸ OUT

have it out (with someone) to settle something with someone by fighting or arguing. ☐ *Finally, John had it out with Carl, and now they are speaking to one another again.* ☐ *Elaine had been at odds with Sam for a long time. She finally decided to have it out.*

have something out to have something, such as a tooth, stone, tumor, removed surgically. ☐ *You are going to have to have that tumor out.* ☐ *I don't want to have my tooth out!*

HAVE ▸ OVER

have control over someone or something to have the power to direct or manage someone or something. ☐ *I have no control over Mary. I can't stop her from running away.* ☐ *I have control over what goes on in this house!*

have it (all) over someone (in something) to surpass someone in something. ☐ *I have it over him in strength.* ☐ *When it comes to musical ability, Elaine has it all over David.*

have someone over a barrel to have one in a position where one must give in. (Figurative.) ☐ *I'm afraid that we have you over a barrel. You have to do what we ask or you will face trouble.* ☐ *They have me over a barrel and I have to pay them to get my car back.*

have someone over (for something) to invite someone to come to one's home for a meal, party, visit, cards, the evening, etc. ☐ *We will have you over for dinner some day.* ☐ *We will have you over soon.*

HAVE ► TO

have a right to something AND **have the right to something** **1.** to have a privilege or license to have something. ☐ *I have the right to have the kind of house I want.* ☐ *You have a right to any house you can afford.* **2.** to have a privilege or license to do something. ☐ *We all have a right to move freely about our country.* ☐ *I have the right to buy any house I can afford.*

have a score to settle (with someone) to have a disagreement to resolve with someone; to be obliged to get revenge on someone. ☐ *I have a score to settle with you. Why do you want the walls painted green?* ☐ *I am mad at you and I have a score to settle with you.* ☐ *He said he wouldn't do that to me, but he did. I've got a score to settle with him, and I'll get even.*

have access to someone or something to have the privilege of using or approaching someone or something. ☐ *Karen will let you have access to her secretary for a while.* ☐ *Do you have access to a computer?*

have recourse to something to be able to use something for help; to be able to fall back on something. ☐ *You will always have recourse to the money your grandfather left you.* ☐ *You will not have recourse to that money until you are over 21 years of age.*

HAVE ► UNDER

have someone or something under control to have made someone, something, or some creature manageable. (*Someone* includes *oneself*.) ☐ *At last we have the children under control.* ☐ *Is the ice maker under control yet?* ☐ *Please get your dog under control.* ☐ *Finally, she had herself under control.*

have someone under one's spell See under *HAVE ► IN.*

HAVE ► UP

have a leg up on someone to have an advantage that someone else does not have. ☐ *I have a leg up on Walter when it comes to getting around town, since I have a car.* ☐ *I want to get a leg up on Ken, since he thinks he can beat me at tennis.*

have someone up (for something) to invite someone to a place that is on a higher level or in the north, for a meal, party, cards, etc. ☐ *We would like to have you up for dinner some evening.* ☐ *We will have you up soon.*

HAVE ► WITH

have a way with someone or something to have a special and effective way of dealing with someone or something. ☐ *She has a way with Jeff. She can get him to do anything.* ☐ *Sarah has a way with flowers. She can arrange them beautifully.*

have a word with someone (about something) to speak to someone about something. (Often to persuade or criticize.) ☐ *Can I have a word with you about your report?* ☐ *I have to have a word with Andrew.*

have something with someone **1.** to have a meeting with someone. (The *something* is literal.) ☐ *I have something with Walter at noon.* ☐ *We have something with Michael Friday night.* **2.** to eat a meal with someone. (The *something* is literal.) ☐ *Come and have something with me at the cafeteria.* ☐ *Would you like to have lunch with me sometime?*

have words with someone (over someone or something) to quarrel with someone over someone or something. ☐ *I had words with John over Mary and her friends.* ☐ *Elaine had words with Tony over his driving habits.* ☐ *We had words with Joe.*

HEAD ► AT

head someone or something at someone or something to point or aim someone or something toward someone or something. □ *He headed the boat at the island and sped off.* □ *I headed Rachel at her brother, whom she hadn't seen for thirty years.*

HEAD ► AWAY

head away from someone or something to turn and move away from someone or something. □ *The car headed away from Andrew and he knew he was stranded for at least an hour.* □ *We headed away from the store, not knowing that my purse was riding on the roof of the car.*

HEAD ► BACK

head back (some place) to start moving back to some place. □ *I walked to the end of the street and then headed back home.* □ *This is far enough. Let's head back.*

HEAD ► FOR

See *be headed for something* under *BE ► FOR.*

head for someone or something to go directly toward someone or something. □ *She came in and headed right for her grandfather.* □ *She headed for the refrigerator the minute she got home.*

head for the hills **1.** to flee to higher ground. (Folksy cliché. See also *take to the hills* under *TAKE ► TO.*) □ *The river's rising. Head for the hills!* □ *Head for the hills! Here comes the flood!* **2.** to flee. (Cliché.) □ *Here comes crazy Joe. Head for the hills.* □ *Everyone is heading for the hills because that boring Mr. Simpson is coming here again.*

HEAD ► INTO

head someone or something into someone or something **1.** to direct someone or something into someone or something. □ *Jill headed the car into the parking place.* □ *I headed Rachel into the ice cream store and left her on her own.* **2.** to crash someone or something into someone or something. (*Someone* includes *oneself.*) □ *One of the fighting boys headed his opponent into the wall, and that nearly killed him.* □ *Roger headed the boat into the dock and dented the bow.* □ *Running out of control, he headed himself into the wall and made a loud thud.*

HEAD ► IN(TO)

head in(to something) to move into something head or front end first. □ *Head into that parking space slowly. It is quite narrow.* □ *I turned the boat toward shore and headed in.*

HEAD ► OFF

head someone off at the pass to intercept someone. (Informal. Originally a Western movie cliché.) □ *I need to talk to John before he gets into the boss's office. I'll head him off at the pass.* □ *The sheriff set out in a hurry to head Jed off at the pass.*

head someone or something off to intercept and divert someone or something. □ *I think I can head her off before she reaches the police station.* 🅃 *I hope we can head off trouble.* □ *We can head it off. Have no fear.*

HEAD ► OUT

head out after someone or something to start pursuing someone, something, or some creature. □ *The sheriff and his men headed out after the bank robbers.* □ *We headed out after the runaway boat.* □ *Tex headed out after the escaped cattle.*

head out (for something) to set out for something or some place; to begin a journey to something or some place. □ *We headed out for Denver very early in the morning.* □ *What time do we head out tomorrow morning?*

head something out to aim something outward; to move something outward, head or front first. □ *Head the boat out and pull out the throttle.* □ *I headed the car out and we were on our way.*

HEAD ► TOWARD

head toward someone or something to point at and move toward someone, something, or some place. □ *Head toward Mary and don't stop to talk to anyone else.* □ *Sharon headed toward the parking lot, hoping to get home soon.*

head toward something to be developing into something; to be moving toward a specific result. ☐ *The problem will head toward a solution when you stop making the situation worse than it is.* ☐ *I believe that you are heading toward severe health problems if you don't stop smoking.*

HEAD ▸ UP

head something up **1.** to get something pointed in the right direction. (Especially a herd of cattle or a group of covered wagons.) ☐ *Head those wagons up—we're moving out.* 🅃 *Head up the wagons!* **2.** to be in charge of something; to be the head of some organization. ☐ *I was asked to head the new committee up for the first year.* 🅃 *Will you head up the committee for me?*

HEAL ▸ OF

heal someone of something to cure someone's ailments. (*Someone* includes *oneself*.) ☐ *Are you the doctor who healed me of my wounds?* ☐ *Can physicians heal themselves of a common cold?*

HEAL ▸ OVER

heal over [for the surface of a wound] to heal. ☐ *The wound healed over very quickly and there was very little scarring.* ☐ *I hope it will heal over without having to be stitched.*

HEAL ▸ UP

heal up [for an injury] to heal. ☐ *The cut healed up in no time at all.* 🄰 *The healed-up wounds were still very sensitive.*

HEAP ▸ ON

See under *HEAP ▸ (UP)ON.*

HEAP ▸ UP

heap something up to make something into a pile. ☐ *He heaped the mashed potatoes up on my plate, because he thought I wanted lots.* 🅃 *Heap up the leaves in the corner of the yard.* 🄰 *The children were jumping into the heaped-up leaves.*

HEAP ▸ (UP)ON

heap something (up)on someone or something **1.** to pile something up on someone or something. (*Upon* is formal and less commonly used than *on*.) ☐ *Please don't heap so much trouble upon me!* ☐ *Wally heaped leaves on the flower bed.* **2.** to give someone too much of something, such as homework, praise, criticism, etc. (Figurative. *Upon* is formal and less commonly used than *on*.) ☐ *Don't heap too much praise on her. She will get conceited.* ☐ *The manager heaped criticism on the workers.*

HEAP ▸ WITH

heap something with something to pile something onto something. ☐ *Karen heaped Jeff's plate with way too much food.* ☐ *We heaped the driveway with leaves and then put them into bags.*

HEAR ▸ ABOUT

hear about someone or something to learn about someone or something. (Not necessarily by hearing.) ☐ *Have you heard about Tom and what happened to him?* ☐ *I heard about the accident.*

HEAR ▸ FROM

hear from someone or something to get a message from someone or a group. ☐ *I want to hear from you every now and then.* ☐ *We hear from the county clerk every year or so about jury duty.*

HEAR ▸ OF

hear of someone or something to learn of the existence of someone or something. ☐ *Did you ever hear of such a thing?* ☐ *I have heard of Sharon Wallace and I would like to meet her.*

HEAR ▸ OUT

hear someone out **1.** to hear all of what someone has to say. ☐ *Please hear me out. I have more to say.* ☐ *Hear him out. Don't jump to conclusions.* **2.** to hear someone's side of the story. ☐ *Let him talk! Hear him out! Listen to his side!* 🅃 *We have to hear out everyone in this matter.*

HEAR ▸ THROUGH

hear something through to listen to all of something. ☐ *I would like you to hear this explanation through before making your decision.* ☐ *I won't have an opinion until I hear this through.*

HEARKEN ▶ TO

hearken to someone or something to listen to someone or something; to pay attention to someone or something. (Stilted.) □ *Please hearken to me. I speak the truth.* □ *Hearken to the call of the nightingale.*

HEAT ▶ UP

heat someone up to make someone angry. (One old [now folksy] past tense is *het*.) □ *This kind of nonsense really heats me up.* □ *She is really heated up about the new law.* □ *Jed is really het up.*

heat something up (to something) to raise the temperature of something to a certain level. □ *Please heat this room up to about seventy degrees.* 🅃 *Can you heat up the room a little more?* □ *I'll heat some soup up for dinner.* 🄰 *Would you like some heated-up tomato soup?*

heat up **1.** to get warmer or hot. □ *It really heats up in the afternoon around here.* □ *How soon will dinner be heated up?* **2.** to grow more animated or combative. □ *The debate began to heat up near the end.* □ *Their argument was heating up, and I was afraid there would be fighting.*

HEAVE ▶ AT

heave something at someone or something to throw something at someone or something. □ *Fred heaved a huge snowball at Roger.* □ *The thug heaved the rock at the window and broke it to pieces.*

HEAVE ▶ IN(TO)

heave in(to) sight to move into sight in the distance. □ *As the fog cleared, a huge ship heaved into sight.* □ *After many days of sailing, land finally heaved in sight.*

HEAVE ▶ TO

heave to to stop a sailing ship by facing it directly into the wind. □ *The captain gave the order to heave to.* □ *The ship hove to and everyone had a swim.*

HEAVE ▶ UP

heave something up **1.** to lift something up. □ *With a lot of effort, they heaved the heavy lid up* 🅃 *The workers heaved up the huge boulder.* **2.** to vomit something up. □ *The dog heaved most of the cake up on the kitchen floor.* 🅃 *It heaved up the cake it had eaten.*

HEDGE ▶ AGAINST

hedge against something to do something to lessen the risk of something happening; to bet against something bad happening. □ *I want to hedge against something going wrong.* □ *We will hedge against any risk we can detect.*

hedge something against something to protect investments against a decline in value by making counterbalancing bets or investments. □ *The investor hedged his portfolio against a drop in stock prices.* □ *I have to hedge my bets against losing.*

HEDGE ▶ IN

hedge someone in to restrict someone. (*Someone* includes *oneself*.) □ *Our decision hedged Jill in so she could not have any flexibility.* □ *She hedged herself in by her own behavior.*

hedge someone or something in to enclose someone or something in a hedge. □ *Their overgrown yard has almost hedged us in.* 🅃 *Their bushes hedged in our yard.*

HELL ▶ AROUND

hell around to go around raising hell. (Slang.) □ *Who are those kids who are out there helling around every night?* □ *They hell around because it's fun.*

HELP ▶ ALONG

help someone along **1.** to help someone move along. □ *I helped the old man along.* □ *Please help her along. She has a hurt leg.* **2.** to help someone advance. (*Someone* includes *oneself*.) □ *I am more than pleased to help you along.* □ *She helped herself along by studying hard.*

HELP ▶ BACK

help someone back (to something) to help someone return to something or some place. □ *The ushers helped him back to his seat.* □ *When she returned, I helped her back.*

HELP ▸ DOWN

help someone down (from something) to help someone climb down from something. ☐ *Sharon helped the boy down from the horse.* ☐ *Elaine helped the children down.*

HELP ▸ IN

help someone in something to help someone with some task; to aid someone in the doing of something. ☐ *Please help me in my efforts to win the contest.* ☐ *Will you help me in my reelection?*

HELP ▸ IN(TO)

help someone in(to something) to help someone get into something. ☐ *I will help my grandfather into the car.* ☐ *We all had to help him in.*

HELP ▸ OFF

help someone off ((of) something) to help someone get off something. (The *of* is colloquial.) ☐ *Please help me off this horse!* ☐ *Do help him off!*

help someone off with something to help someone take off an article of clothing. ☐ *Would you please help me off with my coat?* ☐ *We helped the children off with their boots and put their coats in the hall.*

HELP ▸ ON

help someone on with something to help someone put on an article of clothing. ☐ *Would you help me on with my coat?* ☐ *Please help her on with her coat.*

HELP ▸ OUT

help out some place to help [with the chores] in a particular place. ☐ *Would you be able to help out in the kitchen?* ☐ *Sally is downtown, helping out at the shop.*

help out (with something) to help with a particular chore. ☐ *Would you please help out with the dishes?* ☐ *I have to help out at home on the weekends.* ☐ *I'll come over and help out before the party.*

help someone or something out (of something) **1.** to help someone or some creature get out of something or some place. ☐ *Please help your grandmother out of the car.* ☐ *I will help her out.* ☐ *Please help the cat out of the carton.* **2.** to help someone or some creature get out of a garment. ☐ *She helped the dog out of its sweater.* ☐ *I helped her out of her coat when we got inside.* ☐ *She was stuck in her huge parka, so I helped her out.* **3.** to help someone or some creature get out of trouble. ☐ *Can you please help me out of this mess that I got myself into?* ☐ *You are in a real mess. We will help you out.* ☐ *The rabbit was in trouble, so I helped it out of the mess it had gotten itself into.*

help someone or something out with someone or something **1.** to aid someone or a group by providing someone or something. ☐ *I need some salt. Would you help me out with a little bit of salt?* ☐ *Can you help our department out with a secretary?* ☐ *Could you help our department out with some secretarial help?* 🅃 *Could you help out our department with some secretarial help?* **2.** to aid someone or a group deal with the problems posed by someone or something. ☐ *Please help me out with Tommy. He is more than I can handle.* ☐ *Can you help me out with this problem?* 🅃 *I would be happy to help out the committee with some typing.*

help (someone) out to help someone do something; to help someone with a problem. ☐ *I am trying to raise this window. Can you help me out?* 🅃 *I'm always happy to help out a friend.* ☐ *This calculus assignment is impossible. Can you help out?*

HELP ▸ OVER

help someone or something (get) over something **1.** to aid someone or some creature climb over something. ☐ *I helped him get over the wall.* ☐ *I helped the puppy over the barrier.* **2.** to aid someone or a group recover from something. ☐ *Sharon wanted to help Roger get over his illness.* ☐ *We try to help the families get over the loss of their loved ones.*

HELP ▸ TO

help oneself to something to take more of something; to take as much of something as one wants. □ *Tell Roger to help himself to the sweet potatoes.* □ *Please help yourself. There's plenty.*

help someone to something to serve something to someone. (*Someone* includes *oneself.*) □ *Please help yourself to the food. Don't stand on ceremony.* □ *Help yourself to more turkey.* □ *Shall I help myself or do you want to serve everyone?*

HELP ▶ UP

help someone up (from something) to help someone rise up from something; to help someone get up from something. (Also without *up,* but not eligible as an entry.) □ *She offered to help him up from the chair.* □ *Elaine helped Tony up.*

HELP ▶ WITH

help someone or something with someone or something to give aid to someone or something in dealing with someone or something. □ *Please help your father with your little sister.* □ *I helped the committee with the problem.* □ *I helped Roger with the committee.*

HEM ▶ IN

hem someone or something in to get someone in a bind; to constrain someone. □ *He is hemmed in and can't get his car out of the parking place.* □ *Please don't hem me in this space again.*

HERD ▶ TOGETHER

herd someone or something together to bunch people or creatures together. □ *Let's herd all the kids together and take them in the house for ice cream and cake.* □ *I herded all the puppies together and put them in a box while I cleaned their play area.*

HESITATE ▶ OVER

hesitate over something to pause before acting on something; to suspend action about someone or something. □ *We are hesitating over the final decision because we have some doubts about the competitors.* □ *Do not hesitate too long over this matter.*

HET ▶ UP

het up See *heat someone up* under *HEAT ▶ UP.*

HEW ▶ DOWN

hew something down to fell something wooden, usually a tree. □ *We will have to hew most of this forest down.* 🅃 *They hewed down the tree.*

HEW ▶ OUT

hew something out of something to carve the shape of something out of something wooden. (The *of*-phrase is paraphrased with a *from*-phrase when the particle is transposed. See the 🄵 example.) □ *Dan hewed each of the posts out of a tree trunk.* 🅃 *He hewed out a number of posts.* 🄵 *He hewed out a fence post from the tree trunk.*

HEW ▶ TO

hew to something to conform to a rule or principle. □ *I wish you would hew to the rules a little better.* □ *Sarah refuses to hew to the company policies.*

HIDE ▶ AWAY

hide away to hide somewhere. □ *Ted? Oh, he's hiding away somewhere.* □ *I want to hide away for the first few days of my vacation.* 🄽 *I know just the perfect hideaway for a vacation.*

hide someone or something away (some place) to conceal someone or something somewhere. (*Someone* includes *oneself.*) □ *Please hide Randy away where no one can find him.* □ *Rachel hid the cake away, hoping to save it for dessert.* 🅃 *Mary hid away the candy so the kids wouldn't eat it all.* □ *He hid himself away in his study until Mrs. Bracknell had gone.* 🄽 *His wife found out about his little hideaway.*

HIDE ▶ BEHIND

hide behind someone or something to conceal oneself behind someone or something. □ *The child hid behind his father.* □ *Rachel hid behind a tree.*

hide someone or something behind something to use something to conceal someone or something. □ *We hid the guests for the surprise party behind a large Oriental screen.* □ *I will hide the cake behind the screen too.*

HIDE ▸ FROM

hide from someone or something to conceal oneself from someone or some creature. □ *Are you hiding from me?* □ *The rabbit was trying to hide from the fox.*

HIDE ▸ IN

hide one's head in the sand to ignore things that are negative or threatening; to pretend that nothing is wrong. (Figurative. From an image of an ostrich sticking its head in the sand and assuming that no can see it.) □ *Stop hiding your head in the sand.* □ *The government is hiding its head in the sand when it refuses to recognize its financial problems.*

hide something in something to conceal something inside something. □ *She hid her money in a book.* □ *Let's hide the cake in this closet.*

HIDE ▸ OUT

hide out (from someone or something) to hide oneself so that one cannot be found by someone or something. □ *Max was hiding out from the police in Detroit.* □ *Lefty is hiding out too.* [N] *The crook spent the night in the hideout.*

HIGH-PRESSURE ▸ INTO

high-pressure someone into something to compel someone into doing something. □ *Here comes Jill. Watch out. She will try to high-pressure you into working on her committee.* □ *You can't high-pressure me into doing anything! I'm too busy!*

HIKE ▸ UP

hike something up to raise something, such as prices, interest rates, a skirt, pants legs, etc. □ *The grocery store is always hiking prices up.* [T] *She hiked up her skirt so she could wade across the creek.*

HINDER ▸ FROM

hinder someone from something to prevent someone from doing something. □ *Please don't hinder me from my appointed tasks.* □ *You can't hinder me from doing what I want!*

HINGE ▸ (UP)ON

hinge (up)on someone or something to depend on someone or something; to depend on what someone or something does. (*Upon* is formal and less commonly used than *on*.) □ *The success of the project hinges upon you and how well you do your job.* □ *It all hinges on the weather.*

HINT ▸ AT

hint at something to refer to something; to insinuate something. □ *What are you hinting at?* □ *I am not hinting at anything. I am telling you to do it!*

HINT ▸ FOR

hint for something to give a hint that something is wanted. □ *I could tell she was hinting for an invitation.* □ *Are you hinting for a second helping of fried chicken?*

HINT ▸ TO

hint something to someone to give a hint or clue to someone. □ *I thought she was leaving. She hinted that to me.* □ *She wasn't hinting anything to you! You made it all up!*

HIRE ▸ AWAY

hire someone away (from someone or something) [for one] to get someone to quit working for someone or something and begin working for one. □ *We hired Elaine away from her previous employer, and now she wants to go back.* [T] *The new bank hired away all the tellers from the old bank.* □ *They tried to hire them all away.*

HIRE ▸ OUT

hire someone or something out to grant someone the use or efforts of someone or something for pay. (*Someone* includes *oneself*.) □ *I hired my son out as a lawn-care specialist.* [T] *I hire out my son to mow lawns.* □ *I hired my cottage out for the winter.* □ *Shall I hire myself out as a baby-sitter?*

HISS ▸ AT

hiss at someone or something **1.** [for a reptile] to make a hissing sound as a warning. □ *The snake hissed at me. Otherwise I wouldn't have known it was there.* □ *The lizard hissed at the snake.*

2. [for someone] to make a hissing sound at someone to show disapproval. □ *The audience hissed at the performer, who was not all that bad.* □ *They hissed at all three acts.*

HISS ▸ OFF

hiss someone off ((of) the stage) [for the audience] to hiss and drive a performer off the stage. (The *of* is colloquial.) □ *The boys in the front row tried to hiss her off the stage.* □ *The audience, angry with the quality of the singers, tried to hiss them all off.*

HISS ▸ OUT

hiss something out to say something with a hissing voice, usually in anger or disgust. □ *The disgusted manager hissed his appraisal out.* [T] *He hissed out his criticism.*

HIT ▸ AGAINST

hit against someone or something to strike against someone or something. □ *The door hit against me as I went through.* □ *The door hit against my foot as I went out.*

HIT ▸ AT

hit at someone or something to strike at someone or something. □ *The injured man hit at the nurses who were trying to help him.* □ *I hit at the wall to see how solid it was.*

HIT ▸ BACK

hit back (at someone or something) to strike someone or something back. □ *Tom hit Fred, and Fred hit back at Tom.* □ *I have to hit back when someone hits me.*

HIT ▸ BELOW

hit below the belt to do something unfair in a competition. (Both literal and figurative uses. See the following entry.) □ *Stop that! That's hitting below the belt.* □ *When Henry said that, he was really hitting below the belt.*

hit someone below the belt **1.** [for a boxer] to strike an opponent below the belt. (An unfair blow.) □ *The champ hit the contender below the belt and the crowd began to boo like fury.* □ *Fred was hit below the belt and suffered considerably.* **2.** to deal someone an unfair blow. (Figurative.) □ *That's not fair! You told them I was the one who ordered the wrong-size carpet. That's hitting me below the belt.* □ *Todd hit her below the belt when he said it was all her fault because she had become ill during the trip.*

HIT ▸ BETWEEN

hit someone between the eyes **1.** to strike someone on the nose between the eyes. □ *The punk kid hit the old man between the eyes.* □ *Max hit Lefty between the eyes.* **2.** [for the reality of something] to strike one suddenly and hard. (Figurative.) □ *Suddenly, the terribleness of what I had done hit me between the eyes.* □ *The realization of what had happened hit me between the eyes.*

HIT ▸ FOR

hit someone (up) for something to ask someone for the loan of money or for some other favor. □ *The tramp hit me up for a dollar.* □ *My brother hit me for a couple of hundred bucks.*

HIT ▸ IN

hit someone in something to strike someone on a particular part of the body. (*Someone* includes *oneself.*) □ *She hit him in the face by accident.* □ *Watch out or you'll hit yourself in the leg with the hammer.*

HIT ▸ OF

hit the (broad) side of a barn to hit an easy target. (Folksy. Usually negative.) □ *He can't park that car! He can't hit the broad side of a barn, let alone that parking place.* □ *He's a lousy shot. He can't hit the side of a barn.*

HIT ▸ OFF

hit it off (with someone) to start a good and friendly relationship with someone from the first meeting. □ *I really hit it off with my new boss.* □ *From the moment I met her, we really hit it off.* □ *They hit it off with each other from the start.*

hit something off to begin something; to launch an event. □ *She hit off the fair* *with a speech.* 🅃 *The mayor hit the fair off by giving a brief address.*

HIT ▶ ON

See also under *HIT ▶ (UP)ON.*

hit on someone to make sexual advances toward someone. ☐ *Sam hit on Clara and she became enraged.* ☐ *Nobody ever hits on me.*

hit someone or something on something to strike someone or some creature in a particular place. (*Someone* includes *oneself.*) ☐ *The stone hit me on the leg.* ☐ *I hit the beaver in the side and it didn't seem to feel it.* ☐ *She hit herself on her left cheek.*

hit the nail on the head to state something exactly and truly. (Figurative.) ☐ *You are exactly right! You hit the nail on the head!* ☐ *She hit the nail on the head when she said that the economy was getting weak.*

HIT ▶ OUT

hit out (at someone or something) (in something) to strike out at someone or something in some state, such as anger, revenge, etc. ☐ *The frightened child hit out at the teacher in sheer terror.* ☐ *He hit out in terror.* ☐ *Andy hit out at the threat.*

hit out (for something or some place) to set out for something or some place. (Colloquial.) ☐ *We hit out for the top of the hill early in the morning, and it was noon before we got there.* ☐ *We'll hit out about noon.*

HIT ▶ UP

hit someone (up) for something See under *HIT ▶ FOR.*

HIT ▶ (UP)ON

hit (up)on someone or something **1.** to discover someone or something. ☐ *I think I have hit upon something. There is a lever you have to press in order to open this cabinet.* ☐ *I hit on Tom in an amateur play production. I offered him a job in my nightclub immediately.* **2.** to strike or pound on someone or something. (Colloquial. *Upon* is formal and less commonly used than *on.*) ☐ *Jeff hit upon the mugger over and over.* ☐ *I hit on the radio until it started working again.*

HIT ▶ WITH

hit someone with something **1.** to strike someone with something. (*Someone* includes *oneself.*) ☐ *Max hit Lefty with a club.* ☐ *She hit herself with the door handle.* **2.** to charge someone with an amount of money. (Colloquial.) ☐ *The government hit us with a big fine.* ☐ *The tax people hit us with a huge tax bill.* **3.** to present someone with shocking or surprising news. ☐ *He was shocked when she hit him with the news that she was leaving.* ☐ *Don't hit me with another piece of bad news!*

HITCH ▶ TO

hitch someone or something (up) (to something) to attach someone or something to something. (*Someone* includes *oneself.*) ☐ *Please hitch the horse up to the wagon, and let's get going.* 🅃 *Please hitch up the horse.* ☐ *The farmer hitched his wife to the plow and got the field plowed.* ☐ *Hitch yourself up to the wagon and see if you can pull it.*

HITCH ▶ UP

See the previous entry.

HOARD ▶ UP

hoard something up to accumulate a large store of something against bad times. ☐ *Scott was hoarding caviar up for the hard times ahead.* 🅃 *He hoarded up many pounds of canned caviar.*

HOBNOB ▶ WITH

hobnob with someone or something to associate with someone or a group. ☐ *I'm not used to hobnobbing with such luminaries.* ☐ *Walter is spending a lot of time hobnobbing with the very rich.*

HOLD ▶ AGAINST

hold a grudge against someone See *bear a grudge against someone* under *BEAR ▶ AGAINST.*

hold something against someone or something **1.** to press something against someone, a group, or something. ☐ *Max held the gun against Lefty and threatened to pull the trigger.* ☐ *Fred* *held the drill against the wall and turned it on.* **2.** to think badly of someone, a group, or something because of something. ☐ *I am the one who dented your fender. I'm sorry. I hope you don't hold it against me.* ☐ *I hold all this mess against the government.*

HOLD ▸ AT

hold someone or something at bay to make someone, a group, or an animal stay at a safe distance. (Originally referred only to animals.) ☐ *I held the attacker at bay while Mary got away and called the police.* ☐ *The dogs held the bear at bay while I got my gun loaded.*

hold someone or something at something to keep someone or something at some distance, such as an arm's length, respectful distance, comfortable distance, etc. ☐ *I held the child at an arm's length until he could be calmed.* ☐ *The police held the crowd at a distance from the injured man.*

hold the line at someone or something not to exceed a certain limit regarding someone or something. ☐ *Having your wife on the payroll is one thing, but I will hold the line at her.* ☐ *We have to hold the line at this kind of expenditure.*

HOLD ▸ BACK

hold back (on something) to withhold something; to give only a limited amount. ☐ *Hold back on the gravy. I'm on a diet.* ☐ *That's enough. Hold back. Save some for the others.*

hold someone or something back (from someone or something) to restrain someone, something, or some creature from getting at or getting to someone or something. (*Someone* includes *oneself.*) ☐ *The parents held the children back from the cake and ice cream until the hostess said she was ready.* ☐ *Please hold your dog back.* 🆃 *Please hold back your dog.* ☐ *I was so hungry that, when I saw the food, I could hardly hold myself back.*

HOLD ▸ BY

hold by something to stick by a promise. ☐ *I hope that you will hold by our agreement.* ☐ *I will hold by everything I said.*

hold someone or something by something to grasp someone or something by a particular part. ☐ *I held him by the shoulder while I talked to him.* ☐ *Donna held the dog by the collar.*

HOLD ▸ DOWN

hold someone or something down **1.** to keep someone, something, or some creature down. ☐ *The heavy beam held him down, and he could not rise.* ☐ *The hunter held the animal down until the porters arrived.* ☐ *Hold him down until I get out my handcuffs.* **2.** to prevent someone or something from advancing. ☐ *I had a disability that held me down in life.* ☐ *The company had a lot of debt that held it down, even in prosperous times.*

HOLD ▸ FOR

hold good for someone or something [for an offer] to remain open to someone or a group. ☐ *Does your offer of help still hold good for us?* ☐ *Does it hold good for the entire membership?* ☐ *Does your offer of help hold good for my brother, who is not a member?*

hold no brief for someone or something not to tolerate someone or something; to be opposed to someone or something. ☐ *I hold no brief for Wally and his friends.* ☐ *Rachel holds no brief for that kind of thing.*

hold someone for ransom to demand money for the return of a person who has been kidnapped. ☐ *The kidnappers held me for ransom, but no one would pay.* ☐ *We will hold Timmy for ransom and hope that the police don't find us.*

hold something for someone **1.** to keep something safe for someone. ☐ *I will hold your money for you.* ☐ *Do you want me to hold your wallet for you while you swim?* **2.** [for a merchant] to set something aside for a purchaser who will pay for it and take delivery at a later date. ☐ *I will hold it for you until you get the money.* ☐ *We can hold it right here and give it to you when you have accumulated the money.*

hold still for someone or something AND **keep still for someone or something** to remain motionless for someone or something. □ *Hold still for the doctor and the shot won't hurt.* □ *Please keep still for the doctor.* □ *Hold still for the shot.*

hold still for something to tolerate something; to put up with something. □ *I will not hold still for any more of your antics.* □ *They refused to hold still for her antics.*

hold terror for someone [for something] to be frightening to a person. □ *The thought of flying to Rio by myself held great terror for me.* □ *Nothing holds terror for me. I am a daredevil.*

hold true for someone or something to prove to be true for someone or something. □ *The rule holds true for you too.* □ *This one is too big, and the same holds true for that one.*

HOLD ▶ FORTH

hold forth (on someone or something) to speak at great length about someone or something. □ *Sadie held forth on the virtues of home cooking.* □ *Sharon is holding forth and everyone is paying close attention.*

HOLD ▶ IN

hold someone or something in check AND **keep someone or something in check** to restrain someone or something. □ *Please try to hold your brother in check. He must not start another fight.* □ *Keep your dog in check if you can.*

hold someone or something in high regard to think well of someone or something. (*Someone* includes *oneself*.) □ *All of us hold the vice president in high regard.* □ *We hold these policies in high regard.* □ *You could tell that he held himself in high regard.*

hold someone or something in low regard to think poorly of someone or something. □ *I'm afraid that Hazel holds you in low regard.* □ *I'm afraid we hold this establishment in low regard.*

hold someone or something in reserve AND **keep someone or something in reserve** to hold back someone or something for future needs. □ *I am holding the frozen desserts in reserve, in case we run out of cake.* □ *We are holding Sharon in reserve.* □ *Keep a few good players in reserve.*

hold something in AND **keep something in** to hold in one's stomach, gut, belly, etc. □ *Hold your belly in so you don't look like a blimp.* 🅃 *Hold in your stomach.* □ *Keep your stomach in!* 🄰 *His held-in stomach still hung out over his belt.*

hold something in abeyance to stall or postpone something. □ *This is a good plan but not at this time. Let's just hold it in abeyance until things get better.* □ *We will hold the matter in abeyance until we hear from you.*

HOLD ▶ IN(SIDE)

hold something in(side (of) one(self)) AND **keep something in(side (of) one(self))** to keep one's emotions inside oneself. (The *of* is colloquial.) □ *You really shouldn't hold those feelings inside of you.* □ *Don't hold it in.* □ *Don't try to keep it in.* □ *I have kept all this inside myself too long.* 🅃 *You shouldn't hold in all that anger.* 🄰 *Her held-in emotions had to come out somehow.*

HOLD ▶ OFF

hold off ((from) doing something) to avoid doing something; to postpone doing something. □ *Can you hold off from buying a new car for another few months?* □ *I will hold off firing him until next week.*

hold off (on someone or something) to delay doing something concerning someone or something. □ *Please hold off on Tom until we interview the other candidates.* □ *I will hold off on this job for a while.*

hold someone or something off **1.** to make someone or something wait. □ *I know a lot of people are waiting to see me. Hold them off for a while longer.* 🅃 *See what you can do to hold off the reporters.* **2.** AND **keep someone or something off** to stave someone or something off. □ *Tom was trying to rob us, but we managed to hold him off.* 🅃

We held off the attackers. 🅃 *I couldn't keep off the reporters any longer.*

HOLD ▸ ON

hold on **1.** to wait. □ *Hold on a minute! Let me catch up!* □ *Hold on and wait till I get there.* □ *Hold on. I'll call her to the phone.* **2.** to be patient. □ *Just hold on. Everything will work out in good time.* □ *If you will just hold on, everything will probably be all right.*

hold on (to someone or something) See under *HANG ▸ ON.*

Hold on to your hat! See under *HANG ▸ ON.*

HOLD ▸ OUT

hold out to survive; to last. □ *I don't know how long we can hold out.* □ *They can probably hold out for another day or two.*

hold out (against someone or something) to continue one's defense against someone or something. □ *We can hold out against them only a little while longer.* □ *Dave can hold out forever.* 🄽 *The soldier found himself a holdout against a long-dead enemy.*

hold out (for someone or something) to strive to wait for someone or something. □ *I will hold out for someone who can do the job better than your last suggestion.* □ *I want to hold out for a better offer.* 🄽 *Tom is a holdout for a better offer.*

hold someone or something out (of something) **1.** to keep someone or something out of something. □ *We held the kids out of the party room as long as we could.* □ *We couldn't hold them out any longer.* **2.** to set someone or something aside from the rest; to prevent someone or a group from participating. □ *Her parents held her out of sports because of her health.* □ *The school board held the team out of competition as punishment for something.* 🅃 *They held out every player.*

hold something out (from something or oneself) to hold something or some creature out or away from one's body. □ *You ought to hold the snake out from your body in case it decides to bite.* □ *Hold your arm out from yourself to avoid spreading the poison ivy.*

hold (something) out on someone or something to keep news or something of value from someone or a group. (Slang.) □ *What's going on? Are you holding something out on me?* □ *Don't hold out on the city council. They have ways of finding out everything.*

hold something out (to someone) to offer something to someone. □ *I held an offer of immunity out to her.* 🅃 *I held out an offer of immunity to prosecution to her, but she would not cooperate.* □ *The court held out an offer of leniency, but the defendant turned it down.*

HOLD ▸ OVER

hold someone or something over to keep a performer or performance for more performances. (Because the performance is a success.) □ *The manager held Julie over for a week because she was so well received.* □ *They held our act over too.*

hold something over someone('s head) to have knowledge of something about a person and to use that knowledge to control the person. (As if someone were holding this information like a club over someone's head, threatening to strike the person with it.) □ *So I made a mistake when I was young. Are you going to hold that over my head all my life?* □ *Please don't hold that over me anymore.*

HOLD ▸ TO

hold a candle to someone or something to be equal to someone or something. (Idiomatic. Usually negative.) □ *Tom doesn't hold a candle to Jane when it comes to running.* □ *Our team doesn't hold a candle to yours.*

hold someone to something to make someone adhere to an agreement. (*Someone* includes *oneself.*) □ *You promised me that you would buy six of them, and I'm going to hold you to your promise.* □ *It was difficult, but he held himself to the terms of the contract.*

HOLD ▸ TOGETHER

hold oneself together to maintain one's sanity. (*Someone* includes *oneself.*) □ *I* *don't know if I can hold myself together through another horrible day like this one.* □ *I don't know how she held herself together through all her troubles.*

hold someone or something together to keep a group of people or things together. □ *She worked at two jobs in order to hold her family together.* □ *Our club was failing despite our efforts to hold it together.*

hold something together to keep the parts of an object together. □ *Hold this broken vase together until I get back with the glue.* □ *What can I use to hold this together?*

hold together [for something] to keep from falling apart. □ *Don't run the engine too fast because it won't hold together.* □ *Do you think that this book will hold together much longer?*

HOLD ▸ UP

hold one's end of the bargain up to adhere to a bargain one has made. (See also *hold one's end up.*) □ *I hope you will hold your end of the bargain up.* 🅃 *I hope you will hold up your end of the bargain.*

hold one's end up **1.** to *hold up one's end of the bargain.* □ *I expect you to hold your end up like the rest of us.* □ *You made the agreement and you have to hold your end up.* **2.** to carry one's share of the burden; to do one's share of the work. □ *You're not holding your end up. We're having to do your share of the work.* □ *Get busy. You have to hold your end up.* 🅃 *You have to hold up your end.*

hold one's head up to be confident of the respect of other people; to hold up one's head with pride. □ *Now I know that I can hold my head up again. I feel completely vindicated.* □ *I am so embarrassed. I will never be able to hold my head up again.* 🅃 *Now I can hold up my head with pride.*

hold someone or something up **1.** to keep someone or something upright. □ *Johnny is falling asleep. Please hold him up until I prepare the bed for him.* □ *Hold the window up while I prop it open.* **2.** to rob someone or a group. □ *Some punk tried to hold me up.* □ *The mild-looking man held up the bank and shot a teller.* 🄽 *The crooks pulled a holdup nearly every night that week.* **3.** to delay someone or something. □ *Driving the kids to school held me up.* 🅃 *An accident on Main Street held up traffic for thirty minutes.* □ *We were stuck in traffic and I couldn't see what the holdup was.*

hold someone or something up as an example to single out someone or something as a person or thing worthy of imitation. (*Someone* includes *oneself.*) □ *No one has ever held me up as an example.* 🅃 *Jane held up Doris as an example.* □ *I hate to hold myself up as an example, but if you would do what I do, at least I wouldn't criticize you.*

hold someone or something up to ridicule to single out someone or something for ridicule. □ *They must stop holding Matt up to ridicule! Who do they think they are?* 🅃 *She held up Donald to ridicule.* □ *They held our team up to ridicule.*

hold someone or something up to scorn to single out someone or something for repudiation. (*Someone* includes *oneself.*) □ *The entire crowd held Randy up to scorn for his part in the riot.* □ *We held the losing team up to scorn.* □ *At his most neurotic, he held himself up to scorn and ridiculed his own accomplishments.*

hold someone up to something to lift someone up to the level of something. □ *I held little Mary up to the window so she could see out.* □ *She was held up to the window so she could see better.*

hold up (for someone or something) to wait; to stop and wait for someone. □ *Hold up for Wallace. He's running hard to catch up to us.* □ *Hold up a minute.*

hold up (on someone or something) to delay or postpone further action on someone or something. □ *I know you are getting ready to choose someone, but hold up on Tom. There may be someone better.* □ *Hold up on the project, would you?* □ *We need to hold up for a while* *longer.* [N] *What's the holdup? Get moving!*

HOLD ► WITH

hold with something to agree with something; to tolerate something. (Folksy.) ☐ *I don't hold with what you are saying.* ☐ *We don't hold with that kind of thing around here.*

HOLE ► UP

hole up in something to hide in something or some place. (Colloquial.) ☐ *Max holed up in Lefty's place for a few days until the coast was clear.* ☐ *The snake holed up with a gopher for the winter.*

HOLLER ► OUT

holler something out to yell something out. ☐ *The guard hollered a warning out.* [T] *They hollered out a warning.*

HOLLOW ► OUT

hollow something out to make the inside of something hollow. ☐ *Martha hollowed the book out and put her money inside.* [T] *She hollowed out a book.*

HOME ► IN

home in (on someone or something) to aim directly at someone or something. ☐ *She came into the room and homed in on the chocolate cake.* ☐ *She saw the cake and homed in.*

HOME ► ON(TO)

home on(to something) to aim directly at something; to fix some type of receiver on a signal source. ☐ *The navigator homed onto the radio beam from the airport.* ☐ *The navigator located the beam and homed on.*

HONK ► AT

honk at someone or something to blow a horn at someone or something. ☐ *Is someone honking at me?* ☐ *The motorists honked at the sheep that were clogging the roadway.*

HONOR ► AS

honor someone as something to praise someone as something; to praise someone for being something. ☐ *Aren't you going to honor Kevin as a hero?* ☐ *We will honor Henry as the most promising scholar of the year.*

HONOR ► FOR

honor someone for something to praise someone for doing something. ☐ *The committee agreed to honor Laurel for her role in the benefit dance.* ☐ *I want to honor you for your efforts on behalf of our cause.*

HONOR ► WITH

honor someone with something to show one's respect for someone with something, such as a gift, party, ceremony, a response, etc. ☐ *We would like to honor you with a little reception.* ☐ *We chose to honor you with a little gift.*

HOODWINK ► INTO

hoodwink someone into something to deceive someone into doing something. ☐ *She will try to hoodwink you into driving her to the airport. Watch out.* ☐ *You can't hoodwink me into doing that!*

HOODWINK ► OUT

hoodwink someone out of something to get something away from someone by deception. ☐ *Are you trying to hoodwink me out of my money?* ☐ *Max tried to hoodwink the old lady out of all her money.*

HOOK ► DOWN

hook something down **1.** to attach something down with a hook. ☐ *Please hook the lid down so it doesn't fall off.* [T] *Please hook down the lid.* **2.** to toss something down to someone. (Slang.) ☐ *Hook another can of pop down to me, will you?* [T] *Hook down another can of pop.* **3.** to eat something; to gobble something up. (Slang.) ☐ *Wally hooked the first hamburger down and ordered another.* [T] *He hooked down two more burgers in a few minutes.*

HOOK ► INTO

hook something into something to connect something to something. ☐ *I want to hook another communication line into the system.* ☐ *Is it possible to hook my computer into your network?*

HOOK ► IN(TO)

hook in(to something) to connect into something. □ *We will hook into the water main tomorrow morning.* □ *We dug the pipes up and hooked in.*

HOOK ► ON

See also *HOOK ► ON(TO).*

hook oneself on someone or something to become enamored of someone or something. (Slang.) □ *I'm afraid I've hooked myself on Alice.* □ *He hooked himself on Bach organ music.*

hook someone on something to addict someone to a drug or alcohol. (Slang. *Someone* includes *oneself.*) □ *Careful, or you'll hook yourself on those tranquilizers.* □ *Some friend at school hooked Roger on dope.* □ *Sharon has hooked herself on cocaine.*

HOOK ► ON(TO)

hook something on(to someone or something) to attach something to someone or something by a hook. □ *Hook this sign on her and let her walk around advertising our play.* 🅃 *Hook on the sign and hope that it stays.* □ *Hook it onto the tree carefully.*

HOOK ► UP

hook someone or something up (to someone or something) AND **hook someone or something up (with someone or something)** to attach someone or something to someone or something. (*Someone* includes *oneself.*) □ *The nurse hooked the patient up to the oxygen tubes.* 🅃 *They hooked up the patient with the tubes.* □ *Let's hook the dog up to the post.* □ *We hooked the dog up.* □ *She hooked herself up to the machine, and began her biofeedback session.*

hook something up to set something up and get it working. (The object is to be connected to electricity, gas, water, telephone lines, etc.) □ *Will it take long to hook the telephone up?* 🅃 *As soon as they hook up the telephone, I can call my friends.* 🄽 *Let's get all these hookups made before quitting time.*

HOOT ► AT

hoot at someone or something See under *HOWL ► AT.*

HOOT ► DOWN

hoot someone down See under *HOWL ► DOWN.*

HOOT ► OFF

hoot someone off the stage [for an audience] to boo and hiss until a performer leaves the stage. □ *The rude audience hooted Carl off the stage.* □ *Carl was hooted off the stage.*

HOP ► IN(TO)

hop in(to something) to jump into something; to get into something. □ *Hop into your car and drive over to my house.* □ *I hopped in and drove off.*

HOP ► OFF

hop off ((of) something) to jump off something. (The *of* is colloquial.) □ *She hopped off her bike and came into the house.* □ *The bird on the branch hopped off.*

HOP ► ON

hop on the bandwagon See under *GET ► ON.*

HOP ► ON(TO)

hop on(to something) to jump or get onto something that is moving. □ *Sometimes you have to hop onto the cable car after it has started to move.* □ *I ran to the cable car and hopped on.* □ *I will hop on a plane and be there in an hour.*

HOP ► TO

hop to it to get going; to start doing what one was told to do. (Informal.) □ *Get moving! Faster! Hop to it!* □ *I want you to hop to it and get the job done.*

HOP ► UP

hop something up to make a machine, especially a car, run extra fast or give it extra power. (Slang.) □ *He will take that junk heap home and hop it up.* 🅃 *He spent nearly every evening hopping up his old car.* 🄰 *What a neat hopped-up car.*

hop up (to someone or something) [for an animal] to come close to someone or something by hopping. □ *The bunny hopped up to me and just sat there.* □ *It hopped up and stared.*

HOPE ▸ AGAINST

hope against (all) hope (for something) to hope even when everything is hopeless. □ *I'm afraid that I am hoping against all hope for his safe return.* □ *We hoped against hope, and everything worked out.*

HOPE ▸ FOR

hope for something to be optimistic that one's wish for something will come true. □ *I still hope for her return.* □ *We hope for good weather on Friday.*

hope for the best to desire the best to happen. □ *Good luck. You know we all hope for the best.* □ *Mary is worried, but she hopes for the best.*

HORN ▸ IN

horn in (on someone or something) to interfere with someone or something. (Informal.) □ *Are you horning in on us?* □ *Please don't horn in on our conversation.* □ *I'm not horning in!*

HORSE ▸ AROUND

horse around to play around boisterously, perhaps physically or roughly. □ *Stop horsing around, you guys!* □ *You spend too much time horsing around.*

horse around (with someone or something) **1.** to play around roughly with someone or something, possibly abusing someone or something. □ *Stop horsing around with your little brother. Leave him alone.* □ *Will you kids stop horsing around?* **2.** to join someone in boisterous play; to participate in rough play with someone. □ *He's horsing around with his little brother. They are really having a good time.* □ *We spent the entire afternoon just horsing around.*

HOSE ▸ DOWN

hose someone or something down to wash something down with water from a hose. (*Someone* includes *oneself*.) □ *Hose her down to cool her off and maybe she will do the same for you.* 🅃 *Please hose down the driveway.* □ *Hose it down.* □ *He hosed himself down for an hour, but the smell of the skunk was impossible to get off.*

HOUND ▸ DOWN

hound someone or something down to pursue and capture someone or some creature. □ *I will hound the killer down if it takes me the rest of my life.* 🅃 *I will hound down that killer if it takes years.* □ *The bear hounded down the hunter.*

HOUND ▸ FROM

hound someone from some place AND **hound someone out (of something or some place)** to chase someone out of some place; to force someone out of something or some place. □ *They hounded Joel and his friends from the town.* □ *The sheriff hounded Tex out of town.*

HOUND ▸ OUT

hound someone out (of something or some place) See the previous entry.

hound something out of someone to force someone to give information. □ *We are going to have to hound the information out of her.* □ *We hounded the combination to the safe out of them.*

HOVER ▸ AROUND

hover around (someone or something) to hang or wait around someone or something. □ *The mugger hovered around the side door to the theater, waiting for a victim.* □ *The birds hovered around the bird feeder.*

HOVER ▸ BETWEEN

hover between someone and someone else to waver in the choosing of one person or another. (Figurative.) □ *I am hovering between Tom and Terry for the job.* □ *Don't hover between the two for so long. Just choose one!*

hover between something and something else **1.** to float or hang between things. □ *The helicopter hovered between the buildings and lowered a rescue chair.* □ *The hummingbird hovered between the blossoms, sipping from one and then the other.* **2.** to waver between one thing and another. (Figurative.) □ *I hovered between chocolate and vanilla.* □ *Uncle Jed hovered between life and death for days.*

HOVER ▶ OVER

hover over someone or something **1.** to remain suspended over someone or something. □ *The rescue helicopter hovered over the floating sailor.* □ *A huge blimp hovered over the football stadium.* **2.** [for someone] to stay close to someone or something, waiting, ready to advise or interfere. (Figurative.) □ *Please don't hover over me, watching what I am doing.* □ *I have to hover over this project or someone will mess it up.*

HOWL ▶ AT

howl at someone or something **1.** [for a canine] to bay at someone or something. □ *The dog howls at me when I play the trumpet.* □ *The wolves howled at the moon and created a terrible uproar.* **2.** AND **hoot at someone or something** to yell out at someone or something. □ *The audience howled at the actors and upset them greatly.* □ *We hooted at the singer until he stopped.* **3.** to laugh very hard at someone or something. □ *Everyone just howled at Tom's joke.* □ *I howled at the story Alice told.*

HOWL ▶ DOWN

howl someone down AND **hoot someone down** to yell at or boo someone's performance; to force someone to stop talking by yelling or booing. □ *The audience howled the inept magician down.* [T] *They howled down the musician.* □ *We all hooted them down.* □ *The crowd howled the speaker down and he left the platform.*

HOWL ▶ WITH

howl with something to yell or holler because of something, such as pain. □ *Roger howled with pain as the needle went into his arm.* □ *Mary howled with grief when she saw what had happened to her roses.*

HUDDLE ▶ AROUND

huddle around someone or something to gather or bunch around someone or something. □ *The girls huddled around Mary to hear what she had to say.* □ *The kids huddled around the cake and consumed it almost instantaneously.*

HUDDLE ▶ TOGETHER

huddle someone together to bunch people together. □ *The scoutmaster huddled the boys together to give them a pep talk.* □ *Let's huddle everyone together to keep warm.*

See the following entry.

HUDDLE ▶ UP

huddle (up) (together) to bunch up together. □ *The children huddled up together to keep warm.* □ *They huddled up to keep warm.* □ *The newborn rabbits huddled together and squirmed hungrily.*

HUM ▶ WITH

hum with activity [for a place] to be busy with activity. □ *The kitchen hummed with activity as usual.* □ *Our main office was humming with activity during the busy season.*

HUNCH ▶ OVER

hunch over [for someone] to bend over. □ *The wounded man hunched over and staggered to the window.* □ *He was hunched over with pain.*

HUNCH ▶ UP

hunch something up to raise up or squeeze up some body part, usually the shoulders. □ *He hunched his shoulders up in his effort to get warm.* [T] *He hunched up his shoulders to keep warm.*

hunch up to squeeze or pull the parts of one's body together. □ *He hunched up in a corner to keep warm.* □ *Why is that child hunched up in the corner?*

HUNGER ▶ AFTER

hunger after something to crave for something, not necessarily food. □ *I hunger after some old-fashioned gospel music.* □ *Mary hungered after something fattening, such as ice cream or even a baked potato with sour cream.*

HUNGER ▶ FOR

hunger for someone or something to desire someone or something; to yearn for someone or something. □ *I hunger for you. I want you madly.* □ *He looked at the cake and you could see he was hungering for it.*

HUNKER ▶ DOWN

hunker down (on something) to squat down on one's heels, a stool, a stone, etc. (Folksy.) □ *Jeff hunkered down on the pavement and watched the world go by.* □ *He hunkered down to take a rest.*

HUNT ▶ AFTER

hunt after someone or something to seek or pursue someone or something. □ *I'm hunting after a tall man with straight black hair.* □ *Elaine is hunting after a place to store her bicycle.*

HUNT ▶ DOWN

hunt someone or something down **1.** to chase and catch someone or something. □ *I don't know where Amy is, but I'll hunt her down. I'll find her.* T *I will hunt down the villain.* **2.** to locate someone or something. □ *I don't have a big enough gasket. I'll have to hunt one down.* T *I have to hunt down a good dentist.*

HUNT ▶ FOR

hunt for someone or something **1.** to chase someone or something for sport. □ *The demented hunter hunted for kidnap victims on his human game preserve.* □ *Frank likes to hunt for deer.* **2.** to look for someone or something. □ *I am hunting for someone to help me with the piano.* □ *I am hunting for a new piano.*

HUNT ▶ OUT

hunt someone or something out to find someone or something even if concealed. □ *We will hunt them all out and find every last one of those guys.* T *We will hunt out all of them.* T *They hunted out the murderer.*

HUNT ▶ THROUGH

hunt through something to search through the contents of something; to search among things. □ *Joel hunted through his wallet for a dollar bill.* □ *I will have to hunt through my drawers for a pair of socks that match.*

HUNT ▶ UP

hunt someone or something up to seek someone or something. □ *I don't know where Jane is. I'll hunt her up for you, though.* T *I'll help you hunt up Jane.* T *Will someone please hunt up a screwdriver?*

HURL ▶ AROUND

hurl something around to throw something, such as words, around carelessly. □ *Don't just go hurling words around like they didn't mean anything.* T *You are just hurling around words!*

HURL ▶ AT

hurl someone or something at someone or something to throw someone or something at someone or something. □ *The huge man actually hurled me at the tree.* □ *Larry hurled his shoe at me.*

HURL ▶ AWAY

hurl something away (from someone or something) to throw or push something away from someone or something. □ *She hurled the bricks away from the partially buried child.* □ *Hurl the bricks away as fast as you can.*

HURL ▶ DOWN

hurl someone or something down to throw or push someone or something downward to the ground. (*Someone* includes *oneself*.) □ *Roger hurled the football down and it bounced away wildly.* T *He hurled down the football in anger.* □ *The angry player hurled the ball down.* □ *Fred hurled himself down and wept at the feet of the queen.*

HURL ▶ INTO

hurl someone or something into something to throw someone or something into something. (*Someone* includes *oneself*.) □ *She hurled the little boys into the storm cellar and went back to the house for the dog.* □ *Sharon hurled her belongings into the suitcase and jammed it closed.* □ *In the deepest despair, the shadowy figure hurled himself into the torrential current.*

HURL ▶ OUT

hurl someone or something out (of some place) to throw someone or something out of some place. (The *of*-phrase is paraphrased with a *from*-phrase when the particle is transposed. See the F example.) □ *The manager hurled them out of the tavern.* T *The manager hurled out the annoying people.* F *The* *manager hurled out the annoying people from the café.* ☐ *I opened the window and hurled the burning wastebasket out.*

HURRY ▸ ALONG

hurry someone or something along to make someone or something go faster. ☐ *Go hurry your mother along. We're almost late.* ☐ *Why don't you hurry the meeting along?*

HURRY ▸ AWAY

hurry away AND **hurry off** to leave in a hurry. ☐ *I have to hurry away. Excuse me, please. It's an emergency.* ☐ *Don't hurry off. I need to talk to you.*

HURRY ▸ BACK

hurry back to return sometime soon. (A formula heard in retail shops.) ☐ *Please hurry back. Good-bye.* ☐ *I want you to hurry back here right away.*

hurry back (to someone or something) to return to someone or something immediately or as fast as possible. ☐ *Oh, please hurry back to me as soon as you can.* ☐ *Hurry back!*

HURRY ▸ DOWN

hurry down to descend rapidly. ☐ *We need you down here in the basement. Hurry down.* ☐ *Please hurry down and help us.*

HURRY ▸ IN(TO)

hurry someone or something in(to something) to make someone or something go into something fast. ☐ *She hurried the chickens into the coop and closed the door on them for the night.* ☐ *It was beginning to rain, so Jerry hurried the children in.* ☐ *Please don't hurry me into a decision.*

HURRY ▸ OFF

hurry off See under *HURRY ▸ AWAY.*

HURRY ▸ ON

hurry on See under *HURRY ▸ UP.*

hurry on (toward something) to move quickly to or toward something. ☐ *Please hurry on toward gate number ten. That's where our plane is.* ☐ *We finished our business and hurried on.*

hurry one on one's way to help someone to hasten on. ☐ *Mary hurried Joel on his way so he could catch his train.* ☐ *There is no need to hurry me on my way. I am leaving.*

HURRY ▸ UP

hurry someone or something up to make someone or something go or work faster. ☐ *Please hurry them all up. We are expecting them very soon.* ☐ *See if you can hurry this project up a little.*

hurry up AND **hurry on** to move faster. ☐ *Hurry up! You're going to be late.* ☐ *Please hurry on. We have a lot to do today.*

hurry up and wait to do some things in a series fast and then have to wait a long time to do the next things in the series. (Idiomatic. Originally military.) ☐ *That's all we ever do. Rush to stand in line somewhere. We just hurry up and wait all day long.* ☐ *Hurry up and wait! That's the army for you.*

HURT ▸ FOR

hurt for someone or something See under *ACHE ▸ FOR.*

HURTLE ▸ THROUGH

hurtle through something to travel through something at great speed or with great force, possibly causing breakage. ☐ *A brick hurtled through the window and fell on the floor.* ☐ *The rocket hurtled through space toward Mars.*

HUSH ▸ UP

hush someone or something up to make someone or something be quiet. ☐ *Please hush the children up. I have a telephone call.* ☐ *Can you hush that radio up, please?*

hush something up to keep something from public knowledge. ☐ *The company moved quickly to hush the bad news up.* 🅃 *They wanted to hush up the bad financial report.*

hush up to be quiet; to get quiet; to stop talking. ☐ *You talk too much. Hush up!* ☐ *I want you to hush up and sit down!*

HUSTLE ▸ UP

hustle up to hurry up. (Informal.) ☐ *Hustle up, you guys. We have to get* *moving.* □ *Hustle up. We are almost late.*

HYPE ▸ UP

hype someone or something up to promote, advertise, or boost someone or something, often in exaggeration. (Also without *up,* but not eligible as an entry.) □ *No matter how much they hyped it up, it was still a very dull movie.* □ *Her agent hyped her up as a great actress.* Ⓐ *That movie was just a hyped-up piece of trash.*

hype someone up to get someone excited. □ *Who hyped you up? Why are you so excited?* Ⓐ *Who is that hyped-up guy jumping around?*

HYPOTHESIZE ▸ ABOUT

hypothesize about something to speculate about something; to make guesses about something. □ *Don't waste time hypothesizing about what happened.* □ *There is no point in hypothesizing about what happened when we don't know the actual truth.*

HYPOTHESIZE ▸ ON

hypothesize on something to conjecture on the origin or nature of something. □ *We sat around hypothesizing on the origin of life.* □ *I refuse to hypothesize on her real motive.*

I

ICE ▶ DOWN

ice something down to cool something with ice. □ *They are icing the champagne down now.* [T] *They are icing down the champagne now.* [A] *Four iced-down bottles of champagne sat in buckets, waiting for the party to start.*

ICE ▶ OVER

ice over [for water] to freeze and develop a covering of ice. □ *I can't wait for the river to ice over so we can do some ice fishing.* [A] *Is the iced-over pond really safe to skate on?*

ICE ▶ UP

ice something up to cause something to become icy. □ *I hope the cold doesn't ice the roads up.* [T] *The wind and rain iced up the roads.*

ice up to become icy. □ *Are the roads icing up?* [A] *The iced-up roads are terribly dangerous. Don't go out.*

IDENTIFY ▶ AS

identify someone as someone **1.** to determine that someone is a certain person. □ *Can you identify Fred as the perpetrator?* □ *Fred was identified as the thief.* **2.** to reveal one's identity or name. (*Someone* includes *oneself*.) □ *Will you identify the man as Tom?* □ *The stranger identified himself as a meter reader from the gas company.*

IDENTIFY ▶ BY

identify someone or something by something to recognize someone or something because of something. □ *Can you identify your baggage by any special marks?* □ *You can identify me by the red carnation in my lapel.*

IDENTIFY ▶ WITH

identify (oneself) with someone or something to classify oneself with someone or something; to relate to someone or something; to see part of oneself represented in someone or something. □ *I identify myself with the others.* □ *I identify with the birds and animals of the forest.* □ *She had always identified herself with the downtrodden.*

identify someone or something with someone or something to associate people and things, in any combination. (*Someone* includes *oneself*.) □ *I tend to identify Wally with big cars.* □ *We usually identify green with greed.* □ *We tend to identify big cars with greedy people.* □ *We always identify Tom with the other kids from Toledo.*

IDLE ▶ ABOUT

idle about to loiter around, doing nothing. □ *Please don't idle about. Get busy!* □ *Andy is idling about today.*

IDLE ▶ AWAY

idle something away to waste one's time in idleness; to waste a period of time, such as an afternoon, evening, ones's life. □ *She idled the afternoon away and then went to a party.* [T] *Don't idle away the afternoon.*

IDOLIZE ▶ AS

idolize someone or something as something to worship or adore someone or something as being something. □ *We all idolized Jim as our hero.* □ *They idolized wealth as a cure for all their ills.*

ILLUMINATE ▸ WITH

illuminate something with something 1. to light up something with something. □ *The lights illuminated the monument with a bright glow.* □ *The monument was illuminated with mercury vapor lamps.* 2. to explain or elucidate something with explanation. □ *Please try to illuminate this matter with an explanation.* □ *Could you illuminate your answer with a little more detail?* 3. to decorate a manuscript with pictures or designs. □ *The monks spent all their days illuminating manuscripts with pictures.* □ *No one has the patience to illuminate books with tiny designs.*

ILLUSTRATE ▸ WITH

illustrate something with something 1. to provide pictorial examples for a book or other document. □ *She illustrated her book with clever line drawings.* □ *We need someone to illustrate this book with drawings.* 2. to use something to show how something works, how something is meant to be, or how to do something. □ *Would you please illustrate how to do it with a drawing or two?* □ *I think I can illustrate what I mean with a little more explanation.*

IMAGINE ▸ AS

imagine someone or something as someone or something to think of someone or something as another person or another type of thing. (*Someone* includes *oneself.*) □ *I really can't imagine you as a sailor.* □ *When I imagine that statue as John, I get all fidgety inside.* □ *I just can't imagine you as an expert skier.*

IMBUE ▸ WITH

imbue someone with something to indoctrinate someone with something; to build something into someone. □ *I tried to imbue my children with a strong sense of justice.* □ *Her thinking and attitudes had been imbued with childhood fears.*

IMMERSE ▸ IN

immerse someone or something in something 1. to submerge someone or something beneath the surface of a liquid; to soak someone or something in a liquid. (*Someone* includes *oneself.*) □ *The preacher immersed the baptism candidate in the water.* □ *We immersed all the dirty plates in the soapy water and left them to soak.* □ *She immersed herself in the bathwater.* 2. to saturate or steep someone or a group in information or some type of instruction. (*Someone* includes *oneself.*) □ *The trainers immersed us in details day after day.* □ *The teachers will immerse the entire class in nothing but the Spanish language, day after day.* □ *He immersed himself in his studies.*

IMMIGRATE ▸ (IN)TO

immigrate (in)to some place (from some place) to migrate into a place from some other place. □ *Many of them immigrated into Minnesota from the northern lands.* □ *My family immigrated to Chicago.*

IMMUNIZE ▸ AGAINST

immunize someone against something to vaccinate someone against some disease; to do a medical procedure that causes a resistance or immunity to a disease to develop in a person. □ *They wanted to immunize all the children against the measles.* □ *Have you been immunized against polio?*

IMPACT ▸ (UP)ON

impact (up)on someone or something [for something] to have an effect on someone or something. (*Upon* is formal and less commonly used than *on.*) □ *This event will impact upon the seashore for years to come.* □ *The day's troubles impacted on Rachel quite seriously.*

IMPALE ▸ ON

impale someone or something on something to put someone or something on a pointed object and press down. (*Someone* includes *oneself.*) □ *The insect impaled the spider on a twig.* □ *The waves almost impaled me on a submerged tree branch.* □ *The robber impaled himself on the top of the iron fence surrounding the house.*

IMPART ▸ TO

impart something to someone or something 1. to bestow a quality on someone or a group. □ *That hat imparts an aura of grandeur to her presence.* □

Walnut paneling imparts an expensive seriousness to a law office. **2.** to tell something to someone or a group. ☐ *My professor tried to impart her knowledge to us.* ☐ *The speaker imparted a great deal of wisdom to the group.*

IMPEACH ► FOR

impeach someone for something **1.** to charge someone with doing something illegal. ☐ *You can't impeach her for just disagreeing!* ☐ *We tried to impeach Gus for failing to attend sessions.* **2.** to criticize or discredit someone for something. ☐ *The opposition impeached him for his position in no uncertain terms.* ☐ *Liz was impeached by the press for her views.*

IMPEL ► INTO

impel someone or something into something **1.** to urge or force someone or something into something. ☐ *The strong words impelled us into the arena.* ☐ *The sheriff impelled the crowd into the storm shelter.* **2.** to urge or force someone or something into doing something. ☐ *We were not able to impel them into returning.* ☐ *Sam impelled the committee into extending its meeting time.*

IMPINGE ► (UP)ON

impinge (up)on someone or something to interfere with someone or something. (*Upon* is formal and less commonly used than *on*.) ☐ *This will not impinge upon me at all.* ☐ *Will this matter impinge on my policies in any way?*

IMPLANT ► IN(TO)

implant something in(to) someone or something to embed something into someone or something. ☐ *The surgeon implanted a pacemaker into Fred.* ☐ *They implanted the device in Fred's chest.*

IMPLICATE ► IN

implicate someone in something to say that someone is involved in something. (*Someone* includes *oneself*.) ☐ *Dan implicated Ann in the crime.* ☐ *Ted refused to implicate himself in the affair.*

IMPORT ► FROM

import something (from something) ((in)to something) to buy and transport something from a foreign place into a country. ☐ *We imported the carpets from the Orient into this country.* ☐ *They imported wine into this country from France.* ☐ *I imported this from Germany.*

IMPORT ► (IN)TO

See the previous entry.

IMPOSE ► (UP)ON

impose something (up)on someone to force something on someone. (*Upon* is formal and less commonly used than *on*.) ☐ *Don't try to impose your ideas upon me!* ☐ *The colonists tried to impose their values on the indigenous peoples.*

impose (up)on someone to be a bother to someone; to make a request of something of someone. (*Upon* is formal and less commonly used than *on*.) ☐ *I don't mean to impose upon you, but could you put me up for the night?* ☐ *Don't worry, I won't let you impose on me.*

IMPREGNATE ► WITH

impregnate something with something **1.** to saturate something with something; to penetrate something with some fluid. ☐ *They impregnated the boards with a wood preservative.* ☐ *The process impregnated the fibers with a bright yellow dye.* **2.** to infuse something into something. (Figurative.) ☐ *You have impregnated the entire matter with unpleasantness.* ☐ *The whole scheme has been impregnated with needless flaws.*

IMPRESS ► AS

impress someone as something to be memorable to someone as a particular type of person. ☐ *She didn't impress me as a particularly wise individual.* ☐ *Liz impressed us all as a skilled artisan.*

IMPRESS ► BY

impress someone by something to make someone notice one's good qualities. ☐ *You impress me by your willingness to serve.* ☐ *We were all impressed by your candor.*

IMPRESS ▸ INTO

impress something into something to press something into something. □ *I impressed the key into the wax, making a perfect copy.* □ *Andy impressed his thumb into the pie.*

IMPRESS ▸ (UP)ON

impress something (up)on someone to make someone fully aware of something. (*Upon* is formal and less commonly used than *on*.) □ *You must impress these facts upon everyone you meet.* □ *She impressed its importance on me.*

impress something (up)on something to press something into the surface of something, leaving a mark. □ *The ribbing of my socks impressed a pattern upon my calves.* □ *The heavy vase impressed its outline on the pine tabletop.*

IMPRESS ▸ WITH

impress someone with someone or something to awe someone with someone or something. □ *Are you trying to impress me with your wisdom?* □ *She impressed him with her friend, who was very tall.*

IMPRINT ▸ INTO

See under *IMPRINT ▸ ON(TO).*

IMPRINT ▸ ON(TO)

imprint something on(to) something **1.** to print something onto something. □ *We imprinted your name onto your stationery and your business cards.* □ *Please imprint my initials on this watch.* **2.** AND **imprint something into something** to record something firmly in the memory of someone. □ *The severe accident imprinted a sense of fear onto Lucy's mind.* □ *Imprint the numbers into your brain and never forget them!* **3.** AND **imprint something into something** to make a permanent record of something in an animal's brain. (As with newly hatched fowl, which imprint the image of the first moving creature into their brains.) □ *The sight of its mother imprinted itself on the little gosling's brain.* □ *Nature imprints this information into the bird's memory.*

IMPRINT ▸ WITH

imprint something with something to print something with a message. □ *Amy imprinted each bookmark with her name.* □ *Each bookmark was imprinted with her name.*

IMPRISON ▸ IN

imprison someone in something to lock someone up in something. □ *The authorities imprisoned him in a separate cell.* □ *Bob imprisoned Timmy in the closet for an hour.*

IMPROVE ▸ (UP)ON

improve (up)on something to make something better. (*Upon* is formal and less commonly used than *on*.) □ *Do you really think you can improve upon this song?* □ *No one can improve on my favorite melody.*

IMPROVISE ▸ ON

improvise on something [for a musician] to create a new piece of music on an existing musical theme. □ *For an encore, the organist improvised on "Mary Had a Little Lamb."* □ *She chose to improvise on an old folk theme.*

IMPUTE ▸ TO

impute something to someone or something to ascribe something to someone or something; to attribute something to someone or something. □ *I didn't mean to impute a bad intention to your company.* □ *The lawyer imputed perjury to the witness.*

INAUGURATE ▸ AS

inaugurate someone as something to launch or introduce someone as something. □ *The club inaugurated Amy as the new president.* □ *We will inaugurate Ken as vice president.*

INCAPACITATE ▸ FOR

incapacitate someone (for something) (for a period of time) to make someone physically unfit to do something for a period of time. □ *The accident incapacitated Rick for further work for a year.* □ *Sam's carelessness incapacitated Frank for a month.*

INCARCERATE ▸ IN

incarcerate someone in something to imprison someone in something. □ *The sheriff incarcerated Lefty in the town jail.* □ *He had wanted to incarcerate Max in the jail too.*

INCH ▸ ACROSS

inch one's way across something AND **inch oneself across something** to creep slowly across something. □ *The little green worm inched its way across the branch.* □ *It inched itself across the leaf.* □ *Fred inched himself across the damaged bridge.*

INCH ▸ ALONG

inch one's way along something AND **inch oneself along something** to creep slowly on or along something. □ *I inched my way along the ledge and almost fell off.* □ *Sharon inched herself along the side of the bridge.* □ *The group of climbers inched themselves along the narrow ledge.*

INCH ▸ BACK

inch back to move back very slowly. □ *The trainer inched back from the angry tiger.* □ *The tiger inched back and sprang.*

INCH ▸ FORWARD

inch forward to move forward very slowly. □ *Inch forward very slowly, and try not to make any noise.* □ *The tiger inched forward, taking care not to alert the cow to its presence.*

INCH ▸ OVER

inch over to move over a tiny bit. □ *Could you inch over a little? I need just a little more room.* □ *Please inch over a little.*

INCITE ▸ TO

incite someone to something to excite or provoke someone to something. □ *The radicals tried to incite the students to violence.* □ *The students were incited to violent behavior by the lecturer.*

INCLINE ▸ AWAY

incline away (from someone or something) to lean or slope away from someone or something. □ *I inclined away from her to avoid her alcohol breath.* □ *The land inclined away from the house.* □ *The platform inclined away from the rear wall of the stage.* □ *The major area of the stage inclined away from Terri, making it hard for her to stand up.*

INCLINE ▸ FORWARD

incline forward to lean forward; to slant forward. □ *The earthquake-ravaged building inclined forward a little bit more and looked as if it was going to fall.* □ *My chair inclined forward and I kept feeling as if I were going to fall off.*

incline something forward to lean something forward; to make something slant forward. □ *Incline the light forward a little bit, so you can see better.* □ *The fence had been inclined slightly forward to make it harder to climb.*

INCLINE ▸ TOWARD

incline toward someone or something **1.** to lean or slant toward someone or something. □ *The piece of scenery inclined toward Roger very slowly and stopped its fall just in time.* □ *The tree inclined toward the flow of the wind.* **2.** to favor or "lean" toward choosing someone or something. □ *I don't know which to choose. I incline toward Terri but I also favor Amy.* □ *I'm inclining toward chocolate.*

INCLUDE ▸ AMONG

include someone or something among something to count someone or something as a member of a group or collection. (*Someone* includes *oneself.*) □ *I am happy to include you among my friends.* □ *I include Roger among my group of close friends.* □ *Do you include chocolate among your favorite flavors?* □ *Sally included herself among those needing better housing.*

INCLUDE ▸ IN

include someone in (something) to invite someone to participate in something. (*Someone* includes *oneself.*) □ *Let's include Terri in the planning session.* □ *I will include her in.* □ *Without asking, Henry included himself in the group going on a picnic.*

INCLUDE ▸ OUT

include someone out (of something) to exclude someone from something. (Colloquial.) ☐ *I'm not interested in your games. Include me out of them.* ☐ *Include me out too.*

INCORPORATE ▸ IN(TO)

incorporate someone or something in(to) something to build someone or something into something; to combine someone or something into something. (*Someone* includes *oneself.*) ☐ *We want to incorporate you into our sales force very soon.* ☐ *The prince had incorporated himself into the main governing body.*

INCREASE ▸ BY

increase something by something to enlarge something by an amount or degree. ☐ *They increased the size of the house by two hundred square feet.* ☐ *The house size has been increased by a small amount.*

INCREASE ▸ FROM

increase something (from something) (to something) to enlarge something from something to something bigger; to enlarge something from one size to a larger size. ☐ *We plan to increase sales from four million to six million dollars.* ☐ *I increased my bid to two thousand from one thousand.*

INCREASE ▸ IN

increase in something to grow or expand in some quality. ☐ *He increased in stature and wisdom.* ☐ *The tree increased in size every year.*

INCREASE ▸ TO

increase something (from something) (to something) See under *INCREASE ▸ FROM.*

INCREMENT ▸ BY

increment something by something to increase a sum by a supplement [of a certain figure]. ☐ *Increment the numbering by ten so that 1, 2, 3 becomes 10, 20, 30.* ☐ *The base number was incremented by 4.*

INCULCATE ▸ IN(TO)

inculcate something in(to) someone to instill specific knowledge into someone; to teach something to someone so that it will be remembered. ☐ *They inculcated good manners into their children all their lives.* ☐ *We tried to inculcate good morals into our students.*

INCULCATE ▸ WITH

inculcate someone with something to impress someone with some specific knowledge. ☐ *The teacher sought to inculcate the students with the knowledge they needed.* ☐ *Her parents inculcated her with good manners.*

INDEMNIFY ▸ AGAINST

indemnify someone or something against something to agree to protect someone or something against something, such as damage or a lawsuit. (*Someone* includes *oneself.*) ☐ *Their employer indemnified them against legal action.* ☐ *We indemnified the publisher against legal trouble.* ☐ *Jane was asked to indemnify herself against legal action for as much as one million dollars.*

INDICATE ▸ TO

indicate something to someone to signify something to someone. (By speech, writing, or some other sign.) ☐ *Karen indicated her agreement to the lawyer.* ☐ *Fred indicated his assent to me.*

INDICT ▸ FOR

indict someone for something [for a legal body] to arraign someone for a crime or name someone formally as the doer of a crime. ☐ *The grand jury indicted her for murder.* ☐ *Then they indicted Max for grand larceny.*

INDOCTRINATE ▸ INTO

indoctrinate someone into something to teach someone the ways of a group or some activity. ☐ *The military staff sought to indoctrinate Walter into the ways of the intelligence detail.* ☐ *Todd indoctrinated Ken into camp life.*

INDOCTRINATE ▸ WITH

indoctrinate someone with something to teach someone the official or fundamental knowledge about something. ☐ *They indoctrinated all their spies with* *the importance of being loyal to the death.* □ *Ken indoctrinated Todd with revolutionary thinking.*

INDUCE ▸ IN

induce labor in someone to cause the onset of childbirth in a mother-to-be. □ *They decided to induce labor in the mother-to-be.* □ *They decided not to induce labor in Alice.*

INDUCT ▸ INTO

induct someone into something **1.** to conscript someone into the armed services; to bring a non-volunteer into the armed services. □ *They inducted Wally into the army in a little ceremony.* □ *They inducted a number of new members into the group.* **2.** to draft someone into something. □ *The government inducted Sam into the army.* □ *They inducted him into a new platoon.* **3.** to install someone in an office or position. □ *They inducted her into the presidency.* □ *The college inducted a new president into office last week.*

INDULGE ▸ IN

indulge in something **1.** to take pleasure in doing something; to do something habitually. □ *No, I don't indulge in contact sports anymore.* □ *We don't indulge in strenuous activity.* **2.** to choose to eat food or drink something, usually alcohol. □ *I don't usually indulge in hard spirits, but just this once.* □ *I indulge in chocolate until I can't hold any more.*

INDULGE ▸ WITH

indulge someone with something to grant someone the favor or privilege of something. (*Someone* includes *oneself.*) □ *Please indulge me with this one favor.* □ *He always indulged himself with a candy bar when he went into town.*

INFATUATE ▸ WITH

See *be infatuated with someone or something* under *BE ▸ WITH.*

INFECT ▸ WITH

infect someone with something **1.** to transmit disease-causing organisms to someone. (*Someone* includes *oneself.*) □ *Please don't infect me with your cold germs.* □ *Somehow, she infected herself with the virus she was studying.* **2.** to affect someone with something, such as excitement, joy, desires, etc. (Figurative.) □ *She infected everyone she worked with with her happiness.* □ *Her explosive laughter infected everyone with good spirits.*

INFER ▸ FROM

infer something from something to reach a conclusion from something; to deduce facts from something, such as someone's words, a situation, etc. □ *What can we infer from the experience we have just had?* □ *You should not infer anything from Sue's remarks.*

INFEST ▸ WITH

See *be infested with something* under *BE ▸ WITH.*

INFILTRATE ▸ INTO

infiltrate into something **1.** to permeate something; to filter into something. □ *The sour smell infiltrated into everything in the refrigerator.* □ *The paint smell infiltrated into every room in the house.* **2.** to penetrate a group, secretly, for the purposes of spying or influencing the activities of the group. (Also without *into*, but not eligible as an entry.) □ *The spy infiltrated into the city council.* □ *They infiltrated into the government.*

INFLATE ▸ WITH

inflate something with something **1.** to fill up something with air or some other gas. □ *Jerry has to inflate all the balloons with helium.* □ *Ken inflated the balloons with gas.* **2.** to fill something with air, using a pump or similar device. □ *We inflated the balloons with the pump.* □ *Liz inflated the rubber raft with a hand pump.* **3.** to make a sum appear larger by including additional irrelevant amounts. □ *I think that she has inflated her expense report with too many miles of travel.* □ *Don't inflate your expense report with extra costs.*

INFLICT ▸ (UP)ON

inflict someone (up)on someone to burden someone with the care or keeping of someone else. (*Upon* is formal and less commonly used than *on*. *Someone* includes *oneself.*) □ *Please don't in-*

flict Bob upon me. ☐ *My brother inflicted his children on us for the weekend.* ☐ *Well, I certainly don't want to inflict myself on you for the weekend, but I do need a place to stay.*

inflict something (up)on someone or something to impose something, such as pain, a burden, a problem, etc., on someone or something. (*Upon* is formal and less commonly used than *on*.) ☐ *I hate to inflict an additional burden upon you, but someone has to clean the oven.* ☐ *Please don't inflict that on me.*

INFORM ▸ ABOUT

inform someone about someone or something to tell someone about someone or something. ☐ *How is my friend Tom getting on? I asked you to inform me about him from time to time.* ☐ *Please inform me about the state of the contract for the book.*

INFORM ▸ OF

inform someone of something to tell someone a fact. ☐ *Please inform Sally of my decision.* ☐ *Sally has been informed of your decision.*

INFORM ▸ ON

inform on someone to tell the authorities about someone; to tattle on someone. ☐ *I am going to have to inform on you.* ☐ *Liz informed on Ken.*

inform someone on someone to *tattle (on someone) (to someone)* ☐ *I will inform the teacher on you!* ☐ *Billy informed his mother on Bobby.*

INFRINGE ▸ (UP)ON

infringe (up)on something to interfere with the rights of someone or with someone's property rights; to encroach on something. (*Upon* is formal and less commonly used than *on*.) ☐ *You are infringing upon my right to free speech.* ☐ *I am not infringing on anything.*

INFUSE ▸ INTO

infuse something into someone to put specific knowledge into a person's brain; to teach someone something very well. ☐ *The boss infused a lot of company information into the new assistant before she took another job.* ☐ *The teacher infused a lot of knowledge into the students in a short time.*

infuse something into something to mix something into something. ☐ *You should infuse this mixture into the tea.* ☐ *The tea was infused into the water very slowly.*

INFUSE ▸ WITH

infuse someone with something to teach someone a body of knowledge or a perspective on a body of knowledge. ☐ *The schools sought to infuse the children with a sense of history.* ☐ *Children should be infused with a sense of history.*

infuse something with something to make something mix into some liquid. ☐ *He infused the mixture with a strong solution of soap.* ☐ *The chemical mixture was infused with the other solution.*

INGRATIATE ▸ INTO

ingratiate oneself into something to work hard to bring oneself into the favor of someone. ☐ *Oh, how he fawns over the guests! Isn't it terrible the way he tries to ingratiate himself into their favor?* ☐ *You will never succeed in ingratiating yourself into my good graces.*

INGRATIATE ▸ WITH

ingratiate oneself with someone to work oneself into someone's favor. ☐ *Why do you have to ingratiate yourself with everyone? Don't you know how to be just plain friends?* ☐ *She was very obvious in her effort to ingratiate herself with the boss.*

INHERIT ▸ FROM

inherit something from someone **1.** to fall heir to something from someone; to receive something from the estate of a person who has died. ☐ *I inherited this silver bowl from my aunt.* ☐ *Liz inherited her house from her parents.* **2.** to receive a genetic or behavioral trait from a relative. ☐ *I inherited my stubbornness from my father's side of the family.* ☐ *My stubbornness was inherited from my grandfather.*

INHIBIT ▸ FROM

inhibit someone from something to keep someone from doing something.

☐ *We will attempt to inhibit Karen from doing it, but we have no control over her.* ☐ *A serious case of shyness inhibited Harry from participating in things.*

inhibit something from something to keep something from happening. ☐ *We need to inhibit the weeds from further growth.* ☐ *The weeds were inhibited from spreading by the application of a pesticide.*

INITIATE ▸ INTO

initiate someone into something **1.** to induct someone into an organization or activity, usually in a ceremony. ☐ *They will initiate me into the fraternity next week.* ☐ *They initiated all their new members into the club at once.* **2.** to introduce someone to the activities associated with a job or other situation. ☐ *The personnel department will initiate you into our office routines.* ☐ *Our procedures are complicated and it takes weeks to initiate a new employee into all our procedures.*

INJECT ▸ INTO

inject something into something **1.** to squirt something, such as oil, water, etc., into something. ☐ *The pump injected the oil into the wheel bearings when I squeezed the lever.* ☐ *The mechanic injected a solvent into the lock.* **2.** AND **inject someone or something with something** to give a hypodermic injection of something to someone or some creature. ☐ *The nurse injected the medicine into my arm.* ☐ *He injected a very large dose into the patient.* ☐ *The nurse injected me with the serum.* **3.** to put something, such as humor, excitement, etc., into a situation. ☐ *Let's inject a little humor into this dismal affair.* ☐ *She likes to inject a lot of excitement into her books.*

INJECT ▸ WITH

inject someone or something with something See under the previous entry.

INK ▸ IN

ink something in **1.** to fill in an outline with ink. ☐ *Please ink the drawing in with care.* 🅃 *Ink in the drawing carefully.* **2.** to write something in ink. ☐ *Please ink your name in on the dotted line.* 🅃 *Now, ink in your signature on this line right here.*

INLAY ▸ WITH

inlay something with something to decorate something by cutting in a design and filling the cut with some decorative substance. ☐ *The workers inlaid the tabletop with bits of polished seashell.* ☐ *The tabletop was inlaid with a lovely design.*

INOCULATE ▸ AGAINST

inoculate someone against something to immunize someone against a disease. ☐ *We need to inoculate all the children against whooping cough.* ☐ *Have you been inoculated against measles?*

INOCULATE ▸ WITH

inoculate someone with something to use a particular substance in immunizing someone against a disease. ☐ *Donna inoculated Richard and Nancy with yellow fever vaccine for their trip.* ☐ *She also inoculated Sam with something to prevent seasickness.*

INQUIRE ▸ ABOUT

inquire about someone or something to ask about someone or something. ☐ *I inquired about Tom and was told that he doesn't live here anymore.* ☐ *You will have to inquire about that at the front desk.*

INQUIRE ▸ AFTER

inquire after someone to ask about the well-being of someone. ☐ *Jerry inquired after you when I saw him at the store today.* ☐ *I will inquire after his wife the next time I see him.*

INQUIRE ▸ FOR

inquire for someone to ask to see someone. ☐ *Mr. Franklin, there is a man out here inquiring for you. What shall I tell him?* ☐ *Who is inquiring for me?*

INQUIRE ▸ INTO

inquire into something to look into something; to investigate something by asking questions. ☐ *I will inquire into your complaint. It sounds as if some-*

thing is wrong. □ *We have not inquired into it yet.*

INQUIRE ▸ OF

inquire something of someone to ask some information of someone. □ *I need to inquire something of you.* □ *May I inquire something personal of you?*

INQUIRE ▸ WITHIN

inquire within to ask questions of a person inside [some place, such as a store or office]. (Formula. On a sign posted outside.) □ *"Help wanted. Inquire within," read the sign on the door.* □ *If you want to apply, you must inquire within.*

INSCRIBE ▸ INTO

inscribe something into something to write or engrave a dedication on something. (Emphasis is on the act of inscribing.) □ *It was a lovely watch. I asked them to inscribe something into the back, so I could remember the occasion.* □ *My initials were inscribed into the wristband.*

INSCRIBE ▸ ON(TO)

inscribe something on(to) something to write or engrave certain information on something. (Emphasis is on the message that is inscribed.) □ *The jeweler inscribed Amy's good wishes onto the watch.* □ *I inscribed my name on my tools.*

INSCRIBE ▸ WITH

inscribe something with something to engrave something with a message. □ *Could you please inscribe this trophy with the information on this sheet of paper?* □ *I inscribed the bracelet with her name.*

INSERT ▸ BETWEEN

insert something between something and something else to put something in between things. □ *Insert this marker between pages ten and eleven.* □ *A marker was inserted between the pages.*

INSERT ▸ IN

insert something in(to) something to push or stick something into something. □ *Insert the card into the slot and pull the lever.* □ *Insert the coins in the machine.* □ *I need to insert another paragraph into this article.*

INSINUATE ▸ INTO

insinuate oneself into something to work oneself into a group or situation. □ *She had sought for years to insinuate herself into Terry's organization.* □ *Must you always insinuate yourself into my set of friends?*

INSINUATE ▸ TO

insinuate something to someone to hint at something to someone; to imply something to someone. □ *You think I am interested in you for your money! Is that what you are insinuating to me?* □ *I did not insinuate anything to you!*

INSIST ▸ (UP)ON

insist (up)on something to demand something. (*Upon* is formal and less commonly used than *on*.) □ *I want you here now! We all insist upon it!* □ *I insist on it too.* Ⓐ *I believe I can satisfy all your insisted-upon conditions.*

INSPIRE ▸ IN

inspire something in someone to stimulate a particular quality in someone. □ *You do not particularly inspire trust in me.* □ *She inspires fear in me.*

INSPIRE ▸ WITH

inspire someone with something to use something to inspire someone; to stimulate or encourage someone with something. □ *The president inspired us all with patriotic speeches.* □ *She inspired us all with her story of heroism.*

INSTALL ▸ AS

install someone as something to inaugurate or launch someone into the role of something. (*Someone* includes *oneself*.) □ *The board installed Jerry as the new parliamentarian.* □ *She installed herself as the boss of the kitchen and wouldn't allow anyone else in.*

INSTALL ▸ IN

install something in someone or something to insert or build something into someone or something. □ *We are going to install a trash compactor in our kitchen.* □ *The doctors installed a pacemaker in Donald.*

INSTIGATE ▸ TO

instigate someone to do something to prompt someone to do something; to urge or cause someone to do something. ☐ *Are you the one who instigated Terry to start all this trouble?* ☐ *Did you instigate the children to do this?*

INSTILL ▸ IN(TO)

instill something in(to) someone to impress something into someone's mind. ☐ *You need to remember your manners. I want to instill that into you.* ☐ *Good manners were instilled in me at home.*

instill something in(to) something to add something to a situation. ☐ *The presence of the mayor instilled a legitimacy into the proceedings.* ☐ *Sharon sought to instill a little levity in the meeting.*

INSTILL ▸ WITH

instill someone with something to indoctrinate someone with something. ☐ *Her story instilled us all with courage.* ☐ *She instilled us with courage.*

INSTITUTE ▸ AGAINST

institute something against someone or something to initiate something against someone or something. ☐ *The hospital decided to institute proceedings against her for failing to pay her bill.* ☐ *The prosecutor instituted a case against the county board.*

INSTRUCT ▸ IN

instruct someone in something to teach someone about something. ☐ *Amy will instruct you in the way to hang paper.* ☐ *The manager instructed Ken in the best method of entering data into the computer.*

INSULATE ▸ AGAINST

insulate someone or something against someone or something AND **insulate someone or something from someone or something** to protect someone or something against the effect of someone or something. (*Someone* includes *oneself.*) ☐ *Use an extra blanket to insulate the baby against the cold.* ☐ *John is a bad influence on the children, and I've taken care to insulate them against him.* ☐ *We insulated the children from the effects of John and his bad habits.* ☐ *She learned to insulate herself against the effects of the constant attacks.*

INSULATE ▸ FROM

insulate someone or something from something See the previous entry.

INSURE ▸ AGAINST

insure against something to guard or protect against something. ☐ *You must insure against theft and fire.* ☐ *I will insure against all risks.*

insure someone or something (against something) (for something) to provide insurance for someone or something against certain perils up to a certain amount of money. (*Someone* includes *oneself.*) ☐ *I insured my wife against accidental death for $100,000.* ☐ *We insured the car for its current value against all losses.* ☐ *They were advised to insure themselves against theft.*

INSURE ▸ FOR

See the previous entry.

INSURE ▸ WITH

insure someone or something with something to provide insurance for someone or something from a specific company. ☐ *I insured Amy with a fine old insurance company.* ☐ *We insured the car with Acme Insurance in Adamsville.*

INTEGRATE ▸ INTO

integrate someone or something into something to combine someone or something into something; to work someone or something into something. (*Someone* includes *oneself.*) ☐ *We sought to integrate Amy into the everyday affairs of the company.* ☐ *We sought to integrate the new family into the ways of the community.* ☐ *We integrated ourselves into the community in no time at all.*

INTEGRATE ▸ WITH

integrate someone with someone to mix people together; to unify people into one group. (*Someone* includes *oneself.*) ☐ *We are going to integrate the Yankees and the Confederates one of these days.* ☐ *They integrated them-*

selves with the people already in attendance.

integrate something with something to merge things together; to join things into one. ☐ *I want to integrate the accounting department with the auditing department to save a little money.* ☐ *They integrated your department with mine.*

INTEND ▶ AS

intend something as something to mean something to serve as something. ☐ *We intend this money as a gift. Do not even think about paying it back.* ☐ *This money is intended as a gift.*

INTEND ▶ FOR

intend something for someone or something to mean for someone or something to get something. ☐ *I intended this one for you. I'm sorry I failed to give it to you in time.* ☐ *Aunt Em intended this cake for the county fair, but you can have it instead.* ☐ *I intended this one for you all along.*

INTER ▶ IN

inter someone in something to bury someone in something or in some place. ☐ *They chose to inter her in the family burial plot.* ☐ *She was interred in the vault with the rest of the family.*

INTERACT ▶ WITH

interact with someone to converse with and exchange ideas with someone. (*Someone* includes *oneself.*) ☐ *In act two, I want Terri to interact with Amy a little more. They act as if they never even met each other.* ☐ *The students will interact with one another in their study projects.*

interact with something to have a reciprocal action with something; to react with something. (Often refers to the negative consequences of interaction.) ☐ *Will this drug interact with coffee?* ☐ *This drug will not interact with anything.*

INTERCEDE ▶ FOR

intercede (for someone) (with someone or something) to intervene on behalf of someone with someone or a group; to plead someone's case with someone or a group. ☐ *I will intercede for Charlotte with the council.* ☐ *Tom interceded with Fred for Sharon, who was too shy to speak for herself.*

INTERCEDE ▶ WITH

See the previous entry.

INTERCHANGE ▶ WITH

interchange someone with someone else to exchange one person for another. ☐ *I interchanged Sally with Roger for the honor of being first speaker.* ☐ *Roger has been interchanged with Sally.*

interchange something with something to exchange one thing for another. ☐ *Please interchange the orange one with the purple one.* ☐ *The orange one has been interchanged with the red one.*

INTEREST ▶ IN

interest someone in someone or something to arouse the interest of someone in someone or something. ☐ *Yes, I can recommend someone for you to hire. Could I interest you in Tom? He's one of our best workers.* ☐ *Can I interest you in checking out a book from the library?*

interest someone in something to cause someone to wish to purchase something. ☐ *Could I interest you in something with a little more style to it?* ☐ *Can I interest you in some additional insurance on your life?*

INTERFACE ▶ WITH

interface someone or something with someone or something to bring about a complex connection of people and things, in any combination. (*Someone* includes *oneself.* Originally having to do with computers.) ☐ *Let's interface Walter with the staff from the main office.* ☐ *I want to interface my computer with Sam, who is located down the hall.* ☐ *Roger needs to interface himself better with his staff.*

interface with someone or something to develop a connection or interaction with someone or something. ☐ *Call Walter and set up a meeting so we can interface with him.* ☐ *This computer is meant to interface with as many as five others just like it.*

INTERFERE ► IN

interfere in something to meddle in something; to become involved in someone else's business. ☐ *Don't interfere in my business!* ☐ *Are you interfering in this matter again?*

INTERFERE ► WITH

interfere with someone or something to meddle with something or someone's affairs. ☐ *Please do not interfere with us.* ☐ *Are you interfering with my project?*

INTERJECT ► INTO

interject oneself into something to force oneself into something, usually into someone else's business. ☐ *I am going to have to interject Fred into this matter before it gets out of hand.* ☐ *I hate to interject myself into your affairs, but I have something to say.*

interject something into something to volunteer information or a comment into a conversation. ☐ *We can always count on Liz to interject something sensible into our discussions.* ☐ *At last, something sensible has been interjected into our discussions.*

INTERLACE ► WITH

interlace something with something to weave something into something else. ☐ *I will interlace some silver thread with the white yarn.* ☐ *The manufacturer had interlaced a silver thread into the yarn.*

INTERMARRY ► WITH

intermarry with someone [for members of a group] to marry into another group or clan. ☐ *Our people don't intermarry with people of that clan.* ☐ *They do not intermarry with other groups on purpose.*

INTERMINGLE ► WITH

intermingle something with something to mingle or merge things with things. ☐ *Don't intermingle the U.S. mail with the interoffice mail.* ☐ *The office mail had been intermingled with the regular mail!*

intermingle with someone to mingle or merge with people. ☐ *The mugger intermingled with the people on the street and could not be recognized.* ☐ *Let's intermingle with the guests.*

INTERN ► IN

intern someone in something to detain or imprison a person in something. ☐ *The government interned the citizens in the camps for a few months.* ☐ *He was interned in a prison camp during the war.*

INTERPOSE ► BETWEEN

interpose someone or something between people or things to put someone or something between people or things, in any combination. (*Someone* includes *oneself.*) ☐ *I do not wish to interpose Randy between the twins.* ☐ *We will not interpose our own standards between these two tribes.* ☐ *Is there any point in interposing these bright colors between the two major areas already done in muted shades?* ☐ *Rudely, he interposed himself between Lady Bracknell and the door.*

INTERPOSE ► IN(TO)

interpose something in(to) something to introduce something into something; to put a question into a conversation. ☐ *The chairman interposed a question into the discussion.* ☐ *May I interpose an observation in the proceedings?*

INTERPRET ► AS

interpret something as something to assume that something means something. ☐ *Don't interpret what I just said as criticism.* ☐ *It will be interpreted as criticism no matter what you say.*

INTERPRET ► FOR

interpret for someone to translate speech in a foreign language for someone. (Interpreting is done in real time.) ☐ *Nina interpreted for Michael, since he understood very little Russian.* ☐ *Is there someone who can interpret for me?*

interpret something for someone **1.** to translate a foreign language for someone. (Interpreting is done in real time.) ☐ *Could you interpret the ambassador's address for me.* ☐ *Nina interpreted the director's greetings for the visitors.* **2.** to explain something to someone. ☐ *Let* *me interpret the instructions for you.* ☐ *The instructions have been interpreted for me by the manager.*

INTERSPERSE ▸ AMONG

intersperse something among something to place something among things at random. ☐ *We interspersed a few chocolate ones among all the plain ones.* ☐ *Some chocolate ones had been interspersed among the plain ones.*

INTERSPERSE ▸ BETWEEN

intersperse something between something to place things between other things, perhaps regularly or in a pattern. ☐ *We interspersed an onion plant between each pair of plants.* ☐ *Onions had been interspersed between every two marigold plants.*

INTERSPERSE ▸ THROUGHOUT

intersperse something throughout something to put things throughout something. ☐ *He interspersed his ideas for a better life throughout the book.* ☐ *Good advice had been interspersed throughout the book.*

INTERSPERSE ▸ WITH

intersperse something with something to provide or bestow something with something. ☐ *You should intersperse some red ones with the orange ones.* ☐ *The book was interspersed with good advice.*

INTERTWINE ▸ WITH

intertwine something with something to mingle or twist something together with something else. ☐ *She intertwined the flowers with the sprigs of greenery, making a lovely wreath.* ☐ *The flowers were intertwined with sprigs of greenery.*

intertwine with something to twist together with something else. ☐ *The vines intertwined with the ropes and cables that had once held the beached raft together.* ☐ *The ropes intertwined with each other, causing many problems.*

INTERVENE ▸ BETWEEN

intervene between someone and someone to intercede between someone and someone. ☐ *I decided to intervene between Ralph and his brother, who were arguing endlessly.* ☐ *There was no point in intervening between Bill and Bob.*

INTERVENE ▸ IN

intervene in something to get involved in something. ☐ *I will have to intervene in this matter. It's getting out of hand.* ☐ *I want to intervene in this before it gets out of hand.*

INTERVENE ▸ WITH

intervene with someone or something to step into a matter concerning someone or something. ☐ *Megan said she would intervene with the bank manager on our behalf.* ☐ *Do I need to intervene with this process?*

INTERVIEW ▸ FOR

interview someone for something [for an employer] to discuss employment in a particular job with a person seeking employment. ☐ *We will interview her for the manager's job.* ☐ *We will interview the rest of them for the position tomorrow.*

INTERVIEW ▸ WITH

interview with someone for something [for a person seeking employment] to discuss employment in a particular job with an employer. ☐ *She interviewed with the civic opera company for a job in the business department.* ☐ *I interviewed with Roger for the job.*

INTIMATE ▸ TO

intimate something to someone to suggest or imply something to someone. ☐ *What are you intimating to me?* ☐ *I intimated nothing at all to you.*

INTIMIDATE ▸ INTO

intimidate someone into something to threaten someone into doing something. ☐ *Do you think you can intimidate me into working for you?* ☐ *We weren't intimidated into doing it.*

INTIMIDATE ▸ WITH

intimidate someone with something to threaten or frighten someone with something. ☐ *Please don't try to intimidate me with your silly threats!* ☐ *We hadn't been intimidated with their threats.*

INTOXICATE ▸ WITH

intoxicate someone with someone or something to enthrall or entrance someone with someone or something. (Figurative.) ☐ *She intoxicated him with her smiling eyes.* ☐ *The king intoxicated the dignitaries with his beautiful daughter, whom he offered in marriage to the bravest of them all.*

intoxicate someone with something to make someone drunk with alcohol. (*Someone* includes *oneself.*) ☐ *I think that the plaintiff set out to intoxicate the defendant with liquor and then fake a crime.* ☐ *Jed set out to intoxicate Max with gin and then rob him.* ☐ *Alice intoxicated herself with too much whiskey.*

INTRIGUE ▸ AGAINST

intrigue (with someone) (against someone) See under *INTRIGUE ▸ WITH.*

INTRIGUE ▸ WITH

intrigue someone with someone or something to fascinate someone with someone or something. ☐ *Walter intrigued the baby with his keys and funny faces.* ☐ *The king intrigued the guests with a seductive dancer who had trained in the Far East.*

intrigue (with someone) (against someone) to conspire with someone against someone. ☐ *You are guilty of intriguing with Terry against William and Mary.* ☐ *I did not intrigue against anyone.* ☐ *Roger intrigued with Fred, and all this threatened David, who figured out it was directed at him.*

INTRODUCE ▸ INTO

introduce someone into something to bring someone into something; to launch someone into something. (*Someone* includes *oneself.*) ☐ *Tony introduced Wally into his club.* ☐ *You do not wish me to introduce myself into local social life, do you?*

introduce something into something to bring something into something or some place; to bring something into something as an innovation. ☐ *The decorator introduced a little bit of raspberry into the conference room.* ☐ *After I introduced the new procedures into the factory, production increased enormously.*

INTRODUCE ▸ TO

introduce someone to someone to make someone acquainted with someone else. (*Someone* includes *oneself.*) ☐ *I would like to introduce you to my cousin, Rudolph.* ☐ *Allow me to introduce myself to you.*

INTRUDE ▸ INTO

intrude into something to get involved in something that is someone else's business. ☐ *I don't want to intrude into your affairs, but I see that you're short of money.* ☐ *Please don't intrude into this matter.*

intrude oneself into something to work oneself into some matter that is someone else's business. ☐ *I hate to intrude myself into your conversation, but don't I know you?* ☐ *Please do not intrude yourself into this matter.*

INTRUDE ▸ (UP)ON

intrude (up)on someone or something to encroach on someone or something or matters that concern only someone or something. (*Upon* is formal and less commonly used than *on*.) ☐ *I didn't mean to intrude upon you.* ☐ *Please don't intrude on our meeting. Please wait outside.*

INUNDATE ▸ WITH

inundate someone or something with something **1.** to flood someone or something with fluid. ☐ *The river inundated the fields with three feet of water.* ☐ *The storm inundated us with buckets of water.* **2.** to overwhelm someone with someone or something. (Figurative.) ☐ *They inundated us with requests.* ☐ *The children inundated us with requests for their favorite songs.* ☐ *The citizens inundated the legislature with demands for jobs.* ☐ *We were inundated with applicants for the job.*

INURE ▸ TO

inure someone or something to something to accustom someone to someone or something. (*Someone* includes *oneself.*) ☐ *We wanted to inure you to this kind of problem, but here it is and you* *must face it.* □ *The coach inured the team to the thought of losing.* □ *She had long ago inured herself to attacks of this type.*

INVEIGH ▸ AGAINST

inveigh against someone or something to attack someone or something verbally. □ *Why must you always inveigh against Dan whenever I mention his name?* □ *Stop inveighing against the government all the time.*

INVEIGLE ▸ INTO

inveigle someone into something to coax or trick someone into doing something. □ *We tried to inveigle her into attending, but she caught on to us.* □ *I was inveigled into doing it.*

INVEIGLE ▸ OUT

inveigle someone out of something to deceive someone into giving something up. □ *Are you trying to inveigle me out of my money?* □ *I was inveigled out of my money.*

inveigle something out of someone to get something away from someone, usually by deception or persuasion. □ *They inveigled a large donation out of Mrs. Smith.* □ *The crooks tried to inveigle a fortune out of the old lady.*

INVEST ▸ IN

invest in someone or something to put resources into someone or something in hopes of increasing the value of the person or thing. (The emphasis is on the act of investing.) □ *We invested in Tom and we have every right to expect a lot from him.* □ *She invested in junk bonds heavily.*

invest something in someone or something to put money, time, effort, etc., into someone or something, hoping for a return. (The emphasis is on what is invested.) □ *We will invest time and effort in Fred and make him into a movie star.* □ *Sharon invested a lot of money in the stock market.*

INVEST ▸ WITH

invest someone or something with something to place some quality into someone or something. □ *His family fortune and connections invested him with an automatic acceptance wherever he went.* □ *Sheer power invested the committee with an enormously effective voice in politics.*

INVITE ▸ IN(TO)

invite someone in(to some place) to bid or request someone to enter a place. (*Someone* includes *oneself.*) □ *Don't leave Dan out there in the rain. Invite him into the house!* 🅃 *Oh, do invite in the visitors!* □ *Yes, invite them in.* □ *To my horror, he invited himself in.*

INVITE ▸ OUT

invite someone out to ask someone out on a date. □ *I would love to invite you out sometime. If I did, would you go?* □ *Have you been invited out this week?*

INVITE ▸ OVER

invite someone over (for something) to bid or request someone to come to one's house for something, such as a meal, party, chat, cards, etc. □ *Let's invite Tony and Nick over for dinner.* 🅃 *Let's invite over some new people.* □ *I will invite Amy over for a talk.*

INVITE ▸ TO

invite someone to something to bid or request someone to come to an event. (*Someone* includes *oneself.*) □ *Shall we invite Sally to the party?* □ *I didn't invite her. She invited herself to this affair.*

INVOKE ▸ (UP)ON

invoke something (up)on someone or something to call something, such as judgment, power, wrath of God, etc., to deal with someone or something. (*Upon* is formal and less commonly used than *on.*) □ *The charlatan invoked the power of Catherine the Great upon his enemies—to no avail.* □ *Walter invoked the wrath of God on the proceedings, which weren't going very well anyway.*

INVOLVE ▸ IN

involve someone in something to draw someone into a matter or problem. (*Someone* includes *oneself.*) □ *Please don't involve me in this mess.* □ *I do not wish to involve myself in Alice's business.* □ *I didn't want to involve you in the problem we are having with the police.*

INVOLVE ▸ WITH

involve someone with someone or something 1. to cause someone to associate with someone or something. (*Someone* includes *oneself*.) □ *Don't try to involve me with John. I can't stand him.* □ *We will try to involve all the teachers with the new association.* □ *I will not involve myself with such goings-on.* 2. to connect someone or someone's name to wrongdoing associated with someone or something. □ *Don't try to involve Amy with the crime. She is innocent.* □ *We involved the committee with the intense lobbying effort, and everyone began to see the extent of its influence.*

IRON ▸ OUT

iron something out 1. to use a flatiron to make cloth flat or smooth. □ *I will iron the drapes out, so they will stay flat.* 🅃 *I ironed out the drapes.* 2. to ease a problem; to smooth out a problem. (Figurative. Here *problem* is synonymous with *wrinkle*.) □ *It's only a little problem. I can iron it out very quickly.* 🅃 *We will iron out all these little matters first.*

ISOLATE ▸ FROM

isolate someone or something from someone or something to keep people or things separated from one another, in any combination. (*Someone* includes *oneself*.) □ *They isolated everyone from Sam, who was ill with malaria.* □ *We isolated the children from the source of the disease.* □ *I need to isolate myself from things like that.*

ISSUE ▸ AS

issue something as something to release or send out something as something. □ *They issued this month's magazine as a special double issue.* □ *The publisher issued this month's magazine as the very last one.*

ISSUE ▸ FORTH

See the following entry.

ISSUE ▸ FROM

issue (forth) from some place to go out or come out of a place. □ *The news releases issued forth from the pressroom on a regular basis.* □ *Clear water issued from the side of the hill.*

issue from something to come out or flow out of something. □ *A delicious perfume issued from Sally's hair as she passed.* □ *A wonderful odor issued from the kitchen. Something good was happening there.*

ISSUE ▸ TO

issue something to someone to distribute or dispense something to someone. □ *The front office issued new room assignments to everyone today.* □ *New keys were issued to everyone.*

ISSUE ▸ WITH

issue someone with something to provide someone with something; to distribute something to someone. □ *We issued them with the clothes they needed for the trip.* □ *Everyone was issued with supplies.*

ITCH ▸ FOR

itch for something to desire something. (Colloquial.) □ *I'm just itching for a visit from Amy.* □ *We are itching for some chocolate.*

J

JAB ▸ AT

jab at someone or something to poke at someone or something. ☐ *Tom jabbed at Fred.* ☐ *Don't jab at the cat!*

jab something at someone or something to poke someone or something with something. ☐ *Tom jabbed the stick at the dog.* ☐ *I jabbed my fist at Walter.*

JAB ▸ IN

jab someone in something to poke someone in a particular location on the body. (*Someone* includes *oneself.*) ☐ *Fred jabbed Tom in the side.* ☐ *He jabbed himself in the hand.*

JAB ▸ IN(TO)

jab something in(to something) to stab something into something. ☐ *Billy jabbed his spoon into the gelatin.* 🅃 *He jabbed in his spoon.* ☐ *He jabbed it in.*

JAB ▸ OUT

jab something out to thrust something out. ☐ *Molly jabbed her fist out suddenly.* 🅃 *She jabbed out her fist.*

JAB ▸ WITH

jab someone with something to poke or stick someone with something. ☐ *He jabbed Henry with the rake handle on purpose.* ☐ *The mugger jabbed the victim with a knife.*

JABBER ▸ ABOUT

jabber about someone or something **1.** to talk or chat very informally about someone or something. ☐ *Who are they jabbering about?* ☐ *Those kids are jabbering about school again.* **2.** to talk unintelligibly about someone or something. ☐ *Is she jabbering about anybody who comes to mind?* ☐ *She is jabbering about something, but we can't understand her.*

JACK ▸ AROUND

jack around AND **jerk around** to waste time. (Slang.) ☐ *Stop jacking around, you jerk.* ☐ *The kids spend most of the day jerking around.*

jack someone around AND **jerk someone around** to give someone a difficult time; to harass someone. (Slang.) ☐ *Come on! Stop jacking me around!* ☐ *Max started jerking Lefty around, and it looked as if there was going to be trouble.*

JACK ▸ UP

jack someone up to excite or stimulate someone, possibly with drugs. (Slang. *Someone* includes *oneself.*) ☐ *Tom jacked up his buddy by talking to him.* 🅃 *Tom jacked up Fred with a lot of encouragement.* ☐ *Max jacked himself up with a dose.*

jack something up **1.** to raise something up on a mechanical lifting device. ☐ *Now I have to jack the car up, so I can change the tire.* 🅃 *Please jack up the car.* 🄰 *A jacked-up car is unstable and dangerous.* **2.** to raise the price of something. (Slang.) ☐ *The store keeps jacking prices up.* 🅃 *The grocery store jacked up the prices again last night.* 🄰 *I won't pay your jacked-up prices!*

JAM ▸ IN(TO)

jam someone or something in((to) something) to force or compress someone or something into something or some place. (*Someone* includes *oneself.*) ☐ *Sam jammed all his clothes into the canvas bag.* ☐ *The conductor jammed all* *the passengers into one tiny rail coach.* □ *Don't jam us all in!* □ *They had to jam themselves into the tiny room, because there was no other place to meet.* [T] *Don't jam in all those books.*

JAM ▸ ON

jam something on **1.** to cram on an article of wearing apparel, such as a hat, shoes, socks, a ring, etc., in haste or anger. □ *Todd jammed his hat on.* [T] *Todd jammed on his hat and left the room.* **2.** to press down hard on an automobile control, such as brakes or accelerator. □ *Alice jammed the brakes on and the car skidded all over the place.* [T] *She jammed on the brakes.*

JAM ▸ TOGETHER

jam someone or something together to pack people or things close together. (*Someone* includes *oneself*.) □ *The usher jammed everybody together so more people could be seated.* □ *Don't just jam the boxes together! Sort them out first.* □ *They jammed themselves close together on the narrow bench.*

jam something together to assemble something hastily and with force, possibly in anger. □ *The automobile workers jammed the car together and it barely ran.* □ *The thing was just jammed together with no care at all.*

JAM ▸ UP

jam someone or something up to clog up someone or something; to impede or block the movement of or through someone or something; to make someone or some creature constipated. □ *Rachel jammed traffic up when her car stalled.* [T] *Rachel jammed up the sewer by running too much shampoo down the drain.* □ *The strange foods jammed us up.*

jam something up to force something upwards in haste or anger. □ *Who jammed the window up?* [T] *Wally jammed up the window and nearly broke it.*

jam something up (something) to thrust something up something. □ *She poked the broom handle up the chimney, hoping to force the bird to fly out.* □ *She jammed it up a few times, but it had no effect.*

See the following entry.

JAM ▸ WITH

jam something (up) with something to clog something with something. □ *Time had jammed the pipe up with rust.* [T] *Time had jammed up the pipe with rust.* □ *Jam the hole with a cloth so nothing else will leak out.*

jam with someone to play music in an improvised band with someone. □ *Andy loves to jam with the other students.* □ *Let's set up a time when we can jam with the others.*

JANGLE ▸ ON

jangle on something **1.** to ring a bell incessantly. □ *Will you stop jangling on that doorbell!* □ *Who is jangling on that bell?* **2.** to irritate someone's nerves; to make someone nervous. (Informal.) □ *All that noise jangles on my nerves.* □ *Too much chattering jangles on Ken's nerves.*

JAR ▸ AGAINST

jar against someone or something to bump against someone or something. □ *The guest jarred against the wall, knocking a picture askew.* □ *Someone jarred against Fran, almost knocking her over.*

JAR ▸ ON

jar on someone or something to bother someone or someone's nerves. (Similar to *jangle on something*.) □ *Her voice really jars on me.* □ *My brash manner jars on her, I guess.* □ *Your voice jars on my nerves.*

JAR ▸ WITH

jar with something to clash [mismatch] with something. □ *This color really jars with the color of the room.* □ *The sounds of the kitchen jarred with the music being performed in the main hall.*

JAW ▸ ABOUT

jaw about someone or something to talk aimlessly about someone or something. (Slang.) □ *Do we have to keep jawing about Tom all day?* □ *Stop jawing about your problems and set about fixing them.*

JAW ▸ AT

jaw at someone to lecture at someone; to talk endlessly to someone. (Slang.) ☐ *Please stop jawing at me.* ☐ *You are jawing at me too much lately.*

JAW ▸ DOWN

jaw someone down to talk someone down; to wear someone down talking. (Slang.) ☐ *We'll try to jaw him down. If that doesn't work, I don't know what we will do.* 🅃 *We will jaw down the objectors.*

JAZZ ▸ UP

jazz someone up to make a person appear to be more contemporary and exciting. (*Someone* includes *oneself*.) ☐ *She jazzed up the model.* 🅃 *She used makeup and a new hairstyle to jazz up the model.* 🄰 *Who is that jazzed-up blond trying to sing a torch song?* ☐ *She bought some new clothes with which she jazzed herself up considerably.*

jazz something up to make something more exciting or livelier. ☐ *Let's jazz this musical number up a bit.* 🅃 *We will jazz up the number.* 🄰 *The jazzed-up version is definitely better.*

JEER ▸ AT

jeer at someone or something to poke fun at someone; to make rude sounds at someone. ☐ *Please stop jeering at my cousin!* ☐ *The others just jeered at my idea.*

JERK ▸ AROUND

See the entries under *JACK ▸ AROUND.*

JERK ▸ AWAY

jerk something away (from someone or something) to snatch something away or pull something back from someone or some creature. ☐ *I jerked the bone away from the dog.* ☐ *Kelly jerked the ant poison away from the child.* ☐ *Mary jerked her hand away from the fire.*

JERK ▸ OFF

jerk something off ((of) someone or something) to snatch something off someone or something. (The *of*-phrase is paraphrased with a *from*-phrase when the particle is transposed. See the 🄵 example. The *of* is colloquial.) ☐ *Alice jerked the top off the box and poured out the contents.* 🅃 *She jerked off the box top.* 🄵 *She jerked off the top from the box.* ☐ *She jerked the socks off of Jimmy and put clean ones on him.*

JERK ▸ OUT

jerk someone or something out of something to pull someone or something out of something sharply and quickly. ☐ *She jerked the baby out of the crib and ran from the burning room.* ☐ *I jerked the puppy out of the mud.*

jerk something out (of someone or something) to pull something out of someone or something, quickly. (The *of*-phrase is paraphrased with a *from*-phrase when the particle is transposed. See the 🄵 example.) ☐ *The doctor jerked the arrow out of Bill's leg.* 🅃 *He jerked out the arrow.* 🄵 *He jerked out the arrow from his hip.* ☐ *Ted jerked the sword out of Max and wiped it off.*

JERK ▸ UP

jerk something up **1.** to pull something up quickly. ☐ *He jerked his belt up tight.* 🅃 *He jerked up the zipper to his jacket.* **2.** to lift up something, such as ears, quickly. ☐ *The dog jerked its ears up.* 🅃 *The dog jerked up its ears when it heard the floor creak.* ☐ *The soldier jerked his binoculars up to try to see the sniper.*

JEST ▸ ABOUT

jest about someone or something to make jokes about someone or something. ☐ *There is no need to jest about Lady Bracknell.* ☐ *I wish you would not jest about that.*

JEST ▸ AT

jest at someone or something to make fun of someone or something. ☐ *Please don't jest at my cousin.* ☐ *Is someone jesting at my hairdo?*

JEST ▸ WITH

jest with someone to joke with someone. ☐ *Surely you are jesting with me.* ☐ *Don't jest with me!*

JET ▸ FROM

jet (from some place) (to some place) to travel from some place to some other place by jet airplane. □ *They jetted from here to there.* □ *They jetted to here from there.* □ *We will have to jet from Amsterdam to Frankfurt.*

jet from something to spurt from something. □ *Water jetted from the broken pipe.* □ *A column of water jetted from the top of the fountain.*

JET ▸ TO

See *jet (from some place) (to some place)* under *JET ▸ FROM.*

JIBE ▸ WITH

jibe with something [for something] to agree with something. □ *Your story doesn't jibe with what we heard from the arresting officer.* □ *Her tale jibes with yours quite well.*

JIMMY ▸ UP

jimmy something up pry something up. (Informal.) □ *See if you can jimmy this window up.* 🅃 *Can you jimmy up this window?*

JOCKEY ▸ AROUND

jockey around to move around as if trying to get into a special position. □ *I spent most of the movie jockeying around, trying to get comfortable.* □ *She always has to jockey around a bit when she is getting into a parking place.*

jockey something around to maneuver something around; to manage something. □ *We had to jockey our bikes around a number of stalled cars.* □ *A few cars had to be jockeyed around to get to where we wanted to park.*

JOCKEY ▸ FOR

jockey for position **1.** to work one's horse into a desired position in a horse race. □ *Three riders were jockeying for position in the race.* □ *Ken was behind, but jockeying for position.* **2.** to work oneself into a desired position. □ *The candidates were jockeying for position, trying to get the best television exposure.* □ *I was jockeying for position but running out of campaign money.*

JOCKEY ▸ INTO

jockey someone or something into position to manage to get someone or something into a chosen position. (*Someone* includes *oneself.*) □ *The rider jockeyed his horse into position.* □ *Try to jockey your bicycle into position so you can pass the others.* □ *With much effort, she jockeyed herself into position to peek over the transom.*

JOG ▸ ALONG

jog along to trot or run along at a slow pace. □ *She was jogging along quite happily.* □ *I had been jogging along for a few minutes when my shoelaces broke.*

JOG ▸ TO

jog to the right or left [for a road, path, etc.] to turn to the right or left. □ *The road jogs to the right here. Don't run off.* □ *Keep going until the road jogs to the left. Our driveway is on the right side.*

JOIN ▸ IN

join in (with someone) to join someone in doing something. □ *Do you mind if we join in with you?* □ *Please join in.*

join in ((with) something) to participate in doing something. □ *The older boys joined in with the singing.* □ *I'm glad they joined in. We needed basses.*

JOIN ▸ TO

join something to something else to connect something to something else. □ *We joined our club to the other club.* □ *We joined our chorus to the other chorus, making a huge singing group.* □ *Please join this part onto that part with glue.*

JOIN ▸ TOGETHER

join something and something together to connect or unite things. (Also without *together*, but not eligible as an entry.) □ *We joined the pipe and the hose together.* □ *The parts of the hose were joined together with a special cement.* 🅃 *He joined together all the blue wires and the red ones.*

JOIN ▸ UP

join up to join some organization. □ *The club has opened its membership* *roles again. Are you going to join up?* ☐ *I can't afford to join up.*

join ((up) with someone or something) See under *JOIN ▸ WITH.*

JOIN ▸ WITH

join forces with someone to combine one's efforts with someone else's efforts. ☐ *The older boys joined forces with the younger ones to serenade the teachers.* ☐ *Let's join forces with the other members and run our own slate of candidates.*

join someone with someone else or something with something else to connect things or people. (See also *JOIN ▸ TO.*) ☐ *I joined Fred with the others.* ☐ *We joined the older puppies with the full-grown dogs.*

join ((up) with someone or something) to bring oneself into association with someone or something. ☐ *I decided to join up with the other group.* ☐ *Our group joined with another similar group.*

JOKE ▸ ABOUT

See the following entry.

JOKE ▸ WITH

joke (with someone) (about someone or something) to quip with someone about someone or something; to make verbal fun with someone about someone or something. ☐ *I was joking with Tom about the performance.* ☐ *I joked about Andy with Fran.* ☐ *You are joking with me, aren't you?*

JOLT ▸ OUT

jolt someone out of something to startle someone out of inertness. (*Someone* includes *oneself.*) ☐ *The cold water thrown in her face was what it took to jolt Mary out of her deep sleep.* ☐ *At the sound of the telephone, he jolted himself out of his stupor.*

JOSTLE ▸ AROUND

jostle someone around to push or knock someone around. ☐ *Please don't jostle me around.* ☐ *Lee has been jostled around enough.* 🅃 *Don't jostle around everyone!*

JOSTLE ▸ ASIDE

jostle someone aside to push or nudge someone aside. ☐ *The crowd jostled the beggar aside.* ☐ *Poor little Timmy was jostled aside every time he got near the entrance.* 🅃 *The big kids jostled aside all the little ones.*

JOSTLE ▸ WITH

jostle with someone to struggle with someone. ☐ *Andy jostled with Fred for access to the door.* ☐ *Timmy and Bobby jostled with one another while they were waiting to get in.*

JOT ▸ DOWN

jot something down to make a note of something. ☐ *This is important. Please jot this down.* 🅃 *Jot down this note, please.*

JUDGE ▸ BETWEEN

judge between someone or something and someone or something to decide between people or things, in any combination. ☐ *You can't expect me to judge between apples and oranges, can you?* ☐ *I can't judge between poor Fred and the honesty of the witnesses.* ☐ *Can you judge between the prosecution and the defense?*

JUDGE ▸ BY

judging by something AND **judging from something** to make a decision or judgment based on something. (The phrase is not variable.) ☐ *Judging by the amount of food eaten, everyone must have been very hungry.* ☐ *Judging from the mess that's left, the party must have been a good one.*

JUDGE ▸ FROM

judging from something See the previous entry.

JUDGE ▸ ON

judge one on one's own merits to evaluate one on one's own good and bad points and no one else's. ☐ *Please judge Janet on her own merits.* ☐ *I was judged on my own merits.*

judge something on its own merits to evaluate something on its own good and bad points and nothing else's. ☐ *You must judge this proposal on its own mer-*

its. ☐ *The proposal has not been judged on its own merits.*

JUGGLE ▸ AROUND

juggle someone or something around to alter the position or sequence of someone or something. ☐ *We will juggle everyone around so that no one always gets the same good seat.* ☐ *I think I can juggle my schedule around so I can have lunch with you.*

JUICE ▸ BACK

juice something back to drink all of something, quickly. (Slang.) ☐ *He juiced a beer back.* 🅃 *Max juiced back another beer.*

JUICE ▸ UP

juice something up **1.** to make something more powerful. (Slang.) ☐ *How much did it cost to juice this thing up?* 🅃 *Wally juiced up his car.* 🄰 *Where did you get that juiced-up car?* **2.** to turn on the electricity to something. (Slang.) ☐ *It's time to juice the stage lights up.* 🅃 *Juice up the stage lights.*

juice up to drink one or more alcoholic drinks. (Slang.) ☐ *Hey, man, let's go out and juice up tonight.* ☐ *Stop juicing up every night.*

JUMBLE ▸ TOGETHER

jumble someone or something together to mix people or things together randomly into a hodgepodge. ☐ *They just jumbled everything together and made a real mess.* ☐ *The army just jumbled everybody together, no matter what their skills and talents were.*

jumble something together to assemble something clumsily and hastily. ☐ *They just jumbled this car together. It's a pile of junk.* ☐ *I hope this airplane hasn't been jumbled together as badly as this meal.*

JUMBLE ▸ UP

jumble something up to make a hodgepodge out of things. ☐ *Who jumbled my papers up?* 🅃 *Who jumbled up all my papers?* 🄰 *I can't make heads or tails of this jumbled-up mess.*

JUMP ▸ ACROSS

jump across something to leap over something that is flat rather than tall. ☐ *The frog jumped across the puddle.* ☐ *Timmy tried but failed to jump across the puddle.*

JUMP ▸ AT

jump at someone or something to jump in the direction of someone or something. ☐ *The frog jumped at me, but I dodged it.* ☐ *The cat jumped at the leaf as it fell from the tree.*

jump at something to accept an opportunity eagerly. (Figurative.) ☐ *Sally jumped at the chance to go to the opera.* ☐ *I knew she would jump at the chance.*

JUMP ▸ DOWN

jump (down) (from something) See under *JUMP ▸ FROM.*

jump down someone's throat to attack someone verbally; to scold someone severely. (Figurative.) ☐ *There's no need to jump down my throat.* ☐ *Please don't jump down his throat.*

jump down something to leap downward into or through something. ☐ *The rats jumped down the manhole.* ☐ *Timmy jumped down the stairs on the morning of his birthday party.*

JUMP ▸ FROM

jump (down) (from something) to jump downward off something. ☐ *A small mouse jumped down from the shelf.* ☐ *A mouse jumped down.* ☐ *A tiny mouse jumped from the shelf.* ☐ *Timmy jumped down from the ladder and sprained his ankle.*

jump from something to something to leap from one place to another. ☐ *A frog jumped from lily pad to lily pad.* ☐ *The child jumped from stone to stone.*

JUMP ▸ IN(TO)

jump in((to) something) to leap into something, such as water, a bed, a problem, etc. ☐ *She was so cold she just jumped into bed and pulled up the covers.* ☐ *I jumped in and had a refreshing swim.*

JUMP ▸ OF

jump clear of something to get out of the way of something; to leap off something before it crashes. ☐ *I barely had time to jump clear of the oncoming truck.* ☐ *I jumped clear of the ball as it came my way.* ☐ *Somehow, Todd was able to jump clear of the motorcycle before it crashed.*

JUMP ▸ OFF

jump off ((of) something) to leap off something. (The *of* is colloquial.) ☐ *Rachel lost her balance and jumped off the diving board instead of diving.* ☐ *Better to jump off than to fall off.*

jump off the deep end (over someone or something) to get deeply involved with someone or something. (Often refers to romantic involvement.) ☐ *Jim is about to jump off the deep end over Jane.* ☐ *Jane is great, but there is no need to jump off the deep end.*

JUMP ▸ ON

See also under *JUMP ▸ ON(TO).*

jump on someone or something to pounce on someone or something. ☐ *The cat jumped on the mouse.* ☐ *Max jumped on the unsuspecting tourist and robbed him.*

jump on the bandwagon AND **leap on the bandwagon** to begin to do or think what everyone else is doing or thinking. (Figurative.) ☐ *Aren't you going to jump on the bandwagon with the others?* ☐ *She didn't want to leap on the bandwagon just to be stylish.*

JUMP ▸ ON(TO)

jump on((to) something) **1.** to get onto something. ☐ *The cat jumped onto the sofa and took a nap.* ☐ *I was sitting on the sofa and the cat jumped on it and scared me.* **2.** to get involved in something very quickly. (Colloquial.) ☐ *Jump onto that story now and get it done for tonight's edition.* ☐ *I'll jump on the story right now, boss.*

JUMP ▸ OUT

jump out of one's skin to be very startled or shocked. (Figurative.) ☐ *I was so frightened that I nearly jumped out of my skin.* ☐ *Ken frightened Katie and she nearly jumped out of her skin.*

jump out of something to leap from something. ☐ *A mouse jumped out of the cereal box.* ☐ *I jumped out of bed and ran to answer the telephone.*

JUMP ▸ OVER

jump all over someone to scold someone. (Figurative.) ☐ *The teacher jumped all over the student.* ☐ *She jumped all over me for being late.*

jump over something to leap over or across something. ☐ *The fellow named Jack jumped over a candle placed on the floor.* ☐ *Puddles are to be jumped over, not waded through.*

JUMP ▸ THROUGH

jump through hoops to do what one is told; to do whatever is necessary to appease someone. (Figurative.) ☐ *She expects all of us to jump through hoops for her.* ☐ *Do you want me to jump through hoops for you?*

JUMP ▸ TO

jump to conclusions to move too quickly to a conclusion; to form a conclusion from too little evidence. (Idiomatic.) ☐ *Please don't jump to any conclusions because of what you have seen.* ☐ *There is no need to jump to conclusions!*

JUMP ▸ UP

jump up (from something) to leap upward from something. ☐ *The dog jumped up from its resting place.* ☐ *The dog jumped up and ran to the door.*

jump up (on someone or something) to leap upward onto someone or something. ☐ *A spider jumped up on me and terrified me totally.* ☐ *The cat jumped up on the sofa.*

jump up (to something) to leap upward to the level of something. ☐ *The child jumped up to the next step.* ☐ *The dog couldn't reach the piece of meat on the edge of the table, so it jumped up and got it.*

JUMP ▸ WITH

jump with something to be very active with excitement or enthusiasm. ☐ *The* *crowd was jumping with enthusiasm.* ☐ *The bar was jumping with young people.*

JUSTIFY ▸ BY

justify something by something to try to explain why something needs doing or why it is acceptable to do something. ☐ *You cannot justify violence by quoting proverbs.* ☐ *Your action was totally justified by the circumstances.*

JUSTIFY ▸ TO

justify something to someone to explain something to someone and show why it is necessary. ☐ *Please try to justify this to the voters.* ☐ *I can justify your action to no one.*

JUT ▸ OUT

jut out (from something) to stick outward from something. ☐ *The flagpole juts out from the side of the building.* ☐ *His nose juts out sharply.*

jut out (into something) to stick outward into an area. ☐ *The back end of the truck jutted out into the street.* ☐ *The back end jutted out.*

jut out (over someone or something) to stick out over someone or something. ☐ *The roof of the house jutted out over the patio.* ☐ *I'm glad the roof jutted out and kept us dry during the brief storm.*

JUXTAPOSE ▸ TO

juxtapose someone or something to someone or something to place people or things next to each other, in any combination. (Also implies that the placing or arranging is done carefully.) ☐ *The teacher juxtaposed himself to the principal.* ☐ *I juxtaposed the chair to the view out the window.*

K

KEEL ▸ OVER

keel over to fall over; to capsize. □ *The boat keeled over.* □ *Tom was so surprised he nearly keeled over.*

KEEP ▸ ABOUT

keep one's wits about one to remain alert. (Idiomatic.) □ *Please keep your wits about you while you give the interview.* □ *You should keep your wits about you at all times.*

keep quiet about someone or something AND **keep still about someone or something** to say nothing about someone or something. □ *Can you keep quiet about Tom?* □ *You must keep quiet about the surprise party.* □ *Please keep still about our plans.*

keep someone or something about AND **keep someone or something around** to have someone or something nearby habitually. □ *Try to keep some spare parts about.* □ *He doesn't work very hard, but we keep him around anyway.* □ *I like to keep some coffee around in case anyone wants it.*

keep still about someone or something See *keep quiet about someone or something.*

KEEP ▸ ABOVE

keep one's head above water **1.** to manage to survive, especially financially. (Figurative. Also literal.) □ *We have so little money that we can hardly keep our heads above water.* □ *It's hard to keep your head above water on this much money.* **2.** to keep up with one's work. (Figurative. Also literal.) □ *It's all I can do to keep my head above water with the work I have. I can't take on any more.* □ *We can hardly keep our heads above water.*

KEEP ▸ AFTER

keep after someone (about something) to nag someone about something. □ *I'll have to keep after him about getting the roof repaired.* □ *He'll get it done if you keep after him.*

KEEP ▸ AHEAD

keep ahead of someone or something **1.** to remain in advance of someone or something. □ *Kelly kept ahead of Ken throughout the race.* □ *The runner kept ahead of the pack.* **2.** to be ready to accept whatever product someone or something has turned out. □ *Claire works faster than I do, and I couldn't keep ahead of her.* □ *I couldn't keep ahead of the very rapid productive powers of the machine.*

keep ahead of something See *stay ahead of something* under *STAY ▸ AHEAD.*

keep one step ahead of someone or something to function slightly in advance of someone or something. □ *Al kept one step ahead of Detective Rogers.* □ *Try to keep one step ahead of the investigators.*

KEEP ▸ APART

keep someone or something apart to keep someone away from someone else; to keep something away from something else. □ *Try to keep the dogs and cats apart.* □ *Can you keep Bill and Bob apart?*

KEEP ► AROUND

keep someone or something around See under *KEEP ► ABOUT.*

KEEP ► AT

keep at arm's length from someone or something to retain a degree of physical or social remoteness from someone or something. (Usually figurative.) □ *I try to keep at arm's length from Larry, since our disagreement.* □ *You should keep at arm's length from the committee.*

keep at someone (about something) to harass someone about something. □ *I will keep at Megan about the meeting until she sets it up.* □ *You will have to keep at her if you want to get anything done.*

keep at something to continue to do something; to continue to try to do something. □ *Keep at it until you get it done.* □ *I have to keep at this.*

keep someone at something to make sure someone continues to work at something. (*Someone* includes *oneself.*) □ *Please keep Walter at his chores.* □ *I was so sick I couldn't keep myself at my work.*

keep someone or something at a distance to retain some amount of physical distance from someone or something. □ *Please try to keep Tom at a distance. He just gets in the way.* □ *I wanted to keep the smelly plant at a distance.*

keep someone or something at arm's length to retain a degree of physical or social distance from someone or something. (Usually figurative.) □ *I keep Tom at arm's length because we don't get along.* □ *Try to keep that committee at arm's length. It's best they don't know what you are doing.*

keep someone or something at bay to hold off someone or something. □ *She managed to keep the bill collectors at bay.* □ *The dogs kept the raccoon at bay for an hour.*

KEEP ► AWAY

keep away (from someone or something) to avoid someone or something; to maintain a physical distance from someone or something. □ *Please keep away from me if you have a cold.* □ *Keep away from the construction site, Timmy.*

keep someone or something away (from someone or something) to maintain a physical distance between someone or something and someone or something, in any combination. (*Someone* includes *oneself.*) □ *I will try to keep the smokers away from you.* □ *Try to keep the dog away from the roast.* □ *Try to keep the roast away from Timmy, who has a cold.* □ *Keep yourself away from me if you are going to smoke.*

KEEP ► BACK

keep back (from someone or something) to continue to stay in a position away from someone or something. □ *You must keep back from the edge of the crater.* □ *Keep back! It's really dangerous.*

keep behind someone or something **1.** to remain hidden behind someone or something. □ *Keep behind me, and maybe they won't notice you.* □ *Keep behind the pillar, and no one will know you are there.* **2.** to follow someone or something. □ *Keep behind me as we pass through this narrow passage.* □ *Please keep behind me as we go across this bridge.*

keep someone back **1.** to hold a child back in school. □ *We asked them to keep John back a year.* □ *John was kept back a year in school.* **2.** to keep someone from advancing in life. □ *I think that your small vocabulary is keeping you back.* □ *Her vocabulary kept her back in life.*

keep someone or something back to hold someone or something in reserve. □ *Keep some of the food back for an emergency.* □ *We are keeping Karen back until the other players have exhausted themselves.*

keep someone or something back (from someone or something) to make someone or some creature stay in a position away from someone or something. □ *Keep everyone back from the injured lady.* □ *Please keep the dogs back from the turtle.* □ *Can you keep your bicycle back from the hole, please?*

KEEP ▸ BY

keep someone or something by someone to make someone or something stay next to someone. ☐ *Try to keep the twins by you until we have taken a few more pictures.* ☐ *Please keep this package by you until we are ready to present it.*

keep something by to keep something handy; to keep something in reserve, ready to be used. (Folksy.) ☐ *Keep this extra glue by in case you need it.* ☐ *This money had been kept by for just such an emergency.*

KEEP ▸ DOWN

keep someone down to prevent someone from advancing or succeeding. ☐ *His lack of a degree will keep him down.* ☐ *I don't think that this problem will keep her down.*

keep someone or something down to hold someone or something in a hidden or protected position. (*Someone* includes *oneself.*) ☐ *Try to keep Sam down where no one can see him.* ☐ *Please keep the party hats down so Fred won't know it's a party when he comes in.* ☐ *Keep yourself down so you won't be seen.*

keep something down **1.** to make the level of noise lower and keep it lower. ☐ *Please keep it down. You are just too noisy.* ☐ *Keep the noise down, or I will call the police.* **2.** to retain food in one's stomach rather than throwing it up. ☐ *I'm not hungry and I can't keep any food down.* ☐ *She couldn't keep the milk down.* **3.** to keep something under control. ☐ *I work hard to keep expenses down.* ☐ *Please try to keep the cost of the new project down.*

KEEP ▸ FOR

keep one's eyes open for someone or something AND **keep one's eyes peeled for someone or something; keep an eye out for someone or something** to remain alert for the sight of someone or something. ☐ *Please keep your eyes open for Amy. She is due at any moment.* ☐ *It would be a good idea to keep your eyes peeled for the bus. It is sometimes ahead of schedule.* ☐ *Keep an eye out for the mail.*

keep one's fingers crossed for someone or something to hope for good luck in a matter relating to someone or something. ☐ *Here I go. Please keep your fingers crossed for me.* ☐ *I'm keeping my fingers crossed for the outcome of the game.*

keep someone or something for someone **1.** to retain and care for someone or something. ☐ *I would be happy to keep Teddy for you while you are away.* ☐ *Would you keep my dog for me?* **2.** to keep someone or something in reserve for someone. ☐ *John wanted to return to the accounting department, but I will keep him here for you for last-minute changes.* ☐ *I am keeping some here for you, since you will miss the party.*

keep still for someone or something See under *HOLD ▸ FOR.*

KEEP ▸ FROM

keep aloof from someone or something to remain remote or distant from someone or something. ☐ *She tends to keep aloof from the rest of us.* ☐ *Ken keeps aloof from the committee he chairs.*

keep from something to refrain from doing something. ☐ *See if you can keep from coughing for a while.* ☐ *I will keep from doing it if I can.*

keep one's distance from someone or something to remain at a safe distance from someone or something. ☐ *I'm keeping my distance from Donna.* ☐ *You had better keep your distance from that bear!*

keep someone from someone or something to hold someone away from someone or something; to prevent someone from getting at someone or something. (*Someone* includes *oneself.*) ☐ *You must keep the child from her mother until the mother is infection free.* ☐ *It is hard to keep a child from the playground, even a sick child.* ☐ *I could hardly keep myself from the dessert table.*

keep someone or something from doing something to prevent someone or something from doing something. ☐ *Would you please keep your dog from* *digging in my garden?* ☐ *Her lack of a degree kept her from advancing.*

keep something from someone not to tell something to someone. ☐ *Why did you keep the news from me? I needed to know.* ☐ *This matter shouldn't have been kept from me.*

keep the wolf from the door to remain strong enough or financially sound enough to fight off threats to one's well-being. (Figurative.) ☐ *We have enough money to keep the wolf from the door, but not a cent more.* ☐ *We can hardly keep the wolf from the door.*

KEEP ▸ IN

keep in good with someone to remain in someone's favor. ☐ *I always try to keep in good with the boss's secretary.* ☐ *It's also good to keep in good with the boss.*

keep in touch (with someone or something) to retain lines of communication with someone or something. ☐ *I want to keep in touch with you after the conference.* ☐ *Please keep in touch while you are away.*

keep in training to preserve oneself in good physical condition. ☐ *I try to keep in training so I will live longer.* ☐ *Try to keep in training.*

keep one in one's place to make someone stay in the proper rank or station. (*One* includes *oneself.*) ☐ *I guess you want to keep me in my place, is that right?* ☐ *I know enough to keep myself in my place.*

keep one's hand in (something) to remain involved in something, perhaps only a token involvement. ☐ *I want to keep my hand in things even after I retire.* ☐ *I always have to keep my hand in so I will feel a part of things.*

keep someone in (a state of) suspense to make someone wait anxiously for something. ☐ *Tell us what happened. Don't keep us in a state of suspense.* ☐ *Don't keep me in suspense!*

keep someone in ignorance to prevent someone from learning in general; to keep someone in an uneducated state. (*Someone* includes *oneself.*) ☐ *I think they are trying to keep us in ignorance on purpose.* ☐ *He left school and kept himself in ignorance.*

keep someone in ignorance (about someone or something) to prevent someone from learning specific information about someone or something. (*Someone* includes *oneself.*) ☐ *I think we had better keep them all in ignorance about the money for a while.* ☐ *I want to know about the accident. Don't keep me in ignorance.* ☐ *I don't know about her. I have kept myself in ignorance on purpose.*

keep someone in sight to make sure that a person is visible at all times. ☐ *He looks suspicious. Keep him in sight at all times.* ☐ *I cannot keep him in sight day and night.*

keep someone in stitches to keep someone laughing. (Figurative.) ☐ *She is so funny. She always keeps us in stitches.* ☐ *The audience was kept in stitches by the comedian.*

keep someone in the dark (about someone or something) to make sure someone stays ignorant about someone or something. (Figurative.) ☐ *We will have to keep Sally in the dark about the plans for a while longer.* ☐ *You are keeping me in the dark about your boyfriend.* ☐ *Tell me what's going on. Don't keep me in the dark.*

keep someone or something in to make someone or some creature stay inside. (*Someone* includes *oneself.*) ☐ *I will have to keep Billy in until his cold is better.* ☐ *Keep the dog in. It's too cold for her to go out.* ☐ *She decided to keep herself in until she got well.*

keep someone or something in check See under *HOLD ▸ IN.*

keep someone or something in line to make someone or some creature behave properly. (Figurative. Also literal.) ☐ *Try to keep the children in line during the service.* ☐ *Please keep the dogs in line at the pet show.*

keep someone or something in mind (for someone or something) to remember to bring up someone or something in regard to someone or something. ☐

Would you keep me in mind for the vice president job? ☐ *I will keep a watch in mind for John, since he is graduating soon.*

keep someone or something in order to keep people or things in the proper sequence. ☐ *Please try to keep the children in order until their turn to perform comes.* ☐ *Can you keep these books in order for me?*

keep someone or something in reserve See ***hold someone or something in reserve*** under *HOLD ▸ IN.*

keep someone or something in some place to house or maintain someone or something in some place. ☐ *We keep the boys in an apartment just off campus. It's cheaper than three dormitory rooms.* ☐ *We can keep your dog in the garage until you return.*

keep someone or something in with someone or something to locate people or things together, in any combination. ☐ *I will keep Tom in with me until he gets his own room.* ☐ *We will keep the cat in with Tom until there is room elsewhere.*

keep something in See under *HOLD ▸ IN.*

KEEP ▸ INSIDE

keep inside ((of) something) to remain inside of something, usually a shelter, house, etc. (The *of* is colloquial.) ☐ *Please keep inside of the house while it's raining.* ☐ *I want you to keep inside.*

keep something in(side (of) one(self)) See under *HOLD ▸ IN.*

KEEP ▸ IN(SIDE)

keep in(side (of)) something to remain inside something. (The *of* is colloquial.) ☐ *Keep inside the house until it stops raining.* ☐ *Please keep in the house.*

KEEP ▸ OF

keep abreast of someone or something to make certain that one is informed about someone or something. ☐ *Fred is so busy lately. I can't keep abreast of him.* ☐ *You ought to keep abreast of all the news.*

keep clear of someone or something to remain well away from someone or something; to avoid someone or something. ☐ *Keep clear of the dancer. She needs lots of space.* ☐ *Keep clear of this machine. It is dangerous.* ☐ *Please keep clear of the man in the green jacket. He is in a very bad mood.*

keep sight of someone or something to keep someone or something in view. ☐ *Try to keep sight of the skier.* ☐ *I want to keep sight of the children at all times.*

keep someone abreast of something to make certain that someone is well informed about something. ☐ *Your job is to keep the boss abreast of the latest news.* ☐ *Please keep me abreast of what is going on.*

keep something of someone's or something's to retain something that belongs to or is associated with someone or something. ☐ *I would love to keep this handkerchief of yours.* ☐ *I want to keep a memento of the occasion.*

keep track of someone or something AND **keep an eye on someone or something** to take notice of what happens to someone or something; to monitor someone or something. (The main entry is often in the negative.) ☐ *Please try to keep track of Walter.* ☐ *I can hardly keep track of expenses these days.* ☐ *Please keep an eye on Timmy for a moment.* ☐ *You need to keep an eye on your accounts.*

KEEP ▸ OFF

keep off (of) someone's back AND **keep off someone's case** to leave someone alone; to stop criticizing or scolding someone. (Idiomatic slang.) ☐ *Keep off of my back! Leave me alone.* ☐ *Keep off my case!*

keep off ((of) something) to remain off something; not to trespass on something. (The *of* is colloquial.) ☐ *Please keep off the grass.* ☐ *This is not a public thoroughfare! Keep off!*

keep one's hands off someone or something not to touch someone or something. ☐ *Keep your hands off me!* ☐ *Please keep your hands off the cake!*

keep someone or something off See under *HOLD ▸ OFF.*

keep someone or something off ((of) someone or something) to make sure that someone or something remains off someone or something. (*Someone* includes *oneself*. The *of* is colloquial.) □ *Keep that woman off of me! She's obsessed with me!* □ *Please keep Timmy off the couch.* □ *Keep him off!* □ *Keep yourself off my property!*

KEEP ▸ ON

keep a close watch on someone or something to watch someone or something very carefully. □ *Let's keep a close watch on Fred and his friends.* □ *I want to keep a close watch on the house across the street.*

keep a firm grip on someone or something AND **keep a tight grip on someone or something** **1.** to hold on to someone or something tightly. □ *As they approached the edge, Sally kept a firm grip on little Timmy.* □ *She kept a tight grip on him.* □ *Keep a firm grip on my hand as we cross the street.* **2.** to keep someone or something under firm control. □ *The manager keeps a firm grip on all the employees.* □ *I try to keep a firm grip on all the accounts.*

keep an eye on someone or something See under *KEEP ▸ OF.*

keep (going) on about someone or something to continue to talk excessively about someone or something. □ *I wish you would not keep going on about Tom and Jill.* □ *Don't keep on about my haircut. It's perfect!*

keep (going) on at someone or something to continue to lecture or scold someone, a group, or some creature. □ *Don't keep going on at him. Give him the dickens and be done with it.* □ *Please don't keep on at the committee. They did the best they could.*

keep on (doing something) to continue to do something. □ *Are you going to keep on singing all night?* □ *Yes, I'm going to keep on.*

keep on someone (about something) to nag someone about something. □ *We will have to keep on him about the report until he turns it in.* □ *Don't worry. I'll keep on him.*

keep on (something) to work to remain mounted on something, such as a horse, bicycle, etc. □ *It's really hard for me to keep on a horse.* □ *It's hard to keep on when it's moving all over the place.*

keep on something to pay close attention to something. (See *keep on top of someone or something.*) □ *Keep on that story until everything is settled.* □ *This is a problem. Keep on it until it's settled.*

keep on the left(-hand) side (of something) to stay on the left-hand side of something. □ *In England, they have to keep on the left-hand side of the street.* □ *Please don't keep on the left side all the time when everyone else is on the right!* □ *In England you keep on the left-hand side.*

keep on the right side of someone AND **keep on the good side of someone** to remain in someone's favor. (This has nothing to do with the right-hand side.) □ *You had better keep on the right side of Mr. Franklin. He's very particular.* □ *I will keep on the good side of him.*

keep on the right(-hand) side (of something) to stay on the right-hand side of something. □ *Please keep on the right-hand side of the hallway.* □ *We always keep on the right side of the road on this country.* □ *Please keep on the right-hand side.*

keep on the track to stay on the path that one is on; to continue doing the things one is doing. □ *Keep on the track and you will end up where you want to be.* □ *I know I can keep on the track.*

keep on top (of someone or something) to stay well informed about the status of someone or something. □ *I need to keep on top of the president, because I am doing a report on him.* □ *News is easy to get these days, and I do what I can to keep on top.* □ *I try to keep on top of world events.*

keep on trucking to continue to do well; to continue to try. (Slang.) □ *Just keep on trucking, man.* □ *All I can do is keep on trucking.*

keep on with something to continue with something. □ *Just keep on with your work. Don't pay any attention to me.* □ *Can I keep on with this while you are talking?*

keep one on one's toes to keep someone or oneself alert. (Figurative.) □ *They monitor what I do, and that tends to keep me on my toes.* □ *I know something that will keep you on your toes.*

keep one's eye on the ball 1. to watch the ball in any kind of a ball game. □ *The key to good Ping-Pong playing is to keep your eye on the ball.* □ *The coach told Rachel to keep her eye on the ball.* 2. to pay attention to what is happening. (Figurative.) □ *You have to keep your eye on the ball! Pay attention to detail if you want to succeed.* □ *Keep your eye on the ball and don't worry about anything else.*

keep one's eye(s) on someone or something to monitor someone or something. (Figurative.) □ *Would you keep your eye on the door while I have some coffee?* □ *I'll keep my eyes on the telephone, but I hope no one calls.*

keep one's feet on the ground to remain calm and stable. (Figurative.) □ *You will do all right if you keep your feet on the ground. Don't get carried away.* □ *Just keep your feet on the ground and you will do fine.*

keep one's finger on the pulse of something to monitor the current state of something frequently. (Figurative.) □ *I have to keep my finger on the pulse of the city if I want to be a good reporter.* □ *It is hard to keep your finger on the pulse of Washington, D.C., but you must do it.*

keep one's mind on someone or something to concentrate on someone or something. □ *He is keeping his mind on Jane instead of his work.* □ *I find it hard to keep my mind on my reading.*

keep one's shirt on AND **keep one's pants on** to be patient. (Figurative. Often a command.) □ *Wait a minute! Keep your shirt on!* □ *Keep your pants on! I'll be with you in a minute.*

keep someone on to retain someone in employment longer than is required or was planned. □ *She worked out so well that we decided to keep her on.* □ *Liz was kept on as a consultant.*

keep someone on something 1. to make or help someone stay mounted on something, such as a horse, bicycle, etc. (*Someone* includes *oneself.*) □ *Her father kept her on the bicycle as she was learning to ride it.* □ *I couldn't keep myself on the horse.* 2. to retain someone on the payroll. □ *We can't keep you on the payroll any longer.* □ *Ken could not be kept on the payroll any longer.*

keep someone on tenterhooks to keep someone in suspense. (Figurative.) □ *Don't keep me on tenterhooks! Tell me your news!* □ *We were all kept on tenterhooks too long.*

keep someone or something on the (right) track to make sure that someone or some process continues to progress properly. (*Someone* includes *oneself.*) □ *You have to watch him and keep him on the right track.* □ *I will do what I can to keep the process on the track.* □ *Pay attention to what you are doing. Try to keep yourself on the track.*

keep something on to continue to wear an article of clothing. □ *I'm going to keep my coat on. It's a little chilly in here.* 🅃 *I'll keep on my coat, thanks.*

keep something on its feet to keep something stable and viable. (Figurative.) □ *It takes a lot of effort to keep this old firm on its feet. We may have to go out of business.* □ *Can we keep this business on its feet another year?*

keep something on track to manage to keep something moving along on schedule. (Figurative.) □ *Try to keep these procedures on track this time.* □ *Please keep the discussion on track. Time is limited.*

keep the lid on something 1. to leave a lid on something, such as a pot, pan, etc. □ *Keep the lid on the pot until the stew is almost done.* □ *Keep the lid on the skillet for just a little while.* 2. to keep a scandalous or embarrassing situation secret. (Figurative.) □ *We can't* *keep the lid on this any longer. The press has got wind of it.* ☐ *The lid could not be kept on the scandal any longer.*

keep watch on someone or something AND **keep tabs on someone or something** to monitor someone or something. ☐ *Keep watch on the lady in the big coat. She may be a shoplifter.* ☐ *Try to keep tabs on the committee's work.*

KEEP ▸ OUT

keep an eye out for someone or something See under *KEEP ▸ FOR.*

keep one's nose out of something to stay out of something, such as someone else's business. (Figurative.) ☐ *Try to keep your nose out of stuff that doesn't concern you.* ☐ *Keep your nose out of my business.*

keep out from under someone's feet to stay out of someone's way. (Figurative.) ☐ *Please keep out from under my feet. I'm very busy.* ☐ *Try to keep out from under Tom's feet while he is working.*

keep out (of something) **1.** to remain uninvolved with something. ☐ *Keep out of this! It's my affair.* ☐ *It's not your affair. Keep out!* **2.** to remain outside something or some place. ☐ *You should keep out of the darkroom when the door is closed.* ☐ *The door is closed. Keep out!*

keep someone or something out (of something) **1.** to prevent someone or something from getting into something or some place. (*Someone* includes *oneself.*) ☐ *Keep your kids out of my yard.* ☐ *Please keep the loose papers out of the room.* ☐ *She just couldn't keep herself out of the cookie jar.* **2.** to keep the subject of someone or something out of a discussion. (*Someone* includes *oneself.*) ☐ *Keep the kids out of this! I don't want to talk about them.* ☐ *They kept Dorothy out of the discussion.*

KEEP ▸ OVER

keep watch over someone or something to supervise someone or something; to take care of someone or something. ☐ *Please keep watch over the project.* ☐ *Will you keep watch over Timmy for a minute?*

KEEP ▸ STILL

keep still for someone or something See *hold still for someone or something* under *HOLD ▸ FOR.*

KEEP ▸ TO

keep one's ear to the ground to be alert for news or signals. (Figurative.) ☐ *I don't know what's next, so keep your ear to the ground.* ☐ *Please keep your ear to the ground for news.*

keep one's hands to oneself not to touch anything or anyone; not to punch or poke someone. ☐ *Won't you keep your hands to yourself?* ☐ *Keep your hands to yourself while we are in the toy store.*

keep one's nose to the grindstone to work very hard; to keep busy. (Figurative.) ☐ *I have to keep my nose to the grindstone if I want to get ahead.* ☐ *I always keep my nose to the grindstone.*

keep something to a minimum to make something as small, few, or little as possible. ☐ *Do what you can to keep construction dust to a minimum.* ☐ *The dust should be kept to a minimum.*

keep something to oneself to keep something a secret. ☐ *I want you to keep this news to yourself.* ☐ *This should be kept to yourself.*

keep to oneself to remain secluded. ☐ *She keeps to herself a lot and doesn't have many friends.* ☐ *I keep out of trouble by keeping to myself.*

keep to something to adhere to an agreement; to follow a plan; to keep a promise. ☐ *Please keep to the agreed-upon plan.* ☐ *Can you keep to what we agreed on?*

keep to the straight and narrow to behave properly and correctly; to stay out of trouble. ☐ *If you keep to the straight and narrow, you can't help but win in the end.* ☐ *I always keep to the straight and narrow.*

KEEP ▸ TOGETHER

keep body and soul together to manage to keep existing, especially when one has very little money. (Idiomatic. Compare to *keep the wolf from the door.*) ☐ *We hardly had enough to keep body and* *soul together.* □ *I don't earn enough money to keep body and soul together.*

keep someone or something together to keep things or a group of people together; to keep something, including a group of people, from falling apart. □ *I hope we can keep our club together for a few more years.* □ *We will keep it together for a while longer.* □ *Keep your toys together. Don't scatter them all over the house.*

keep together to remain as a group. □ *We will keep together to the very end.* □ *Our group decided to keep together.*

KEEP ▸ UNDER

keep someone or something under control to cause someone or something to remain controlled. □ *Try to keep your child under control.* □ *I am unable to keep my dog under control when a cat is around.*

keep someone or something under something to store, hide, or cache someone or something beneath something. □ *Keep Max under the packing crate until the police go away.* □ *I keep a box of extra sweaters under the bed.*

keep something under wraps to keep something concealed, originally under some kind of wrapper. (Idiomatic.) □ *The car company kept the new models under wraps until the last minute.* □ *The car was kept under wraps.*

keep under something to remain beneath something. □ *Keep under the packing crate, Max.* □ *I ordered the dog to keep under the table.*

KEEP ▸ UNTIL

keep something until something to retain something until a certain time. □ *Can you keep this box until I call for it next week?* □ *The package will be kept until Monday.*

KEEP ▸ UP

keep an act up AND **keep one's act up** to maintain behavior that is a facade; to continue with one's facade. (The *an* can be replaced with *the, this, that,* etc.) □ *How long do I have to keep this act up? I am tired of fooling people.* 🅃 *I am weary of keeping up my act.* □ *I will keep my act up until I get what I want.*

keep one's chin up to remain brave. (Figurative.) □ *Things are bad, but keep your chin up.* □ *I'll keep my chin up no matter what happens.*

keep one's end up to carry one's share of the burden; to carry through on one's part of a bargain. □ *You have to keep your end up like the rest of us.* □ *Don't worry, I'll keep my end up.*

keep someone up **1.** to hold someone upright. □ *Try to keep him up until I can get his bed turned down.* □ *Keep her up for a few minutes longer.* **2.** to prevent someone from going to bed or going to sleep. □ *I'm sorry, was my trumpet keeping you up?* □ *We were kept up by the noise.*

keep something up **1.** to hold or prop something up. □ *Keep your side of the trunk up. Don't let it sag.* 🅃 *Keep up your side of the trunk.* **2.** to continue doing something. □ *I love your singing. Don't stop. Keep it up.* 🅃 *Please keep up your singing.* **3.** to maintain something in good order. □ *I'm glad you keep the exterior of your house up.* 🅃 *You keep up your house nicely.* 🄰 *This is a nicely kept-up house you have.*

keep up appearances to make things look all right whether they are or not. □ *We must keep up appearances even if it means little sacrifices here and there.* □ *Things may be unpleasant, but we will keep up appearances.*

keep up with someone or something **1.** to stay even with someone or something; to be just as productive as someone or something. □ *Don't work so fast. I can't keep up with you.* □ *I can't keep up with the runner ahead of me.* **2.** to pay attention to the news about someone or something. □ *I don't see the Smiths a lot since they moved, but I keep up with them by phone.* □ *I try to keep up with current events.*

keep up with the Joneses to make all the financial expenditures that the neighbors make. □ *I am tired of trying to keep up with the Joneses. Let's just move if we can't afford to live here.* □

We never try to keep up with the Joneses.

keep up with the times to work to appear contemporary and fashionable. □ *I am too old-fashioned. I have to keep up with the times better.* □ *I don't care about keeping up with the times.*

KEEP ▸ WITH

keep company with someone **1.** to associate with someone. □ *I understand you have been keeping company with a jazz musician. Is this correct?* □ *Do you mind if I keep company with you and your friends?* **2.** to associate with someone in courtship. □ *Mary has been keeping company with Tom for a number of weeks.* □ *They have been keeping company with each other for over a month.*

keep faith with someone to be loyal to someone. □ *I intend to keep faith with my people and all they stand for.* □ *We could not keep faith with them any longer.*

keep pace with someone or something to move at the same rate as someone or something; to keep up with someone or something. □ *Try to keep pace with the other workers.* □ *I can't keep pace with that machine that keeps spitting out things for me to do.*

keep something with someone **1.** to leave something in the care of someone. □ *Can I keep my bicycle with you while I am gone?* □ *Please keep your bicycle with me.* **2.** to celebrate a festival with someone, such as Christmas. (Stilted.) □ *I prefer to keep Christmas with my parents.* □ *We keep Christmas with people from our church.*

KEEP ▸ WITHIN

keep (someone or something) within bounds to cause someone or something to remain constrained or be reasonable; to cause someone to act or something to be in good taste. (*Someone* includes *oneself.*) □ *I know you want artistic freedom, but if you want an audience, you are going to have to keep within bounds.* □ *Try to keep the children within bounds.* □ *Do keep things within bounds.*

keep within something to remain within a thing or within the boundaries of something. □ *If you keep within the tourist area, you will be safe.* □ *Please keep within the yard.*

KEY ▸ UP

See *be keyed up (about something)* under *BE ▸ UP.*

key someone up to cause someone to be anxious or excited. □ *The excitement of the moment really keyed me up.* □ *Thoughts of their vacation keyed up the children.*

KICK ▸ ABOUT

kick about someone or something to complain about someone or something. (Figurative.) □ *Why are you kicking about your cousin? What has he done now?* □ *They kicked about our regulations, but they finally accepted them.*

KICK ▸ AGAINST

kick against someone or something to give someone or something a blow with the foot. □ *I kicked against the side of the television set, and it came on.* 🅃 *He kicked against the giant of a man, but it had no effect.*

KICK ▸ AROUND

kick some ass around to show people who is in charge; to show people that someone is in charge. (Slang. Use *ass* with discretion. Also without *around,* but not eligible as an entry.) □ *I'm going to go down to accounting and kick some ass around.* □ *He said he was going to kick some ass around in the election campaign.*

kick someone around to harass someone; to give someone trouble and treat them badly. (Figurative.) □ *Stop kicking me around if you know what's good for you.* □ *I have been kicked around enough!*

kick something around **1.** to move something around by kicking it, as in play. □ *Kick the ball around awhile and then try to make a goal.* □ *The boys kicked a can around, making a lot of noise.* 🅃 *Don't kick around all the dirt. You'll make a mess.* **2.** to discuss something; to chat about an idea. □ *We got* *together and kicked her idea around.* 🅃 *Fred and Bob kicked around some plots for a new movie.*

KICK ▶ ASIDE

kick someone or something aside **1.** to get someone or something out of the way by kicking. □ *The bully kicked Timmy aside and grabbed our cake.* □ *I kicked the cat aside and came into the room.* **2.** to get rid of someone or something. (Figurative.) □ *He simply kicked his wife aside and took up with some young chick.* □ *I kicked the old car aside and got a new one.*

KICK ▶ AT

kick at someone or something to make kicking motions toward someone or something. □ *The horse kicked at me, but I knew it was just a threat.* □ *The boys kicked at the can aimlessly.*

KICK ▶ AWAY

kick someone or something away to force someone or something away by kicking. □ *Fred kicked the intruder away from the gun he had dropped on the floor.* 🅃 *Then he kicked away the gun.* □ *The kickboxer kicked the mugger away.*

KICK ▶ BACK

kick back **1.** to relax; to lean back and relax. (Slang. See also *lie back.*) □ *I really like to kick back and relax.* □ *It's time to kick back and enjoy life.* **2.** [for an addict] to return to an addiction or a habit, after having "kicked the habit." (Slang.) □ *Lefty kicked back after only a few days of being clean.* □ *A lot of addicts kick back very soon.*

kick back (at someone or something) to kick at someone or something in revenge. □ *She kicked at me, so I kicked back at her.* □ *If you kick me, I'll kick back.*

kick something back (to someone or something) to move something back to someone, something, or some place by kicking. □ *I kicked the ball back to Walter.* □ *He kicked it to me and I kicked it back.*

KICK ▶ DOWN

kick something down to break down something by kicking. □ *I was afraid they were going to kick the door down.* 🅃 *Don't kick down the door!*

KICK ▶ IN

kick in (on something) (for someone or something) to contribute to something for someone or something. (Slang.) □ *Would you like to kick in on a gift for Joel?* □ *I'll be happy to kick in on a gift.* □ *Sure, I would like to kick in for the gift.* □ *Sure, I would like to kick in for Joel.*

kick something in to break through something by kicking. □ *Tommy kicked the door in and broke the new lamp.* 🅃 *He kicked in the door by accident.*

kick something in (on something) (for someone or something) to contribute something, such as money, on something for someone or something. □ *I will kick a few bucks in on some flowers for the receptionist.* 🅃 *I will kick in a few bucks on the gift for Marge.* □ *Sharon kicked a dollar in on the gift for Marge.* □ *Alice kicked something in too.*

KICK ▶ OFF

kick off **1.** to begin a football game by kicking the ball. □ *When do they kick off?* 🄽 *We missed the kickoff.* **2.** to die. (Slang.) □ *The old lady kicked off last Monday.* □ *Max thought he was going to kick off.*

kick something off to begin something. (Figurative slang.) □ *The city kicked the centennial celebration off with a parade.* 🅃 *They kicked off the celebration with a parade.*

kick something off ((of) someone or something) to knock something off someone or something by kicking. (The *of*-phrase is paraphrased with a *from*-phrase when the particle is transposed. See the 🄵 example. The *of* is colloquial.) □ *The baby must have kicked her covers off herself in the night.* 🅃 *She kicked off her covers in the night.* 🄵 *She kicked off the covers from most of her body.*

KICK ▸ OUT

kick out (at someone or something) to thrust one's foot outward at something. □ *The ostrich kicked out at the men trying to catch her.* □ *The mule kicked out and just missed me.*

kick someone out (of something) to eject someone from something or some place brusquely. (Figurative. The *of*-phrase is paraphrased with a *from*-phrase when the particle is transposed. See the [F] example.) □ *The usher kicked the boys out of the movie.* [T] *The usher kicked out the noisy boys.* [F] *The usher kicked out the noisy boys from the theater.* □ *I would have kicked them out too.*

kick something out (of something) to move something out of something or some place by kicking. (The *of*-phrase is paraphrased with a *from*-phrase when the particle is transposed. See the [F] example.) □ *The soccer player kicked the ball out of the tangle of legs.* [T] *She got into the fracas and kicked out the ball.* [F] *She kicked out the ball from the tangle of legs.* □ *It looked trapped, but Todd kicked it out.*

KICK ▸ OVER

kick over the traces to do what one is meant not to do; to rebel against authority. (Idiomatic. Refers to a horse that steps on the wrong side of the straps that link it to whatever it is pulling.) □ *At the age of sixty, Walter kicked over the traces and ran away to Brazil.* □ *All these young kids seem to want to kick over the traces.*

KICK ▸ UP

kick up to give trouble; to cause pain. (Informal.) □ *My arthritis is kicking up again.* □ *It always kicks up in this weather.*

kick up a fuss (about someone or something) to complain about or object to someone or something. □ *What are you kicking up such a fuss about?* □ *Molly kicked up a fuss about Alice.* □ *I'm not kicking up a fuss.*

kick up a row (with someone) to start a fight or quarrel with someone. □ *Andrew is kicking up a row with his roommate again.* □ *Stop kicking up a row every time things don't go your way.*

kick up a storm to create a disturbance; to raise a noisy objection. □ *The whole committee kicked up such a storm that we had to withdraw the proposal.* □ *Wally kicked up a storm when he was fired.*

kick up one's heels to celebrate and have a good time. (Figurative.) □ *Let's go out tonight and kick up our heels.* □ *It's good to kick up your heels every now and then.*

KID ▸ ABOUT

kid someone about someone or something to tease someone about someone or something. □ *You wouldn't kid me about Jody, would you?* □ *Please don't kid me about my long hair!*

KID ▸ AROUND

kid (around) (with someone) to quip and joke with someone. □ *Don't kid around with me, buster!* □ *We are just kidding around.*

KID ▸ WITH

See *kid (around) (with someone)* under *KID ▸ AROUND.*

KILL ▸ OFF

kill someone or something off to kill all of a group of people or creatures. □ *Lefty set out to kill Max and his boys off.* [T] *Something killed off all the dinosaurs.*

KILL ▸ WITH

kill someone with kindness to be enormously kind to someone. (Figurative.) □ *You are just killing me with kindness. Why?* □ *Don't kill them with kindness.*

kill two birds with one stone to accomplish two things with only one deed. (Figurative.) □ *I'd like to kill two birds with one stone, if possible, and save some money in the process.* □ *I like to kill two birds with one stone. It saves time and effort.*

KINDLE ▸ WITH

kindle with something [for the eyes] to begin to light with some quality, such as joy, pleasure, evil, etc. (Stilted.) □ *Her eyes kindled with recognition, and I* *knew she would be all right.* □ *The child's eyes kindled with joy as she saw her mother.*

KINK ▶ UP

kink up [for something] to develop kinks or tangles. □ *The leather parts tend to shrink and kink up in the damp weather.* □ *My hair kinks up in this weather.*

KISS ▶ AWAY

kiss something away (from something) to kiss something and make something bad go away, such as tears, grief, pain, etc. □ *She kissed the tears of pain and disappointment away from his smudgy face.* 🅃 *She kissed away his tears.* □ *She kissed the tears away.*

KISS ▶ OFF

kiss someone off to kill someone. (Slang.) □ *Max kissed Lefty off with a small gun he carried in his boot.* 🅃 *He kissed off Lefty with a small gun.*

kiss someone or something off to dismiss someone or something lightly; to abandon or write off someone or something. (Informal.) □ *I kissed off about $200 on that last deal.* □ *They kissed me off and that was the end of it.*

KISS ▶ ON

kiss someone on something to kiss someone on a particular place. □ *He kissed her right on the tip of her nose.* □ *She was kissed on the tip of her nose.*

KISS ▶ UP

kiss up to someone to flatter someone; to curry favor with someone. (Slang.) □ *Edgar is in kissing up to the boss again.* □ *Stop kissing up to me.*

KLUTZ ▶ AROUND

klutz around to go about acting stupidly. (Slang.) □ *Stop klutzing around and get your act together.* □ *Why are you klutzing around so much?*

KNEEL ▶ DOWN

kneel down to get down on one's knees. □ *Please kneel down and fold your hands.* □ *You should at least kneel down and be quiet.*

kneel down (before someone or something) to show respect by getting down on one's knees in the presence of someone or something. □ *We were told to kneel down in front of a statue of a golden calf.* □ *I'm too old to kneel down comfortably.*

KNIT ▶ TOGETHER

knit something together to join things together by knitting. □ *Terry knitted the parts of the sweater together.* 🅃 *Sally knitted together the two parts of the glove.*

knit together to join or grow together. (Said of broken bones.) □ *The bones are knitting together exactly as expected.* □ *If the bones don't knit together properly, we will have to do something a little more drastic.*

KNOCK ▶ ABOUT

knock about (some place) (with someone) AND **knock around (some place) (with someone)** to hang around some place with someone; to wander idly about some place with someone. (Slang.) □ *Sally was knocking about France with her friends.* □ *I knocked around town with Ken for a while.*

knock someone or something about AND **knock someone or something around** **1.** to jostle someone or something. □ *The bumpy road was knocking everyone in the truck about.* □ *The bumpy road knocked the old truck around a lot.* □ *Don't knock the grocery bags around. You'll break the eggs.* **2.** to strike someone or something; to beat on someone or something. □ *Max knocked Judy about.* □ *Stop knocking me around.*

KNOCK ▶ AGAINST

knock against someone or something to bump against someone or something. □ *Mickey knocked against Mary and said he was sorry.* □ *I didn't mean to knock against your sore knee.*

knock one's head (up) against a brick wall to be totally frustrated. (Figurative.) □ *Trying to get a raise around here is like knocking your head up against a brick wall.* □ *No need to knock your head against a brick wall.*

knock something against something to strike something against something. □

He knocked a chair against the table and tipped both pieces of furniture over. □ *A chair was knocked against the table, upsetting a vase.*

knock (up) against someone or something to bump against someone or something. □ *The loose shutter knocked up against the side of the house.* □ *The large branch knocked against the garage in the storm.* □ *The child's bicycle knocked up against me.*

KNOCK ► AROUND

knock around (some place) (with someone) See under *KNOCK ► ABOUT.*

KNOCK ► AT

knock at something to knock [on something] at a particular location. □ *I could hear someone knocking at the door next to mine.* □ *Who is knocking at the door?*

KNOCK ► AWAY

knock away (at something) to continue to knock at something. □ *The banging shutter kept knocking away at the side of the house.* □ *It knocked away all night, keeping me awake.*

KNOCK ► BACK

knock back a drink AND **knock one back; knock one over** to swallow a drink of alcoholic beverage. (Idiomatic slang.) □ *Todd knocked back one drink, and then had another.* □ *Kelly knocked one back.* □ *She knocked one over and left the bar.*

KNOCK ► DOWN

knock someone down to size to strike one, making one more humble. (Both literal and figurative uses.) □ *The other kids will knock him down to size. Have no fear.* □ *Max was finally knocked down to size.*

knock someone or something down to thrust someone to the ground by hitting. □ *The force of the blast knocked us down.* 🅃 *It knocked down everyone in the room.* □ *The wind knocked the fence down.*

KNOCK ► FOR

knock someone for a loop 1. to strike someone hard. □ *You really knocked me for a loop. I hope that was an accident.* □ *I was really knocked for a loop by the falling branch.* **2.** to stun or shock someone with some news. (Slang.) □ *What he told me knocked me for a loop, and it took me a while to recover.* □ *I was really knocked for a loop by the bad news.*

KNOCK ► INTO

knock someone into something to strike one, sending one into something. □ *The blow knocked him into the wall.* □ *Max knocked Lefty into a lamp post.*

knock something into a cocked hat to upset or ruin something. (Figurative.) □ *The news knocked all my plans into a cocked hat.* □ *This weather has knocked everything into a cocked hat.*

KNOCK ► IN(TO)

knock some sense in(to someone) to strike one, making one smarter, or at least obedient. □ *I think his father finally knocked some sense into him.* 🅃 *The accident finally knocked in some sense.* □ *I thought that last week's experience would knock some sense in.*

KNOCK ► OFF

knock it off to stop talking; to be silent. (Usually a rude command.) □ *Shut up, you guys! Knock it off!* □ *Knock it off and go to sleep!*

knock off doing something to stop doing something. (Informal.) □ *Knock off shoveling snow now, and come in for a hot drink.* □ *I wish he would knock off practicing for a while.*

knock off (work) to finish work for a short period or for the day. (Colloquial.) □ *I knock off work about five, and then I usually go out with the boys.* □ *When do you knock off?*

knock one off one's feet 1. to strike one, sending one to the ground. □ *The blow knocked me off my feet.* □ *The force of the wind knocked me off my feet.* **2.** to surprise or shock someone with some news. (Figurative.) □ *The news of the wedding knocked Andrew off his feet.* □ *The news knocked me off my feet.*

knock someone off to kill someone. (Slang.) □ *Max was told to knock Lefty off.* 🅃 *He really wanted to knock off Lefty.*

knock someone's block off to strike someone very hard. (Idiomatic slang.) □ *I'm going to knock your block off!* □ *Max knocked Lefty's block off.*

knock someone's socks off AND **knock the socks off (of) someone** to surprise someone thoroughly. (Idiomatic slang. The *of* is colloquial.) □ *The exciting news just knocked my socks off!* □ *The news knocked the socks off of everyone in the office.*

knock something off **1.** to finish something hastily. (Slang.) □ *I knocked a quick paper off for my history class.* 🅃 *I knocked off a paper for history in two hours.* **2.** to copy or reproduce a product. □ *The manufacturer knocked off a famous designer's coat.* 🅃 *They are well known for knocking off cheap versions of expensive watches.* 🄽 *The knockoffs were much cheaper than the originals.*

knock something off (of) someone or something to remove something from someone or something by striking. (The *of* is colloquial.) □ *I knocked the hat off of Wally when I hit him accidentally with the ladder.* □ *My elbow knocked the book off the table.*

KNOCK ▸ ON

knock on something to rap or tap, often with the knuckles, on something. □ *She knocked on the door several times.* □ *Knock on it again. Maybe she didn't hear you.*

knock on wood to rap on something made of wood. (For good luck. Usually a phrase attached to another statement.) □ *I think I am well at last—knock on wood.* □ *I knock on wood when I wish something were true.*

KNOCK ▸ OUT

knock oneself out (to do something) (for someone or something) to make a great effort to do something for someone or some group. □ *I knocked myself out to plan this party for you!* □ *She knocked herself out for us.* □ *He knocked himself out to get there on time.* □ *Please don't knock yourself out.*

knock someone out **1.** to knock someone unconscious. (*Someone* includes *oneself.*) □ *Max knocked Lefty out and left him there in the gutter.* 🅃 *Max knocked out Lefty.* □ *She fell and knocked herself out.* **2.** to make someone unconsciousness. (*Someone* includes *oneself.*) □ *The drug knocked her out quickly.* 🅃 *The powerful medicine knocked out the patient.* 🄰 *The bartender slipped in some knockout drops.* **3.** to surprise or please someone. (Figurative.) □ *I have some news that will really knock you out.* 🄰 *I have a knockout recipe for tomato soup.* 🄽 *That new dress of yours is a real knockout.* **4.** to wear someone out; to exhaust someone. □ *All that exercise really knocked me out.* □ *The day's activities knocked the kids out and they went right to bed.*

knock something out **1.** to create something hastily. (Slang.) □ *He knocked a few out as samples.* 🅃 *He knocked out a few of them quickly, just so we could see what they were going to look like.* **2.** to put something out of order; to make something inoperable. □ *The storm knocked the telephone system out.* 🅃 *The high winds will probably knock out electrical service all over town.*

knock something out of someone to beat someone until something emerges or dissipates. □ *Max knocked the truth out of the spy.* □ *Lefty knocked the sense out of Max.*

knock something out of something to beat or knock on something until something comes out. □ *Timmy knocked the stuffing out of his pillow.* □ *Someone knocked the coins out of my piggy bank.*

knock the bottom out of something [for something] to go down so low as to knock out the bottom. (Figurative.) □ *The bad news knocked the bottom out of the stock market.* □ *The recession knocked the bottom out of our profits.*

knock the hell out of someone or something to strike someone or something very hard. (Idiomatic and informal. Use *hell* with discretion.) □ *The bully knocked the hell out of Sam.* □ *You really knocked the hell out of my front bumper.*

knock the living daylights out of someone to beat someone severely. (Figurative.) □ *If you do that again, I will knock the living daylights out of you.* □ *Max wants to knock the living daylights out of his enemy, Lefty "Fingers" Moran.*

knock the wind out of someone's sails 1. to bring someone to an abrupt halt by a heavy blow to the body, presumably knocking the person's wind out. □ *Max hit Lefty and really knocked the wind out of his sails.* □ *Fred ran into the side of the garage and knocked the wind out of his sails.* **2.** to humiliate someone. (Figurative.) □ *The sharp rebuke from the boss knocked the wind out of his sails.* □ *That really knocked the wind out of her sails.*

KNOCK ▸ OVER

knock one over See under *KNOCK ▸ BACK.*

knock over something 1. to steal something. (Slang.) □ *Lefty knocked over a truckload of broccoli.* □ *Some cheap crook knocked over a load of television sets.* **2.** to rob a place. (Slang.) □ *Max knocked over two banks in one week.* □ *He was the kind of punk who would try to knock over a filling station.*

knock someone or something over to tip someone or something over. □ *Fred bumped into a lady and knocked her over.* □ *I turned and knocked the flower vase over by accident.* 🅃 *Who knocked over this vase?* 🄽 *He's so easy to fool. A real knockover!*

knock someone over to surprise or overwhelm someone. □ *His statement simply knocked me over.* □ *When she showed me what happened to the car, it nearly knocked me over.*

knock someone over with a feather to have a powerful effect on someone. (Said about someone who is stunned and surprised by news. Figurative.) □ *I was so surprised that you could have knocked me over with a feather.* □ *Todd could have knocked me over with a feather when he told me his news.*

knock something over to tip something over. (See also *knock over something.*) □ *Someone knocked the chair over.* 🅃 *Who knocked over the flower pot?*

KNOCK ▸ THROUGH

knock through something to break through something. □ *They knocked through the wall and put in a doorway.* □ *The wall had to be knocked through before we could install a doorway.*

KNOCK ▸ TO

knock something to someone to hit something, such as a ball, to someone. □ *The coach knocked the ball to each player in turn.* □ *The ball was knocked to the guy out in center field.*

KNOCK ▸ TOGETHER

knock one's knees together [for one's knees] to shake together from fright. □ *I stood there freezing for ten minutes, knocking my knees together in the cold.* □ *It takes a lot of energy to knock your knees together.*

knock some heads together to show someone who's boss; to make people do their jobs. (Figurative.) □ *I am going to knock some heads together around here.* □ *I think I'm going to have to knock some heads together to get things done.*

knock something together to assemble something hastily. □ *I knocked this model together so you could get a general idea of what I had in mind.* □ *This thing has just been knocked together!*

KNOCK ▸ UP

knock one's head (up) against a brick wall See under *KNOCK ▸ AGAINST.*

knock someone up to get a woman pregnant. (Slang.) □ *He thinks he knocked her up.* 🅃 *He didn't knock up anybody.*

knock (up) against someone or something See under *KNOCK ▸ AGAINST.*

KNOT ▸ TOGETHER

knot something together to tie something together in a knot. □ *Knot these strings together and trim the strings off* *the knot.* □ *Are the ropes knotted together properly?*

KNOW ▸ ABOUT

know about someone or something to have information about someone or something. □ *I know about John and what he does.* □ *I know about cars, but I can't fix this one!*

KNOW ▸ APART

know people or things apart to be able to distinguish one person from another or one thing from another. □ *You two sure look alike. How is one to know you and your sister apart?* □ *Is there a way to know Fred and Bob apart?* □ *He doesn't know Japanese food and Chinese food apart.*

KNOW ▸ AROUND

know one's way around **1.** to know how to get from place to place. □ *I can find my way. I know my way around.* □ *I don't know my way around yet.* **2.** to know how to deal with people and situations; to have had much experience at living. (Slang.) □ *I can get along in the world. I know my way around.* □ *Do you think I don't know my way around?*

KNOW ▸ AS

know someone as someone to know someone by a different name. □ *I know her as Candy La Tour.* □ *She is known as Fifi La Tour.*

know someone or something as something to recognize someone or something as something. □ *I know Mr. Franklin as a fine man.* □ *I know this name as a very fine brand.*

KNOW ▸ AT

know where something is at **1.** to know where something is located. (Colloquial, folksy, or nonstandard. Without *at,* this sense is standard English, and it would be ineligible as an entry.) □ *Do you know where the hammer is at?* □ *I don't know where my glasses are at.* **2.** to be alert and know how the world—or some part of it—really works. (Slang. Usually with *it*. Not concerned with location.) □ *Man, you just don't know where it's at!* □ *I don't know where cool jazz is at.*

KNOW ▸ BY

know someone by sight to recognize a person's face, but not know the name. □ *I'm afraid I don't know her by sight.* □ *I know all my employees by sight.*

know someone or something by name to recognize the name but not the appearance of someone or something. □ *I only know her by name. I have no idea what she looks like.* □ *I know this brand of sausage by name, but I have never tasted it.*

know someone or something by something to recognize someone or something by a certain characteristic. □ *I know her by her perfume.* □ *I know this committee only by its reputation, which is not good, by the way.*

know something by heart to have memorized something perfectly. □ *I know the Gettysburg Address by heart.* □ *Do you know it by heart?*

KNOW ▸ FOR

know one for what one is to recognize someone as some type of person or thing. □ *I know you for what you are, you devil.* □ *We know him for the thief he is.*

KNOW ▸ FROM

know from something to know about something. (Slang and regional.) □ *Do you know from thermostats?* □ *You don't know from anything!*

know someone from someone to tell the difference between one person and another. □ *I don't know Fred from his twin brother.* □ *I know Bill from Bob, but I can't tell most identical twins apart.*

know something from memory to have something stored in one's memory. □ *I know the opera from memory. I don't need a copy of the score.* □ *I don't know my part from memory yet.*

know something from something to tell the difference between one thing and another. □ *You don't know a smoked herring from a squid!* □ *She didn't know a raven from a writing box, and who does?*

KNOW ▸ INSIDE

know something inside out to know something thoroughly. (Figurative.) □ *I know my multiplication tables inside out.* □ *Fred knows his part in the play inside out.*

KNOW ▸ OF

know of someone or something to be aware of the existence of someone or something. □ *I think I know of someone who can help you.* □ *I didn't know of Wally's arrival.*

KNOW ▸ ON

know where someone stands on someone or something to know what someone thinks about someone or something; to know someone's position on someone or something. □ *Tom is up for promotion. I want to know where you stand on him.* □ *I want to know where you stand on this matter.*

KNOW ▸ THROUGH

know something through and through to know something very well. □ *I want you to know this project through and through before the staff meeting.* □ *I know my part in the play through and through.*

KNUCKLE ▸ DOWN

knuckle down (to something) to get busy doing something. □ *I want you to knuckle down to your work and stop worrying about the past.* □ *Come on. Knuckle down. Get busy.*

KNUCKLE ▸ UNDER

knuckle under (to someone or something) to yield to someone; to acquiesce to someone's wishes. □ *I'm afraid you have to knuckle under to the boss. That's part of your job.* □ *You really need to knuckle under.*

KOWTOW ▸ TO

kowtow to someone or something to grovel to someone or something. □ *I won't kowtow to anyone!* □ *You don't expect me to go in there and kowtow to that committee, do you?*

L

LABEL ▸ AS

label someone or something as something to designate someone or something as something. ☐ *She labeled him as an uncouth person.* ☐ *We labeled the committee as a worthless organization.*

LABEL ▸ WITH

label someone or something with something to mark or identify someone or something with something. ☐ *They labeled each person who had paid the admission fee with a symbol stamped on the hand.* ☐ *I labeled each book with my name.*

LABOR ▸ AT

labor at something to work hard at something. ☐ *He is laboring at his gardening and won't be back in the house until dinnertime.* ☐ *What are you laboring at so intensely?*

LABOR ▸ FOR

labor for someone or something to work on behalf of someone or something. ☐ *I labored for them all day, and they didn't even thank me.* ☐ *I have labored for this cause for many years.*

labor for something to work in order to get something, such as money. ☐ *I was laboring for a pittance, so I decided to get another job.* ☐ *I labor for the love of it.*

LABOR ▸ OVER

labor over someone or something to work hard on someone or something. ☐ *The surgeon labored over the patient for four hours.* ☐ *I labored over this painting for months before I got it the way I wanted it.*

LABOR ▸ UNDER

labor under something **1.** to work beneath something. ☐ *He is laboring under his automobile and he has been hard at work there all afternoon.* ☐ *They labored under the hot sun all day.* **2.** to function believing something; to go about living while assuming something [that may not be so]. ☐ *I was laboring under the idea that we were going to share the profits equally.* ☐ *Are you laboring under the notion that you are going to be promoted?*

LACE ▸ INTO

lace into someone or something to set to work on someone or something; to "attack" someone or something. ☐ *Todd laced into Ralph and scolded him severely.* ☐ *Elaine laced into the job with the intention of finishing it within an hour.*

lace someone into something to tighten the laces of something someone is wearing. (*Someone* includes *oneself.*) ☐ *Sally helped Billy lace himself into his boots.* ☐ *The maid laced Gloria into her corset.*

LACE ▸ UP

lace someone up to tie someone's laces; to help someone get dressed in a garment having laces. (*Someone* includes *oneself.*) ☐ *Would you please lace me up? I can't reach the ties in the back.* 🅃 *I laced up Sally, as she requested.* ☐ *She got herself into the ancient costume but could not lace herself up.*

lace something up to tie the laces of something. ☐ *Lace your shoes up, Tommy.* 🅃 *Lace up your shoes.*

LACE ▸ WITH

lace something with something to adulterate something with something, often with something alcoholic. ☐ *Someone laced the punch with strong whiskey.* ☐ *Who laced my coffee with brandy?*

LACK ▸ FOR

lack for something to lack something. (Stilted.) ☐ *We don't lack for new ideas.* ☐ *We lack for nothing, thank you.*

LADLE ▸ OUT

ladle something out (of something) to scoop something out of something with a spoon or ladle. (The *of*-phrase is paraphrased with a *from*-phrase when the particle is transposed. See the 🄵 example.) ☐ *Marie ladled the last of the gravy out of the gravy boat and went to the kitchen for more.* 🅃 *She ladled out the soup.* 🄵 *She ladled out the soup from the pot.* ☐ *Roger will ladle the soup out.*

LADLE ▸ UP

ladle something up to scoop something up in a ladle. ☐ *Jerry ladled a cool dipper of water up and quenched his thirst.* 🅃 *Please ladle up the soup and serve it.*

LAG ▸ BEHIND

lag behind in something to fall behind in something. ☐ *I am lagging behind in my car payments.* ☐ *She is lagging behind in her homework assignments.*

lag behind (someone or something) to linger behind someone or something; to fall behind someone or something. ☐ *Come on up here. Don't lag behind us or you'll get lost.* ☐ *Please don't lag behind the donkeys. Come up here with the rest of the hikers.* ☐ *Don't lag behind too much.*

LAID ▸ BACK

See *be laid-back* under *BE ▸ BACK.*

LAM ▸ INTO

lam into someone or something to attack someone or some creature. ☐ *Paul was so angry that he lammed into his friend and struck him in the side.* ☐ *The angry coachman lammed into the poor horses.*

LAMENT ▸ FOR

lament for someone or something See the following entry.

LAMENT ▸ OVER

lament over someone or something AND **lament for someone or something** to sorrow over someone or something. ☐ *There is no need to lament over Sam. There is nothing that crying will do for him now.* ☐ *She is still lamenting for her cat.*

LAND ▸ AT

land at some place **1.** [for a ship] to come to port at a place. ☐ *The ship landed at the wharf and the passengers got off.* ☐ *We landed at the island's main city and waited for customs to clear us.* **2.** [for an airplane] to return to earth at an airport. ☐ *We landed at O'Hare at noon.* ☐ *We were to land at Denver, but there was bad weather.*

land something at some place to bring a boat, ship, or airplane to rest or to port at or near a place. ☐ *The captain landed the boat at a small island in hopes of finding a place to make repairs.* ☐ *They had to land the plane at a small town in an emergency.*

LAND ▸ IN

land in something **1.** [for someone] to end up in something, such as a mess, jail, trouble, etc. ☐ *If you don't mend your ways, you're going to land in jail!* ☐ *Andy is going to land in hot water if he doesn't start paying his bills.* **2.** [for an airplane] to make a landing in something, such as bad weather, darkness, daylight, fog, etc. ☐ *You can't land this plane in fog like this.* ☐ *The pilot is not capable of landing in the dark.* **3.** [for an airplane] to return to earth in or near a particular city. ☐ *We landed in Chicago on time.* ☐ *They could not land in San Francisco, so they flew on to Los Angeles.*

land someone in something to cause someone to end up in something. (*Someone* includes *oneself.*) ☐ *His criminal activity finally landed him in jail.* ☐ *You really landed yourself in a fine mess!*

LAND ▸ ON

See under *LAND ▸ (UP)ON.*

LAND ▸ UP

land up somehow to end up in some way. (Colloquial.) □ *If you keep eating all those sweets, you'll land up sick.* □ *Do you want to land up without a job?*

LAND ▸ (UP)ON

land (up)on both feet AND **land (up)on one's feet** **1.** to end up on both feet after a jump, dive, etc. (*Upon* is formal and less commonly used than *on.*) □ *She jumped over the bicycle and landed upon both feet.* □ *Donna made the enormous leap and landed on her feet.* **2.** to come out of something well; to survive something satisfactorily. (Figurative. *Upon* is formal and less commonly used than *on.*) □ *It was a rough period in his life, but when it was over he landed on both feet.* □ *At least, after it was over I landed on my feet.*

land (up)on someone or something to light on someone or something. (*Upon* is formal and less commonly used than *on.*) □ *A bee landed upon her and frightened her.* □ *A butterfly landed on the cake and ruined the icing.*

LANGUISH ▸ IN

languish in some place **1.** to become dispirited in some place; to weaken and fade away in some place. □ *Claire languished in prison for her crime.* □ *I spent over three days languishing in a stuffy hotel room.* □ *We languished in the airport waiting room while they refueled the plane.* **2.** to suffer neglect in a place. □ *The bill languished in the Senate for months on end.* □ *The children languished in the squalid conditions until the courts intervened.*

LANGUISH ▸ OVER

languish over someone or something to pine over someone or something. □ *There is no point in languishing over Tim. He'll never come back.* □ *She wasted half her life languishing over her lost opportunities.*

LAP ▸ AGAINST

lap (up) against something [for waves] to splash gently against something. □ *The waves lapped up against the shore softly.* □ *The waves lapped against the shore all night long and I couldn't sleep.*

LAP ▸ OVER

lap over (something) [for something] to extend or project over the edge or boundary of something. □ *The lid lapped over the edge of the barrel, forming a little table.* □ *The blanket did not lap over enough to keep me warm.* Ⓝ *There was not enough overlap to keep the cold out of my side of the bed.*

LAP ▸ UP

lap something up **1.** [for an animal] to lick something up. □ *The dog lapped the ice cream up off the floor.* Ⓣ *The dog lapped up the ice cream.* **2.** [for someone] to accept or believe something with enthusiasm. (Figurative.) □ *Of course, they believed it. They just lapped it up.* Ⓣ *They lapped up the lies without questioning anything.*

lap (up) against something See under *LAP ▸ AGAINST.*

LAPSE ▸ FROM

lapse from grace **1.** to fall out of favor with God. □ *The child was told that if he ever smoked even one cigarette, he would lapse from grace, for certain.* □ *It is easy, these days, to lapse from grace.* **2.** to fall out of favor. □ *Everyone is getting into trouble with the boss at the office. Ted lapsed from grace when he left the lobby door unlocked all weekend.* □ *I have to be there on time every day or I will lapse from grace for sure.*

LAPSE ▸ INTO

lapse into something to weaken or slip into something, especially a coma. □ *After suffering for a few hours, she lapsed into a coma and died.* □ *Uncle Herman lapsed into a state of unconsciousness.*

LASH ▸ ABOUT

lash something about to whip or fling something about violently. □ *The big cat lashed its tail threateningly.* □ *The strong wind lashed the tall grass about.*

LASH ▸ AGAINST

lash against something [for something, such as wind or water] to beat or whip heavily against something. □ *The angry waves lashed against the hull of the boat, frightening the people huddled inside.* □ *The wind lashed against the house and kept us awake all night.*

LASH ▸ AT

lash at someone or something to thrash or beat someone or something violently. □ *The rain lashed at the windows.* □ *The mule driver lashed at his beasts with his whip.*

LASH ▸ BACK

lash back (at someone or something) to strike or fight back against someone or something—physically or verbally. □ *Randy lashed back at his attackers and drove them away.* □ *If you threaten Fred, he'll lash back.*

LASH ▸ DOWN

lash down on someone or something [for rain] to beat down on someone or something. □ *The wind and rain lashed down on us.* □ *The rain lashed down on the young plants and pounded them into the soil.*

lash someone or something down to tie someone or something down. (*Someone* includes *oneself.*) □ *The villain lashed Nell down to the railroad tracks.* 🅃 *He lashed down the innocent victim.* □ *Lash that cask down so it doesn't wash overboard.* 🄰 *We will have to sit on the lashed-down cargo. There are no other seats.* □ *They lashed themselves down to the bolts on the deck, hoping they would not wash overboard.*

LASH ▸ INTO

lash into someone or something to attack someone or some creature—physically or verbally. □ *Max lashed into Lefty, who had messed up a robbery again.* □ *Walter lashed into the cat for tearing the upholstery.*

lash into something to begin to eat something with vigor. □ *Mary lashed into the huge ice cream concoction, and ate almost the whole thing.* □ *The workers lashed into their lunches and did not say a word until they had finished.*

LASH ▸ OUT

lash out (at someone or something) AND **lash out (against someone or something)** to strike out in defense or attack—physically or verbally. □ *Amy was angry with Ed and lashed out at him just to show who was boss.* □ *She was so angry with him that she just lashed out against him.* □ *Gretchen was fed up with the cat and lashed out savagely in her anger.*

LASH ▸ TO

lash someone or something to something to tie someone or something to someone or something. (*Someone* includes *oneself.*) □ *The boys lashed one of their number to a tree and danced around him like savages.* □ *Abe lashed the cask to the deck.* □ *Frank lashed himself to the mast.*

LASH ▸ TOGETHER

lash something together to tie something or things together. □ *Let's lash these logs together and make a raft.* □ *Lash two or three of the poles together to make them stronger.*

LAST ▸ FOR

last for something **1.** to exist for a period of time; to serve or function for a period of time. □ *This condition has lasted for some time.* □ *Enjoy it while you can. It won't last forever.* **2.** to hold out or survive for a period of time. □ *It's so hot in here. I don't think I can last for another minute.* □ *Can you last for another few minutes while I get this window open?*

LAST ▸ FROM

See under *LAST ▸ UNTIL.*

LAST ▸ OUT

last out to hold out; to endure. (Colloquial.) □ *How long can you last out?* □ *I don't think we can last out much longer without food and water.*

last something out to endure until the end of something. □ *Ed said that he didn't think he could last the opera out and left.* 🅃 *He couldn't last out the first act.*

LAST ▸ UNTIL

last (from something) until something to endure from one point in time to another. ☐ *The meeting lasted from noon until midnight.* ☐ *It lasted until the universal exhaustion of the members.*

LATCH ▸ ON(TO)

latch on(to someone or something) to grasp onto someone or something; to get hold of someone or something. (Colloquial.) ☐ *I don't know where Jane is. Let me try to latch onto her.* ☐ *I could not latch onto a copy of the book.* ☐ *Toss me another one. The last one slipped through my fingers. I didn't quite latch on.*

LATHER ▸ UP

lather something up to apply thick soapsuds to something, such a part of the body or all of it. ☐ *He lathered his face up in preparation for shaving.* 🅃 *He lathered up his face.*

lather up 1. [for a horse] to develop a foam of sweat from working very hard. ☐ *The horses lathered up heavily during the race.* ☐ *Don't let your horse lather up!* **2.** [for soap] to develop thick suds when rubbed. ☐ *This soap won't lather up, even when I rub it hard.* ☐ *When the soap lathers up, spread the lather on your face and rub.* **3.** AND **lather (oneself) up** [for one] to apply soap lather to one's body. ☐ *He will spend a few minutes lathering himself up before he rinses.* ☐ *He lathered up and then shaved.*

LAUGH ▸ ABOUT

laugh about someone or something to chuckle or giggle loudly about someone or something. ☐ *Please don't laugh about Sue. It's not funny.* ☐ *They were laughing about my haircut.*

LAUGH ▸ AT

laugh at someone or something to chuckle or giggle loudly at someone or something, perhaps in ridicule. ☐ *Thank goodness, the audience laughed at all my jokes.* ☐ *Don't laugh at me! I'm doing my best!* ☐ *Everyone laughed at the love scene because it was so badly done.*

LAUGH ▸ AWAY

laugh away at someone or something to continue to laugh and laugh at someone or something. ☐ *They laughed away at Sue until she fled the room in embarrassment.* ☐ *While they laughed away at the Punch and Judy show, their pockets were picked.*

laugh something away 1. to spend an amount of time laughing. ☐ *We laughed the hour away listening to the comedian.* 🅃 *We laughed away the evening.* **2.** to get rid of something negative by laughing. ☐ *Kelly knows how to laugh her problems away, and it cheers up the rest of us too.* 🅃 *She laughed away her problems.*

LAUGH ▸ DOWN

laugh someone or something down to cause someone to quit or cause something to end by laughing in ridicule. ☐ *Her singing career was destroyed when the audience laughed her down as an amateur.* 🅃 *The cruel audience laughed down the amateur singer.* ☐ *They laughed down the magic act also.*

LAUGH ▸ IN

laugh in someone's face to laugh in derision directly to someone's face; to show displeasure or ridicule at something one has said by laughing directly into one's face. ☐ *It is very impolite to laugh in someone's face!* ☐ *After I heard what she had to say, I just laughed in her face.*

LAUGH ▸ OFF

laugh one's head off to laugh very hard and loudly, as if one's head might come off. (Figurative.) ☐ *The movie was so funny I almost laughed my head off.* ☐ *I laughed my head off at Mary's joke.*

laugh someone off something to laugh rudely, forcing a person to leave a stage. ☐ *The rude audience laughed the politician off the platform.* ☐ *The children laughed the soprano off the stage. She really wasn't very good, you know.*

laugh something off to treat a serious problem lightly by laughing at it. ☐ *Although his feelings were hurt, he just laughed the incident off as if nothing* *had happened.* Ⓣ *He laughed off the incident.*

LAUGH ▸ OUT

laugh oneself out of something to lose out on something because one has made light of it or laughed at it. ☐ *While you were howling with laughter about my hat, you laughed yourself out of a ride to town. The bus just pulled away.* ☐ *You laugh too much. You just laughed yourself out of a job.*

laugh out of the other side of one's face to be forced to take a different or opposite view of something, humbly; to sing a different tune. (Cliché. After having been rebuked or put down.) ☐ *When you get the kind of punishment you deserve, you'll laugh out of the other side of your face.* ☐ *A real appraisal of your potential will make you laugh out of the other side of your face!*

laugh someone out of something to force someone to leave a place by laughing in ridicule. ☐ *The citizens laughed the speaker out of the hall.* ☐ *We laughed the city council out of the auditorium.*

LAUGH ▸ WITH

laugh with something to laugh in a particular manner. ☐ *Everyone was laughing with glee at the antics of the clown.* ☐ *Max laughed with malice as he saw his plan beginning to work.*

LAUNCH ▸ AGAINST

launch something against someone or something to set something going against someone or something. ☐ *The general launched an attack against the town.* ☐ *Claire launched a gossip attack against James.*

LAUNCH ▸ FORTH

launch forth ((up)on something) to set out on something; to begin on something, such as a journey or a long lecturing or sermon. (*Upon* is formal and less commonly used than *on*.) ☐ *We launched forth on our trip before dawn.* ☐ *What time shall we launch forth tomorrow morning?*

LAUNCH ▸ INTO

launch into something to start in doing something. ☐ *Now, don't launch into lecturing me about manners again!* ☐ *Tim's mother launched into a sermon about how to behave at a concert.*

LAUNCH ▸ OUT

launch out on something to start out to do something or go somewhere. ☐ *When are you going to launch out on your expedition?* ☐ *Ted and Bill launched out on their trip through the mountains.*

LAVISH ▸ (UP)ON

lavish something (up)on someone to give something freely to someone; to squander something on someone. (*Upon* is formal and less commonly used than *on*.) ☐ *The manager lavished all sorts of favors upon the new employee.* ☐ *Susan lavished compliments on the cook.*

LAY ▸ ABOUT

See under *LAY ▸ AROUND.*

LAY ▸ AGAINST

lay something against something to lean or place something against something. ☐ *They laid the Christmas tree against the house where they could get to it easily when the time came.* ☐ *Lay this hot cloth against the sore place and hold it there.*

LAY ▸ ALONGSIDE

lay alongside something [for a ship] to rest afloat next to something. ☐ *The ship lay alongside a lovely island while a shore party searched for fresh water.* ☐ *Our ship lay alongside the narrow wooden pier.*

lay something alongside ((of) something) to place something next to something else, lengthwise. ☐ *Please lay the spoon alongside the knife.* ☐ *Find the knife and lay the spoon alongside.*

LAY ▸ AROUND

lay around AND **lay about** to *lie around.* (Commons errors for *lie about, lie around.*) ☐ *Don't just lay around all day!* ☐ *I need to lay around for a few days.* Ⓝ *You are a worthless layabout!*

LAY ▶ ASIDE

lay something aside to set something aside; to place something to one side, out of the way. □ *He laid his papers aside and went out to welcome the visitor.* 🅃 *He laid aside his papers.*

lay something aside for someone or something to put something aside, in reserve, for someone or something. □ *I laid some cake aside for Tom, and someone else got it.* 🅃 *I laid aside some cake for Tom.* □ *I will lay a tiny bit of hamburger aside for the cat.*

LAY ▶ AT

lay something at someone's door AND **put something at someone's door** **1.** to blame a problem on someone or something; to hold someone responsible for something. □ *I'm laying responsibility for this mess at your door!* □ *Don't put this at my door!* **2.** to give or assign a problem to someone for solving. □ *I am going to lay this problem right at your door. You are the one who can settle it.* □ *I will put this business at your door and hope you can do something about it.*

lay something at someone's feet AND **put something at someone's feet** **1.** to place something on the ground in front of someone. □ *The cat came up to me and laid a mouse at my feet.* □ *The dog put a rabbit at my feet.* **2.** to hold someone responsible for something. (Figurative.) □ *I am going to lay this matter at your feet. You are clearly to blame.* □ *I will put this matter at your feet. It is your fault.*

LAY ▶ AWAY

lay someone away to bury someone. (Euphemism.) □ *Yes, he has passed. We laid him away last week.* 🅃 *He laid away his uncle in a simple ceremony.*

lay something away (for someone) to put something in storage for someone to receive at a later time. (Often said of a purchase that is held until it is paid for.) □ *Please lay this away for me. I'll pay for it when I have the money.* 🅃 *Please lay away this coat until I can get the money together.* □ *I will lay it away for you.*

lay something away (for something) to set something aside or put something in storage for a special occasion or purpose. □ *She laid the lovely dress away for the next party.* 🅃 *She laid away the dress.* □ *Hoping there would be a chance to use it, she laid it away.*

LAY ▶ BACK

See *be laid-back* under *BE ▶ BACK.*

LAY ▶ BEFORE

lay something before someone **1.** to present something to someone. □ *The cat laid the mouse before her mistress.* □ *Dave laid the present before her as a peace offering.* **2.** to present something for someone to judge. □ *All you can do is lay the matter before the teacher and hope for a favorable response.* □ *I want to lay this before you and let you decide.*

LAY ▶ BY

lay something by to set something aside; to hold something in reserve. □ *I will have to lay some money by in case things don't go as planned.* □ *We laid our best clothes by, saving them for a very special occasion.*

LAY ▶ DOWN

lay down on the job to fail to do one's job efficiently; to fail to do one's job. (Colloquial. In error for *lie down on the job.* Figurative.) □ *You guys have been laying down on the job! Get busy!* □ *If you lay down on the job, you will be fired.*

lay down one's arms to put one's gun, sword, club, etc., down; to stop fighting; to surrender. □ *The prisoners were instructed to lay down their arms.* □ *The soldiers laid down their arms and surrendered.*

lay down one's life for someone or something to die willingly for the sake of someone or a cause. □ *The mother said she was willing to lay down her life for her child.* □ *Gerald refused to lay down his life for his principles.*

lay down the law (to someone) (about something) to scold someone; to make something very clear to someone in a very stern manner. (Figurative.) □ *Wow, was she mad at Ed. She really laid down* *the law about drinking to him.* □ *She laid down the law to Ed.* □ *She laid down the law about drinking.*

lay (oneself) down to lie down. (Colloquial.) □ *Just lay yourself down there and try to sleep.* □ *I'll lay down here for just a few minutes.*

lay someone down to ease someone into a reclining position; to ease someone into bed. □ *The baby woke up when I tried to lay him down.* □ *The nurse laid the disturbed patient down time and time again.*

lay something down (on something) to place something down on something. □ *Lay the plates down on the table gently.* [T] *Please lay down your book and listen to me.* □ *Lay your books down right there.*

LAY ▸ FOR

lay for someone to wait in ambush for someone. (Slang or nonstandard.) □ *The robbers were laying for me and attacked me as I walked by their hiding place.* □ *They were laying for me, but I sensed that they were there and I escaped.*

lay something for someone or something to prepare something (for a meal) for the benefit of someone or a group. □ *She laid a lovely picnic dinner for the two of them.* □ *Would you lay the table for dinner for my guests?* □ *Please lay the table for twelve for dinner.*

lay the blame (for something) on someone See under *LAY ▸ ON.*

LAY ▸ IN

lay something in to build up a supply of something. □ *We had better lay some firewood in for the winter.* [T] *I will lay in a supply.*

LAY ▸ INTO

lay into someone or something to attack someone or some creature; to go to work on someone or some creature. □ *The angry father laid into the frightened child.* □ *The angry farmer laid into the stubborn mule.*

LAY ▸ IN(TO)

lay someone or something in(to) something to place someone or something in something. □ *The women laid the king into the coffin and the funeral procession assembled.* □ *The cook laid the salmon in the poaching liquid.*

LAY ▸ OF

lay hold of someone or something to take hold of someone or something. □ *Just wait till I lay hold of you!* □ *She lay hold of the checkbook and ran off to spend some money.*

LAY ▸ OFF

lay off ((from) something) to cease doing something. □ *Lay off from your hammering for a minute, will you?* □ *That's enough! Please lay off.*

lay off ((of) someone or something) to stop doing something to someone or something; to stop bothering someone or something. (The *of* is colloquial.) □ *Lay off of me! You've said enough.* □ *Please lay off the chicken. I cooked it as best I could.*

lay someone off (from something) to put an end to someone's employment at something. □ *The automobile factory laid five hundred people off from work.* [T] *They laid off a lot of people.* □ *We knew they were going to lay a lot of people off.* [A] *There were long lines of tired workers, waiting to get unemployment checks.* [N] *There were many layoffs at the auto plant.*

LAY ▸ ON

lay a finger on someone or something to touch or get involved with someone or something. □ *Don't you dare lay a finger on me, you brute!* □ *Please don't even lay a finger on this cake.*

lay a guilt trip on someone to try to make someone feel guilty. (Slang.) □ *Don't lay that guilt trip on me! I play no part in your problems.* □ *I am not laying a guilt trip on anyone!*

lay a (heavy) trip on someone to reveal serious or devastating information to someone. (Slang.) □ *That's a powerful story. I didn't know you were going to* *lay a heavy trip like that on me.* □ *Man, you really laid a trip on me.*

lay emphasis on something AND **lay stress on something** to place emphasis on something; to emphasize something. □ *When you present this explanation, lay emphasis on the matter of personal responsibility.* □ *I'm afraid I laid too much stress on the notion of good attendance. If you are really sick, stay home!*

lay eyes on someone or something to see someone or something, often for the first time. □ *I've never seen her before. This is the first time I have laid eyes on her!* □ *I didn't take your book! I've never even laid eyes on it!*

lay it on the line AND **put it on the line** to make something very clear. (Figurative.) □ *I am going to lay it on the line and you had better listen to me. If you eat any of these mushrooms you will die.* □ *I've said it before, but this time I'm going to put it on the line. Don't eat the mushrooms!*

lay it on thick to exaggerate one's praise, flattery, or compliments. (Informal.) □ *Oh, you are such an old flatterer. You really know how to lay it on thick.* □ *She really lays it on thick.*

lay one on to get drunk. (Slang.) □ *Sally went out and laid one on over the weekend.* □ *Tom and the guys lay one on almost every night.*

lay one's cards on the table AND **place one's cards on the table** to be very candid about one's position on some issue. (Figurative. As if one were laying playing cards on the table, face up, to show one's hand.) □ *All right. Let's lay our cards on the table and speak very candidly about this matter.* □ *It's time we placed our cards on the table and spoke honestly.*

lay one's hands on someone or something See *put one's hands on someone or something* under *PUT ▸ ON.*

lay something on to supply something in abundance. (Informal.) □ *Look at him lay that butter on! What do you suppose the insides of his arteries look like?* 🅃 *He really laid on the butter!* 🅃 *They laid on a beautiful buffet lunch.*

lay something on someone to tell something to someone. (Slang.) □ *I want to hear the whole thing! Lay it on me!* □ *Lay it on her. Tell her everything.*

lay something on someone or something to place something on someone or something; to cover someone or something with something. □ *As soon as he breathed his last, the nurse laid a cloth on him.* □ *Ken laid the bundle of flowers on the coffee table.*

lay stress on something See *lay emphasis on something.*

lay the blame (for something) on someone to place the blame for something on someone. □ *We could not possibly lay the blame for the accident on you.* □ *Don't try to lay the blame on me!*

lay the finger on someone AND **put the finger on someone** to identify or incriminate someone. (Slang.) □ *Max is going to lay the finger on Lefty about the bank robbery.* □ *Don't you lay the finger on me! I wasn't even in town the night of the bank robbery.*

LAY ▸ OUT

lay someone or something out to arrange someone or something on a surface. (Refers to preparations for burial when said of a person.) □ *The older women laid George out while the preacher comforted his wife.* 🅃 *They laid out the body carefully.* 🄰 *She chose from among the nicely laid-out gowns the one she would wear to the formal dinner.*

lay someone out to knock someone to the ground, perhaps unconscious. □ *The champ laid the contender out in the second round.* 🅃 *Mike really laid out his challenger.*

lay someone out in lavender to scold someone severely. (Informal.) □ *She was really mad. She laid him out in lavender and really put him in his place.* □ *If you ever feel like you need to lay me out in lavender again, just forget it.*

lay something out to explain something; to go over details of a plan carefully. □ *They laid the sales campaign out after many meetings.* 🅃 *She laid out exactly what she had been thinking so they all could discuss it.*

lay something out (for someone) to explain something in great detail to someone. (Colloquial.) □ *Let me lay it out for you so you can understand it.* 🅃 *She laid out the details for Roger.* □ *This is very confusing. Listen carefully and I'll lay it out.* 🄽 *Now here's the layout. Is it clear?*

lay something out on someone or something AND **lay something out for someone or something** to spend an amount of money on someone or something. □ *We laid out nearly ten thousand dollars on that car.* 🅃 *We laid out a fortune on the children.* □ *I won't lay out another cent for that car!* 🄽 *I can't afford that kind of layout.*

LAY ▸ OVER

lay over (some place) to wait somewhere between segments of a journey. □ *We were told we would have to lay over in New York.* □ *I don't mind laying over if it isn't for very long.* 🄽 *We had a two-hour layover in Atlanta.*

lay something over someone or something to cover someone or something with something. □ *Here, lay this blanket over the baby.* □ *Please lay a napkin over the bread before you take it to the table.*

LAY ▸ TO

lay claim to something to place a claim on something. □ *Do you really think you can lay claim to that money after all these years?* □ *Someone came by and laid claim to the wallet you found.*

lay someone to rest to bury someone. □ *We laid Uncle Carl to rest over a year ago.* □ *We laid her to rest in the family vault.*

lay something to rest AND **put something to rest** to put an end to a rumor; to allay a suspicion. □ *It's time to lay these rumors to rest and tell the truth.* □ *I want to put this business to rest once and for all.*

lay something to something to attribute something to something. □ *I lay all our problems to the inadequacy of our training.* □ *Mary laid her success to a good upbringing.*

lay something to waste to destroy something or some place. □ *The army marched in and laid the city to waste.* □ *The deer got into my garden and laid it to waste.*

lay to to begin doing something, such as fighting or eating. □ *All right, you guys. Lay to. The stuff will get cold if you don't eat it.* □ *Lay to! Let's get on with it.*

LAY ▸ TOGETHER

lay something together to lay things side by side. □ *Lay all the logs together and stack them as high as you can.* □ *Lay the red ones together and put all the others over there in a pile.*

LAY ▸ UNDER

lay something under something to place something beneath something. □ *Please lay a cloth under your cutting to catch the scraps.* □ *Would you mind laying a sheet of plastic over the table?*

LAY ▸ UP

lay someone up (with something) to make someone ill abed with something; to debilitate someone with something. □ *This cold has laid me up all winter.* 🅃 *The flu laid up a lot of people this winter.* □ *A nagging cough laid me up for months.*

lay something up **1.** to acquire and store something. □ *Try to lay as much of it up as you can.* 🅃 *I am trying to lay up some firewood for the winter.* **2.** [for something] to disable something. □ *The accident laid up the ship for repairs.* □ *The ship was laid up by engine trouble and a number of other defects.*

LAZE ▸ AWAY

laze something away to spend a period of time being lazy. □ *I just love to sit here and laze the day away.* 🅃 *I will laze away the entire day.*

LEACH ▸ AWAY

leach away [for something] to erode away by leaching. ☐ *The soft sandstone leached away under the constant rains.* ☐ *The flowerpots sat out in the rain, where all the nutrients leached away.*

leach something away (from something) AND **leach something out (of something)** to remove something from something by leaching. ☐ *The heavy rains leached nutrients away from the soil.* 🆃 *The rains leached away the nutrients.* ☐ *The water leached the minerals out of the soil.* ☐ *The water leached the nutrients away.*

LEACH ▸ IN(TO)

leach in(to something) [for a substance] to seep or penetrate into something. ☐ *The salt leached into the soil and ruined it.* ☐ *A tremendous amount of salt leached in.*

LEACH ▸ OUT

leach out of something [for a substance] to seep or drain out of something. ☐ *All the nutrients leached out of the soil and nothing would grow.* ☐ *The phosphorus leached out of the soil after a few years.*

leach something out of something See *leach something away from something* under *LEACH ▸ AWAY.*

LEAD ▸ AGAINST

lead someone or something against someone or something to manage someone or a group in an attack on someone or something. ☐ *The general led the entire company against the troops holding the city.* ☐ *The general led Bill and Dave against Roger.*

LEAD ▸ ASTRAY

lead someone astray to direct or guide someone in the wrong direction. ☐ *I am afraid that this young man has been leading you astray. I think you had better stop seeing him.* ☐ *No one can lead me astray. I am too alert.*

LEAD ▸ AWAY

lead someone or something (away) (from someone or something) to direct or guide someone or something away from someone or something. ☐ *The officer led the victim's wife away from the accident.* 🆃 *The trainer led away the dog from the other animals.* ☐ *We led them away.*

LEAD ▸ BACK

lead back (to some place) [for a pathway] to return to a place. ☐ *This path leads back to the camp.* ☐ *I hope it leads back. It seems to be going the wrong way.*

lead someone or something back (to someone or something) to guide someone or something back to someone or something. ☐ *Someone will have to lead me back to camp. I just know I'll get lost if I go by myself.* 🆃 *The park ranger led back the hikers to their tent.* ☐ *I will lead them back.*

LEAD ▸ BY

lead someone by something to guide someone by grasping a part and moving. ☐ *Do you expect me to lead you around by the hand, showing you everything to do in your job?* ☐ *The cop grabbed Max and led him around by the collar.*

lead someone by the nose to guide someone very carefully and slowly. (As if the person were not very smart. Figurative.) ☐ *He will never find his way through the tax form unless you lead him by the nose.* ☐ *Don't lead me by the nose! I'm coming!*

LEAD ▸ DOWN

lead down to something [for a pathway or other trail] to run downward to something. ☐ *The trail led down to a spring at the bottom of the hill.* ☐ *These stairs lead down to the furnace room.*

lead someone down (something) to help someone down something, such as stairs, a steep path, a ladder, etc. ☐ *The usher led the couple down the aisle and seated them at the front.* ☐ *I am going to the cellar myself. Let me lead you down.*

lead someone down the garden path to deceive someone. (Figurative.) ☐ *Don't believe what he is telling you. He is just leading you down the garden path.* ☐ *Toby was led down the garden path by Mary, who had plans for him.*

lead someone down to something to guide someone downward to something. □ *She led us down to a little room in the cellar, where the old trunk had been kept for all these years.* □ *Would you please lead me down to the wine cellar?*

LEAD ► FORTH

lead forth [for someone] to go on ahead; to precede someone. □ *You lead forth, and I will follow.* □ *Wallace led forth, but no one came after him.*

lead someone or something forth to bring or usher someone or something forward. □ *The captain led the soldiers forth to the parade ground.* 🅃 *They led forth the army into battle.*

LEAD ► FROM

lead someone or something (away) (from someone or something) See under *LEAD ► AWAY.*

LEAD ► IN(TO)

lead in(to something) **1.** to begin something; to work into something. □ *Let me lead into the first number with a little talk about the composer.* □ *I'll lead in, then you pick up the melody.* 🄽 *The lead-in was too long, and people got bored.* **2.** to make a transition into something; to *segue into* something. □ *Now, we will lead into the second scene with a little soft orchestral music.* □ *The soft music will lead in, then the curtains will open.* 🄽 *After a short lead-in, the band played for an hour.*

lead someone in(to something) to guide someone into something or some place. □ *The usher led us into the darkened theater and showed us our seats.* 🅃 *She led in the children.* □ *We led them in.*

LEAD ► OFF

lead off to be the first one to go or leave. □ *You lead off. I'll follow.* □ *Mary led off and the others followed closely behind.*

lead off (with someone or something) to begin with someone or something. □ *The musical revue led off with a bassoon trio.* □ *Sharon, the singer, will lead off tonight.*

lead someone or something off to guide someone or something away. □ *The guide led the hikers off on the adventure of their lives.* 🅃 *The dog owners led off their animals and they awaited the decision of the judges.*

LEAD ► ON

lead on to continue to lead onward. □ *The guide led on and we followed.* □ *Lead on, my friend. We are right behind you!*

lead someone on **1.** to guide someone onward. □ *We led him on so he could see more of the gardens.* □ *Please lead Mary on. There is lots more to see here.* **2.** to tease someone; to encourage someone's romantic or sexual interest. □ *You are just leading me on!* □ *It's not fair to continue leading him on.* 🅃 *It's easy to lead on teenage boys.*

lead someone on a merry chase to cause someone to follow a circuitous route. (Also without *on,* but not eligible as an entry.) □ *There you are! We couldn't find you anywhere. You've led us on a merry chase!* □ *Our dog got out of its pen and led us on a merry chase.*

LEAD ► OUT

lead someone or something out (of something) to guide someone or some creature out of something or some place. (The *of*-phrase is paraphrased with a *from*-phrase when the particle is transposed. See the 🄵 example.) □ *Someone finally led the hikers out of the valley or they would still be there now.* 🅃 *She led out the workers.* 🄵 *She led out the workers from the office.* □ *I led the weary dog out of the house.*

LEAD ► TO

lead someone or something to something to guide someone or some creature to something or some place. □ *Would you lead Paul to the place where the trunks are kept?* □ *The cat is so old that we had to lead her to her food.*

lead someone to believe something to cause someone to believe something; to influence someone to infer something. (Idiomatic.) □ *But you led me to believe that this work would not cost very much* *money.* ☐ *Don't lead them to believe anything that isn't true.*

lead someone to do something to cause someone to do something. ☐ *What led you to do a thing like that?* ☐ *Your comments almost led me to leave the country.*

LEAD ▸ UP

lead someone up something to guide someone upward along some route. ☐ *Would you please lead Tom up the path so he can leave his things at the cabin on the hill?* ☐ *Mary led the visitors up the stairs to the loft, which she had recently redecorated.*

lead someone up the garden path to deceive someone; to cause someone to be deceived. (Idiomatic.) ☐ *They are just leading you up the garden path. Don't believe a word any of them says.* ☐ *Don't let them lead you up the garden path.*

lead up to something **1.** to aim at or route movement to something. ☐ *A narrow path led up to the door of the cottage.* ☐ *This road leads up to the house at the top of the hill.* **2.** to prepare to say something; to lay the groundwork for making a point. (Typically with the present participle.) ☐ *I was just leading up to telling you what happened when you interrupted.* ☐ *I knew she was leading up to something, the way she was talking.*

LEAD ▸ WITH

lead with someone or something to start out with someone or something. ☐ *The coach led with Walter as pitcher and Sam on first base.* ☐ *We will lead with our best players.*

lead with something to tend to strike with a particular fist—the right, the left, the best, etc. (Boxing.) ☐ *Watch that guy, Champ, he always leads with his right.* ☐ *Get in there and lead with your left.*

LEAF ▸ OUT

leaf out [for a plant] to open its leaf buds. ☐ *Most of the bushes leaf out in mid-April.* ☐ *The trees leafed out early this year.*

LEAF ▸ THROUGH

leaf through something to look through something, turning the pages. ☐ *Jan leafed through the catalog, looking for a suitable winter coat.* ☐ *Leaf through this and see if there is anything you like.*

LEAK ▸ IN(TO)

leak in(to something) [for a fluid] to work its way into something. ☐ *Some of the soapy water leaked into the soil.* ☐ *The rainwater is leaking in!*

LEAK ▸ OUT

leak out [for information] to become known. ☐ *I hope that news of the new building does not leak out before the contract is signed.* ☐ *When the story leaked out, my telephone would not stop ringing.*

leak out (of something) [for a fluid] to seep out of something or some place. ☐ *Some of the brake fluid leaked out of the car and made a spot on the driveway.* ☐ *Look under the car. Something's leaking out.*

leak something out to permit [otherwise secret] information to become publicly known. ☐ *Please don't leak this out. It is supposed to be a secret.* 🅃 *Someone leaked out the report.*

LEAK ▸ THROUGH

leak through something [for a fluid] to seep through something. ☐ *Rainwater leaked through the roof.* ☐ *I was afraid that the crushed orange would leak through the paper bag.*

LEAK ▸ TO

leak something to someone to tell [otherwise secret] information to someone. ☐ *The government leaked a phony story to the press just to see how far it would travel.* ☐ *The government leaks things to the press occasionally, just to make sure their channels of communication are open.*

LEAN ▸ ACROSS

lean across someone or something to incline oneself across someone or something. ☐ *She leaned across me to reach the telephone and spilled my wine.* ☐

Laura leaned across the table and knocked my coffee over.

LEAN ▸ AGAINST

lean against someone or something to prop oneself against someone or something. □ *The child leaned against her sister to keep warm.* □ *I leaned against the back of the chair and went right to sleep.*

lean something against someone or something to prop something against someone or something. □ *She leaned her spade against the house and wiped the sweat from her brow.* □ *Bill leaned the mirror against Ted while he screwed the hook into the wall.*

LEAN ▸ BACK

lean back [for someone] to recline backwards, usually in a chair. □ *Lean back and make yourself comfortable.* □ *Let's lean back and be comfortable.*

lean back (against someone or something) to recline backwards, putting weight on someone or something. □ *Just lean back against me. I will prevent you from falling.* □ *Relax and lean back. Nothing bad is going to happen.*

lean back (on someone or something) to recline backwards, pressing on someone or something. □ *Don't lean back on me! I'm not a chair!* □ *Lean back on the couch and tell me what you are thinking.*

LEAN ▸ DOWN

lean down to bend over. □ *Lean down and tie your shoe before you trip.* □ *He leaned down and picked something up from the floor.*

LEAN ▸ FORWARD

lean forward to bend forward. □ *Lean forward a minute so I can put a cushion behind your back.* □ *When Betsy leaned forward, she lost her balance and fell.*

lean something forward to tilt or bend something forward. □ *Lean the board forward a little bit, please.* □ *Someone leaned this panel forward a little too much.*

LEAN ▸ IN(TO)

lean in(to something) to incline or press into something. □ *You have to lean into the wind when you walk or you will be blown over.* □ *As you walk into the wind, lean in a little bit.* □ *The north wall of the barn leans in a little. Is it going to fall?*

LEAN ▸ ON

lean on someone to put pressure on someone to do something. (Figurative.) □ *If he won't do it, lean on him a little bit till he agrees.* □ *Don't lean on me! I won't do it if I don't want to.*

lean on someone or something **1.** to incline or press on someone or something. □ *Don't lean on me. I'm not strong enough to support both of us.* □ *Lean on the wall and rest a little while.* **2.** to depend on someone or something. □ *You lean on your parents too much. You must be more independent.* □ *You can't lean on the government forever.*

LEAN ▸ OUT

lean out of something to hang or bend out of something or some place. □ *She leaned out of the window so she could watch what was going on.* □ *Don't lean out of the car window. You will fall.*

LEAN ▸ OVER

lean over **1.** to bend over. □ *Lean over and pick the pencil up yourself! I'm not your servant!* □ *As Kelly leaned over to tie her shoes, her chair slipped out from under her.* **2.** to tilt over. □ *The fence leaned over and almost fell.* □ *As the wind blew, the tree leaned over farther and farther.*

lean over backwards (to do something) to make a great effort to do something. (Figurative.) □ *I've leaned over backwards to do everything you wanted and you still aren't happy!* □ *I did everything I could. I leaned over backwards.*

LEAN ▸ TOWARD

lean toward someone or something **1.** to incline toward someone or something. □ *Tom is leaning toward Randy. I think he is going to fall on him.* □ *The tree is leaning toward the edge of the cliff. It will fall eventually.* **2.** to tend to favor [choosing] someone or something. □ *I am leaning toward Sarah as the new committee head.* □ *I'm leaning toward a new committee.*

LEAP ▸ AT

leap at someone or something **1.** to jump toward someone or something. □ *The grasshopper leapt at me and scared me to death.* □ *The cat leapt at the mouse and caught it.* **2.** to accept or choose someone or something eagerly. □ *We leapt at Carl when his department offered him to us.* □ *When we had the chance to hire Carl, we leapt at it.*

leap at the opportunity (to do something) AND **leap at the chance (to do something)** to accept an opportunity eagerly. □ *Frank leapt at the opportunity to become a commercial artist.* □ *It was a great idea and we leapt at the opportunity.* □ *I would leap at the chance to go to Moscow.*

LEAP ▸ DOWN

leap down (from something) to hop down from something or some place. □ *The performer leapt down from the stage and ran up the aisle.* □ *She leapt down and ran away.*

LEAP ▸ FOR

leap for joy to jump up because one is happy; to be very happy. (Usually figurative.) □ *Tommy leapt for joy because he had won the race.* □ *We all leapt for joy when we heard the news.*

LEAP ▸ FORWARD

leap forward to jump or hop forward. □ *The little creature leapt forward and looked carefully at us.* □ *As the frog leapt forward, the kitten jumped straight up and fled.*

LEAP ▸ ON

leap on the bandwagon See under *JUMP ▸ ON.*

LEAP ▸ OUT

leap out (of something) to jump outward from something. □ *A mouse leapt out of the cereal box and frightened everyone.* □ *I opened the box and a mouse leapt out.*

LEAP ▸ OVER

leap over something to jump over something. □ *The dog leapt over the hedge and chased the rabbit around the corner of the house.* □ *Please don't leap over my roses. You'll injure them.*

LEAP ▸ TO

leap to conclusions to form conclusions hastily, without sufficient evidence. □ *Now, now, don't go leaping to conclusions!* □ *There is no point in leaping to conclusions.*

LEAP ▸ UP

leap up to jump upwards. □ *The dog leapt up and licked my cheek.* □ *I leapt up so I could see over the wall for just a second.*

LEARN ▸ ABOUT

learn about someone or something to find out about someone or something. □ *What have you learned about Mr. Franklin and his business dealings?* □ *I learned about what causes rain.*

LEARN ▸ BY

learn by something to learn [something] from some kind of experience. □ *The best way to learn is to learn by doing.* □ *The best way to learn to sail is to learn by sailing.*

learn something by heart to learn something so well that it will never be forgotten. □ *You will have to learn your lines by heart if you want to be in this play.* □ *I learned the Gettysburg Address by heart.*

learn something by rote to learn something by memorizing. □ *You must learn your lines by rote if you want to be in the school play.* □ *You must learn the multiplication tables by rote.*

LEARN ▸ FROM

learn from someone or something to learn [something] from the experience of someone or something. □ *Pay attention to what Sarah does. I think you can learn from her.* □ *This was quite an experience, and we all can learn from it.*

learn something from someone or something to find out something from someone or something. □ *I don't know* *when the children are due to arrive. See what you can learn from Walter.* ☐ *I am sure we can learn something from this experience.*

learn something from the bottom up to learn about something by starting at the lowest level and finding out all the details. ☐ *You can't get into this business unless you learn it from the bottom up. No one starts at the top.* ☐ *The best way to find out how the newspaper business works is to learn it from the bottom up.*

LEARN ▸ OF

learn of someone or something to find out about someone or something. ☐ *I'm not in the telephone book. How did you learn of me?* ☐ *How did you learn of our company?*

LEASE ▸ BACK

lease something back to sell something, then rent it from the buyer. ☐ *We sold the building to a real estate firm and then leased it back. There was some tax saving involved.* 🅃 *We leased back the building.* 🄽 *The leaseback was a fine idea, and we really save on taxes.*

LEASE ▸ FROM

lease something from someone to rent something from someone. ☐ *We decided to lease the building from the owner rather than buying it.* ☐ *The company always leases its cars from the dealership.*

LEASE ▸ OUT

See the following entry.

LEASE ▸ TO

lease something (out) to someone to rent something to someone. ☐ *The company leases cars out to its customers.* ☐ *Can you lease this building to me for two years?*

LEAVE ▸ ABOUT

See the following entry.

LEAVE ▸ AROUND

leave something (lying) around AND **leave something (lying) about** to permit something to lie around unguarded; to leave something somewhere carelessly. ☐ *Don't leave your clothes lying around. Hang them up.* ☐ *Don't leave stuff lying about!* ☐ *Who left these books lying about?*

LEAVE ▸ ASIDE

leave something aside **1.** to leave something in reserve. ☐ *Leave some of the sugar aside for use in the icing.* ☐ *Leave a bit of cake aside for the children.* 🅃 *Leave aside some cookies too.* **2.** to ignore something, especially a fact. ☐ *Let's leave the question of who will pay for it aside for a while.* ☐ *Leaving money aside, do you think this purchase is basically a good idea?* 🅃 *We will leave aside the current situation and talk about the future.*

LEAVE ▸ AT

leave it at that to leave a situation as it is. ☐ *This is the best we can do. We'll have to leave it at that.* ☐ *I can do no more. I will have to leave it at that.*

leave someone or something at some place **1.** to abandon someone or something at some place. ☐ *Don't leave me here by myself!* ☐ *Betty left her newspaper at the table, hoping someone else would enjoy it.* **2.** to allow someone or something to remain at some place. ☐ *You leave me here and go on ahead.* ☐ *Please leave your packages at the door.* **3.** to allow someone or something to stay behind through forgetfulness. ☐ *I left my glasses behind on my desk.* ☐ *I was left at the movie theater by mistake.*

LEAVE ▸ DOWN

leave something down to leave something in a lowered or low position. ☐ *Leave the window down, please. It's hot in this car.* ☐ *Leave the window down. This house is cold enough as it is.*

LEAVE ▸ FOR

leave for some place to depart for some place. ☐ *We will leave for Denver at dawn.* ☐ *When do we leave for Grandmother's house?*

leave someone for dead to leave a severely injured person, assuming death. ☐ *The dog was so severely injured that we almost left her for dead.* ☐ *Jim's buddies went off and left him for dead, but he came dragging along after them with his rifle, pack, and everything.*

leave something for someone or something to allow something to remain for the use of someone or some creature. ☐ *I will leave this bread here for you, so you won't starve.* ☐ *Don't clean it up. Leave it for the dog.*

leave word for someone to do something to leave a message or a request for someone. (See also *leave word with someone* under *LEAVE ► WITH.*) ☐ *I left word for you to come to my office.* ☐ *We left word for her to hurry up and come home.*

LEAVE ► IN

leave someone or something in (something) to permit someone or something to remain in something. ☐ *We left the children in the house while we went out to greet the guests.* ☐ *Did you leave the dog in the car?* ☐ *Poor puppy! I didn't mean to leave you in.*

LEAVE ► OF

leave go of someone or something to let go of someone or something. (Colloquial and usually considered nonstandard.) ☐ *Leave go of me!* ☐ *Leave go of my hand!*

LEAVE ► OFF

leave off something to quit something. ☐ *I have to leave off working for a while so I can eat.* ☐ *I left off reading and went downstairs for supper.*

LEAVE ► ON

leave something on **1.** to allow something [that can be turned off] to remain on. ☐ *Who left the radio on?* 🅃 *Please leave on the light for me.* **2.** to continue to wear some article of clothing. ☐ *I think I will leave my coat on. It's chilly in here.* 🅃 *I'll leave on my coat.*

leave something on someone or something to allow something to remain on someone or something. ☐ *Leave the coats on the children. We are taking them out to a movie almost immediately.* ☐ *Who left this book on the table?*

LEAVE ► OUT

leave someone or something out in the cold **1.** to allow someone or some creature to remain outside in the cold air. ☐ *He accidentally left his grandfather out in the cold.* ☐ *Don't leave the dog out in the cold.* **2.** to omit someone or some creature totally. (Figurative.) ☐ *There was a party last night, but my friends left me out in the cold.* ☐ *When it came to the final prizes in the dog show, they left our animals out in the cold.*

leave someone or something out (of something) to neglect to include someone or something in something. (The *of*-phrase is paraphrased with a *from*-phrase when the particle is transposed. See the 🄵 example.) ☐ *Please leave me out of it.* 🅃 *Can I leave John out this time?* 🄵 *Can I leave John out from our list this time?* ☐ *Don't leave out Fred's name.*

leave someone or something out (of something) to omit someone or something from something. (*Someone* includes *oneself*. The *of*-phrase is paraphrased with a *from*-phrase when the particle is transposed. See the 🄵 example.) ☐ *Please leave me out of your group.* 🅃 *We left out Tom.* 🄵 *We left out Tom from the list of participants.* ☐ *Don't leave me out!* ☐ *She left herself out of the group she was criticizing.*

LEAVE ► TO

leave one to one's own devices AND **leave one to one's own resources** to make one rely on oneself. ☐ *I am sure that she will manage if we leave her to her own devices.* ☐ *I will leave her to her own resources and everything will turn out fine.*

leave someone or something to someone to give or abandon someone or something to someone. ☐ *I leave Mr. Franklin to you. Good luck in dealing with him.* ☐ *I leave the whole problem to you. Good luck.*

leave someone to it to withdraw and allow someone to finish something alone. (Idiomatic.) ☐ *I hate to leave before the job is finished, but I'll have to leave you to it.* ☐ *I will leave them to it. I have to go home now.*

leave something to chance to allow something to be settled by chance. (Idiomatic.) ☐ *Plan your day. Don't leave* *anything to chance.* □ *It is not a good idea to leave any of this to chance.*

leave something to someone 1. to will something to someone. □ *My grandfather left his house to my mother.* □ *I will leave this watch to one of my grandchildren.* 2. to assign work to or reserve a task for someone. □ *I will leave this last little bit of the job to you.* □ *Can I leave this last part to Carl to finish?* 3. to depend on someone to behave in a certain way. (Idiomatic. Almost always with *it*.) □ *Leave it to Harry to mess things up.* □ *She did it wrong again. Leave it to Janet!*

LEAVE ▸ UP

leave someone up in the air to leave someone waiting for a decision. □ *Please don't leave me up in the air. I want to know what's going to happen to me.* □ *Nothing was decided, and they left me up in the air.*

leave something up to leave something in a raised or high position. □ *It's still warm in here. Please leave the window up.* 🆃 *Please leave up the window. It's so hot!*

leave something up in the air to leave a matter undecided. (Idiomatic.) □ *Let's get this settled now. I don't want to leave anything up in the air over the weekend.* □ *The whole matter was left up in the air for another week.*

leave something up to someone or something to allow someone or something to make a decision about something. □ *We will try to leave that decision up to you.* □ *Can we leave this up to the committee?*

LEAVE ▸ WITH

leave someone or something with someone or something to allow someone or something to remain with someone or something. □ *Can I leave Jimmy with you while I shop?* □ *Do you mind if I leave my papers with the committee, just in case they have time to look at them?*

leave with someone to depart in the company of someone. □ *I left with Frank early in the evening and did not see what happened to Tom and Edna.* □ *Mary is gone. She left with Gerald.*

leave word with someone to leave a message with someone. □ *Please leave word with my secretary if you can't be there on time.* □ *Will you leave word with John if you cannot come to the party?*

LECTURE ▸ ABOUT

lecture ((to) someone) about someone or something AND **lecture ((to) someone) on someone or something** 1. to give an instructional speech to someone about someone or something. □ *He always lectured his children about their duty to vote.* □ *She lectured to all her classes on employment opportunities.* 2. to scold someone about someone or something. □ *Please don't lecture me about my behavior. Can't you accept that I am just wicked?* □ *I like Ted! Don't lecture about him.*

LECTURE ▸ AT

lecture at someone (about something) to talk to someone about something in the manner of a lecture. □ *There is no need to lecture at me about the problem. I know how serious the matter is.* □ *Don't lecture at me all the time!*

LECTURE ▸ FOR

lecture someone for something to give someone a talking-to about something. □ *Please don't lecture me for being late. It won't help now, will it?* □ *There is no point in lecturing us for something we didn't do.*

LECTURE ▸ ON

lecture ((to) someone) on someone or something See under *LECTURE ▸ ABOUT.*

LECTURE ▸ TO

lecture ((to) someone) about someone or something See under *LECTURE ▸ ABOUT.*

LEER ▸ AT

leer at someone to gaze at someone flirtatiously or with lust. □ *Why are you leering at that woman in the bikini?* □ *Stop leering at me!*

LEGISLATE ▶ AGAINST

legislate against something to prohibit something; to pass a law against something. ☐ *You can't just legislate against something. You have to explain to people why they shouldn't do it.* ☐ *The Congress has just legislated against insolvent banks.*

LEGISLATE ▶ FOR

legislate for something to pass a law that tries to make something happen. ☐ *The candidate pledged to legislate for tax relief.* ☐ *We support your efforts to legislate for lower taxes.*

LEND ▶ OUT

lend something out (to someone) to allow someone to borrow something. ☐ *I lent my tuxedo out to a friend who was going to a dance, and now I haven't anything to wear to the opera.* 🅃 *I lent out my copy of the book.* ☐ *Sorry, I lent it out.*

LEND ▶ TO

lend an ear to someone or something AND **lend your ear to someone or something** to listen to someone or what someone has to say. (Figurative.) ☐ *Lend an ear to me and I will tell you a story.* ☐ *Lend your ear to what I am saying.*

lend itself to something [for something] to be suitable for something. ☐ *I don't think that this gown lends itself to outdoor occasions.* ☐ *This room lends itself to small, intimate gatherings.*

lend something to someone to make a loan of something to someone. ☐ *Never lend money to a friend.* ☐ *Would you be able to lend your coat to Fred?*

LEND ▶ WITH

lend someone a hand with something to help someone with something. (This need not involve "hands.") ☐ *Could you please lend us a hand with this?* ☐ *Can I lend you a hand with that?*

LENGTHEN ▶ OUT

lengthen out to stretch or grow longer. ☐ *The days began to lengthen out and we knew summer was upon us.* ☐ *As we approached the end of the trail, the distance seemed to lengthen out.*

LET ▶ AT

let someone or something at someone or something to permit someone or something to attack or get at someone or something. ☐ *He did that? Just let me at him!* ☐ *Let the committee at her, then she'll change her tune.*

LET ▶ BY

let someone (get) by to permit someone to pass. (*Get* can be replaced with *pass.*) ☐ *Please let me get by. I am in a hurry.* ☐ *Let me by, please.*

let someone get by with something to allow someone to do something wrong and not be punished or reprimanded. (An elaboration of *get by with something* under *GET ▶ AWAY.*) ☐ *She lets those kids get by with anything.* ☐ *They won't let you get by with that!*

let someone slide by to permit someone to get past a barrier or a challenge too easily. ☐ *You let too many people slide by. You need to be more rigorous.* ☐ *Don't let even one unqualified person slide by!*

let something slip by to let a deadline pass unnoticed. ☐ *I'm afraid you let the final deadline slip by, and you will have to pay a penalty.* ☐ *We let the proper time slip by without a thought.*

let the chance slip by to miss taking advantage of an opportunity. ☐ *It's too late. You let the chance slip by.* ☐ *Don't let the chance slip by. This may be your last chance.*

LET ▶ DOWN

let down to relax one's efforts or vigilance. ☐ *Now is no time to let down. Keep on your guard.* ☐ *After the contest was over, Jane let down a bit so she could relax.*

let one's hair down to tell [someone] everything; to tell one's innermost feelings and secrets. ☐ *Let your hair down and tell me all about it.* 🅃 *Come on. Let down your hair and tell me what you really think.*

let someone or something down to fail someone or something; to disappoint someone or a group. ☐ *Please don't let me down. I am depending on you.* 🅃 *I* *let down the entire cast of the play.* □ *I'm sorry I let you down.* [N] *Your efforts were a real letdown.*

LET ► IN

See also under *LET ► IN(TO).*

let oneself in for something to make oneself vulnerable to some difficulty. □ *I don't want to let myself in for a lot of extra work.* □ *You really let yourself in for some problems!*

let someone in on something to permit someone to share in something, such as profits, a secret, a scheme, etc. □ *Please let me in on your secret. I won't tell anyone.* □ *Don't let Henry in on our deal.*

LET ► IN(TO)

let someone or something in(to something) to permit someone or something to enter something or some place; to make it possible for someone or something to enter something or some place. (*Someone* includes *oneself.*) □ *Would you let Ed into his room? He forgot his key.* [T] *Please let in the dog.* □ *Let the dog in.* □ *The maid used her key to let herself into the room.*

LET ► OF

let go of someone or something to release someone or something. □ *Please let go of me. I have to get to class.* □ *Let go of my hand!*

let loose of someone or something **1.** to loosen the grasp on someone or something. □ *Please let loose of me!* □ *Will you let loose of the doorknob?* **2.** to become independent from someone or something. □ *She is nearly forty years old and has not yet let loose of her mother.* □ *Dave can't let loose of his childhood.*

LET ► OFF

let off (some) steam **1.** [for something] to release steam. □ *The locomotive let off some steam after it came to a halt.* [T] *The locomotive let some steam off and frightened the children.* □ *With a great hiss, it let off steam and frightened the children.* **2.** to work or play off excess energy. □ *Those boys need to get out and let off some steam.* □ *Go out and let off steam!* **3.** to release one's anger, usually verbally. □ *I'm sorry I yelled at you. I guess I needed to let off some steam.* □ *She's not mad. She's just letting off steam.*

let someone (get) off (something) to permit someone to debark, dismount, or leave something. □ *Please move and let me get off the bus.* □ *Let her off!*

let someone off the hook to permit someone to get out of some responsibility; to release someone from a pending responsibility. (*Someone* includes *oneself.*) □ *I can't serve as usher at your wedding. I hope you will let me off the hook.* □ *Now can I let myself off the hook on this matter?*

let someone off (with something) to give someone a light punishment [for doing something]. □ *The judge let the criminal off with a slap on the wrist.* [T] *The judge would not let off the criminal with a small fine.* □ *This judge lets too many of these petty crooks off.*

LET ► ON

let on (about someone or something) to confirm or reveal something about someone or something. □ *You promised you wouldn't let on about Sally and her new job!* □ *I didn't let on. She guessed.*

let on something to pretend something. □ *She let on that she was a college graduate.* □ *He looked quite tired, but that wasn't how he let on.*

let on (to someone) (about someone or something) to reveal knowledge about someone or something to someone. □ *Please don't let on to anyone about what happened last night.* □ *I won't let on to anyone.* □ *I won't let on about Kate.*

let someone get on with something to permit someone to continue something. (*Someone* includes *oneself.*) □ *I will leave now and let you get on with your work.* □ *She had to settle the matter first. She would not let herself get on with life until the matter was settled.*

LET ► OUT

let it all hang out to become totally relaxed and unpretentious. (Slang.) □ *I need to get away somewhere where I can* *let it all hang out.* □ *Ted tends to let it all hang out when he gets a little melancholy.*

let out [for an event that includes many people] to end. (The people are then permitted to come out.) □ *What time does the movie let out? I have to meet someone in the lobby.* □ *The meeting let out at about seven o'clock.* □ *School lets out in June.*

let out (with) something **1.** to state or utter something loudly. □ *The man let out with a screaming accusation about the person whom he thought had wounded him.* □ *She let out a torrent of curses.* **2.** to give forth a scream or yell. □ *She let out with a blood-curdling scream when she saw the snake in her chair.* □ *They let out with shouts of delight when they saw the cake.*

let someone or something (get) out (of something) **1.** to permit someone or some creature to exit or escape from something or some place. □ *Please let the president get out of the car.* □ *Let the bear get out of the trap.* □ *Don't let the snake get out!* N *They were trapped! There was no outlet.* **2.** to permit someone or some creature to evade something. □ *I will not let you get out of your responsibilities.* □ *They wouldn't let me out of the contract.*

let someone or something (get) out (of something) to allow someone or some creature to avoid [doing] something. □ *I will not let you get out of your responsibilities.* □ *They wouldn't let me out of the contract.*

let someone or something out (of something) to permit someone or some creature to exit from something or some place. (*Someone* includes *oneself*. The *of*-phrase is paraphrased with a *from*-phrase when the particle is transposed. See the F example.) □ *Would you please let Ed out of the closet?* T *Please let out Ed.* F *Please let out Ed from the closet.* □ *Do let the dog out.* □ *She let herself out of the room.*

let something out **1.** to reveal something; to tell about a secret or a plan. □ *It was supposed to be a secret. Who let it out?* T *Who let out the secret?* **2.** to enlarge the waist of an article of clothing. □ *She had to let her shirts out because she had gained some weight.* T *I see you have had to let out your trousers.*

let something out (to someone) to rent something to someone. □ *I let the back room out to a college boy.* T *I let out the back room to someone.*

let something slip out to reveal secret information by accident. □ *I tried to keep it a secret, but somehow I let it slip out.* □ *Who let the secret slip out?*

let the cat out of the bag to allow a surprise or secret to become known. (Cliché.) □ *Please don't let the cat out of the bag. This party is supposed to be a surprise.* □ *Who let the cat out of the bag? Now everybody knows.*

LET ▸ PAST

let someone (get) past to allow someone to pass; to get out of the way so someone can pass. □ *Please let me get past. I'm in a hurry.* □ *Do let me past.*

LET ▸ THROUGH

let someone or something through (something) to permit someone or something to move through an opening or through a congested area. □ *The usher wouldn't let me through the door.* □ *Please let the ambulance through the crowd.* □ *Let the doctor through!*

LET ▸ UNDER

let the grass grow under one's feet to stay in one place for a long time; to be sluggish and ineffectual. (Cliché. Usually negative.) □ *He is always on the move. He never lets the grass grow under his feet.* □ *I have always thought that I ought not to let the grass grow under my feet.*

LET ▸ UP

let up **1.** to diminish. □ *I hope this rain lets up a little soon.* □ *When the snow lets up so I can see, I will drive to the store.* **2.** to stop [doing something] altogether. □ *The rain let up about noon, and the sun came out.* N *The rain continued without any letup.*

let up (on someone or something) to reduce the pressure or demands on someone or something. □ *You had better let up on Tom. He can't handle any more work.* □ *Please let up on the committee. It can only do so much.* □ *Do let up. You are getting too upset.*

LET ▸ WITH

let fly with something to throw or thrust something, such as a rock, ball, punch, hard right fist to the nose, etc. □ *The pitcher wound up and let fly with a strike—right over the plate.* □ *Max let fly with a blow to Lefty's chin.*

let go with something AND **let loose with something** **1.** to deliver a strong verbal reprimand. □ *Molly let loose with a tremendous scolding at Dave.* □ *Dave let loose with a vengeful retort.* **2.** to give out a scream or yell. □ *Sam let go with a rebel yell that scared everyone in the room.* □ *Jed let loose with a savage scream.*

let loose with something See the previous entry.

LEVEL ▸ AGAINST

level something against someone to place a charge against someone; to accuse someone of something. □ *The neighbors leveled a disturbance of the peace charge against us.* □ *The cops leveled an assault charge against Max.*

LEVEL ▸ AT

level something at someone or something to direct something at someone or something. □ *Why did you think you had to level that barrage of words at me? I didn't make the problem.* □ *Sam leveled an acid comment or two at the committee.* □ *The sheriff leveled his rifle at the fleeing bandit.* □ *The angry teacher leveled her gaze at me and smiled grimly.*

LEVEL ▸ DOWN

level something down to make something level or smooth. □ *The soil is very uneven in this part of the garden. Would you please level it down?* □ *The huge earth-moving machines leveled the hill down in preparation for the building of the highway.*

LEVEL ▸ OFF

level off [for variation or fluctuation in the motion of something] to diminish; [for a rate] to stop increasing or decreasing. □ *The plane leveled off at 10,000 feet.* □ *After a while the work load will level off.* □ *Things will level off after we get through the end of the month.*

level something off to make something level or smooth. □ *You are going to have to level the floor off before you put the carpet down.* [T] *Please level off the floor.* [A] *Move the furniture over to that leveled-off place, please.*

LEVEL ▸ OUT

level out [for something that was going up and down] to assume a more level course or path. □ *The road leveled out after a while, and driving was easier.* □ *As we got down into the valley, the land leveled out, and traveling was easier.*

level something out to cause something to assume a more level course or path. □ *Level this path out before you open it to the public.* [T] *They have to level out this roadway.*

LEVEL ▸ TO

level something to the ground to crush or demolish something down to the ground. □ *They were forced to level the building to the ground, because they could not afford to maintain it.* □ *The house was leveled to the ground by the tornado.*

LEVEL ▸ UP

level something up to move something into a level or plumb position. □ *Use a piece of wood under the table's leg to level it up.* [T] *I will level up the table.*

LEVEL ▸ WITH

level with someone (about someone or something) to be honest about something with someone. (Informal.) □ *I insist that you level with me about this. This is no time for deception.* □ *Please level with me. Tell the truth.*

LEVY ▸ (UP)ON

levy something (up)on someone or something to place a tax on someone or something. (*Upon* is formal and less commonly used than *on*.) □ *The Congress was very straightforward. It levied heavy taxes upon rich people.* □ *The* *city council levied a heavy tax on junky old cars.*

LIBERATE ▸ FROM

liberate someone or something from someone or something to free someone or something from someone or something; to set someone or something free from the control of someone or something. □ *The police hoped to liberate the child from his kidnappers.* □ *We liberated the town from the enemy.* □ *I liberated the cat from the trap.*

LICK ▸ AT

lick at something to draw the tongue over something repeatedly. □ *Jimmy was just licking at the ice cream cone, and soon it began to melt and drip off his elbow.* □ *I don't just lick at the ice cream. I take big bites of it.* □ *The dog licked at the sore on its leg.*

LICK ▸ INTO

lick someone or something into shape to press or force someone or something into good shape or condition. (Colloquial.) □ *The drama coach will try to lick her into shape by performance time.* □ *Please try to lick this report into shape by tomorrow morning.*

LICK ▸ OFF

lick something off ((of) something) to remove something from something by licking with the tongue. (The *of*-phrase is paraphrased with a *from*-phrase when the particle is transposed. See the 🄵 example. The *of* is colloquial.) □ *The dog licked the grease off of the floor where the meat had dropped.* 🅃 *The dog licked off the grease.* 🄵 *The dog licked off the grease from the plate.* □ *The grease is gone. The dog licked it off.*

LICK ▸ UP

lick something up to clean up all of some substance by licking with the tongue. (Usually said of an animal.) □ *Don't worry about the spilled milk. The dog will lick it up.* 🅃 *The dog licked up the milk.*

LIE ▸ ABOUT

lie about **1.** [for someone] to recline lazily somewhere. □ *She just lay about through her entire vacation.* □ *Don't lie about all the time. Get busy.* **2.** [for something] to be located somewhere casually and carelessly, perhaps for a long time. □ *This hammer has been lying about for a week. Put it away!* □ *Why are all these dirty dishes lying about?*

lie about someone or something (to someone) to say something untrue about someone or something to someone. □ *I wouldn't lie about my boss to anyone!* □ *I wouldn't lie about anything like that!*

LIE ▸ AHEAD

lie ahead of someone or something AND **lie before someone or something** **1.** to exist in front of someone or something. □ *A small cottage lay ahead of us near the trail.* □ *A huge mansion lay before the car at the end of the road.* **2.** to be fixed in the future of someone or something. □ *I just don't know what lies ahead of me.* □ *We don't know what lies before our country.*

LIE ▸ ALONGSIDE

lie alongside ((of) someone or something) to lie next to someone or some creature. (The *of* is colloquial.) □ *Jimmy came in to lie alongside of his father in bed.* □ *The puppy lay alongside its mother.*

LIE ▸ AROUND

lie around (some place) to recline some place; to spend some time lazily in some place. □ *I think I will just lie around the house all day.* □ *I need to lie around every now and then.*

LIE ▸ AT

lie at anchor [for a ship] to wait or rest at anchor. □ *The ship lay at anchor throughout the day while a shore party searched for the runaway.* □ *We lay at anchor overnight, waiting for the tide.*

lie at death's door to be close to dying. (Figurative.) □ *She lay at death's door for over a month.* □ *I do not intend to lie at death's door suffering. I'll just get up and go in without knocking.*

LIE ▸ BACK

lie back to relax; to lean back in a chair and relax. (See also *kick back.*) □ *Just lie back and try to get comfortable.* □ *I* *really need to get home and lie back and relax.*

LIE ► BEFORE

lie before someone or something See under *LIE ► AHEAD.*

LIE ► BEHIND

lie behind someone or something **1.** [for something] to be positioned to the rear of someone or something. □ *A wide expanse of water lay behind the sentry, and a narrow roadway lay in front.* □ *A vast field lies behind the house.* **2.** [for something] to be in someone's or a group's past. □ *Now that all of our difficulties lie behind us, we can get on with our business.* □ *The busy season lay behind the company and people could take their vacations.*

LIE ► BEYOND

lie beyond someone or something **1.** to be located on the other side of someone or something. □ *The stream lies beyond those men you see working in the field.* □ *The village lies just beyond that hill there.* **2.** to be outside the grasp or the ability of someone or a group. □ *I am afraid that this matter lies beyond Dave.* □ *The solution lies beyond the power of the committee.*

LIE ► DOWN

lie down to recline. □ *Why don't you lie down for a while?* □ *I need to lie down and have a little snooze.*

lie down on something to recline on something. □ *Don't lie down on that couch!* □ *I will just lie down on my bed for a few minutes.*

lie down on the job to fail to do one's job efficiently; to fail to do one's job. □ *I haven't been lying down on the job! I am not the reason things are slow!* □ *Mary had been lying down on the job and not getting her work done.*

lie down under something to lie down beneath something. □ *She was tired, so she lay down under a willow tree by the brook.* □ *The dog lay down under a lawn chair and slept.*

LIE ► IN

lie in [for a woman] to lie in bed awaiting the birth of her child. □ *The child is due soon and the mother is lying in at the present time.* □ *All the women in that particular hospital are lying in.* [N] *He stayed with her during her lying-in.*

lie in ruins to exist in a state of ruin, such as a destroyed city, building, scheme, plan, etc. □ *The entire city lay in ruins.* □ *My garden lay in ruins after the cows got in and trampled everything.*

lie in something to recline in something, such as a bed, a puddle, etc. □ *I found my wallet lying in a puddle. My money was soaked!* □ *We found Jimmy lying in a pile of leaves, napping.*

lie in state [for a corpse] to remain on public display in a formal and dignified setting. □ *The body of the prime minister lay in state for three days.* □ *Some rulers are kept lying in state for a long time.*

lie in store for someone [for something] to await someone in the future. □ *None of us knows what lies in store for us tomorrow.* □ *Some good lies in store for me, I think.*

lie in wait for someone or something to remain secluded, waiting to set upon someone or something. □ *The robbers were lying in wait for Mr. Franklin.* □ *The hijackers lay in wait for the armored truck.*

LIE ► OUT

lie out (in something) to remain out in something. □ *Who left my screwdriver lying out in the rain?* □ *It's not lying out. It's in the drawer.*

LIE ► THROUGH

lie through one's teeth to tell blatant lies. (Colloquial.) □ *That's not true. You are just lying through your teeth.* □ *Don't believe Mary. She is lying through her teeth.*

LIE ► TO

lie to someone (about someone or something) to tell an untruth about someone or something to someone. □ *You wouldn't lie to me about Sarah, would you?* □ *I'm not lying to you!*

LIE ▸ WITH

lie with someone **1.** to recline with someone. □ *Come and lie with me and we will keep warm.* □ *Jimmy and Franny were lying with each other to keep warm.* **2.** to recline with someone and have sex. □ *She claimed he asked her to lie with him.* □ *Do you mean to imply that she lay with him?*

LIE ▸ WITHIN

lie within something to remain within a defined area or domain. □ *The boundaries of the village lie completely within the river valley.* □ *The cost you cited lies within the range I was considering.*

LIFT ▸ AGAINST

lift a hand against someone or something AND **lift a hand to someone or something; raise a hand against someone or something; raise a hand to someone or something** to make a move against someone or some creature. (Usually negative.) □ *You wouldn't lift a hand against me, would you?* □ *I would never lift a hand to a dumb animal.* □ *I never raised a hand against any of my children when they were growing up.* □ *He would never raise a hand to an animal.*

LIFT ▸ DOWN

lift someone or something down (from something) to help someone or something down (from something or some place) by lifting and carrying. □ *Would you please lift Jimmy down from the top bunk?* [T] *Frank lifted down the heavy box.* □ *Can you lift me down?*

LIFT ▸ FROM

lift something from someone or something to raise something off someone or something. □ *Please lift this burden from me.* □ *I lifted the glass from the tray carefully.*

LIFT ▸ OFF

lift off [for a plane or rocket] to move upward, leaving the ground. □ *The rocket lifted off exactly on time.* [N] *We have a lift-off! There it goes!*

lift something off (of) someone or something to raise something and uncover or release someone or something. (The *of*-phrase is paraphrased with a *from*-phrase when the particle is transposed. See the [F] example. The *of* is colloquial.) □ *Lift the beam off of him and see if he is still breathing.* [T] *Please lift off the heavy lid.* [F] *Jake lifted off the heavy lid from the kettle.* □ *I lifted the fallen branch off of Tim and helped him up.*

LIFT ▸ TO

lift a hand to someone or something See *lift a hand against someone or something* under *LIFT ▸ AGAINST.*

LIFT ▸ UP

lift someone or something up to raise someone or something. □ *I helped lift him up and put him on the stretcher.* [T] *Please lift Tommy up.* □ *I lifted the lid up.*

lift someone or something up to someone or something to elevate someone or something to the same level as someone or something. □ *Please lift Tommy up to the window, so he can see in.* [T] *Please lift up Tommy.* □ *Could you lift the cup up to my mouth?* □ *Please lift the child up to me.*

lift up to raise up. □ *Suddenly, the top of the box lifted up and a hand reached out.* □ *Bill's hand lifted up and fell back again.*

LIGHT ▸ INTO

light into someone or something to attack someone or something physically or verbally. (Informal.) □ *The teacher lit into the pupil without really knowing what had happened.* □ *The farmer lit into the dog.*

LIGHT ▸ ON

See under *LIGHT ▸ (UP)ON.*

LIGHT ▸ OUT

light out (of some place) (for some place) to leave a place in a great hurry for some place. (Folksy.) □ *I lit out of there for home as fast as I could.* □ *I lit out for home.* □ *I lit out of there as fast as I could go.*

LIGHT ▸ UNDER

light a fire under someone to motivate someone; to force someone into action.

(Figurative.) □ *I had hoped that her experiences in Europe would light a fire under her and that she would begin to paint again.* □ *You had better light a fire under your staff. Either that or fire some of them.*

LIGHT ▸ UP

light someone or something up to shine lights on someone or something. □ *We lit Fred up with the headlights of the car.* 🅃 *Light up the stage and let's rehearse.*

light something up to light smoking tobacco. □ *She lit the cigarette up and took in a great breath of the smoke.* 🅃 *She lit up a cigarette.*

light up **1.** to become brighter. □ *Suddenly, the sky lit up like day.* □ *The room lit up as the fire suddenly came back to life.* **2.** [for someone] to become interested and responsive in something. □ *We could tell from the way Sally lit up that she recognized the man in the picture.* □ *She lit up when we told her about our team's success.*

LIGHT ▸ (UP)ON

light (up)on someone or something **1.** to land on someone or something; to settle on someone or something. (*Upon* is formal and less commonly used than *on*.) □ *Three butterflies lit on the baby, causing her to shriek with delight.* □ *The bees lit on the clover blossom and pulled it to the ground.* □ *Her glance lit upon a dress in the store window.* **2.** to arrive at something by chance; to happen upon something. (Figurative. Close to sense 1.) □ *The committee lit upon a solution that pleased almost everyone.* □ *We just happen to light upon this idea as we were talking to each other.*

LIGHT ▸ WITH

light something with something **1.** to set something afire with something else. □ *Kelly lit the fire with her last match.* □ *I will light the fire with a cigarette lighter.* **2.** to illuminate something. □ *She lit the room with a few candles.* □ *We lit the Christmas tree by turning on a switch.*

LIGHTEN ▸ UP

lighten something up to make something lighter or brighter. □ *Some white paint will lighten this room up a lot.* 🅃 *The sunlight came in and lightened up the kitchen.*

lighten up to become lighter or brighter. □ *We applied a new coat of white paint to the walls, and the room lightened up considerably.* □ *The sky is beginning to lighten up a little.*

lighten up (on someone or something) to be less rough and demanding or rude with someone or something. (Colloquial.) □ *Please lighten up on her. You are being very cruel.* □ *You are too harsh. Lighten up.*

LIKEN ▸ TO

liken someone or something to someone or something to compare someone or something to someone or something, concentrating on the similarities. (*Someone* includes *oneself*.) □ *He is strange. I can only liken him to an eccentric millionaire.* □ *The poet likened James to a living statue of Mercury.* □ *She likened herself to the queen once too often.*

LIMBER ▸ UP

limber someone or something up to make someone or something more flexible or loose. (*Someone* includes *oneself*.) □ *Let me give you a massage; that will limber you up.* 🅃 *I need to limber up my arms.* □ *She did lots of exercises to limber herself up.*

LIMIT ▸ TO

limit someone to something **1.** to limit someone to a certain amount or number of something. (*Someone* includes *oneself*.) □ *I will have to limit you to two helpings of mashed potatoes.* □ *I limit myself to cola drinks only.* **2.** to restrict someone to a certain area. (*Someone* includes *oneself*.) □ *Please try to limit your children to your own yard.* □ *They limited themselves to the north side of town.*

limit something to something to restrict something to a limited set, a certain amount, or a specific number of something. □ *Please limit your com-*

ments to five minutes. ☐ *Can you limit your remarks to the subject at hand?*

LINE ▶ UP

line someone or something up 1. to put people or things in line. (*Someone* includes *oneself.*) ☐ *Line everyone up and march them onstage.* 🅃 *Line up the kids, please.* ☐ *Please line these books up.* ☐ *Hey, you guys! Line yourselves up!* 2. to schedule someone or something [for something]. ☐ *Please line somebody up for the entertainment.* 🅃 *We will try to line up a magician and a clown for the party.* 🅃 *They lined up a chorus for the last act.*

line someone or something up against something to put people or things into a row in front of or against something. (*Someone* includes *oneself.*) ☐ *We lined everyone up against the wall for the photograph.* 🅃 *Please line up everyone against the wall.* ☐ *Please line yourselves up against the wall.*

line someone or something up behind someone or something to put people or things into a line behind someone or something. (*Someone* includes *oneself.*) ☐ *Please line all the children up behind the tallest child.* 🅃 *Line up everyone behind the curtain.* 🅃 *Line up the books behind the biggest one.* ☐ *Tell them to line themselves up behind me.*

line someone or something up (in something) to put people or things into some kind of formation, such as a row, column, ranks, etc. (*Someone* includes *oneself.*) ☐ *The teacher lined the children up in two rows.* 🅃 *Please line up the children in a row.* ☐ *Yes, line them up.* ☐ *Let's line ourselves up into two columns.*

line someone or something up on something to place people or things into a line oriented on one or more things. (*Someone* includes *oneself.*) ☐ *Line them all up on the flagpole and the church steeple.* 🅃 *Line up the children on the white line.* 🅃 *Line up the books on the edge of the shelf.* ☐ *The birds lined themselves up neatly on the wire.*

line someone or something up with someone or something 1. to place people or things into a line with other people or things. (*Someone* includes *oneself.*) ☐ *Line Fred up with the others.* 🅃 *Line up Fran with everyone else.* ☐ *Line the children up with Fran.* 🅃 *Line up these books with the others.* ☐ *Please line yourselves up with the others.* 2. to place people or things into a line that is oriented on someone or something. ☐ *Line everyone up with the flagpole so we can march into the hall.* 🅃 *Please line up everyone with the flagpole straight ahead.* 🅃 *Line up these books with the back of the cabinet.* 3. to schedule a meeting date with someone or a group of people. ☐ *Will you line everyone up with us for a Monday morning meeting?* 🅃 *See if you can line up a meeting with Todd and Frank.* ☐ *I will line the committee up with our management for a meeting.*

line someone up behind someone or something to organize people in support of someone or something. (*Someone* includes *oneself.*) ☐ *I will see if I can line a few supporters up behind our candidate.* 🅃 *I can line up everyone behind you.* ☐ *We will line them up behind our party.* ☐ *The rest of the city council lined itself up with the mayor.*

line someone up for something to find and schedule someone for something. ☐ *I need someone to help park cars. I have to line someone up for the party tomorrow.* 🅃 *I will line up someone to help.*

line up to form a line; to get into a line. ☐ *All right, everyone, line up!* 🄽 *The men in the lineup just stood there, waiting for things to quiet down.*

line up against someone or something to organize against someone or something. ☐ *Our people lined up against the candidate and defeated her soundly.* ☐ *We will line up against the opposing party as we did during the last election.*

line up alongside someone or something to form or get into a line beside someone or something. ☐ *Can you line up alongside the other people?* ☐ *Line up alongside the wall and get ready to be photographed.*

line up behind someone or something **1.** to form or get into a line behind someone or something. ☐ *Please line up behind Kelly.* ☐ *Please go and line up behind the sign.* **2.** to organize in support of someone or something. ☐ *We all lined up behind Todd and got him elected.* ☐ *We lined up behind the most active political party.*

line up for something to form or get into a line and wait for something. ☐ *Everyone lined up for a helping of birthday cake.* ☐ *Let's line up for dinner. The doors to the dining room will open at any minute.*

line up in(to) something to form or get into a line, row, rank, column, etc. ☐ *Please line up in columns of two.* ☐ *I wish you would all line up into a nice straight line.*

line up on something to form a line oriented on something. ☐ *Line up on the white line painted on the pavement.* ☐ *Please line up on the marks on the floor.*

line up with someone to get into a line with someone. ☐ *Go over and line up with the others.* ☐ *Would you please line up with the other students?*

LINE ▸ WITH

line something with something to place a layer of something over the inside surface of something. ☐ *You should line the drawers with clean paper before you use them.* ☐ *I want to line this jacket with new material.*

LINGER ▸ AROUND

linger around to wait around; to be idle some place. ☐ *Don't linger around. Get going!* ☐ *All the students were lingering around, waiting until the last minute to go into the building.*

LINGER ▸ ON

linger on to remain for a long time; to exist longer than would have been thought. ☐ *This cold of mine just keeps lingering on.* ☐ *Some of the guests lingered on for a long time after the party was over.*

linger on (after someone or something) AND **stay on (after someone or something)** to outlast someone or something; to live longer than someone else or long after an event. ☐ *Aunt Sarah lingered on only a few months after Uncle Herman died.* ☐ *She lingered on and was depressed for a while.* ☐ *She stayed on after her husband for a short time.*

linger on something to delay moving on to the next thing; to remain at something and not move on. ☐ *Don't linger on that note so long.* ☐ *I don't want to waste a lot of time lingering on this question.*

LINGER ▸ OVER

linger over something **1.** to dawdle or idle over something, such as a meal, a cup of coffee, etc. ☐ *I could linger over coffee all morning, given the chance.* ☐ *Don't linger over your soup. It will get cold.* **2.** to dawdle over the doing of something. ☐ *You shouldn't linger over eating your dinner.* ☐ *It would be best not to linger over making up your mind.*

LINK ▸ TO

link someone or something to someone or something AND **link someone or something and someone or something together; link someone or something together with someone or something; link someone or something with someone or something** **1.** to discover a connection between people and things, in any combination. ☐ *I would never have thought of linking Fred to Tom. I didn't even know they knew each other.* ☐ *I always sort of linked Tom with honesty.* ☐ *I never linked Bill together with Ted until they made their movie.* **2.** to connect people and things, in any combination. (*Someone* includes *oneself*.) ☐ *We have to link each person to one other person, using this colored paper to tie them together.* ☐ *We linked each decoration together with another one.* ☐ *They linked themselves to each other in a support network.*

LINK ▸ TOGETHER

link someone or something together with someone or something See the previous entry.

LINK ▸ UP

link someone or something up (to something) to connect someone or something to something, usually with something that has a type of fastener or connector that constitutes a link. □ *They promised that they would link me up to the network today.* 🅃 *They will link up my computer to the network today.* □ *Have you linked it up yet?* □ *Have you linked Sarah up yet?*

link up to someone or something AND **link (up) with someone or something** to join up with someone or something. □ *I have a computer modem so I can link up to Bruce.* □ *Now my computer can link up with a computer bulletin board.*

LINK ▸ WITH

link someone or something with someone or something See under *LINK ▸ TO.*

link (up) with someone or something See *link up to someone or something* under *LINK ▸ UP.*

LIQUOR ▸ UP

liquor someone up to get someone tipsy or drunk. (Colloquial.) □ *He liquored her up and tried to take her home with him.* 🅃 *They liquored up the out-of-town visitors.*

liquor up to drink an alcoholic beverage, especially to excess. □ *Sam sat around all evening liquoring up.* □ *They seem to liquor up almost every night of the week.*

LIST ▸ AMONG

list someone or something among something to include someone or something in a particular category. □ *I list George among the all-time greats.* □ *I have to list the budget committee as the most efficient ever.*

LIST ▸ AS

list someone as something to categorize someone as something, usually in a written list. (*Someone* includes *oneself.*) □ *I will list you as a contributor to the Preservation Fund, if you don't mind.* □ *Although she was not registered as such, she listed herself as a stockbroker.*

LIST ▸ OFF

list someone or something off to recite a list of people or things, one by one. □ *She listed everyone off in order without having to look at her notes.* 🅃 *She listed off the names of the people who are always late.* □ *Dale listed each one off.*

LIST ▸ TO

list to something to lean to one side; to lean toward a specific direction. □ *The ship had listed to one side since being struck by the speedboat.* □ *The huge ship listed a tiny bit to starboard.*

LISTEN ▸ FOR

listen for someone or something to try to hear someone or something. □ *I will have to let you in the front door if you come home late. I will listen for you.* □ *I am listening for the telephone.*

LISTEN ▸ IN

listen in (on someone or something) **1.** to join someone or a group as a listener. □ *The band is rehearsing. Let's go listen in on them.* □ *It won't hurt to listen in, will it?* **2.** to eavesdrop on someone. □ *Please don't try to listen in on us. This is a private conversation.* □ *I am not listening in. I was here first. You are conversing carelessly.*

LISTEN ▸ TO

listen to someone or something **1.** to pay attention to and hear someone or something. □ *Listen to me! Hear what I have to say!* □ *I want to listen to his speech.* **2.** to heed someone, orders, or advice. □ *Listen to me! Do what I tell you!* □ *You really should listen to his advice.*

LISTEN ▸ UP

listen up to listen carefully and obey. (Colloquial.) □ *Listen up, you guys! Pay attention to me!* □ *All right, you guys, listen up!*

LITTER ▸ ABOUT

litter something about AND **litter something around** to cast around something, such as trash, clothing, personal possessions, etc. □ *Don't litter all that stuff about.* □ *I wish you wouldn't litter your trash around.*

LITTER ▸ AROUND
See the previous entry.

LITTER ▸ UP
litter something up to mess something up with litter, trash, possessions, etc. □ *Who littered this room up?* 🅃 *Who littered up this room?* 🄰 *Please help clean up the littered-up yard.*

LIVE ▸ ABOVE
live above someone or something AND **live over someone or something** to live in a place that is at a higher level than someone or something; to dwell directly over someone or something. □ *We used to live above a small grocery store.* □ *Now we live over a seamstress.*

LIVE ▸ AFTER
live (on) after someone to outlive someone. □ *Aunt Sarah lived on after Uncle Herman only a short time.* □ *She had hoped to live after him and have some fun.*

LIVE ▸ AMONG
live among someone to live in a community with someone or a community made up of certain people. □ *The anthropologist lived among the small tribe for two years.* □ *They lived among the Jivaro Indians for a brief period.*

LIVE ▸ APART
live apart (from someone) to live separated from a person whom one might be expected to live with. □ *John lives apart from his wife, who has a job in another city.* □ *He lives apart, but they are still married.*

LIVE ▸ BEYOND
live beyond one's means to live in conditions that are more than one can afford. □ *We just cannot continue to live beyond our means.* □ *Andy is still trying to live beyond his means.*

LIVE ▸ BY
live by one's wits to survive by one's cleverness. □ *He was orphaned at an early age and learned to live by his wits in the streets of the town.* □ *It is amazing how such a young boy can live by his wits.*

live by something **1.** to live near something. □ *We live by a lovely park that is filled with children in the summer.* □ *I would love to live by the sea.* **2.** to survive by doing or using something in particular. □ *She lives by her wits.* □ *We live by the skills that we have—and hard work, of course.*

LIVE ▸ DOWN
live something down to overcome some embarrassing or troublesome problem or event. □ *It was so embarrassing! I will never live it down.* 🅃 *I will never live down this incident.*

LIVE ▸ FOR
live for someone or something **1.** to exist for the benefit of someone or something. □ *She just lives for her children.* □ *Roger lives for his work.* **2.** to exist to enjoy someone or something. □ *She lives for her vacations in Acapulco.* □ *Sam loves his grandchildren. He just lives for their visits.*

live for the moment to live only for the pleasures of the present time without planning for the future. □ *You need to make plans for your future. You cannot live just for the moment!* □ *He lives only for the moment.*

LIVE ▸ FROM
live from day to day to survive one day at a time with no plans or possibilities for the future. □ *The Simpsons just live from day to day. They never plan for the future.* □ *I can't live from day to day. I have to provide for the future.*

live from hand to mouth to live with only enough to eat. □ *Last month was a bad one financially for us. We ended the final week living from hand to mouth.* □ *Fred's family was quite used to living from hand to mouth.*

LIVE ▸ IN
live in hope(s) of something to live with the hope that something will happen. □ *I have been living in hopes that you would come home safely.* □ *Greg lives in hope of winning a million dollars in the lottery.*

live in sin to live with and have sex with someone to whom one is not married.

(Sometimes serious and sometimes jocular.) □ *Would you like to get married, or would you prefer that we live in sin for a few more years?* □ *Let's live in sin. There's no risk of divorce.*

live in something to dwell within something or some place. □ *They live in the village.* □ *She lives in a large house in the country.* [A] *This house has a nice, lived-in look.*

live in the past to live with past memories without participating in the present or planning for the future. □ *You are just living in the past. Join us in the twentieth century.* □ *Living in the past has its advantages.*

live in the present to experience contemporary events and not be dominated by events of the past or planning for the future. □ *Forget the past; live in the present.* □ *It was no longer possible to get Uncle Herman to live in the present.*

live in (with someone) to live in a residence that one might be expected only to visit rather than reside in. (Said of servants and lovers.) □ *Their maid lives in with them.* □ *She lives in.* [A] *We cannot afford a live-in maid.* [N] *Is Bill her live-in?*

LIVE ▸ OFF

live high off the hog AND **live high on the hog** to live and eat very well. (Folksy or colloquial.) □ *They have been living rather high off the hog in the last few months. Where do they get their money?* □ *How do you manage to live so high on the hog?*

live off campus [for a student] to live in a dwelling that is not part of or regulated by a university. □ *I wanted to live off campus this year, but my parents refused.* □ *Most students want to live off campus in their third year.*

live off (of) someone or something to obtain one's living or means of survival from someone or something. (The *of* is colloquial.) □ *You can't live off your uncle all your life!* □ *I manage to live off of my salary.*

live off the fat of the land to live by eating of the rich harvest of good farmland. □ *We lived off the fat of the land until the horrible drought that started three years ago.* □ *I have always wanted to settle down on a nice farm and live off the fat of the land.*

live off the land to live by eating only the food that one produces from the land; to survive by gathering or stealing food, fruits, berries, eggs, etc., while traveling through the countryside. □ *We lived off the land for a few years when we first started out farming.* □ *The unemployed wandered about, living off the land.*

LIVE ▸ ON

live high on the hog See *live high off the hog* under *LIVE ▸ OFF.*

live on to continue to live, especially after death was thought to be certain. □ *She lived on for many years after the diagnosis.* □ *Uncle Herman lived on for a very long time.*

live (on) after someone See under *LIVE ▸ AFTER.*

live on (after someone or something) to be remembered long after someone or something might otherwise be forgotten or dead, in the case of persons. □ *His good works will live on long after him.* □ *Fears of war will live on after the actual conflict.* □ *I hope my memory lives on.*

live on borrowed time to exist only with good fortune; to live on when death was expected. □ *The doctors told him he was living on borrowed time.* □ *You are living on borrowed time, so make the best of it.*

live on one's own to live independently, in a separate dwelling. □ *I moved out of my parents' house because I wanted to live on my own for a while.* □ *It's time you were out living on your own.*

live on something to live on a specific amount of money; to manage to live on a specific amount of money. □ *Can you live on only that much money?* □ *I can live on a very small amount of money.*

LIVE ▸ OUT

live out of a suitcase to live temporarily, as a traveler, in many places without ever unpacking. □ *I really can't stand to live out of a suitcase.* □ *I lived out of a suitcase for months at a time when I traveled for the company.*

live out of cans to eat only canned food. □ *You have to have some fresh fruit and vegetables. You can't just live out of cans.* □ *We lived out of cans for the entire camping trip.*

live out one's days AND **live out one's life** to live for the remainder of one's life. □ *Where do you plan to live out your days?* □ *I will live out my life in sunny Florida.*

live out something to act out something such as one's fantasies. □ *She tried to live out a strange dream that she kept having.* □ *He has a tendency to try to live out his fantasies.*

LIVE ▸ OVER

live over someone or something See under *LIVE ▸ ABOVE.*

live something over to go back and live a part of one's life again in order to do things differently. □ *I wish I could go back and live those days over again. Boy, would I do things differently!* □ *I would like to live that period of my life over again.*

LIVE ▸ THROUGH

live through something to endure something; to survive an unpleasant or dangerous time of one's life. □ *I almost did not live through the operation.* □ *I know I can't live through another attack.*

LIVE ▸ TO

live to do something **1.** to survive long enough to do something. □ *I just hope I live to see them get married and have children.* □ *Bill wants to live to see the turn of the century.* **2.** to exist only to do something. □ *He lives to work.* □ *One shouldn't live to eat.*

live to the (ripe old) age of something to survive to a specific [advanced] age. (Cliché.) □ *Sally's aunt lived to the ripe old age of one hundred.* □ *Ken lived to the age of sixty-two.*

LIVE ▸ TOGETHER

live together **1.** [for two people] to dwell in the same place. □ *I live together with my sister in the house my parents left us.* □ *Henry and Jill live together in their parents' house.* **2.** [for two people, male and female] to dwell together unmarried, having sex. □ *I heard that Sally and Sam are living together.* □ *They are living together and may get married.*

live (together) with someone See under *LIVE ▸ WITH.*

LIVE ▸ UNDER

live under someone or something to dwell directly beneath someone or something. □ *We live under the Johnsons. They are fairly quiet.* □ *We lived under a law firm for a few years.*

live under something to exist under some kind of worry or threat. □ *I can't continue to live under the threat of bankruptcy all the time.* □ *It is hard to live under the worry of another war.*

live under the same roof with someone to share a dwelling with someone. (Implies living in close harmony, as with husband and wife.) □ *I don't think I can go on living under the same roof with her.* □ *She was quite happy to live under the same roof with him.*

LIVE ▸ UP

live it up to have a good time; to enjoy oneself. □ *I want to have enough money to live it up every now and then.* □ *Let's live it up while we can.*

live up to something to be equal to expectations or goals. □ *The dinner did not live up to my expectations.* □ *We will live up to your first impressions of us.*

LIVE ▸ WITH

live (together) with someone [for someone] to live with someone else. □ *She lives together with her sister in a condo.* □ *He lives with his family.*

live with something to put up with something. (Does not mean "to dwell with.") □ *That is not acceptable. I can't live with that. Please change it.* □ *Mary* *refused to live with the proposed changes.*

LIVE ▸ WITHIN

live within something **1.** to live within certain boundaries. ☐ *Do you think you can live within your space, or are we going to argue over the use of square footage?* ☐ *Ted demanded again that Bill live within his assigned area.* **2.** to keep one's living costs within a certain amount, especially within one's budget, means, etc. ☐ *Please try to live within your budget.* ☐ *You must learn to live within your means.*

LIVE ▸ WITHOUT

live without something to survive, lacking something. ☐ *I just know I can't live without my car.* ☐ *I am sure we can live without vegetables for a day or two.*

LIVEN ▸ UP

liven something up to make something more lively or less dull. ☐ *Some singing might liven things up a bit.* 🅃 *The songs livened up the evening.*

LOAD ▸ DOWN

load someone or something down (with someone or something) to burden someone or something with someone or something. (*Someone* includes *oneself*.) ☐ *Please don't load me down with all your relatives.* ☐ *Load Ted down with the packages. He's strong.* 🅃 *Don't load down my car with too many people.* ☐ *Tom loaded himself down with work every weekend.*

LOAD ▸ INTO

load into something [for people] to get into something. ☐ *Everyone loaded into the bus, and we set off for Denver.* ☐ *The kids all loaded into the station wagon for the trip.*

load someone or something into something to put someone or something into something. ☐ *Load all the boxes into the truck.* ☐ *Would you load the dishes into the dishwasher?* ☐ *Let's load the kids into the car and go to the zoo.*

LOAD ▸ ONTO

load something onto someone or something to lift something onto someone or something. ☐ *We loaded the trunk onto Sam, and he carried it up the stairs into the house.* ☐ *Please help me load the boxes onto the cart.*

LOAD ▸ UP

load someone or something up (with someone or something) to burden someone or something to the maximum with someone or something. (*Someone* includes *oneself*.) ☐ *I loaded her up with a number of books on investments, so she could learn what to do with her money.* 🅃 *Don't load up your shelves with books you will never look at.* ☐ *She loaded her car up with people and took off for the weekend.* ☐ *Don't load yourself up with debt.*

load up (with something) to take or accumulate a lot of something. ☐ *Don't load up with cheap souvenirs. Save your money.* ☐ *Whenever I get into a used bookstore, I load up.*

LOAD ▸ WITH

load something with something to burden something with something; to put a lot of something onto or into something. ☐ *Load this box with all the clothing you can get into it.* ☐ *Don't load these drawers with so much stuff.*

LOAF ▸ AROUND

loaf around to waste time; to idle the time away doing almost nothing. ☐ *Every time I see you, you are just loafing around.* ☐ *I enjoy loafing around on the weekend.*

LOAF ▸ AWAY

loaf something away to waste away a period of time. ☐ *You have loafed the entire day away!* 🅃 *He loafed away the entire day.*

LOAN ▸ TO

loan something to someone to lend something to someone. (Considered to be an error for *lend*. Colloquial.) ☐ *Can you loan a few bucks to Sam and me?* ☐ *I will not loan anything to you.*

LOB ▸ AT

lob something at someone or something to throw or toss something at someone or something. ☐ *Who lobbed this thing* *at me?* □ *They lobbed a stone at the cat, but that only made it mad.* □ *Ted lobbed a stone at the window.*

LOBBY ▸ AGAINST

lobby against something to solicit support against something, such as a piece of legislation or a government regulation. □ *We sent a lot of lawyers to the state capital to lobby against the bill, but it passed anyway.* □ *They lobbied against the tax increase.*

LOBBY ▸ FOR

lobby for something to solicit support for something among the members of a voting body, such as the Congress. □ *Tom is always lobbying for some bill or other.* □ *The manufacturers lobbied for tax relief.*

LOCK ▸ AWAY

lock someone or something away to put someone or something away in a locked container or space. □ *You will have to lock all the medications away when the grandchildren come to visit.* 🅃 *They locked away some cash for a rainy day.* □ *They locked it away.*

LOCK ▸ IN

lock in on someone or something AND **lock on(to) someone or something** to focus on someone or something; to fix some kind of electronic sensing device on someone or something. □ *The enemy pilot was flying just ahead of us. Aiming the laser, we locked in on him and shot him down.* □ *We locked onto the satellite and got an excellent TV picture.*

lock someone or something (up) in (something) to fasten the opening to something so someone, a group, or some creature cannot get out. (*Someone* includes *oneself*.) □ *Take Chuck and lock him up in the cell.* 🅃 *Lock up Chuck and throw away the key.* □ *Don't lock me in there!* □ *Don't lock me up!* 🄰 *The accidentally locked-in guard pounded on the door loudly.* □ *Jane locked herself up in her inner office.*

lock something in to take action to fix a rate or price at a certain figure. □ *I can lock the price in for a week.* 🅃 *If you put down a deposit now, I can lock in the price for you for a week.*

LOCK ▸ ON

lock on(to) someone or something See *lock in on someone or something* under *LOCK ▸ IN.*

LOCK ▸ ONTO

lock something onto someone or something to attach or fix something onto someone or something. □ *The cop locked the handcuffs onto the mugger and led him away.* □ *Andy locked his bicycle onto the signpost.*

LOCK ▸ ON(TO)

lock on(to someone or something) **1.** to fasten or grab onto someone or something. □ *She locked onto the child and wouldn't leave his side for an instant.* □ *I saw the thing I wanted and locked on.* **2.** to *lock in on someone or something,* as with tuning in someone or something. □ *I locked onto a ham radio operator in Argentina.* □ *Lock onto the strongest signal you can pick up.*

LOCK ▸ OUT

lock someone or something out (of something) to lock something to prevent someone or something from getting into it. (*Someone* includes *oneself*. The *of*-phrase is paraphrased with a *from*-phrase when the particle is transposed. See the 🄵 example.) □ *Someone locked me out of my office.* 🅃 *Who locked out Fred?* 🄵 *Who locked out Fred from the office?* □ *Don't lock me out!* 🄰 *On the front steps we discovered a very cold, locked-out little girl who had forgotten her key.* □ *Careful, Sally! You'll lock yourself out!*

LOCK ▸ UP

lock someone or something (up) in something See under *LOCK ▸ IN.*

lock someone or something up (somewhere) to lock someone or something within something or some place. (*Someone* includes *oneself*.) □ *The captain ordered the sailor locked up in the brig until the ship got into port.* 🅃 *The sheriff locked up the crook in a cell.* □ *Don't lock me up.* □ *She locked herself* *up in her office where no one could get to her.*

LOCK ▸ WITH

lock horns with someone to come into conflict with someone or something. (Figurative.) □ *Don't lock horns with me! I'll beat you in any conflict.* □ *There is no point in locking horns with your teacher.*

LODGE ▸ AGAINST

lodge something against someone to place a charge against someone. □ *The neighbors lodged a complaint against us for parking on their grass.* □ *I want to lodge an assault charge against Max.*

lodge something against something to place or prop something against something. □ *We lodged the chest against the door, making it difficult or impossible to open.* □ *Let's lodge the stone against the side of the barn to help support it.*

LODGE ▸ IN

lodge something in something to get something stuck in something or some place. □ *She lodged a fish bone in her throat.* □ *He lodged a screwdriver in the machine's gears by accident.*

LODGE ▸ WITH

lodge someone with someone to have someone stay with someone as a guest. □ *We lodged the visitor with George for the weekend.* □ *Would it be possible for us to lodge Mary with you?*

lodge with someone to stay or reside with someone. □ *I lodged with my cousin while I was in Omaha.* □ *Tricia plans to lodge with us while she is here.*

LOG ▸ FOR

log someone for something **1.** to schedule someone for something. □ *I am going to log you for sentry duty on the weekends.* □ *We will have to log Bill for service as a parking attendant.* **2.** to make a note in a ship's log about someone's bad behavior. □ *The captain logged the first mate for the navigation error.* □ *I will have to log you for that.*

LOG ▸ OFF

log off AND **log out** to record one's exit from a computer system. (This action may be recorded, or logged, automatically in the computer's memory.) □ *I closed my files and logged off.* □ *What time did you log out?*

log someone off AND **log someone out** [for someone] to cause someone to exit from a computer system. (This exit may be recorded, or logged, automatically in the computer's memory. *Someone* includes *oneself*.) □ *Mary had to rush off to an appointment, so I logged her off.* □ *Do I have to log you out again?* □ *Mary will log herself off when she finishes this stuff.*

LOG ▸ ON

log on to attach oneself up to use a computer system. (This action may be recorded, or logged, automatically in the computer's memory.) □ *What time did you log on to the system this morning?* □ *I always log on before I get my first cup of coffee.*

log someone on (to something) to attach someone to a computer system. (*Someone* includes *oneself*. This action may be recorded, or logged, automatically in the computer's memory.) □ *I will log you on to the system if you forgot how to do it.* 🆃 *I will log on Jill, who is late.* □ *I'm tired of logging her on.* □ *I can't help you. You will have to log yourself on.*

LOG ▸ OUT

log out See *log out* under *LOG ▸ OFF.*

log someone out See *log someone off* under *LOG ▸ OFF.*

LOG ▸ UP

log something up to record an amount of something. □ *The ship logged many nautical miles up on its last voyage.* 🆃 *It logged up a lot of miles.* □ *The plane had logged only a few miles before it needed servicing.* □ *I logged up a lot of overtime last week.*

LOITER ▸ AROUND

loiter around to idle somewhere; to hang around. □ *Stop loitering around! Get going!* □ *The kids were loitering around for most of the summer.*

LOITER ▸ AWAY

loiter something away to idle away a period of time. □ *Those boys will loiter half their lives away.* T *They loitered away their summer vacation.*

LOITER ▸ OVER

loiter over something to dawdle or linger over something. □ *Don't loiter over your meal. I want to start the dishwasher.* □ *I wish you wouldn't loiter over your chores.*

LOLL ▸ ABOUT

loll about (some place) to lie, lounge, or "droop" some place. □ *The tired travelers lolled about all over the hotel lobby until their rooms were ready.* □ *They were still lolling about at three in the afternoon.*

LOLL ▸ AROUND

loll around to roll, flop, or hang around. □ *The dog's tongue lolled around as it rolled on its back, trying to keep cool.* □ *Stop lolling around and get to work.*

LOLL ▸ BACK

loll back [for a head] to fall or droop backwards. □ *As he passed out, his head lolled back and struck the corner of the table.* □ *Her head lolled back and suddenly she was fast asleep.*

LOLL ▸ OUT

loll out [for a tongue] to hang or flop out. □ *The dog's tongue lolled out as it lay sleeping.* □ *Since the dog's tongue lolled out every time it opened its mouth, it is a wonder it didn't bite it when it closed its mouth.*

LONG ▸ FOR

long for someone or something to desire or pine for someone or something. □ *She is longing for her old friends.* □ *Walter longed for his hometown in the mountains.*

LOOK ▸ ABOUT

look about (for someone or something) to try to locate someone or something. □ *I have to look about for someone to serve as a baby-sitter.* □ *I don't see it here. I'll have to look about.*

LOOK ▸ AFTER

look after someone or something to take care of someone or something. □ *Please look after my little boy.* □ *Will you look after my cat while I'm away?* □ *Do you want me to look after your car?*

LOOK ▸ AHEAD

look ahead to something to try to foresee something; to think into the future about something. □ *She looked ahead to a bright future in sales.* □ *I look ahead to a new job when I graduate.*

LOOK ▸ ALIKE

look alike to appear similar. □ *All these cars look alike these days.* □ *The twins look alike and not many people can tell them apart.* N *They say that everyone has a look-alike somewhere.*

LOOK ▸ AROUND

look around (at something) to investigate something; to study something visually. □ *Go into the room and look around at the way they have fixed it up.* □ *I went in and looked around.*

look around for someone or something to seek someone or something out. □ *Look around for Ted and tell him to come home.* □ *I looked around for the can opener, but it's not there.*

look around some place to investigate some place. □ *Look around in the kitchen. You will find what you want.* □ *Tell her to look around in the attic. Maybe the camping gear is there.*

LOOK ▸ ASIDE

look aside to look to one side; to turn one's head aside so as not to see someone or something. □ *As I approached, he looked aside, pretending not to recognize me.* □ *She looked aside, hoping I wouldn't see her.*

LOOK ▸ ASKANCE

look askance at someone or something to be surprised or shocked at someone or something. □ *The teacher looked askance at the student who had acted so rudely.* □ *Everyone had looked askance at her efforts as an artist.*

LOOK ▶ AT

look at someone cross-eyed to [even] appear to question, threaten, or mock someone. (Idiomatic. Often in the negative.) ☐ *You had better be on your best behavior around Tony. Don't even look at him cross-eyed!* ☐ *If you so much as look at me cross-eyed, I will send you to your room.*

look at someone or something to examine someone or something. ☐ *The doctor needs to look at the wound before you leave.* ☐ *You had better have the doctor look at you. That is a nasty wound.*

look daggers at someone to display anger at someone, as evidenced by one's gaze. ☐ *I knew she was mad from the way she was looking daggers at me.* ☐ *Mary was looking daggers at Tom throughout the evening.*

LOOK ▶ AWAY

look away (from someone or something) to turn one's gaze away from someone. ☐ *She looked away from him, not wishing her eyes to give away her true feelings.* ☐ *In embarrassment, she looked away.*

LOOK ▶ BACK

look back (at someone or something) AND **look back (on someone or something)** **1.** to gaze back and try to get a view of someone or something. ☐ *She looked back at the city and whispered a good-bye to everything she had ever cared for.* ☐ *I went away and never looked back.* **2.** to think about someone or something in the past. ☐ *When I look back on Frank, I do remember his strange manner, come to think of it.* ☐ *When I look back, I am amazed at all I have accomplished.*

look back (on someone or something) See the previous entry.

LOOK ▶ BEFORE

look before you leap to make a visual check before doing something. (Cliché. Rarely literal.) ☐ *You should have investigated the company before you invested. Always look before you leap.* ☐ *Look before you leap and you won't get into trouble.*

LOOK ▶ BEYOND

look beyond someone or something **1.** to try to see to a point farther than someone or something. ☐ *Look beyond Claire at the forest in the distance.* ☐ *Look beyond the house and see what you can spot in the trees behind it.* **2.** to try to think or plan further than someone or something. (Figurative.) ☐ *Sally will be gone soon. Look beyond Sally and decide whom you want to hire.* ☐ *Look beyond Tom. Think about how you will deal with the next person who has Tom's job.*

LOOK ▶ DOWN

look down (at someone or something) **1.** to turn one's gaze downward at someone or something. ☐ *She looked down at me and giggled at the awkward position I was in.* ☐ *She looked down and burst into laughter.* **2.** AND **look down on someone or something** to view someone or something as lowly or unworthy. ☐ *She looked down at all the waiters and treated them badly.* ☐ *They looked down on our humble food.*

look down on someone or something See under *look down (at someone or something).*

look down one's nose at someone or something to hold someone or something to be beneath one; to consider someone or something lowly and unworthy. ☐ *Don't look down your nose at me like that!* ☐ *Ted looked down his nose at the humble food.*

LOOK ▶ FOR

look for someone or something to seek someone or something. ☐ *I am looking for Mr. William Wilson. Do you know where he lives?* ☐ *I am looking for the address of Bill Wilson.*

look for someone or something high and low to search everywhere for someone or something. ☐ *Where were you? I looked for you high and low.* ☐ *I looked for my passport high and low.*

look for trouble to seek out trouble; to try to cause trouble. (Usually with the present participle.) □ *What are you doing here? Are you looking for trouble?* □ *Somebody around here is looking for trouble.*

LOOK ▸ FORWARD

look forward to something to anticipate something eagerly. □ *I look forward to seeing you again in the near future.* □ *We all look forward to your arrival.*

LOOK ▸ IN

look a gift horse in the mouth to be ungrateful to someone who gives you something; to treat someone who gives you a gift badly. (Usually negative.) □ *Never look a gift horse in the mouth.* □ *I advise you not to look a gift horse in the mouth.*

look in (on someone or something) to check on someone or something. □ *I will look in on her from time to time.* □ *I looked in and everything was all right.*

look someone in the eye to face someone forthrightly; to stare right into someone's eyes. □ *She looked him in the eye and told him to get out.* □ *Why don't you look me in the eye and say that?*

look someone in the face to face toward someone when speaking or listening; to face someone while being scolded. □ *Look me in the face when you speak to me!* □ *He looked her right in the face and told her what he thought of her.*

LOOK ▸ INTO

look into something **1.** to gaze into the inside of something. □ *Look into the box and make sure you've gotten everything out of it.* □ *Look into the camera's viewfinder at the little red light.* **2.** to investigate something. □ *I will look into this matter and see what I can do about it.* □ *Please ask the manager to look into it.*

LOOK ▸ LIKE

look like a million dollars to look very, very good. (Colloquial.) □ *Wow! You look like a million dollars!* □ *This room looks like a million dollars. What did you do to it?*

look like someone or something to resemble someone or something. □ *You look like my cousin Fred.* □ *This one looks like an apple.*

LOOK ▸ ON

See also under *LOOK ▸ (UP)ON; LOOK ▸ ON(TO).*

look on to be a spectator. □ *The beating took place while a policeman looked on.* □ *While the kittens played, the mother cat looked on contentedly.*

look on (with someone) to share and read from someone else's notes, paper, book, music, etc. □ *I don't have a copy of the notice, but I will look on with Carlo.* □ *Carla has a copy of the music. She doesn't mind if I look on.*

LOOK ▸ ON(TO)

look (out) on(to) something [for something] to face onto something or some place. □ *The balcony looks out onto the meadow.* □ *My window looks onto the street.*

LOOK ▸ OUT

look out to be careful; to think and move fast because something dangerous is about to harm one. (Usually a command.) □ *Look out! Don't trip over that board!* □ *Look out!*

look out for someone or something **1.** to be watchful for the appearance of someone or something. □ *Look out for Sam. He is due any minute.* □ *Look out for the bus. We don't want to miss it.* Ⓝ *The lookout warned Max when the police arrived.* **2.** to be alert to the danger posed by someone or something. □ *Look out for that last step. It's loose.* □ *Look out for that truck!*

look out (of) something to gaze outward from inside something. (The *of* is colloquial.) □ *Look out of the window and see if it is raining.* □ *I looked out of the door to see what the weather was like.*

look (out) on(to) something See under *LOOK ▸ ON(TO).*

LOOK ▸ OVER

look someone or something over to examine someone or something. (*Someone* includes *oneself*.) □ *I think you had better have the doctor look you over.* 🅃 *Please look over these papers.* □ *They looked themselves over and declared themselves beautiful.*

LOOK ▸ THROUGH

look through something **1.** to gaze through something. □ *Look through the window at what the neighbors are doing.* □ *Look through the binoculars and see if you can get a better view.* **2.** to examine the parts, pages, samples, etc., of something. □ *Look through this report and see what you make of it.* □ *I will look through it when I have time.*

LOOK ▸ TO

look to someone or something (for something) to expect to get something from someone or something. □ *I always look to my uncle for financial help in times like these.* □ *We look to the government to get us out of trouble.* □ *When everyone looks to the government for money, we have a real problem.*

LOOK ▸ TOWARD

look toward someone or something to face in the direction of someone or something. □ *Look toward Sarah and see where she is standing. Isn't that a lovely garden?* □ *Look toward the sea and see what a sunset is meant to look like.*

LOOK ▸ UP

look someone or something up **1.** to seek someone, a group, or something out. □ *I lost track of Sally. I'll try to look her up and get in touch with her.* 🅃 *I am going to look up an old friend when I am in Chicago.* □ *I am going to look that old gang up.* 🅃 *Ted came into town and looked up his favorite pizza place.* **2.** to seek information about someone or something in a book or listing. (*Someone* includes *oneself*.) □ *I don't recognize his name. I'll look him up and see what I can find.* 🅃 *I'll look up this person in a reference book.* 🅃 *Can I use the directory to look up an address?* □ *She looked herself up in the telephone book to make sure her name was spelled correctly.*

look up to show promise of improving. □ *My prospects for a job are looking up.* □ *Conditions are looking up.*

look up and down (for someone or something) to look everywhere for someone or something. □ *Where is Kelly? I looked up and down for her.* □ *I can't find her. I looked up and down, but no Kelly.*

look up and down something to gaze up and then down something, such as a street. □ *We looked up and down the street and saw no cars, no houses, and no people.* □ *Mary looked up and down the highway, but she could not find her lost hubcap.*

look up at someone or something to raise one's gaze to someone or something. □ *Would you please look up at me while I am talking to you? I hate to be ignored.* □ *Look up at the top of that building.*

look up (from something) to gaze upwards; to stop reading or working and lift one's gaze upward. □ *She looked up from her reading and spoke to us.* □ *Mary looked up as we came into the room.*

look up to someone to admire someone. □ *We all look up to Roger. He's authoritative but kind.* □ *I am glad they look up to me.*

LOOK ▸ (UP)ON

look (up)on someone or something as something to view someone or something as something; to consider someone or something to be something. □ *I look upon Todd as a fine and helpful guy.* □ *I look on these requests as an annoyance.*

look (up)on someone or something with something to view someone or something with an attitude, such as scorn, favor, anger, disgust, etc. □ *She looked upon all of us with scorn.* □ *Bill looked on the food set before him with disgust.*

LOOM ▸ OUT

loom out of something to appear to come out of or penetrate something. □ *A truck suddenly loomed out of the fog* *and just missed hitting us.* □ *A tall building loomed out of the mists.*

LOOM ▸ UP

loom up to appear to rise up [from somewhere]; to take form or definition, usually threatening to some degree. □ *A great city loomed up in the distance. It looked threatening in the dusky light.* □ *A ghost loomed up, but we paid no attention, since it had to be a joke.* □ *The recession loomed up and the stock market reacted.*

LOOSEN ▸ UP

loosen someone or something up **1.** to make someone's muscles and joints move more freely by exercising them. (*Someone* includes *oneself.*) □ *The exercise loosened me up quite nicely.* 🅃 *It loosened up my legs.* □ *I have to do some exercises to loosen myself up.* **2.** to make someone or a group more relaxed and friendly. (*Someone* includes *oneself.*) □ *I told a little joke to loosen the audience up.* 🅃 *I loosened up the audience with a joke.* □ *Loosen yourself up. Relax and try to enjoy people.*

loosen something up to make something less tight. □ *Loosen the freshly oiled hinges up by swinging the door back and forth.* 🅃 *Try to loosen up those hinges.*

loosen up to become loose or relaxed. □ *Loosen up. Relax.* □ *We tried to get Mary to loosen up, but she did not respond.*

LOP ▸ OFF

lop something off ((of) something) to chop or cut something off something. (The *of*-phrase is paraphrased with a *from*-phrase when the particle is transposed. See the 🄵 example. The *of* is colloquial.) □ *Lop that long branch off the tree before you put the saw away, will you?* 🅃 *Please lop off that branch.* 🄵 *Please lop off the dead branch from the other side of the tree.* □ *I'll lop it off.*

LOPE ▸ ALONG

lope along to move along, bounding. □ *The dog loped along at a very even pace, traveling to the place where he was born.* □ *The horses loped along, eager to get home.*

LORD ▸ OVER

lord (it) over someone to dominate someone; to act superior to someone. □ *You shouldn't lord it over your fellow workers.* □ *Please don't lord over me all the time!*

LOSE ▸ ABOUT

lose sleep about someone or something See *lose sleep over someone or something* under *LOSE ▸ OVER.*

LOSE ▸ AT

lose at something to be defeated at a particular game or activity. □ *We lost at basketball but we won at football this weekend.* □ *I hate to lose at checkers.*

lose something at something to lose a wager at playing something or at gambling. □ *I lost a fortune at gambling.* □ *We lost all our money at dice.*

LOSE ▸ BY

lose by something to be defeated by a certain amount. □ *Our team lost by ten points.* □ *I only lost by a few points.*

LOSE ▸ IN

See *be lost in something* under *BE ▸ IN.*

lose oneself in someone or something to be thoroughly absorbed in someone or something; to become engrossed in someone or something. □ *Frank loses himself in his children when he is at home.* □ *When I lose myself in my work, time just rushes by.* □ *Jane had a tendency to lose herself in thought during warm weather.*

lose something in something to misplace something in something. □ *I lost my wallet in the barn.* □ *Did someone lose something in the dining room?*

LOSE ▸ OF

lose count of someone or something to fail to be able to count someone or something, because there are so many. □ *I have lost count of the people who have asked that question.* □ *I am afraid I have lost count of all the times we have run out of money.*

lose sight of someone or something **1.** to have one's vision of someone or something fade because of distance or an obstruction. ☐ *I lost sight of Alice as she walked into the distance.* ☐ *We lost sight of the ship as it sailed out of the harbor.* **2.** to forget to consider someone or something. ☐ *Don't lose sight of Alice and her basic contributions.* ☐ *Don't lose sight of the basic value of the land on which the house sits.*

lose the use of something to be deprived of the use of something. ☐ *After the accident, I lost the use of my left arm for a few days.* ☐ *Andy lost the use of the car for a week.*

lose trace of someone or something to fail to maintain a way of finding someone or something. (A little folksy.) ☐ *I lost trace of Walter after we left high school.* ☐ *I lost trace of the stock certificates after about twenty years.*

lose track of someone or something to misplace someone or something; to fail to keep an accounting of someone or something. ☐ *I lost track of Sam years ago.* ☐ *I lost track of my glasses.* ☐ *I lost track of my expenditures, and some of my checks bounced.*

LOSE ▸ ON

See *be lost on someone* under *BE ▸ ON.*

lose money on something to have a net loss on something, such as an investment. ☐ *I lost thousands on that deal.* ☐ *I don't want to lose money on any investment.*

lose one's hold on someone or something AND **lose one's grip on someone or something** **1.** to relax one's handhold on someone or something. ☐ *I lost my hold on the child, and she nearly slipped away.* ☐ *She lost her grip on the bag of jewels and it fell overboard.* **2.** to give up control over someone or something. ☐ *The manager lost her hold on her employees and was fired.* ☐ *Fred is losing his grip on his workers.*

LOSE ▸ OUT

lose out to lose in competition; to lose one's expected reward. ☐ *Our team lost out because our quarterback broke his leg.* ☐ *I ran my best race, but I still lost out.* ☐ *I was hoping for a promotion, but I lost out because of my bad attendance record.*

lose out (on something) to miss enjoying something; to miss participating in something. ☐ *I would hate to lose out on all the fun.* ☐ *We'll lose out if we don't get there on time.*

lose out to someone or something to lose in a competition to someone or something. ☐ *I didn't want to lose out to the other guys.* ☐ *Our firm lost out to the lowest bidder.*

LOSE ▸ OVER

lose one's head over someone or something to do something foolish because of someone or something; to act foolishly over someone or something. ☐ *Don't lose your head over Walter. He isn't worth it.* ☐ *You shouldn't lose your head over your success. It may not last.*

lose one's hold over someone or something to lose one's dominance over someone or something. ☐ *She is fearful of losing her hold over her children.* ☐ *He is losing his hold over his empire.*

lose sleep over someone or something AND **lose sleep about someone or something** to worry about someone or something a lot, sometimes when one should be sleeping. ☐ *Yes, Kelly is in a little bit of trouble, but I'm not going to lose any sleep over her.* ☐ *Don't lose any sleep over the matter.* ☐ *I refuse to lose sleep about it.*

LOSE ▸ TO

lose ground to someone or something to lose out to someone or something. ☐ *I am losing ground to Wendy in the sales contest.* ☐ *We were losing ground to the opposite team in our quest for the trophy.*

lose something to someone to yield or give up something in defeat to someone. ☐ *We lost the case to the opposing lawyers.* ☐ *Mary lost her title to the runner-up.*

lose to someone or something to be defeated by someone or something. ☐ *I lost to Wendy in the sales contest.* ☐ *Our team lost to the Adamsville Raiders for the seventh year in a row.*

LOSE ▶ WITH

lose contact with someone or something AND **lose touch with someone or something** [for communication with someone or a group] to fail or fade away; to let one's friendship or relationship with someone or a group lapse. □ *I hope I don't lose contact with you.* □ *I don't want to lose touch with my old friends.* □ *I have lost contact with Ed. I haven't seen him in ages.*

lose touch with someone See the previous entry.

LOSE ▶ WITHOUT

See *be lost without someone or something* under *BE ▶ WITHOUT.*

LOST ▶ IN

See *be lost in something* under *BE ▶ IN.*

LOST ▶ ON

See *be lost on someone* under *BE ▶ ON.*

LOST ▶ WITHOUT

See *be lost without someone or something* under *BE ▶ WITHOUT.*

LOUNGE ▶ AROUND

lounge around (some place) to lie about some place. □ *I am going to lounge around the house this morning.* □ *Don't lounge around all day.*

LOUSE ▶ UP

louse someone or something up to ruin something; to *mess someone or something up.* (Slang. *Someone* includes *oneself.*) □ *You really loused me up! You got me in a real mess!* [T] *Who loused up my scheme?* [A] *I don't know what to do with a loused-up stereo.* □ *I really loused myself up in French class.*

LOWER ▶ ON

lower the boom on someone to become stern or severe with someone; to become more strict with someone. (See also *crack down (on someone or something).*) □ *The boss is going to lower the boom on those people who have been taking long lunch hours.* □ *They finally lowered the boom on shoplifters.*

LUCK ▶ INTO

luck into something to find something by luck; to get involved in something by luck. □ *I lucked into this apartment on the very day I started looking.* □ *We lucked into a good deal on a used car.* □ *I lucked into this job when I answered a want ad.*

LUCK ▶ OUT

luck out (of something) to get out of something by luck alone. (Slang.) □ *I lucked out of taking a driving test. I only had to pass a vision test to get my license.* □ *Man, I really lucked out.*

LULL ▶ INTO

lull someone into something to calm someone into a deceptive sense of something, such as well-being, safety, etc. (*Someone* includes *oneself.*) □ *The prosperous economic conditions lulled investors into a false sense of security.* □ *Tom lulled himself into a false sense of security.*

LULL ▶ TO

lull someone or something to sleep to quiet and comfort someone or some creature to sleep. □ *The sound of the waves lulled me to sleep.* □ *The dog's heartbeat lulled her puppies to sleep.*

LUMBER ▶ ALONG

lumber along to lope or walk along heavily and awkwardly. □ *The horses were lumbering along very slowly because they were tired out.* □ *They were lumbering along, hoping to get there on time.*

LUMBER ▶ OFF

lumber off to move or lope away heavily and awkwardly. □ *The angry farmer lumbered off, and we left in a hurry.* □ *He lumbered off, leaving us there alone.*

LUMP ▶ TOGETHER

lump someone and someone else or something and something else together to classify people or things as members of the same category. □ *You just can't lump Bill and Ted together. They are totally different kinds of people.* □ *I tend to lump apples and oranges together.*

LUNCH ▶ OFF

lunch off something to make a lunch by eating something or part of something. □ *We will be able to lunch off the leftover turkey for days!* □ *I can lunch off what is in the refrigerator. Don't worry about me.*

LUNCH ▶ OUT

lunch out to eat lunch away from one's home or away from one's place of work. □ *I think I'll lunch out today. I'm tired of carrying lunches.* □ *I want to lunch out today.*

LUNGE ▶ AT

lunge at someone or something to jump or dive at someone or something. □ *The dog lunged at the man, but he got out of the way without getting bitten.* □ *The dog lunged at the bicycle.*

LUNGE ▶ FOR

lunge for someone or something to charge at someone or something; to attack someone or something. □ *The mugger lunged for her, but she dodged him.* □ *Ted lunged for the door, but Bill beat him to it.*

LURCH ▶ AT

lurch at someone or something AND **lurch toward someone or something** to sway or turn quickly toward someone or something. □ *Todd lurched at the door and got it open just as the guard saw him.* □ *Bill lurched toward the ship's rail and hung on.*

LURCH ▶ FORWARD

lurch forward to jerk or sway forward. □ *The car lurched forward and shook us around.* □ *When the train lurched forward, we were pushed back into our seats.*

LURCH ▶ TOWARD

lurch toward someone or something See under *LURCH ▶ AT.*

LURE ▶ AWAY

lure someone or something away (from someone or something) to entice or draw someone away from someone or something. □ *Do you think we could lure her away from her present employment?* 🅃 *They were not able to lure away many of the employees of the other companies.* □ *They finally managed to lure her away.*

LURE ▶ IN(TO)

lure someone or something in(to something) to entice someone or something into something or a place. □ *The thief tried to lure the tourist into an alley to rob him.* □ *The thief led the tourist to an alley and lured him in.* 🅃 *Using an old trick, the thief lured in the tourist.*

LURK ▶ AROUND

lurk around to slink or sneak around somewhere. □ *Who is that guy lurking around the building?* □ *Stop lurking around.*

LUST ▶ AFTER

lust after someone to desire someone sexually. □ *You could see that Sam was lusting after Sally.* □ *All those guys are just lusting after the girls.*

LUST ▶ FOR

lust for someone to desire someone sexually. □ *They say that Roger lusts for Sue, but I think it's just a rumor.* □ *Roger claims that he does not lust for anyone.*

lust for something to desire something. (Colloquial and jocular.) □ *He says he lusts for a nice cold can of soda pop.* □ *Mary lusts for rich and fattening ice cream.*

LUXURIATE ▶ IN

luxuriate in something to indulge oneself in something; to enjoy the luxury of something. □ *She stood in front of the mirror, luxuriating in her lovely new coat.* □ *They were all luxuriating in their fine new clothes in front of the mirrors.*

M

MAC ▸ OUT

mac out to overeat on MacDonald's Big Mac sandwiches. (Slang.) □ *I just want to get back to the U.S. and mac out.* □ *I mac out every weekend.*

MADE ▸ FOR

See *be made for someone* under *BE ▸ FOR.*

See *be made for something* under *BE ▸ FOR.*

MAIL ▸ FROM

mail something from some place to send something by mail from a particular place. □ *I mailed the check from my office.* □ *I will mail it from the main post office.*

MAIL ▸ TO

mail something to someone to send something to someone by mail. □ *I mailed the check to you yesterday.* □ *I mailed a gift to my niece.*

MAINTAIN ▸ AT

maintain something at something to keep something at a certain level, setting, degree, amount, etc. □ *You must maintain the temperature at 30 degrees Celsius.* □ *We have to maintain the temperature at a very high level.*

MAINTAIN ▸ IN

maintain someone in something to keep someone in a certain style or condition. (*Someone* includes *oneself.*) □ *I insist that you maintain me in the style to which I have become accustomed.* □ *He had hoped to maintain himself in comfort.*

MAJOR ▸ IN

major in something to specialize in a certain subject in college. □ *I majored in history in college.* □ *I want to major in math.*

MAKE ▸ ABOUT

make a big deal about something to make a big event or problem out of something. (Slang.) □ *There is no need to make a big deal about it. I'm sorry.* □ *She made such a big deal about it, you'd have thought somebody died.*

make a (big) stink about someone or something to make trouble about someone or something. (Slang.) □ *Why did you make a big stink about it?* □ *Jim is making a stink about Alice.*

make cracks about someone or something to make jokes or smart remarks about someone or something. (Informal.) □ *Stop making cracks about my cousin.* □ *Ken made a few cracks about the movie.*

make no bones about something to be very specific about something; to spare no words in expressing one's feelings about something. (Informal and idiomatic.) □ *This one is great. Make no bones about it.* □ *She made no bones about the fact that she was unhappy.*

make no mistake about something to be very certain about something. (Folksy and informal.) □ *This is really good soup, make no mistake about it.* □ *Make no mistake about it. She will do an excellent job.*

make something about someone or something to make comments, remarks, a furor, a fuss, etc., about someone or something. □ *Why are you making such a furor about such a minor matter?* □ *You are making too many negative remarks about Sue.*

MAKE ▸ AFTER

make (out) after someone or something to run after someone or something; to start out after someone or something. □ *Paul made out after Fred, who had taken Paul's hat.* □ *The police officer made after the robber.*

MAKE ▸ AGAINST

make something against someone or something to build a legal case, argument, speech, etc., against someone or something. □ *The prosecutor made a strong case against Tim.* □ *I made a strong speech against the proposed legislation.*

MAKE ▸ ALONG

make one's way along something to move along something slowly or carefully. □ *Todd made his way along the slippery walk.* □ *The old man made his way along the street carefully.*

MAKE ▸ AS

make good as something to succeed as something. □ *I hope you make good as a bank teller.* □ *I know you will make good as an accountant.*

MAKE ▸ AT

make a grab at someone or something to grasp at someone or something. □ *Don made a grab at Betsy, but she eluded him.* □ *Kelly made a grab at the ball, but it went on past her.*

make a pass at someone to flirt with or suggest having sex with someone. □ *Can you believe? Larry made a pass at me!* □ *No one ever makes a pass at me.*

make a pass at something **1.** to fly over or close by something. □ *The plane made a pass at the landing field and pulled up at the last minute.* □ *The bird made a pass at me because I got too close to its nest.* **2.** to try to do something. □ *I don't know if I can do it, but I'll make a pass at it.* □ *You did not do a careful job. You only made a pass at it.*

make eyes at someone to flirt with someone. (Idiomatic.) □ *Mother, he's making eyes at me!* □ *Jed tried to make eyes at all the girls.*

make good at something to succeed at a particular task. □ *We all want you to make good at whatever you choose to do.* □ *Mary hopes to make good at her new job.*

make something at someone to make some sign or signal at or to a person. □ *Carlo made a sign at Bill, who seemed to know just what to do.* □ *Jimmy made a face at me!*

MAKE ▸ AWAY

make away with someone or something to take or carry someone or something away. □ *The kidnapper made away with little Jimmy in the dead of night.* □ *The kids made away with all the cookies.*

MAKE ▸ BACK

make one's way back (to something) to work one's way back to something or some place. □ *I made my way back to the little town in the densest fog I have ever seen.* □ *I went for a walk and got lost. It took hours for me to make my way back.*

MAKE ▸ FOR

See *be made for someone* under *BE ▸ FOR*.

See *be made for something* under *BE ▸ FOR*.

make a beeline for someone or something to go straight for someone or something in a hurry. □ *The child made a beeline for her mother.* □ *She came in and made a beeline for the bathroom.*

make a bolt for someone or something to run quickly to or at someone or something. □ *The child came into the room and made a bolt for her mother.* □ *The dog made a bolt for the door.*

make a break for someone or something to run suddenly toward someone or something; to seize an opportunity to run toward someone or something. □ *The crook made a break for the cop in order to get his gun.* □ *Max made a break for the door.*

make a dash for someone or something to run quickly for someone or something. ☐ *Suddenly Max made a dash for Lefty and punched him in the stomach.* ☐ *John made a dash for the bathroom as soon as they arrived home.*

make a name for oneself to become well known because of one's efforts. ☐ *When I grow up, I want to make a name for myself.* ☐ *Tom really made a name for himself in show business.*

make a pitch for someone or something to speak in support of someone or something; to promote someone or something. ☐ *I want to make a pitch for my favorite candidate, Gerald.* ☐ *The announcer was making a pitch for some kind of cereal, so I changed the channel.*

make a play for someone to try to win someone's attention or romantic favor. ☐ *She tried to make a play for him, but he didn't even notice her.* ☐ *Jenny made a play for Tony and was rebuffed.*

make allowances for someone or something to excuse someone or something; to rationalize someone's behavior or some situation. ☐ *Sorry. You will have to make allowances for my cousin. He's from Kansas.* ☐ *Please make allowances for her behavior.*

make amends (to someone) (for someone or something) See under *MAKE ▸ TO.*

make an exception for someone to make a special case for someone; to break a rule or amend a policy for one person only. ☐ *We can't make an exception for anyone.* ☐ *They decided to make an exception for you.*

make application (to someone or something) (for something) See under *MAKE ▸ TO.*

make arrangements (with someone) (for something) See under *MAKE ▸ WITH.*

make change (for someone) (for something) **1.** to return change [coins] for someone to use for some purpose. ☐ *Will you please make change for me for the telephone?* ☐ *I will make change for the telephone for you.* **2.** to return change [coins] to someone for a paper bank note. ☐ *The clerk refused to make change for her for the dollar bill.* ☐ *I will be happy to make change for a ten for you.*

make life miserable for someone to give someone a life of misery. ☐ *This nagging backache is making life miserable for me.* ☐ *I wish you would stop making life miserable for me.*

make (out) for someone or something to run toward someone, something, or some place. ☐ *They made out for Sam as soon as they saw him coming.* ☐ *The boys made for the swimming pool as soon as the coach blew the whistle.*

make room for someone or something to provide space for someone or something. ☐ *Make room for Sam. He needs a place to sit.* ☐ *Can you make room for this package?*

make something for someone or something to prepare something for someone or something. ☐ *I made a big bowl of fruit salad for the visitors.* ☐ *James made a cake for the party.*

make time for someone or something to provide time in one's schedule to deal with someone or something. ☐ *Can you make time for me today?* ☐ *The teacher could not make time for a meeting with me yesterday.*

make tracks for something to move rapidly toward something or some place. (Informal. From Western movies.) ☐ *The cowboys all made tracks for the chuck wagon.* ☐ *Let's make tracks for the hills. Here comes the sheriff.*

make way for someone or something to clear a path for someone or something. ☐ *We need to make way for the mayor and his people.* ☐ *Would you please make way for the trunk? They are bringing it through.*

MAKE ▸ FROM

make something from scratch to make something from the basic ingredients. (Idiomatic.) ☐ *Did you make this cake from scratch?* ☐ *I prefer to make things from scratch rather than use boxed mixes.*

make something from something to make something from certain parts or ingredients. ☐ *I made this cake from fresh butter and eggs.* ☐ *They made the fences from the stones of a ruined Roman fort.*

MAKE ▸ IN

make a dent in something **1.** to make a depression in something. ☐ *I kicked the side of the car and made a dent in it.* ☐ *Please don't make a dent in the side of the house.* **2.** to use only a little of something; to make a small amount of progress with something. (Informal.) ☐ *Look at what's left on your plate! You hardly made a dent in your dinner.* ☐ *They made a pretty big dent in our ice cream supply.* ☐ *I've been slaving all day, and I have hardly made a dent in my work.*

make a difference in someone or something to cause a noticeable change in someone or something. ☐ *Getting a job made a big difference in my life-style.* ☐ *His mother's death made a difference in his attitudes toward doctors.*

make one's way in the world to succeed in the world independently. ☐ *I intend to prepare myself to make my way in the world by getting a college degree.* ☐ *I know that all my children can make their way in the world.*

make something in something to make money in a particular enterprise. ☐ *She made a lot of money in real estate.* ☐ *I hope to make some money in the stock market.*

MAKE ▸ INTO

make inroads into something to succeed in getting something done or at least started. ☐ *George was unable to make inroads into solving the problem.* ☐ *We are making no inroads into the high priority project.*

make someone or something into something to turn someone or something into something. (*Someone* includes *oneself.*) ☐ *I will make you into a Hollywood star!* ☐ *We made our garage into a family room.* ☐ *She made herself into a goddess by dieting and skillful makeup.*

MAKE ▸ LIKE

make like someone or something to act like someone or something. (Slang.) ☐ *I have a cousin who can make like Frank Sinatra.* ☐ *I have a dog that can make like a cat.*

MAKE ▸ OF

make a believer (out) of someone to cause someone to believe in God; to convince someone decisively about something. (Informal.) ☐ *The harrowing experience we had made a believer out of me.* ☐ *It was an interesting discussion, but it did not make a believer out of me.*

make a clean breast of something (to someone) to admit something to someone. ☐ *You should make a clean breast of the matter to someone.* ☐ *You'll feel better if you make a clean breast of the incident.*

make a day of it to spend a full day at something. ☐ *We intended to be at the zoo for only an hour, but we had such a good time that we decided to make a day of it.* ☐ *Let's plan to leave after lunch. I don't want to make a day of it.*

make a fool of someone to make someone look stupid or foolish. ☐ *Are you trying to make a fool of me?* ☐ *Please don't make a fool of me!*

make a go of something to succeed at something. ☐ *She just didn't have the energy or inclination to make a go of her marriage.* ☐ *I did everything I could to make a go of it.*

make a habit of something to do something so often that it becomes a habit. ☐ *You mustn't make a habit of interrupting.* ☐ *I make a habit of counting my change.*

make a man of someone to make a young male into an adult male. (Often idiomatic.) ☐ *The experience will make a man of Ted.* ☐ *Send Wally into the army. That'll make a man of him.*

make a meal of something **1.** to eat something. ☐ *The cat made a meal of the fish.* ☐ *They made a meal of the roast beef and enjoyed it very much.* **2.** to eat enough of something to consider it a full meal. □ *I really don't want to make a meal of lettuce alone.* □ *Can we make a meal of this turkey, or should we use it for sandwiches?*

make a mental note of something to remember something. □ *So, you want to be considered for a job. I'll make a mental note of that.* □ *Please make a mental note of my telephone number.*

make a mess of something to mess something up; to ruin something. □ *Give it a try, but don't make a mess of it.* □ *Jerry made a mess of the kitchen.*

make a mockery of something to make a deliberate parody or a poor imitation of something. □ *What a mess. You made a mockery of the task.* □ *You have made a mockery of my position!*

make a night of it to spend the entire evening or night doing something. (Especially when one had intended to devote only a little time to the outing.) □ *We went out to have a bite to eat and were having such a good time that we decided to make a night of it.* □ *I did not want to make a night of it, so I left early.*

make a note of something **1.** to write something down as a reminder. □ *Please make a note of it so you will remember.* □ *I will make a note of it and try to remember where I put the note.* **2.** to make a mental note of something. □ *You want to be considered for promotion. I'll make a note of it.* □ *Please make a note of it.*

make a nuisance of oneself to be annoying. □ *I don't want to make a nuisance of myself, but I really need to see Alice Wilson.* □ *I was tired of seeing Claire. She was really beginning to make a nuisance of herself.*

make a pig of oneself to eat too much; to eat more than one's share. □ *Don't make a pig of yourself!* □ *Sam is making a pig of himself and taking more than his share.*

make a point of something **1.** to make a special effort to do or say something. □ *I will make a point of telling her what you said.* □ *Make a point of it to do it soon.* **2.** to make something into an important point or example. □ *That is very important. I will make a point of it in my speech.* □ *I will try to make a point of it in my discussion.*

make a practice of something to do something frequently. □ *It's all right this time, but please don't make a practice of it.* □ *We don't usually make a practice of doing this, but we will do it just this one time.* □ *Our company makes a practice of sending money to charities.*

make a secret of something to act as if something were a secret. □ *I'm not making a secret of it. I am quitting this job.* □ *Mary made a secret of her intentions.*

make an example of someone to do something to someone that shows the bad results of bad behavior; to point to someone as a bad example. □ *The judge said that he would make an example of Sally and would fine her the maximum amount.* □ *The same judge had made an example of Max a number of times.*

make an exhibition of oneself to show off; to try to get a lot of attention for oneself. □ *She is not just dancing, she is making an exhibition of herself.* □ *Whenever Rudy drinks, he makes an exhibition of himself.*

make an honest woman of someone to marry a woman. (Intended as jocular.) □ *So you finally made an honest woman out of Denise.* □ *She had wanted Max to make an honest woman of her, but you can't depend on Max to do anything right.*

make certain of something to check something in order to be sure. □ *Please make certain of what you want to do.* □ *Would you please make certain of the number of things you want to order?*

make demands of someone or something AND **make demands on someone or something** to expect someone or something to do something or act in a particular way. □ *Please don't make demands of everyone in the shop.* □ *The boss is making a lot of demands on the new machinery.*

make fast work of someone or something to use up or finish off someone or something. □ *The barber worked rapidly on John's hair and made fast work of him.* □ *I can make fast work of this pie!*

make fun of someone or something to ridicule someone or something. □ *Are you making fun of me?* □ *I am making fun of your hat.*

make (good) use of something to use something well. □ *I am sure I can make good use of the gift you gave me.* □ *We will make use of this book.*

make heads or tails of someone or something to understand someone or something that someone has said. (Usually negative.) □ *I can't make heads or tails of Fred.* □ *No one can make heads or tails of this problem.*

make light of something to treat something as less important than it really is. □ *She was disturbed by the event, but she just made light of it.* □ *I did not mean to make light of your problems.*

make mention of someone or something to mention someone or something. □ *Did you have to make mention of Sally? I'm angry with her.* □ *I will have to make mention of your failure to secure additional business.*

make mincemeat (out) of someone AND **make hamburger (out) of something** to beat or pound someone or something; to treat someone or something roughly. (Informal and figurative.) □ *If you don't behave, I'll make mincemeat out of you.* □ *Do you want Max to make hamburger out of you?*

make nonsense of something to make something appear to be silly or nonsensical. □ *You are just making nonsense of everything I have tried to do.* □ *Your statement makes nonsense of everything you have said before.*

make nothing of something to ignore something bad [that has happened]. □ *Don had ruined the whole vacation, but Doris made nothing of his bad behavior.* □ *I was surprised that they made nothing of the disaster.*

make sense (out) of someone or something to understand someone or something. □ *I can't make sense out of Doris and what she has done!* □ *No one can make sense out of Tom's story.*

make short work of someone or something to finish with someone or something quickly. □ *Max made short work of the poor guy who had gone to the cops.* □ *Danny and Elaine made short work of the pie.*

make something of someone or something to succeed with improving someone or something; to turn someone or something into someone or something worthwhile. □ *I tried to make something of you, but you had to do things the way you saw fit.* □ *I think I can make something of this script.*

make something of something 1. to make an interpretation of something. □ *What do you make of this letter?* □ *Look through this and see what sense you make of it.* **2.** to turn an incident into a dispute. (Usually with *it*. Often as an invitation to fight.) □ *Do you want to make something of it?* □ *He looks like he wants to make something of it.*

make sure of something to check something and be certain about it. □ *Please make sure of your facts before you write the report.* □ *We made sure of the route we had to follow before we left.*

make the best of something to do as well as possible with something that is not too promising. (Especially with *a bad job.*) □ *I don't like doing it, but I will try to make the best of a bad job.* □ *I will make the best of it, for a while anyway.*

make the most of something to exploit something as much as possible. □ *Please try to make the most of your opportunities.* □ *Larry made the most of the short amount of time he had at home.*

make (too) much of someone or something to pay too much attention to someone or something. □ *We all believe you are making much of Tom when he has done no more than anyone else.* □

Don't make too much of it. It was really nothing.

make use of someone or something to utilize someone or something; to do something useful with someone or something. ☐ *Can you make use of these papers?* ☐ *We were unable to make use of the items you shipped to us.*

MAKE ▸ OFF

make off with someone or something to leave and take away someone or something. ☐ *The kidnappers made off with the baby in the night.* ☐ *Max made off with Lady Bracknell's jewels.*

make something off (of) someone or something to make money from someone or something. (The *of* is colloquial.) ☐ *Are you trying to make your fortune off of me?* ☐ *We think we can make some money off the sale of the house.*

MAKE ▸ ON

make a move on someone to attempt to seduce someone; to ask someone to have sex. (Slang or colloquial.) ☐ *Was he making a move on me? I think he was.* ☐ *Jed is known for making moves on girls.*

make a start on something to set out to do something; to make a beginning on something. ☐ *See if you can make a start on the project.* ☐ *I will try to make a start on the cleaning before I leave today.*

make an impression on someone to make oneself noticed by someone. ☐ *Your presentation really made an impression on the people who make the decisions.* ☐ *Do you think I made an impression on Donna?*

make book on something to feel confident enough about something to accept wagers on it. (Slang.) ☐ *Of course the delivery date is certain. You can make book on it!* ☐ *It might be done on time, but I wouldn't make book on it.*

make demands on someone or something See *make demands of someone or something* under *MAKE ▸ OF.*

make good on something to pay a sum that is owed; to reimburse [someone] for the cost of damages, goods, a loan, etc. ☐ *She promised to make good on her debts.* ☐ *I know my payment is late, but I will make good on it.*

make something on something to make a certain amount of profit on something. ☐ *I am sure I can make something on the deal.* ☐ *Can I make any money on this sale?*

MAKE ▸ OUT

make a believer (out) of someone See under *MAKE ▸ OF.*

make a check out (to someone or something) to write a check to someone or a group. ☐ *Please make the check out to Bill Franklin.* 🅃 *Make out a check to me.* ☐ *Please make a check out to the bank.*

make a monkey out of someone to make someone appear silly. (Figurative.) ☐ *Are you trying to make a monkey out of me?* ☐ *I can't decide whether they were trying to help me or make a monkey out of me.*

make a mountain out of a molehill to make something seem to be more important than it is. (Figurative.) ☐ *It is not that important. You are just making a mountain out of a molehill.* ☐ *There is no big problem here. Someone has made a mountain out of a molehill.*

make hamburger (out) of someone or something See *make mincemeat (out) of someone or something* under *MAKE ▸ OF.*

make mincemeat (out) of someone or something See under *MAKE ▸ OF.*

make (out) after someone or something See under *MAKE ▸ AFTER.*

make (out) for someone or something See under *MAKE ▸ FOR.*

make out [that] something to pretend something. ☐ *He made out that he hadn't seen me.* ☐ *We all made out that we hadn't heard the sound.*

make out (with someone) to kiss and pet with someone. ☐ *All evening long, he was trying to make out with me.* ☐ *Sharon was trying to make out with Bill.* ☐ *Sam and Sally were in the corner, making out with each other.*

make out (with someone or something) to manage satisfactorily with someone or something. ☐ *I know you are negotiating with George on that Franklin deal. How are you making out with him?* ☐ *How are you making out with school?* ☐ *He is making out okay.*

make sense (out) of someone or something See under *MAKE ▶ OF.*

make something out to see, read, or hear something well enough to understand it. ☐ *What did you say? I couldn't quite make it out.* 🅃 *Can you make out what he is saying?* ☐ *I could just make out the ship in the fog.*

make something out of nothing to create something from nothing. ☐ *You are just making a big argument out of nothing!* ☐ *Please don't make such a to-do out of nothing!*

make something out of something to make something out of parts or raw materials. ☐ *I will make the cake out of the very best ingredients.* ☐ *Can you make a salad out of these vegetables?*

make something out to be something else to portray something as something else. ☐ *You are trying to make this tragedy out to be a minor matter.* ☐ *They made the disease out to be something far more serious than it really is.*

MAKE ▶ OVER

make a fuss over someone or something **1.** to pay too much attention to someone or something. ☐ *She always makes a fuss over my sister, but ignores me altogether.* ☐ *There's no need to make a fuss over dinner.* **2.** to create a disturbance over someone or something. ☐ *They are making a silly fuss over that talentless singer.* ☐ *Why are they making a fuss over that silly book?*

make over someone or something to pay a lot of attention to someone or something. ☐ *Why does she make over your sister so much?* ☐ *Aunt Em made over the wedding gifts as if they were for her instead of Susan.*

make someone or something over to convert someone or something into a new or different person or thing. (*Someone* includes *oneself.*) ☐ *The hairstylist tried to make Carla over, but she wanted to be the way she has always been.* 🅃 *She made over Carla.* ☐ *I would really like to make this house over.* 🄰 *This family room is a made-over garage.* ☐ *He tried to make himself over into a gentleman.* 🄽 *She looked just great after the make-over.*

make something over to someone or something to endorse a check, making it payable to someone or a group. ☐ *Please make the check over to Bill Franklin.* ☐ *Would you make the check over to my bank?*

MAKE ▶ THROUGH

make one's way through something **1.** to travel, usually on foot, through an area of heavy vegetation or through a crowd of people or things. ☐ *Slowly, the little group made its way through the jungle.* ☐ *We made our way through the weeds to the shore of the lake.* ☐ *The politician made his way through the crowd, shaking hands and forgetting names.* **2.** to work through something long and complex. ☐ *He made his way through the book with a dictionary. The vocabulary was arcane and mystical.* ☐ *I could hardly make my way through her argument.*

MAKE ▶ TO

make a difference to someone [for one choice or another] to matter to someone. ☐ *The big one or the little one—does it really make a difference to anyone?* ☐ *It makes quite a difference to me!*

make advances to someone to flirt with someone; to begin to seduce someone. ☐ *She began making advances to me, and I left the room.* ☐ *Mary made advances to every male she encountered.*

make amends (to someone) (for someone or something) to make up to someone for something that someone or something did. ☐ *Don't worry. I will make amends to her for my sister, who behaved so badly.* ☐ *I will try to make amends for the accident.* ☐ *I can make amends to Sam, I'm sure.*

make application (to someone or something) (for something) to apply to a person or an office for something. □ *You must make application to the committee for admission.* □ *Can I make application for a scholarship to this office?* □ *You must make application to a different office for that.*

make arrangements to do something to plan to do something; to facilitate the doing of something. □ *Please make arrangements to have all this stuff hauled away.* □ *We will make arrangements to be there on time.*

make it to some place to reach some place; to be able to attend an event at a place. (Also without *to some place*, but not eligible as an entry.) □ *I couldn't make it to the party.* □ *He didn't think his car could make it to Cleveland.*

make love to someone **1.** to kiss and caress someone. □ *Ernest made love to Linda in the garden in the moonlight.* □ *She liked the way he made love to her—all that poetry.* **2.** to have sex with someone. □ *I really think that he wanted to make love to me.* □ *She did not want to make love to him.*

make no difference to someone [for a choice] not to matter to someone. (*Any* is used with negative nouns or verbs.) □ *Pick whom you like. It makes no difference to me.* □ *It doesn't make any difference to me.* □ *Nothing much makes any difference to them anymore.*

make someone or something available to someone to allow someone to use or consult someone or something. (*Someone* includes *oneself*.) □ *I will make my assistant available to you for the afternoon.* □ *Can you make your car available to me this evening?* □ *The boss always made herself available to all her managers.*

make something clear to someone to help someone understand something. □ *Let me help make the contract clear to you.* □ *I want to make it clear to you, so ask questions if you want.* □ *Didn't I make it clear to you the first time we talked about it?*

make something to order to custom-make an item; to make an item to fit someone's specifications. □ *The tailor made the jacket to order for me.* □ *Were your shoes made to order?*

make something to someone or something to write a check to someone. (See also *make a check out (to someone or something)* under *MAKE ▸ OUT*.) □ *The check should be for fifty dollars. Please make it to me.* □ *Make the check to Jim.* □ *She made the check to the bank, and sent it off in the mail.*

MAKE ▸ UP

make one's mind up (about someone or something) to decide about someone or something. □ *Please make your mind up about Ralph. Will you pick him or not?* [T] *Make up your mind about her!* □ *I just couldn't make my mind up.*

make someone up to put makeup on someone. (*Someone* includes *oneself*.) □ *You have to make the clowns up before you start on the other characters in the play.* [T] *Did you make up the clowns?* [A] *The poorly made-up actor ruined the whole play.* □ *He made himself up for the play.*

make someone's mind up to do something that decides something for someone. □ *Will you please make up your mind?* [T] *I will help make up your mind.*

make something up (See also *make up something*.) **1.** to make a bed. □ *We have to make all the beds up and then vacuum all the rooms.* [T] *Did you make up the beds?* [A] *This is a nicely made-up bed. Well done.* **2.** to fabricate something, such as a story or a lie. □ *That's not true. You are just making that up!* [T] *You made up that story!* [A] *I don't want to hear any more made-up tales about ghosts and elves.* **3.** to redo something; to do something that one has failed to do in the past. □ *Can I make the lost time up?* [T] *Can I make up the test that I missed?* [A] *Can I turn in this made-up work for a grade?* [N] *I had to take a makeup test.* **4.** to assemble something. □ *They will make up the train in Chicago, and it will leave on time.* [T] *Have they finished making up the pages for the next edition of the magazine?*

make something up from something to create something from something. □ *I will make some stew up from the ingredients available in the fridge.* 🅃 *I will make up a stew from the leftovers.*

make something up out of whole cloth to fabricate a story or a lie. □ *That's a lie. You just made that up out of whole cloth.* 🅃 *That's a lie. You just made up that story out of whole cloth.*

make something up to someone to make amends to someone. □ *I'm so sorry. I will do what I can to make it up to you.* □ *I will make it up to them. Don't worry.*

make up to put on makeup. □ *I have to go make up before Joe comes to pick me up.* 🄽 *I haven't even put on my makeup yet.*

make up a foursome to assemble into a team of four people. □ *We have three people now. Who can we get to make up a foursome?* □ *Let's make up a foursome and play bridge.*

make up for lost time to catch up; to go fast to balance a period of going slow. □ *We drove as fast as we could, trying to make up for lost time.* □ *Hurry. We have to make up for lost time.*

make up for someone or something to compensate for something or something someone did. □ *We all had to do extra work to make up for Harry, who was very tired from being out late the night before.* □ *We will certainly make up for what we failed to do.*

make up something to constitute something. (See also *make something up.*) □ *Two chapters make up this volume.* □ *Over forty freight cars made up the train.*

make up to someone **1.** to apologize to someone. □ *It's too late to make up to me.* □ *I think you should go make up to Jerry.* **2.** to try to become friends with someone. □ *Look how the cat is making up to Richard!* □ *Jimmy is making up to Donna, and she doesn't even notice.*

make up with someone to reconcile with someone; to offer an apology to someone. □ *I'm sorry I argued with Fred. I will make up with him.* □ *Todd and Jed made up with each other.*

MAKE ▶ WITH

make a deal with someone to strike a bargain with someone. □ *I want to buy your car and I think I can make a deal with you.* □ *I will make a deal with you that you will like.*

make a hit with someone to please someone; to impress someone. □ *The dessert you served really made a hit with the guests.* □ *Her talk made a hit with the audience.*

make an appointment with someone to set a time for a meeting with someone. □ *I will make an appointment with the doctor so I can get this cough cleared up.* □ *Did you make an appointment with the decorator?*

make arrangements (with someone) (for something) to make plans with someone for something. □ *I will make arrangements with Fred for the loan.* □ *We can make arrangements for a car with the manager.* □ *I will make arrangements with Walter.*

make do with someone or something to get along with only someone or something; to do as well as possible with only someone or something. (See *do with someone or something.*) □ *I think we can make do with Karen for a while. We will need an additional person soon.* □ *We will have to make do with the ones you have brought.*

make free with someone to exploit someone; to take advantage of someone. □ *You shouldn't make free with your employees. They are liable to take you to court.* □ *He was making free with his secretary, having her do his private business.*

make free with something to use something freely; to exploit something. □ *You can make free with the hot water. We have a huge tank.* □ *Sally is making free with the sugar I was saving for breakfast cereal.*

make friends with someone to work to become a friend of someone. □ *I want to make friends with all the people I am* *going to be working with.* ☐ *Let's try to make friends with each other.*

make (one's) peace with someone to set things right with someone; to make amends with someone. ☐ *I will make my peace with Jane. You needn't be the one to patch things up.* ☐ *Let's go make peace with Karen.*

make points with someone to impress someone. (Slang.) ☐ *You are just trying to make points with me. You really don't believe what you say.* ☐ *Harry is always trying to make points with the boss.*

make something with something to make something out of something. ☐ *I will make the cake with margarine rather than butter.* ☐ *Can you make our coffee with springwater, please?*

make time with someone to flirt and be romantic with someone. (Colloquial.) ☐ *Jane has been making time with Fred.* ☐ *Who is Paul making time with lately?*

make with something to deliver something. (Slang.) ☐ *Come on, make with the stuff you promised!* ☐ *Make with the information, Max, or you will stay in jail even longer!*

MANAGE ▸ WITH

manage with someone or something to do as well as possible with only someone or something. ☐ *We wanted Kelly to help us, but we will manage with Larry.* ☐ *I am sure we can manage with the money that we have.*

MANAGE ▸ WITHOUT

manage without someone or something to do as well as possible without someone or something. ☐ *Carla said that she just can't manage without Jerry.* ☐ *We just can't manage without some more money.*

MANEUVER ▸ FOR

maneuver for something to get into position for something. ☐ *Sally is maneuvering for a shot at a promotion.* ☐ *Todd maneuvered for some attention, but they ignored him.*

MANEUVER ▸ INTO

maneuver someone into something to lure, position, or deceive someone into (doing) something. (*Someone* includes *oneself*.) ☐ *I will see if I can maneuver him into accepting the offer.* ☐ *He was maneuvered into accepting the offer.* ☐ *I maneuvered myself into the vice president's confidence.*

MANEUVER ▸ OUT

maneuver someone out of something to trick someone out of getting or achieving something. (*Someone* includes *oneself*.) ☐ *Are you trying to maneuver me out of the running for the job?* ☐ *The runner maneuvered her opponent out of first place.* ☐ *It took a lot of scheming, but I finally maneuvered myself out of having to serve on the committee.*

MAP ▸ OUT

map something out to plot something out carefully, usually on paper. ☐ *I have a good plan. I will map it out for you.* [T] *I will map out the plan for you.*

MAR ▸ UP

mar something up to dent or scratch something; to harm the smooth finish of something. ☐ *Please don't mar the furniture up.* [T] *Don't mar up my desk.* [A] *She planned to sand down the marred-up desk and refinish it.*

MARCH ▸ AGAINST

march against someone or something to march in a demonstration against someone or something. ☐ *The demonstrators marched against the mayor.* ☐ *The citizens got together and marched against crime and injustice.*

MARCH ▸ FROM

march (from some place) (to some place) to move along, walking with purposeful steps, from some place to some place. ☐ *The army marched from one town to another.* ☐ *They marched to the battlefield from town.*

MARCH ▸ ON

march on **1.** to continue marching. ☐ *Please march on. Don't stop here; there are other parts of the parade coming along behind you.* ☐ *Let's march on. We have a long way to go.* **2.** [for time] to continue. ☐ *Time marches on. We are* *all getting older.* □ *As the day marches on, try to get everything completed.*

MARCH ▸ PAST

march past someone or something to move in a file past someone or something. □ *The people in the parade marched past the children standing on the curb.* □ *The soldiers marched past the general.*

MARCH ▸ TO

march (from some place) (to some place) See under *MARCH ▸ FROM.*

march to something to move along, walking with purposeful steps, to something or some place. □ *The entire class marched to the dean's office to complain.* □ *We marched to the site of the celebration.*

MARK ▸ AS

mark something as something to make a mark next to the name of something on a list indicating what the thing is. □ *I will mark this one as expired.* □ *This one is marked as needing repair work.*

MARK ▸ DOWN

mark someone down to give someone a low grade in school because of something. □ *The teacher marked me down because I wrote the assignment in pencil.* T *The teacher marked down the student.*

mark something down **1.** to reduce the price of something. □ *We are going to mark all this merchandise down next Monday.* T *We marked down the merchandise.* N *How much markdown is there on this dress?* **2.** to write something down on paper. □ *She marked the number down on the paper.* T *She marked down the number.*

MARK ▸ FOR

mark someone for life to affect someone for life. (Figurative.) □ *The event marked her for life and she was never the same.* □ *She was marked for life.*

MARK ▸ IN

mark something in to write or make a mark on something, perhaps in a box or on a line. □ *I will mark an* X *in the box by your name.* T *I'll mark in the* X.

MARK ▸ OFF

mark someone or something off AND **mark someone or something out** to cross off the name of someone or something. □ *They were late, so I marked them off.* T *I marked off the late people.* □ *Could you mark that title out? It has been discontinued.*

MARK ▸ OUT

mark someone or something out See the previous entry.

MARK ▸ UP

mark something up **1.** to make marks all over something. □ *Who marked my book up?* T *I did not mark up the book.* A *The teacher handed back the marked-up papers.* **2.** to raise the price of something. □ *I think that they mark everything up once a week at the grocery store.* T *They marked up the prices again last night.* **3.** to raise the wholesale price of an item to the retail level. □ *How much do you mark cabbage up?* T *They marked up the cabbage too much.* N *How much markup is there on this washer?*

MARK ▸ WITH

mark someone or something with something **1.** to use something with which to mark someone or something. (*Someone* includes *oneself.*) □ *She marked one of the twins with a blob of ink so she could identify him later.* □ *Jill marked the ones that were sold with a wax pencil.* □ *She marked herself with the felt pen, just to see if it would work.* **2.** to place a particular kind of mark on someone or something. □ *The attendant marked the concert-goers who had paid with a rubber stamp.* □ *Frank marked the book with his initials.*

MAROON ▸ ON

maroon someone on something to strand someone on something; to abandon someone on something, such as an island. (*Someone* includes *oneself.*) □ *The pirate chief marooned his first mate on a small island in the Caribbean.* □ *Through a navigation error, I marooned myself on a tiny island east of Guam.*

MARRY ▸ ABOVE

marry above oneself to marry someone better than oneself. □ *They say she married above herself, but who cares?* □ *Scott thought it would not be possible to marry above himself.*

MARRY ▸ BELOW

marry below oneself AND **marry beneath oneself** to marry someone who is not as good as oneself. □ *He married beneath himself, but he is happy, and what more is required of a marriage?* □ *He did not want to marry beneath himself.*

MARRY ▸ BENEATH

marry beneath oneself See the previous entry.

MARRY ▸ INTO

marry into something to become a part of a family or a fortune by marriage. □ *She married into money, they say.* □ *I always wanted to marry into a large family until I found out what that means in terms of buying gifts.*

MARRY ▸ OFF

marry someone off (to someone) to manage to get someone married to someone and out of the house or family. □ *Her parents wanted nothing more than to marry her off to a doctor.* 🅃 *They married off their children soon.* □ *They were very happy to marry Mary off.*

MARRY ▸ OUT

marry one's way out of something to get out of something, such as poverty, by marrying someone. □ *She was able to marry her way out of poverty but regretted it in the long run.* □ *Sally married her way out of one unhappy home into another one.*

MARSHAL ▸ TOGETHER

marshal someone or something together to "herd" or gather someone or something together. □ *The leader marshaled all his people together in preparation for the parade.* □ *Let's marshal the troops together for the attack.*

MARVEL ▸ AT

marvel at someone or something to express wonder or surprise at someone or something. □ *I can only marvel at Valerie and all she has accomplished.* □ *We all marveled at the beauty of the new building.*

MASH ▸ ON

mash on something to press on something, such as a button. (Southern.) □ *He kept mashing on the button until someone responded.* □ *Just mash on this button if you want someone to come.*

MASH ▸ UP

mash something up to crush something into a paste or pieces. □ *Mash the potatoes up and put them in a bowl.* 🅃 *Mash up the potatoes and put them on the table.* 🄰 *Put a little of the mashed-up red pepper in the sauce—just a little.*

MASH ▸ WITH

mash something with something **1.** to use something to mash something up. □ *Vernon mashed the potatoes with a spoon because he couldn't find the masher.* □ *Gerald used the heel of his shoe to mash the wasp.* **2.** to combine ingredients while mashing. □ *Mash the turnips with the butter.* □ *She mashed the potatoes with sour cream, cream cheese, and a little garlic salt.*

MASK ▸ OUT

mask someone or something out to conceal or cover part of someone or something from view. □ *The trees masked the city dump out, so it could not be seen from the street.* 🅃 *The trees masked out the dump.* □ *When I enlarged the photograph, I masked my ex-husband out.*

mask something out to make a noise that covers up some other noise. □ *The sound of the waves on the shore masked the traffic sounds out.* 🅃 *The music masked out the traffic.*

MASQUERADE ▸ AS

masquerade as someone or something to appear disguised as someone or something; to pretend to be someone or something. □ *We decided to masquerade as Mutt and Jeff for the party.* □ *Mr. Wilson, who is a bit overweight, masqueraded as Cinderella's coach.*

MATCH ► AGAINST

match someone against someone or something against something else to challenge someone with someone else in a contest; to challenge something with something else in a contest. (*Someone* includes *oneself*.) □ *I will match my boxer against your boxer any day.* □ *I'll match myself against you any day!* □ *Do you want to match your car against mine?*

MATCH ► IN

match someone or something in something to equal someone or something in some quality. □ *I am sure I match her in wisdom if not in grace and beauty.* □ *You do not match her in any way.* □ *Our house does not match Roger's in a single feature.*

MATCH ► UP

match someone (up) (with someone) or something (up) (with something) to pair people or things. (*Someone* includes *oneself*.) □ *I will match Carl up with Kelly and George with Jane.* [T] *I will match up Carl with Kelly.* □ *Let's match the red plates up with the blue cups.* □ *Each one matched himself up with a player from the opposite team.*

match up [for things or people] to match, be equal, or complementary. □ *These match up. See how they are the same length?* □ *Sorry, but these two parts don't match up.*

match up to something [for something] to match, be equal to, or complementary to something. □ *This sock does not match up to the other one.* □ *This one matches up to all the others.*

MATCH ► WITH

match someone or something (up) (with someone or something) See under *MATCH ► UP.*

MATE ► WITH

mate someone with someone or something with something to pair or breed people or things. □ *The king sought to mate his daughter with the son of a magician.* □ *Harry wanted to mate his guppies with June's guppies.*

mate with someone to marry with someone, and presumably, to copulate with someone. □ *Jed did not care to mate with a total stranger, so they had dinner before the wedding.* □ *Did you meet anyone you would like to mate with and spend the rest of your life with?*

mate with something [for some creature] to copulate with its own kind. □ *The gander mated with the goose in the barnyard.* □ *The coyote acted as if it wanted to mate with the dog.*

MATTER ► TO

matter to someone to be important to someone. □ *Does money really matter to you?* □ *Yes, it matters to me a lot.*

MEAN ► AS

mean something as something to intend something to be understood as something. □ *Do you mean your remarks as criticism?* □ *I meant my comment as encouragement.*

MEAN ► BY

mean by something to intend a certain meaning by words or deeds. □ *What do you mean by that?* □ *I did not mean anything special by my remarks.*

MEAN ► FOR

mean something for someone or something **1.** to imply something important for someone or something; to be important or meaningful for someone or something. □ *Are your comments supposed to mean something special for me?* □ *I mean these remarks for the government.* **2.** to intend for someone or something to have or receive something. □ *Do you mean this gift for me?* □ *I mean this gift for the entire community.*

MEAN ► TO

mean something to someone to be meaningful to someone. ("Something" can be literal, here, meaning something good.) □ *Does this mean anything to you?* □ *You really mean something to me.*

MEASURE ► AGAINST

measure someone against someone or something against something to compare someone with someone else; to compare something with something else. (*Someone* includes *oneself*.) □ *Daniel measured his brother against the boy next door.* □ *We measured the new building against the older ones and found the new one lacking in many respects.* □ *I measured myself against Tom and found him superior in almost everything.*

MEASURE ▸ OFF

measure something off 1. to determine the length of something. □ *He measured the length of the room off and wrote down the figure in his notebook.* 🅃 *Fred measured off the width of the house.* 2. to distribute something in measured portions. 🅃 *He measured off two feet of the wire.* □ *Fred measured a few feet of string off, and cut it with a knife.*

MEASURE ▸ OUT

measure something out to measure and distribute something as it is being taken out, unwrapped, unfolded, etc. □ *Carl measured the grain out a cup at a time.* 🅃 *He measured out the grain little by little.*

MEASURE ▸ UP

measure someone up against someone or something to place someone up against someone or something else for the purpose of comparing size or other qualities. □ *Please measure Fred up against Tom and see who has the best qualifications.* □ *Can you measure Brian up against the mark on the wall to see how he is growing?*

measure up (to someone or something) to compare well to someone or something. □ *He just doesn't measure up to Sarah in intelligence.* □ *He measures up fairly well.*

measure up to someone's expectations to be what was expected or desired. □ *Sorry, you just don't measure up to my expectations.* □ *Her efforts measured up to no one's expectations.*

MEDDLE ▸ IN

meddle in something to intrude [oneself] into something. □ *I wish you wouldn't meddle in my affairs.* □ *Go meddle in someone else's business.*

MEDDLE ▸ WITH

meddle with someone or something to interfere with someone or something; to mess around with someone or something. □ *Please don't meddle with me. I am in a bad mood.* □ *Would you please stop meddling with my computer?*

MEDIATE ▸ BETWEEN

mediate between someone and someone else to negotiate an agreement between people. □ *I will have to mediate between Mary and Vernon.* □ *No one wants to mediate between them.*

MEDITATE ▸ ON

meditate on someone or something to reflect on someone or something. □ *Judy was instructed to meditate on a flower.* □ *I will meditate on that happy thought.*

MEET ▸ UP

meet up with someone or something to meet someone or something, usually by accident. (Colloquial.) □ *I met up with Don on the street yesterday.* □ *James met up with a strange accident.*

MEET ▸ WITH

meet with someone to have a meeting with someone. □ *I will meet with all of them on Monday.* □ *When can I meet with you?*

meet with something 1. [for someone] to experience something, such as an accident. □ *Poor Carlo met with a serious accident.* □ *Henry always feared meeting with a horrible fate.* 2. [for someone or something] to strike or touch something. □ *That board is supposed to meet perfectly with the surface of the wall.* □ *Her head met with the top of the car a number of times during the journey.*

meet with something to encounter some kind of response. □ *The proposal met with unexpected opposition.* □ *Her speech was met with universal approval.*

MELLOW ▸ OUT

mellow out to become more relaxed and calmer. (Slang.) □ *I need some time* *to get away and mellow out.* □ *Just mellow out, man. Relax.*

MELT ▸ AWAY

melt away to melt into a liquid. □ *The ice cubes melted away quickly in the intense heat.* □ *When the wax candles melted away, they ruined the lace tablecloth.*

melt something away to cause something to melt into a liquid. □ *The sun melted the ice away.* 🅃 *The sun melted away the ice.*

MELT ▸ DOWN

melt down **1.** [for something frozen] to melt. □ *The glacier melted down little by little.* □ *When the ice on the streets melted down, it was safe to drive again.* **2.** [for a nuclear reactor] to become hot enough to melt through its container. □ *The whole system was on the verge of melting down.* 🄽 *We were afraid of a meltdown for a while.*

melt something down to cause something frozen to melt; to cause something solid to melt. □ *The rays of the sun melted the candle down to a puddle of wax.* 🅃 *The heat melted down the ice.*

MELT ▸ IN

melt in someone's mouth to be tasty enough to dissolve in one's mouth, as would sugar. □ *The cake was so good it melted in my mouth.* □ *I have always wanted to cook food that would melt in people's mouths.*

melt in something **1.** [for something] to melt to a liquid at a high temperature. □ *Surely the plastic cup will melt in such heat.* □ *This tray will melt in the oven, so keep it out of there.* **2.** [for something] to dissolve in a particular liquid. □ *Sugar melts in hot water easily.* □ *Will this substance melt in heated water?*

MELT ▸ INTO

melt into something to melt and change into a different state. □ *All the ice cream melted into a sticky soup.* □ *The candles melted into a pool of colored wax in all the heat we had last summer.*

melt something into something to cause something to change its state when melting. □ *The ice melted into a cold liquid that we could drink.* □ *We melted the fat into a liquid that we could deep-fry in.*

MENTION ▸ IN

mention someone or something in something **1.** to name someone or something in a particular context. □ *We mentioned you in regard to nominations for the congress.* □ *Everyone mentioned your book in the discussions.* **2.** to name someone or something in a will, lecture, story, article, etc. □ *They mentioned your name in the discussion.* □ *Uncle Herman mentioned you in his will.*

MENTION ▸ TO

mention something to someone to refer to something while talking to someone. □ *Please mention it to your father.* □ *You had better not mention that to anyone.* □ *I mentioned the book to John, but he had never heard of it.*

MERGE ▸ IN(TO)

merge in(to something) to join into something. □ *The stream merged into the main channel of the river.* □ *Another little stream came from the south and merged in.*

merge someone or something in(to something) to route someone or something into something else. □ *They merged the marchers into the parade and no one ever knew they were late.* 🅃 *We merged in the latecomers to the parade at an intersection.* □ *We slowed up a little and let them merge in.*

MERGE ▸ WITH

merge something with something to join two things together. □ *The management merged the sales division with the marketing division.* □ *We merged the accounting department with the auditing department.*

merge with someone or something to join with someone or something. □ *Ted merged with Fred and they created a very profitable partnership.* □ *Our company merged with a larger one, and we all kept our jobs.*

merge with something to join into something. □ *This stream merges with a larger stream about two miles to the west.* □ *We will merge with a similar company located in Ohio.*

MESH ▸ TOGETHER

mesh together to fit together. □ *The various gears mesh together perfectly.* □ *Their ideas don't mesh together too well.*

MESH ▸ WITH

mesh with something to fit with something. □ *Your idea just doesn't mesh with my plans.* □ *Currently, things don't mesh at all well with our long-range planning.*

MESS ▸ ABOUT

mess about See under *MESS ▸ AROUND.*

mess (about) with someone or something See under *MESS ▸ WITH.*

MESS ▸ AROUND

mess around AND **mess about** to waste time; to do something ineffectually. (Colloquial.) □ *Stop messing around and get busy.* □ *I wish you wouldn't mess about so much. You waste more time that way.*

mess (around) with someone or something See under *MESS ▸ WITH.*

mess around with something to experiment with something; to use and learn about something. (Colloquial. See also *mess (around) with someone or something* under *MESS ▸ WITH.*) □ *We had been messing about with some new video techniques when we made our discovery.* □ *The people in this lab are messing around with all kinds of polymers.*

MESS ▸ OVER

mess someone over to treat someone badly; to beat or harm someone. (Slang.) □ *Max messed Lefty over and sent him to the hospital.* 🆃 *Max messed over Lefty.*

MESS ▸ UP

mess someone or something up 1. to put someone or something into disarray; to make someone or something dirty or untidy. (*Someone* includes *oneself.*) □ *A car splashed water on me and really messed me up.* 🆃 *The muddy water messed up my shirt.* □ *Don't mess up the living room.* 🅰 *She combed her messed-up hair and went on in.* □ *I messed myself up when I fell.* **2.** to interfere with someone or something; to misuse or abuse someone or something. □ *You really messed me up. I almost got fired for what happened.* 🆃 *The new owners messed up the company.* 🆃 *Dropping out of school really messed up my life.* □ *Mess him up good so he won't double-cross us again.*

mess someone's face up to beat someone about the face. (Slang.) □ *Max threatened to mess Lefty's face up.* 🆃 *Max did mess up Lefty's face.*

mess up to do something badly; to make errors. □ *Oh, I really messed up!* □ *Try not to mess up so often.*

MESS ▸ WITH

mess (around) with someone or something AND **mess (about) with someone or something** to tinker with someone or something; to play with someone or something; to handle someone or something carelessly. (See also *mess around with something.*) □ *Don't mess around with me.* □ *I wish you wouldn't mess with the clocks.* □ *Please don't mess about with the guys all day.* □ *Don't mess around with my camera.*

METAMORPHOSE ▸ INTO

metamorphose into something to transform into something. □ *This ugly caterpillar will surely metamorphose into something beautiful.* □ *At about eighteen, Wally metamorphosed into a reasonably handsome young man.*

METE ▸ OUT

mete something out to measure something out. □ *She meted the water out carefully since there was hardly any left.* 🆃 *She meted out the cookies to each of them.*

MIGRATE ▸ BETWEEN

migrate between some place and some place else to leave some place and resettle in another, perhaps repeatedly. □

These birds migrate between the north and the south. ☐ *They migrate between their cottage in the North in the summer and their condo in Florida in the winter.*

MIGRATE ▸ FROM

migrate (from some place) (to some place) [for a population] to move from some place to another. ☐ *The birds all migrate from Europe to Africa.* ☐ *They migrate to Canada from South America.*

MIGRATE ▸ TO

See the previous entry.

MILITATE ▸ AGAINST

militate against something [for something] to work against something. ☐ *Everything you have said today militates against an early settlement to our disagreement.* ☐ *This really militates against my going to college.*

MILL ▸ ABOUT

mill about See the following entry.

MILL ▸ AROUND

mill around AND **mill about** to wander or move around aimlessly within a small area. ☐ *Everyone was milling around, looking for something to do.* ☐ *The students milled about between classes.*

MINE ▸ FOR

mine for something to dig into the ground in search of a mineral, a metal, or an ore. ☐ *The prospectors ended up mining for coal.* ☐ *What are they mining for in those hills?*

MINGLE ▸ IN

mingle in (with someone) to join in with someone; to mix with people. ☐ *I am going to go into the hall and mingle in with the rest of the guests.* ☐ *Ken came into the room and mingled in at once.*

MINGLE ▸ WITH

mingle someone with someone else or something with something else to mix people together; to mix things together. ☐ *Try to mingle your friends with mine.* ☐ *You had better not mingle your money with that of the corporation.*

mingle with someone to mix with people. ☐ *Try to mingle with the guests.* ☐ *I would like to get out and mingle with people more.*

MINISTER ▸ TO

minister to someone or something to take care of someone or someone's needs. ☐ *Sarah tried to minister to the people of the village.* ☐ *He sought to minister to the grief of the widow.* ☐ *It is difficult to minister to the religious needs of thousands of people who have not had a decent meal in months.*

MINOR ▸ IN

minor in something to study a secondary subject in college. (Compare to *major in something.*) ☐ *I minored in math in college.* ☐ *I decide to minor in history.*

MISLEAD ▸ ABOUT

mislead someone about something to misrepresent something to someone. (*Someone* includes *oneself.*) ☐ *I hope you are not trying to mislead me about the price.* ☐ *I'm afraid I misled myself on this matter.* ☐ *The broker misled the customer very badly about the growth potential of the stock.*

MISS ▸ OUT

miss out (on something) not to do something because one is unaware of the opportunity; to fail to or neglect to take part in something. ☐ *I hope I don't miss out on the January linen sale.* ☐ *I really don't want to miss out.*

MIST ▸ OVER

mist over AND **mist up** [for glass] to fog up; [for glass] to develop a coating of water vapor so that one cannot see. ☐ *The windshield misted over and we could hardly see out.* ☐ *The glass misted up and we had to wipe it off.* 🄰 *Henry wiped the misted-over window clean.*

MIST ▸ UP

mist up See the previous entry.

MISTAKE ▸ FOR

mistake someone for someone to think or assume that someone is someone else. ☐ *I'm sorry. I mistook you for your brother.* ☐ *Someone has mistaken me for a famous movie star.*

mistake something for something to think or assume that something is something else. □ *I think you have mistaken the appetizer for the salad.* □ *I would never mistake a snake for a stick.*

MIX ▸ IN

mix in (with someone or something) to mix or combine with people or substances. □ *The band came down from the stage and mixed in with the guests during the break.* □ *The eggs won't mix in with the shortening!*

MIX ▸ IN(TO)

mix someone or something in(to something) to combine someone or something into something. □ *We will try to mix the new people into the group.* 🅃 *We will mix in the new people a few at a time.* □ *Ted mixed the flour into the egg mixture slowly.* □ *The cook mixed it in slowly.*

MIX ▸ UP

See *be mixed up with someone else* under *BE ▸ UP.*

mix it up (with someone) to get into a fight or argument with someone. (Slang.) □ *Max was in a mood to mix it up with Lefty.* □ *Max looked at Lefty and really wanted to mix it up.*

mix someone up to confuse someone. (*Someone* includes *oneself.*) □ *Please don't mix me up!* 🅃 *You mixed up the speaker with your question.* 🄰 *She is one mixed-up kid.* □ *I was so tired I mixed myself up as I spoke.*

mix someone up in something to get someone involved in something. (*Someone* includes *oneself.*) □ *Please don't mix me up in this problem.* 🅃 *Walter mixed up his daughter in the sordid affair.* □ *I don't want to mix myself up in this.*

mix someone up with someone to confuse one person with another. □ *I'm sorry. I mixed you up with your brother.* 🅃 *I mixed up Ted with his brother.* 🄽 *I'm sorry about the mix-up. You sure do look like Fred.*

mix something up to bring something into disorder; to throw something into a state of confusion. □ *He mixes things up in his eagerness to speak.* □ *Don't mix up the papers on my desk.*

mix something up (with something) to mix or stir something with a mixing or stirring device. □ *He mixed the batter up with a spoon.* 🅃 *Please mix up the batter with a spoon.* □ *I will mix it up, if you wish.*

mix something up with something 1. to combine substances and mix them together. □ *Please mix the egg up with the sugar first.* 🅃 *Please mix up the egg with the sugar.* **2.** to confuse something with something else. □ *I am afraid that you have mixed the green up one with the blue one.* 🅃 *I mixed up the green one with the blue one.* 🄽 *Sorry about the mix-up, Tom.*

MIX ▸ WITH

mix with someone or something to mix socially with someone or a group. □ *Tom dislikes Bill and Ted so much that he could never mix with them socially.* □ *She finds it difficult to mix with friends.*

mix with something [for a substance] to combine with a substance. □ *Will this pigment mix with water?* □ *Water will not mix with oil.*

MOAN ▸ ABOUT

moan about something to complain about something. □ *What are you moaning about?* □ *I am not moaning about anything.*

MOAN ▸ OUT

moan something out to say something in a moan. □ *The injured woman moaned the name of her assailant out.* 🅃 *She moaned out the name.*

MOAN ▸ WITH

moan with something to groan because of pain or pleasure. □ *The patient moaned with pain and fear.* □ *Ken moaned with pleasure.*

MOCK ▸ UP

mock something up to make a model or simulation of something. □ *The engineers mocked the new car design up for the managers to see.* 🅃 *They mocked up the new car design.* 🄽 *The* *mock-up looked good, so they went ahead with the production model.*

MODEL ▸ AFTER

model someone after someone or something after something AND **model someone on someone or something on something** to use something as a pattern for something; to use someone as a pattern for someone. (*Someone* includes *oneself.*) ☐ *I will model my house after the style we saw in the Mediterranean.* ☐ *We modeled our garage after a French villa.* ☐ *She tried to model herself after her mother.* ☐ *Todd modeled his behavior on his best friend's behavior.* ☐ *I modeled my plan on one I saw in Spain.* ☐ *We modeled our house on a dwelling we saw on our vacation.*

MODEL ▸ IN

model something in something to make a model of something in a particular substance. ☐ *She modeled the figure in clay.* ☐ *I modeled a bear in modeling clay.*

MODEL ▸ ON

model something on something or someone on someone See *model something after something or someone after someone* under *MODEL ▸ AFTER.*

MODULATE ▸ TO

modulate to something to change from one musical key to another by means of a musical transition. ☐ *Suddenly, the organist modulated to a key that was too high for most of the singers.* ☐ *I will have to modulate to a lower key before I start the next hymn.*

MOLD ▸ FROM

mold something from something See the following entry.

MOLD ▸ OUT

mold something out of something AND **mold something from something** to form something, using a substance, such as clay, plastic, terra cotta. ☐ *She molded a small turtle out of the moist clay.* ☐ *Elaine molded a turtle from the clay.*

MONKEY ▸ AROUND

monkey around to waste time; to idle away time. (Colloquial.) ☐ *Stop monkeying around and get busy!* ☐ *I wish you wouldn't monkey around so much.*

monkey (around) (with someone or something) to fiddle with, interfere with, or tamper with someone or something. ☐ *I wish you guys would stop monkeying around with Chuck. He has to finish his homework.* ☐ *Please stop monkeying with the stereo.*

MONKEY ▸ WITH

See the previous entry.

MOOCH ▸ FROM

mooch (something) from someone to beg something from someone. ☐ *Can I mooch a match from you?* ☐ *Go mooch it from Fred.* ☐ *Why do you always mooch from people?*

MOON ▸ ABOUT

moon about someone or something AND **moon over someone or something** to pine or grieve about someone or something. ☐ *Stop mooning about your cat. Cats always come back eventually.* ☐ *Jill is still mooning over Robert.*

MOON ▸ AWAY

moon something away to waste time pining. ☐ *Don't moon the whole year away!* 🅃 *You have mooned away half the year. Now pull yourself together!*

MOON ▸ OVER

moon over someone or something See under *MOON ▸ ABOUT.*

MOP ▸ DOWN

mop something down to clean a surface with a mop. ☐ *Please mop this floor down now.* 🅃 *Please mop down this floor.*

MOP ▸ OFF

mop something off to wipe the liquid off something. ☐ *Please mop the counter off.* 🅃 *Mop off the counter.*

MOP ▸ UP

mop something up to clean up something, such as a spill, with a mop or with a mopping motion. ☐ *Please mop this mess up.* 🅃 *I will mop up this mess.*

mop something up with something ☐ *I can mop the mess up with this old rag mop.* 🅃 *She will mop up the mess with the rag.*

mop the floor up with someone to beat someone up. (Slang.) ☐ *He will mop the floor up with you!* 🅃 *Max said he was going to mop up the floor with Lefty.*

MOPE ▸ AROUND

mope around to wander around depressed. ☐ *Please stop moping around. You are depressing me.* ☐ *I wish you wouldn't mope around all the time.*

MORALIZE ▸ ABOUT

moralize about someone or something to utter moral platitudes about someone or something. ☐ *There is no point in moralizing about Carlo. He can't be changed.* ☐ *Why are you moralizing about the election? The people are always right.*

MOTION ▸ ASIDE

motion someone aside to give a hand signal someone to move aside. ☐ *He motioned her aside and had a word with her.* 🅃 *I motioned aside the guard and asked him a question.*

MOTION ▸ AWAY

motion someone away from someone or something to give a hand signal to someone to move away from someone or something. ☐ *She motioned me away from Susan.* ☐ *The police officer motioned the boys away from the wrecked car.*

MOTION ▸ FOR

motion (for) someone to do something See under *MOTION ▸ TO.*

MOTION ▸ TO

motion (for) someone to do something to give someone a hand signal to do something. ☐ *The minister motioned the organist to begin playing.* ☐ *I motioned Ken to raise the curtain so the play could begin.* ☐ *Sally motioned for the waiter to bring the check.* ☐ *I will motion to the usher and try to get him to come over here and help us.*

motion someone to one side AND **motion someone to the side** to give someone a hand signal to move to the side of something, such as the road. (Very close to motion someone aside.) ☐ *The cop motioned her to the side of the road.* ☐ *Claire motioned Fred to one side, where she spoke to him.*

motion to someone to make some sort of hand signal to a person. ☐ *Did you motion to me? What do you want?* ☐ *I did not motion to you.*

MOUND ▸ UP

mound something up to form something into a mound. ☐ *Mound the dirt up around the base of the shrub.* 🅃 *Please mound up the leaves around the rosebushes.*

MOUNT ▸ AGAINST

mount something against someone or something to create or instigate something against someone or something. ☐ *The prosecutor mounted a questionable case against Robert.* ☐ *The state mounted a very complex case against the company.*

MOUNT ▸ ON

mount something on something to place something on something. ☐ *Mount the butterflies on plain white paper.* ☐ *Sue mounted her favorite stamps on a display board.*

MOUNT ▸ UP

mount up **1.** to get up on a horse. ☐ *Mount up and let's get out of here!* ☐ *Please mount up so we can leave.* **2.** [for something] to increase in amount or extent. ☐ *Expenses really mount up when you travel.* ☐ *Medical expenses mount up very fast when you're in the hospital.*

MOURN ▸ FOR

mourn for someone or something AND **mourn over someone or something** to grieve for someone or something. ☐ *Everyone will mourn for you when you go.* ☐ *We all mourned over the end of the holiday.* ☐ *There is no point in mourning over your cat. It won't come back.*

MOURN ▸ OVER

mourn over someone or something See the previous entry.

MOUTH ▸ OFF

mouth off to make smart-aleck remarks; to speak out of turn. (Slang.) □ *Stop mouthing off and get busy.* □ *That kid has to mouth off about everything!*

MOUTH ▸ ON

mouth on someone to inform the authorities on someone; to tattle on someone. (Slang.) □ *Max mouthed on Lefty and got him arrested.* □ *You had better not mouth on me!*

MOVE ▸ ABOUT

move about See under *MOVE ▸ AROUND.*

MOVE ▸ AHEAD

move ahead of someone or something to advance beyond someone or something. □ *All my coworkers are moving ahead of me in salary. What am I doing wrong?* □ *The police moved ahead of the parade, pushing back the crowd.*

MOVE ▸ ALONG

move along to continue to move; to start moving out of the way. (Often a command.) □ *The crowd moved along slowly.* □ *Please just move along. There is nothing to see here.*

MOVE ▸ AROUND

move around AND **move about** to move here and there a bit; to stir; to walk around a bit. □ *Stay where you are. Don't move around at all!* □ *I wish you would stop moving about.*

move someone or something around to move someone or something from place to place. □ *I wish that the army would stop moving me around. I have moved ten times in eight years.* □ *Let's move the furniture around and see how this room looks.*

MOVE ▸ ASIDE

move aside to step or move out of the way. □ *Please move aside.* □ *Could you please move aside so we can get this cart through?*

MOVE ▸ AWAY

move away (from someone or something) **1.** to withdraw from someone or something. □ *Please don't move away from me. I like you close.* □ *I have to move away from the smoking section.* □ *There was too much smoke there, so I moved away.* **2.** to move, with one's entire household, to another residence. □ *Timmy was upset because his best friend had moved away.* □ *They moved away just as we were getting to know them.*

move someone or something away (from someone or something) to cause someone or something to withdraw from someone or something. (*Someone* includes *oneself.*) □ *Move Billy away from Tommy so they will stop fighting.* □ *Move the cake away from Billy.* □ *Move Billy away from the cake.* □ *They moved themselves away from the smokers.*

MOVE ▸ BACK

move back (from someone or something) to move back and away. (Often a command.) □ *Please move back from the edge.* □ *Please move back!*

move someone or something back (from someone or something) to cause someone or something to move back and away from someone or something. □ *Please move your child back from the lawn mower.* 🅃 *Move back everyone from the street.* □ *Move the crowd back from the injured woman.*

MOVE ▸ DOWN

move down to move oneself farther down a line of things. □ *Someone else needs to sit on this bench. Please move down.* □ *Could you move down a little so we can have some more room?*

move someone or something down to cause someone or something to move farther down or along [something]. □ *Move Tom down. We need more space here.* 🅃 *Move down all these people. We need more space.* □ *Could you move the cart down the hall where it will be out of the way?*

MOVE ▸ FOR

move for something to make a parliamentary or legal motion in favor of something. □ *I move for dismissal of the case against my client.* □ *My lawyer moved for a recess.*

MOVE ▸ FORWARD

move forward with something to advance with something; to make progress with something. ☐ *Let us try to move forward with this matter at once.* ☐ *I want to move forward with the project at a fast pace.*

move someone or something forward to cause someone or something to advance. ☐ *Move her forward. She is too far back.* ☐ *Please move the chair forward.*

MOVE ▸ FROM

move (from some place) (to some place) to travel from one place to another. ☐ *The whole family moved from Denver to Chicago.* ☐ *We moved from the city.* ☐ *We moved to the country.*

MOVE ▸ IN

See also under *MOVE ▸ IN(TO).*

move in (for something) to get closer for some purpose, such as a kill. ☐ *The big cat moved in for the kill.* ☐ *As the cat moved in, the mouse scurried away.*

move in (on someone) to come to live with someone. ☐ *My brother moved in on me without even asking.* ☐ *I don't mean to move in on you. I just need a place for a few days.* ☐ *We really didn't want Mary's brother moving in.*

move in (on someone or something) **1.** to move closer to someone or something; to make advances or aggressive movements toward someone or something. (Both literal and figurative senses.) ☐ *The crowd moved in on the frightened guard.* ☐ *They moved in slowly.* **2.** to attempt to take over or dominate someone or something. ☐ *The police moved in on the drug dealers.* ☐ *Max tried to move in on Lefty's territory.* ☐ *So, you're trying to move in?*

move in with someone to take up residence with someone. ☐ *Sally moved in with Sam.* ☐ *Jimmy moved in with his brother and shared expenses.*

MOVE ▸ IN(TO)

move in(to something) **1.** [for someone] to come to reside in something or some place. ☐ *I moved into a new apartment last week.* ☐ *When did the new family move in?* **2.** to enter something or some place. ☐ *The whole party moved into the house when it started raining.* ☐ *All the children just moved in and brought the party with them.* **3.** to begin a new line of activity. ☐ *After failing at real estate, he moved into house painting.* ☐ *It looked like an area where he could make some money, so he moved in.*

move someone or something in(to something) to cause someone or something to enter something or some place. ☐ *We moved Carla into the spare room.* [T] *We found a vacant room and moved in the piano.* ☐ *He moved the piano in.*

MOVE ▸ OFF

move off (from someone or something) to move away from someone or something. ☐ *The doctor moved off from the patient, satisfied with her work.* ☐ *The officer stopped for a minute, looked around, and then moved off.*

move someone or something off ((from) someone or something) AND **move someone or something off ((of) someone or something)** to remove someone or something from on top of someone or something. (The *of* is colloquial.) ☐ *The referee moved the wrestler off from the body of his opponent.* ☐ *I moved the beam off of the leg of the man.* ☐ *Please move the books off the table.*

MOVE ▸ ON

move on to continue moving; to travel on; to move away and not stop or tarry. ☐ *Move on! Don't stop here!* ☐ *Please move on!* ☐ *There was no more for him to do in Adamsville, and so he moved on.*

move on something to do something about something. ☐ *I will move on this matter only when I get some time.* ☐ *I have been instructed to move on this and give it the highest priority.*

move on (to something) to change to a different subject or activity. ☐ *Now, I will move on to a new question.* ☐ *That is enough discussion on that point. Let's move on.*

move someone or something on to cause someone or something to move onward. □ *Please move those people on. They are in the way.* □ *The officers worked hard to move the crowd on.*

MOVE ▸ OUT

move out (of some place) **1.** to leave a place; to leave; to begin to depart. (Especially in reference to a large number of persons or things.) □ *The crowd started to move out of the area about midnight.* □ *They had moved out by one o'clock.* **2.** to leave a place of residence permanently. □ *We didn't like the neighborhood, so we moved out of it.* □ *We moved out because we were unhappy.*

move someone or something out (of some place) to cause someone to depart or leave; to carry someone or something out of a place. □ *Move those people out of here. They are cluttering up the room.* □ *Please move all that stuff out.*

MOVE ▸ OVER

move over to move a bit [away from the speaker]. □ *Move over. I need some space.* □ *Please move over. Part of this space is mine.*

move someone or something over to cause someone or something to move a little way away. □ *Move Tom over a little bit. He is taking too much space.* □ *Would you move your foot over a little?*

MOVE ▸ TO

move (from some place) (to some place) See under *MOVE ▸ FROM.*

move someone or something to something to make someone or something shift toward something. (*Someone* includes *oneself.*) □ *Can you move your foot to the right a little?* □ *Would you move yourself to the right?*

move someone to something to bring someone to the point of something, such as tears, crying, laughter, etc. (*Someone* includes *oneself.*) □ *The story moved me to tears.* □ *As she spoke, she moved herself to tears.*

move to some place to go to some place, perhaps permanently. □ *When we retired, we moved to Arizona.* □ *I hope we can move to a larger house.*

MOVE ▸ TOWARD

move toward someone or something to move in the direction of someone or something. (Both literal and figurative.) □ *The car is moving toward Roger!* □ *We are moving toward making the proper decision.*

MOVE ▸ UP

move someone or something up to cause someone or something to go higher or more forward. □ *She is too far down. Move her up.* □ *Would you move the sofa up a little? It is too far back.*

move someone up to advance or promote someone. □ *We are ready to move you up. You have been doing quite well.* □ *How long will it be before they can move me up?*

move up to advance; to go higher. □ *Isn't it about time that I move up? I've been an office clerk for over a year.* □ *I had hoped that I would move up faster than this.*

move up in the world to experience success and perhaps fame in the world. □ *I am moving up in the world and making enough to live on.* □ *Some people just don't ever move up in the world.*

move up into something to advance into something. □ *I moved up into administration and I like it fine.* □ *When I move up into management, I will get a bigger office.*

move up through something to advance through something. □ *He moved up through the ranks at a very rapid pace.* □ *We want you to move up through various titles as fast as you can.*

move up (to something) to advance to something; to purchase a better quality of something. □ *We are moving up to a larger car.* □ *There are too many of us now for a small house. We are moving up.*

MOW ▸ DOWN

mow someone or something down to cut, knock, or shoot someone or something down. □ *The speeding car almost* *mowed us down.* Ⓣ *The car mowed down the pedestrian.* Ⓣ *The lawn mower mowed down the tall grass.* □ *Machine guns mowed the attackers down.*

MUDDLE ▸ ALONG

muddle along to progress in confusion; to continue awkwardly. □ *I will just have to muddle along as best I can until things get straightened out.* □ *The project muddled along until the new manager got hold of it.*

MUDDLE ▸ AROUND

muddle around to work inefficiently. □ *I can't get anything done today. I'm just muddling around.* □ *Jed is not doing his job well. He is muddling around and getting nothing done.*

MUDDLE ▸ THROUGH

muddle through (something) to manage to get through something awkwardly. □ *We hadn't practiced the song enough, so we just muddled through it.* □ *We didn't know what we were meant to do, so we muddled through.*

MUDDLE ▸ UP

muddle something up to mix something up; to make something confusing. □ *You really muddled the language of this contract up.* Ⓣ *Who muddled up the wording?* Ⓐ *What am I going to do about this muddled-up contract?*

MUDDY ▸ UP

muddy something up **1.** to make water muddy; to stir up the mud in water. □ *Don't muddy the water up. It will clog our filters.* Ⓣ *Don't muddy up the water.* **2.** to make something unclear. □ *You have really muddied this issue up. I thought I understood it.* Ⓣ *You sure muddied up this issue.*

MUFFLE ▸ UP

muffle something up to deaden or stifle a sound. □ *Betty tried to muffle the sounds up, but everyone heard what was going on.* Ⓣ *She muffled up the sounds.*

MULCT ▸ OUT

mulct something out of someone to cheat something away from someone. □ *Are you trying to mulct my inheritance out of me?* □ *Max tried to mulct every last cent out of his victim.*

MULL ▸ OVER

mull something over to think over something; to ponder something. □ *Let me mull this over a little while.* Ⓣ *Mull over this matter for a while and see what you think.*

MULTIPLY ▸ BY

multiply by something to use the arithmetic process of multiplication to expand numerically a certain number of times. □ *To get the amount of your taxes, multiply by .025.* □ *Can you multiply by sixteens?*

multiply something by something □*Multiply the number of dependents you are claiming by one thousand dollars.* □ *Multiply 12 by 16 and tell me what you get.*

MUNCH ▸ OUT

munch out to overeat. (Slang.) □ *I can't help it. Whenever I see french fries, I just have to munch out.* □ *I try not to munch out more than once a week.*

MUNG ▸ UP

mung something up to mess something up; to ruin something. (Slang.) □ *You really munged this report up!* Ⓣ *You munged up the report.*

MURMUR ▸ AGAINST

murmur against someone or something to grumble about someone or something. □ *Everyone was murmuring against the manager.* □ *The citizens will begin murmuring about the government soon.*

MURMUR ▸ AT

murmur at someone or something to say something softly or indistinctly to someone or some creature. □ *Stop murmuring at me.* □ *Gene sat alone, murmuring at his favorite cat for over an hour.*

MUSCLE ▸ IN

muscle in (on someone or something) to interfere with someone or something; to intrude on someone or something. □ *Max tried to muscle in on Lefty, and that made Lefty's gang really mad at Max.*

☐ *You're not trying to muscle in, are you?*

MUSCLE ▸ OUT

muscle someone out (of something) to force someone out of something; to push someone out of something. (The *of*-phrase is paraphrased with a *from*-phrase when the particle is transposed. See the Ⓕ example.) ☐ *Are you trying to muscle me out of my job?* Ⓣ *The younger people are muscling out the older ones.* Ⓕ *The younger people are muscling out the older ones from their jobs.* ☐ *Lefty "Fingers" Moran had had enough competition, and he wanted to muscle Max out.*

MUSE ▸ OVER

muse over someone or something to reflect or meditate on someone or something. ☐ *We were just now musing over Sarah and the way she has changed.* ☐ *Tom is so strange. I was musing over his behavior just yesterday.*

MUSHROOM ▸ INTO

mushroom into something to grow suddenly into something large or important. ☐ *The question of pay suddenly mushroomed into a major matter.* ☐ *The unpaid bill mushroomed into a nasty argument and, finally, a court battle.*

MUSS ▸ UP

muss someone or something up to put someone or something into disarray. (*Someone* includes *oneself*.) ☐ *Don't muss me up!* Ⓣ *You mussed up my hair.* ☐ *I'm afraid I mussed myself up a little.*

MUSTER ▸ OUT

muster out of something to be discharged from military service. ☐ *He mustered out of the service before his time was up.* ☐ *I want to know how I can muster out too.*

MUSTER ▸ UP

muster something up to call up some quality, such as courage. ☐ *Do you think you can muster enough courage up to do the job?* Ⓣ *Can you muster up enough strength to do the job?*

MUTINY ▸ AGAINST

mutiny against someone or something **1.** to rebel against a ship's captain or the captain's authority. ☐ *The crew mutinied against the officers.* ☐ *They know better than to mutiny against an authority as great as that held by Captain Bligh.* **2.** to rebel against someone or something. ☐ *It does no good to mutiny against the professor.* ☐ *The students mutinied against the school's administration.*

MUTTER ▸ ABOUT

mutter about someone or something to grumble or complain about someone or something. ☐ *Are you muttering about me? What is your complaint?* ☐ *Why is everyone muttering about the food here? It is excellent.*

mutter something about someone or something to say something softly and indistinctly about someone or something. ☐ *I heard him mutter something about being late.* ☐ *Sharon is muttering something about Dave. What does she mean?*

N

NAG ▸ AT

nag at someone (about someone or something) to pester someone about someone or something. □ *Don't keep nagging at me about her.* □ *Stop nagging at me!*

NAIL ▸ BACK

nail someone's ears back to scold someone severely. (Idiomatic slang.) □ *I'm going to nail your ears back for doing that!* □ *Who's going to nail my ears back?*

nail something back to secure something back out of the way by nailing it. □ *Please nail the shutters back so they won't bang against the house.* 🅃 *I'll nail back the shutters.* 🄰 *The nailed-back shutters broke loose and began banging on the house.*

NAIL ▸ DOWN

nail someone down (on something) See *pin someone down (on something)* under *PIN ▸ DOWN.*

nail something down **1.** to secure something down by nailing it. □ *Please nail the flooring down or someone will trip over it.* 🅃 *I'll nail down these floorboards.* **2.** See *pin something down* under *PIN ▸ DOWN.*

NAIL ▸ INTO

nail something into something to drive a nail or something similar into something. □ *She nailed the nail into the wall to hold the picture up.* □ *Please nail in this tack.*

NAIL ▸ ON(TO)

nail something on(to something) AND **nail something to something** to attach something onto something by nailing. □ *Suzy nailed the hose bracket onto the side of the house.* 🅃 *She nailed on the bracket.* □ *Laura nailed the bracket to the wall.* □ *Laura nailed it on.* 🄰 *Remove all the nailed-on boards carefully. Some are glued. Just rip them down.*

NAIL ▸ TO

nail someone to a cross to punish someone much too severely for the wrong committed. (Cliché.) □ *I only broke your vase. Are you going to nail me to a cross?* □ *She nailed me to a cross for doing practically nothing.*

nail someone('s hide) to the wall to scold or punish someone severely. (Idiomatic slang.) □ *I'll nail your hide to the wall if you do that again.* □ *The boss really nailed her to the wall.*

nail something to something See under *NAIL ▸ ON(TO).*

NAIL ▸ UP

nail something up **1.** to put something up, as on a wall, by nailing. □ *Please nail this up.* 🅃 *I'll nail up this picture for you.* 🄰 *The nailed-up pictures were not anything that anyone would want to take.* **2.** to nail something closed; to use nails to secure something from intruders. □ *Sam nailed the door up so no one could use it.* 🅃 *Who nailed up the door? I can't get in!*

NAME ▸ AFTER

name someone after someone to name someone, usually a child, using someone else's name. □ *I would be pleased if you would name your child after me.* □ *I was named after an uncle.*

NAME ▸ AS

name someone as something to select someone as something. (*Someone* includes *oneself*.) ☐ *The mayor named Karen as corporate council.* ☐ *The president named himself as chairman of the board.*

NAME ▸ FOR

name someone or something for someone or something to name someone or something, using the name of someone or something, in any combination. ☐ *I named her for the beauty of the rising sun.* ☐ *They named the mountain for the first person to see it.* ☐ *The town's founders named it for a village that once stood on this site.*

NARROW ▸ DOWN

narrow something down (to people or things) to reduce a list of possibilities from many to a selected few. ☐ *We can narrow the choice down to green or red.* 🅃 *We narrowed down the choice to you or Paul.* ☐ *We can't seem to narrow the choice down.*

NAUSE ▸ OUT

nause someone out to make someone ill; to disgust someone. (Slang. From *nauseate. Someone* includes *oneself*.) ☐ *That's awful. I bet it nauses Jennifer out.* 🅃 *This day naused out everybody I know.* ☐ *He naused himself out just thinking of the accident.*

NECK ▸ WITH

neck with someone to engage in amorous kissing and caressing with someone. (Informal.) ☐ *Ted is over there necking with Molly.* ☐ *Molly is necking with Ted and thinking of Ken.*

NEEDLE ▸ ABOUT

needle someone about someone or something to pester or bother someone about someone or something. ☐ *Please don't needle me about Jane.* ☐ *Stop needling me about eating out.*

NEGLECT ▸ TO

neglect to do something to fail to do something. ☐ *I hope you do not neglect to tack down the carpet.* ☐ *He neglected to water the plants.*

NEGOTIATE ▸ ABOUT

negotiate (with someone or something) (about someone or something) See under *NEGOTIATE ▸ WITH.*

NEGOTIATE ▸ OVER

See the following entry.

NEGOTIATE ▸ WITH

negotiate (with someone or something) (over someone or something) AND **negotiate (with someone or something) (about someone or something)** to bargain with someone or a group about someone or something. ☐ *We decided to negotiate with them over the terms of the contract.* ☐ *We want to negotiate with them about the cost of the goods.* ☐ *They refused to negotiate with our purchasing agent.* ☐ *I have to negotiate over price with a committee.* ☐ *Can we negotiate about this?*

NEIGHBOR ▸ ON

neighbor on something to be directly adjacent to something. ☐ *Our house neighbors on a park.* ☐ *The park neighbors on a stretch of beach.*

NEST ▸ IN

nest in something to build a nest in something and live in it. ☐ *Some mice nested in a corner of the garage.* ☐ *The birds nested in the eaves.*

NEST ▸ TOGETHER

nest together to fit together or within one another compactly. ☐ *These mixing bowls nest together.* ☐ *I want some of those Russian wooden dolls that nest together.*

NESTLE ▸ AGAINST

nestle (up) against someone or something AND **nestle up (to someone or something)** to lie close to someone or something; to cuddle up to someone or something. ☐ *The kitten nestled up against its mother.* ☐ *It nestled up to Kathy.* ☐ *Kathy nestled against the back seat of the car.*

NESTLE ▸ DOWN

nestle down (in something) to settle down in something; to snuggle into something, such as a bed. ☐ *They nes-*

tled down in their warm bed. ☐ *Please nestle down and go to sleep.*

NESTLE ▸ UP

nestle (up) against someone or something See under *NESTLE ▸ AGAINST.*

nestle up (to someone or something) See under *NESTLE ▸ AGAINST.*

NIBBLE ▸ AT

nibble at something to take tiny bites of some kind of food. (See also the following entry.) ☐ *The children nibbled at their dinner because they had eaten too much candy.* ☐ *Stop nibbling at that candy.*

NIBBLE ▸ AWAY

nibble away at something to eat at something in tiny bits; to erode away tiny bits of something. (See also the previous entry.) ☐ *The waves nibbled away at the base of the cliff, year after year.* ☐ *The action of the waves continued to nibble away at the cliff.* ☐ *The mice nibbled away at the huge cheese.*

NICK ▸ UP

nick something up to make little dents or nicks in something, ruining the finish. ☐ *Someone nicked the kitchen counter up.* 🅃 *Who nicked up the coffeepot?*

NIGGLE ▸ ABOUT

niggle about something to make constant petty complaints about something. (See also under *NIGGLE ▸ OVER.*) ☐ *Please don't niggle about little things like this. This is just not important.* ☐ *Let's not niggle about it.*

NIGGLE ▸ OVER

niggle (over something) (with someone) to have a petty disagreement over some minor thing. ☐ *Stop niggling over this with me!* ☐ *I don't want to niggle with you over this.* ☐ *I won't niggle over price.* ☐ *The merchant refused to niggle with me anymore.*

NIGGLE ▸ WITH

See the previous entry.

NIP ▸ AT

nip at someone or something to bite at someone or something. ☐ *The dog nipped at the visitor, but didn't cause any real harm.* ☐ *A small dog nipped at my heels.*

NIP ▸ IN

nip something in the bud to put an end to something while it is still a minor problem. (Cliché. Refers to destroying a flower bud before it blooms.) ☐ *I wanted to nip that little romance in the bud.* ☐ *The whole idea was nipped in the bud.*

NIP ▸ OFF

nip something off ((of) something) to clip or cut something off something. (The *of*-phrase is paraphrased with a *from*-phrase when the particle is transposed. See the 🄵 example. The *of* is colloquial.) ☐ *Let me nip a few blossoms off the rosebush.* 🅃 *I nipped off a few blossoms and made a bouquet.* 🄵 *I nipped off a few blossoms from the rosebush.* ☐ *Laura nipped some blossoms off.*

NOD ▸ AT

nod at someone to make a motion to someone with one's head indicating a greeting, agreement, or something else. ☐ *I nodded at Fred, but I really didn't agree.* ☐ *Molly nodded at Fred, and Fred, knowing she wanted to leave the party, went for their coats.* ☐ *Todd nodded at Ralph as he passed by.* ☐ *When she offered him some ice cream, he only nodded. She thought he was rude and decided not to give him any.*

NOD ▸ OFF

nod off to fall asleep. (Slang.) ☐ *I usually nod off about midnight.* ☐ *After the second act, I nodded off.*

NOISE ▸ ABOUT

noise something about AND **noise something abroad; noise something around** to spread around a secret; to gossip something around. ☐ *Now don't noise it about, but I am going to Houston next week to see my girl.* ☐ *Please don't noise this abroad.* ☐ *Stop noising that gossip around.*

NOISE ▶ ABROAD

noise something abroad See the previous entry.

NOISE ▶ AROUND

noise something around See under *NOISE ▶ ABOUT.*

NOMINATE ▶ AS

nominate someone as something to suggest someone to be the person to serve as something. (*Someone* includes *oneself.*) □ *I would like to nominate Karen as our representative.* □ *She nominated herself as the one most likely to do the job.*

NOMINATE ▶ FOR

nominate someone for something to suggest someone to hold a particular office. (*Someone* includes *oneself.*) □ *I will nominate Carolyn for president.* □ *You cannot nominate yourself for this office.*

NOMINATE ▶ TO

nominate someone to something to suggest someone to become a member of a group. (*Someone* includes *oneself.*) □ *I am the one who nominated her to the board.* □ *The president nominated herself to the position of chairman of the board.*

NOSE ▶ ABOUT

nose about (for someone or something) AND **nose around (for someone or something)** to search here and there to find someone or something. □ *We spent an hour nosing about for a newspaper.* □ *I will nose around for someone to help you.* □ *We nosed about for a while, but found no one.*

NOSE ▶ AROUND

nose around (for someone or something) See the previous entry.

nose around (something) to pry into something; to snoop around something. □ *I caught her nosing around my desk.* □ *Wally is always nosing around.*

NOSE ▶ IN(TO)

nose in(to something) [for a car or boat] to move or be moved into something or some place carefully, nose first. □ *The captain nosed into the channel, and our journey had begun.* □ *He nosed in and we sailed on.*

nose something in(to something) to steer something, such as a car or a boat, into something or some place, nose first. □ *She nosed her car into the parking place and turned off the engine.* 🅃 *She nosed in the car.* □ *Liz nosed the car in.*

NOSE ▶ OUT

nose out (of something) to move cautiously out of something or some place, nose first. □ *She nosed out of the little room, hoping she hadn't been observed.* □ *She nosed out quickly and stealthily.*

nose someone or something out to defeat someone or something by a narrow margin. (Alludes to a horse winning a race "by a nose.") □ *Karen nosed Bobby out in the election for class president.* □ *Our team nosed out the opposing team in last Friday's game.*

nose something out (into something) to drive or push something into the midst of something carefully, nose first. □ *She nosed the car out into traffic cautiously.* 🅃 *She nosed out the car.* □ *She nosed it out.*

nose something out (of something) 1. [for an animal] to force something out of something gently and cautiously. (As if pushing with the nose. The *of*-phrase is paraphrased with a *from*-phrase when the particle is transposed. See the 🄵 example.) □ *The cat nosed her kitten out of the corner.* 🅃 *The cat nosed out her kittens where we could see them.* 🄵 *The dog nosed out her pups from the basket.* □ *She nosed them out.* **2.** to move something cautiously out of something or some place, nose first. (Figurative. The *of*-phrase is paraphrased with a *from*-phrase when the particle is transposed. See the 🄵 example.) □ *Todd nosed the car out of the parking place carefully.* 🅃 *He nosed out the car with skill.* 🄵 *He nosed out the car from the parking space.* □ *Ted nosed it out.*

nose something out (onto something) to drive or push something carefully out onto the surface of something, nose first. □ *I nosed the car out onto the highway, looking both ways.* 🅃 *She* *nosed out the car.* ☐ *She nosed it out carefully.*

NOTE ▸ DOWN

note something down to write down a note about something. ☐ *Please note these words down.* 🅃 *Note down the following facts.*

NOTE ▸ FOR

See *be noted for something* under *BE ▸ FOR.*

NOTIFY ▸ ABOUT

notify someone about someone or something to inform someone about someone or something. (Compare to the following entry.) ☐ *Please notify the insurance company about the accident.* ☐ *I have to notify the doctor about Ed, who is ill.*

NOTIFY ▸ OF

notify someone of something to inform someone about something. (Compare to the previous entry.) ☐ *Can you notify my parents of my arrival at the airport?* ☐ *We were notified of it last night.*

NUDGE ▸ ASIDE

nudge someone or something aside to push or bump someone or something out of the way. ☐ *We nudged the old man aside and went on ahead.* 🅃 *She nudged aside the cat to make room on the sofa.* ☐ *The attendant nudged the teenager aside.*

NUMBER ▸ AMONG

number someone or something among something to include someone or something in a group of something. (*Someone* includes *oneself.*) ☐ *I number her among my best friends.* ☐ *I number this product among the most popular developed during the past year.* ☐ *I number myself among the more accomplished pianists.*

NUMBER ▸ IN

number in something to total up to a certain figure. ☐ *The birds numbered in the thousands.* ☐ *These ants number in the million. Let's go home.*

NUMBER ▸ OFF

number off (by something) to say out a number in a specified sequence when it is one's turn. ☐ *Please number off by tens.* ☐ *Come on, number off!*

number someone off to provide people with numbers. ☐ *I had to number the children off.* 🅃 *I numbered off the contestants.*

NUMBER ▸ WITH

number someone with something to include someone in a list of people. (*Someone* includes *oneself.*) ☐ *I number Clara Wilson with the all-time greats.* ☐ *Todd numbered himself with the heroes of the age.* ☐ *The police numbered both Lefty and Max with the most likely of the suspects.*

NURSE ▸ AGAINST

nurse a grudge against someone to harbor a resentment against someone. (Idiomatic.) ☐ *I hope you aren't nursing a grudge against your ex-wife.* ☐ *I do not nurse a grudge against anyone.*

NURSE ▸ ALONG

nurse someone or something along to tend to the welfare of someone or some creature; to aid or encourage the well-being or return to health of someone or some creature. (*Someone* includes *oneself.*) ☐ *She nursed the old man along for a few years until he died.* 🅃 *She nursed along the invalid.* ☐ *The vet nursed the horse along for the rest of the night.* ☐ *He nursed himself along with chicken noodle soup and hot baths until the virus ran its course.*

nurse something along to manage something with care and thrift. (Figurative.) ☐ *She nursed the business along until it was showing a profit.* ☐ *The board of directors agreed to nurse the firm along for a while and then sell it.*

NURSE ▸ BACK

nurse someone back to health to care for a sick person until good health is obtained. (*Someone* includes *oneself.*) ☐ *Sally was glad to help nurse her mother back to health.* 🅃 *She nursed back her mother to health.* ☐ *Henry—all alone* *in the house—had to nurse himself back to health.*

NURSE ▸ THROUGH

nurse someone through (something) to care for a sick person during the worst part of a sickness or recovery. ☐ *There was no one there to nurse him through the worst part of his illness.* ☐ *It was a horrible ordeal, but John nursed her through.*

NUT ▸ UP

nut up to go crazy. (Slang. See also *crack up* under *CRACK ▸ UP*.) ☐ *I knew I would nut up if I didn't quit that job.* ☐ *I almost nutted up at the last place I worked.*

NUZZLE ▸ UP

nuzzle up against someone or something AND **nuzzle up (to someone or something)** [for an animal] to rub its nose against someone or something; to rub against someone or something, softly, in the manner of rubbing the nose against someone or something; to snuggle up to someone or something. (*Nuzzle* is related to *nose*.) ☐ *The dog nuzzled up against my leg, wanting to be friends.* ☐ *The dog nuzzled up to me and licked my hand.* ☐ *The cat nuzzled up against my leg and demanded food.*

O

OBJECT ▸ TO

object to someone or something to disapprove of someone or something. ☐ *I object to him as your choice.* ☐ *I object to Fred on general principles.*

OBLIGATE ▸ TO

obligate someone to someone to force someone to do something for someone. (*Someone* includes *oneself.*) ☐ *This obligates you to me for life!* ☐ *I don't wish to obligate myself to anyone.*

OBLIGE ▸ BY

oblige someone by something to accommodate someone by doing something. ☐ *Please oblige me by closing the window.* ☐ *Would you oblige me by accompanying me to the dance?*

OBLIGE ▸ TO

oblige someone to do something to require someone to do something. ☐ *You are obliged to arrive on time and enter by the side door.* ☐ *The lateness of the hour obliged Tony to enter by the back door.*

OBLIGE ▸ WITH

oblige someone with something to accommodate someone with something. ☐ *He obliged her with a willing attitude.* ☐ *Please oblige me with a big piece of cake.*

OBLITERATE ▸ FROM

obliterate someone or something from something to destroy or wipe out someone or something from something. ☐ *Karen obliterated the writing from the wall.* ☐ *Max set out to obliterate Lefty "Fingers" Moran from the face of the earth.*

OBSESS ▸ WITH

See *be obsessed with someone or something* under *BE ▸ WITH.*

OBTAIN ▸ FOR

obtain something for someone or something to get or receive something from someone or something. ☐ *I promised I would obtain a pet for Becky.* ☐ *I obtained a new part for the vacuum cleaner.*

OCCUPY ▸ BY

occupy oneself by something to keep busy by doing something. ☐ *Don't worry. I can occupy myself by knitting or sewing.* ☐ *While waiting, I occupied myself by knitting a scarf.*

OCCUPY ▸ WITH

occupy someone with something to keep someone busy with something. (*Someone* includes *oneself.*) ☐ *Can you occupy the child with this toy?* ☐ *Here, occupy yourself with this.*

OCCUR ▸ TO

occur to someone to come to someone's mind; to be remembered by someone. ☐ *It occurs to me that you might be the one.* ☐ *Did it ever occur to you that I might have a say in what is done here?*

OFFEND ▸ AGAINST

offend against someone or something to anger or affront someone or something. ☐ *We do not wish to offend against anyone.* ☐ *He didn't realize that he offended against their cultural values.*

OFFEND ▸ WITH

offend someone with something to anger or affront someone with something.

☐ *Don't offend us with your bad jokes.* ☐ *I offended Ralph with my constant niggling.*

OFFER ▸ FOR

offer something for something to suggest a certain amount of money as a purchase price for something. ☐ *I'll offer you ten bucks for that watch.* ☐ *They offered me very little for my car.*

OFFER ▸ TO

offer something to someone (as something) to propose giving something to someone as a gift, peace offering, payment, etc. ☐ *They offered us a bunch of flowers as a peace offering.* ☐ *As an apology, I offered a gift to the hostess.*

OFFER ▸ UP

offer something up (to someone or something) to offer to give something to someone or something. (Stilted.) ☐ *We offered our gratitude up to the ruler.* 🅃 *We offered up our gratitude to the queen.* ☐ *We offered our thanks up.*

OFFICIATE ▸ AS

officiate (as something) (at something) to serve as an official or moderator at some event. ☐ *They asked me to officiate as a judge at the contest.* ☐ *Laura will officiate as parade marshal.* ☐ *Who will officiate at the parade?*

OFFICIATE ▸ AT

See the previous entry.

OGLE ▸ AT

ogle at someone or something to stare at someone or something, usually with amorous or erotic relish. (Also without *at*, but not eligible as an entry.) ☐ *Don't just stand there and ogle at me!* ☐ *Stop ogling at those magazines.*

OMIT ▸ FROM

omit someone or something from something to leave someone or something out of something. (*Someone* includes *oneself*.) ☐ *You omitted Carol from the list.* ☐ *I think that you omitted our company from the bidding.* ☐ *She omitted herself from the list of participants.*

OOZE ▸ FROM

ooze (out) (from someone or something) AND **ooze out (of someone or something)** to seep out of someone or something. ☐ *The heavy oil oozed out from the hole in the barrel.* ☐ *Something was oozing out of him.* ☐ *Some sticky stuff oozed out.* ☐ *At the base of the barrel, black stuff oozed out.*

OOZE ▸ OUT

ooze (out) (from someone or something) See the previous entry.

ooze out (of someone or something) See under *OOZE ▸ FROM.*

OOZE ▸ WITH

ooze with something **1.** to flow or seep with something; to be covered with some oozing substance. ☐ *The wound oozed with blood.* ☐ *The roast beef oozed with juices.* **2.** [for someone] to exude an ingratiating or insincere manner. (Figurative.) ☐ *The used-car salesman oozed with insincerity.* ☐ *The young woman oozed with charm.*

OPEN ▸ INTO

open into something to open inward to something. ☐ *The passageway opened into a dining room.* ☐ *Our kitchen opens into a bright breakfast nook.*

OPEN ▸ ON

open fire on someone or something to begin shooting at someone or something. ☐ *The troops opened fire on the enemy.* ☐ *The trainees opened fire on the target.*

OPEN ▸ ON(TO)

See the following entry.

OPEN ▸ OUT

open (out) on(to) something [for a building's doors] to exit toward something. ☐ *The french doors opened out onto the terrace.* ☐ *The doors opened on a lovely patio.*

open something out to unfold or expand something; to open and spread something out. ☐ *When she opened the fan out, she saw it was made of plastic.* ☐ *The peacock opened its tail feathers out and delighted the children.*

OPEN ▸ TO

open one's heart to someone or something **1.** to tell all of one's private thoughts to someone. □ *I didn't mean to open my heart to you.* □ *She opened her heart to the wrong magazine, and it published a scandalous story.* **2.** to become loving and solicitous toward someone; to donate money generously to someone or some cause. □ *We opened our hearts to Fred, who was soliciting for a good cause.* □ *We hope you will all open your hearts to our plea.* □ *We opened our hearts to the refugees.*

open someone's eyes to someone or something to cause someone, including oneself, to become aware of someone or something. □ *We finally opened our eyes to what was going on around us.* □ *The events of last night opened my eyes to Tom.*

open the door to someone **1.** to permit someone to enter. □ *The butler opened the door to the guests and they all entered.* □ *I opened the door to Mr. Wilson.* **2.** to make a move or passage easier for a person. □ *Ann opened the door to Fred, who wanted to start a new career in writing.* □ *Mark opened the door to her, and she was always grateful to him.*

open the door to something **1.** to permit something or some creature to enter. □ *Molly opened the door to the family dog.* □ *The door was opened to the cat, which then refused to enter.* **2.** to invite something to happen. □ *This opened the door to further discussion.* □ *The door was opened to further discussion.*

OPEN ▸ UP

open someone up to perform a surgical operation requiring a major incision on someone. (Informal.) □ *The doctor had to open George up to find out what was wrong.* 🅃 *They opened up George, seeking the cause of his illness.*

open something up **1.** to open something that was closed. □ *They opened Peru's border up recently.* 🅃 *They opened up the border.* **2.** to begin working on something for which there are paper records, such as a case, investigation, file, etc. □ *I'm afraid we are going to have to open the case up again.* 🅃 *They opened up the case again.*

open something up (to someone) to make something available to someone; to permit someone to join something or participate in something. □ *We intend to open the club up to everyone.* 🅃 *We will open up our books to the auditors.* □ *We had to open the books up.*

open up (about someone or something) (with someone) AND **open up (on someone or something) (with someone)** to speak freely about someone or something; to speak a great deal about someone or something. (Compare to *dilate on someone or something.*) □ *After a while, he began to open up about the accident with me.* □ *He opened up with us about the accident.* □ *She opened up on Fred with Alice.* □ *At last, Tony opened up on Jerry.* □ *Please open up with me.*

open up on someone or something to begin shooting bullets or throwing things at someone or something. (Colloquial.) □ *The enemy opened up on the retreating troops.* □ *The cops opened up on Max.*

open up (to someone) **1.** to tell [everything] to someone; to confess to someone. □ *If she would only open up to me, perhaps I could help her.* □ *She just won't open up. Everything is "private."* □ *After an hour of questioning, Thomas opened up.* **2.** [for opportunities] to become available to someone. (Figurative.) □ *After Ann's inquiries, doors began to open up to me.* □ *An agent helps. After I got one, all sorts of doors opened up.*

open up (to someone or something) **1.** [for doors] to become open so someone, something, or some creature can enter; to open for someone or something. □ *The doors to the supermarket opened up to me, so I went in.* □ *The automatic doors opened up to the dog, and it came into the store.* **2.** [for someone] to become more accepting of someone or something. □ *Finally, he opened up to the suggestion that he should leave.* □ *Finally the boss opened up to Tom as a* *manager.* **3.** to become available to someone or something. □ *Harry had to recruit a few people for the new jobs that opened up.* □ *A number of directions opened up to the committee.*

OPEN ▸ WITH

open with someone or something to begin a season, session, series, or performance with someone or something. □ *The season will open with a series of speakers.* □ *The performance opened with Donna, who played the flute.*

OPERATE ▸ AGAINST

operate against someone or something to work against someone or something; to have a negative effect on someone or something. □ *All of this operates against our idea of fixing the garage up as a family room.* □ *The new vacation policy operates against me.*

OPERATE ▸ FROM

operate from something to work out of something or some place. □ *I'm in business for myself. I operate from my home.* □ *We operate from a garage in the back of City Hall.*

OPERATE ▸ ON

operate on someone to perform a surgical operation on someone. □ *They decided not to operate on her.* □ *She wasn't operated on after all.*

operate on something **1.** to work on something; to work with the insides of something. (As a surgeon might operate.) □ *He tried to operate on his watch and ruined it.* □ *Todd operated on the doorlock and fixed it.* **2.** to function or conduct business on a certain principle or assumption. □ *The company has always operated on the theory that the president is always right.* □ *Sam operates on the assumption that everyone is out to get him.*

OPPOSE ▸ TO

See *be opposed to something* under *BE ▸ TO.*

OPT ▸ FOR

opt for something to choose a particular option. □ *I opted for the orange one.* □ *I opt for not doing it at all.*

OPT ▸ IN

opt in favor of someone or something to choose a particular person; to choose a particular thing. □ *Do you think she will opt in favor of this one or that?* □ *We will opt in favor of David.*

OPT ▸ IN(TO)

opt in(to something) to choose to join in. (Informal.) □ *She opted into our plans.* □ *She opted in almost immediately.*

OPT ▸ OUT

opt out (of something) to choose not to be in something. □ *If you do that, I'm going to have to opt out of the club.* □ *Then go ahead and opt out.*

ORBIT ▸ AROUND

orbit around someone or something to circle around something in an orbit. (Also without *around*, but not eligible as an entry.) □ *The flies orbited around Fred and his ice cream cone.* □ *The moon, Luna, orbits around our planet.*

ORDAIN ▸ AS

ordain someone as something **1.** to establish someone as something. (Both senses also without *as,* but not eligible as an entry.) □ *They ordained the poor old man as a deputy sheriff.* □ *Was he duly ordained as a Mercedes mechanic?* **2.** to establish someone as a priest or minister. □ *In a lovely ceremony, they ordained David as a priest.* □ *He was ordained as a priest in a lovely service.*

ORDER ▸ ABOUT

order someone about AND **order someone around** to give many orders to someone; to boss someone around. □ *You have no right to order me about.* 🅃 *The general ordered about all the soldiers.* □ *You can't order me around!*

ORDER ▸ AROUND

order someone around See the previous entry.

ORDER ▸ FROM

order something from someone or something to agree to purchase something from someone or a group. □ *We ordered some plants from the mail-order company.* □ *I will order some of those* *clever little things from you as soon as I can.*

ORDER ▸ IN

order something in to have something, usually food, brought into one's house or place of business. □ *Do you want to order pizza in?* [T] *Shall I order in pizza?*

ORDER ▸ IN(TO)

order someone in(to something) to command someone to get into something. □ *The officer ordered Ann into the wagon.* □ *She didn't want to go, but the cop ordered her in.*

ORDER ▸ OFF

order someone off ((of) something) to command someone to get off something. □ *The teacher ordered Tom off the steps.* □ *He ordered him off.*

order someone off the field [for a games official] to command a player to leave the playing area. □ *The referee will order you off the field.* □ *He ordered us off the field.*

ORDER ▸ OUT

order someone out (of some place) to command that someone leave a place. □ *The cook ordered Judy out of the kitchen.* [T] *The cook ordered out all the kids.*

ORDER ▸ TO

order something to go to request food to be prepared to be taken away and eaten elsewhere. (*To go* is an adjective here.) □ *Order everything to go so we can eat while we travel.* □ *The meal was ordered to go.*

ORIENT ▸ TO

orient someone to something **1.** to help someone locate a compass direction or other similar location. (*Someone* includes *oneself.*) □ *Try to orient Karen to the light so I can photograph her.* □ *It took time, but I oriented myself to north at last.* **2.** to help someone adjust to something, a position, or a relationship. (*Someone* includes *oneself.*) □ *Will you please orient Bill to our routine?* □ *She found it difficult to orient herself to the new procedures.*

ORIGINATE ▸ FROM

originate from something to come from something or some place. □ *Did you originate from around here?* □ *I originated from a different area of the country.* □ *Some of our customs originate from old beliefs.*

ORIGINATE ▸ IN

originate in something to have had a beginning in something or some place. □ *The river originates in the Andes Mountains.* □ *All your troubles originate in your lungs.*

ORIGINATE ▸ WITH

originate with someone or something to have been started by someone or during a time period or event. □ *Did this policy originate with you?* □ *This idea originated with the committee.*

ORNAMENT ▸ WITH

ornament something with something to decorate something with something. □ *The driver ornamented his truck with lots of chrome.* □ *The room was ornamented with velvet drapes, ferns, and photographs—a den of Victorian virtue.*

OSCILLATE ▸ BETWEEN

oscillate between someone or something and someone or something to swing between choosing someone and someone else; to swing between choosing something and something else. □ *Fred oscillated between going to college and getting a job.* □ *The boss oscillated between John and Roger.*

OUST ▸ FROM

oust someone from something to force someone to leave something or some place; to throw someone out of something or some place. □ *They ousted the boys from the bar.* □ *The underage kids were ousted from the tavern quickly.*

OVERDOSE ▸ ON

overdose someone on something AND **overdose someone with something** to give someone too much of some substance, usually a drug. (*Someone* includes *oneself.*) □ *Sam overdosed his sister on the cough medicine.* □ *She overdosed herself with aspirin.* □ *Tom overdosed himself with the drug.*

OVERDOSE ► WITH

overdose someone with something See the previous entry.

OVERFLOW ► INTO

overflow into something to spill over into something. □ *The river overflowed into the surrounding farmland.* □ *The water in the bowl overflowed into the sink.*

OVERFLOW ► WITH

overflow with someone or something to have so many people or things that they spill over. □ *The kitchen overflowed with the guests.* □ *My cup overflowed with strong coffee.* Ⓝ *More people showed up than the hall could hold, and we didn't know what to do with the overflow.* Ⓐ *We had an overflow crowd and no place to put all the people.*

OWE ► FOR

owe someone for something to be under obligation to someone for something. □ *I'll have to owe you for it.* □ *You owe me for plenty already.*

See the following entry.

OWE ► TO

owe something (to someone) (for something) to be under obligation to pay or repay someone for something. □ *I owe forty dollars to Ann for the dinner.* □ *I owe money for the gift to Ann.* □ *I still owe money for the gift.* □ *Do you still owe money to Ann?*

OWN ► UP

own up to someone to confess or admit something to someone. □ *Finally, he owned up to his boss.* □ *We had hoped he would own up to us sooner.*

own up to something to admit something; to confess to something. □ *He refused to own up to doing it.* □ *I will own up to my mistakes.*

P

PACE ▸ ABOUT

pace about See the following entry.

PACE ▸ AROUND

pace around AND **pace about** to walk around nervously or anxiously. □ *Stop pacing around and sit down.* □ *There is no need to pace about.*

PACE ▸ BACK

pace back and forth AND **pace up and down** to walk over and over the same short route nervously or anxiously. □ *The leopard paced back and forth in its cage.* □ *I paced up and down, worrying about a variety of things.*

PACE ▸ OFF

pace something off to mark off a distance by counting the number of even strides taken while walking. □ *The farmer paced a few yards off and pounded a stake into the soil.* 🅃 *He paced off a few yards.* □ *Walter paced the distance off quickly.*

PACE ▸ OUT

pace something out **1.** to deal with a problem by pacing around. □ *When she was upset, she walked and walked while she thought through her problem. When Ed came into the room, she was pacing a new crisis out.* 🅃 *She usually paced out her anxiety.* **2.** to measure a distance by counting the number of even strides taken while walking. □ *He paced the distance out and wrote it down.* 🅃 *He paced out the distance from the door to the mailbox.*

PACE ▸ UP

pace up and down See under *PACE ▸ BACK.*

PACK ▸ AWAY

pack something away to pack something up and put it away. □ *Pack this mirror away where it will be safe.* 🅃 *Please pack away this mirror carefully.*

PACK ▸ DOWN

pack down [for something] to settle down in a container; [for gravity] to pack something down in a container. □ *The cereal has packed down in the box so that it seems that the box is only half full.* □ *Everything was packed down carefully inside.*

pack something down to make something more compact; to press something in a container down so it takes less space. □ *The traffic packed the snow down.* □ *Pack the grass down in the basket so the basket will hold more.* 🅃 *She packed down the grass in the basket.* 🄰 *The packed-down dirt serves well as a floor.*

PACK ▸ IN

See also under *PACK ▸ IN(TO).*

pack it in to quit trying to do something; to give up trying something and quit. (Idiomatic.) □ *I was so distressed that I almost packed it in.* □ *I've had enough! I'm going to pack it in.*

pack someone or something (in) like sardines See under *PACK ▸ LIKE.*

pack something in something to surround or enclose something in something □ *They packed his wounded hand in ice, then took him to the hospital.* □ *Pack the vase in shredded paper before you close the box.*

PACK ▸ IN(TO)

pack someone or something in(to something) to press or push someone or something into something; to manage to get a lot of things or people into a place. (*Someone* includes *oneself*.) □ *The boys packed a lot of kids into a telephone booth as a gag.* 🅃 *They packed in a lot of kids.* □ *They packed us all in.* □ *Please pack all your clothes into the suitcase.* □ *All of the boys packed themselves into the tiny car.*

PACK ▸ LIKE

pack someone or something (in) like sardines to squeeze in as many people or things as possible. (From the efficient way that sardines are packed into a can. *Someone* includes *oneself*.) □ *They packed us in like sardines. There was no room to breathe.* 🅃 *They packed in the people like sardines.* □ *Dave got a box and packed his books in like sardines.* □ *They packed themselves in like sardines.*

PACK ▸ OFF

pack someone off (to someone or something) to send someone away to someone or some place. □ *Laura just packed all the kids off to summer camp.* 🅃 *She packed off the kids to their camp.* □ *After a lot of planning and a few tears, she packed them all off.*

pack something off (to someone or something) to send something to someone or something. □ *I will pack the books off to you immediately.* 🅃 *She packed off the books to my home address.* □ *Harry found the books I wanted and packed them off.*

PACK ▸ TOGETHER

pack someone or something together to press or squeeze people or things together. (*Someone* includes *oneself*.) □ *The ushers packed the people together as much as they dared.* 🅃 *They packed together all the people standing in the room.* □ *They packed the cups together too tightly.* □ *They packed themselves together as tightly as they could.*

PACK ▸ UP

pack something up (in something) to prepare something to be transported by placing it into a container. □ *Gerry will pack the dishes up in a strong box, using lots of crumpled paper.* 🅃 *Please pack up the dishes carefully.*

pack up to prepare one's belongings to be transported by placing them into a container; to gather one's things together for one's departure. □ *If we are going to leave in the morning, we should pack up now.* □ *I think you should pack up and be ready to leave at a moment's notice.* □ *He didn't say good-bye. He just packed up and left.*

PAD ▸ DOWN

pad down (some place) to make one's bed somewhere, usually a casual or temporary bed. (Slang.) □ *Do you mind if I pad down at your place for the night?* □ *Can I pad down tonight?*

PAD ▸ OUT

pad out to go to bed; to go to sleep. (Slang.) □ *Where are you going to pad out tonight?* □ *I want to pad at out Fred's place if there's room.*

pad something out to make something appear to be larger or longer by adding unnecessary material. □ *If we pad the costume out here, it will make the person who wears it look much older.* 🅃 *Let's pad out this paragraph a little.*

PAINT ▸ IN

paint something in to paint something extra onto a painted area. □ *I know that there is supposed to be a big white spot here. We will have to paint it in.* 🅃 *We will have to paint in the spot.*

PAINT ▸ ON

paint on something to apply paint to the surface of something. □ *He painted on the fence a while and then went inside to rest.* □ *Please don't paint on the area that is not sanded down.*

PAINT ▸ ON(TO)

paint something on(to something) to apply a design or picture to something, using paint. □ *Joel painted the portrait onto a large sheet of plywood.* 🅃 *He painted on some leaves and flowers too.* □ *There was plenty of room on the sign, so he painted the phone number on.*

PAINT ▸ OUT

paint something out to cover something up or obliterate something by applying a layer of paint. ☐ *The worker painted the graffiti out.* 🅃 *They had to paint out the graffiti.*

PAINT ▸ OVER

paint over something to cover something up with a layer of paint. ☐ *Sam painted over the rusty part of the fence.* ☐ *The work crew was told to paint over the graffiti.*

PAIR ▸ OFF

pair off [for two people or other creatures] to form a couple or pair. ☐ *All of them paired off and worked as teams to solve the puzzle.* ☐ *Everyone should pair off and discuss the issue for a while.*

pair off with someone to join with someone to make a couple or pair. ☐ *Sally paired off with Jane, and they set up the tent they were going to share.* ☐ *Tom paired off with Donna, and they entered the dance contest.*

PAIR ▸ UP

pair up (with someone) to join with someone to make a pair. ☐ *Sally decided to pair up with Jason for the dance contest.* ☐ *Sally and Jason paired up with each other.* ☐ *Sally and Jason paired up.* ☐ *All the kids paired up and gave gifts to one another.*

PAL ▸ AROUND

pal around (with someone) to associate with someone as a good friend. ☐ *I like to pal around with my friends on the weekends.* ☐ *They like to pal around.* ☐ *They often palled around with each other.*

PAL ▸ UP

pal up (with someone) to join with someone as a friend. ☐ *I palled up with Henry and we had a fine time together.* ☐ *We palled up and had a fine time together.* ☐ *They palled up with each other.*

PALE ▸ AT

pale at something to become weak, frightened, or pale from fear of something or the thought of something. (Often figurative.) ☐ *Bob paled at the thought of having to drive all the way back to get the forgotten suitcase.* ☐ *We paled at the notion that we would always be poor.*

PALE ▸ BESIDE

pale beside someone or something to appear to be weak or unimportant when compared to someone or something. ☐ *He is competent, but he pales beside Fran.* ☐ *My meager effort pales beside your masterpiece.*

PALM ▸ OFF

palm someone or something off (on someone) (as someone or something) AND **pass someone or something off (on someone) (as someone or something); pawn someone or something off (on someone) (as someone or something)** to give someone or something to someone as a gift that appears to be someone or something desirable. (As if the gift had been concealed in one's palm until it was gotten rid of.) ☐ *Are you trying to palm that annoying client off on me as a hot prospect?* 🅃 *Don't palm off that pest on me.* ☐ *Please don't pass that problem off on me as a challenge.* ☐ *Don't pass it off on me!* ☐ *Don't pawn it off on me as something of value.*

PAN ▸ ACROSS

pan across to someone or something to move a film or television camera sideways so that the picture moves to and settles on someone or something. ☐ *The camera panned across to Mary, who was sitting, looking out the window.* ☐ *The camera operator panned across to the window on the opposite side of the room.*

PAN ▸ FOR

pan for something to search for a precious metal, usually gold, by using a pan to locate the bits of metal in sand and gravel. ☐ *When I was in Alaska, I panned for gold in a little stream set aside for tourists.* ☐ *The old prospector spent many hours panning for gold.*

PAN ▸ IN

pan in (on someone or something) See under *ZOOM ▸ IN*.

PAN ▸ OUT

pan out AND **zoom out** to move back to a wider angle picture using a zoom lens. □ *The camera zoomed out.* □ *Pan out at this point in the script and give a wider view of the scene.*

pan out (somehow) to *turn out* somehow; to succeed. (If no *somehow* is expressed, success is assumed.) □ *Things will pan out all right in the end.* □ *Don't worry. Things will pan out.* □ *The experiment didn't pan out as we had hoped.*

PAN ▸ OVER

pan over someone or something to move a film or television camera sideways so that the picture moves across a view of someone or something. □ *The camera panned over the skyline, picking up interesting cloud formations.* □ *It panned over Roger as if he weren't there—which is exactly the effect the director wanted.*

PANDER ▸ TO

pander to someone or something to cater toward undesirable tastes or people with undesirable tastes. □ *All your writing seems to pander to persons with poor taste.* □ *You are pandering to the lowest personal tastes.*

PANIC ▸ AT

panic at something to lose control in a frightening or shocking situation. □ *Try not to panic at what you see. It will be a shock.* □ *Don't panic at the price of food. It will be worse next week.*

PANIC ▸ BY

panic someone by something to make someone lose control by doing something. □ *She panicked Denise by describing the event too vividly.* □ *She panicked her horse by jerking the reins too tightly.*

PANT ▸ FOR

pant for someone or something to desire or long for someone or something. □ *My heart is panting for you!* □ *I am just panting for some interesting news.*

pant for something to breathe fast and hard in need of something, such as oxygen, fresh air, etc. □ *The dog was panting for air.* □ *I was panting for oxygen after my long climb.*

PANT ▸ OUT

pant something out to tell something while panting for breath. □ *Laura had been running but she was able to pant the name of the injured person out.* 🅃 *She panted out the name.*

PAPER ▸ OVER

paper over something **1.** to put a layer of wallpaper on a wall. □ *We papered over the wall, giving the room a bright, new look.* □ *We papered over the old plaster on the wall.* **2.** to cover up some sort of blemish on a wall with wallpaper. □ *We papered over a lot of little cracks.* □ *Sam papered over all the flaws in the plaster wall.* **3.** to conceal something; to cover something up. (Figurative.) □ *Don't try to paper over the mess you have made.* □ *George tried to paper over all his mistakes.*

PARADE ▸ BY

parade by (someone) to march past someone in a parade or as if in a parade. □ *The soldiers paraded by the commander in chief.* □ *Looking quite sharp, they paraded by.*

PARADE ▸ IN

parade someone or something in front of someone or something to exhibit someone or something in front of someone or something, as if in a parade. (*Someone* includes *oneself*.) □ *One by one, the teacher paraded the honor students in front of the parents.* □ *The sheriff paraded the suspects in front of the camera.* □ *The sheriff paraded the suspects in front of the victim.* □ *The children paraded themselves in front of all the guests.*

PARADE ▸ OUT

parade someone or something out to bring or march someone or some creature out in public. □ *He parades his children out every Sunday as they go to church.* 🅃 *He paraded out all his children.* □ *The owners paraded their dogs out, and the judge got ready to choose the best one.*

PARCEL ▶ OUT

parcel someone or something out to divide up and send or give away people or things. □ *Carla parceled all the costumes out so everyone would have something to wear to the parade.* [T] *We will parcel out the children for the summer.*

PARCEL ▶ UP

parcel something up to wrap something up in a package. □ *Would you parcel the papers up and set them in the corner?* [T] *Parcel up the papers and place them on top of the file cabinet.*

PARDON ▶ FOR

pardon someone for something **1.** to excuse someone for doing something. □ *Will you please pardon me for what I did?* □ *I can't pardon her for that.* **2.** to excuse and release a convicted criminal. □ *The governor pardoned Max for his crime.* □ *The governor did not pardon Lefty for the same crime.*

PARE ▶ DOWN

pare something down (to something) to cut someone down to something or a smaller size. □ *I will have to pare the budget down to the minimum.* [T] *I hope we can pare down the budget.* □ *After much arguing, we pared it down.*

PARE ▶ OFF

pare something off ((of) something) to cut something off something. (The *of*-phrase is paraphrased with a *from*-phrase when the particle is transposed. See the [F] example. The *of* is colloquial.) □ *See if you can pare a bit of this extra wood off the edge of the base of this pillar.* [T] *Pare off some of the wood.* [F] *Pare off some of the dead wood from the tree.* □ *You should pare the skin off before you eat it.*

PARLAY ▶ INTO

parlay something into something to exploit an asset in such a way as to increase its value to some higher amount. □ *She is trying to parlay her temporary job into a full-time position.* □ *Alice parlayed her inheritance into a small fortune by investing in the stock market.*

PARLEY ▶ WITH

parley with someone to talk with someone. □ *I need to parley with my brother before making a financial commitment.* □ *We need to parley with each other sometime soon.*

PART ▶ FROM

part from someone to leave someone. □ *I just hate parting from you.* □ *I must part from her now.*

part someone or something from someone or something to take someone or some creature away from someone or some creature. □ *It was difficult to part the mother dog from her puppies.* □ *I hated to part the mother from her child.*

PART ▶ OVER

part over something [for people] to separate because of something. □ *We had to part over our disagreement.* □ *They parted over a very small matter.*

PART ▶ WITH

part company with someone to end an association with someone. □ *He parted company with Mary over a year ago.* □ *Tom and I parted company with each other quite some time ago.*

part with someone or something to give up or let go of someone or something. □ *She did not want to part with her friend.* □ *I could never part with my books.*

PARTAKE ▶ IN

partake in something to participate in something. □ *Valerie does not care to partake in those childish games.* □ *I would like to partake in the fun.*

PARTAKE ▶ OF

partake of something **1.** to have a portion of something, such as food or drink. □ *Would you care to partake of this apple pie with me?* □ *I would like to partake of that fine dinner I see set out on the table.* **2.** to take part in or experience something. □ *Sarah had always wanted to partake of the good life.* □ *Roger had no intention of partaking of the events offered at the fair.*

PARTICIPATE ▶ IN

participate (in something) (with someone or something) to take part in something with someone or a group. □ *I will not participate in this activity with you.* □ *They don't participate with our team in this contest.*

PARTICIPATE ▶ WITH

See the previous entry.

PARTITION ▶ INTO

partition something into something to divide or separate something into something [smaller]. □ *I will partition this room into two separate spaces.* □ *Do you think you can partition this box into four compartments so we can store all our old computer discs?*

PARTITION ▶ OFF

partition something off to divide off a section of something. □ *They planned to partition the basement off.* 🅃 *We will partition off a larger area.*

PASS ▶ ALONG

pass something along (to someone) 1. to give or hand something to someone. □ *Would you kindly pass this along to Hillary?* 🅃 *Please pass along my advice to Wally over there.* □ *I would be happy to pass it along.* **2.** to relay some information to someone. □ *I hope you don't pass this along to anyone, but I am taking a new job next month.* 🅃 *Could you pass along my message to Fred?* □ *I will pass it along as you ask.*

PASS ▶ AROUND

pass something around (to someone) to offer something to everyone. □ *Please pass the snacks around to everyone.* 🅃 *Would you pass around the snacks?* □ *Harry will pass them around.*

pass the hat around (to someone) to collect donations of money from people. □ *Jerry passed the hat around to all the other workers.* 🅃 *He passed around the hat to everyone.* □ *I'll pass the hat around.*

PASS ▶ AS

pass as someone or something to be accepted as an authentic type of person or thing. □ *Frank was very often able to pass as his twin brother.* □ *This car could pass as a valuable antique.*

PASS ▶ AWAY

pass away to die. (Euphemistic.) □ *Uncle Herman passed away many years ago.* □ *He passed away in his sleep.*

PASS ▶ BACK

pass something back (to someone) to return something by hand to someone. □ *Kelly passed the pictures back to Betty.* □ *They weren't Betty's and she passed them back to Beth.*

PASS ▶ BETWEEN

pass between people or things to move between people and things, in any combination. □ *The huge dog passed between Jerry and Dave and nearly knocked them over.* □ *The car had to pass between two large pillars in order to enter the ancient city.*

PASS ▶ BY

pass by (someone or something) to move or travel past someone, something, or some place. □ *Please don't pass by me so fast.* □ *If you pass by a large white house with a red roof, you have gone too far.*

PASS ▶ DOWN

pass something down (to someone) AND **pass something on (to someone) 1.** to send something down a line of people to someone. (Each person hands it to the next.) □ *Please pass this down to Mary at the end of the row.* 🅃 *Pass down this box to Mary.* □ *Mary wants this. Please pass it down.* □ *Mary is expecting this. Please pass it on.* **2.** to will something to someone. □ *My grandfather passed this watch down to me.* 🅃 *He passed on the watch to me.* □ *I have always wanted it and I'm so glad he passed it down.*

PASS ▶ FOR

pass for someone or something to be accepted as someone, some type of person, or something. □ *You could pass for your twin brother.* □ *This painting could almost pass for the original.*

PASS ▶ FORWARD

pass something forward to send something toward the front of a group of people. (Each person hands it to the next.) ☐ *Please pass this forward to the front of the room.* ☐ *Would you pass this book forward, please?*

PASS ▸ FROM

pass from something to fade away from something; to go away gradually. ☐ *The larger trees had passed from the scene years ago.* ☐ *The correct numbers passed from Harry's memory some time ago.*

PASS ▸ IN

pass in review [for marchers] to move past an important person for a visual examination. ☐ *All the soldiers passed in review on the Fourth of July.* ☐ *As they passed in review, each of them saluted the officers on the reviewing stand.*

pass something in (to someone) AND **hand something in (to someone)** to turn in or hand in something, such as a school assignment, paper, etc., to someone. ☐ *They were told to pass their papers in to the teacher.* 🅃 *Hand in your papers to me.* ☐ *Please hand your papers in.*

PASS ▸ INTO

pass into something to move into something; to fade away into something. ☐ *Thoughts about the accident, little by little, passed into oblivion.* ☐ *All her old school chums passed into oblivion.*

PASS ▸ OFF

pass someone or something off (on someone) (as someone or something) See under *PALM ▸ OFF.*

PASS ▸ ON

pass judgment on someone or something to render a judgment of someone or something; to act as judge of someone or something. ☐ *I hope you are not going to pass judgment on all of us.* ☐ *Don't pass judgment on the food until you have eaten the entire meal.*

pass on to die. ☐ *When did your uncle pass on?* ☐ *Uncle Herman passed on nearly thirty years ago.*

pass on someone or something to accept or approve someone or something. ☐ *She refused to pass on Ted, so he will not be appointed.* ☐ *The committee passed on the proposal and work can begin.*

pass on (to someone or something) to leave the person or thing being dealt with and move on to another person or thing. ☐ *I am finished with Henry. I will pass on to Jerry.* ☐ *I will pass on when I am finished.*

pass sentence on someone **1.** [for a judge] to read out the sentence of punishment for a convicted criminal. ☐ *It is my job as judge to pass sentence on you.* ☐ *The judge was about to pass sentence on Max when Lefty broke into the courtroom and took the foreman of the jury hostage.* **2.** [for someone] to render a judgment on another person in the manner of a judge. ☐ *You have no right to pass judgment on me!* ☐ *I wish you wouldn't pass judgment on everyone around you.*

pass someone on (to someone) to send, hand, or conduct a person to someone else. ☐ *I passed the baby on to the next admiring relative.* 🅃 *She passed on the baby to her aunt.* ☐ *She passed the applicant on to another department head.*

pass something on (to someone) See under *PASS ▸ DOWN.*

PASS ▸ OUT

pass out to faint; to lose consciousness. ☐ *It was so hot in there that I nearly passed out.* ☐ *Sarah nearly passed out from the heat.*

pass something out (to someone) to distribute something to someone. ☐ *Please pass these out to everyone.* 🅃 *Pass out these papers to everyone.* ☐ *Please pass them out.*

PASS ▸ OVER

pass over (someone or something) **1.** to skip over someone or something; to fail to select someone or something. ☐ *I was next in line for a promotion, but they passed over me.* ☐ *I passed over the bruised apples and picked out the nicest ones.* **2.** to pass above someone or something. ☐ *A cloud passed over our little group, cooling us a little.* ☐ *The* *huge blimp passed over the little community.*

pass something over (to someone) to send something to someone farther down in a line of people. (Each person hands it to the next.) □ *Please pass this paper over to Jane.* 🅃 *Would you pass over this paper to Jane?* □ *I would be happy to pass it over.*

PASS ▸ THROUGH

pass through someone to work through the bowels of someone. □ *This lovely piece of fruit should pass through you in no time at all.* □ *He will be better when the offending food passes through him.*

pass through someone's mind [for an idea] to occur in someone's mind. □ *You wouldn't believe what just passed through my mind.* □ *An interesting thought just passed through my mind.*

pass through something to travel through something or some place. □ *I passed through the countryside and breathed the good clean air.* □ *Perhaps I will stop and visit Joe the next time I pass through Adamsville.*

PASS ▸ TO

pass something to someone to hand or send something to someone, usually by way of a number of other people. □ *Please pass this paper to Betty.* □ *Who passed this to me?*

pass the hat (around) (to someone) See under *PASS ▸ AROUND.*

PASS ▸ UNDER

pass under something to move or travel beneath something. □ *The ship slowly passed under the bridge.* □ *Harry counted the cars as they passed under the bridge.*

PASS ▸ UP

pass someone or something up **1.** to fail to select someone or something. □ *The committee passed Jill up and chose Kelly.* 🅃 *They passed up Jill.* □ *We had to pass your application up this year.* **2.** to travel past someone or something. □ *We had to pass her up, thinking we could visit her the next time we were in town.* 🅃 *We passed up a hitchhiker.* 🅃 *You passed up a nice restaurant near the edge of town when you left.*

PASTE ▸ DOWN

paste something down to secure something down [onto something] with paste or glue. □ *The poster will look better if you will paste the loose edges down.* 🅃 *Please paste down the edges.*

PASTE ▸ ON

paste something on someone **1.** to affix something to someone with paste or glue. □ *We had to paste a mustache on her for the last scene of the play.* 🅃 *They pasted on a beard too.* **2.** to charge someone with a crime. (Slang.) □ *You can't paste that charge on me! Max did it!* □ *The cops pasted a robbery charge on Lefty "Fingers" Moran.* **3.** to land a blow on someone. (Slang.) □ *If you do that again, I'll paste one on you.* □ *Max pasted a nasty blow on Lefty's chin.*

PASTE ▸ UP

paste something up **1.** to repair something with paste. □ *See if you can paste this book up so it will hold together.* 🅃 *Paste up the book and hope it holds together for a while.* **2.** to assemble a complicated page of material by pasting the parts together. □ *There is no way a typesetter can get this page just the way you want it. You'll have to paste it up yourself.* 🅃 *Paste up this page again and let me see it.* 🄰 *You need to make a pasted-up version before you do the real thing.* 🄽 *Take this pasteup back to the art department.*

PAT ▸ DOWN

pat something down to tap something down with the open hand. □ *I heaped some soil over the seeds and patted it down.* 🅃 *I patted down the soil.*

PAT ▸ ON

pat someone on the back (for something) to praise someone for something. (Literal and figurative uses. *Someone* includes *oneself.*) □ *The teacher patted all the students on the back for their good work.* □ *If she does her work well, you need to pat her on the back.* □ *They were patting them-*

selves on the back for winning when the final whistle blew.

pat someone or something on something to tap someone or something on a particular place with the open hand. □ *She patted the child on the bottom.* □ *I patted the car on its hood to show how proud I was of it.*

PATCH ▸ TOGETHER

patch something together (with something) to use something to repair something hastily or temporarily. □ *I think I can patch the exhaust pipe together with some wire.* □ *See if you can patch this engine together well enough to run for a few more hours.*

PATCH ▸ UP

patch a quarrel up to put an end to a quarrel; to reconcile quarreling parties. □ *Tom and Fred were able to patch their quarrel up.* 🅃 *I hope we can patch up this quarrel.*

patch someone up to give medical care to someone. (Slang.) □ *That cut looks bad, but the doc over there can patch you up.* 🅃 *The doc patched up my friend.* 🄰 *The patched-up soldier returned immediately to combat.*

patch something up to repair something in a hurry; to make something temporarily serviceable again. □ *Can you patch this up so I can use it again?* 🅃 *I'll patch up the hose for you.* 🄰 *I don't want an old patched-up car. I want a new one.*

PATTERN ▸ AFTER

pattern something after something to use something as an example or model when making something. □ *I patterned my house after one I saw in England.* □ *She wanted to pattern her coat after her mother's.*

PATTERN ▸ ON

pattern something on something to use something as a model for something else. □ *Try to pattern your sales speech on Jane's. She's got it just right.* □ *We patterned our approach on Bob's.*

PAVE ▸ FOR

pave the way (for someone or something) (with something) to prepare the way with something for someone to come or something to happen. □ *I will pave the way for her with an introduction.* □ *I am sure I can pave the way for your success.* □ *I will pave the way with an introduction.*

PAVE ▸ WITH

See the previous entry.

PAWN ▸ OFF

pawn someone or something off (on someone) (as someone or something) See under *PALM ▸ OFF.*

PAY ▸ BACK

pay someone back **1.** to return money that was borrowed from a person. □ *You owe me money. When are you going to pay me back?* □ *You must pay John back. You have owed him money for a long time.* **2.** to get even with someone [for doing something]. (Figurative.) □ *I will pay her back for what she said about me.* □ *Max will pay Lefty back. He bears a grudge for a long time.*

pay something back to repay a debt. □ *I hope to be able to pay the loan back next month.* 🅃 *I will pay back the debt.*

pay something back (to someone) to repay someone. □ *I paid the money back to Jerry.* 🅃 *Can I pay back the money to George now?* □ *Please pay the money back now.*

PAY ▸ BY

pay by something **1.** to use something as a medium of payment. □ *Will you pay by cash or check?* □ *The bill was paid by check.* **2.** to pay by a certain time. □ *You will have to pay by the end of the month or we will cancel your lease.* □ *I promise I will pay by the end of the month.*

PAY ▸ DOWN

pay something down to make a deposit of money on a purchase. □ *You will have to pay a lot of money down on a car that expensive.* 🅃 *I only paid down a few thousand dollars.*

pay something down to reduce a bill by paying part of it, usually periodically. □ *I think I can pay the balance down by half in a few months.* 🅃 *I will pay down the balance a little next month.*

PAY ▸ FOR

pay for someone to pay someone's admission, charges, bill, etc. □ *Put your money away! You are my guest and I will pay for you.* □ *Who will pay for my friend?*

pay for something **1.** to pay the cost of something. □ *Where do I pay for this merchandise? I don't see a cashier.* □ *How much did you pay for that?* **2.** to be punished for something. (Figurative.) □ *You will pay for doing that to me!* □ *Max paid for his wicked ways.*

pay someone (for something) (with something) to make payment with something to someone for something or for doing something. □ *I will pay you for the loan you made me with the money I get for selling my car.* □ *I will pay you with a check.* □ *I can't pay for this!* □ *I will pay with cash for my share of the bill.*

PAY ▸ IN

pay in advance to make payment before receiving goods or services. □ *Since this is a special order, you will have to pay in advance.* □ *It was a mistake to pay in advance.*

PAY ▸ IN(TO)

pay into something to pay money into an account. □ *I intend to pay into my vacation account until I have enough for a nice vacation.* □ *We paid a lot into our savings account this month.*

pay something in(to something) to pay an amount of money into an account. □ *Mary paid forty dollars into my account by mistake.* 🅃 *She paid in a lot of money.* □ *I have an account here and I want to pay something in.*

PAY ▸ OFF

pay off to yield profits; to result in benefits. □ *My investment in those stocks has really paid off.* □ *The time I spent in school paid off in later years.*

pay someone off **1.** to pay what is owed to a person. □ *I can't pay you off until Wednesday when I get my paycheck.* 🅃 *I have to use this money to pay off Sarah.* **2.** to bribe someone. (Slang.) □ *Max asked Lefty if he had paid the cops off yet.* 🅃 *Lefty paid off the cops on time.* 🄽 *The crook tried to give the cop a payoff.*

pay something off to pay the total amount of a bill; to settle an account by paying the total sum. □ *You should pay the total off as soon as possible to avoid having to pay more interest.* 🅃 *I will pay off the entire amount.* 🄰 *Here is a record of a paid-off loan in your name.*

PAY ▸ ON

pay on something to make a payment against a bill. □ *You have to pay on this every month or we will repossess it.* □ *How much do you plan to pay on the car per month?*

PAY ▸ OUT

pay something out to unravel or unwind wire or rope as it is needed. □ *One worker paid the cable out and another worker guided it into the conduit.* 🅃 *The worker paid out the cable.* 🄰 *The paid-out rope lashed against the side of the truck.*

pay something out (for someone or something) to disburse money for something or something. □ *We have already paid too much money out for your education.* 🅃 *We paid out too much money.* □ *How much did you pay out?* 🄽 *My monthly payout is too high.*

pay something out (to someone) to pay money to someone. □ *The grocery store paid one hundred dollars out to everyone who had become ill.* 🅃 *They paid out money to people who claimed illness.* □ *Alice, the cashier, paid the money out as it was requested.* 🄽 *I want my payout now!*

PAY ▸ THROUGH

pay through something to make payment through an intermediary, such as a bank. □ *I will pay the bill through my bank in New York.* □ *Sam had to pay through his brokerage account.*

pay through the nose (for something) to pay a great amount of money for something. (A cliché.) □ *Yes, I managed to get the kind of shoes I wanted, but I had to pay through the nose for them.* □ *I got it, but I had to pay through the nose.*

PAY ▸ TO

pay attention to someone or something to heed someone or something; to concentrate on someone or something. □ *Please pay attention to me.* □ *Please pay attention to what you are doing.*

pay court to someone to solicit someone's attention; to woo someone. □ *The lawyer was thought to be paying court to too many politicians.* □ *The lobbyist paid court to all the influential members of Congress.*

pay heed to someone to listen to and accommodate someone. □ *You had better pay heed to your father!* □ *They are not paying heed to what I told them.*

pay homage to someone or something to honor or worship someone or something. □ *Do you expect me to pay homage to your hero?* □ *I refuse to pay homage to your principles.*

pay lip service to someone or something to give insincere support to someone or something. □ *You are just paying lip service to Jane. You are not really supporting her candidacy at all.* □ *You don't care about the election! You are just paying lip service to this exercise in democracy.*

pay tribute to someone or something to salute someone or something; to give public recognition to someone or something. □ *Many of Judy's friends gathered to pay tribute to her.* □ *We will have a reception to pay tribute to the work of the committee.*

PAY ▸ UP

pay something up to pay all of whatever is due; to complete all the payments on something. □ *Please pay all your bills up.* 🅃 *Would you pay up your bills, please?* □ *Your dues are all paid up.*

pay up to pay what is owed. (Often a command: **Pay up!**) □ *I want my money now. Pay up!* 🄰 *This is a paid-up account. I owe nothing.*

PAY ▸ WITH

pay someone (for something) (with something) See under *PAY ▸ FOR.*

PEAL ▸ OUT

peal out [for bells or voices] to sound forth musically. □ *The bells pealed out to announce that the wedding had taken place.* □ *All six of the bells seemed to peal out at once.*

PECK ▸ AT

peck at someone or something [for a bird] to poke someone or something with its beak. □ *The bird pecked at the ground, snatching up the ants.* □ *I tried to hold on to the bird but it pecked at me hard.*

peck at something [for someone] to eat just a little bit of something, being as picky as a bird. □ *Are you well, Betty? You are just pecking at your food.* □ *Please don't peck at your food. You should eat everything.*

PECK ▸ UP

peck something up [for a bird] to eat something up by pecking at it. □ *The chickens pecked all the grain up.* 🅃 *The birds pecked up the grain.*

PEEK ▸ AT

peek at someone or something to sneak a glimpse at someone or something. □ *Now, don't peek at me while I am changing my shirt.* □ *I peeked at the dessert you made. It looks delicious.*

PEEK ▸ IN

peek in (on someone or something) to glance quickly into a place to see someone or something. □ *Would you please peek in on the baby?* □ *Yes, I'll peek in in a minute.*

PEEK ▸ IN(TO)

peek in(to something) to steal a quick glimpse into something. □ *Sam peeked into the oven to see what was cooking.* □ *Laura opened the oven door and peeked in.*

PEEK ▶ OUT

peek out (from behind someone or something) **1.** to look outward from behind someone or something. ☐ *A shy kitten peeked out from behind the sofa.* ☐ *I looked toward the back of the sofa just as a little cat face peeked out.* **2.** to show just a little bit with the rest concealed behind someone or something. ☐ *A bit of yellow peeked out from behind the tree, so we knew Frank was hiding there.* ☐ *We saw a flash of Frank's yellow shirt peek out.*

peek out (from underneath someone or something) **1.** to look outward from beneath someone or something. ☐ *A small furry face peeked out from underneath the sofa.* ☐ *At the base of the sofa, a cat peeked out.* **2.** to show just a little bit with the rest concealed under someone or something. ☐ *Her petticoat peeked out from underneath her skirt.* ☐ *Her skirt was a tad too short and a little bit of lace peeked out.*

peek out of something (at someone or something) **1.** to be inside of something and take a look out. ☐ *A pair of glimmering eyes peeked out of the darkened room at the two people standing at the door.* ☐ *I peeked out of my room at the eerie shadows in the hallway.* ☐ *Jerry peeked out of the bathroom to see if anyone was looking.* **2.** [for a little bit of something] to be revealed with the rest concealed within. ☐ *A band of white skin peeked out of his shirt sleeve at us. He had had his watch on when he got his suntan.* ☐ *A bit of white skin peeked out.*

PEEK ▶ OVER

peek over something **1.** to examine something with a quick glance. ☐ *I really can't say how good the story was. I only peeked over it.* ☐ *I peeked over your manuscript, and it looks good.* **2.** to raise up and look over some barrier. ☐ *I peeked over the wall and saw the lovely garden.* ☐ *Don't peek over the sofa and let Roger see you. It will ruin the surprise.*

PEEK ▶ THROUGH

peek through (something) **1.** to peer or glimpse through something. ☐ *I'll just peek through your picture album. I'll study it more carefully later.* ☐ *I only have time to peek through. I would like to spend more time with it later.* **2.** [for something] to become slightly visible through something. ☐ *Mary, the lace of your slip is peeking through your blouse!* ☐ *Some lace is peeking through.*

PEEK ▶ UNDER

peek under something to sneak a little glance beneath something. ☐ *I peeked under the table, hoping to see the dog waiting there for the part of my dinner I wasn't going to eat.* ☐ *Peek under the chair and see if the cat is there.*

PEEL ▶ AWAY

peel something away (from something) to peel something from the surface of something. ☐ *Peel the label away from the envelope and place it on the order form.* 🅃 *Peel away the label carefully.* ☐ *I peeled it away and disposed of it.*

PEEL ▶ BACK

peel something back (from something) to lift something away from the surface of something. ☐ *He peeled the sheets back from the bed and got in.* 🅃 *He peeled back the sheets and got into the bed.* ☐ *When he peeled the banana skin back, he found that the banana was not ripe.*

PEEL ▶ OFF

peel off (from something) [for one or more airplanes] to separate from a group of airplanes. ☐ *The lead plane peeled off from the others, and soon the rest followed.* ☐ *The lead plane peeled off and dived into the clouds.*

peel off ((of) something) [for a surface layer] to come loose and fall away from something. (The *of* is colloquial.) ☐ *The paint is beginning to peel off the garage.* ☐ *The paint is peeling off.*

peel something off ((of) something) AND **peel something off from something** to remove the outside surface layer from something. (The *of*-phrase is paraphrased with a *from*-phrase when the particle is transposed. See the [F] example. The *of* is colloquial.) □ *She carefully peeled the skin off the apple.* [T] *She peeled off the apple's skin.* [F] *She peeled off the skin from the apple.* □ *Please peel the skin off.*

PEEL ▸ OUT

peel out [for a driver] to speed off in a car with a great screeching of tires. (As if the rubber were being peeled off the tires.) □ *Dave got in his car and peeled out, waking the neighbors.* □ *I wish he would stop peeling out!*

PEEP ▸ AT

peep at someone or something to get a glimpse of someone or something, as if looking through a hole. □ *I peeped at Tom through the venetian blinds.* □ *Look in the microscope and peep at this bacterium.*

PEEP ▸ IN(TO)

peep in(to something) to get a quick look into something, as through a hole in the wall or something similar. □ *I peeped into the oven to see what was cooking for dinner.* □ *She opened the oven door and peeped in.*

PEEP ▸ OUT

peep out (of something) (at someone or something) to sneak a glimpse of someone or something out of something, as through a hole. □ *A little mouse peeped out of its hole at the bright lights in the room.* □ *Johnny, hiding in the closet, peeped out at the guests through the partly opened door.*

PEEP ▸ OVER

peep over something to raise up and sneak a glance over some barrier; to look over the top of something. □ *The child peeped over the wall to get a look at the yard next door.* □ *Grandfather peeped over his glasses to look at the television set for a moment.*

PEEP ▸ THROUGH

peep through something to take a quick glance through something, such as a hole, telescope, etc. □ *Sam peeped through the keyhole and saw that the room was dark.* □ *Peep through the telescope and have a look at the moon!*

PEEP ▸ UNDER

peep under something to take a quick little glance under something. □ *Would you please peep under the table and see if my shoes are there?* □ *Dave peeped under the bed, looking for the cat.*

PEER ▸ ABOUT

peer about to stare around; to look at everything about. □ *She came into the room and peered about.* □ *Mary peered about, looking for a place to sit.*

PEER ▸ AT

peer at someone or something to look at someone or something closely; to stare at and examine someone or something. □ *The child peered at me for a while in a strange way.* □ *The owl peered at the snake for a moment before grabbing it.*

PEER ▸ IN(TO)

peer in(to something) to stare into something; to look deep into something. □ *I peered into the room, hoping to get a glimpse of the lovely furnishings.* □ *I only had time to peer in.*

PEER ▸ OUT

peer out at someone or something to stare out at someone or something. □ *A little puppy peered out at them from the cage.* □ *When I looked under the box, Timmy peered out at me with a big smile.*

PEER ▸ OVER

peer over something to stare out or look over something, such as one's glasses. □ *The old man peered over his glasses and looked off into the distance.* □ *She peered over the wall to see what she could see.*

PEER ▸ THROUGH

peer through something **1.** to view or look through glasses, spectacles, binoculars, etc. □ *From the way she peered through her glasses at me, I knew I was in trouble.* □ *Claire stood on the balcony, peering through her binoculars.* **2.** to stare through a partial barrier, such as a window, drapes, the haze, the fog, etc.

☐ *George peered through the drapes and spied on the party next door.* ☐ *Sally peered through the haze as best she could, trying to see if the way was clear.*

PEER ► UNDER

peer under something to look underneath something. ☐ *She peered under the bed, hoping to find her slippers.* ☐ *When she peered under the bed, she found nothing but lint.*

PEG ► AS

peg someone or something as something to appraise someone or something to be something. (Informal.) ☐ *I pegged you as a more sedate character than you turned out to be.* ☐ *We had pegged him as a real pest, and then we learned how helpful he is.*

PEG ► AWAY

peg away at something to keep trying to do something. (Slang.) ☐ *You should just keep pegging away at the task. You'll get it done sooner or later.* ☐ *She had pegged away at the task for an hour, and then she quit.*

PEG ► DOWN

peg something down to fasten something to the ground with pegs. ☐ *After he had finished pegging the tent down, he built a fire.* 🅃 *He pegged down the tent before building a fire.*

PEG ► OUT

peg out to die. (Slang.) ☐ *I was so scared, I thought I would peg out for sure.* ☐ *Uncle Herman almost pegged out last week.*

PELT ► DOWN

pelt down (on someone or something) [for something] to fall down on someone or something. (Typically rain, hail, sleet, stones, etc.) ☐ *The rain pelted down on the children as they ran to their school bus.* ☐ *The ashes from the volcanic eruption pelted down on the town, covering the houses in a gray shroud.*

PELT ► WITH

pelt someone or something with something to hit or strike someone or something with something. ☐ *The citizens pelted Max with rocks.* ☐ *The boys pelted the mad dog with a hail of stones.*

PEN ► IN

pen someone or something in (some place) to confine someone or some creature in a pen. ☐ *We penned all the kids in in the backyard while we got the party things ready in the house.* 🅃 *We had to pen in the kids to keep them away from the traffic.* ☐ *Alice penned her dog in.*

PEN ► UP

pen someone or something up to confine someone or something to a pen. (Implies more security than the previous entry.) ☐ *He said he didn't want them to pen him up in an office all day.* 🅃 *They penned up the dog during the day.* 🄰 *These penned-up animals must be given some exercise immediately.*

PENALIZE ► FOR

penalize someone for something to punish someone for something. (*Someone* includes *oneself*.) ☐ *It's not fair to penalize her for being late.* ☐ *You needn't penalize yourself for the failure. It wasn't all your fault.*

PENCIL ► IN

pencil someone or something in to write in something with a pencil. (Implies that the writing is not final.) ☐ *I will pencil you in for a Monday appointment.* ☐ *This isn't the final answer, so I will just pencil it in.* 🅃 *I penciled in a tentative answer.* 🄰 *This is just a penciled-in figure. I want all figures final and written in ink.*

PENETRATE ► INTO

penetrate into someone or something to pierce into someone or something; to stick deep into someone or something. ☐ *The lance penetrated into the knight, right through his armor.* ☐ *The bullet penetrated into the wall.*

PENETRATE ► THROUGH

penetrate through something to pierce all the way through something. (Some people will view the *through* as redundant.) ☐ *The bullet could not penetrate through the metal plating.* ☐ *It did not* *have enough force to penetrate through the steel.*

PENETRATE ► WITH

penetrate something with something to pierce something with something. □ *I could not even penetrate the steel door with a cold chisel.* □ *It was easy to penetrate the lid with a can opener.*

PENSION ► OFF

pension someone off to retire someone with a pension. □ *The company tried to pension me off before I was ready to retire.* 🅃 *They pensioned off the loyal workers.*

PEOPLE ► WITH

people something with someone to provide population for something or some place, using someone or some kind of people. □ *The government decided to people the frontier with a variety of races.* □ *The island had been peopled with marooned sailors.*

PEP ► UP

pep someone or something up to make someone or something more vigorous. □ *Nancy needs to take some vitamins to pep her up.* 🅃 *The vitamins pepped up the tired workers.* □ *Better food might pep your cat up.* □ *After the play's first performance, the author pepped up the second act.*

PEPPER ► WITH

pepper someone or something with something to shower someone or something with something, such as stones, bullets, etc. □ *The angry crowd peppered the police with stones.* □ *The sheriff's posse peppered the bandit's hideout with bullets.*

PERCEIVE ► AS

perceive someone or something as something to think of someone or something as something or as displaying certain characteristics. □ *I perceive Randy as sort of hotheaded.* □ *We all perceive this problem as solvable.*

PERCH ► ON

perch on something **1.** [for a bird] to stand at rest on something. □ *A robin perched on the branch by my window.* □ *We saw a parrot perched on some kind of flowering tree.* **2.** to sit or balance on something. □ *I can't perch on this fence forever. Let's go.* □ *Sam was perched on the bicycle and he looked very uncomfortable.*

perch someone or something on something □ *She perched the little girl on the edge of the tub.* □ *Walter perched his hat on the top shelf.*

PERCOLATE ► THROUGH

percolate through something [for a liquid] to seep down through something. □ *The water percolated through the coffee grounds too slowly for Fred, who was just dying for a hot cup of the stuff.* □ *The water percolated through the subsoil and appeared again at the bottom of the hill.*

PERFORM ► ON

perform something on someone or something to do something to someone or something; to carry out a procedure on someone or something. □ *The surgeon performed a simple office procedure on the patient.* □ *Do you expect me to perform magic on this problem?*

PERISH ► FROM

perish from something to die from a particular cause, such as a disease. □ *Nearly all the fish perished from the cold.* □ *I was afraid that I would perish from hunger.*

PERISH ► IN

perish in something to die because of involvement in something. □ *Four people perished in the flames.* □ *Our cat perished in an accident.*

PERISH ► WITH

perish with something to feel bad enough to die because of something, such as heat, hunger, etc. □ *I was just perishing with hunger when we arrived at the restaurant.* □ *Mary felt as if she would perish with the intense heat of the stuffy little room.*

PERK ► UP

perk someone or something up to refresh someone or something. □ *Have a drink of cool water. That ought to perk* *you up.* 🅃 *The cool water perked up the thirsty hikers.* □ *A bit of bright yellow here and there will perk this room up a lot.*

perk up to be invigorated; to become more active. □ *After a bit of water, the plants perked up nicely.* □ *About noon, Andy perked up and looked wide-awake.*

PERMEATE ▸ THROUGH

permeate through something to seep in and saturate something. (The *through* is redundant.) □ *The paint spilled on the desk and permeated through all the papers and stuff.* □ *The strong odor permeated through the walls and nearly suffocated us.*

PERMEATE ▸ WITH

permeate something with something to saturate something with something. □ *The comedian permeated his act with smutty jokes.* □ *The evening air was permeated with the smell of jasmine.*

PERMIT ▸ IN(TO)

permit someone in(to something) to allow someone to enter something or some place. □ *They would not permit me in the dining room since I had no tie.* 🅃 *They would not permit in any of her friends.* □ *Do not permit Larry in. He is being a pest.*

PERMIT ▸ OUT

permit someone out (of something) to allow someone to go out of something or some place. □ *His mother won't permit him out of his room all weekend.* □ *I didn't do anything, but she won't permit me out!*

PERMIT ▸ THROUGH

permit someone through (something) to allow someone to pass through something. □ *Would you permit me through the door? I have to get into this building.* □ *Janet said she was in a hurry, but they wouldn't permit her through.*

PERMIT ▸ UP

permit someone up (something) to allow someone to come up something. □ *She would not permit me up the ladder.* □ *I wanted to climb the ladder to be with Walter, but he wouldn't permit me up.*

permit someone up to something to allow someone to come up to something or some place. □ *The teacher would not permit the smallest children up to the edge.* □ *They would not permit us up to the gate before our turn came.*

PERSECUTE ▸ FOR

persecute someone for something to harass or repress someone for something. □ *They were persecuting the native people for being underdeveloped.* □ *They were persecuted for being simple and unsuspecting.*

PERSEVERE ▸ AT

persevere at something to keep trying to do something. □ *I will persevere at my studies and I'm sure I will succeed.* □ *Todd persevered at his job and got promoted in no time.*

PERSEVERE ▸ IN

persevere in something to persist in [doing] something. □ *I will persevere in my efforts to win election.* □ *Kelly persevered in her studies and graduated with honors.*

PERSEVERE ▸ WITH

persevere with something to continue to try to accomplish something. □ *Do you really think it is wise to persevere with your plan?* □ *Sally persevered with her scheme to earn a million dollars.*

PERSIST ▸ IN

persist in something to continue doing or thinking something. □ *I wish you would not persist in your efforts.* □ *Mary persisted in her questioning.*

PERSIST ▸ WITH

persist with something to continue with some activity or plan. □ *I assume that you intend to persist with your efforts to learn to play chess.* □ *Surely she will not persist with this any longer.*

PERSUADE ▸ OF

persuade someone of something to convince someone of something. □ *Laura was unable to persuade me of the truth of her statement.* □ *We were all persuaded of the need for higher taxes.*

PERSUADE ► TO

persuade someone to do something to convince someone to do something. □ *Are you sure I can't persuade you to have another piece of cake?* □ *Richard was easily persuaded to have another piece of his favorite cake.*

PERTAIN ► TO

pertain to someone or something to relate to someone or something; to have something to do with someone or something. □ *I don't think that anything discussed in this meeting pertained to me.* □ *It really doesn't pertain to the matter at hand.*

PESTER ► ABOUT

pester someone about someone or something to bother someone about someone or something. □ *Please don't pester me about Frank.* □ *Stop pestering me about money.*

PESTER ► INTO

pester someone into something to annoy someone into doing something. □ *We are trying to pester her into accepting the position.* □ *I don't want to be pestered into losing my temper!*

PESTER ► OUT

pester someone out of something **1.** to annoy someone out of doing something. □ *Dave pestered Mary out of going away for the weekend.* □ *He pestered her out of leaving without him.* **2.** to annoy one out of one's mind, senses, good manners, etc. □ *You are pestering me out of my typically polite decorum! Stop it!* □ *I was pestered out of my mind by a series of silly questions.*

pester the life out of someone to annoy someone excessively. (Figurative.) □ *Leave me alone. You are pestering the life out of me.* □ *Stop pestering the life out of me!*

PESTER ► WITH

pester someone with something to annoy someone with something. □ *Don't pester me with your constant questions!* □ *I was pestered with phone call after phone call.*

PETER ► OUT

peter out to fade away; to dwindle away. □ *All my energy peters out at about three o'clock.* □ *The party sort of petered out about midnight.*

PETITION ► FOR

petition someone or something for something to make a formal request of someone or a group for something. □ *They petitioned us for an end to unpaid overtime.* □ *We had to petition the upper administration for a revision in the policy.* 🄰 *We regret to inform you that your petitioned-for change cannot be made.*

PHASE ► IN(TO)

phase someone or something in(to something) to work someone or something into use or service gradually. (*Someone* includes *oneself*.) □ *They decided to phase Ruth into the job little by little.* 🅃 *They phased in Ruth over a long period of time.* □ *We will phase the new machine in gradually.* 🄰 *Your smoothly phased-in changes were almost unnoticed.* □ *Cleverly, she phased herself into the committee without offending anyone.*

PHASE ► OUT

phase someone or something out (of something) to work someone or something out of use or service or out of a group gradually. □ *We are going to have to phase you out of the job of treasurer.* 🅃 *They phased out the unneeded workers.* □ *The manufacturer is planning to phase this model out.* 🄰 *The phased-out model was available nowhere.* □ *He phased himself out of office instead of quitting all at once.*

PHONE ► IN

phone in (to someone or something) to call in by telephone to a central person or central point. □ *I will phone in to my secretary and report the change in schedule.* □ *I have to phone in and report the changes.*

phone something in (to someone or something) to transmit information to a central person or central point by telephone. □ *I will phone this order in to* *the plant right away.* 🅃 *I will phone in the order to my secretary right now.* □ *Don't worry. I'll phone it in.* 🄰 *I am sorry, but we cannot accept phoned-in orders.*

PHONE ▸ UP

phone someone up to call someone on the telephone. □ *I don't know what he will do. I will phone him up and ask him.* 🅃 *Phone up your brother and ask his advice.*

PICK ▸ APART

pick someone or something apart **1.** to peck at and pull someone or something to pieces. □ *The storks attacked the hunger-weakened man and tried to pick him apart.* 🅃 *They tried to pick apart the body.* □ *Harry picked the whole cake apart, looking for the lost diamond ring.* **2.** to analyze and criticize someone or something negatively. □ *You didn't review her performance; you just picked her apart.* 🅃 *The critics picked apart the performers.*

PICK ▸ AT

pick at someone or something **1.** to try to pull away bits of someone or something. □ *The vultures picked at the dead convict. At last he was serving a purpose in life.* □ *Don't pick at the bookbinding. It will fall apart.* **2.** to criticize someone or something. (Figurative.) □ *I wish you would stop picking at me!* □ *The critics picked at the little things, missing the serious problems.*

pick at something to eat just a tiny bit of a meal or some kind of food. □ *You are just picking at your food!* 🄰 *Just put her picked-at food in the refrigerator. We'll heat it up for her supper.*

PICK ▸ AWAY

pick something away to pull or pinch something loose from something. □ *Tim picked the burrs away from his pants legs.* □ *Mary picked the meat away from the bones.* 🅃 *He picked away the burrs.*

PICK ▸ FROM

pick someone or something from someone or something to choose someone from a group of people; to choose something from a group of things. □ *I picked Joe from all the other boys.* □ *Tony picked this one from the collection.*

PICK ▸ IN

pick holes in something **1.** to poke or pinch little holes in something. □ *Look! You've picked holes in the bread! How can I make sandwiches?* □ *Who picked holes in the blanket?* **2.** to find all the weak points in an argument or case. (Figurative.) □ *The lawyer picked holes in the witness's testimony and won the case.* □ *Stop picking holes in everything I say!*

PICK ▸ OFF

pick someone or something off to shoot someone or something with a gun, especially from a distance or from a place of concealment. □ *The bandits picked the members of the sheriff's posse off one by one.* 🅃 *The hunter went into the forest, hoping to pick off a rabbit or even a deer.* □ *The hunter picked two rabbits off in the first hour.*

pick someone or something off ((of) someone or something) to pull or gather someone or something off something. (The *of*-phrase is paraphrased with a *from*-phrase when the particle is transposed. See the 🄵 example. The *of* is colloquial.) □ *The teacher picked the little boys off the jungle gym and hurried them back into the school building before the storm hit.* 🅃 *Pick off the ripe tomatoes and leave the rest.* 🄵 *Pick off the ripe tomatoes from the other vines.* □ *King Kong picked the man off the tree as if he were a gnat.*

PICK ▸ ON

pick on someone or something to harass or bother someone or something, usually unfairly. □ *Please stop picking on me! I'm tired of it.* □ *You shouldn't pick on the cat.* 🄰 *The frequently picked-on child was always nervous.*

PICK ▸ OUT

pick someone or something out (for someone or something) to choose someone or something to serve as someone or something. □ *I picked one of the new people out for Santa Claus this year.*

T *I picked out several large potatoes for the stew.* T *Sally picked out a ripe one.* □ *I picked her out myself.*

pick someone or something out (of something) **1.** to lift or pull someone or something out of something. (The *of*-phrase is paraphrased with a *from*-phrase when the particle is transposed. See the F example.) □ *The mother picked her child out of the fray and took him home.* T *I picked out the mushrooms before eating the soup.* F *I picked out the mushrooms from the soup.* □ *Larry fell off the boat into the water, and I picked him out.* **2.** to select someone or something out of an offering of selections. □ *I picked Jerry out of all the boys in the class.* T *I picked out Jerry.* □ *I picked Jerry out.*

PICK ► OVER

pick something over to look through something carefully, looking for something special. □ *The shoppers who got here first picked everything over, and there is not much left.* T *They picked over all the merchandise.* □ *Everything in the store is picked over.* A *She found nothing she wanted in the picked-over goods.*

PICK ► THROUGH

pick one's way through something **1.** to work carefully through something, handling or examining every piece or part. □ *Sam had to pick his way through report after report to find the information.* □ *She picked her way through the store, looking at every product.* **2.** to walk through something carefully. □ *Valerie picked her way through the swamp, step by step.* □ *I had to pick my way carefully through the piles of papers scattered about on the floor.*

PICK ► TO

pick someone or something to pieces **1.** to pull or pinch at someone or something until only pieces are left. □ *The savage birds picked the injured man to pieces.* □ *The mice seem to have picked the stuffed doll to pieces.* **2.** to criticize someone or something until nothing is left uncriticized. (Figurative.) □ *You have just picked her to pieces. Leave her alone!* □ *The critic picked the play to pieces.*

PICK ► UP

pick someone or something up (from something) **1.** to lift up or raise someone or something from a lower place. (*Someone* includes *oneself*.) □ *Please help me pick this guy up from the pavement. He passed out and fell down.* T *Help me pick up this guy from the ground, will you?* □ *Please pick the papers up.* □ *Slowly, she picked herself up from the ground.* **2.** to fetch someone or something from something or some place. □ *I picked her up from the train station.* T *Please pick up my cousin from the airport.* □ *I have to pick my dog up from the vet.* T *The police picked Max up for questioning.* □ *I have to pick up some eggs at the store.* □ *Please go to the post office and pick my package up, will you?* N *I've got to make a pickup on Maple Street now. Good-bye.* **3.** to acquire someone or something. □ *They picked up some valuable antiques at an auction.* □ *She picked up a cold last week.* □ *I picked up a little German while I was in Austria.* □ *The team picked up a good third baseman through a trade.*

pick someone up to acquire a date spontaneously or casually. □ *He picked her up at a bar.* □ *She set out to pick him up, but he would have nothing to do with her.* N *She is nothing but a pickup.*

pick the tab up (for something) to accept the bill for something and pay it. (Informal.) □ *Who will pick the tab up for dinner?* T *Do you think she will pick up the tab for the dinner?* □ *I'll pick it up.*

pick up to increase, as with business, wind, activity, etc. □ *Business is beginning to pick up as we near the holiday season.* N *We are hoping for a pickup in business activity this month.*

pick up (after someone or something) to tidy up after someone or a group. (*Someone* includes *oneself*.) □ *I refuse to pick up after you all the time.* □ *I refuse to pick up after your rowdy friends.* □ *Why do I always have to pick* *up?* □ *You have to learn to pick up after yourself.*

pick up on something to understand and process mentally facts or information very rapidly. □ *He really picked up on that part about getting a new car.* □ *Mary didn't pick up on what he had said for a minute or two.*

pick up speed to increase speed. □ *The train began to pick up speed as it went downhill.* □ *The car picked up speed as we moved into the left lane.*

pick up the pieces (of something) **1.** to gather up each piece or part. □ *Norma picked up the pieces of the broken lamp.* □ *She stooped down to pick up the pieces.* **2.** to try to repair emotional, financial, or other damage done to one's life. □ *I need some time to pick up the pieces of my life after the accident.* □ *After a while, Fred was able to pick up the pieces and carry on.*

PICK ► WITH

pick a fight with someone to start a fight with someone. □ *Are you trying to pick a fight with me?* □ *Max intended to pick a fight with Lefty.*

pick a quarrel with someone to start an argument with someone. □ *Let's not argue. I didn't mean to pick a quarrel with you.* □ *Max picked a quarrel with Lefty.*

PICTURE ► AS

picture someone as someone or something to imagine someone as someone or a type of person; to form a mental picture of someone as someone or a type of person. (*Someone* includes *oneself.*) □ *Just picture me as Santa Claus!* □ *I can't picture you as a doctor.* □ *I really can't picture myself as a grandfather.*

PICTURE ► IN

picture someone in something **1.** to form a mental picture of someone wearing something. (*Someone* includes *oneself.*) □ *I can just picture Tony in that baseball uniform.* □ *Can you picture yourself in a dress like this?* **2.** to form a mental picture of someone inside something or some place. (*Someone* includes *oneself.*) □ *I can just picture you in that car!* □ *Can you picture yourself in jail?*

PIDDLE ► AROUND

piddle around to waste time doing little or nothing. (Colloquial.) □ *Stop piddling around and get busy.* □ *I'm not piddling around. I am experimenting.*

PIDDLE ► AWAY

piddle something away to waste away money or a period of time. (Slang or colloquial.) □ *Please don't piddle all your money away.* [T] *Jane piddled away most of the day.*

PIECE ► OUT

piece something out **1.** to add patches or pieces to something to make it complete. □ *There is not quite enough cloth to make a shirt, but I think I can piece it out with some scraps of a complementary color for the collar.* [T] *We managed to piece out the material that we needed.* **2.** to add missing parts to a story, explanation, or narrative to make it make sense. □ *Before she passed out she muttered a few things and we were able to piece the whole story out from that.* [T] *We pieced out the story from the few bits we heard from her.*

PIECE ► TOGETHER

piece something together to fit something together; to assemble the pieces of something, such as a puzzle or something puzzling, and make sense of it. □ *The police were unable to piece the story together.* [T] *The detective tried to piece together the events leading up to the crime.* [A] *The pieced-together explanation of how things happened would be discussed for a long time to come.*

PIERCE ► THROUGH

pierce through something to poke through something; to penetrate something. □ *He pierced through the meat with a spike and then put it in a spicy marinade.* [T] *Mary pierced the yarn through with the knitting needles.*

PIG ► OUT

pig out (on something) to eat too much of something; to make a pig of oneself. (Slang.) □ *I intend to really pig out on pizza.* □ *I love to pig out on anything.*

PILE ▸ IN(TO)

pile in(to something) to climb into something in a disorderly fashion. □ *Everyone piled into the car, and we left.* □ *Come on. Pile in!*

pile someone in(to something) to bunch people into something in a disorderly fashion. (*Someone* includes *oneself.*) □ *She piled the kids into the van and headed off for school.* [T] *She piled in the kids and closed the doors.* □ *Pile them in and let's go.* □ *They piled themselves into the car and sped off.*

PILE ▸ OFF

pile off (something) to get down off something; to clamber down off something. □ *All the kids piled off the wagon and ran into the barn.* □ *She stopped the wagon and they piled off.*

PILE ▸ ON

pile the work on (someone) to give someone a lot of work to do. (Informal.) □ *The boss really piled the work on me this week.* [T] *The boss piled on the work this week.* □ *She really piles the work on!*

PILE ▸ ON(TO)

pile on((to) someone or something) to make a heap of people on someone or something. □ *The football players piled onto the poor guy holding the ball.* □ *They ran up to the ballcarrier and piled on.*

pile someone or something on((to) someone or something) to heap people or things onto someone or something. □ *The wrestler piled the referee onto the inert form of Gorgeous George, his opponent.* □ *We piled some more wood on the fire and stood back.* □ *We piled the kids on the heap of leaves we had raked up.*

PILE ▸ OUT

pile out (of something) to climb out of something, such as a car. □ *All the kids piled out of the van and ran into the school.* □ *The van pulled up and the kids piled out.*

PILE ▸ UP

pile something up to make something into a heap. □ *Carl piled all the leaves up and set them afire.* [T] *Please pile up the leaves.* [A] *All the piled-up leaves waited to be picked up and hauled away.*

pile up 1. to gather or accumulate. □ *The newspapers began to pile up after a few days.* □ *Work is really piling up around here.* **2.** [for a number of vehicles] to crash together. □ *Nearly twenty cars piled up on the tollway this morning.* [N] *We saw a horrible pileup on the expressway.*

PILFER ▸ FROM

pilfer from someone or something to steal from someone or a group. □ *The petty thief had pilfered from practically everyone in town.* □ *Someone has pilfered from the petty-cash drawer.*

pilfer something from someone or something to steal something from someone or something. □ *Did you pilfer this money from your parents?* □ *Who pilfered some money from the cash box?*

PILOT ▸ IN(TO)

pilot something in(to something) to steer or guide something into something. (Usually refers to steering a ship.) □ *We need to signal for a pilot to pilot our ship into the harbor.* [T] *Fred piloted in the freighter.* □ *Mary piloted the ship in.*

PILOT ▸ OUT

pilot something out (of something) to steer or guide something out of something. (Usually refers to steering a ship.) □ *The chubby little man with a pipe piloted the huge ship out of the harbor.* □ *The storm made it very difficult to pilot the ship out.*

PILOT ▸ THROUGH

pilot someone or something through (something) to guide or steer someone or something through something, especially through a waterway. (Literal or figurative with people or things.) □ *We hired someone to pilot us through the harbor entrance.* □ *The channel was treacherous and we hired someone to pilot the ship through.* □ *John offered to pilot us through the bureaucracy when we went to the court house.*

PIN ▸ AGAINST

pin someone or something against something to press and hold someone or something against something. □ *The police pinned the mugger against the wall and put handcuffs on him.* □ *The wildlife veterinarian pinned the rhino against the walls of the enclosure and subdued it so it could be treated.*

PIN ▸ BACK

pin someone's ears back **1.** to beat someone, especially about the head. (Slang.) □ *Don't talk to me like that or I will pin your ears back!* □ *Max wanted to pin Lefty's ears back for making fun of him.* **2.** to give someone a good scolding. (Slang.) □ *Did you hear him? He really pinned Chuck's ears back.* 🅃 *He pinned back Chuck's ears.*

pin something back to hold something back by pinning. □ *I will pin the curtains back to let a little more light in.* 🅃 *Jane pinned back the curtains.*

PIN ▸ BENEATH

pin someone or something beneath someone or something to trap someone or something beneath someone, some creature, or something. □ *The mine cave-in pinned four miners beneath a beam.* □ *I held the alligator's mouth closed and pinned it beneath me.*

PIN ▸ DOWN

pin someone down (on something) AND **nail someone down (on something)** to demand and receive a firm answer from someone to some question. □ *I tried to pin him down on a time and place, but he was very evasive.* 🅃 *Don't try to pin down the mayor on anything!* □ *I want to nail her down on a meeting time.* □ *It's hard to pin her down. She is so busy.*

pin something down AND **nail something down** to determine or fix something, such as a date, an agreement, an amount of money, a decision, etc. □ *It will be ready sometime next month. I can't pin the date down just yet, however.* 🅃 *I can't pin down the date just now.* □ *I hope I can nail something down soon.* □ *We nailed down the contract yesterday.*

pin something down (on(to) something) to attach something down onto something with pins. □ *She pinned the butterfly down onto the cardboard.* 🅃 *She pinned down the butterfly onto the board.* □ *I pinned the notice down on the picnic table where everyone could see it.*

PIN ▸ ON

pin one's faith on someone or something AND **pin one's hopes on someone or something** to fasten one's faith or hope to someone or something. □ *Don't pin your faith on Tom. He can't always do exactly what you want.* □ *He pinned his hopes on being rescued soon.*

pin one's hopes on someone or something See the previous entry.

pin something on someone to blame something on someone; to frame someone for a crime; to make it appear that an innocent person has actually committed a crime. (Slang.) □ *Don't try to pin that crime on me! I didn't do it.* □ *Lefty tried to pin the crime on Max.*

pin something on someone or something to hang something on someone or something by pinning. □ *The mayor pinned the medal on the boy who had rescued the swimmer.* □ *I pinned a yellow ribbon on my lapel.*

PIN ▸ (ON)TO

pin something (on)to something to attach or fix something to someone or something by pinning. □ *The mayor pinned the medal onto the lapel of the brave young hero.* □ *She pinned a medal to his lapel.*

PIN ▸ TO

See the previous entry.

PIN ▸ UNDER

pin someone or something under someone or something to trap someone or something under someone or something. □ *Someone knocked Gerry down and pinned Randy under him.* □ *The accident pinned Maggie under the car.*

PIN ▸ UP

pin something up to raise something and hold it up with pins. □ *I will pin* *this hem up and then sew it later.* Ⓣ *Please pin up the hem so I can see where to sew it.*

pin something up (on(to) something) to attach something to something, for display, with pins. □ *I pinned the picture up onto the bulletin board where everyone could see it.* Ⓣ *I pinned up the picture onto the wall.* □ *Please pin this up.*

PINCH ▶ BACK

pinch something back to pinch off a bit of the top of a plant so it will branch and grow more strongly. □ *You should pinch this back so it will branch.* Ⓣ *Pinch back the new leaves at the top.*

PINCH ▶ FOR

pinch someone for something to arrest someone for something. (Slang.) □ *The cops pinched Max for driving without a license.* □ *Max was pinched for speeding.*

PINCH ▶ FROM

pinch something from someone or something to steal something from someone or something. (Slang.) □ *Sam pinched an apple from the produce stand.* □ *We saw a pickpocket pinch a wallet from an old man.*

PINCH ▶ OFF

pinch something off ((of) something) to sever something from something by pinching. (The *of*-phrase is paraphrased with a *from*-phrase. See the Ⓕ example. The *of* is colloquial.) □ *Pinch the buds off the lower branches so the one at the top will bloom.* Ⓣ *Pinch off the lower buds.* Ⓕ *Pinch off the buds from the lower part of the plant.* Ⓕ *Pinch them off from the lower branches.* □ *Pinch the buds off, please.*

PINCH-HIT ▶ FOR

pinch-hit for someone **1.** to bat for someone else in a baseball game. □ *Wally Wilson will pinch-hit for Gary Franklin.* □ *Rodney Jones is pinch-hitting for Babe DiMaggio.* **2.** to substitute for someone in any situation. □ *Bart will pinch-hit for Fred, who is at another meeting today.* □ *Who will pinch-hit for me while I am on vacation?*

PINE ▶ AFTER

pine after someone or something AND **pine for someone or something, pine over someone or something** to long for or grieve for someone or something. □ *Bob pined after Doris for weeks after she left.* □ *Dan is still pining for his lost dog.* □ *There is no point in pining over Claire.*

PINE ▶ AWAY

pine away (after someone or something) to waste away in melancholy and longing for someone or something. □ *A year later, he was still pining away after Claire.* □ *Still, he is pining away.*

PINE ▶ FOR

pine for someone or something See under *PINE ▶ AFTER.*

PINE ▶ OVER

pine over someone or something See under *PINE ▶ AFTER.*

PIPE ▶ AWAY

pipe something away to conduct a liquid or a gas away through a pipe. □ *We will have to pipe the excess water away.* Ⓣ *They piped away the water.*

PIPE ▶ DOWN

pipe down to be quiet; to become more quiet. (Often a command. Informal.) □ *Hey! Pipe down, you guys.* □ *Please pipe down!*

PIPE ▶ FROM

pipe something from some place (to some place) to conduct a liquid or a gas from one place to another place through a pipe. □ *One oil company wanted to pipe oil all the way from Alaska to Chicago.* □ *The company pipes gas from the storage tanks in the middle of the state.*

PIPE ▶ IN(TO)

pipe something in(to some place) **1.** to conduct a liquid or a gas into some place through a pipe. □ *An excellent delivery system piped oxygen into every hospital room.* Ⓣ *They piped in oxygen to every room.* □ *They piped it in.* **2.** to bring music or other sound into a place over wires. □ *They piped music into the stairways and elevators.* Ⓣ *The eleva-*

tors were nice except that the management had piped in music. □ *I wish they hadn't piped that horrible music into my office.* Ⓐ *I cannot stand piped-in music.*

PIPE ▸ UP

pipe up (with something) to interject a comment; to interrupt with a comment. □ *Nick piped up with an interesting thought.* □ *You can always count on Alice to pipe up.*

PIT ▸ AGAINST

pit someone or something against someone or something to match someone or something against someone or something in a competition. (*Someone* includes *oneself.*) □ *The coach pitted his best players against the other team.* □ *I'll pit my fastest horse against that jalopy of yours in a race.* □ *They were unwilling to pit themselves against such a dangerous opponent.*

PITCH ▸ AT

pitch something at someone or something **1.** to throw something at someone or something. □ *The boys pitched cans at the tree.* □ *We all pitched rocks at the soldiers.* **2.** to aim advertising at a particular group. □ *They pitched the ad campaign at teenagers.* □ *These comedy programs are pitched at the lowest level of mentality.*

PITCH ▸ AWAY

pitch something away to toss or throw something away. □ *He pitched the broken stick away, and looked around for something stronger.* Ⓣ *He pitched away the stick.*

PITCH ▸ FORWARD

pitch forward to jerk or thrust forward. □ *Suddenly the car pitched forward, jerking the passengers around.* □ *We pitched forward inside the car as we went over the bumpy road.*

PITCH ▸ IN

pitch in (and help) (with something) to join in and help someone with something. □ *Would you please pitch in and help with the party?* □ *Come on! Pitch in!* □ *Please pitch in with the dishes!* □ *Can't you pitch in and help?*

PITCH ▸ IN(TO)

pitch something in(to something) to toss or throw something into something. □ *Please pitch your aluminum cans into this container.* Ⓣ *She pitched in the can.* □ *She pitched it in.*

PITCH ▸ OUT

pitch someone or something out ((of) something) to throw someone or something out of something or some place. (The *of*-phrase is paraphrased with a *from*-phrase when the particle is transposed. See the Ⓕ example.) □ *The usher pitched the drunk out of the theater.* Ⓣ *The usher pitched out the annoying person.* Ⓕ *The bartender pitched out the annoying person from the tavern.* □ *The officer arrested the driver because he pitched a can out the car window.*

pitch something out to throw something away; to discard something. □ *This cottage cheese is so old, I'm going to pitch it out.* Ⓣ *They pitched out the bad food.*

PITCH ▸ OVER

pitch someone or something over something to toss someone or something over something. □ *Then Max tried to pitch Lefty over the railing onto the tracks.* □ *Billy pitched the stone over the wall.* □ *Barry pitched the ball over home plate.*

PIVOT ▸ ON

pivot on something to rotate on something; to spin around, centered on something. □ *This part spins around and pivots on this little red spot, which is what they call a jewel.* □ *If the lever will not pivot on the bar, it needs some lubrication.*

PLACE ▸ ABOVE

place someone or something above someone or something **1.** to put someone or something in a place that is higher than someone or something else. □ *I placed Sally above everyone else in a place where she could see everything.* □ *I placed the book above Sally on a shelf.* □ *Who placed the mirror above the fireplace?* **2.** to hold someone or something in higher regard than someone or something else. (*Someone* includes *oneself*.) ☐ *I place her above all others.* ☐ *She seems to place money above her family.* ☐ *She placed herself above almost everyone else.*

PLACE ▸ ASIDE

place something aside to set something aside or out of the way. ☐ *Place this one aside and we'll keep it for ourselves.* ☐ *This one had been placed aside for an occasion such as this.*

PLACE ▸ AT

place someone or something at something **1.** to put someone or something somewhere. ☐ *The king placed extra guards at the door for the night.* ☐ *I placed the wine bottle at the left of the host.* **2.** to figure that someone or something was in a certain place. ☐ *The detective placed Randy at the scene of the crime about midnight.* ☐ *I place the getaway car at the first tollbooth at dawn.*

place something at a premium to force up the value of something so that its price is higher. ☐ *The rapid changes in the market placed all the medical stocks at a premium.* ☐ *The goods had been placed at a premium by the changing market conditions.*

PLACE ▸ BACK

place something back **1.** to move something backwards. ☐ *Place this chair back a little. It is in the walkway.* ☐ *Would you please place the boxes back so there is more room to get through?* **2.** to return something to where it was. ☐ *You found it on the table. Place it back when you finish.* ☐ *When you finish examining the book from the shelf, place it back.*

PLACE ▸ BEFORE

place someone or something before someone or something AND **put someone or something before someone or something** **1.** to put someone or something in front of someone or something, especially in a line. (*Someone* includes *oneself*.) ☐ *The teacher placed George before Bob, because Bob was a little taller.* ☐ *Ted put the nasturtium before the iris, taking full advantage of the contrast in the shapes of their leaves.* ☐ *Tom placed himself before the door and began to speak.* **2.** to consider someone or something more important than someone or something. ☐ *I am sorry, but I place my wife and her welfare before yours!* ☐ *He places his job before his family!*

PLACE ▸ BEHIND

place someone or something behind someone or something **1.** to move someone or something to a place behind or to the rear of someone or something else. (*Someone* includes *oneself*.) ☐ *Place the taller boy behind John in the second row.* ☐ *Place the iris behind the nasturtium.* ☐ *Place the boxes behind the bride for the photograph.* ☐ *The police officer placed himself behind the pillar to watch what was going on.* **2.** to guess that someone or something is lagging behind someone or something else. ☐ *I would place George behind Fred in this contest.* ☐ *Frank placed the white horse well behind the black one in the race.* ☐ *Believe it or not, I place the sprinter behind the bicycle at the finish line.*

PLACE ▸ DOWN

place something down (on something) to put something down on something. ☐ *Place the book down on the top of the table.* 🅃 *Please place down the book on the table.* ☐ *Place it down gently.*

PLACE ▸ IN

place one's trust in someone or something to trust someone or something. ☐ *If you place your trust in me, everything will work out all right.* ☐ *You should place your trust in the upper administration.*

place someone in an awkward position to put someone in an embarrassing or delicate position. (*Someone* includes *oneself*.) ☐ *Your decision places me in an awkward position.* ☐ *I'm afraid I have put myself in sort of an awkward position.*

place someone or something in jeopardy to put someone or something at risk.

(*Someone* includes *oneself.*) ☐ *Do you realize that what you just said places all of us in jeopardy?* ☐ *She has placed the entire project in jeopardy.* ☐ *I really don't want to place myself in jeopardy.*

place something in something to put something inside something. ☐ *Place the rabbit in the pen with the others.* ☐ *Please place your dishes in the sink when you finish.*

PLACE ▸ NEXT

place someone or something next to someone or something to put someone or something immediately adjacent to someone or something. (*Someone* includes *oneself.*) ☐ *Please don't place Donna next to Betty for the class photograph. They are wearing identical dresses.* ☐ *Please don't place the flowers next to me. I have hay fever.* ☐ *The police officer placed himself next to the doorway, where he could watch everything that was happening.*

PLACE ▸ ON

place a strain on someone or something to tax the resources or strength of someone, a group, or something to the utmost. (Literal and figurative uses.) ☐ *All of the trouble at work placed a strain on Kelly.* ☐ *The heavy trucks placed a strain on the bridge.*

place one's cards on the table See *lay one's cards on the table* under *LAY ▸ ON.*

place someone or something on someone or something to put or lay someone or something on someone or something. ☐ *The archbishop placed the crown on the new queen.* ☐ *The police officer placed Timmy on the sergeant's desk and gave him an ice cream cone.*

place the blame on someone or something (for something) to blame someone or something for something. ☐ *Please don't try to place the blame on me for the accident.* ☐ *The insurance company placed the blame on the weather.* ☐ *Please don't place the blame for the problem on me.*

PLACE ▸ UNDER

place something under someone or something to put something beneath someone or something. ☐ *Bill was in the tree trying to get down, so we placed a ladder under him.* ☐ *I placed my wallet under my pillow.*

PLACE ▸ WITH

place someone with someone or something to get someone a job with someone or some company. ☐ *The agency was able to place me with Dave, who runs a small candy store on Maple Street.* ☐ *They placed me with a firm that makes doghouses.*

place something with someone or something to leave something in the care of someone or something. ☐ *We placed the trunk with Fred and his wife.* ☐ *Mary placed the problem with the committee, hoping a solution could be found.*

PLAGUE ▸ WITH

plague someone or something with something to bother or annoy someone or something with something. ☐ *Stop plaguing me with your requests.* ☐ *We plagued the committee with ideas.*

PLAN ▸ FOR

plan for someone to prepare enough [of something] for someone. ☐ *Fred just called and said he can show up for dinner after all. Please plan for him.* ☐ *Tony wasn't planned for, and there is no place for him to sit.*

plan for something **1.** to prepare for something. ☐ *I need to take some time and plan for my retirement.* ☐ *We carefully planned for almost every possibility.* Ⓐ *The long-planned-for event was canceled at the last minute.* **2.** to prepare for a certain number [of people or things]. ☐ *I am planning for twelve. I hope everyone can come.* Ⓐ *The planned-for number of guests was too low.*

PLAN ▸ ON

plan on someone to be ready for someone; to anticipate someone's arrival. ☐ *Don't plan on Sam. He has a cold and* *probably won't come.* □ *We are planning on Ted and Bill.*

plan on something to prepare for something; to be ready for something; to anticipate something. □ *If I were you, I would plan on a big crowd at your open house.* □ *This was not planned on.* □ *I was planning on going to the game, but I couldn't make it.*

PLAN ► OUT

plan something out to make thorough plans for something. □ *Let us sit down and plan our strategy out.* [T] *We sat down and planned out our strategy.*

PLANE ► AWAY

plane something away to smooth off bumps or irregularities with a plane. □ *Please plane the bumps away so that the board is perfectly smooth.* [T] *Sam planed away the bumps.*

PLANE ► DOWN

plane something down to smooth something down with a plane. □ *I will have to plane the door down before I hang it again.* [T] *I planed down the edge of the door for you.*

PLANE ► OFF

plane something off to remove bumps, nicks, or scrapes by planing. □ *Plane the rough places off so the surface will be as smooth as possible.* [T] *Sam planed off the bumps.*

PLANK ► OVER

plank over something to cover something over with wood planking. □ *The county planked over the old bridge so bicyclists could use it.* [A] *People could walk easily through the planked-over bog and see all the wildlife.*

PLANT ► IN

plant something in something **1.** to set out a plant in something; to sow seeds in something. □ *Are you going to plant tomatoes in these pots?* □ *What have you planted in the garden?* **2.** to put an idea in someone's brain, head, or thinking. (Figurative.) □ *Who planted that silly idea in your head?* □ *I want to plant this concept in her thinking.* **3.** to conceal something in something. (Slang.) □ *The crook planted the money in the back of the refrigerator.* □ *What did the cops plant in your pockets?*

PLANT ► ON

plant something on someone to conceal something on someone's person. □ *The police planted some drugs on him and then arrested him.* □ *Roger planted a counterfeit dollar bill on Tom and called the police.*

PLASTER ► DOWN

plaster one's hair down to use water, oil, or cream to dress the hair for combing. (The result looks plastered to the head.) □ *Tony used some strange substance to plaster his hair down.* [T] *He plastered down his hair with something that smells good.* [A] *The man with the plastered-down hair turned out to be the king in disguise.*

PLASTER ► ON

plaster something on to lay on a substance as if it were plaster. □ *Look at him plaster the butter on! Hasn't he heard of cholesterol?* [T] *Wow! He really plastered on the marmalade.* [A] *The lady wearing the plastered-on makeup was said to be a beauty consultant.*

PLASTER ► ON(TO)

plaster something on(to something) to spread a substance onto something. □ *She plastered great globs of the jam onto the toast.* [T] *She plastered on lots of butter.* □ *Mary plastered the butter on.*

PLASTER ► OVER

plaster over something to cover over something with plaster. □ *I think that we will just plaster over the cracks in the wall.* [A] *You could just make out the outline of a plastered-over opening where the door had been.*

PLASTER ► UP

plaster something up to close something up with plaster; to cover over holes or cracks in a wall with plaster. □ *He plastered the cracks up and then painted over them.* [T] *You have to plaster up the cracks.* [A] *All the plastered-up cracks were visible less than six months after the repairs.*

PLASTER ▸ WITH

plaster something with something to spread some substance onto something. □ *Jane plastered each slice of bread with butter and then heaped on a glob of jam.* □ *She plastered the wall with a thin coat of fine white plaster.*

PLAY ▸ ABOUT

play about See under *PLAY ▸ AROUND.*

play about (with someone or something) See under *PLAY ▸ AROUND.*

PLAY ▸ AGAINST

play against someone or something to compete against someone or something in a team sport. □ *We won't be ready to play against the other team this weekend.* □ *We refuse to play against you until each of you is in a proper uniform.*

play both ends against the middle to cause two parties to quarrel with one another; to pit one side against the other. □ *Her style is to say one thing to one person and the opposite to another and then play both ends against the middle.* □ *You can't play both ends against the middle successfully.*

play someone against someone to cause someone to dispute with someone else. □ *Don tried to play George against David, but they figured out what he was up to.* □ *Alice never managed to play Tom against Fred.*

PLAY ▸ ALONG

play along (with someone or something) **1.** to play a musical instrument with someone or a group. □ *The trombonist sat down and began to play along with the others.* □ *Do you mind if I play along?* **2.** to pretend to cooperate with someone or something in a joke, scam, etc. □ *I decided that I would play along with Larry for a while and see what would happen.* □ *I don't think I want to play along.*

PLAY ▸ AROUND

play around (with someone or something) AND **play about (with someone or something)** **1.** to play and frolic with someone or something. □ *Kelly likes to play around with the other kids.* □ *The boys are out in the yard, playing about with the neighbor girls.* □ *Will you kids stop playing about and get busy?* □ *Stop playing around and get busy!* **2.** to have a romantic or sexual affair with someone or persons in general. □ *Kelly found out that her husband had been playing around with Susan.* □ *I can't believe that Roger is playing about!*

PLAY ▸ AS

play something as something to deal with something as if it were something else. □ *I will play this matter as a simple case of mistaken identity.* □ *We will play this lapse as an instance of forgetfulness and not make too much of it.*

PLAY ▸ AT

play at something to pretend to be doing something. □ *You are not fixing the car, you are just playing at repair work!* □ *Stop playing at doing the dishes and get the job done.*

PLAY ▸ BACK

play something back (to someone) to play a recording to someone. □ *Can you play the speech back to me?* 🅃 *Please play back the speech to me, so I can hear how I sound.* □ *Let me play it back.* 🄽 *We listened to the playback for a while, then we left.*

PLAY ▸ BY

play by ear to play music through hearing, not through musical instruction or from musical scores. (Idiomatic.) □ *Do you play by ear or did you take lessons?* □ *I can't read music, but I can play by ear.*

play something by ear to play a particular piece of music from having heard it, not from having seen the musical score. □ *I can play the Moonlight Sonata by ear.* □ *Jane can play "Happy Birthday" by ear, but not very well.*

PLAY ▸ DOWN

play down to someone to condescend to one's audience. □ *Why are you playing down to the audience? They will walk out on you!* □ *Don't play down to the people who have paid their money to see you.*

play someone or something down to diminish the importance of someone or something. ☐ *We tried to play him down so the scandal he caused wouldn't ruin everyone else's chance at election.* 🅃 *They played down the scandal.*

PLAY ▸ FOR

play for keeps to do things that are permanent; to be serious in one's actions. (Informal. From the game of marbles, where the winner actually keeps all the marbles won.) ☐ *Are we playing for keeps or can we give everything back at the end of the game?* ☐ *We are playing for keeps, so be careful of what you do.*

play for something **1.** to gamble for something; to use something as the medium of exchange for gaming or gambling. ☐ *Let's just play for nickels, okay?* ☐ *We will play for dollar bills.* **2.** to play for a particular reason, other than winning. ☐ *We are just playing for fun.* ☐ *They are not competing. They are playing for practice.*

play for time to stall; to temporize. ☐ *I'll play for time while you sneak out the window.* ☐ *The lawyers for the defense were playing for time while they looked for a witness.*

play someone for something to treat someone like something, especially a fool; to assume someone is something or a particular kind of person. ☐ *Are you playing me for some kind of rural curiosity?* ☐ *Don't play me for a fool. I won't have it.* ☐ *You are playing me for a fool! Stop it!*

PLAY ▸ IN

play a part in something AND **play a role in something** **1.** to participate in something in a specific way. ☐ *I hope to play a part in the development of the new product.* ☐ *I want to play a role in this procedure.* **2.** to portray a character in a performance. ☐ *He played a part in* The Mikado, *but it was not a major role.* ☐ *Larry wanted to play a role in the next play.*

play a role in something See the previous entry.

play in something **1.** to play a musical instrument in some musical organization. ☐ *I used to play in a band.* ☐ *I wanted to play in the orchestra but I wasn't good enough.* **2.** [for someone] to play the action of a game in a particular position or location. ☐ *Fred played in left field for the rest of the game.* ☐ *I will play in the backfield for the rest of the game.* **3.** to perform in a specific production. ☐ *She played in the Broadway production of* Major Barbara. ☐ *Once, I played in* The Mikado.

PLAY ▸ INTO

play into someone's hands to do exactly as someone wants or has planned. ☐ *Good! Let him tell the manager! He's playing right into my hands.* ☐ *I will try to get her to play into my hands.*

PLAY ▸ LIKE

play like someone or something to pretend to be someone or a type of a person. (Colloquial.) ☐ *Sam is playing like Mr. Watson, the teacher.* ☐ *He is playing like a teacher and helping Mary with her homework.*

PLAY ▸ OFF

play someone off against someone or something to manage to get someone to combat someone or something. ☐ *I played the bill collectors off against one another.* 🅃 *She played off Fred against Walter.* ☐ *Do you think I can play my creditors off against the bank?*

play something off to play a game to break a tied score. ☐ *They decided not to play the tie off because it had grown so late.* 🅃 *They went ahead and played off the tie after all.* 🄽 *We went to the play-offs and enjoyed them a lot.*

PLAY ▸ ON

See also under *PLAY ▸ (UP)ON.*

play on to continue to play. ☐ *The band played on and the dance continued until the wee hours of the morning.* ☐ *We played on and on until the last guests left the party.*

play something on someone or something to aim a light or a hose on someone or something. ☐ *The fireman played water on the burning building.*

☐ *The stagehand played a spotlight on the singer.*

play tricks on someone 1. to pull pranks on someone. ☐ *You had better not play any tricks on me!* ☐ *Stop playing tricks on people!* **2.** [for something, such as the eyes] to deceive someone. ☐ *Did I see him fall down or are my eyes playing tricks on me?* ☐ *My brain is playing tricks on me. I can't remember a word you said.*

PLAY ▸ OUT

See *be played out* under *BE ▸ OUT.*

play out to run out; to finish. ☐ *The whole incident is about to play out. Then it all will be forgotten.* ☐ *When the event plays out, everything will return to normal.*

play something out 1. to play something, such as a game, to the very end. ☐ *I was bored with the game, but I felt I had to play it out.* 🅃 *She played out the rest of the game.* **2.** to unwind, unfold, or unreel something. ☐ *Please play some more rope out.* 🅃 *They played out many feet of cable.*

PLAY ▸ OVER

play something over to replay something, such as a game, a video tape, an audio recording, etc. ☐ *There was an objection to the way the referee handled the game, so they played it over.* ☐ *Let's play that play over again.* ☐ *Would you rewind the movie and play it over?*

PLAY ▸ THROUGH

play something through to play something, such as a piece of music or a record, all the way through. ☐ *I played the album through, hoping to find even one song I liked.* 🅃 *As I played through the album, I didn't hear anything I liked.*

play through [for golfers] to pass someone on the golf course. ☐ *Do you mind if we play through? We have to get back to the courtroom by two o'clock.* ☐ *We let them play through because they were moving so fast.*

PLAY ▸ TO

play one's cards close to one's chest AND **play one's cards close to one's vest** to keep to oneself in one's dealing with people. (Informal. As if one were playing cards and not permitting anyone to see any of the cards.) ☐ *He is very cautious. He plays his cards close to his chest.* ☐ *You seem to be playing your cards close to your vest.*

play to someone or something 1. to perform something for someone or a group. ☐ *The cast played to one of their classmates who was confined to the hospital.* ☐ *Gerald Watson will play to a small gathering of wealthy socialites this Saturday evening.* **2.** to aim one's performance only toward a particular person, group, or a particular taste. ☐ *The comedian was playing only to the juveniles in the audience.* ☐ *It was clear that she was playing to the people in the cheaper seats.*

play to the gallery to aim one's performance toward the persons with the poorest taste in the audience; to aim one's remarks toward the populace in general. ☐ *Those politicians always play to the gallery when they are trying to get votes.* ☐ *The comedian played to the gallery, hoping to get the loudest laughs from the crudest jokes.*

PLAY ▸ UP

play someone or something up to emphasize someone or something; to support or boost someone or something. ☐ *Her mother kept playing Jill up, hoping she would get chosen.* 🅃 *She played up her daughter to anyone who would listen.* ☐ *Don't play our weak points up so much.*

play up to someone to flatter someone; to try to gain influence with someone. ☐ *It won't do any good to play up to me. I refuse to agree to your proposal.* ☐ *I played up to him and he still wouldn't let me go.*

PLAY ▸ (UP)ON

play (up)on something 1. to make music on a musical instrument. (*Upon* is formal and less commonly used than *on*.) ☐ *Can you play upon this instrument, or only the one you are holding?* ☐ *I can't play on this! It's broken.* **2.** to exploit something—including a word—for some purpose; to develop something for some purpose. (*Upon* is formal and less commonly used than *on*.) □ *You are just playing on words!* □ *You are playing on a misunderstanding.* **3.** to play a game on a field or court. □ *Shall we play on the floor or on the table?* □ *Let's play on the field. It's dry enough now.* **4.** [for light] to sparkle on something. □ *The reflections of the candles played on the surface of the soup.* □ *The lights played on the crystal goblets.*

PLAY ▸ WITH

play ball with someone **1.** to toss a ball back and forth with someone. □ *Carla is out playing ball with the little kids.* □ *Will you play ball with us?* **2.** to play baseball or some other team sport with someone. □ *Do you want to play ball with our team?* □ *I decided I wouldn't play ball with the home team anymore.* **3.** to cooperate with someone. (Figurative.) □ *Why can't you guys play ball with us?* □ *Max won't play ball with the gang anymore.*

play cat and mouse with someone to be coy and evasive with someone. □ *I know what you are up to. Don't play cat and mouse with me!* □ *I wish that they wouldn't play cat and mouse with me!*

play fast and loose with someone or something to be careless or deceitful with someone or something. □ *Don't play fast and loose with me!* □ *You had better not try to play fast and loose with the bank's money.*

play footsie with someone **1.** to get romantically or sexually involved with someone. (Refers literally to secretly pushing or rubbing feet with someone under the table.) □ *Someone said that Ruth is playing footsie with Henry.* □ *Henry and Ruth are playing footsie with each other.* **2.** to get involved in a scheme with someone; to cooperate with someone. (Colloquial.) □ *The guy who runs the butcher shop was playing footsie with the city meat inspector.* □ *Henry was playing footsie with the mayor in order to get the contract.*

play hardball with someone to be tough in one's dealings with someone. (Colloquial.) □ *Now he's playing hardball with me, and I'll have to get a little more difficult to deal with.* □ *Don't play hardball with Max unless you know what you are getting into.*

play havoc with someone or something to mess someone or something up; to devastate someone or something. □ *Karen's policies are really playing havoc with me.* □ *The date you picked for the banquet really played havoc with my calendar.*

play hell with someone or something to cause enormous disruptions with someone or something. (Colloquial. Use discretion with *hell*.) □ *Your proposal would play hell with Gerry and his plans.* □ *This new event really plays hell with my schedule.*

play hob with something to mess something up; to foul something up. □ *The wind was playing hob with the efforts of the pitcher, and we almost lost the game.* □ *The bottom of the door was playing hob with the carpet, so we had to trim some wood off.*

play something with someone or something **1.** to play a game with someone or a group. □ *Do you want to play checkers with me?* □ *Fran played ball with the dog for a while.* **2.** to assume a particular role with someone or some group. □ *Don't play the fool with me!* □ *Don always tried to play the successful entrepreneur with the board of directors.*

play the devil with something to cause disruption with something; to foul something up. □ *Your being late really played the devil with my plans for the day.* □ *This weather is really playing the devil with my arthritis.*

play with a full deck to be completely sane or mentally sound. (Slang. Usually negative.) □ *You'll have to excuse Laura. She's not playing with a full deck.* □ *Are you playing with a full deck? You don't act like it.*

play with fire to do something dangerous. (Figurative.) □ *Be careful with that knife! You are playing with fire!* □ *If you mess with Max, you are playing with fire.*

play with someone or something 1. to play games with someone or a group. □ *I love to play Ping-Pong. Will you play with me?* □ *They won't play with our team. We are too good.* 2. to toy with someone or something. □ *You are just playing with me. Can't you take me seriously?* □ *Please don't play with that crystal vase.*

PLEAD ▸ FOR

plead for someone to beg for someone to be spared. □ *Tom pleaded for Dave, but is was no use. They took Dave away.* □ *She pleaded for her husband, but the judge sentenced him to ten years in prison.*

plead for something to beg for something. □ *I don't want to have to plead for what's already mine.* □ *The children were pleading for ice cream, so we got some for them.*

PLEAD ▸ TO

plead guilty to something to state that one is guilty of a crime before a court of law. □ *Gerald refused to plead guilty to the crime and had to stand trial.* □ *Max pleaded guilty to the charge and then fled town.*

plead to something to enter an admission of guilt to a specific crime. □ *Max pleaded to the lesser charge of larceny.* □ *Lefty pleaded to the grand larceny charge.*

PLEAD ▸ WITH

plead with someone to beg something of someone; to make an emotional appeal to someone. □ *Do I have to plead with you to get you to do it?* □ *You can plead with me as much as you want. I won't permit you to go.*

PLEASE ▸ FOR

See *be pleased for someone or something* under *BE ▸ FOR.*

PLEASE ▸ WITH

See *be pleased with someone or something* under *BE ▸ WITH.*

PLEDGE ▸ TO

pledge something to someone to promise something to someone. □ *I pledged one hundred dollars to Ralph for his cause.* □ *We pledged a lot of money to our favorite charity.*

PLIGHT ▸ TO

plight one's troth to someone to become engaged to be married to someone. (Stilted and formulaic.) □ *I chose not to plight my troth to anyone who acts so unpleasant to my dear aunt.* □ *Alice plighted her troth to Scott.*

PLOD ▸ ALONG

plod along to move along slowly, but deliberately. □ *I'm just plodding along, but I am getting the job done.* □ *The old man plodded along, hardly able to stand.* □ *The movie plodded along putting most of the audience to sleep.*

PLOD ▸ AWAY

plod away at something to keep trying to do something. □ *He continues to plod away at his novel. It's been three years now.* □ *How long have you been plodding away at that book?*

PLOD ▸ THROUGH

plod through something to work one's way through something laboriously. □ *I just plodded through my work today. I had no energy at all.* □ *This is certainly a lot of papers to have to plod through.*

PLONK ▸ DOWN

plonk something down to slap something down; to plop something down. □ *He plonked a dollar down and demanded a newspaper.* 🅃 *He plonked down a dollar.*

PLOT ▸ AGAINST

plot against someone or something to make a scheme against someone or something. □ *All the counselors plotted against the czar.* □ *We plotted against the opposing party.*

PLOT ▸ ON

plot something on something to draw a route or outline on something. □ *He plotted the course they would be taking on a map of the area.* □ *The captain plotted the course on a chart of the upper reaches of the Nile.*

PLOT ▸ OUT

plot something out to map something out; to outline a plan for something. □

I have an idea about how to remodel this room. Let me plot it out for you. [T] *I plotted out my ideas for the room.*

PLOT ▸ WITH

plot with someone to scheme with someone. □ *Mary looks as though she is plotting with Jerry to make some sort of mischief.* □ *I am not plotting with anyone. I am planning everything myself.*

PLOW ▸ BACK

plow something back into something to put something, such as a profit, back into an investment. □ *We plowed all the profits back into the expansion of the business.* [T] *Bill and Ted plowed back everything they earned into the company.*

PLOW ▸ IN

plow something in to work something into the soil by plowing. □ *Lay the fertilizer down and plow it in.* [T] *Plow in the fertilizer as soon as you can.*

PLOW ▸ INTO

plow into someone or something to run into someone or something. □ *The truck almost plowed into the children waiting by the road.* □ *The car plowed into the side of the building and knocked in a few bricks.*

PLOW ▸ THROUGH

plow through something to work through something laboriously. □ *I have to plow through all the paperwork this weekend.* □ *Will you help me plow through all these contracts?*

PLOW ▸ UNDER

plow something under (something) to push something under the surface of the soil or of water. □ *The farmer plowed the wheat stubble under the surface of the soil.* □ *The farmer plowed the stubble under.*

PLOW ▸ UP

plow something up to uncover something by plowing. □ *The farmer plowed some old coins up and took them to the museum to find out what they were.* [T] *He plowed up some valuable coins.* [A] *He picked up his plowed-up treasure and went back to the house to hide it.*

PLUCK ▸ AT

pluck at someone or something to pull or pick at someone or something. □ *Kelly plucked at Ed, picking off the cockleburrs that had caught on his clothing.* □ *Kelly plucked at the burrs.*

PLUCK ▸ FROM

pluck something from someone or something to pick, grab, or snatch something from someone. □ *Wally plucked the book from Dave and ran over to the window.* □ *Sally plucked a chocolate from the box and popped it into her mouth.*

pluck something from something to pick a blossom or a fruit from a plant. □ *He stooped over and plucked a rose from the bush.* □ *Who plucked the blossoms from my lily plants?*

PLUCK ▸ OFF

pluck something off ((of) someone or something) to pick something off someone or something. (The *of*-phrase is paraphrased with a *from*-phrase when the particle is transposed. See the [F] example. The *of* is colloquial.) □ *She plucked the mosquito off his back before it could bite him.* [T] *She plucked off the bud.* [F] *She plucked off the bud from the plant.* □ *There is an unnecessary branch on the plant. Please pluck it off.*

PLUCK ▸ OUT

pluck something out (of something) to snatch something out of something. (The *of*-phrase is paraphrased with a *from*-phrase when the particle is transposed. See the [F] example.) □ *She plucked the coin out of his hand and put it in her shoe.* [T] *Reaching into the fountain, Jane plucked out the coin.* [F] *She plucked out the coin from the fountain.* □ *Mary plucked it out.*

PLUCK ▸ UP

pluck up someone's courage to bolster someone's, including one's own, courage. □ *I hope you are able to pluck up your courage so that you can do what has to be done.* □ *Some good advice* *from a friend helped pluck up my courage.*

PLUG ▸ AWAY

plug away (at someone or something) to keep working at someone or something. ☐ *I will just keep plugging away at Fred. I will convince him yet.* ☐ *I won't leave him alone. I'll keep plugging away.*

PLUG ▸ IN(TO)

plug (oneself) in(to something) to become attached to something; to become attached to some sort of network or system. ☐ *As soon as I have plugged myself into the local network, I will have access to the large computer.* ☐ *I will be connected as soon as I plug in.* ☐ *I plugged myself into the computer network and began to communicate quickly and efficiently.*

plug something in(to something) to connect something to something else, usually by connecting wires together with a plug and socket. ☐ *Plug this end of the wire into the wall.* 🅃 *Plug in the lamp and turn it on.* ☐ *Please plug this in.* ☐ *Is the vacuum cleaner plugged in?*

PLUG ▸ UP

plug something up to fill up a hole; to block a hole or opening. ☐ *Please plug this hole up so the cold air doesn't get in.* 🅃 *Can you plug up the hole?*

PLUMMET ▸ TO

plummet to earth to fall rapidly to earth from a great height. ☐ *The rocket plummeted to earth and exploded as it struck.* ☐ *As the plane plummeted to earth, all the people on the ground were screaming.*

plummet to something to drop or fall to some level or low point. ☐ *Stock prices plummeted to record low levels.* ☐ *The rock plummeted to the river at the base of the cliff.*

PLUMP ▸ DOWN

plump something down **1.** to drop a heavy load of something. ☐ *She plumped the load of groceries onto the bench and looked through her purse for the keys.* 🅃 *Jill plumped down her packages.* **2.** to drop something as if it were a heavy load. ☐ *He plumped the potatoes down on each plate, making a funny noise each time.* 🅃 *Dave plumped down a huge slab of meat onto the grill.*

PLUMP ▸ FOR

plump for someone or something to support or promote someone or something. ☐ *Henry spent a lot of energy plumping for Bill, who was running for vice president.* ☐ *She spent a lot of time plumping for our candidate.*

PLUMP ▸ UP

plump something up to pat or shake something like a pillow into a fuller shape. ☐ *Todd plumped his pillow up and finished making the bed.* 🅃 *He plumped up his pillow.* 🄰 *Jane dropped her head back onto the freshly plumped-up pillow and tried to go back to sleep.*

PLUNGE ▸ DOWN

plunge down something to run or fall down something. ☐ *The car plunged down the hill and ran into a tree at the bottom.* ☐ *The bicyclist plunged down the side of the hill at a great speed.*

PLUNGE ▸ FROM

plunge from something to flee or run from something or some place. ☐ *The people plunged from the burning building as fast as they could run.* ☐ *Lily plunged from the room in embarrassment.*

PLUNGE ▸ IN(TO)

plunge in(to something) to dive or rush into something; to immerse oneself in something. ☐ *Ned took off his shoes and plunged into the river, hoping to rescue Frank.* ☐ *He plunged into his work and lost track of time.* ☐ *Barry strode to the side of the pool and plunged in.*

plunge something in(to someone or something) to drive or stab something into someone or something. ☐ *The murderer plunged the knife into his victim.* 🅃 *She plunged in the dagger.* ☐ *Ken plunged the cooked pasta into cold water.*

PLUNGE ▸ TO

plunge to something **1.** to fall or drop down to something. ☐ *The temperature* *plunged to zero last night.* ☐ *The burning car plunged to the floor of the canyon.* **2.** to dive or fall to one's death. ☐ *She walked straight to the edge of the cliff and plunged to her death.* ☐ *The burro slipped and plunged to an untimely end.*

PLUNK ▸ DOWN

plunk down to fall or drop down hard. ☐ *The tree plunked down right in the middle of the road. We were stuck.* ☐ *Please don't come in here and plunk down. These seats are reserved.*

plunk (oneself) down to sit or fall down hard. ☐ *Nancy pulled up a chair and plunked herself down.* ☐ *She pulled the chair up and plunked down.* ☐ *She plunked herself down in the middle of the kids and began to sing.*

plunk someone or something down to place, drop, or plop someone or something down hard. ☐ *He picked her up and plunked her down in a chair and began to shout at her.* 🅃 *Sally plunked down the book in anger.*

plunk something down (for something) to slap or drop down a sum of money in payment for something. ☐ *Dave plunked a dollar down for the coffee.* 🅃 *He plunked down a dollar for the coffee and left the cafe.* ☐ *Sir, did you plunk this money down for something?*

PLY ▸ BETWEEN

ply between something and something to travel between things or places regularly or constantly. ☐ *There are a number of small craft that ply between Santerem and Manaus on a regular basis.* ☐ *Our little ship was unable to ply the entire distance between the two towns.*

PLY ▸ WITH

ply someone with something to keep supplying something to someone. (Implies an attempt to influence or fawn upon someone.) ☐ *We plied the mayor with gifts and favors, but it got us nowhere.* ☐ *Don't try to ply the police officer with any gift, especially money. That is considered a bribe.* ☐ *He plied her with alcoholic beverages, hoping to take advantage of her.*

POCK ▸ WITH

pock something with something to cause dents or small craters by shooting or throwing something at something. ☐ *The hail pocked the roof of the car with dents.* ☐ *The side of the house was pocked with tiny dents where the hail had struck.* ☐ *My car was pocked with dents where little stones had hit it.*

POINT ▸ AT

point at someone or something **1.** [for someone] to direct an extended finger at someone or something; to point one's finger at someone or something. ☐ *You should not point at people.* ☐ *Harry pointed at the mess Jerry had made and scowled.* **2.** [for something] to aim at someone or something. ☐ *The gun pointed directly at him. He was frightened.* ☐ *The sign pointed at a small roadside cafe, populated by truck drivers.*

point something at someone or something to aim or direct something at someone or something. ☐ *Don't ever point a gun at anyone!* ☐ *Point the rifle at the target and pull the trigger.*

POINT ▸ DOWN

point down to something to aim downward to something. ☐ *The sign pointed down to the little bell sitting on the counter.* ☐ *The room clerk pointed down the stairs to a little cafe on the lower level.*

POINT ▸ OUT

point someone or something out to identify someone or something in a group; to select someone or something from a group. ☐ *I don't know what June looks like, so you will have to point her out.* 🅃 *Will you point out June, please?* ☐ *I pointed the door out to her.*

point something out to identify a fact; to remind someone of a fact. ☐ *I didn't know that. Thanks for pointing it out.* 🅃 *You pointed out something very important.*

POINT ▸ TO

point to someone or something to aim at someone or something. ☐ *Who is she pointing to?* ☐ *He pointed to the door.*

point to something to indicate, reveal, or suggest something ☐ *All the evidence seems to point to his guilt.* ☐ *The signs point to a very cold winter.*

point to something as something to identify something as something. ☐ *All the indications pointed to Jill as the next president.* ☐ *The sign pointed to a small service station as the last chance to fill up on cheap gasoline.*

POINT ▸ TOWARD

point toward someone or something to direct an extended finger toward someone or something. ☐ *The teacher pointed toward Laura and asked her to come to the front of the room.* ☐ *Randy pointed toward the door and frowned at the dog.*

POINT ▸ UP

point something up **1.** to emphasize something; to emphasize one aspect of something. ☐ *This is a very important thing to learn. Let me point it up one more time by drawing this diagram on the board.* 🅃 *This points up what I've been telling you.* **2.** to tuck-point something. ☐ *I hired someone to point the chimney up.* 🅃 *Carl pointed up the brick wall.*

POISE ▸ FOR

poise oneself for something to get ready for something. ☐ *She poised herself for her dive.* ☐ *Fred poised himself for a fall, but everything worked out all right.*

POISE ▸ OVER

poise over someone or something to hover or hang over someone or something. ☐ *She spent the entire afternoon poised over her desk, pouting.* ☐ *The dog poised over the downed duck, waiting for the hunter.*

POISON ▸ AGAINST

poison someone against someone or something to cause someone to have negative or hateful thoughts about someone, a group, or something. ☐ *You have done nothing more than poison Gerald against all of us! Stop talking to him!* ☐ *Your comments poisoned everyone against the proposal.*

POISON ▸ WITH

poison someone or something with something to render someone or some creature sick or dead with a poison. (*Someone* includes *oneself.*) ☐ *He intended to poison his wife with arsenic.* ☐ *Barry wanted to poison the cat with something that left no trace.* ☐ *He poisoned himself with the cleaning compound.*

poison something with something to render something poisonous with something. ☐ *She poisoned the soup with arsenic.* ☐ *They are poisoning our water supply with pollutants.*

POKE ▸ ABOUT

poke about (in something) AND **poke around (in something)** to rummage around in something or some place; to look through things in something or some place. ☐ *I'll have to go up and poke about in the attic to see if I can find it.* ☐ *Janet went to the attic and spent the rest of the afternoon poking about.* ☐ *I will poke around in the garage and see if I can find a wrench.*

POKE ▸ ALONG

poke along to move along slowly; to lag or tarry. ☐ *Get moving. Stop poking along.* ☐ *I was just poking along, not paying attention to what was going on around me.*

POKE ▸ AROUND

poke around to move slowly or aimlessly; to waste time while moving about. ☐ *I just poked around all afternoon and didn't accomplish much.* ☐ *Stop poking around and get moving.*

poke around (in something) See under *POKE ▸ ABOUT.*

POKE ▸ AT

poke at someone or something to thrust or jab at someone or something. ☐ *Stop poking at me!* ☐ *Don't poke at the turtle. It might bite you.*

poke fun at someone or something to make fun of someone or something. □ *You shouldn't poke fun at me for my mistakes.* □ *They are just poking fun at the strange architecture.*

poke something at someone or something to jab or thrust something at someone or something. □ *Don't poke that thing at me!* □ *The hunter poked his spear at the pig one more time and decided it was dead.*

POKE ▸ IN

poke someone in something to strike or jab someone in some body part. (*Someone* includes *oneself.*) □ *Billy poked Bobby in the tummy and made him cry.* □ *She poked herself in the eye accidentally.*

POKE ▸ IN(TO)

poke one's nose in(to something) to get involved in something; to pry into something that may not concern one. □ *Must you always poke your nose into my business?* [T] *Do you have to poke in your nose?* □ *Stop poking your nose in all the time.*

poke something in(to something) to stick or cram something into something. □ *He poked his finger into the jam, pulled it out again, and licked it.* [T] *Jeff poked in his finger.* □ *Don't poke your finger in!*

POKE ▸ OUT

poke out (of something) to stick out of something; to extend out of something. □ *The bean sprouts were beginning to poke out of the soil of the garden.* □ *I knew there were little birds in the birdhouse, because a little head poked out now and then.*

poke something out (of something) to thrust something out of something. (The *of*-phrase is paraphrased with a *from*-phrase when the particle is transposed. See the [F] example.) □ *The lobster poked its antennae out of the little cave and wiggled them around.* [T] *It poked out its antennae.* [F] *It poked out its antennae from the little cave.* □ *An eel poked its head out.*

POKE ▸ THROUGH

poke something through someone or something to jab or stab something through someone or something. □ *The evil knight poked his weapon through Arthur and withdrew it again.* □ *Danny poked his finger through the plastic pool liner by mistake.*

poke through (something) to stick through something; to extend through something. □ *The tips of Tommy's toes poked through his sneakers and looked very cold.* □ *The end of the lost spoon poked through the piecrust on the freshly baked pie. Now we knew where it had disappeared to.*

POLARIZE ▸ INTO

polarize something into something to divide a group into two segments. □ *Your actions have just polarized the students into two opposing groups!* □ *We polarized the entire population into two factions.*

POLISH ▸ OFF

polish something off to eat, consume, exhaust, or complete all of something. □ *Who polished the cake off?* [T] *Who polished off the cake?* [T] *She polished off her chores in record time.*

POLISH ▸ UP

polish something up to rub something until it shines. □ *Polish the silver up and make it look nice and shiny.* [T] *If you will polish up the silver, I will put it away.*

POLLUTE ▸ WITH

pollute something with something to adulterate something with something; to dirty something with something. □ *You should not pollute the stream with chemicals.* □ *Someone polluted the sewer with automotive oil.*

PONDER ▸ (UP)ON

ponder (up)on something to think on something; to consider something. (*Upon* is formal and less commonly used than *on.*) □ *Ponder upon this awhile. See what you come up with.* □ *I need to ponder on this.*

POONTIFICATE ▸ ON

pontificate on something to speak and act dogmatically and pompously. ☐ *Must you pontificate on your own virtues so much?* ☐ *The speaker was pontificating on the virtues of a fat-free diet.*

POOCH ▸ OUT

pooch out to stick or bulge out, as with a belly. (Slang.) ☐ *His tummy pooched out when he relaxed.* Ⓐ *Who is that guy with the pooched-out tummy?*

POOP ▸ OUT

poop out to become exhausted; to quit or give out. ☐ *I'm about ready to poop out. This running is too much.* ☐ *I'm really pooped out.* Ⓐ *At about three in the morning, four pooped-out Cub Scouts appeared at the door, saying that their tent had collapsed.*

poop someone or something out to cause someone to become exhausted or give out. (*Someone* includes *oneself*.) ☐ *All that exercise really pooped everyone out.* ☐ *A full day of play at the beach had pooped the dog out.* Ⓣ *The activity pooped out the dog.* ☐ *Bill pooped himself out by running too fast.*

POP ▸ AROUND

pop around (for a visit) AND **pop by (for a visit), pop in (for a visit), pop over (for a visit)** to come by [one's residence] for a visit. ☐ *You simply must pop around for a visit sometime.* ☐ *I will pop by about noon.* ☐ *I can pop in for only a minute.* ☐ *Why don't you pop over for a few minutes?*

POP ▸ BACK

pop back (for something) to come back for just a moment. ☐ *Okay, I think I can pop back for a minute.* ☐ *I have to pop back for something I forgot.*

POP ▸ BY

pop by (for a visit) See under *POP ▸ AROUND.*

POP ▸ DOWN

pop down (for a visit) to come or go to someone's home that is downstairs or in a place on a lower level. ☐ *You simply must pop down for a visit whenever you get a chance.* ☐ *I'll try to pop down tomorrow evening after dinner.*

POP ▸ FOR

pop for something to pay for a treat. (Slang.) ☐ *Come on. Let's go out. I'll pop for pizza.* ☐ *Who will pop for the treats today?*

POP ▸ IN

pop in (for a visit) See under *POP ▸ AROUND.*

POP ▸ IN(TO)

pop in(to something) **1.** to come or go into some place, such as a store, shop, etc., for a moment. ☐ *Let me pop into the bakery for a minute.* ☐ *I have to pop into the drugstore for some shampoo.* ☐ *Here's a drugstore. I have to pop in for a minute.* **2.** to snap into place in something. ☐ *The little plastic thing popped into its slot, and the model plane was finished.* ☐ *It pops in and holds tight if you do it right.*

pop something in(to something) to fit, snap, or press something into place in something. ☐ *Lee popped the lever into place, and the machine began to function.* Ⓣ *Lee popped in the plastic part, and the toy ran beautifully.* ☐ *He popped the part in.*

POP ▸ OFF

pop off **1.** to die. (Slang.) ☐ *Lee was so scared that he thought he was going to pop off.* ☐ *I'm not ready to pop off yet!* **2.** to depart. (Slang.) ☐ *I must pop off. It's getting late.* ☐ *Don't you think it's time we popped off?*

pop off (about someone or something) (at someone) to take out one's anger or frustration about someone or something on someone else. (Slang.) ☐ *There is no need to pop off about Fred at me! I am innocent!* ☐ *Why are you popping off at me? I didn't do it!* ☐ *She is always popping off about something.*

pop off (about someone or something) (to someone) to speak carelessly or in anger about someone or something to someone. ☐ *Don't pop off about this mess to me! Talk to someone who can straighten it out.* ☐ *I am a little tired of your popping off all the time.*

pop someone off to kill someone. (Slang.) □ *Max was told to pop Lefty off because he was trying to muscle in on the gang's turf.* 🅃 *Max intended to pop off Lefty.*

POP ▸ ON

pop someone on something to strike someone on some body part. (Slang.) □ *If you don't sit down, I'll pop you on the chin!* □ *Max popped Lefty on the nose.*

POP ▸ ON(TO)

pop something on((to) something) to snap something onto something. □ *Denise took one more sip of the medicine and popped the lid onto the bottle.* 🅃 *She popped on the lid when she was finished.* □ *Mary popped the top on and put the box away.*

POP ▸ OUT

pop out (of something) to jump out of something; to burst out of something. □ *Suddenly, a little mouse popped out of the drawer.* □ *I opened the drawer and a mouse popped out.*

pop something out (of something) to release something from something so that it jumps or bursts out, possibly with a popping sound. □ *Sue popped the cork out of the champagne bottle.* □ *It took a little effort to pop the cork out.*

POP ▸ OVER

pop over (for a visit) See under *POP ▸ AROUND.*

POP ▸ UP

pop something up to remove something by making it jump or burst upwards. □ *Henry popped the lid up and helped himself to the strawberry preserves.* 🅃 *He popped up the lid and cleaned out the jam jar.*

pop up (some place) to appear suddenly and unexpectedly some place. □ *I never know where Henry is going to pop up next.* □ *A new problem has popped up.* □ *Guess who popped up at the office today?*

PORE ▸ OVER

pore over something to look over something carefully. □ *She pored over the reports, looking for errors.* □ *I need to take a few hours to pore over these contracts and see if they are ready to be signed.*

PORK ▸ OUT

pork out (on something) to overeat on something; to become fat as a pig from eating something. (Slang.) □ *I pork out on French fries whenever I get the chance.* □ *I wish I didn't pork out all the time.*

PORTION ▸ OUT

portion something out to give out shares of something. □ *Who will portion the cake out?* 🅃 *She portioned out the chocolate carefully, making sure everyone got an equal share.*

PORTRAY ▸ AS

portray someone as someone or something to represent or describe someone as someone or a type of person. (*Someone* includes *oneself.*) □ *Fred portrayed his political opponent as an evil man.* □ *She tried to portray herself as a grand lady, but she fooled no one.*

portray someone or something as someone to develop a character that one is playing in a stage production as a kind of person or someone having certain characteristics or a particular personality. □ *Tom portrayed Scrooge as an evil old man.* □ *Randy hopes to portray his character as a sympathetic friend.*

POSE ▸ AS

pose as someone or something to pretend to be someone or a type of person. □ *I posed as Gerald and got the job.* □ *I posed as a nurse and got a job at a summer camp.*

POSE ▸ FOR

pose for someone or something to assume a posture appropriate to the subject of a photograph or painting. □ *Paul wanted me to pose for him, but I declined.* □ *Will you pose for my painting?*

POSE ▸ TO

pose something to someone to suggest something to someone. □ *Let me pose this question to you.* □ *She posed a very difficult question to us.*

POSSESS ▸ BY

See *be possessed by something* under *BE ▸ BY.*

POSSESS ▸ OF

See *be possessed of something* under *BE ▸ OF.*

POST ▸ AT

post someone at something to place someone, as if on guard, at something or some place. (*Someone* includes *oneself.*) □ *The police chief posted a guard at the hospital door.* □ *The boss posted himself at the water cooler to catch up on the gossip.*

POST ▸ ON

post something on something to fasten a notice onto something. □ *Please post this notice on the door where everyone will see it.* □ *I will post this on the bulletin board.*

POST ▸ TO

post something to someone to mail something to someone. □ *I posted it to him over a month ago. I can't imagine where it is now.* □ *The letter was posted last week.*

POST ▸ UP

post something up to record a transaction in an account. □ *I'll post this charge up right away, and then you can check out.* 🅃 *Please post up the charges a little later.*

POSTPONE ▸ UNTIL

postpone something until something to delay something until something happens or until a later time. □ *Can we postpone our meeting until tomorrow?* □ *The picnic was postponed until Saturday.*

POSTURE ▸ AS

posture as someone or something to pretend to be someone or a particular type of person. □ *Why is the secretary posturing as the manager? Putting on airs?* □ *Carla entered the ballroom, posturing as a grand duchess of somewhere or another.*

POT ▸ UP

pot something up to put plants into pots. □ *If you would like one of these tomato plants, I'll pot one up for you.* 🅃 *Jan potted up a plant for me.*

POUNCE ▸ (UP)ON

pounce (up)on someone or something to spring or swoop upon someone or something; to seize someone or something. (*Upon* is formal and less commonly used than *on.*) □ *As Gerald came into the room, his friend Daniel pounced on him and frightened him to death.* □ *The cat pounced upon a mouse.* □ *The preacher pounced on me after church and talked my ear off.* □ *The teacher pounced on all my spelling errors immediately.*

POUND ▸ ALONG

pound along something **1.** to walk or run along something awkwardly or heavily. □ *As the horse pounded along the street, the rider tried hard to get it to slow down.* □ *Tom pounded along the pavement, looking a bit angry.* **2.** to tap or hammer along something. □ *The worker pounded along the edge of the roof, looking for rotten places.* □ *I pounded along the wall, looking for a board to nail into.*

POUND ▸ AWAY

pound away (at someone or something) to hammer or batter constantly on someone or something. □ *The cops pounded away at the poor guy, and then they put him in handcuffs.* □ *The jackhammer kept pounding away at the pavement.* 🅃 *Two jackhammers pounded away all morning.*

POUND ▸ DOWN

pound something down to hammer, flatten, or batter something. □ *Please pound that nail down so that no one gets hurt on it.* 🅃 *Yes, please pound down that nail!* □ *The butcher pounded the chicken breasts down.*

POUND ▸ IN

pound someone's head in to beat someone, especially about the head. (Figurative slang.) □ *Max looked like he wanted to pound Lefty's head in; he was so mad!* 🅃 *You want me to pound in your head?*

POUND ▶ IN(TO)

pound something in(to someone) See *hammer something in(to someone)* under *HAMMER ▶ IN(TO).*

pound something in(to something) See *hammer something in(to something)* under *HAMMER ▶ IN(TO).*

POUND ▶ ON

pound on someone or something to beat or hammer on someone or something. □ *She kept pounding on him until he released her.* □ *Will you please stop pounding on that drum?*

pound something on someone or something to hit or strike someone or something with something. □ *Sarah pounded the vase on the robber until it broke.* □ *Betty stood pounding her shoe on the radiator, hoping the racket would magically bring heat.*

POUND ▶ OUT

pound something out **1.** to flatten something by pounding. □ *He pounded the gold leaf out very thin.* 🅃 *He pounded out the gold leaf.* **2.** to type something out with vigor and enthusiasm. □ *The reporter pounded out the story, racing to meet the deadline.* □ *It's not a great piece of work. I pounded it out in an hour or two.*

POUND ▶ UP

pound something up to break something up by pounding. □ *Pound the crackers up into crumbs and use them to coat the chicken before you fry it.* 🅃 *Pound up the crackers and put the crumbs in a jar.* 🄰 *They poured the pounded-up pottery into the bin for future use.*

POUR ▶ ALONG

pour along something to rush along something in great numbers or in a great amount. □ *Hundreds of people poured along the street during the lunch hour.* □ *The rainwater poured along the side of the house, heading toward the gutter.*

POUR ▶ BACK

pour something back (in(to something)) to replace a liquid into something. □ *Larry poured the extra glass of orange juice back into the pitcher.* 🅃 *Pour back the extra juice into the pitcher.* □ *Lily took too much and poured some back.* □ *Please pour it back in.*

POUR ▶ DOWN

pour down (on someone or something) [for something] to shower down on someone or something. (Typically water, but also blessing, criticism, praise, kudos.) □ *The rain poured down on all of us.* □ *It poured down like that for hours.*

POUR ▶ FORTH

pour forth to gush out; to gush forth. □ *The milk gushed out of the hole in the container.* □ *A tremendous amount of water poured forth when the pitcher was knocked over.*

POUR ▶ IN

pour in(to something) to flow or flood into something. (Both literal and figurative senses.) □ *The rain poured into the open window.* □ *I left the window open and the rain just poured in.* □ *Complaints poured into the television station after the broadcast.* □ *Cards and letters are still pouring in.*

POUR ▶ INTO

pour oneself into something to get deeply involved with something. □ *He distracted himself from his grief by pouring himself into his work.* □ *She poured herself into the project and got it done on time.*

POUR ▶ IN(TO)

pour oneself in(to something) to fit someone into something very tight. (Usually jocular.) □ *I will go pour myself into my gown and I will be ready to leave in a moment.* □ *Marilyn didn't put that dress on, she poured herself in!* □ *She looks as if she poured herself into that dress.*

pour something in(to something) to guide a flow of liquid into something. □ *She poured the lemonade into the pitcher and carried it to the porch.* 🅃 *She held the glass and poured in the lemonade.* □ *Mary took a cup and poured some juice in.*

POUR ▸ OFF

pour something off ((of) something) to spill liquid off the top of something. (The *of*-phrase is paraphrased with a *from*-phrase when the particle is transposed. See the F example. The *of* is colloquial.) □ *Valerie poured the cream off the milk.* T *Valerie poured off the cream.* F *Valerie poured off the water from the boiled potatoes.* □ *She poured the water off.* A *The poured-off fat is discarded or saved for other uses.*

POUR ▸ ON

See also under *POUR ▸ ON(TO).*

pour cold water on something **1.** to douse something with cold water. □ *Pour cold water on the vegetables to freshen them.* □ *I poured cold water on my hands to cool myself off.* **2.** to be very discouraging about something. (Figurative.) □ *I hate to pour cold water on your suggestion, but it will never work.* □ *She always pours cold water on my ideas.*

pour it on thick to flatter someone excessively. □ *Ken really pours it on thick! What an apple-polisher.* □ *You really pour it on thick!*

pour oil on troubled water(s) to calm someone or something down. (Figurative. A thin layer of oil will actually calm a small area of a rough sea.) □ *Don can calm things down. He's good at pouring oil on troubled waters.* □ *Alice is very good at pouring oil on troubled water.*

POUR ▸ ON(TO)

pour something on(to) something to discharge a vessel of something onto something. □ *Don broke open the piggy bank and poured the money onto the kitchen table.* T *Don spread out a towel on the table and poured the money on it.*

POUR ▸ OUT

pour one's heart out (to someone) to tell one's personal feelings to someone else. □ *I didn't mean to pour my heart out to you, but I guess I just had to talk to someone.* T *She poured out her heart to her friend.* □ *I found someone to whom I could pour out my heart.*

pour out (of something) [for someone or something] to stream or gush out of something or some place. □ *The water poured out of the broken pipe and flooded the basement.* □ *The pipe split and the water just poured out.*

pour something out (on(to) someone or something) to empty something onto someone or something. □ *She poured the pitcher of ice water out onto Dave, making him scream.* T *Sarah poured out the pitcher on Dave.* □ *She held the pitcher over Dave's head and poured it out.*

POUR ▸ OVER

pour (all) over someone or something to flood over someone or something. (Compare to *pore over something.*) □ *The water from the broken dam poured over all the spectators standing at its base.* □ *The spilled milk poured over my lap.*

pour something over someone or something to cover someone or something with something. □ *As I poured the cooling water over myself, I felt relaxed for the first time since I began the long hike.* □ *Mary poured some milk over her cereal.*

POUR ▸ THROUGH

pour something through something to cause a liquid to flow through something, such as a filter. □ *The chemist poured the mixture through the filter.* □ *I can't get the syrup into the bottle without pouring it through a funnel.*

pour through something to flow freely through something. □ *The water poured through the leak in the window frame.* □ *The rain poured through the hole in the roof.*

POUR ▸ WITH

pour with rain to rain heavily. (Said of the sky, day, morning, night, the weather, etc.) □ *The sky was pouring with rain and the sun never shone from dawn to dusk.* □ *It poured with rain the entire night.*

POUT ▸ ABOUT

pout about someone or something to be sullen about someone or something.

☐ *There is no need to pout about Sally. She'll come back.* ☐ *Sally is pouting about her lost dog.*

POWER ▸ UP

power something up to start something, such as an engine. ☐ *You should power the engine up and let it run awhile before you drive away.* [T] *Power up the engine and mow the grass.*

power up to start an engine. ☐ *Well, let's power up so we will be ready to leave with the others.* ☐ *It's time to power up and get going.*

POWER ▸ WITH

power something with something to provide something as the source of energy for something to operate. ☐ *The government decided to power its vans with natural gas engines.* ☐ *We will power the generators with coal as long as it is cheap.*

PRACTICE ▸ (UP)ON

practice (up)on someone or something to train or drill on someone or something. (In preparation for the real thing. *Upon* is formal and less commonly used than *on*.) ☐ *I do not want anyone practicing upon me.* ☐ *I want to learn how to braid hair. Can I practice on you?* ☐ *If you want to learn how to give injections, you should practice on an orange, not on me.*

PRAISE ▸ FOR

praise someone or something for something to commend someone for something. ☐ *I like to praise a person for doing very good work.* ☐ *Alice praised the committee for its work.*

PRAISE ▸ TO

praise someone or something to the skies to praise someone or something enormously. (Figurative.) ☐ *The coach praised the players to the skies.* ☐ *I didn't think the play was very good, but Jerry praised it to the skies.*

PRANCE ▸ AROUND

prance around to dance, jump, or strut around. ☐ *The little deer were prancing around, enjoying the spring air.* ☐ *Stop prancing around and get to work.*

prance around something to dance or jump in celebration around something or throughout some place. (Compare to *waltz around something*.) ☐ *The kids pranced around the room, celebrating.* ☐ *They pranced around the table that held the ice cream and cake.*

PRATTLE ▸ ABOUT

prattle (away) about someone or something to chatter idly and endlessly about someone or something. ☐ *The little girl sat down and prattled away about her school, her friends, and her toys.* ☐ *I wish you would stop prattling about your friends.*

PRATTLE ▸ AWAY

See the previous entry.

PRAY ▸ FOR

pray for someone or something 1. to beseech God, or some other deity, on behalf of someone or something. ☐ *I will pray for you.* ☐ *As the fire spread throughout the old church, the congregation prayed for its preservation.* **2.** to ask God, or some other deity, to grant something. ☐ *They prayed for David's safety.* ☐ *All the people prayed for peace.* [A] *The prayed for rain fell in torrents.*

PRAY ▸ OVER

pray over something 1. to say grace over a meal. ☐ *Do you pray over your meals?* ☐ *We prayed over dinner so long that everyone was starved by the time we ate.* **2.** to seek divine guidance about something through prayer. ☐ *I will have to think about it and pray over it awhile. I'll have an answer next week.* ☐ *She prayed over the problem for a while and felt she had a solution.*

PRAY ▸ TO

pray to someone or something to utter prayers of praise or supplication to some being or something. ☐ *I pray to God that all this works out.* ☐ *The high priest prayed to the spirits of his ancestors that the rains would come.*

pray to the porcelain god to kneel at the toilet bowl and vomit. (Slang.) ☐ *Wally spent a while praying to the porce-*

lain god last night. □ *I think I have to go pray to the porcelain god.*

PREACH ► ABOUT

preach about something to give a moral discourse on something. □ *Please don't preach about the evils of fried food. I like the stuff, and people eat it all the time and don't die!* □ *She was preaching about the value of a fat-free diet.*

PREACH ► AGAINST

preach against someone or something to exhort against someone or something. □ *The evangelist preached against the operator of the town's only saloon.* □ *The principal kept preaching against drinking and drugs.*

PREACH ► AT

preach at someone to lecture or moralize at someone. □ *Don't preach at me! I don't need any of your moralizing.* □ *I really don't wish to be preached at.*

PREACH ► TO

preach to someone to give a moral discourse to someone. □ *Please don't preach to me. A scolding will do just fine.* □ *When you preach to us like that, we don't pay any attention to you.*

PRECIPITATE ► INTO

precipitate into something **1.** [for a chemical] to go out of solution into solid form. □ *The sodium chloride precipitated into a salt.* □ *Will this compound precipitate into anything if I cool it?* **2.** [for something] to become a more serious matter. □ *By then, the incident had precipitated into a riot.* □ *We were afraid that the argument would precipitate into a fight.*

precipitate something into something **1.** to cause a chemical to go out of a solution into a solid form. □ *Adding just one salt grain at the right time will precipitate the salt dissolved into the water into large crystals.* □ *One grain precipitated the dissolved salt into crystals.* **2.** to cause something to become more serious. □ *The police precipitated the incident into a riot.* □ *The rally was precipitated into a serious brawl.*

PRECLUDE ► FROM

preclude someone or something from something to prevent someone or something from being included in something; to eliminate someone from something, in advance. □ *Your remarks do not preclude me from trying again, do they?* □ *These facts do not preclude my company from consideration, do they?*

PREDICATE ► (UP)ON

predicate something (up)on something to base something on something. □ *There is no need to predicate my promotion upon the effectiveness of my secretary!* □ *You can hardly predicate the picnic on the weather, can you?*

PREDISPOSE ► TO

predispose someone or something to(ward) something to make someone or something susceptible to something. □ *Your comments will not predispose me toward a favorable treatment of your case.* □ *Your comments will not predispose me toward your case.* □ *Do you think that this weather will predispose me to catching a cold?*

PREFACE ► BY

preface something by something to begin something by saying, writing, or reading something. □ *I would like to preface my prepared remarks by making a personal observation.* □ *Her remarks were prefaced by the reading of a poem.*

PREFACE ► WITH

preface something with something to begin something with a particular message. □ *She prefaced her speech with a recitation of one of her favorite poems.* □ *Alice prefaced her remarks with a few personal comments.*

PREFER ► AGAINST

prefer something against someone to file charges against someone [with the police]; to file a complaint or a charge against someone. □ *The neighbors preferred charges against the driver of the car who ruined their lawns.* □ *I will not prefer charges against the driver, since it was partly my fault.*

PREFER ▸ TO

prefer someone or something to someone or something to rank the desirability of someone or something over someone or something else. □ *For the post of treasurer, I prefer Don to Jill.* □ *I prefer Jill to death.* □ *I prefer starvation to Jill's cooking.* □ *I prefer death to Jill.*

PREFIX ▸ TO

prefix something to something to place something at the beginning of a word or part of a word. □ *If you prefix a* re- *to some verbs, you get an entirely different meaning.* □ *You can't prefix anything to some verbs.*

PREJUDICE ▸ AGAINST

prejudice someone or something against someone or something to turn someone or a group against someone or something. □ *I believe that the lawyer was trying to prejudice the jury against the defendant.* □ *The discussion prejudiced me against eating veal.* □ *The proceedings prejudiced the prospective juror against the legal system.*

PREPARE ▸ FOR

prepare someone for something to build someone up for shocking news. (*Someone* includes *oneself.*) □ *I went in and had a talk with her to prepare her for the report.* □ *You should prepare yourself for the worst.*

prepare someone or something for something to get someone or something ready for something. (*Someone* includes *oneself.*) □ *I prepared her for the bad news by talking to her beforehand.* □ *I prepared the garden for planting.* [A] *The prepared-for war never occurred.* □ *We will prepare ourselves for the winter weather.*

PRESCRIBE ▸ FOR

prescribe something for someone to order a medication to be given to or sold to someone. □ *I asked the doctor to prescribe a painkiller for me.* □ *What can you prescribe for me for this illness?*

prescribe something for something to suggest or recommend something for a particular disease. □ *Could you prescribe something for my cold?* □ *What can you prescribe for this illness?*

PRESENT ▸ AT

present someone (to someone) (at something) to introduce someone to someone at some event. □ *They presented him to the queen at her birthday party.* □ *I will present you to the rest of the committee.* □ *Don presented Donna at the monthly meeting.*

PRESENT ▸ TO

See the previous entry.

present something to someone AND **present someone with something** to give something to someone, especially if done ceremoniously. □ *They presented a watch to me when I retired.* □ *They presented me with a watch when I retired.*

PRESENT ▸ WITH

present someone with something See the previous entry.

PRESERVE ▸ AGAINST

preserve someone or something against something to guard or protect someone or something against something. (Stilted or old-fashioned in reference to people.) □ *I hope that the vaccine will preserve us against influenza.* □ *There is nothing in the jam to preserve it against spoilage.*

PRESERVE ▸ FOR

preserve something for someone or something to save, maintain, or protect something for someone or something. □ *Try to preserve some of these memories for your grandchildren.* □ *We learned how to preserve leaves for future reference.*

PRESERVE ▸ FROM

preserve someone or something from someone or something to protect or guard someone or something from someone or something. □ *Please help preserve our people from the attacks of our enemies.* □ *Is there any way to preserve my skin against the harmful rays of the sun?*

PRESIDE ▸ AT

preside at something to manage or control a meeting or a ceremony. □ *The* *mayor presided at the meeting, assuring that the speeches would be very short.* □ *She presided at the ceremony.*

PRESIDE ▸ OVER

preside over something to be in control of the order and procedures of a meeting or ceremony. □ *The vice president will have to preside over the next meeting.* □ *I will be glad to preside over the discussion.*

PRESS ▸ AGAINST

press against someone or something to push or bear upon someone or something. □ *I pressed against Henry, trying gently to get him to move out of the way.* □ *Don't press against the glass door!*

press something against someone or something to push or force something against someone or something. □ *The person in line behind Betty kept pressing his elbow against her.* □ *I pressed my hand against the door and it opened.*

PRESS ▸ DOWN

press down on someone or something to push down on someone or something. □ *The weight of all the covers was pressing down on me, and I couldn't sleep.* □ *Press down on this lever and the recorder will start.*

PRESS ▸ FOR

See *be pressed for money* under *BE ▸ FOR.*

See *be pressed for time* under *BE ▸ FOR.*

press for something **1.** to press a button for service. □ *If you need any help, just press for service.* □ *Here is the steward's button. Just press for immediate service.* **2.** to request something. □ *The citizens are pressing for an investigation of the incident.* □ *The boss is pressing for an explanation.* **3.** to urge for something to be done. □ *The mayor is pressing for an early settlement to the strike.* □ *I will press her for an answer.*

PRESS ▸ FORWARD

press forward to move forward; to struggle forward; to continue. □ *Do not be discouraged. Let us press forward.* □ *We must press forward and complete this on time.*

PRESS ▸ INTO

press someone or something into service to force someone or something to serve or function. □ *I don't think you can press him into service just yet. He isn't trained.* □ *I think that in an emergency, we could press this machine into service.*

PRESS ▸ IN(TO)

press something in(to something) **1.** to force something into something, such as a mold. □ *Now, you need to press the clay into the mold carefully.* 🅃 *Now, hold the mold with one hand and press in the clay.* □ *Press it in.* **2.** to force or drive something into the surface of something. □ *You are standing on my chewing gum, and you have pressed it into the carpet!* 🅃 *Don't press in the gum by standing on it.* □ *You pressed the gum in!*

PRESS ▸ ON

See also under *PRESS ▸ (UP)ON.*

press on something to push or depress something, such as a button, catch, snap, etc. □ *Press on this button if you require room service.* □ *Don't press on this because it rings a loud bell.*

PRESS ▸ ON(TO)

press something on(to something) to put pressure on something and cause it to stick to the surface of something. □ *I pressed the label onto the envelope and took it to the post office.* 🅃 *I pressed on the label.* □ *With much effort, I pressed the label on so it would stick.*

PRESS ▸ ON(WARD)

press on(ward) to continue; to continue to try. (Formal.) □ *Don't give up! Press onward!* □ *I have lots to do. I must press on.*

PRESS ▸ OUT

press something out (of something) to squeeze something out of something by applying pressure. (The *of*-phrase is paraphrased with a *from*-phrase when the particle is transposed. See the 🄵 example.) □ *The Indians press the acid out of the manioc before they use it as* *food.* □ *Gene used an iron to press the wrinkles out of his suit coat.* 🅃 *They pressed out the acid.* 🄵 *They pressed out the acid from the manioc root.* □ *Gerald pressed the wrinkles out.*

PRESS ▶ TO

press someone to the wall to make as many demands as possible on someone; to place enormous social or financial pressure on someone. □ *The bills I had to face after I got out of the hospital really pressed me to the wall.* □ *We were pressed to the wall with all our medical bills.*

PRESS ▶ TOGETHER

press something together to use pressure to close or unite things. □ *He pressed his lips together and would say no more.* □ *Why are his lips pressed together so tightly?*

PRESS ▶ (UP)ON

press something (up)on someone to urge something on someone; to try to get someone to accept something. (*Upon* is formal and less commonly used than *on.*) □ *He always presses second helpings upon his guests.* □ *She pressed a gift on us that we could not refuse.*

press (up)on someone or something to put pressure on someone or something. (*Upon* is formal and less commonly used than *on.*) □ *The crowd pressed upon the child, squeezing out all his breath.* □ *The load presses on your car's springs very heavily.*

PRESSURE ▶ INTO

pressure someone into something to force someone into doing something. □ *Please don't try to pressure me into doing it.* □ *You can't pressure me into it. I won't do it!*

PRESUME ▶ (UP)ON

presume (up)on someone or something to take unwelcome advantage of someone or something. □ *I didn't mean to seem to presume upon you. I apologize.* □ *I did not feel that you presumed on me.*

PRETEND ▶ TO

pretend to something to claim to have a skill or quality. □ *I can hardly pretend to the artistry that Wally has, but I can play the piano a bit.* □ *I can't pretend to that level of skill.*

PRETTY ▶ UP

pretty oneself or something up to make oneself or something more attractive; to tidy oneself or something up. (Folksy.) □ *I tried to pretty myself up for him, but he didn't notice.* 🅃 *Let's try to pretty up this room.*

PREVAIL ▶ AGAINST

prevail against someone or something to win out over someone or something; to dominate someone or something. □ *You will not prevail against me!* □ *I am sure that our team will prevail against the challengers.*

PREVAIL ▶ (UP)ON

prevail (up)on someone or something (to do something) to appeal to someone or a group to do something. (*Upon* is formal and less commonly used than *on.*) □ *I will prevail upon her to attend the meeting.* □ *I prevailed on the committee to no avail.*

PREVENT ▶ FROM

prevent someone from doing something to keep someone from doing something. □ *You can't prevent me from doing it!* □ *We must try to prevent her from going back there.*

PREY ▶ ON

prey on something [for an animal] to feed on another animal as a matter of habit or preference. □ *Owls prey on mice.* □ *Many birds prey on snakes.*

PREY ▶ (UP)ON

prey (up)on someone or something to take advantage of someone or something. (*Upon* is formal and less commonly used than *on.*) □ *The people of that island prey on tourists and do not give them good treatment.* □ *I really don't want to seem to prey on your kindness.*

PRICE ▸ DOWN

price something down to lower the price of something. □ *When they start pricing this stuff down at the end of the season, I'll come in and buy something.* 🅃 *I hope to price down the merchandise soon.* 🄰 *The priced-down coats sold out almost at once.*

PRICE ▸ OUT

price someone or something out of the market to raise a price and drive someone or something out of the marketplace. (*Someone* includes *oneself.*) □ *You are a very good singer, but your agent has priced you out of the market.* □ *The price changes posted by the chain store were meant to price us out of the market.* □ *They priced themselves out of the market.*

PRICE ▸ UP

price something up to raise the price of something. □ *They have priced oranges up so high that I can't afford any.* 🅃 *Why do they price up these common foods so high?*

PRICK ▸ UP

prick its ears up [for an animal] to move its ears into alert position to hear better. □ *The sound made the dog prick its ears up.* 🅃 *The dog pricked up its ears when it heard the window break.*

prick one's ears up [for someone] to start paying attention. (Figurative.) □ *She pricked her ears up when she heard her name.* 🅃 *When she heard her name mentioned, she pricked up her ears.*

PRIDE ▸ IN

pride oneself in something AND **pride oneself on something** to take pride in one of one's qualities or accomplishments. □ *She prides herself in her ability to spot a shoplifter.* □ *I pride myself on my ability to find compromises.* □ *Larry prides himself in his neatness.*

PRIDE ▸ ON

pride oneself on something See the previous entry.

PRIME ▸ WITH

prime something with something to enable something to start working or functioning with something. □ *Larry primed the pump with a little water, and it began to do its work.* □ *We will prime the market for our product with a free coupon offer.*

PRIMP ▸ UP

primp (oneself) up to get dressed up; to fix oneself up, combing, brushing, adjusting, etc. □ *Let me stop in the powder room and primp myself up a bit.* □ *I have to go in here and primp up.*

PRINT ▸ IN

print something in something **1.** to draw letters in a specific location on a paper. □ *Please print your name in the box.* □ *Would you please print the information in the space provided?* **2.** to publish something in a publication. □ *They printed my letter in today's paper.* □ *Her stories have been printed in several magazines.*

PRINT ▸ OUT

print something out **1.** to write something out by drawing letters. □ *Please print it out. I can't read your handwriting.* 🅃 *Print out your name, please.* **2.** to use a computer printer to print something. □ *I will print a copy out and send it to you.* 🅃 *Please print out another copy.*

PRINT ▸ UP

print something up to set something in type and print it; to print something by any process. □ *This looks okay to me. Let's print it up now.* 🅃 *Print up the final version.*

PRIZE ▸ ABOVE

prize someone or something above someone or something to value someone or something more than anyone or anything else. □ *He prized his only daughter above everyone else in the world.* □ *Scott seemed to prize his sports car above all the members of his family.*

PROBE ▸ FOR

probe something for something to poke around in something for something. □ *He probed his memory for some clue as to where he had been on* *that date.* ☐ *Sam probed the darkened space for the tool that he had mislaid.*

PROBE ▸ INTO

probe into something to investigate something. ☐ *The police will probe into the matter and report to the commissioner.* ☐ *We will take some time and probe into that for you.*

PROCEED ▸ AGAINST

proceed against someone or something **1.** to begin to move against someone or something. ☐ *The entire platoon proceeded against the single enemy soldier who refused to surrender.* ☐ *The army proceeded against the fortress as planned.* **2.** to start legal action against someone or something. ☐ *The district attorney will proceed against the woman next week.* ☐ *The state prosecutor will proceed against the company as soon as one of the witnesses is located.*

PROCEED ▸ FROM

proceed (from something) (to something) to go from something or some place to something or some place. ☐ *Next, we will proceed from Vienna to Budapest.* ☐ *We proceeded from Detroit, passing through rural Michigan.*

PROCEED ▸ TO

See the previous entry.

PROCEED ▸ WITH

proceed with something to start with something; to continue something. ☐ *Now, we will proceed with the reading of the minutes of the last meeting.* ☐ *When will you proceed with the needed action?*

PROCURE ▸ FOR

See the following entry.

PROCURE ▸ FROM

procure something (from someone or something) (for someone or something) to get something from someone or something for someone or some purpose. ☐ *I will procure a copy of the paper from Kelly for you.* ☐ *I have to procure a book for my sister.* ☐ *Can I procure the proper form from you?*

PROD ▸ AT

prod at someone or something to poke at someone or something. ☐ *The boys prodded at the prone body of the man to see if he was dead or sleeping.* ☐ *If you prod at the turtle, it will never come out of its shell.*

PROD ▸ INTO

prod someone into something to motivate someone into doing something; to provoke someone into action. (Informal.) ☐ *Do I have to prod you into going? Can't you volunteer for once?* ☐ *We will prod her into getting it done on time.*

PRODUCE ▸ FOR

produce something for something **1.** to make something for some purpose. ☐ *This production line produces brackets for the installation of the circuit boards in the next production line.* ☐ *We produce the seats for the trucks that they manufacture on the other side of town.* **2.** to bring something out for some purpose. ☐ *Lee quickly produced a penknife for cutting the string on the package.* ☐ *Ruth can always produce the right tool for the job.*

PRODUCE ▸ FROM

produce something from something to create something from something; to make something out of something. ☐ *We are able to produce a high-quality writing paper from the scraps we trim off the edges of the books as we bind them.* ☐ *Jane produces an excellent jelly from the grapes she grows in her backyard.*

PROFIT ▸ BY

profit by something AND **profit from something** **1.** to gain money from something. ☐ *You will surely profit by investing in this stock.* ☐ *I know I will profit from this investment.* **2.** to learn from something. ☐ *I am sure you will profit by your unpleasant experience.* ☐ *Yes, I will profit from my failure.*

PROFIT ▸ FROM

profit from something See the previous entry.

PROGRESS ▸ TO

progress to something to reach all the way to something or some place. □ *The crisis has progressed to its final stage.* □ *Things had progressed to a serious stage where nothing more could be done for him.*

PROGRESS ▸ TOWARD

progress toward something to move partway toward some goal. □ *Nancy is progressing toward her degree quite nicely.* □ *We are progressing toward the end of the project.*

PROGRESS ▸ WITH

progress with something to continue to move toward something or completing something. □ *I can't seem to progress with this project.* □ *How are you progressing with your model ship?*

PROHIBIT ▸ FROM

prohibit someone from something **1.** to prevent someone from doing something. □ *The committee voted to prohibit people from leaving before the meeting was over.* □ *They will prohibit anyone from being seated after the first act has started.* **2.** to keep someone out of some place. □ *Our policy is to prohibit people from the beach area after dark.* □ *State law prohibits children from this dangerous area while the machines are running.*

prohibit something from something **1.** to prevent something from happening or from doing something. □ *You can't prohibit the sun from rising. You cannot make rules like that.* □ *Why do you want to prohibit the cars from traveling on this street during rush hour?* **2.** to keep something out of or away from something or some place. □ *The law prohibited the cars from the sidewalks.* □ *The city council prohibits dogs from the public parks.*

PROJECT ▸ INTO

project into something to extend into something. □ *The end of the grand piano projected into the next room, but she had to have a grand, nonetheless.* □ *The front of the car projected into the flower bed when it was parked, but that was all right.*

PROJECT ▸ ON

See under *PROJECT ▸ ON(TO).*

PROJECT ▸ ONTO

project something onto someone to imagine that someone else experiences one's feelings, especially one's guilt or anger. □ *Since you project your anger onto your best friends, you imagine you have gathered a number of angry people around you.* □ *You should not project your feelings onto other people.*

PROJECT ▸ ON(TO)

project something on(to) someone or something AND **project something upon someone or something** to show a picture, such as from a film, transparency, etc., onto something, such as a screen, wall, etc., or even onto a person. □ *Henry projected the pictures onto the screen as he discussed each one.* □ *The teacher had to project the slides upon the wall.* □ *As an experiment, Todd projected a fanciful face onto Scott.*

PROJECT ▸ UPON

See the previous entry.

PROMISE ▸ TO

promise something to someone to pledge something to someone. □ *I promised this vase to my niece.* □ *Is this book promised to anyone?*

PROMOTE ▸ FROM

promote someone (from something) (to something) to raise someone's rank from something to something. □ *They promoted her from teller to vice president.* □ *Carl promoted his daughter to head teller.*

PROMOTE ▸ TO

See the previous entry.

PRONOUNCE ▸ ON

pronounce something on someone or something to make a statement, usually a judgment, about someone or something. □ *The judge pronounced final judgment on the prisoner.* □ *The family all pronounced a positive judgment on the cake.*

PROP ▸ AGAINST

prop someone or something (up) (against someone or something) to stand or lean someone or something against someone or something. (*Someone* includes *oneself*.) □ *He was so tired I had to prop him up against the wall while I looked for the door key.* Ⓣ *I propped up the man against the wall.* □ *I propped the mop against the wall.* □ *She was so tired that she propped herself up against the wall.*

PROP ▸ UP

See the previous entry.

PROPOSE ▸ TO

propose something to someone to suggest something to someone. □ *I have an idea I would like to propose to you.* □ *Sam wanted to propose a new plan to Sarah.*

propose to someone to suggest marriage to someone, usually a male to a female. □ *Guess who proposed to me last night?* □ *Do you think that Sam will propose to Mary?*

PROSPECT ▸ FOR

prospect for something to search for something, especially for metals or minerals. □ *The old men said they were prospecting for gold.* □ *What are they prospecting for out in the desert?*

PROSPER ▸ FROM

prosper from something to gain wealth from something. □ *Carla prospered from trading on the options exchange.* □ *I hope you prosper from your new enterprise.*

PROSTRATE ▸ BEFORE

prostrate oneself before someone or something 1. to spread oneself out in respect or obedience in front of someone or something. □ *The members of the cult prostrated themselves before their leader.* □ *They prostrated themselves before the altar.* 2. to submit to someone's dominance. (Figurative.) □ *If you think I'm going to prostrate myself before you and do as you ask, you are wrong.* □ *I will not prostrate myself to your power, no matter how great it is.*

PROTECT ▸ AGAINST

protect someone or something against someone or something AND **protect someone or something from someone or something** to shield or preserve someone or something against someone or something. (*Someone* includes *oneself*.) □ *Please come along and protect us against muggers as we walk home.* □ *What will protect my car against thieves?* □ *What will protect my car from the heavy hailstones?* □ *You must protect yourself against the cold.*

PROTECT ▸ FROM

protect someone or something from someone or something See the previous entry.

PROTEST ▸ ABOUT

protest about someone or something AND **protest against someone or something** 1. to complain about someone or something. □ *Valerie is always protesting about something.* □ *She filed a complaint that protested against her supervisor.* 2. to rally or demonstrate against someone or something. □ *A number of people protested about the war.* □ *They were mainly protesting against the draft.*

PROTEST ▸ AGAINST

protest against someone or something See the previous entry.

PROTRUDE ▸ FROM

protrude from someone or something to stick out from someone or something. □ *Even in the dark, I knew he was hurt because I could see the knife protruding from him.* □ *A knife protruded from the victim's back.*

PROVE ▸ AS

prove oneself as something to demonstrate that one can serve in a certain office or capacity. □ *It's time to promote her. She has proved herself as a teller.* □ *I proved myself as an investor by making a lot of money in the stock market.*

PROVE ▸ TO

prove something to someone to substantiate a claim about something to someone; to make someone believe or accept a statement about something. □ *What do I have to do to prove my innocence to you?* □ *Nothing you say will prove it to me.*

PROVIDE ▸ AGAINST

provide against something to plan against something happening. □ *Have you provided against the possible collapse of the agreement?* □ *We have not provided against financial disaster.*

PROVIDE ▸ FOR

provide for someone or something to supply the needs of someone or something. □ *Don't worry, we will provide for you.* □ *We will provide for the committee.* Ⓐ *The well-provided-for children grew up to be surprisingly frugal.*

provide something for someone or something to supply something for someone or something. □ *I will provide salad for the guests.* □ *Ted provided food for his dog.*

PROVIDE ▸ UNDER

provide something under something to supply something in keeping with a contract, rule, guideline, agreement, etc. □ *We have agreed to provide two tons of coal per month under our contract. Do you want more?* □ *We will agree to provide ample insurance for our employees under union guidelines.*

PROVIDE ▸ WITH

provide someone with something to supply something to someone. (*Someone* includes *oneself*.) □ *I will provide you with an escort to your car.* □ *Jane provided herself with just enough food to get through the weekend.*

PROVOKE ▸ INTO

provoke someone into something to incite someone into doing something. □ *The soldiers sought to provoke the demonstrators into starting something.* □ *They provoked us into leaving.*

PROWL ▸ ABOUT

prowl about AND **prowl around** to sneak around, looking for someone or something. □ *Something is prowling about out there.* □ *There is someone outside prowling around.*

PROWL ▸ AROUND

prowl around See the previous entry.

PRUNE ▸ AWAY

prune something away to cut away something unwanted or unneeded. □ *Please prune the lower branches of the trees away. They are starting to annoy pedestrians.* Ⓣ *We pruned away the dead branches.*

PRUNE ▸ OF

prune something of something to clear, clean, or groom something of something by pruning. □ *Sally was out in the orchard pruning the apple trees of dead branches.* □ *They pruned the roses of their unneeded branches.*

PRUNE ▸ OFF

prune something off ((of) something) to cut something off something. (The *of*-phrase is paraphrased with a *from*-phrase when the particle is transposed. See the Ⓕ example. The *of* is colloquial.) □ *Claire pruned the dead branch off the apple tree.* Ⓣ *She pruned off the dead branch.* Ⓕ *She pruned off the branch from the tree.* Ⓐ *A bunch of pruned-off branches lay beside the curb, waiting to be picked up.*

PRY ▸ AROUND

pry around to sneak or prowl around looking for something. □ *Why are you prying around? Mind your own business!* □ *Please don't pry around. You might find out something you don't want to know.*

PRY ▸ FROM

pry something from someone AND **pry something out of someone** to work information out of someone; to force someone to reveal information. □ *I couldn't even pry her name from her.* □ *The police tried to pry the name of the killer out of Max.*

pry something from something AND **pry something out (of something)** to remove something from something as if with a lever. □ *See if you can pry this wedge from its slot.* □ *I pried the bad board out of the side of the house.*

PRY ▸ INTO

pry into something to snoop into something; to get into someone else's business. □ *Why are you prying into my* *affairs all the time?* □ *I wish you wouldn't pry into things.*

PRY ▸ OFF

pry something off ((of) something) to use a lever to get something off something. (The *of*-phrase is paraphrased with a *from*-phrase when the particle is transposed. See the Ⓕ example. The *of* is colloquial.) □ *Tom pried the top off the jelly jar.* Ⓣ *He pried off the jar top.* Ⓕ *He pried off the top from the jar.* □ *Tom pried it off.*

PRY ▸ OUT

pry something out of someone See *pry something from someone* under *PRY ▸ FROM.*

pry something out (of something) See *pry something from something* under *PRY ▸ FROM.*

PRY ▸ UP

pry something up to raise something, as with a lever. □ *See if you can pry that trapdoor up.* Ⓣ *Pry up that lid.*

PSYCH ▸ OUT

psych out to become very excited; to lose mental control. (Slang.) □ *I was so angry I almost psyched out.* □ *The kids were psyching out over the rock star.*

psych someone out **1.** to get someone very excited; to cause someone to lose mental control. (Slang. *Someone* includes *oneself.*) □ *Wow! What you just said really psyched me out!* Ⓣ *He psyched out his friends.* □ *Sally worked so hard that she psyched herself out.* **2.** to figure someone out. □ *It took me a while to psych Fred out, but I have him figured out now.* □ *Don't waste time trying to psych me out. I am an enigma.*

PSYCH ▸ UP

psych someone up to get someone mentally prepared to do something, such as take a test or participate in an athletic event. (Slang. *Someone* includes *oneself.*) □ *The coach talked to the team and tried to psyche the players up before the game.* Ⓣ *The coach psyched up the players.* Ⓐ *The psyched-up players waited for the starting bell.* □ *Tom psyched himself up for the concert.*

psych up to get mentally ready for something. (Slang.) □ *I have to psych up before the game tonight.* □ *We want to psych up so we can play a good game.*

PUCKER ▸ UP

pucker something up to cause something to wrinkle up, especially the edges of the mouth, as when tasting something very sour. □ *She puckered her lips up and pouted for a while.* Ⓣ *She puckered up her lips.* □ *The hot water puckered up the seam of the shirt.*

pucker up **1.** to tighten one's lips together into a hard circle. □ *He puckered up and kissed her once, and then again.* Ⓐ *He looked longingly at her puckered-up lips.* **2.** [for something] to shrink up and get tight. □ *The material puckered up when I washed it.* □ *The top edge of the drapes puckered up and I don't know how to straighten it out.*

PUFF ▸ ALONG

puff along **1.** [for someone] to run along, puffing to breathe. □ *Sam puffed along, jogging on his morning route.* □ *As Wally puffed along, he thought again about going on a diet.* **2.** [for an engine] to move along, putting out puffs of smoke or steam. □ *The old engine puffed along, driving the small boat slowly up the river.* □ *The locomotive puffed along, not making very much headway up the hill.*

PUFF ▸ AT

puff (away) at something **1.** to blow at or into something in puffs. □ *She puffed away at the beach ball, blowing it up as fast as she could.* □ *Todd puffed at the fire until it grew larger.* **2.** AND **puff (away) on something** to smoke something, such as a cigar, cigarette, or pipe. □ *Scott was puffing away at his pipe.* □ *All the old men were puffing away on cigars.* □ *She is always puffing on a cigarette.*

PUFF ▸ AWAY

See the previous and the following entries.

PUFF ▸ ON

puff (away) on something See under *PUFF ▸ AT.*

PUFF ▸ OUT

puff out to swell out. □ *The frog's throat puffed out, and we expected to hear a croak.* □ *The sail puffed out and the boat began to move.*

puff something out to cause something to swell out or expand outward. □ *The frog puffed its throat out and croaked.* 🅃 *The frog puffed out its throat and croaked a mighty croak.* 🄰 *A very loud noise came from the frog's puffed-out throat.*

PUFF ▸ UP

puff someone or something up to boost or promote someone or something. (*Someone* includes *oneself.*) □ *Judy puffed Nell up so much that Nell could not begin to live up to her own reputation.* 🅃 *Don't puff up your own interests so much.* □ *Wally puffed himself up so much that he couldn't live up to his own image.*

puff up to swell up. □ *Her finger puffed up and she thought she might have an infection.* □ *His eyelids had puffed up during the night.*

puff up (into something) to assume a larger shape by filling up with air or water; to swell up into something. □ *The strange-looking fish puffed up into a round ball.* □ *The fish puffed up and stuck out its spines.* 🄰 *The general pinned a medal on Charlie's puffed-up chest.*

PULL ▸ ABOUT

pull someone about **1.** to drag someone around. □ *The boys were pulling one another about and playing very rough.* □ *Don't pull your little brother about so!* **2.** to give someone a hard time. (Slang.) □ *I'm tired of your double-talk! Stop pulling me about!* □ *You can't believe what she tells people. She is always pulling people about.*

PULL ▸ ALONGSIDE

pull (up) alongside ((of) someone or something) to move to a point beside someone or something. (The *of* is colloquial.) □ *The car pulled up alongside the truck and honked and the people inside waved and waved.* □ *Please pull alongside the curb.* □ *Pull alongside carefully. Don't scrape my tires.*

PULL ▸ APART

pull someone apart **1.** to separate people who are entangled. □ *The teacher pulled the fighting boys apart and sent them home.* □ *They hugged each other so tightly that no one could have pulled them apart.* □ *They stopped fighting and pulled themselves apart.* **2.** to upset someone very much; to cause someone grief and torment. (Figurative.) □ *This whole terrible affair has just pulled me apart.* □ *Don't let this matter pull you apart. Things won't always be this bad.*

pull someone or something apart to separate or dismember someone or something. (*Someone* includes *oneself.*) □ *The murderer pulled his victim apart and sought to dispose of the parts.* 🅃 *He pulled apart his victim.* □ *Nick pulled the parts of the box apart.*

PULL ▸ AROUND

pull around to something to drive around to something or some place. □ *Please pull around to the back and deliver the furniture there.* □ *We told the driver to pull around to the service entrance.*

pull someone or something around to drag or haul someone or something around. □ *The woman had pulled her children around all day while she did the shopping. All of them were glad to get home.* □ *Nick pulled his wagon around and collected discarded aluminum cans.*

PULL ▸ ASIDE

pull someone aside to grasp and pull a person to one side. □ *I pulled the child aside and scolded him for trying to sneak into the theater.* 🅃 *I pulled aside the child to say something to him.*

PULL ▸ AT

pull at someone to vie for someone's attention or concern. □ *There are too many demands pulling at me. I need to cut down on my responsibilities.* □ *I don't see how I can function with so many different things pulling at me.*

pull at someone or something to tug at someone or something. □ *The child* *kept pulling at her mother to get her attention.* □ *Don't keep pulling at your hair. It will come out.*

PULL ► AWAY

pull away from someone or something to jerk away or draw away from someone or something. □ *Suddenly, she pulled away from me and fled.* □ *The car pulled away from the curb and drove off.*

pull someone or something away (from someone or something) to grasp and haul someone or something away from someone or something. □ *The lady pulled the child away from the edge of the well.* □ *Please pull your dog away from my hedge.* □ *Pull your foot away from the dirty spot so I can clean it up.*

PULL ► BACK

pull back (from someone or something) to move back from someone or something. □ *When I saw how sick he looked, I pulled back from him in shock.* □ *I took one look at it and pulled back.* □ *I pulled back from the curb just in time.* [N] *The troops accomplished the pullback in a week.*

pull someone or something back (from someone or something) to grasp and haul someone or something away from someone or something. □ *The cop pulled the kid away from the other kid and made them stop fighting.* [T] *I pulled back the child from the dangerous hole.* □ *Joan pulled the plate back from the rude child.* [A] *She slipped quickly under the pulled-back sheet and tried to get warm again.*

PULL ► BY

pull someone or something by something to grasp someone or something by something and tug or haul. □ *I pulled him by the hand, trying to get him to follow me.* □ *Timmy pulled the toy duck by its string and it quacked as it waddled along.*

PULL ► DOWN

pull down an amount of money to earn a certain amount of money. (Slang.) □ *I bet he pulls down about two hundred thousand a year.* □ *How much do you think she pulls down?*

pull someone or something down to drag or force someone or some creature down. □ *The wolves pulled the hunter down and set upon him.* [T] *They pulled down the hunter.* □ *The wolf pulled the moose calf down.*

pull something down to tear something down; to raze something, such as a building. □ *The developers decided not to pull the historic house down.* [T] *They tried to pull down the old house.*

pull something down over someone or something to draw something down over someone or something. □ *Lucy's mother pulled the dress down over Lucy and buttoned it up in back.* □ *Sarah pulled the cover down over the birdcage and turned out the lights.*

PULL ► FOR

pull for someone or something to support and cheer on someone, a group, or something. □ *We're pulling for you. We know you can do it!* □ *All the students were pulling for the team.*

PULL ► IN

See also under *PULL ► IN(TO)*.

pull in one's ears to stop listening in on someone or something. (Figurative. The opposite of *prick up one's ears*.) □ *Now, pull in your ears. This is none of your business.* □ *Pull in your ears and mind your own business.*

pull in one's horns to cease being aggressive or threatening; to temper one's manner or behavior. □ *Flatter him a little, and then he'll pull in his horns.* □ *I wish she would pull in her horns and act civil.*

pull in some place to steer or drive to a point off the main route. (Said of almost any wheeled vehicle.) □ *Let's pull in at the next motel and get some rest.* □ *I want to pull in at a service station and have my tires checked.*

pull one's belt in (a notch) **1.** to tighten one's belt a bit. (Probably because one has not eaten recently or because one has lost weight.) □ *He pulled his belt in a notch and smiled at his success at losing* *weight.* 🆃 *He pulled in his belt a notch and wished he had something to eat.* 🆃 *Time to pull in my belt!* **2.** to reduce expenditures; to live or operate a business more economically. □ *They had to pull their belts in a notch budgetarily speaking.* 🆃 *The people at city hall will have to pull in their belts a notch unless they want to raise taxes.* 🆃 *It's time that government pulled in its belt too.*

pull (out) in front of someone or something to drive out into the road in front of someone or some vehicle. □ *A car pulled out in front of me, and I almost hit it.* □ *The car pulled in front of a truck and there was a terrible wreck.*

pull someone in to bring someone into a place; to draw someone into a place; [for the police] to bring someone to the police station. □ *Advertising will pull hundreds of customers in.* □ *The cops pulled Max in and booked him.* 🆃 *They pulled in Max.* □ *The sale pulled a lot of customers in.*

PULL ▸ IN(TO)

pull in(to some place) to drive into some place. □ *A strange car just pulled into our driveway.* □ *Some stranger just pulled in.*

pull someone in(to something) to get someone involved in something. □ *Please don't pull me into this argument.* 🆃 *Don't pull in anyone else.* □ *It's not my affair. Don't pull me in!*

pull someone or something in(to something) to haul or drag someone or something into something or some place. □ *She pulled him into the room and closed the door.* 🆃 *Lisa pulled in her friend and closed the door.* □ *Sammy opened the door to the shed and pulled all the bags of grass clippings in.*

PULL ▸ OFF

pull off (something) to steer or turn a vehicle off the road. □ *I pulled off the road and rested for a while.* □ *I had to pull off and rest.*

pull something off to succeed with something. (Informal.) □ *He wants to get the Johnson account. I hope he can pull it off.* 🆃 *Will he be able to pull off the plan?*

pull something off ((of) something) to tug or drag something off something else. (The *of*-phrase is paraphrased with a *from*-phrase when the particle is transposed. See the 🅵 example. The *of* is colloquial.) □ *Sam pulled the covers off the bed and fell into it, dead tired.* 🆃 *He pulled off the covers.* 🅵 *He pulled off the covers from the bed.* □ *Sam pulled them off.*

PULL ▸ ON

pull a stunt on someone AND **pull a trick on someone** to perform a trick on someone. □ *Who decided that it was a good idea to pull a stunt on Mrs. Franklin?* □ *Please don't pull a trick like that on me again.*

pull a trick on someone See *pull a stunt on someone.*

pull on something to tug something. □ *I pulled on the rope, hoping to get it loose.* □ *Please help me pull on the anchor chain so we can raise the anchor.*

pull rank on someone to use one's rank or power to overrule or dominate someone. □ *Are you trying to pull rank on me?* □ *She pulled rank on him and ordered him to do it.*

pull something on to draw on an article of clothing. □ *He pulled his pants on.* 🆃 *He pulled on his pants quickly and ran outside while putting on his shirt.*

pull the plug on someone or something **1.** to terminate the functions of someone or something by pulling a connector from a socket. □ *While she was working at the computer, I accidentally pulled the plug on her.* □ *I pulled the plug on the vacuum because the switch was broken.* **2.** to disable someone or something. (Figurative.) □ *I was doing just fine until Mark pulled the plug on me.* □ *David pulled the plug on all our plans.*

PULL ▸ OUT

pull all the stops out to do everything possible; to use everything possible; to go all out. (Refers to drawing all the stops on a pipe organ, resulting in the loudest possible sound.) ☐ *Todd pulled all the stops out for his exhibition and impressed everyone with his painting artistry.* 🅃 *He pulled out all the stops.*

pull (out) in front of someone or something See under *PULL ▸ IN.*

pull out (of something) **1.** to withdraw from something. ☐ *For some reason, he pulled out of the coalition and went his own way.* ☐ *The other side got impatient with the negotiations and pulled out.* 🄽 *The pullout was to begin in mid-January.* **2.** to drive out of something, such as a driveway, parking space, garage, etc. ☐ *The car pulled out of the driveway and nearly hit a truck.* ☐ *Look out! A car is about to pull out!*

pull something out to withdraw something. ☐ *Arthur pulled his sword out and saluted the knight.* 🅃 *He pulled out his sword.*

pull something out of a hat AND **pull something out of thin air** to produce something seemingly out of nowhere. (Usually figurative.) ☐ *Where am I going to get the money? I can't just pull it out of a hat!* ☐ *I don't know where she found the book. She pulled it out of thin air, I guess.*

pull something out of someone to manage to get information out of someone. ☐ *The cops finally pulled a confession out of Max.* ☐ *I thought I would never pull her name out of her.*

pull something out (of someone or something) to withdraw something from someone or something. (The *of*-phrase is paraphrased with a *from*-phrase when the particle is transposed. See the 🄵 example.) ☐ *I pulled the arrow out of the injured soldier and tried to stop the bleeding.* 🅃 *I pulled out the arrow.* 🄵 *I pulled out the arrow from his leg.* ☐ *I found a dandelion growing in the garden and pulled it out.*

pull something out of the fire to rescue something; to save something just before it's too late. (Figurative.) ☐ *Can we rescue this project? Is there time to pull it out of the fire?* ☐ *There is no way we can pull this one out of the fire.*

pull something out of thin air See *pull something out of a hat.*

pull the rug out (from under someone) to make someone or someone's plans fall through; to upset someone's plans. (Figurative.) ☐ *Don pulled the rug out from under me in my deal with Bill Franklin.* ☐ *I was doing great until Don came along and pulled the rug out.*

PULL ▸ OVER

pull over (to something) to steer over to something, such as the side of the road. ☐ *Betty pulled over to the side of the road and waited for the traffic to thin.* ☐ *The police officer ordered her to pull over.*

pull someone or something over (to something) to cause someone or a vehicle to drive over to something, such as the side of the road. ☐ *The cop pulled Betty over to the side of the road.* ☐ *I pulled the car over to the side.*

pull something over someone or something to drag something over someone or something. ☐ *The doctor pulled a sheet over Gerald and left the room.* ☐ *Sharon pulled the cover over the birdcage for the night.*

pull the wool over someone's eyes to deceive someone. (Figurative.) ☐ *That is not so! Are you trying to pull the wool over my eyes?* ☐ *You can't pull the wool over my eyes! I'm too clever.*

PULL ▸ THROUGH

pull someone or something through (something) to help someone or some creature survive a difficult time or situation. (*Someone* includes *oneself*.) ☐ *All her friends worked hard to pull her through the crisis.* ☐ *The vet worked hard to pull the cat through the illness.* ☐ *The vet pulled the cat through.* ☐ *I think I can pull myself through this time, but I don't know if I can do it again.*

pull through (something) to survive something. ☐ *I am sure that your uncle will pull through the illness.* ☐ *I'm glad he pulled through.*

PULL ▸ TO

pull someone or something to pieces to pull someone or something apart; to separate someone or something into pieces. ☐ *The machine almost pulled him to pieces when he got his arm caught in it.* ☐ *It almost pulled his arm to pieces.*

pull something to to close something, usually a door of some type. ☐ *The door is open a little. Pull it to so no one will hear us.* ☐ *Please pull the door to.*

PULL ▸ TOGETHER

pull oneself together **1.** to compose oneself; to gather one's wits about one. ☐ *I have to pull myself together and try it again.* ☐ *Now try to pull yourself together and get through this thing.* **2.** to gather up one's things. ☐ *I'll be ready to leave as soon as I pull myself together.* ☐ *I want to pull myself together and leave.*

pull something together **1.** to assemble something, such as a meal. ☐ *I will hardly have time to pull a snack together.* ☐ *I will pull a light snack together for the two of us.* **2.** to close something, such as a pair of drapes or sliding doors. ☐ *Please pull the doors together when you finish in the closet.* ☐ *Would you pull the drapes together before you turn on the lights?*

pull together to cooperate; to work well together. ☐ *Let's all pull together and get this done.* ☐ *If we pull together, we can get this job done on time.*

PULL ▸ TO(WARD)

pull something toward oneself to draw something closer to oneself. ☐ *He pulled his plate toward himself and began eating like a starving man.* ☐ *Mary pulled the basket of fruit toward herself and chose a nice juicy peach.*

PULL ▸ UNDER

pull someone or something under **1.** to drag someone or something beneath the surface of something. ☐ *The strong undertow pulled John under.* ☐ *The whirlpool nearly pulled the boat under.* **2.** to cause someone or something to fail. ☐ *The heavy debt load pulled Don under. He went out of business.* ☐ *The recession pulled his candy shop under.*

PULL ▸ UP

pull oneself up by one's (own) bootstraps to become a success by one's own efforts. ☐ *If Sam had a little encouragement, he could pull himself up by his bootstraps.* ☐ *Given a chance, I'm sure I can pull myself up by my own bootstraps.*

pull someone or something up to drag or haul someone or something upward or to an upright position. (*Someone* includes *oneself.*) ☐ *Bob had slipped down into the creek, so I reached down and pulled him up.* [T] *I pulled up Bob and nearly fell in myself.* ☐ *Nick pulled the cushion up and propped it against the back of the sofa.* ☐ *The injured soldier pulled himself up with the greatest of difficulty.*

pull someone up short to cause someone to stop short. ☐ *My scream pulled him up short.* ☐ *The sudden thought that everything might not be all right pulled Tom up short.*

pull something up (out of something) to draw something upward out of something. ☐ *The worker pulled a cold wet dog up out of the well.* [T] *He pulled up the dog out of the well.* ☐ *Sam reached down and pulled the dog up.*

pull something up (to something) to draw something close to something else. ☐ *She pulled the chair up to the table and began to examine the papers.* [T] *She pulled up a chair.* ☐ *Please pull a chair up.*

pull (up) alongside (of someone or something) See under *PULL ▸ ALONGSIDE.*

pull up (some place) to arrive at a place in a vehicle; [for a vehicle] to arrive some place. ☐ *She pulled up at the front door exactly on time.* ☐ *Alice pulled up exactly on time.*

pull up stakes to end one's ties to a particular place; to get ready to move away from a place where one has lived or worked for a long time. (As if one were removing tent stakes.) ☐ *Even after all* *these years, pulling up stakes is easier than you think.* □ *It's time to pull up stakes and move on.*

pull up to something to drive up close to something. □ *I pulled up to the drive-in window and placed my order.* □ *When the taxi pulls up to the curb, open the door and get in.*

PULSE ▸ THROUGH

pulse through someone or something to flow or surge through someone or something. □ *A jolt of electricity pulsed through Sam, causing him to jerk his hand away from the wire.* □ *They repaired the power lines and electricity began to pulse through the wires again.*

PUMP ▸ FOR

pump someone for something to try to get information about something out of someone. (Figurative.) □ *The representative of the other company pumped Harry for information, but he refused to say anything.* □ *Are you trying to pump me for company secrets?*

PUMP ▸ IN(TO)

pump something in(to someone or something) to try to force something, such as a gas, liquid, information, or money into someone or something. □ *First you have to pump some air into the ball to make it hard.* 🅃 *I pumped in the air.* □ *The hospital oxygen system pumped life-giving oxygen into Karen's lungs.* □ *The small pump near the aquarium pumped air in.* □ *I helped pump anatomical terms into Fred for the big test he was having the next day.* 🅃 *I pumped in the knowledge.* □ *Congress tried to pump money into the economy, but only created inflation.* □ *The young teacher worked hard to pump new life into the classroom.*

PUMP ▸ OUT

pump something out to empty something by pumping. □ *I need to buy a large pump to pump my basement out.* 🅃 *I have to pump out my basement.*

pump something out (of someone or something) to remove something from someone or something by force or suction. (The *of*-phrase is paraphrased with a *from*-phrase when the particle is transposed. See the 🄵 example.) □ *The doctors pumped the poison out of her.* 🅃 *They pumped out the poison.* 🄵 *They pumped out the poison from her stomach.* □ *The workers pumped the water out of the basement.* □ *They used electric pumps to pump the water out.*

PUMP ▸ THROUGH

pump something through something to force something, such as a gas or fluid, through something. □ *They pumped hot oil through this pipeline, all the way to the south shore.* □ *They pumped fresh air through the sewers while the workers were working inside.*

PUMP ▸ UP

pump someone up (for something) to get someone, including oneself, mentally ready for something. (Slang.) □ *The coach tried to pump the team up so they would win.* □ *The coach talked and talked to pump them up.* 🄰 *There I was, in the midst of a bunch of pumped-up football players getting ready to go out on the field.* □ *Frank pumped himself up for the game.*

pump something up 1. to inflate something. □ *Do you have something with which I can pump my basketball up?* 🅃 *I pumped up the ball just an hour ago.* **2.** to make a muscle get as big as it can be. (Slang.) □ *The bodybuilder pumped her muscles up in preparation for the competition.* 🅃 *She pumped up her muscles.*

PUNCH ▸ DOWN

punch something down to press something down. □ *Punch this lever down and then try to place your telephone call.* 🅃 *Punch down this lever and push this button.*

PUNCH ▸ IN

punch in to record one's arrival at one's workplace at a certain time. □ *What time did you punch in?* □ *I punched in at the regular time.*

punch someone in something to strike someone in some body part. □ *Tony punched Nick in the side.* □ *Why didn't you punch that mean guy in the nose?*

punch something in to crush or smash something in. ☐ *Who punched the cereal box in?* 🅃 *Who punched in the cereal box?*

PUNCH ▸ IN(TO)

punch something in(to something) to stick or press something into something. ☐ *She punched her finger into the cake and ruined my lovely icing job.* ☐ *He finally punched a spoon into the cereal box to get it open.* ☐ *She punched her finger in, just to see what was inside.*

PUNCH ▸ ON

punch someone on something to strike someone on some body part, typically the shoulder. (Not with the intention of causing harm.) ☐ *Sally punched Frank on the shoulder just to show they were still friends.* ☐ *Tom punched Fred on the shoulder in a friendly way.*

PUNCH ▸ OUT

punch out to record that one has left one's workplace at a certain time. ☐ *Why didn't you punch out when you left last night?* ☐ *I punched out at the regular time.*

punch someone out to beat someone up. (Slang.) ☐ *Max threatened to punch the guy out if he said it again.* 🅃 *Max finally punched out the guy who was annoying him.*

punch someone's lights out to knock someone out. (Slang.) ☐ *You had better stop that, or I will punch your lights out!* ☐ *Do you want me to punch your lights out?*

punch something out (of something) to press on something and make it pop out of something. (The *of*-phrase is paraphrased with a *from*-phrase when the particle is transposed. See the 🄵 example.) ☐ *She punched the stickers out of the page and stuck them onto her schoolbooks.* 🅃 *Jane punched out the stickers.* 🄵 *She punched out the sticker from the page of colorful designs.* ☐ *Punch another one out for me.*

PUNCH ▸ UP

punch something up to register a figure on a cash register. ☐ *Jake punched the total up and the register drawer opened.* 🅃 *He punched up the total too carelessly.*

PUNCTUATE ▸ WITH

punctuate something with something **1.** to add a particular punctuation mark to a piece of writing. ☐ *You have punctuated this report with enough exclamation points to last a lifetime.* ☐ *This letter is punctuated with too many commas.* **2.** to add emphasis to one's speaking by adding phrases, exclamations, or other devices. ☐ *Her comments were punctuated with a few choice swearwords.* ☐ *Tom punctuated his address with a few choice comments about politicians.*

PUNISH ▸ BY

punish someone by something to discipline someone by doing something. (*Someone* includes *oneself*.) ☐ *The cruel headmaster punished the children by forcing them to go without supper.* ☐ *She punished herself by not eating.*

PUNISH ▸ FOR

punish someone for something to discipline someone for [doing] something. ☐ *Someone will punish you for what you did.* ☐ *Please don't punish me for doing it. I'm sorry.*

PUNISH ▸ WITH

punish someone with something to use something to discipline someone. ☐ *The captain punished the sailor with the lash.* ☐ *Sally threatened to punish Timmy with a spanking.*

PURCHASE ▸ FOR

purchase something for someone to buy something for someone else; to buy something to give to someone. ☐ *Tony purchased a number of toys for the children in the orphanage.* ☐ *Who did you purchase this for?*

PURGE ▸ AWAY

purge something away to wash or flush something away. ☐ *We will purge the rusty water away and then start up the pump again. We will have fresh, clean water again in no time.* 🅃 *Laura purged away the rusty water.*

PURGE ► FROM

purge someone or something from something to rid something of someone or something. (Compare to the following entry.) □ *We are going to purge the delinquent members from the list.* □ *The court purged her arrest from the records.* □ *Kelly purged the outdated files from the computer's memory.*

PURGE ► OF

purge someone or something of someone or something to rid someone or something of someone or something. (Compare to the previous entry.) □ *The witch doctor proceeded to purge the patient of the ghost of his dead mother.* □ *We purged the list of the delinquent members.* □ *They purged her records of all previous arrests.*

PURR ► LIKE

purr like a cat [for a person] to be very pleased, and perhaps moan or purr with pleasure. (Possibly literal.) □ *She was so pleased that she purred like a cat.* □ *Sarah really purrs like a cat when she is happy.*

PURSE ► UP

purse something up to bunch or pucker something up. (Usually the lips.) □ *When he tasted the stew, he pursed his lips up and spat it out.* [T] *Don pursed up his lips as if to spit it out.* [A] *She stood there, arms akimbo, with her pursed-up lips covered with the brightest of red lipstick, demanding to know where I had been.*

PUSH ► ABOUT

push someone or something about AND **push someone or something around** to jostle someone around. □ *The crowd pushed the visitors around and made them feel unwelcome.* □ *People on the sidewalk pushed the delegation about during the noon rush hour.*

push someone or something about (in something) AND **push someone or something around (in something)** to propel someone or something about on wheels. □ *Freddie pushed his brother about in the wagon.* □ *The nurse pushed Aunt Mary around in her wheelchair.* □ *Freddie pushed his brother around for a while and then demanded to be pushed around himself.*

PUSH ► ACROSS

push someone or something across (something) to move or propel someone or something across something. □ *Jill pushed Fred across the ice. He simply could not skate at all.* □ *The old car stalled just before the bridge, so we pushed it across.*

PUSH ► AGAINST

push something (up) against someone or something to press something against someone or something. □ *I pushed the chair up against the door to prevent the robber from getting in.* □ *Accidentally, I pushed the door against Donna and hurt her sore elbow.*

push (up) against someone or something to put pressure on someone or something. □ *The small dog pushed up against me, wagging its tail.* □ *Push up against the ceiling tile while I try to tack it back in place.*

PUSH ► AHEAD

push ahead (on something) See *push ahead (with something).*

push ahead (with something) **1.** to go on ahead, pushing with something. □ *The worker pushed ahead with the plow, moving the snow to the side of the road.* □ *Our car followed the snowplow, which was pushing ahead at a fast clip.* **2.** AND **push ahead (on something)** to keep moving forward with something; to continue to progress with something. □ *Let's push ahead with this project immediately.* □ *I want to push ahead on this project.* □ *Let's push ahead. We must finish soon.*

push someone or something ahead of someone to push someone or something forward from behind. □ *I pushed Gerald ahead of me, hoping that the soldiers would recognize him as a friend.* □ *Sally pushed the cart ahead of her and filled it from the supermarket shelves.*

PUSH ▸ ALONG

push along to move along; to travel along as with a purpose. ☐ *We must push along. We have a long way to travel before morning.* ☐ *They pushed along at a steady clip until they arrived at their destination.*

push someone or something along to apply pressure to move someone or something along. ☐ *The mother tried to push her child along, but he wouldn't go.* ☐ *Jane pushed the cart along, down the supermarket aisle.*

PUSH ▸ AROUND

push someone around to harass someone; to jostle someone. (See also *push someone or something around* under *PUSH ▸ ABOUT*.) ☐ *I wish you would stop pushing me around all the time.* ☐ *Stop pushing Max around if you know what's good for you.*

push someone or something around See *push someone or something about* under *PUSH ▸ ABOUT.*

PUSH ▸ ASIDE

push someone or something aside to shove someone or something to one side. ☐ *Martha pushed Bill aside and went in ahead of him.* ☐ *He pushed the papers aside and laid his books on the desk.*

PUSH ▸ AT

push at someone or something to apply pressure to and try to move someone or something. ☐ *She pushed at him, trying to get him to get out of the way, but he wouldn't budge.* ☐ *Mary pushed at the door, trying to open it against the wind.* ☐ *There is no need for you to push at me so hard.*

PUSH ▸ AWAY

push (oneself) away (from something) to move oneself back and away from something. ☐ *The skater pushed herself away from the wall.* ☐ *Tom pushed himself away from the table when he had eaten enough.*

push someone or something (away) (from someone or something) to move or force someone or something away from someone or something. ☐ *The police pushed the crowd away from the movie star.* 🅃 *They pushed away the hecklers from the stage.* ☐ *The guards pushed them away.*

PUSH ▸ BACK

push someone or something back (from someone or something) to move or force someone or something back from someone or something. (*Someone* includes *oneself*.) ☐ *I quickly pushed her back from the edge. She almost fell over.* 🅃 *There wasn't enough room, so we pushed back the furniture.* ☐ *Tony pushed Jane back from the edge.* ☐ *Ken pushed Tony back.* ☐ *Sally placed her cards on the table and pushed herself back.*

PUSH ▸ BY

push (oneself) by (someone or something) to shove or thrust oneself past someone or something. ☐ *In a hurry, I pushed myself by the security guard, and almost got arrested for doing so.* ☐ *I pushed by Jane and went in first.* ☐ *Sally pushed herself by the two people blocking the hallway.*

PUSH ▸ DOWN

push down on something to press down on something, such as a button, stamp, typewriter key, etc. ☐ *Push down on this button if you want room service.* ☐ *Don't push down on the door handle too hard. It will break.*

push someone or something down to force someone or something downward. ☐ *Every time he tried to get up, the other boys pushed him down again.* ☐ *I pushed the button down and the machine began to operate.*

PUSH ▸ FOR

be pushed for money See *be pressed for money* under *BE ▸ FOR.*

be pushed for time See *be pressed for time* under *BE ▸ FOR.*

push for something to request or demand something. ☐ *The citizens are pushing for an investigation of the police department.* ☐ *My secretary is pushing for a raise.*

PUSH ▶ FORWARD

push forward to move forward; to move onward toward a goal. □ *We have lots to do. We must push forward!* □ *They are pushing forward, hoping to complete the project on time.*

push someone or something forward to shove or move someone or something to the front. (*Someone* includes *oneself.*) □ *Mary's mother pushed her forward where she would be seen.* □ *Let me push the piano bench forward for you.* □ *The child pushed herself forward and began to shout.*

PUSH ▶ FROM

push someone or something (away) (from someone or something) See under *PUSH ▶ AWAY.*

PUSH ▶ IN

push something in to crush something in; to make something cave in. □ *He ran at the door and pushed it in.* [T] *He pushed in the door.* [A] *They stood and looked at the pushed-in car door and wondered what had happened.*

PUSH ▶ INTO

push someone into something to force someone into a situation; to force someone to do something. □ *They are trying to push me into signing the contract.* □ *Please don't push me into it!*

push someone or something in(to someone or something) to guide, shove, or press someone or something inside of someone or something. □ *The magician claimed he could push one twin into the other so that they would become one person.* □ *I pushed the lawn mower into the garage and closed the door.* □ *I opened the garage door and pushed the lawn mower in.*

push someone or something into someone or something to cause someone or something to bump into someone or something. □ *Todd accidentally pushed Marlene into Bill.* □ *I pushed the lawn mower into the tree by accident.*

PUSH ▶ OFF

push off to depart. (Informal.) □ *It's late. I have to push off.* □ *We're going to push off early in the morning.*

push (oneself) off (on something) [for someone in a boat] to apply pressure to something on the shore, thus propelling the boat and oneself away. □ *The weekend sailor pushed himself off on the boat he had been moored to.* □ *We pushed off on the dock.* □ *Grabbing onto the boathook, Roger pushed off.* □ *Wally pushed himself off on the dock.*

push someone or something off ((of) someone or something) to apply pressure to and force someone or something off someone or something. (The *of*-phrase is paraphrased with a *from*-phrase when the particle is transposed. See the [F] example. The *of* is colloquial.) □ *He continued the attack, but I managed to push him off me and escape.* [T] *I pushed off the attacker from the victim.* □ *The victim pushed the attacker off.* □ *I pushed the creature off of her and shot it with my ray gun.*

push something off on(to) someone to place one's task onto another person; to make someone else do an unwanted job. □ *Don't push the dirty work off onto me.* □ *Kelly pushed her job off on me.* □ *I will try to push the cleaning off onto Sally and Todd.*

PUSH ▶ ON

push on someone or something to put pressure on someone or something. □ *Don't push on me! I can't move any faster than the person in front of me!* □ *Push on this button if you want the steward to come.* □ *Push on the door a little. It will open.*

push on (to something) **1.** to move on to another topic; to stop doing one thing and move on to another. □ *Okay. Let's push on to the next topic.* □ *Let us push on. We are nearly finished with the list.* **2.** to travel onward to something or some place. □ *We left Denver and pushed on to Omaha.* □ *Let us push on. We are nearly there.*

push on (with something) to continue to try to make progress with something. □ *Let's push on with this project. We must finish it soon.* □ *Yes, let's push on and finish.*

push someone or something on ahead (of someone or something) to move or propel someone or something ahead. ☐ *He did not want to go in with me, but I pushed him on ahead of me.* ☐ *I went into each room to clean it, pushing the laundry cart on ahead.* ☐ *Mary pushed Fran on ahead.*

PUSH ▸ OUT

push out to spread out; to expand outward. ☐ *The sides of the box pushed out, and I was afraid it would break.* ☐ *His little tummy pushed out when he was full.*

push someone or something out (of something) to force someone or something out of something. (*Someone* includes *oneself.*) ☐ *Nick pushed the intruder out of the house.* 🅃 *Nick pushed out the intruder.* ☐ *Elaine opened the door and pushed the dog out.* ☐ *He pushed himself out of the door of the plane and parachuted to the ground.*

PUSH ▸ OVER

push someone or something over to make someone or something fall over or fall down. ☐ *When you ran against me, you nearly pushed me over.* 🅃 *You nearly pushed over your friend.* ☐ *Who pushed over the lawn chairs?*

push someone or something over (something) to cause someone or something to get over something. ☐ *The convict pushed his buddy over the wall and followed after him.* ☐ *He worked up to the top and I pushed him over.*

PUSH ▸ PAST

push past (someone or something) to force one's way past someone or something. (Considered a rude act.) ☐ *Nick pushed past the others and made himself first in line.* ☐ *I pushed past the gate and went right in.*

PUSH ▸ THROUGH

push something through (something) **1.** to force something to penetrate something. ☐ *Tony pushed the needle through the cloth, and drew the thread tight.* ☐ *He pushed the needle through just like a pro.* **2.** to force passage of a motion or law. ☐ *The committee chairman managed to push the bill through the committee.* ☐ *With a little lobbying, they pushed it through.*

push through (something) to work through or force one's way through something. ☐ *I pushed through the snow, trying to get to the post office on time.* ☐ *The snow was very deep, but I pushed through.*

PUSH ▸ TO

push someone or something to someone or something to propel someone or something to or as far as someone or something. ☐ *Max pushed Lefty to the window and made him look out.* ☐ *I pushed the chair to the window.* ☐ *I pushed the chair to Sam so he could sit down.*

push someone to something to try to drive or force a person to do something. ☐ *At almost every meeting the committee pushed the president to resign.* ☐ *We pushed her to reconsider, but her mind was made up.*

push someone to the wall to drive or force someone into a defenseless position. ☐ *Only after they pushed him to the wall did he admit being at the scene of the crime.* ☐ *We were pushed to the wall, but we still did not give in.*

push something to to close something, such as a door. ☐ *The door is open a little. Please push it to.* ☐ *Todd came in and pushed the door to.*

PUSH ▸ TOWARD

push someone or something toward someone or something to propel someone or something to someone or something. ☐ *The drama coach got behind the shy young actor playing Romeo and pushed him toward Juliet.* ☐ *Clyde pushed Bonnie toward the edge of the cliff.*

push toward someone or something to move or struggle toward someone or something. ☐ *The crowd pushed toward the convicted man, but the police held them back.* ☐ *The horses pushed toward the corral gate.*

PUSH ▸ UP

push someone or something up to raise or lift someone or something. □ *Jake is sliding down again. Push him up.* [T] *Push up the window, please.* [N] *Fred could do over fifty push-ups.*

push something (up) against someone or something See under *PUSH ▸ AGAINST.*

push (up) against someone or something See under *PUSH ▸ AGAINST.*

push up daisies to be dead and buried. (Slang or colloquial. Usually with *pushing.*) □ *I'll be pushing up daisies before the national debt stops growing.* □ *Don't make Max mad unless you want to end up pushing up daisies.*

push up on something to raise something upward; to push something up from below. □ *Larry pushed up on the trapdoor and lifted it so he could climb out.* □ *Push up on this lever if you want the lights to get brighter.*

PUSSYFOOT ▸ AROUND

pussyfoot around to go about timidly and cautiously. □ *Stop pussyfooting around! Get on with it!* □ *I wish that they would not pussyfoot around when there are tough decisions to be made.*

PUT ▸ ABOVE

put someone or something above someone or something to place someone or something at a higher level than someone or something. □ *The captain put one soldier above the wall so he could see trouble coming.* □ *In the painting, the artist put an angel above the small shed.*

put something above someone to think of some deed as unworthy of a person; to think that someone is too good to do something bad. □ *I put that kind of behavior above Dave. I wonder why he did it.* □ *Sam had put that kind of childish action above Sarah, but he was wrong.*

PUT ▸ ACROSS

put something across (to someone) to make something clear to someone. □ *I don't know how to put this point across to my class. Can you help?* □ *Can you help me put this across?*

PUT ▸ AHEAD

put someone or something ahead (of someone or something) **1.** to move or place someone or something in front of someone or something. □ *The teacher put Freddie ahead of Mike, because Mike had been disrespectful.* □ *Don't put him ahead! I didn't do anything.* **2.** to think of someone or something as more important than someone or something. (*Someone* includes *oneself.*) □ *I put Gerry ahead of Betty as far as strength is concerned.* □ *Yes, I would put Gary ahead.* □ *She put herself ahead of everyone else and expected special treatment.*

PUT ▸ AMONG

put someone or something among someone or something to place someone or something in the midst of people or things. □ *The martial arts instructor put Fred among the strongest students to see what he would do.* □ *The shopkeeper put the green pears among the ripe ones and tried to sell them.*

PUT ▸ ASIDE

put something aside to set or place something to the side. □ *I put the magazine aside and began reading a book.* □ *Put your work aside for a minute and listen to what I have to tell you.*

put something aside (for something) to hold something in reserve for some purpose. □ *You should put a little of the sugar aside for your coffee in the morning.* [T] *Please put aside some money for me.* □ *I can put a little aside.*

PUT ▸ AT

put one at (one's) ease to cause someone to relax or feel welcome. □ *She usually tells a little joke to put you at your ease.* □ *Please do something to put me at ease.*

put someone or something at someone's disposal to make someone or something available for someone's use or service. (*Someone* includes *oneself.*) □ *I will put my secretary at your disposal for the day.* □ *Could you please put your car at my disposal?* □ *I am happy to put myself at your disposal.*

put something at a premium to make something available only at an extra cost or through extra effort. □ *The scarcity of fresh vegetables at this time of year puts broccoli at a premium.* □ *The high demand for apples puts them at a premium.*

put something at an amount to price something at a certain amount of money; to estimate something at a certain figure. □ *I would put the charges at about two hundred dollars.* □ *She put the damages at nearly two hundred thousand dollars.*

put something at one's door See under *LAY ▸ AT.*

put something at someone's feet See under *LAY ▸ AT.*

PUT ▸ AWAY

put someone or something away to kill someone or some creature. (Usually slang, but also euphemism.) □ *Max set out to put Lefty away.* □ *We were forced to put our ailing cat away.* 🅃 *It's kind to put away terminally ill animals.*

put something away to put something where it belongs; to return something to where it is stored. □ *When you finish with this book, please put it away.* 🅃 *Put away your books this instant!*

PUT ▸ BACK

put something back **1.** to return something to where it was before. □ *Please put the book back when you finish it.* 🅃 *Put back the book when you finish.* **2.** See *set something back* under *SET ▸ BACK.*

PUT ▸ BEFORE

put someone or something before someone or something See under *PLACE ▸ BEFORE.*

put the cart before the horse to do things in the wrong order; to do things backwards. (A cliché.) □ *You should not buy a house before you have sold the old one. That's putting the cart before the horse.* □ *Don't put the cart before the horse. Do things in order.*

PUT ▸ BEHIND

put someone behind bars to put someone in jail. (Slang.) □ *The cops put Lefty behind bars, but he didn't stay there long.* □ *Max needs to be put behind bars too.*

put something behind one to try to forget about something. □ *I look forward to putting all my problems behind me.* □ *She will be happier when all this can be put behind her.*

put something behind someone or something to place something in back of someone or something. □ *I put the box behind Mary, and she didn't even know it was there.* □ *Please put the present behind the couch where Janet will not see it.*

PUT ▸ BETWEEN

put some distance between someone and oneself or something to move or travel away from someone or something. (Informal.) □ *Jill and I aren't getting along. I need to put some distance between her and me.* □ *I drove fast to put some distance between Max and me.*

PUT ▸ BY

put something by (for something) to set something aside for some purpose. □ *Remove some of the cooking juices and put them by for the gravy.* □ *I collected some of the cooking juices and put them by.* □ *I put some money by for our vacation.*

PUT ▸ DOWN

put one's foot down (about someone or something) to assert something strongly. (Informal.) □ *Finally, I got so mad that I put my foot down about Walter. I had had enough!* □ *She put her foot down and refused to accept any more changes.* □ *I finally put my foot down and insisted that we go to Acapulco.*

put roots down (some place) to settle down somewhere; to make some place one's permanent home. □ *I'm not ready to put roots down anywhere yet.* 🅃 *I'm ready to put down roots someplace.* □ *I want to settle down. I want to put roots down and buy a house.*

put someone down for something to write down someone's name, indicating that someone is going to do something. (*Someone* includes *oneself.*) □ *Put me down for Friday. I'll be there.* 🅃 *Put down Roger for Tuesday.* □ *I put myself down for a contribution of ten dollars.*

put someone or something down **1.** to disparage someone or something. (Informal. *Someone* includes *oneself.*) □ *Stop putting him down! He is doing his best!* 🅃 *Why are you always putting down my efforts?* □ *Tom had a tendency to put himself down in public.* 🄽 *Mary was shocked by the clever putdown.* **2.** to lower or set down someone or something. □ *Put me down!* 🅃 *Put down that child!* □ *Please put that vase down. It cost a fortune.*

put someone or something down as something to write down the name of someone or a group as something. (*Someone* includes *oneself.*) □ *I will put you down as cook for the benefit luncheon.* 🅃 *I put down John as a likely prospect.* □ *We put your company down as a big contributor. Would your company like to contribute now?* □ *I'll put myself down as a volunteer.*

put something down to take the life of a creature mercifully. □ *We put down our old dog last year.* □ *It's kind to put down fatally ill animals.*

put something down to something to attribute the cause of something to something else. □ *I don't know why he did it. I put it down to haste.* 🅃 *I put the messy writing down to haste.*

PUT ▸ FORTH

put (something) forth to exert effort. □ *You are going to have to put more effort forth if you want to succeed.* □ *You need to put forth. You are not carrying your load.*

PUT ▸ FORWARD

put one's best foot forward to try to make a good impression. (Figurative.) □ *Please remember your manners. You should always put your best foot forward.* □ *I will put my best foot forward when I meet my new boss.*

put someone or something forward **1.** to move someone or something forward. □ *The director put all the players forward during the last scene, leaving more room for the chorus to come on for the finale.* □ *Could you put your left foot forward a little?* **2.** to suggest someone or something; to advance the name of someone or something. (*Someone* includes *oneself.*) □ *I put Henry forward as a possible nominee.* 🅃 *I would like to put forward a plan.* □ *If you don't mind, I'll put myself forward.*

PUT ▸ IN

See also under *PUT ▸ IN(SIDE); PUT ▸ IN(TO).*

put a bee in someone's bonnet (about someone or something) to give someone an idea about someone or something. (A cliché.) □ *Julie put a bee in my bonnet about a way to solve our money problems.* □ *Sam put a bee in my bonnet about having a party for Jane.* □ *He put a bee in my bonnet about Jane.* □ *I'm glad he put a bee in my bonnet.*

put a plug in (for someone or something) to say something favoring someone or something; to advertise someone or something. □ *I hope that when you are in talking to the manager, you put a plug in for me.* 🅃 *I could use some help. While you're there, put in a plug.* □ *Put a plug in for me.*

put a sock in it See *stuff a sock in it* under *STUFF ▸ IN.*

put all one's eggs in one basket to make everything dependent on only one thing. (Figurative. If the basket is dropped, all is lost.) □ *Don't invest all your money in one company. Never put all your eggs in one basket.* □ *I advise you not to put all your eggs in one basket.*

put in a good word (for someone) to say something favorable to someone about someone. (Cliché.) □ *When you talk to the boss, put in a good word for me.* □ *I could use some help too. Please put in a good word.*

put in an appearance (at something) to appear briefly some place or at some event. □ *I only wanted to put in an ap-*

pearance at the reception, but I ended up staying for two hours. ☐ *Do we have to stay a long time, or can we just put in an appearance?*

put in for something to apply for something; to place an order for something. ☐ *I put in for a transfer, but I bet I don't get it.* ☐ *She put in for a new file cabinet, but she never got one.*

put in one's oar AND **put in one's two cents (worth)** to add one's comments or opinion. (Cliché.) ☐ *Do you mind if I put in my oar? I have a suggestion.* ☐ *There is no need for you to put in your two cents worth.*

put in one's two cents (worth) See the previous entry.

put in some place to dock temporarily some place. ☐ *The ship put in at Bridgetown, Barbados, for repairs.* ☐ *We will put in at Honolulu for a few hours.*

put one foot in front of the other **1.** to walk deliberately. ☐ *I was so tired that I could hardly even put one foot in front of the other.* ☐ *She was putting one foot in front of the other so carefully that I thought she must be ill.* **2.** to do things in their proper order. (Figurative.) ☐ *Let's do it right now. Just put one foot in front of the other. One thing at a time.* ☐ *All I need to do is put one foot in front of the other. Everything else will take care of itself.*

put one in one's place to rebuke someone. ☐ *I heard what you said to Joe. I guess you really put him in his place.* ☐ *Someone needs to put Alice in her place.*

put one's foot in it to make a serious mistake; to say something that should not have been said. (Either to *put one's foot in one's mouth*—figurative—or to step in dung—literal but evasive.) ☐ *You really put your foot in it when you told her off.* ☐ *I put my foot in it when I mentioned what Tom was giving her for her birthday.*

put one's foot in one's mouth to say something that should not have been said. (Figurative.) ☐ *When you said that, you really put your foot in your mouth.* ☐ *Sam put his foot in his mouth when he told the price of Tom's car.*

put one's nose in (where it's not wanted) to interfere. (Figurative.) ☐ *Please don't put your nose in where it's not wanted.* ☐ *Why do you always have to put your nose in?*

put one's (own) house in order to make one's own affairs right, before or instead of criticizing someone else. (Figurative.) ☐ *You should put your own house in order before criticizing someone else.* ☐ *I have to put my house in order before I criticize yours.*

put one's trust in someone or something to trust someone or something. ☐ *Will I never be able to put my trust in you?* ☐ *You can put your trust in the bank. Its deposits are insured.*

put oneself in someone else's place to pretend that one is another person and think how the other person feels. ☐ *I put myself in her place and imagined what she must have felt like.* ☐ *If you would just put yourself in my place, you would see things quite differently.*

put someone in an awkward position to make it difficult for someone; to make it difficult for someone to evade or avoid acting. (*Someone* includes *oneself.*) ☐ *Your demands have put me in an awkward position. I don't know what to do.* ☐ *I'm afraid I've put myself in sort of an awkward position.*

put someone in the picture to include someone in something. ☐ *Let's put another child in the picture and see how that affects our housing needs.* ☐ *If you put Sam in the picture, it changes things all around, doesn't it?*

put someone in touch with someone or something to cause or help someone to communicate with someone or something. ☐ *Can you put me in touch with Liz?* ☐ *Would you please put me in touch with the main office?*

put something in a nutshell to state something very concisely. ☐ *The explanation is long and involved, so let me put it in a nutshell for you.* ☐ *To put it in a nutshell: you are fired!*

put something in quotes to put quotation marks around writing or printing. ☐ *Please put this word in quotes, since* *it means something special the way you have used it here.* □ *They put it in quotes so people would know it means something different.*

put something in the way of someone or something to place a barrier in the way of someone or something. □ *You know I don't want to put anything in the way of your happiness.* □ *I would never put anything in the way of you and Donna.*

Put that in your pipe and smoke it! See how you like that! (A cliché.) □ *Here is your hat, squashed flat when you sat on it! Put that in your pipe and smoke it!* □ *I don't care whether you like it or not! Put that in your pipe and smoke it!*

PUT ▸ IN(SIDE)

put someone in(side) (something) to place or insert someone inside something. □ *The sheriff put Roger inside the cell and locked the door.* □ *He opened the cell door and put Roger in.*

put something in((side) someone or something) to place or insert something inside someone or something. □ *The surgeon put a sponge inside Chuck and left it there by mistake.* □ *While you have the closet door open, will you put this in?*

PUT ▸ INTO

put one's back into something to apply some effort to something, especially, but not necessarily to lifting or moving something. □ *Push! Come on! Put your back into the job!* □ *Put your back into it! It will move!*

put one's heart and soul into something to put all of one's sincere efforts into something. □ *You have to put your heart and soul into a song if you want to be convincing.* □ *She put her heart and soul into the singing of the national anthem.*

put something into effect AND **put something into force** to make something take effect; to begin a policy or procedure. □ *When will the city council put this law into effect?* □ *We will put it into force tomorrow.*

put something into force See the previous entry.

put something into practice to make a suggested procedure the actual procedure. □ *That is a good policy. I suggest you put it into practice immediately.* □ *I plan to put the new technique into practice as soon as I can.*

put something into words to form an idea into sentences that can be spoken or written. □ *I find it hard to put my thoughts into words.* □ *She put it into words quite nicely.*

PUT ▸ IN(TO)

put someone in(to power) to elect or appoint someone to office or a position of power. □ *The election put an unknown from the country into power.* T *They put in a complete unknown.* □ *They don't care who they put in.*

put someone or something in(to) jeopardy to put someone or something into danger. (*Someone* includes *oneself*.) □ *What you just said puts Bill into jeopardy.* □ *It puts his plans in jeopardy.* □ *Have I put myself into jeopardy by doing this?*

put someone or something into order to put people or things into a proper sequence. □ *Would you please put these people into order so we can march into the auditorium?* □ *Could you put these magazines into order?*

put someone or something in(to something) to insert or install someone or something into something. □ *The magician put the woman into the cabinet and locked the door.* T *She put in the woman and locked the cabinet.* □ *I put the key in and turned it.*

put something in(to) order to make something tidy. □ *Please put this room into order.* □ *I will put it in order as soon as I have a minute.*

put something in(to) print to publish something; to record something spoken in printed letters. □ *The article looks good. We will put it into print as soon as possible.* □ *We'll put it in print as soon as we can.*

put something in(to) service AND **put something into use** to start to use a thing; to make a device operate and function. □ *I hope that they are able to put the elevator into service again soon. I am tired of climbing stairs.* □ *We will put it in service within an hour.* □ *We can put it into use as soon as we finish the repairs.*

put something in(to) someone's head to give ideas to someone who might not have thought of them without help. □ *Who put that idea into your head?* □ *No one put it in my head. I thought of it all by myself.*

put something in(to) use See *put something in(to) service.*

put teeth in(to) something See *give teeth to something* under *GIVE ▸ TO.*

put the fear of God in(to) someone to frighten someone severely; [for something] to shock someone into contrite behavior. (Folksy.) □ *A near miss like that really puts the fear of God into you.* □ *Yes, it puts the fear of God in you.*

put words in(to) someone's mouth to interpret what someone says so that the words mean what you want and not what the speaker wanted. □ *I didn't say that! You are putting words into my mouth.* □ *Stop putting words in my mouth!* □ *No, I don't mean that at all! You are trying to put words into my mouth.*

PUT ▸ OFF

put one off one's stride to interfere with one's normal and natural progress or rate of progress. (Both literal and figurative uses.) □ *Your startling comments put Larry off his stride for a moment.* □ *He was put off his stride by an interruption from the audience.*

put someone off 1. to delay action with someone. □ *I hate to keep putting you off, but we are not ready to deal with you yet.* 🅃 *I had to put off the plumber again. He really wants his money.* 2. to repel someone. □ *You really put people off with your scowling face.* 🅃 *You put off people with your frown.*

put someone off something to force someone to get off a conveyance. □ *The conductor put the offensive boys off the train.* □ *Some of the passengers hoped that the rude person would be put off the bus.*

put someone or something off the scent to distract someone, a group, or an animal from following a scent or trail of some other creature, including humans. (Both literal [for animals] and figurative [for people].) □ *The clever maneuvers of the bandits put the sheriff's posse off the scent.* □ *The loud noise put the dogs off the scent.*

put someone or something off the track AND **put someone or something off the trail** to cause someone or some creature to lose a trail that is being followed. □ *A distraction put me off the track and I almost got lost in the jungle.* □ *I was following an escaped convict and something put me off the trail.* □ *Your hints put me off the track for a while, but I finally saw through your deception.*

put something off (until something) to postpone or delay something until something happens or until some future time. □ *I can't put this off until tomorrow.* 🅃 *I will put off the review until next week.* □ *I can put it off forever if you want.*

PUT ▸ ON

put a damper on something to have a dulling or numbing influence on something. □ *The bad news really put a damper on everything.* □ *The weather put a damper on our celebration.*

put a premium on something to make something harder or more expensive to obtain or do. □ *The recent action of the bank directors put a premium on new home loans.* □ *The scarcity of steel put a premium on the cost of new cars.*

put a strain on someone or something to burden or overload someone or something. □ *All this bad economic news puts a strain on everyone's nerves.* □ *The epidemic put a strain on the resources of the hospital.*

put hair on someone's chest to do something to invigorate or virilize someone, always a male, except in jest. (Folksy.) □ *Here, have a drink of this stuff! It'll put hair on your chest.* □

That stuff is powerful. It will really put hair on your chest.

put it on the line See *lay it on the line* under *LAY ► ON.*

put on to pretend; to deceive. ☐ *She is not really that way. She is just putting on.* ☐ *Stop putting on. Act yourself.*

put on a brave face See *put up a brave front* under *PUT ► UP.*

put on airs to act better than one really is; to pretend to be good or the best. ☐ *Pay no attention to her. She is just putting on airs.* ☐ *Stop putting on airs and act like the rest of us.*

put on an act to pretend. ☐ *She's not upset. She's just putting on an act.* [N] *The whole affair was just a put-on.*

put on one's thinking cap to ponder or concentrate. (A cliché. Usually said to children.) ☐ *That's a real problem. I'll have to put on my thinking cap to figure it out.* ☐ *Put on your thinking caps, and let's see who can come up with the correct answer first.*

put on the dog to dress up in fancy clothing; to make plans to do something as elegantly as possible. (Slang.) ☐ *Who are you putting on the dog for? Somebody special?* ☐ *They put on the dog for the out-of-town guests.*

put on the ritz to do something as elegantly as possible; to dress up in fancy clothing. ☐ *You are really putting on the ritz! Where are you going tonight?* ☐ *We put on the ritz when the boss came to dinner.*

put on weight to gain weight; to get fat. ☐ *I think I am putting on a little weight. I had better go on a diet.* ☐ *I'm not putting on any weight for the moment.*

put one on one's feet See *get one on one's feet* under *GET ► ON.*

put one on one's guard to make one wary or cautious. ☐ *The menacing growl by the watchdog put me on my guard.* ☐ *Every time the boss comes around, it puts me on my guard.*

put one on one's honor to inform one that one is trusted to act honorably, legally, and fairly without supervision. ☐ *I'll put you on your honor when I have to leave the room during the test.* ☐ *They put us on our honor to take no more than we had paid for.*

put one's cards on the table (about someone or something) to reveal what one has planned; to be honest and straightforward about someone or something. (Cliché. From cardplaying.) ☐ *It's time you put your cards on the table about the Smith deal.* ☐ *It's time to stop messing around and put our cards on the table.*

put one's dibs on something to lay a claim to something; to announce one's claim to something. ☐ *She put her dibs on the last piece of cake.* ☐ *I put my dibs on the seat by the window.*

put one's finger on something **1.** to touch something with one's finger. ☐ *I put my finger on the button and pressed.* ☐ *Put your finger on this spot and push hard.* **2.** to identify and state the essence of something. (Idiomatic.) ☐ *That is correct! You have certainly put your finger on the problem.* ☐ *When she mentioned money, she really put her finger on the problem.*

put one's hands on someone or something AND **lay one's hands on someone or something** **1.** to lay one's hands on someone or some creature. ☐ *He put his hands on the sick woman and proclaimed her cured. This act of faith healing failed, alas.* ☐ *He lay his hands on the dog and gently felt for broken bones.* **2.** AND **get one's hands on someone or something** to get hold of someone or something with punishment or harm as a goal. ☐ *Just wait till I put my hands on you!* ☐ *When I lay my hands on Ken, he will be sorry he ever did that.* ☐ *I can't wait to get my hands on that cat! Will I ever teach it a lesson!* ☐ *You watch what happens when I get my hands on Greg.* **3.** AND **get one's hands on someone or something** to locate and get hold of someone or something. (Sometimes figurative.) ☐ *As soon as I can lay my hands on him, I'll get him right over here.* ☐ *I can't seem to get my hands on a dictionary.* ☐ *I'm trying to get my hands on that messenger.* ☐ *I am* *trying to put my hands on the book you suggested.*

put one's money on someone or something (to do something) **1.** to bet money that someone or something will accomplish something. □ *I put my money on Bob to win the race.* □ *Donna put her money on the most popular political party.* **2.** to predict the outcome of an event involving someone or something. (Figurative. This is not a wager.) □ *I put my money on Bob to get elected this time.* □ *Alice put her money on the most promising horse to win.* □ *She put her money on the best horse.*

put pressure on something to apply weight or pressure to something. □ *Put pressure on the wound to stop the bleeding.* □ *Put some pressure on the papers to flatten them out.*

put (some) years on someone or something to cause someone or something to age prematurely; to cause deterioration in the state of someone or something. (The *some* may be replaced with a specific number or period of time.) □ *The events of the last week have really put a lot of years on Gerald.* □ *The severe weather put many years on the roof of the house.*

put someone on to tease or deceive someone. □ *You can't be serious! You're just putting me on!* □ *Stop putting me on!* N *It was not a real robbery. It was just a put on.*

put someone on a pedestal to worship someone; to elevate someone to a position of honor or reverence. □ *He puts his wife on a pedestal. She can do no wrong.* □ *There is no point in putting me on a pedestal!*

put someone on the spot to put one in a position where one must act or speak decisively; to put one in a position where one cannot avoid speaking or acting decisively. (*Someone* includes *oneself*.) □ *Please don't put me on the spot. I don't know the answer.* □ *I seem to have put myself on the spot, and I have nothing to say on the matter.*

put someone or something on hold **1.** to put someone or someone's telephone call on an electronic hold. □ *Please don't put me on hold! I'm in a hurry!* □ *I am going to have to put this call on hold.* **2.** to postpone action on someone or something. □ *I know he keeps asking, but we will just have to put him on hold.* □ *We will have to put this project on hold.*

put someone or something on ice **1.** to put a person's body on ice to preserve it; to put a foodstuff on ice to cool it. □ *The small-town undertaker had so many customers that he had to put some of them on ice.* □ *Please put the soda pop on ice.* **2.** to postpone acting on someone or something. □ *I know he keeps pestering you for an answer, but we'll just have to put him on ice until we have more facts to go on.* □ *Let's put this project on ice till we find out how well it's financed.*

put someone or something on something to place someone or something on top of something. □ *The man put the child on the pony and led it about.* □ *June put the lid on the pickle jar and put it in the fridge.*

put someone or something on the back burner to postpone acting on or dealing with someone or something. (Figurative.) □ *I can't deal with her now. We'll just have to put her on the back burner.* □ *Let's put this business on the back burner.*

put something on to dress in an article of clothing. □ *Put your coat on, and let's go.* T *Put on your coat, and let's go.*

put something on its feet See *get something on its feet* under *GET ▶ ON.*

put something on paper to write something down. (Said of information that is important and must be preserved in its exact wording.) □ *If it is important, you should put it on paper!* □ *I will put it on paper so there will be no doubt about what I mean.*

put something on someone or something **1.** to place or set something on someone or something. □ *She put sand on Tom as he lay napping on the beach.* □ *Please put the paper on the coffee table.*

2. to clothe someone or some creature in something. ☐ *The mother put a little jacket on her child.* ☐ *Alice puts a silly little garment on her poodle during the winter.*

put something on the map to make some place famous. (A cliché.) ☐ *The good food you serve here will really put this place on the map.* ☐ *Nothing like a little scandal to put an otherwise sleepy town on the map.*

put something on the street to tell something to everyone. (Slang.) ☐ *There is no need to put all this gossip on the street. Keep it to yourself.* ☐ *Now, please don't put this on the street, but I am going to get married.*

put the bite on someone (for something) to pressure someone for a loan of money. (Slang.) ☐ *I'll put the bite on Sam for some money.* ☐ *Max is trying to put the bite on Sam.*

put the blame on someone or something (for something) to blame someone or something for something. ☐ *Don't try to put the blame on me for everything that went wrong.* ☐ *Donna put the blame on the weather for the cancellation.* ☐ *They put the blame on me.*

put the brakes on someone to block someone's activities; to cause someone to stop doing something. ☐ *The boss put the brakes on Gerald, who was trying too aggressively to get promoted.* ☐ *We are going to have to put the brakes on you if you make any more difficulties.*

put the brakes on something to halt or impede some process. ☐ *The manager had to put the brakes on the Wilson project due to lack of funds.* ☐ *We will put the brakes on this project because it is costing too much money.*

put the chill on someone AND **put the freeze on someone** to ignore someone; to end social contact with someone. (Slang.) ☐ *Max put the chill on the guys who threatened him.* ☐ *Max put the freeze on Lefty.*

put the clamps on (someone or something) AND **put on the clamps** (Slang.) to impede or block someone or something. ☐ *Fred had to put the clamps on Tony, who was getting too eager about getting his money back.* 🅃 *Tony is getting a little anxious. Time to put on the clamps.*

put the feed bag on AND **put the nose-bag on** to eat a meal. (Folksy and slang. Both refer to a method of feeding a horse by attaching a bag of food at its nose and mouth.) ☐ *It's time to put the feed bag on! I'm starved!* 🅃 *When do we put on the nose-bag?*

put the finger on someone See under *LAY ▸ ON.*

put the freeze on someone See *put the chill on someone.*

put the hard word on someone See *put the make on someone.*

put the heat on to turn on central heating; to increase the amount of heat in a room or house. ☐ *It's going to get cold tonight. I'd better put the heat on.* ☐ *Let's put the heat on to take off the chill.*

put the heat on someone to put pressure on someone. (Slang.) ☐ *The cops are putting the heat on the motorists who show any signs of driving while under the influence of alcohol.* ☐ *I want to put the heat on Jerry so he will meet our terms.*

put the kibosh on someone or something to squelch someone or something. (Informal.) ☐ *I hate to put the kibosh on Randy, but he isn't doing what he is supposed to.* ☐ *Your comments put the kibosh on the whole project.*

put the make on someone AND **put the hard word on someone** to attempt to seduce or proposition someone. (Slang.) ☐ *I think he was beginning to put the make on me. I'm glad I left.* ☐ *James tried to put the hard word on Martha.*

put the moves on someone to attempt to seduce someone. (Slang.) ☐ *About midnight he started putting the moves on Carla, and boy, was she mad!* ☐ *Are you putting the moves on me?*

put (the) pressure on someone (to do something) to make demands on someone; to try to get someone to do something. ☐ *Please don't put pressure on* *me to go there!* □ *There is no use putting pressure on me.*

put the squeeze on someone **1.** to put pressure on someone. (Slang.) □ *The cops are putting the squeeze on the speeders around here.* □ *It's time someone started putting the squeeze on the cheaters.* **2.** to attempt to get money out of someone. (Slang.) □ *Max put the squeeze on all the merchants, threatening to break their windows if they didn't pay.* □ *Are you trying to put the squeeze on me for more money?*

put too fine a point on something to make too much out of something; to dwell overly long on a small detail of a complaint or argument. (Usually with *not*. Formal or stilted.) □ *Not to put too fine a point on it, but did you really mean to say that Paul was the former secretary of the organization? Wasn't he the corresponding secretary?* □ *When he said that everyone was angry, he put too fine a point on it.*

put wear (and tear) on something to cause deterioration in the state of something. (There can be various amounts of *wear and tear*. See the examples.) □ *This cold weather puts a lot of wear on cars.* □ *All this wave action puts too much wear and tear on the boat dock.*

PUT ▸ ONTO

put someone onto someone or something to alert someone to the existence of someone or something; to lead someone to someone or something. □ *Nancy put Elaine onto George, who knew of a job that Elaine might be interested in.* □ *Nancy put Elaine onto a good job lead.*

PUT ▸ OUT

put oneself out to inconvenience oneself. □ *I just don't know why I put myself out for you!* □ *No, I did not put myself out at all. It was no trouble, in fact.* □ *She refused to put herself out even one little bit.*

put out to generate lots of something. (Colloquial.) □ *What a great machine. It really puts out!* □ *The outlet of the dam really puts out!*

put out a warrant (on someone) AND **send out a warrant (on someone)** to issue a warrant for the arrest of someone. □ *The police put out a warrant on Max.* □ *We sent out a warrant on Lefty "Fingers" Moran at the same time.* □ *Max has gone too far. It's time to put out a warrant.*

put out (some) feelers (on someone or something) to arrange to find out about something in an indirect manner. □ *I put out some feelers on Betty to try and find out what is going on.* □ *I will put out feelers on what's going on with June.*

put someone or something out of one's mind to force oneself to forget someone or something. □ *I tried to put her out of my mind, but I couldn't do it.* □ *See if you can put all these problems out of your mind.*

put someone or something out (of something) to get rid of someone or some creature; to eliminate someone or some creature from something or some place. □ *The usher put the noisy boys out of the theater.* [T] *He put out the boys.* □ *Please put the dog out.*

put someone or something out of the way **1.** to move someone or something out of a pathway. □ *Please put that chair out of the way before someone falls on it.* □ *Put the baby out of the way so the noise doesn't bother her.* **2.** to kill someone or some creature that is a burden. □ *Frederick actually threatened to put his wife out of the way.* □ *Max really wanted to put Lefty out of the way once and for all.*

put someone or something out to pasture to retire someone or something. (Figurative except when used with horses.) □ *They can't put me out to pasture! I'm too young.* □ *They plan on putting half the office staff out to pasture.* □ *They put the old horse that used to pull the milk wagon out to pasture.*

put someone out to annoy or irritate someone. (See also *put someone's nose out of joint*.) □ *He really put me out when he used a saucer for an ashtray.* □

I didn't mean to put you out. I had no idea you were so touchy.

put someone's nose out of joint to make someone resentful. (Colloquial.) □ *What's wrong with Jill? What put her nose out of joint?* □ *Don't put your nose out of joint. I didn't mean anything by what I said.*

put something out **1.** to send a creature, such as a pet, outdoors. □ *Did you put the cat out?* 🅃 *Yes, I put out the cat.* **2.** to publish something. □ *When was this book put out?* 🅃 *We put out both books last year.* **3.** to emit something. □ *The factory put a lot of fumes out.* 🅃 *It put out nasty fumes.* **4.** to extinguish something. □ *He used flour to put the grease fire out.* 🅃 *He put out the fire with flour.* **5.** to manufacture or produce something. □ *That factory puts electrical supplies out.* 🅃 *We put out some very fine products.* 🄽 *The output fell far below average this year.*

PUT ▸ OVER

put someone or something over to succeed in making someone or something be accepted. (*Someone* includes *oneself*.) □ *The public relations expert helped put John over to the public.* □ *Do you think we can put this over?* □ *Do you think I put myself over all right?*

put something over on someone to play a trick on someone; to deceive someone with something. □ *We really put one over on the teacher and boy, was he mad.* □ *I'm too observant. You can't put anything over on me.*

PUT ▸ PAST

put it past someone to think that someone would not do something. (Usually negative.) □ *He might run away from school. I wouldn't put it past him.* □ *I wouldn't put it past Roger to arrive unannounced.*

PUT ▸ THROUGH

put one through one's paces AND **put something through its paces** to give someone or something a thorough test; to show what someone or something can do. (Both literal and figurative senses.) □ *I brought the young gymnast out and put her through her paces.* □ *She wanted to put her horse through its paces, but it was already getting dark.*

put someone or something through (to someone) to put someone's telephone call through to someone. □ *Will you please put me through to the long-distance operator?* □ *Please put my call through.*

put someone through the wringer to give someone a difficult time; to interrogate someone thoroughly. (Figurative. Refers to an old-fashioned clothes wringer.) □ *The lawyer really put the witness through the wringer!* □ *The teacher put the students through the wringer.*

put something through its paces See *put one through one's paces.*

PUT ▸ TO

See *be put to it* under *BE ▸ TO.*

put a stop to something AND **put an end to something** to stop something from happening. □ *That's terrible. I'll put a stop to it once and for all.* □ *I am going to put an end to all this noise!*

put one's hand to the plow to get busy; to help out; to start working. (Figurative.) □ *You should start work now. It's time to put your hand to the plow.* □ *Put your hand to the plow and get the job done!*

put one's mind to something AND **set one's mind to something** to concentrate on doing something; to give the doing of something one's full attention. □ *I know I can do it if I put my mind to it.* □ *I will set my mind to it and finish by noon.*

put one's nose to the grindstone to get busy; to apply some effort. (Figurative.) □ *You have to put your nose to the grindstone and accomplish something.* □ *It's time for me to put my nose to the grindstone and get the job done!*

put one's shoulder to the wheel to apply some effort; to push hard at something. (Figurative.) □ *Come on! Move it! Put your shoulder to the wheel!* □ *Things won't get done around here until I put my shoulder to the wheel.* □ *Put* *your shoulder to the wheel and let's get this thing moved.*

put someone or something to the test to test someone or something. □ *All right. I'll find out if you can do what you say. I'll put you to the test.* □ *Let's put this new medication to the test.*

put someone to bed to send someone, usually a child, to bed; to put a child into bed. □ *It's time to put Don to bed.* □ *The children were put to bed very late last night.*

put someone to shame to shame someone. □ *I couldn't hit him, so I put him to shame.* □ *They were all put to shame by the health inspectors.*

put someone wise to someone or something to inform someone about someone or something. (Slang.) □ *Valerie put me wise to you.* □ *I put Valerie wise to what was going on.*

put something to bed to finish something and set it aside or send it on for the next step. (Figurative.) □ *This project looks okay to me. Let's put it to bed.* □ *We put it to bed because we were sure we were done with it.*

put something to (good) use to use something well; to be able to use something. □ *Thank you for the birthday gift. I am sure I will put it to good use.* □ *I look forward to putting this clock to use.*

put something to rest See *lay something to rest* under *LAY ▸ TO.*

put something to sleep to have a living creature, such as a pet, killed. (Figurative.) □ *We had to put the cat to sleep, because she was very sick.* □ *The ailing dog had to be put to sleep.*

put the pedal to the metal to press the accelerator of a car all the way to the floor. (Slang.) □ *Come on, Fred. Put the pedal to the metal and let's get going.* □ *He put the pedal to the metal and sped off.*

PUT ▸ TOGETHER

put people or things together to join or combine people or things. □ *We will put Sam and Trudy together at the dinner table.* □ *Let's put all the crystal goblets together.*

put someone's heads together to join together with someone to confer. (Informal.) □ *Let's put our heads together and come up with a solution to this problem.* □ *Mary and Ted put their heads together, but failed to provide anything new.*

put something together to assemble something. □ *How long will it take to put dinner together?* □ *This was put together incorrectly.*

put two and two together to figure something out. (Figurative.) □ *I know what's going on here! I can put two and two together!* □ *If you would put two and two together, you could figure this out!*

PUT ▸ UNDER

put someone or something under something to place someone or something beneath something. □ *Dave put Sam under the loft in the barn, hoping no one would find him there.* □ *Alice put the birthday present under the couch, where she could get to it in a hurry.*

put someone under to anesthetize someone. □ *They put him under with ether.* □ *After you put her under, we will begin the operation.*

put the skids under someone or something to cause someone or something to fail. □ *Her lateness put the skids under our presentation to the board of directors.* □ *He thought he could get promoted if he put the skids under the vice president.*

put the skids under someone or something to make someone or something move or operate more efficiently. (Colloquial.) □ *The new law put the skids under the people who wanted to make cigarettes illegal.* □ *It put the skids under their efforts.*

PUT ▸ UP

put one's hand up to raise one's hand to get attention from whomever is in charge. □ *The student put his hand up to ask a question.* 🅃 *She put up her hand to ask a question.*

put someone up against someone to place someone into competition with someone else. (*Someone* includes *oneself*.) ☐ *The coach put his best wrestler up against the champ from the other team.* ☐ *The team members put themselves up against the other team in a game to benefit charity.*

put someone up (for something) to nominate or offer someone for some office or task. ☐ *I put Henry up for dogcatcher.* 🅃 *We put up Shannon for treasurer.*

put someone up for the night to provide overnight lodging for someone. ☐ *I would be happy to put your friend up for the night.* 🅃 *I will put up your friend for the night.*

put someone up some place to provide someone housing some place. ☐ *I think I can put you up at my place for the night.* ☐ *Could you put me up at a nearby hotel?* ☐ *He put up the whole family in his apartment.*

put someone up to something to persuade someone to do something. ☐ *Why did you do this? Who put you up to it?* ☐ *No one put me up to it. I did it myself.*

put someone up with someone to house someone with someone. ☐ *I will put her up with my cousin, who has an extra bedroom.* 🅃 *We will put up the lady with us.*

put someone's back up to make someone angry or resentful. (Figurative. Refers to the raised back of an angry cat.) ☐ *I'm sorry. I didn't mean to put your back up.* ☐ *There is no need to put your back up. It is a mistake.*

put something up (for auction) to offer something for sale through an auction. ☐ *I will have to put the house up for auction to pay the taxes that are due.* ☐ *I hate to put it up, but we need the money.*

put something up (for sale) to offer something for sale. ☐ *We had to put the farm up for sale because the crops failed once too often.* 🅃 *They put up their house for sale.* ☐ *They are going to sell the house themselves. They put it up last Saturday.*

put up a brave front AND **put on a brave face** to appear to be brave when one is really frightened. ☐ *He was frightened, but he put up a brave front.* ☐ *I have to put on a brave face before I do anything like that.*

put up a front to appear to be what one is not; to pretend. ☐ *She is not really mean. She is just putting up a front.* ☐ *I am not putting up a front.*

put up or shut up to deliver or produce something or be quiet about it. (Colloquial. Usually a command.) ☐ *I've heard enough. Do something! Put up or shut up!* ☐ *Put up or shut up! Words are worth nothing.*

put up with someone or something to endure or tolerate someone or something. ☐ *I can't put up with her anymore.* ☐ *I cannot put up with this mess anymore.*

PUT ▸ WITH

put someone or something with someone to place someone or something with someone; to assign someone or something to someone. ☐ *I will put David with you and let you two work together for a while.* ☐ *I will put this project with you for the time being.*

PUTT ▸ ALONG

putt along to move along rapidly, usually in a motorized vehicle. ("Putt-putt" is the sound made by engines, especially small engines.) ☐ *The little car was putting along down the highway, when one of the tires went flat.* ☐ *We were putting along very smoothly all the way into town.*

PUTTER ▸ ABOUT

putter about See the following entry.

PUTTER ▸ AROUND

putter around AND **putter about** to do little things of little consequence; to do small tasks as found around the house. ☐ *I spent all of Saturday just puttering around, not really getting anything done.* ☐ *I stayed home and puttered about during my vacation.*

PUZZLE ▸ OUT

puzzle something out to figure something out. □ *It took me a while to puzzle it out.* [T] *I puzzled out the answer to the question.*

PUZZLE ▸ OVER

puzzle over someone or something to consider or ponder someone or something. □ *Anne is a bit strange. I've spent some time puzzling over her.* □ *While I was puzzling over why she had slapped me, she did it again.*

Q

QUAIL ▸ AT

quail at someone or something to show fear at someone or something; to shrink from someone or something. ☐ *Todd quailed at the thought of what he had to do.* ☐ *The students quailed at the teacher who had been so hard on them in the past.*

QUAIL ▸ BEFORE

quail before someone or something to cower before or at the threat of someone or something. ☐ *The students quailed before the angry dean.* ☐ *They quailed before the thought of punishment.*

QUAKE ▸ IN

quake in one's boots to shake from fear. (Rarely literal.) ☐ *They were so frightened they were quaking in their boots.* ☐ *I was quaking in my boots from fear.*

QUAKE ▸ WITH

quake with something to shake as with fear, terror, etc. ☐ *Alice was quaking with fear as the door slowly opened.* ☐ *Todd quaked with terror when he saw Alice at the door.*

QUALIFY ▸ AS

qualify as something to fulfill the requirements to be something. ☐ *Tom qualified as a mechanic.* ☐ *I have been qualified as a mechanic since I was fifteen.*

qualify someone as something to cause someone to fulfill the requirements for something. (*Someone* includes *oneself.*) ☐ *Does this qualify me as a stockbroker?* ☐ *She qualified herself as a realtor.*

QUALIFY ▸ FOR

qualify for something to meet the requirements for something. ☐ *I'm sorry, you do not qualify for this job.* ☐ *I don't qualify for it.*

qualify someone for something to enable someone to meet the requirements for something. ☐ *His years with the company qualified him for pension.* ☐ *Does this ticket qualify me for the drawing?*

QUARREL ▸ ABOUT

quarrel (with someone) (about someone or something) to have an argument with someone about the subject of someone or something. ☐ *Please don't quarrel with me about money.* ☐ *You are always quarreling with Claire.* ☐ *They are quarreling about Donna.* Ⓐ *The quarreled-about proposition was taken off the ballot.*

QUARREL ▸ OVER

quarrel (with someone) (over someone or something) to have an argument with someone about who is going to have someone or something. ☐ *Todd quarreled with Carl over who was going to get the new secretary.* ☐ *They are quarreling over Sally.* ☐ *Don't quarrel over money.*

QUARREL ▸ WITH

See also under both *QUARREL ▸ ABOUT* and *QUARREL ▸ OVER.*

quarrel with something to argue against something; to have a complaint about something. ☐ *I can't quarrel with that.* ☐ *Does anyone want to quarrel with that last remark?*

QUEST ▸ FOR

quest for someone or something to seek after someone or something. □ *Martin is off questing for a book on baroque organ building.* □ *She is questing for a better way to do it.*

QUESTION ▸ ABOUT

question someone about someone or something to ask someone about someone or something. □ *The police questioned Roger about the crime.* □ *Then they questioned Claire about Roger.*

QUEUE ▸ UP

queue up (for something) to line up for something. (Typically British.) □ *We had to queue up for tickets to the play.* □ *You must queue up.* [A] *All the queued-up people stood there in the rain.*

QUIBBLE ▸ ABOUT

quibble (about someone or something) (with someone) AND **quibble (over someone or something) (with someone)** to be argumentative or contentious with someone about someone or something. □ *Let's not quibble about it.* □ *Please don't quibble with your sister.* □ *No need to quibble about it.* □ *Let's not quibble over this matter.* □ *I refuse to quibble with Sally over this matter.*

QUIBBLE ▸ OVER

quibble (over someone or something) (with someone) See the previous entry.

QUIBBLE ▸ WITH

See under *QUIBBLE ▸ ABOUT.*

QUIET ▸ DOWN

quiet down to become quiet; to become less noisy. □ *Please quiet down.* □ *Ask them to quiet down.*

quiet someone or something down to make someone or some creature more quiet. (*Someone* includes *oneself*.) □ *Please go and quiet the children down.* [T] *Try to quiet down the children.* □ *Please quiet that dog down.* □ *He was able to quiet himself down by taking a tranquilizer.*

QUIP ▸ ABOUT

quip about someone or something to joke about someone or something. □ *The kids were quipping about the principal's hairpiece.* □ *It is rude to quip about an elderly person.*

QUIT ▸ ON

quit on someone **1.** [for something] to quit while someone is using it. □ *This stupid car quit on me.* □ *I hope this thing doesn't quit on me.* **2.** [for one] to leave one's job, usually suddenly or unannounced. □ *Wally, the mayor, quit on us at the last minute.* □ *My boss quit on me.* □ *I don't know what to do. Both of my waitresses quit on me over the weekend.*

QUIT ▸ OVER

quit over someone or something to stop working or doing something because of someone or something; to quit because of a dispute over someone or something. □ *Please don't quit over a silly thing like that.* □ *She quit over one of her fellow workers.*

QUIVER ▸ WITH

quiver with something **1.** to shake or shiver from something, such as cold, fear, anticipation, etc. □ *On seeing the bear, the dogs quivered with fear.* □ *Todd quivered with the cold.* **2.** to experience eagerness or joy. (Figurative.) □ *I quivered with delight when I saw the dessert.* □ *Tom quivered with eagerness as the door opened.*

QUIZ ▸ ABOUT

quiz someone about someone or something to ask someone many questions about someone or something. □ *The general quizzed the soldier about the incident.* □ *The officer quizzed her about Randy.*

QUIZ ▸ ON

quiz someone on someone or something to give someone a quiz or test over the subject of someone or something. □ *The teacher quizzed the students on the chapter she had assigned for homework.* □ *I hope they quiz me on George Washington. I am prepared.*

QUIZ ▸ OUT

quiz out (of something) to earn permission to waive a college course by successful completion of a quiz or exam. (Informal.) □ *Andrew was able to quiz out of calculus.* □ *After studying very hard, he quizzed out.*

QUOTE ▸ FROM

quote (something) from someone or something to recite something verbatim that someone else has said; to recite something verbatim from a printed source. □ *May I quote from your letter of the tenth?* □ *Do you mind if I quote a line from Keats?* Ⓐ *The often-quoted-from book of poetry lay beside the armchair.*

R

RACE ► AGAINST

race against someone or something to attempt to win a trial of speed against someone or something. □ *I don't want to race against Kelly. She is too fast.* □ *I had to race against time to get there before the baby got worse.*

RACE ► AROUND

race around to run or move around in a great hurry. □ *Stop racing around and calm down!* □ *I have been racing around all morning, trying to get some things done.*

race around (after someone or something) to rush here and there to find or fetch someone or something. □ *I had to race around after Tom. I couldn't seem to catch up to him.* □ *I wish I could find the dog without having to race around all over the neighborhood.*

RACE ► FOR

race for something to run or drive fast to get to something in a hurry. □ *I raced for the door to see who was there.* □ *The children raced for the best seats in front of the television set.*

race someone for something to compete against someone for a prize; to try to outrun someone to get to something first. □ *I will race you for the grand prize.* □ *Ned raced his sister for the breakfast table every morning.*

RACE ► INTO

race into someone or something to bump or crash into someone or something. □ *The boys raced into the side of the car, and one of them was hurt.* □ *We raced into Mary and knocked her over.*

race into something to run into a place. □ *The children raced into the room and headed straight for their presents.* □ *Please don't race into the garden. You will trample the flowers.*

RACE ► THROUGH

race through someone or something to run or chase through a group of people or a place. □ *The children raced through the group of ladies standing by the door.* □ *They raced through the room, upsetting a lamp.*

race through something to perform some task very rapidly. □ *They raced through their prayers and jumped into bed.* □ *The children raced through dinner, in a hurry to get outside to play.*

RACE ► TO

race someone to some place to compete against someone to see who gets to a place first. □ *I will race you to the door.* □ *Tim wanted to race me to the corner.*

race to someone or something to run to someone or something. □ *The girls raced to the front room.* □ *We all raced to Mary, who had the candy.*

RACE ► UP

race up to someone or something to run to someone or something. □ *Molly raced up to Paul and kissed him on the cheek.* □ *We raced up to the door and opened it cautiously.*

RACE ► WITH

race with someone or something to enter a speed contest with someone or something. □ *I refuse to race with Carla. She is much too fast for me.* □ *I can't race with a horse!*

RACK ▸ OUT

rack out to go to bed and to sleep. (Slang.) □ *I'm really tired. I've got to go rack out for a while.* □ *I racked out until nearly noon.*

RACK ▸ UP

rack someone or something up to damage someone or something. (Slang. *Someone* includes *oneself*.) □ *The accident racked Ann up seriously.* [T] *She racked up her foot badly.* □ *Mary racked her car up.* □ *How did your car get racked up like that?* □ *He had an accident and really racked himself up.* [A] *We saw his racked-up bike at the side of the road.*

rack something up **1.** to place something onto or into its rack. □ *You had better rack the billiard balls up when you finish this time.* [T] *Please rack up the balls.* **2.** to accumulate a number of things, particularly a score, a win, etc. □ *The Bears racked their fourth victory up.* [T] *They hope to rack up a few more points before the end of the game.*

RADIATE ▸ FROM

radiate from someone or something to spread out from someone or something, as with rays. □ *Happiness radiated from Mary. She was so proud!* □ *The heat radiated from the wall next to the furnace room.*

RAFFLE ▸ OFF

raffle something off to dispose of something by a drawing or raffle. □ *They will raffle a television set off.* [T] *They are going to raffle off a television set this weekend at the school.*

RAG ▸ ABOUT

rag someone about someone or something **1.** to complain to someone about someone or something. □ *Why are you always ragging me about Mary?* □ *Stop ragging me about being late.* **2.** to tease someone about someone or something. □ *I wish you would stop ragging me about my hat.* □ *Why do you always rag me about my funny walk? I can't help it.*

RAGE ▸ AGAINST

rage against someone or something to vent one's anger about someone or something; to criticize someone or something severely. □ *She exhausted herself raging against Judy.* □ *Mary is raging about the office rules again.*

RAGE ▸ AT

rage at someone or something to direct one's anger at someone or something. □ *Why are you raging at me? What on earth did I do?* □ *Nothing can be solved by raging at the police department.*

RAGE ▸ OUT

rage out of control to become uncontrollable. □ *The fire raged out of control and threatened the residential area.* □ *If we didn't do something soon, the fire would be raging out of control.*

RAGE ▸ OVER

rage over someone or something to fight furiously over someone or something. □ *The two managers both wanted to hire the same prospective employee. They raged over her for nearly an hour.* □ *The bears raged over that one fish for a long time.*

RAGE ▸ THROUGH

rage through something **1.** [for a fire] to burn rapidly through an area or a building. □ *The fire raged through the unoccupied building.* □ *When the fire began to rage through the forest, we knew we had better head for the river.* **2.** [for someone] to move rapidly through some sequence or process, as if in a rage. □ *Harry raged through the contract, looking for more errors.* □ *She raged through the book, angry with everything she read.*

RAIL ▸ AGAINST

rail against someone or something to complain vehemently about someone or something. □ *Why are you railing against me? What did I do?* □ *Leonard is railing against the policies again.*

RAIL ▸ AT

rail at someone or something to scold someone or something. □ *Why are you railing at me? What is wrong with you?* □ *Gerald was in the backyard railing at* *his dogs. They don't even understand English.* □ *You can rail at the door all you want. It still won't open.*

RAILROAD ▸ INTO

railroad someone into something to force someone into doing something in great haste. □ *The committee tried to railroad me into signing the contract.* □ *You can't railroad me into doing anything!*

RAILROAD ▸ THROUGH

railroad something through (something) to force something through some legislative body without due consideration. □ *The committee railroaded the new constitution through the ratification process.* □ *Mary felt she could railroad the legislation through.*

RAIN ▸ DOWN

rain down on someone or something to fall or drop down on someone or something like rain. □ *The ashes from the incinerator rained down on us, getting our clothes dirty.* □ *The hail rained down on us—some of it quite large.*

rain something down (on someone or something) to pour something, such as criticism or praise, onto someone or something. □ *The employees rained criticism down on the manager for the new policy on sick leave.* 🅃 *The audience rained down compliments on the performers.*

RAIN ▸ IN

rain in on someone or something [for rain] to enter a window or other opening and get someone or something wet. □ *Carol left the window open and it rained in on her in the night.* □ *The storm rained in on my carpet!*

RAIN ▸ ON

See under *RAIN ▸ (UP)ON.*

rain on someone's parade to dampen someone's spirits; to ruin someone's plans. (Figurative.) □ *I don't want to rain on your parade, but the hall you reserved for the party isn't big enough.* □ *You always rain on my parade.*

RAIN ▸ OUT

rain something out [for rain] to force the cancellation of an outdoor event. □ *It looked as if the storm would rain the picnic out, but it blew over before causing any trouble.* 🅃 *The storm rained out the game.*

RAIN ▸ (UP)ON

rain (up)on someone or something [for rain, or something similar] to fall on someone or something. (*Upon* is formal and less commonly used than *on*.) □ *The ashes from the erupting volcano rained on all the people fleeing the village.* □ *It rained on the fields until they were flooded.*

RAISE ▸ ABOUT

raise a stink about someone or something to cause a commotion about someone or something; to turn someone or something into a major issue. □ *I wish you wouldn't raise a stink about Carl.* □ *Do you have to raise a stink about everything that happens?*

RAISE ▸ AGAINST

raise a hand against someone or something See *lift a hand against someone or something* under *LIFT ▸ AGAINST.*

raise one's voice against someone or something to speak out angrily against someone or something; to complain about someone or something. □ *Tony was very polite and did not raise his voice against Roger.* □ *I was too timid to raise my voice against the injustices of the day.*

RAISE ▸ FROM

raise someone from something to help someone up from a lowly state. □ *They hoped for someone to raise them from their poverty.* □ *They raised me from the depressed state I was in.*

raise someone from the dead to bring a dead person back to life. □ *How great are your magic powers? Can you raise people from the dead?* □ *They say her singing could raise people from the dead.*

raise someone or something from something to bring up someone or some creature from a young state. □ *My* *grandmother raised me from a baby.* ☐ *We raised all these parrots from babies.*

RAISE ▶ TO

raise a hand to someone or something See *lift a hand against someone or something* under *LIFT ▶ AGAINST.*

raise an objection to someone or something to object to someone or something. ☐ *I hope that no one raises an objection to Donald.* ☐ *I wish to raise an objection to your decision.*

raise one's glass to someone or something to propose a drinking toast in salute to someone or something. ☐ *Let us all raise our glasses to George Wilson!* ☐ *They raised their glasses to the successful campaign.*

raise someone or something to something to elevate someone or something to something at a higher level. ☐ *Dan raised Alice up to the window.* ☐ *I helped raise the lookout tower to the top of the wall.*

raise someone or something to the surface (of something) to bring someone or something up to the surface of a body of water. ☐ *The pull of the inflatable life vest raised Tom to the surface of the water.* ☐ *The divers were able to raise the sunken ship to the surface.*

raise someone to something to promote or advance someone to a higher rank. ☐ *The boss raised her to vice president after one year.* ☐ *I hope she raises me to head clerk.*

RAISE ▶ UP

raise someone or something up to lift someone or something up. (*Someone* includes *oneself.*) ☐ *The aides raised the dying man up while the nurse spread clean linen beneath him.* 🅃 *Jane raised up the lid.* ☐ *He raised himself up with the greatest of difficulty.*

raise up to lift oneself up; to get up or begin to get up. ☐ *She raised up and then fell back onto her bed. She was too weak to get up.* ☐ *I could not raise up enough to see out the window.*

RAISE ▶ WITH

raise havoc with someone or something to create chaos with someone or something. ☐ *The new policy on travel raised havoc with the people in the accounting department.* ☐ *All this activity is raising havoc with our housepainting.*

raise hell with someone or something **1.** to create serious problems with someone or something. (Use discretion with *hell.*) ☐ *This schedule is going to raise hell with me this week.* ☐ *This new policy is raising hell with our cash flow.* **2.** to chastise severely someone or a group. ☐ *The coach came in and raised hell with Sally for her error in the first quarter of the game.* ☐ *I'm going to raise hell with him!*

raise hob with someone or something to create trouble with someone or something. ☐ *We are going to go raise hob with her right now!* ☐ *The new policy will raise hob with my budget.*

raise something with someone to bring up a matter with someone. ☐ *I will raise that question with Mary when she comes in.* ☐ *Please raise the question with the boss.*

RAKE ▶ AROUND

rake something around to spread something around with a rake. ☐ *She raked the leaves around, spreading them over the flower beds as natural fertilizer.* ☐ *I need to rake the soil around and stir it up.*

RAKE ▶ IN

rake something in to draw or pull something in, as with a rake. ☐ *He raked the money in with both hands.* 🅃 *Jane's really raking in the money.*

RAKE ▶ OFF

rake something off ((of) something) to remove something from something by raking. (The *of*-phrase is paraphrased with a *from*-phrase when the particle is transposed. See the 🄵 example. The *of* is colloquial.) ☐ *Please rake the leaves off the lawn.* 🅃 *Rake off the leaves.* 🄵 *Rake off the leaves from the lawn, please.* ☐ *Please rake them off.*

RAKE ▶ OUT

rake something out to clean something by raking. ☐ *Please rake the gutter out.*

🅃 *You ought to rake out the flower beds. They are a mess.*

rake something out (of something) to clean something out of something by raking. (The *of*-phrase is paraphrased with a *from*-phrase when the particle is transposed. See the 🄵 example.) □ *You ought to rake the leaves out of the gutter so the water will flow.* 🅃 *Please rake out the leaves.* 🄵 *Please rake out the leaves from the gutter.*

RAKE ▸ OVER

rake someone over the coals to chastise someone severely. (Figurative.) □ *She raked him over the coals for making the costly error.* □ *Fred raked Tom over the coals for being late all the time.*

RAKE ▸ THROUGH

rake through something [for someone] to rummage through something, as with a rake. □ *She quickly raked through the mass of loose papers, looking for the right one.* □ *I will have to rake through everything in this drawer to find a red pencil.*

RAKE ▸ UP

rake something up **1.** to gather and clean up something with a rake. □ *Would you please rake these leaves up before it rains?* 🅃 *Please rake up the leaves.* 🄰 *The raked-up leaves were to be burned.* **2.** to clean something up by raking. □ *Would you rake the yard up?* 🅃 *I will rake up the yard.* **3.** to find some unpleasant information. □ *His opposition raked an old scandal up and made it public.* 🅃 *That is ancient history. Why did you have to rake up that old story?*

RALLY ▸ AROUND

rally around someone or something to unite or assemble in support of someone or something. □ *All the other workers rallied around Fred in his fight with management.* □ *They rallied around the principle that Fred stood for.*

RALLY ▸ TO

rally to someone or something to unite in support of someone or something. □ *The students rallied to Betty, their elected president.* □ *We all rallied to the cause.*

RAM ▸ DOWN

ram someone or something down someone's throat to force someone to accept someone or something. □ *Why do you keep trying to ram Laura down my throat? I can make my own choices.* □ *Don't ram all that political stuff down my throat.*

ram something down to pack something down by pounding, as with a ram. □ *The worker used a pole to ram the earth down and pack it tight.* 🅃 *The worker rammed down the earth.*

ram something down something to pound something down into something. □ *The zookeeper rammed the food down the snake's gullet.* □ *Max threatened to ram his fist down Lefty's throat.*

RAM ▸ INTO

ram into someone or something to crash into someone or something. □ *Mary accidentally rammed into a fence as she rode along.* □ *The car rammed into the tree and was totally wrecked.*

RAM ▸ IN(TO)

ram something in(to someone or something) to pound something into someone or something. □ *He rammed his fist into Bill's side and shouted something angry at him.* 🅃 *He rammed in his fist.* □ *Mary put the knife at the top of the pumpkin and rammed it in. That's how you start a jack-o'-lantern.*

RAM ▸ THROUGH

ram something through (something) **1.** to force something through something. □ *He rammed his fist through the window, cutting himself in the process.* □ *Harry put the brick up to the window glass and rammed it through. Next time he would remember his key.* 🅃 *The brick rammed through the glass.* **2.** to force something through a deliberative body, usually not allowing due consideration. □ *They rammed the bill through the city council.* □ *The President was unable to ram the measure through Congress.* 🅃 *They rammed through the bill.*

ram through something to crash or pound through something. □ *The car rammed through the back of the garage.* □ *I was afraid that the truck would ram through the fence.*

RAMBLE ▸ ON

ramble on to go on and on aimlessly; to wander about aimlessly. (Usually figurative. As with a road, a speaker, a speech, etc.) □ *The road rambled on through mile after mile of wilderness.* □ *The speaker rambled on for almost an hour without really saying anything.*

ramble on (about someone or something) [for someone] to talk endlessly and aimlessly about someone or something. □ *I wish you wouldn't ramble on about your first husband all the time.* □ *Must you ramble on so?*

RANGE ▸ FROM

range from something to something to vary from one thing to another. □ *The weather ranges from bad to terrible in this part of the north.* □ *The appraisals of the property ranged from high to low.*

RANGE ▸ OVER

range over something to cover an area; to travel about in one area. □ *The buffalo ranged over vast areas of prairie, grazing and breeding.* □ *These animals range over a very large territory.*

RANK ▸ ABOVE

rank above someone to outrank someone; to rank higher than someone. □ *I think that I rank above you, so I will sit by the window.* □ *The boss ranks above everyone and demands that everyone recognize the fact.*

RANK ▸ AMONG

rank among something to be included in a particular group. □ *In my opinion, Kelly ranks among the very best.* □ *Tom ranks among the most widely known of the contemporary writers.*

rank someone among something to judge someone to be essentially equal to a specific group of people. □ *I don't rank Kelly among the best drivers in the world.* □ *Our committee ranked Fred among the best of the current applicants.*

RANK ▸ AS

rank as something to have a particular rank; to serve in a particular rank. □ *She ranks as a fine pianist in my book.* □ *Don ranks as the top economist of the day.*

rank someone or something as something to assign a particular rank to someone or something. (*Someone* includes *oneself.*) □ *I have to rank Sally as number one. She's the best.* □ *Mary ranked the chocolate as the best she had ever eaten.* □ *She ranked herself as one of the best.*

RANK ▸ WITH

rank someone with someone to judge someone to be equal with someone. (*Someone* includes *oneself.*) □ *Would you rank Tom with Donna?* □ *Fred ranked himself with Tom when it came to diving.*

rank with someone to be equal to someone. □ *Do you think Sarah ranks with Albert?* □ *No one ranks with Albert.*

rank with something to be equal to something. □ *The food at that restaurant ranks with that of the best places in New York.* □ *This book does not rank with the other novels written by the same author.*

RANT ▸ AGAINST

rant against someone or something to rave and yell against someone or something. □ *She spent most of the morning ranting against her mother-in-law.* □ *Leonard spent the entire morning ranting against the government.*

RANT ▸ AT

rant at someone or something to rave and yell at someone or something. □ *Stop ranting at me!* □ *The boss would never rant at the office staff.*

RAP ▸ ACROSS

rap someone across the knuckles AND **rap someone on the knuckles** to strike someone on the knuckles. □ *As punishment, she rapped him across the knuckles.* □ *The teacher rapped the student on the knuckles.*

RAP ▸ AT

rap at something to tap on something to attract someone's attention. ☐ *Who is that rapping at my door?* ☐ *Someone is rapping at the window, trying to get my attention.*

RAP ▸ ON

rap on something to tap on something, such as a door. ☐ *I will rap on her window and try to wake her.* ☐ *Rap on the door a few times, and someone will let you in.*

rap someone on the knuckles See *rap someone across the knuckles* under *RAP ▸ ACROSS.*

RAP ▸ OUT

rap something out (on something) to tap out the rhythm of something on something. ☐ *Try to rap the rhythm out on the table.* 🅃 *He rapped out the rhythm on the table.* ☐ *Rap it out and hum the song as you do.*

RAP ▸ WITH

rap with someone to have a chat with someone or a group of people. ☐ *Come in, sit down, and rap with me for a while.* ☐ *Let's get together and rap with one another sometime.*

RASP ▸ OUT

rasp something out to carve something out with a rasp. ☐ *You should use this tool to rasp the inside of the bowl out. Use sandpaper to make the inside smoother.* 🅃 *Rasp out the inside carefully.*

RAT ▸ ON

rat on someone to tattle on someone. (Slang.) ☐ *You had better not rat on me!* ☐ *Tom ratted on his brother and made him angry.*

RATE ▸ ABOVE

rate someone or something above someone or something to judge someone to be better than someone else; to judge something to be better than something else. (*Someone* includes *oneself.*) ☐ *Do you rate Alice above Valerie?* ☐ *I rate chocolate above vanilla.* ☐ *In fact, I rate chocolate above Alice and Valerie.* ☐ *Do you rate yourself above the rest of the group?*

RATE ▸ AMONG

rate someone or something among something to judge someone or something to be essentially equal to something. (*Someone* includes *oneself.*) ☐ *I rate Polly among the best of this year's class.* ☐ *We rate these contestants among the best ever.* ☐ *I rate her among the others of her age group.*

RATE ▸ AS

rate someone or something as something to assign a particular rating to someone or something. (*Someone* includes *oneself.*) ☐ *I rate her as a number four.* ☐ *The judge rated my cake as second place.* ☐ *I rate you as a one.*

RATE ▸ AT

rate something at something to assign a particular level of rating to something. ☐ *I rate this brand at about a B-.* ☐ *The broker rated this stock at a buy.*

RATE ▸ BELOW

rate someone below someone else or something below something else to judge someone to rank lower than someone else; to judge something to rank lower than something else. (*Someone* includes *oneself.*) ☐ *I have to rate Carol below Donna in this regard.* ☐ *We all rate plain chocolate ice cream below rocky road ice cream.* ☐ *We rated Tom below Mary.*

RATE ▸ WITH

rate someone or something with someone or something to judge someone or something to be equal to someone or something else. (*Someone* includes *oneself.*) ☐ *I rate Fred with Don. They are equally good.* ☐ *Alice is very nice, but I don't rate her with chocolate ice cream.* ☐ *Alice is my favorite thing in all the world. I could never rate even the best ice cream with Alice.* ☐ *They rated Sally with the best of the group.*

rate with someone to be liked by someone. (Colloquial.) ☐ *Betty likes you, and you really rate with me too.* ☐ *Betty rates with all the guys.*

RATION ► OUT

ration something out (among someone) to give people small shares of something, attempting to make it last as long as possible. □ *The captain rationed the water out among all the crew, trying to make it last as long as possible.* [T] *Jane rationed out the cookies among the kids.* □ *In no time at all, she had rationed them all out.*

RATTLE ► AROUND

rattle around in something **1.** to make a rattling noise inside something. □ *What is rattling around in this package?* □ *There is something rattling around in my glove compartment.* **2.** to ride about in a rattly vehicle. □ *I am perfectly happy to rattle around in my ten-year-old car.* □ *Todd rattles around in his grandfather's old car.* **3.** to live in a place that is much too big. (Figurative.) □ *We have been rattling around in this big old house for long enough. Let's move to a smaller place.* □ *I can't afford to rattle around in a three-story house any longer.*

RATTLE ► AWAY

rattle away to chatter endlessly and aimlessly. (Colloquial.) □ *The two old men sat there and rattled away at one another.* □ *Tom rattled away at Jane for a few minutes and then left the house.*

RATTLE ► OFF

rattle something off to recite something with ease; to recite a list quickly and easily. □ *He rattled the long list of names off without even taking a breath.* [T] *He rattled off the long list of names without even taking a breath.*

RAVE ► ABOUT

rave about someone or something **1.** to rage in anger about someone or something. □ *Gale was raving about Sarah and what she did.* □ *Sarah raved and raved about Gale's insufferable rudeness.* **2.** to sing the praises of someone or something. □ *Even the harshest critic raved about Larry's stage success.* □ *Everyone was raving about your excellent performance.*

RAVE ► OVER

rave over someone or something to recite praises for someone or something. □ *The students were just raving over the new professor.* □ *Donald raved over the cake I baked. But he'll eat anything.*

RAZE ► TO

raze something to the ground to tear something, usually a building, down to ground level. (The phrase *to the ground* is considered redundant and unnecessary.) □ *The council decided to raze the old city hall to the ground.* □ *This building is to be razed to the ground.*

REACH ► BACK

reach back (in)to something to extend back into a particular period in time. □ *This policy reaches back into the last century.* □ *Our way of making fine candies reaches back to the recipes used by the founder of the company.*

REACH ► DOWN

reach down to extend downward. □ *The stems of the plant reached down almost to the floor.* □ *The drapes don't quite reach down to the floor.*

reach something down to hand something down. (Colloquial.) □ *Please reach the hammer down to me.* [T] *Would you reach down the hammer to Jane?*

REACH ► FOR

reach for someone or something to extend one's grasp to someone or something. □ *I reached for my father, but he wasn't there.* □ *I reached for a pen, but I only had a pencil.*

reach for the sky **1.** to set one's sights high. (Colloquial.) □ *Reach for the sky! Go for it!* □ *You should always reach for the sky, but be prepared for not attaining your goals every time.* **2.** to stick one's hands up, as in a burglary. (Colloquial or slang.) □ *The gunman told the bank teller to reach for the sky.* □ *Reach for the sky and give me all your money!*

REACH ► IN(TO)

reach in(to something) to stick one's hand into something to grasp something. □ *Bob reached into the cookie jar and found it empty.* □ *Bob went to the cookie jar and reached in.*

REACH ▸ OUT

reach out **1.** to extend one's grasp outward. ☐ *He reached out, but there was no one to take hold of.* ☐ *I reached out and grabbed onto the first thing I could get hold of.* **2.** to enlarge one's circle of friends and experiences. ☐ *If you are that lonely, you ought to reach out. Get to know some new friends.* ☐ *I need to reach out more and meet people.*

reach out (after someone or something) to extend one's grasp to someone or something. ☐ *Don reached out after Doris, but she slipped away before he could get a good hold on her.* ☐ *Doris reached out after the door, but it slammed closed.* ☐ *As she reached out, the door closed.*

reach out into something to extend one's grasp out into something, such as the darkness. ☐ *Laura reached out into the darkness, looking for the light switch.* ☐ *Jane reached out in the night, hoping to find a lamp or even a candle.*

reach out to someone **1.** to offer someone a helping hand. ☐ *You reached out to me just when I needed help the most.* ☐ *I reach out to other people in trouble because I would want someone to do that for me.* **2.** to seek someone's help and support. ☐ *When I reached out to Don for help, he turned me down.* ☐ *Jane reached out to her friends for the help and support that she needed.*

REACH ▸ TO

reach to something to extend all the way to something. ☐ *Our property reaches to the bank of the river.* ☐ *The grounds reach all the way to the banks of the river.* ☐ *This carpet doesn't reach to the end of the hall.*

REACH ▸ TOWARD

reach toward someone or something to aim one's reach to someone or something. ☐ *Sam reached toward Walter and took hold of his shoulder.* ☐ *He reached toward the apple but withdrew his hand when he gave it a second thought.*

REACH ▸ UP

reach something up to someone to hand something up to someone. (Colloquial.) ☐ *I reached the hammer up to Jack, who was fixing a loose shingle on the roof.* ☐ *Please reach this soda pop up to your brother.*

REACH ▸ WITH

reach an accord with someone AND **reach an agreement with someone** to come to an agreement with someone. ☐ *I hope that we can reach an accord with the union so work can start again.* ☐ *We will try one more time to reach an agreement with you.*

reach an understanding with someone to come to a settlement or an agreement with someone. ☐ *I hope we are able to reach an understanding with the commissioners.* ☐ *We were able to reach an understanding with Tony.*

reach first base with someone or something to manage to get basic and initial negotiation out of the way with someone or a group. ☐ *I was unable to reach first base with the client.* ☐ *We will never be able to reach first base with the bank on a loan.*

REACT ▸ AGAINST

react against someone or something to respond negatively to someone or something. ☐ *Why did she react against me so strongly?* ☐ *There is no need to react against the plan with such force.*

REACT ▸ TO

react to someone or something to act in response to someone or something. ☐ *You made some very good points. I would like to take some time to react to you.* ☐ *How did Mary react to the news?*

READ ▸ ABOUT

read about someone or something to read information concerning someone or something. ☐ *Did you read about John in the newspaper?* ☐ *I read about bonds, and learned a lot about finance.*

READ ▸ AS

read someone or something as something to interpret someone or something as something. ☐ *I read you as a* *quiet guy who wants to settle down and have kids.* ☐ *Mary read the problem as one that did not require a lot of understanding.*

READ ▶ BACK

read something back (to someone) to read back some information to the person who has just given it. ☐ *Yes, I have written the telephone number down. Let me read it back to you to make sure I have it right.* 🅃 *Please read back the letter to me.* ☐ *Did you copy the number correctly? Please read it back.*

READ ▶ BETWEEN

read between the lines to understand more than is written or stated; to infer something from what is written or stated. ☐ *I know what's going on here. I can read between the lines.* ☐ *You will understand this memo better if you read between the lines.*

READ ▶ FOR

read for something to read, looking especially for something, such as errors, clarity, etc. ☐ *Please read this manuscript for spelling and grammar errors.* ☐ *Read this book for entertainment and nothing more.*

READ ▶ FROM

read from something to read [aloud] from something in particular. ☐ *I will now read from a book of poetry that I like very much.* ☐ *I like that poem very much. What are you reading from?*

READ ▶ IN

read something in something to read something in particular in a particular document. ☐ *I read an interesting article about moose in today's newspaper.* ☐ *Did you read that in today's newspaper?*

READ ▶ IN(TO)

read something in((to) something) to presume inferences as one reads something; to imagine that additional messages, ideas, or biases are present in something that one is reading. ☐ *Just accept the words for what they mean. Don't read something else into it.* ☐ *Don't read anything in.*

READ ▶ OF

read of someone or something (somewhere) to read news about someone or something in something. ☐ *I think I have read of you in the papers.* ☐ *Mary read of the job opening in the newspaper.*

READ ▶ OFF

read something off to read aloud a list. ☐ *Nick read the list of the names off, and I wasn't on the list.* 🅃 *Jane read off the names.*

READ ▶ ON

read on to continue to read. ☐ *Please read on. Don't stop.* ☐ *She read on until she had come to the end of the story.*

READ ▶ OUT

read someone out (for something) to chastise someone verbally for doing something wrong. ☐ *The coach read the player out for making a silly error.* ☐ *She really read the players out.* 🅃 *The coach read out the whole team.*

read someone out of something to make a case for the removal of someone from something. ☐ *The chairman read the absent members out of the organization.* ☐ *Dave was read out of the club.*

read (someone) something out of something to read something [aloud] from something. (*Someone* includes *oneself*.) ☐ *He read us a story out of the book.* ☐ *Mary read the story out of the magazine.* ☐ *Mary read herself a story out of the book.*

read something out to read something aloud. ☐ *Please read it out so everyone can hear you.* 🅃 *Read out the names loudly.*

READ ▶ OVER

read something over to read something, concentrating on form as well as content. ☐ *Please read this over and report back to me when you are finished.* 🅃 *I will read over the report and talk to you later.*

READ ▶ THROUGH

read through something to look through some reading material. ☐ *I read through your proposal and find* *that it has merits.* □ *Please read through this at your convenience.*

READ ▸ TO

read oneself to sleep to read something in preparation for falling asleep. □ *I need a really dull book so I can read myself to sleep.* □ *That's the kind of book I use to read myself to sleep.*

read (something) to someone to read something aloud to someone. □ *Please read a story to me.* □ *Grandpa read to Timmy all afternoon.*

READ ▸ UP

read up (on someone or something) to study about someone or something by reading. □ *I have to read up on Milton Berle for a report I have to write.* □ *I can't write a word about him until I read up.*

READJUST ▸ TO

readjust to someone or something to make a new adjustment to someone or something. □ *Please make an attempt to readjust to Molly after she returns from the hospital.* □ *I don't think I can readjust to this climate.*

REALIZE ▸ FROM

realize something from something 1. to perceive something from some kind of evidence. □ *I just now realized something from what you've been saying.* □ *Tom realized how wrong he had been from what Mary told him.* **2.** to reap a profit by selling an asset that has increased in value. □ *He realized a large profit from the sale of the house.* □ *We hoped to realize a lot of money from the sale from the sale of stock.*

REAP ▸ FROM

reap something from something 1. to harvest something from something. □ *We reaped a fine harvest from our cornfields this year.* □ *They will reap nothing from their flooded fields.* **2.** to gain something from something. (Figurative.) □ *The students reaped a lot of information from their interview with the police chief.* □ *I hope to reap some good advice from the discussion.*

REAPPOINT ▸ AS

reappoint someone as something to select or appoint someone to serve again in the same office. □ *Are they going to reappoint Alan as the chairman again?* □ *Alan was reappointed as the head of the committee.*

REAR ▸ BACK

rear back 1. [for a horse] to pull back onto its hind legs in an effort to move backwards rapidly. □ *The animal reared back in terror.* □ *The horse reared back and almost threw its rider.* **2.** [for a person] to pull back and stand up or sit up straighter. □ *He reared back in his chair and looked perturbed.* □ *Tom reared back in his chair, waiting for something else to happen.*

REAR ▸ UP

rear up 1. [for a horse] to lean back on its hind legs and raise its front part up, assuming a threatening posture or avoiding something on the ground such as a snake. □ *The horse reared up suddenly, throwing the rider onto the ground.* □ *When the horse reared up, I almost fell off.* **2.** [for something, especially a problem] to raise up suddenly. (Figurative.) □ *A new problem reared up and cost us a lot of time.* □ *A lot of new costs reared up toward the end of the month.*

REASON ▸ AGAINST

reason against something to argue against something, using reason. □ *I can hardly be expected to reason against a silly argument like that!* □ *I reasoned against it, but they paid no attention to me.*

REASON ▸ OUT

reason something out to figure something out; to plan a reasonable course of action. □ *Now let's be calm and try to reason this out.* T *Let us reason out our difficulties.*

REASON ▸ WITH

reason with someone to discuss something with someone, seeking a reasonable solution to a problem. □ *Try to reason with Jill. If she won't listen, forget her.* □ *You cannot reason with someone who is so narrow-minded.*

REASSIGN ▶ TO

reassign someone to something to change someone's assignment to something else. ☐ *I will reassign Jill to a different department.* ☐ *I was reassigned to the accounting department.*

REASSURE ▶ ABOUT

reassure someone about something to give someone confidence about something. ☐ *Nancy reassured Betty about her promotion.* ☐ *Betty was reassured about her promotion.*

REASSURE ▶ OF

reassure someone of something to promise or guarantee someone something. ☐ *Kelly reassured her friend of her support in the election.* ☐ *Please reassure Tom of our continued support.*

REBEL ▶ AGAINST

rebel against someone or something to resist and revolt against someone or something. ☐ *Barbara rebelled against the teachers at the school.* ☐ *Most young people have to rebel against authority for a while.*

REBEL ▶ AT

rebel at someone or something to resist and defy someone or something. ☐ *It is natural for teenagers to rebel at their parents.* ☐ *I feel as if I have to rebel at all these rules.*

REBOUND ▶ FROM

rebound from something **1.** to bounce back from something. ☐ *The ball rebounded from the wall and hit Randy hard on the elbow.* ☐ *When the ball rebounded from the backboard, it bounced onto the court and Tom tripped on it.* **2.** to recover quickly from something. (Figurative.) ☐ *Barbara rebounded from her illness in less than a week.* ☐ *I hope I can rebound from this cold quickly.*

REBUKE ▶ FOR

rebuke someone for something to reprimand someone for something. ☐ *There is no need to rebuke me for a simple mistake like that.* ☐ *Sally was rebuked for overspending her budget.*

RECALL ▶ FROM

recall someone from something to call someone back from something or some place. ☐ *The president recalled our ambassador from the war-torn country.* ☐ *I was recalled from retirement to help out at the office.*

recall someone or something from something to remember someone or something from some event or some place. ☐ *I recall someone by that name from my days at the university.* ☐ *Mary recalled the appropriate fact from her history class.*

RECALL ▶ TO

recall something to mind to cause [someone] to remember something. ☐ *The events of the day recall similar days in the past to mind.* ☐ *This book recalls a similar book published some years ago to mind.* ☐ *That recalls to mind a joke I heard the other day.*

recall something to someone to bring something to the mind of someone. ☐ *Your comments recall another event to me—something that happened years ago.* ☐ *What you just said recalled an old saying to me.*

RECAST ▶ IN

recast something in something to rebuild or redevelop something in a different form. ☐ *She recast the sentence in the negative, hoping to make it less blunt.* ☐ *I will recast my request in different language.*

RECEDE ▶ FROM

recede from something to pull back from something. ☐ *The river receded from its banks during the dry season.* ☐ *I think that my hair is receding from my forehead.*

RECEIVE ▶ AS

receive someone as someone or something to welcome and accept someone as someone or something. ☐ *The king received the ambassador as an honored guest.* ☐ *They said they would receive the former resident as an unwelcome pest, so he did not come back.*

RECEIVE ▸ BACK

receive someone or something back to get someone or something back. □ *Martha received her husband back after his escapade.* □ *I sent a letter off with the wrong postage and received it back two weeks later.*

RECEIVE ▸ FROM

receive something from some place to get and accept something from some place. □ *I just received a letter from Budapest!* □ *Mary received a package from Japan.*

receive something from someone to get and accept something from someone. □ *Tony received a sweater from his grandfather for his birthday.* □ *Who did you receive this from?*

RECEIVE ▸ INTO

receive someone into something to welcome someone into something, some place, or some organization. □ *Everyone received the new member into the club with eager congratulations.* □ *We received them into our homes and fed them well.*

RECEIVE ▸ WITH

receive someone with open arms to welcome someone eagerly. □ *He received his guests with open arms.* □ *We received Mary with open arms and did everything we could to make her feel more comfortable.*

RECKON ▸ AMONG

reckon someone or something among something to judge someone or something to belong among a select group. (*Someone* includes *oneself.*) □ *I reckon Donna among the best tennis pros in the country.* □ *We reckon this automobile among the most advanced in the world.* □ *The woman reckoned herself among the best of the entire group.*

RECKON ▸ AS

reckon someone as someone or something to perceive someone as someone or something. □ *I reckoned her as a more thoughtful individual than she turned out to be.* □ *Mary reckoned Scott as a constant irritation, and she was right on the button.*

RECKON ▸ IN(TO)

reckon someone or something in(to something) to figure someone or something in; to include someone or something in one's calculations. (*Someone* includes *oneself.*) □ *I will reckon Jane into the total number of guests.* [T] *I reckoned in a few too many people.* □ *I failed to reckon the electric bill in.* □ *Did you reckon yourself into the cost?*

RECKON ▸ WITH

reckon with someone or something to deal with someone or something; to cope with someone or something. □ *I have to reckon with the troublesome Mr. Johnson this afternoon.* □ *Mary knew just exactly how she had to reckon with the bill collector.*

RECKON ▸ WITHOUT

reckon without someone to fail to think about someone. □ *He thought he'd get away with his crime, but he reckoned without Ford Fairlane.* □ *He had thought he was gone for sure, but he had reckoned without Superman.*

RECLAIM ▸ FROM

reclaim someone or something from someone or something to bring someone or something back from someone or something. □ *The mother reclaimed Sally from her father, who had taken her away in the night contrary to the divorce decree.* □ *Mary reclaimed the book from her brother's desk.* □ *She reclaimed the book from her brother.*

RECOGNIZE ▸ AS

recognize someone as someone or something as something to accept and acknowledge someone to be someone; to accept and acknowledge something to be something. □ *Mary didn't recognize the lawyer as her legal representative.* □ *She didn't recognize the car as her car.*

RECOGNIZE ▸ BY

recognize someone or something by something to know someone or something by some distinguishing sign. □ *You will be able to recognize me by my long mustache.* □ *Mary recognized her car by the flower tied to the antenna.*

RECOGNIZE ▶ FOR

recognize someone or something for something 1. to identify someone or something as something. □ *I recognized the deal for a scam as soon as I heard about it.* □ *Anyone could recognize Max for a common thief.* **2.** to show appreciation to someone or something for something. □ *The organization recognized Laura for her excellent contributions to the philanthropy committee.* □ *The officers recognized the committee for its efforts.*

RECOIL ▶ AT

recoil at the sight (of someone or something) AND **recoil at the thought (of someone or something)** to flinch or cringe at the sight or thought of someone or something. □ *Sally recoiled at the sight of Gerry, who had said something unspeakable.* □ *Mary recoiled at the very thought.*

RECOIL ▶ FROM

recoil from someone or something to draw back from someone or something. □ *I recoiled from Sally when she told me what she had done.* □ *I recoiled from the horror and slammed the door.*

RECOMMEND ▶ AS

recommend someone as something to suggest someone as something. □ *Could you recommend Frank as a good carpenter?* □ *I would like to recommend Jane Smith as a good artist.*

RECOMMEND ▶ FOR

recommend someone for something to suggest someone for something. (*Someone* includes *oneself.*) □ *I would be very glad to recommend you for promotion.* □ *She recommended herself as the best choice.*

RECOMMEND ▶ TO

recommend someone or something to someone to suggest that someone choose someone or something. □ *I would like to recommend Sally to you as a good prospect for membership on the committee.* □ *Could you recommend a good mechanic to me?*

RECOMPENSE ▶ FOR

recompense someone for something to (re)pay someone for something. □ *I am required to recompense Mrs. Wilson for her broken window.* □ *Can I recompense you for your expenses?*

RECONCILE ▶ TO

reconcile oneself to something to adjust one's thinking to accept something. □ *Ted finally reconciled himself to going to a less costly university.* □ *She reconciled herself to what was going to have to happen.*

RECONCILE ▶ WITH

reconcile something with something to bring something into harmony, accord, or balance with something. □ *The accountants were not able to reconcile the expense claims with the receipts that had been turned in.* □ *I can't reconcile your story with those of the other witnesses.*

RECONSTRUCT ▶ FROM

reconstruct something from something **1.** to rebuild something from something. □ *I was not able to reconstruct the garage from the parts that were left after the storm.* □ *Can you reconstruct the damaged part of the house from what's left?* **2.** to recall and restate a story or the details of an event from something. □ *Can you reconstruct the story from the fragments you have just heard?* □ *I cannot reconstruct the chain of events from memory.*

RECORD ▶ FROM

record something from something to make an audio recording of something from some source. □ *Listen to this. I recorded it from a radio broadcast.* □ *From what did you record this?*

RECORD ▶ IN

record something in something to enter a record of something into something. □ *I will record your appointment in my notebook.* □ *Jane recorded the memo in her computer.*

RECORD ▶ ON

record something on something to make a record of something on the surface of something. □ *Nancy recorded the appointment on the calendar that* *served as a blotter on the top of her desk.* □ *Please record this on your calendar.*

RECOUNT ▸ TO

recount something to someone to tell something to someone; to narrate a series of events, in order. □ *Carl recounted the events of the day to his wife.* □ *The strange events were recounted by a number of people.*

RECOUP ▸ FROM

recoup something from someone or something to salvage something from someone or something. □ *I hope I can recoup my losses from the manager.* □ *Mary intended to recoup her money from the investment.*

RECOVER ▸ FROM

recover from someone or something to get over an experience with someone or something. □ *My great-uncle just left, and it will take a week or two to recover from him.* □ *I hope I recover from his visit soon.*

recover from something to recuperate from a disease. □ *I hope I recover from this cough soon.* □ *She recovered from her cold soon enough to go on the trip.*

recover something from someone or something to retrieve or salvage something from someone, something, or some place. □ *The police recovered my purse from the thief who had taken it.* □ *Mary recovered her deposit from the failed bank.*

RECRUIT ▸ FOR

recruit someone for something to seek and engage someone for something. □ *Harry had to recruit a few people for the new jobs that opened up.* □ *We recruited three more people to work with us.*

RECRUIT ▸ FROM

recruit someone from something to convince someone to leave something and join one's own group. □ *Phyllis recruited a new work team from the company she used to work for.* □ *We recruited a number of people from private industry.*

RECRUIT ▸ INTO

recruit someone into something to seek out and induct someone into something. □ *The colonel tried to recruit ten people a week into the army.* □ *The army recruited almost no one during the month of December.*

RECUPERATE ▸ FROM

recuperate from something to recover from something; to be cured or to heal after something. □ *I hope that you recuperate from your illness soon.* □ *Has she recuperated from her surgery yet?*

REDEDICATE ▸ TO

rededicate oneself or something to someone or something to reaffirm the dedication of oneself or something to someone or something. □ *I must ask you to rededicate yourself to our high purposes.* □ *They rededicated their church to God.* □ *Mary rededicated herself to the task.*

REDOUND ▸ ON

redound on someone to have an effect on someone. □ *The hot weather has redounded on all of us in a bad way.* □ *The problems created by your mistake have redounded on the entire company.*

REDUCE ▸ BY

reduce something by something to diminish something by a certain amount. □ *I have to reduce your allowance by two dollars per week until you pay me back for the broken window.* □ *I will reduce the bill by a few dollars.*

REDUCE ▸ FROM

reduce something from something to something to diminish something from one degree to a lower degree. □ *I will reduce the fine from two hundred dollars to one hundred dollars.* □ *Mary reduced her demands from a large sum to a smaller one.*

REDUCE ▸ TO

reduce someone to silence to cause someone to be silent. □ *The rebuke reduced him to silence—at last.* □ *Mary was reduced to silence by Jane's comments.*

reduce someone to tears to cause someone to cry; to harass a person to tears. ☐ *The teacher's rude scolding reduced the student to tears.* ☐ *Jane was reduced to tears as she listened to the story.*

REEF ▸ IN

reef something in to reduce the area of a ship's sail, by folding the sail. ☐ *The first mate ordered the sailors to reef the sails in.* 🅃 *They had to reef in the sails.*

REEK ▸ OF

reek of something **1.** to have the stench or smell of something. ☐ *This whole house reeks of onions! What did you cook?* ☐ *She reeks of a very strong perfume. She must have spilled it on herself.* **2.** to give a strong impression of something. ☐ *The neighborhood reeks of poverty.* ☐ *The deal reeked of dishonesty.*

REEK ▸ WITH

reek with something to stink with some smell. ☐ *This place reeks with some horrible odor.* ☐ *Jane reeks with too much perfume.*

REEL ▸ BACK

reel back (from something) to fall or stagger backwards, as from a blow. ☐ *The boxer reeled back from the blow, stunned.* ☐ *Another blow to the midsection and he reeled back and fell.*

REEL ▸ FROM

See the previous entry.

REEL ▸ IN

reel something in to bring in something, such as a fish, by winding up the line on a reel. ☐ *With great effort, she reeled the huge fish in.* 🅃 *Hurry and reel in the fish!*

REEL ▸ OFF

reel something off to recite a list or sequence of words, rapidly, from memory. ☐ *Jane reeled her speech off flawlessly.* 🅃 *Tony reeled off his speech as fast as he could.*

REEL ▸ UNDER

reel under something **1.** to stagger under the weight of something. ☐ *Tony reeled under the weight of the books.* ☐ *She knew she would reel under the heavy load.* **2.** to stagger because of a blow. ☐ *The boxer reeled under the blow to his chin.* ☐ *Max reeled under the beating that Lefty gave him.* **3.** to suffer because of a burden. (Figurative.) ☐ *Gary reeled under the responsibilities he had been given.* ☐ *I was just reeling under the burdens of my new job.*

REFER ▸ BACK

refer someone back to someone or something to suggest that someone go back to someone or something, such as the source. ☐ *I referred the client back to the lawyer she had originally consulted.* ☐ *Tom referred the customer back to the manufacturer who had made the shoddy product.*

refer something back (to someone or something) to send something back to someone or a group for action. ☐ *The senate referred the bill back to committee.* ☐ *John had not seen it, so I referred it back to him.* ☐ *They referred back all the bills.*

REFER ▸ TO

refer someone to someone or something to direct someone to someone or something; to send someone to someone or something. ☐ *The front office referred me to you, and you are now referring me to someone else!* ☐ *They should have referred you to the personnel department.*

refer to someone or something to mention someone or something. ☐ *Are you referring to me when you speak about a kind and helpful person?* ☐ *I was referring to the personnel department.*

REFLECT ▸ BACK

reflect (back) (up)on someone or something See under *REFLECT ▸ (UP)ON.*

REFLECT ▸ IN

reflect in something **1.** [for something] to be mirrored in something, such as a mirror, water, ice, etc. ☐ *His image was reflected in the mirror, giving him a good view of his sunburn.* ☐ *When the hermit saw his image in the pool, he was amazed.* **2.** [for something] to be shown in a result. ☐ *The extra charges will be reflected in next month's bill.* ☐ *I do* *not understand all the charges reflected in my statement.*

REFLECT ▸ (UP)ON

reflect (back) (up)on someone or something to remember or think about someone or something. (*Upon* is formal and less commonly used than *on*.) □ *When I reflect back on the years I spent with my parents, I think I had a good childhood.* □ *I like to reflect on my great-grandmother.*

reflect credit (up)on someone or something [for some act] to bring credit to someone or something. (*Upon* is formal and less commonly used than *on*.) □ *Your efforts really reflect credit upon you.* □ *Mary's success really reflected credit on the quality of her education.*

REFRAIN ▸ FROM

refrain from something to hold back from doing something; to choose not to do something as planned. □ *I wish you would refrain from shouting.* □ *Please refrain from hollering.*

REFRESH ▸ WITH

refresh someone with something to renew or revive someone with something. (*Someone* includes *oneself*.) □ *Here, let me refresh you with a cool glass of lemonade.* □ *After the game, Wally will probably refresh himself with a bottle of pop.*

refresh something with something to restore or brighten up something. □ *I think we can refresh this drab old room with a coat of fresh paint.* □ *The old house was refreshed with new siding and some landscaping.*

REFUND ▸ TO

refund something to someone to return payment for something to someone. □ *I insist that you refund the money to me at once.* □ *Her money was refunded to her as soon as she asked for it.*

REFUSE ▸ TO

refuse something to someone to deny someone permission to receive or use something. □ *You wouldn't refuse water to me, would you?* □ *Nothing at all was refused to the new employee.*

refuse to do something to reject doing something; to reject a request to do something. □ *I absolutely refuse to go there!* □ *We all refused to break the law.*

REGAIN ▸ FROM

regain something from someone or something to take possession of one's property or right from someone or something. □ *I intend to regain my money from Herb.* □ *The used car agency regained the car from the delinquent buyer.*

REGALE ▸ WITH

regale someone with something to present a great deal of something, such as lavish entertainment or fine food, to someone. □ *They regaled their guests with food and song well into the night.* □ *The committee was regaled with tales of wrongdoing by the government.*

REGARD ▸ AS

regard someone or something as someone or something to look upon someone or something as someone or something; to consider someone or something to be someone or something. (*Someone* includes *oneself*.) □ *I have always regarded you as my friend.* □ *The cult members regarded the stone idol as their dead leader.* □ *Mary regarded herself as the most likely candidate.*

REGARD ▸ WITH

regard someone or something with something to look upon someone or something with a certain attitude or with certain expectations. □ *The child regarded the teacher with a questioning expression.* □ *The kitten regarded the fishbowl with great curiosity.*

REGISTER ▸ AS

register someone as something to record someone's name on a list of a category of people. □ *I will register you as an independent voter.* □ *I am registered as a qualified advisor.*

REGISTER ▸ FOR

register for something to sign up to participate in something. □ *Have you registered for the class yet?* □ *She is registered for the same classes as I am.*

register someone for something to sign someone up to participate in something. (*Someone* includes *oneself.*) □ *Would you please register me for the workshop when you sign up?* □ *Excuse me. I have to go register myself for the contest.*

REGISTER ▸ IN

register in something to enter one's name on a list in something; to sign up to belong to something. □ *Are you going to register in the pie-eating contest?* □ *We registered in the drawing for a new car.*

register someone in something **1.** to enter someone's name on a list in something. (*Someone* includes *oneself.*) □ *I will register you in the competition.* □ *Can I register myself in this contest?* **2.** to sign someone up to belong to something. (*Someone* includes *oneself.*) □ *I registered my cousin in the club.* □ *Mary wanted to register herself in the club.*

REGISTER ▸ ON

register on something [for an effect] to show on something, such as someone's face. □ *Recognition registered on her face when she saw the photograph of Walter.* □ *The total of the votes registered on the large scoreboard at the front of the hall.*

REGISTER ▸ WITH

register something with someone or something to record the existence of something with someone or something. □ *Did you register your new stereo with the manufacturer?* □ *If you bring any packages into this store, please register them with the manager.*

register with someone **1.** to sign up with someone. □ *You will have to register with the lady at the front desk.* □ *I registered with the attendant when I came in.* **2.** [for something] to be realized or understood by someone. □ *Suddenly, the import of what she had said registered with me.* □ *My name did not register with her, and I had to explain who I was.*

REGRESS ▸ TO

regress to something to go back to an earlier, probably simpler, state; to go back to a more primitive state. □ *Bob claimed that Gerald's behavior was regressing to that of a three-year-old.* □ *I tend to regress when I am out with the guys.*

REHEARSE ▸ FOR

rehearse for something to practice for something. □ *We will rehearse for the graduation exercises on Saturday morning.* □ *We rehearsed for the play all weekend.*

REIGN ▸ OVER

reign over someone or something to rule over someone or something. □ *The king reigned over his subjects for over thirty years.* □ *The queen reigned over the country for a long time.*

REIMBURSE ▸ FOR

reimburse someone for something to repay someone for making a purchase. (*Someone* includes *oneself.*) □ *I will reimburse you for whatever it cost you.* □ *The treasurer reimbursed himself for his expenses.*

REIMBURSE ▸ TO

reimburse something to someone to repay money to someone. □ *I will reimburse the money to you. Don't worry.* □ *The full cost was reimbursed to me.*

REIN ▸ BACK

rein back on someone or something to control or diminish the intensity of someone or something. □ *The manager was urged to rein back on her employees.* □ *She reined back on expenses and demanded that others do likewise.*

REIN ▸ IN

rein someone or something in to bring someone or something under control; to slow down someone or something. □ *Fred is getting out of hand. The boss undertook to rein him in a bit.* T *The boss is trying to rein in Jane's enthusiasm.* T *Can't you rein in the power of the police department?*

REIN ► UP

rein something up to bring something, usually a horse, to a stop. □ *She reined her horse up and stopped for a chat.* 🅃 *Rein up your horse and stop for a while.*

rein up [for a horse rider] to stop. □ *The equestrian reined up and dismounted.* □ *We all reined up and waited for the cars to pass by.*

REINFORCE ► WITH

reinforce someone or something with something to strengthen someone or something with something. □ *The general reinforced his troops with volunteers fresh from working in the wheat fields.* □ *I had to reinforce the garage roof with new boards.*

REINSTATE ► AS

reinstate someone as something to put someone back as a certain officeholder. □ *The city council agreed to reinstate Mr. Wilson as alderman.* □ *Fred was reinstated as the court clerk.*

REINSTATE ► IN

reinstate someone in something to put someone back into a certain office or position. □ *If you will pay your dues, we will reinstate you in the organization.* □ *Fred was reinstated in office.*

REISSUE ► TO

reissue something to someone to release or distribute to someone something that has been distributed before. □ *I plan to reissue the check to you next week.* □ *The check was reissued to Mary the very next day.*

REJOICE ► AT

rejoice at something to celebrate or revel about something. □ *Everyone rejoiced at the lucky events that had saved them.* □ *We all rejoiced at the outcome of the election.*

REJOICE ► IN

rejoice in someone or something to take great joy at someone or something. (Stilted.) □ *I am in love and I rejoice in my beloved!* □ *Roger rejoices in a good night's sleep.*

REJOICE ► OVER

rejoice over something to celebrate because of something. □ *Everyone rejoiced over their good fortune.* □ *What happened to us next was nothing to rejoice over.*

RELAPSE ► INTO

relapse into something to experience a return to a worse condition. □ *Valerie relapsed into a coma in the afternoon.* □ *Mary relapsed into her depression after a brief period of normalcy.*

RELATE ► TO

See *be related to someone* under *BE ► TO.*

relate something to someone to tell something to someone; to narrate something to someone. □ *Very slowly, she related the events of the past week to her parents.* □ *I have an interesting story to relate to you.*

relate something to something to associate something to something. □ *I relate this particular problem to the failure of the company to provide proper training.* □ *This point is related to what I just told you.*

relate to someone or something to understand, accept, or feel kinship with someone or something. □ *He relates to people well.* □ *I really don't relate to your thinking at all.*

RELAX ► INTO

relax into something **1.** to sit or lie down in something, relaxing. □ *I want to go home and relax into my easy chair.* □ *I relaxed into the reclining chair and was asleep in a few moments.* **2.** [for something that is tense] to assume a more relaxed shape or condition. □ *His cramped muscle finally relaxed into a soft mass of tissue.* □ *As her tight neck relaxed into yielding muscles, her face brightened.*

RELAX ► ON

relax one's hold on someone or something to lessen one's grasp on someone or something. □ *When she relaxed her hold on me, I got away.* □ *Never relax your hold on an alligator.*

RELAY ▸ TO

relay something to someone to pass something on to someone. □ *Can you relay this to Frank, who is way down the line?* □ *The message was relayed to Frank, who was at the end of the line.*

RELEASE ▸ FROM

release someone or something from something to liberate or let someone or something go from something. □ *The police officer released George from the handcuffs.* □ *I released all the dogs from the city dog pound.*

RELEASE ▸ TO

release someone to someone to discharge or distribute someone to someone. □ *The judge released the defendant to his mother.* □ *Don was released to his father, who was more than a little bit angry.*

RELEGATE ▸ TO

relegate someone to someone or something to assign someone to someone or something. □ *They relegated the old man to a bed in the corner.* □ *The former vice president was relegated to the position of manager of special projects.*

RELIEVE ▸ OF

relieve someone of something **1.** to unburden someone of something. (*Someone* includes *oneself.*) □ *Here, let me relieve you of that heavy box.* □ *At last, he could relieve himself of the problem.* **2.** to lessen someone's responsibilities. (Figurative.) □ *I will relieve you of some of the responsibility you have carried for so long.* □ *Let me relieve you of that job. You have enough to do.*

RELINQUISH ▸ OVER

relinquish something over someone to release the hold on or control of someone. □ *She refused to relinquish control over the operations of the front office.* □ *Mary was ordered to relinquish her hold over the children for a month each year.*

RELINQUISH ▸ TO

relinquish something to someone or something to surrender something to someone or something. □ *Todd refused to relinquish his authority to anyone.* □ *I finally relinquished the car to the bank.*

RELOCATE ▸ IN

relocate someone or something in something to reposition or move someone or something in or at something. (*Someone* includes *oneself.*) □ *I will have to relocate you in a different office.* □ *Can I relocate the copy machine in the other room?* □ *They relocated themselves in a better neighborhood.*

RELY ▸ (UP)ON

rely (up)on someone or something to depend on someone or something; to trust in someone or something. (*Upon* is formal and less commonly used than *on*.) □ *I know I can rely upon you to do a good job.* □ *Can we rely on this old car to get us there?*

REMAIN ▸ AHEAD

remain ahead of someone or something to manage to keep up with someone or something; to maintain a position in front of someone or something. □ *I don't know how long I can remain ahead of Todd in this contest.* □ *We can hardly remain ahead of the orders coming in.*

REMAIN ▸ AT

remain at some place to stay at some place; to stay behind at some place. □ *I will remain at the office until supper time.* □ *Please remain at home until I call you.*

REMAIN ▸ AWAY

remain away (from someone or something) to stay away from someone or something. □ *I must ask you to remain away from my daughter.* □ *I cannot remain away any longer. I must be with her.*

REMAIN ▸ BEHIND

remain behind to stay at a place even when others have left. □ *Can't I go too? Do I have to remain behind?* □ *I will remain behind for a day or two.*

remain behind someone or something to maintain a position in back of someone or something. □ *Jerry remained be-*

hind his wife throughout her argument with the plumber. ☐ *Timmy remained behind the pillar, where he couldn't be seen.*

REMAIN ▶ DOWN

remain down to stay down; to keep down. ☐ *I asked them to remain down until the shooting stopped.* ☐ *Please remain down with me so no one will see us.*

REMAIN ▶ IN

remain in (something) **1.** to stay within something. ☐ *Please remain in the house today. It is too cold to go out.* ☐ *You should remain in because the weather is bad.* **2.** to stay in an organization as a member. ☐ *He remained in the Boy Scouts of America until he was sixteen.* ☐ *I will remain in the Scottish Terrier Club of Michigan for many years.* ☐ *How long will you remain in?*

REMAIN ▶ OF

remain clear of something to continue to avoid something. ☐ *Please remain clear of the machine while it is running.* ☐ *I remained clear of the dangerous area.*

REMAIN ▶ ON

remain on something **1.** to continue to be on something; to continue to serve on a body. ☐ *Will you remain on the board of directors for another year?* ☐ *I will remain on this committee as long as I am needed.* **2.** to continue to take a particular medicine. ☐ *How long should I stay on these pills?* ☐ *I want you to remain on this medication until you run out of medicine.*

remain on (somewhere) to continue to stay in one place. ☐ *Everyone else left, but I decided to remain on there.* ☐ *I remained on for a while during the time they were training my replacement.*

REMAIN ▶ TOGETHER

remain together to stay close together; to stay in association. ☐ *We will have to remain together while we are on this tour. It is very easy to get lost in this town.* ☐ *The two boys remained together throughout college.*

REMAIN ▶ UNDER

remain under something to continue to stay beneath the surface of something. ☐ *Please remain under the umbrella so you don't get wet.* ☐ *A lot of people decided to leave the shelter, but I remained under it.*

REMAIN ▶ UP

remain up to stay awake and out of bed. ☐ *I remained up throughout most of the night.* ☐ *I cannot remain up much longer.*

REMAIN ▶ WITHIN

remain within (something) to stay inside something or some place. ☐ *Please try to remain within the boundaries of the campus.* ☐ *Everyone else went out, but I decided to remain within.*

REMAND ▶ (IN)TO

remand someone (in)to the custody of someone to order someone placed into the custody of someone. ☐ *The court remanded the prisoner into the custody of the sheriff.* ☐ *The judge remanded Mary to the sheriff.*

REMAND ▶ OVER

remand someone over to someone to order someone to be turned over to someone. (And see the previous entry.) ☐ *The judge remanded Gerald over to his father.* ☐ *Gerald was remanded over to the state corrections institution.*

REMARK ▶ (UP)ON

remark (up)on someone or something to comment on someone or something. (*Upon* is formal and less commonly used than *on*.) ☐ *She remarked upon his tardiness and then continued the lesson.* ☐ *There is no need to remark on me or anything I do or don't do.*

REMEMBER ▶ AS

remember someone as something to recall someone as being a particular type of person. ☐ *I remember Terri as a rather cheerful girl, always willing to help out.* ☐ *Terri will be remembered as a grouchy person.*

REMEMBER ▶ IN

remember someone in one's will to bequeath something to someone in one's will. □ *My uncle always said he would remember me in his will.* □ *He failed to remember me in his will.*

REMEMBER ▸ TO

remember someone to someone to carry the greetings of someone to someone else. □ *Please remember me to your uncle.* □ *I will remember you to my brother, who asks of you often.*

REMIND ▸ ABOUT

remind someone about someone or something to cause someone to remember someone or something. (*Someone* includes *oneself*.) □ *Will you please remind me about Fred? He's coming to visit next week.* □ *I will remind you about your appointments for today.* □ *As he was about to eat the pasta, he reminded himself about his diet.*

REMIND ▸ OF

remind someone of someone or something to bring a memory of someone or something into someone's mind. □ *You remind me of my brother.* □ *The happy song reminded us of our cabin on the lake.*

REMINISCE ▸ ABOUT

reminisce about someone or something to think about one's memories of someone or something; to discuss or share memories of someone or something. □ *They were reminiscing about their old friends.* □ *The old men sat and reminisced about the good old days.*

REMINISCE ▸ WITH

reminisce with someone to share memories with someone. □ *I love to reminisce with my sister about old times.* □ *Todd was reminiscing with Alice about the good old days.*

REMIT ▸ TO

remit something to someone or something to send something, especially money, to someone or a group. □ *Please remit your rent to your landlady immediately.* □ *You are requested to remit your loan payment to the bank on time this month.*

REMONSTRATE ▸ ABOUT

See the following entry.

REMONSTRATE ▸ WITH

remonstrate (with someone) (about someone or something) to protest to someone about someone or something. □ *After remonstrating with the manager about the price for a while, Vernon left quietly.* □ *I spent an hour remonstrating about Ted with Alice.*

REMOVE ▸ FROM

remove someone from something to take someone out of an office or position. (*Someone* includes *oneself*.) □ *The county board removed the sheriff from office.* □ *She removed herself from office voluntarily.*

remove someone or something from someone or something to take someone or something away from someone or something. (*Someone* includes *oneself*.) □ *The authorities removed the child from his mother.* □ *They removed the dog from his owner.* □ *Please remove yourself from the premises.*

REMUNERATE ▸ FOR

remunerate someone for something **1.** to pay someone for something. □ *Of course, I will remunerate you for your time.* □ *She was promptly remunerated for the hours she spent working on the project.* **2.** to repay someone for money spent. □ *I will remunerate you for the cost of the book if you will give me the receipt.* □ *Please remunerate me for the charges as soon as possible.*

REND ▸ FROM

rend something from someone or something to tear something from someone or something. □ *Harry rent the burning clothing from the man who had just fled from the burning building.* □ *God rent the veil from the temple.*

REND ▸ INTO

rend something into something to rip or tear something into something. (The past tense and past participle are *rent*.) □ *The tailor rent the garment into shreds in his anger.* □ *The garment was rent into bits and pieces by the machine.*

RENDER ▸ DOWN

render something down (to something) **1.** to cook the fat out of something. □

Polly rendered the chicken fat down to a bit of golden grease that she would use in cooking a special dish. 🅃 *Jane rendered down the fat for use later.* □ *The cook rendered it down.* **2.** to reduce or simplify something to its essentials. □ *Let's render this problem down to the considerations that are important to us.* 🅃 *Can't we render down this matter into its essentials?* □ *Not all of this is important. Let's render it down.*

RENDER ▸ IN
render something in something to translate something into something. □ *Now, see if you can render this passage in French.* □ *Are you able to render this in German?*

RENDER ▸ TO
render something to someone or something to give something to someone or a group. □ *You must render your taxes to the government.* □ *I will render my money to the tax collector.*

RENDER ▸ UP
render something up (to someone) to give something up to someone; to yield something to someone. (Formal and stilted.) □ *I was forced to render my earnings up to my creditors.* 🅃 *I had to render up all my earnings.* □ *There wasn't much, but I had to render it up.*

RENEGE ▸ ON
renege on something to go back on one's promise or commitment. □ *I am mad at you because you reneged on your promise!* □ *I did not renege on what I promised.*

RENOUNCE ▸ FOR
renounce someone for something to repudiate someone for doing something. □ *She renounced her brother for his political orientation.* □ *Jane was renounced for her illegal activities.*

RENT ▸ FROM
rent something from someone to pay someone for the use of something. □ *We rented a small car from one of the rental agencies.* □ *They rented a house from a local realtor.*

RENT ▸ OUT
See the following entry.

RENT ▸ TO
rent something (out) (to someone) to sell temporary rights for the use of something to someone. □ *I rented the back room out to a nice young student.* □ *We rented the back room to someone.* □ *For how long did you rent it out?* 🅃 *Let's rent out the garage.*

REPAIR ▸ TO
repair to some place to move oneself to some place. □ *I will repair to my room until the crisis is over.* □ *She repaired to a safe place for the duration of the storm.*

REPATRIATE ▸ TO
repatriate someone to some place to restore one to one's country of origin. □ *He asked that they repatriate him to the land of his birth.* □ *She was repatriated to her homeland.*

REPAY ▸ BY
repay someone by something to recompense someone by doing something; to end an obligation to someone by doing something; to settle a debt with someone by doing something. □ *I will repay you by cutting your lawn free for a year. How's that?* □ *Can I repay you by taking you to dinner?*

REPAY ▸ FOR
repay someone for something to remunerate someone for doing something. □ *I refused to repay him for his expenses. He had made a mess of the assignment.* □ *She was repaid for her kindnesses many times over.*

REPAY ▸ WITH
repay someone with something to remunerate someone with something. □ *The farmer's wife repaid the banker with fresh eggs and rich cream.* □ *We were repaid with fresh eggs from the farm.*

REPEL ▸ FROM
repel someone from something to push someone back from something; to fight someone off from something. □ *The army repelled the attackers from the en-*

trance to the city. □ *The attacking army was repelled from the city.*

REPLACE ▸ BY

replace someone or something by someone or something AND **replace someone or something with someone or something** to remove someone or something and add someone or something in place of the first. □ *The manager replaced Fred by a machine.* □ *Walter replaced his old lawn mower with a newer one.*

REPLACE ▸ WITH

replace someone or something with someone or something See the previous entry.

REPLENISH ▸ WITH

replenish something with something to rebuild the supply of something with more of it. □ *I will replenish the checking account with more money at the end of the month.* □ *Can I replenish your glass with more iced tea?*

REPLY ▸ TO

reply to someone or something to give a response to someone or something. □ *I replied to her already. There is no reason to do it again.* □ *I will reply to her letter as soon as I can.*

REPORT ▸ ABOUT

report about someone or something to deliver information about someone or something. □ *Isn't it time to report about Frank and how well he is doing?* □ *I want to report about the accident.*

REPORT ▸ BACK

report back (on someone or something) to return with information or an explanation to someone or something. □ *I need you to report back on Walter by noon.* □ *I'll report back as soon as I can.*

report back (to someone or something) **1.** to go back to someone or something and present oneself. □ *Report back to me at once!* □ *I'll report back immediately.* **2.** to present information or an explanation to someone. □ *Please report back to me when you have the proper information.* □ *I'll report back as soon as I have all the information.*

REPORT ▸ FOR

report for something to present oneself for something. □ *Please report for duty on Monday morning at eight sharp.* □ *I can't report for my examination at the time we agreed upon.*

REPORT ▸ IN

report in to present oneself; to make one's presence known. □ *Please report in when you get back in town.* □ *He reported in and his name was taken off the list.*

report in sick to call one's office to say that one will not come to work because one is sick. (See also *call in sick* under *CALL ▸ IN.*) □ *I don't feel well today. I will report in sick.* □ *The phone was busy, so I reported in sick over the fax machine.*

REPORT ▸ ON

See under *REPORT ▸ (UP)ON.*

REPORT ▸ TO

report something to someone to present a body of information to someone. □ *Please report the results to the supervisor.* □ *The event was reported to the proper person.*

report to someone or something **1.** to present oneself to someone or an office. □ *You must report to me for duty at noon.* □ *They told me to report to this office at this time.* **2.** to be supervised by someone or an office. □ *When you start work here you will report to Mrs. Franklin.* □ *I report directly to the home office.* **3.** to return to someone or an office and make a report. □ *Please report to me when you have the results.* □ *If you have any more to say, please report to headquarters and tell the whole story.*

REPORT ▸ (UP)ON

report (up)on someone or something to present an explanation on someone or something. (*Upon* is formal and less commonly used than *on*.) □ *The detective visited Mrs. Jones to report upon Mr. Jones.* □ *I want to report on the events of the day. Do you have time to listen?*

REPOSE ▶ IN

repose in something 1. to lie stretched out in something, such as a bed. ☐ *I think I would like to repose in my own bed for an hour or two before I begin my journey.* ☐ *Tom reposed in a comfortable chair for the rest of the evening.* 2. to lie stretched out in a particular state, such as death or slumber. ☐ *She lay on the cot, reposed in slumber, waiting for Prince Charming to arrive.* ☐ *The ruler reposed in death on public view for over a year.* 3. [for something] to exist in something or be part of the essence of something. ☐ *Much of our cultural heritage reposes in our literature.* ☐ *Considerable important thinking reposes in folktales and myths.*

REPOSE ▶ (UP)ON

repose (up)on something to lie on something. (*Upon* is formal and less commonly used than *on*.) ☐ *I will repose upon these cushions until my bathwater has been drawn.* ☐ *Dawn reposed on the sofa for over an hour.*

REPRESENT ▶ AS

represent someone or something as something to depict or portray someone or something as something; to think of someone or something as something. ☐ *I don't think you should represent me as an angel. After all, I'm human.* ☐ *The artist represented my puppy as a wolflike animal.*

REPRESENT ▶ IN

represent someone in something to act as one's advocate or agent in business or legal proceedings. ☐ *My lawyer represented me in court.* ☐ *His attorney will represent him in all his dealings with the publishing company.*

REPRESENT ▶ TO

represent something to someone 1. to exemplify something to someone. ☐ *What does this represent to you?* ☐ *This represents a lapse in manners to me.* 2. to explain a matter to someone. ☐ *He represented the matter to me in a much more charitable light.* ☐ *I did not represent it properly to you.*

REPRIMAND ▶ FOR

reprimand someone for something to scold someone for something; to admonish someone for something. ☐ *There is no need to reprimand me for a simple accident!* ☐ *Mary was reprimanded for being late.*

REPROACH ▶ FOR

reproach someone for something to rebuke or censure someone for something. (*Someone* includes *oneself*.) ☐ *She reproached Jerry for gambling away all their money.* ☐ *She reproached herself mercilessly for her failure.*

REPROACH ▶ WITH

reproach someone with something to rebuke someone with reference to something. ☐ *I wish you wouldn't continue to reproach me with things that happened long ago.* ☐ *She was reproached with something out of the past.*

REPRODUCE ▶ FROM

reproduce something from something to make a copy of something from something else. ☐ *I think we can reproduce the picture from the copy that you have there. We don't need the negative.* ☐ *Can you reproduce a good copy from this messy page?*

REPROVE ▶ FOR

reprove someone for something to criticize or censure someone for something. ☐ *The boss reproved all the employees for their use of the telephones for personal calls.* ☐ *We were all reproved for being late too often.*

REPULSE ▶ FROM

repulse someone or something from something to resist or repel someone or something from something. ☐ *The royal guard repulsed the rebels from the palace grounds.* ☐ *Only the use of guns could repulse the starving wolves from the area around the cabin.*

REQUEST ▶ FROM

request something from someone to call for something from someone. ☐ *I will request an explanation from the employee in question.* ☐ *A full report was requested from each person present.*

REQUEST ▸ OF

request something of someone to call for someone to give or do something. □ *I have to request a favor of you.* □ *Can I request an early answer from you?*

REQUEST ▸ TO

request someone to do something to ask someone to do something. □ *I am going to request you to turn your radio down.* □ *Mary was requested to arrive a few minutes early.*

REQUIRE ▸ FROM

require something from someone to demand something from someone. □ *The telephone company required a deposit from John and Martha before they would install a telephone.* □ *They required some help from us.*

REQUIRE ▸ OF

require something of someone to expect or demand someone to give or do something. □ *I require absolute loyalty of my employees.* □ *What is required of me in this job?*

REQUISITION ▸ FOR

requisition something for someone or something to present an order for something for someone or some purpose. □ *I will have to requisition a desk for you. You can't work an eight-hour day at a table.* □ *We will requisition catering for the office party.*

REQUISITION ▸ FROM

requisition something from someone or something to send an order to someone or something for something. □ *The general requisitioned food and bedding from the farmer.* □ *We requisitioned a new typewriter from central supply.*

RESCUE ▸ FROM

rescue someone or something from someone or something to save or liberate someone or something from someone or something. □ *I hoped that someone would come and rescue me from this boring person.* □ *Nothing can rescue us from the ravages of time.* □ *Can anyone rescue the tree from this rotting disease?*

RESEARCH ▸ INTO

research into someone or something to study about someone or something thoroughly. □ *I decided that I would research into Queen Elizabeth.* □ *We researched into the period in which she lived.*

RESEMBLE ▸ IN

resemble someone or something in something to look or seem like someone or something. □ *You resemble my Uncle Herman in the way you walk.* □ *This resembles vanilla ice cream in flavor, but not in consistency.*

RESERVE ▸ FOR

reserve something for someone or something to save or set aside something for someone or something. □ *I am reserving this seat for Claire.* □ *We are reserving some of the cake for tomorrow.*

RESIDE ▸ IN

reside in some place to dwell in some place. □ *I reside in a small apartment in the center of town.* □ *The Wilsons resided in a large house on a hill.*

reside in someone or something to be a property or characteristic of someone or something. □ *I never knew such anger could reside in such a calm person.* □ *The finest acoustics that can be found in the world reside in this hall.*

RESIGN ▸ FROM

resign from something to make a written statement that removes one from an office or position of employment. □ *Andy resigned from the fraternity.* □ *I will not resign from my job. You will have to fire me.*

RESIGN ▸ TO

resign oneself to something to surrender to something; to give up and accept something. □ *She gave up and resigned herself to buying the car that she could afford.* □ *He resigned himself to life in the army.*

RESORT ▸ TO

resort to something to turn to something that is not the first choice. □ *I hope they don't resort to a lawsuit to ac-*

complish their goals. ☐ *She will resort to anything to get her way.*

RESOUND ▸ THROUGH(OUT)

resound through(out) something to roar, booming, through a space or an enclosed area. ☐ *An explosion resounded through the busy train station.* ☐ *An explosion resounded throughout the busy train station.*

RESOUND ▸ WITH

resound with something [for something, such as the air or a place] to be filled with sound or sounds. ☐ *The hall resounded with the sounds of the orchestra.* ☐ *The house resounded with the laughter of children.*

RESPECT ▸ AS

respect someone as something to admire someone as something. ☐ *I respect you as a friend and supervisor.* ☐ *We respected them all as colleagues and coworkers.*

RESPECT ▸ FOR

respect someone for something to admire someone for something. ☐ *I really respect George for his courage.* ☐ *Mary respected the company for their fine products.*

RESPOND ▸ TO

respond to someone or something **1.** to answer someone or something. ☐ *Would you please respond to me?* ☐ *When are you going to respond to my letter?* **2.** to react to someone or something. ☐ *You have heard his presentation. How would you respond to him?* ☐ *I need you to respond to the points in the report by the end of the day.* ☐ *The police did not respond to the riot call.*

REST ▸ AGAINST

rest against someone or something to lean against someone or something; to take a rest period positioned against someone or something. ☐ *The child rested against his father until it was time to board the train.* ☐ *A fishing pole rested against the side of the garage, eagerly waiting to go to work.*

rest something against something to lean or position something against something, allowing it to bear part of the weight of the thing being rested. ☐ *Rest the heavy end of the box against the wall and we'll slide it down the stairs.* ☐ *Please rest the board against something solid while you paint it.*

REST ▸ FROM

rest from something to take it easy and recover from something. ☐ *I need to take a few minutes and rest from all that exertion.* ☐ *When you have rested from your running, please come in here and help me.*

REST ▸ IN

rest in something **1.** to take it easy in something, such as a chair or a bed. ☐ *I rested in the chair for a while and then got up and made supper.* ☐ *I will rest in bed until I feel better.* **2.** to take it easy in a particular condition or status, such as death, comfort, or comfortable surroundings. ☐ *I hope that you can rest in comfort for the rest of the night.* ☐ *We rested in the plush surroundings and then went back out into the hot sun to work.* **3.** [for something] to have its source in something. ☐ *The source of her magnetism rests in the way she uses her eyes.* ☐ *His skill rests in his thorough training.*

rest something in someone or something to place or vest something in someone or something. ☐ *The board of directors saw fit to rest the power to hire and fire in the office of the vice president.* ☐ *The president rested the power to hire and fire in the hands of his son, who promptly fired his father.*

REST ▸ ON

See also under *REST ▸ (UP)ON.*

rest on one's laurels to stop trying because one is satisfied with one's past achievements. ☐ *Despite our success, this is no time to rest on our laurels.* ☐ *We rested on our laurels too long. Our competitors took away a lot of our business.*

REST ▸ UP

rest up (for something) to take it easy in advance of something tiring. ☐ *Excuse me, but I have to go rest up for the* *concert tonight.* ☐ *I really need to rest up a while.*

rest up (from something) to recover or recuperate from something tiring. ☐ *I need about a week to rest up from my vacation.* ☐ *I'll need a few days to rest up.*

REST ▶ (UP)ON

rest (up)on something to lie on something; to take it easy on something. (*Upon* is formal and less commonly used than *on*.) ☐ *Here, rest upon this mat.* ☐ *I'll just rest on this chair, thanks.* ☐ *She rested upon the couch for a while and then went out to weed the garden.*

REST ▶ WITH

rest with someone or something to remain with someone or something; to be vested with someone or something. ☐ *The final decision rests with you.* ☐ *The power rests with the board of directors.*

RESTORE ▶ IN

restore someone's something in something to reinstate someone's belief, faith, trust, etc., in something. ☐ *I knew that a good performance on the test would restore my parents' belief in me.* ☐ *Her faith was restored in the government.*

RESTORE ▶ TO

restore something to someone to give something back to someone; to cause something to be returned to someone. ☐ *I will restore the man's wallet to him after we lock the thief up.* ☐ *His wallet was restored to him by a police officer.*

restore something to something to bring something to its original state. ☐ *The state restored the park to its original condition.* ☐ *The government forced the mining company to restore the area to its original state.*

RESTRAIN ▶ FROM

restrain someone from something to prevent someone from doing something. (*Someone* includes *oneself*.) ☐ *I had to restrain her from hurting herself.* ☐ *I am unable to restrain myself from giggling.*

RESTRICT ▶ TO

restrict someone or something to someone or something to limit someone or something to someone or something; to confine someone or something to someone or something. (*Someone* includes *oneself*. The first *something* may typically refer to a choice or selection.) ☐ *When choosing team members, we are restricting them to people they already know.* ☐ *We restricted the choices to Bill, Bob, or Ted.* ☐ *I had to restrict myself to the people in the room when it came to choosing a partner.*

RESULT ▶ FROM

result from something to emerge from something; to be the outcome of something. ☐ *It will be interesting to see what results from your efforts.* ☐ *Nothing resulted from all that work.*

RESULT ▶ IN

result in something to achieve something; to bring about something; to cause something to happen. ☐ *I hope that this will result in the police finding your car.* ☐ *All my effort resulted in nothing at all.*

RESURRECT ▶ FROM

resurrect someone or something from something to restore someone or something from some state to the original state. ☐ *We decided to resurrect Toby from the ranks of the retired.* ☐ *I resurrected my old uniform from its tattered and wrinkled state.*

RETAIL ▶ AT

retail at something to sell at a retail price of something. ☐ *This model normally retails at a much higher price.* ☐ *What does a product like this usually retail at?*

RETAIL ▶ FOR

retail for something to sell for a retail price of an amount of money. ☐ *This item retails for less than ten dollars.* ☐ *How much does this retail for?*

RETAIL ▶ TO

retail something to someone to sell something to someone at a retail price. ☐ *I can retail this merchandise to anybody at half the price of my competitor.*

□ *We are not allowed to retail this to anyone in the state of Maine.*

RETAIN ▸ OVER

retain something over someone or something to keep or maintain something, such as power or control, over someone or something. □ *Tony found a way to retain control over Fred.* □ *I wish to retain veto power over the committee.*

RETALIATE ▸ AGAINST

retaliate against someone or something to take revenge against someone or something. □ *The administration will retaliate against the students by closing down the cafeteria.* □ *The students retaliated against the administration.*

RETIRE ▸ FROM

retire from something to withdraw from something. (Usually to terminate a working career permanently.) □ *I retired from the company early.* □ *When do you intend to retire from your job?*

retire someone or something from something to take someone or something out of service permanently. □ *The company retired the vice president from the job and gave it to someone else.* □ *It is time to retire my automobile from service.*

RETIRE ▸ (IN)TO

retire (in)to something to quit working and move into something or some place. □ *Sam and Ella retired into a Florida condo.* □ *Joe did not want to retire to Florida.*

RETIRE ▸ ON

retire on something to quit working and live on something or a particular amount of money. □ *I already have enough money to retire on.* □ *I cannot retire on a sum like that!*

RETIRE ▸ TO

See also under *RETIRE ▸ (IN)TO.*

retire to some place to quit working permanently and move to a particular location. □ *When I quit working I want to retire to Florida.* □ *We will retire to our place in the country.*

RETOOL ▸ FOR

retool for something **1.** to set up with new or altered tools for a different kind of production. □ *The factory was closed down so they could retool for next year's model.* □ *How soon can we retool for this new line of products?* **2.** to prepare oneself for a different kind of work. □ *He decided to retool for a new job in the computer industry.* □ *I am too old to retool for a job like this.*

retool something for something to set up a factory with new or altered tools for a different kind of production. □ *The manager decided to retool the factory for greater efficiency.* □ *We will retool the plant for next year's models.*

RETREAT ▸ FROM

retreat (from something) (to some place) to withdraw from something to some place. □ *The army retreated from the battlefield to the safety of the forest.* □ *They retreated to the other side of the river.* □ *We retreated from the meeting room, having lost our plea.*

RETREAT ▸ TO

See the previous entry.

RETRIEVE ▸ FROM

retrieve someone or something from some place to recover and bring back someone or something from some place. □ *The mother hurried to the school and retrieved her child from the classroom.* □ *I retrieved my cat from the well into which she had fallen.*

retrieve something from someone to get something back from someone. □ *I hope I can retrieve my book from the person who borrowed it.* □ *We were not able to retrieve the lawn mower from Fred before he moved away and took it with him.*

RETURN ▸ FOR

return something for something to give or pay back something for something. □ *The clerk returned the correct change for a twenty-dollar bill.* □ *I hope that the store returns good value for my money.*

RETURN ► FROM

return from some place to come back from some place. □ *I just returned from the Amazon basin.* □ *When will they return from their vacation?*

RETURN ► TO

return someone or something to someone to give someone or something back to someone. □ *Please return my child to me.* □ *Would you return my book to me soon?*

return to some place to go or come back to some place. □ *When do you plan to return to your home?* □ *I will return there when I have finished here.*

RETURN ► WITH

return with something to come back with something. □ *He went to town and returned with the doctor just in time.* □ *She returned with the material they had requested.*

REUNITE ► WITH

reunite someone or something with someone or something to bring someone or something together with someone or something. □ *Mary was pleased to reunite Sally with her sister.* □ *I reunited Walter with his wallet.* □ *I was happy to reunite the wallet with its owner.*

REV ► UP

rev something up to race an engine in one or more short bursts. □ *George revved the engine up and took off.* 🅃 *He revved up the engine.*

rev up to increase in amount or activity. □ *Production revved up after the strike.* □ *We're hoping business will rev up soon.*

REVEAL ► TO

reveal someone or something to someone to show or disclose someone or something to someone. (*Someone* includes *oneself*.) □ *The magician opened the door of the cabinet and revealed his assistant to the audience.* □ *I revealed my secret to no one.* □ *She stepped out from behind the tree and revealed herself to the hostess.*

REVEL ► IN

revel in something to rejoice or celebrate about something. □ *All the children reveled in the fresh, warm, spring air.* □ *Tony reveled in his success.*

REVENGE ► (UP)ON

revenge oneself (up)on someone or something to retaliate against someone or something. (*Upon* is formal and less commonly used than *on*.) □ *There is no need for you to revenge yourself upon Walter. It was an accident.* □ *I will revenge myself on the whole world!* □ *She did not know how she would revenge herself on Joe, but she knew she would.*

REVERBERATE ► THROUGH

reverberate through something [for sound] to roll through or pass through a space. □ *The thunder reverberated through the valley.* □ *The sound of the organ reverberated through the church.*

REVERBERATE ► THROUGHOUT

reverberate throughout something [for sound] to roll about and fill a space. □ *The thunder reverberated throughout the valley.* □ *The noise of chairs scraping the floor reverberated throughout the room.*

REVERBERATE ► WITH

reverberate with something to echo or resound with something. □ *The hall reverberated with the rich basso voice of Walter Rogers.* □ *The church reverberated with the roar of the pipe organ.*

REVERE ► FOR

revere someone or something for something to admire or venerate someone or something for something. □ *I will always revere my dear aunt for her devotion to all of us.* □ *We have always revered his lovely gift for our little kindnesses.*

REVERT ► TO

revert to someone or something to become the property of someone, a group, or an institution. □ *At the end of ten years, this house and the land it sits on reverts to the youngest living child.* □ *Then the property reverts to the state.*

REVIEW ▸ FOR

review for something to study material again for something, such as an examination. □ *I need some time to review for the examination.* □ *Have you had enough time to review for your speech?*

REVOLT ▸ AGAINST

revolt against someone or something to rebel or rise against someone or something. □ *They had had enough and were planning to revolt against their leader.* □ *The citizens were gathering arms, preparing to revolt against the government.*

REVOLT ▸ AT

See *be revolted at someone or something* under *BE ▸ AT.*

REVOLVE ▸ ABOUT

See the following entry.

REVOLVE ▸ AROUND

revolve around someone or something AND **revolve about someone or something** **1.** to spin or move around someone or something. □ *Do you think that the whole world revolves around you?* □ *The moon revolves about the earth.* **2.** [for people or things] to center upon someone or something or to be primarily concerned with someone or something. □ *The way all of this is going to turn out revolves around Bob.* □ *The success of the picnic revolves around the weather.*

REWARD ▸ FOR

reward someone for something to give someone a prize or a bonus for doing something. (*Someone* includes *oneself.*) □ *I would like to reward you for your honesty.* □ *She wanted to reward herself for her patience but did not know how.*

REWARD ▸ WITH

reward someone with something to honor someone with a gift of something. (*Someone* includes *oneself.*) □ *She rewarded the helpful child with a chocolate chip cookie.* □ *He rewarded himself with a night on the town.*

RHAPSODIZE ▸ OVER

rhapsodize over someone or something to go on and on about the virtues of someone or something. □ *Young Thomas likes to rhapsodize over Francine, his girlfriend.* □ *Please do not rhapsodize over this poem anymore.*

RHYME ▸ WITH

rhyme something with something [for someone] to make one word rhyme with another word. □ *I need to rhyme* tree *with some other word. Any suggestions?* □ *Can I rhyme* good *with* food?

rhyme with something [for a word] to rhyme with another word. □ *You can't use* house *in that line of the poem, because it doesn't rhyme with* moose. □ *The last word in your poem doesn't rhyme with any other word in the poem!*

RICOCHET ▸ OFF

ricochet off something [for some rapidly moving object, such as a bullet] to bounce off something at an oblique angle. □ *The bullet ricocheted off the wall and struck the gunman.* □ *Bullets were ricocheting off the walls from all angles.*

RID ▸ OF

rid oneself or something of someone or something to free oneself or something of someone or something; to deliver oneself or something from someone or something. □ *The boys were not clever enough to rid themselves of Tom's little sister.* □ *Will we ever be able to rid this house of spiders?* □ *I have to rid myself of a number of problems before I can take on any of yours.*

RIDDLE ▸ WITH

riddle someone or something with something to fill someone or something with small holes, such as bullet holes. □ *Max pulled the trigger of the machine gun and riddled Lefty with holes.* □ *Max riddled the wall with holes with the leftover bullets.*

RIDE ▸ AWAY

ride away to depart, riding a bike or a horse or similar animal. □ *She got on her horse and rode away.* □ *They rode away without even saying good-bye.*

RIDE ▸ BY

ride by someone or something to pass by someone or something, riding. (As on a horse or bicycle, or as a passenger in a car.) □ *She rode by me without saying anything.* □ *I rode by the store and forget to stop and go in.*

RIDE ▸ DOWN

ride someone or something down to chase down someone or some creature while riding on horseback. □ *The mounted policeman rode the mugger down and captured him.* 🅃 *The rider rode down the thief.* □ *We had to ride down the runaway horse.*

ride something down to ride on something that is going down, such as an elevator. □ *You take the stairs, and I will ride the elevator down.* □ *I don't want to ride the cable car down. I will walk.*

RIDE ▸ FOR

riding for a fall doing something in which one will fail. (Idiomatic. Always *riding*.) □ *If he thinks he can win the race, he's riding for a fall.* □ *They did not know it at the time, but they were riding for a fall.*

RIDE ▸ OFF

ride off to depart, riding something such as a horse or a bicycle. □ *Betty said good-bye and rode off.* □ *We rode off, each one in a different direction.*

ride off in all directions [for people] to scatter, riding something, such as a horse or a bicycle. (See also *run off in all directions* under *RUN ▸ OFF.*) □ *The boys hopped on their bikes and rode off in all directions.* □ *The sheriff got the posse together and they rode off in all directions, looking for the bank robber.*

RIDE ▸ ON

See also under *RIDE ▸ (UP)ON.*

ride herd on someone or something to keep a close watch or tight control over someone or something, as a cowboy monitors cattle. □ *I have to ride herd on everyone at the office, or they will mess everything up.* □ *We have to ride herd on the staff at all times.*

ride on to continue to ride, traveling onward. □ *We rode on for at least an hour before a rest stop.* □ *They rode on for a while.*

ride on someone's coattails to achieve some degree of success by following someone else. □ *The vice president rode on the president's coattails throughout the election process.* □ *You can't ride on my coattails all the time. Do something for yourself!*

ride on something **1.** to travel on something. □ *Do you like to ride on the train?* □ *I have never ridden on a horse.* **2.** to be borne on something and carried along. (Figurative.) □ *She rode on a wave of popularity to reelection.* □ *He rode on his past laurels as long as he could.*

RIDE ▸ OUT

ride out (of some place) to travel out of a place on something such as a horse or bicycle. □ *All the racers rode out of the starting area and began the bicycle marathon.* □ *At the sound of the starting gun, all the contestants rode out.*

ride something out to endure something; to remain with something to the termination of something. □ *Things are rough in my department at the office, but I think I can ride it out.* 🅃 *I can ride out the storm if I can remember to be patient.*

RIDE ▸ OVER

ride over someone or something to pass over someone or something, riding something such as a horse or a bicycle. □ *Bobby fell down and Susan rode over him with her bicycle, but he wasn't hurt at all.* □ *Tom almost rode over my toe!*

ride roughshod over someone or something to treat someone or something badly; [figuratively] to trample someone or something. □ *Is it really necessary to ride roughshod over your friends?* □ *The boss really rode roughshod over my proposal.*

RIDE ▸ TO

ride to some place to travel to a place, riding something such as a horse or a bicycle. □ *I will ride to town and get the doctor.* □ *Tom will ride to the store on his bike to get a loaf of bread.*

RIDE ▸ UP

ride up (on someone) **1.** [for someone on a horse] to approach someone, riding. ☐ *I rode up on him and frightened him.* ☐ *I guess I was in the house when you rode up.* **2.** [for clothing, especially underpants] to keep moving higher on one's body. ☐ *I don't like it when my pants ride up on me.* ☐ *I hate it when my underpants ride up.*

RIDE ▸ (UP)ON

ride (up)on someone or something to use someone or something as a beast of burden. (*Upon* is formal and less commonly used than *on.*) ☐ *As a game, the children used to ride on their father.* ☐ *We rode upon burros along the narrow mountain trails.*

RIDE ▸ WITH

ride with someone to travel with someone on or in a vehicle or a beast of burden. ☐ *I'm going to the store for some milk. Do you want to ride with me?* ☐ *Can I ride with you to the store?*

RIFLE ▸ THROUGH

rifle through something to ransack something; to search through something looking for something to steal. ☐ *The teenager quickly rifled through the cabinets, looking for something worth eating.* ☐ *The soldiers rifled through every house they could break into.*

RIG ▸ UP

rig someone or something out (in something) to outfit someone or something in something; to decorate or dress someone or something in something. (*Someone* includes *oneself.*) ☐ *Joan rigged her daughter out in a witch's costume for the Halloween party.* 🅃 *He rigged out his car with lights for the parade.* ☐ *Alice rigged her bicycle out in festive colors.* ☐ *She rigged herself out in a clown suit and joined the circus for a day.*

rig something up to prepare something, perhaps on short notice or without the proper materials. ☐ *We don't have what's needed to make the kind of circuit you have described, but I think we can rig something up anyway.* 🅃 *We will rig up whatever you need.*

RING ▸ AROUND

ring around something to circle something. ☐ *The children ringed around the maypole, dancing and singing.* ☐ *The mourners had ringed around the coffin for the final ceremony.*

RING ▸ BACK

ring back to call back on the telephone. ☐ *No, there's no message. I'll ring back later.* ☐ *She's not here now. I suggest you ring back after dinner.*

ring someone back to call someone back on the telephone. ☐ *I will have to ring you back later.* ☐ *Please ring me back when you have a moment.* 🅃 *I will ring back the caller when I have time.*

RING ▸ DOWN

ring the curtain down (on someone or something) **1.** to bring down the curtain on someone or something in a theater. (The ringing down refers to sending the signal to have the curtain lowered.) ☐ *They had to ring the curtain down on Fred because he fainted.* ☐ *At the end of the play, they rang the curtain down too soon.* 🅃 *When was I supposed to ring down the curtain?* **2.** to put an end to the activities or story of someone or something. (Figurative.) ☐ *That seems to ring the curtain down on the Wilson project.* 🅃 *At the end of a long career, Gene felt it was time to ring down the curtain.*

RING ▸ FOR

ring for someone or something to summon someone or something with a signal, such as a bell. ☐ *Would you ring for the steward, please? I need a cooling drink.* ☐ *I think I will ring for a drink.*

RING ▸ IN

ring in something [for words or a sound] to linger in one's ears [mind]. ☐ *Her words rang in my ears for days.* ☐ *The sound of the choir rang in their minds long after they had finished their anthem.*

ring in the new (year) to celebrate the new year; to welcome in the new year. ☐ *I plan to ring in the new year at home* *with friends and family.* ☐ *Where are you going to ring in the new year this year?*

RING ▸ OFF

ring off the hook [for a telephone] to ring incessantly and repeatedly. ☐ *What a busy day! The telephone has been ringing off the hook all day long.* ☐ *The telephone has been ringing off the hook ever since the ad appeared in the paper.*

RING ▸ OUT

ring out [for a loud sound] to go out. ☐ *The bells rang out at the end of the wedding ceremony.* ☐ *The bells were ringing out their welcome to the new mayor.* ☐ *Loud cheers rang out at the end of the game.* ☐ *A shot rang out and started all the dogs barking.*

ring out the old to celebrate the end of a year while celebrating the beginning of a new one. ☐ *I don't plan to ring out the old this year. I'm just going to go to bed.* ☐ *We never ring out the old because it's too dismal.*

RING ▸ UP

ring someone up to call someone on the telephone. (Chiefly British.) ☐ *I will ring her up when I get a chance.* 🅃 *I have to ring up a whole list of people.*

ring something up (on something) to record the amount of a sale on a cash register. ☐ *Jane rang the purchases up one by one on the cash register.* 🅃 *She rang up the purchases on the register as quick as lightning.* ☐ *She rang them up and collected the money.*

ring the curtain up **1.** to raise the curtain in a theater. (Refers to sending the signal to raise the curtain.) ☐ *The stagehand rang the curtain up precisely on time.* 🅃 *Let's ring up the curtain. It's time to start.* **2.** to start a series of activities or events. (Figurative.) ☐ *I am set to ring up the curtain on a new lifestyle.* 🅃 *It's a little late to ring up the curtain for a new career.*

RING ▸ WITH

ring with something **1.** to resound with something. ☐ *The morning air rang with the sound of church bells.* ☐ *The canyon rang with the sound of gunfire.* **2.** [for a bell] to ring in some characteristic way. ☐ *The bells seemed to ring with unusual clarity on this fine Sunday morning.* ☐ *The doorbell rang with an urgency that could not be ignored.*

RINSE ▸ DOWN

rinse someone or something down to wash or clean someone or something with water or other fluid. ☐ *I rinsed him down for an hour and still didn't get the smell of skunk off him.* 🅃 *I had to rinse down the driveway.* 🄰 *Please don't track up the freshly rinsed-down floor.*

rinse something down (with something) to wash something down one's throat with a liquid; to follow something that one has eaten with a drink to aid its going down. (Informal.) ☐ *Alice rinsed the cheeseburger down with a milkshake.* 🅃 *She rinsed down the sandwich with a drink.* ☐ *She rinsed it down quickly.*

RINSE ▸ OFF

rinse someone or something off to wash or clean someone or something by flushing with water or other fluid. (*Someone* includes *oneself*.) ☐ *Mother rinsed the baby off and dried him with a soft towel.* 🅃 *She rinsed off the baby.* ☐ *Coming out of the sea, she rinsed herself off with fresh water.*

RINSE ▸ OUT

rinse someone's mouth out (with soap) to punish one by washing one's mouth out with soap. (Figurative. Usually a jocular threat.) ☐ *If you say that again, I'll rinse your mouth out with soap.* 🅃 *I will rinse out your mouth.*

rinse something out **1.** to clean cloth or clothing partially by immersing it in water and squeezing it out. ☐ *Can you please rinse this rag out? It's all dirty.* 🅃 *Please rinse your clothes out to make sure there is no soap left in them.* **2.** to launder something delicate, such as feminine underwear, using a mild soap. ☐ *I have to go rinse a few things out.* 🅃 *After I rinse out some things, I will be right with you.* **3.** to clean the inside of a container partially by flushing it out with water. ☐ *Rinse the bottle out and throw* *it away.* 🅃 *Rinse out the bottle and throw it away.*

rinse something out (of something) to remove something from something by flushing it with water. (The *of*-phrase is paraphrased with a *from*-phrase when the particle is transposed. See the 🄵 example.) □ *See if you can rinse the dirt out of this jacket.* 🅃 *I can't rinse out the dirt.* 🄵 *She can't rinse out the dirt from my jacket.* □ *Then I'll rinse it out.* 🄰 *Take a rinsed-out rag and wipe down the counter.*

RINSE ▸ WITH

rinse something with something to flush something with some fluid. □ *Your should rinse your clothes in milk or tomato juice to remove the smell of the skunk.* □ *Please rinse the meat with cold water.*

RIP ▸ APART

rip someone or something apart to tear someone or something apart into pieces. □ *The automobile accident ripped the driver apart.* 🅃 *Don't rip apart the newspaper!*

RIP ▸ AWAY

rip something away (from someone) to grab or snatch something away from someone. □ *Betty ripped the box away from Frank and walked away with it.* 🅃 *She ripped away the box and opened it.* □ *Frank was angry about the way she ripped it away.*

rip something away (from something) to tear or strip something away. □ *Billy ripped the wrapping paper away from the box.* 🅃 *He ripped away the paper.* □ *Eagerly, he ripped the paper away.*

RIP ▸ DOWN

rip something down to tear something down. (Refers to something that has been posted or mounted.) □ *The custodian ripped all the posters down at the end of the day.* 🅃 *He ripped down the posters.*

RIP ▸ IN

rip something in half AND **rip something in two** to tear something into two parts. □ *Did you know that Ed can rip a telephone book in half?* □ *I can rip a textbook in two.*

rip something in two See the previous entry.

RIP ▸ INTO

rip into someone or something **1.** to attack someone or something. □ *The raccoons ripped into the trash bags, scattering papers and stuff all over the street.* □ *The horrid murderer ripped into the helpless victim.* **2.** to criticize or censure someone or something severely. □ *The drama critic ripped into Larry.* □ *The critics really ripped into Larry's poor performance.*

RIP ▸ OFF

rip off [for something] to tear or peel off. □ *My pocket ripped off and my money is gone now!* □ *A piece of the bumper ripped off my car.*

rip someone off to steal from someone; to cheat someone. (Slang.) □ *That merchant ripped me off!* 🅃 *She rips off everyone.* 🄽 *This movie is a rip-off.*

rip something off ((of) someone) to steal something from someone. (Slang.) □ *The mugger ripped my purse off of me.* 🅃 *Jane ripped off a lot of money.* □ *Somebody ripped my wallet off.*

rip something off ((of) someone or something) to tear something away from someone or something. (The *of*-phrase is paraphrased with a *from*-phrase when the particle is transposed. See the 🄵 example. The *of* is colloquial.) □ *I ripped the cover off of the book accidentally.* 🅃 *I ripped off the book cover.* 🄵 *I ripped off the covers from the bed.* □ *He ripped the shirt off the injured man and began to treat the wound.* □ *Alice ripped the cover off.*

RIP ▸ ON

rip on someone to give someone a hard time; to hassle someone. (Slang.) □ *Stop ripping on me! What did I do to you?* □ *Tim is ripping on Mary and she is getting really mad.*

RIP ▸ OUT

rip something out (of someone or something) to tear someone out of someone or something. (The *of*-phrase is paraphrased with a *from*-phrase when the particle is transposed. See the 🄵 example.) ☐ *The high priest ripped the beating heart out of the sacrificial victim.* 🅃 *The priest ripped out the victim's heart.* 🄵 *The priest ripped out the heart from the victim's chest.* ☐ *He ripped the heart out and kicked the victim down the steep side of the pyramid.*

RIP ▸ TO

rip someone or something to something **1.** to tear someone or something into small pieces, expressed as bits, pieces, shreds, etc. ☐ *If you fall into that lawn mower, it will rip you to pieces.* ☐ *The lawn mower ripped the newspaper to tiny bits.* **2.** to criticize someone or something mercilessly. (*Someone* includes *oneself*.) ☐ *The critics ripped Gerald to pieces even though the audience just loved his show.* ☐ *They ripped the whole production to pieces.* ☐ *He felt he had done badly. In fact he just ripped himself to pieces.*

RIP ▸ UP

rip someone or something up to tear someone or something into bits; to mutilate someone or something. (*Someone* includes *oneself*.) ☐ *Careful! That machine will rip you up if you fall in.* 🅃 *I ripped up the contract and threw the pieces in the air.* ☐ *I got mad and ripped the contract up.* 🄰 *Don't spread that ripped-up paper all over the place.* ☐ *The dog fell into the lawn mower and ripped itself up badly.*

rip something up to take something up by force and remove it. (Usually refers to something on the floor or ground, such as carpeting or pavement.) ☐ *They are going to rip all the broken sidewalk up.* 🅃 *The workers ripped up the pavement and loaded the pieces into a truck.* 🄰 *What shall I do with the ripped-up carpet?*

RIPEN ▸ INTO

ripen into something to mature into something. (Figuratively and literally.) ☐ *This problem is going to ripen into a real crisis if we don't do something about it right now.* ☐ *The small matter ripened into a large problem in a short time.*

RIPPLE ▸ THROUGH

ripple through something **1.** to move through liquid so as to cause ripples or tiny waves. ☐ *The canoe rippled through the still water.* ☐ *A tiny snake rippled through the swamp water.* **2.** to move through something or a group of people in a ripple or wave motion. ☐ *A murmur of excitement rippled through the crowd.* ☐ *Some giggling rippled through the group of children sitting by the door.*

RISE ▸ ABOVE

rise above something **1.** to move up above something. ☐ *The huge sun rose above the horizon and spread its red glow across the sea.* ☐ *The bear rose above the stone it was behind and scared us to death.* **2.** [for one] to ignore petty matters and do what one is meant to do in spite of them. ☐ *He was able to rise above the squabbling and bring some sense to the proceedings.* ☐ *Jane was never able to rise above her petty dislikes.*

RISE ▸ AGAINST

rise (up) against someone or something to challenge someone or something; to rebel against someone or something. ☐ *The citizens rose up against their elected officials.* ☐ *They rose against the abusive power of the government.*

RISE ▸ FROM

rise from someone or something to emanate from someone or something in the manner of a cloud of dust or a cheer. ☐ *After the singer finished, a loud cheer rose from the crowd.* ☐ *A cloud of smoke rose from the burning barn.*

rise from the ashes to be rebuilt after destruction. (Figurative.) ☐ *The entire west section of the city was destroyed and a group of new buildings rose from the ashes in only a few months.* ☐ *Will the city rise again from the ashes? No one knows.*

rise from the dead to come back to life after being dead. ☐ *Albert didn't rise from the dead. He wasn't dead in the* *first place.* □ *How many people do you know who have risen from the dead?*

rise from the grave to return to life after dying and being buried. □ *The movie was about a teenager who rose from the grave and haunted his high school friends.* □ *I would not care to rise from the grave. Everyone needs a good rest.*

rise from the ranks to achieve position or office, having worked up from the masses. □ *He rose from the ranks to become president of the company.* □ *Most of the officers of the company have risen from the ranks.*

RISE ▶ IN

rise in something to increase in something. □ *I hope that this land rises in value over the next few years.* □ *Her expensive antique car actually rose in value during the first year.*

RISE ▶ TO

rise to one's feet to stand up. □ *The entire audience rose to its feet, applauding wildly.* □ *We rose to our feet when the bride came down the aisle.*

rise to something to move or float to something, such as the top, surface, etc. □ *The cream will rise to the top.* □ *The lighter oil rose to the top and we scooped it up and saved it.*

rise to the bait to respond to an allurement; to fall for an enticement or fall into a trap. (As a fish might come up from deep water to seize bait.) □ *You can get him here easily. Tell him that there will be lots of food and he will rise to the bait.* □ *He rose to the bait and did just as he was expected to do.*

rise to the challenge to accept a challenge. □ *You can depend on Kelly to rise to the challenge.* □ *We were not able to rise to the challenge and we lost the contract.*

rise to the occasion to be able to deal well with something difficult as the occasion to do so arises. □ *Your speech was excellent, George. You really rose to the occasion.* □ *George rose to the occasion and gave an excellent speech.*

RISE ▶ UP

rise up 1. to come up; to ascend. (Also without *up*, but not eligible as an entry.) □ *The water is rising up fast. You had better get to higher ground.* □ *As the water rose up, it covered the houses and streets.* **2.** to get up from lying down. □ *The deer rose up and darted off into the woods.* □ *I rose up and brushed my clothing.*

rise (up) against someone or something See under *RISE ▶ AGAINST.*

RISK ▶ ON

risk something on someone or something to chance losing something on someone or something. □ *I wouldn't risk any money on him. He's a poor credit risk.* □ *Don't risk your life on his being there to help you.*

RIVAL ▶ IN

rival someone in something to have a quality or status that is comparable to that of someone else. □ *I would say that Jane rivals Dave in the ability to find the essential elements of a problem and deal with them swiftly.* □ *No one rivals Ted in pitching a baseball.*

RIVET ▶ ON

rivet something on someone or something to fasten something, such as one's gaze, onto someone or something. (Figurative.) □ *He riveted his gaze on the surly young man.* □ *Walter riveted his hateful glare on the last page of the contract and sneered.*

RIVET ▶ ON(TO)

rivet something on(to) something to attach something to something with rivets. □ *The pockets of these jeans are riveted onto the body of the pants.* 🅃 *You should rivet on this part of the frame to the wall.* □ *Okay. I'll rivet it on the wall.*

RIVET ▶ TO

See *be riveted to the ground* under *BE ▶ TO.*

ROAM ▶ ABOUT

roam about AND **roam around** to wander or range about freely. □ *Stay where* *you are and don't roam about.* ☐ *I'm too tired to roam around very much.*

ROAM ▸ AROUND

roam around See the previous entry.

ROAR ▸ AT

roar at someone or something **1.** to bellow or bawl at someone or something. ☐ *Don't roar at me! Control your temper.* ☐ *The lion roared at the hyena, who just laughed.* **2.** to laugh very hard at someone or something. ☐ *The audience roared at the clown.* ☐ *The children roared at Dad's jokes.*

ROAR ▸ AWAY

roar away to speed away, making a loud clamor. ☐ *The car with screeching tires roared away into the night.* ☐ *The train roared away, carrying Andy to Canada.*

ROAR ▸ OUT

roar something out to bellow something out loudly. ☐ *Walter roared his protest out so everyone knew how he felt.* 🅃 *Jane roared out her criticism.*

ROB ▸ OF

rob someone of something to deprive someone of something, not necessarily by theft. (*Someone* includes *oneself.*) ☐ *What you have done has robbed me of my dignity!* ☐ *If you do that, you will rob yourself of your future.* ☐ *The crooks robbed me of every cent I have.*

ROCK ▸ AROUND

rock around to tilt or totter about. ☐ *The boat rocked around, tossing the passengers to and fro.* ☐ *The road was bumpy and the huge car rocked around.*

ROCK ▸ TO

rock someone to something to help someone, usually an infant, get to sleep by rocking in a rocking chair, cradle, or carriage. (*Someone* includes *oneself.*) ☐ *It is best to rock the baby to sleep after you feed her.* ☐ *Somehow she learned to rock herself to sleep.*

ROCKET ▸ (IN)TO

rocket (in)to something **1.** [for a projectile] to ascend into the sky or into space; [for something] to shoot rapidly into something. ☐ *The space shuttle rocketed into space.* ☐ *The locomotive rocketed into the darkness.* **2.** to ascend rapidly into something, such as fame or prominence. (Figurative.) ☐ *Jill rocketed into prominence after her spectacular performance on the guitar.* ☐ *She will undoubtedly rocket to success.*

ROCKET ▸ INTO

rocket something into something to send something somewhere—usually into space—by rocket. ☐ *The government rocketed the satellite into space.* ☐ *Someone suggested rocketing our waste into space.*

ROLL ▸ ABOUT

roll about to move about, turning or rotating, as a wheel or a ball. ☐ *The ball rolled about awhile and then came to rest.* ☐ *His eyes rolled about in amazement before he spoke.*

ROLL ▸ ALONG

roll along **1.** [for wheels or something on wheels] to move along, smoothly and rapidly. ☐ *The wheels of the cart rolled along, making a grinding noise as they went.* ☐ *Our car rolled along rapidly toward our destination.* **2.** [for something] to progress smoothly. (Figurative.) ☐ *The project is rolling along nicely.* ☐ *I hope that things are rolling along quite well.*

ROLL ▸ AROUND

roll around to move about, rotating, turning over, turning, or moving on wheels. ☐ *The baby rolled around on the floor, giggling and cooing.* ☐ *The ball rolled around and finally came to rest.* 🅃 *The toy truck won't roll around anymore.*

ROLL ▸ AWAY

roll away to move away, rotating, turning over, turning, or moving on wheels. ☐ *The ball rolled away and fell down a storm sewer.* ☐ *The cart rolled away and we had to chase it down the hill.*

roll something away to cause something to move away, rotating, turning over, turning, or moving on wheels. ☐ *Jane rolled the ball away and it was lost.* 🅃 *Jane rolled away the ball.* ☐ *Please* *roll the cart away.* [A] *It's a smaller apartment with a roll-away bed.*

ROLL ▸ BACK

roll back [for something] to return, rotating or turning or moving on wheels. □ *I rolled the ball away, thinking it would roll back. It didn't.* □ *I struck the golf ball away from the sand trap, but it rolled back.*

roll something back **1.** to return something to someone by rotating it, as with a wheel or a ball, or moving it back on wheels. □ *I intercepted the ball and rolled it back.* [T] *Jane rolled back the ball.* **2.** to reduce prices. □ *The store rolled all its prices back for the sale.* [T] *The protesters demanded that they roll back their prices.* [N] *There was a roll-back in car prices, but people still did not buy them.*

ROLL ▸ BY

roll by **1.** to pass by, rotating, as a wheel or a ball; to move past, rolling on wheels. □ *The wheel of a car rolled by, all by itself. It must have come off a car somewhere down the road.* □ *The traffic rolled by relentlessly.* **2.** to move past, as if rolling. □ *The years rolled by, and soon the two people were old and gray.* □ *The clouds were rolling by, spreading patterns of light and dark across the land.*

ROLL ▸ DOWN

roll down to move downward, rotating, as a wheel or a ball, or to move downward on wheels. □ *I pushed the wagon up the driveway, and it rolled down again.* □ *Don't place the cart at the top of the hill. It will roll down.*

roll down something to move downward, along something, rotating, as a wheel or a ball, or moving downward on wheels. □ *The ball rolled down the hall to the end.* □ *The cart went rolling down the hill all by itself.*

roll something down **1.** to move something down, making it rotate like a wheel or a ball, or moving it on wheels. □ *Don't carry the ball down; roll it down!* [T] *I rolled down the ball as you asked.* **2.** to crank down something, such as a car window. □ *Please roll the window down and get some air in this car.* [T] *Please roll down the car window.*

roll something down something to cause something to move down along something, rotating it like a wheel or a ball. □ *Claire rolled the bowling ball down the alley for a strike.* □ *Roll the barrel down the ramp carefully. It is heavy.*

ROLL ▸ IN

See also under *ROLL ▸ IN(TO).*

roll in something **1.** to rotate about in something. □ *What is that dog rolling in?* □ *We had fun rolling in the leaves.* **2.** to have lots of something, such as money—enough to roll in. □ *She is just rolling in cash.* □ *Mary is rolling in money because she won the lottery.*

roll in the aisles to fall into and rock about in the aisles with laughter. (Figurative.) □ *The audience rolled in the aisles when the comedian told her best jokes.* □ *We were rolling in the aisles, laughing at the movie.*

roll someone or something (up) in something to turn or spin someone or something so as to contain someone or something in something. □ *Roll this painting up in a sheet of heavy wrapping paper.* □ *They rolled Cleopatra in a rug.* □ *They rolled the burning man up in a blanket to put out the flames.*

roll something in to bring something in by rotating it like a wheel or a ball or by moving it on wheels. □ *She put the table on its edge and rolled it in. Then she went out and got the chairs before the rain started.* □ *Jane rolled the table in.* [T] *The waiters rolled in the table with the wedding cake on it.*

roll something in something to turn something over and over in something, as if to coat the thing being rolled. □ *Tony rolled each of the meatballs in flour and popped them into the hot oil.* □ *Roll each of these cookies in powdered sugar.*

ROLL ▸ IN(TO)

roll in(to some place) to arrive at a place; to come into some place. (Figurative.) ☐ *The two cars rolled into the parking lot at about the same time.* ☐ *What time did they roll in?*

ROLL ▸ OFF

roll off (someone or something) to flow or fall off someone or something. (Both literal and figurative.) ☐ *The ball rolled off the shelf and bounced across the room.* ☐ *The ball rolled off and struck the lampshade.* ☐ *The insults rolled off Walter like water off a duck's back.*

roll something off ((of) someone or something) to cause something to roll away, off someone or something. (The *of*-phrase is paraphrased with a *from*-phrase when the particle is transposed. See the 🄵 example. The *of* is colloquial.) ☐ *The other workers quickly rolled the wheel off of the injured man.* 🅃 *Please roll off the wheel quickly!* ☐ *We had to roll the heavy stone off the neighbor's lawn.*

ROLL ▸ ON

roll on **1.** [for something] to continue rolling. ☐ *The ball rolled on and on.* ☐ *The cart came rolling down the hill and rolled on for a few yards at the bottom.* **2.** [for something] to be applied by rolling. ☐ *This kind of deodorant just rolls on.* ☐ *She rolled on too much paint and it dripped from the ceiling.* **3.** to move on slowly and evenly. (Figurative.) ☐ *The years rolled on, one by one.* ☐ *As the hours rolled on, I learned just how bored I could get without going to sleep.*

ROLL ▸ ON(TO)

roll something on(to something) to apply something or a coat of a substance by rolling something saturated with the substance on the thing to be coated. ☐ *You should roll another coat of paint onto this wall over here.* 🅃 *Roll on another coat.* ☐ *Okay, I'll roll it on.*

ROLL ▸ OUT

roll out the red carpet (for someone) to unwind a roll of red carpet for someone important; to give someone a royal treatment. (Can be either figurative or literal.) ☐ *The city council voted to roll out the red carpet for the visit of the crown prince.* ☐ *The citizens of the small community enjoyed rolling out the red carpet.*

roll something out **1.** to bring or take something out by rolling it; to push something out on wheels. ☐ *Jane rolled her bike out to show it off.* 🅃 *Alice rolled out her bicycle for us to see.* **2.** to flatten something by rolling it. ☐ *You should roll the pastry out first.* 🅃 *They rolled out the steel in a huge mill.*

ROLL ▸ OVER

roll over to turn over; to rotate once. ☐ *The old man rolled over and started snoring again.* ☐ *Please roll over and give me some more space in the bed.*

roll over something [for something that rolls] to pass over something. (See also *roll something over*.) ☐ *The wheelbarrow rolled over the hose, making the water squirt off and on.* ☐ *After all the traffic had rolled over Timmy's ball, there was very little left to it.*

roll someone or something over to turn someone or something over. ☐ *Bobby rolled Billy over and began tickling him ruthlessly in the tummy.* ☐ *Mary rolled the stone over, hoping to find a snake underneath.*

roll something over to renew a financial instrument as it expires. (See also *roll over something*.) ☐ *Do you plan to roll this certificate of deposit over?* 🅃 *Are you going to roll over your certificates of deposit?* ☐ *Should I do a rollover with my certificates of deposit?*

ROLL ▸ TO

roll something to someone or something to send something revolving toward someone or something or moving toward someone or something on wheels. ☐ *I rolled the ball to the baby, who just sat and looked at it.* ☐ *The blow with the mallet rolled the croquet ball to the wicket.* ☐ *Sally rolled the toy truck to the baby.*

ROLL ▸ UP

roll one's sleeves up **1.** to twist one's sleeves upward, exposing the arms. ☐ *He rolled his sleeves up and began to wash the dishes.* 🅃 *Don rolled up his* *sleeves so he would be cooler.* **2.** to prepare to get to work. (Literal or figurative.) □ *Let's roll our sleeves up and get this job done!* 🅃 *Jane rolled up her sleeves and got to work.*

roll (oneself) up in something to spin or swivel oneself so as to be contained in a coil of something. □ *Roll yourself up in some cloth and go to the costume party as a mummy.* □ *The caterpillar rolled up in a leaf.* □ *Sam rolled himself up in the carpet, trying to hide from Maggie.*

roll someone or something (up) in something See under *ROLL ► IN.*

roll something up to coil or rotate something into a coil or roll of something. □ *I rolled the poster up and put it back in its mailing tube.* 🅃 *I have to roll up this paper.*

roll something up into something **1.** to include something into something that is being rotated into a coil. □ *I guess I accidentally rolled the letter up into the poster that was lying on my desk.* 🅃 *I rolled up the letter into the poster.* **2.** to make something into a shape by rolling it. □ *He rolled the gum up into a ball and tossed it away.* 🅃 *Jane rolled up the dough into a ball.*

ROLL ► WITH

roll with the punches to absorb the force of a blow, as in boxing. (Usually figurative.) □ *You have to learn to roll with the punches. Accept what is dealt to you.* □ *Paul could never roll with the punches. He always had to get even.*

ROMP ► AROUND

romp around to run and bounce around playfully. □ *The horses were in the meadow, romping around in the crisp autumn air.* □ *The children need to get out and romp around.*

ROMP ► ON

romp on someone AND **romp all over someone** **1.** to scold someone. □ *The teacher romped on the students for their behavior.* □ *He romped all over all of them.* **2.** to beat or win over, as in a sports contest. □ *Our team romped on our opponents and beat them 10 to 1.* □ *We romped all over them.*

ROMP ► OVER

romp (all) over someone See the previous entry.

ROMP ► THROUGH

romp through something to run through something fast and playfully. □ *The conductor romped through the slow movement of the symphony as if it were a march.* □ *The cast romped through the last act, knowing that the play would be closed that very night.*

ROOF ► OVER

roof something over to build a roof over something; to provide something with a roof. □ *After the destructive storm they had to roof the shed over so that the cow would have some shelter.* 🅃 *We will roof over the patio and turn the area into a porch.*

ROOM ► TOGETHER

room together [for two or more people] to share a room, as in a college dormitory. □ *Sarah and I roomed together in college.* □ *We don't want to room together anymore.*

ROOM ► WITH

room with someone to share a room with someone. □ *I need someone to room with me next year.* □ *No one wants to room with Kelly.*

ROOT ► AROUND

root around (for something) to dig or shuffle in or through something, looking for something. □ *Alice rooted around in her desk drawer for a pen.* □ *I'll root around here and see if I can find it.* □ *The pigs rooted around, looking for something to eat.* □ *I opened the drawer and began to root around to see if I could find a screwdriver.*

ROOT ► FOR

root for someone or something to cheer for someone or something. □ *They were all rooting for the quarterback.* □ *The students rooted loudly for their team.*

ROOT ▸ IN

root something in something to start a plant growing roots in something. □ *I tried to root the plants in sand, but they died.* □ *You have to root this kind of tree in very rich soil.*

ROOT ▸ OUT

root someone or something out (of something) to seek and remove someone or something from something or some place; to seek to discover or bring something to light. (The *of*-phrase is paraphrased with a *from*-phrase when the particle is transposed. See the Ⓕ example.) □ *The committee wanted to root all the lazy people out of the club.* Ⓣ *The manager rooted out all the deadwood.* Ⓣ *We rooted out all the problem files and gave them to Walter to fix.* Ⓣ *We spent many hours rooting out the cause of the problem.* Ⓕ *The manager rooted out all the deadwood from the office staff.*

ROOT ▸ TO

See *be rooted to something* under *BE ▸ TO.*

ROOT ▸ UP

root something up [for a pig] to find something in the ground by digging with its nose. □ *The pigs will root your plants up if they get out of their pen.* Ⓣ *The pigs will root up your plants if they get out of their pen.*

ROPE ▸ IN(TO)

rope someone in(to something) to persuade or trick someone into doing something. □ *You can't rope me into doing it. I'm wise to your tricks.* Ⓣ *The con artists roped in the unsuspecting tourist.* □ *They tried to rope me in.*

ROPE ▸ OFF

rope something off to isolate something with a rope barrier. □ *The police roped the scene of the accident off.* Ⓣ *The police roped off the scene of the accident.* Ⓐ *Please do not go into the roped-off area.*

ROPE ▸ TOGETHER

rope something together to tie or bind up a thing or things with rope. □ *Rope this carton together and put it in the trunk of the car.* Ⓣ *Rope together these two packages and take them to the truck.*

ROPE ▸ UP

rope someone or something up to tie someone or some creature up with a rope. □ *Rope this guy up tight so he won't get away.* Ⓣ *The sheriff roped up the bandit.* Ⓣ *The cowboy roped up the calf in a few seconds.*

ROT ▸ AWAY

rot away to decompose; to decompose and fall away. □ *The fallen trees rotted away and surrendered their nutrients to the soil.* □ *As the wood rotted away, it became rich humus.*

ROT ▸ OFF

rot off to decompose and fall off. □ *If you don't clean your smelly feet, they'll rot off!* □ *A few old branches finally rotted off, but the ancient tree looked as if it would survive the wet spell.*

ROT ▸ OUT

rot out to decompose and fall out. □ *If you don't wash your teeth, they'll rot out!* □ *Some of the rafters in the shed rotted out, but we replaced them easily.*

ROTATE ▸ ON

rotate on something to spin on something; to pivot on something. □ *This wheel rotates on this little red jewel on the main frame of the watch.* □ *The record rotates on this device, which is called a turntable.*

ROUGH ▸ IN

rough something in to construct or draw something initially, temporarily, or crudely. □ *The carpenter roughed the doorways in without consulting the plans.* Ⓣ *The carpenter roughed in the doorways without consulting the plans.*

ROUGH ▸ OUT

rough something out to make a rough sketch of something. □ *I will rough it out and have one of the staff artists attend to the details.* Ⓣ *Jane roughed out a picture of the proposed building.*

ROUGH ▸ UP

rough someone up to treat someone roughly. □ *Max wanted to rough Lefty* *up a bit, but the boss said no.* 🅃 *Lefty roughed up Max.*

rough something up to scrape or rub something in a way that makes it rough. □ *All you have to do is rough the ground up, sow the seeds, and then water them.* 🅃 *Rough up the surface a little before you paint it.*

ROUND ▸ DOWN

round down to something to discard a fractional part of a number. □ *You should round down to whole numbers.* □ *Round down to the next number if the sum is less than half.*

round something down to reduce a fractional part of a number to the next lowest whole number. □ *You can round this figure down if you want. It won't affect the total all that much.* 🅃 *Please round down all figures having fractions less than one-half.*

ROUND ▸ OFF

round something off to change a fractional part of a number to the closest whole number. □ *Please round all your figures off.* 🅃 *Round off everything.* 🄰 *Change this to a rounded-off figure and add everything up again.*

round something off (with something) to finish something with something; to complement something with something. □ *We rounded the meal off with a sinful dessert.* 🅃 *We rounded off the meal with a sinful dessert.*

ROUND ▸ OUT

round something out to complete or enhance something. □ *We will round the evening out with dessert at a nice restaurant.* 🅃 *They rounded out the meal with dessert.* 🅃 *That's a fine way to round out a meal.*

ROUND ▸ UP

round someone or something up to locate and gather someone or something. □ *Please round the suspects up for questioning.* 🅃 *The police rounded up the usual suspects.* □ *They failed to round Max and Lefty up, however.* 🅃 *The cowboys rounded up all the cattle for market.* □ *It takes many reporters to round the news up for television.* 🄽 *The new roundup is at ten this evening.* 🄽 *The cattle roundup was delayed by the rains.*

ROUSE ▸ FROM

rouse someone from something to awaken someone from something; to cause someone to come out of something. □ *I roused Tom from his nap and sent him on his way.* □ *We could not rouse her from her deep sleep.*

ROUSE ▸ OUT

rouse someone out of something to awaken someone out of a state, such as sleep. □ *It was almost impossible to rouse George out of his sleep.* □ *They could not rouse us out of our drowsy state.*

ROUSE ▸ TO

rouse someone to something to stir someone to something. □ *I will rouse the workers to action. They will work or find other jobs.* □ *The speech by the president roused the citizens to action.* □ *The absence of any bread threatened to rouse the populace to rebellion.* □ *We were roused to anger by the news reports.*

ROUST ▸ OUT

roust someone out (of something) to force someone out of something. □ *Bob's brother rousted him out of bed just in time for the school bus.* □ *Bill went up to Bob's bed and rousted him out.*

ROUT ▸ OUT

rout someone or something out (of some place) to vanquish someone or something from some place. (The *of*-phrase is paraphrased with a *from*-phrase when the particle is transposed. See the 🄵 example.) □ *The soldiers routed the snipers out of the deserted buildings.* 🅃 *They routed out the snipers.* 🄵 *They routed out the snipers from the buildings.* □ *After a lot of gunfire, they routed Harry out.*

ROUTE ▸ AROUND

route someone or something around something to send someone or something on a path that avoids something. (*Someone* includes *oneself*.) □ *The tra-*

vel agent routed us around the congestion of the big city. □ *Due to the storm, they routed the trains around the fallen bridge.* □ *The pilot routed himself around the storm.*

ROUTE ▸ TO

route something to someone to send something along a particular path to someone. □ *Try to route this to Walter, who is on a ship at sea. I'll get the name of the ship for you.* □ *I will route a copy of the invoice to you.*

ROW ▸ OUT

row (someone or something) out to something to carry someone or something in a rowboat from the shore out to something. (*Someone* includes *oneself.*) □ *Will you row me out to the island?* 🅃 *I rowed out all the visitors to the little island.* □ *Mary rowed out to the little island.* □ *Do I have to row myself out to the island?*

RUB ▸ AGAINST

rub something against someone or something to scrape or chafe something against someone or something repeatedly. □ *The cat kept rubbing its tail against me.* □ *The cat kept rubbing its tail against my leg.*

rub (up) against someone or something to bump or scrape against someone or something. □ *The cat rubbed up against me and seemed friendly.* □ *The side of the car rubbed against the fence.*

RUB ▸ AT

rub (away) at something to chafe or scrape something, repeatedly. □ *The side of his shoe rubbed away at the side of his desk until the paint wore off.* □ *Don't rub at your sore. It will get worse.*

RUB ▸ AWAY

See the previous entry.

rub something away to remove something by chafing or rubbing. □ *See if you can rub some of the dirt away.* 🅃 *Rub away the dirt if you can.*

RUB ▸ DOWN

rub someone or something down to stroke or smooth someone or some creature, for muscular well-being. □ *Sam rubbed his horse down after his ride.* 🅃 *He rubbed down his horse.* □ *The trainer rubbed Sam down.* 🄽 *Sam got a good rubdown.*

RUB ▸ IN(TO)

rub something in(to something) to cause something to penetrate a surface by rubbing it against the surface. □ *Rub this lotion into your muscles. It will stop the aching.* 🅃 *Try rubbing in this lotion.* □ *Please rub it in.*

RUB ▸ OFF

rub off ((of) something) [for something] to become detached from something because of incidental rubbing or scraping. (The *of* is colloquial.) □ *The label rubbed off this can. What do you think it is?* □ *I can't tell what it is. The label rubbed off.*

rub off on(to) someone [for a trait] to transfer from one person to another. □ *I hope that your good humor rubs off on our children.* □ *I wish it would rub off on Mary.*

rub off on(to) someone or something [for something, such as a coating] to become transferred to someone or something through the contact of rubbing. □ *Look what rubbed off on me!* □ *The wet paint rubbed off onto my pants leg.*

rub something off ((of) something) to remove something from something by rubbing. (The *of*-phrase is paraphrased with a *from*-phrase when the particle is transposed. See the 🄵 example. The *of* is colloquial.) □ *The butler rubbed the tarnish off the pitcher.* 🅃 *The butler rubbed off the dark tarnish.* 🄵 *He rubbed off the dark tarnish from the silverware.* □ *Yes, please rub that stuff off.*

RUB ▸ ON(TO)

rub something on(to something) to apply something onto the surface of something by rubbing. □ *Alice rubbed suntan lotion onto her arms and legs.* 🅃 *Rub on some of this lotion.* □ *Rub it on and see how you feel.*

RUB ▸ OUT

rub someone out to kill someone. (Slang.) □ *Max threatened to rub Lefty out.* 🅃 *Max rubbed out Lefty.*

rub something out to obliterate something by rubbing. □ *See if you can rub those stains out.* 🅃 *Rub out the graffiti on the side of the car if you can.*

RUB ▸ OVER

rub something over something to cover something with something, spreading it by rubbing. □ *The chef rubbed the herbal butter over the skin of the turkey.* □ *Please rub the lotion over my back.*

RUB ▸ TOGETHER

rub something together to press two things together and chafe. □ *Sam rubbed his fingers together, indicating that he needed some money before he could continue.* □ *Mary rubbed her hands together to get them warmed up.*

RUB ▸ UP

rub something up to raise something, such as the nap of a rug, by rubbing. □ *When you scuff your feet across the floor, you rub the nap of the rug up and get the carpet dirtier than ever!* 🅃 *Don't rub up the nap.*

rub (up) against someone or something See under *RUB ▸ AGAINST.*

RUB ▸ WITH

rub elbows with someone AND **rub shoulders with someone** to come into working contact with someone whose knowledge or status is important to one. □ *Betty enjoys the job because she gets to rub elbows with the rich and famous.* □ *They enjoy rubbing elbows with working folks.* □ *Hillary likes to rub shoulders with the very rich.* □ *We rubbed shoulders with all the famous authors.*

rub someone or something with something to chafe or wipe someone or something with something. (*Someone* includes *oneself.*) □ *The mother rubbed the baby gently with a soft cloth.* □ *Todd rubbed the surface of the car with a rag to polish it.* □ *Tom rubbed himself briskly with a towel.*

RUFFLE ▸ UP

ruffle something up to raise something, such as feathers, up or outward. □ *The bird ruffled its feathers up and started to preen.* 🅃 *It ruffled up its feathers.*

RULE ▸ AGAINST

rule against someone or something to give a judgment against someone or something. □ *The judge ruled against the prosecutor.* □ *The judge ruled against my motion.* □ *I hope the board doesn't rule against my proposal.*

RULE ▸ FOR

rule for someone or something See *rule in favor of someone or something* under *RULE ▸ IN.*

RULE ▸ IN

rule in favor of someone or something AND **rule for someone or something** [for a judge or deliberating body] to award a decision to someone or something or to render a decision favoring someone or something. □ *The judge ruled for the defendant.* □ *The examining board ruled in favor of dismissing George.*

RULE ▸ ON

rule on something to give a decision or judgment about something. □ *How long will it be before the court rules on your petition?* □ *The boss will rule on your request tomorrow.*

RULE ▸ OUT

rule someone or something out to eliminate someone or something from consideration. (*Someone* includes *oneself.*) □ *I can rule Tom out as a suspect. He was in Denver.* 🅃 *Don't rule out Tom.* □ *You can rule this one out.* □ *I'll have to rule myself out. I can't run for office.*

RULE ▸ OVER

rule over someone or something to serve as the boss or chief over someone or something. □ *I guess you could say that the boss rules over me.* □ *The president of a democracy doesn't really rule over the country.*

RUMINATE ▸ ABOUT

ruminate about something to ponder and think about something. ☐ *He sat, ruminating about the events of the day, humming and eating peanuts.* ☐ *I need some more time to ruminate about this matter.*

RUMINATE ▸ ON

ruminate on something to occupy one's thinking with a particular topic. ☐ *Let me ruminate on this a little bit.* ☐ *She ruminated on his request for a few days and sent him a reply.*

RUMMAGE ▸ AROUND

rummage around (somewhere) (for something) to toss things about while looking for something somewhere. ☐ *Alice rummaged around in the drawer for a candy bar she had been saving.* ☐ *After she rummaged around for the candy bar, she found it.* ☐ *She rummaged around in the old trunk.*

RUMMAGE ▸ THROUGH

rummage through something to toss things about while searching through something. ☐ *I rummaged through my top drawer, looking for any two socks that matched.* ☐ *Mary spent some time rummaging through the toolbox before she found what she was looking for.*

RUMPLE ▸ UP

rumple someone or something up to bring disorder to someone['s clothing] or something. (*Someone* includes *oneself*.) ☐ *One of the little boys knocked another boy down and rumpled him up.* 🅃 *He rumpled up Dan's shirt.* 🄰 *The bird shook itself and smoothed its rumpled-up feathers.* ☐ *I have to keep from rumpling myself up before the party.*

RUN ▸ ACROSS

run across someone or something to discover someone or something by accident. (See also the following entry.) ☐ *I ran across Ted Walters the other day.* ☐ *Guess what I ran across today.*

run across something to cross something, running. ☐ *The joggers all ran across the bridge together.* ☐ *The mice ran across the floor, not knowing that a cat was watching them.*

RUN ▸ AFTER

run after someone or something to chase someone or something. ☐ *The cops ran after the mugger, but he got away.* ☐ *The dogs ran after the truck.*

RUN ▸ AGAINST

run against someone to compete against someone for elective office. ☐ *Eisenhower ran against Adlai Stevenson in 1952.* ☐ *Not many people run against an incumbent.*

run against someone or something **1.** to run into and be stopped by someone or something. ☐ *The little car ran against my uncle, who was napping on the floor by the chair.* ☐ *I ran against the wall and fell down.* **2.** to race against someone or something on foot. ☐ *I will run against Sarah in the 100-yard dash Saturday.* ☐ *I can't run against a horse! I'm fast, but not that fast!*

run one's head against a brick wall to come up against an insurmountable obstacle. ☐ *There is no point in running your head against a brick wall. If you can't succeed in this case, don't even try.* ☐ *I have been running my head against a brick wall about this problem long enough.*

RUN ▸ AGROUND

run aground (on something) [for a ship] to ram its hull into something beneath the water and get stuck. ☐ *The ship ran aground on a reef and had to wait for high tide to get free.* ☐ *I was afraid we would run aground in the storm.*

RUN ▸ ALONG

run along to leave. ☐ *Please run along and leave me alone.* ☐ *I have to run along now. Good-bye.*

RUN ▸ AROUND

run around **1.** to run here and there. ☐ *Why are you running around? Sit down and be quiet.* ☐ *Please stop running around. You are making me nervous.* **2.** to go here and there, as if doing errands. ☐ *I've been running around all day, shopping for the party tonight.* ☐ *I am so tired of running around, carting children to various places.*

run around after someone or something to chase after someone or something; to seek after someone or something. □ *Where have you been? I've run around after you all over town!* □ *I have been running around after the right-sized shoes all morning.*

run around like a chicken with its head cut off to go about aimlessly and futilely. (A cliché.) □ *Calm down! You are running around like a chicken with its head cut off!* □ *I have been running around like a chicken with its head cut off, unable to get organized.*

run around someone to run in circles around someone. □ *The children ran around the ice cream man, trying to distract him.* □ *The dogs ran around their master, eager for their food.*

run around someone or something to avoid someone or something while running. □ *I ran around the boys who were standing there.* □ *We had to run around the lamppost to avoid hitting it.*

run around with someone to go places with someone; to socialize with someone. □ *I used to run around with Alice and Jill before we all graduated.* □ *Carl and Jane used to run around with each other.*

run circles around someone AND **run rings around someone** to outdo someone; to do much better than someone. (Not necessarily in racing.) □ *Jane is much better than Ned. She runs circles around him.* □ *I can run rings around Ned!*

run rings around someone See the previous entry.

RUN ▸ AS

run as something to run for office in a certain party. □ *Do you suppose I can run as an independent?* □ *Fred ran as a Democrat and won a seat in the legislature.*

RUN ▸ AT

run at someone or something to run toward someone or something; to charge someone or something. □ *The bull started to run at us, but changed its mind—thank heavens.* □ *The huge crocodile ran at the goat, but the goat leapt away.*

RUN ▸ AWAY

run away (from someone or something) to flee someone or something. □ *Please don't run away from me. I mean you no harm.* □ *Our dog ran away from the lawn mower.* Ⓐ *The runaway train finally crashed.* Ⓝ *The child was a runaway and very frightened.*

run away with someone **1.** to flee in the company of someone. □ *Frank arrived on the scene, saw what had happened, and ran away with the other boys.* □ *Tom ran away with Bill to a place where they could hide.* **2.** [for two people] to elope. □ *Jill ran away with Jack, much to her father's relief.* □ *Jill and Jack ran away with each other.*

run away with something **1.** to flee with something in one's possession. □ *The crook ran away with the watch.* □ *Someone ran away with that lady's purse.* **2.** to capture or steal a performance by being the best performer. (Idiomatic.) □ *Henry ran away with the show, and everyone loved him.* □ *The dog ran away with the whole performance.*

RUN ▸ BACK

run back to come back, running. □ *She ran to the barn and then ran back.* □ *Tom ran back, very much afraid.*

run back over something to review something. □ *Would you please run back over that last part again?* □ *Let me run back over the hard part for you.*

run back to someone or something to return to someone or something in a hurry. □ *The child ran back to her mother.* □ *We all ran back to the house.*

run something back to wind something back to the beginning. □ *Run the tape back and listen to it again.* Ⓣ *Run back the tape and listen again.*

RUN ▸ BEHIND

run behind to be late; to run late. □ *We are running behind. You had better hurry.* □ *Things are running behind, and we will not finish on time.*

run behind someone or something to travel along behind someone or something, running. □ *I will run behind you in the race.* □ *Mary ran behind the bicycle until she could not run anymore.*

RUN ▸ BETWEEN

run between something and something **1.** to travel between someone or something, running. □ *I spent all afternoon running between my office and the conference room.* □ *We ran between the two quarreling people all day long, trying to settle the argument.* **2.** to pass between someone or something, running. □ *The child ran between the two ladies, giving them quite a start.* □ *Please don't run between the bushes. You will make a path there.*

RUN ▸ BY

run something by (someone) (again) to explain something to someone again; to say something to someone again. (Colloquial.) □ *I didn't hear you. Please run that by me again.* □ *Please run it by so we can all hear it.*

RUN ▸ DOWN

run down **1.** to come down, running; to go down, running. □ *I need to talk to you down here. Can you run down?* □ *I will run down and talk to you.* **2.** [for something] to lose power and stop working. □ *The clock ran down because no one was there to wind it.* □ *The toy ran down and wouldn't go again until it had been wound.* **3.** to become worn or dilapidated. □ *The property was allowed to run down and it took a lot of money to fix it up.* □ *The old neighborhood has certainly run down since we moved away.* Ⓐ *I won't live in a run-down house like that!*

run down to someone or something to come or go down to someone or something, rapidly. □ *Sally ran down the slope to Bob, who stood waiting for her with outstretched arms.* □ *I ran down to the well to get some water for Ed, who had the hiccups.*

run down to something to travel to a place. (By running or any other means. Idiomatic.) □ *I have to run down to the store and get some bread.* □ *I want to run down to the bank, but my car is out of gas.* □ *Rachel asked Chuck to get on his bike and run down to the corner for a paper.*

run someone or something down **1.** to criticize or deride someone or something. (*Someone* includes *oneself*.) □ *Please stop running me down all the time. I can't be that bad!* Ⓣ *You run down everybody!* □ *All the critics ran the play down.* □ *Poor Sally is always running herself down.* **2.** to collide with and knock down someone or something. □ *The driver ran three pedestrians down.* Ⓣ *Mary ran down a stop sign.* **3.** to hunt for and locate someone or something. □ *Could you run some information down for me?* Ⓣ *I was finally able to run down my old friend.*

run something down to use something having batteries, a motor, or an engine until it has no more power and it stops. □ *Who ran my electric toothbrush down?* Ⓣ *Someone ran down my batteries.*

RUN ▸ FOR

run for it to escape by running. (See also *swim for it* under *SWIM ▸ FOR*.) □ *The dogs were coming after me fast. There was nothing I could do but run for it.* □ *I ran for it when I saw the farmer coming.*

run for one's life to run to escape a deadly danger; to run as fast as if one's life were at stake. □ *Run for your life! The lion is loose.* □ *We told them to run for their lives because the dam had broken.*

run for something to travel quickly by running to a place of safety. □ *The picnickers ran for the shelter when the rain started to fall.* □ *Tom and Jane ran for the house as soon as they heard your call.*

run for something to try to be elected to a particular office. □ *Who's going to run for president?* □ *I am running for mayor.*

RUN ▸ FROM

run from someone or something to flee someone or something, usually on foot. ☐ *She ran from the mugger who had accosted her.* ☐ *Mary ran from the dog and jumped over a fence to safety.*

run from something to something to travel on foot from one thing or place to another, running. ☐ *Do you think you can run from the bank downtown to the post office on Maple Street?* ☐ *I ran from door to door, telling people what had happened.*

RUN ▸ IN

See also under *RUN ▸ IN(TO).*

run in circles **1.** to run in a circular path. ☐ *The horses ran in circles around the corral for their daily exercise.* ☐ *The children ran in circles around the tree.* **2.** to waste one's time in aimless activity. ☐ *Stop running in circles and try to organize yourself so that you are more productive.* ☐ *I have been running in circles over this matter for days.*

run in something to compete in something, such as a race or an election. ☐ *I will run in the one-hundred-yard dash.* ☐ *I will not run in a race this time.* ☐ *Who will run in this year's election?*

run in the family [for a trait] to be genetic or to be typical of a family. ☐ *Red hair runs in the family.* ☐ *Her strange personality runs in the family.*

run someone in to arrest one and take one to the police station. ☐ *The cop ran George in so they could question him extensively.* 🆃 *They ran in George to protect him from the rioters.*

run something in to break in a new machine or electronic device. (See also *break something in* under *BREAK ▸ IN.*) ☐ *I have to run this press in slowly.* 🆃 *Have you run in your car yet?*

run something in for something to bring or drive something quickly into a place for some purpose. ☐ *I have to run my car in for an oil change.* ☐ *I will run the truck in for the mechanic to take a look at it.*

RUN ▸ INTO

run into a stone wall to be stopped by an insurmountable barrier. (Usually figurative.) ☐ *Progress on the project has run into a stone wall.* ☐ *I ran into a stone wall on the task you set me to.*

run into someone or something **1.** to bump into someone or something. ☐ *I didn't mean to run into you. I'm sorry.* ☐ *Mary ran into the fence and scraped her elbow.* **2.** to discover someone or something by accident. ☐ *Guess whom I ran into yesterday!* ☐ *I ran into an interesting problem the other day.*

run something in(to something) to guide or route something, such as a wire or a pipe, into something or a place. ☐ *The worker ran the circuit into each room.* ☐ *He ran the circuit in as instructed.* 🆃 *He ran in the circuit as specified.*

run something into something to drive or steer something into something else. ☐ *Bobby ran his bicycle into the wall, bending the front wheel.* ☐ *Please don't run your car into the wall!*

run something into the ground to overdo something; to carry something too far or to great extremes. (Figurative.) ☐ *That joke isn't funny anymore. You're running it into the ground.* ☐ *There is no point in running it into the ground. Just forget it!*

RUN ▸ IN(TO)

run in(to something) **1.** [for a liquid] to flow into something or a place. ☐ *The water is running into the basement!* ☐ *It's running in very fast.* **2.** to enter something or a place on foot, running. ☐ *The boys ran into the room and out again.* ☐ *They ran in and knocked over a lamp.* **3.** to stop by a place for a quick visit or to make a purchase quickly. ☐ *I have to run in the drugstore for a minute.* ☐ *I ran into the store for some bread.* ☐ *I want to visit Mrs. Potter. I can't stay long. I can only run in for a minute.* ☐ *All right. If you just run in.*

run someone or something in(to something) to take or drive someone or something into something or some place. (*Someone* includes *oneself.*) ☐ *Let me run you into the city this morning. I need the car today.* 🆃 *Do you want to go to town? I have to run in George and you can come along.* ☐ *As* *soon as I run George in, I'll talk to you.* ☐ *Bill ran himself into town to get the medicine.*

RUN ▸ OF

run a risk of something AND **run the risk of something** to take a chance that something will happen. ☐ *If you don't get your shots, you run a risk of contracting a serious disease.* ☐ *You run the risk of getting malaria in the Amazon basin.*

run afoul of someone or something to infringe upon someone or something; to get in trouble with someone or something. ☐ *Be careful that you don't run afoul of the manager.* ☐ *Mary ran afoul of one of the company rules and was reprimanded.*

run short of something to use up all of something and not have enough. ☐ *I hope I don't run short of something after the grocery store closes.* ☐ *We ran short of eggs while we were baking cookies.*

RUN ▸ OFF

run off 1. to flee. ☐ *The children rang our doorbell and then ran off.* ☐ *They ran off as fast as they could.* **2.** to have diarrhea. ☐ *He said he was running off all night.* ☐ *One of the children was running off and had to stay home from school.* **3.** [for a fluid] to drain away from a flat area. ☐ *By noon, all the rainwater had run off the playground.* 🄽 *The runoff from the driveway leaked into the basement.*

run off at the mouth to speak far more than is necessary. (Colloquial. To have "diarrhea of the mouth." Use with discretion.) ☐ *You'll have to excuse me. I always run off at the mouth.* ☐ *Fred runs off at the mouth all the time.*

run off in all directions [for people] to set out to do something or go somewhere in an aimless and disorganized fashion. (Can also apply to one person. See also *ride off in all directions* under *RIDE ▸ OFF.*) ☐ *The people in the marketing department need some organization. They are always running off in all directions.* ☐ *Stop running off in all directions and focus your energy.*

run off something to drive or travel off something, such as rails, tracks, a road, etc. ☐ *The train ran off its rails and piled up in a cornfield.* ☐ *We almost ran off the road during the storm.*

run off with someone or something 1. to take someone or something away, possibly running. ☐ *Fred ran off with Ken. They'll be back in a minute.* ☐ *Who ran off with my dictionary?* **2.** to capture and take away someone or something; to steal someone or something. ☐ *The kidnappers ran off with little Valerie.* ☐ *The kids ran off with a whole box of candy and the storekeeper is going to press charges.*

run one's feet off to run very hard and fast. (Figurative.) ☐ *I ran my feet off and I'm really tired now that the race is over.* ☐ *I almost ran my feet off getting over here to see you!*

run someone or something off to drive someone or something away from something. ☐ *The defenders ran the attackers off time after time.* 🅃 *We had to run off the attackers.* ☐ *The police came and ran off the raccoons.*

run someone or something off (of) something to drive someone or something off something. (The *of*-phrase is paraphrased with a *from*-phrase when the particle is transposed. See the 🄵 example. The *of* is colloquial.) ☐ *Go out and run those dogs off the lawn.* 🅃 *Go run off the dogs from the lawn.* ☐ *Go run those kids off of the street.*

run something off 1. to duplicate something, using a mechanical duplicating machine. ☐ *If the master copy is ready, I will run some other copies off.* 🅃 *I'll run off some more copies.* **2.** to get rid of something, such as fat or energy, by running. ☐ *The little boys are very excited. Send them outside to run it off.* 🅃 *They need to run off their energy.*

RUN ▸ ON

run low on something to have only a small amount of something left. ☐ *I'm running low on gas and I have to stop at the first chance.* ☐ *We are running low* *on milk and we had better get some at the store.*

run on 1. to continue running. ☐ *I wanted to stop her and ask her something, but she just ran on.* ☐ *The joggers had a chance to stop and rest, but they just ran on.* **2.** to continue on for a long time. ☐ *The lecture ran on and bored everyone to tears.* ☐ *How long is this symphony likely to run on?*

run on all cylinders 1. [for an engine] to run well and smoothly. ☐ *This car is now running on all cylinders, thanks to the tune-up.* ☐ *You can hear if an engine is not running on all cylinders.* **2.** to function well or energetically. (Figurative.) ☐ *Our department seems to be running on all cylinders. Congratulations.* ☐ *I am back at my desk after my illness—running on all cylinders.*

RUN ▸ ONTO

run something onto something to drive or guide something onto the surface of something. ☐ *He ran the car onto the grass and washed it.* ☐ *Please run your bicycle onto the porch and I will try to fix it for you.*

RUN ▸ OUT

run out at someone or something to come out of a place and charge or attack someone or something. ☐ *The badger ran out at us and then went back to its den.* ☐ *The dogs ran out at the speeding car.*

run out of gas 1. to use up the last of one's gasoline and stop. ☐ *I have to get fuel before I run out of gas.* ☐ *We are just about to run out of gas.* **2.** to falter and fail. (Figurative.) ☐ *The whole project ran out of gas when Dave left the company.* ☐ *Our enthusiasm for this project is about to run out of gas.*

run out of some place to leave a place quickly, on foot; to flee a place. ☐ *He ran out of the room as fast as he could.* ☐ *We ran out of the building as soon as we felt the first signs of the earthquake.*

run out (of something) 1. to leave something or a place, running. ☐ *Everyone ran out of the theater when they smelled smoke.* ☐ *They ran out screaming.* **2.** to use all of something and have none left. ☐ *I am afraid that we have run out of eggs.* ☐ *Check again. I don't think we have run out.*

run out of time to have used up most of the allotted time; to have no time left. ☐ *You have just about run out of time.* ☐ *I ran out of time before I could finish the test.*

run out on someone to depart and leave someone behind. ☐ *My date ran out on me at the restaurant, and I had to pay the bill.* ☐ *Her boyfriend ran out on her when she needed him the most.*

run someone or something out (of something) to chase someone or something out of something or some place. (The *of*-phrase is paraphrased with a *from*-phrase when the particle is transposed. See the 🄵 example.) ☐ *The old man ran the kids out of his orchard.* 🅃 *He ran out the kids.* 🄵 *He ran out the pesky kids from his garden.* ☐ *We had to run the raccoons out of our backyard. They are getting very brave.*

run something out to produce a complete mathematical computation; to produce a complete total. ☐ *Run this out and see what you get for a total.* 🅃 *Run out the totals again.*

run something out (of something) to drive or steer something out of something or some place. ☐ *The cowboys ran the cattle out of the corral.* 🅃 *They ran out the cattle.* ☐ *They ran the horses out too.*

RUN ▸ OVER

run one's eye over something to gaze at the whole of something; to glance at all of something. ☐ *She ran her eyes over the lines of the automobile and nodded her approval.* ☐ *He ran his eyes over the drawing and decided that he had to have it.*

run over 1. to come by for a quick visit. ☐ *Can you run over for a minute after work?* ☐ *I will run over for a minute as soon as I can.* **2.** to overflow. ☐ *The bathtub ran over and there was water all over the floor.* ☐ *She poured the coffee until the cup ran over.*

run over someone or something to drive, steer, or travel so as to pass over someone or something. ☐ *The bus ran over the fallen man.* ☐ *That car almost ran over my toe.*

run over (something) to exceed a limit. ☐ *The lecture ran over the allotted time.* ☐ *The students ran over the time allotted for the exam.* ☐ *I thought I had our order for food exactly right, but when the people showed up, we ran over.*

run over something with someone to review something with someone. ☐ *I would like to run over this with you one more time.* ☐ *I want to run over the proposal with Carl again.*

run over to something to go to something or some place, running or by any independent mode of transportation. ☐ *Would you run over to the store and get me some eggs?* ☐ *I have to run over to the bank to cash a check.* ☐ *Please get on your bike and run over to Mrs. Potter's for some eggs.*

run over with something to drop over for a visit, bringing something. ☐ *Do you mind if I run over with the cup of sugar I borrowed last week?* ☐ *Mary ran over with the papers you requested.*

run something over (to someone or something) to carry something to someone or something. ☐ *Would you please run this package over to Mrs. Franklin?* 🅃 *Do you know where Bill lives? Please run over this package.* ☐ *I'll run it over in just a minute.*

RUN ▸ THROUGH

run a comb through something to comb one's hair, quickly. ☐ *Run a comb through your hair after you come back in the house.* ☐ *She ran a comb through Timmy's hair, and tried to make him look presentable.*

run one's fingers through one's hair AND **run one's hand through one's hair** to comb one's hair with one's fingers. ☐ *I came in out of the wind and ran my fingers through my hair to straighten it out a bit.* ☐ *He ran his hand through his hair and tried to make himself presentable.*

run someone through something 1. to guide a person through a process. ☐ *Let me run you through the process so you will know what is happening to you.* ☐ *Can I run you through this business again?* **2.** to rehearse someone. (*Someone* includes *oneself*.) ☐ *The director ran the cast through the last act three times.* ☐ *She ran herself through the part at home between rehearsals.* 🄽 *The run-through went very well.*

run someone through (with something) to stab a person all the way through with something, such as a sword. ☐ *The knight ran the attacker through with his own sword.* ☐ *He ran him through and stole his horse.*

run something through something 1. to drive or propel something through the midst of something or a group. ☐ *The cowboys ran the cattle right through the crowd of people standing at the station.* ☐ *He ran his truck through the bushes at the end of the driveway.* **2.** to process something in a machine, procedure, deliberative body, or department. ☐ *Would you please run these clothes through the washer for me?* ☐ *I will have to run this through the board of directors.* ☐ *She ran the invoice through the accounting department.*

run through something 1. to go through a procedure or sequence; to rehearse a procedure or sequence. ☐ *I want to run through act two again before we end this rehearsal.* 🄽 *Let's give it another run-through and then go home.* **2.** to read or examine something quickly. ☐ *I ran through your report this afternoon.* ☐ *Sally ran through the list, checking off the names of the people who had already paid for tickets.* **3.** to spend or use something wastefully and rapidly. ☐ *He ran through his inheritance in two years.* ☐ *Have we run through all the peanut butter already?*

RUN ▸ TO

run someone or something to something 1. to run someone or something to some extreme extent, such as death. ☐ *The villain's idea was to run his victim to death by chasing him.* ☐ *He nearly ran* *his horse to death.* **2.** to drive someone or something to some place. □ *Could you run me to the store?* □ *Please run these clothes to the cleaners.* □ *Would you be able to run this package to the post office?*

run to seed to become unkempt, as a lawn that has gone to seed from lack of care. (See also *go to seed.*) □ *Please go mow the lawn before it runs to seed.* □ *All our furniture has run to seed.*

run to someone or something to travel quickly on foot to someone or something; to go to someone or something with some urgency. □ *Mary ran to Alice and greeted her.* □ *I ran to the door and fled.* □ *She ran to the teacher to tattle on the boys.*

RUN ► UP

run something up **1.** to raise or hoist something, such as a flag. □ *Harry ran the flag up the flagpole each morning.* 🅃 *Will you please run up the flag today?* **2.** to cause something to go higher, such as the price of stocks or commodities. □ *A rumor about higher earnings ran the price of the computer stocks up early in the afternoon.* 🅃 *They ran up the price too high.* 🄽 *Coffee has had quite a run-up in the last week.* **3.** to stitch something together quickly. □ *She's very clever. I'm sure she can run up a costume for you.* □ *The seamstress ran up a party dress in one afternoon.* **4.** to accumulate indebtedness. □ *I ran up a huge phone bill last month.* □ *Walter ran up a bar bill at the hotel that made his boss angry.*

run up against someone or something **1.** to bump into someone or something and stop, while running. □ *Betty ran up against Randy while she was jogging. She nearly knocked him over.* □ *Mary ran up against the wall and hurt her arm.* **2.** to encounter someone or something as a barrier to progress. □ *I'm afraid we have run up against a little problem here.* □ *Everything was going well until we ran up against Walter, who objected to everything.*

run up (to someone or something) to run as far as someone or something and stop; to run to the front of someone or something. □ *I ran up to the mailman and said hello to him.* □ *I ran up and said hello.*

RUN ► WITH

run with someone or something to stay in the company of someone or some group. □ *Fred was out running with Larry when they met Vernon.* □ *Let's go out and run with the other guys this morning.* □ *He runs with a bad crowd and is bound to get in trouble.*

run with something **1.** to run, showing a particular characteristic. □ *Sally runs with speed and grace.* □ *Fred runs with tremendous speed.* **2.** to take over something and handle it aggressively and independently. (Figurative.) □ *I know that Alice can handle the job. She will take it on and run with it.* □ *I hope she runs with this next project.*

RUSH ► AT

rush at someone or something to run at or charge toward someone or something. □ *The dog rushed at us and scared us to death.* □ *Mary rushed at the door, but it slammed shut before she got there.*

RUSH ► FOR

rush for something to hurry to something. □ *All the people rushed for the exits when the game was over.* □ *We rushed for the picnic tables as soon as they said that lunch was ready.*

RUSH ► INTO

rush someone into something to hurry someone into doing something. □ *We rushed Harry into taking the job.* □ *Sally has always hated that dress. Sam rushed her into buying it.*

rush something into print to print up something hastily. □ *The story was so timely that the newspaper editor rushed it into print without checking all the details.* □ *We will rush the book into print as soon as it is finished.*

RUSH ► IN(TO)

rush in(to something) **1.** to run or hurry into a thing or a place. □ *Everyone rushed into the shelter when the rain started.* □ *They all rushed in at once.* **2.**

to begin doing something without the proper preparation. □ *Don't rush into this job without thinking it through.* □ *Mary rushed in without thinking.*

rush someone or something in(to something) to lead or carry someone into something or some place hurriedly. □ *I rushed her into the hospital emergency room, and everything was soon all right.* 🅃 *The nurse rushed in the emergency medical equipment.*

RUSH ▸ OFF

rush off (from some place) to hurry away from some place. □ *I'm sorry, but I will have to rush off from this meeting before it's over.* □ *Mary had to rush off before the party was over.*

rush something off (to someone or something) to send something quickly to someone or something. □ *I will rush your order off to you immediately.* 🅃 *I need to rush off this package to Walter.*

RUSH ▸ OUT

rush out (of something) to exit in a hurry. □ *Everyone rushed out of the room at the same time.* □ *They rushed out because they smelled smoke.*

rush someone or something out (of something) to lead or guide someone or something out of something or some place hurriedly. □ *The ushers rushed everyone out of the church so they could clean the place before the next wedding.* 🅃 *They rushed out another edition of the newspaper that afternoon.* □ *We will have to rush another edition out.*

RUSH ▸ THROUGH

rush something through (something) to move something through some deliberative body in a hurry. □ *He was in a hurry so we rushed his order through the order department.* □ *He asked us to rush it through.*

rush through something to hurry to get something finished; to race through something. □ *Please don't rush through this business. Get it right.* □ *Timmy rushed through dinner so he could go out and play.*

RUSH ▸ TO

rush someone to the hospital to lead or carry someone to the hospital. □ *They had to rush her to the hospital because she had stopped breathing.* □ *We rushed Uncle Harry to the hospital after he complained of chest pains.*

rush to conclusions to try to reach a conclusion too fast, probably with insufficient evidence. □ *I hope that you don't rush to any conclusions. I can explain this.* □ *I'm afraid you are rushing to conclusions when you speak of canceling the performance.*

rush to someone or something to hurry to get to someone, something, or some event. □ *I rushed to the injured man to try to help him.* □ *We all rushed to the office to see what had happened.*

RUST ▸ AWAY

rust away to dissolve away into rust. □ *In a few years, this car will rust away if you don't take care of it.* □ *The bridge is rusting away, little by little.*

RUSTLE ▸ UP

rustle something up to manage to prepare a meal, perhaps on short notice. (Folksy.) □ *I think I can rustle something up for dinner.* 🅃 *I'll rustle up some ham and eggs.*

S

SACK ▸ OUT

sack out to go to bed; to take a nap. (Slang.) □ *It's time to sack out. I'm tired.* □ *I have to go sack out for a while.*

SACK ▸ UP

sack something up to put something into bags or sacks. □ *Please sack the groceries up and put them in the cart.* 🅃 *I will sack up your groceries.*

SACRIFICE ▸ FOR

sacrifice someone or something for someone or something to forfeit someone or something for the sake of someone or something. (*Someone* includes *oneself.*) □ *Surely you won't sacrifice your dear wife for a silly twit like Francine!* □ *Would you sacrifice your fine car for a chance to go to Europe?* □ *You don't expect me to sacrifice myself for this cause, do you?*

SACRIFICE ▸ TO

sacrifice someone or something to someone or something to make an offering of someone or something to someone or some power. □ *The high priest prepared to sacrifice the prisoner to the gods.* □ *I sacrificed a lot of money to my own pride.*

SADDLE ▸ UP

saddle something up to put a saddle on a horse or some other beast of burden. □ *Please saddle my horse up. I have to leave.* 🅃 *Would you saddle up my horse for me?*

SADDLE ▸ WITH

saddle someone with someone or something to burden someone with someone or something. (*Someone* includes *oneself.*) □ *I apologize for saddling you with my young cousin all day.* □ *I didn't mean to saddle you with my problems.* □ *I refuse to saddle myself with any of your problems.*

SAFEGUARD ▸ AGAINST

safeguard against someone or something to protect against someone or something. □ *We will try to safeguard against accidents.* □ *How can I safeguard against prowlers?* □ *Tom is threatening me, and I need to safeguard against him.*

safeguard someone or something against someone or something to protect someone or something against someone or something. (*Someone* includes *oneself.*) □ *We will take action that will safeguard you against a recurrence of the unpleasantness.* □ *I will safeguard my family against the prowler.* □ *We safeguard ourselves against violence.*

SAG ▸ AWAY

sag away (from something) to settle or droop down or away. □ *The cloth sagged away from the edge of the table.* □ *The cloth sagged away.*

SAG ▸ DOWN

sag down to droop downward. □ *The branch sagged down and nearly touched the ground.* □ *When the rain got the drapes wet, they sagged down and touched the floor.*

SAG ▸ UNDER

sag under something to droop under the burden of something. □ *The porch roof sagged under the weight of the* *snow.* ☐ *The springs of the car sagged under the weight of all the passengers.*

SAIL ▶ AGAINST

sail against something to operate a boat or ship, so as to move against the wind. ☐ *It takes skill and training to sail against the wind.* ☐ *The huge cruise ship sailed against the wind all the way to St. Thomas.*

SAIL ▶ ALONG

sail along (something) to travel on a course in a boat or plane. ☐ *The huge white ship sailed along the Amazon River slowly and peacefully.* ☐ *The boat sailed along peacefully.*

SAIL ▶ AROUND

sail around to travel around or move about in a boat or ship. ☐ *We sailed around for about an hour and then went back to the shore.* ☐ *Let's go out and sail around before dinner.*

SAIL ▶ FOR

sail for some place to depart in a boat or ship for some place. ☐ *This ship sails for Bridgetown, Barbados, at noon today.* ☐ *We will sail for home early in the morning.*

SAIL ▶ FROM

sail from some place to some place to move or travel from one place to another in a boat or ship. ☐ *We sailed from San Juan to Acapulco.* ☐ *The ship sailed from its home port to Baltimore overnight.*

SAIL ▶ INTO

sail into someone to attack someone; to chastise someone. (Figurative.) ☐ *The angry coach sailed into the players.* ☐ *Sally sailed into Timmy for breaking the window.*

sail into someone or something **1.** to crash into someone or something with a boat or ship. ☐ *The boat sailed into the dock, causing considerable damage.* ☐ *I was in my skiff when a larger boat sailed into me.* **2.** to crash into someone or something. ☐ *The missile sailed into the soldiers, injuring a few.* ☐ *The car sailed into the lamppost.*

SAIL ▶ IN(TO)

sail in(to something) **1.** to travel into something or some place in a boat or ship. ☐ *We sailed into the harbor nearly an hour late.* ☐ *We sailed in late.* **2.** to move or proceed into something or some place gracefully or without resistance. ☐ *She sailed into the room wearing a flowing gown.* ☐ *Three or four maidens sailed into the castle and the curtain came down.*

SAIL ▶ THROUGH

sail (right) through something **1.** to travel through something in a boat or ship. ☐ *The line of boats sailed right through the Grenadines in the daylight hours.* ☐ *We sailed through the narrows without a pilot.* **2.** to go through something very quickly and easily. ☐ *The kids just sailed right through the ice cream and cake. There was not a bit left.* ☐ *You have sailed through your allowance already.*

sail through to get through a procedure quickly and easily. ☐ *The proposal sailed through with flying colors.* ☐ *I hope that this matter sails through quickly.*

SAIL ▶ UNDER

sail under false colors **1.** to sail with false identification. (Pirates often sailed under the national flag of the ship they planned on attacking.) ☐ *The ship, sailing under false colors, suddenly started to pursue our ship.* ☐ *Bluebeard the pirate was known for sailing under false colors.* **2.** to function deceptively. (Figurative.) ☐ *You are not who you seem to be. You are sailing under false colors.* ☐ *Tom was sailing under false colors and finally got found out.*

SAIL ▶ UP

sail up something to travel up something in a boat or ship. ☐ *We sailed up the Amazon River in a large, seagoing ship.* ☐ *It was not possible to sail up the Mississippi as far as we wanted.*

SALT ▶ AWAY

salt something away **1.** to store and preserve a foodstuff by salting it. ☐ *The farmer's wife salted a lot of fish and* *hams away for the winter.* [T] *She salted away a lot of food.* **2.** to store something; to place something in reserve. ☐ *I need to salt some money away for my retirement.* [T] *I will salt away some money for emergencies.*

SALT ▸ DOWN

salt something down to place salt on something, such as icy roads. ☐ *I won't go out until midmorning, after they have salted the roads down.* [T] *I hope they salt down the roads soon.* [A] *Travel was easy on the salted-down roads.*

SALT ▸ WITH

salt something with something **1.** to put a variety of salt or a salt substitute onto some food. ☐ *Oscar salts his food with a salt substitute.* ☐ *Did you salt your meat with salt or something else?* **2.** to put something into something as a lure. (As with putting a bit of gold dust into a mine in order to deceive someone into buying the mine.) ☐ *The land agent salted the bank of the stream with a little gold dust and sat back waiting for a land rush to start.* ☐ *Someone salted the mine to fool the prospectors.*

SALUTE ▸ WITH

salute someone with something **1.** to greet someone with a formal hand salute. (Military.) ☐ *He failed to salute the officer with the proper salute and was reprimanded.* ☐ *David saluted the captain with the appropriate salute and passed on by.* **2.** to greet or honor someone with the firing of guns or an overflight of airplanes. (Military or government.) ☐ *The government saluted the visiting dignitary with a twenty-one gun salute.* ☐ *They saluted the president of Dosnia with a flight of acrobatic jets.*

SALVAGE ▸ FROM

salvage something from someone or something to rescue or save something from someone or something. ☐ *The baby got into the eggs, but I was able to salvage about six of them from him before they were spread all over the place.* ☐ *I salvaged a good pair of shoes from the trash.*

SAND ▸ DOWN

sand something down **1.** to make something smooth by rubbing it with sandpaper. (To act on the main body of the object, not the imperfections.) ☐ *You should sand the board down before you paint it.* [T] *Please sand down the board.* **2.** to remove bumps or imperfections on the surface of something by rubbing them with sandpaper. (To act on the imperfections, not the main body of the object.) ☐ *Sand these bumps down, will you?* [T] *Sand down these bumps, please.*

SANDWICH ▸ BETWEEN

sandwich someone or something between things or people to enclose someone or something on both sides between people or things in any combination. (*Someone* includes *oneself.*) ☐ *We had to sandwich the children between us because there were no other seats close by.* ☐ *We had to sandwich the package between Ed and the side of the bus.* ☐ *We sandwiched Ed between the package and me.* ☐ *I had to sandwich myself between two other passengers.*

SATIATE ▸ WITH

satiate someone or something with something to provide enough of something for someone or some creature. (*Someone* includes *oneself.*) ☐ *The waiters set out to satiate the guests with whatever sinful desserts they desired.* ☐ *The keeper satiated the tigress with a huge leg of beef.* ☐ *He satiated himself with the fresh fruit and took a nap.*

SATISFY ▸ BY

satisfy something by something AND **satisfy something with something** to fulfill a requirement, using a particular thing, such as a school or college course. ☐ *Can I satisfy the requirements by taking a course in art?* ☐ *Will I satisfy the requirement with this course?*

SATISFY ▸ WITH

satisfy someone or something with something to use something to please or content someone or some creature. ☐ *Do you think I can satisfy Mrs. Franklin with payment for her broken window?* ☐ *A dog biscuit will satisfy the dog until its regular feeding time.*

satisfy something with something See under *SATISFY ▶ BY.*

SATURATE ▶ WITH

saturate someone or something with something to drench someone or something thoroughly with something. (*Someone* includes *oneself.*) □ *The rain saturated them all with cooling water.* □ *It saturated the field with the moisture they needed.* □ *He saturated himself with seawater when he fell into the sea.*

SAUNTER ▶ ALONG

saunter along to walk along slowly; to ramble along. □ *Bob sauntered along, looking as if he didn't have a care in the world.* □ *I was just sauntering along, minding my own business, when all of a sudden a mugger jumped out and swiped my purse.*

SAVE ▶ FOR

save something for a rainy day to reserve something for a time of greater need. (A cliché.) □ *I can't let you have that money. I'm saving it for a rainy day!* □ *If you were saving this for a rainy day, that day has come!*

save something for someone or something to reserve something for someone or something. □ *Please save some cake for me.* □ *I am saving this cake for tomorrow.*

SAVE ▶ FROM

save someone or something from someone or something to rescue someone or something from someone or something. □ *The cop was able to save the kid from his attackers.* □ *I managed to save some old photographs from the fire.*

SAVE ▶ ON

save (something) on something to save money or some amount of money on the purchase of something. □ *I can save a lot of money on this purchase by buying it somewhere else.* □ *I am sure you can save on a new car if you shop wisely.*

SAVE ▶ TOWARD

save (something) toward something to accumulate money toward the purchase of something. □ *I am saving my money toward the purchase of a CD player.* □ *I'm saving toward a new car.*

SAVE ▶ UP

save something up (for something) to accumulate an amount of money for the purchase of something. □ *I'm saving my money up for a car.* 🅃 *Save up your money for a car.* □ *You should save it up.* 🄰 *She took all her saved-up money out of the bank and gave it to the church.*

save up (for something) to accumulate something for some purpose. □ *I can't buy a car because I am saving up for college.* □ *I don't have the money now, but I am saving up.* 🄰 *What are you going to do with all those saved-up newspapers?*

SAVOR ▶ OF

savor of something to taste like something. □ *This casserole savors of nutmeg.* □ *The meat savors of too much garlic.*

SAW ▶ DOWN

saw something down to cut something down with a saw. □ *We are going to have to saw that dead tree down before it falls on the house.* 🅃 *I'll saw down the tree.*

SAW ▶ INTO

saw into something to cut into something with a saw. □ *The carpenter sawed into the beam, and had it cut in two in no time at all.* □ *Be careful and don't saw into the table.*

SAW ▶ IN(TO)

saw something (up) (in(to) something) to cut something up into pieces with a saw. □ *Jake sawed the logs up into pieces the right size for the fireplace.* 🅃 *Would you saw up the logs into smaller pieces?* □ *Nancy sawed the wood up.*

SAW ▶ OFF

saw something off ((of) something) to cut something off something with a saw. (The *of*-phrase is paraphrased with a *from*-phrase when the particle is transposed. See the 🄵 example. The *of* is colloquial.) □ *He sawed the branch off of the tree.* □ *After a month of putting* *it off, Sam sawed the dead branch off.* 🅃 *He sawed off the branch.* 🄵 *She accidentally sawed off the leg from the table.* 🄰 *The sawed-off limb fell to the ground.*

SAW ▸ THROUGH

saw through something to cut through something with a saw. ☐ *I can't saw through this wood. It's too hard!* ☐ *I can saw through it!*

SAW ▸ UP

saw something (up) (in(to) something) See under *SAW ▸ INTO.*

SAY ▸ ABOUT

say something about someone or something **1.** to make remarks about someone or something. ☐ *What did you say about me?* ☐ *I think that Fran must have said something about me to you.* **2.** to indicate or reveal something about someone or something. ☐ *They all cheered. That really says something about Tom's popularity.* ☐ *The fact that almost no one came to his party says something about Walter, I think.*

SAY ▸ AGAINST

say something against someone or something to speak out against someone or something; to make a case against someone or something. ☐ *I would never say anything against you!* ☐ *No one would say anything against your work.*

SAY ▸ FOR

say something for something [for something] to imply something good about something. ☐ *The speed with which we were able to sell the house says something for the state of the real estate market.* ☐ *The number of new cars on the road says something for the state of the nation's economy.*

SAY ▸ OUT

say something out loud to say something so it can be heard; to say something that others might be thinking, but not saying. ☐ *Yes, I said it, but I didn't mean to say it out loud.* ☐ *If you know the answer, please say it out loud.*

SAY ▸ OVER

say something over (and over (again)) to repeat something, perhaps many times. ☐ *I have said it over and over again! Why don't you listen?* ☐ *Why do you keep saying it over?*

SAY ▸ TO

say something to oneself **1.** to mutter something to oneself. ☐ *He said something to himself, but I didn't catch what it was.* ☐ *I said the answer to myself and no one else was supposed to hear it.* **2.** to think something to oneself. ☐ *When I thought of him as a basketball player, I said to myself that he really isn't tall enough.* ☐ *I said a few choice critical remarks to myself when she presented her talk.*

say something to someone to tell something to someone. ☐ *He didn't say anything to me.* ☐ *Did someone say something to you?*

say something to something to say yes or no to a proposal, request, etc. ☐ *I hope you will say yes to my proposal.* ☐ *Nothing was said to your request at the last meeting.*

SAY ▸ UNDER

say something under one's breath to mutter something softly, so that no one can understand it. (Idiomatic.) ☐ *I heard him say something unpleasant under his breath.* ☐ *Did you say something under your breath that I wasn't supposed to hear?*

SCAB ▸ OVER

scab over [for a wound] to form a scab. ☐ *The wound soon scabbed over and the injury was well on its way to healing.* ☐ *I hope this shaving cut scabs over before I have to leave for work.*

SCALE ▸ DOWN

scale something down to reduce the size or cost of something. ☐ *The bad economy forced us to scale the project down.* 🅃 *Liz scaled down the project.* 🄰 *This is just a scaled-down version of the real thing.*

SCALE ▸ TO

scale something to something to design or adjust the size of one thing to match or complement the size of another thing. □ *The architect sought to scale the office building to the buildings surrounding it.* □ *The playhouse will have to be scaled to the main house.*

SCAMPER ▶ ALONG

scamper along to run along nimbly. (Said of a child or a small animal.) □ *The rabbit scampered along, unaware that a fox was following it.* □ *It is time for Timmy to scamper along home.*

SCAMPER ▶ AWAY

scamper away to run away nimbly. (Said of a child or a small animal.) □ *The rabbit scampered away across the lawn.* □ *The children scampered away when they heard the teacher coming.*

SCAR ▶ OVER

scar over [for an injury] to form and leave a scar. □ *The wound will scar over, but your arm will never be the same as it was before the accident.* [A] *This scarred-over area is still very sensitive to heat.*

SCARE ▶ AWAY

scare someone or something away (from someone or something) to frighten someone or something away from someone or something. □ *He put on a gruff exterior to scare everyone away from him.* [T] *Jeff scared away a lot of people from the store.* □ *The scarecrow was designed to scare the crows away.*

SCARE ▶ INTO

scare someone or something into something **1.** to frighten or intimidate someone or some creature into something or some place. □ *The sudden electrical storm scared the people into their homes.* □ *Please try to scare the chickens into the chicken house.* **2.** to frighten or intimidate someone or some creature into doing something. □ *You can't scare me into leaving town. I know you're bluffing.* □ *I scared the pigs into running away.* □ *I tried to scare the deer into keeping out of our garden.*

SCARE ▶ OFF

scare someone or something off to frighten someone or some creature away. □ *The dog's barking scared the burglar off.* [T] *The barking scared off the prowler.* □ *My dog finally scared the skunk off.*

scare the pants off (of) someone to frighten someone very badly. (Figurative. The *of* is colloquial.) □ *Wow! You nearly scared the pants off me!* □ *The explosion scared the pants off of everyone.*

SCARE ▶ OUT

scare one out of one's wits to cause one to lose mental control from fear. □ *The loud noise scared me out of my wits.* □ *The explosion scared Sam out of his wits.*

scare someone or something out (of something) to frighten someone or some creature out of something or some place. □ *The old man tried to scare the kids out of his orchard by threatening them.* [T] *Karen scared out the intruder.* □ *I went into the garden and scared the deer out.*

scare someone out of something to frighten someone into losing something, such as a year's worth of growth, ten years of life, etc. (Folksy.) □ *You nearly scared me out of my skin!* □ *The bad news scared Roger out of ten years' growth.*

scare something out of someone to frighten someone very badly. (The *something* can be *the living daylights, the wits, the hell, the shit,* etc. Use discretion with *shit.*) □ *Gee, you scared the living daylights out of me!* □ *The police tried to scare the truth out of her.*

SCARE ▶ TO

scare someone or something to death to frighten someone or some creature very much. (Figurative. The literal sense is also used. *Someone* includes *oneself.*) □ *The horrendous noise scared me to death.* □ *You could tell that the fireworks were scaring the dog to death.* □ *We scared ourselves to death by telling horror stories around the fire.*

SCARE ▶ UP

scare someone or something up to seek and find someone or something. (Informal.) □ *I don't know offhand who could do it. I'll try to scare somebody* *up though.* [T] *I'll scare up somebody, don't worry.* □ *I will scare a wrench up, if you still need one.*

SCATTER ▸ ABOUT

scatter something about AND **scatter something around** to throw or distribute something about. □ *The children scattered the books about and left the room in a general mess.* [T] *They scattered about all the books and papers.* □ *Please don't scatter the papers around.*

SCATTER ▸ AROUND

scatter something around See the previous entry.

SCAVENGE ▸ AROUND

See the following entry.

SCAVENGE ▸ FOR

scavenge (around) for someone or something to search everywhere for someone or something. □ *We had to scavenge for a person who would agree to run in my place.* □ *Sam scavenged around for a socket wrench.*

SCHEME ▸ AGAINST

scheme against someone or something to plot or conspire against someone or something. □ *A group of generals was plotting against the government.* □ *They schemed against Roger until he caught them and put an end to it.*

SCHEME ▸ FOR

scheme for something to plot and plan for something, perhaps using deception. □ *She is scheming for a raise.* □ *Ted is always scheming for a way to get a higher salary.*

SCHOOL ▸ IN

school someone in something to train, discipline, or coach someone in something. (*Someone* includes *oneself.*) □ *The voice coach schooled the singer in excellent singing techniques.* □ *We were schooled in oratory and debate.* □ *She schooled herself in patience.*

SCOFF ▸ AT

scoff at someone or something to show ridicule or scorn for someone or something. □ *The directors scoffed at her when she presented her plan.* □ *They scoffed at my new vest, not realizing how stylish it was.*

SCOLD ▸ ABOUT

scold someone about something to rebuke or chastise someone about something. □ *How many times have I scolded you about that?* □ *Please don't scold me about something I didn't do.*

SCOLD ▸ FOR

scold someone for something to rebuke or chastise someone for doing something. □ *The manager scolded the worker for misplacing the door key.* □ *The teacher scolded all the students for their bad behavior.*

SCOOP ▸ OUT

scoop something out (of something) to remove something from something by dipping or scooping. (The *of*-phrase is paraphrased with a *from*-phrase when the particle is transposed. See the [F] example.) □ *She scooped the water out of the bottom of the rowboat.* [T] *Karen scooped out all the water.* [F] *Karen scooped out the water from the boat.* □ *Dave took up a big spoon and scooped the ice cream out.* [A] *The scooped-out pumpkin seeds were placed in the oven to dry.*

SCOOP ▸ UP

scoop something up to gather and remove something by scooping, dipping, or bailing. □ *Karen scooped the nuts up and put them in a bag.* [T] *Jill scooped up all the money she had won and left the poker table.*

SCOOT ▸ DOWN

scoot down (to some place) to go down somewhere in a hurry. (Colloquial.) □ *I want you to scoot down to the store and get me a dozen eggs. Okay?* □ *I'll scoot down as soon as I finish reading the newspaper.*

SCOOT ▸ OVER

scoot over to slide sideways while seated. □ *Scoot over and let me sit down.* □ *If you scoot over, we can get another person in this row.*

scoot over to someone or something to travel or move over to someone or something or some place in a hurry. (Colloquial.) □ *Scoot over to Don and ask him to come here for a minute.* □ *We all scooted over to the stadium for the football game.*

SCORE ▶ AGAINST

score against someone or something to make a point or goal against someone or some team. □ *Because of his bad ankle, Fred was unable to score against Alice.* □ *We never scored against the visiting team.*

score something (up) against someone or something to tally up a score against someone or some team. □ *Score another point up against Sally's team.* □ *Ted scored a few points against Sally.* 🅃 *The Bears scored up thirteen points against the Giants.*

SCORE ▶ FOR

score something for something **1.** to arrange music for one or more musical instruments; to arrange music for a particular type of voice or voices. □ *The arranger scored the music for two pianos.* □ *The arranger scored the song for a four-part chorus.* **2.** to scratch something, such as glass, for breaking. □ *Valerie scored the piece of glass for breaking, and then snapped it off.* □ *The worker scored the pane of glass for snapping off.*

SCORE ▶ UP

score something (up) against someone or something See under *SCORE ▶ AGAINST.*

SCORE ▶ WITH

score with someone or something to please someone or a group. (Slang or colloquial.) □ *Her rendition of "Old Kentucky Home" really scored with the audience.* □ *You really score with me.*

SCOUR ▶ FOR

scour something for someone or something to look carefully in something for someone or something. (Informal.) □ *I scoured the entire roster of members for a person who would agree to run for president.* □ *The police scoured the entire area for any sign of Lefty "Fingers" Moran.*

SCOUR ▶ OFF

scour something off ((of) something) to clean something off something by scouring. (The *of*-phrase is paraphrased with a *from*-phrase when the particle is transposed. See the 🄵 example. The *of* is colloquial.) □ *See if you can scour the rust off the cookie sheet.* 🅃 *I will scour off the rust.* 🄵 *I will scour off the rust from the pans.* □ *Please help me scour it off.*

SCOUR ▶ OUT

scour something out to clean something out by scouring. □ *Would you scour the pans out?* 🅃 *Please scour out the pans—don't just wash them.* 🄰 *She put the scoured-out pots into the cupboard.*

scour something out of something to clean something out of something by scouring. □ *Did you scour the rust out of the pan?* □ *Please scour the burned material out of the bowl.*

SCOUT ▶ AROUND

scout around (for someone or something) to look around for someone or something. □ *I don't know who would do a good job for you, but I'll scout around for a likely candidate.* □ *You stay here. I'll scout around.*

SCOUT ▶ OUT

scout someone or something out to search for and discover someone or something. □ *I will scout a new salesclerk out for you if you want.* 🅃 *I'll scout out a new clerk for you.* □ *I will try to scout Sharon out. I can't imagine where she has gone.* 🅃 *Will you help me scout out a new apartment?*

SCOUT ▶ UP

scout someone or something up to search for and find someone or something. □ *I'll scout up a costume for the Halloween party.* □ *Can you scout up a date for Friday night?*

SCOWL ▶ AT

scowl at someone or something to make a frown of disapproval or displeasure at someone or something. □ *Why are you scowling at me? I didn't do any-*

thing wrong! ☐ *Mary scowled at her cat.*

SCRAMBLE ▸ FOR

scramble for someone or something to push and struggle to get to someone or something. ☐ *All the teenagers scrambled for the rock star but couldn't catch him.* ☐ *The children scrambled for the candy as it fell from the piñata.*

SCRAPE ▸ ALONG

scrape along (on something) AND **scrape along (with something)** to manage just to get along with a minimum amount of something. ☐ *We can just scrape along on the money I earn from my sewing.* ☐ *Do you think you can scrape along with just $400 per month?* ☐ *I can hardly scrape along after I pay all my medical bills.*

SCRAPE ▸ AWAY

scrape something away (from something) to scratch or rasp something off something. ☐ *Ted scraped the rough places away from the fender he was repairing.* 🅃 *Ted scraped away the rough places.* ☐ *Mary couldn't polish her shoes until she scraped the mud away.*

SCRAPE ▸ BY

scrape by (on something) AND **scrape by (with something)** to manage just to get by with something. (Usually applies to a more specific period or time or a more specific event than *scrape along (on something).*) ☐ *There is not really enough money to live on, and we just have to scrape by on what we get.* ☐ *We can't scrape by with only that amount of money.* ☐ *I think we can just scrape by again this month.*

scrape by (something) to manage just to get by something. ☐ *I scraped by the man standing at the gate, and got into the theater without a ticket.* ☐ *Mary scraped by the cart that was blocking the crowded hallway.*

SCRAPE ▸ OFF

scrape something off ((of) someone or something) to rub or stroke something off someone or something. (The *of*-phrase is paraphrased with a *from*-phrase when the particle is transposed. See the 🄵 example. The *of* is colloquial.) ☐ *I sat down and scraped the caked mud off of me. It was everywhere!* 🅃 *Jake scraped off the caked mud.* 🄵 *Jake scraped off the caked mud from his shoes.* ☐ *Mary scraped the mud off.*

SCRAPE ▸ OUT

scrape something out to empty something by scraping. ☐ *Scrape the pan out. Don't leave any of that good sauce inside.* 🅃 *Please scrape out the pan.*

scrape something out (of something) to remove something by scraping. (The *of*-phrase is paraphrased with a *from*-phrase when the particle is transposed. See the 🄵 example.) ☐ *Scrape all the peanut butter out of the jar before you discard it.* 🅃 *Scrape out the peanut butter.* ☐ *Please scrape it out.* 🄵 *Did you scrape out all the sauce from the pan?*

SCRAPE ▸ THROUGH

scrape through (something) **1.** to move through something, scraping or rubbing the sides. ☐ *The car, going at a very high speed, scraped through the tunnel.* ☐ *It just managed to scrape through.* **2.** to get by something just barely; to pass a test just barely. ☐ *Alice passed the test, but she just scraped through it.* ☐ *I just scraped through my calculus test.*

SCRAPE ▸ TOGETHER

scrape someone or something together to put together a group of people or things from a very small selection or on short notice. (Colloquial.) ☐ *I tried to scrape some people together to help with the harvest.* 🅃 *Liz scraped together a few friends to help with the chores.* ☐ *I think we can scrape something together for dinner.*

scrape something together to gather things together by scraping. ☐ *The waiter scraped all the crumbs together and removed them from the table with a little gadget.* 🅃 *Karen scraped together all the trimmings and set them aside.*

SCRAPE ▸ UP

scrape someone or something up to search very hard to find someone or something. (Colloquial.) ☐ *I don't know offhand of anyone who could do* *it, but I'll see if I can scrape somebody up.* 🅃 *I'm sure we can scrape up someone.* □ *I will scrape up some toys to entertain the children.*

SCRATCH ▸ ABOUT

scratch about (for something) AND **scratch around (for something)** to look very hard for something. (Both literal, as with a chicken scratching for food, and someone looking for something.) □ *The chickens were scratching about for something to eat.* □ *They spend most of their lives scratching around.*

SCRATCH ▸ AROUND

scratch around (for something) See the previous entry.

SCRATCH ▸ AT

scratch at something to scratch something. □ *You shouldn't scratch at a chigger bite because it might get infected.* □ *Don't scratch at it!*

SCRATCH ▸ AWAY

scratch something away to rub or knock something off by scratching. □ *Look at the finish on this furniture. The cat has almost scratched it away!* 🅃 *That cat scratched away the finish.*

SCRATCH ▸ FROM

scratch someone or something from something to mark the name of someone or something off a list. □ *We were obliged to scratch Dave from the list.* □ *The judges scratched the large collie from the eligibility list.*

SCRATCH ▸ OUT

scratch someone or something out to mark out the name of someone or something. □ *I scratched John out and wrote in George instead.* 🅃 *I scratched out John and forgot about him.* □ *Donna scratched the name of the defunct company out.*

scratch something out to remove something by scratching. (Refers to scratching something out with a pen point or a fountain pen.) □ *Timmy made a mistake in his writing and scratched it out.* 🅃 *Please scratch out that word and spell it right.* 🄰 *The scratched-out words were still legible.*

SCRATCH ▸ UP

scratch someone or something up to damage or mar someone or something by scratching. □ *Being thrown clear of the car in the accident didn't break any bones, but it scratched her up a lot.* 🅃 *Who scratched up my coffee table?* □ *I didn't scratch it up.* 🄰 *The scratched-up table was sent out to be refinished.*

SCREAM ▸ AT

scream at someone or something to yell or screech at someone or something. □ *Why are you screaming at me?* □ *Go scream at the dog, not me!*

SCREAM ▸ DOWN

scream down (on someone or something) [for something, such as birds or bombs] to dive down on someone or something, screaming. □ *The bombs screamed down on the helpless peasants.* □ *As the bombs screamed down, some people ran and some prayed.*

scream someone down to scream loudly at someone; to outscream someone. (Compare to *shout someone down.*) □ *The angry crowd screamed the politician down.* 🅃 *They screamed her down and drove her from the platform.*

SCREAM ▸ FOR

scream for something to yell or shriek for something. □ *The teenage audience applauded and screamed for more.* □ *The children said they were screaming for ice cream.*

SCREAM ▸ OUT

scream something out to say something out loud in a screaming voice. □ *She screamed his name out for everyone to hear.* 🅃 *Liz screamed out the winner's name.*

SCREAM ▸ WITH

scream with something to scream because of something, such as pain, anger, rage, etc. □ *Frank screamed with pain when the car door closed on his fingers.* □ *The teacher screamed with rage when the student spoke back.*

SCREEN ▸ FROM

screen someone or something (off) (from someone or something) to make someone or something out of sight to someone or something by erecting a screen. □ *We screened her off from the patient in the next bed.* 🅃 *We screened off the yard from the street.* □ *The Wilsons decided to screen their yard from the street.*

SCREEN ▸ OFF

See the previous entry.

SCREEN ▸ OUT

screen someone or something out (of something) to filter someone or something out of something. □ *The test screened all the unqualified candidates out of the group.* 🅃 *We screened out the suppliers who were not financially sound.* □ *We screened some of the applicants out.* 🅃 *Walter screened out the rocks from the soil.*

SCREW ▸ AROUND

screw around **1.** to mess around; to waste time. (Slang.) □ *Stop screwing around and get to work!* □ *I'm not screwing around, I'm thinking.* **2.** to play sexually; to indulge in sexual intercourse. (Slang.) □ *All those kids are out screwing around all the time.* □ *They say that Ted and Alice are screwing around a lot.*

screw (around) with someone or something See under *SCREW ▸ WITH.*

screw someone around to harass or bother someone. (Slang.) □ *Don't screw me around, man! I bite back!* □ *Max got tired of being screwed around by Lefty.*

SCREW ▸ DOWN

screw something down to secure something to the floor or a base by the use of screws. □ *You had better screw these seats down or someone will knock them over.* 🅃 *Please screw down the threshold.*

SCREW ▸ INTO

screw something into something to twist something that is threaded into something. □ *I screwed all the screws into the back of the computer and turned it on.* □ *Please screw this bracket into the wall.*

SCREW ▸ OFF

screw off to waste time. (Slang.) □ *Stop screwing off and get busy!* □ *I'm not screwing off. This is my lunch hour.*

SCREW ▸ ON

screw something (on)(to something) to attach something to something by the use of screws or other threaded fasteners. □ *Screw the bracket onto the wall, will you?* 🅃 *Screw on the bracket to the wall.* □ *Please screw this on.*

SCREW ▸ OUT

screw someone out of something to cheat someone out of something. (Slang.) □ *I think you screwed me out of ten bucks on that deal.* □ *Max screwed me out of what was due me.*

SCREW ▸ TO

screw something (on)(to something) See under *SCREW ▸ ON.*

SCREW ▸ UP

screw someone or something up to mess someone or something up; to deal with someone or something badly. (Slang. *Someone* includes *oneself.*) □ *You really screwed me up by being late.* 🅃 *You screwed up this whole project!* □ *I didn't screw it up!* 🄰 *Who is responsible for this screwed-up mess?* □ *I really screwed myself up.* 🄽 *Who is responsible for this screwup?*

screw someone up to confuse someone mentally. (Slang.) □ *Please don't screw me up again!* 🅃 *You screwed up my train of thought.* 🄽 *This kid's a real screwup.*

screw something up to attach something to a higher place by the use of screws. □ *The bracket holding the shelf up has come loose. Will you please screw it up again?* 🅃 *Please screw up this loose bracket.* 🄰 *The tightly screwed-up bracket held up a lot of weight.*

screw up to mess up; to do something badly. (Slang.) □ *Well, I guess I really screwed up, huh?* □ *You really screwed up that time.*

screw up one's courage to build up one's courage; to work up enough courage to do something. (Figurative slang.) □ *She screwed up her courage and en-*

tered the room full of examiners. □ *I had to screw up my courage a lot to go in there.*

SCREW ▸ WITH

screw (around) with someone or something to harass or harm someone or something; to fiddle, play, or toy with someone or something. (Slang.) □ *Don't screw around with my tape recorder.* □ *Hey, don't screw with me!* □ *Come on! Don't screw around with me if you know what's good for you!* □ *He spends most of his time screwing around with Jim.*

SCRIBBLE ▸ AWAY

scribble away (at something) to write hard and fast at some task. □ *He scribbled away at his notes as the lecturer droned on.* □ *Jane sat there scribbling away.*

SCRIBBLE ▸ DOWN

scribble something down to write something down fast and not too neatly. □ *He scribbled the figure down and raced for the telephone.* 🅃 *Liz scribbled down the telephone number.* 🄰 *I can't read your scribbled-down notes.*

SCRIMP ▸ ON

scrimp on something to try to economize on the use of something; to fail to use enough of something. □ *Please don't scrimp on the quality of the food.* □ *There is enough money. You don't have to scrimp on anything.*

SCROUNGE ▸ AROUND

scrounge around (for someone or something) to look around high and low for someone or something. (Informal.) □ *I scrounged around for Jamie, but she was nowhere to be found.* □ *I'm sorry you won't be able to attend. I will scrounge around for a replacement for you.*

SCROUNGE ▸ UP

scrounge someone or something up to find someone or something somewhere; to dig someone or something up. □ *I can't think of anyone, but I will try to scrounge someone up.* 🅃 *They scrounged up an escort for Liz.*

SCRUB ▸ AWAY

scrub something away to clean something away by rubbing. □ *See if you can scrub that rust away.* 🅃 *Scrub away that rust if you can.*

SCRUB ▸ DOWN

scrub someone or something down to clean someone or something thoroughly by rubbing. (*Someone* includes *oneself.*) □ *The mother scrubbed the baby down gently and put lotion on her.* 🅃 *Please scrub down this floor.* 🄽 *Please give the basement floor a good scrub-down.* □ *He scrubbed himself down and put on clean clothes.*

SCRUB ▸ OFF

scrub someone or something off to clean someone or something by rubbing. (*Someone* includes *oneself.*) □ *Mother scrubbed Timmy off.* 🅃 *Liz scrubbed off the countertop.* □ *He scrubbed himself off and went to work.*

scrub something off ((of) something) to clean something off something by scrubbing. (The *of*-phrase is paraphrased with a *from*-phrase when the particle is transposed. See the 🄵 example. The *of* is colloquial.) □ *I have to scrub the mud off the porch steps.* □ *Did you scrub all the grease off?* 🅃 *Tina scrubbed off the grease.* 🄵 *Walter promised to scrub off the mud from the steps.*

SCRUB ▸ OUT

scrub something out to clean out the inside of something by rubbing or brushing. □ *Please scrub these pots out and put them away.* 🅃 *Jim will scrub out the pots.* 🄰 *Please see that a scrubbed-out bathtub is ready for our guest.*

scrub something out (of something) to clean something out of something by scrubbing. (The *of*-phrase is paraphrased with a *from*-phrase when the particle is transposed. See the 🄵 example.) □ *Please scrub the gravy out of the pot.* 🅃 *Are you going to scrub out the burned material?* 🄵 *She promised to scrub out the gravy from the pot.*

SCRUB ▸ UP

scrub up 1. to clean oneself up. □ *You have to scrub up before dinner.* □ *Please go scrub up before you come to the table.* 2. to clean oneself, especially one's hands and arms, as a preparation for performing a surgical procedure. (A special use of sense 1.) □ *The surgeon scrubbed up thoroughly before the operation.* □ *When you finish scrubbing up, someone will help you on with sterile clothing.*

SCRUNCH ▸ DOWN

scrunch down to squeeze or huddle down into a smaller shape. □ *Mary scrunched down, trying to look smaller.* □ *The children scrunched down so they wouldn't be seen.*

scrunch down into something to squeeze down into a small area or container. □ *Fred scrunched down into his seat, hoping no one would see him there.* □ *Don't scrunch down into your seat. It's bad for your posture.*

scrunch something down (into something) 1. to squeeze something into a smaller size or shape. □ *He scrunched the wad of paper down into a hard ball.* 🅃 *Liz scrunched down the cloth into a pad for the hot pan.* □ *Scrunch the boxes down before you throw them away.* 2. to pack something tightly into something. □ *Dave scrunched his clothing down into the drawer and closed it.* 🅃 *Dave scrunched down his clothing into the suitcase.* □ *Francine scrunched everything down, but her clothes still would not fit in the trunk.*

SCUFF ▸ UP

scuff something up to scrape or scratch something. □ *Who scuffed my floor up?* 🅃 *Please don't scuff up my freshly polished floors!* 🄰 *Don't you dare show up in scuffed-up shoes again!*

SCUFFLE ▸ WITH

scuffle with someone to struggle or have a fight with someone. □ *Max scuffled with Lefty a little till a cop came along and saw them.* □ *The cowboys scuffled with each other when they came out of the saloon.*

SCURRY ▸ ALONG

scurry along to run or scamper along fast. □ *The children scurried along, trotting to school.* □ *We scurried along, keeping watch out for bears and things like that.*

SCUTTLE ▸ ACROSS

scuttle across something to hurry across something. (Especially of a small animal.) □ *A tiny mouse scuttled across the kitchen floor and startled me.* □ *A rabbit scuttled across my path.*

SCUTTLE ▸ AWAY

scuttle away [for a small animal] to run away. □ *The otters scuttled away as we approached.* □ *A skunk scuttled away quickly—thank heavens.*

SEAL ▸ OFF

seal something off (from someone or something) to make something inaccessible to someone or something. □ *The police sealed the building off from everyone.* 🅃 *They sealed off the building from all the reporters.* □ *We sealed the room off from the outside air.* 🄰 *We cannot get into the sealed-off chamber.*

SEAL ▸ UP

seal something (up) (with something) to fasten something closed with something. □ *Please seal this box up with twine.* 🅃 *Would you seal up this box with tape?* □ *I will seal it with packing tape.* 🄰 *The herbs were stored in sealed-up containers.*

SEAL ▸ WITH

See the previous entry.

SEAM ▸ WITH

seam something with something to join the edges of something together with something. □ *The worker seamed the two parts of the carpet with a special tool.* □ *She seamed the material with a strip of cloth to strengthen the seam.*

SEARCH ▸ AFTER

search after someone or something to look for someone or something. (Perhaps over a long period of time.) □ *We searched after a suitable candidate for weeks.* □ *I am searching after a part for my stereo.*

SEARCH ▸ FOR

search for someone or something to look very hard for someone or something. ☐ *I searched for Ted everywhere, but he was already gone.* ☐ *I have searched for my glasses high and low.*

search someone for something to feel, touch, pat, frisk, or examine electronically a person's body, looking for something hidden underneath the clothes. ☐ *The police searched Max for hidden weapons.* ☐ *The airport guard used an electronic instrument to search the passengers for weapons.*

search something for someone or something to examine something, looking for someone or something. ☐ *Everyone searched the house for little Wally, but he was not to be found.* ☐ *I searched all my coat pockets for the note, but I didn't find it.*

SEARCH ▸ OUT

search someone or something out to seek and find someone or something. ☐ *I will search Fred out. I know he's here somewhere.* 🅃 *We have to search out the key to the safe-deposit box.*

SEARCH ▸ THROUGH

search through something to examine all the things found in something. ☐ *I searched through my books for the answer.* ☐ *My drawers were searched through thoroughly.*

SEASON ▸ WITH

season something with something to make something more flavorful with specific spices and herbs. ☐ *I always season my stews with lots of freshly ground black pepper.* ☐ *The chili was seasoned with cumin and allspice, among other things.*

SECEDE ▸ FROM

secede from something to withdraw from something. ☐ *Which was the first state to secede from the Union?* ☐ *We do not want to secede from the organization, but we will if we must.*

SECURE ▸ AGAINST

secure something against someone or something **1.** to fasten something against the entry of someone, some creature, or something. ☐ *Jane secured the doors and windows against the prowler who was roving around the neighborhood.* ☐ *You had better secure the henhouse against coyotes.* ☐ *The house was secured against invaders.* **2.** to obtain a legal order involving someone or something. ☐ *I secured an injunction against Harry. If he bothers you again, he'll have to go into court to explain himself.* ☐ *We can't secure an injunction against this law.*

SEDUCE ▸ FROM

seduce someone from something to lure someone away from something. (Stilted.) ☐ *The devilish agent seduced Jerry from his usual quiet behavior.* ☐ *Frank was seduced from his proper ways by the offer of money.*

SEE ▸ ABOUT

see about someone or something to investigate someone or something. ☐ *I don't know who is going on the trip. You ask Jill, and I'll see about Jerry.* ☐ *I will see about your request.*

see someone about someone or something to confer with someone about someone or something. ☐ *Jill has to see the boss about one of her office staff members.* ☐ *I will have to see Jill about getting permission to go.*

SEE ▸ ACROSS

see someone across something to accompany someone across a dangerous area. ☐ *Paul saw his mother across the pasture, which contained a number of hazards.* ☐ *Timmy offered to see the elderly lady across the street.*

SEE ▸ AFTER

see after someone or something to take care of someone or something. (The same as but less common than *look after someone or something*.) ☐ *Would you please see after Walter? He looks a little pale.* ☐ *I will see after the committee while they are meeting.* ☐ *I asked the vet to see after my kittens.*

SEE ▸ AGAINST

see something against something **1.** to view something against something else. ☐ *I can't see the cars against the evening* *sky if their lights aren't on.* ☐ *The cars can't be seen against the evening sky.* **2.** to view or consider something within the context of something else. ☐ *If you can see this issue against the background of a long series of problems, perhaps you will understand how concerned we are.* ☐ *You really need to see this matter against the background of what has happened before.*

SEE ▸ AHEAD

see ahead (of someone or something) to be able to see into the distance in front of someone or something. ☐ *The fog was so thick I couldn't see ahead of the car.* ☐ *I can't see ahead, so I will have to stop.*

SEE ▸ AROUND

see around something **1.** to see what is on the other side of or partially concealed by something. ☐ *I could not see around the truck in front of me.* ☐ *Do you think I can see around corners?* **2.** to perceive someone's deception. ☐ *I see around your trickery!* ☐ *We all see around your stated purpose!*

see someone around to see someone again sometime. (A type of colloquial good-bye.) ☐ *Bye. See you around.* ☐ *I will see you around sometime.*

see someone or something around something to notice someone or something in the vicinity of something or near something. ☐ *I saw the boys around the swings on the playground.* ☐ *Did you see my cat around the neighborhood anywhere?*

SEE ▸ AS

see someone as someone or something to visualize someone as some other person or type of person. (*Someone* includes *oneself.*) ☐ *I see you as a perfect candidate for the job.* ☐ *I don't see you as mayor.* ☐ *Do you see yourself as a basically good person?*

see something as something to visualize or fantasize something as something else. ☐ *I see this as a wonderful way to interest some new people in our organization.* ☐ *We all see this as a golden opportunity to get to know one another better.*

SEE ▸ BACK

see someone back (to something) to accompany someone back to something or some place. ☐ *I saw her back to her apartment.* ☐ *I will see her back safely.*

SEE ▸ BEYOND

see beyond something **1.** to be able to perceive into the distance beyond something. ☐ *Can you see beyond the big tree there, where the barn is on the horizon?* ☐ *I can't see beyond the end of the road. I think I need glasses.* **2.** to be able to imagine the future beyond a certain time or event. ☐ *He can't see beyond the next day—no sense of the future.* ☐ *Todd is usually able to see beyond his immediate situation. I do not know what happened this time.*

see beyond the end of one's nose **1.** to see only a short distance. (Usually negative.) ☐ *My eyes are getting so bad, I can hardly see beyond the end of my nose.* ☐ *Unless I have my glasses on, I can't see beyond the end of my nose.* **2.** to be perceptive about things or people. (Usually negative.) ☐ *Carl is so self-centered that he can't see beyond the end of his nose.* ☐ *She has no sense of what is going on around her. She can't see beyond the end of her nose.*

SEE ▸ DOWN

see someone down to something to accompany or escort someone to a lower level. ☐ *I will see you down to the front door.* ☐ *Would you please see Mrs. Bracknel down to the door?*

SEE ▸ IN

See also under *SEE ▸ IN(TO).*

see one's hand in front of one's face to see something very close to one. (Usually negative.) ☐ *It was so dark I couldn't see my hand in front of my face.* ☐ *With the electricity out, Ann could not see her hand in front of her face.*

see someone or something in a new light to understand someone or something in a different way [than before]. (Figurative. *Someone* includes *oneself.*) ☐ *After we had a little discussion, I began to* *see Fred in a new light.* ☐ *I can now see the problem in a new light.* ☐ *After her experience, Maggie began to see herself in a new light.*

see something in someone or something to appreciate a certain quality in someone or something. ☐ *I see a strong sense of dignity in Fred. That's good.* ☐ *I now see the strong points in your proposal.* ☐ *What does she see in him?*

SEE ▸ INTO

see into something **1.** to view into the depth of something. ☐ *He couldn't see into the smoky room.* ☐ *The water was muddy and we could not see into it.* **2.** to examine something. (Similar to but not as common as *look into something*.) ☐ *I will see into the problem tomorrow.* ☐ *Someone will see into this matter immediately.*

SEE ▸ IN(TO)

see someone in(to something) to usher or accompany someone into something or some place. ☐ *Please see her into the room and make sure she is seated where she can hear the speaker.* 🅃 *Please see in the speaker.* ☐ *I will see the guests in and get them seated.*

SEE ▸ OF

see something of someone or something to know, experience, or visit with someone or some group for some amount of time. (*Something* can be used literally.) ☐ *I hope we are able to see something of you while you are in town.* ☐ *We don't see enough of the town council. What does it do?* ☐ *We want to see more of them.*

see the last of someone or something to have experienced the last visit, episode, adventure, etc., with someone or something. ☐ *I hope I have seen the last of Robert Ellis!* ☐ *We have seen the last of the strawberry jam.*

SEE ▸ OFF

see someone off to accompany one to the point of departure for a trip and say good-bye upon departure. ☐ *We went to the train station to see Andy off.* 🅃 *We saw off all the scouts going to camp.*

see someone off something to accompany someone who is leaving something; to escort someone away from something. ☐ *I saw the elderly lady off the station platform safely.* ☐ *The emcee saw the contestants off the stage.*

SEE ▸ OUT

see someone out (of something) to accompany or escort someone out of something or some place. ☐ *Please see our guest out of the factory.* 🅃 *Please see out our guest.* ☐ *I will see you out.*

see something out to stay with a project all the way to its completion. ☐ *I am very tired of this matter, but I will see it out.* 🅃 *I will see out this project to the very end.*

SEE ▸ OVER

see over something to be able to have a view over something such as a wall, fence, etc. ☐ *I couldn't see over the fence, but I could hear what was going on.* ☐ *We could not see over the wall.*

SEE ▸ THROUGH

see something through to stay with a project all the way to its completion. ☐ *They will see the job through.* ☐ *I will see this whole thing through, don't worry.*

see through someone or something to recognize the deception involved with someone or something. ☐ *I know what you're up to! I see through you!* ☐ *I see through this proposal.*

SEE ▸ TO

see eye to eye (about someone or something) (with someone) AND **see eye to eye (on someone or something) (with someone)** [for someone] to agree about someone or something with someone else. ☐ *I'm glad we see eye to eye about Todd with Mary.* ☐ *I see eye to eye with Mary.* ☐ *We see eye to eye on this, don't we?* ☐ *Todd and I see eye to eye about this proposal.*

see fit to do something to think it proper to do something; to agree to do something. ☐ *I hope you will see fit to come and visit us again.* ☐ *Jane saw fit to ask that the children leave the house.*

see someone to something to accompany or escort someone to something or some place. □ *I will see you to the door.* □ *Would you please see your aunt to her car?*

see to someone or something to tend to or care for someone or something. □ *Please go see to the baby. She's crying again.* □ *Ted went to see to whoever was at the door.*

SEE ▸ UP

see someone up to something to accompany or escort someone to a higher level. □ *That is the end of the tour of the wine cellar. I will see you up to the exit.* □ *Ted saw Mary up to her apartment.*

SEEK ▸ AFTER

seek after someone or something to keep looking for someone or something. □ *I will continue to seek after the thief who stole my car.* □ *The thief was seeking after a late-model sedan.* [A] *This is a much-sought-after type of antique.*

SEEK ▸ FROM

seek something from someone or something to pursue something from someone or something. □ *We will seek an injunction from the judge.* □ *My lawyer sought an injunction from the court to try to stop the building project.*

SEEK ▸ OUT

seek someone or something out to search for and find someone or something. □ *We will seek someone out to do the work for us.* [T] *Liz sought out a helper for Karen.* [T] *I will seek out a suitable apartment for you.*

SEEM ▸ LIKE

seem like someone or something to appear to be like some kind of person or something. (Colloquial.) □ *You seemed like such a nice person when I met you.* □ *This seems like a nice day.*

SEEP ▸ AWAY

seep away [for a fluid] to escape little by little, as through a leak. □ *All the oil seeped away, leaving none in the engine.* □ *The water seeped away after a while.*

SEEP ▸ IN(TO)

seep in(to something) [for a fluid] to trickle or leak out of something. □ *Water is seeping into the basement.* □ *Water is seeping in very slowly.*

SEEP ▸ OUT

seep out (of something) [for a fluid] to trickle or leak out of something. □ *A lot of oil has seeped out of the car onto the driveway.* □ *There is oil seeping out. There must be a leak.*

SEEP ▸ THROUGH

seep through something [for a fluid] to permeate something and escape. □ *The oil seeped through the gasket onto the ground.* □ *Some water seeped through the ceiling, ruining our carpet as well as the ceiling.*

SEETHE ▸ WITH

seethe with someone or something to swarm or seem to "boil" with someone or something. □ *The wedding reception was seething with guests and well-wishers.* □ *The room was just seething with flies and other flying creatures.*

seethe with something [for someone] to be agitated with anger, hatred, scorn, disgust, etc. □ *Laura was seething with rage as she entered the tax office.* □ *We were seething with disgust at the way they treated the people who had just moved in.*

SEGREGATE ▸ FROM

segregate someone from someone else or something from something else to separate someone from someone else or something from something else. (*Someone* includes *oneself*.) □ *I was asked to segregate the swimmers from the non-swimmers.* □ *Let's segregate the larger fish from the smaller ones.* □ *They chose to segregate themselves from the others.*

SEGREGATE ▸ INTO

segregate someone or something into something to isolate someone, a creature, or something into something or a special place. (*Someone* includes *oneself*.) □ *We segregated the infected people into a separate room.* □ *Let's segregate the white pigs into a different pen.* □ *They* *segregated themselves into a separate room.*

SEGUE ▸ INTO

segue into something to make a smooth transition into something. (From filmmaking and broadcasting. Rhymes with *egg - day*.) □ *At this point in the script, you should segue into the next scene.* □ *Don't segue here, this is where a commercial goes.*

SEIZE ▸ ON

See under *SEIZE ▸ (UP)ON.*

SEIZE ▸ ONTO

seize onto someone or something to grab onto someone or something. □ *The beggar seized onto the well-dressed gentleman and demanded money.* □ *Tony seized onto the doorknob and gave it a hard jerk.*

SEIZE ▸ UP

seize something up to grab or take something. □ *The crow seized the freshly hatched chick up and flew away.* 🅃 *The huge bird seized up the tiny chick.*

seize up to freeze or halt; to grind suddenly to a stop. □ *The engine seized up and we were almost thrown out of the car.* □ *My knee seized up in the middle of a football game.*

SEIZE ▸ (UP)ON

seize (up)on something **1.** to grasp something tightly. (*Upon* is formal and less commonly used than *on*.) □ *Dave seized upon the knob of the door and yanked hard.* □ *I seized on the railing and held on tight.* **2.** to take hold of something, such as a plan, idea, etc. (Figurative.) □ *I heard her ideas and seized upon them immediately.* □ *The committee seized on the idea at once.* □ *The plan was seized upon at once.*

SEIZE ▸ WITH

See *be seized with something* under *BE ▸ WITH.*

seize someone or something with something to grab someone or something with something. □ *The robot seized Roger with its mechanical claws.* □ *Jane seized an ice cube with the tongs.*

SELECT ▸ AS

select someone or something as something to choose someone or something to be something. □ *The voters selected Alice as the county treasurer.* □ *We selected Acme as our main distributor.*

SELECT ▸ FOR

select someone or something for someone or something to choose someone or something for the benefit of someone or something. □ *You need a helper, so I will select someone for you.* □ *Jane selected a car for her husband.* □ *Jane selected a carpet for the living room.*

SELECT ▸ FROM

select from someone or something to make a choice from a group of people or things. □ *You will have to select from the people we have asked to interview with you today.* □ *They told me that I had to select from what you have in stock.*

select someone from something to choose someone from a group of people. □ *You will have to select a new secretary from the available pool of workers.* □ *I selected Ted from the applicants I had at the time.*

SELL ▸ AS

sell someone or something as something to put someone or something up for consideration as something. (*Someone* includes *oneself*.) □ *The political party tried to sell the candidate as a responsible administrator.* □ *The sales force was told to sell the paint as the best available anywhere.* □ *She sold herself as a computer consultant.*

SELL ▸ AT

sell at something [for something] to be marketed at a particular price. □ *This coat formerly sold at twice this price.* □ *Next month, this will sell at a 60 percent markup.*

sell something at something **1.** to market something at a particular price. □ *Do you think we can sell these things at four dollars each?* □ *We cannot sell these at ten times what we paid for them!* **2.** to market something at something or some place. □ *We will try to* *sell our old kitchen sink at the flea market in Adamsville.* □ *He sold all his watermelons at the farmers market in town.*

SELL ▸ DOWN

sell someone down the river to betray someone. (Slang.) □ *Why did you sell your best friend down the river?* □ *Max sold Lefty down the river to save his own skin.*

SELL ▸ FOR

sell something for something to market something at a certain price. □ *I think I can sell this for twice what I paid for it.* □ *This is selling for twice the price at the shop down the street.*

SELL ▸ OFF

sell something off to sell all of something. □ *We ended up with a large stock of out-of-style coats and we had to sell them all off at a loss.* 🅃 *We sold off all the excess stock.*

SELL ▸ ON

sell someone on something to convince someone of something. (Informal.) □ *Now, I have to try to sell the board of directors on the idea.* □ *They were not sold on the idea by your presentation.*

sell something (to someone) on credit to market something on a plan where the purchaser receives the merchandise at the time of sale and pays for it over a period of time, with interest. □ *Sorry. We don't sell anything on credit here.* □ *Is there a chance you could sell this to me on credit?*

SELL ▸ OUT

sell out [for an item] to be sold until there is no more. □ *All the plastic hangers have sold out.* 🄽 *It was a sellout! There's nothing left.*

sell out (to someone) **1.** to sell everything to someone. □ *The farmer finally gave up and sold out to a large corporation.* □ *I refuse to sell out no matter what they offer me.* **2.** to betray someone or something to someone. □ *I think that you have sold out to the enemy!* 🄽 *What a sellout! I thought he was more loyal!*

sell someone or something out to betray someone or something. (*Someone* includes *oneself*.) □ *The small country didn't know how to conduct espionage. They sold their own agent out.* 🅃 *They sold out their own agent.* □ *The agent sold her country out.* □ *You're asking me to sell myself out!* 🄽 *My best friend pulls a sellout like that!*

sell something out to sell all of something. □ *Have they sold their supply out yet?* 🅃 *The stores sold out their stocks of that game long before Christmas.*

SELL ▸ TO

sell something to someone to convey something to someone for money. □ *The shopkeeper refused to sell the medicine to me.* □ *Who did you sell your car to?*

SEND ▸ ABOUT

send one about one's business to brush someone off; to tell someone to leave or get out. (Informal.) □ *Jill was annoyed with Roger and sent him about his business.* □ *Please send those boys about their business. They are being pests.*

SEND ▸ ACROSS

send someone or something across (something) to cause someone or something to cross something. □ *The coach sent the player across the field to give a message to someone on the other side.* □ *We sent the taxi across the river to pick up Gerald on the other side.*

SEND ▸ AFTER

send after someone or something to request that someone or something be brought; to *send for someone or something.* □ *You really ought to send after a doctor.* □ *Let's send after a taxi to take us to the airport.*

send someone after someone or something to send someone to get someone or something. □ *Please send someone after the doctor. This is an emergency.* □ *The telephone was out so we sent someone after an ambulance.*

SEND ▸ AHEAD

send ahead for something to send a message for something to be ready or available when one arrives. □ *I will send* *ahead for a taxi to meet us at the station.* ☐ *We sent ahead for room reservations at the hotel.*

SEND ▶ ALONG

send someone or something along to help someone or something continue along; to send someone. ☐ *I knew it was time for Johnny to go home, so I sent him along.* ☐ *You left your hair spray behind, so I will send it along later.*

SEND ▶ AROUND

send someone or something around to cause someone or something to go from place to place. ☐ *I sent my secretary around to look for the missing book.* 🅃 *I will send around some papers for you to sign.*

send someone or something around for someone or something to make someone or something go somewhere to pick up someone or something. ☐ *I will send my driver around for you at about six.* ☐ *We sent a taxi around for Jane.* ☐ *We sent a truck around for the package.*

SEND ▶ AWAY

send away (for something) to order something to be brought or sent from some distance. ☐ *I sent away for a new part to replace the one that was broken.* ☐ *I couldn't find the part locally. I had to send away for it.*

send someone away with something to make someone leave and carry something away. ☐ *I sent him away with a message for his mother.* ☐ *She sent Ted away with a little booklet about manners.*

send someone or something away to cause someone, a group, or something to leave. ☐ *I sent the solicitor away.* 🅃 *I sent away all the petitioners.*

SEND ▶ BACK

send someone back for something to cause someone to return to get something. ☐ *He came without it, so I sent him back for it.* ☐ *Ted sent Roger back for the rest of the groceries.*

send someone or something back to cause someone or something to return. ☐ *He came to apologize, but I sent him back.* 🅃 *Send back these goods. They are defective.*

SEND ▶ BEFORE

send someone before someone or something to cause someone to appear before someone or a group. ☐ *I sent my lawyer before the mayor to plead my cause.* ☐ *Donna sent a friend before the committee.*

SEND ▶ BELOW

send someone below to send someone to one of the lower decks of a ship. ☐ *The first mate sent the sailor below to shovel coal into the boiler.* ☐ *The captain sent Mr. Wallace below, where he would be out of the way during the storm.*

SEND ▶ BY

send something by something **1.** to dispatch something by a particular carrier. ☐ *I will send it to you by special messenger.* ☐ *We sent the package by air freight.* **2.** to deliver something to something or some place. (Informal.) ☐ *I will send the parcel by your office this afternoon.* ☐ *We sent your order by your house, but no one was there to receive it.*

SEND ▶ DOWN

send someone down for something to request someone to go to a place on a lower level to get something. ☐ *I sent the butler down for another bottle of wine.* 🅃 *I sent down the butler for more of this vintage.*

send someone or something down to dispatch someone or something to some place on a lower level. ☐ *They wanted someone downstairs to help with the moving, so I sent John down.* 🅃 *I sent down John to help.* ☐ *They are hungry down there. Can you send some sandwiches down?*

SEND ▶ FOR

send for someone or something to make a request that someone or something be brought. ☐ *Mr. Franklin sent for his secretary.* ☐ *I think we should send for an ambulance.*

send someone for someone or something to cause someone to go and get someone or something. □ *Please send Jerry for the doctor. This is an emergency.* □ *Could you send someone for pizza?*

SEND ▸ FROM

send someone from pillar to post to send someone to many different places, none of which is the correct place. (Compare to *send someone on a wild goose chase.*) □ *Jill sent Roger from pillar to post to look for a special kind of paper.* □ *Roger was sent from pillar to post with his problem.*

send something from something to dispatch something from something or some place. □ *Ted sent the package from the downtown post office.* □ *The gifts were sent off in a large box from the company's shipping dock.*

SEND ▸ IN

See also under *SEND ▸ IN(TO).*

send in for something to dispatch one's request for something to a company or other body making a public offer of goods. □ *I sent in for a new vitamin that is supposed to make my hair grow back.* □ *Did you send in for that country and western compact disc as you said you would?*

send someone in for someone to send someone into a game as a replacement for someone else. □ *The coach sent Jill in for Alice, who was beginning to tire.* □ *Ted sent Bill in for Wally.*

send something in (to something) to dispatch something, such as an order, to a company or other body making a public offer of goods. □ *I sent the order in to the home office.* 🅃 *I sent in the order.* □ *I sent it in.*

SEND ▸ IN(TO)

send someone in(to something) to make someone go into something or some place. □ *George sent me into the house for a hammer.* 🅃 *The boys know where it is. He should have sent in the boys.* □ *George sent me in.*

SEND ▸ OFF

send off for something to dispatch an order for something to a distant place. □ *I sent off for the proper contest entry forms.* □ *Did you send off for a new license?*

send someone off (to something) to send someone away to something or some place, especially away on a journey; to be present when someone sets out on a journey to something or some place. □ *We sent both kids off to camp this summer and had peace in the house for the first time in years.* 🅃 *Liz sent off Karen to the store.* □ *I had to send them off. They were getting to be annoying.* 🄽 *The committee gave me a fine send-off.*

send something off (to someone or something) to dispatch something to someone, something, or some place. □ *I will send the package off to you in tomorrow's mail.* 🅃 *Karen sent off a letter to her aunt.* □ *She sent it off only yesterday.*

SEND ▸ ON

send someone on a wild-goose chase to send someone on a pointless or futile search. □ *You sent me on a wild-goose chase! There are no straw hats for sale anywhere in town!* □ *Fred was sent on a wild-goose chase while his friends prepared a surprise party for him.*

send someone or something on (ahead) (of someone or something) to dispatch someone or something to arrive before someone or something else. □ *I sent my valet on ahead of me to get the rooms ready.* 🅃 *Jeff sent on his luggage.* □ *I sent her on ahead to get things ready.* □ *I sent my secretary on ahead of me.*

send someone (out) on an errand to dispatch someone to perform an errand. □ *Jerry will be back in a minute. I sent him out on an errand.* □ *Who sent you on an errand?* 🅃 *I sent out Kenny on an errand.*

SEND ▸ OUT

send out a warrant (on someone) See *put out a warrant (on someone)* under *PUT ▸ OUT.*

send out (for someone or something) to send an order by messenger, telephone, cable, or fax that someone or something is to come or be delivered. □

We sent out for a public stenographer to record the will as Uncle Herman dictated it. □ *There was no one there who could take dictation, so we had to send out.* □ *We sent out for sandwiches.*

send someone out (for someone or something) to send someone out to search for someone or something. □ *We sent Gerald out for Walter, who was supposed to have been there already.* 🅃 *Karen sent out Liz for some medicine.*

send someone out (of something) to command someone to leave something or some place. □ *The teacher sent the student out of the room.* 🅃 *The teacher sent out the troublesome students.* □ *Harold sent Thomas out.* □ *Thomas was sent out of the room while we discussed him.*

send someone (out) on an errand See under *SEND ▸ ON.*

SEND ▸ OVER

send someone over ((to) some place) to order someone to go to some place. □ *I sent Dave over to the main office.* □ *I will send someone else over.* 🅃 *Please send over someone else.*

send something over ((to) some place) to cause something to be taken to some place. □ *I sent the package over to your home.* □ *Did you get the package I sent over?* 🅃 *Please send over the rest of the mail.*

SEND ▸ TO

send one to one's death to order one to go on an errand or journey that will result in one's death. □ *The general sent many fine young men to their deaths that day.* □ *They were sent to their death by the act of a madman.*

send someone to someone or something to order someone to go to someone, something, or some place. □ *I sent him to the boss for an answer.* □ *We sent Roger to Detroit.*

send someone to the locker room See the following entry.

send someone to the showers AND **send someone to the locker room** to order a player from the playing field, thus ending the player's participation for the day. □ *The coach had sent four players to the showers before the end of the game.* □ *He was angry enough to send them all to the locker room.*

send something to someone or something to dispatch something to someone, something, or some place. □ *I will send the books to my parents.* □ *I sent the order to Detroit.*

send word to someone to get a message to someone by any means. □ *I will send word to her as soon as I have something to report.* □ *Tom sent word to Bill just in time.*

SEND ▸ UNDER

send someone or something under something to force someone or something under something. □ *The accident sent poor Roger under the wheels of a truck.* □ *Mary kicked the ball and sent it under a bush.*

SEND ▸ UP

send someone or something up 1. to order someone to go upwards to a higher level; to command that something be taken upwards to a higher level. □ *If you need someone else to help you up there, I'll send Gary up.* 🅃 *I'll send up Gary.* □ *They are hungry on the tenth floor. Let's send some sandwiches up.* **2.** to parody or ridicule someone or something. (Informal.) □ *Comedians love to send the president or some other famous person up.* 🅃 *The comedian sent up the vice president.* □ *The skit sent the entire government up.* 🄽 *The prime minister enjoyed the send-up.*

send someone up the river to send someone to prison; to sentence someone to a prison term. (Slang.) □ *The judge tried to send Lefty up the river for a few years, but Lefty had a clever lawyer who got him off with probation.* □ *Max was sent up the river, but his lawyers got him off.*

send someone up the wall to annoy and irritate someone; to drive someone crazy. (Figurative.) □ *Don't scratch your fingers on the blackboard. It sends me up the wall!* □ *That noise sends me up the wall!*

send up a trial balloon to test the validity of something on a small scale. (Cliché.) ☐ *It sounds good to me. Let's send up a trial balloon and see what we find out.* ☐ *We will send up a trial balloon to see what people think.*

SENSITIZE ▸ TO

sensitize someone to something **1.** to make a person have an allergic reaction to something. ☐ *Frequent exposure to the chemical sensitized Harry to it and made him get a rash.* ☐ *He was sensitized to the strong chemical.* **2.** to make someone more thoughtful and receptive to something. ☐ *We want to sensitize you to the feelings of other people.* ☐ *He never became sensitized to the needs of others.*

SENTENCE ▸ TO

sentence someone to something (for something) to order someone to suffer confinement, death, or labor for committing a crime. ☐ *The judge sentenced Roger to three years in prison for the crime.* ☐ *The judge sentenced him to hard labor.* ☐ *The judge sentenced Max to ten years.*

SEPARATE ▸ FROM

separate someone from someone else or something from something else to segregate people or things. (*Someone* includes *oneself.*) ☐ *The nurse separated the infected people from the healthy ones.* ☐ *Please separate the spoiled apples from the good ones.* ☐ *They separated themselves from the rest of the group.*

SEPARATE ▸ INTO

separate someone or something into something to divide people or things into subdivisions. (*Someone* includes *oneself.*) ☐ *We had to separate the kids into smaller groups.* ☐ *Jane separated the apples into three groups.* ☐ *They separated themselves into a number of small groups.*

SEPARATE ▸ OFF

separate off (from something) to go away from something. ☐ *The road to the cabin separates off from the main road and goes along for a mile or two.* ☐ *It separates off about a mile from here.*

separate something off (from something) to remove something from something. ☐ *Frank separated the cream off from the milk.* 🅃 *Separate off the hens from the rooster.* ☐ *All right. I will separate them off.*

SEPARATE ▸ OUT

separate something out (of something) to remove something out from something. (The *of*-phrase is paraphrased with a *from*-phrase when the particle is transposed. See the 🄵 example.) ☐ *She used a filter to separate the dirt particles out of the water.* 🅃 *A filter separated out the impurities.* 🄵 *The filter separated out the dirt from the water.* ☐ *It separated the sand out.*

SERVE ▸ AROUND

serve something around to distribute something to eat or drink to everyone present. ☐ *Please serve the snacks around so that everyone gets some.* 🅃 *Serve around the little cheese things, would you?*

SERVE ▸ AS

serve as someone or something to act in the capacity of someone or something. ☐ *I served as the mayor's assistant for a number of years.* ☐ *This brick will not serve as a doorstop.*

SERVE ▸ FOR

serve something for something to distribute something to eat or drink for a particular purpose. ☐ *We served smoked salmon for an appetizer.* ☐ *What will you serve for a main course?*

SERVE ▸ IN

serve something in something to present something to eat or drink in a particular container. ☐ *Kelly served the lemonade in paper cups.* ☐ *What will you serve the soup in?*

SERVE ▸ ON

serve on something to carry out one's duty or responsibility on something, such as a committee or a board. ☐ *Will you be able to serve on this committee next year also?* ☐ *Sarah refused to serve* *on the committee again.* □ *He served on an aircraft carrier during World War II.*

serve something on someone to deliver something, such as a subpoena, to someone. □ *A little old lady served the subpoena on Max.* □ *The document was served on the plaintiff by a sheriff's deputy.*

SERVE ▸ OUT

serve something out to carry out one's duty or responsibility for the whole time, all the way to the end. □ *She was unable to serve her term out.* 🅃 *The convict served out his sentence in solitary confinement.*

SERVE ▸ TO

serve something to someone **1.** to present someone with something to eat or drink. □ *The host served the snacks to everyone and left the room to work on the salad.* □ *The snacks were served to everyone in attendance.* **2.** to deliver something, such as a subpoena, to someone. □ *The little old lady at the door was there to serve a subpoena to Fred.* □ *She served the papers to the person who lived there.*

SERVE ▸ UNDER

serve under someone or something to carry out one's responsibility under the direction or in the employment of someone. □ *I served under the president of the company as special assistant.* □ *Jane served under the court as an investigator.*

SERVE ▸ UP

serve something up to distribute or deliver food for people to eat. □ *The cook served the stew up and then passed around the bread.* 🅃 *Can you serve up the food now?* 🄰 *The served-up food tasted better than it looked in the pot.*

SERVE ▸ WITH

serve someone with something to deliver something, such as a subpoena, to someone. □ *He served her with papers from the circuit court.* □ *Has Tom been served with the subpoena?*

serve with someone to perform military service alongside or with someone. □ *I served with Harry when we were both in the army.* □ *At the reunion, I met a lot of the guys I served with in the navy.*

SET ▸ ABOUT

set about doing something to begin to do something. □ *When are you going to set about fixing the roof?* □ *We will set about painting the house when the weather gets a little cooler.*

set someone about something to make someone begin doing something. (*Someone* includes *oneself.*) □ *I set the boys about raking up the leaves.* □ *She set herself about repairing the damaged machine.*

SET ▸ ABOVE

set someone or something above someone or something **1.** to place someone or something in a physical location higher than someone or something. □ *Timmy's dad set him above the others so he could see better.* □ *I set the trophy above the television on a little shelf.* **2.** to regard someone or something as better than someone or something else. (*Someone* includes *oneself.*) □ *Fred set his wife and children above everyone else.* □ *Gene set his job above his family.* □ *Why do you set yourself above the others?*

SET ▸ AGAINST

set something against someone or something **1.** to place or lean something against someone or something. □ *Dave set the chair against Fred and had to move it away.* □ *I set the rake against the side of the house.* **2.** to make someone hate or oppose someone or something. □ *His second wife set him against his former in-laws.* □ *The Civil War set brother against brother.* □ *The politician's speech set the populace against him.*

SET ▸ APART

set someone apart from someone to make someone stand out when compared to someone else. (*Someone* includes *oneself.*) □ *Her flaming red hair sets her apart from all the others in her class.* □ *They set themselves apart from* *the rest due to their superb accomplishments.*

set something apart from something **1.** to make something stand out when compared to something else. ☐ *The bright green really sets this one apart from the others.* ☐ *Her golden hair sets her apart from all the others.* **2.** to move something so it is away from something else. ☐ *Set the old ones apart from the others so we can sell them first.* ☐ *The stale loaves were set apart from the fresh ones.*

SET ▸ ASIDE

set something aside to place something in a place that is out of the way. ☐ *Betty set the manuscript aside until she had more time to work on it.* 🅃 *Liz set aside her book for a while.*

set something aside (for someone or something) to reserve something for someone or some purpose. ☐ *I will set a piece of cake aside for you.* 🅃 *Liz set aside some cake for Karen.* ☐ *I will set some of this roast aside for tomorrow's lunch.* ☐ *Oh, yes. Set some aside.* 🅃 *Did you set aside enough money for the rent?*

SET ▸ AT

set someone's mind at ease (about someone or something) to make someone feel mentally comfortable about someone or something. ☐ *Alice is upset. I will have to do something to set her mind at ease about the accident.* ☐ *Please set your mind at ease. Everything will be all right.*

set something at something to fix something at a particular value or amount. ☐ *Please set the thermostat at a lower temperature.* ☐ *Who set the refrigerator at freezing?*

SET ▸ BACK

See *set one (back) on one's feet* under *SET ▸ ON.*

set one back on one's heels to surprise or shock someone. (Colloquial.) ☐ *I'll bet that news really set her back on her heels!* ☐ *The bill for the repairs set me back on my heels.*

set something back AND **put something back** to set something, like a timepiece, to a lower number. ☐ *It's that time of year when you must set your clocks and watches back!* 🅃 *Set back your clock tonight.* ☐ *I have to put all the clocks back.* ☐ *We will have to set the schedule back by a week or more.* 🄽 *The project suffered another setback.*

set something back (from something) to place something at some distance from something else. ☐ *Set the glasses back from the edge or they will get knocked off.* 🅃 *You should set back the glasses a little from the edge.* ☐ *Set them back or they will get broken.*

SET ▸ BEFORE

set something before someone or something to place something in front of someone, a creature, a group, or something. ☐ *I set the plate of sandwiches before the children and they were gone in a few minutes.* ☐ *Jane set the bowl of food before the cats.*

SET ▸ BESIDE

set something beside something to place something near or next to something. ☐ *Please set the chair beside the window.* ☐ *I set the suitcase beside the door so I would not forget it.*

SET ▸ BY

set great store by someone or something to view someone or something with great favor and high expectations. (Idiomatic.) ☐ *I set great store by my accountant.* ☐ *We set great store by our insurance company.*

SET ▸ DOWN

set someone down (on(to) something) to place a person one is carrying or lifting onto something. ☐ *I set the small boy down onto the desk, and gave him a piece of candy.* 🅃 *I set down the child on the chair.* ☐ *Jane set her down.*

set something down as something to regard something as something. ☐ *I set his behavior down as an event that would not repeat itself.* ☐ *Please just set the whole afternoon down as an exercise in patience.*

set something down (on something) **1.** to place something on the surface of something. □ *Andy set the hot skillet down on the countertop and burned a hole in it.* 🅃 *He set down the skillet on the counter.* □ *Please set it down carefully.* **2.** to write something on paper. □ *Let me set this down on paper so we will have a record of what was said.* 🅃 *I will set down this note on paper.* □ *She set it down in a very neat hand.* **3.** to land an airplane in something. □ *The pilot set the plane down on the runway.* □ *I can't set the plane down on this field!*

set something down to something to blame something on something; to regard something as the cause of something. □ *She set his rude behavior down to indigestion.* □ *I just set her crankiness down to lack of sleep.*

SET ▸ FOR

set sail for some place to leave in a ship or boat for some place. (Not limited to ships having sails.) □ *We set sail for Grenada at noon.* □ *When do we set sail for St. Louis?*

set something for something to adjust something for a particular setting. □ *I set the thermostat for a lower temperature.* □ *Please set the air-conditioning for about 75 degrees.*

set the stage for something **1.** to arrange a stage for an act or scene of a production. □ *The stage crew set the stage for the first act.* □ *They set the stage for the second scene while the orchestra played.* **2.** to prepare something for some activity. □ *The agreement set the stage for further negotiations.* □ *Your comments set the stage for another big argument.*

SET ▸ FORTH

set forth on something to start out on something, such as a journey. □ *We will set forth on the trip next Thursday.* □ *What time did you set forth?*

set something forth to explain something; to present some information. □ *She set her ideas forth in an organized and interesting manner.* □ *Please set your thoughts forth quickly and concisely.*

SET ▸ FORWARD

set something forward **1.** to move something to a more forward position. □ *Please set the chair forward a little bit. It is in the walkway.* □ *If you set the vase forward, it will show up better against the dark background.* **2.** to reset a timepiece to a later time. □ *You are supposed to set your clock forward at this time of year.* □ *Did you set your watch forward?*

SET ▸ FROM

set someone or something free from something to release someone or something from something. (*Someone* includes *oneself*.) □ *The commando set the secret agent free from the prison.* □ *Who set the chickens free from their pens?* □ *At last, he set himself free from the things that held him back.*

SET ▸ IN

set foot in some place to enter into some place; to begin to enter some place. □ *The judge ordered him never to set foot in her house again.* □ *I would never set foot in a place like that.*

set in to begin; to become fixed for a period of time. □ *A severe cold spell set in early in November.* □ *When high temperatures set in, the use of electricity went up considerably.*

set one's house in order to make certain that one's affairs are in proper legal order. □ *Before we can ask for a bank loan, we have to set our house in order.* □ *I found an accountant who would help me set my house in order.*

set something in a place to locate the action of a play or movie in a place. □ *The author set the second act in a wooded glade.* □ *The opera was set in a forest outside Moscow.*

set something in motion to start something moving. □ *The mayor set the project in motion by moving the first shovelful of soil.* □ *I cannot set the procedure in motion until I receive a purchase order.*

set something in something to set something in type, a particular style of type, or a particular font. □ *Why not* *set this section in italics to make it stand out from the rest?* □ *Why was this paragraph set in bold type?*

SET ▶ IN(TO)

set something in(to something) to install something into its place. □ *The movers set the stove into its proper place and the plumber hooked it up two weeks later.* 🅃 *They set in the stove.* □ *It was difficult, but they set it in properly.*

SET ▶ OFF

set off (for something) to leave for something or some place. □ *We set off for Springfield three hours late.* □ *It was after noon before we could set off.*

set off on something to begin on a journey or expedition. □ *When do you plan to set off on your journey?* □ *We will set off on our adventure tomorrow morning.*

set someone off 1. to cause someone to become very angry; to ignite someone's anger. □ *That kind of thing really sets me off!* 🅃 *Your behavior set off Mrs. Franklin.* □ *When I mentioned high taxes it really set Walter off. He went into a rage.* 2. to cause someone to start talking or lecturing about a particular subject. □ *When I mentioned high taxes it really set Walter off. He talked and talked.* 🅃 *The subject set Karen off, and she talked on endlessly.*

set something off 1. to ignite something, such as fireworks. □ *The boys were setting firecrackers off all afternoon.* 🅃 *They set off bomb after bomb.* 2. to cause something to begin. □ *The coach set the race off with a shot from the starting pistol.* 🅃 *She set off the race with a gunshot.* 3. to make something distinct or outstanding. □ *The lovely stonework sets the fireplace off quite nicely.* 🅃 *The white hat really sets off Betsy's eyes.*

SET ▶ ON

See also under *SET ▶ ON(TO).*

set eyes on someone or something to catch sight of someone or something. □ *I loved her from the moment I first set eyes on her.* □ *I had never set eyes on a glacier before.*

set one (back) on one's feet AND **set one on one's feet again** to reestablish someone; to help someone become active and productive again. □ *Gary's uncle helped set him back on his feet.* □ *We will all help set you on your feet again.*

set one's heart on someone or something to be determined to get someone or something. □ *I am sorry you didn't get to pick the one you wanted. I know you had set your heart on Fred.* □ *Andy had his heart set on a car as a graduation present.*

set one's hopes on someone or something to have one's hopes or expectations dependent on someone or something. □ *Please don't set your hopes on me in the race. I can't run as fast as I used to.* □ *I have set my hopes on the effectiveness of the new law.*

set one's mind on someone or something to be determined to get or have someone or something. □ *I've set my mind on Dave. I have to have him on my team.* □ *Jamie set her mind on the red sports car.*

set one's sights on someone or something to regard having someone or something as one's goal. □ *He wanted a wife and he had set his sights on Alice.* □ *James set his sights on a college degree.*

set someone on fire to excite someone; to make someone passionate. (Figurative.) □ *Her oratory set everyone on fire.* □ *Ted's presentation didn't exactly set me on fire, but I didn't go to sleep either.*

set someone or something on fire to ignite someone or something. (*Someone* includes *oneself*.) □ *The torturer finished off by setting his victim on fire.* □ *The students set the mountain of wood on fire and had a party.* □ *He set himself on fire in protest of the war.*

set someone or something on someone or something to command someone or some creature to attack someone or some creature. □ *The gang leader set his thugs on the unwary tourists.* □ *Scott set his hounds on the cocker spaniel.*

set someone's teeth on edge 1. [for a scraping sound] to irritate someone's nerves. □ *That noise sets my teeth on edge!* □ *Tom's teeth were set on edge by the incessant screaming of the children.* 2. [for a thought or idea] to upset someone very much. □ *Her ideas usually set my teeth on edge.* □ *The very thought of doing that set her teeth on edge.*

SET ► ON(TO)

set something (up)on something to place something on the surface of something. □ *Mrs. Franklin set a bowl of fruit upon the table.* □ *I set my empty glass on the counter.*

SET ► OUT

set out (for some place) (from some place) to leave from some place on a journey for some place. □ *We set out for home from the cabin on the very next morning.* □ *We set out from the cabin at dawn.* □ *We set out for the lake at dawn.*

set out (on something) to begin a journey; to begin a project. □ *We set out on our trip exactly as planned.* □ *We set out as planned.* Ⓝ *It was a lot of fun at the outset. Then it became quite dull.*

set out to do something to begin to do something; to intend to do something. □ *Jill set out to weed the garden, but pulled up a few valuable plants in the process.* □ *I set out to repair the door, not rebuild the whole house.*

set something out (for someone or something) to remove something and place it so that it is available for someone or some purpose. □ *I set a piece of cake out for you to eat whenever you get home.* Ⓣ *Liz set out some cake for Karen.* □ *I set some cake out. Where is it now?*

SET ► OVER

set something over something to place something in a position above something else. □ *Toby set the plate over the hole in the tablecloth.* □ *Please set this kettle over the fire.*

SET ► TO

See *be set to do something* under *BE ► TO.*

set fire to someone or something to cause someone or something to ignite and burn. □ *The torturers ended their activities by setting fire to their victim.* □ *Who set fire to the leaves? Burning leaves is illegal.*

set one's mind to something See *put one's mind to something* under *PUT ► TO.*

set someone or something to work to start someone or something working; to cause someone or something to begin functioning. (*Someone* includes *oneself.*) □ *The captain set everyone to work repairing the tears in the fabric of the balloon.* □ *We will set the machines to work at the regular time.* □ *They set themselves to work on the task.*

set to to begin; to attack or commence. □ *The two boys set to almost as soon as they met each other.* □ *They set to and fought for about ten minutes, cursing and screaming.* Ⓝ *The set-to lasted about ten minutes.*

set to work (on someone or something) to begin working on someone or something. □ *We have finished questioning Tom, so we will set to work on Fred.* □ *We set to work on dinner at noon.* □ *It was 2:00 P.M. before we set to work.*

SET ► UP

set someone or something up to place someone or something in an upright position. □ *He was asleep, but we tried to set him up anyway.* Ⓣ *I set up the lamp, which had fallen over again.*

set someone or something up against someone or something to put someone or something into competition against someone or something. □ *The coach set his team up against the Lions.* □ *Walter set his brother up against the town bully.* Ⓣ *He set up Will against a very fast runner.*

set someone or something up as something 1. to equip someone or something to be or work as something. (*Someone* includes *oneself.*) □ *His uncle set him up as a tax consultant.* Ⓣ *Lee set up his uncle as a tax consultant.* □ *Ken set the company up as a partnership.* □ *She set herself up as a consult-*

ant. **2.** to make someone, oneself, or something appear to be something. ☐ *You have set yourself up as judge, jury, and executioner!* Ⓣ *The boss set up his nephew as vice president.* ☐ *Ken set his firm up as a trading company.* ☐ *He set himself up as some sort of spiritual advisor.*

set someone up (for something) **1.** to prepare someone for a deception. (*Someone* includes *oneself.*) ☐ *The crooks set the old lady up for their standard scam.* Ⓣ *They set up their victim for the scam.* ☐ *It didn't take much to set Max up.* ☐ *They set themselves up to be cheated.* **2.** to make someone become part of a joke. (*Someone* includes *oneself.*) ☐ *The comedian was highly skilled at setting members of the audience up for a gag.* Ⓣ *The joker set up a friend for the butt of the joke.* ☐ *So, you thought you could set me up!* ☐ *You really set yourself up for that one!*

set someone up in something to equip someone for business or a particular business. (*Someone* includes *oneself.*) ☐ *My uncle set me up in business for myself.* Ⓣ *He set up Fred in a candy shop.* ☐ *He set himself up for business as a tax advisor.*

set someone up with someone to arrange a date or rendezvous for someone with someone. ☐ *I set my cousin up with Jill for a movie Saturday night.* Ⓣ *I set up my cousin with Jill.*

set something up against something to prop or lean something against something. ☐ *Set the table up against the wall. Make sure it is firmly against the wall.* ☐ *Tom set the couch up against the door to try to keep Max and Lefty out.*

set something up (for something) to arrange something for a particular time or event. ☐ *I will set a meeting up for tomorrow.* Ⓣ *Can you set up a meeting for tomorrow?* ☐ *Yes, I'll set it up.*

set up housekeeping to begin living in a particular place. ☐ *I am anxious to settle down and set up housekeeping.* ☐ *We set up housekeeping in a small apartment on Maple Street.*

set up shop (some place) to open one's business or trade in a place. ☐ *The merchant set up shop right on the street corner and was doing quite well until the police came along.* ☐ *I heard you went into business for yourself. Where did you set up shop?*

SET ▸ UPON

set upon someone or something to attack someone or some creature. ☐ *The dogs set upon the man and injured him severely.* ☐ *The gulls set upon the helpless kitten.*

SETTLE ▸ BACK

settle (back) (in(to) something) to sit and relax comfortably in a soft place to sit. ☐ *She settled back into her chair and kicked off her shoes.* ☐ *Just sit down and settle back.*

SETTLE ▸ DOWN

settle down **1.** to become calm. ☐ *Please settle down. Relax.* ☐ *I will try to settle down so I can think straight.* **2.** to get quiet. ☐ *Will you all please settle down so we can begin?* ☐ *Settle down! Let's get this meeting over with!* **3.** to abandon a free life-style and take up a more stable and disciplined one. (Often with thoughts of marriage, homeownership, and child bearing.) ☐ *I wish Charles would settle down.* ☐ *Haven't you ever thought of settling down and raising a family?*

settle down somewhere to establish a residence somewhere. (Also without *down,* but not eligible as an entry.) ☐ *After retiring, they settled down in a little cabin near a lake.* ☐ *We really wanted to settle down in a small town in the South.*

settle down to something to begin in earnest to do something. ☐ *Now, let's settle down to business.* ☐ *I want to settle down to a nice calm meal.*

settle someone down to make someone become quiet. (*Someone* includes *oneself.*) ☐ *The principal had to go into the classroom and settle the students down.* ☐ *At last the little boys settled themselves down and went to sleep.*

SETTLE ▸ FOR

settle for someone or something to accept or be satisfied with someone or something. □ *I wanted Fred on my team, but I will have to settle for Don.* □ *We will settle for a smaller car, considering the cost of a large one.*

SETTLE ▸ IN(TO)

settle (back) (in(to) something) See under *SETTLE ▸ BACK.*

settle in(to something) 1. to become accustomed to something, such as a new home, job, status, etc. □ *By the end of the first week he had settled into his new job.* □ *He settled in with no problems.* 2. to *settle (back) (in(to) something).* □ *I love to settle back into my new reclining chair.* □ *Jan sat down in the chair and settled in.*

settle someone or something in(to something) to ease someone or something into something or some place. (*Someone* includes *oneself.*) □ *I helped settle the new residents into their apartments.* 🅃 *We helped settle in the Wilsons, who had just arrived.* □ *Jan settled her new puppy in with no problems.* □ *The newlyweds settled themselves into their new home.*

SETTLE ▸ ON

See under *SETTLE ▸ (UP)ON.*

SETTLE ▸ TO

settle to something [for something suspended in a liquid] to work down to the lowest point. □ *The dirt finally settled to the bottom of the bottle.* □ *All the stuff that was suspended in the aquarium water finally settled to the bottom.*

SETTLE ▸ UP

settle (something) up (with someone) to divide the cost of something with someone. □ *I will settle the bill up with you later.* 🅃 *Can I settle up the bill with you later?* □ *Let's settle up later.* □ *We'll settle this up later.*

SETTLE ▸ (UP)ON

settle (up)on someone or something 1. [for a flying creature] to light upon someone or something. (*Upon* is formal and less commonly used than *on.*) □ *The bee settled upon Mary, who sat very still until it flew away.* □ *The plane settled on the runway gently.* 2. [for something] to cover and press down on someone or something. □ *The heavy blankets settled upon Fred, and he began to feel a little too warm.* □ *The snow settled on the ground gently.* 3. [for someone] to accept the choice of someone or something. (*Upon* is formal and less commonly used than *on.*) □ *She finally settled on Fred as her choice.* □ *I finally settled on a red car with power windows.*

SETTLE ▸ WITH

settle a score with someone to get even with someone for something; to get revenge on someone. □ *I'm glad to see you. I want to settle a score with you.* □ *Lefty had to settle a score with Max.*

settle (something) with someone to bring a legal contest with someone to an end, usually by one side paying money to the other. □ *Have you settled the suit with Bill Wilson yet?* □ *I have not settled with Wilson yet.*

settle something with someone to conclude a matter, such as an argument, with someone. □ *I need to settle this argument with you.* □ *Have you settled your disagreement with Ed?*

SEW ▸ AROUND

sew around something to stitch the edges of something. □ *Sew around the edge to keep it from unraveling.* □ *Ted sewed around the bottom of his pants leg where the puppy had chewed a hole.*

SEW ▸ DOWN

sew something down to attach something down to something else by sewing or stitching. □ *The edge of the pocket was coming loose, so I sewed it down.* 🅃 *Nancy sewed down the loose pocket.*

SEW ▸ TO

sew something to something to attach something to something with stitches. (The things are usually cloth.) □ *She sewed the sleeve to the jacket.* □ *I sewed the pocket to the wrong side of the apron.*

SEW ► UP

sew someone or something up 1. to stitch together an opening in someone or something. ☐ *The surgeon sewed the patient up and pronounced the operation a success.* 🅃 *This is torn. Can you sew up this rip?* 2. to complete one's dealings with someone or something. (Figurative.) ☐ *It's time to sew this up and go home.* ☐ *I think we can sew up Charles this afternoon and get on to someone else.* 🅃 *Let's sew up this last matter and go.* 3. to secure someone or something, as in a business deal. (Figurative.) ☐ *I think I have sewed the Wilson contract up.* ☐ *We will sew him up and have him under contract for three years.* 🅃 *Can we sew up the other matter next?*

SHACKLE ► TO

shackle someone to someone or something 1. to attach someone to someone or something with a chain. ☐ *The jailkeeper shackled the prisoner to the wall, where he could cause little trouble.* ☐ *He shackled Ted to Wally.* ☐ *A huge dog had been shackled to the wall with a heavy chain.* 2. to burden someone with something. (*Someone* includes *oneself.*) ☐ *Please don't shackle me to the out-of-town visitors all weekend! I have other things to do.* ☐ *They don't want to shackle themselves to a child.*

SHACKLE ► WITH

shackle someone with someone or something to burden someone with someone or something. (*Someone* includes *oneself.*) ☐ *Immediately after they got married, he shackled her with a child and then another and then another.* ☐ *Let's not shackle ourselves with a big, expensive car.*

shackle someone with something to fetter or hobble someone with something, such as chains, etc. (Both literal and figurative uses.) ☐ *The sheriff shackled the prisoner with handcuffs and leg irons.* ☐ *The robbers were shackled with leg irons.*

SHADE ► FROM

shade (from something) into something See under *SHADE ► INTO.*

shade someone or something from something to provide a barrier between a light source and someone or something. ☐ *She shaded her child from the bright sun.* ☐ *We should shade the young plants from the sun.*

SHADE ► INTO

shade (from something) into something [for the density of the colors in a picture or design] to change gradually from one to another. ☐ *A deep purple shaded from the dark shadows of the mountains into the lighter areas of the sky.* ☐ *The gray shaded into white.*

shade something into something to blend one color or design into another. ☐ *The artist very skillfully shaded the purple into the dark mountains in the background.* ☐ *See how skillfully the artist has shaded the sky into the sea.*

SHADE ► WITH

shade someone or something with something to use something to ward off heat or light from someone or something. (*Someone* includes *oneself.*) ☐ *The mother shaded her baby with her hand because the sun was so bright.* ☐ *Let's shade the young plants with cheesecloth.* ☐ *She shaded herself the best she could with her hand.*

SHAG ► OUT

shag someone out to make someone exhausted. (Informal.) ☐ *All that work really shagged me out.* ☐ *What have you been doing to shag you out so much?*

SHAKE ► BY

shake someone by the hand to grasp someone's hand and shake it in greeting or congratulation; to shake someone's hand. ☐ *He came up and shook me by the hand as if he hadn't seen me for ages.* ☐ *They shook each other by the hand and walked off together.*

SHAKE ► DOWN

shake someone down 1. to search someone's person for contraband, a gun, or other weapon. (Slang.) ☐ *The cops shook Max down but didn't find anything but a knife.* 🅃 *They shook down all the members of the street gang.* 🄽

The cops gave Lefty the shakedown and found his gun. **2.** to attempt to extort money from someone; to blackmail someone. (Slang.) □ *Max tried to shake Mr. Wilson down to prevent Mrs. Wilson from knowing what was going on.* 🅃 *Max tried to shake down the wrong victim and got arrested.* 🄽 *You want money for these pictures? Is this a shakedown?*

shake someone or something (down) from something See under *SHAKE ▸ FROM.*

shake something down See under *shake something out* under *SHAKE ▸ OUT.*

SHAKE ▸ FROM

shake someone or something (down) (from something) to shake something and cause someone or something to fall out of or down from it. □ *The kids shook Timmy down from the tree.* □ *They shook the Frisbee from the tree.* □ *They shook the Frisbee down.*

shake something from something to get something, such as crumbs, off of something by shaking. □ *Paul shook the crumbs from the tablecloth and folded it up and put it away.* □ *Please shake the lint from the blanket before you put it away.*

SHAKE ▸ IN

shake in one's boots to tremble from fear. (Figurative.) □ *I was so scared I was shaking in my boots.* □ *She was shaking in her boots in anticipation of what she thought would happen.*

SHAKE ▸ OFF

shake oneself or itself off [for someone or some creature] to shake to get something off of one. (As an animal might do.) □ *The pillow burst and covered Terry with feathers. He tried to shake himself off, but it didn't work.* □ *The dog came out of the water and shook itself off.* □ *Don got up from the dusty road and shook himself off the best he could.*

shake someone off to get rid of someone; to get away from someone who is following one. (Figurative.) □ *The cops had a guy following me, but I managed to shake him off.* 🅃 *Max shook off the guy who was following him.*

shake something off **1.** to shake [oneself] and make something fall off. □ *She shook the dust off before coming into the house.* 🅃 *Please shake off some of that dust.* **2.** to fight off a cold or other disease. (Informal.) □ *I'm coming down with a cold, but I think I can shake it off.* 🅃 *I hope I can shake off this cold.*

shake something off something to shake something until something falls off. □ *I shook the dust off my coat before I went in the house.* □ *Please shake the dirt off the doormat.*

SHAKE ▸ ON

shake (hands) on something to seal an agreement about something by shaking hands. □ *Let's shake hands on this agreement.* □ *Okay, let's shake on it.*

SHAKE ▸ OUT

shake someone or something out (of something) to cause someone or something to fall out of a tree. (Does not refer to things that grow on trees, such as fruit or nuts. See under *SHAKE ▸ FROM.*) □ *They tried shaking the cat out of the tree.* 🅃 *They couldn't shake out the cat.* □ *The boys tried to shake Tim out of the tree.*

shake something out **1.** to clean something of dirt or crumbs by shaking. □ *Please shake the tablecloth out.* 🅃 *Can you shake out your coat? It's really dusty.* **2.** AND **shake something down** to test something to find out what the problems are. (Figurative.) □ *I need to spend some time driving my new car to shake it out.* 🅃 *We need to shake out this car before I make the final payment.* □ *The ship ran well when I shook it down.* 🄰 *We took the boat on a shakedown cruise.* 🄽 *We gave it a good shakeout. It runs fine.*

shake something out (of someone) to get a person to give information by shaking the person. (Refers to holding a person, often a child, by the shoulders and shaking.) □ *I want to know his name! Am I going to have to shake it out* *of you?* □ *I'll get the truth out of you if I have to shake it out.*

shake something out of something to get something out of the inside of something else by shaking. (The *of*-phrase is paraphrased with a *from*-phrase when the particle is transposed. See the F example.) □ *Please shake the dirt out of your cuffs before you come in the house.* T *Please shake out the dirt.* F *Will you shake out the dirt from your cuffs?*

SHAKE ▸ UP

shake someone up to startle or upset someone. (Slang.) □ *Loud noises shake me up.* T *The explosion shook up everyone.*

shake something up **1.** to mix something by shaking. □ *I am going to shake the salad dressing up before I serve it.* T *Please shake up the salad dressing.* **2.** to upset an organization or group of people by some administrative action. □ *The board of directors shook middle management up by firing a few of the old-timers.* T *They shook up the firm by taking the company public.* N *The president lost his job during the shake-up.*

SHAKE ▸ WITH

shake hands with someone to greet or congratulate someone by shaking hands. □ *The politician went around shaking hands with everyone.* □ *He refused to shake hands with me, so I left.*

shake with something to tremble because of something such as fear, cold, anger, anticipation, etc. □ *The clerk shook with rage and threatened to quit immediately.* □ *Tom was shaking with anger as he saw the results of the robbery.*

SHAME ▸ INTO

shame someone into something to use guilt or embarrassment to make someone do something. □ *They shamed me into agreeing to go with them.* □ *Please don't try to shame me into it. I can be reasoned with, you know.*

SHAME ▸ OUT

shame someone out of something to use guilt or embarrassment to make someone give up something. (Colloquial.) □ *I shamed him out of the stolen candy bar.* □ *They tried to shame me out of a donation, but I resisted.*

shame something out of someone to use guilt or embarrassment to make someone tell something or give something. □ *At first, she refused to tell, but the boss managed to shame it out of her.* □ *They tried to shame a donation out of him, but he resisted.*

SHAMPOO ▸ OUT

shampoo something out of something to clean something out of something, such as hair, carpet, etc., using soap or shampoo. □ *Fred used some sort of liquid to shampoo the stain out of the carpet.* T *He shampooed out the stain.*

SHAPE ▸ INTO

shape someone into something to groom or coach someone for a particular job or purpose. □ *I think I can shape you into a fine accountant.* □ *Teachers have always tried to shape me into whatever I didn't happen to be at the time.*

shape something into something to mold something into something; to form something into something. □ *I shaped the clay into a small turtle.* □ *Can you shape this balloon into a dog?*

SHAPE ▸ UP

shape someone up **1.** to cause someone to get into good physical condition. □ *The jogging shaped him up, but it harmed his joints.* T *The jogging shaped up Karen in about three weeks.* **2.** to cause someone to become productive, efficient, competent, etc. □ *The manager decided she had to shape everyone in the office up.* T *The new director shaped up the salespeople virtually overnight.*

shape up **1.** to get into good physical condition. □ *I really need to shape up. I get out of breath too easily.* □ *If you don't shape up, you might develop heart trouble.* **2.** to become productive, efficient, competent, etc. □ *You are going to have to shape up if you want to keep your job.* □ *The boss told her to shape up or find another job.*

shape up or ship out to start functioning properly or leave. (Fixed phrase. Originally naval. Usually a command.) □ *The boss told Sally to shape up or ship out.* □ *You have to become more productive. It's either shape up or ship out.*

SHARE ▸ AMONG

share something among someone to divide or apportion something among a number of people. □ *The people in the lifeboat shared the remaining food among themselves politely.* □ *Please share this among yourselves.* □ *He shared the cookies among the children.*

SHARE ▸ BETWEEN

share something between people to apportion something between two people or two groups of people. □ *Please share this between the two groups of people.* □ *The teacher wanted the candy shared between the boys and the girls.*

SHARE ▸ IN

share in something 1. to receive a share of something. □ *I hope I am allowed to share in the fruits of our labor.* □ *Everyone should share in the profits.* 2. to participate in some activity. □ *I would like to share in the planning of the party.* □ *Would you like to share in the evaluation of the public library staff?*

SHARE ▸ OUT

share something out (to someone or something) to apportion something among people or a group. □ *Will you please share out the pie?* 🅃 *Karen shared out the pie to everyone.* □ *We have to share out the orders to various supply companies.*

SHARE ▸ WITH

share something with someone or something to give something or part of something that one has to someone or members of a group. □ *I shared the cake with my brother.* □ *Can you share your information with the committee?*

SHAVE ▸ AWAY

shave something away (from something) to remove something from the surface of something by shaving or scraping. □ *The carpenter shaved the rough places away from the windowsill.* 🅃 *The carpenter shaved away the rough area from the edge of the door.* □ *Walter shaved his mustache away.*

SHAVE ▸ OFF

shave something off ((of) someone or something) to cut something off someone or something by shaving. (The *of*-phrase is paraphrased with a *from*-phrase when the particle is transposed. See the 🄵 example. The *of* is colloquial.) □ *The barber shaved the beard off of Jake.* 🅃 *The barber shaved off Don's beard.* 🄵 *The barber shaved off the whiskers from Don's face.* □ *He shaved them off.*

SHEAR ▸ OF

shear someone or something of something to remove something from someone or something by cutting or trimming. □ *The barber sheared Tom of his curly locks.* □ *The barber sheared Tom's head of lots of thick brown hair.*

SHEAR ▸ OFF

shear something off ((of) something) to cut or trim something off something. (The *of*-phrase is paraphrased with a *from*-phrase when the particle is transposed. See the 🄵 example. The *of* is colloquial.) □ *Vincent sheared the wool off of the sheep in record time.* 🅃 *He sheared off the wool.* 🄵 *He sheared off the wool from the sheep.* □ *Carla sheared many pounds of wool off in one afternoon.*

SHED ▸ ON(TO)

shed (some) light on(to) someone or something 1. to shine or direct light onto someone or something. □ *The glow of the old-fashioned lantern shed a dim light on Tony, who sat there immobile.* □ *The single hanging bulb shed very little light on her work.* 2. to provide insight or special knowledge about someone or something. □ *I have some information that will shed some light on Fred and his whereabouts.* □ *This letter should shed light on the problem.*

SHED ▸ OVER

shed tears over someone or something to cry about someone or something; to be sympathetic about someone or something. □ *I might miss him a little, but I won't shed any tears over him.* □ *There is little use in shedding tears over a lost shoe.*

SHEER ▸ OFF

sheer off (from something) to turn sharply away from something. □ *The speedboat sheered off from the shore and headed out into the lake.* □ *The bullet sheered off and went into a tree harmlessly.*

SHELL ▸ OUT

shell out an amount of money (for something) (to someone) to pay money out, perhaps unwillingly, for something to someone. (Colloquial.) □ *I refuse to shell out forty dollars for a book to anyone!* 🅃 *Liz shelled a fortune out for the stereo.* □ *I won't shell out any more money for electronic equipment.* □ *Fred refuses to shell out even one cent to that store.*

SHELTER ▸ FROM

shelter someone or something from something to protect someone or something from something, such as weather. (*Someone* includes *oneself*.) □ *We had to shelter Bill and Ted from the night.* □ *The mother bird sheltered her chicks from the storm.* □ *She pulled up her collar to shelter herself from the rain.*

SHIELD ▸ AGAINST

shield someone or something against someone or something AND **shield someone or something from someone or something** to protect or shelter someone or something against someone or something, in any combination. (*Someone* includes *oneself*.) □ *The father shielded his child against the attacker.* □ *He shielded her against the rain.* □ *He shielded the puppy from the cold.* □ *He shielded the crystal goblet against harm.* □ *They tried to shield themselves against the attackers.*

SHIELD ▸ FROM

shield someone or something from someone or something See the previous entry.

SHIFT ▸ DOWN

shift down to shift into a lower automotive gear. □ *The engine is laboring. It's time to shift down.* □ *I had to shift down twice as I was going up the hill.*

SHIFT ▸ FOR

shift for oneself to make one's own way in the world; to survive for oneself. □ *I was left alone to shift for myself when I was fifteen.* □ *I had to shift for myself for dinner, because it was the cook's night off.*

SHIFT ▸ FROM

shift from something to something to transfer or change from one thing or place to another. □ *Alice shifted from one foot to the other as she stood in line.* □ *Tom had to shift from desk to desk while his office was being painted.*

shift someone or something from something to something to transfer or change someone or something from one thing or place to another. □ *Tom shifted Alice from her long-time job to a different assignment.* □ *We shifted the committee from one room to another.*

SHIFT ▸ INTO

shift into something to change into a different mode, time, gear, attitude, etc. □ *The conductor shifted into a much slower tempo for the rest of the piece.* □ *I shifted into a higher gear when we got on level ground.*

SHIFT ▸ OUT

shift out of something to change out of a particular mode, time, gear, attitude, etc. □ *She quickly shifted out of second gear into third.* □ *I hope you can shift out of that bad attitude into a more pleasant state before the guests arrive.*

SHIFT ▸ TO

shift something to something to transfer or change something to a different position or orientation. □ *Laura shifted the table to the left.* □ *Can you shift the picnic table to a place closer to the lake?*

SHIN ▸ DOWN

shin down something to climb down something like a pole, using one's legs to hold on while letting oneself down with one's hands. ☐ *I couldn't shin down the pole as fast as I wanted.* ☐ *Tom shinned down the downspout and ran off into the night.*

SHIN ▸ UP

shin up something to climb up something like a pole, using one's legs to hold on while pulling with one's arms. ☐ *He had to shin up a pole as the last part of his test.* ☐ *We shinned up the downspout to get to the roof.*

SHINE ▸ AT

shine at someone or something [for a light, such as the sun] to radiate or beam at someone or something. ☐ *The spotlight shone at Don and blinded him temporarily.* ☐ *The car lights shone at the approaching traffic in the opposite lane. They needed adjustment.*

shine something at someone or something to direct a light at someone or something. ☐ *Shine the light at Tony and see if he's awake.* ☐ *Would you shine your light at the house number to see if we are in the right block?*

SHINE ▸ DOWN

shine (down) (up)on someone or something See under *SHINE ▸ (UP)ON.*

SHINE ▸ ON

See under *SHINE ▸ (UP)ON.*

SHINE ▸ OUT

shine out **1.** to shine or radiate light; to shine forth. ☐ *She snapped on the flashlight and a reassuring light shone out.* ☐ *The hallway was cheery and a bright light shone out, inviting us in.* **2.** [for a characteristic] to make itself very evident. ☐ *His good humor shone out, especially when he was surrounded by grouches.* ☐ *Sarah's basically good character shone out almost all the time.*

shine out (of something) [for light] to radiate out of some enclosed thing. ☐ *The lamp Tony was reading with shone out of his room, under the door.* ☐ *Under his door, a light shone out.*

SHINE ▸ THROUGH

shine something through something to direct a beam of light through something. ☐ *Tom shone a beam of light through the darkness.* ☐ *Fred shone the flashlight through the water, but could not see anything.*

shine through (something) **1.** [for rays of light] to penetrate something. ☐ *The bright light of day shone through the windows.* ☐ *The light shone through and lit up the room.* **2.** [for something that was obscured or hidden] to become visible or evident. ☐ *Her basic intelligence shone through in spite of her country ways.* ☐ *Her intelligence shone through in most instances.*

SHINE ▸ UP

shine something up to polish something. (Also without *up*, but not eligible as an entry.) ☐ *Tom shined his shoes up.* 🅃 *Fred shined up the furniture.*

shine up to someone to flatter someone; to try to get into someone's favor. ☐ *The cat shined up to the man every day, but it still got thrown out of the house every night.* ☐ *Are you trying to shine up to me? What will that accomplish?*

SHINE ▸ (UP)ON

shine (down) (up)on someone or something [for a light, such as the sun] to radiate downward onto someone or something. (*Upon* is formal and less commonly used than *on.*) ☐ *I hope that the sun will shine down on us all day long.* ☐ *The sun shone down on the cornfields all summer long.*

shine something (up)on someone or something to cast a beam of light onto someone or something. (*Upon* is formal and less commonly used than *on.*) ☐ *Please shine your flashlight on Sam so we can see him.* ☐ *The sun shone its rays on the fields.*

SHINE ▸ WITH

shine with something **1.** to be bright with something, such as light. ☐ *The day shone with the bright sunlight.* ☐ *The room shone with the light that came through the window.* **2.** to show a pleased look with something. ☐ *Betty's face shone with pride after receiving the award.* ☐ *His eyes shone with recognition.*

SHINNY ▸ UP

shinny up something to climb up something such as a pole, using the legs to hold on. ☐ *Tony shinnied up the pole, trying to get as high as he could get.* ☐ *How long did it take him to shinny up the downspout?*

SHIP ▸ OFF

ship someone or something off (to someone or something) to send someone or something away to someone or something. ☐ *We shipped the kids off to their grandmother for the whole summer!* 🅃 *We shipped off the kids to camp.* ☐ *Have you shipped my order off yet?*

SHIP ▸ OUT

ship out 1. to leave with the ship that one has boarded or to which one has been assigned. ☐ *When do you ship out?* ☐ *I ship out tomorrow at high tide.* **2.** to leave. (Colloquial.) ☐ *Man, it's late. I have to ship out!* ☐ *We had better ship out if we are going to get up early tomorrow.*

ship something out 1. to send something out on a ship. ☐ *The little fruit company shipped more than seventy tons of bananas out last year.* 🅃 *They shipped out a lot of bananas.* **2.** to dispatch something, such as goods for sale. ☐ *The factory shipped fewer orders out this year than last.* 🅃 *They used a lot of trucks to ship out the goods.*

SHIVER ▸ AT

shiver at something to tremble because of something, such as a thought or mental picture. ☐ *Alice shivered at the thought of having to drive all the way to Springfield in the rain.* ☐ *I shivered at the idea of going there alone.*

SHIVER ▸ FROM

shiver from something to tremble because of something, such as cold. ☐ *After a few minutes outside, Ellen began to shiver from the freezing wind.* ☐ *Ted and Bill were shivering from the icy cold.*

SHIVER ▸ WITH

shiver with something to tremble because of something, such as fear, cold, anticipation. ☐ *Don shivered with the cold because his coat was so thin.* ☐ *The children shivered with fear, not knowing what was going to happen to them.*

SHOCK ▸ INTO

shock someone into something to jar or jolt someone into doing something. ☐ *The cold air shocked her into her senses.* ☐ *I will try to shock him into realizing what's good for him.*

SHOCK ▸ OUT

shock someone out of something to bring someone out of a mental state by shock or surprise. ☐ *The excitement of the last few minutes shocked her out of her boredom.* ☐ *The sudden realization of where I was shocked me out of my senses.*

SHOO ▸ AWAY

shoo someone or something away (from someone or something) to brush or chase someone or something away from someone or something. ☐ *Aunt Maude shooed the children away from the cookies.* 🅃 *She shooed away all the pesky birds from the corn.* ☐ *Maude shooed them away.*

SHOO ▸ OFF

shoo someone or something off to chase or drive someone or some creature away. ☐ *The farmer shooed the hikers off because they were frightening the cows.* 🅃 *Liz shooed off the chickens.* ☐ *She shooed them off.*

SHOOT ▸ AS

shoot someone as something to shoot and kill someone for being something, such as a traitor. ☐ *The general shot the sergeant as a traitor.* ☐ *Mr. Allen was shot as a common traitor.*

SHOOT ▸ AT

shoot a glance at someone or something to direct a quick glance at someone or something. ☐ *Jill shot a glance at Jerry, embarrassing him considerably.* ☐ *Jan shot a glance at the report and smiled.*

shoot (something) at someone or something to fire something, such as a gun, at someone or something. ☐ *Dave shot* *his gun at me!* ☐ *He shot at me!* ☐ *He shot it at the target, not at you!*

SHOOT ▸ AWAY

shoot away to run away; to escape very quickly. ☐ *The boy who stole the apples shot away when the farmer came into the orchard.* ☐ *The assailant shot away when he heard the police sirens.*

shoot something away to break something off by shooting at it. ☐ *The gunfire shot the woodwork around the door away and broke all the windows.* 🅃 *They shot away the windows.* 🄰 *They tripped over a shot-away piece of the building.*

SHOOT ▸ BETWEEN

shoot someone between the eyes to fire a bullet right between someone's eyes. ☐ *Max threatened to shoot Lefty between the eyes, but Lefty wasn't scared a bit.* ☐ *The soldiers were trained to shoot the enemy between the eyes.*

SHOOT ▸ DOWN

shoot someone or something down **1.** to bring down someone or some creature by gunfire. ☐ *Max shot Lefty down in the street.* 🅃 *Max tried to shoot down Lefty.* ☐ *The hunter shot the deer down.* **2.** to render someone's idea or plan invalid. (Figurative.) ☐ *He raised a good point, but the others shot him down almost immediately.* 🅃 *Liz shot down Jeff's best idea.* ☐ *She shot the idea down.*

SHOOT ▸ FOR

shoot for something **1.** to aim for or at something. (Usually in reference to basketball.) ☐ *The center shot for the basket just before the end of the game.* ☐ *Wally shot for the basket, but missed.* **2.** to aim for something; to set something as one's goal. (Figurative.) ☐ *You have to shoot for the very best. Don't be satisfied with less.* ☐ *She shot for the highest attainable goal.*

shoot for the sky to aim very high; to set one's goals very high. ☐ *Shoot for the sky! Set your sights as high as you can!* ☐ *I want to shoot for the sky, but I don't want to be disappointed.*

SHOOT ▸ FROM

shoot from the hip **1.** to fire a gun from the level of the hip, without sighting down the barrel of the gun. ☐ *Actually, very few of the classic cowboys could shoot from the hip. It is more of a circus stunt.* ☐ *Anne shot from the hip at a moving target.* **2.** to react verbally to something very quickly and without much thought. (Figurative.) ☐ *She is a real loudmouth. She always shoots from the hip.* ☐ *Don't shoot from the hip. Hear what I have to say.*

SHOOT ▸ INTO

shoot something into someone or something **1.** to fire something, such as a bullet or an arrow, into someone or something. ☐ *The hunter accidentally shot an arrow into his partner.* ☐ *He shot the arrow into the bull's-eye.* **2.** to inject something into someone, something, or some creature. ☐ *She shot the vaccine into my arm and rubbed the spot.* ☐ *The vet shot some sort of medicine into the horse.*

SHOOT ▸ IN(TO)

shoot in(to something) to run or dart into something or some place. ☐ *A mouse shot into the crack in the wall of the barn.* ☐ *A little mouse shot in.*

SHOOT ▸ OFF

shoot one's mouth off (about someone or something) **1.** to brag publicly about someone or something. ☐ *He's always shooting his mouth off about his daughter.* 🅃 *Stop shooting off your mouth about your success.* ☐ *I wish you wouldn't shoot your mouth off!* **2.** to tell secret information about someone or something. ☐ *Stop shooting your mouth off about how much the car cost!* 🅃 *Liz is always shooting off her mouth about Fred's problems.* ☐ *It's not any of her business! She's just shooting her mouth off!*

shoot something off to fire a gun; to set off fireworks. ☐ *The fireworks crew shot the rockets off.* 🅃 *The crew shot off the rockets.*

SHOOT ▸ OUT

shoot out to pop or dart out. □ *A car shot out right in front of me.* □ *The frog's tongue shot out.*

shoot out of something to rush out of something; to be expelled from something. □ *The bullet shot out of the gun.* □ *The children shot out of the schoolroom door.*

shoot something out **1.** to extinguish something by shooting at it. □ *The archer shot out the candle flame.* □ *He shot out the light.* **2.** to dart or lash something out. □ *The frog shot its tongue out and caught a fly.* 🅃 *It shot out its tongue.*

shoot something out (with someone) to settle an argument with someone by shooting. (Western or gangster contexts.) □ *Tex finally shot it out with Jed in front of the saloon.* □ *Tex and Jed finally shot it out.* 🄽 *There is a shoot-out at the saloon almost every night.*

SHOOT ▸ OVER

shoot over someone or something **1.** [for someone] to fire bullets over someone or something. □ *The soldiers shot over the crowd in an effort to disperse them.* □ *Jan shot over the target and missed it altogether.* **2.** [for something] to dart or rush above someone or something. □ *The missile shot harmlessly over the spectators.* □ *The rocket shot over the water and headed off into the sky.*

shoot something over someone or something [for someone] to fire or launch something above someone or something. □ *Dave and Al shot the skyrockets over the crowd, scaring them half to death.* □ *You should shoot these things over vacant land, not living people!*

shoot something (over) (to someone) See under *SHOOT ▸ TO.*

SHOOT ▸ THROUGH

See *be shot through with something* under *BE ▸ THROUGH.*

SHOOT ▸ TO

shoot someone or something (all) to hell **1.** to destroy someone or something with gunfire. (Colloquial. Use discretion with *hell.*) □ *Max shot Lefty to hell with his machine gun.* □ *The farm boys had shot the stop sign to hell.* □ *Lefty is all shot to hell.* **2.** to destroy or damage someone or something. (Figurative.) □ *The hard work in the morning shot me all to hell for the rest of the day.* □ *You shot my ideas to hell.*

shoot something (over)(to someone) to send something to someone in a hurry. (Informal. The optional elements are not transposable.) □ *I will shoot the package over to you as soon as it arrives.* □ *Please shoot the letter to me immediately.*

SHOOT ▸ UP

shoot someone or something up to damage someone or something with gunfire. □ *Max threatened to shoot Lefty up if he didn't get out of town.* 🅃 *He shot up Lefty a bit.* □ *The farm boys shot the road signs up.* 🄰 *We looked out on all the shot-up buildings and knew that last night's battle was a bad one.* 🄽 *The sheriff was ill-prepared for the shoot-up.*

shoot up to grow rapidly. □ *The seeds germinated and sprouts shot up almost overnight.* □ *Tim shot up just after he turned twelve.*

shoot up (on something) to inject oneself with an addictive drug. (Slang.) □ *The addict shot up on heroin and took the rest of the day off.* □ *The addict shot up and went back to her desk.*

SHOOT ▸ UPWARD

shoot someone or something upward to fire or launch someone or something upward. □ *The force of the wreck shot him upward, over the fence.* □ *Jed shot the gun upward, not knowing where the lead would fall.*

SHOOT ▸ WITH

shoot someone or something with something to discharge or shoot a weapon at someone. (*Someone* includes *oneself.*) □ *Max shot Lefty with his automatic.* □ *The hunter shot the deer with a bow and arrow.* □ *Todd shot himself with his own gun accidentally.*

SHOP ▸ AROUND

shop around (for something) (for someone or something) to go from merchant to merchant examining merchandise, and possibly to buy something for someone, some creature, or some purpose. □ *I am going to shop around for a gift for my nephew.* □ *I have to shop around for Walter.* □ *We need to shop around for a gift.*

SHORE ▸ UP

shore something up to brace or prop something up. □ *The workers shored the wall up with heavy timbers.* 🅃 *The workers shored up the wall with heavy timbers.* 🄰 *They examined the shored-up foundation and were forced to condemn the building.*

SHORT ▸ OUT

short out [for an electrical circuit] to go out because of a short circuit. □ *All the lights in the house shorted out when lightning struck.* □ *This radio has shorted out, I think.*

SHORTEN ▸ BY

shorten something by something to reduce the length of something by a specified amount. □ *The teacher shortened the class by ten minutes.* □ *The lecture was shortened by ten minutes so we could get to the meeting on time.* □ *She shortened the skirt by four inches.*

SHORTEN ▸ TO

shorten something to something to reduce the length of something to a specified amount. □ *Andrew shortened his name to Andy.* □ *Can you shorten this board to about three feet?*

SHOT ▸ THROUGH

See *be shot through with something* under *BE ▸ THROUGH.*

SHOULDER ▸ ASIDE

shoulder someone aside to push or nudge someone aside, usually with one's shoulder. □ *The busy little cleaner shouldered me aside, muttering, "'Scuse me, 'scuse me."* □ *Max shouldered everyone aside in his effort to get in the door first.*

SHOULDER ▸ THROUGH

shoulder (one's way) through something to push one's way through a crowd of people, perhaps by leading with one's shoulder. □ *I shouldered my way through the crowd, hoping to reach her before it was too late.* □ *Ted shouldered through the line of people to get to where Bill was standing.*

SHOUT ▸ ABOUT

shout about someone or something 1. to yell about someone or something. □ *Alice is shouting about Tom, the guy who stood her up.* □ *What are you shouting about?* **2.** to show one's pride or enthusiasm about someone or something. (Idiomatic and figurative. Usually with the object shifted to the front of the sentence.) □ *That's really something to shout about.* □ *She's something to shout about.*

SHOUT ▸ AT

shout at someone or something to yell at someone or something. □ *Nancy can't hear you. Shout at her and see if you can get her attention.* □ *There is no point in shouting at a cat!*

SHOUT ▸ DOWN

shout someone down to stop someone from speaking by shouting, yelling, or jeering. □ *The audience shouted the politician down.* 🅃 *They shouted down the speaker.*

SHOUT ▸ FOR

shout for someone or something to call or yell for someone or something. □ *I shouted for Gary, but he was not anywhere close by.* □ *Mary shouted for help.*

SHOUT ▸ OUT

shout something out (at someone or something) to yell something at someone or something. □ *Someone in the audience shouted a funny remark out at the speaker.* 🅃 *Someone shouted out a rude remark.* □ *Who shouted that word out?*

SHOVE ▸ AROUND

shove someone around 1. to push someone around. □ *The bigger boys shoved him around by accident because* *he is so small.* 🅃 *Karen shoved around the little kids until they got mad at her.* **2.** to harass someone. (Figurative.) □ *Stop shoving me around! Who do you think you are?* 🅃 *Do you think you can shove around just anybody?*

SHOVE ▸ ASIDE

shove someone or something aside to push someone or something to one side, out of the way. □ *The guards shoved the spectators aside as the president's car approached.* 🅃 *The guard shoved aside the curtain and came right in.* □ *They shoved the furniture aside.*

SHOVE ▸ AWAY

shove someone or something away to push someone or something back, out of the way. □ *He came toward me, but I shoved him away.* 🅃 *I shoved away the drink. I didn't want it at all.*

SHOVE ▸ BACK

shove someone back to push someone in return. □ *She shoved me and I shoved her back.* □ *There is no need to shove her back.*

shove someone or something back **1.** to push someone or something backwards and away or out of the way. □ *He wandered close enough to the edge to fall off, but I shoved him back.* 🅃 *I shoved back the door as it started to close on me.* **2.** to return someone or something back to where it was. □ *This lady in the supermarket line kept shoving me forward, and I kept shoving her back.* 🅃 *I shoved back the cart as it rolled toward me.* □ *I shoved it back.*

SHOVE ▸ BY

See under *SHOVE ▸ PAST.*

SHOVE ▸ DOWN

shove someone or something down to force someone or something downward. □ *Todd shoved Mary down hard to get her out of the way of the flying glass.* □ *I shoved the planter down by accident.*

shove someone or something down someone's throat to force someone to accept someone or something. (Figurative. Also used literally.) □ *I wish that Ralph didn't always try to shove his visiting relatives down our throats.* □ *Don't try to shove all that classical music down my throat.*

shove someone or something down something to push someone or something down into something. □ *Tony accidentally pushed his brother down the laundry chute.* □ *I almost shoved the chair down the stairs by mistake.*

SHOVE ▸ IN(TO)

shove something in(to someone or something) to force something into someone or something. □ *As he ran away, Frank shoved the table into his pursuers, trying to slow them down.* 🅃 *He opened the oven and shoved in the pizza.* □ *He shoved the pizza in and closed the oven door.*

SHOVE ▸ OFF

shove off (for something) **1.** to begin a journey to something or some place by pushing a boat or ship out onto the water. □ *We will shove off at about noon, headed for Barbados.* □ *Go to the bow of the boat and shove off when I tell you.* **2.** to depart for something or some place, using any form of transportation. □ *The car is all warmed up and ready to go. Let's shove off.* □ *Let's shove off pretty soon.*

shove someone or something off ((of) something) to push someone or something off something. (The *of* is colloquial.) □ *Tom was tempted to shove Gale off of the cliff, but restrained himself.* 🅃 *He did not shove off Gale.* □ *He shoved a medium-sized boulder off.*

SHOVE ▸ OVER

shove someone or something over to push someone or something some distance to one side. □ *I shoved him over a little so I could get by, and he got angry.* □ *I shoved the books over and stuck a few more on the shelf.*

shove someone or something over (something) to push someone or something over something, such as a wall, cliff, etc. □ *What am I supposed to do to get rid of that pest? Shove him over a cliff?* □ *I just wanted to drive that old car to a cliff and shove it over.*

SHOVE ▸ PAST

shove past someone or something AND **shove by someone or something** to push oneself past someone or something. ☐ *The lady shoved past the cart that was blocking her way.* ☐ *Please don't shove by me. I was here first.*

shove past someone or something to push one's way past someone or something. ☐ *Alice shoved past everyone else so she could be first in line.* ☐ *Jamie shoved past the barrier and ran down the hall.*

SHOVEL ▸ DOWN

shovel something down to eat something very fast in enormous bites. (Informal. Also used literally.) ☐ *Dave shoveled his breakfast down and ran to catch the school bus.* 🅃 *Karen shoveled down her lunch and ran to class.*

SHOVEL ▸ INTO

shovel something into something to load something into something with a shovel. ☐ *The deckhand had to shovel coal into the fiery-hot boiler.* ☐ *Please shovel all this gravel into the wheelbarrow.*

SHOW ▸ AROUND

show someone around (something) to give someone a tour of something or some place; to lead someone in an examination of something or some place. (*Someone* includes *oneself*.) ☐ *I would be happy to show you around the factory.* ☐ *Can I show you around?* ☐ *I'll show myself around. Don't worry. I can find the way.*

show someone or something around to take someone or something around to be seen by many people. ☐ *Would you be so kind as to show our friend around so people can meet her?* ☐ *Please show this proposal around and see what people think of it.*

SHOW ▸ IN(TO)

show someone in((to) something) to usher someone into something or some place. ☐ *The butler showed the guest into the main hall.* 🅃 *Please, James, show in our guest.* ☐ *Show our guest in.*

SHOW ▸ OF

show signs of something to give the characteristic visual indications of something. ☐ *This carpet is showing signs of wear.* ☐ *Timmy is showing signs of tiring. Shouldn't we go home now?*

SHOW ▸ OFF

show off (to someone) to make an exhibition of oneself to someone. ☐ *Ed was making a nuisance of himself, showing off to the girls.* ☐ *Stop showing off, Ed.* 🄽 *Don't be such a show-off, Ed.*

show someone or something off (to someone) to show someone or something to someone proudly. ☐ *She was very pleased to show her daughter off to everyone.* 🅃 *Liz showed off her daughter to Karen.* ☐ *Richard showed off his new shoes to everyone in the office.*

SHOW ▸ OUT

show someone out (of something) to usher or escort someone out of something or some place. ☐ *The butler showed Roger out of the main hall into the orangery.* ☐ *May I show you out, sir?*

SHOW ▸ THROUGH

show someone through (something) to give someone a tour of something or some place. ☐ *I would be happy to show you through the office complex.* ☐ *This is our office area. Let me show you through.*

show through (something) [for something] to be visible through something. ☐ *Fred's undershirt showed through his shirt, and everyone except Fred learned that he had a big hole in it.* ☐ *The hole in her slip showed through.*

SHOW ▸ TO

show something to someone to demonstrate something to someone; to permit someone to examine something. ☐ *Let me show this handy device to my husband.* ☐ *I want to show my new shoes to everyone.*

SHOW ▸ UP

show someone up (as something) to make someone appear fraudulent, inadequate, or deficient. ☐ *You didn't* *need to say that! You are just trying to show me up!* 🅃 *Don't show up your employer.* □ *The test showed Walter up as ignorant.*

show up 1. to become apparent. □ *A mild reaction to the drug is beginning to show up.* □ *The kinds of problems I expected are beginning to show up.* 2. to arrive. (Informal.) □ *What time do you think you will show up?* □ *He showed up about midnight, full of apologies.*

SHOWER ► DOWN

shower down on someone or something [for something, not necessarily liquid] to rain down on someone or something. □ *Upon completion of her circumnavigation of the globe, offers for television appearances showered down on Nancy.* □ *The much-needed rain showered down on the fields.*

shower something down (up)on someone or something to rain something, not necessarily a liquid, down onto someone or something. (*Upon* is formal and less commonly used than *on*.) □ *The crowd showered curses down upon the city council.* 🅃 *They showered down curses on the politicians.* □ *The storm showered hail down on the cars that were parked outdoors.*

SHOWER ► WITH

shower someone or something with something to cover someone or something with cascades of something. (Figurative.) □ *Mary's friends showered her with gifts on her twenty-first birthday.* □ *The guests showered the bride and groom with confetti and rice.*

SHRIEK ► AT

shriek at someone or something to scream or yell at someone or something shrilly. □ *Dana shrieked at Tom, who had frightened her half to death.* □ *Richard shrieked at the cat, but it did no good.*

SHRIEK ► OUT

shriek something out to scream something out shrilly. □ *She shrieked someone's name out and became silent.* 🅃 *Liz shrieked out a warning.*

SHRIEK ► WITH

shriek with something to scream or yell with something such as glee, laughter, joy, etc. □ *The children all shrieked with joy at the antics of the clown.* □ *We shrieked with glee when the evil sorcerer got what he deserved.*

SHRINK ► BACK

shrink (back) (from someone or something) to pull back from someone or something; to recoil at someone or something. □ *Frank looked so drawn and haggard that Gary shrank back from him.* □ *Tom shrank from the blazing barbecue grill.* □ *He moved closer, then shrank back again.*

SHRINK ► FROM

See the previous entry.

SHRINK ► UP

shrink up to shrivel; to recede. □ *My shirt shrank up when you washed it!* □ *The bruise on Tom's arm shrank up when he put ice on it.*

SHRIVEL ► UP

shrivel something up to cause something to shrink or contract. □ *The bathwater shriveled Tony's fingertips up.* 🅃 *The water shriveled up his fingertips.* 🄰 *There was nothing left to eat but a shriveled-up sausage.*

shrivel up to contract; to shrink. □ *The goldfish must have jumped out of its bowl during the night. Anyway, it's on the floor all shriveled up this morning.* □ *The new plants shriveled up in the burning sun.*

SHROUD ► IN

shroud someone or something in something to wrap or conceal someone or something in something. (Both literal and figurative senses.) □ *The sailmaker shrouded Mr. Carlson in sailcloth and prepared him for burial at sea.* □ *They shrouded the brand-new car model in canvas in preparation for its presentation.* □ *They shrouded the decision in a series of formalities.*

SHRUG ► AT

shrug at someone (about someone or something) to indicate to someone that one is ignorant about someone or something. □ *She shrugged at me about Tom. She didn't know where he was either.* □ *He just shrugged at me when I asked him about the date of his wedding.*

shrug at someone or something to make a sign of not knowing or caring about someone or something. □ *When Jill asked Dave what time it was, he just shrugged at her, making her quite angry.* □ *The boss just shrugged at the idea.*

SHRUG ▶ OFF

shrug something off to ignore something; to dismiss something. □ *No, you didn't hurt my feelings. I just shrugged your comment off.* 🅃 *Liz couldn't shrug off the remark.*

shrug something off as something to dismiss something as something. □ *Jill simply shrugged his anger off as something unavoidable.* 🅃 *I shrugged off the incident as meaningless.*

SHUCK ▶ DOWN

shuck down to take one's clothes off. (Slang.) □ *The boys shucked down and went swimming in the creek.* □ *I have to shuck down and take a shower before I can even think about going out for dinner.*

SHUCK ▶ OFF

shuck something off **1.** to take something off. (Slang.) □ *Tom shucked his jacket off and sat on the arm of the easy chair.* 🅃 *He shucked off his jacket.* **2.** to get rid of someone or something. (Figurative slang.) □ *She shucked all her bad habits off.* 🅃 *Tom shucked off one girlfriend after another.*

SHUDDER ▶ AT

shudder at something to shake or quiver at something. □ *I shudder at the thought of getting a disease like malaria.* □ *We shuddered at the idea of going there alone.*

SHUFFLE ▶ OFF

shuffle off to depart, scraping or rubbing one's feet on the floor. □ *The old tramp shuffled off into the dusk.* □ *The boys shuffled off, looking for some way to spend the rest of the afternoon.*

shuffle something off (on someone) to burden someone with something. □ *I know you have a lot of work to do, but don't shuffle it off on me.* 🅃 *Don't shuffle off your problems on me.* □ *He just shuffles his work stress off in laughter.*

SHUFFLE ▶ OUT

shuffle out of something to leave something or some place, scraping or rubbing one's feet on the floor. □ *The exhausted hikers shuffled out of the cabin for another day of hiking.* □ *The office staff shuffled out of the door after another hard day at work.*

SHUFFLE ▶ UP

shuffle something up to place something, such as playing cards, in random order. □ *Shuffle these cards up so that they are thoroughly mixed.* 🅃 *Please shuffle up the cards one more time.*

SHUNT ▶ INTO

shunt someone or something into something to guide or divert someone or something into something. □ *The camp counselor shunted most of the younger kids into the shallow swimming pool.* □ *We shunted most of the cars into the field, where there was a lot of room to park.*

SHUNT ▶ ONTO

shunt someone or something onto something to guide or divert someone or something onto something. □ *The leader shunted all the weaker people onto an easier trail.* □ *The police officer shunted the traffic onto a side street until the accident was removed.*

SHUSH ▶ UP

shush someone up to cause someone to stop talking, crying, etc.; to request someone to stop talking, crying, etc. □ *Don't shush me up when I'm talking!* □ *They shushed me up, so I stopped talking altogether.*

shush up to stop talking, crying, etc. (Informal.) □ *You are too noisy. Shush up!* □ *Shush up, you guys!*

SHUT ▶ AWAY

shut someone away to confine someone in a place. (*Someone* includes *one-*

self.) □ *I think that my mind is going. I feel like some day they are going to shut me away.* 🅃 *They had to shut away the disturbed person.* □ *Sally shut herself away in her room so she could finish her homework.*

SHUT ▸ DOWN

shut down to stop operating. □ *The plant shut down for a week so everyone could go on vacation.* 🄽 *A lot of workers quit during the shutdown.*

shut someone or something down to close a business; to force someone who runs a business to close. □ *Sam's business was failing, and finally the bank shut him down.* 🅃 *The bank shut down Tom's shop.* 🄽 *The mayor ordered a shutdown of all businesses.*

shut something down to turn something off. □ *They shut the machine down so they could repair it.* 🅃 *They had to shut down the machine.* 🄽 *The shutdown of the engine came just in time.*

SHUT ▸ IN(TO)

shut someone or something in((to) something) to enclose and confine someone or something in something or some place. □ *Tom shut his brother into the closet.* 🅃 *He shut in his brother.* □ *Please don't shut me in! There's no air in there!*

SHUT ▸ OF

shut oneself of someone or something to get rid of someone or something; to eliminate the burden of someone or something. □ *Larry shut himself of his wife once and for all.* □ *I will shut myself of this problem.* □ *I will be very happy to shut myself of Roger.*

SHUT ▸ OFF

shut off to stop operating; to turn off. □ *The machine shuts off automatically.* □ *What time do the lights shut off?*

shut someone off to make someone stop speaking or doing something. (Informal.) □ *Kelly kept talking on and on, and finally we had to shut her off.* 🅃 *We shut off the speaker.*

shut someone or something off from someone or something to place some sort of a barrier between things or people, in any combination. □ *Why do you always shut yourself off from everyone else?* □ *Tom shut Mary off from access to the refrigerator.* □ *He shut the refrigerator off from Mary.*

shut something off to turn something off. (Folksy if referring to a light.) □ *Shut the light off and go to bed!* 🅃 *Please shut off the lights!* □ *Did you shut the water off?* 🄰 *The shutoff valve was stuck.* 🄽 *The machine has an automatic shutoff.*

SHUT ▸ ON

See under *SHUT ▸ (UP)ON.*

SHUT ▸ OUT

shut someone or something out (of something) to place a barrier that prevents someone or something from getting into something or some place. □ *The guards shut the late arrivals out of the building.* 🅃 *Mary used a heavy curtain to shut out the light.* □ *She shut the sunlight out.*

SHUT ▸ TO

shut one's eyes to something See *close one's eyes to something* under *CLOSE ▸ TO.*

SHUT ▸ UP

shut someone or something up (in something) to confine someone or something in something or some place. (*Someone* includes *oneself.*) □ *Please don't shut me up in that little room with no windows!* 🅃 *Liz shut up the dog in the garage.* □ *Todd shut himself up in his office to escape the reporters.*

shut someone up to cause someone to stop talking or making other noise. □ *I don't know how to shut him up. He just talks on and on.* 🅃 *Shut up that loudmouth!*

shut something up **1.** to close one's mouth and stop talking. (Slang.) □ *Shut your yap up, you chatterbox!* 🅃 *Shut up that noisy mouth of yours!* **2.** to stop saying something in particular. (Slang.) □ *Shut that nonsense up!* 🅃 *Shut up your constant talking!*

shut up to be quiet. (Slang. Rude.) ☐ *Shut up! You talk too much!* ☐ *Please shut up when I am on the phone.*

SHUT ▶ (UP)ON

shut something (up)on someone or something **1.** to close something, such as a door, preventing someone or something from passing. (*Upon* is formal and less commonly used than *on*.) ☐ *They shut the door upon me, and I couldn't get in!* ☐ *We quickly shut the door on the smoke.* **2.** to eliminate an opportunity for someone or something. (Figurative.) ☐ *The board of directors shut the door on me, and there was no further opportunity for me to pursue.* ☐ *They shut the door on further discussions.*

SHUTTLE ▶ BETWEEN

shuttle between someone or something and someone or something to come and go between people or things, in any combination. ☐ *Kelly shuttled between the vice president and the president all day long, carrying urgent messages.* ☐ *The secretary shuttled between her boss and the watercooler all day.* ☐ *The secretary shuttled between the watercooler and her typewriter all day long.*

SHY ▶ AWAY

shy away (from someone or something) to draw away from someone or something that is frightening or startling; to avoid dealing with someone or something. ☐ *The child shied away from the doctor.* ☐ *I won't hurt you. Don't shy away.*

SIC ▶ ON

sic someone or something on someone or something to urge or direct someone or some creature to attack someone or something. ☐ *The boss sicced his hatchet man on the supplier who was late with his deliveries.* ☐ *Nancy sicced her dog on the attacker.*

SICKEN ▶ AT

sicken at something to become repulsed by something, especially a thought. ☐ *Jane sickened at the thought of the boat sinking.* ☐ *We all sickened at the idea of having to kill the rabbit in order to eat it.*

SICKEN ▶ OF

sicken of someone or something to tire or grow bored of someone or something. ☐ *I have really sickened of the Johnsons. They are so rude!* ☐ *We are beginning to sicken of all these extra charges.*

SIDE ▶ AGAINST

See the following entry.

SIDE ▶ WITH

side (with someone) (against someone or something) to join with someone against someone or something. ☐ *Why do you always side with them against me?* ☐ *I don't side against you!* ☐ *You always side with them.* ☐ *Will you side against the new law with me?*

SIDLE ▶ AWAY

sidle away (from someone or something) to avoid someone or something by moving to the side; to ease away from someone or something. ☐ *The cowboy sidled away from the bar and drew his gun.* ☐ *He sidled away and snuck out the door.*

SIDLE ▶ UP

sidle up (to someone or something) to move close to someone or something cautiously or furtively; to move closer to someone or something obliquely. ☐ *Tex sidled up to Dolly and said howdy in a soft, shy voice.* ☐ *Dolly sidled up and picked the cowboy's pocket.*

SIFT ▶ FROM

sift something from something to remove something from something by sifting. ☐ *Fran sifted all the impurities from the flour before using it.* ☐ *Timmy sifted all the leaves from the sand in his sandbox.*

SIFT ▶ OUT

sift something out (of something) to get rid of something in something else by sifting. (The *of*-phrase is paraphrased with a *from*-phrase when the particle is transposed. See the 🄵 example.) ☐ *Dan sifted the impurities out of the flour.* 🅃 *Walter sifted out the foreign matter.* 🄵 *Dan sifted out the sand from the beans.* ☐ *He sifted the sand out.*

SIFT ▸ THROUGH

sift something through something to make something pass through something like a sieve. ☐ *She sifted the powdered sugar through a strainer.* ☐ *Please sift the soil through this screen and watch for bits of pottery.*

sift through something to examine all parts of something. ☐ *The fire inspector sifted through the rubble, looking for clues to the start of the fire.* ☐ *We sifted through all the papers in the old trunk, but we did not find what we were looking for.*

SIGH ▸ ABOUT

sigh about something to release a deep breath, indicating anxiety, distress, or relief about something. ☐ *What are you sighing about?* ☐ *She sighed about her illness and then shifted her thoughts to something else.*

SIGH ▸ FOR

sigh for someone to release a deep breath, indicating anxiety about one's emotional attachment for someone. (Sometimes figurative.) ☐ *Dave spent a lot of his time sighing for Laura, on whom he had a crush.* ☐ *Laura has been sighing for some as-yet-unnamed young man.*

SIGN ▸ AWAY

sign something away to sign a paper in which one gives away one's rights to something. ☐ *Valerie signed her rights away.* 🅃 *She signed away her claim to the money.*

SIGN ▸ FOR

sign for someone to sign something, using one's signature in place of someone else's signature; to sign something, using another person's name, adding the phrase "by [one's own name]." ☐ *He's not here. I will sign for him. Where do I sign?* ☐ *Who will sign for Mr. Wilson?*

sign for something to sign a piece of paper indicating that one has received something. ☐ *Would you sign for this, please?* ☐ *Ted signed for the package and opened it up.*

sign something for someone **1.** to sign one's signature on a paper in place of someone else's signature. ☐ *Would you please sign this for me?* ☐ *I can't sign it right now. Would you sign it for me?* **2.** to sign a paper, using another person's name, adding the phrase "by [one's own name]." (The *for me* means "on my behalf.") ☐ *When the delivery comes, will you please sign my name for me?* ☐ *I signed Ted's name for him.*

SIGN ▸ IN

sign in to indicate that one has arrived somewhere and at what time by signing a piece of paper or a list. ☐ *Please sign in so we will know you are here.* ☐ *Did you remember to sign in this time?*

sign someone in to record that someone has arrived somewhere and at what time by recording the information on a paper or a list. (*Someone* includes *oneself*.) ☐ *I will sign you in. What is your name?* 🅃 *Do I have to sign in everyone?* ☐ *I'll sign myself in. You don't need to.*

sign something in to record that something has been received at a particular time by recording the information on a paper or a list. ☐ *I have to sign this tape recorder in, then I will be right with you.* 🅃 *Should I sign in this tape recorder now?*

SIGN ▸ OFF

sign off **1.** [for a broadcaster] to announce the end of programming for the day; [for an amateur radio operator] to announce the end of a transmission. ☐ *Wally signed off and turned the transmitter off.* ☐ *Wally failed to sign off at the scheduled time last night.* 🄽 *The sign-off was late.* **2.** to quit doing what one has been doing and leave, go to bed, quit trying to do something, etc. (Figurative.) ☐ *I have to sign off and get to bed. See you all.* ☐ *When you finally sign off tonight, please turn out all the lights.*

sign off on something to sign a paper, indicating that one has finished with something or agrees with the state of something. ☐ *Michael signed off on the book and sent it to be printed.* ☐ *I refuse to sign off on this project until it is done correctly.*

SIGN ▸ ON

sign on to announce the beginning of a broadcast transmission. ☐ *The announcer signed on and then played "The Star-Spangled Banner."* ☐ *We usually sign on at six in the morning.*

sign on the dotted line **1.** to indicate one's agreement or assent by placing one's signature on a special line provided for that purpose. (The line may be solid or dotted.) ☐ *I agreed to the contract, but I haven't signed on the dotted line yet.* ☐ *When you have signed on the dotted line, please give me a call.* **2.** to indicate one's agreement to something. (Figurative.) ☐ *Okay. I agree to your terms. I'll sign on the dotted line.* ☐ *He is thinking favorably about going with us to Canada, but he hasn't signed on the bottom line.*

sign on (with someone or something) (as something) to join up with someone or something in a particular capacity by signing a contract or agreement. ☐ *I signed on with the captain of the* Felicity Anne *as first mate.* ☐ *Roger signed on as captain with a steamship line.* ☐ *When did you sign on with this project?*

SIGN ▸ OUT

sign out to indicate in writing that one is leaving or going out temporarily. ☐ *I forgot to sign out when I left.* ☐ *Please sign out every time you leave.*

sign someone out (of some place) to make a record of someone's departure from someplace. (*Someone* includes *oneself.*) ☐ *Did someone sign you out of the factory, or did you just open the door and leave?* 🅃 *I signed out those two who just left.* ☐ *Please sign me out. I have to leave in a hurry.* ☐ *Do I have to sign myself out?*

sign something out (of some place) to make a record of the borrowing of something from some place. ☐ *Dave signed the tape recorder out of the library.* 🅃 *Dave signed out the tape recorder.* ☐ *Mary signed a projector out.*

SIGN ▸ OVER

sign something over (to someone) to sign a paper granting the rights to or ownership of something to a specific person. ☐ *Larry signed all the rights to his book over to the publisher.* 🅃 *He signed over all the rights to the publisher.* ☐ *Steve signed all rights over.*

SIGN ▸ UP

sign someone up (for something) to record the agreement of someone, including oneself, to participate in something. (*Someone* includes *oneself.*) ☐ *Has anyone signed you up for the party?* 🅃 *Can you sign up Liz for the party?* ☐ *I would be happy to sign her up.* ☐ *I signed myself up for the class.*

sign someone up (with someone or something) to record the agreement of someone to join a group of people or an organization. (*Someone* includes *oneself.*) ☐ *I found Tom in the hall, and we went to sign him up with Alice.* 🅃 *Tom signed up his friends with the agency.* ☐ *Tom signed all his friends up with his newly started bicycle club.* ☐ *I signed myself up with the crew of the* Felicity Ann.

sign up (for something) to record one's agreement to participate in something. ☐ *I want to sign up for guitar lessons.* ☐ *We will sign up as soon as possible.* 🄰 *Where is the sign-up sheet?* 🄽 *When does the official sign-up begin?*

SIGN ▸ WITH

sign (up) with someone or something to enter into an agreement with someone or a group. ☐ *I signed up with Tom and John to crew their ship in the regatta.* ☐ *Did you sign with the office equipment supplier yet?*

SIGNAL ▸ FOR

signal for someone to make a sign for someone to come. ☐ *I signaled for the waiter and got the check.* ☐ *Ted signaled for the parking lot attendant.*

signal for something to make a sign that something should be done. ☐ *I caught the waiter's eye and signaled for the check.* ☐ *The director signaled for applause.* ☐ *Fred signaled for the houselights to be dimmed.* ☐ *The police officer signaled for the car in front of me to turn to the left.*

SIGNAL ▸ TO

signal to someone to make a sign or send a signal to someone. □ *The conductor signaled to the engineer to start moving again.* □ *Ted signaled to the waiter, who then brought the check.*

SILT ▸ UP

silt up [for a body of water] to become filled with silt. □ *The river moved too fast to silt up.* □ *The lake silted up in a very few years.*

SIMMER ▸ DOWN

simmer down **1.** to decrease in intensity. □ *The hectic activity of the day finally simmered down.* □ *When things simmer down in the fall, this is a much nicer place.* **2.** [for someone] to become calm or less agitated. (Figurative.) □ *I wish you would simmer down.* □ *Please simmer down, you guys!*

SIN ▸ AGAINST

sin against someone or something to offend or desecrate someone or something sacred or revered. (Literary.) □ *The critic said that Walter sinned against the poet when he read the poem in a sarcastic manner.* □ *I would say that Walter sinned against poetry, not just one poet.*

SING ▸ ALONG

sing along (with someone or something) to sing with someone or with the accompaniment of some instrument(s). □ *Harry played all the old songs and everybody sang along.* □ *Let's sing along with Mary. She knows some good songs.*

SING ▸ OF

sing of someone or something to tell about or sing a song about someone or something. □ *The folksinger sang of Paul Bunyan.* □ *They all sang of happier times in the past.*

SING ▸ OUT

sing out to sing more loudly. □ *Sing out, please. This is a very large hall.* □ *The sopranos will have to sing out more.*

sing something out to sing or announce something loudly. □ *He sang the names out loud and clear.* 🅃 *She sang out "The Star-Spangled Banner" in a loud voice.*

SING ▸ TO

sing someone to sleep to sing softly and sweetly to someone until sleep comes. □ *The mother sang her baby to sleep.* □ *Please sing Timmy to sleep. He is very restless.*

sing to someone or something to sing a song and direct it at someone or something. □ *The singer sang to a man in the front row, and he was very embarrassed by it.* □ *Claire sang to an older audience and put many of them to sleep.*

SING ▸ TOGETHER

sing something together [for people] to sing something as a group. □ *Let's sing this together.* □ *If we all sing it together, we can make a sound that will fill the hall.*

sing together [for people] to coordinate their singing. □ *Let's sing together now. Everyone should watch the conductor and follow the beat.* □ *You have to sing together if you want your words to be understood.*

SINGLE ▸ OUT

single someone or something out (for something) to choose or pick someone or something for something; to select an eligible person or thing for something. □ *The committee singled her out for a special award.* 🅃 *We singled out Liz for special honors.* □ *They singled out my entry for special mention.*

SINK ▸ BACK

sink back (into something) to lean back and relax in something, such as a soft chair. □ *I can't wait to get home and sink back into my easy chair.* □ *He sank back and went to sleep almost immediately.*

SINK ▸ BELOW

sink below something to descend below a certain level. □ *The boat sank below the surface of the water and was gone.* □ *The temperature sank below the freezing mark again today.*

SINK ▸ DOWN

sink down to sink or submerge. ☐ *The sun sank down and darkness spread across the land.* ☐ *She sat in the chair and sank down, enjoying her moment of relaxation.*

sink down into something to descend downward into something. ☐ *Sue sank down into the soft, comfortable chair.* ☐ *As he sank down into the bed, he fell asleep immediately.*

SINK ▸ INTO

sink into despair to become depressed; to become completely discouraged. ☐ *After facing the hopelessness of the future, Jean Paul sank into despair.* ☐ *Mary sank into despair upon learning of the death of her voice coach.*

sink into oblivion to fade into obscurity. ☐ *She may be famous now, but in no time she will sink into oblivion.* ☐ *In his final years, Wally Wilson sank into oblivion and just faded away.*

sink one's teeth into something **1.** to bite into something. ☐ *I can't wait to sink my teeth into a crisp, juicy apple.* ☐ *I would really like to sink my teeth into a nice hamburger.* **2.** to start to work on something. (Figurative.) ☐ *I can't wait to sink my teeth into the new job.* ☐ *Alice wanted to sink her teeth into the project, but it was assigned to Mary instead.*

SINK ▸ IN(TO)

sink in(to someone or something) to penetrate someone or something. (Used figuratively in reference to someone's brain or thinking.) ☐ *It finally began to sink into me that we were really, totally lost.* ☐ *When what she said finally sank in, I was shocked and amazed.*

sink something in((to) someone or something) **1.** to drive or push something into someone or something. ☐ *The brave hero sank the wooden stake into the vampire.* 🅃 *The hero sank in the stake.* ☐ *Jamie sank it in, and the movie ended.* **2.** to invest time or money in someone or something. (Sometimes implying that it was wasted.) ☐ *You would not believe how much money I've sunk into that guy!* ☐ *She sank a lot of money in the stock market.*

SINK ▸ TO

sink to something to lower oneself to doing something low or mean. ☐ *I never thought he would sink to doing that.* ☐ *There is nothing that Max wouldn't sink to.*

SINK ▸ UNDER

sink under (something) to submerge. ☐ *The small boat turned over and sank under the surface.* ☐ *It sank under and went straight to the bottom.*

SIPHON ▸ OFF

siphon something off (from something) to suck or draw a liquid off from something. ☐ *Harry siphoned the cream off the milk.* 🅃 *He siphoned off the cream.* ☐ *He siphoned it off.* ☐ *Frank siphoned all the water off from the fish tank.* 🄰 *What shall I do with the siphoned-off water?*

SIT ▸ AROUND

sit around to relax sitting; to waste time sitting. ☐ *Don't just sit around! Get moving!* ☐ *I need to sit around every now and then and reorganize my thoughts.*

sit around something to be seated at the edge or perimeter of something. ☐ *They sat around the campfire for hours.* ☐ *We used to sit around the big kitchen table and talk.*

SIT ▸ AT

sit at something to be seated in front of something, such as a table. ☐ *He sat at the table, taking his tea.* ☐ *Please sit at your desk and finish your work before taking a break.*

sit at the feet of someone to pay homage to someone; to pay worshipful attention to someone. (Figurative. Literal uses are also possible.) ☐ *The graduate student sat at the feet of the famous professor for years.* ☐ *I do not intend to sit at the feet of an incompetent for years and years.*

SIT ▸ BACK

sit back to push oneself back in one's seat; to lean against the back of one's seat. □ *Please sit back. I can't see around you.* □ *I sat back and made myself comfortable, assuming that the movie would bore me to sleep.*

sit back and let something happen to allow something to happen without trying to interfere. (Figurative.) □ *Just sit back and let me take care of things.* □ *The doctor sat back and let the illness run its course.*

SIT ▸ BY

sit by someone to sit next to someone. □ *May I sit by you?* □ *Come over here and sit by me.*

sit (idly) by to refrain from interfering in something. □ *I can't just sit idly by while things fall apart.* □ *While everything was going to pieces, James sat by and did nothing.*

SIT ▸ DOWN

sit down to be seated; to sit on something, such as a chair. □ *Please sit down and make yourself comfortable.* □ *Can I sit down here?*

sit down on something to be seated on something. □ *Please sit down on this chair and wait until you are called.* □ *I don't want to sit down on this hard bench.*

sit down to something to sit down at a table to do something, such as eat a meal or attend to some business. □ *I look forward to going home and sitting down to a quiet supper.* □ *Ted looked forward to sitting down to a big Thanksgiving dinner.*

SIT ▸ FOR

sit for someone **1.** to care for someone in the role of baby-sitter. □ *I sit for Timmy sometimes. I like him. He's a good little kid.* □ *Mary doesn't sit for anyone anymore. It leaves no time for a social life.* **2.** to serve as a baby-sitter in someone's employ. □ *I sit for Mrs. Franklin every now and then.* □ *Ted used to sit for the Wilsons.* **3.** to serve as a model or subject for someone, such as an artist. (See also the following entry.) □ *She sat for the portrait painter every day for a week.* □ *She is looking for someone to sit for her so she can develop her skills.*

sit for something **1.** to take an exam, such as a bar exam. (Formal and chiefly British.) □ *When do you sit for the bar exam?* □ *I will sit for the exam next week.* **2.** to serve as a model or subject for a portrait painter or photographer. (See also the previous entry.) □ *I sat for the picture for two hours.* □ *Do you mind sitting for the painter all day? It will be easier if you get it over with all at once.*

sit still for something **1.** to remain seated without fidgeting during something. □ *The child could hardly be expected to sit still for the opera.* □ *Timmy would not sit still for his haircut.* **2.** to remain idle rather than act to prevent something; to endure or tolerate something. (Figurative.) □ *I won't sit still for that kind of treatment.* □ *She would not sit still for an insult like that.* □ *I will not sit still for any more of this nonsense. I'm leaving.*

SIT ▸ IN

sit in (for someone) to act as a substitute for someone. □ *I am not a regular member of this committee. I am sitting in for Larry Smith.* □ *Do you mind if I sit in? My representative can't be here.*

sit in judgment (up)on someone or something to make a judgment about someone or something. (*Upon* is formal and less commonly used than *on*.) □ *I don't want to sit in judgment upon you or anyone else, but I do have some suggestions.* □ *There is no need to sit in judgment on the proposal at this time.*

sit in (on something) to attend something as a visitor; to act as a temporary participant in something. □ *Do you mind if I sit in on your discussion?* □ *Please do sit in.*

SIT ▸ ON

See also under *SIT ▸ (UP)ON.*

sit on a gold mine to be in control of something very valuable; to be in control of something potentially very valuable. (Figurative. Usually in the progressive aspect.) □ *When I found out how much* *the old book was worth, I realized that I was sitting on a gold mine.* □ *That land is valuable. She is sitting on a gold mine.*

sit on its hands AND **sit on their hands** [for an audience] to refuse to applaud. □ *The performance was really quite good, but the audience sat on its hands.* □ *They sat on their hands during the first act.*

sit on one's ass to sit idle; to sit around doing nothing. (Use *ass* with discretion.) □ *Don't just sit on your ass! Get busy!* □ *He just sat on his ass, watching what was going on.*

sit on someone to hold someone back; to hold someone down. (Colloquial and idiomatic. Can also be used literally.) □ *The manager is sitting on Fred, trying to keep him from advancing in his job.* □ *It's hard to do your best when you know that someone is sitting on you, and no matter what you do, it won't help your advancement.*

sit on someone or something to place oneself in a sitting position on someone or something. □ *The enormous woman knocked Max out and sat on him until the police came.* □ *I need to sit on this chair for a minute and catch my breath.*

sit on the fence to be unable to choose; to refuse to choose. (Figurative. Also with the obvious literal use.) □ *He can't seem to decide. He's been sitting on the fence for over a month.* □ *I am sitting on the fence on this matter. I can't decide what to do about it.* Ⓝ *Ted is such a fence sitter. He's very indecisive.*

SIT ▸ OUT

sit (something) out to elect not to participate in something. □ *I think I will not join in this game. I'll sit it out.* Ⓣ *I'll sit out this round.* □ *I'm not playing, thanks. I'll just sit out.*

SIT ▸ THROUGH

sit through something to remain seated and in attendance for all of something. □ *I can't stand to sit through that class one more time!* □ *Do I have to sit through the whole lecture?*

SIT ▸ UP

sit up **1.** to rise from a lying to a sitting position. □ *When the alarm went off, he sat up and put his feet on the floor.* □ *She couldn't sleep, so she sat up and read a book.* **2.** to sit more straight in one's seat; to hold one's posture more upright while seated. □ *Please sit up. Don't slouch!* □ *You wouldn't get backaches if you would sit up.*

sit up and take notice to become alert and observe something. □ *The loud music and bright lights made everyone in the audience sit up and take notice.* □ *I knew you would sit up and take notice when you heard the announcement.*

sit up with someone to remain awake and attend someone throughout the night. □ *I sat up with a sick friend all night.* □ *I had to sit up with Timmy because he had a tummyache.*

SIT ▸ (UP)ON

sit (up)on someone or something to seat oneself on a person or thing. (*Upon* is formal and less commonly used than *on*.) □ *When I finally got the mugger to the ground, I conked him and then sat on him so he couldn't get away.* □ *Claire sat upon the edge of the couch and took her tea in a very practiced manner.*

SIT ▸ WITH

sit right with someone to be acceptable or understandable to someone. (Figurative. Very close to *sit well with someone*.) □ *What you just said doesn't really sit right with me. Let's talk about it.* □ *It didn't sit right with the boss.*

sit well with someone to be acceptable to someone. (Figurative.) □ *Your explanation of your absence doesn't sit well with the president.* □ *The whole affair didn't sit well with the manager.*

sit with someone **1.** to baby-sit with someone. □ *I have to sit with my little brother tonight.* □ *Who is sitting with Timmy tonight?* **2.** to stay with someone, especially a sick person. □ *I sat with her while she recovered.* □ *His mother sat with him in the hospital.*

SIZE ▸ UP

size someone or something up to scrutinize someone or something and form a judgment. □ *The boxer had sized up his opponent by watching videotapes of previous fights.* 🅃 *He came into the house and sized up the kitchen and dining room.*

SKATE ▸ AROUND

skate around to skate here and there in no particular direction. □ *Let's go over to the pond and skate around.* □ *We will skate around for a while until we get too cold.*

skate around someone or something **1.** to skate to one side or the other of someone or something. □ *Somehow I managed to skate around the child without knocking her down.* □ *I skated around the tree limb and avoided an accident.* **2.** to circle someone or something while skating. □ *The children skated around their instructor until she was satisfied with their form.* □ *We skated around the post in a circle.*

SKATE ▸ ON

skate on something to skate on a particular surface. □ *You can't skate on that ice! It's too thin.* □ *Don't skate on the ice until it has been scraped smooth.*

skate on thin ice to move very cautiously; to be in a very precarious position. (Figurative.) □ *This is a very delicate situation. You are skating on thin ice when you try to tamper with the traditions of the company.* □ *Now you are skating on thin ice. You really don't know what you are talking about.*

SKATE ▸ OVER

skate over something **1.** to move over something, skating. □ *I love to be the first one to skate over newly frozen ice.* □ *I skated over the pond too soon and the ice cracked while I was on it.* **2.** to move over or deal with something quickly. (Figurative.) □ *The speaker skated over the touchy issues with discretion.* □ *I will skate over the things that I am not sure about.*

SKETCH ▸ IN

sketch something in to draw in the image of someone or something. □ *I sketched a figure of a woman in so that she appears to be standing beneath the tree.* 🅃 *I'll sketch in the house in the upper left corner.*

SKETCH ▸ OUT

sketch something out to create a rough idea of something by sketching or some other means. □ *Sally sketched the furniture arrangement out so we could get an idea of what it was to look like.* 🅃 *Would you sketch out your ideas, please?*

SKID ▸ ACROSS

skid across something to slip or glide across something, such as ice or wet pavement. □ *The car skidded across the pavement and crashed into a tree.* □ *Our bus skidded across the bridge and ran into a ditch on the other side.*

SKID ▸ INTO

skid into someone or something to slip or glide into someone or something. □ *The bicycle skidded into a pedestrian.* □ *The car skidded into a light pole.*

SKIM ▸ OFF

skim something off ((of) something) **1.** to scoop something off the surface of something. (The *of*-phrase is paraphrased with a *from*-phrase when the particle is transposed. See the 🄵 example. The *of* is colloquial.) □ *The cook skimmed the fat off the stew.* 🅃 *The cook skimmed off the fat.* 🄵 *The cook skimmed off the fat from the pan.* □ *Larry skimmed it off.* 🄰 *The skimmed-off froth should be discarded.* **2.** to remove a portion of something of value, such as money, from an account. (The *of*-phrase is paraphrased with a *from*-phrase when the particle is transposed. See the 🄵 example.) □ *The teller was skimming a few dollars a day off the bank's cash flow.* 🅃 *Kelly skimmed off a few dollars each day.* 🄵 *Kelly skimmed off a few dollars each day from her cash drawer.* □ *She was skimming money off every day.* 🄰 *The skimmed-off funds were found in a Swiss bank account.*

SKIM ▸ OVER

skim over something 1. to glide across something. □ *The sailboat skimmed over the waves like a bird.* □ *The bird skimmed over the treetops, darting and dodging.* 2. to go over or review something hastily. □ *I just skimmed over the material and got an A on the test!* □ *Please skim over chapter four for Thursday.*

SKIM ▸ THROUGH

skim through something to go through something hastily; to read through something hastily. □ *She skimmed through the catalogs, looking for a nice gift for Gary.* □ *I will skim through your manuscript and see if it looks promising.*

SKIMP ▸ ON

skimp on something to use too little of something; to save something by using less of it than needed for something. □ *Please don't skimp on the gravy. I like my potatoes swimming in it.* □ *They skimped on quality a little when they furnished the lobby.*

SKIP ▸ OFF

skip off (with something) to leave and take something with one. □ *The little kid with the freckles skipped off with a candy bar.* □ *He took the candy bar I offered him and skipped off.*

SKIP ▸ OUT

skip out (on someone or something) to abandon someone or something. (Slang.) □ *I heard that Max skipped out on his wife.* □ *Yes, he skipped out.* □ *Lefty skipped out on the waiter.* □ *He skipped out without paying the bill.*

skip out with something to leave and take something with one; to steal something. (Slang.) □ *The hotel guest skipped out with the towels.* □ *Someone skipped out with the petty cash box.*

SKIP ▸ OVER

skip over someone or something not to choose someone or something next in line. □ *She skipped over me and chose the next one in line.* □ *I skipped over the red ones and took a blue one.*

SKIP ▸ THROUGH

skip through something to go through a book or a stack of papers without dealing with every page. □ *I skipped through the book, just looking at the pictures.* □ *Ted skipped through the report, not bothering to read it.*

SKIRMISH ▸ WITH

skirmish with someone or something to have a minor fight with someone, a group, or something. □ *Tim skirmished a bit with his brother and then ran into the house.* □ *I don't want to skirmish with the committee.*

SKIRT ▸ AROUND

skirt around someone or something to move around and avoid someone or something. (Figurative. *Something* can be a topic of conversation.) □ *We talked the whole evening and managed to skirt around Fred.* □ *We had to skirt around the subject.*

SLACK ▸ OFF

slack off to wane or decline; to decrease in intensity. □ *Finally the rains slacked off, and we could go outside and walk around.* □ *When business slacks off a bit, we have a sale.*

SLACK ▸ UP

slack up (on something) AND **slack off (on something)** to release the pressure or tension on something. □ *Slack up on the rope a bit, will you?* □ *Please slack up!* □ *Slack off, will you?*

SLAM ▸ DOWN

slam someone or something down to push or strike someone or something downward. □ *The wrestler slammed his opponent down hard.* 🅃 *He slammed down his opponent and injured him.* □ *Jane slammed the book down.*

slam something down (on something) to bang something down onto something. □ *She slammed her fist down on the table.* 🅃 *Karen slammed down her fist onto the table.*

SLAM ▸ IN

slam the door in someone's face 1. to swing a door closed with force while someone is standing in the doorway. □ *I* *didn't know Todd was behind me and I slammed the door in his face.* □ *Please don't slam the door in my face!* **2.** suddenly to withdraw an opportunity from someone. (Figurative.) □ *The events of the last week effectively slammed the door in my face for future employment.* □ *We slammed the door in Bill's face since he was so rude when we interviewed him.*

SLAM ▸ INTO

slam into someone or something to crash into someone or something. □ *The race car—out of control—slammed into the crowd.* □ *The bus slammed into a truck.*

SLAM ▸ ON

slam the brakes on to push on a vehicle's brakes suddenly and hard. (Informal. *The* can be replaced by a possessive pronoun.) □ *The driver in front of me slammed her brakes on and I nearly ran into her.* 🅃 *Don't slam on your brakes when the road is wet.*

SLANT ▸ AGAINST

slant against something to rest obliquely against something. □ *The bookcase slants against the wall, and it should be straight.* □ *The lumber was left slanted against the garage.*

slant something against someone or something to bias something against someone or something; to twist information so it is against someone or something. (Figurative.) □ *The writer slanted the story against the innocent people of the town.* □ *The reporter slanted her story against one political party.*

SLANT ▸ IN

slant something in favor of someone or something See *slant something toward someone or something* under *SLANT ▸ TOWARD.*

SLANT ▸ TOWARD

slant something toward someone or something AND **slant something in favor of someone or something** to bias something toward someone or something; to twist information so it favors someone or something. (Figurative.) □ *The writer slanted the story toward the cruel boys.* □ *The reporter slanted her story in favor of one political party.*

slant toward someone or something to incline toward someone or something. □ *The scenery slanted toward the actors and looked as if it would fall.* □ *Everything in your sketch slants toward the right.*

SLAP ▸ AGAINST

slap against someone or something [for something] to flap or strike against someone or something. □ *The flag kept slapping against Ed, making it hard for him to remain at attention.* □ *The awning slapped against the side of the house.*

slap something against someone or something to flap or strike something onto someone or something. □ *The wind slapped the branch against Walter.* □ *The gusts from the storm slapped the shutters against the side of the house.*

SLAP ▸ DOWN

slap someone down **1.** to cause someone to fall by striking with the open hand. □ *She became enraged and slapped him down when he approached her again.* 🅃 *Liz slapped down the insulting wretch.* **2.** to squelch someone. □ *I had a great idea, but the boss slapped me down.* □ *Don't slap me down every time I say something!*

slap something down to strike downward with something flat in one's hand. □ *She slapped the dollar bill down in great anger and took her paper cup full of water away with her.* 🅃 *Karen slapped down the money that the bailiff demanded.*

SLAP ▸ IN

slap someone in something to put or throw someone in jail or prison. (Figurative.) □ *The sheriff slapped the crooks in jail.* □ *Do you want me to slap you in jail?*

SLAP ▸ ON

See also under *SLAP ▸ ON(TO).*

slap someone on something to slap a particular part of someone. (*Someone* includes *oneself.*) □ *Gerald was always slapping his friends on the back.* □ *He* *slapped himself on the knee and laughed very loudly.*

slap someone on the wrist **1.** to strike someone's wrist with the open hand, as a punishment. ☐ *Aunt Maude slapped Tony on the wrist when he grabbed a couple of her freshly baked cookies.* ☐ *Tony was slapped on the wrist when he tried to swipe some cookies.* **2.** to administer only the mildest of punishments to someone. (Figurative.) ☐ *The judge did nothing but slap the mugger on the wrist.*

slap something on to dress in something hastily. ☐ *Henry slapped a shirt on and went out to say something to the garbage hauler.* 🅃 *He slapped on a shirt and ran to the bus stop.*

slap something on someone to serve someone with a legal paper or citation. (Colloquial.) ☐ *The strange man came into the office and slapped a subpoena on Mary.* ☐ *I will slap a citation on you for speeding if you don't stop arguing.*

SLAP ▸ ON(TO)

slap something on(to someone or something) to place something onto someone or something by slapping. ☐ *Tim slapped a sign onto Gary that said "kick me."* 🅃 *Tim came up to Gary's back and slapped on a sign.* ☐ *Tim slapped a sign on.*

SLAP ▸ TOGETHER

slap something together to make up something very quickly. ☐ *This is very carelessly done. Someone has just slapped it together.* ☐ *This house was just slapped together. It is really poorly constructed.*

SLASH ▸ AT

slash (out) at someone to thrust out at someone with a knife or something similar, with the intent of cutting. ☐ *The attacker slashed out at his victim and then ran away.* ☐ *Max slashed at Lefty.*

SLASH ▸ OUT

See the previous entry.

SLATE ▸ FOR

slate someone or something for something to schedule someone or something for some thing or a particular time. (*Someone* includes *oneself.*) ☐ *They slated me for a trip to Columbia, Missouri, in August.* ☐ *Wally slated the meeting room for his presentation.* ☐ *Are you slated to perform soon?* ☐ *She slated herself for the first shift.*

SLATE ▸ TO

See *be slated to do something* under *BE ▸ TO.*

SLAVE ▸ AWAY

slave away (at something) to work at something very hard. ☐ *I am tired of slaving away at this work all day.* ☐ *I can't remember why I slave away all the time.*

SLAVE ▸ OVER

slave over something to stand over something, working at it very hard, typically cooking over a hot stove. (A cliché.) ☐ *I've been slaving over this hot stove all day to cook this meal!* ☐ *Ted slaved over his special dessert for hours.*

SLED ▸ DOWN

sled down something to ride down something on a sled. ☐ *I love to sled down the hill in the winter.* ☐ *This hill is too steep to sled down safely.*

SLED ▸ OVER

sled over something to travel over something, such as snow, in a sled. ☐ *We sledded rapidly over the fresh snow, scooting down the hill.* ☐ *We wanted to sled over the new snow, but we had to wait until Uncle Herman had taken a picture of it for his scrapbook.*

SLEEP ▸ AROUND

sleep around the clock to sleep for a full twenty-four hours; to sleep for a very long time. ☐ *I was so tired I could have slept around the clock.* ☐ *When I got home, I lay down and slept around the clock.*

sleep around (with someone) to practice promiscuous sex with a number of people. (Colloquial.) ☐ *They say she sleeps around with just anybody all the time.* ☐ *Yes, she sleeps around.*

SLEEP ▸ AWAY

sleep something away to spend or waste a specific period of time sleeping. ☐ *You can't sleep the whole day away!* 🅃 *Jim slept away his whole vacation.*

SLEEP ▸ IN

sleep in to remain in bed, sleeping past one's normal time of arising. ☐ *I really want to sleep in this morning.* ☐ *I slept in both Saturday and Sunday.*

SLEEP ▸ LIKE

sleep like a log to sleep very soundly. (A cliché.) ☐ *After all the exercise I did, I slept like a log all night long.* ☐ *I always sleep like a log.*

SLEEP ▸ OFF

sleep something off to sleep away the effect of alcohol or drugs. ☐ *Jeff is in his room, sleeping it off.* 🅃 *Jeff is sleeping off the effects of the night before.*

SLEEP ▸ ON

sleep on something **1.** to recline on something and slumber. ☐ *I like to sleep on a firm bed.* ☐ *Mary had to sleep on the floor because her sister was visiting.* **2.** to postpone a decision until one has slept through the night. (Figurative. As if one were going to think through the decision while sleeping.) ☐ *It sounds like a good idea, but I'd like to sleep on it before giving you my response.* ☐ *You go home and sleep on it and give me your answer in the morning.*

SLEEP ▸ OUT

sleep out to sleep away from one's home. ☐ *Can I sleep out tonight?* ☐ *Didn't you sleep out last night?*

SLEEP ▸ OVER

sleep over (with someone) (some place) to spend the night sleeping at someone else's home. (Typically said by teenagers or younger children who spend the night with a friend.) ☐ *Mom, can I sleep over with Tony?* ☐ *Can I sleep over at Tony's house?* ☐ *No, you can't sleep over.*

SLEEP ▸ THROUGH

sleep through something to remain sleeping through some event. ☐ *I didn't hear the storm. I guess I slept through it.* ☐ *Wally slept through the entire opera—even the loud part.*

SLEEP ▸ TOGETHER

sleep together **1.** [for two or more people] to share a bed. ☐ *Do you mean that Fred and Dave have to sleep together?* ☐ *My brother and I used to have to sleep together.* **2.** [for two people] to copulate. ☐ *Do you think they slept together?* ☐ *Ted and Alice slept together a lot when they were in college.*

SLEEP ▸ WITH

sleep with someone **1.** to share a bed with someone. ☐ *Do I have to sleep with my little brother?* ☐ *Many little boys have to sleep with their brothers.* **2.** to copulate with someone. ☐ *I hear Sam's sleeping with Sally now.* ☐ *Whom did you say he slept with?*

SLICE ▸ INTO

slice someone or something into something to cut someone or something into strips of something. ☐ *The villain threatened to slice the helpless maiden into bits.* ☐ *Slice the meat into thin strips and saute it quickly.*

SLICE ▸ IN(TO)

slice in(to something) to cut into something, usually with a knife or something similar. ☐ *Betty sliced into the cake and discovered it was chocolate all the way through.* ☐ *It wasn't until she sliced in that she found out what kind of cake it was.*

SLICE ▸ OFF

slice something off to cut something off with slicing motions. ☐ *Sue sliced the dead branches off with a rusty machete.* 🅃 *Karen sliced off a nice piece of turkey.*

SLICE ▸ THROUGH

slice through something to cut through something with slicing motions. ☐ *The chef sliced through the ham as if it were butter.* ☐ *The knife was too dull to slice through the tomato.*

SLICE ▸ UP

slice someone or something up to cut someone or something up into slices. (*Someone* includes *oneself*.) ☐ *The* *blades of the lawn mower can slice you up if you get too close.* 🅃 *The sharp blades sliced up Bobby's rubber ball.* □ *She had an accident with a hedge trimmer, and she sliced herself up badly.*

SLICK ▸ DOWN

slick something down to brush or comb down hair, usually with some sort of dressing or water. □ *He used something gooey—grease or something—to slick his hair down.* 🅃 *Please slick down your hair. You look a mess.*

SLICK ▸ UP

slick something up to tidy up something or some place. (Colloquial.) □ *I have to slick this house up a little.* 🅃 *Please slick up this room before company gets here.*

SLIDE ▸ ALONG

slide along to slip or glide along. □ *The sled slid along at a good clip down the gently sloping hill.* □ *We slid along on the icy roads, going primarily where gravity and centrifugal force sent us.*

SLIDE ▸ AROUND

slide around to slip or skid around. □ *Many cars slide around on the roads when they are icy.* □ *The pedestrians were sliding around on the pavement.*

slide something around to push, twist, or turn something around. (The thing must be movable, but not on wheels.) □ *Please slide the carton around and look at the address on the other side.* □ *Can you slide the refrigerator around so I can clean the back of it?*

SLIDE ▸ BY

slide by to get along with a minimum of effort. □ *She didn't do a lot of work—she just slid by.* □ *Don't just slide by. Put in some effort.*

SLIDE ▸ DOWN

slide down from something to slip down on something from a higher place. □ *Beth slid down from the top of the mound.* □ *The boys slid down from the roof of the shed and got their pants all dirty.*

slide down something to slip down something, such as a pole. □ *The fire captain slid down the pole and ran to the engine.* □ *Please don't slide down the stairs. You'll ruin the carpet.*

SLIDE ▸ INTO

slide into something to slip or glide into something, such as a car going into a ditch. □ *It was raining hard, and car after car slid into the ditch at the sharp turn near Wagner Road.* □ *Mary's car slid right into the side of a bus.*

SLIDE ▸ IN(TO)

slide something in(to something) to insert something into something effortlessly. □ *Henry slid the end of the seat-belt buckle into its holder and started the car.* 🅃 *Slide in the buckle and make sure it's tight.* □ *Slide it in quickly so we can start up.*

SLIDE ▸ OUT

slide out of something to slip or glide out of something without much effort. □ *Mary slid out of the car and ran to the front door.* □ *The floppy disk slid out of the computer.*

slide something out (of something) to cause something to slip or glide out of something without much effort. (The *of*-phrase is paraphrased with a *from*-phrase when the particle is transposed. See the 🄵 example.) □ *The hunter slid his knife out of its sheath and got ready to skin the deer.* 🅃 *He slid out the heavy box.* 🄵 *Liz slid out the machine from its storage place.* □ *Tony slid the box out.*

SLIDE ▸ OVER

slide over something to slip or glide over something. □ *The car almost slid over the edge of the cliff.* □ *We almost slid over the edge.*

SLIM ▸ DOWN

slim down to become thinner; to become narrower. □ *You have really slimmed down a lot since I last saw you.* □ *I need to eat less so I can slim down.* □ *He slimmed down quite a bit after he had his health problem.*

slim someone down to cause someone to lose weight. □ *They started to slim her down in the hospital, but she gained the weight back as soon as she got out.*

🅃 *The dietician slimmed down all the patients under his care.*

SLING ▸ AT

sling something at someone or something to heave or toss something at someone or something. □ *The child slung a handful of mud at his playmate.* □ *Who slung this muddy mess at the side of the house?*

SLING ▸ OUT

sling something out **1.** to toss or heave something outward. □ *The fishermen slung their nets out into the water.* 🅃 *They slung out their nets.* **2.** to throw something away. □ *Just sling all that old junk out, if you will.* 🅃 *Sling out that stuff!*

SLINK ▸ AROUND

slink around to creep or slither around furtively. □ *The cat slunk around, waiting for a chance to get at the bird.* □ *Don't slink around like that. Someone is likely to take you for a robber.*

SLINK ▸ AWAY

slink away to creep or slither away furtively. □ *The fox slunk away, leaving the henhouse as quietly as such a thing is possible.* □ *I hope that the skunk will slink away as quietly as it came.*

SLINK ▸ IN(TO)

slink in(to something) to creep into something. □ *The cat slunk into the hallway and lay down in the middle of the bathroom door.* □ *I left the door ajar and a cat slunk in.*

SLINK ▸ OFF

slink off to creep away furtively. □ *Carl was embarrassed and tried to slink off, but the ushers spotted him.* □ *The boys slunk off from the picnic and smoked some cigarettes.*

SLINK ▸ OUT

slink out (of some place) to creep out of some place furtively. □ *The fox slunk out of the henhouse just as the farmer came out.* □ *It slunk out and got away.*

SLIP ▸ AROUND

slip around to slide or skid around. □ *The pedestrian slipped around and finally fell on the ice.* □ *The dog slipped around on the ice and finally made it to shore.*

SLIP ▸ AWAY

slip away (from someone or something) to creep away from someone or something furtively; to fall or escape from the hold of someone or something. □ *The child slipped away from her brother and wandered about the store on her own.* □ *Mary slipped away and got lost.* □ *The prisoner slipped away from the bailiff and escaped into the streets of the city.*

SLIP ▸ BACK

slip back (to someone or something) to move quietly and cautiously back to someone or something. □ *Walter slipped back to Sally when her parents weren't looking.* □ *He slipped back and then Mary's parents slipped back, and there was quite a scene.*

slip something back **1.** to pull or place something back. □ *Alice slipped the gearshift lever back and away they went.* 🅃 *She slipped back the gearshift and sped away.* **2.** to return something secretively. □ *Someone took my textbook away and slipped it back later.* 🅃 *The thief slipped back my book.*

SLIP ▸ BETWEEN

slip between the cracks [for someone or something] to be forgotten or neglected. (Idiomatic and figurative. Taken literally, this is nonsense.) □ *Where is Alice? I guess we neglected her and she slipped between the cracks.* □ *This issue seems to have slipped between the cracks and become forgotten.*

SLIP ▸ BY

slip by [for time] to pass quickly or unnoticed. □ *Goodness, almost an hour has slipped by! How time flies.* □ *The entire workday slipped by before I knew it.*

slip by (someone or something) to sneak past someone or something. □ *We slipped by the guard and got in.* □ *We slipped by, but the next people who tried it got caught.*

SLIP ► DOWN

slip down to slide or glide downward. □ *His socks kept slipping down.* □ *He lost so much weight that his pants almost slipped down.*

slip something down to slide something downward. □ *I slipped my pants down a little so the doctor could give me a shot in what they call your "hip."* 🅃 *He slipped down his pants a little.*

SLIP ► FROM

slip (away) from someone or something See under *SLIP ► AWAY.*

slip from something to fall away from something; to lose one's grasp and fall from something. □ *He slipped from the top step and bumped down the other three.* □ *Ted slipped from the stool and fell on the floor.*

SLIP ► IN

slip in (some place) to sneak or go into a place quietly and unnoticed. □ *I think we can slip in the rear door unnoticed.* □ *We slipped in and crept up the stairs.*

SLIP ► IN(TO)

slip in(to something) to slide or glide into something, such as clothing, a sleeping bag, a tight place, etc. □ *I don't want to slip into a cold sleeping bag. How can I warm it up?* □ *I opened the bag and slipped in.*

slip something in((to) something) to cause something to slide or glide into something. □ *Max slipped the bullets into their chambers and got ready to face Lefty.* 🅃 *He slipped the bullets in silently.* □ *Max slipped them in.*

SLIP ► OFF

slip off ((of) someone or something) to fall away from or off someone or something. (The *of* is colloquial.) □ *The jacket slipped off of Sally, but she grabbed it before it hit the floor.* □ *She hung the jacket on the back of the chair, but it slipped off.*

slip off (to some place) to sneak away to some place. □ *Judy and Jeff slipped off to the movies unnoticed.* □ *They slipped off and no one cared.*

slip something off to let an item of clothing slide off one's body; to remove an item of clothing. □ *He slipped his coat off and put it on a chair.* 🅃 *She slipped off her shoes and relaxed.*

SLIP ► ON

slip on something to step on and slide on something. □ *Valerie slipped on a banana peel and hurt her back.* □ *Don't slip on that wet spot on the floor!*

slip something on to put on an article of clothing, possibly in haste or casually. □ *I will go in and slip my bathing suit on and join you in a minute.* 🅃 *She slipped on her shoes and we left.*

SLIP ► OUT

slip out (of something) **1.** to sneak out of a place unnoticed. □ *Gloria slipped out of the theater at intermission.* □ *She slipped out and went home.* **2.** to slide out of an article of clothing. □ *She slipped out of her dress and hung it neatly in the closet.* □ *Ted slipped out of his T-shirt and left it on the floor where it fell.*

SLIP ► OVER

slip something over on someone or something AND **slip one over on someone or something** to deceive someone. (Idiomatic. The *something* is used unchanged.) □ *Are you trying to slip something over on me?* □ *I think he tried to slip one over on me.*

slip something over someone or something to cause something to slide or glide over and onto someone or something. □ *Mother slipped the covers over Timmy and kissed him good night.* □ *Jane slipped the cover over the birdcage for the night.*

SLIP ► PAST

slip past someone or something to sneak or move past someone or something unnoticed. □ *It is impossible to slip past a U.S. Immigration and Naturalization officer.* □ *Do you think I can slip past the doorway without being seen?*

slip someone or something past someone or something to cause someone or something to move past someone or something unnoticed; to manage to get something past the scrutiny of someone. ☐ *I slipped another one of my friends past the usher into the theater.* ☐ *Do you think I can slip this sausage past the customs officers?* ☐ *I slipped a note past the guard.*

SLIP ▸ THROUGH

slip something through (something) **1.** to cause something to slide or glide through something. ☐ *The nickel I dropped slipped through the crack in the floor.* ☐ *It rolled toward a crack in the floor and slipped through.* **2.** to get something approved without much fuss by a group of people, perhaps by deception. (Figurative.) ☐ *I will try to slip this through the committee.* ☐ *I can slip it through for you.*

slip through someone's fingers **1.** to slide through and out of one's grasp. ☐ *The glass slipped through his fingers and crashed to the ground.* ☐ *The rope slipped through his fingers and followed the anchor to the bottom of the lake.* **2.** to escape from someone; to elude someone's capture or control. (Figurative.) ☐ *The prisoner slipped through the sheriff's fingers.* ☐ *Don't let Max slip through your fingers again this time!*

slip through something to slide or slither through something narrow or crowded. ☐ *Gerald slipped through the narrow opening and got away.* ☐ *The dog slipped through the door and ran out into the street.*

SLIP ▸ UP

slip up to make an error. ☐ *I hope you don't slip up again. Try to be more careful.* 🄽 *I think I've made another careless slipup.*

slip up on someone or something to sneak up on someone, a creature, or something quietly. ☐ *I slipped up on Harry and scared him to death.* ☐ *The cat slipped up on a mouse and grabbed it.*

slip up on something to make an error in something ☐*I guess I slipped up on that last job.* ☐ *Fred slipped up on that list—there are a lot of names missing.*

slip up something to climb something, slipping along the way. ☐ *The hikers slipped up the wet slope.* ☐ *Ted slipped up the stairs, tracking mud and water as he went along.*

SLITHER ▸ ALONG

slither along to slink or crawl along. ☐ *The snake slithered along, unmindful of our presence.* ☐ *A pair of otters slithered along playfully.*

SLITHER ▸ AWAY

slither away to sneak or crawl away, like a snake. ☐ *The little lizards slithered away soundlessly.* ☐ *The snake slithered away while Maggie was still screaming.*

SLOBBER ▸ OVER

slobber (all) over someone or something to drool on someone or something. ☐ *The dog slobbered over the child. It was just being friendly.* ☐ *Jenny has slobbered all over her dress.*

slobber over someone or something to drool with delight or eagerness at the thought of someone or something. (Figurative.) ☐ *Fred was slobbering over Donna as she lay sunbathing in a tiny bikini.* ☐ *Jamie was slobbering over Mary's new car.*

SLOG ▸ THROUGH

slog through something to wade or trudge through something, such as mud or snow. ☐ *Do I have to slog through snow to go to school? Can't you drive me?* ☐ *When I was your age, I slogged through snow twice this deep almost every day to get to school.*

SLOP ▸ AROUND

slop around **1.** [for someone] to splash around in a body of liquid, such as a bath. ☐ *Timmy was in his bath, slopping around and singing.* ☐ *Bob is out in the pool, slopping around.* **2.** [for a liquid] to splash or rush around in a container. ☐ *The water was slopping around in the bottom of the boat even though the lake we were traveling on was calm.* ☐ *There is some coffee left. I hear it slopping around in the bottom of the pot.*

slop something around to spill portions of a liquid here and there. ☐ *Don't slop the milk around as you pour it.* ☐ *Please don't slop the paint all around while you work.*

SLOP ▸ ON(TO)

slop something on(to) someone or something to spill or splash a liquid onto someone or something. ☐ *Don't slop the pancake batter onto yourself.* ☐ *Who slopped paint on the floor?*

SLOP ▸ OUT

slop out (of something) [for a liquid] to spill or splash out of a container. ☐ *Some of the orange juice slopped out of the container, making a mess on the table.* ☐ *Some milk slopped out. Please clean it up.*

SLOP ▸ OVER

slop over [for a liquid] to splash out of or overflow a container. ☐ *The milk slopped over and messed up the carpet.* ☐ *Her cup slopped over and discharged its contents on the kitchen table.*

slop something over something to spill or splash some liquid all over something. ☐ *He slopped the starting fluid over the charcoal and lit it.* ☐ *The artist slopped some grape juice over the canvas and proceeded to spread it around in an artistic fashion.*

SLOPE ▸ AWAY

slope away from something to slant downward and away from something. ☐ *The lawn sloped away from the patio toward the riverbank.* ☐ *The porch sloped away from the house at a very acute angle.*

SLOPE ▸ DOWN

slope down (to something or some place) to slant downward toward something or some place from a higher level. ☐ *The wide white beach sloped down to the azure water.* ☐ *The yard sloped down, making a lovely view from the living room.*

slope (down) toward something See the following entry.

SLOPE ▸ TOWARD

slope (down) toward something to slant downward toward something. ☐ *The backyard slopes down toward the river.* ☐ *It slopes toward the water.*

SLOPE ▸ UP

slope up (to something) to slant upwards in the direction of something. ☐ *The ramp sloped up to the door, allowing wheelchairs to enter.* ☐ *It sloped up rather steeply.*

SLOSH ▸ AROUND

slosh around (in something) **1.** [for a liquid] to rush or splash around in an enclosure or container. ☐ *The milk sloshed around in the pitcher and splashed over a little bit.* ☐ *The fluid sloshed around, making a horrible sound.* **2.** to move or splash through a liquid, usually standing on one's feet. ☐ *Billy sloshed around in the wading pool.* ☐ *The kids have been sloshing around in puddles again.*

slosh something around to cause a liquid to rush or splash in a container. ☐ *The chef sloshed the dressing around a few times and poured it on the salad.* 🅃 *The chef sloshed around the dressing and poured it on the salad.*

SLOSH ▸ ON(TO)

slosh something on(to) someone or something to splash or spill a liquid onto someone or something. ☐ *Betty sloshed the charcoal lighter fluid on Fred, and he went in to wash it off.* ☐ *Then she sloshed the fluid onto the charcoal.*

SLOSH ▸ OVER

slosh over [for a liquid] to splash over its container. ☐ *The water in the wading pool sloshed over and made the grass slippery.* ☐ *Don't fill the glass too full. It will slosh over.*

slosh something (all) over someone or something to spill or splash a liquid over someone or something. ☐ *Laura tripped and sloshed the grape juice all over Martha.* ☐ *Martin sloshed pancake batter over the side of the stove.*

SLOSH ▸ THROUGH

slosh through something [for a person] to wade or splash through something. □ *The little kids sloshed through every puddle on their way home.* □ *We sloshed through the stream, ruining our shoes and soaking our cuffs.*

SLOUCH ▸ AROUND

slouch around to move around with a stooped or bent body. (One may slouch because of depression, fear, or with the intention of not being observed.) □ *She is slouching around because she is tired.* □ *Don't you slouch around when you are tired?*

SLOUCH ▸ BEHIND

slouch behind something to remain behind something, slouching with depression, fear, or the intent of not being observed. □ *Jim slouched behind a chair, where no one could see him.* □ *A weary clerk slouched behind the counter, wanting a nap more than anything else.*

SLOUCH ▸ DOWN

slouch down to slump or droop down. □ *Don't always slouch down, Timmy! Stand up straight.* □ *I slouch down because I am tired.*

slouch down (in something) to sink or snuggle down into something, trying to become less visible or more comfortable. □ *Please don't slouch down in your chair, Tim.* □ *He can't sit in anything without slouching down.*

SLOUCH ▸ OVER

slouch over to lean or crumple and fall to one side; [for someone] to collapse in a sitting position. □ *He slouched over and went to sleep in his chair.* □ *When he slouched over, I thought something was wrong.*

SLOUGH ▸ OFF

slough something off **1.** to brush or rub something off. □ *The snake sloughed its old skin off.* 🅃 *It sloughed off its skin.* **2.** to ignore or disregard a negative remark or incident. □ *I could see that the remark had hurt her feelings, but she just pretended to slough it off.* 🅃 *Liz sloughed off the remark.*

SLOW ▸ DOWN

slow down to decrease speed; to go slower. □ *Please slow down. You are going too fast.* 🄽 *The slowdown on the highway was caused by a large truck.*

slow someone or something down to cause someone or something to decrease speed or go slower. (*Someone* includes *oneself*.) □ *Slow him down if you can. He is going too fast.* 🅃 *Slow down that car!* □ *Please slow your car down!* 🄽 *Who is responsible for this slowdown in production?* □ *Slow yourself down a little. You are working too hard and too fast.*

SLOW ▸ UP

slow someone or something up to impede someone or something; to deter someone or something from going at full or normal speed. □ *The wet highway slowed us up quite a bit.* 🅃 *The rain slowed up the trip a little.*

slow up to go slower; to go more slowly in order for someone or something to catch up. □ *Slow up a little! I can't keep up with you!* □ *Please slow up. I can't follow your lecture when you talk so fast.*

SLUG ▸ OUT

slug something out (with someone) to fight about something; to settle a disagreement by fighting. □ *Max wanted to slug it out with Lefty.* 🅃 *Lefty "Fingers" Moran was always ready to slug out an argument with Max.* □ *Finally, they slugged it out once and for all.*

SLUICE ▸ DOWN

sluice something down to rinse something down; to flood the surface of something with water or other liquid to clean it. □ *John sluiced the driveway down.* 🅃 *Karen sluiced down the garage floor.*

SLUICE ▸ OUT

sluice something out to rinse something out; to flood the inside of something to clean it. □ *Sluice the wheelbarrow out, will you?* 🅃 *Please sluice out the wheelbarrow.*

SLUMP ► DOWN

slump down [for someone] to collapse and fall down; [for someone] to crumple. ☐ *The shot hit Max and he slumped down.* ☐ *Suddenly, Mr. Wilson slumped down in his chair.*

slump down (in something) [for someone] to bend down or collapse on something, such as a chair. ☐ *Gary grabbed at his chest and slumped down in his chair.* ☐ *He slumped down and draped himself over the arm of the chair.*

SLUMP ► OVER

slump over [for someone] to collapse and fall over in a sitting position. ☐ *Just after the gunshot, Bruno slumped over and slid from his chair.* 🄰 *The slumped-over figure was motionless and gave us a fright.*

slump over to fall over heavily; to collapse and droop from an upright position. ☐ *How can you work when you slump over your desk that way?* ☐ *He slumped over suddenly and we were afraid that he was ill.*

SLUR ► OVER

slur over something **1.** to avoid saying difficult or crucial words by mumbling them; to slide or slip over words. ☐ *The speaker slurred over so many words that we didn't know what she was saying.* ☐ *Unfortunately, Ted slurred over many of the important parts of his speech.* **2.** to avoid talking about or mentioning an issue. (Figurative.) ☐ *The mayor slurred over the major issue of the day.* ☐ *She slurred over the major problems.*

SLUSH ► UP

slush up to become messy with slush. ☐ *As the storm increases in intensity, the roads will slush up and become impassable.* ☐ *After an hour of snow and rain, the roads were so slushed up that we could not travel.*

SMACK ► DOWN

smack someone down **1.** to knock a person down or cause a person to retreat with a slap or a blow. ☐ *He tried to touch her again and she smacked him down.* 🅃 *She smacked down the rude fellow.* **2.** to rebuke someone. (Figurative.) ☐ *She smacked him down by telling him that he didn't live there anymore.* 🅃 *He has a way of smacking down people who ask stupid questions.*

smack something down (on(to) something) to slap something down onto something. ☐ *He smacked his bet down onto the table, angry with his mounting losses.* 🅃 *Todd smacked down his hand on the table.* ☐ *She smacked her dollar down and grabbed up the newspaper.*

SMACK ► OF

smack of something to be reminiscent of something; to imply something. ☐ *The whole scheme smacked of dishonesty and deception.* ☐ *All of this smacks of illegal practices.*

SMART ► AT

smart at something to suffer the pains of something. ☐ *Over an hour later she was still smarting at his cruel remarks.* ☐ *For many days Ted smarted at the scolding he got.*

SMART ► FROM

smart from something **1.** to get a stinging pain from something. ☐ *His arm smarted from many mosquito bites.* ☐ *Her legs smarted from the scratches she got from walking through the weeds.* **2.** to suffer mental distress from something. (Figurative.) ☐ *She smarted from wounded vanity.* ☐ *He smarted from the rude rebuff.*

SMART ► UNDER

smart under something to suffer stinging pain under something. ☐ *The sailor's back smarted under the blows of the lash.* ☐ *Ted smarted under the lash for his wrongdoings.*

SMARTEN ► UP

smarten up to get smarter; to become more alert and knowing. (Colloquial.) ☐ *You had better smarten up if you want to survive around here.* ☐ *I knew he would smarten up sooner or later.*

SMASH ► IN

smash someone's face in **1.** to crush someone's face. ☐ *The accident smashed Harry's face in, and he had to have extensive surgery.* 🅃 *The accident smashed in* *his face.* **2.** to strike someone in the face. (Slang.) ☐ *You had better stop that or I will smash your face in.* 🅃 *Max tried to smash in Lefty's face.*

smash something in to crush something inward; to make something collapse inward by striking it. ☐ *Andy gave one good kick and smashed the drum in.* 🅃 *Liz smashed in the window.* 🄰 *The police were examining the smashed-in window.*

SMASH ▸ INTO

smash into something to crash into something; to bump or crash into something. ☐ *Judy smashed into the coffee table and hurt her leg.* ☐ *The car smashed into the side of a bus and caused a lot of damage.*

SMASH ▸ OUT

smash out of something to break [one's way] out of something. ☐ *The prisoner smashed out of his cell.* ☐ *The horse smashed out of its stable.*

SMASH ▸ THROUGH

smash through something to break [one's way] through some sort of barrier. ☐ *The fleeing car smashed through the police barrier.* ☐ *Max got angry and smashed through the office door.*

SMASH ▸ UP

smash something up to break something up; to destroy something. ☐ *I hope the children don't smash the good china up if we use it tonight.* 🅃 *The angry worker smashed up the bucket.* 🄰 *Where shall I put the smashed-up bicycle?*

SMEAR ▸ ON(TO)

smear something on(to someone or something) to spread or rub something onto someone or something. ☐ *Judy asked Jeff to smear the sun lotion onto her, and he was very happy to do so.* 🅃 *She smeared on the lotion.* ☐ *Jane smeared a little on.*

SMEAR ▸ WITH

smear someone or something with something **1.** to spread or rub someone or something with some substance. (*Someone* includes *oneself.*) ☐ *Billy smeared Bobby with mud and made him very angry.* ☐ *You should smear that burn with lotion.* ☐ *He smeared himself with grease and ruined his shirt.* **2.** to damage the reputation of someone or something by spreading serious charges or rumors. ☐ *He smeared his opponent with all sorts of charges.* ☐ *The speaker smeared the entire city with his accusations.*

SMELL ▸ OF

smell of something to have the smell of something; to smell like something. ☐ *This house smells of onions.* ☐ *Her cooking always smells of entirely too much garlic.*

SMELL ▸ OUT

smell someone or something out to locate someone, a creature, or something by smelling or as if by smelling. ☐ *The dog smelled the crook out from the place in the alley where he was hiding.* 🅃 *The dog smelled out the raccoon.* ☐ *The sheriff hoped he could smell out the bandits before they struck again.*

SMELL ▸ TO

smell to high heaven to smell very bad; to smell with a smell so bad that it would not disperse even high in the sky. ☐ *This place smells to high heaven! What have you been cooking?* ☐ *Can't we air the house out? It smells to high heaven.*

SMELL ▸ UP

smell something up to cause a bad odor in a place or on something. ☐ *Your cooking sure smelled this place up!* 🅃 *Those onions really smelled up the house!*

SMILE ▸ AT

smile at someone to make a smiling face at someone. ☐ *I love the way you smile at me.* ☐ *I am glad you smile at me occasionally.*

SMILE ▸ (UP)ON

smile (up)on someone or something to bestow approval on someone or something. (*Upon* is formal and less commonly used than *on*.) ☐ *Fate has smiled upon me at last!* ☐ *I wish Alice would smile on me.*

SMIRK ► AT

smirk at someone or something to smile in a smug or sneering way at someone or something. ☐ *Why are you smirking at me like that?* ☐ *Jane looked at the report and smirked at it.*

SMITE ► WITH

smite someone with something to strike someone with something. (Literary or biblical.) ☐ *The silver knight approached the black knight and smote him with his sword.* ☐ *Please go and smite the dragon with your sword.*

SMOKE ► OUT

smoke someone or something (out of something) **1.** to force someone, a creature, or something out of something or a place, using smoke. (In cowboy movies, there is also an implication that the smoke is gunsmoke from the gunpowder used in trying to drive someone or something out.) ☐ *The police used tear gas to smoke the kidnappers out of the house.* T *They smoked out the crooks.* ☐ *We smoked them out.* **2.** to drive someone, a creature, or something out into public view, as if using smoke or something similar. (Figurative.) ☐ *What will it take to smoke these crooks out of government?* T *We will smoke out the corrupt officials yet.* ☐ *We plan to smoke them out.*

SMOKE ► UP

smoke something up to cause something or a place to become smoky. ☐ *Get out of here with that cigarette! I don't want you smoking my house up!* T *The burning beans sure smoked up the house.* A *I refuse to stay in a smoked-up room like that.*

SMOOTH ► AWAY

smooth something away to remove something, such as wrinkles or other unevenness, by pressing or smoothing. ☐ *Jeff put the cloth on the table and smoothed the wrinkles away with his hand.* T *Jeff smoothed away the wrinkles.*

SMOOTH ► BACK

smooth something back to flatten and position something by pressing or smoothing. ☐ *He smoothed his hair back out of his eyes.* T *Jeff smoothed back his hair.*

SMOOTH ► DOWN

smooth something down to make something flat or smooth by pressing. ☐ *She smoothed her skirt down, fluffed her hair, and went into the boardroom.* T *Karen smoothed down the bedclothes.*

SMOOTH ► ON(TO)

smooth something on(to someone or something) to spread or flatten something onto someone or something. ☐ *Ted smoothed the suntan lotion onto Alice, who lay on a towel in the sand.* T *He smoothed on some lotion.*

SMOOTH ► OUT

smooth something out **1.** to flatten or even something by smoothing or pressing. ☐ *Wally smoothed the bedspread out.* T *Wally finished making the bed by smoothing out the spread.* **2.** to polish and refine something. (Figurative.) ☐ *The editor smoothed John's style out.* ☐ *You need to smooth out your delivery when you are speaking.*

SMOOTH ► OVER

smooth something over to ease a bad situation by careful and gentle actions or words. ☐ *The boss tried to smooth the matter over, but did not succeed.* T *Let me try to smooth over this affair.*

SMOTHER ► IN

smother someone or something in something **1.** to kill someone or a creature by smothering in something. (*Someone* includes *oneself.*) ☐ *Max tried to smother Lefty in the Persian carpet.* ☐ *You really wouldn't try to smother that cat in the rug, would you?* ☐ *He almost smothered himself in the huge pile of leaves.* **2.** to cover or bury someone, a creature, or something with something. ☐ *Her mother smothered her in kisses.* ☐ *Fred smothered the steak in mushrooms and catsup.*

SMOTHER ► WITH

smother someone or something with something **1.** to suffocate someone or something with something. ☐ *The vil-*

lain tried to smother his victim with a pillow. □ *Max tried to smother the cat with a plastic bag.* **2.** to cover or bury someone or something with something. (Figurative.) □ *She smothered him with kisses.* □ *Aunt Margaret almost smothered us with the ruffles on the front of her dress when she hugged us.*

SMUGGLE ► ACROSS

smuggle someone or something across something to move someone or something across a border illegally and in secret. □ *The patriots smuggled one of their number across the border last night.* □ *Larry helped smuggle a computer across the border.*

SMUGGLE ► IN(TO)

smuggle someone or something in(to some place) to move someone or something across a border into a place illegally and in secret. □ *The secret agent smuggled his family into the country and then defected.* 🅃 *He smuggled in his family.* □ *Don't try to smuggle contraband into that country.*

SMUGGLE ► OUT

smuggle someone or something out (of some place) to move someone or something across a border out of a place illegally and in secret. (The *of*-phrase is paraphrased with a *from*-phrase when the particle is transposed. See the 🄵 example.) □ *Judy smuggled her cousin out of the country in a van.* 🅃 *She smuggled out her cousin.* 🄵 *Judy smuggled out her cousin from that troubled land.* □ *I smuggled a few pieces of paper currency out, just for my collection.*

SMUGGLE ► PAST

smuggle someone or something past (someone or something) to move something past a guard or monitor illegally and in secret. □ *We failed in our attempt to smuggle Mary past the border.* □ *It is easy to smuggle wine past the border guards.* □ *While they weren't looking, we smuggled some wine past.*

SMUGGLE ► THROUGH

smuggle someone or something through (something) to move something through a guard post or other barrier illegally and in secret. □ *The officers smuggled the child through the barrier so he could be with his mother.* □ *We smuggled some other goods through too.*

SNACK ► OFF

snack off (of) something to eat food, bit by bit, in little snacks. (The *of* is colloquial.) □ *Please don't snack off the turkey so we can get another meal out of it.* □ *Who has been snacking off of last night's roast beef?*

SNAKE ► ALONG

snake along to move along in a line, looking like a snake; to move along in a line, moving as a snake moves. □ *The train snaked along, gaining speed as it went downhill.* □ *The line of people waiting to buy tickets snaked along slowly.*

SNAP ► AT

snap at someone to speak sharply or angrily to someone. □ *Don't snap at me. What did I do?* □ *Why did you snap at me? What did I do?*

snap at someone or something to bite at someone or something. □ *The dog snapped at my pants leg, but I escaped the attack unharmed.* □ *The fox snapped at the chicken and finally caught hold of it.* □ *The dog snapped at the judge and was disqualified.*

snap at something to seize an opportunity. (Figurative.) □ *It is such a good deal, I knew you would snap at it.* □ *Just as I thought, Ted snapped at my final offer.*

SNAP ► BACK

snap back (after something) to return to normal after an accident or similar event. □ *He is upset now, but he will snap back after things settle down.* □ *Things will snap back in no time at all.*

snap back (at someone) to give a sharp or angry response to someone. □ *The telephone operator, unlike in the good old days, snapped back at the caller.* □ *Please don't snap back. I've had a bad day.*

snap back (on someone or something) [for something] to be jerked back onto someone or something. □ *The branch* *snapped back on Tim and left a welt on his arm.* □ *The whip snapped back and stung Tex's hand.* □ *I got this cut when a branch snapped back.*

snap something back to cause something to jerk back. □ *The force of the crash snapped his head back and injured his neck.* [T] *The crash snapped back his head.*

SNAP ▶ INTO

snap into something [for something] to be put or fit into an opening with an audible snap. □ *The larger edge of the card snaps into the slot at the base.* □ *This part snaps right into the other part.*

snap something into something to put or press something into something with an audible snap. □ *Next, you snap this little part into this slot here.* □ *Snap these legs into the bottom of the tray.*

SNAP ▶ OFF

snap someone's head off to speak very sharply to someone. (Figurative.) □ *How rude! Don't snap my head off!* □ *Mary snapped Ted's head off because he had come in late.*

snap something off to break off something brittle. □ *Liz snapped a bit of the rock off and put it in her bag.* [T] *Carl snapped off a piece of the candy and gave it to Timmy.*

SNAP ▶ ON

snap something on to attach something to something else, causing an audible snap. □ *Dawn took two pills from the bottle and snapped the lid on.* [T] *She snapped on the lid.*

SNAP ▶ OUT

snap out of something to return quickly to normal after a period of illness, inactivity, or disorientation. □ *I seemed to have a little cold, but I snapped out of it quickly.* □ *Come on, snap out of it! I need your complete attention.*

snap something out (of something) to remove something from something, causing an audible snap. (The *of*-phrase is paraphrased with a *from*-phrase when the particle is transposed. See the [F] example.) □ *Jeff snapped the plastic plug out of socket.* [T] *He snapped out the plug.* [F] *Jeff snapped out the plug from the socket.* □ *He snapped the plug out and reeled in the cord.*

SNAP ▶ TO

snap to (attention) to move quickly to military attention. □ *The troops snapped to attention when they saw the general appear.* □ *Snap to when I tell you!*

SNAP ▶ UP

snap something up **1.** to grasp something quickly. □ *Karen snapped the bargain up.* [T] *Teddy walked through the kitchen and snapped up two cookies on the way.* **2.** to believe something eagerly; to believe a lie readily. □ *They are so irrational that you can say anything bad about refuse disposal and they'll snap it up.* [T] *They will snap up anything that sounds good.*

SNARL ▶ AT

snarl at someone or something to growl at someone, a creature, or something angrily and threateningly. □ *The dog snarled at everyone who passed by.* □ *Our dog used to sit in front of the washing machine and snarl at it.*

SNARL ▶ OUT

snarl something out to utter something by snarling or growling. □ *Lefty snarled a naughty word out at Max.* [T] *Max snarled out a curse as the cop grabbed his coat collar.*

SNARL ▶ UP

snarl someone or something up to tangle someone or something; to mess something up. (Both literal and figurative uses.) □ *The wind snarled my hair up terribly.* [T] *The wind snarled up my hair.* □ *Your intervention snarled our procedures up terribly.*

SNATCH ▶ AT

snatch at someone or something to grasp at someone or something. □ *The mugger snatched at Jane just as she maced him.* □ *He snatched at the Mace, but it was too late.*

SNATCH ▶ AWAY

See the following entry.

SNATCH ▸ FROM

snatch someone or something (away) from someone or something to grab and take someone or something from someone or something. ☐ *The mother snatched her child away from the doctor and fled.* ☐ *She snatched the candy from the child.* ☐ *The board of directors snatched power away from the committee.*

SNATCH ▸ OUT

snatch something out of something to grab something out of something. ☐ *The police officer snatched the gun out of Don's hand.* ☐ *Mary snatched the piece of chicken out of the fire as soon as it fell in.*

SNATCH ▸ UP

snatch something up **1.** to grasp something and lift it up. ☐ *Tom snatched the last cookie up and popped it into his mouth.* 🅃 *He snatched up the last piece of cake.* **2.** to collect or acquire as many of something as possible. ☐ *The shoppers snatched the sale merchandise up very quickly.* 🅃 *The shoppers snatched up the sale merchandise very quickly.*

SNAZZ ▸ UP

snazz something up to make something more contemporary and appealing; to make something more jazzy. (Slang.) ☐ *This act is too dull. Let's do something to snazz it up.* 🅃 *Snazz up this music a bit.*

SNEAK ▸ AROUND

sneak around (some place) to move about a place in a sneaky fashion. ☐ *Please don't sneak around the house. It makes me nervous.* ☐ *Please stop sneaking around!*

sneak around someone or something **1.** to creep around or past someone or something. ☐ *The cat sneaked around Molly and ran out the door.* ☐ *We had to sneak around the corner so we wouldn't be seen.* **2.** to circumvent the control or censorship of someone or some group. (Figurative.) ☐ *I think we can sneak around the board of directors and authorize this project ourselves.* ☐ *Yes, let's sneak around it.*

SNEAK ▸ AWAY

sneak away (from some place) to go away from a place quietly and in secret. ☐ *Jeff tried to sneak away from the party, but Judy saw him.* ☐ *They sneaked away together.*

SNEAK ▸ IN(TO)

sneak in(to some place) to enter a place quietly and in secret, perhaps without a ticket or permission. ☐ *The kids tried to sneak into the rock concert, but they were stopped by the guards.* ☐ *Never try to sneak in. Sometimes they arrest you for trespassing.*

SNEAK ▸ OUT

sneak out (of some place) to go out of a place quietly and in secret. ☐ *I sneaked out of the meeting, hoping no one would notice.* ☐ *Jamie saw me and sneaked out with me.*

SNEAK ▸ UP

sneak up on someone or something to approach someone or something quietly and in secret. ☐ *Please don't sneak up on me like that.* ☐ *I sneaked up on the cake, hoping no one would see me. Someone did.*

sneak up to someone or something to move close to someone or something quietly and in secret. ☐ *I sneaked up to Don and scared him to death.* ☐ *Don sneaked up to the punch bowl and helped himself before the party began.*

SNEER ▸ AT

sneer at someone or something to make a haughty or deprecating face at someone or something; to show one's contempt for someone or something. ☐ *I asked her politely to give me some more room, and she just sneered at me.* ☐ *Jamie sneered at the report that Ken had submitted.*

SNEEZE ▸ AT

sneeze at someone to sneeze in someone's direction. ☐ *Please don't sneeze at me! Cover your mouth!* ☐ *You should never sneeze at anyone. It is very bad manners.*

sneeze at something to indicate one's disapproval of something; to belittle someone or something. (Figurative.) ☐

I wouldn't sneeze at that amount of money if I were you. It's better than nothing. □ *I though it was a good offer, but the customer just sneezed at it.*

SNEEZE ▸ INTO

sneeze into something to aim a sneeze into something. □ *You should always sneeze into a handkerchief.* □ *Please sneeze into a tissue or something.*

SNEEZE ▸ ON

sneeze on someone or something to aim a sneeze onto someone or something. □ *Don't sneeze on me!* □ *Don't sneeze on anything. Cover your mouth!*

SNIFF ▸ AT

sniff at someone or something **1.** to try to get the smell of someone or something by smelling. □ *The dog sniffed at the visitor.* □ *The cat sniffed at almost every inch of the rug that the dog had walked on.* **2.** to show one's disapproval of someone or something by sniffing. □ *I made one suggestion, but Claire just sniffed at me.* □ *Gale just sniffed at the idea and would say nothing.*

SNIFF ▸ OUT

sniff someone or something out to locate someone or something by sniffing or as if by sniffing. □ *The dog sniffed the intruder out and the police captured him.* 🅃 *The dog sniffed out the mole in the lawn.*

SNIP ▸ OFF

snip something off ((of) something) to cut something off something. (The *of*-phrase is paraphrased with a *from*-phrase when the particle is transposed. See the 🄵 example. The *of* is colloquial.) □ *She snipped a dead blossom off the rosebush.* 🅃 *Jane snipped off a bud.* 🄵 *Jane snipped off a dead bud from the rosebush.* □ *She snipped it off.*

SNIPE ▸ AT

snipe at someone or something **1.** to fire a weapon at someone or something from a concealed position. □ *Someone with a rifle sniped at the troops as they went through the jungle.* □ *A rifleman was busy sniping at the platoon.* **2.** to make petty complaints about someone or something. (Figurative.) □ *Stop sniping at me and everything I do.* □ *Ken is always sniping at my reports.*

SNITCH ▸ ON

snitch on someone to tattle on someone. □ *You wouldn't snitch on me, would you?* □ *Timmy snitched on his older brother.*

SNOOP ▸ AROUND

snoop around (something) to look around in a place, trying to find out something secret or about someone else's affairs. □ *Why are you snooping around my house?* □ *I am not snooping around.*

SNOOP ▸ INTO

snoop into something to pry into something or someone else's affairs. □ *I wish you would stop snooping into my business!* □ *Whose affairs are they snooping into now?*

SNORT ▸ AT

snort at someone or something to show one's displeasure with someone or something by snorting. □ *The customer snorted at the waiter for his surliness.* □ *The customer snorted at the prices and walked out.*

SNOW ▸ IN

snow someone or something in [for heavy snowfall] to block someone or something in a place. □ *The sudden storm snowed us in.* 🅃 *The storm snowed in most of the people in town.* 🅃 *We hoped it hadn't snowed in the fire engines.*

SNOW ▸ UNDER

snow someone or something under (with something) to burden someone or something with something. (Usually too much work.) □ *The busy season snowed us all under with too much work.* 🅃 *The heavy work load snowed under the office staff.* □ *The billing period often snows the computer under.* □ *We are really snowed under!*

SNOWBALL ▸ INTO

snowball into something [for something] to become larger or more serious by growing like a snowball. □ *This* *whole problem is snowballing into a crisis very rapidly.* □ *The argument soon snowballed into a full-blown riot.*

SNUFF ▶ OUT

snuff someone out to kill someone. (Slang.) □ *Max really wanted to snuff Lefty out, once and for all.* 🅃 *Lefty wanted to snuff out Max.*

snuff something out to extinguish something, such as a flame. □ *She snuffed all the candles out and went to bed.* 🅃 *Karen snuffed out the flames one by one.*

SNUG ▶ DOWN

snug down (some place) to become comfortable and warm in a place. □ *The cat snugged down at the foot of the bed.* □ *Finally the children snugged down and we could go to sleep.*

SNUGGLE ▶ AGAINST

snuggle (up) against someone or something to press or cuddle against someone or something, as if to keep warm. □ *Tiffany snuggled up against Tad and asked him to give her some chewing gum.* □ *He snuggled against the warm wall on the other side of the fireplace.*

SNUGGLE ▶ DOWN

snuggle down (into something) to nestle into something, such as a warm bed. □ *Toby snuggled down into his nice warm bed.* □ *He got into bed and snuggled down.*

snuggle down (with someone) to nestle [into something] with someone else. □ *Billy snuggled down with his sister in the big feather bed.* □ *They snuggled down and went to sleep.*

snuggle down (with something) to nestle [into something] with something, such as a book. □ *The baby snuggled down with her blanket and was asleep in no time.* □ *Sally grabbed onto her favorite blanket and snuggled down for the night.*

SNUGGLE ▶ UP

See under *SNUGGLE ▶ AGAINST.*

snuggle up (to someone or something) to cuddle up close to someone or something. □ *Kelly snuggled up to Jeff.* □ *She snuggled up and said she wanted some pizza.*

SOAK ▶ IN

soak something in something to leave something immersed in a liquid, intending for it to be absorbed. □ *Soak your feet in Epsom salts to make them feel better.* □ *I had to soak my elbow in ice water to take down the swelling.*

SOAK ▶ IN(TO)

soak in(to something) [for moisture] to penetrate something. □ *The rain soaked into the parched ground as fast as it fell.* □ *I'm glad it soaked in. I was afraid it would run off.*

SOAK ▶ OFF

soak something off ((of) something) to remove something, such as a label or surface soil, from something by soaking in a liquid. (The *of*-phrase is paraphrased with a *from*-phrase when the particle is transposed. See the 🄵 example. The *of* is colloquial.) □ *She soaked the labels off the bottles and jars.* 🅃 *Please soak off the label.* 🄵 *Karen soaked off the labels from all the jars.* □ *Soak the labels off, don't scrape them off.*

SOAK ▶ OUT

soak something out (of something) to remove something, such as a stain, from something by soaking in a liquid. (The *of*-phrase is paraphrased with a *from*-phrase when the particle is transposed. See the 🄵 example.) □ *Dan soaked the stain out of his shirt and then washed it.* 🅃 *Dan soaked out the stain.* 🄵 *He soaked out the stain from his pants.* □ *I couldn't soak the stain out.*

SOAK ▶ THROUGH

soak through something [for liquid] to work its way through something, such as cloth or paper. □ *Please wipe up that mess before it soaks through the tablecloth.* □ *It's too late. The grape juice has soaked through the carpet into the mat.*

SOAK ▶ TO

soak someone to the skin [for water, rain, or other liquid] to work its way through someone's clothing to the skin.

(*Someone* includes *oneself.*) ☐ *The storm soaked us all to the skin.* ☐ *She soaked herself to the skin in the storm.*

SOAK ▸ UP

soak something up 1. to gather up moisture or a liquid, using an absorbent cloth, paper, etc. ☐ *Alice soaked the spill up with a sponge.* Ⓣ *She soaked up the spilled milk.* 2. [for cloth, paper, or other absorbent material] to absorb moisture or a liquid. ☐ *Please get some paper towels to soak the spill up.* Ⓣ *The sponge soaked up the orange juice.* 3. to learn or absorb some information; to learn much information. ☐ *I can't soak information up as fast as I used to be able to.* Ⓣ *Liz can soak up an amazing number of facts.* 4. to believe something; to be gullible enough to believe something. (Colloquial.) ☐ *This is all nonsense, but the customers will soak it up anyway.* Ⓣ *The tourists will soak up anything you tell them.*

SOAK ▸ WITH

soak someone or something with something to get someone or something thoroughly wet with some liquid. (*Someone* includes *oneself.*) ☐ *The rain soaked us all with icy-cold drops of water.* ☐ *It soaked the land with much-needed moisture.* ☐ *He soaked himself with the bucket of paint.*

SOAP ▸ DOWN

soap someone or something down to cover someone or something thoroughly with soap or suds. (*Someone* includes *oneself.*) ☐ *Mother soaped Timmy down and rinsed him off in warm water.* Ⓣ *She soaped down the floor.* ☐ *He soaped himself down and then rinsed off.*

SOB ▸ OUT

sob one's heart out to cry very hard in great sorrow. (Figurative.) ☐ *She suffered such grief—alone and sobbing her heart out.* ☐ *He sobbed his heart out for the characters in the movie who had suffered so much.*

sob something out to speak something out while sobbing. ☐ *Wally sobbed his story out while the police made notes.* Ⓣ *He sobbed out his tale.* Ⓐ *His sobbed-out words were heard by only a few.*

SOB ▸ TO

sob oneself to sleep to cry until one falls asleep. ☐ *He sobbed himself to sleep almost every night.* ☐ *The child sobbed himself to sleep night after night.*

sob something to someone to cry and tell one's troubles to someone. ☐ *He is always sobbing his sad tale to anyone who will listen.* ☐ *Timmy sobbed his story to the teacher.*

SOBER ▸ UP

sober someone up 1. to take actions that will cause a drunken person to become sober. (*Someone* includes *oneself.*) ☐ *Some coffee ought to sober him up.* ☐ *He tried to sober himself up because he had to drive home.* Ⓣ *They tried to sober up the guys who had been out all night.* 2. to cause someone to face reality. ☐ *The harsh reality of what had happened sobered him up immediately.* Ⓣ *The lecture sobered up all the revelers.*

sober up to return to sobriety from a drunken state. ☐ *Jeff sobered up in an hour and could function again.* ☐ *I don't think that Tex has sobered up since the early 1960s.*

SOCK ▸ AWAY

sock something away to place something, such as money, into reserve; to store something in a secure place. (Colloquial.) ☐ *I try to sock a little money away each month for my vacation.* Ⓣ *I will sock away some money.*

SOCK ▸ IN

sock someone or something in [for fog] to cause someone or something to remain in place. ☐ *The heavy fog socked us in for six hours.* Ⓣ *The fog socked in the airport for an hour.*

SOCK ▸ TO

sock it to someone 1. to punch someone; to punch one's fist at someone. (Colloquial.) ☐ *Max really socked it to Lefty!* ☐ *Lefty socked it to Roger and knocked him down.* 2. to tell bad news to someone in a straightforward manner. (Slang.) ☐ *I can take it. Sock it to me!*

☐ *I don't care how bad it seems. Sock it to me!*

SOFTEN ▸ UP

soften someone up to prepare to persuade someone of something. ☐ *I will talk to Fred and soften him up for your request.* 🅃 *I will soften up your father before you ask him about it.*

soften something up to take actions that will make something softer. ☐ *Soften the butter up before you add it to the sauce.* 🅃 *Please soften up the ice cream before you try to serve it.*

soften up 1. [for something] to become softer. ☐ *The butter softened up in the heat of the day.* ☐ *The candles will probably soften up and bend over in this hot weather.* **2.** [for someone] to adopt a more gentle manner. ☐ *After a while, she softened up and was more friendly.* ☐ *It was weeks before Ted softened up and treated us more kindly.*

SOLICIT ▸ FOR

solicit for someone or something to seek money or other contributions for someone or something, such as a charitable cause. ☐ *I am soliciting for crippled children. Would you care to contribute?* ☐ *Are you soliciting for a good cause?*

solicit someone for something to attempt to persuade someone to give something, such as money, for a specific purpose. ☐ *The little group solicited the owners of the business for a contribution.* ☐ *Fred solicited everyone in his department for at least a dollar.*

SOP ▸ UP

sop something up to mop or soak up a liquid. ☐ *Use this rag to sop the spilled milk up.* 🅃 *The rag will sop up the mess a little at a time.*

SORROW ▸ OVER

sorrow over someone or something to grieve or feel sad about someone or something. ☐ *There is no need to sorrow over Tom. He will come back.* ☐ *He is sorrowing over the business he has lost because of the weather.*

SORT ▸ OUT

sort oneself out to pull oneself together; to figure out what to do about one's problems. ☐ *I need a few days to sort myself out.* ☐ *I need some time to sort myself out.*

sort something out 1. to sort something; to arrange according to class or category. ☐ *Let's sort these cards out.* ☐ *Would you please sort out your socks?* **2.** to study a problem and figure it out. ☐ *I can't sort this out without some more time.* 🅃 *Let's sort out this mess and settle it once and for all.*

sort something out from something to separate something away from something else. ☐ *You really ought to sort the pebbles out of the rice before you cook it.* 🅃 *I will sort out the good ones from the bad ones.*

SOUND ▸ OFF

sound off to speak something loudly; to call out one's name or one's place in a numerical sequence. ☐ *All right, sound off, you guys!* ☐ *Each one sounded off.*

sound off (about something) to complain loudly about something; to make a fuss over something. ☐ *She is always sounding off about something.* ☐ *Betty sounds off all the time.*

SOUND ▸ OUT

sound someone out to discuss a matter and try to figure out where someone stands on the matter. ☐ *I don't know what she thinks. I will sound her out.* 🅃 *I will sound out Fred and Liz to see what they think.*

SOUP ▸ UP

soup something up to make something more powerful. (Colloquial.) ☐ *Tony spent a lot of time souping the engine up in his old car.* 🅃 *Tony souped up his old car.* 🄰 *That souped-up car of his is sure noisy.*

SPACE ▸ OUT

space out to become giddy or disoriented. (Slang.) ☐ *Judy spaced out during the meeting and I didn't understand a word she said.* ☐ *I have a tendency to space out at the end of the day.*

space someone out to cause someone to become giddy or disoriented. (Slang.) □ *The excitement of the emergency simply spaced her out.* 🅃 *The movie spaced out every member of the audience.* 🄰 *Who is that spaced-out kid over there?*

SPADE ▸ UP

spade something up to turn over the soil in a garden plot with a spade. □ *Please go out and spade the garden up so I can plant the potatoes and onions.* 🅃 *I will spade up the garden.*

SPAR ▸ WITH

spar with someone **1.** to box with someone. □ *The champ needs someone to spar with every day.* □ *Ted was sparring with his brother when the phone rang and saved him from further exertion.* **2.** to argue or quibble with someone. (Figurative.) □ *I think you really enjoy sparring with people just to irritate them.* □ *Stop sparring with me! I am not here to argue.*

SPARK ▸ OFF

spark something off **1.** to ignite something explosive. □ *The lightning sparked a fire off.* 🅃 *The match sparked off a raging inferno.* **2.** to foment some violent activity. □ *We were afraid there would be a riot and the speaker nearly sparked it off.* 🅃 *The speaker sparked off quite a discussion.*

SPARKLE ▸ WITH

sparkle with something to glitter or twinkle because of something. □ *The crystal goblets sparkled with the light from the flickering candles.* □ *Her eyes sparkled with the reflection of the candles.*

SPATTER ▸ AROUND

spatter something around to scatter bits or drops of a liquid or something moist here and there. □ *Ted spattered paint around everywhere when he redecorated his kitchen.* 🅃 *Don't spatter around the paint.*

SPATTER ▸ ON

spatter on someone or something [for a liquid or something moist] to splash onto someone or something. □ *When Kelly painted the hallway, a lot of paint spattered on the floor.* □ *The hot fat spattered on me.*

SPATTER ▸ ON(TO)

spatter something on(to) someone or something to scatter or splash bits or drops of a liquid or something moist onto someone or something. □ *Who spattered barbecue sauce on the wall?* □ *The paint can fell and spattered paint on everyone.*

SPATTER ▸ UP

spatter someone or something up to get drops of a liquid or bits of something moist onto someone or something. (*Someone* includes *oneself*.) □ *The painter spattered up his partner when he dropped the paint bucket accidentally.* 🅃 *The falling paint bucket spattered up the wall.* □ *The painter spattered himself up with various colors.*

SPATTER ▸ WITH

spatter someone or something with something to splash someone or something with drops of a liquid or bits of something moist. □ *Frank spattered us with grapefruit juice as he was eating a half of grapefruit.* □ *He even spattered the wall with juice.* □ *He spattered himself with paint.*

SPAZ ▸ AROUND

spaz around to go about acting giddy or disoriented. (Slang.) □ *Stop spazzing around and get organized!* □ *I am not spazzing around. I am as organized as I can get.*

SPAZ ▸ OUT

spaz out **1.** to become giddy or disoriented. (Slang.) □ *Freddie nearly spazzed out when he saw the new car.* □ *After the long plane ride, I just spazzed out.* **2.** to lose one's self control. (Slang.) □ *Jeff spazzed out and made a fool of himself.* □ *Ted was having such a good time that he spazzed out and had to be taken home.*

SPEAK ▸ ABOUT

speak about someone or something to mention someone or something. □ *And now I will speak about Abraham Lincoln.* □ *Let us speak about what happened yesterday.*

SPEAK ▸ AGAINST

speak against someone or something **1.** to criticize someone or something. ☐ *Many people are speaking against the mayor. She will not be reelected.* ☐ *Please don't speak against cats in my presence.* **2.** to testify or argue against someone or something. ☐ *Judy spoke against the candidate at length.* ☐ *The next speaker spoke against waste.*

SPEAK ▸ DOWN

speak down to someone to address someone in simpler terms than necessary; to speak condescendingly to someone. ☐ *There is no need to speak down to me. I can understand anything you are likely to say.* ☐ *Sorry. Sometimes I tend to speak down to people over the telephone.*

SPEAK ▸ FOR

speak for oneself **1.** to speak on one's own behalf. ☐ *I can speak for myself. I don't need you to speak for me.* ☐ *Speak for yourself. What you say does not represent my thinking.* **2.** to recognize that one is expressing only one's own opinion. (Always in the *ing* form.) ☐ *Speaking for myself, I am ready to cancel the contract.* ☐ *Sally is speaking for herself. She is not expressing our opinions.*

speak for someone or something **1.** to testify or argue for someone or something. ☐ *I would be happy to speak for you in court. Just tell me when.* ☐ *My attorney will speak for our position.* **2.** to lay claim to someone or something. ☐ *Fred is spoken for.* ☐ *I want to speak for the red one.* Ⓐ *The spoken-for goods were set to one side until the end of the auction.*

SPEAK ▸ FROM

speak from something to draw authority or credibility in one's speaking from something such as knowledge or experience. ☐ *Believe me, I speak from experience.* ☐ *Listen to her. She speaks from a lot of knowledge and training.*

SPEAK ▸ OF

speak highly of someone or something **1.** [for someone] to say good things about someone or something. ☐ *She always speaks highly of you.* ☐ *Everyone spoke highly of this movie, but it is not good.* **2.** [for a fact] to reflect well on someone or something. (Figurative. See also *speak of something*.) ☐ *The success of your project speaks highly of you.* ☐ *All of this good news speaks highly of your ability to influence people.*

speak of someone or something to mention or discuss someone or something. ☐ *Were we speaking of Judy? I don't recall.* ☐ *We were speaking of the new law.*

speak of something [for a type of behavior or action] to reflect a particular quality. (Figurative. See also *speak highly of someone or something*.) ☐ *Jeff's behavior spoke of a good upbringing.* ☐ *Her good singing voice speaks of years of training.*

speak of the devil [a catchphrase said when a person who has been discussed suddenly appears.] ☐ *Speak of the devil—the guy we were talking about just walked into the room.* ☐ *Speak of the devil—look who's here!*

SPEAK ▸ OFF

speak off the cuff to speak without preparing a speech; to speak extemporaneously; to render a spoken opinion or estimate. (As if one's notes had been written hastily on one's cuff.) ☐ *She is capable of making sense and being convincing even when she speaks off the cuff.* ☐ *I find it very difficult to speak off the cuff.*

SPEAK ▸ ON

See under *SPEAK ▸ (UP)ON.*

SPEAK ▸ OUT

speak out to speak loudly; to speak to be heard. ☐ *Please speak out. We need to hear you.* ☐ *They won't hear you in the back row if you don't speak out.*

speak out (about someone or something) to express oneself about someone or something; to tell what one knows about someone or something. ☐ *I could keep silent no longer. I had to speak out* *about the alleged accident.* □ *I had to speak out!*

speak out (against someone or something) to speak negatively and publicly about someone or something; to reveal something negative, in speech, about someone or something. □ *I don't want to speak out against my friends, but I am afraid I have to.* □ *The citizens spoke out against corruption in government.* □ *They felt that they had to speak out.*

speak out of turn to say something improper about someone or something. □ *I'm sorry. I spoke out of turn. I regret saying that.* □ *I wish you wouldn't speak out of turn.*

speak out on something to express one's opinion about something; to reveal information one has about something. □ *You would expect that Judy would speak out on an issue like that.* □ *You really should speak out on matters that concern us all.*

SPEAK ► TO

speak to someone to talk to someone. □ *I am angry with him and I refuse to speak to him.* □ *Were you speaking to me?*

speak to something [for something] to address, indicate, or signal something. □ *This event speaks to the need for good communication.* □ *Your present state of employment speaks to the need for a better education.*

SPEAK ► UP

speak up to speak loudly. □ *Please speak up. I can't hear you.* □ *No one will be able to hear you if you do not speak up.*

speak up for someone or something to speak in favor of someone or something; to come forward and express favorable things about someone or something. □ *I hope you will speak up for me when the time comes.* □ *I will speak up for the proposed legislation.*

SPEAK ► (UP)ON

speak (up)on something to talk about a particular topic. (*Upon* is formal and less commonly used than *on*.) □ *This evening, I will speak upon the subject of Plato's thoughts on the universe.* □ *What will you speak on today?*

SPEAK ► WITH

speak with someone (about someone or something) **1.** to talk with someone about someone or something; to discuss someone or something with someone. □ *I was speaking with Fred about Don, who is a mutual friend.* □ *I need to know something about Don. I will speak with his friend Fred.* **2.** to reprimand one about one's dealing with someone or something. □ *He should not have insulted Kelly. I will speak with him about her.* □ *He what? I will speak with him!*

SPEAR ► OUT

spear something out (of something) to bring something forth from something by sticking it with something sharp and pulling. (The *of*-phrase is paraphrased with a *from*-phrase when the particle is transposed. See the F example.) □ *Walter speared the pickle out of the jar.* T *He speared out a pickle.* F *Richard speared out a pickle from the jar.* □ *He speared it out.*

SPECIALIZE ► IN

specialize in something to limit oneself to one particular thing. □ *I specialize in tropical medicine.* □ *What do you specialize in?*

SPECULATE ► ABOUT

speculate about someone or something to make guesses about someone or something; to hypothesize about someone or something. □ *I refuse to speculate about Sally. I don't presume to guess what she will do.* □ *We don't speculate about failure.*

SPECULATE ► IN

speculate in something to make risky business deals in the buying and selling of something. □ *Jeff made a fortune speculating in cotton.* □ *I do not wish to speculate in anything. It is too risky.*

SPECULATE ► ON

speculate on something to make a hypothesis about something. □ *I really don't want to speculate on what might happen next.* □ *Would you care to spec-*

ulate on what might happen if you quit your job?

SPEED ▶ AWAY

speed away (from someone or something) to move or drive away very fast from someone or something. ☐ *The taxi sped away from the passenger who had just alighted.* ☐ *The car sped away from the accident.* ☐ *The train sped away.*

SPEED ▶ UP

speed someone or something up to cause someone or something to move faster. ☐ *We tried to speed him up, but he is just a very slow person.* 🅃 *We sped up the process, but it still took too long.* 🄰 *The sped-up machine soon broke down and stopped.* 🄽 *The boss ordered a speedup in the production line.*

speed up to go faster. ☐ *Please speed up. We are late.* 🄽 *Just past the accident, there was a speedup in traffic.*

SPELL ▶ DOWN

spell someone down to win over someone in a spelling match. ☐ *Frank spelled everyone else down and won the spelling bee.* 🅃 *He spelled down almost everyone.*

SPELL ▶ FOR

spell something for someone to spell a word for someone's benefit. ☐ *I don't recognize that word. Would you please spell it for me?* ☐ *It is a difficult name. I will have to spell it for you.*

SPELL ▶ OUT

spell something out **1.** to spell a word. ☐ *Please spell it out. I don't recognize the word the way you pronounced it.* 🅃 *Please spell out all the abbreviations.* **2.** to make something clear. ☐ *Let me spell it out to you. It is really quite simple.* 🅃 *I will spell out all the details to you.*

SPEND ▶ FOR

spend something for something to pay out an amount of money for something. ☐ *I spent nearly forty dollars for that vase!* ☐ *How much did you spend for this house—if I may ask?*

SPEND ▶ IN

spend time in something to stay in something or some place for a period of time. ☐ *I spent time in Barbados when I was younger.* ☐ *I am afraid that you will have to spend some time in the hospital until the matter is cleared up.*

SPEND ▶ ON

spend something on someone or something to pay out an amount of money for the benefit of someone or something. ☐ *How much did you spend on him for his birthday?* ☐ *I spent a lot on Mary's gift.*

SPEW ▶ OUT

spew one's guts out to vomit. (Slang.) ☐ *I was so sick. I spent all night spewing my guts out.* 🅃 *I was up all night, spewing out my guts.*

spew something out to gush something forth. (Figurative.) ☐ *The faucet spewed a little yellowish water out and stopped altogether.* 🅃 *The faucet spewed out some yellowish water.*

SPEW ▶ UP

spew something up to gush something upward. ☐ *The geyser spewed hot water and steam up every hour on the hour.* 🅃 *The fountain spewed up a thin stream of pure water.*

SPICE ▶ UP

spice something up **1.** to make some food more spicy. ☐ *Judy spiced the cider up by adding cinnamon and nutmeg.* 🅃 *She spiced up the chili too much.* **2.** to make something more interesting, lively, or sexy. (Figurative.) ☐ *I'm afraid that they spiced the musical up too much. Some people walked out.* ☐ *Judy liked to spice her lectures up by telling jokes.* 🅃 *She spiced up each lecture with a joke.* 🅃 *They spiced up the play too much.*

SPIEL ▶ OFF

spiel something off to recite a list of things very rapidly; to recite something very rapidly. ☐ *I used to be able to spiel the names of the presidents off.* 🅃 *Liz spieled off her gift list to the clerk.*

SPIFF ► OUT

See *be spiffed out* under *BE ► OUT.*

SPIFF ► UP

spiff something up to polish and groom something very well. (Informal.) □ *See if you can spiff this place up a little.* 🅃 *I will spiff up the room a little.*

SPILL ► INTO

spill (out) into something AND **spill (over) into something** to be so great in number or volume as to expand into another area. □ *The crowd spilled out into the street.* □ *The well-wishers spilled over into the neighbor's yard.*

SPILL ► OUT

spill (out) into something See under *SPILL ► INTO.*

spill out (of something) to scatter, flow, or drop out of something. □ *All the rice spilled out of the box onto the floor.* □ *The rice spilled out on the floor.*

spill something out (of something) to cause something to scatter, flow, or drop out of something. (The *of*-phrase is paraphrased with a *from*-phrase when the particle is transposed. See the 🄵 example.) □ *She spilled all her orange juice out of her cup.* 🅃 *She spilled out all her juice.* 🄵 *Carla spilled out the paper clips from the box.* □ *Carla spilled the contents of the box out.*

SPILL ► OVER

spill over **1.** [for a container] to overflow. □ *I hope your bucket of water doesn't spill over.* □ *The milk glass spilled over because it was filled too full.* **2.** [for the contents of a container] to overflow. □ *The bucket is too full. I don't know why the water doesn't spill over.* □ *The milk spilled over because you overfilled the glass.* 🄽 *Todd wiped up the spillover quickly.*

spill (over) into something See under *SPILL ► INTO.*

spill over on(to) someone or something [for something] to scatter, flow, or drop (out of something) onto someone or something. □ *The bowl of milk spilled over onto the children when they jarred the table.* □ *The bowl spilled over on the floor.*

spill something over to tip something over and spill out the contents. □ *Please don't spill the glass of milk over.* 🅃 *Jimmy spilled over the whole pitcher of milk.*

SPIN ► AROUND

spin around **1.** to turn around to face a different direction. □ *Jill spun around to face her accuser.* □ *Todd spun around in his chair so he could see who was talking to him.* **2.** to rotate, possibly a number of times. □ *The propellers spun around and the old plane began to taxi down the runway.* □ *The merry-go-round spun around at a moderate speed.*

SPIN ► OFF

spin off [for something] to part and fly away from something that is spinning; [for something] to detach or break loose from something. □ *The blade of the lawn mower spun off, but fortunately no one was injured.* □ *The lid to the pickle jar spun off easily after I got it loosened.*

spin something off **1.** [for something rotating] to release a part that flies away. □ *The propeller spun one of its blades off and then fell apart all together.* 🅃 *It spun off one of its blades.* **2.** [for a business] to divest itself of one of its subparts. □ *The large company spun one of its smaller divisions off.* 🅃 *It spun off an asset and used the cash to pay down its debt.* 🄽 *Our company was a spin-off of a larger company that wanted to sell some of its assets.* **3.** [for an enterprise] to produce useful or profitable side effects or products. □ *We will be able to spin off a number of additional products.* 🅃 *The development of this product will allow us to spin off dozens of smaller, innovative products for years to come.* □ *Do you think we can spin a children's cereal off from this movie?* 🄽 *The spin-offs of this research should be very profitable.*

SPIN ► OUT

spin out [for a vehicle] to go out of control, spinning. □ *You nearly spun out on that last turn!* □ *Cars were spinning out all over the highway when the* *ice storm hit.* N *David almost had a nasty spinout.*

spin something out to prolong something. □ *Was there really any need to spin the whole process out so long?* T *Why did they spin out the graduation ceremony for such a long time?*

spin something out (of something) to remove liquid from something by spinning. (The *of*-phrase is paraphrased with a *from*-phrase when the particle is transposed. See the F example.) □ *The washer spun the water out of the load of clothing.* T *The washer spun out all the water in the clothes.* F *The washer spun out all the water from the clothes.* □ *It spun the water out.*

SPIRAL ▸ DOWN

spiral down to descend in a spiral path. □ *The ancient trail spiraled down the mountain peak.* □ *A path spiraled down and at the bottom was a small refreshment stand.*

SPIRAL ▸ UP

spiral up to ascend in a spiral path. □ *The smoke spiraled up to the sky.* □ *The trail spiraled up the slope to the top.*

SPIRIT ▸ AWAY

spirit someone or something away (somewhere) to sneak someone or something away to another place. □ *The police spirited the prisoner away before the crowd assembled in front of the jail.* T *They spirited away the celebrity.* □ *The guards spirited the prisoner away.* □ *Wally spirited the best pieces of candy away to his desk drawer.*

SPIRIT ▸ OFF

spirit someone or something off (to some place) to hurry someone or something away, presumably unnoticed, to another place. □ *Aunt Jane spirited the children off to bed at half-past eight.* T *She spirited off the leftover roast beef.* □ *The police had spirited Jeff off to a cabin in the mountains.* □ *They spirited him off in the night.*

SPIT ▸ AT

spit at someone or something to expectorate on someone or something or in the direction of someone or something. □ *The angry crowd cursed and spit at the prisoner as he was being taken back to jail.* □ *Max actually spit at the police station door as he was dragged in.*

SPIT ▸ IN(TO)

spit something in((to) something) to cast something from the mouth into something. □ *He spit his gum into the toilet.* T *He opened the toilet and spit in his gum.* □ *Scott spit his gum in.*

SPIT ▸ ON

See under *SPIT ▸ (UP)ON.*

SPIT ▸ ON(TO)

spit something on(to) something to cast something from the mouth onto something. □ *You shouldn't spit your gum onto the sidewalk!* □ *Don't spit your gum on the pavement.*

SPIT ▸ OUT

spit something out **1.** to cast something from the mouth. □ *The food was so terrible that I spit it out.* T *I spit out the sweet potatoes.* **2.** to manage to say something. (Slang.) □ *Come on! Say it! Spit it out!* □ *Spit it out! Get it said!* **3.** to say something scornfully. □ *He spit out his words in utter derision.* □ *She spit out the most unpleasant string of curse words I have ever heard from anyone.*

SPIT ▸ UP

spit something up to vomit something. □ *She almost spit her dinner up.* T *Sally was afraid she was going to spit up her dinner.* A *The spit-up mess was cleaned up by the janitor.*

spit up to vomit. □ *The food was so bad, she was afraid she would spit up.* □ *Mommy, I have to spit up!*

SPIT ▸ (UP)ON

spit (up)on someone or something **1.** to eject spit onto someone or something. (*Upon* is formal and less commonly used than *on.*) □ *The angry crowd spit on the convict.* □ *Don't spit on the sidewalk.* **2.** to spew spittle onto someone or something while talking. (*Upon* is formal and less commonly used than *on.*) □ *I always have a fear of accidentally spitting on someone in the first row* *while I am talking.* □ *I regret spitting on the first row.*

SPLASH ▸ ABOUT

splash about AND **splash around** **1.** [for a creature] to move about in a volume of a liquid, splashing. □ *The children splashed about in the pool.* □ *They splashed around for an hour.* **2.** [for a liquid] to move about, splashing. □ *The water splashed about in the bucket.* □ *It splashed around as I carried the bucket.*

splash something about to scatter or slosh a liquid about. □ *Please don't splash that about. It will stain anything you spill it on.* 🅃 *Don't splash about that stuff.*

SPLASH ▸ AROUND

splash around See *splash about* under *SPLASH ▸ ABOUT.*

SPLASH ▸ DOWN

splash down [for a space capsule] to land in the water. □ *The capsule splashed down very close to the pickup ship.* 🄽 *When is splashdown?*

SPLASH ▸ ON

splash on someone or something to scatter [a liquid] on someone or something. □ *Try to keep from splashing on anybody.* □ *Don't splash on the wall!*

SPLASH ▸ ON(TO)

splash something on(to) someone or something to make a liquid scatter onto someone or something. □ *Accidentally, the lab assistant splashed acid onto the visitor.* □ *He splashed something on the counter.*

SPLASH ▸ OVER

splash over [for a volume of liquid] to overflow its container. □ *A lot of the coffee splashed over before I got to the table with the cup.* □ *Don't fill it so full and it won't splash over.*

splash something (all) over someone or something to cause a liquid to overflow or engulf someone or something. □ *Tony splashed water all over Nick.* □ *Who splashed milk all over the table?*

SPLASH ▸ UP

splash someone or something up to scatter a liquid onto someone or something. □ *Don't get that stuff all over me! Don't splash me up!* 🅃 *She splashed up the kitchen when she washed the dishes.*

SPLASH ▸ WITH

splash someone or something with something to scatter or slosh someone or something with a liquid. (*Someone* includes *oneself.*) □ *The whales at Sea World splashed everyone in the audience with water.* □ *I splashed the side of the stove with pancake batter when I dropped the bowl.* □ *She splashed herself with a few drops of the acid.*

SPLATTER ▸ UP

splatter someone or something up to cover someone or something with drops of a liquid. (*Someone* includes *oneself.*) □ *The painter splattered his coworker up with both red and blue.* 🅃 *Don't splatter up the wall!* □ *The child splattered herself up with mud and other stuff.*

SPLAY ▸ OUT

splay out to spread out; to lean out at an angle. □ *His feet splayed out so much that it was hard to see how he could stand up.* □ *The legs of the table splayed out and gave it sturdy support.*

SPLICE ▸ TO

splice something to something to connect something to something; to weave something into something to connect the two. □ *The workers spliced the small wires into the main cable.* □ *Let's splice this rope into the larger one at the halfway point.*

SPLICE ▸ TOGETHER

splice something together to connect things together, usually by weaving a joint between the two. □ *I spent over an hour splicing the two ends of the ropes together, and it didn't hold for even a minute.* □ *When will they finish splicing the wire together?* 🅃 *He carefully spliced together the two ropes.*

SPLINTER ▸ OFF

splinter off ((of) something) AND **splinter off (from something)** [for a bit of something] to tear off or separate from something. (The *of* is colloquial.) □ *A* *piece of wood splintered off of the oar and dropped into the water.* □ *A tiny bit splintered off and stuck in my hand.* □ *A bit of glass splintered off from the corner of the table.*

SPLIT ▸ BETWEEN

split something between someone and someone else or something and something else to divide something between two people or things. □ *The cook split the last pie between the two girls.* □ *We have to divide the copies of the reports between the two committees.*

SPLIT ▸ IN

split in something to divide into a certain number of groups. (The *something* can be *half, thirds, two, quarters,* etc.) □ *Lightning struck the big tree and the trunk split in half.* □ *The vase dropped and split in quarters.*

SPLIT ▸ INTO

split something into something to divide or sever something into something. □ *Jeff split the log into four parts.* □ *Please split this log in half so it will burn better.* □ *Split the cake in two parts and give half to Sam.* □ *Please split the cake into two parts and give half to me.*

SPLIT ▸ OFF

split off (from something) to separate away from something; to sever connection with and separate from something. □ *A large iceberg split off from the glacier and made an enormous splash.* □ *A giant ice cube split off and floated away.*

split something off ((of) something) to sever connection with something and separate. (The *of*-phrase is paraphrased with a *from*-phrase when the particle is transposed. The *of* is colloquial.) □ *Dave split a piece of wood off the log to use for kindling.* 🅃 *He split off a stick of wood.* 🄵 *He split off a stick of wood from the log.* □ *Jamie took a log and split a stave of wood off.*

SPLIT ▸ UP

split people up to separate two or more people. □ *I am going to have to split you two up if you don't stop talking to each other.* 🅃 *I will have to split up those two.*

split someone or something up (into something) to divide people or things up into something, such as groups. (*Someone* includes *oneself.*) □ *I had to split the group up into two sections—there were so many who showed up.* 🅃 *I split up the class into two discussion sections.* □ *I split them up.* □ *They split themselves up into smaller groups.* 🄽 *Everything has been great since the split-up.*

split up to divide, separate, or fall apart. □ *The couple split up because they couldn't get along.* □ *They didn't want to split up, but there was nothing else that could be done.* □ *They were still unhappy after the split-up.*

split up with someone [for someone] to separate from someone; to break up a marriage or love affair. □ *Jeff split up with Judy.* □ *I had heard that they had split up with each other.*

SPLIT ▸ WITH

split someone or something with someone or something to divide someone or something with someone or a group of people. □ *I will split the campers with you. You lead your half on the hike, and I will lead my half.* □ *Will you split your candy bar with me?*

SPLURGE ▸ ON

splurge on someone or something to spend a lot of money on someone or something. □ *I really splurged on my wife for her birthday.* □ *Mary really splurged on that dinner!*

SPOIL ▸ FOR

spoil for a fight to be ready and anxious for a fight; to be eager to fight or argue. (Idiomatic.) □ *Are you in a bad mood? Are you spoiling for a fight?* □ *You could see that Max was really spoiling for a fight.*

SPONGE ▸ AWAY

sponge something away to absorb, wipe up, and wipe away something. □ *Try sponging the stain away with some soda water.* 🅃 *I will sponge away the mess.*

SPONGE ▸ DOWN

sponge someone or something down to remove the [excess] moisture from someone or something. ☐ *The fight manager sponged his boxer down.* 🅃 *I will sponge down the countertop.*

SPONGE ▸ FROM

sponge something from someone to beg or borrow money or food from someone. (Slang.) ☐ *Gary tried to sponge a few bucks from me.* ☐ *I can't continue sponging food from my relatives.*

sponge something from something to remove moisture from something, as with a sponge. ☐ *Liz sponged the sauce from her blouse.* ☐ *We gently sponged the splattered paint from the carpet.*

SPONGE ▸ OFF

sponge something off (of someone or something) to beg or borrow money or food from someone or a group. (Colloquial. The *of*-phrase is paraphrased with a *from*-phrase when the particle is transposed. See the 🄵 example.) ☐ *Please stop sponging food and money off your relatives!* 🅃 *Stop sponging off food and money all the time!* 🄵 *He keeps sponging off money from his relatives.* ☐ *I wish my brother-in-law would quit sponging off me.*

SPONGE ▸ UP

sponge something up to absorb or take up moisture, as with a sponge. ☐ *I had to sponge the spilled milk up from the floor, the chair, the table, and the baby. What a mess!* 🅃 *Liz sponged up the water.*

SPOON ▸ OUT

spoon something out to serve something out, as with a spoon; to give something out, as with a spoon. ☐ *The cook spooned the beans out, giving not quite enough to each camper.* 🅃 *The cook spooned out the beans.*

SPOON ▸ UP

spoon something up to serve something that requires finding and bringing up out of a pot with a spoon. ☐ *The cook spooned the hard-cooked eggs up one by one.* 🅃 *The cook spooned up the eggs.*

SPORT ▸ WITH

sport with someone or something to tease or play with someone or something. ☐ *What a tease you are! You are just sporting with me!* ☐ *The dog was sporting with a turtle down by the stream.*

SPOT ▸ AS

spot someone as something to recognize someone to be something; to realize that someone is something. ☐ *I spotted you as a troublemaker from the very beginning.* ☐ *The guard spotted Max as a potential thief the moment he saw him.*

SPOUT ▸ FROM

spout from something [for a liquid] to gush from something. ☐ *A plume of water vapor spouted from the head of the whale.* ☐ *Water spouted from the top of the fountain and flowed down the sides.*

SPOUT ▸ OFF

spout off (about someone or something) **1.** to brag or boast about someone or something. ☐ *Stop spouting off about Tom. Nobody could be that good!* ☐ *Alice is spouting off about her new car.* **2.** to speak out publicly about someone or something; to reveal information publicly about someone or something. ☐ *I wish you wouldn't spout off about me in public.* ☐ *There is no point in spouting off about this problem.*

SPOUT ▸ OUT

spout something out **1.** to exude a liquid. ☐ *The hose spouted the cooling water out all over the children.* 🅃 *It spouted out cooling water.* **2.** to blurt something out; to speak out suddenly, revealing some important piece of information. ☐ *She spouted the name of the secret agent out under the effects of the drug.* 🅃 *She spouted out everything we wanted to know.*

SPRAWL ▸ ABOUT

sprawl about AND **sprawl around** to slouch or lounge somewhere; to spread oneself out casually while lounging. (Usually refers to habitual action, perhaps in a number of places. See also *SPRAWL ▸ OUT.*) ☐ *He sprawled about, loafing the afternoon away.* ☐ *When I came into the room, four teenage boys sprawled on the furniture, watching television.*

SPRAWL ▸ AROUND

sprawl around See the previous entry.

SPRAWL ▸ OUT

sprawl out to spread oneself out casually while lounging. (Usually done one time, not habitually. Compare to *SPRAWL ABOUT.*) ☐ *He sprawled out and took up most of the space.* ☐ *I need more room so I can sprawl out.*

SPRAY ▸ ON(TO)

spray something on(to someone or something) to direct a mist or splatter of a liquid onto someone or something. ☐ *Danny sprayed cold water onto the boys and cooled them off.* 🅃 *Dan sprayed on some cold water.* ☐ *I sprayed the paint on and it dried almost immediately.*

SPRAY ▸ WITH

spray someone or something with something to coat someone or something with a mist or splatter of liquid. (*Someone* includes *oneself.*) ☐ *The elephant sprayed us with water.* ☐ *I sprayed the fence with white paint.* ☐ *He sprayed himself with some of the cologne.*

SPREAD ▸ AROUND

spread someone or something around to distribute people or things. (*Someone* includes *oneself.*) ☐ *Spread the good singers around so they can help the others in the choir.* 🅃 *Liz spread around the seeds so they would dry.* ☐ *They planned to spread themselves around so they could talk to everyone.*

spread something around to distribute news or gossip. ☐ *Please don't spread this around, but Don ran away from home!* 🅃 *Don't spread around that story!*

SPREAD ▸ LIKE

spread like wildfire [for something, including fire] to spread rapidly. ☐ *The blaze spread like wildfire.* ☐ *This disease will spread like wildfire when it gets going.*

SPREAD ▸ ON

spread something on thick **1.** to distribute a thick layer of something. ☐ *This paint will cover well if you spread it on thick.* ☐ *If you spread the paint on thick, you will only need one coat.* **2.** to inundate someone with flattery. (Always with *it.* See also *butter someone up* under *BUTTER ▸ UP.*) ☐ *Listen to all that flattery! She is really spreading it on thick!* ☐ *Jeff always spreads it on thick. No one believes a word he says.*

SPREAD ▸ ON(TO)

spread something on(to something) to distribute a coating of something onto something. ☐ *Spread the butter onto the bread evenly.* 🅃 *Spread on the butter evenly.* ☐ *Donna spread the paint on with a roller.*

SPREAD ▸ OUT

spread out to separate and distribute over a wide area. ☐ *The sheriff told the members of the posse to spread out and continue their search.* ☐ *The grease spread out and stained a large area of the carpet.*

spread something out to open, unfold, or lay something over a wider area. ☐ *Spread the wet papers out so they will dry.* 🅃 *She spread out the papers to dry them.*

SPREAD ▸ OVER

spread over someone or something [for something] to cover someone or something gradually. ☐ *The shade slowly spread over the picnickers.* ☐ *Dusk spread its final shadows over the land.*

spread something over someone or something to cause something to cover or be distributed over someone or something. ☐ *The cloud spread its shadow over everyone at the picnic.* ☐ *We spread fertilizer over the prepared ground.* ☐ *He spread the work over a few weeks.* ☐ *She spread the frosting over the cake.* ☐ *Mary spread the blanket over the sleeping children.*

SPREAD ▸ TO

spread to someone or something to expand or extend to reach someone or something. ☐ *The epidemic finally spread to me and my family.* ☐ *The business slowdown spread to the West Coast.*

SPREAD ▸ UNDER

spread something under someone or something to extend or unfold something, such as a tarpaulin, beneath someone or something. ☐ *Please spread some newspapers under Jimmy while he is working this clay.* ☐ *Would you spread some newspapers under your work, please?*

SPREAD ▸ WITH

spread something with something to cover something with a coat of something. ☐ *Using the roller, Judy spread the wall with a thick coat of pink paint.* ☐ *Spread the lasagna with a layer of cheese mixture and cover that with another layer of lasagna.*

SPRING ▸ AT

spring at someone or something to jump at someone or something. ☐ *The cat sprang at me, but could not sink in its claws.* ☐ *The spider sprang at the moth and captured it.*

SPRING ▸ BACK

spring back (to some place) to jump, bounce, or recoil back to a place. ☐ *The cat sprang back to its original place on the top of the table.* ☐ *The lid sprang back to a closed position.*

SPRING ▸ FOR

spring for something to agree to pay for something; to treat someone to something. (Slang.) ☐ *Let me spring for dinner. Okay?* ☐ *I would be happy to spring for treats for everyone.*

SPRING ▸ FORTH

See the following entry.

SPRING ▸ FROM

spring (forth) from someone or something to come forth from someone or something; to gush out of someone or something, as with a spring of water; to jump from or out of someone or something. (Stilted.) ☐ *The best ideas spring forth from the mind of Mary!* ☐ *What new example of pure genius can we expect to spring from Mary today?*

SPRING ▸ ON

See also under *SPRING ▸ (UP)ON.*

spring something on someone **1.** to surprise someone with something. ☐ *I hate to spring this on you at the last moment, but I will need some money to travel on.* ☐ *Please don't spring any other demands on me.* **2.** to pull a trick on someone. (Slang.) ☐ *Let me tell you about the trick I sprang on Sally.* ☐ *What are you going to spring on her this time?*

SPRING ▸ OUT

spring out at someone to jump out at someone. ☐ *A grasshopper sprang out at me when I peered into the hollow log.* ☐ *I was afraid that something would spring out at me, so I opened the cupboard carefully.*

spring out of something to jump out of something. ☐ *The cat sprang out of the closet when I opened the door.* ☐ *The boys sprang out of the cold water as fast as they could.*

SPRING ▸ TO

spring to life to become suddenly alive or more alive. ☐ *The party sprang to life after midnight.* ☐ *The city sprang to life at dawn.*

spring to one's feet to stand up quickly. ☐ *He sprang to his feet and demanded that the chair recognize him.* ☐ *The audience sprang to its feet and cheered madly when the soprano finished.*

spring to someone's defense to go quickly to defend someone. (Can be against physical or verbal attack.) ☐ *Fred was attacked and Ralph sprang to his defense.* ☐ *We sprang to Mary's defense when she was accused of doing wrong.*

spring to something to move quickly to assume a certain position or posture. ☐ *The recruit sprang to attention.* ☐ *We all sprang to action the minute the boss appeared.*

SPRING ▸ UP

spring up to appear or develop suddenly; to sprout, as with a seedling. □ *We knew it was really spring when all the flowers sprang up.* □ *It seems as if the tulips sprang up overnight.* □ *The dog's ears sprang up when the refrigerator opened.* □ *A little breeze sprang up and cooled things off.*

SPRING ▸ (UP)ON

spring (up)on someone or something to jump on someone, a creature, or something; to pounce on someone, a creature, or something. (*Upon* is formal and less commonly used than *on*.) □ *The lion sprang upon him and knocked him down.* □ *The cat sprang on the mouse and captured it.*

SPRINKLE ▸ ON(TO)

sprinkle something on(to) someone or something to scatter or dribble something onto someone or something. □ *The minister sprinkled the water onto the baby.* □ *Larry sprinkled powdered sugar on his grapefruit.*

SPRINKLE ▸ WITH

sprinkle someone or something with something to cover someone or something with something by scattering or sprinkling. □ *The storm sprinkled us with a few droplets of water and then blew away.* □ *Larry sprinkled his grapefruit with powdered sugar.*

SPROUT ▸ UP

sprout up to grow upward quickly, as do newly sprouted seedlings. (Also without *up*, but not eligible as an entry.) □ *The seeds sprouted up in the warm rains.* □ *Many of the newly planted seeds failed to sprout up on time.*

SPRUCE ▸ UP

spruce someone or something up **1.** to tidy up and groom someone or something. (*Someone* includes *oneself*.) □ *Laura's mother took a few minutes to spruce her daughter up for the party.* 🅃 *She spruced up her daughter.* □ *Let's spruce the house up this spring.* □ *He spruced himself up a bit and then rang the doorbell.* **2.** to refurbish or renew someone or something. (*Someone* includes *oneself*.) □ *Do you think we should spruce this room up a little?* 🅃 *Yes, let's spruce up this room.* □ *We spruced up the house for the holidays.* 🄰 *I find this spruced-up little restaurant quite nice.* □ *She bought all new clothes so she could spruce herself up for her new job.*

SPUR ▸ ON

spur someone on to urge someone onward; to egg someone on. (As if applying spurs to a horse.) □ *The crowd spurred the runners on throughout the race.* 🅃 *The cheering spurred on the runners.*

spur someone on (to something) to urge someone to do something or to achieve a valued status. □ *The thought of a big profit spurred Susan on to even greater efforts.* 🅃 *The thought of more money spurred on the workers to greater productivity.* □ *The proper kind of incentive will spur me on.*

SPURT ▸ FROM

spurt (out) (from something) See the following entry.

SPURT ▸ OUT

spurt out (of someone or something) AND **spurt (out) (from someone or something)** to squirt out of someone or something; to erupt in a stream out of someone or something. □ *Hot lava spurted out of the volcano.* □ *Hot lava spurted out from the volcano.* □ *The blood spurted out from Walter wherever he had been slashed by the blades of the machine.* □ *Blood spurted out.* □ *Blood spurted from the wound.* □ *The fountain had a fish with water spurting from its mouth.*

spurt something out to eject something in a stream. □ *The octopus spurted its ink out as the scuba diver approached it.* 🅃 *It spurted out all its ink.*

SPUTTER ▸ OUT

sputter out [for a flame] to go out in little puffs. □ *The candle flame flickered and sputtered out.* □ *The fire sputtered out after midnight and we all got very cold before down.*

sputter something out to utter something while stuttering or faltering. (As when one is physically or mentally disoriented.) □ *She was so excited she could hardly sputter her name out.* 🅃 *He could only sputter out a few words.*

SPY ▸ ON

See under *SPY ▸ (UP)ON.*

SPY ▸ (UP)ON

spy (up)on someone or something to watch someone or something to learn secret or concealed information. (*Upon* is formal and less commonly used than *on*.) □ *Are you spying upon me?* □ *I wasn't spying on you! I was just trying to see who you were.*

SQUABBLE ▸ ABOUT

squabble about someone or something to quarrel and disagree about someone or something. □ *Please stop squabbling about Jeff, or I'll put him on my team so neither of you can have him.* □ *There is no need to squabble about the last piece of pie. There's more in the kitchen.*

SQUABBLE ▸ OVER

squabble over someone or something to fight over someone or something. □ *Please don't squabble over me. I don't want to be chosen by any of you!* □ *Stop squabbling over money and go out and get a job.*

SQUABBLE ▸ WITH

squabble with someone to argue with someone. □ *Please don't squabble with your sister!* □ *I wish that everyone would stop squabbling with me!*

squabble with something to argue about something. □ *I won't squabble with what you said, but you are wrong.* □ *One political party will squabble with anything the other party says.*

SQUANDER ▸ AWAY

squander something away to waste something; to dispose of something valuable wastefully. □ *Where is all the money I gave you last month? Did you squander it all away?* 🅃 *Frank squandered away all his assets.*

SQUANDER ▸ ON

squander something on someone or something to waste all of something on someone or something. □ *I am tired of squandering money on this house.* □ *I squandered a fortune on Roger and what did it get me?*

SQUARE ▸ AWAY

square someone away (on something) to explain something carefully to someone until the person understands. (Colloquial.) □ *I will square her away on the operation of the camera.* 🅃 *I will square away my staff on this matter.* □ *I squared them away and now they understand.* □ *Are you squared away on this now?*

square someone or something away to get someone or something taken care of properly; to attend to someone or something. □ *The manager did everything possible to square everyone away for the night.* 🅃 *I will square away the immediate problems and get back to you.* □ *When you are squared away, come back and we'll talk.*

SQUARE ▸ OFF

square off (for something) to prepare for a fight. □ *Are those two squaring off for a fight?* □ *Max and Lefty squared off and everybody got out of the way.*

square something off to make something square; to trim something until it is square. □ *You will have to square this corner off a bit so it will match the part it will be attached to.* 🅃 *Please square off this corner.*

SQUARE ▸ UP

square something up to cause something to have right angles. □ *Please square the door frames up better before you nail them in.* 🅃 *Can you square up this box a little better?*

square up to something to move up to something and face it head on. □ *Carl squared up to the mirror and studied himself carefully.* □ *The fighters squared up to each other and prepared to begin the match.*

SQUARE ▸ WITH

square accounts with someone 1. to settle outstanding financial accounts with someone. □ *I have to square accounts with the loan company.* □ *Sam promised to square accounts with the people he owed money to.* 2. to settle outstanding disagreements with someone. □ *I regretted that I was unable to square accounts with Valerie before she left.* □ *Max intended to square accounts with Lefty once and for all.*

square something with someone to make certain that something is approved by a particular person. □ *I am sure I can square this matter with Sally.* □ *Sam intended to square everything with Henry when he had time.*

square with someone 1. to settle a disagreement with someone. □ *I will try to square with Fred before the end of the school year.* □ *Max refused to square with Lefty and they are still feuding.* 2. to apologize to someone. □ *I will try to square with Harold. I really am sorry, you know.* □ *Finally, Mary squared with Alice and they forgave each other.*

square with something to agree, match, or correspond to something. □ *Your answer doesn't square with mine.* □ *The figures I have don't square with those the government has.*

SQUASH ▸ DOWN

squash something down to crush something down; to pack something down. □ *Squash the ice cream down so the air will be pushed out.* 🅃 *Who squashed down my hat?*

SQUASH ▸ IN

squash something in to make something concave by squashing or mashing. □ *The children squashed the Halloween jack-o'-lantern in and ruined it.* 🅃 *Someone squashed in the lampshade.*

SQUASH ▸ IN(TO)

squash something in(to something) to press or mash something into something. □ *She squashed the clay into the mold.* 🅃 *She squashed in the clay and started to make a bowl.*

SQUASH ▸ UP

squash someone or something up to grind someone or something up; to mash someone or something up. □ *You had better stay out of the traffic, or some big truck will squash you up!* 🅃 *The truck squashed up the tiny car.* 🄰 *Now, put the squashed-up apple mixture into the sauce.*

squash up against someone or something to press hard up against someone or something. □ *The door of the car squashed up against Walter's leg and nearly broke it.* □ *The pumpkin squashed up against the side of the truck.*

SQUAWK ▸ ABOUT

squawk about something to complain about something. (Colloquial.) □ *Stop squawking about how much money you lost. I lost twice as much.* □ *What are you squawking about now?*

SQUEAK ▸ BY

squeak by (someone or something) 1. to manage just to squeeze past someone or something. □ *I squeaked by the fat man in the hallway only to find myself blocked by another.* □ *I just barely squeaked by.* 2. to manage just to get past a barrier represented by a person or thing, such as a teacher or an examination. □ *Judy just squeaked by Professor Smith, who has a reputation for flunking just about everyone.* □ *I took the test and just squeaked by.*

SQUEAK ▸ THROUGH

squeak something through to manage just to get something accepted or approved. □ *I just managed to squeak the proposal through.* □ *Tom squeaked the application through at the last minute.*

squeak through (something) 1. to manage just to squeeze through an opening. □ *The child squeaked through the opening and escaped.* □ *Sally squeaked through and got away.* 2. to manage just to get past a barrier, such as an examination or interview. □ *Sally just barely squeaked through the interview, but she got the job.* □ *I wasn't too alert and I just squeaked through.*

SQUEAL ▸ ON

See the following entry.

SQUEAL ▸ TO

squeal (on someone) (to someone) to report someone to someone. (Slang.) □ *Max was afraid that Lefty would squeal on him to the cops.* □ *Sally threatened to squeal to the boss.* □ *Please promise you won't squeal on me!* □ *Lefty threatened to squeal on Max to his wife.*

SQUEAL ▸ WITH

squeal with something to shriek or squeak, exhibiting some characteristic emotion or experience, such as delight, pain, glee, etc. □ *The baby saw the bright picture and squealed with delight.* □ *Timmy squealed with excitement when he saw the presents and the birthday cake.*

SQUEEZE ▸ BY

squeeze by (someone or something) to manage just to press oneself past someone or something. □ *The hall was crowded and I had to squeeze by a number of rotund gentlemen.* □ *I squeezed by and ran on to my appointment.*

SQUEEZE ▸ FROM

squeeze something from something **1.** to press something out of something; to press on something until something comes out. □ *Betty squeezed some toothpaste from the tube.* □ *Don't squeeze so much mustard from the bottle.* **2.** to get a little more of something from something. □ *Let's see if we can squeeze a few more miles from this tank of gas before we fill up again.* □ *I think I can squeeze another few minutes from this candle before I have to light a new one.*

SQUEEZE ▸ IN(TO)

squeeze someone or something in(to something) to press or push someone or something into something small. (*Someone* includes *oneself*.) □ *Let's see if we can squeeze everyone into the car.* 🅃 *Let's squeeze in one more.* □ *Can you squeeze another pair of shoes into the suitcase?* □ *Tom tried to squeeze himself into the tiny area, but he couldn't.*

SQUEEZE ▸ OUT

squeeze something out (of something) to press something until something is expelled from something. (The *of*-phrase is paraphrased with a *from*-phrase when the particle is transposed. See the 🄵 example.) □ *Claire squeezed some toothpaste out of the tube.* 🅃 *She squeezed out some toothpaste.* 🄵 *She squeezed out some toothpaste from the fresh tube.* □ *Jamie pressed hard and squeezed some more out.*

SQUEEZE ▸ THROUGH

squeeze someone or something through (something) to push and compress until someone or something passes through something. (*Someone* includes *oneself*.) □ *John's cellmate managed to squeeze John through the window just before the guards walked by.* □ *I squeezed some food through the crack and the trapped explorer was glad to get it.* □ *He just managed to squeeze himself through the gate on time.*

squeeze through something to manage to press oneself through an opening. □ *I think I can squeeze through the window and get out of this place.* □ *The cat squeezed through a hole in the fence and got away.*

SQUEEZE ▸ TOGETHER

squeeze someone or something together to press people or things together. □ *The driver squeezed us together so he could get more people in the taxi.* □ *See if you can squeeze the vegetables together a little so we can get more in the basket.*

squeeze (themselves) together [for creatures] to press close together. □ *The little pigs squeezed themselves together to get a better chance at some food.* □ *They squeezed together and gobbled their dinner.* □ *They squeezed themselves together to keep warm.*

SQUEEZE ▸ UP

squeeze someone or something up to press people or things close together. □ *The usher tried to squeeze us up so she could seat more people.* 🅃 *Don't squeeze up the cars too tight in the parking area.*

squeeze (themselves) up [for people] to press themselves closely together. (Also in other persons.) ☐ *Everyone squeezed themselves up in the tiny car so there would be room for one more.* ☐ *Let's squeeze up so Jamie can sit down.* ☐ *They squeezed themselves up so they would take less space.* ☐ *Let's squeeze ourselves up to make more room.*

squeeze up against someone or something to press close up against someone or something. ☐ *He squeezed up against me, trying to keep warm.* ☐ *The puppies squeezed up against their mother.*

SQUINT ▶ AT

squint at someone or something to look at someone or something with the eyes partly closed. (When squinting, the eyes are partly closed by pressing the upper and lower eyelids toward one another.) ☐ *Why are you squinting at me?* ☐ *I had to squint at the small print in order to read it.*

SQUINT ▶ OUT

squint out of something **1.** to cast one's gaze from something, such as a place of concealment, with one's eyes partly closed. ☐ *The prisoner squinted out of the little hatch in the door to his cell.* ☐ *You could see that many people were squinting out of the windows, trying to get a good view of the movie star who was visiting.* **2.** to cast one's gaze through something, such as glasses, one eye, etc., with one's eyes partly closed. ☐ *She squinted out of one eye in the bright sun.* ☐ *Tony squinted out of his glasses and his mother decided that he needed to have his eyes checked again.*

SQUIRM ▶ IN(TO)

squirm in(to something) to press into something that is tight; to crawl or wiggle into something tight. (For people, this is often clothing that is too tight. For other creatures, it is more variable.) ☐ *Dave squirmed into his jeans and pledged to himself that he would lose some weight.* ☐ *He squirmed in and knew he could never eat another bite.*

SQUIRM ▶ OUT

squirm out (of something) **1.** to crawl or wiggle out of something. ☐ *The worm squirmed out of its hole and was gobbled up by a bird.* ☐ *The worm squirmed out.* **2.** to escape doing something; to escape the responsibility for having done something. ☐ *You can't squirm out of it. You have to do it.* ☐ *He agreed to go but squirmed out at the last minute.* ☐ *You did it and you can't squirm out of it by denying it!*

SQUIRM ▶ WITH

squirm with something to fidget or move around restlessly, showing irritation of some type. ☐ *The children squirmed with impatience, but they kept quiet.* ☐ *I squirmed with discomfort, hoping that the time on the aircraft would pass rapidly.*

SQUIRREL ▶ AWAY

squirrel something away to hide something or store something in the way that a squirrel stores nuts for use in the winter. ☐ *I squirreled a little money away for an occasion such as this.* 🅃 *Liz squirreled away a lot of money while she was working.*

SQUIRT ▶ AT

squirt something at someone or something **1.** to direct a narrow stream of liquid onto someone or something. ☐ *They squirted the water at the cat and it ran away.* ☐ *Who is squirting catsup at people?* **2.** to direct a device for squirting liquid at someone or something. ☐ *Tom squirted the hose at the cat.* ☐ *Who is squirting the firehose at the front of the house?*

SQUIRT ▶ FROM

squirt from something [for a liquid] to be ejected in a spurt from something. ☐ *The water squirted from the hose.* ☐ *Juice squirted from the orange when I squeezed it.*

SQUIRT ▶ OUT

squirt out (of someone or something) [for something, especially a liquid] to gush or spurt forth from someone or something. ☐ *In the horror movie, black stuff squirted out of this guy* *whenever he got angry.* ☐ *Something horrible squirted out and I closed my eyes.*

squirt something out of something to cause something to spurt out of something. (The *of*-phrase is paraphrased with a *from*-phrase when the particle is transposed. See the 🄵 example.) ☐ *He squirted a bit of the vaccine out of the syringe, making sure the needle was not clogged.* 🅃 *He squirted out a bit of the vaccine.* 🄵 *He squirted out a bit of the vaccine from the syringe.*

STAB ▸ AT

stab at someone or something to thrust at someone or something with something sharp, such as a knife. ☐ *The horrid man stabbed at me and missed.* ☐ *The stork stabbed at the frog with its beak.*

stab something at someone or something to thrust something at someone or something. ☐ *The hunter stabbed a stick at the bear to see if there was any life at all left in it.* ☐ *The stork tried to stab its beak at me as I held it, but I held tight while the vet examined it.*

STAB ▸ IN

stab someone in something to stab someone in a particular place. (*Someone* includes *oneself*.) ☐ *Max stabbed Lefty in the belly and left him to die.* ☐ *Tom stabbed himself in the thigh by accident.*

stab someone in the back **1.** to thrust a knife into someone's back. ☐ *Max planned to stab Lefty in the back.* ☐ *The murderer stabbed his victim in the back and fled.* **2.** to betray someone. (Figurative.) ☐ *I wish you would not gossip about me. There is no need to stab me in the back.* 🄽 *Fred has turned into a real back-stabber. He can't be trusted.*

STACK ▸ AGAINST

stack something against someone or something **1.** to make a pile of something that leans against someone or something. ☐ *Watch what you are doing! Why are you stacking the books against me? They will fall when I move.* ☐ *Stack the books against the wall.* **2.** to cause a situation to develop that works against someone or something; to affect a situation so that it is highly unfavorable for someone or something. (Typically with *the cards, the deck*, referring to the source of this expression, card playing.) ☐ *My competitor stacked the cards against me with that client.* ☐ *The prosecutor had stacked the case against our side by not following the rules of evidence.*

STACK ▸ UP

stack something up to make a stack of some things. ☐ *Please stack these books up.* 🅃 *Liz stacked up the papers and took them to the garage.* 🄰 *All of the hastily stacked-up boxes fell over at the same time.*

stack up [for something] to accumulate, as in stacks. (Often used in reference to vehicular traffic.) ☐ *Your work is stacking up. You will have to work late to finish it.* ☐ *I hate to let my work stack up. I have to do it sooner or later.*

stack up to someone or something [for someone or something] to measure up favorably to someone or something. (Colloquial.) ☐ *How do you think I stack up to Liz?* ☐ *My car stacks up pretty well to yours.*

STAGGER ▸ AROUND

stagger around to go about tottering or wobbling, especially as if drunk. ☐ *The wounded man staggered around and then fell.* ☐ *A lot of people came out of the party and staggered around.*

STAGGER ▸ FROM

stagger from something to move out of a place, tottering. ☐ *The drunk staggered from the tavern and fell into the gutter.* ☐ *The wounded man staggered from the door and called for help.*

STAGGER ▸ IN(TO)

stagger in(to some place) to walk into some place, tottering. ☐ *The old man staggered into the room and collapsed.* ☐ *He staggered in and fell down.*

STAGGER ▸ OUT

stagger out (of some place) to walk out of some place, tottering. ☐ *The drunk staggered out of the tavern and fell* *down.* □ *She staggered out and sat on the curb.*

STAGGER ▶ UNDER

stagger under something to struggle or totter under a serious burden, either a heavy object or a serious problem or responsibility. □ *The budget is staggering under the burden of having to care for many people.* □ *Sam staggered under the heavy load and finally fell.*

STAIN ▶ WITH

stain something with something **1.** to cause a blemish or blotch on something with something. (Usually an accident.) □ *Judy stained the carpet with some grape juice.* □ *You will stain your clothing with that food if you drop any of it.* **2.** to affect the coloring of something through the use of a chemical stain. (A purposeful act, much the same as painting.) □ *Walter stained the house with a long-lasting reddish stain.* □ *We decided to stain the doors with a special varnish rather than paint them.* **3.** to injure or blemish someone's reputation. □ *They stained his reputation with their charges.* □ *I don't want to do anything that would stain my reputation.*

STAKE ▶ OFF

stake something off to mark out the boundaries of an area of land with stakes. □ *The prospectors staked an area off for themselves.* [T] *The prospectors staked off an area in which they would look for gold.* [A] *The staked-off area is where the new building will be built.*

STAKE ▶ ON

stake one's reputation on someone or something to risk harming one's reputation on someone or something. (Idiomatic.) □ *Of course Denise is great. I will stake my reputation on her!* □ *It may be so, but I wouldn't stake my reputation on it.*

STAKE ▶ OUT

stake out a claim to something AND **stake out a claim on something** to lay claim to something. □ *The prospector staked out a claim to the promising piece of land.* □ *We staked out a claim on two seats at the side of the auditorium.*

stake someone out (on someone) to assign someone to watch someone or to spy on someone. □ *The police staked a detective out on Fred.* [T] *They staked out a detective on Fred.* □ *Fred needed watching, so the police staked someone out.* [N] *The stakeout kept a close watch on Fred.*

STAKE ▶ TO

stake a claim to someone or something to state or record one's claim on someone or something. (Alludes to marking off an area by pounding in wooden stakes.) □ *She staked a claim to Jeff and told all her rivals to stay away.* □ *The prospector staked a claim to the gold-rich area.*

stake someone to something to make a loan of something to someone. □ *I will stake you to a hundred bucks if that will help.* □ *Jed refused to stake Tex to a loan.*

STALK ▶ IN(TO)

stalk in(to some place) to stride into a place, perhaps indignantly. □ *Carl stalked into the manager's office and began his tirade.* □ *He stalked in and began to complain.*

STALK ▶ OUT

stalk out of some place to stride out of a place indignantly. □ *Jeff stalked out of the store and went straight to the police.* □ *Mary got angry and stalked out of the meeting.*

STALL ▶ FOR

stall for time to cause a delay. □ *You are just stalling for time. Please hurry.* □ *She is stalling for time, hoping someone will rescue her.*

stall someone or something for something to delay someone or something for a period of time. □ *I stalled him for as long as I could.* □ *I could not stall the proceedings for another second.*

STALL ▶ OFF

stall someone or something off to hold someone or something off; to postpone the action of someone or something. □

Please stall them off while I try to get out the back door. 🅃 *I will stall off the bill collector for a while.*

STAMMER ► OUT

stammer something out to manage to say something, but only haltingly. □ *Fred stammered the words out haltingly.* 🅃 *He stammered out the name of the winner.*

STAMP ► AS

stamp someone or something as something to label someone or something as something; to mark someone or something as something. (Figurative.) □ *His manner stamped him as a fool.* □ *The committee stamped the proposal as wasteful.*

STAMP ► ON

See also under *STAMP ► (UP)ON.*

stamp on someone or something to attempt to crush someone or something by striking with the bottom of the foot. □ *The attacker stamped on his victim after he had knocked him down.* □ *Walter stamped on a spider.*

STAMP ► ONTO

stamp something onto something to affix an informative label onto something, as with a rubber stamp. □ *She stamped her name and address onto all her books.* □ *Tom stamped his identification onto all his papers and books.*

STAMP ► OUT

stamp someone or something out to destroy someone or something; to obliterate someone or something. □ *The king decided to stamp his enemy out.* 🅃 *They tried to stamp out yellow fever.*

stamp something out of someone or something to eliminate a characteristic of someone or something; to destroy a characteristic of someone or something. (Figurative.) □ *I would really like to stamp that mean streak out of you.* □ *We were not able to stamp the excess costs out of the proposal and had to reject it.*

STAMP ► (UP)ON

stamp something (up)on someone or something to affix an informative label onto someone or something, as with a rubber stamp. (*Upon* is formal and less commonly used than *on*.) □ *The attendant stamped a date upon each person who entered the dance hall.* □ *The person at the door stamped something on my hand when I came in.* □ *Who stamped the wrong price on this can of beans?*

STAMP ► WITH

stamp someone or something with something to affix a label onto someone or something with something; to apply a particular message or symbol onto someone or something, as with a rubber stamp. □ *Judy stamped everyone who went into the dance with a symbol that showed that each had paid admission.* □ *Mary stamped the bill with the* paid *symbol.* □ *Judy stamped each visitor with a big* X.

STAMPEDE ► INTO

stampede someone or something into something to cause people or other creatures to move rapidly into a place, in panic or as if in panic. □ *The loud noises stampeded the crowd into the parking lot across from the stadium.* □ *The cowboys stampeded the cattle into the corral.* □ *Please avoid stampeding the crowd into violence.*

STAMPEDE ► IN(TO)

stampede in(to some place) [for a crowd of people or other creatures] to move rapidly into a place, as if in panic. □ *The shoppers stampeded into the store the minute the doors opened.* □ *The doors opened and the shoppers stampeded in.*

STAMPEDE ► OUT

stampede out of some place [for a crowd of people or other creatures] to move rapidly out of a place, as if in panic. □ *The patrons stampeded out of the smoky theater.* □ *The cattle stampeded out of the corral.*

STAND ► ABOVE

stand head and shoulders above someone or something [for someone or something] to be considerably superior to someone or something. (Both literal and figurative senses.) ☐ *Alice stands head and shoulders above all the rest of them.* ☐ *Your proposal stands head and shoulders above the rest.*

STAND ▸ AGAINST

stand against someone or something to take a position against someone or something; to stand up to someone or something. ☐ *We will stand against the new owners, and we will quit before we are fired.* ☐ *We have to stand against this new policy!*

STAND ▸ APART

stand apart (from someone or something) **1.** to stand, separated from someone or something. ☐ *Please stand apart from the person next to you. We want to see the table between you.* ☐ *Stand apart. Leave some space between you.* **2.** to appear clearly different from other things or people. ☐ *Alice really stands apart from her peers.* ☐ *This book really stands apart. It is much better than the others.*

STAND ▸ AROUND

stand around to wait around, standing; to loiter. ☐ *Please don't stand around. Get busy!* ☐ *Why are all these people standing around doing nothing?*

STAND ▸ ASIDE

stand aside **1.** to step aside; to get out of the way. ☐ *Please stand aside while the bridal party passes by.* ☐ *The guests stood aside while the bride and groom left.* **2.** to withdraw and ignore something; to remain passive while something happens. ☐ *He just stood aside and let his kids get away with murder.* ☐ *She stood aside and did not try to come between them.*

STAND ▸ AT

stand at something **1.** to stand in front of something; to stand in the vicinity of something. ☐ *I stood at the window, watching the traffic.* ☐ *Tom stood at the door, counting people as they came in.* **2.** to stand or remain in a particular state, such as attention or readiness. ☐ *The troops stood at attention for a very long time.* ☐ *The entire platoon is standing at readiness, awaiting further orders.*

STAND ▸ BACK

stand back (from someone or something) to stand or move well away and to the rear of someone or something. ☐ *Stand back from Sam. He is really angry.* ☐ *Would you please stand back from the edge?* ☐ *Stand back!*

stand back of someone or something AND **stand behind someone or something** to guarantee someone or something; to guarantee the performance or worth of someone or something. ☐ *I will stand back of Elaine. I trust her totally.* ☐ *The manufacturer stands back of this product.* ☐ *The manufacturer stands behind this product.*

STAND ▸ BEHIND

stand behind someone or something **1.** to stand in the back of someone or something; to remain behind someone or something, standing. ☐ *Tom stood behind Alice for the photograph because he is taller.* ☐ *Please stand behind the table.* **2.** See *stand back of someone or something* under *STAND ▸ BACK.*

STAND ▸ BETWEEN

stand between someone or something and someone or something to position oneself between things and people, so as to act as a barrier. ☐ *I don't want to stand between you and your family.* ☐ *We won't stand between you and your goals.*

STAND ▸ BY

stand by to wait in a state of readiness. ☐ *I may need your help in a minute. Please stand by.* ☐ *Stand by while I find your records in this computer.* [A] *I have a standby computer if this one fails.* [N] *I think its time to start using the standby.*

stand by someone to support and encourage someone. ☐ *I will stand by you, no matter what.* ☐ *Tom promised to stand by his friend and help in any way that was needed.*

stand by someone or something to stand next to someone or something. ☐ *Jeff, please stand by Judy. I want to take* *your picture.* □ *Can I stand by the window and watch the birds?*

STAND ▸ DOWN

stand down to step down, particularly from the witness stand in a courtroom. □ *The bailiff told the witness to stand down.* □ *Please stand down and take your seat.*

STAND ▸ FOR

stand for something 1. to endure something; to tolerate something. □ *I will not stand for any more of this nonsense.* □ *She would not stand for further questioning.* 2. to represent something; to symbolize something. □ *I know that not everyone in this business stands for honesty and forthrightness.* □ *We stand for truth and justice and other good things.* □ *Each star on the American flag stands for a state.* □ *The* X *stands for her name.*

stand still for something 1. to remain still while standing for some purpose. □ *Please stand still for the photograph.* □ *It was hard to get Timmy to stand still for the fitting of his new suit.* 2. to endure and accept something, especially something that is wrong or unacceptable. (Figurative.) □ *I won't stand still for any more of this nonsense.* □ *She refused to stand still for any more abuse.*

STAND ▸ IN

stand in awe of someone or something to be in wonder or reverence of someone or something. (Both literal and figurative uses.) □ *Jeff saw Judy in her formal and just stood in awe of her.* □ *We stood in awe of the grand scenery.*

stand in (for someone) to represent someone; to substitute for someone. □ *I will stand in for Roger in tonight's performance of the play. He is sick.* □ *He is sick, so I will stand in.* N *He was sick, so his stand-in performed for him.*

stand in someone's way 1. to be in someone's pathway. □ *I'm sorry. I didn't realize I was standing in your way.* □ *There is a chair standing in my way. Please move it.* 2. to prevent someone from doing something by one's very existence. (Figurative.) □ *Do what you want. Don't let me stand in your way.* □ *I won't stand in your way if you want to leave.*

stand someone in good stead [for something] to be of great use and benefit to someone. □ *I know that my reference books will always stand me in good stead at college.* □ *Any experience you can get in dealing with the public will stand you in good stead no matter what line of work you go into.*

STAND ▸ OFF

stand off from someone or something to be or remain at some distance from someone or something. □ *Charles stood off from the group.* □ *Mary stood off from the fireside, where all the excitement was taking place.*

stand off some place [for a ship] to wait some distance from a point on shore. □ *The ship stood off at some distance, waiting for its berth.* □ *We stood off about a mile from shore and went to land in small boats called tenders.*

stand someone or something off to repel the attack of someone or something; to defend against someone or something; to stave someone or something off. □ *It was all we could do to stand them off.* □ *The soldiers stood off the attackers as long as they could.*

STAND ▸ ON

See also under *STAND ▸ (UP)ON.*

stand on ceremony to behave in a cautious and reserved manner socially, especially to wait to be introduced to people rather than introducing oneself. □ *Don't stand on ceremony. Mingle.* □ *There is no need to stand on ceremony. Make yourself at home.*

stand on one's dignity to remain dignified in spite of difficulties. □ *I will stand on my dignity to the very end.* □ *She stood on her dignity and ignored all the nonsense going on around her.*

stand on one's head to stand or balance vertically with one's head and hands—rather than one's feet—touching the floor. □ *Can you stand on your head?* □ *Todd stood on his head as a form of exercise.*

stand on one's (own) two feet to act in an independent and forthright manner. (Figurative.) □ *I can stand on my own two feet without any help from you!* □ *Dave will be better off when he gets a job and can stand on his own feet.*

stand on something **1.** to step or tread on something, perhaps by accident. □ *I didn't mean to stand on the cat's tail.* □ *Please don't stand on the nice carpet with muddy shoes.* **2.** to elevate oneself by standing on something, such as a chair or stool. □ *Tony stood on a stool so he could reach the cookie jar.* □ *Don't stand on that box. It won't hold you and it's not tall enough.*

stand one on one's head to confuse, baffle, or surprise someone. (Figurative.) □ *The accident stood the people in the office on their heads for the rest of the day.* □ *This will really stand them on their heads!*

stand pat on something to remain firm on something; to refuse to negotiate one's position on something. □ *I am going to stand pat on my last offer. There will not be a further offer.* □ *We have to stand pat on this business. We can't keep changing our policies.*

stand something on its head to confuse, baffle, or surprise a group or organization. (Figurative.) □ *The new owners came into the company and stood it on its head. Nothing will ever be the same.* □ *The mayor set out to stand the town on its head, but after one month, it was business as usual.*

STAND ▸ OUT

stand out against someone or something to be prominent or conspicuous against a background of someone or something. □ *Your red coat really stands out against all those dull brown ones.* □ *With that deep tan, you really stand out against the others.* □ *Sally was a real standout in the school play.*

stand out (from someone or something) to be prominent when compared to someone or something. □ *As a programmer, she stands out from all the others.* □ *This one stands out from all the rest.* □ *It really stands out.*

stand out (from something) to protrude from something. □ *One very straight branch in particular stood out from the tree and looked suitable for a post.* □ *The branch stood out and made a perfect place to hang my shirt while I worked.*

STAND ▸ OUTSIDE

stand outside ((of) something) to remain outside of a place, standing. (The *of* is colloquial.) □ *Judy stood outside the shop, waiting for it to open.* □ *How long have you been standing outside the door in this cold wind?* □ *She has been standing outside for a long time.*

STAND ▸ OVER

stand over someone or something to hover over someone or something; to monitor or keep close watch on someone or something. □ *Please don't stand over me while I work!* □ *Dave stood over the machine, making sure it did what it was supposed to do.*

STAND ▸ TO

stand someone to a treat to pay for a treat for someone. □ *Come on. Let's go out and eat. I'll stand you to a treat.* □ *It seems as if I am always standing someone to a treat.*

stand to reason to be reasonable or rational. □ *It simply stands to reason that everything will work out eventually.* □ *It always stands to reason that people will do the easiest things first.*

STAND ▸ TOGETHER

stand together **1.** to stand in a group. □ *All the members of the family stood together for a photograph.* □ *Please stand together so I can count you.* **2.** to remain united. □ *We must stand together if we want to defeat this enemy.* □ *If we don't stand together, we will be defeated one by one.*

STAND ▸ UP

stand someone up **1.** to place someone into a standing position. □ *I tried to stand him up, but he was just too tired.* □ *Let's stand Timmy up and try to get him awake.* **2.** to fail to show up for a meeting or a date. (Figurative.) □ *He stood her up once too often, so she* *broke up with him.* □ *Tom stood Mary up and she never forgave him.*

stand up **1.** to arise from a sitting or reclining position. □ *He stood up and looked across the valley.* □ *She had been sitting for so long that it was a pleasure to stand up.* **2.** to be in a standing position. □ *I've been standing up all day and I'm exhausted.* □ *I stood up throughout the whole trip because there were no more seats on the train.* **3.** to wear well; to remain sound and intact. □ *This material just doesn't stand up well when it's washed.* □ *Her work doesn't stand up under close scrutiny.* **4.** [for an assertion] to remain believable. (Figurative.) □ *His testimony will not stand up in court.* □ *When the police checked the story, it did not stand up.*

stand up against someone or something to challenge or hold one's own against someone or something. □ *He's good, but he can't stand up against Jill.* □ *Can this tent stand up against the wind?*

stand up and be counted to make one's allegiance publicly known. (Figurative.) □ *Make your feelings known. Stand up and be counted.* □ *I decided to stand up and be counted, so I wrote a letter to my state senator.*

stand up for someone or something to take the side of someone or something; to defend someone or something. □ *I hope you will stand up for me if the going gets rough.* □ *We will have to stand up for our rights someday.*

stand up in court [for a case] to survive a test in a court of law. □ *Do you think that this case will stand up in court?* □ *These charges will never stand up in court. They are too vague.*

stand up to someone or something to take a stand against someone or something; to hold one's ground or principles in the face of a challenge by someone or something. □ *He is a dragon, and you have to learn to stand up to him.* □ *Can the witness stand up to questioning by the prosecution?*

stand up with someone to attend someone who is being married. (Usually refers to males.) □ *I agreed to stand up with my buddy at his wedding.* □ *Tom stood up with Harry when the latter got married.*

STAND ► (UP)ON

stand (up)on someone or something to be on someone or something, standing. (*Upon* is formal and less commonly used than *on*.) □ *To help his back pain, he lay down on his tummy and Jill stood upon him, digging her toes into his back.* □ *Please don't stand on the bed.*

STAND ► WITH

stand well with someone to be acceptable or agreeable to someone. □ *That idea doesn't stand well with the management.* □ *I hope my suggestions stand well with you.*

stand with someone to unite with someone, as in defense. □ *Don't worry. I'll stand with you to the end.* □ *He stood with her and they faced the threat together.*

STAR ► AS

star as someone or something [for someone] to be a featured performer, representing a particular person, or play in a particular role. □ *Judy starred as Evita in the broadway production of the same name.* □ *Mary starred as an aging countess.*

STAR ► IN

star in something to be a featured actor in a play, movie, opera, etc. □ *Roger starred in an off-Broadway play last season.* □ *Mary always wanted to star in her own movie, but it was not to be.*

STARE ► AT

stare at someone or something to look fixedly at someone or something. □ *Why are you staring at me?* □ *I was staring at the scenery behind you.*

STARE ► DOWN

stare someone down to pressure someone to capitulate, back down, or yield by staring. □ *Don't try to stare me down. I have nerves of steel.* 🅃 *I tried to stare down my opponent, but it didn't work.*

STARE ► IN

stare someone in the face **1.** to stare directly at someone's face. □ *I stared her* *in the face and told her no.* ☐ *You can't just stare me in the face and tell me you hate me!* **2.** [for evidence] to confront someone directly. ☐ *Finally, the truth stared me in the face, and I had to realize what had really happened.* ☐ *When the facts in the case stared the jury in the face, there was nothing they could do but acquit.*

STARE ▶ INTO

stare into something to gaze fixedly into something. ☐ *She just sat there, staring into space.* ☐ *Tom stared into the water, hoping to see a fish or maybe a turtle.*

STARE ▶ OUT

stare out at someone or something **1.** to be in a place staring outward at someone or something. ☐ *I stayed in my little room and stared out at the others having fun in the crisp fall air.* ☐ *We stared out at the deep snow.* **2.** [for a face or eyes visible in a place] to be seen staring outward from that place. ☐ *Two bright little cat eyes stared out at me from the basket.* ☐ *Her faced stared out of the tiny window.*

START ▶ AS

start as something to begin in some original condition or status. ☐ *Every forest fire starts as a small spark.* ☐ *The argument started as a small disagreement.*

START ▶ BACK

start back (to some place) to begin the journey back to a place. ☐ *When do we start back to Chicago?* ☐ *It's time to start back.*

START ▶ FOR

start for some place to begin a journey to some place. ☐ *When shall we start for Springfield?* ☐ *We will start for Detroit before dawn.*

START ▶ FROM

start from scratch to begin from the beginning; to begin to make something from the raw materials. ☐ *Do I have to start from scratch, or has some of this work been done by someone else?* ☐ *We started from scratch and made a completely new one.*

start from some place **1.** [for someone] to begin a journey at some place. (The emphasis is on the location of the start of the journey.) ☐ *We started from Chicago.* ☐ *Where will you start from?* **2.** [for a journey] to begin from a particular point. ☐ *The journey started from Chicago.* ☐ *Our trip started from the airport in New York.*

START ▶ IN

start in on someone or something to begin dealing with, discussing, or chastising someone or something. ☐ *Please don't start in on me again! You said enough the previous three times.* ☐ *When will you be ready to start in on painting the house?*

start someone in as something to give someone a starting job as something. ☐ *I will start you in as a clerk, and you can work your way up.* ☐ *I want to be started in as a junior partner.*

START ▶ OFF

start off to begin; to set out on a journey. ☐ *When do you want to start off?* ☐ *We will start off as soon as we can get ready.*

start off as someone or something to begin in a particular status, character, rank, etc. ☐ *I started off as a waiter and ended up as the owner of the restaurant.* ☐ *This tree started off as a tiny seedling only a few years ago.*

start off (by doing something) to begin a process by doing a particular thing first. ☐ *Can I start off by singing the school song?* ☐ *That's a good way to start off.*

start off from some place to begin a journey from some place. (The emphasis is on the inception of the journey.) ☐ *We will start off from Detroit and drive to Chicago.* ☐ *He started off from work rather than home.*

start off (on something) **1.** to begin a series or sequence. ☐ *Today I start off on the first volume of my trilogy.* ☐ *I am ready to start off now.* **2.** to begin a journey. ☐ *When do we start off on our trip?* ☐ *I'm ready to start off. What about you?*

start off on the wrong foot AND **step off on the wrong foot** to begin things incorrectly. (As if one were beginning to march and began on the right rather than the left foot.) □ *Give me some advice. I don't want to start off on the wrong foot.* □ *Tim stepped off on the wrong foot in his new job.*

start off with a bang to begin with considerable excitement. (Figurative.) □ *The program started off with a bang and the whole show was great.* □ *The day started off with a bang and kept going that way.*

start (off) with a clean slate See under *START ▸ WITH.*

start (off) with someone or something See under *START ▸ WITH.*

start someone off (on something) to cause someone to begin on a task or job. □ *I have to start Jeff off on this task, then I will talk to you.* 🅃 *I will start off my workers on the job tomorrow.* □ *Let me know what time to start them off.*

START ▸ ON

start on someone or something to begin dealing with someone or something. □ *We have finished talking about Gary, and now we will start on Bob.* □ *We will start on dessert after you have finished your broccoli.*

start on someone or something to begin to castigate someone or something □*Don't start on me! I didn't do anything wrong!* □ *The politician started on the opposing party, and everyone in the audience cheered.*

START ▸ OUT

start out to begin. □ *Whenever you are ready, we will start out.* □ *We can't start out until Tom is here.*

start out as something to begin one's career as something. □ *I started out as a clerk and I'm still a clerk!* □ *I wanted to start out as an assistant manager.*

start out (on something) to begin something, such as a trip, a career, an investigation, etc. □ *When we started out on this investigation, I never dreamed we would uncover so much.* □ *What time did you start out this morning?* □ *I hear you are starting out on a new career.* □ *There never seems to be enough money when you are just starting out.*

start out with someone or something to begin something in association with someone or something. □ *I started out with Jeff, but he had to be replaced.* □ *We started out with the Acme company, but they could not handle all our work.* □ *I started out with three other climbers, but only two of us made it to the top.*

start someone out as something to start someone working in a particular capacity. □ *I will start you out as a clerk and see what you can do.* □ *But I want to be started out as an assistant manager.*

start someone out at something to start someone working at a particular salary. □ *We will start you out at $30,000.* □ *I wanted to be started out at $35,000.*

START ▸ OVER

start over to begin again. □ *I have messed this up so much that there is nothing to do now but start over.* □ *When you start over, try to do it right this time.*

start (over) with a clean slate See under *START ▸ WITH.*

start someone over to cause someone to begin again; to lead someone to begin again. □ *The orchestra messed up the first few bars, so the conductor started them over again.* □ *I hope the conductor doesn't start us over again. This is getting boring to play.*

START ▸ UP

start someone up (in something) to help someone get a start in some enterprise. □ *My uncle started me up in business.* 🅃 *I started up my niece in the candy business.* □ *I was glad I could help start her up.*

start something up to start something, such as an engine or a motor. □ *Start your lawn mower up and get that grass cut!* 🅃 *Start up your car and let's go.* 🄽 *The start-up was easy in spite of the temperature.*

start something up with something to use something in the process of starting something else. □ *Do you have to start this old car up with a crank?* Ⓣ *Do you start up this car with a crank?*

start up to begin; to begin running, as with an engine. □ *The car started up without a problem.* □ *The engines of the plane started up one by one.*

start up with someone or something to begin by using someone or something. □ *We will start up with two clerks and add more as we grow.* □ *We started up with one old cash register, and now we have six.*

START ▸ WITH

start (off) with a clean slate to begin freshly with all previous problems solved. □ *In her new job, Sherri plans to start off with a clean slate.* □ *Jamie tried to start with a clean slate.*

start (off) with someone or something to begin a task or a process with someone or something. □ *I will start off with the first volunteer and then add others as we go along.* □ *I will start off with one hot dog and get another later if I want it.*

start (over) with a clean slate to begin again; to have a fresh start. (As if one had erased the writing from a slate. See also *start (off) with a clean slate* under *START ▸ WITH.*) □ *I look forward to starting my new job. It's like starting over with a clean slate.* □ *Jamie tried to start over with a clean slate after some problems before.*

STARTLE ▸ OUT

startle someone out of something to frighten someone very badly. (The *something* that may be lost is *wits, senses, ten years' growth,* etc. *Someone* includes *oneself.*) □ *The explosion startled Polly out of her senses.* □ *I frightened myself out of ten years' growth.*

STARVE ▸ FOR

starve for someone or something to have a strong desire or need for someone or something. (Both literal and figurative uses.) □ *I am starved for Jane. I miss her so!* □ *Nancy was starved for some ice cream.* □ *Claire was starved for affection.*

starve for something to be very hungry for something. (The *something* is food in general or a particular food.) □ *I am just starved for some fresh peaches.* □ *We were starved for dinner by the time we finally got to eat.*

STARVE ▸ INTO

starve someone or something into something to force someone or some creature to do something by starvation. □ *The torturers finally starved the prisoner into telling the battle plans.* □ *They starved the water buffalo into a state of weakness.*

STARVE ▸ OUT

starve someone or something out (of some place) to force a living creature to come out of a hiding place or a place of security by starvation. (The *of*-phrase is paraphrased with a *from*-phrase when the particle is transposed. See the Ⓕ example.) □ *The attackers tried to starve the people out of the walled city.* Ⓣ *We tried to starve out the mice.* Ⓕ *We tried to starve out the mice from the attic.* □ *We never starved them out.*

STASH ▸ AWAY

stash something away to hide something; to set something aside for use at a later time. □ *Please stash this away somewhere. You may need it someday.* Ⓣ *You should stash away some money for later.* Ⓐ *Her stashed-away twenty-dollar bills came in handy after she lost her job.*

STASH ▸ IN

stash something in something to put or shove something into something; to store or hide something in something. □ *You should stash your food in a place that is safe from bears when you go camping.* □ *I stashed my clothes in my suitcase and called a taxi.*

STATION ▸ AT

station someone at something to position or place someone near something. □ *The manager stationed a receptionist at the door.* □ *Would you station a guard at the back door to keep people out?*

STAVE ▶ IN

stave something in to crush something in. (The past tense is usually *stove* with ships, and otherwise, *staved*.) ☐ *The rocks on the reef staved the hull of the ship in.* 🅃 *The angry sailor staved in cask of rum.* 🅃 *The rocks will stave in the hull.*

STAVE ▶ OFF

stave someone or something off to hold someone or something off; to defend against the attack of someone or something. ☐ *The citizen was not able to stave the mugger off.* 🅃 *The army staved off the attackers for three hours without letup.* 🅃 *The hunters were able to stave off the wolves.*

stave something off to delay or postpone something, such as hunger, foreclosure, death, etc. ☐ *He could stave his thirst off no longer. Despite the enemy sentries, he made a dash for the stream.* 🅃 *The lost hiker could not stave off her hunger any longer.*

STAY ▶ AFTER

stay after someone to continue to urge someone to do something. ☐ *I will stay after you until you get it done.* ☐ *There is no need to stay after me. I can get it done on my own.*

stay after (someone or something) to remain behind someone or something. ☐ *I will stay after the others and clean up.* ☐ *I would be happy to stay after.*

stay after something **1.** to remain in a place after an event has finished. ☐ *He was told he had to stay after school as a punishment.* ☐ *A number of people stayed after the meeting to discuss what had happened.* **2.** to continue to urge that something get done. (Figurative.) ☐ *Please stay after that project. We have to finish it soon.* ☐ *I will stay after this matter until it is completed.*

STAY ▶ AHEAD

stay ahead (of someone or something) **1.** to remain in front of someone or something. ☐ *The photographer almost had to run to stay ahead of the marchers.* ☐ *She had to run to stay ahead.* **2.** to keep informed about someone or something. ☐ *My grandchildren are doing so many things that I can hardly stay ahead of them.* ☐ *The children are doing so many things that I can hardly stay ahead.* **3.** to outthink or outguess someone or something. ☐ *It's hard to stay ahead of a clever gal like Sue!* ☐ *I've given up trying to stay ahead.*

stay ahead of something AND **keep ahead of something** to keep up with one's work or financial responsibilities; to have one's work and financial responsibilities under control. ☐ *I can't seem to keep ahead of my bills.* ☐ *They can't stay ahead of their work and production is falling behind schedule.*

STAY ▶ AT

stay at some place **1.** to remain at a place. ☐ *Have you ever tried to make a cat stay at one place?* ☐ *Please stay at home until I call you.* **2.** to live at a place temporarily. ☐ *I am staying at the Statler Hotel.* ☐ *At what hotel are you staying while you are in town?*

stay at something to keep working at something. ☐ *You should stay at something until you finish it.* ☐ *She couldn't seem to stay at her place of work for a whole day.*

STAY ▶ AWAY

stay away (from someone or something) to avoid someone or something. ☐ *Stay away from me!* ☐ *Please stay away!*

STAY ▶ BACK

stay back (from something) to keep one's distance from someone or something. ☐ *Stay back from the lawn mower!* ☐ *This is dangerous. Stay back!*

STAY ▶ BEHIND

stay behind [for someone] to remain in a place when others have left. ☐ *I will stay behind and tell the late people where you have gone.* ☐ *Fred always stayed behind to clean up.*

stay behind (someone or something) to remain in back of someone or something. ☐ *Please stay behind me where it is safe.* ☐ *Stay behind the curtain until I signal you.* ☐ *Don't come out. Stay behind.*

STAY ▶ BY

stay by someone or something to remain close to someone or something. ☐ *Please stay by me until we get through this crowd of rough-looking people.* ☐ *Stay by the wall and move along slowly.*

STAY ▶ DOWN

stay down to remain in a prone, squatting, or sitting position. ☐ *Stay down until the danger is over.* ☐ *Stay down so they won't see you.*

STAY ▶ FOR

stay for something to remain in a place to participate in something. ☐ *Would you please stay for dinner?* ☐ *I am sorry, but we cannot stay for dinner.*

STAY ▶ IN

stay in (something) to remain inside a place or thing; to stay indoors. ☐ *Please stay in the house. It's too cold to go outside.* ☐ *You should stay in when it's this cold.*

stay in touch with someone to keep up one's contact with someone. ☐ *I hope you will stay in touch with me.* ☐ *I have stayed in touch with my godson all these years.*

STAY ▶ OF

stay abreast of someone or something **1.** to keep even with someone or something. ☐ *I had to run hard to stay abreast of Sally.* ☐ *My car could not stay abreast of Roy's in the race.* **2.** to keep informed about someone or something. ☐ *Sally's career is of great interest to me. I intend to stay abreast of her.* ☐ *I have to work hard to stay abreast of my field.*

stay clear of someone or something to keep one's distance from something, usually something dangerous. ☐ *Please stay clear of me. I have the flu.* ☐ *Stay clear of that machine. It is dangerous.*

STAY ▶ OFF

stay off (something) to keep off of something. ☐ *Please stay off my lawn!* ☐ *Stay off!*

STAY ▶ ON

stay on (after someone or something) See *linger on (after someone or something)* under *LINGER ▶ ON.*

stay on (some place) to remain at a place longer than had been planned. ☐ *I stayed on in Paris for nearly two years.* ☐ *Mary liked it there and decided to stay on.*

stay on something **1.** to remain on something, such as a horse, road, stool, etc. ☐ *The first time I rode, I could hardly stay on the horse.* ☐ *It was so rainy that I had trouble staying on the road.* **2.** to continue to pursue something. ☐ *I will stay on this problem until it is settled.* ☐ *She stayed on the matter for weeks until it had been dealt with.*

stay on top of someone or something to keep well informed about someone or something; to keep watch over someone or something. ☐ *You have to stay on top of her if you want her to do it right.* ☐ *I will stay on top of this project.*

STAY ▶ OUT

stay out (of something) **1.** to keep out of something or some place. ☐ *Stay out of here!* ☐ *Please stay out until we are ready.* **2.** to remain uninvolved in some piece of business. ☐ *I decided to stay out of it and let someone else handle it.* ☐ *My help wasn't needed there, so I just stayed out.*

STAY ▶ OVER

stay over (somewhere) to stay overnight in a dwelling other than one's own. ☐ *Can I stay over at Jimmy's tonight?* ☐ *No, you can't stay over.*

STAY ▶ TO

stay to something to remain in a place for something, such as dinner. ☐ *I hope you will stay to dinner.* ☐ *I stayed to lunch because they were having fried shrimp.*

STAY ▶ UNDER

stay under (something) to remain concealed or protected beneath something. ☐ *You had better stay under the blankets until I get the fire started in the fireplace.* ☐ *Stay under and keep warm.*

STAY ▸ UP

stay up (for something) to remain awake and out of bed for some nighttime event. ☐ *I will stay up for her arrival.* ☐ *I can't stay up that late.*

stay up late to remain awake and out of bed. ☐ *I am in the practice of staying up late.* ☐ *I can't stay up late three nights in a row.*

stay up until something to remain awake and out of bed until a particular time. ☐ *I stayed up until long past midnight last night.* ☐ *Do you think Susie should stay up until midnight?*

STAY ▸ WITH

stay with someone or something to remain in the company of someone or something. ☐ *Please stay with me for a little while.* ☐ *How long did you stay with the company?*

STAY ▸ WITHIN

stay within something to remain inside something. ☐ *You will have to stay within the resort area until things return to normal in the town.* ☐ *Our dog just can't seem to stay within our yard.*

STEAL ▸ AT

steal a glance at someone or something to sneak a peek at someone or something. ☐ *He stole a glance at his brother, who appeared to be as frightened as he was.* ☐ *Karen stole a glance at her watch and yawned.*

STEAL ▸ AWAY

steal away to sneak away quietly. ☐ *She stole away in the still of the night.* ☐ *I plan to steal away during the second act because I have to get to bed early.*

steal away from someone or something to sneak away from someone or something. ☐ *The thief stole away from the policeman.* ☐ *We stole away from the boring lecture.*

STEAL ▸ FROM

steal from someone or something to rob someone or something. ☐ *You wouldn't steal from a poor man, would you?* ☐ *Max didn't feel bad about stealing from a bank.*

steal something from someone or something to take the property belonging to someone or something without permission; to commit the theft of something from someone or something. ☐ *Max stole $50 from Henry.* ☐ *Lefty stole an apple from the fruit stand.*

STEAL ▸ OFF

steal something off someone to rob something from someone. (Colloquial.) ☐ *I think that guy who walked past me stole my wallet off me!* ☐ *Max stole a lot of money off tourists last season.*

STEAL ▸ ON

steal a march on someone or something to precede someone; to accomplish something before someone else does. ☐ *Jeff stole a march on all of us when he had his story published.* ☐ *Our competitor stole a march on us and got the big contract.*

STEAL ▸ OUT

steal out of some place to sneak quietly out of some place. ☐ *The critic stole out of the theater, unable to endure any more of the abysmal play.* ☐ *I stole out of the lecture and went back to my room.*

STEAL ▸ OVER

steal over someone or something **1.** [for a covering of some sort] to move slowly over someone or something. (As with the sun or the shade of a cloud.) ☐ *The shade stole over the sunbathers and ended their day.* ☐ *Darkness stole over the land.* **2.** [for a feeling] to spread through someone gradually. ☐ *A feeling of gloom stole over the crowd.* ☐ *A sense of high excitement stole over the boys as they waited.*

STEAL ▸ UP

steal up on someone or something to sneak up on someone or something. ☐ *We will steal up on Tony and give him a start.* ☐ *The fox stole up on the hen and grabbed it.*

STEAM ▸ ACROSS

steam across something [for a ship] to cross a body of water under power, originally steam power. ☐ *How long does it take to steam across the Atlantic these* *days?* ☐ *We steamed across the bay in less than an hour.*

STEAM ▸ IN(TO)

steam in((to) something) [for a vehicle, usually a ship] to enter something under power, originally steam power. ☐ *The ship steamed into the harbor and headed for the pier.* ☐ *Right on time, the ship steamed in.*

STEAM ▸ OFF

steam something off ((of) something) to loosen and remove something by an application of steam. (The *of*-phrase is paraphrased with a *from*-phrase when the particle is transposed. See the Ⓕ example. The *of* is colloquial.) ☐ *Toby steamed the old paper off the wall.* Ⓣ *Toby steamed off the old paper.* Ⓕ *Toby steamed off the old paper from the walls of the living room.* ☐ *It is hard to steam the paper off.*

STEAM ▸ OUT

steam out (of some place) [for a conveyance, usually a ship] to exit something under power, originally steam power. ☐ *The huge diesel engines began to labor, and the ship steamed out of its berth.* ☐ *It shuddered a couple of times and steamed out.*

steam something out (of something) to remove something embedded, through an application of steam. (The *of*-phrase is paraphrased with a *from*-phrase when the particle is transposed. See the Ⓕ example.) ☐ *The cleaner was not able to steam the wrinkles out of my jacket.* Ⓣ *I tried to steam out the gum.* Ⓕ *Do you think I can steam out the wrinkles from these pants?* ☐ *I will try to steam them out.*

STEAM ▸ UP

steam something up to cause something to be covered with water vapor due to the presence of steam. ☐ *Our breaths steamed the windows up.* Ⓣ *Our breaths steamed up the windows.* Ⓐ *The steamed-up mirror was of no use.*

steam up to become covered with a film of steam or water vapor. ☐ *The windows steamed up and we had to wipe them so we could see out.* ☐ *The window has steamed up, and I can't see.*

STEEL ▸ AGAINST

steel someone against someone or something to fortify someone against someone or something; to prepare someone to endure someone or something. (*Someone* includes *oneself.*) ☐ *I tried to steel Liz against Carl, who was bringing her some very bad news.* ☐ *We steeled her against the bad news.* ☐ *We will steel ourselves against all possibilities.*

STEEL ▸ FOR

steel oneself for someone or something to prepare oneself for someone or something; to get ready to face someone or something. (Compare to *steel oneself against* under *STEEL ▸ AGAINST.*) ☐ *Aunt Helen is coming for a visit. We should steel ourselves for her.* ☐ *I think something is going wrong. We had better steel ourselves for a shock.* ☐ *I knew I would have to steel myself for the trouble I would have to face.*

STEEP ▸ IN

steep someone in something to immerse someone in some kind of knowledge or other experience; to saturate someone with some kind of experience or training. (*Someone* includes *oneself.*) ☐ *Her parents steeped her in good literature and music.* ☐ *She steeped herself in the legends of her people.*

steep something in something to soak something in a liquid. ☐ *I steeped the shirt in red dye.* ☐ *You have to steep these herbs in steamy hot water for five minutes.*

STEER ▸ AWAY

steer away from someone or something to move or turn away from someone or something. ☐ *You had better steer away from Jeff. He is in a terrible mood.* ☐ *Try to steer away from the potholes. The road is full of them.*

STEER ▸ FOR

steer something for something to aim oneself or one's vehicle toward something. ☐ *Jeff steered the car for the entrance to the tunnel and stepped on the* *gas.* ☐ *The driver steered the bus for the center lane just in time.*

STEER ▸ INTO

steer into something to turn or drive into something. ☐ *Try to steer into the right parking space this time.* ☐ *Poor Wally steered into the curb.*

STEER ▸ OF

steer clear of someone or something to avoid someone or something. ☐ *Todd has been in a very bad mood. I would steer clear of him for a while if I were you.* ☐ *Could you steer clear of the living room for a while? I am doing my taxes there.*

STEER ▸ THROUGH

steer someone or something through something to guide someone or something through something that is confusing or treacherous. ☐ *I tried to steer Judy through the registration procedure, but I really didn't know what I was doing.* ☐ *Should I try to steer my car through all this foot traffic or take a different route?*

steer through something to maneuver through something that is confusing or treacherous. ☐ *Do you think you can steer through this flooded tunnel?* ☐ *I can't steer through this mess of leaves and mud on the road.*

STEER ▸ TOWARD

steer something toward someone or something to guide something in the direction of someone or something. ☐ *The farmer steered the tractor toward the sheriff, who had come to talk to the farmer.* ☐ *Please steer the car toward the right side.*

steer toward someone or something to turn or drive toward someone or something. ☐ *He steered toward the empty parking space, but someone got there before he did.* ☐ *Steer toward the house with the red door.*

STEM ▸ FROM

stem from something to grow out of something; to result from something. (Not used literally for plants.) ☐ *These problems all stem from your mismanagement.* ☐ *Our difficulties stem from the bad weather we have been having.*

STEP ▸ ASIDE

step aside to step out of the way. ☐ *Please step aside. You are in the way.* ☐ *I stepped aside just in time.*

step aside for someone **1.** to move out of someone's way. ☐ *Would you step aside for my uncle and his walker?* ☐ *We had to step aside for the people in wheelchairs to get by.* **2.** to step down from something (for someone). (Figurative.) ☐ *The president retired and stepped aside for someone else.* ☐ *Walter stepped aside for a younger person to take over.*

STEP ▸ BACK

step back (from someone or something) to move back from someone or something; to move back so as to provide space around someone or something. ☐ *Please step back from the injured woman. Give her some air.* ☐ *Step back and give her some air.*

step back on someone or something to move back and tread on someone or something in the process. ☐ *Jeff stepped back on Judy and made her yelp with pain.* ☐ *Jeff stepped back on the cat.*

STEP ▸ BETWEEN

step between someone or something and someone or something to move between things or people. ☐ *Jeff stepped between Judy and the gunman.* ☐ *He stepped between Judy and the wall.* ☐ *Jamie stepped between the wall and a large planter.*

STEP ▸ DOWN

step down to move down one step. ☐ *Please step down now.* ☐ *Step down and make room for someone behind you.*

step down (from something) to come down from something; to alight from something. ☐ *Please step down from the platform.* ☐ *She stepped down and went back to her chair.*

step down (from something) (for someone) to retire or resign from something, allowing someone else to take over. ☐ *The old man stepped down* *from the presidency for his daughter.* □ *He stepped down for his daughter.* □ *He stepped down from his leadership role.* □ *He became weak and had to step down.*

step something down to reduce the intensity or amount of something by one step or grade. □ *See if you can step the lights down a little.* 🅃 *Step down the lights just a little more.*

STEP ▶ FORWARD

step forward **1.** to move forward one step. □ *The volunteer stepped forward.* □ *I stepped forward and someone moved up behind me immediately.* **2.** to volunteer to present important information. □ *When I go into court, I will have to step forward and present evidence. It is my civic duty.* □ *If you have evidence to present, you should step forward and seek recognition to do so.*

STEP ▶ IN

step in something to walk into something, such as a puddle. □ *Careful. Don't step in that puddle.* □ *I think I stepped in some mud.*

STEP ▶ INSIDE

step inside (some place) to walk into a place. □ *Please step inside my office, and we will discuss this matter.* □ *Please step inside.*

STEP ▶ INTO

step into someone's shoes to take over a task for someone; to take over someone's job or official position. (Figurative.) □ *Do you think you can step into Jeff's shoes?* □ *I could never step into Donna's shoes. I just don't have the skills to do her job.*

step into something to involve oneself in some matter to intervene in an affair or dispute. □ *I will have to step into the business and settle the problem.* □ *Please don't step into something that does not concern you.*

step into the breach [for someone] to assume a position or take on a responsibility when there is an opportunity to do so. □ *The person who was supposed to help didn't show up, so I stepped into the breach.* □ *The manager stepped into the breach when Jane got sick.*

STEP ▶ IN(TO)

step in(to some place) to walk into a place. □ *Tiffany stepped into the room and said hello to everyone.* □ *She stepped in to say hello.*

STEP ▶ OFF

step off to come off something by taking a step. □ *She came to the bottom step and stepped off.* □ *Ed was afraid to dive in from the side of the pool, so he just stepped off.*

step off (of) something to leave something that is elevated on one's first step. (The *of* is colloquial.) □ *She stepped off the bottom step and walked down the street.* □ *Tony stepped off of the bank and waded across the stream.*

step off on the wrong foot See *start off on the wrong foot* under *START ▶ OFF.*

step something off to measure a distance by counting the paces required to cover it. □ *She stepped the distance off and noted it on her pad.* 🅃 *Liz stepped off the number of feet from the window to the opposite wall.*

STEP ▶ ON

step on someone or something to tread on someone or something. □ *Ouch! You stepped on me!* □ *Don't step on the flooring in that spot. It's weak.*

step on someone's toes AND **tread on someone's toes** to offend someone. (Also the obvious literal meaning.) □ *You're sure I won't be stepping on her toes if I talk directly to her supervisor?* □ *I didn't mean to tread on your toes.*

step on the gas AND **step on it** to hurry up. (Slang. As if stepping on an automobile's accelerator. □ *Step on the gas. We are going to be late!* □ *Step on it! Let's go!*

STEP ▶ OUT

step out into something to go out from a place into a different set of conditions. □ *Julie stepped out of her previous job into a whole new world.* □ *Wally stepped out into the bright sunlight.*

step out of line 1. to move out of a line of people. ☐ *If you step out of line, you will lose your place in it.* ☐ *I had to step out of line to sit down on the curb and rest for a minute.* 2. to misbehave. (Figurative.) ☐ *If you step out of line again, I'll slap you.* ☐ *Tom stepped out of line once too often and got yelled at.*

step out (of something) 1. to go out of a place. ☐ *She stepped out of the house without a coat and nearly froze to death.* ☐ *Jamie stepped out and nearly froze her nose.* 2. to take one step to get out of pants of some type that have been dropped. ☐ *He stepped out of his pants and pulled off his shirt.* ☐ *He dropped his pants and stepped out.*

step out (on someone) to be unfaithful to a spouse or lover. ☐ *Jeff has been stepping out on Judy.* ☐ *I was not stepping out!*

STEP ▸ OUTSIDE

step outside 1. to go outside, as to get some fresh air. ☐ *I need to step outside for a minute to get a breath of air.* ☐ *Tom and Harry stepped outside for a moment.* 2. to go outside to fight or settle an argument. ☐ *I find that insulting. Would you care to step outside?* ☐ *Max invited Lefty to step outside.*

STEP ▸ OVER

step over someone or something to walk so as to avoid stepping on someone or something. ☐ *I stepped over Tom, who was napping on the floor.* ☐ *Please step over the things on the floor. We are doing the spring cleaning.*

step over (to) some place to move to a place a few steps away. ☐ *Please step over here and I'll show you some other merchandise.* ☐ *If you will step over to the display case, I will show you some earrings.*

STEP ▸ UP

step right up to come right to where the speaker is; to come forward to the person speaking. (Used by people selling things.) ☐ *Please step right up and buy a ticket to see the show.* ☐ *Don't be shy! Step right up and buy one of these.*

step something up 1. to make something more active. ☐ *I hope we can step the pace of business up in the next few days.* 🅃 *We can step up business considerably by putting out a larger sign.* 🄰 *The stepped-up battle was very costly in terms of lives.* 2. to make something go or run faster. ☐ *The engineer stepped the motors up and the production line moved even faster.* 🅃 *Please step up the speed of your activity.* ☐ *The new manager stepped production up considerably.* 🄽 *He could not achieve a step-up in production without sacrificing quality.*

step up to increase. ☐ *Industrial production stepped up a large amount this last quarter.* ☐ *Traffic has stepped up since the road was paved.*

step up to something to walk to something, especially a counter or a bar. ☐ *Jake stepped up to the ticket counter and bought a single ticket for the balcony.* ☐ *When Wally stepped up to the ticket window, he learned that the show was sold out.*

STEW ▸ IN

stew in one's own juice to suffer the torment of one's own anger or resentment. (Figurative.) ☐ *He is such a sourpuss. Just let him stew in his own juice.* ☐ *She stewed in her own juice for a while and then decided to make up with Ted.*

STICK ▸ AROUND

stick around to remain in the general vicinity. (Colloquial.) ☐ *Please stick around. I need to talk to you after the meeting.* ☐ *I will stick around for a while, but I have another appointment.*

STICK ▸ AT

stick at something to keep trying to do something; to stay on the job. ☐ *I hope he can stick at this job.* ☐ *He doesn't seem to be able to stick at anything for very long.*

STICK ▸ BY

stick by someone or something to remain close to and supportive of someone or something. ☐ *Stick by me and I will help you.* ☐ *Stick by the committee and they will take care of you later.*

STICK ▸ DOWN

stick something down to fasten something down, as with glue or paste. ☐ *Get some glue and stick down this wallpaper, please.* Ⓣ *Stick down this wallpaper, would you?*

STICK ▸ IN

stick in someone's mind to remain in someone's thinking. ☐ *The events of that day stuck in my mind for a very long time.* ☐ *The image of her smiling face stuck in Henry's mind for a long time.*

stick in something to remain embedded in something; to remain held in something. ☐ *Do you think this will stick in the hole, or is it too small?* ☐ *A fish bone stuck in his throat for a while.*

stick one's foot in one's mouth to say something foolish or embarrassing. (Figurative.) ☐ *You really stuck your foot in your mouth that time.* ☐ *I'm afraid I stuck my foot in my mouth that time.*

stick one's nose in (where it's not wanted) to get involved in something that is not part of one's own business. (Figurative. See also *poke one's nose in(to something)* at *POKE ▸ IN(TO)*.) ☐ *Please stop sticking your nose in where it's not wanted!* ☐ *I was not sticking my nose in!*

STICK ▸ IN(TO)

stick something in(to someone or something) to insert something into someone or something. ☐ *The technician stuck a needle into my arm and took some blood out.* Ⓣ *She stuck in the needle.* ☐ *Harry stuck the needle in with great care.*

STICK ▸ ON

See *be stuck on someone or something* under *BE ▸ ON.*

STICK ▸ ON(TO)

stick something on(to) someone or something to affix something onto someone or something. ☐ *The baggage clerk stuck a label onto Jimmy as a joke.* ☐ *Jimmy stuck the label on his bag.* Ⓐ *The baggage was covered with stick-on labels.*

STICK ▸ OUT

stick one's neck out (to do something) to take a risk to do something. ☐ *I refuse to stick my neck out to try to save his reputation.* Ⓣ *I won't stick out my neck again.*

stick out to project outward. ☐ *You can't lock your suitcase because there is a bit of cloth sticking out.* ☐ *Some cloth stuck out of the top of the drawer.*

stick out a mile to project outward very obviously. (Colloquial.) ☐ *My nose sticks out a mile! I hate it!* ☐ *His stomach sticks out a mile. What do you suppose is in there?*

stick out against something to be highly visible against a background of something. ☐ *Your cold, red nose sticks out against your white, frozen face.* ☐ *The red vase sticks out against the pale blue wallpaper.*

stick out (from someone or something) to project outward from someone or something. ☐ *His right arm, which was in a cast, stuck out from him like a crane.* ☐ *His arm stuck out.*

stick out like a sore thumb [for someone or something] to be very obvious. ☐ *Please don't wear plaid trousers. You stick out like a sore thumb!* ☐ *I stick out like a sore thumb in a crowd because I am so tall.*

stick out (of someone or something) to protrude from someone or something. ☐ *The arrow stuck out of him, wobbling as he staggered.* ☐ *A dollar bill stuck out of the book. What a strange bookmark.*

stick something out **1.** to cause something to project outward. ☐ *Don't stick your tongue out at me!* Ⓣ *She stuck out her tongue at me!* **2.** to endure something; to stay with something. (The *something* is usually *it*.) ☐ *I will stick it out as long as I can.* ☐ *She stuck it out as long as she could; then she started looking for another job.*

stick something out to someone to hold something, such as one's hand, out where someone can grasp it. ☐ *She stuck her hand out to him, intending* *that he shake it.* ☐ *Ted stuck his hand out to Bill, but withdrew it suddenly.*

STICK ▸ THROUGH

stick something through someone or something to push something so that it penetrates someone or something. ☐ *The good knight stuck his lance through the bad knight.* ☐ *I stuck my fist through the flimsy wall.*

STICK ▸ TO

stick it to someone to burden someone with extra or excessive costs or with harsh treatment. (Slang.) ☐ *The bill was much higher than I thought. They really stick it to you with all the little extras.* ☐ *I guess I looked as if I had a lot of money and they decided to really stick it to me.*

stick to one's guns to maintain one's position through adversity; to stand on one's own. (Figurative.) ☐ *I know I am right, and I'm going to stick to my guns.* ☐ *Don't give up. Stick to your guns.*

stick to someone or something 1. to adhere to someone or something; to remain affixed to someone or something. ☐ *The tape stuck to me and I couldn't get it off.* ☐ *This stamp won't stick to the envelope.* ☐ *The blob of glue stuck to me for almost three days before falling off.* **2.** to continue to accompany someone or something. (Colloquial.) ☐ *Stick to me and I'll lead you out of here.* ☐ *Stick to the group of us, and you'll be okay.* **3.** to continue to use or employ someone or something. ☐ *I'll stick to Jill. She does a good job and she's my friend.* ☐ *We decided to stick to our present supplier.*

stick to someone's fingers to remain in someone's possession; to be stolen by someone. (Slang or colloquial.) ☐ *Other people's watches tend to stick to Max's fingers.* ☐ *Watch that clerk. Your change tends to stick to his fingers.*

STICK ▸ TOGETHER

stick something together 1. to glue or paste something together. ☐ *Use glue to stick these pieces together.* ☐ *Please stick the pieces of the broken vase together with glue.* **2.** to assemble something, perhaps in haste. ☐ *He just stuck the model plane together, making a mess of it.* ☐ *Don't stick the parts together so fast. It won't look good.*

stick together 1. to adhere to one another. ☐ *The noodles are sticking together. What shall I do?* ☐ *You need to keep the pieces separate while you fry them or else they will stick together.* **2.** to remain in one another's company. (Figurative.) ☐ *Let us stick together so we don't get lost.* ☐ *They stuck together through thick and thin.*

STICK ▸ UP

Stick 'em up! to raise one's hands in the face of a loaded gun. (Always the command of a robber.) ☐ *The armed robber ordered the clerk to stick 'em up.* ☐ *Stick 'em up! This is a robbery!*

stick one's nose up in the air to behave in a haughty manner. ☐ *Jeff stuck his nose up in the air and walked out.* ☐ *Don't stick your nose up in the air. Come down to earth with the rest of us.*

stick someone or something up to rob someone or a business establishment. (Presumably with the aid of a gun.) ☐ *Max tried to stick the drugstore up.* 🅃 *Max stuck up the store.* ☐ *He stuck the store up.* 🄽 *Tom was almost killed in a stickup.*

stick something up to fasten something to a place where it can be seen; to put something on display, especially by gluing, tacking, or stapling. ☐ *Stick this notice up. Put a copy on every bulletin board.* 🅃 *Please stick up this notice.*

stick something up to raise something; to hold something up. ☐ *She stuck her hand up because she knew the answer.* ☐ *The elephant stuck its trunk up and trumpeted.*

stick up to stand upright or on end; to thrust upward. ☐ *The ugly red flower stuck up from the bouquet.* ☐ *Why is the worst-looking flower sticking up above all the rest?* ☐ *The porcupines quills stuck up and rattled in the wind.*

stick up for someone or something to take the side of and support someone or something. ☐ *Don't worry. I will stick* *up for you!* □ *We all stuck up for our school.*

STICK ▸ WITH

stick someone with someone or something to burden someone with someone or something. □ *Please don't stick me with your little nephew for the day!* □ *I'm sorry I had to stick you with the problem.*

stick with someone or something to remain with or accompany someone or a group. □ *Stick with me and do what I do.* □ *I will have to stick with the tour group or I will get lost.*

STIFFEN ▸ UP

stiffen something up to make something rigid or tense. □ *He added a little starch to the rinse water to stiffen his collars up a bit.* 🆃 *The cold draft has stiffened up my neck.*

stiffen up to become stiff. □ *The bread dough stiffened up as it got cold.* □ *My knees began to stiffen up after I sat still for an hour.*

STIGMATIZE ▸ AS

stigmatize someone as something to brand or label someone as something. □ *The opposition will try to stigmatize you as a spendthrift.* □ *Tony was stigmatized as a poor loser.*

STIMULATE ▸ INTO

stimulate someone or something into something to excite or cause someone or some creature to do something. □ *They stimulated the workers into higher productivity for the week.* □ *The morning light stimulates the birds into singing.*

STING ▸ FOR

sting someone for something to cheat someone of a particular amount. (Slang.) □ *That guy stung me for twenty bucks!* □ *Toby was stung for the lunch bill.*

STING ▸ WITH

sting someone with something to use something to sting someone. □ *The bee stung me with its stinger.* □ *The wasp can sting you with its poisonous barb.*

STINK ▸ ON

stink on ice to be really rotten. (Slang. Refers to something that is rotten [or simply undesirable] even though it has been kept on ice.) □ *This play really stinks on ice.* □ *This whole business stinks on ice.*

STINK ▸ TO

stink to high heaven to smell very bad. (Colloquial.) □ *What are you cooking? It stinks to high heaven!* □ *This place stinks to high heaven. Open some windows and air it out.*

STINK ▸ UP

stink something up to make something or some place smell very bad. □ *Your cooking really stunk the place up!* 🆃 *The onions will stink up the whole house.*

STINK ▸ WITH

stink with something to smell very bad with the smell of something. □ *The room stinks with a garlicky smell.* □ *Our garden stinks with the smell of something rotting.*

STIR ▸ AROUND

stir something around to agitate or mix a liquid substance by moving it in a circular motion. □ *Stir the mixture around to mix it up.* □ *You should stir the dressing around a bit before you serve it.*

STIR ▸ (IN)TO

stir someone (in)to something to excite someone into doing something. (*Someone* includes *oneself*.) □ *The events of the day stirred everyone into action.* □ *The danger stirred them to action.* □ *Finally, they stirred themselves to action.*

STIR ▸ IN(TO)

stir something in(to something) to mix something into something. □ *The painter stirred too much red pigment into the paint.* 🆃 *The painter stirred in the pigment.* □ *When should I stir the eggs in?*

STIR ▸ UP

stir someone up to get someone excited; to get someone angry. □ *The march music really stirred the audience* *up.* [T] *The march stirred up the audience.*

stir something up 1. to mix something by stirring. □ *Please stir the pancake batter up before you use it.* [T] *Please stir up the batter.* 2. to foment trouble. □ *Why are you always trying to stir trouble up?* [T] *Are you stirring up trouble again?*

stir up a hornet's nest to create a lot of trouble. □ *If you say that to her, you will be stirring up a hornet's nest.* □ *There is no need to stir up a hornet's nest.*

STITCH ▶ ON(TO)

stitch something on(to something) to sew something onto the surface of something else. □ *Fred stitched the badge onto his jacket.* [T] *Fred stitched on the badge.* □ *He stitched the badge on.*

STITCH ▶ UP

stitch something up to sew something together; to mend a tear or ripped seam. □ *I tore my shirt. Would you stitch it up, please?* [T] *Please stitch up my shirt.*

STOCK ▶ UP

stock something (up) with something See under *STOCK ▶ WITH.*

stock up (on something) to build up a supply of something in particular. □ *I need to stock up on food for the party.* □ *We need fresh vegetables. We will have to stock up before the weekend.*

stock up (with something) to build up a supply of something. □ *You had better stock up with firewood before the first snowstorm.* □ *Yes, I will stock up today.*

STOCK ▶ WITH

stock something (up) with something to load something with a supply of something. □ *Let's stock the wine cellar with good vintages this year.* □ *They stocked their cellars up with the finest of wines.* [T] *We will stock up our wine cellar with whatever is on sale.*

STOKE ▶ ON

See *be stoked on someone or something* under *BE ▶ ON.*

STOKE ▶ UP

stoke something up 1. to poke a fire to make it burn hotter. □ *Grandpa had to go down each winter morning to stoke the fire up.* [T] *He stoked up the furnace every morning during the winter.* 2. to start something, such as an engine. (Slang.) □ *Stoke this old car up so we can leave.* [T] *Stoke up your motorcycle and let's get going.*

STOMP ▶ ON

stomp on someone 1. to stamp someone down. □ *The angry crowd knocked him down and stomped on him.* □ *The crowd stomped on the mugger.* 2. to repress someone. (Figurative.) □ *Every time I get a good idea, the boss stomps on me.* □ *Don't stomp on her every time she says something.*

STOOP ▶ DOWN

stoop down to dip, duck, or squat down. □ *I had to stoop down to enter the tiny door.* □ *Stoop down so you don't bump your head.*

STOOP ▶ OVER

stoop over to bend over. □ *Carl stooped over to pick up his napkin and lost his balance.* □ *As he stooped over, he lost his balance and fell.*

STOOP ▶ TO

stoop to doing something to lower oneself to doing something that ought to be beneath one. □ *I wouldn't stoop to doing anything so horrible.* □ *She wouldn't stoop to running away without paying!*

STOP ▶ AT

stop at nothing to fail to keep oneself from doing things that are illegal or immoral. □ *Tom will stop at nothing to get his own way.* □ *Max would stop at nothing to win the race.*

stop at something 1. to go as far as something and then stop. □ *I will stop at the end of the road.* □ *The road stopped at the base of a mountain.* 2. to stop briefly at something and then continue. (See also under *STOP ▶ OFF.*) □ *I have to stop at the store for a minute.* □ *Do you mind if I stop at a drug store?* 3. to spend the night at something. (Typically with *motel, inn, bed and breakfast,* and *hotel.*) □ *We stopped at a nice little inn for the night.* □ *When we travel, we like to stop at hotels that are run by one of the national chains.*

STOP ▶ BEHIND

stop behind someone or something to bring oneself or one's vehicle to a stop behind someone or something. □ *I stopped behind Fred at the red light.* □ *Fred stopped behind a minivan.*

STOP ▶ BY

stop by (some place) to go to a place and stop and then continue. (The *some place* may be any expression of a location.) □ *Stop by my place for dinner sometime.* □ *Please stop by before the end of the day.*

STOP ▶ FOR

stop for someone to halt one's vehicle to allow someone to get in. □ *I stopped for Jeff, but he didn't want a ride.* □ *I didn't have time to stop for you. I hope you will forgive me.*

stop for something to halt one's vehicle because of something or the need of something. □ *I had to stop for a red light.* □ *We stopped for some gas.*

STOP ▶ FROM

stop someone from doing something to prevent someone from doing something. (*Someone* includes *oneself.*) □ *I can't stop her from running away.* □ *They couldn't stop themselves from eating.*

STOP ▶ IN

stop dead in one's tracks to stop suddenly because of fear. (The creature that stops is not dead.) □ *I stopped dead in my tracks when I heard the scream.* □ *The deer stopped dead in its tracks when it heard the hunter step on a fallen branch.*

stop in (some place) to pay a brief visit to a place. □ *Do you want to stop in Adamsville or just drive on through?* □ *Let's stop in for a few minutes.*

stop one or something dead in one's or something's tracks to stop someone or something suddenly and completely. □ *The gunshot stopped the killer dead in her tracks.* □ *The arrow stopped the deer dead in its tracks.* □ *The sound of gunfire stopped me dead in my tracks.*

STOP ▶ OF

stop short of something **1.** to stop before reaching something. □ *She stopped short of the back wall of the garage.* □ *The train stopped short of the end of the track.* **2.** to stop before doing something. □ *She stopped short of crashing through the wall.* □ *Ted stopped short of striking his brother.*

STOP ▶ OFF

stop off (some place) (for a period of time) to halt or pause for a certain period of time. □ *I need to stop off for a rest.* □ *Let's find a little town and stop off.* □ *I have to stop off at the store for a minute.* □ *We stopped off for a while at the park.*

STOP ▶ ON

stop on a dime to stop suddenly. (Figurative.) □ *This car will stop on a dime.* □ *My bicycle will stop on a dime except when it's raining.*

stop on something to go as far as something [on the floor or the ground] and then stop. □ *Please stop on the line.* □ *You are supposed to stop on the white line or behind it.*

STOP ▶ OVER

stop over (some place) to stay one or more nights at a place. □ *We stopped over in Miami for one night.* □ *We had to stop over, but we stayed in a very nice hotel.* Ⓝ *We had a brief stopover in Atlanta.*

STOP ▶ TO

stop to do something to stop briefly to do something. □ *I have to stop to tie my shoes.* □ *Tex stopped to water his horse.*

STOP ▶ UP

stop something up [for something] to clog something; [for something] to plug something up. □ *The leaves that had fallen in the night clogged the storm sewer up.* Ⓣ *The leaves stopped up the sewer.* Ⓣ *The bacon grease stopped up the sink.*

stop something up (with something) to plug something with something. □ *Gary stopped the sink up with bacon grease.* 🅃 *He stopped up the sink with bacon grease.* □ *Try not to stop the sink up.*

stop up [for something] to become clogged. □ *The sink stopped up again!* 🄰 *What am I going to do with this stopped-up sink?*

STORE ▸ AWAY

store something away to put something away for future use; to set something aside. □ *Store the extra rice away for use next week.* 🅃 *Please store away the extra food.*

STORE ▸ IN

store something in something to set something aside in something. □ *Can I store my bicycle in your garage?* □ *Do you mind if I store my coat in your locker?*

STORE ▸ UP

store something up to build up and lay away a supply of something. □ *The bears will store fat up for the long winter.* 🅃 *They store up fat for the winter.*

STORM ▸ AROUND

storm around to go about in a fury. (Figurative.) □ *What is he storming around about?* □ *Martin was storming around all morning because he lost his car keys.*

STORM ▸ AT

storm at someone or something to direct one's anger at someone or something. (Figurative.) □ *She stormed at him because he was late again.* □ *Richard was storming at the cat again.*

STORM ▸ IN(TO)

storm in(to some place) to burst into something or some place angrily. □ *The army stormed into the town and took many of the citizens as prisoners.* □ *Leonard stormed in, shouting at everyone.*

STORM ▸ OUT

storm out (of some place) to burst out of some place angrily. □ *Carol stormed out of the office in a rage.* □ *She got mad and stormed out.*

STOW ▸ AWAY

stow away to conceal oneself in a vehicle, originally a ship, in order to travel without paying. □ *Don got to this country by stowing away on a cargo ship.* 🄽 *The crew found a stowaway in the engine room.*

stow something away to pack something away. □ *I have to stow my clothes away before I go to bed.* 🅃 *Please stow away your things and get right to work.*

STRAIGHTEN ▸ OUT

straighten out 1. to become straight. □ *The road finally straightened out.* □ *The train tracks straightened out on the plain.* **2.** to improve one's behavior or attitude. □ *I hope he straightens out before he gets himself into real trouble.* □ *Fred had better straighten out soon if he wants to get a job.*

straighten someone or something out to make someone's body or something straight or orderly. (*Someone* includes *oneself*.) □ *The undertaker straightened Sam out in his coffin.* 🅃 *The undertaker straightened out the corpse in the coffin.* □ *Can you straighten this spoon out?* □ *Straighten yourself out and see if your bed is going to be long enough.*

straighten someone out 1. to cause someone to behave better or to have a better attitude. (*Someone* includes *oneself*. See also the previous entry.) □ *You are terrible. Someone is going to have to straighten you out!* 🅃 *The principal straightened out the troublesome boys.* □ *If you don't straighten yourself out, I'll have to ask you to leave.* **2.** to help someone become less confused about something. □ *Can you straighten me out on this matter?* 🅃 *I will do what I can to straighten out the office staff on this question.*

straighten something out 1. to make something straighter. □ *I can't straighten this row of books out.* 🅃 *Please straighten out this line of people.* **2.** to bring order to something that is disorderly. □ *See if you can straighten this* *mess out.* 🅃 *Will you straighten out this mess?*

STRAIGHTEN ► UP

straighten someone or something up to make someone or something become close to vertical. □ *The nurse straightened the invalid up and gave him some soup.* 🅃 *Try to straighten up the tree before you pack in the dirt around its roots.*

straighten something up to make something less messy. □ *This room is a mess. Please straighten it up.* 🅃 *Can you straighten up this room?*

straighten up **1.** to sit or stand more vertically. □ *Please straighten up. Don't slouch.* □ *I have to remind Timmy constantly to straighten up.* **2.** to behave better. □ *Come on! Straighten up or I will send you home!* □ *I wish you would straighten up. Your behavior is very bad.*

straighten up and fly right to improve one's behavior or attitude and perform better. (Colloquial. Originally referred to an airplane.) □ *If you want to keep out of trouble, you had better straighten up and fly right.* □ *Straighten up and fly right or I will send you to the principal.*

STRAIN ► AFTER

strain after something [for a singer] to work very hard to reach a very high or a very low note. □ *Don't strain after the note. Let it come naturally, like a cooling breeze.* □ *She was straining after each note as if it hurt her to sing, which it probably did.*

STRAIN ► AT

strain at the leash **1.** [for a dog] to pull very hard on its leash. □ *It's hard to walk Fido, because he is always straining at the leash.* □ *I wish that this dog would not strain at the leash. It's very hard on me.* **2.** [for a person] to want to move ahead with things, aggressively and independently. (Figurative.) □ *She wants to get started right away. She is straining at the leash to get started.* □ *Paul is straining at the leash to get on the job.*

STRAIN ► AWAY

strain away (at something) to work very hard, continuously, at doing something. □ *She strained away at her weights, getting stronger every day.* □ *She was straining away when we came in.*

STRAIN ► FOR

strain for an effect to work very hard to try to achieve some effect. □ *The actors were straining so hard for an effect that they forgot their lines.* □ *Don't strain for effect so much. The authors of this drama knew what they were doing, and it's in the lines already.*

STRAIN ► OFF

strain something off (of something) to remove the excess liquid from something. (The *of*-phrase is paraphrased with a *from*-phrase when the particle is transposed. See the 🄵 example.) □ *The cook strained the grease off the cooking juices.* 🅃 *The cook strained off the grease.* 🄵 *The cook strained off the grease from the pan.*

STRAIN ► THROUGH

strain something through something to filter a liquid or a watery substance by pouring it through something. □ *Tony strained the strawberry jelly through cheesecloth.* □ *We will have to strain the clabber to take out the curds.*

STRAND ► ON

strand someone on something to abandon someone on something from which there is no escape. □ *The shipwreck stranded our little group on a deserted beach.* □ *We were stranded on the little island by a storm.*

STRAP ► DOWN

strap someone or something down to tie or bind someone or something down to something. □ *The nurses strapped Gary down in preparation for the operation.* 🅃 *They strapped down the patient and gave him a sedative.* □ *The vet strapped the dog down.*

STRAP ► FOR

See *be strapped for something* under *BE ► FOR.*

STRAP ▶ IN(TO)

strap someone or something in((to) something) to tie or bind someone, a creature, or something into something. (*Someone* includes *oneself*.) ☐ *Mother strapped little Jimmy into his seat.* 🅃 *She strapped in Jimmy.* ☐ *Jamie opened the car trunk and strapped the tire jack in where she had found it.* ☐ *Please strap yourself into your seat.*

STRAP ▶ ON(TO)

strap something on(to someone or something) to tie or bind something onto someone or something. ☐ *The hiker strapped the load onto her partner.* 🅃 *She strapped on the load.* ☐ *Jane strapped the load onto the top of the car.*

STRAY ▶ AWAY

See the following entry.

STRAY ▶ FROM

stray (away) (from something) to drift away from or wander away from a particular topic or location. (The option elements cannot be transposed.) ☐ *Please don't stray from the general area of discussion.* ☐ *Sally strayed from her topic a number of times.* ☐ *Don't stray away from the tourist areas of the city.* ☐ *Please don't stray away. Stay right here.* ☐ *The cat strayed away, but that's okay.* ☐ *I tried to keep her to her topic, but she kept straying away.* ☐ *Jane strayed away and got lost.*

STRAY ▶ IN(TO)

stray in(to something) to wander into something. ☐ *The cows strayed into the town and ruined almost everyone's garden.* ☐ *We left the gate open, and the cows strayed in and drank from the pond.*

STRAY ▶ ONTO

stray onto something to wander onto an area, such as a parcel of land. ☐ *Your cows strayed onto my land and ate my marigolds!* ☐ *If your horse strays onto my land one more time, it's my horse!*

STREAK ▶ ACROSS

streak across something to move across something very fast. ☐ *A comet streaked across the night sky.* ☐ *Tom streaked across the street to get a cup of coffee.*

STREAM ▶ DOWN

stream down (on someone or something) [for a liquid or light] to flow downward onto someone or something. ☐ *The water streamed down on all of them.* ☐ *The light broke through the clouds and streamed down on all of them.* ☐ *It streamed down and soaked them all.*

STREAM ▶ IN(TO)

stream in(to something) to flow or rush into something. ☐ *The people streamed into the hall, each seeking the best possible seat.* ☐ *Water streamed into the room from the broken pipe.* ☐ *Complaints about the performance streamed in.*

STRETCH ▶ AWAY

stretch away (from something) to extend away from something. ☐ *A vast plain stretched away from the riverbank.* ☐ *The plain stretched away as far as we could see.*

stretch away to some place to extend as far as some place. ☐ *The forest stretched away to the horizon.* ☐ *The river stretched away to the sea.*

STRETCH ▶ FORTH

stretch forth (from something) to extend out or forth from something. ☐ *A path stretched forth from the cabin, leading deep into the woods.* ☐ *Outside the cabin door, a path stretched forth.*

STRETCH ▶ OUT

stretch out [for one] to extend and stretch one's body to its full length. ☐ *She lay down, stretched out, and relaxed for the first time in days.* ☐ *I need a bigger bed. I can't stretch out in this one.*

stretch out to someone or something to extend as far as someone or something. ☐ *His arm stretched out to the guy next to him and established the correct amount of separation in the ranks.* ☐ *The beach stretched out to the horizon.*

stretch someone or something out to extend or draw out someone or something. (*Someone* includes *oneself*.) ☐ *Molly stretched the baby out to change* *his clothes.* 🅃 *She stretched out the baby, who had rolled into a ball.* ☐ *Stretch the chicken out and skin it.* 🄰 *Please stay off the stretched-out parachute.* ☐ *Stretch yourself out and be comfortable.*

stretch something out (to someone or something) to reach something out to someone or something. ☐ *Jeff stretched his hand out to Tiffany.* 🅃 *He stretched out his hand to the visitor.* ☐ *The visitor approached and stretched her hand out.* 🄰 *She fell into his outstretched arms.*

STREW ▸ ON

strew something on someone or something to sow or spread something on someone or something. ☐ *The wind strewed the dandelion seeds on Fred and his friends.* ☐ *A child went down the aisle, strewing flowers on the white walkway ahead of the bride.*

STREW ▸ OVER

strew something (all) over something to sow or spread something over an area. ☐ *Clean this place up! You have strewn your clothing all over the place.* ☐ *The wind strewed the leaves over the lawns.*

strew something over someone or something to spread or scatter something over someone or something. ☐ *The silo explosion strewed the grain over everyone in the vicinity.* ☐ *The explosion strewed wreckage over a two-block area.*

STREW ▸ WITH

strew something with something to cover something with bits of something. ☐ *Who strewed the sidewalk with rice and confetti?* ☐ *The yards were strewn with leaves and branches after the storm.*

STRICKEN ▸ WITH

See *be stricken with something* under *BE ▸ WITH.*

STRIDE ▸ IN(TO)

stride in(to some place) to walk with long steps into some place. ☐ *Jeff strode into the restaurant and demanded the best table.* ☐ *He strode in and ordered roast chicken.*

STRIDE ▸ OUT

stride out of some place to walk with long steps out of some place. ☐ *The angry customer strode out of the shop without purchasing anything.* ☐ *We strode out of the restaurant, pledging never to go there again.*

STRIKE ▸ AGAINST

strike (out) against someone or something to hit against someone or something. ☐ *The frightened child struck out against the teacher.* ☐ *He struck against what he perceived as a threat.*

STRIKE ▸ AS

strike someone as something to impress someone as something or a type of person. (Figurative.) ☐ *You strike me as thoughtful.* ☐ *You don't strike me as the type of person to do something like that.*

STRIKE ▸ AT

strike at someone or something to hit at or toward someone or something. ☐ *She struck at him, but he parried the blows.* ☐ *The bear struck at the branch, hoping to break it and get at the honey.*

STRIKE ▸ BACK

strike back (at someone or something) to return the blows of someone or something; to return the attack of someone or something. ☐ *The victim struck back at the mugger and scared him away.* ☐ *The victim struck back in the courts.*

STRIKE ▸ DOWN

strike someone or something down to knock someone or something down by striking. ☐ *Max struck Lefty down with one blow.* 🅃 *He struck down the weeds with a scythe.*

strike something down [for a court] to invalidate a law. ☐ *The higher court struck the ruling of the lower court down.* 🅃 *The court struck down the ruling.*

STRIKE ▸ FOR

strike for something to conduct a work stoppage in order to gain something. ☐ *The workers were striking for longer vacations.* ☐ *We are striking for fundamental human rights.*

STRIKE ▸ FROM

strike someone or something from something to remove someone or something from something, such as a list. □ *I will have to strike David from our rolls. He never shows up.* □ *We struck the red car from the list of eligible racers.*

STRIKE ▸ INTO

strike something into something to knock something, such as a ball, into something. □ *Johnny struck the ball into the vacant lot.* □ *Ted struck golf ball after golf ball into the water.*

STRIKE ▸ OFF

strike something off ((of) someone or something) to knock something off someone or something. (The *of*-phrase is paraphrased with a *from*-phrase when the particle is transposed. The *of* is colloquial.) □ *She accidentally struck John's hat off of him.* T *She struck off a chunk.* F *Sarah struck off a chunk from the wall.* □ *She struck a chunk off.*

STRIKE ▸ ON

strike someone or something on something to hit someone or something on a particular place or part. (*Someone* includes *oneself*.) □ *The ball struck me on my elbow, causing a great deal of pain.* □ *I struck the bear on the paw, and that only made it madder.* □ *She almost struck herself on her head.*

strike something (up)on something to hit or bang something on something else. □ *She struck her head upon the side of the bed.* □ *Mary struck her elbow on the doorjamb.*

STRIKE ▸ OUT

strike out 1. [for a baseball player] to accumulate three strikes. □ *Jeff struck out for the fourth time this season.* □ *I knew I would strike out this inning.* **2.** to have a series of failures. (Figurative.) □ *It was a hard job. Finally I struck out and had to go into another line of work.* □ *I keep striking out when it comes to the opposite sex.*

strike (out) against someone or something See under *STRIKE ▸ AGAINST.*

strike out (at someone or something) to hit at someone or something with the intention of threatening or harming. □ *Dave would strike out at anyone who came near him, but it was all bluff.* □ *He was mad, and when anyone came close, he struck out.*

strike out for some place to begin a journey to some place; to set out on a journey for some place. □ *We struck out for Denver, hoping to get there in a few hours.* □ *The hikers struck out for the cabin, but were delayed by a sudden storm.*

strike someone out [for a baseball pitcher] to pitch three strikes on a batter. □ *Jeff struck batter after batter out.* T *He struck out another batter.* A *The second Walter had pitched the strikeout pitch, the crowd began to cheer.* N *After the third strikeout, Walter left the mound.*

strike something out to cross something out of a section of printing or writing. □ *This is wrong. Please strike it out.* T *Strike out this sentence.*

STRIKE ▸ OVER

strike over something [for a typist] to blot out a section of typing by typing over it. □ *Please don't strike over your errors. Erase them altogether.* □ *Betty struck over most of the misspellings.* N *There are too many strikeovers on this page.*

STRIKE ▸ UP

strike something up to begin something; to cause something to begin. (Typically, the band, a conversation, or a friendship.) □ *We tried to strike a conversation up—to no avail.* T *I struck up a conversation with Molly.*

STRIKE ▸ WITH

See *be stricken with something* under *BE ▸ WITH.*

strike home with someone [for something] to awaken recognition and acceptance in a person. (Idiomatic.) □ *What you said really strikes home with me.* □ *Her comments struck home with her audience.*

strike someone or something with something to hit someone or something with something. (*Someone* includes *oneself*.) ☐ *Max struck Lefty with his fist.* ☐ *The mayor struck the table with his fist.* ☐ *He struck himself with the hammer by accident.*

STRING ▸ ALONG

string along (with someone) 1. to follow with someone. ☐ *Do you mind if I string along with you?* ☐ *I don't mind if you string along.* 2. to agree with someone's policies and actions. ☐ *Okay. I will string along with you this time, but I don't know about the future.* ☐ *I would appreciate it if you would string along just this one time.*

string someone along to maintain someone's attention or interest, probably insincerely. ☐ *You are just stringing me along because you like to borrow my car. You are not a real friend.* ☐ *Rachel strung her along for the sake of old times.*

STRING ▸ OUT

string something out 1. to unravel something, such as string, and extend it. ☐ *The workers strung the wires out before installing them.* 🅃 *They strung out the wires first.* 2. to cause something to be longer than it ought to be. ☐ *Is there any good reason to string this meeting out any longer?* 🅃 *Don't string out the meetings so long.*

STRING ▸ TOGETHER

string something together to connect things, such as beads, together, as with string. ☐ *I spent all afternoon stringing beads together.* ☐ *My pearls broke and I had to take them to a jeweler to have them strung together again.*

STRING ▸ UP

string someone up to hang someone. (Colloquial.) ☐ *The sheriff swore he would string Tex up whenever he caught him.* 🅃 *He never strung up Tex.*

STRIP ▸ AWAY

strip something away (from someone or something) to remove or peel something from someone or something. ☐ *The emergency room nurse stripped the clothing away from the burn victim.* 🅃 *He stripped away the victim's clothing.* 🅃 *Jamie stripped away the old paint from the bathroom wall.* ☐ *He stripped it away.*

STRIP ▸ DOWN

strip down to remove one's clothing. ☐ *The doctor told Joe to strip down for his examination.* ☐ *Joe stripped down for the examination.*

strip someone or something down (to something) to remove the covering of someone or something down to the lowest level. (*Someone* includes *oneself*.) ☐ *The emergency room nurse stripped the unconscious patient down to his shorts.* 🅃 *He stripped down the patient to his underwear.* ☐ *He stripped the patient down.* ☐ *He stripped himself down and went for a swim.* ☐ *Ruth stripped the turkey down to the bones.*

STRIP ▸ FOR

strip for something to take off one's clothing for something. ☐ *Todd went into the locker room and stripped for his shower.* ☐ *All the recruits stripped for their medical examination.*

STRIP ▸ IN

strip something in to insert something into a line of print. ☐ *You will have to strip the accent in.* 🅃 *Strip in a grave accent right here.*

STRIP ▸ OF

strip someone or something of something to take something, such as status or property, away from someone or something. ☐ *The court stripped him of all his property.* ☐ *We stripped him of his rights when we put him in jail.*

STRIP ▸ OFF

strip something off ((of) someone or something) to tear something from someone or something. (The *of*-phrase is paraphrased with a *from*-phrase when the particle is transposed. See the 🄵 example. The *of* is colloquial.) ☐ *The paramedic stripped the shirt off the burn victim and began to treat her burns.* 🅃 *The medic stripped off the patient's shirt.* 🄵 *The medic stripped off the shirt from the victim.* ☐ *She stripped the* *shirt off.* Ⓐ *The stripped-off clothes were piled in the corner.*

STRIP ▸ TO

strip to something to take off one's clothing down to a particular level, usually to one's skin, the waist, or some euphemistic way of expressing nudity or near nudity. ☐ *Tom stripped to the waist and continued to labor in the hot sun.* ☐ *Tom stripped to the bare essentials and got ready to be examined by the doctor.*

STRIVE ▸ AFTER

strive after something to try very hard to obtain something. ☐ *I am always striving after perfection.* ☐ *Ted was striving after a promotion and finally got it.*

STRIVE ▸ AGAINST

strive against something to work against something. ☐ *He worked hard, striving against failure at every turn.* ☐ *Things were difficult. I had to strive against quitting almost every day.*

STRIVE ▸ FOR

strive for something to try to obtain or bring about something. ☐ *I am striving for the best possible result.* ☐ *Mary strives for perfection in everything she does.*

STRIVE ▸ TO

strive to do something to try hard to do something. ☐ *She strove very hard to do what she had set out to do.* ☐ *Please strive to do it as best you can.*

STRIVE ▸ TOWARD

strive toward something to work toward a goal. ☐ *I always strive toward perfection.* ☐ *Mary strove toward doing her best at all times.*

STROLL ▸ AROUND

stroll around to walk around casually. ☐ *I think I will stroll around a bit this evening.* ☐ *Would you like to stroll around a little and see the sights?*

STROLL ▸ THROUGH

stroll through something to walk casually through something or some place. ☐ *Would you like to stroll through the park with me?* ☐ *Let's stroll through a few shops and see what the prices are like here.*

STRUGGLE ▸ AGAINST

struggle against someone or something to strive or battle against someone or something. ☐ *There is no point in struggling against me. I will win out.* ☐ *He struggled against the disease for a year before he died.*

STRUGGLE ▸ ALONG

struggle along under something to make do as well as one can under a particular burden. ☐ *I will have to struggle along under these poor conditions for quite a while.* ☐ *I am sorry you have to struggle along under such burdens.*

struggle along (with someone or something) to make do as well as one can with someone or something. ☐ *I really need someone who can type faster, but I'll struggle along with Walter.* ☐ *We struggled along the best we could.*

STRUGGLE ▸ FOR

struggle for something to strive to obtain something. ☐ *I was struggling for a law degree when I won the lottery.* ☐ *I had to struggle for everything that came my way.*

STRUGGLE ▸ ON

struggle on with something to make do as well as one can with something. ☐ *I will have to struggle on with the car that I have.* ☐ *We will struggle on with what we have, hoping for better someday.*

STRUGGLE ▸ THROUGH

struggle through (something) to get through something in the best way possible. ☐ *I am going to struggle through this dull book to the very end.* ☐ *The book was dull, but I struggled through.*

STRUGGLE ▸ TO

struggle to do something to strive or battle to do something. ☐ *She struggled hard to meet her deadlines.* ☐ *We had to struggle to make ends meet.*

STRUGGLE ▸ WITH

struggle with someone for something to fight with someone to obtain something. ☐ *Max struggled with Lefty for the gun, and it went off.* ☐ *Timmy* *struggled with Bobby for the bicycle, and finally David took it away from both of them.*

struggle with someone or something to fight or battle with someone or something. □ *Fred struggled with Tom for a while and finally gave in.* □ *Tom struggled with the disease for a while and finally succumbed to it.*

STRUM ▸ ON

strum something on something to brush or play with the fingers some stringed instrument, such as a guitar. □ *She strummed a nice little melody on her guitar.* □ *He strummed the accompaniment on the guitar with one hand and picked the melody out on the piano with the other.*

STRUT ▸ AROUND

strut around to stride around pompously. □ *Stop strutting around in your new jeans and get to work!* □ *Tex was strutting around, showing off his new boots.*

STRUT ▸ IN(TO)

strut in(to some place) to stride pompously into a place. □ *He strutted into the house as if he owned the place.* □ *Betty strutted in and sat down.*

STRUT ▸ OUT

strut out of some place to stride pompously out of some place. □ *The clowns strutted out of the tent and joined the parade through the big top.* □ *Tex strutted out of the saloon and got on his horse.*

STUB ▸ AGAINST

stub one's toe against something to ram one's toe accidentally against some hard object. □ *Don't stub your toe against that brick in the path.* □ *Claire stubbed her toe against one of the legs of the sofa.*

STUB ▸ ON

stub one's toe on something to ram one's toe accidentally into some hard object. □ *I stubbed my toe on the bottom step.* □ *Don't stub your toe on the broken sidewalk.*

STUB ▸ OUT

stub something out to put out something, such as a cigarette or cigar, by butting the burning end against a hard object. □ *Max stubbed his cigar out and tossed it into the street.* 🅃 *He stubbed out his cigar.*

STUCK ▸ ON

See *be stuck on someone or something* under *BE ▸ ON.*

STUDY ▸ FOR

study for something to try to learn in preparation for an examination. □ *I have to study for my calculus exam.* □ *Have you studied for your exam yet?*

STUDY ▸ UP

study up on someone or something to learn all one can about someone or something. □ *I have to study up on Abraham Lincoln in preparation for my speech.* □ *John studied up on seashells.*

STUFF ▸ DOWN

stuff something down someone's throat to force someone to hear, learn, endure, etc., some kind of information. (Colloquial.) □ *I don't like the nonsense they are stuffing down our throats.* □ *Please don't try to stuff those lies down our throats.*

stuff something down something to force something down inside of something. □ *Don stuffed the cauliflower leaves down the garbage disposal and turned it on.* □ *Timmy stuffed the extra toothpaste down the drain and turned the water on to wash it away.*

STUFF ▸ IN

stuff a sock in it AND **put a sock in it** to be quiet; to shut up. (Slang.) □ *Shut up! Stuff a sock in it!* □ *Be quiet! Put a sock in it!*

STUFF ▸ IN(TO)

stuff someone or something in(to someone or something) to force someone or something into someone or something. (*Someone* includes *oneself.*) □ *The sheriff stuffed Tex into the tiny cell.* 🅃 *He stuffed in some other prisoners too.* □ *Donna got down her suitcase and stuffed her clothes in.* □ *The nurse* *stuffed the oatmeal into the old man faster than he could swallow it.* □ *She really stuffed in the oatmeal.* □ *He stuffed himself into his costume and ran on stage.*

STUFF ▸ UP

stuff something up to plug something by stuffing something in its opening. □ *He stuffed the hole up with old newspapers.* 🅃 *Liz stuffed up the hole with paper.*

stuff something up something to force something upwards or up into something. □ *He tried to hide the book by stuffing it up the chimney.* □ *Sam stuffed the money he found up the downspout, where he thought no one would find it.*

STUFF ▸ WITH

stuff someone or something with something to fill up someone or something with something. (*Someone* includes *oneself.*) □ *She stuffed the kids with pancakes and sent them to school.* □ *Dale stuffed the doll with fluffy material and gave it back to Timmy.* □ *He was afraid he would stuff himself with food as he usually did.*

stuff someone's head with something to fill someone's brain with certain kinds of thoughts. □ *Who has been stuffing your head with that nonsense?* □ *Tex thought that the government was stuffing peoples' heads with all sorts of propaganda.*

STUMBLE ▸ ACROSS

stumble across someone or something to find or discover someone or something. (As if one were walking along and tripped on the thing discovered. Not necessarily while walking.) □ *Guess whom I stumbled across today.* □ *I stumbled across an interesting little store today.*

STUMBLE ▸ INTO

stumble into someone or something to trip and lurch into someone or something. □ *Not seeing the brick in the path, Carl tripped and stumbled into Alice.* □ *Jamie stumbled into the wall.*

STUMBLE ▸ ON

See also under *STUMBLE ▸ ON(TO).*

stumble on someone or something to trip on someone or something. □ *I stumbled on Jeff, who was sleeping on the floor.* □ *I stumbled on a brick and fell.*

STUMBLE ▸ ON(TO)

stumble on(to) someone or something to find someone or something by accident. □ *I stumbled onto Jeff, who had come to town to shop for shoes.* □ *We stumbled on a new route while we were driving the other day.*

STUMBLE ▸ OVER

stumble over someone or something to trip over someone or something. □ *Tom stumbled over Bill, who was napping on the floor.* □ *Don't stumble over the laundry basket.*

STUMBLE ▸ THROUGH

stumble through something to get through a sequence of something awkwardly and falteringly. □ *The cast stumbled through the first act and barely finished the second.* □ *Mary stumbled through her speech and fled from the stage.*

STUMP ▸ FOR

stump for someone to go about making political speeches in support of someone. □ *The vice president was out stumping for members of Congress who were running this term.* □ *Since all the politicians were out stumping for one another, there was no one in the capital to vote on important legislation.*

SUB ▸ FOR

sub for someone or something to substitute for someone or something. □ *I have to sub for Roger at work this weekend.* □ *Will pliers sub for the wrench you wanted?*

sub someone for someone else or something for something else to substitute someone for someone else or something for something else. □ *I will sub Chuck for Roger for this next play only.* □ *We will sub the red ones for the blue ones.*

SUBDIVIDE ▸ INTO

subdivide something into something to divide something into parts. □ *They subdivided the land into several valuable parcels.* □ *Sam tried to subdivide his large lot into three smaller lots, but the zoning commission wouldn't let him do it.*

SUBJECT ▸ TO

subject someone or something to something to cause someone to endure someone or something. (*Someone* includes *oneself.*) □ *I didn't mean to subject you to Uncle Harry.* □ *I am sorry I have to subject you to all this questioning.* □ *They are unwilling to subject themselves to any further abuse.*

SUBJUGATE ▸ TO

subjugate someone to someone to suppress someone in someone else's favor. (*Someone* includes *oneself.*) □ *The army sought to subjugate everyone to the king.* □ *She had had to subjugate herself to her mother most of her life.*

SUBMERGE ▸ IN

submerge someone or something in something to immerse someone or something in a liquid. (*Someone* includes *oneself.*) □ *The preacher submerged Jeff in the water of the river as part of the baptism ceremony.* □ *Submerge the fish in the marinade for at least two hours.* □ *He looked forward to submerging himself in the hot bathwater.*

SUBMERGE ▸ UNDER

submerge someone or something under something to put someone or something below the surface of a liquid. (The *under* is considered redundant. *Someone* includes *oneself.*) □ *The maid submerged her mistress under the surface of the water for a moment and brought her up and dried her off.* □ *They submerged themselves under the surface of the water and had a look around.*

SUBMIT ▸ TO

submit someone or something to something to allow someone or something to undergo the effects of something. (*Someone* includes *oneself.*) □ *I hate to submit you to all this questioning, but that is the way we do things here.* □ *Don't submit your car to a lot of misuse.* □ *We did not want to submit the cat to a lot of pain.* □ *She will probably refuse to submit herself to surgery.*

submit to something to surrender to something; to agree to something. □ *He submitted to the cross examination.* □ *She will probably refuse to submit to surgery.*

SUBORDINATE ▸ TO

subordinate someone or something to someone or something else to put someone in an inferior position to someone else; to put something in an inferior position to something else. (*Someone* includes *oneself.*) □ *I am going to have to subordinate you to the other manager, because she has more experience.* □ *The first thing you learn is that you must subordinate yourself to your boss.* □ *Fred never learned to subordinate his needs to anyone else's.*

SUBPOENA ▸ TO

subpoena someone to do something to deliver a document forcing someone to do something. □ *The attorney subpoenaed a number of witnesses to testify.* □ *I subpoenaed four witnesses to appear and none of them showed up.*

SUBSCRIBE ▸ TO

subscribe to something **1.** to agree with a policy. □ *I don't subscribe to the scheme you have just described.* □ *You don't have to subscribe to the policy to accept it.* **2.** to hold a standing order for a magazine or other periodical. □ *I subscribe to three magazines, and I enjoy them all.* □ *I don't subscribe to any of them anymore.*

SUBSIST ▸ ON

subsist on something to exist on something; to stay alive on something. □ *We can only subsist on this amount of money. We need more!* □ *They are able to do no more than subsist on what Mrs. Harris is paid.*

SUBSTITUTE ▸ FOR

substitute for someone or something to serve as a replacement for someone or something. ☐ *I have to substitute for Roger at work this weekend.* ☐ *Do you think that this will substitute for the one you wanted?*

substitute someone for someone else or something for something else to exchange someone or something for someone or something; to replace someone or something with someone or something. ☐ *Shall I substitute Fred for Mary in the front office?* ☐ *Please substitute fish for beef on my dinner order.*

SUBTRACT ▸ FROM

subtract something from something to deduct or take away something from something else. ☐ *Please subtract the cost of the meal from my fee.* ☐ *I demanded that they subtract the extra charge from my bill.*

SUCCEED ▸ AS

succeed as something to flourish or prosper as a type of person. ☐ *I hope I succeed as a bank teller.* ☐ *Jamie succeeded as an investigator.*

succeed someone as something to take the place of someone as something; to supplant someone in something. (*Someone* includes *oneself*.) ☐ *Jeff will succeed Claude as president of the organization.* ☐ *You are not allowed to succeed yourself as president.*

SUCCEED ▸ AT

succeed at something to prosper or flourish in some task. ☐ *I hope I can succeed at the task you have assigned me.* ☐ *I am sure you will succeed at it.*

SUCCEED ▸ IN

succeed in something to prosper or flourish in some position or office. ☐ *I hope you succeed in your new job.* ☐ *We knew you would succeed in doing what you wanted to do.*

SUCCEED ▸ TO

succeed to something to fall heir to something; to take something over. ☐ *Carl will succeed to the throne when he is of age.* ☐ *Mary succeeded to the throne at the age of three months.*

SUCCUMB ▸ TO

succumb to something to yield to something, especially a temptation, fatal disease, a human weakness, etc. ☐ *He finally succumbed to his pneumonia.* ☐ *She did not succumb to the disease until the last.*

SUCK ▸ DOWN

suck someone or something down [for a vacuum or water currents] to drag someone or something downward. ☐ *The savage currents sucked the swimmers down to their death.* 🅃 *The current sucked down the floating trees.*

SUCK ▸ FROM

suck something from something to draw something out of something by the application of a vacuum. ☐ *Freddie used his straw to suck the last of the soda pop from the can.* ☐ *The machine sucked the water from the bottom of the barrel.*

SUCK ▸ IN

See also under *SUCK ▸ IN(TO).*

suck someone in to deceive someone; to convince someone to participate in a deceptive scheme. (Colloquial.) ☐ *Those crooks really sucked you in!* 🅃 *The con artists sucked in a number of people.*

suck something in **1.** to draw something into one's mouth by sucking. ☐ *She sucked the soda pop in so hard she nearly collapsed the straw.* 🅃 *Liz sucked in the fresh air.* **2.** to draw in one's belly, gut, or stomach. (Informal.) ☐ *Suck that belly in!* 🅃 *Suck in that gut!*

SUCK ▸ IN(TO)

suck someone or something in(to something) [for a vacuum] to draw someone or something into something. ☐ *The whirlpool sucked the swimmers into the depths of the river.* 🅃 *The whirlpool sucked in a swimmer.* ☐ *A whirlpool nearly sucked our canoe in.* ☐ *The vacuum cleaner sucked the dirt in well.*

SUCK ▸ UNDER

suck someone or something under [for current or waves] to pull someone or something beneath the surface of the water. ☐ *The strong current almost* *sucked me under!* □ *It almost sucked our boat under.*

SUCK ▸ UP

suck something up to pick something up by suction, as with a vacuum cleaner, or through a straw. □ *Will this vacuum suck all this dirt up?* 🅃 *The vacuum cleaner sucked up all the dirt.*

suck up to someone to act in a deferent or servile manner to someone. □ *Bob sucks up to the boss all the time.* □ *The candidates suck up to the voters.*

SUCKER ▸ IN(TO)

sucker someone in(to something) to deceive someone into some sort of scam or confidence game. (Colloquial.) □ *Surely you don't think you can sucker me into doing something as stupid as that, do you?* 🅃 *The con artist suckered in an unsuspecting tourist.* □ *You can't sucker me in again!*

SUE ▸ FOR

sue for something to file a lawsuit in order to get something. □ *If you so much as harm a hair on my head, I will sue for damages.* □ *Ted sued for back pay in his dispute with a former employer.*

sue someone for something to file a lawsuit against someone in order to get something. □ *I will sue you for damages if you do anything else to my car!* □ *She sued her employer for failure to provide a safe workplace.*

SUFFER ▸ FROM

suffer from something to endure or experience unpleasantness, a disease or a health condition. □ *Jeff is suffering from the flu.* □ *I'm afraid that you must suffer from the disease until it has run its course.* □ *Toby is really suffering from the cold.*

SUFFER ▸ UNDER

suffer under someone to endure the punishments or bad treatment of someone. □ *The citizens suffered badly under the rule of the cruel king.* □ *We suffered under Carlos and we will suffer under his successor.*

SUFFICE ▸ FOR

suffice for someone or something to be sufficient for someone or something. □ *This will suffice for me. Did you get enough?* □ *Will this suffice for you?* □ *That will suffice for the time being.*

SUFFIX ▸ ONTO

suffix something onto something to add an inflection or other part of a word onto another word. □ *The students were told to suffix the correct plural marker onto all the nouns in the list.* □ *What do you get when you suffix* -ed *onto a verb like* talk?

SUFFUSE ▸ WITH

suffuse something with something to saturate something with something, usually a color. □ *The sun suffused the afternoon sky with orange and yellow.* □ *The bright light suffused the leaves with a golden glow.*

SUGGEST ▸ TO

suggest itself to someone [for an idea] to seem to present itself to someone. □ *A new scheme suggested itself to Alice as she looked at the records of the last attempt.* □ *As you read this, does anything suggest itself to you?*

suggest something to someone to make a suggestion of something to someone. □ *The waiter suggested the roast beef to all his customers.* □ *What did you suggest to the people at the other table? They look quite pleased with their meal.*

SUIT ▸ FOR

See *be suited for something* under *BE ▸ FOR.*

SUIT ▸ TO

suit someone or something to something to match someone or something to something. □ *I am sorry, but we don't suit the worker to the job. We find a job that suits the worker.* □ *Let's try to suit a new sports jacket to the slacks you have on.*

SUIT ▸ UP

suit (oneself) up to get into one's uniform, especially an athletic uniform. □ *The coach told the team to suit up for the game by three o'clock.* □ *It's time to* *suit up!* □ *She suited herself up and went out on the court.*

SULK ▸ ABOUT

sulk about someone or something AND **sulk over someone or something** to pout or be sullen about someone or something. □ *What are you sulking about now?* □ *There is no need to sulk over Mary.*

SULK ▸ OVER

sulk over something See the previous entry.

SUM ▸ UP

sum (something) up to give a summary of something. □ *I would like to sum this lecture up by listing the main points I have covered.* □ *It is time for me to sum up.* 🅃 *She summed up the president's speech in three sentences.*

SUMMON ▸ BEFORE

summon someone before someone or something to request or order someone to appear before someone or a group. □ *The president summoned the committee before her.* □ *The judge summoned Donna before the court.*

SUMMON ▸ TO

summon someone to someone or something to order or request someone to come to someone or something. □ *Uncle Fred summoned the waitress to him.* □ *He summoned her to our table.*

SUMMON ▸ UP

summon something up to call forth particular qualities, such as strength, courage, wisdom, etc. □ *She summoned her courage up and went into the room.* 🅃 *Liz summoned up all her courage.*

SUPERIMPOSE ▸ ON(TO)

superimpose something on(to) someone or something to cover an image of someone or something with an image of something. □ *We superimposed a mustache onto Toby's face, and he looked just like the suspect.* □ *When we superimposed the mustache on him, we knew he was guilty.*

SUPPLY ▸ FROM

See the following entry.

SUPPLY ▸ TO

supply something (to someone or something) (from something) to provide someone or something with something from some source. □ *I supplied ice cream to the new restaurant from a very expensive source.* □ *We supplied nuts from a pushcart.* □ *Frank supplied nothing at all to them.*

SUPPLY ▸ WITH

supply someone or something with something to provide something to someone or something. □ *We will supply you with all the pencils you need.* □ *We supplied the committee with ice water.*

SURGE ▸ IN

surge in(to something) to burst or gush into something or some place. □ *The water surged into the valley after the dam broke.* □ *The doors opened and the people surged in.*

SURGE ▸ OUT

surge out (of something) to burst forth or gush out of something or some place. □ *The water surged out of the huge crack in the dam.* □ *We saw the crack where the water surged out.*

SURGE ▸ UP

surge up to rush or gush upwards. □ *A spring of fresh water surged up under the stone and flowed out on the ground.* □ *The oil surged up and blew out into the open air in a tall column of living blackness.*

SURPASS ▸ IN

surpass someone or something in something to exceed someone or something in some deed or quality. □ *I will never be able to surpass Jill in speed or agility.* □ *My car surpasses yours in almost every respect.*

SURPRISE ▸ BY

surprise someone by something to astonish someone by doing or being something. □ *You surprised me by your forthrightness.* □ *No one was surprised by the way it happened.*

SURPRISE ▸ WITH

surprise someone with something to astonish someone by presenting or showing something. (*Someone* includes *oneself.*) □ *I surprised her with a bouquet of roses.* □ *He surprised Roger with a new car.*

SURRENDER ▸ TO

surrender someone or something to someone or something to give up someone or something to someone or something. (*Someone* includes *oneself.*) □ *You must surrender your child to the nurse for the child's own good. She will give her right back.* □ *He surrendered his car to the bank.* □ *He surrendered his car to Mr. Wilson at the bank.* □ *She surrendered her child to the court.* □ *She surrendered herself to the police.*

surrender to someone or something to give in to someone or something; to yield to someone or something. □ *The robber surrendered to the cops.* □ *I will never surrender to my baser passions.*

SURROUND ▸ WITH

surround someone or something with someone or something to encircle or enclose someone or something with people, something, or things. (*Someone* includes *oneself.*) □ *We surrounded him with his friends as he lay in the hospital bed.* □ *We surrounded the tree with wire netting to protect it against rabbits.* □ *They surrounded the display of jewels with guards.* □ *She surrounded herself with her friends and made the announcement.*

SUSPECT ▸ OF

suspect someone of something to think or believe that someone has done something. □ *I suspect the clerk of stealing.* □ *Ted was suspected of leaving the door unlocked when he left last Friday.*

SUSPEND ▸ BY

suspend something by something to hang something by something. □ *The workers suspended the stone by a steel cable.* □ *Will suspended the decoration by a fine thread.*

SUSPEND ▸ FROM

suspend someone from something to prevent someone from participating in something. □ *The principal suspended the student from classes for a week.* □ *Ted was suspended from school for three days.*

suspend someone or something from something to hang someone or something from something. □ *The hangman suspended the thief from a gibbet as a warning to others.* □ *Jill suspended each decoration from a different branch.*

SUSTAIN ▸ IN

sustain someone in something to stand by or support someone through some problem. □ *She knew she could count on her friends to sustain her in time of trouble.* □ *We will sustain you in the difficult times the best we can.*

SWAB ▸ DOWN

swab something down to wash or scrub something, such as the deck of a ship. □ *The sailors were told to swab the deck down each day.* 🅃 *Swap down the deck!*

SWAB ▸ OUT

swab something out to wash or wipe something out. □ *The doctor swabbed my ear out carefully.* 🅃 *The doctor swabbed out my ear carefully.*

swab something out of something to wipe or mop something out of something. □ *The doctor swabbed the wax out of my ear.* □ *I swabbed the last of the cereal out of the bowl.*

SWALLOW ▸ DOWN

swallow something down to swallow something. □ *Here, take this pill and swallow it down.* 🅃 *Liz swallowed down the pill.*

SWALLOW ▸ UP

swallow someone or something up **1.** to eat or gobble up someone or something. □ *The fairy-tale wolf threatened to swallow Gwen up in one bite.* 🅃 *The wolf swallowed up the meat in one bite.* **2.** to engulf or contain something. (Figurative.) □ *The garage seemed to swallow the cars up.* 🅃 *The huge sweater swallowed up the tiny child.*

SWAMP ► WITH

swamp someone or something with something to cover or deluge someone or something with something. ☐ *The flood swamped our property with river water.* ☐ *The many orders for their product swamped the small business with too much to do.* ☐ *They swamped us with orders.*

SWAP ► FOR

swap someone or something for someone or something to trade someone or something for someone or something. ☐ *I will swap my shortstop for your second baseman.* ☐ *There are times when I would gladly swap you for a new car—even an old car!* ☐ *The spy swapped a car for a political prisoner.*

SWAP ► ON

swap notes on someone or something to exchange bits of information about someone or something. ☐ *We need to swap notes on Jeff sometime. I can't figure him out.* ☐ *Can we swap notes on stereo systems?*

SWAP ► WITH

swap someone or something with someone to exchange a person or thing for someone else's person or thing. ☐ *The representatives of the two countries swapped spies with each other.* ☐ *Can I swap jackets with you?*

swap with someone to exchange someone or something with someone. ☐ *I like yours better. I'll swap with you.* ☐ *If you don't want the one you have, I will swap with you.*

SWARM ► AROUND

swarm around someone or something to gather or crowd around someone or something, in the manner of a swarm of bees. ☐ *The little children swarmed around the lady with the candy.* ☐ *The bees swarmed around the flowers.*

SWARM ► IN(TO)

swarm in(to something) [for a throng] to crowd into something or some place. ☐ *People were swarming into the auditorium to hear the guitarist.* ☐ *They swarmed in and ran for the best seats.*

SWARM ► OUT

swarm out of something to move out of something in great numbers. ☐ *The bees swarmed out of the hive.* ☐ *People swarmed out of the park at the end of the picnic.*

SWARM ► OVER

swarm (all) over someone or something to gather and move all about on someone or throughout something or some place. ☐ *The ants swarmed all over us.* ☐ *The children swarmed over the furniture.*

SWARM ► THROUGH

swarm through something to gather in a crowd and move through something or some place. ☐ *The shoppers swarmed through the store, buying everything in sight.* ☐ *The deer swarmed through the field, eating the entire harvest.*

SWARM ► WITH

swarm with someone or something to be abundant or crowded with moving people or things. ☐ *The playground was swarming with children, and I couldn't find my own.* ☐ *The picnic blanket swarmed with ants.*

SWATHE ► IN

swathe someone or something in something to wrap or drape someone or something in something. (*Someone* includes *oneself.*) ☐ *Molly swathed her children in sheets to turn them into ghosts on Halloween.* ☐ *She swathed the statue in black velvet, just for a change.* ☐ *She swathed herself in fine silks and satins.*

SWATHE ► WITH

swathe someone or something with something to wrap or drape someone or something with something. (*Someone* includes *oneself.*) ☐ *The sculptor swathed his subjects with heavy drapes.* ☐ *The designer swathed the window with billows of taffeta.* ☐ *She swathed herself with beautiful silks.*

SWAY ► BACK

sway back and forth to swing or bend from one direction to another. ☐ *The pendulum swayed back and forth, counting off the seconds.* ☐ *Mary was* *swaying back and forth, keeping time to the music.*

SWAY ► FROM

sway from side to side to swing or bend from one side to the other. □ *The car swayed from side to side as we started out, indicating that something was seriously wrong.* □ *He swayed from side to side with the rhythm of the music.*

SWAY ► TO

sway someone to something to convince someone to do something. (Figurative.) □ *I think I can sway her to join our side.* □ *We could not sway Ted to our position.*

SWEAR ► AT

swear at someone or something to curse someone or something. □ *Please don't swear at the children.* □ *Scott swore at the police station as he drove by.*

SWEAR ► BY

swear by someone or something **1.** to utter an oath on someone or something. □ *I swear by Jupiter that I will be there on time.* □ *She swore by her sainted mother that she would never do it again.* □ *The sheriff swore by his badge that he would lock her up if she ever did it again.* **2.** to announce one's full faith and trust in someone or something. □ *I would swear by Roger any time. He is a great guy, and anything he does is super.* □ *I swear by this computer. It has always served me well.*

SWEAR ► IN

swear someone in (as something) to administer an oath to someone who then becomes something. □ *The judge swore Alice in as street commissioner.* 🅃 *The judge swore in Alice as the new director.* □ *She swore Alice in.* 🄰 *What time is the swearing-in ceremony?* 🄽 *I don't want to be late for my swearing-in.*

SWEAR ► OFF

swear off (something) to pledge to avoid or abstain from something. □ *I've sworn off desserts. I start tomorrow.* □ *No dessert for me. I've sworn off.*

SWEAR ► ON

See under *SWEAR ► (UP)ON.*

SWEAR ► OUT

swear something out against someone to file a criminal complaint against someone. □ *Walter swore a warrant out against Jeff.* 🅃 *He swore out a warrant against Tony.*

SWEAR ► TO

swear someone to something to cause someone to take an oath pledging something, such as silence or secrecy, about something. □ *I swore Larry to secrecy, but he told anyway.* □ *We were sworn to silence about the new product.*

swear something to someone to pledge or promise something to someone. □ *I had to swear my allegiance to the general before I could become one of his revolutionary guerrillas.* □ *We swore our loyalty to our country.*

swear to something to claim that what one says is absolutely true. □ *It is true. I swear to it.* □ *I think I have remembered it all, but I couldn't swear to it.*

SWEAR ► (UP)ON

swear (up)on someone or something to take an oath on someone or something. (*Upon* is formal and less commonly used than *on*.) □ *He swore upon the Bible to tell the truth.* □ *I swear on the memory of my sainted mother that I am telling the truth.*

SWEAT ► FOR

sweat for something to work very hard for something. (Informal.) □ *I sweat for every dollar I bring in.* □ *Ted really sweats for his salary.*

SWEAT ► OFF

sweat something off to get rid of excess moisture or fat by using heat to produce sweat. □ *I think I can sweat a lot of this fat off.* 🅃 *Tony tried to sweat off some of his excess weight.*

SWEAT ► OUT

sweat something out **1.** to get rid of something in one's body by sweating. □ *I have a bit of a cold, and I am going to try to sweat it out.* 🅃 *I took a steamy shower, trying to sweat out my cold.* **2.**

to endure something unpleasant. □ *It was an ordeal, but I sweated it out.* 🅃 *I managed to sweat out the exam.* **3.** to endure suspense about something. □ *She sweated the two-hour wait out until she heard the results of her bar exams.* 🅃 *Karen sweated out the long wait peacefully.*

sweat something out of someone **1.** to apply enough heat to cause someone to sweat, with the goal of removing bodily poisons or the cause of a disease. (The *of*-phrase is paraphrased with a *from*-phrase when the particle is transposed. See the 🄵 example.) □ *They used the ancient treatment of sweating the disease out of me. It worked!* 🅃 *They used steam to sweat out the flu.* 🄵 *They used steam to sweat out the flu from the sick people.* **2.** to force someone to reveal information under pressure. (Informal. The *of*-phrase is paraphrased with a *from*-phrase when the particle is transposed. See the 🄵 example.) □ *The cops couldn't sweat the information out of Max.* 🅃 *They couldn't sweat out the information.* 🄵 *They tried to sweat out the information from Max.*

SWEEP ▸ ALONG

sweep along to glide along smoothly, as if flying. □ *The sailboat swept along, pushed by the strong wind.* □ *Johnny Appleseed swept along, sowing apple seeds as he went.*

SWEEP ▸ ASIDE

sweep someone or something aside to push or brush someone or something aside. □ *The guards swept the spectators aside as the king's coach approached.* 🅃 *They swept aside the spectators.* □ *Let's sweep the papers and discards aside.*

SWEEP ▸ AWAY

sweep someone or something away to dispose of someone or something by pushing or brushing away. □ *The waves nearly swept us away.* 🅃 *The waves caused by the storm swept away all the debris on the beach.*

SWEEP ▸ BACK

sweep something back to push or move something backwards in the shape of a curve. □ *He took the brush and swept his hair back in a huge wave.* 🅃 *She swept back her hair in a striking arrangement.*

SWEEP ▸ DOWN

sweep down on someone or something to flow or rush down onto someone or something. □ *The storm swept down on the campers.* □ *A flash flood swept down on the stream bed.*

sweep something down to clean something by sweeping. □ *Please sweep this floor down whenever you make a mess here.* 🅃 *Jeff will sweep down the floor before he goes home.*

SWEEP ▸ IN

sweep in (from some place) AND **breeze in (from some place)** to arrive suddenly from some place. □ *Tom just swept in from his vacation to face a pile of work on his desk.* □ *Max breezed in from Vegas and asked about Lefty.* □ *When did Max breeze in?*

SWEEP ▸ IN(TO)

sweep in(to some place) to dash or run into some place. □ *The kids swept into the candy store and bought little bits of things.* □ *They swept in and spent all of a dollar before they left.*

sweep someone in(to something) to place someone into an elective position decisively. □ *The decisive victory swept all the candidates of the reform party into office.* 🅃 *The victory swept in the candidates.* □ *The political climate swept a lot of challengers in.*

sweep something in(to something) to move something into something or some place by sweeping. □ *Liz swept the crumbs into the dish.* 🅃 *Liz held the dish and swept in the crumbs.* □ *She swept the dust in.*

SWEEP ▸ OFF

sweep off to exit quickly. □ *He stopped only briefly, then swept off again.* □ *Mary swept off, leaving Ted standing there confused.*

sweep one off one's feet **1.** to knock or blow someone down. □ *The wind nearly swept me off my feet.* □ *Ted was swept off his feet by the force of the door closing on him.* **2.** to impress and overwhelm someone. □ *His suave manners swept her off her feet.* □ *She was swept off her feet by his wittiness.*

sweep something off ((of) something) to clean something by sweeping. (The *of* is colloquial.) □ *The waiter swept the crumbs off the tablecloth.* □ *Jake swept the counter off and wiped it clean.* 🅃 *He swept off the back porch.* 🅃 *He swept off the crumbs from the tablecloth.*

SWEEP ▸ OUT

sweep out of some place to exit from some place quickly with grand flourishes. □ *The famous actress swept out of the room in a grand fashion.* □ *She swept out of her dressing room and walked on stage just as her cue was uttered.*

sweep someone or something out (of something) to remove or brush someone or something from something or some place. (Literal or figurative. The *of*-phrase is paraphrased with a *from*-phrase when the particle is transposed. See the 🄵 example.) □ *The voters swept the crooks out of office.* 🅃 *We swept out the dirt.* 🄵 *We swept out the dirt from the garage.* □ *The next election will sweep them out.*

sweep something out to clean something out by sweeping. □ *Someone has to sweep the garage out.* 🅃 *Don't sweep out this room. I'll do it.*

SWEEP ▸ OVER

sweep over someone **1.** to pass over and cover someone. □ *The waves swept over us and nearly drowned us.* □ *The flood swept over the farmers who would not leave their homes.* **2.** [for something] to overwhelm someone. □ *A wave of nausea swept over me and I guess I slumped to the floor.* □ *The need for fresh air swept over all of us trapped in that room.*

SWEEP ▸ THROUGH

sweep through (something) **1.** to move through something or some place quickly and with grand flourishes. □ *She swept through the room, speaking to no one.* □ *She swept through in a great hurry.* **2.** to perform some task quickly. □ *She swept through the musical number and ran offstage.* □ *It required a slower tempo, but she just swept through.*

sweep through something to rush or move quickly through something. □ *The fire swept through the small frame houses, one by one.* □ *She swept through the room, greeting the people she knew.*

SWEEP ▸ UNDER

sweep something under the carpet **1.** to hide dirt by brushing it away under the edge of a carpet. □ *He was in such a hurry with the cleaning that he just swept the dirt under the carpet.* □ *She swept the dirt under the carpet, hoping no one would find it.* **2.** to hide or ignore something. (Figurative.) □ *You made a mistake that you can't sweep under the carpet.* □ *Don't try to sweep it under the carpet. You are wrong!*

SWEEP ▸ UP

sweep something up **1.** to clean up and remove something, such as dirt, by sweeping. □ *Please sweep these crumbs up.* 🅃 *Can you sweep up these crumbs?* 🄰 *Where shall I put the swept-up glass?* **2.** to clean up some place by sweeping. □ *Please sweep this room up.* 🅃 *Can you sweep up this room, please?* **3.** to arrange something, such as hair, into a curve or wave. □ *The hairstylist swept her hair up over the top. No one liked it.* 🅃 *Sweep up my hair the way it looks in this picture.* 🄰 *I don't care for this new style of upswept hair.*

sweep up to clean up by sweeping. □ *Would you sweep up this time?* □ *Please give me a few minutes to sweep up before you come to visit.*

sweep up after someone to clean up the dirt left on the floor by someone. □ *Do you mind sweeping up after the kids?* □

I had to sweep up after your party and I am not happy about it!

SWEETEN ▸ UP

sweeten someone up to make someone more pleasant. □ *I had hoped that a week in the Caribbean would sweeten him up.* 🅃 *The trip sweetened him up, but not for long.*

sweeten something up **1.** to make something taste sweeter. □ *Where is the sugar? I need to sweeten this up a little.* 🅃 *A little sugar will sweeten up the coffee.* **2.** to make a deal or bargain more attractive to someone. □ *The car dealer took off another hundred dollars to sweeten the deal up a little.* 🅃 *She sweetened up the deal with a little money.*

SWELL ▸ OUT

swell out to bulge outward; to expand outward. □ *The sides of the box swelled out because it was too full.* □ *The west wall of the garage swelled out just before the building collapsed.*

SWELL ▸ UP

swell up to enlarge; to inflate; to bulge out. □ *I struck my thumb with a hammer and it swelled up something awful.* 🄰 *His swollen-up hand hurt him badly.*

SWELL ▸ WITH

swell with something **1.** to expand from a particular cause. □ *My knee joints swelled with arthritis.* □ *His nose swelled after it was struck with the door.* **2.** to seem to swell with a feeling such as pride. □ *His chest swelled with pride at the thought of his good performance.* □ *Ted swelled with pride at the announcement.*

SWERVE ▸ AWAY

swerve (away) (from someone or something) to turn sharply away from someone or something. □ *The car swerved away from Carla just in time.* □ *It swerved away just in time.* □ *We swerved from the shoulder of the highway and straightened out.*

SWERVE ▸ FROM

See the previous entry.

SWERVE ▸ INTO

swerve into someone or something to turn sharply and directly into someone or something. (Usually an accident.) □ *The car almost swerved into a pedestrian.* □ *The bus swerved into a truck.*

SWILL ▸ DOWN

swill something down to drink something, especially an alcoholic drink, in great gulps. □ *The guy took a quart of beer and swilled it down in a few seconds.* 🅃 *He swilled down a quart of beer.*

SWIM ▸ AGAINST

swim against the tide AND **swim against the current** **1.** to swim in a direction opposite to the flow of the water. □ *She became exhausted, swimming against the tide.* □ *If you really want strenuous exercise, go out in the stream and swim against the current.* **2.** to do something that is in opposition to the general movement of things. □ *Why can't you cooperate? Do you always have to swim against the tide?* □ *You always seem to waste your energy swimming against the current.*

SWIM ▸ AROUND

swim around to swim here and there. □ *I just like to get into the pool and swim around.* □ *I saw only one fish swimming around in your aquarium.*

SWIM ▸ BEFORE

swim before someone's eyes [for something, such as spots or visions] to appear in one's field of vision. □ *I was getting feverish and spots swam before my eyes.* □ *Visions of total destruction swam before my eyes as the bus sped along.*

SWIM ▸ FOR

swim for it to escape by swimming. (See also *run for it*.) □ *I escaped from the guard, dived into the river, and swam for it.* □ *Max swam for it, but he didn't get away.*

swim for someone or something to travel toward someone or something by swimming. □ *I swam for George, who was farther out, holding onto a float.* □ *I am going to swim for the island.*

SWIM ▶ IN

swim in something **1.** to swim in a body of water. ☐ *Is it safe to swim in this water?* ☐ *Can we swim in your pool?* **2.** to experience an overabundance of something. (Figurative.) ☐ *We are just swimming in orders right now. Business is good.* ☐ *Mr. Wilson is swimming in money.*

SWIM ▶ INTO

swim into something to enter something, swimming. ☐ *They swam into a lovely grotto.* ☐ *Ted swam into the cove and got out on the beach.*

SWIM ▶ TOWARD

swim toward someone or something to swim in the direction of someone or something. ☐ *Jeff swam toward the drowning man and helped him.* ☐ *I swam toward the boat.*

SWIM ▶ WITH

swim with something **1.** to swim in the same direction as the movement of water. ☐ *Fred had no trouble swimming with the current.* ☐ *Please swim with the current and not against it.* **2.** to be engulfed with something. ☐ *The scene of the crime was swimming with cops and reporters.* ☐ *The hotel with swimming with out-of-town visitors.* ☐ *This place is swimming with cops!*

SWINDLE ▶ OUT

swindle someone out of something AND **swindle something out of someone** to cheat something away from someone. ☐ *The crooks tried to swindle her out of her inheritance.* ☐ *The crooks swindled $3,000 out of the old woman.* ☐ *Don't try to swindle me out of my hard-earned money!*

SWING ▶ AROUND

swing around (to something) to move around to another position. ☐ *She swung around to the left, where she could see better.* ☐ *The bear suddenly swung around and charged.*

SWING ▶ AT

swing at someone or something to strike at someone or something. ☐ *Max swung at the cop—a serious mistake.* ☐ *The batter swung at the ball and missed.*

SWING ▶ FOR

swing for something [for someone] to die by hanging for some crime. ☐ *The sheriff swore that Tex would swing for the killing.* ☐ *Max said he would not swing for something that Lefty had done.*

SWING ▶ FROM

swing from something to hang or dangle from something. ☐ *The child was swinging from an exercise bar on her swing set.* ☐ *Ted was swinging from the edge of the cliff, waiting to be rescued.*

SWING ▶ INTO

swing into high gear to become more active; to start operating at the maximum. (Idiomatic.) ☐ *Things swung into high gear at about midnight. What a party!* ☐ *Things don't swing into high gear before noon.*

swing into something to enter something by swinging. ☐ *The monkey swung into its cage, and I quickly locked the cage door.* ☐ *I grabbed a rope and swung into the cave, where my pursuer couldn't see me.*

SWING ▶ TO

swing to something to change to a different position or attitude. ☐ *The mood of the country is swinging to conservatism.* ☐ *Soon the attitudes of the people will swing to the opposite side.*

SWIRL ▶ ABOUT

swirl about someone or something [for something, such as dust or a fluid] to circle and wind about someone or something. ☐ *The snow swirled about me as I walked along.* ☐ *The smoke swirled about the tiny campfire.*

SWIRL ▶ AROUND

swirl around [for dust or a fluid] to circle around. ☐ *The liquid swirled around in the flask as Toby shook it up.* ☐ *Dust swirled around the room in the sunlight.*

SWISH ▶ AROUND

swish around [for a fluid] to slosh or rush around. ☐ *All that water I drank is swishing around in my stomach.* ☐ *I can hear the water swishing around in the pipes.*

SWISH ▸ OFF

swish something off ((of) someone or something) to brush something off someone or something. (The *of*-phrase is paraphrased with a *from*-phrase when the particle is transposed. See the F example. The *of* is colloquial.) □ *The barber swished the loose hairs off of Paul's collar.* T *The barber swished off the loose hairs.* F *The barber swished off the loose hairs from Paul's collar.* □ *Jamie swished the hairs off.*

SWITCH ▸ AROUND

switch around to change, swing, or turn around. □ *The horse switched around and ran the other way.* □ *I switched around and sat looking the other way for a while.*

switch (around) (with someone or something) to exchange or trade with someone or something. (The optional elements cannot be transposed.) □ *I liked Jill's, and she liked mine, so I switched around with her.* □ *I liked Jill's, and she liked mine, so we switched around with each other.* □ *We switched around and were satisfied.*

switch someone or something around to change, swing, or turn someone or something. □ *I was prepared for a late flight out of Miami, but they switched me around at the last minute.* T *They switched around my flights.* □ *Switch these two around so the big one is in the back.*

SWITCH ▸ BACK

switch back (to something) **1.** to return to using or doing something. □ *I decided to switch back to my old shampoo.* □ *I switched back and was glad I did.* **2.** [for a road] to reverse upon itself. □ *The road switched back twenty times in three miles.* □ *It switched back every now and then.* A *I hate these old switchback roads.*

switch something back (to something) to return something to the way it was. □ *I switched the television back to the previous channel.* T *I switched back the channel to what I was watching before.* □ *I switched it back and then went to sleep.*

SWITCH ▸ FROM

switch from someone to someone to change one's choice from one person to another. □ *I had chosen Jeff, but I will switch from him to Judy.* □ *Tom wanted to try a new barber, so he switched from Nick to Bruno.*

switch from something to something to change one's choice from one thing to another. □ *We switched from oil to gas in our house.* □ *I don't like to switch from one brand to another.*

switch something (from something) (in)to something to change something from one thing into another. □ *The magician switched the silk scarf from red into green.* □ *I would love to be able to switch lead into gold.*

SWITCH ▸ INTO

switch into something to change [one's clothes] into something else. □ *Let me switch into something a little more dressy if we are going to a nice restaurant.* □ *I have to switch into something more comfortable.*

SWITCH ▸ OFF

switch off **1.** [for something] to turn itself off. □ *At midnight, all the lights switched off automatically.* □ *The television switched off after I went to sleep.* **2.** [for someone] to stop paying attention. □ *I got tired of listening and switched off.* □ *You could see that the audience was switching off.*

switch someone or something off to cause someone or something to be quiet or stop doing something. □ *I got tired of listening to her, so I punched the button and switched her off.* T *I switched off the television set.* A *The switched-off machine was still very hot.*

SWITCH ▸ ON

switch on **1.** [for something] to turn itself on. □ *Exactly at midnight, the lights switched on.* □ *The radio switched on early in the morning to wake us up.* **2.** [for someone] to become alert or excited. (Slang.) □ *The wild music made all the kids switch on and start to dance.* □ *About midnight, Ed switches on and becomes a real devil.*

switch something on to close an electrical circuit that causes something to start functioning or operating. ☐ *Please switch the fan on.* [T] *I switched on the fan.*

SWITCH ► OUT

switch something out to remove something from a circuit by turning it off. ☐ *Please switch the light out.* [T] *I switched out the light.*

SWITCH ► OVER

switch over (to someone or something) to change to or choose someone or something else. ☐ *That newscaster is too contentious. Switch over to Walter.* ☐ *Okay, I'll switch over.* [N] *The new workers refused to make the switchover.*

switch someone or something over to someone or something to transfer electronically a signal from someone or something to someone or something. ☐ *Tom is on the line. Shall I switch him over to Jeff?* ☐ *Please switch the call over to my other line.*

switch someone or something over to something to reassign, change, or convert someone or something to something. ☐ *They switched me over to a later flight.* ☐ *I want to switch my furnace over to gas.* [N] *The switchover was done in the night to cause the least trouble.*

switch something over (to something) to convert something to something else. ☐ *We are switching our furnace over to gas.* [T] *We switched over our furnace to gas.* ☐ *We will switch it over next fall.* [N] *We made a switchover from oil to natural gas.*

SWITCH ► THROUGH

switch someone or something through to connect someone or something with something else. (*Someone* includes *oneself.*) ☐ *I will switch you through the priority network.* ☐ *The operator switched the call through.* ☐ *She switched herself through to the central network.*

SWITCH ► TO

switch something to something to change something to something else. ☐ *It was hot so I switched the thermostat from heating to cooling.* ☐ *Mary switched the controls to automatic so she wouldn't have to worry about them constantly.*

switch to something to change to something. ☐ *I am going to switch to a cheaper brand of tissues.* ☐ *We switched to a different long-distance telephone company to save some money.*

SWITCH ► WITH

switch (around) (with someone or something) See under *SWITCH ► AROUND.*

SWOON ► OVER

swoon over someone or something to pass out about someone or something. (Stilted or jocular.) ☐ *The kids swooned over the rock star like the kids of thirty years ago.* ☐ *Evangeline swooned over the frightful news.*

SWOOP ► DOWN

swoop down (up)on someone or something to dive or plunge downward on someone or something. (Both literal and figurative uses.) ☐ *The eagle swooped down upon the lamb.* ☐ *The children swooped down on the ice cream and cake.*

SWOOP ► ON

See the previous entry.

SYMPATHIZE ► WITH

sympathize with someone (about someone or something) to share someone else's sorrow or anger about someone or something; to comfort someone who is sad or angry (about someone or something). ☐ *I sympathize with you about what you are going through.* ☐ *I really sympathize with you.*

SYNCHRONIZE ► WITH

synchronize something with something to set or adjust something to coordinate its timing with something else. ☐ *Would you please synchronize your watch with mine?* ☐ *We could never synchronize our schedules so that we could get together.*

T

TAB ► FOR

tab someone for something to choose someone for something. □ *The director tabbed Sam for a walk-on part.* □ *I wanted her to tab me for a part.*

TACK ► DOWN

tack something down to fasten something down with small nails. □ *Someone had better tack this carpet down.* 🅃 *Please tack down this carpet.*

TACK ► ON(TO)

tack something on(to something) to add something onto something. (Colloquial.) □ *The waiter kept tacking charges onto my bill.* 🅃 *He tacked on charge after charge.* 🅃 *He tacked on an unnecessary charge.*

TACK ► UP

tack something up to fasten something onto something with tacks. □ *The drapes started to fall, so we tacked them up again.* 🅃 *Please tack up these posters.*

TAG ► ALONG

tag along (after someone) AND **tag along (behind someone)** to follow along after someone; to go along with someone. □ *The family dog tagged along after the children wherever they went.* □ *Can I tag along?* □ *Do you mind if I tag along behind you?*

TAG ► OUT

tag someone out [in baseball] to touch with the ball, and thereby put someone out. □ *The shortstop tagged the runner out and retired the side.* 🅃 *He tagged out the runner.*

TAIL ► AFTER

tail after someone to follow after someone. (Colloquial.) □ *Why do you always have to tail after me?* □ *There is someone tailing after you.*

TAIL ► OFF

tail off to dwindle to nothing. □ *The number of people filing for unemployment insurance is beginning to tail off.* □ *As the storms tailed off, we began to realize how much damage had been done.*

TAILOR ► TO

tailor someone or something to someone or something to fit or revise someone or something to fit someone or something. □ *The coach tailored his defensive players to the opposition.* □ *We can tailor service to your company very easily.* □ *I will tailor this suit to you for no extra charge.*

TAINT ► WITH

taint something with something to spoil or debase something with something. □ *The flood tainted the drinking water with disease germs.* □ *The food had been tainted with germs.*

TAKE ► ABACK

See *be taken aback* under *BE ► ABACK.*

TAKE ► ABOARD

take someone or something aboard to load someone or something onto a ship. □ *The ship was in its berth, taking passengers aboard.* □ *The ship took many tons of cargo aboard.*

TAKE ► ACROSS

take someone or something across (something) to carry or lead someone or something across something. □ *Tim took Liz across the bridge.* □ *We took a lot of food and medicine across before the flooded river washed the bridge out.*

TAKE ▸ AFTER

take after someone to behave in the same way as someone else; to have the characteristics of a family member. □ *Doesn't he take after his father?* □ *I think she takes after her Aunt Mabel.*

TAKE ▸ AGAINST

take a stand against someone or something to establish and announce one's opposition to someone or something. □ *I had to take a stand against Bill. We just do not agree.* □ *We all took a stand against the land development project.*

take action against someone or something to begin activity against someone or something. □ *The city council vowed to take action against the mayor.* □ *I will take action against the company for its negligence.*

take revenge against someone to get even with someone. □ *Linda planned to take revenge against Ellen.* □ *The prime minister took revenge against the general.*

take sides against someone or something to join a faction opposing someone or something; to establish a faction against someone or something. □ *Both of them took sides against me. It wasn't fair.* □ *We took sides against the bank.*

TAKE ▸ ALOFT

take something aloft to take an aircraft into the air. □ *The pilot took the plane aloft and tested it out.* □ *When will you take this aloft for a test flight?*

TAKE ▸ ALONG

take someone or something along to bring someone or something along with one. □ *Can I take my friend along?* 🆃 *You should take along your own drinking water.*

TAKE ▸ APART

take someone or something apart to criticize someone or something mercilessly. □ *The critics took the star apart in the morning papers.* 🆃 *They took apart the entire production.* □ *They took Larry apart for his singing.*

take something apart to break something to pieces; to disassemble something. □ *Tim took his watch apart, and that was the end of it.* 🆃 *Don't take apart every mechanical device you own!*

TAKE ▸ AROUND

take someone around to show someone the premises; to introduce someone to the people on the premises. □ *Mr. Franklin needs a plant tour. Would you take him around?* 🆃 *Would you kindly take around our guests?*

take something around to take something from here to there. □ *Would you take the pictures around and show them to everyone?* 🆃 *I will take around this stack of pictures and show them to each person.*

TAKE ▸ AS

take someone as someone to assume that someone is someone or a type of person. □ *I took her as some sort of crank.* □ *She didn't want to be taken as some sort of busybody.*

take something as something **1.** to swallow something, expecting a particular benefit. □ *I took some aspirin as a painkiller.* □ *Tony took calcium tablets as a bone builder.* **2.** to assume that something is something else. □ *I took your comments as a severe criticism.* □ *Sam's actions were taken as constructive.*

TAKE ▸ ASIDE

take someone aside to remove someone temporarily from the group for the purposes of discussing something privately. □ *I'm sorry he insulted you. I'll take him aside and talk to him about it.* 🆃 *I took aside my secretary and explained the procedure.*

TAKE ▸ AT

take a crack at someone or something to have a try at someone or something. □ *I'm sure I can persuade her. Let me take a crack at her.* □ *I think I can do it. Let me take a crack at it.*

take a dig at someone or something to make a rude comment about someone or something. (Colloquial. Also with *dig.*) ☐ *While she was talking, she took a dig at Roger for being late all the time.* ☐ *She is always taking digs at my old car.*

take a gander at someone or something to take a peek or a glance at someone or something. (Slang.) ☐ *Hey, take a gander at Liz!* ☐ *Take a gander at Liz's new car!*

take a jab at someone AND **take a punch at someone** to hit at someone. ☐ *Max took a jab at Lefty and missed.* ☐ *Lefty took a punch at Max.*

take a jab at someone or something to make a rude or hurtful comment about someone or something. (Figurative. Also in plural.) ☐ *He took another jab at Gary, and Gary got really mad at him.* ☐ *Please stop taking jabs at me all the time.* ☐ *He took a jab at my cooking once too often.*

take a look at someone or something to inspect someone or something. ☐ *Take a look at Fred. Isn't his haircut great?* ☐ *Would you take a look at that new sports car?*

take a potshot at someone or something **1.** to shoot at someone or something, as with a shotgun. ☐ *The hunters were taking potshots at each other in the woods.* ☐ *Someone has been taking potshots at my mailbox!* **2.** to criticize or censure someone or something, often just to be mean. (Figurative.) ☐ *Why are you taking potshots at me? What did I do to you?* ☐ *Everyone in the audience was taking potshots at the comedian's toupee.*

take a punch at someone See under *take a jab at someone.*

take a shot at someone or something **1.** to fire a shot at someone or something. ☐ *The hunter took a shot at the deer.* ☐ *He almost took a shot at me by mistake.* ☐ *Who took a shot at my mailbox?* **2.** to have a try at someone or something. (Figurative slang.) ☐ *I'm sure I can convince her. Let me take a shot at her.* ☐ *I guess I'll take a shot at fixing the radio.*

take a swipe at someone or something **1.** to hit at someone or something. (Slang.) ☐ *Max took a swipe at the cop by mistake.* ☐ *Lefty took a swipe at the punching bag—and missed.* **2.** to have a try at someone or something. (Slang.) ☐ *I think I can persuade him. I'll take a swipe at him and see.* ☐ *I will probably fail, but I'll take a swipe at it.*

take a try at someone or something to try to deal with someone or something. ☐ *He is hard to convince, but I'll take a try at him.* ☐ *I will take a try at doing it.*

take a whack at someone or something **1.** to try to do something with someone or something. (Slang.) ☐ *I'll get Danny to agree. Let me take a whack at him.* ☐ *I'm sure I can do it. Let me take a whack at fixing it.* **2.** to hit at someone or something. (Colloquial.) ☐ *Tim took a whack at Roger and Roger clobbered him in return.* ☐ *Roger took a whack at the dog and sent her off howling.*

take aim at someone or something **1.** to aim a weapon at someone or something. ☐ *Max took aim at Lefty and fired the gun.* ☐ *Jamie took aim at the target.* **2.** to focus on someone or something with the intention of criticism or exposure. (Figurative.) ☐ *The critics took aim at the star of the musical and tore her to pieces.* ☐ *Next, they took aim at the theater because of its bad acoustics.*

take offense at someone or something to be insulted by someone or something. ☐ *He means no harm. Don't take offense at him.* ☐ *I hope you don't take offense at Jan's jokes.*

take one at one's word to believe what one has said with no further evidence or with no proof. ☐ *Can I take you at your word?* ☐ *You will just have to take me at my word.*

take someone or something at face value to accept someone or something on appearances; to believe that the way things appear is the way they really are. ☐ *He means what he says. You have to take him at face value.* ☐ *I take everything he says at face value.*

take turns at doing something [for two or more creatures] to alternate at doing something or to do something each in turn. ☐ *We will have to take turns at* *cooking. Neither of us wants to do it every day.* ☐ *Do you want to take turns at answering the telephone?*

take umbrage at something to resent something. ☐ *Unfortunately, she took umbrage at my remarks.* ☐ *I hope you didn't take umbrage at my remarks.*

TAKE ▸ AWAY

take away from someone or something to lessen the value or esteem of someone or something; to detract from someone or something. ☐ *The fact that she is quiet does not take away from her one bit.* ☐ *The huge orange spot in the center of the painting takes away from the intense green of the rest of the work.*

take someone or something away to remove someone or something. ☐ *The police came and took her away.* 🅃 *He took away the extra food.*

take someone or something away (from someone or something) to remove someone or something to some distance away from someone or something else; to remove someone or something from the possession of someone or something else. ☐ *Take her away from me!* 🅃 *Take away that horrible food.* ☐ *Take it away!* ☐ *Do you really think you can take her away from me?* 🅃 *You can't take away my car from me just because I missed a payment!*

take someone's breath away to surprise or astound someone. (Figurative.) ☐ *When the curtain opened on the lovely stage setting, the view took the audience's breath away.* ☐ *When you see what I have to show you, it will take your breath away.*

take something away (from someone or something) to detract from someone or something. ☐ *The bright costume on the soprano takes a lot away from the tenor, who is just as important.* ☐ *The overall picture is good, but the busy background takes a lot away.*

TAKE ▸ BACK

take one back (to sometime) to cause one to think of a time in the past. ☐ *This takes me back to the time I spent the summer in Paris.* ☐ *What you said really takes me back.*

take something back to retract a statement; to rescind one's remark. ☐ *You had better take back what you said about my sister.* ☐ *I won't take it back!*

take something back (from someone) to take possession of something that one had previously given away. ☐ *I took my sweater back from Tim, since he never wore it.* 🅃 *I took back my money from the child.* ☐ *It was mine, so I took it back.*

take something back to someone or something to carry or transport something from someone or something. ☐ *Please take this report back to Liz.* 🅃 *Take back this book to Karen.* ☐ *Would you take this book back to the library?*

TAKE ▸ BEFORE

take someone or something before someone or something to bring someone or something in front of someone or a group for judgment. ☐ *I will have to take Tom before the manager and let Tom tell his story.* ☐ *I took the invention before the committee.* ☐ *I took John before the committee.*

TAKE ▸ BELOW

take someone below to guide someone to a lower deck on a ship. ☐ *The captain told the first mate to take the passengers below.* ☐ *Please take Mr. Wilson below, where he will not be in the way.*

TAKE ▸ BETWEEN

take the bit between one's teeth to begin a task eagerly and with determination; to seize control of a task. ☐ *You've got to take the bit between your teeth and get this project going.* ☐ *Alice took the bit between her teeth and got the job done.*

TAKE ▸ BY

take someone or something by something to grasp someone or something by holding on to some part. ☐ *She took him by the hand and helped him up.* ☐ *Tom took the dog by the collar and led it out.*

take someone or something by storm 1. to conquer someone or something in a fury. □ *The army took city after city by storm.* □ *They crashed in and took the general by storm.* **2.** to succeed overwhelmingly with someone, some place, or a group. □ *The singing star took the audience in each town by storm.* □ *The star took us all by storm.*

take someone or something by surprise to surprise someone or a group. □ *Oh! You took me by surprise!* □ *The boss took the board of directors by surprise.*

take the bull by the horns to begin a vigorous and direct attempt to solve a problem. (A cliché.) □ *It's time to take the bull by the horns and solve this problem.* □ *She took the bull by the horns and got things moving.*

TAKE ▸ DOWN

take someone down a notch (or two) AND **take someone down a peg (or two)** to rebuff someone; to put one in one's place. □ *He is getting sort of arrogant. It's time to take him down a notch or two.* □ *I really wanted to take Wally down a peg.*

take someone down a peg (or two) See the previous entry.

take someone down to size to put one in one's place, possibly by violence. (Figurative.) □ *The boss decided that she would take the troublesome worker down to size.* □ *Am I going to have to take you down to size, or can you straighten yourself out?*

take someone or something down to move someone or something to a lower position or level. □ *The boss is downstairs and wants to meet our visitor. Will you take her down?* 🅃 *The way down to the lobby is confusing. Let me take down our visitor.* □ *Let me take the sandwiches down.* 🅃 *Please take down the flag.* □ *He took his pants down and got his injection in the hip.*

take something down to take some large or complicated things apart. □ *They plan to take all these buildings down and turn the land into a park.* 🅃 *Do they plan to take down the television broadcasting tower?*

take something down (in something) to write something down in something, such as writing, a notebook, etc. □ *Please take these figures down in your notebook.* 🅃 *Take down these figures in your record of this meeting.* □ *I will ask my secretary to take some notes down about what happens at this meeting.* 🅃 *Please take down some notes on this.* □ *I will take them down and type them later.*

take something down on paper to write something on paper, often as one is hearing it said. □ *Please take this information down on paper.* 🅃 *Take down this name on paper so you won't forget it.*

TAKE ▸ FOR

take credit for something to allow people to believe that one has done something praiseworthy, whether or not one has actually done it. □ *I can't take credit for the entire success. Toby helped a lot.* □ *Mary took credit for everything that Dave did.*

take revenge (on someone) (for something) to get even for someone's past misdeed. □ *I intend to take revenge on Paul for what he did.* □ *I would not take revenge on anyone.* □ *I would not take revenge for that!*

take someone for a fool to assume that someone is a fool, probably in error. □ *Do you take me for a fool?* □ *I hope you don't take me for a fool.*

take someone for a ride **1.** to carry someone about, usually for recreation, in a car, plane, boat, etc. □ *Would you take us for a ride in your boat?* □ *Please take me for a ride in your new car.* **2.** to deceive someone. (Figurative.) □ *You really took those people for a ride. They really believed you.* □ *I was taken for a ride on this matter.* **3.** to take away and murder a person. □ *Mr. Big told Lefty to take Max for a ride.* □ *Mr. Gutman had said he thought Lefty had better take Walter for a ride.*

take someone for an idiot to assume that someone is an idiot, probably in error. □ *Do you take me for an idiot?* □

At first, I took her for an idiot, and then I realized my mistake.

take someone for dead to assume that someone who is still alive is dead. □ *When we found her, we took her for dead, but the paramedics were able to revive her.* □ *He was taken for dead and abandoned.*

take someone for someone to mistake someone for someone else. □ *Sorry. I took you for my cousin, who looks something like you.* □ *I think that you took me for someone else.*

take someone for something **1.** to perceive someone as something. □ *I took you for a fairly even-tempered person. You aren't.* □ *Alice took Jim for a gentleman—which he was.* **2.** to escort someone to and through some activities, such as a walk, a swim, a ride, etc. □ *Can I take you for a ride?* □ *He took me for a walk in the park, and then we came home.* **3.** to cheat someone by a certain amount of money. (Slang.) □ *That crook took me for a hundred bucks.* □ *How much did he take you for?*

take someone or something for granted to expect someone or something to be always available to serve in some way without thanks or recognition; to value someone or something too lightly. □ *I wish you didn't take me for granted.* □ *I guess that I take a lot of things for granted.*

take someone's word for something to believe what someone says about something without seeking further information. □ *It's true! Take my word for it.* □ *I can't prove it. You will have to take my word for it.*

take something for something to accept something, such as a price, for something; to charge a certain amount for something. (Colloquial.) □ *I'll take four thousand for that car there.* □ *How much will you take for a big bag of flour?*

take the rap for someone or something to take the blame for doing something for someone else. (Slang.) □ *Do you really think I am going to take the rap for you?* □ *I don't want to take the rap for what Max did.*

TAKE ► FROM

take a page from someone's book to follow someone's example. (Figurative.) □ *Why don't you take a page from Sam's book and do what he does?* □ *Take a page from my book. Do whatever you want.*

take heart from something to receive courage or comfort from some fact. □ *I hope that you will take heart from what we told you today.* □ *Sam was not able to take heart from the news he heard from his hometown.*

take it from someone to accept the statement of someone; to believe someone. (Usually with *me*.) □ *It's true! Take it from me!* □ *Take it from me. This is a very good day for this part of the country.*

take it from the top to begin [again] at the beginning, especially the beginning of a piece of music. (Originally in reference to the top of a sheet of music.) □ *The conductor stopped the band and had the players take it from the top again.* □ *Let's take it from the top and play it a bit softer this time.*

take something from someone **1.** to remove something from someone's possession. □ *Jimmy took Tim's cookie from him.* □ *Please don't take my money from me.* **2.** to endure abuse from someone. □ *I cannot take any more from you!* □ *Tom could not take any more bad treatment from Alice.*

take something from something to subtract something from something; to remove something from something. □ *Take ten from twenty and see what you have left.* □ *If you take the lettuce out of the salad, what do you have left?*

TAKE ► IN

See also under *TAKE ► IN(TO)*.

take a hand in something to help with something; to participate in something. □ *Would you take a hand in this work? We need your efforts.* □ *Ted refused to take a hand in the preparations for the evening meal.*

take an interest in someone or something to become concerned or interested in someone or something. □ *Do you take an interest in your children?* □ *You should take an interest in everything your child does.*

take part in something to participate in something. □ *I hope you agree to take part in our play.* □ *I would like to take part in the conference.*

take pride in someone or something to be proud of someone or something. □ *I take a great deal of pride in my children.* □ *She takes pride in her work and it shows in her product.*

take refuge in something to hide in something; to seek safety or the comfort of being safe in something. □ *The rabbits took refuge in a hole in the ground.* □ *The children took refuge in the house as soon as the storm began.*

take someone in 1. to give someone shelter. (See also *take something in.*) □ *Do you think you could take me in for the night?* 🅃 *I don't take in strangers.* 2. to deceive someone. □ *Those crooks really took me in. I was a fool.* 🅃 *The con artists took in a lot of innocent people.*

take someone in as something to make someone a member of an organization. □ *We took her in as an associate at first.* 🅃 *I took in Karen as an associate.*

take someone in hand to take control of someone; to assume the responsibility of guiding someone. □ *Someone is going to have to take Tim in hand and help him out.* □ *Alice decided that she would take the new worker in hand.*

take someone's life in one's hands to risk someone's life. □ *If you go there, you will be taking your life in your hands.* □ *Ted didn't want to take his life in his hands by going there alone.*

take something in 1. to reduce the size of a garment. □ *This is too big. I'll have to take it in around the waist.* 🅃 *I'll have to take in these pants.* 2. to bring something or a creature into shelter. □ *I didn't want Joan to take the stray cat in, but she did it anyway.* 🅃 *Joan always takes in stray animals.* 3. to view and study something; to attend something involving viewing. □ *The mountains are so beautiful! I need an hour or so to take it all in.* 🅃 *I want to sit here a minute and take in the view.* 🅃 *Would you like to take in a movie?* 4. to receive money as payment or proceeds. □ *How much did we take in today?* 🅃 *The box office took in nearly a thousand dollars in just the last hour.* 5. to receive something into the mind, usually visually. □ *Could you take those explanations in? I couldn't.* 🅃 *I could hardly take in everything she said.*

take something in (one's) stride to accept advances or setbacks as the normal course of events. □ *She faced a serious problem, but she was able to take it in her stride.* □ *I'll just take it in stride.* □ *We were afraid that success would spoil her, but she just took it in stride.*

take stock in something to believe something. (Usually negative.) □ *I take no stock in anything he says.* □ *No one took any stock in the reports that were coming out of Egypt.*

TAKE ▸ INTO

take someone into one's confidence to tell something confidential to someone. □ *I want to say something that is sort of secret. Can I take you into my confidence?* □ *Fred was taken into Sally's confidence and told all about the surprise party for Andrew.*

take someone or something into one's heart to grow to love and trust someone or some creature; to receive a newcomer graciously and lovingly. □ *He was such a cute little boy. We took him into our hearts immediately.* □ *We loved the puppy instantly and took her into our hearts at once.*

take something into account AND **take something into consideration** to consider something to be an important factor in some decision. □ *We will take your long years of service into account when we make our final decision.* □ *You can be certain that we will take it into consideration.*

take something into consideration See the previous entry.

take something into one's head to get an obsession or overpowering idea into one's thinking. ☐ *George took this strange idea into his head about fixing the car himself.* ☐ *I don't know why she took that strange idea into her head.*

take the law into one's own hands to act as judge, jury, and executioner. ☐ *You are not supposed to take the law into your own hands. You had no right to punish the offender.* ☐ *I don't want to take the law into my own hands.*

TAKE ▸ IN(TO)

take something in(to some place) to carry something into a place. ☐ *Fred took the birthday cake into the dining room.* Ⓣ *Liz took in the cake for us.* ☐ *Jamie took the ice cream in.*

TAKE ▸ OF

take a dim view of someone or something to disapprove of someone or something. ☐ *Of all the boys, the teacher likes Dave the least. She takes a dim view of him.* ☐ *I take a dim view of that law.*

take a lot of nerve to demonstrate a lot of audacity or brashness. ☐ *It takes a lot of nerve to be so rude to people!* ☐ *How cruel! That takes a lot of nerve!*

take account of someone or something to pay attention to someone or something. ☐ *You should take account of Tom. He has some good advice.* ☐ *Do I have to take account of the new policies?*

take advantage of someone **1.** to deceive someone. ☐ *I knew that you wouldn't take advantage of me! I trusted you.* ☐ *Please don't take advantage of me the way you took advantage of Carl.* **2.** to impose on someone. ☐ *I am glad of your help. I hope I am not taking advantage of you.* ☐ *I am glad to do it. You are not taking advantage of me.*

take advantage of someone or something to utilize someone or something to the fullest extent. ☐ *Please take advantage of the people who have worked here for a long time.* ☐ *I hope you can take advantage of our free offer.*

take care of someone **1.** to tip someone. ☐ *I took care of the doorman as we left.* ☐ *Did you remember to take care of the waiter?* **2.** to kill or dispose of someone. (Underworld slang.) ☐ *Max said he was going to take care of Lefty once and for all.* ☐ *The crime king ordered Max to take care of a certain private detective.*

take care of someone or something to oversee and protect someone or something; to care for someone or something. ☐ *Please take care of my child while I am away.* ☐ *I will take care of everything for you.*

take charge of someone or something to assume direction of someone or something; to achieve dominion over someone or something. ☐ *Will you please take charge of your children and ask them to be quiet?* ☐ *I am going to ask Richard to take charge of this project.*

take control of someone or something to get the power and right to direct someone or something. ☐ *I will take control of him and see that he does what I want.* ☐ *Will you take control of the Wilson project?*

take heed of someone or something to pay attention to someone or something. ☐ *We will have to take heed of Wendy and see what she will do next.* ☐ *You will learn to take heed of these little signs that things are not going well.*

take hold of someone or something to grasp someone or something. ☐ *He took hold of the child, which frightened her very much.* ☐ *Terry took hold of the doorknob and turned it.*

take leave of one's senses to go crazy; to do something very foolish. ☐ *What are you doing? Have you taken leave of your senses?* ☐ *She took leave of her senses and had the bathroom painted royal purple.*

take leave of someone or something to go away from someone or something. ☐ *It is time for me to take leave of all of you.* ☐ *It saddened me to take leave of the city I grew up in.*

take note of someone or something to commit something about someone or something to one's memory, possibly by making a note on paper. ☐ *I took note* *of her when she came in. I thought she had left the company.* □ *Please take note of the hour. It is late.*

take notice of someone or something to notice the presence or existence of someone or something. □ *They didn't take notice of me, so I left.* □ *I took notice of the amount of the bill.*

take (one's) leave of someone to depart, leaving someone. □ *Tom took his leave of his guests and departed.* □ *I must take leave of all of you. My train departs soon.*

take one's pick of someone or something to be able to have one's choice of someone or something. □ *Can I take my pick of anyone in the group?* □ *Please take your pick of desserts.*

take the liberty of doing something to do something for someone voluntarily; to do something slightly personal for someone that would be more appropriate if one knew the person better. (Often used as an overly polite exaggeration in a request.) □ *Do you mind if I take the liberty of flicking a bit of lint off your collar?* □ *May I take the liberty of removing your wrap?* □ *I took the liberty of ordering an entree for you. I hope you don't mind.*

TAKE ▸ OFF

take a load off (of) someone's mind AND **take a lot off (of) someone's mind** to relieve one's mind of a problem or a worry. (The *of* is colloquial.) □ *I'm glad to hear that. It sure takes a load off of my mind.* □ *This will take a load off her mind.* □ *It sure takes a lot off my mind.*

take a load off one's feet to relax and rest one's feet by sitting down. □ *Please sit down and take a load off your feet.* □ *Sally sat in a comfortable chair and took a load off her feet.*

take off **1.** to take flight. □ *When does this plane take off?* Ⓝ *The takeoff was flawless.* **2.** [for someone] to leave. (Colloquial.) □ *It's late. I've got to take off.* □ *We will have to take off about midnight, since we have to get up early in the morning.* **3.** to become active and exciting. (Colloquial.) □ *Did the party ever take off, or was it dull all night?* □ *Things began to take off about midnight.*

take off after someone or something to set out to chase someone or something. □ *Fred took off after Jim, running as fast as he could.* □ *The dog took off after the rabbit.*

take off (for some place) **1.** to take flight, heading for some place. □ *We took off for Moscow early in the evening.* □ *We took off at dawn.* **2.** to leave for some place. (Figurative.) □ *The girls took off for home when they heard the dinner bell.* □ *It's late. I have to take off now.*

take off from something to take flight from something or some place. □ *The plane took off from the busy airport right on schedule.* □ *We will take off from the airport on one side of town, fly across the city, and land at our destination within three hours.*

take off from work AND **take ((some) time) off from work; take off (from work)** not to appear at one's place of work for a period of time, hours or days. □ *I will have to take off from work to go to the doctor.* □ *I want to take some time off from work and paint the house.* □ *Ken took off from work when he was ill.* □ *I'm going to have to take off this afternoon because I have an appointment with my dentist.*

take one's eyes off (of) someone or something to cease looking at someone or something. (Usually negative. The *of* is colloquial.) □ *I couldn't take my eyes off of the usher.* □ *Ken couldn't take his eyes off Judy.* □ *Don't take your eyes off the children for even a minute!*

take one's hands off (of) someone or something to let go of someone or something. (The *of* is colloquial.) □ *Take your hands off of me!* □ *Please take your hands off the cake plate.*

take one's hat off to someone to salute or pay an honor to someone. □ *Good work. I take my hat off to you.* Ⓣ *I take off my hat to you! What an excellent job!*

take oneself off some place to go away to some place more private. □ *I need to* *take myself off someplace and think all this over.* ☐ *She kept her sanity by taking herself off to her bedroom for a few hours each day.*

take someone or something off someone's hands to relieve someone of the burden or bother of someone or something. (Figurative.) ☐ *I would be happy to take your uncle off your hands for a few hours.* ☐ *Will you please take some of this food off my hands?*

take someone or something off (something) to remove someone or something from the surface of something. ☐ *Bob helped take his children off the merry-go-round.* ☐ *Please take your books off the table.* ☐ *I'll take them off.*

take something off to remove something, such as an article of clothing. ☐ *Please take your coat off and stay awhile.* 🅃 *Please take off your coat.*

take the day off not to go to work for a day. ☐ *I am going to take the day off tomorrow.* ☐ *I need to take the day off and do some things at home.*

take the edge off ((of) something) to decrease the effect of something. (As one might dull a knife. The *of* is colloquial.) ☐ *He did not mean to insult the guest, and he quickly thought of something to say that would take the edge off his remark.* ☐ *Her comments were quite cruel and nothing could be said to take the edge off of them.*

take the heat off (of) someone or something to relieve the pressure on someone or something. (Figurative. The *of* is colloquial.) ☐ *That really takes the heat off of all of us.* ☐ *The change in the deadline takes the heat off the office staff.*

take the lid off ((of) something) **1.** to remove the lid from something. (The *of* is colloquial.) ☐ *I took the lid off the box and set it aside.* 🅃 *Karen took off the lid.* **2.** to become involved in some problems; to reveal a set of previously concealed problems. (Figurative. The *of* is colloquial.) ☐ *You took the lid off this mess. You straighten it out!* 🅃 *You took off the lid, so you have to settle it.*

take years off (of) someone or something to make someone seem younger; to take years off some part of someone. (The *of* is colloquial.) ☐ *My exciting vacation took years off of me.* ☐ *Your shorter haircut has taken years off of your face.*

TAKE ▸ ON

See also under *TAKE ▸ (UP)ON.*

take a bath on something to accumulate large losses on a business transaction or an investment. (Colloquial. Refers to "getting soaked," a slang expression meaning "being heavily charged for something.") ☐ *Sally took a bath on that stock that she bought. Its price went down to nothing.* ☐ *I'm afraid that I will take a bath on any investment I make.*

take a chance on someone or something to gamble that something good might happen or that someone might do well; to take a risk that something would go wrong or that someone would do badly. ☐ *I just couldn't take a chance on Walter, so I picked David.* ☐ *I would never take a chance on that horse!*

take a firm grip on someone or something **1.** to grasp someone or something tightly. ☐ *The police officer took a firm grip on Max and led him to the squad car.* ☐ *Mary took a firm grip on the handle and pulled hard.* **2.** to gain control of someone or something. (Figurative.) ☐ *You will have to take a firm grip on Andrew. He has a mind of his own.* ☐ *Someone needs to take a firm grip on this department and get it organized.*

take a (firm) stand on something to express and maintain a strong opinion of something. ☐ *I hope you take a firm stand on the need for more insurance.* ☐ *Yes, I will take a stand on it.*

take a rain check on something **1.** to accept a piece of paper allowing one to see an event—that has been canceled—at a later time. ☐ *I took a rain check on the game. It looked like the rain would never stop.* ☐ *We all had to take rain checks on the game since they couldn't play very much of it.* **2.** to accept a piece of paper allowing one to purchase on sale something that is temporarily out of stock during the period of the sale. (Originally said of sporting events that had to be canceled because of rain.) ☐ *I will take a rain check on the bottle of vitamins.* ☐ *Do you want to take a rain check on this sale item?*

take action on someone or something to act on someone or something; to do what has to be done on someone or something. ☐ *We still have to discuss what to do with Sam. I hope we can take action on him today.* ☐ *Do we still have time to take action on this proposal?*

take fuel on to refuel; to be refueled. (Usually said of a large conveyance, such as a ship or a plane.) ☐ *We need to land at the next major airport to take fuel on.* 🅃 *We will land somewhere to take on fuel.*

take it easy on someone or something to treat someone or something gently. ☐ *Please take it easy on me. I just got out of the hospital.* ☐ *Please take it easy on this chair. It's very old.*

take it on the lam to run away; to escape from or elude the police. (Slang.) ☐ *Max took it on the lam just after he robbed the bank.* ☐ *He had to take it on the lam to avoid getting picked up by the cops.*

take it on the nose to take the brunt of something; to accept the full force of something oneself. (Figurative.) ☐ *It was a terrible scolding, and poor Jerry took it on the nose.* ☐ *I really took it on the nose and I didn't even do anything wrong.*

take on (so) to behave very emotionally. ☐ *Stop crying. Please don't take on so.* ☐ *I wish you wouldn't take on about this matter.*

take pity on someone or something to show pity for someone or some creature. ☐ *She took pity on us and let us come in.* ☐ *Jan took pity on the kitten.*

take revenge (on someone) (for something) See under *TAKE ▸ FOR.*

take someone or something on to agree to deal with someone or something; to begin to handle someone or something. ☐ *I did not agree to take him on.* 🅃 *I wouldn't have taken on this project if I had thought there would be no help.*

take someone's word on something to accept that what someone says is true without checking further. ☐ *Can I take your word on that?* ☐ *I can't prove it, but you can take my word on it.*

take something on the chin to absorb the full brunt of something. (Figurative.) ☐ *We all got bawled out, but Roger really took it on the chin.* ☐ *Sam took it on the chin and didn't complain at all.*

take something on trust to accept that something is true through trust. ☐ *I don't know if it's so, but I'll take it on trust.* ☐ *You will have to take it on trust because I can't prove it.*

take too much on to accept too many tasks; to accept a task that is too big a burden for one. ☐ *Nancy has a tendency to take too much on and then get exhausted.* 🅃 *I always take on too much and then I have no time of my own.*

TAKE ▸ OUT

take a lot out of someone to drain a lot of energy from someone. ☐ *This kind of work takes a lot out of one.* ☐ *Hot days like this take a lot out of me.*

take out after someone or something to set out chasing or running after someone or something. ☐ *Mary took out after Claire but couldn't catch her.* ☐ *The dog took out after the rabbit.*

take someone or something out (of something) to carry, lead, or guide someone or something out of something or some place. (The *of*-phrase is paraphrased with a *from*-phrase when the particle is transposed. See the 🄵 example.) ☐ *He was becoming quite ill from the smoke, and I had to take him out of the room.* 🅃 *They took out the people.* 🄵 *They took out the coughing people from the burning room.* ☐ *Let's take them out as soon as we can.* 🄽 *I have take-out order for twelve hamburgers.*

take someone out **1.** to block out a player in football. ☐ *You take Joe out and I'll carry the ball.* 🅃 *Who was sup-*

posed to take out that huge guy? **2.** to kill someone. (Slang.) □ *Mr. Gutman told Lefty to take Max out.* 🅃 *One more word out of you, and I'm going to take you out.*

take someone out to something to take someone as one's guest to a meal or an event outside one's home. □ *Can I take you out to dinner sometime?* 🅃 *We will take out the visitors to dinner tonight.*

take something out in trade to accept someone's goods or services in payment of a bill. (Colloquial and idiomatic.) □ *The grocer told the plumber that he would pay the plumber by allowing him to take his bill out in trade.* □ *I don't have any cash right now. Can you take it out in trade?*

take something out of someone or something to remove something from the inside of someone or something. (The *of*-phrase is paraphrased with a *from*-phrase when the particle is transposed. See the 🄵 example.) □ *The doctors took a large intestinal tumor out of Wally.* 🅃 *She took out a sheet of paper.* 🄵 *Karen took out a sheet of paper from her walnut-topped desk.*

take something out of someone's hands **1.** to remove something from someone's grasp. □ *The police officer took the gun out of Max's hands.* □ *The heavy tray was taken out of my hands just in time.* **2.** to assume control of something from someone. (Figurative.) □ *The boss decided to take the project out of Roger's hands.* □ *The contract had to be taken out of Alice's hands because she announced that she was leaving.*

take something out on someone or something to punish someone or something because of something, such as anger, hurt feelings, frustration, etc. □ *I know you're angry, but don't take it out on me!* 🅃 *Don't take out your anger on me.* □ *Ken wanted to take his anger out on the dog.*

take the easy way out (of something) to get free of something by taking the path of least resistance. □ *You can depend on Kelly to take the easy way out of a tough situation.* □ *I'm not the type that takes the easy way out.*

take the words out of someone's mouth to say something just before someone else was going to say the same thing; to say something that someone who agrees with you might have said. □ *That is exactly right! You took the words right out of my mouth!* □ *When you said* expensive, *you took the words right out of my mouth!*

TAKE ▶ OVER

take over (from someone) to assume the role or job of someone. □ *I take over for the manager next month.* □ *Liz takes over and will be in charge.*

take pains over something to deal with something with great care. (See also *take pains with someone or something.*) □ *She certainly takes pains over her work.* □ *You will have to take pains over this if you want it to be done right.*

take someone or something over (to someone or something) to deliver someone or something to someone or something. (*Someone* includes *oneself.*) □ *Would you take this over to Tiffany?* □ *Would you take Tiffany over to the office?* □ *Can you take the flowers over to room 234?* □ *I would be happy to take them over.* □ *She took herself over to the clerk.*

take something over **1.** to assume responsibility for a task. □ *It looks as if I'm going to have to take the project over.* 🅃 *I will take over the project.* **2.** to acquire all of an asset. □ *Carl set out to take the failing airline over.* 🅃 *He took over the failing company.* 🄽 *The takeover of the company was accomplished with the help of a number of investment bankers.*

TAKE ▶ THROUGH

take someone through (something) to escort someone through something or some place. □ *Would you mind taking Jerry through the factory?* □ *I would be happy to take him through.*

TAKE ▶ TO

take a fancy to someone or something AND **take a liking to someone or some-**

thing; take a shine to someone or something to develop fondness for someone or something. (*Take a shine* is colloquial.) ☐ *Fred took a fancy to Tiffany and started dating her.* ☐ *Ann really took a liking to Ken.* ☐ *I think Jed has taken a shine to Molly-Jo.*

take a liking to someone or something See the previous entry.

take a shine to someone or something See *take a fancy to someone or something.*

take exception to something **1.** to take offense at something. ☐ *I must take exception to your remark.* ☐ *Sue took exception to Fred's characterization of Bill as a cheapskate.* **2.** to disagree with something. ☐ *I have to take exception to the figure you quoted.* ☐ *The manager took exception to the statement about having only three employees.*

take someone to court to sue someone; to get a court injunction affecting someone. ☐ *I will take you to court if you persist in pestering my client.* ☐ *Don was taken to court in a negligence suit.*

take someone to one side to lead someone to a relatively private place, to say something private or give private instructions. (See also *take someone aside.*) ☐ *Gary took Fran to one side to talk to her.* ☐ *I will take Sue to one side and have a word with her about this matter.*

take someone to task to scold someone. ☐ *Alice took Greg to task for his manners.* ☐ *Sue was taken to task for her behavior.*

take someone to the cleaners to get all of someone's money. (Slang. Refers to cleaning all the money out of someone's pockets.) ☐ *I went to the clinic with a simple cold and they took me to the cleaners!* ☐ *Roger was taken to the cleaners when he bought that new luxury car.*

take something to heart to consider that some comment is relevant to oneself. ☐ *Mary listened to Bob's advice and took it all to heart.* ☐ *All Sue's advice was taken to heart by the show committee.*

take something to pieces to disassemble something. (Colloquial.) ☐ *I will have to take the vacuum cleaner to pieces to find out what's wrong with it.* ☐ *The machine was taken to pieces again in an effort to find where the left-over part belonged.*

take something to someone or something to carry something to someone or something. ☐ *Should I take this package to Carol?* ☐ *Would you take this to the post office?*

take to one's bed to go to bed, as with an illness. ☐ *I feel a little ill, so I'll take to my bed for a day or so.* ☐ *Sam took to his bed with a fever.*

take to one's heels to run. ☐ *Liz took to her heels and got out of there.* ☐ *I took to my heels and ran away as fast as I could.*

take to someone or something to develop an affinity for someone or something; to like someone or something. ☐ *We will see how Timmy takes to the new baby-sitter.* ☐ *The puppy seems to take to this new food just fine.*

take to the hills to run away, as if escaping a flood. (Figurative. See also *head for the hills* under *HEAD ▸ FOR.*) ☐ *If Carl is elected president, everyone had better take to the hills.* ☐ *We will take to the hills if the tax agents come calling.*

TAKE ▸ UNDER

take someone under one's wing to become the mentor and protector of someone. ☐ *David took Frank under his wing to train him in the policies of the company.* ☐ *I think I will take Sue under my wing and help her understand how to get along around here.*

take something under advisement to hear an idea and think about it carefully. ☐ *It's a good idea, but I'll have to take it under advisement.* ☐ *The suggestion was taken under advisement, and a reply was not expected for at least a month.*

TAKE ▸ UP

take a position up some place to occupy a position at a place. ☐ *They took a position up near the house.* 🅃 *The* *troops took up a position at the foot of the mountain.*

take someone up to discuss or deal with someone. ☐ *What are we going to do about Bill? Are we going to take Bill up today at the board meeting?* 🅃 *Let's take up the applicants in our next meeting.*

take someone up on something to accept an offer that someone has made. ☐ *That's a good offer. I'll take you up on it.* ☐ *Tom took Sue up on her offer of dinner.*

take something up **1.** [for someone or a group] to deliberate something. ☐ *When will the board of directors take this up?* 🅃 *Let's take up that matter now.* **2.** to raise something, such as the height of a hem. ☐ *The skirt is too long. I'll have to take it up.* 🅃 *Can you take up this skirt for me?* **3.** to continue with something after an interruption. ☐ *They took it up where they left off.* 🅃 *Let's take up this matter at the point we were at when we were interrupted.* 🅃 *We must take up our work again.* **4.** to begin something; to start to acquire a skill in something. ☐ *When did you take this hobby up?* 🅃 *I took up skiing last fall.* **5.** to absorb something. ☐ *This old sponge doesn't take much water up.* 🅃 *It used to take up more.* **6.** to adopt something new. ☐ *I see you've taken a new life-style up.* 🅃 *Toby took up the life of a farmer.*

take something up to someone to deliver something to a person on a higher level. ☐ *I will take this up to the boss and try to get it approved.* ☐ *Please take this up to Sue on the next floor and see what she thinks about it.*

take something up with someone to open a discussion about something with someone. ☐ *I would like to take a very important matter up with you.* 🅃 *I will have to take up this question with my supervisor.*

take the slack up **1.** to tighten a rope that is holding something loosely. ☐ *Take the slack up if you can.* 🅃 *This clothesline is too loose. Do something to take up the slack.* **2.** to do what needs to be done; to do what has been left undone. (The 🅃 *example has the most typical order.)* ☐ *Do I have to take the slack up?* 🅃 *Jill did her job poorly and I have to take up the slack.*

take up a collection (from someone) (for someone or something) to collect money from people for someone or something. ☐ *I am taking up a collection from everyone for a gift for Mark.* 🅃 *Karen took a collection up from everyone in the office for Bill.* ☐ *Karen took a collection up for Bill from everyone in the office.* ☐ *She took up a collection for a gift.*

take up arms against someone or something to begin an armed battle with someone or something. (Both literal and figurative uses.) ☐ *The people finally took up arms against their overlords.* ☐ *They were afraid to take up arms against the government.*

take up one's abode some place to make some place one's home. ☐ *I am going to take up my abode in a different city.* ☐ *I will take up my abode in this place and hope to find a job close by.*

take up residence some place to make a residence of a place. ☐ *Ed took up residence in a small efficiency apartment.* ☐ *It looks as if a family of mice has taken up residence in the cupboard.*

take up room AND **take up space** to fill space; to serve no purpose other than to fill space. ☐ *Let's get rid of this old trunk. It just takes up space.* ☐ *You are just taking up room. Please leave.* ☐ *I want to get rid of this. It's just taking up space.*

take up someone's time to use up one's time, probably wastefully. ☐ *Please hurry. You are taking up my time and my time is valuable.* ☐ *I don't want to take up too much of your time, but I have a quick question.*

take up something to occupy something such as space, time, or a period of time. ☐ *The old business took up the entire meeting. The meeting took up an hour.*

take up the challenge to respond to a challenge and do what the challenge asks. ☐ *I am not prepared to take the challenge up.* 🅃 *Dave took up the challenge without much urging.*

take up time to require time; to fill time; to waste time. ☐ *These silly questions of yours just take up time.* ☐ *The little problems seem to take up more time than the big ones.*

take up with someone to become close with someone; to become friends with someone. ☐ *I think that Albert may have taken up with the wrong people.* ☐ *I did not want Lefty to take up with Max, but he did, and look where it's gotten him.*

TAKE ▸ (UP)ON

take something (up)on oneself to accept the entire burden of something on oneself. (*Upon* is formal and less commonly used than *on*.) ☐ *You didn't need to take it all upon yourself. There are others here who can help, you know.* ☐ *Jan takes too much on herself.*

TAKE ▸ UPON

take something upon oneself (to do something) to make it one's exclusive job to do a task; to do something without authorization. ☐ *She took it upon herself to do the whole project.* ☐ *Yes, it needs to be done, but you don't need to take it on yourself.*

TAKE ▸ WITH

See *be taken with someone or something* under *BE ▸ WITH.*

take a hard line with someone to be firm with someone. ☐ *We will have to take a hard line with the students, I'm afraid.* ☐ *The boss took a hard line with the employees who kept coming in late.*

take issue with someone to argue with someone. ☐ *I heard your last statement and I have to take issue with you.* ☐ *Tom took issue with Maggie about the cost of the house.*

take issue with something to disagree with or argue about something. ☐ *I have to take issue with that statement.* ☐ *I want to take issue with the last statement you made.*

take it with one to take possessions with you when you die. (Usually negative.) ☐ *Spend it. You can't take it with you, you know.* ☐ *He knew he couldn't take it with him, so he spent it all.*

take liberties with someone or something to act too freely with someone or something. ☐ *You are taking too many liberties with the office staff. They are not supposed to do your personal work.* ☐ *Who is taking liberties with the office supplies? They are disappearing at a fast rate.*

take pains with someone or something to deal with someone or something with great care. ☐ *He really took pains with me to make sure I understood it all.* ☐ *Ken took pains with the model plane.*

take someone or something with one to take away someone or something when one leaves. ☐ *When you go, take Liz with you.* ☐ *Please take your dog with you.*

take something with a grain of salt to be very skeptical about something. ☐ *I don't know if she is telling the truth. You have to take everything she says with a grain of salt, anyway.* ☐ *He told me how much money I could get for the car, but I took it with a grain of salt.*

take something with one to take something [away] with one. ☐ *I am going to take this food with me.* ☐ *Can I take one of these catalogs with me?*

take something with something to eat or swallow something, such as medicine, with something. ☐ *You have to take this medicine with milk or soda water.* ☐ *I will take this pill with milk.*

take the bitter with the sweet to accept the bad things in life along with the good things. (Idiomatic.) ☐ *Life is not always pleasant, and you have to learn to take the bitter with the sweet.* ☐ *We took the bitter with the sweet, year after year. What choice did we have?*

take turns with someone to alternate [doing something] with someone. ☐ *We both can't be there at the same time. I'll take turns with you.* ☐ *You have to take turns with your brother.*

TALK ▶ ABOUT

talk about someone or something to discuss someone or something. □ *I don't want to talk about Jerry anymore.* □ *Let's not talk about it now.*

TALK ▶ AROUND

talk around something to talk, but avoid talking directly about the subject. □ *You are just talking around the matter! I want a straight answer!* □ *He never really said anything. He just talked around the issue.*

TALK ▶ AT

talk at someone to say words at someone; to talk to someone in a desultory manner. □ *You are just talking at her and she isn't paying attention.* □ *Talk to me, not at me. I want to communicate with you.*

TALK ▶ BACK

talk back (to someone) to challenge verbally a parent, an older person, or one's superior. □ *Please don't talk back to me!* □ *I've told you before not to talk back!* [N] *I've had enough of your backtalk!*

TALK ▶ DOWN

talk down to someone to speak to someone condescendingly. □ *You would be more convincing if you didn't talk down to your audience.* □ *Please don't talk down to me. I can understand anything that you are likely to say.*

talk someone down **1.** to win at debating someone. □ *Liz was able to talk her opponent down.* [T] *She talked down her opponent.* **2.** to direct a pilot to make a safe landing by giving spoken instructions over the airplane's radio. □ *The people on the ground talked the amateur pilot down successfully.* □ *I wonder how many movies have been made about someone talking a pilot down.*

TALK ▶ FOR

talk for something to give a speech for a group. □ *I am going to talk for the City Women's Club in March.* □ *Fred talked for the Chamber of Commerce last month.*

TALK ▶ INTO

talk someone into something to convince someone to do something through discussion. (*Someone* includes *oneself.*) □ *I think I can talk June into it.* □ *She finally talked herself into making the dive.*

TALK ▶ OF

talk of someone or something to speak about someone or something. □ *Weren't we talking of old Mrs. Watson just now?* □ *We were just talking of old times—happier times.*

TALK ▶ ON

talk on to continue to talk. □ *The lecturer talked on for hours.* □ *How can anyone talk on so long without saying anything?*

talk on someone or something to speak on the subject of someone or something. □ *Today, I will talk on Abraham Lincoln.* □ *Ann is going to talk on the subject of manners.*

TALK ▶ OUT

talk one's way out of something to get out of something by verbal persuasion. □ *You are in a mess and you can't talk your way out of it.* □ *If I get into some sort of problem, I will try to talk my way out of it.*

talk oneself out to talk until one can talk no more. □ *She talked herself out and was silent for the rest of the day.* □ *I talked until I talked myself out.*

talk someone out of doing something to convince someone not to do something by talking and arguing. (*Someone* includes *oneself.*) □ *You can't talk me out of doing it. My mind is made up!* □ *I knew I would talk myself out of doing it.*

talk someone out of something to convince someone to give up something. □ *They were trying to talk me out of my inheritance.* □ *Timmy tried to talk Mary out of her ice cream cone.*

talk something out to settle something by discussion. □ *Let's not get mad. Let's just talk it out.* [T] *Please, let's talk out this matter.*

TALK ▸ OVER

talk over someone's head to say things that someone cannot understand; to speak on too high a level for one's audience. ☐ *The speaker talked over our heads and we learned nothing.* ☐ *It is not a good idea to talk over your audience's heads.*

talk over something to use something, such as a microphone, intercom, or telephone, to talk. ☐ *I don't mind talking over the telephone.* ☐ *I will talk to Jeff over the intercom and see what he thinks about the idea.*

talk someone or something over (with someone) to discuss someone or something with someone. ☐ *I want to talk John over with my staff.* 🅃 *I will talk over this matter with Sam.* ☐ *Let's talk it over with Fred.* ☐ *I think we should talk this over.*

TALK ▸ THROUGH

talk something through to get something approved by talking convincingly. ☐ *The board was reluctant to approve it, but I talked it through.* 🅃 *We will talk through this matter in the board meeting.*

talk through one's hat to brag or exaggerate; to talk nonsense. (Colloquial.) ☐ *That can't be so! You are just talking through your hat!* ☐ *Pay no attention to Mary. She is just talking through her hat.*

TALK ▸ TO

talk to someone **1.** to speak to someone; to confer with someone. ☐ *Talk to me!* ☐ *I will have to talk to Mark to see what he thinks.* **2.** to lecture to someone; to reprimand someone. ☐ *I wish you would talk to your son. He is creating havoc in the classroom.* ☐ *I am going to have to talk to Roberta. She is not getting things clean.* 🄽 *Give Sam a good talking-to!*

TALK ▸ UNTIL

talk until one is blue in the face to talk a great deal, futilely. ☐ *I talked until I was blue in the face and got nowhere.* ☐ *She wasted a lot of time, talking herself blue in the face about this silly business.*

TALK ▸ UP

talk something up to promote or advertise something by saying good things about it to as many people as possible. ☐ *Let's talk the play up around campus so we can get a good audience.* 🅃 *I will talk up the play all I can.*

talk up a storm to talk a great deal. ☐ *Whenever we get together, we always talk up a storm.* ☐ *Everyone was talking up a storm and didn't hear the chairman come in.*

TALK ▸ WITH

talk with someone (about someone or something) to hold a discussion with someone or a group. ☐ *Could I talk with you about Alice?* ☐ *Can I talk with you about my salary?* ☐ *I need to talk with you about Walter.* ☐ *I want to talk with you about money.*

TALLY ▸ UP

tally something up to add something up. ☐ *Please tally everything up and tell me the total.* 🅃 *Let's tally up everything and ask for donations.*

TALLY ▸ WITH

tally with something **1.** [for one set of figures] to match another set of figures. ☐ *Your figures don't tally with mine. Let's add them up again.* ☐ *The total Sam got didn't tally with what the tax agent had come up with.* **2.** [for one thing] to agree or correlate with another. ☐ *What you just said doesn't tally with what you told me before.* ☐ *His story doesn't tally with what I already know.*

TAMP ▸ DOWN

tamp something down to pat or pack something down. ☐ *Tamp the soil down over the seeds after you plant them.* 🅃 *Please tamp down the soil firmly.*

TAMPER ▸ WITH

tamper with someone or something to fiddle with someone or something; to meddle with someone or something. ☐ *I've got him believing just what I want him to believe. Don't tamper with him.* ☐ *Please don't tamper with the thermostat.*

TANGLE ▸ OVER

tangle (with someone or something) (over someone or something) See under *TANGLE ▸ WITH.*

TANGLE ▸ UP

tangle someone or something up to entangle someone or something. (*Someone* includes *oneself.*) □ *Please don't tangle me up in your ropes.* 🅃 *I tangled up my feet in the roots of the trees.* □ *We almost tangled ourselves up in the ropes.*

TANGLE ▸ WITH

tangle with someone or something (over someone or something) to battle against someone or something about someone or something. □ *Tim tangled with Karen over the children.* □ *I hope I don't have to tangle with the bank over this loan.* □ *I don't want to tangle with city hall.*

TANK ▸ UP

tank up (on something) AND **tank up with something** **1.** to fill one's fuel tank with something. □ *I need to tank up on premium gas to stop this engine knock.* □ *It's time to tank up.* □ *We need to tank up with gas.* **2.** to drink some kind of alcoholic beverage. (Slang.) □ *Toby spent the evening tanking up on bourbon.* □ *Jerry tanked up with gin and went to work.*

TAP ▸ AT

tap at something to aim one or more light blows at something. □ *Fred tapped at the door, but no one heard him.* □ *Who is tapping at my window?*

TAP ▸ DOWN

tap something down to pound something down with light blows. □ *Please tap that nail down so no one gets hurt on it.* 🅃 *Tap down the tack, if you would.*

TAP ▸ FOR

tap someone for something to choose someone for something. (As if tapping someone on the shoulder.) □ *The coach tapped Linda for a place on the team.* □ *Tom tapped Roger for his replacement.*

TAP ▸ IN(TO)

tap something in(to something) to move something in with light blows. □ *The mechanic tapped the bracket into place.* 🅃 *The worker tapped in the bracket.* □ *He used a little hammer to tap it in.*

TAP ▸ ON

tap on something to make one or more light blows on something. □ *Who is that tapping on my windowpane?* □ *I wish you would stop tapping on the tabletop.*

tap someone or something on something to make one or more light blows on some part of someone or something. □ *Someone tapped me on the shoulder, and I turned around to see who it was.* □ *I tapped the drum on the top to find its pitch.*

TAP ▸ OUT

tap something out **1.** to send a message in Morse code, as on a telegraph. □ *The telegraph operator tapped a message out and waited for a reply.* 🅃 *The operator tapped out a message.* **2.** to thump the rhythm of a piece of music [on something]. □ *Tap the rhythm out until you get it right.* 🅃 *Let's tap out the rhythm together.* **3.** to get the ashes out of a pipe by tapping. □ *He took the pipe out of his mouth and tapped the ashes out.* 🅃 *He tapped out the ashes on his heel.*

TAP ▸ WITH

tap something with something to make light blows on something with something. □ *Alice tapped the table with her keys in an annoying fashion..* □ *Just tap the thing lightly with your hammer.*

TAPER ▸ OFF

taper off to slacken off gradually; to cease something gradually; to reduce gradually. □ *Activity finally tapered off in the middle of the afternoon.* □ *I hope that business doesn't taper off in the summer this year.*

taper off doing something gradually to stop doing something; to do less and less of something until there is no more to do. □ *Bob tried to taper off smoking again.* □ *I can't taper off overeating. I have to stop all at once by going on a strict diet.*

TARGET ▶ AS

target someone or something as something to aim at someone or something as something; to choose someone or something as someone or something. ☐ *The board targeted Alice as a potential candidate.* ☐ *We targeted the first of August as the starting date.*

TASTE ▶ LIKE

taste like something to have the same taste as something. ☐ *This stuff tastes like watermelon.* ☐ *What do you think this tastes like?*

TASTE ▶ OF

taste of something **1.** to have a taste similar to something; to have the hint of a certain flavor. ☐ *This ice cream tastes of apricots.* ☐ *Why does this wine taste of vinegar?* **2.** to take a taste of something. (Typically southern.) ☐ *Here, taste of this pie.* ☐ *Can I taste of your apple?*

TATTLE ▶ ON

tattle (on someone) (to someone) to tell on someone to someone. ☐ *Are you going to tattle on me to my mother?* ☐ *Please don't tattle on me.* ☐ *Are you going to tattle to my father?*

TATTLE ▶ TO

See the previous entry.

TAUNT ▶ ABOUT

taunt someone about something to mock, tease, or torment someone about something. ☐ *Stop taunting me about something that happened years ago!* ☐ *Terry was being taunted about his gaudy tie, so he took it off.*

TAUNT ▶ INTO

taunt someone into something to mock, tease or torment someone into doing something. ☐ *The gang taunted Liz into taking unnecessary chances.* ☐ *Don was taunted into leaving the room.*

TAUNT ▶ WITH

taunt someone with something to tease or tantalize someone with something. ☐ *Jerry taunted Fran with the plate of fudge.* ☐ *Please don't taunt me with food I shouldn't eat.*

TAX ▶ WITH

tax someone or something with something to burden or tire someone or something with something. ☐ *Please don't tax me with any more requests for my immediate attention.* ☐ *You are continuing to tax this body with your constant complaints.*

TEAM ▶ UP

team up against someone or something to join with someone else against someone or something. ☐ *Let's team up against Paul and Tony in the footrace.* ☐ *We teamed up against the group from the other school.*

team up (with someone) to join with one or more persons; to collaborate with two or more persons. ☐ *I intend to team up with a friend and go into the painting business.* ☐ *I do better by myself. I don't want to team up.*

TEAR ▶ ACROSS

tear across something to run across some area. ☐ *The boys tore across the lawn to the swimming pool.* ☐ *As the plane tore across the sky it made a horrendous roar.*

TEAR ▶ ALONG

tear along to go along very fast, as in running, driving, cycling, etc. ☐ *The cars tore along the road, raising dust and making noise.* ☐ *Andy tore along on his bicycle, trying to see how fast he could go.*

TEAR ▶ APART

tear someone apart **1.** to cause two people, presumably lovers, to separate unwillingly. (*Someone* includes *themselves*.) ☐ *The enormous disruption of the accident tore them apart and they separated.* 🅃 *The incident tore apart the engaged couple.* ☐ *They kissed and tore themselves apart.* **2.** to cause someone enormous grief or emotional pain. (*Someone* includes *oneself*.) ☐ *The death of her dog tore her apart.* 🅃 *It was the dog's death that tore apart Barbara.* ☐ *He tore himself apart because of his guilt.*

tear someone or something apart **1.** to pull someone or something apart. ☐

Max threatened to tear Lefty apart. Ⓣ *Karen tore apart the roast chicken and served it angrily.* **2.** to criticize someone or something mercilessly. (*Someone* includes *oneself.*) □ *The critics tore her apart in their reviews.* Ⓣ *They tore apart the entire production.* □ *Why do you have to tear yourself apart for making a little error?*

tear something apart to divide something or the members of a group, citizens of a country, etc. □ *The financial crisis tore the club members apart.* Ⓣ *The crisis tore apart the organization.*

TEAR ▸ AROUND

tear around (some place) to move or run around rapidly and perhaps recklessly. □ *The kids were tearing around through the house all day. They've made a real mess.* □ *Please don't tear around the house.*

TEAR ▸ AT

tear at someone or something to rip at someone or something; to try to tear someone or something up. □ *The badger tore at me, but I dodged it and ran away fast.* □ *Timmy tore at the package, struggling to get the paper off.*

TEAR ▸ AWAY

tear away (from someone or something) to leave someone or something, running. □ *Dave tore away from Jill, leaving her to find her own way home.* □ *Roger tore away from the meeting, trying to make his train.*

tear (oneself) away (from someone or something) to force oneself to leave someone or something. □ *Do you think you can tear yourself away from your friends for dinner?* □ *I could hardly tear myself away from the concert.*

tear something away (from someone or something) **1.** to peel something from someone or something. □ *The paramedic tore the clothing away from the burn victim and began to treat the wounds immediately.* Ⓣ *She tore away the clothing from the victim.* □ *She tore the clothing away.* Ⓐ *The torn-away poster flapped in the breeze.* **2.** to snatch something away from someone or something. □ *I tore the grenade away from the child and threw it in the lake.* Ⓣ *Liz tore away the cover from the book.* □ *She tore it away.*

TEAR ▸ BETWEEN

See *be torn between someone and someone else or something and something else* under *BE ▸ BETWEEN.*

TEAR ▸ DOWN

tear down something to race down something very fast. (Compare to *tear something down.*) □ *The girls tore down the hallway as fast as they could run.* □ *They tore down the stairs and ran out the door.*

tear someone or something down to criticize someone or something mercilessly. (*Someone* includes *oneself.*) □ *What is the point in tearing Frank down? He is doing his best and it's as good as anyone else can do, too.* Ⓣ *Don't tear down Frank or the others!* □ *Ann tore down our efforts mercilessly.* □ *You are always tearing yourself down!*

tear something down to raze something. □ *The workers tore the building down and carried the debris away.* Ⓣ *They tore down the building.* Ⓐ *There was little left but one partially torn-down building after another.*

TEAR ▸ FROM

tear something away (from someone or something) See under *TEAR ▸ AWAY.*

tear something from something to rip or peel something from something. □ *He tore the wrapping from the gift.* □ *The monkey tore the peel from the banana and took a bite of it.*

TEAR ▸ INTO

tear into some place to run or race into a place. □ *The kids tore into the house and knocked over a lamp.* □ *Kelly tore into the boss's office and put the papers on the desk.*

tear into someone or something to attack someone or something; to attack someone or something with the intent of eating someone or something. □ *The wolves tore into the hunter and injured* *him severely.* ☐ *The kids tore into the cake and ate it all.*

TEAR ▶ IN(TO)

tear someone or something into something to rip or divide someone or something into parts. ☐ *The wolves looked as if they were going to tear us all into little bits.* ☐ *We tore the contract into bits and threw it away.*

TEAR ▶ OFF

tear off (from someone or something) to leave someone or something in a great hurry. ☐ *I hate to tear off from you guys, but I'm late for dinner.* ☐ *It's time for me to go. I have to tear off.*

tear something off ((of) someone or something) to peel or rip something off someone or something. (The *of*-phrase is paraphrased with a *from*-phrase when the particle is transposed. The *of* is colloquial.) ☐ *Max tore the tie off his victim and ran away with it.* 🅃 *He tore off the tie.* 🄵 *He tore off the tie from his victim.* ☐ *Max tore the label off the can.* 🄰 *That's not a stamp collection! That's just a lot of torn-off stamps.*

TEAR ▶ ON

tear something on something to rip something on something sharp or jagged. ☐ *I tore my pants on the corner of the desk.* ☐ *Mary tore her new skirt on something sharp on the side of the car.*

TEAR ▶ OUT

tear out (of some place) to leave a place in a great hurry. ☐ *The kids tore out of the house after they broke the window.* ☐ *They saw what they had done and tore out.*

tear something out (of something) to remove something from something by ripping or tearing. (The *of*-phrase is paraphrased with a *from*-phrase when the particle is transposed. See the 🄵 example.) ☐ *Tear the coupons out of the magazine and save them.* 🅃 *Please tear out the coupons.* 🄵 *Please tear out the coupons from all the magazines.* ☐ *I tore them all out.* 🄰 *The torn-out pages are completely missing.*

TEAR ▶ TO

tear someone or something to pieces AND **tear someone or something to shreds** to rip or shred someone or something into bits. ☐ *Careful of that dog. It will tear you to pieces!* ☐ *The dog tore the newspaper to pieces.* ☐ *It tore my shoes to shreds.*

TEAR ▶ UP

tear someone or something up to rip someone or something into many pieces. ☐ *Don't get close to that machine. It can tear you up.* 🅃 *The lawn mower tore up the paper left in the yard.* 🄰 *Please place all the torn-up pages in the trash.*

tear someone up to cause someone to grieve seriously. (See also the previous entry.) ☐ *The news of the accident really tore her up.* 🅃 *The news tore up the whole family.*

TEASE ▶ ABOUT

tease someone about someone or something to make fun of someone about someone or something; to poke fun at someone about someone or something. ☐ *The boys teased Don about his girlfriend.* ☐ *Stop teasing me about it!*

TEASE ▶ INTO

tease someone into doing something to force someone to do something through teasing or tormenting. ☐ *Sam teased her into doing what he wanted.* ☐ *Perhaps you can tease him into leaving, but he won't go if you ask him.*

TEASE ▶ OUT

tease something out to separate threads or hairs by combing. ☐ *The hairdresser teased Jill's hair out carefully.* 🅃 *The hairdresser teased out Jill's hair.*

tease something out of something to lure something out of something by teasing or tempting. (The *of*-phrase is paraphrased with a *from*-phrase when the particle is transposed. See the 🄵 example.) ☐ *I managed to tease the cat out of the tree with a bit of fish.* 🅃 *I teased out the cat.* 🄵 *I teased out the frightened cat from the tight place it had crawled into.*

TEE ▸ OFF

tee off 1. to start the first hole in a game of golf. □ *It's time to tee off. Let's get on the course.* □ *What time do we tee off?* 2. to begin [doing anything]; to be the first one to start something. (Colloquial.) □ *The master of ceremonies teed off with a few jokes and then introduced the first act.* □ *Everyone is seated and ready to begin. Why don't you tee off?*

tee someone off to make someone angry. (Slang.) □ *What you said really teed me off!* 🅃 *Her comments teed off the others.* □ *Todd is teed off and looking for you.*

TEEM ▸ WITH

teem with someone or something to swarm with someone or something; to be abundant with someone or something. □ *The porch was teeming with flies, so we couldn't eat there.* □ *The park teemed with people enjoying the sunny weather.*

TELEPHONE ▸ IN

telephone something in (to someone) to call someone on the telephone, usually to give information. (The person called is in a special location, such as one's workplace or headquarters.) □ *I will telephone my report in to my secretary.* 🅃 *I telephoned in my report.* □ *I will telephone it in tomorrow.*

TELESCOPE ▸ INTO

telescope into something [for one part] to fit down inside another part, thereby reducing the length of the whole. □ *This part telescopes into this part.* □ *The tent poles telescoped into a small, compact unit.*

TELL ▸ ABOUT

tell someone about someone or something to give information to someone about someone or something. □ *Please tell me about Wallace.* □ *You were going to tell me about the old neighborhood.*

TELL ▸ APART

tell people or things apart to distinguish one from another. □ *I can't tell Bob and Bill apart.* 🅃 *I find it easy to tell apart Bill and Bob.* □ *The two cakes look different, but in taste, I can't tell this one and that one apart.*

TELL ▸ BETWEEN

tell the difference between someone and someone else or something and something else to recognize the things that distinguish people or things. □ *I can't tell the difference between Billy and Bobby.* □ *Sam can't tell the difference between Granny Smith and Royal Gala apples.*

TELL ▸ BY

tell someone or something by something to identify someone or something by something. □ *You can tell Jim by the old-fashioned shoes he wears.* □ *I can tell the newer car models by the brake light in the rear window.*

TELL ▸ FROM

tell someone from someone else or something from something else to distinguish one from another. □ *I can't tell Chuck from Roger. They look so much alike.* □ *I can't tell orange from yellow.*

tell something from something to know something because of something, such as evidence, signs, experience, etc. □ *I can tell that she's lying from the way she holds her eyebrows.* □ *I can't tell anything from what you told me.*

TELL ▸ OF

tell of someone or something to speak of someone or something. □ *The messenger told of great destruction, hunger, and disease in the northern part of the country.* □ *I want you to tell of Jane and how she is doing.*

TELL ▸ OFF

tell someone off to dismiss someone with a scolding. □ *I am going to tell Jerry off once and for all.* 🅃 *I told off Jerry today.*

TELL ▸ ON

tell (someone) on someone to tattle to someone about someone. (Actually, to "tell on someone to someone.") □ *I'm going to tell your mother on you!* □ *I'll tell on you!*

TELL ▸ TO

tell someone where to get off to rebuke someone; to put one in one's place. (Idiomatic. Also literal uses, as with a train conductor indicating a debarkation point to a passenger.) □ *You really told him where to get off!* □ *If she keeps acting like that to me, I will tell her where to get off.*

tell something to someone to say something to someone. □ *Please tell the whole truth to me.* □ *Please tell your explanation to Mary.*

TEMPER ▸ WITH

temper something with something **1.** to soften something, such as news, with something. □ *We can temper this disaster story a bit with a picture of the happy survivors.* □ *The news story was tempered with a paragraph of explanation and justification.* **2.** to harden something, such as metal, with something. □ *You have to temper the metal pieces with very high heat.* □ *The sheet of metal was tempered by the application of great pressure.*

TEMPT ▸ INTO

tempt someone into something to lure or seduce someone into something. □ *Could I tempt you into going swimming?* □ *She would not be tempted into eating the rich and fattening cake.*

TEMPT ▸ TO

tempt someone to do something to entice someone to do something. □ *You can't tempt me to eat any of that cake!* □ *I wasn't even tempted to go into town with the others.*

TEMPT ▸ WITH

tempt someone with something to entice someone with someone. □ *Can I tempt you with a bit of chocolate cake?* □ *I was tempted with a free book if I sent in my name, but I decided against it.*

TEND ▸ TO

tend to do something to have a tendency to do something. □ *Jill tends to chew on her tongue while she works.* □ *Sam tends to say things like that when he is upset.*

TEND ▸ TOWARD

tend toward something to have a tendency to display a certain characteristic. □ *Roger tends toward the dramatic.* □ *We all tend toward bad humor during bad weather.*

TENDER ▸ FOR

tender something for something to offer something for something. □ *The shareholders were asked to tender one of their shares for two of the offering company's.* □ *I decided not to tender my shares.*

tender something (to someone) (for something) See the following entry.

TENDER ▸ TO

tender something (to someone) (for something) to offer or present something to someone for something. □ *Laura tendered payment to Gary for the tickets.* □ *Walter tendered the old shares to the company for new shares.*

TENSE ▸ UP

tense up (for something) to become rigid or firm; to become anxious and ready for something. (Both literal and figurative uses.) □ *Liz tensed up for the game and was very nervous.* □ *He tensed up and that made it hard to give him the injection he needed.*

TERRIFY ▸ INTO

terrify someone into something AND **terrorize someone into something** to threaten someone into doing something. □ *The salesman is just trying to terrify you into buying a new one.* □ *They tried to terrorize people into saving water.*

TERRIFY ▸ OUT

terrify someone or something out of something **1.** to terrify someone or some creature to leave something or some place. □ *The attackers terrified the farmers out of their homes.* □ *The snake terrified the gophers out of their burrow.* **2.** to cause someone or some creature to lose something through fear. □ *They tried to terrify the old lady out of her money, but she refused to tell where it was.* □ *The eagle terrified the hawk out of the food it was holding.*

TERRORIZE ▸ INTO

terrorize someone into something See under *TERRIFY ▸ INTO.*

TEST ▸ FOR

test for something to try to find out about something by testing. □ *We are testing for weak places in your roof. That's the noise you hear up there.* □ *They are testing for some sort of infection.*

test someone or something for something to apply a test to someone or something to try to determine something or identify something. □ *They tested me for all sorts of diseases.* □ *Ken tested the roof for weak spots.*

TEST ▸ IN

test someone in something to test someone in a particular subject. □ *The committee decided to test her in her knowledge of the laws of the state.* □ *We were all tested in math and English.*

TEST ▸ OUT

test out (of something) to score high enough on a placement test that one does not need to take a particular course. □ *I tested out of calculus.* □ *I don't know enough to test out.*

test something out to try something out; to test something to see if it works. □ *I can't wait to test my new stereo out.* 🅃 *I will test out the stereo.*

TESTIFY ▸ AGAINST

testify against someone or something to bear witness against someone or something. □ *Who will testify against him in court?* □ *I cannot testify against the company I work for.*

TESTIFY ▸ FOR

testify for someone to present evidence in favor of someone; to testify on someone's behalf. □ *I agreed to testify for her at the trial.* □ *Max testified for Lefty, but they were both convicted.*

TESTIFY ▸ TO

testify to something to swear to something. □ *I will testify to your whereabouts if you wish.* □ *I think I know what happened, but I would not testify to it.*

THANK ▸ FOR

thank someone for something to show or state one's gratitude to someone for something. □ *We would all like to thank you for coming tonight.* □ *Thank you for inviting me.*

THAW ▸ OUT

thaw out to warm up from being frozen. □ *How long will it take for the chicken to thaw out?* □ *I can't wait for the cake to thaw out. I want some now!*

thaw someone or something out to raise the temperature of someone or something above freezing. □ *We need to get inside so I can thaw my brother out. His toes are almost frozen.* 🅃 *Did you thaw out the chicken?* 🄰 *My poor thawed-out toes are still terribly cold.*

THEORIZE ▸ ABOUT

theorize about someone or something to hypothesize about someone or something; to conjecture about someone or something. □ *Let's not waste time theorizing about Ted. He won't change.* □ *I can only theorize about what happened.*

THEORIZE ▸ ON

theorize on something to make a theory about something. □ *There is no point in theorizing on something when you have all the empirical evidence you need to draw a conclusion.* □ *He spent the afternoon theorizing on the origin of the universe.*

THICKEN ▸ UP

thicken something up **1.** to make something, such as a fluid, thicker. □ *I have to thicken this gravy up before we can serve dinner.* 🅃 *Please thicken up the gravy before you serve it.* **2.** to make something wider. □ *See this line here? You need to thicken it up so that it shows more clearly.* 🅃 *Try to thicken up the line a little.*

THIN ▸ DOWN

thin down to become thinner or slimmer. □ *He stopped eating altogether so he could thin down.* □ *I have to thin down so I can get into my new suit.*

thin someone down to make someone thinner or slimmer. (*Someone* includes *oneself*.) □ *What you need to thin you* *down is less, not more.* [T] *The hospital dietician tried to thin down the obese man.* □ *He hoped to thin himself down for the summer season.*

thin something down to dilute a fluid. □ *You should thin this down with a little water.* [T] *Try to thin down this paint a little.* [A] *She poured the thinned-down gravy over the meat.*

THIN ▶ OUT

thin out to spread out; to become less dense. □ *The trees began to thin out as we got higher up the mountain.* □ *The crowd began to thin out as we got a little farther from the theater.*

thin something out to make something less dense; to scatter something. □ *You will have to thin the young plants out, because there is not room for all of them.* [T] *Can you thin out these young plants?* [A] *The thinned-out plants will grow better.*

THINK ▶ ABOUT

think about someone or something to contemplate someone or something. □ *Whenever I think about him, I get goose bumps.* □ *I don't want to think about it.*

think twice about someone or something to give careful consideration to someone or something. □ *Ed may be a good choice, but I suggest that you think twice about him.* □ *You will want to think twice about it.*

THINK ▶ AHEAD

think ahead to plan for the future. □ *I need to think ahead more.* □ *If you had thought ahead, none of these things would have happened.*

think ahead (to something) to have thoughts about something that is to happen in the future. □ *I began to think ahead to next year when the same thing might happen.* □ *You must learn to think ahead if you want to get ahead.*

THINK ▶ BACK

think back (on someone or something) to contemplate someone or something in the past. □ *I like to think back on my family and the way we used to do things together.* □ *It makes me feel good to think back on those things.* □ *I like to think back and relive those days.*

think back (to something) to remember back to something in the past. □ *Now, try and think back to the night of January 16.* □ *I can't think back. My mind is preoccupied with other things.*

THINK ▶ BEFORE

think before doing something to consider the consequences before doing something. □ *You really ought to think before you take on a job like that.* □ *I finally learned to think carefully before accepting jobs like the one I just took on.*

THINK ▶ FOR

think for oneself to do one's own thinking; to think independently. □ *I think for myself. I don't need anyone to tell me what to do, do I?* □ *Sam has to learn to think for himself. He can't let other people make his decisions for him all his life.*

think someone fit for something to judge someone to be in condition or healthy enough for something. □ *Do you think me fit for the race?* □ *She is not fit for the game Friday night.*

think someone or something fit for someone or something to judge someone or something to be suitable for someone or something. □ *I do not think this book fit for young readers.* □ *You are not fit for the office of mayor!* □ *This plate is not fit for further use.*

THINK ▶ OF

think better of someone or something to raise one's opinion of someone or something. □ *I think better of him since I saw how well he does in the sales meetings.* □ *I hope that you will think better of the plan now.*

think better of something to reconsider doing something and end up not doing it. □ *I hope that you will think better of what you are doing and how many people you are hurting.* □ *I will think better of making such a careless remark next time.*

think little of someone or something to hold a low opinion of someone or something. □ *Liz thinks little of Tom and his efforts to interest her.* □ *Ann thinks little of the new plan.*

think nothing of it to pay no attention to something; to forget or ignore something. □ *No harm was caused by what you did. Think nothing of it.* □ *I was pleased to help you. Think nothing of it.*

think nothing of something to give no thought to doing something. □ *She thinks nothing of helping other people at any time of day or night.* □ *Toby thinks nothing of driving one block to the store.*

think of someone or something to contemplate someone or something. □ *I think of you whenever I go to the restaurant where we used to eat.* □ *Whenever I see a frog, I think of Susan.*

think something of someone or something to hold a particular kind of opinion of someone or something; to hold someone or something in a particular kind of regard. (Such as ill, good, highly, bad, much, a lot, a great deal.) □ *Please don't think ill of me. It was a silly mistake. That's all.* □ *We think quite highly of your plan.*

THINK ▶ ON

See also under *THINK ▶ (UP)ON.*

think on one's feet to be able to speak and reason well while (standing and talking) in front of an audience. □ *She really thinks on her feet well.* □ *I am not able to think on my feet too well before a bunch of people.*

THINK ▶ OUT

think out loud to speak one's thoughts aloud. □ *I didn't mean to say anything. I was just thinking out loud.* □ *He was thinking out loud when he made those silly remarks.*

think something out to go through something in one's mind; to think through something. □ *I have to take some time and think this out before I can respond to you.* [T] *I thought out this proposal very carefully before I presented it to you.*

THINK ▶ OVER

think something over to think about something and whether one will choose to do it. □ *I need a few minutes to think it over.* [T] *Let me think over your request for a day or so.*

THINK ▶ THROUGH

think something through to run over and try to settle something in one's mind. □ *Let me think this through and call you in the morning.* [T] *I will think through this matter and get back to you.*

THINK ▶ TO

think to do something to remember to do something. □ *Sorry. I didn't think to call you in time.* □ *I will try to think to bring everything with me next time.*

THINK ▶ UP

think something up to invent something. □ *I don't have a good answer, but I'll think something up.* [T] *I'll think up a good answer.*

THINK ▶ (UP)ON

think (up)on someone or something to contemplate someone or something; to muse or reflect on someone or something. (*Upon* is formal and less commonly used than *on*.) □ *I thought upon Abraham Lincoln and how much we all owe him.* □ *I thought on all the fine things we used to do.*

THIRST ▶ FOR

thirst for something **1.** to desire something to drink. (Formal or stilted.) □ *The entire company thirsted for something cooling.* □ *You could see that everyone there was thirsting for water, or even coffee, but there was no refreshment in sight.* **2.** to have a strong desire for something. (Figurative. Refers neither to food nor drink.) □ *In the old days, students were said to thirst for knowledge.* □ *The warriors thirsted for new battles to be fought.*

THRASH ▶ AROUND

thrash around to move about restlessly or violently. □ *Settle down and stop thrashing around.* □ *Timmy thrashed around all night when he had the high fever.*

THRASH ▸ OUT

thrash something out to argue something through to a settlement. □ *We will have to get together and thrash this out.* 🅃 *We will thrash out this business together.*

thrash something out of someone to beat something out of someone. □ *The sheriff really wanted to thrash the truth out of Tex, but that is illegal.* □ *Max wanted to know where the money was hidden and he tried to thrash it out of Lefty.*

THREAD ▸ THROUGH

thread one's way through something to weave and dodge one's way through something, such as a crowd or a maze. □ *He threaded his way through the crowd and managed to get to the exit.* □ *The line of boys threaded its way through the restaurant to the special room that had been reserved for them.*

thread through something to weave and dodge through something. □ *The little sports car threaded through traffic at high speed.* □ *The little dog threaded its way through the forest of human legs on its way to its master.*

THREATEN ▸ WITH

threaten someone with someone or something to warn someone that there will be punishment in the form of someone or something if conditions are not met. □ *No, no! Your Uncle Herman is not coming here! Please don't threaten me with Uncle Herman!* □ *Are you threatening me with bodily harm?*

THRILL ▸ AT

thrill at someone or something to become excited by someone or something. □ *The opera was mystically intoxicating, and the audience thrilled at the tenor lead.* □ *We thrilled at the agility of the dancers.*

THRILL ▸ TO

thrill someone to death to excite someone a great deal. (Figurative.) □ *This lovely party just thrills me to death!* □ *I was just thrilled to death by what the letter said.*

thrill someone to pieces to cause someone much joy. □ *Your gift just thrilled her to pieces.* □ *Donna was thrilled to pieces by the letter you sent.*

thrill to something to become excited by something; to experience rapture while experiencing something. □ *I always thrill to the sound of a marching band.* □ *The crowd thrilled to the sight of the winning team parading down Main Street.*

THRILL ▸ WITH

thrill someone with something to create or use something to cause someone much joy. □ *The famous singer thrilled us with a lovely song.* □ *Sally was thrilled with the praise heaped upon her daughter.*

THRIVE ▸ (UP)ON

thrive (up)on something to grow vigorously because of something. (*Upon* is formal and less commonly used than *on*.) □ *These plants thrive upon neglect.* □ *Children thrive on love.*

THRONG ▸ AROUND

throng around someone or something to crowd around someone or something. □ *The children thronged around the lady with the bags of candy.* □ *Everyone thronged around the piano for the group sing.*

THRONG ▸ IN(TO)

throng in(to something) [for a crowd] to swarm into some place. □ *The eager crowd thronged into the department store to partake in the advertised sale.* □ *The doors opened and they thronged in.*

THRONG ▸ OUT

throng out (of something) [for a crowd] to swarm out of something or some place. □ *The people thronged out of the concert hall at the end of the program.* □ *At half past ten, the crowd thronged out.*

THROTTLE ▸ DOWN

throttle something down to reduce the speed of an engine by adjusting the throttle. □ *She throttled her engine* *down and came to a stop.* T *She throttled down her engine.*

THROW ▸ ACROSS

throw something across someone or something to toss or spread something, such as a blanket, over someone or something. □ *Tom threw a blanket across Martha.* □ *Tom threw a blanket across his knees.*

throw something across something to toss something over something, from one side of it to the other. □ *Can you throw this stone across the river?* □ *Walter threw the ball across the court to Michael.*

THROW ▸ AFTER

throw good money after bad to waste money on something that someone has already lost money on. (Figurative.) □ *I won't give you another cent. That would be throwing good money after bad.* □ *I won't spend a cent more on this car. There is no sense in throwing good money after bad.*

THROW ▸ AROUND

throw one's weight around to exercise one's authority; to pull rank. (Figurative.) □ *You can't come in here and throw your weight around! Who do you think you are?* □ *Dan is throwing his weight around over at the foreman's office.*

throw someone or something around to toss or cast someone or something around. □ *The belligerent fellow at the bar threatened to throw me around a little if I didn't get out of his way.* T *Don't throw around your empty cans.*

throw someone's name around to use someone's name, implying that one knows the person whose name is being used, in the hopes that it will work to one's benefit. (Figurative.) □ *I tried throwing her name around, but no one had ever heard of her.* □ *I went into the mayor's office and tried throwing some names around, but it did me no good.*

THROW ▸ ASIDE

throw someone or something aside to toss someone or something away; to toss someone or something to one side. (Figurative.) □ *He threw his wife aside and took up with a younger woman.* T *Don't throw aside material that might still be useful.*

THROW ▸ AT

throw a glance at someone or something to take a quick peek at someone or something. □ *Liz threw a glance at her brother to see what he was going to do.* □ *I threw a glance at my watch and got ready to go.*

throw money at something to spend money on a problem in hopes that the expenditure will solve the problem. (Figurative.) □ *Stop throwing money at the problem!* □ *The government is in the habit of throwing money at a problem instead of curing it.*

throw oneself at someone to try to force one's affections on someone; to make oneself readily available to serve someone's romantic interests. □ *She threw herself at him and he ignored her.* □ *Todd has a bad habit of throwing himself at every girl he meets.*

throw oneself at someone's feet to seek someone's mercy. (Figurative.) □ *He threw himself at her feet and pledged never to do it again.* □ *I throw myself at your feet. Forgive me, please forgive me.*

throw oneself at the mercy of the court AND **throw oneself on the mercy of the court** to seek mercy from a court of law, especially at one's sentencing for a crime. □ *He pleaded guilty and threw himself at the mercy of the court.* □ *It did no good to throw myself on the mercy of the court.* □ *Mary threw herself at the mercy of the court.*

throw something at someone or something to toss or cast something at someone or something. □ *The boy threw a rock at his sister.* □ *He threw the stone at the target.*

throw the book at someone or something to charge someone or something with all possible legal violations. (Figurative. The book is a law book.) □ *The judge threw the book at the speeder.* □ *The courts threw the book at the company.*

THROW ▸ AWAY

throw something away to toss something out; to dispose of something. □ *Should I throw this away?* [T] *Don't throw away anything that might be useful.* [N] *This is just a throwaway. I want something more substantial.*

throw something away on someone or something to waste something on someone or something. □ *I won't throw any more money away on your brother-in-law.* [T] *I've thrown away too much money on that project.*

THROW ▸ BACK

throw someone or something back to return someone or something by tossing. □ *The sailor climbed out of the water into the boat, and his mates grabbed him and threw him back. That was their idea of fun.* [T] *Karen threw back the undersize fish.*

throw something back to eat or drink something quickly. (Slang.) □ *He threw a beer back and got up and left.* [T] *She threw back a beer.*

throw something back at someone to return a problem or difficulty to the person from whom it came. (Colloquial.) □ *He said that the problem was mine alone, and he threw it back at me.* □ *I tried to get someone else to take care of it, but it was thrown back at me.*

throw something back to someone **1.** to return something to someone by throwing. □ *Liz threw the ball back to Kelly.* [T] *She threw back the ball to Kelly.* **2.** to return a problem to someone. □ *I can't do anything about this. I'll throw it back to Roger.* [T] *Karen threw back the problem to Roger, who had caused it.*

THROW ▸ DOWN

throw down the gauntlet to issue a challenge. (Idiomatic.) □ *He finally got fed up with the way his boss was treating him, and he threw down the gauntlet.* □ *She threw down the gauntlet and let us all know that she had had enough of our teasing.*

throw something down to cast something down onto the ground; to cast something to a lower level. □ *Dave took one look at the box and threw it down.* [T] *He threw down the box.*

throw something down something to hurl something downward through something, such as a stairway, a duct, a drain, a hole. □ *Max threw the weapon down the storm sewer.* □ *Someone threw the bucket down the well.*

THROW ▸ FOR

throw someone for a loop to confuse someone. (Figurative.) □ *What you just said really threw me for a loop.* □ *The change in plans threw everyone for a loop.*

throw someone for a loss to confuse and frustrate someone. □ *Your question threw me for a loss for a minute.* □ *Ted was thrown for a loss by the sudden appearance of his sister.*

THROW ▸ IN

See also under *THROW ▸ IN(TO).*

throw in the sponge See *toss in the sponge* under *TOSS ▸ IN.*

throw in the towel to signal that one is going to quit; to quit. □ *It's time to throw in the towel. I've had enough.* □ *Finally, I threw in the towel and called it quits.*

throw in with someone to join with someone; to join someone's enterprise. □ *I will throw in with you and we can all go hunting together.* □ *Do you mind if I throw in with you?*

THROW ▸ INTO

throw oneself into something **1.** to dress in something hurriedly. □ *She threw herself into the dress.* □ *He just threw himself into his tux and ran on stage.* **2.** to enter into or join something eagerly and wholeheartedly. □ *Todd always threw himself into a project wholeheartedly.* □ *She threw herself into the project and helped immensely.*

throw something into sharp relief [for something] to make something plainly evident or clearly visible. □ *The dull, plain background threw the ornate settee into sharp relief.* □ *The red vase was thrown into sharp relief against the black background.*

throw something into the bargain to add money or goods to an exchange. □ *I got the books I wanted, and the bookseller threw this nice calendar into the bargain.* □ *I would like to see something else thrown into the bargain, considering that I am paying a lot of money.*

THROW ▸ IN(TO)

throw someone or something in(to something) to cast or hurl someone or something into something. □ *The cops threw Max into jail again.* 🅃 *The warden opened the cell door and threw in the prisoner.* □ *We threw the aluminum cans in the bin.*

throw something in(to) someone's face **1.** to hurl or splash something into someone's face. □ *Jerry got mad at Bob and threw his pop into Bob's face.* □ *He threw the pie in Ken's face.* **2.** to confront someone with a problem. (Figurative.) □ *Jerry caused this mess. I'll just throw the whole problem into his face and tell him to fix it.* □ *It's her fault. Just throw this problem in her face and make her deal with it.*

THROW ▸ OFF

throw someone off balance **1.** to cause someone to falter (and probably fall). □ *The cyclist bumped into me and threw me off balance.* □ *I was thrown off balance by the gust of wind.* **2.** to confuse or disorient one. (Figurative.) □ *Your last question sort of threw me off balance.* □ *The teacher was thrown off balance by the students' difficult questions.*

throw someone or something off ((of) something) **1.** to cast someone or something off something. (*Someone* includes *oneself*. The *of*-phrase is paraphrased with a *from*-phrase when the particle is transposed. See the 🄵 example. The *of* is colloquial.) □ *The character in the movie wanted to throw the heroine off a cliff.* 🅃 *He came to the cliff and threw off the lawn clippings.* 🄵 *He went out and threw off the lawn clippings from the top of a high cliff.* □ *Ken wanted to throw her off.* □ *In deep despair, she threw herself off the cliff into the sea.* **2.** to divert or confuse someone or some creature away from something, such as the scent, track, or trail. (The *of*-phrase is paraphrased with a *from*-phrase when the particle is transposed. See the 🄵 example.) □ *She put a little detail in her story to throw the cops off her trail.* 🅃 *The diversion threw off the investigation.* 🄵 *Her little diversion threw off the investigators from the otherwise straightforward matter.* □ *It threw them off.*

throw something off to cast something, such as a coat, off one's body. □ *He threw off his jacket and dived into the icy water.* 🅃 *He threw off his jacket.*

THROW ▸ ON

See also under *THROW ▸ ON(TO); THROW ▸ (UP)ON.*

throw cold water on something to make something seem discouraging; to belittle something or some plans. (Figurative.) □ *I hate to throw cold water on your plans, but you can't have a party here next weekend.* □ *The principal threw cold water on the plans for an extra holiday.*

throw light on someone or something to present some revealing information about someone or something. □ *What you have just told me throws a lot of light on George and his motivation.* □ *Will you please throw some light on the problem?*

throw oneself on the mercy of the court See *throw oneself at the mercy of the court* under *THROW ▸ AT.*

throw something on someone or something to toss or sling something over or onto someone or something. (*Upon* is formal and less commonly used than *on.*) □ *Mommy, Jimmy threw some mud on me!* □ *Throw a cloth on the sofa to protect it from paint spatters.*

THROW ▸ ON(TO)

throw someone or something on(to) something to hurl someone or something onto something. (*Someone* includes *oneself.*) □ *The intruder threw Jason onto the floor and began to kick him.* □ *He threw the book on the floor and stalked out.* □ *Wailing her grief,* *the woman threw herself on her husband's funeral pyre.*

THROW ▸ OUT

throw one out on one's ear to eject someone from a place. (Slang.) □ *The bartender threw Roger out on his ear.* □ *I will throw you out on your ear if you don't stop making so much noise.*

throw someone or something out (of something) to eject someone or something from something or a place. (The *of*-phrase is paraphrased with a *from*-phrase when the particle is transposed. See the F example.) □ *The intruder tried to throw Walter out of the window.* T *He went to the window and threw out Walter.* F *He went to the opposite side of the room and threw out the flowers from the window overlooking the potting shed.* □ *Ann threw them out.*

throw the baby out with the bath(water) to cast out something valuable along with something that is not valuable. (Figurative.) □ *Think this thing through. Don't throw the baby out with the bathwater.* T *Don't throw out the baby with the bath.*

THROW ▸ OVER

throw someone or something over someone or something to toss someone or something over someone or something; to lay someone or something across someone or something. □ *The wrestler picked his opponent up and threw him over the referee.* □ *He threw his opponent over the ropes.* □ *He threw the ball over Ken.* □ *Ann threw the Frisbee over the fence.*

throw someone over (for someone else) to break up with a lover. □ *Sarah threw Jason over for Larry.* T *She threw over Jason for Walter.* □ *I knew she would throw him over.*

THROW ▸ TO

throw caution to the wind to stop being cautious. □ *He threw caution to the wind and dived into the rapidly moving water.* □ *It was hard for Henry to throw caution to the wind and go on a vacation to such an exotic place, but he did it.*

throw someone to the wolves to sacrifice someone to save the rest; to abandon someone to harm; to leave someone to take all the blame. (Figurative.) □ *Don't try to throw me to the wolves. I'll tell the truth about the whole affair!* □ *The investigation was going to be rigorous and unpleasant, and I could see they were going to throw someone to the wolves.*

throw something to someone or something to toss something to someone or something. □ *Throw the ball to me!* □ *Gary threw a bit of meat to the dog to quiet it.*

THROW ▸ TOGETHER

throw someone together **1.** to bring or put two or more people together. □ *The crisis threw complete strangers together, and they became fast friends before it was over.* □ *They were thrown together by fate.* **2.** to improve the relationship of two people. □ *Ted and Roger had fought for years, but the situation they found themselves in threw them together.* □ *We were thrown together and had to make the best of it.*

throw something together to assemble or create something in a hurry. □ *I think I can throw something acceptable together for dinner.* T *I can throw together something that is quite edible.*

THROW ▸ UP

throw something up **1.** to build or erect something in a hurry. □ *They sure threw that building up in a hurry.* T *They threw up the building in only a few weeks.* **2.** to vomit something. □ *Poor Wally threw his dinner up.* T *He threw up his dinner.*

throw something up to someone to confront someone with something. (Figurative.) □ *I threw the whole matter up to her, but she had nothing to say about it.* □ *I can't figure out what to do. I will just throw the whole business up to the boss.*

throw something up to something to cast something upward to something else. □ *Gary threw a hammer up to the top of the porch roof where Ted could* *get it.* □ *Please throw a can of pop up to the second-floor window. I'll catch it.*

throw up to vomit. □ *I was afraid I would throw up, the food was so horrible.* □ *This food is bad enough to make you throw up.*

throw up one's hands in despair to give up doing something in despair. □ *It was hopeless. She threw up her hands in despair.* 🅃 *Sally threw up her hands in despair.*

throw up one's toenails to vomit heavily. (Slang.) □ *I was so sick. I nearly threw up my toenails.* □ *Frank was in the bathroom, throwing up his toenails.*

THROW ▸ (UP)ON

throw oneself (up)on someone's mercy to seek compassion and mercy from someone. □ *The accused criminal threw himself upon the judge's mercy.* □ *Max threw himself on the judge's mercy.* □ *Please don't! I throw myself upon your mercy!*

THRUST ▸ AGAINST

thrust someone or something against someone or something to drive or shove someone or something against someone or something. □ *The force of the crash thrust Liz against Tiffany.* □ *The crash thrust Liz against the car door.* □ *The crash thrust the package against Liz.*

THRUST ▸ ASIDE

thrust someone or something aside to push someone or something out of the way or to one side. □ *Walter thrust Fred aside and dashed by him into the room.* 🅃 *He thrust aside Fred and came into the room.* □ *She thrust the book aside and went to sleep.*

THRUST ▸ AT

thrust something at someone or something to stab at someone or something with something. □ *The goat thrust its head at the dog.* □ *Ann thrust the pencil at the balloon and popped it.*

THRUST ▸ AWAY

thrust someone or something away from someone or something to push or throw someone or something away from someone or something. □ *The guards thrust the spectators away from the path the rock star was taking.* 🅃 *They thrust away the spectators from the star.*

THRUST ▸ BACK

thrust someone or something back to push someone or something backward and away. □ *Tom moved forward, but the guard thrust him back.* 🅃 *He thrust back the door, which had closed on his foot.*

THRUST ▸ DOWN

thrust something down to jab something downward. □ *Max thrust the knife down and speared a piece of chicken.* 🅃 *He thrust down the fork like a spear.*

thrust something down something to jab or stab something down into something. □ *The keeper quickly thrust the medicine down the lion's throat.* □ *How do you suppose that Santa Claus thrusts all those toys down chimneys?*

THRUST ▸ FORWARD

thrust something forward to jab something forward. □ *She thrust her jaw forward and walked into the room.* □ *Roger thrust his hand forward just in time to stop the child from crossing the street.*

THRUST ▸ IN(TO)

thrust something in(to someone or something) to stab or run something into someone or something. □ *The knight thrust his lance into the villain.* 🅃 *He thrust in his knife.* □ *He thrust it in.*

THRUST ▸ OUT

thrust out to stick out; to stab outward; to protrude outward. □ *A deck thrust out from the back of the house, offering a lovely view of the stream far below.* □ *As he grew angrier, his chin thrust out farther and farther.*

THRUST ▸ THROUGH

thrust someone or something through something to drive or push someone or something through something. □ *I thrust Larry through the open window and followed along quickly.* □ *Ann* *thrust the wad of papers through the opening.*

thrust through something to drive or push through something forcefully. □ *The front end of the car thrust through the side of the house.* □ *The stock clerk's knife thrust through the box, ruining the packages of noodles inside.*

THRUST ▸ UP

thrust up through something to stick or stab upward through something. □ *The tallest of the trees thrust up through the canopy of leaves far overhead.* □ *We heard a ripping sound and saw the tent pole thrust up through the top of the tent.*

THUD ▸ AGAINST

thud against someone or something to thump against someone or something, making a dull noise on impact. □ *The pumpkin thudded against Jerry, breaking open and messing up his clothes.* □ *The ball thudded against the wall and bounced back.*

THUD ▸ INTO

thud into someone or something to bump into someone or something, making a dull noise on impact. □ *The door blew open and thudded into Marie, giving her a bump on the knee.* □ *The ball thudded into the side of the house.*

THUMB ▸ AT

thumb one's nose at someone or something **1.** to show signs of derision at someone or something. □ *Don't thumb your nose at me if you like the way your teeth are arranged.* □ *Max thumbed his nose at the car as it drove off.* **2.** to dismiss someone or something as worthless, verbally. (Figurative.) □ *Walter thumbed his nose at Max and asked the gang to send someone else to do the job.* □ *She thumbed her nose at the whole idea.*

THUMB ▸ THROUGH

thumb through something to turn through the pages of something. □ *I thumbed through the catalog, but didn't find anything I wanted.* □ *I have only thumbed through your manuscript, but it looks good.*

THUMP ▸ DOWN

thump something down to throw something down so it makes a pounding noise. □ *Nancy thumped the parcel down and caught her breath.* 🅃 *She thumped down the parcel.*

THUMP ▸ ON

thump on someone or something to pound on someone or something. □ *Tim was angry with Roger and thumped on him a little, but decided to forgive him.* □ *Andy thumped on the bass drum for an hour.*

THUMP ▸ OUT

thump something out (on the piano) to pound out music on a piano. □ *Joel thumped a happy tune out on the piano.* 🅃 *He thumped out a well-known tune.* □ *Ann can really thump out a tune.*

THUNDER ▸ ACROSS

thunder across something to move across something, making a rumbling sound. □ *The jets thundered across the sky, heading for their home base.* □ *As the race car thundered across the field, people strained to get a better view.*

THUNDER ▸ OUT

thunder something out to respond with words spoken in a voice like thunder. □ *He thundered the words out so everyone could hear them.* 🅃 *He thundered out the words.*

THUNDER ▸ PAST

thunder past someone or something to move past someone or something, rumbling. □ *As the traffic thundered past, I wondered why there was so much of it.* □ *The train thundered past the sleeping town.*

TICK ▸ AWAY

tick away [for seconds or minutes] to go by as the clock ticks. □ *The seconds ticked away as the fateful time got closer.* □ *As time ticked away, the surgeons worked feverishly to repair the walls of Roger's heart.*

TICK ▸ OFF

tick someone off to make someone angry. (Slang.) □ *Todd is always ticking* *me off.* 🅃 *Toby ticked off Sally, who won't speak to him anymore.*

TICKET ▸ FOR

ticket someone for some place to supply a ticket for someone to go to some place. ☐ *The airlines clerk ticketed me for Houston and checked in my baggage.* ☐ *I was ticketed for both flights, saving me some time.*

TICKLE ▸ TO

tickle someone to death **1.** to tickle someone a great deal. (Figurative.) ☐ *Bobby nearly tickled Tim to death. Tim was left breathless.* ☐ *We got him down and tickled him to death.* **2.** AND **tickle someone to pieces** to please someone a great deal. ☐ *What you told her just tickled her to death!* ☐ *That just tickles me to pieces.*

TIDE ▸ OVER

tide someone over (until something) to supply someone until a certain time or until something happens. ☐ *Will this amount tide us over until next week?* 🅃 *There is enough food here to tide over the entire camp until next month.* ☐ *Yes, this will tide us over.*

TIDY ▸ UP

tidy something up to clean something up; to make something more orderly. ☐ *Please tidy this room up.* ☐ *This room needs to be tidied up immediately.*

tidy up to clean up [oneself or a place]. ☐ *Please tidy up. This place is a mess.* ☐ *Please tidy up. You are a mess.*

TIE ▸ BACK

tie something back to bind or fasten something back out of the way. ☐ *George tied the curtains back to let a little more light in.* ☐ *Let me tie the vines back out of the way.*

TIE ▸ DOWN

tie someone down (to someone or something) to encumber something with someone or something; to make someone responsible to or for someone or something. (*Someone* includes *oneself.*) ☐ *Please don't tie me down to your uncle. Let your sister help out.* ☐ *Yes, don't tie me down all week.* ☐ *I'll be tied down until I'm fifty!* ☐ *I don't want to tie myself down to a dog.*

tie someone or something down to fasten someone or something down by tying or binding. (*Someone* includes *oneself.*) ☐ *The robbers tied Gary down so he couldn't get up and get away.* 🅃 *They tied down Gary.* ☐ *Please tie the chairs down so they don't fall off the boat in the storm.* ☐ *It was so windy, I almost had to tie myself down to stay on deck.*

TIE ▸ FOR

tie (with someone) (for something) See under *TIE ▸ WITH.*

TIE ▸ IN

See also under *TIE ▸ IN(TO).*

tie in (with someone or something) to join with someone or something; to connect with someone or something. ☐ *I would like to tie in with you and see if we can solve this together.* ☐ *We would like for you to tie in and share your expertise.* ☐ *I tied in with a manufacturer who will produce the toy I invented.* ☐ *His answer to the committee ties in with what his secretary told us.* 🄽 *Now I understand the tie-in between the two.*

tie in with something to corroborate something; [for a piece of information] to complement other information. ☐ *These figures tie in with what I just said.* ☐ *The crime lab report ties in with our current theory.*

tie someone in knots to make someone very anxious or frustrated. (Figurative. *Someone* includes *oneself.*) ☐ *This suspense really ties you in knots, doesn't it?* ☐ *I just tie myself in knots whenever I have to go on television.*

tie something in a knot to bend something, such as a rope, upon itself to make a knot. ☐ *I ended up tying the rope in a knot.* ☐ *The rope was tied in a knot and no one could get it undone.*

TIE ▸ IN(TO)

tie in(to something) to fasten or connect to something. ☐ *Can you fix it so my computer can tie into Rachel's?* ☐ *This one will not tie into her computer.* ☐ *It just won't tie in.*

tie someone or something in(to something) to seek to establish a connection between someone or something and something. ☐ *The police tried to tie Sarah into the crime.* 🅃 *They tried to tie in Liz, too.* ☐ *Can we tie your computer into the system?* ☐ *Yes, you can tie it in.*

TIE ▸ OFF

tie something off to tie the ends of blood vessels closed to prevent bleeding. ☐ *The surgeons tied all the blood vessels off—one by one—as they were exposed.* 🅃 *They tied off all the vessels very quickly.*

TIE ▸ ON

tie one on AND **hang one on** to get drunk. ☐ *Jed went out to tie one on last night.* ☐ *He hung one on with Tex.*

TIE ▸ ON(TO)

tie something on(to someone or something) to attach something to someone or something by tying or binding. ☐ *I tied his house key onto him so he wouldn't lose it.* 🅃 *I tied on his gloves so he would not lose them.* ☐ *I tied a yellow ribbon on the tree.*

TIE ▸ TO

tie someone or something to something to bind someone or something to something. (*Someone* includes *oneself.*) ☐ *The robber tied the clerk to a chair.* ☐ *I tied colored yarn to the birthday present.* ☐ *They tied themselves to the mast to keep from being washed overboard.*

tie someone to something to associate someone with something; to make a connection between someone and something. ☐ *The police are trying to tie Lefty to the burglary.* ☐ *They'll never tie me to that bunch of crooks!*

TIE ▸ TOGETHER

tie people or things together to bind things or people together. (*People* includes *oneself.*) ☐ *I tied Dave and Chuck together and led them into the initiation ceremonies.* ☐ *The climbers tied themselves together in a special way.*

TIE ▸ UP

tie someone or something up to bind someone or something securely. ☐ *The sheriff tied the crooks up and took them to a cell.* 🅃 *He tied up the bandit.* ☐ *I tied the package up and put a label on it.*

tie someone or something up to keep someone or something busy or occupied. ☐ *Sally tied up the photocopy machine all afternoon.* 🅃 *The well-wishers tied up my telephone all day long.* ☐ *The meeting tied me up all afternoon.*

tie something up to block or impede something, such as traffic or progress. ☐ *The stalled bus tied traffic up for over an hour.* 🅃 *The stalled bus tied up traffic.* 🄽 *The expressway is just one tie-up after another.*

tie up (some place) [for a skipper] to moor a ship or boat some place. ☐ *We need to tie up some place for the night.* ☐ *The captain tied up at the dock and sent the first mate for fuel.* ☐ *The ferry ties up at the end of the harbor road.*

TIE ▸ WITH

tie (with someone) (for something) to have the same score as someone for the prize in some contest. ☐ *I tied with Joel for first place.* ☐ *I tied for the trophy with Joel.* ☐ *I tied with Ann.*

TIGHTEN ▸ ON(TO)

tighten something on(to) something to make something more tightly attached to something. ☐ *Will you please tighten this nut onto the bolt?* ☐ *I tightened the lid on the pickle jar.*

TIGHTEN ▸ UP

tighten something up to make something tighter. ☐ *Tighten your seat belt up. It looks loose.* 🅃 *Can you tighten up all the bolts?*

tighten up 1. [for something] to get tighter. ☐ *The door hinges began to tighten up, making the door hard to open and close.* ☐ *His grip around the handle tightened up and he refused to let go.* **2.** [for someone or a group] to become miserly. ☐ *The government tightened up and our budget was slashed.* ☐ *We almost went out of business when we couldn't get credit because the bank* *tightened up.* **3.** [for someone or something] to become more restrictive. ☐ *The boss is tightening up on matters of this type.* ☐ *There are more rules and the people who enforce them are tightening up.*

TILT ▸ AT

tilt at windmills to seek to destroy nonexistent enemies. (Figurative. From the story of Don Quixote, who attacked windmills with his lance.) ☐ *You don't have a real issue to take on. You are just tilting at windmills.* ☐ *Don't waste your time tilting at windmills. Tackle something you know you can handle.*

TILT ▸ BACK

tilt something back to move something so it leans back. ☐ *Alice tilted her chair back and nearly fell over.* 🅃 *She tilted back her chair and relaxed.*

TILT ▸ TO

tilt to something to lean or slant toward something or in a particular direction. ☐ *The picture tilts to the left.* ☐ *Her head was tilted to the left because she was trying to see around the corner.*

TILT ▸ TOWARD

tilt toward someone or something **1.** to lean toward someone or something. ☐ *The table is tilting toward Roger.* ☐ *The old shed tilted toward the west.* **2.** to favor choosing someone or something. (Figurative. See also *lean toward someone or something* under *LEAN ▸ TO(WARD).*) ☐ *I am tilting toward Roger for my assistant.* ☐ *I am tilting toward the red car, not the black one.*

TIME ▸ IN

time in to record one's arrival time. ☐ *Did you remember to time in this morning?* ☐ *When did she time in?*

time someone in to record someone's arrival time. ☐ *I timed you in at noon. Where were you?* 🅃 *My job is to time in people.*

TIME ▸ OUT

time out to record one's departure time. ☐ *Did you remember to time out when you left work?* ☐ *I timed out at the regular time.*

time someone out to record someone's departure time. ☐ *Harry had to time everyone out because the time clock was broken.* 🅃 *I had to time out everyone.*

TINGE ▸ WITH

tinge something with something to give something a bit of the character, color, state of mind, light, etc., of something. ☐ *The dust in the air had tinged the sunset with orange.* ☐ *The evening air was tinged with the smell of jasmine.*

TINKER ▸ AROUND

tinker (around) (with something) to meddle with something; to play with something, trying to get it to work or work better. ☐ *Let me tinker around with it for a while and see if I can get it to work.* ☐ *Please don't tinker with the controls.* ☐ *I have the stereo set just the way I want it. Don't tinker around.*

TINKER ▸ WITH

See the previous entry.

TIP ▸ AT

tip the scales at something to weigh a particular weight. ☐ *Albert tips the scales at nearly 200 pounds.* ☐ *The champ weighed in and tipped the scales at 180.*

TIP ▸ IN(TO)

tip something in(to something) to spill something into something by raising and tipping. ☐ *He tipped the leaves into the ditch.* 🅃 *He pushed the wheelbarrow to the ditch and tipped in the leaves.*

TIP ▸ OFF

tip someone off (about someone or something) AND **tip someone off (on someone or something)** to give someone a valuable piece of news about someone or something. ☐ *I tipped the cops off about Max and where he was going to be that night.* 🅃 *I tipped off the mayor about the financial crisis.* ☐ *Yes, I am the one who did it. What tipped you off?* ☐ *Somebody gave me a tip-off that you were leaving.*

tip someone off (on someone or something) See the previous entry.

TIP ▸ OUT

tip someone or something out (of something) to tilt something so that someone or something falls or slides out. (The *of*-phrase is paraphrased with a *from*-phrase when the particle is transposed.) □ *Don came up behind Todd's chair and tipped him out of it.* 🅃 *He tipped out Todd.* 🄵 *Jack tipped out the dirt from the wagon.*

TIP ▸ OVER

tip over to topple over and fall. □ *Roger shook the table slightly, and the vase fell over.* □ *The truck was overloaded and looked so heavy that I thought it would tip over.*

tip someone over to cause someone to fall. □ *Oh! You almost tipped me over!* □ *Todd fell against Maggie and tipped her over.*

tip something over to cause something to fall over. □ *Did you tip this chair over?* 🅃 *Who tipped over the chair?*

TIP ▸ UP

tip something up to tilt something so it dumps. □ *Jason tipped the wheelbarrow up and dumped the dirt out.* 🅃 *He tipped up the glass, dumping the orange juice on the table.*

TIP ▸ WITH

tip someone with something to pay a tip of a certain amount to someone. □ *I tipped the headwaiter with a twenty or we would still be waiting.* □ *How much did you tip the waitress with?*

TIRE ▸ OF

tire of someone or something to grow weary of someone or something. □ *She tired of him and left him.* □ *I am beginning to tire of the furniture in the living room.*

TIRE ▸ OUT

tire out to become exhausted. □ *I tire out easily.* □ *When I had the flu, I found that I tired out easily.*

tire someone out to exhaust someone. □ *The extra work tired him out a lot.* 🅃 *Too much work will tire out the horses.*

TOADY ▸ TO

toady (up) to someone to fawn over someone; to try to flatter and impress someone. □ *Carl is always toadying up to people.* □ *He has never toadied to me!*

TOADY ▸ UP

See the previous entry.

TODDLE ▸ ALONG

toddle along to walk along in an unconcerned manner. □ *Kathleen was just toddling along, minding her own business.* □ *Why don't you toddle along now and let me get some work done?*

TODDLE ▸ AWAY

toddle away to walk away. □ *Not even noticing what had happened, the old lady got up and toddled away.* □ *Sam toddled away, leaving us behind to explain things to the boss.*

TODDLE ▸ OFF

toddle off to leave; to walk away. □ *Wally toddled off, leaving his dinner untouched.* □ *Don't just toddle off when I'm talking to you!*

TOIL ▸ FOR

toil for someone **1.** to work on behalf of someone or for someone's benefit. □ *I don't mind toiling for her as long as she thanks me.* □ *I don't know why I toil for you. You are totally ungrateful.* **2.** to do someone else's work. □ *I don't know why I should have to toil for you. Do your own work!* □ *I won't toil for him. He can do his own work.*

toil for something **1.** to work toward a particular goal or ideal. □ *I am willing to toil for something I believe in.* □ *She spent the afternoon toiling for her favorite charity.* **2.** to work for a certain rate of pay. □ *It's hard to toil for slave's wages.* □ *Do you expect me to toil endlessly for such low pay?*

TOIL ▸ OVER

toil over someone or something to work hard on someone or something. □ *The doctors toiled over the patient for hours.* □ *Ken toiled over his model plane well into the night.*

TOIL ▸ UP

toil up something to work hard to climb something steep. □ *The hikers toiled up the slope slowly.* □ *As the bus toiled up the hill, we worried that the engine might be overheating.*

TOLL ▸ FOR

toll for someone [for a bell] to ring for someone. □ *Who are the bells tolling for?* □ *The bells are tolling for old man Green, who died last night.*

TONE ▸ DOWN

tone something down to cause something to have less of an impact on the senses of sight or sound; to lessen the impact of something prepared for public performance or consumption. □ *This is rather shocking. You had better tone it down a bit.* 🅃 *Tone down this paragraph.* 🅃 *Tone down the color of the walls. They're very red.*

TONE ▸ UP

tone someone or something up to make someone or something stronger or more fit, muscularly. (*Someone* includes *oneself.*) □ *I suggested an exercise that would tone him up and make him feel better.* 🅃 *The exercises toned up his tummy muscles.* □ *I need to get busy and tone myself up.*

TOOL ▸ AROUND

tool around (in something) to go around in a car; to speed around in a car. (Slang.) □ *Who is that kid tooling around in that souped-up car?* □ *Ann spends a lot of time tooling around in her new car.*

TOOL ▸ UP

tool something up to equip a factory or production line with tools and machines. □ *The manager closed down the factory so she could tool it up for the new models.* 🅃 *She tooled up the factory in record time.*

tool up to become equipped with tools. □ *I need some money so I can tool up to do the job.* □ *The factory tooled up to make the new cars in only two weeks.*

TOP ▸ OFF

top something off (with something) to celebrate an end to something with something; to complete the top of something, such as a building. □ *They topped the evening off with a bottle of champagne.* 🅃 *They topped off the evening with a bottle of champagne.* □ *The workers topped the building off with a flag.*

TOP ▸ UP

top something up to add a bit of something to replenish the amount that was used. □ *Let me top your drink up.* 🅃 *Can I top up your glass?*

TOP ▸ WITH

top something with something to decorate or finish something by adding something. □ *They topped the new garage with a weather vane.* □ *Molly-Jo topped each sundae with a big red cherry.*

TOPPLE ▸ DOWN

topple down [for a stack of something] to crumple and fall down. □ *The chimney toppled down in the earthquake.* □ *The woodpile toppled down during the night and scared us all to death.*

topple something down to cause a stack of something to crumple and fall down. □ *The earthquake toppled the chimney down.* 🅃 *It toppled down the tallest buildings.*

TOPPLE ▸ FROM

topple from something See the following entry.

TOPPLE ▸ OFF

topple off (of) something AND **topple from something** to fall off the top of something very tall. (The *of* is colloquial.) □ *Careful there! You might topple off of that wall.* □ *I didn't get too close to the edge, because I was afraid of toppling off.* □ *She toppled off the wall.* □ *The vase toppled from its shelf in the quake.* □ *She feared that she would topple from the roof.*

TOPPLE ▸ OVER

topple over [for something very tall] to fall over. □ *I was afraid that Jimmy's* *stack of blocks would topple over.* □ *The stack of books toppled over and ended up as a jumbled mess on the floor.*

TORE ▸ UP

See *tear someone up* under *TEAR ▸ UP.*

TORMENT ▸ INTO

torment someone into something to force someone to agree to do something through threats or maltreatment. □ *You can't torment me into doing something I don't want to do!* □ *Alice was tormented into going on the picnic.*

TORN ▸ BETWEEN

See *be torn between someone and someone else or something and something else* under *BE ▸ BETWEEN.*

TORTURE ▸ INTO

torture someone into something to force someone to do something through the use of torture. (More severe than *torment someone into something.*) □ *The agents threatened to torture me into telling the secrets, so I gave in immediately, of course.* □ *Max tried to torture Lefty into telling where the gold was hidden.*

TOSS ▸ AROUND

toss someone or something around to throw someone or something around. □ *The waves tossed him around and almost dashed him on the rocks.* □ *The waves tossed the boat around.*

TOSS ▸ ASIDE

toss someone or something aside to throw someone or something aside or out of the way. □ *The kidnapper tossed the child aside and reached for his gun.* 🅃 *The soldier tossed aside the helpless civilian and ran into the house.* □ *Fred tossed the pop can aside and Alice picked it up.*

TOSS ▸ AT

toss something at someone or something to throw something at someone or something. □ *Jimmy tossed an apple at Sarah to see what she would do.* □ *John tossed a stone at the wall.*

TOSS ▸ AWAY

toss someone or something away to throw someone or something away; to discard someone or something. □ *You can't just toss me away! I'm your husband!* 🅃 *She tossed away her husband of twenty years.* □ *She tossed the cigarette away.*

TOSS ▸ BACK

toss someone or something back **1.** to throw or force someone or something backwards. □ *The blast tossed me back into the room.* 🅃 *The blast tossed back the emergency personnel.* □ *My kick tossed the dog back into its yard.* **2.** to throw someone or something back to where someone or something came from. □ *My father always threatened to toss me back where I came from, the way a fish is returned to the water.* 🅃 *I will toss back all the undersize fish.*

toss something back and forth **1.** [for two or more people] to toss something to each other. □ *Carol and Kelly tossed the ball back and forth for a few minutes.* □ *We will toss the ball back and forth until we get tired.* **2.** to trade remarks, quips, insults, etc. (Figurative.) □ *They tossed insulting remarks back and forth.* □ *Walter and David spent the evening tossing quips back and forth.*

TOSS ▸ DOWN

toss something down to drink down a drink quickly. (Colloquial.) □ *He tossed a beer down and left the bar.* □ *How many of those did you toss down?* 🅃 *Sam tossed down a couple of shots.*

TOSS ▸ FOR

toss (someone) for something to decide with someone, by tossing a coin, who will get something. □ *Let's see who gets to go first. I'll toss you for it.* □ *I'll toss for it.* □ *Let's toss for it.*

TOSS ▸ IN

toss in the sponge AND **throw in the sponge** to signal that one is going to quit; to quit. (Literal only in boxing. Less common than *throw in the towel.*) □ *I quit. I'm tossing in the sponge.* □ *It's time to throw in the sponge.*

TOSS ▸ IN(TO)

toss something in(to something) to cast or throw something into something. □ *Frank tossed the wood into the fire.* 🅃 *He tossed in the wood.* □ *The chowder* *was ready for the clams, so Ken tossed them in.*

TOSS ▸ OFF

toss someone or something off ((of) something) to hurl someone or something from something. (The *of*-phrase is paraphrased with a *from*-phrase when the particle is transposed. See the Ⓕ example. The *of* is colloquial.) □ *The gigantic ape was going to toss the woman off of the Empire State Building.* Ⓣ *The ape did not toss off the woman.* Ⓕ *It looked as if the ape tossed off the woman from the top of the building.* □ *The ape tossed her off and ruined the movie.*

toss something off **1.** to drink a drink very quickly. □ *He tossed a few beers off and left.* Ⓣ *He tossed off a beer.* **2.** to ignore something. □ *She heard the remark, but she just tossed it off.* Ⓣ *She just tossed off the remark.*

TOSS ▸ OUT

toss someone or something out (of something) to discard someone or something; to throw someone or something out of something or some place. (The *of*-phrase is paraphrased with a *from*-phrase when the particle is transposed. See the Ⓕ example.) □ *The bartender tossed Walter out of the bar.* Ⓣ *The litterbug tossed out the empty can.* Ⓕ *He tossed out the can from the open car window.* □ *He should not have tossed it out.*

TOSS ▸ TOGETHER

toss something together to assemble something hastily. (See also *throw something together.*) □ *This report is useless. You just tossed it together!* □ *This meal was just tossed together, but it was delicious.*

TOSS ▸ UP

toss something up to throw something upward to a higher place or up into the air. □ *He tossed the coin up, calling "heads" and hoping for the best.* Ⓣ *He tossed up the coin.* Ⓝ *It was a toss-up who would go on the trip.*

TOTAL ▸ UP

total something up to add up the total of something. □ *Please total the bill up and let me see the cost.* Ⓣ *Total up the bill and give it to me.*

TOTE ▸ UP

tote something up to add something up. □ *The clerk toted the bill up and asked for an enormous sum.* Ⓣ *Tote up your expense report quickly and submit it to accounts payable.*

TOUCH ▸ AT

touch at some place [for a ship or an airplane] to visit or call at a port. □ *We touched at Aruba for about an hour.* □ *Our little boat touched at a number of different islands during the two-week cruise.*

TOUCH ▸ DOWN

touch down [for an airplane] to come in contact with the ground. □ *Flight twelve is due to touch down at midnight.* □ *When will this plane touch down?* Ⓝ *That was a good touchdown.*

TOUCH ▸ FOR

touch someone for something to approach someone and ask for something; to attempt to beg or borrow something from someone. (Colloquial or slang.) □ *Jerry touched me for twenty bucks, but I didn't have it.* □ *It won't do any good to touch me for money. I don't have any.*

TOUCH ▸ OFF

touch someone or something off to ignite or excite someone or something. □ *She is very excitable. The slightest thing will touch her off.* Ⓣ *The appearance of the fox touched off a furor in the henhouse.*

TOUCH ▸ ON

See under *TOUCH ▸ (UP)ON.*

touch on something come close to something. (Figurative.) □ *Your activities touch on treason.* □ *My thoughts have been touching on retirement lately.*

TOUCH ▸ TO

touch something to something to bring something into contact with something. □ *She touched her hand to her ear to indicate to the speaker to talk louder.* □

The magician touched his wand to the hat and a rabbit jumped out.

TOUCH ▸ UP

touch something up to fix up the minor flaws in something. □ *It's only a little scratch in the finish. We can touch it up easily.* 🅃 *I can touch up the scratch easily.* 🄰 *The room doesn't need painting. We can do a touch-up job.*

TOUCH ▸ (UP)ON

touch (up)on something to mention something; to discuss something briefly. (*Upon* is formal and less commonly used than *on*.) □ *The lecturer only touched upon the question of new technology.* □ *She only touched on the main issue.*

TOUCH ▸ WITH

not touch someone or something with a ten-foot pole not to have anything to do with someone or something. (Idiomatic. Always negative.) □ *No, I won't hire Fred. I wouldn't touch him with a ten-foot pole.* □ *I wouldn't touch that job with a ten-foot pole.*

touch base with someone to make contact with someone to exchange information. (From baseball.) □ *I need to touch base with Ann on a policy question.* □ *I will touch base with you as soon as I can.*

touch someone or something with something to bring something into contact with someone or something. (*Someone* includes *oneself*.) □ *Don't touch me with that filthy stick!* □ *I touched the snake with a stick to make sure it was dead.* □ *Wherever he touched himself with the leaf, his skin blistered.*

TOUGH ▸ OUT

tough something out to endure something; to endure the rigors of something to the very end. □ *I will tough this out to the very end.* 🅃 *I can tough out anything for a few days.*

TOUGHEN ▸ UP

toughen someone or something up to cause someone or something to be stronger, more uncompromising, or more severe. (*Someone* includes *oneself*.) □ *A few days behind the counter at the discount store will toughen her up quickly.* 🅃 *Having to deal with people toughened up the clerk quickly.* □ *She tried to toughen the skin on her palms up.* □ *I need to toughen myself up if I am going to deal with the public.*

toughen up to become tougher, stronger, or more severe. □ *She will toughen up after a while. You have to be tough around here to survive.* □ *You are going to have to toughen up if you want to play on the team.*

TOUT ▸ AROUND

tout someone or something around to promote and boost someone or something publicly. □ *He is touting his favorite candidate around, hoping to get a few votes for her.* □ *Roger is touting his book around, trying to make sales.*

TOUT ▸ AS

tout someone or something as something to present someone or something as a particular type of person or something. □ *Joel touted his candidate as the best of all.* □ *Ann touted her medicine as a cure-all.*

TOW ▸ AWAY

tow someone or something away to pull something, such as a car or a boat, away with another car, boat, etc. (The *someone* refers to the property of someone, not the person.) □ *If I don't get back to my car, they will tow me away.* 🅃 *The truck towed away my car.* □ *A big truck came and towed the illegally parked car away.*

TOW ▸ IN(TO)

tow someone or something in(to something) to pull something, such as a car or a truck, into something, such as a garage. (The *someone* refers to the property of someone, not the person.) □ *They had to tow my car into the garage to be repaired.* 🅃 *They towed in my car.* □ *They towed me in!*

TOW ▸ OUT

tow someone or something out (of some place) to pull something, such as a car, out of something, such as a ditch. (The *someone* refers to the property of someone, not the person. The *of*-phrase is paraphrased with a *from*-phrase when the particle is transposed. See the 🄵 example.) ☐ *The farmer used his tractor to tow Andrew out of the ditch.* ☐ *He towed the car out of the ditch.* 🅃 *He towed out the car.* 🄵 *He towed out the car from the ditch.* ☐ *He towed Andrew out.*

tow someone or something out to something to pull something, such as a boat, or someone in or on something out in the water to something. ☐ *Frank, who was on his surfboard, asked Tony to tow him out to the little island.* ☐ *We towed the raft out to the deepest part of the lake.*

TOWEL ▶ DOWN

towel someone or something down to rub someone or something dry with a towel. (*Someone* includes *oneself.*) ☐ *The mother toweled her child down and dressed her in clean clothes.* 🅃 *She toweled down the child gently.* ☐ *Towel down the dog. He's shaking.* ☐ *She said she would have to towel herself down before leaving.*

TOWEL ▶ OFF

towel someone or something off to dry someone or something with a towel. (*Someone* includes *oneself.*) ☐ *The young mother toweled the baby off with a soft, warm towel.* 🅃 *She toweled off the baby.* 🅃 *I toweled off my brow.* ☐ *Here, towel yourself off.*

TOWER ▶ ABOVE

tower above someone or something to stand or be much taller than someone or something. ☐ *The basketball player towered above everyone else in the room.* ☐ *The new building towered above all the others in town.*

tower head and shoulders above someone or something 1. to stand much taller than someone or something. ☐ *Bob towers head and shoulders above both his parents.* ☐ *The boys towered head and shoulders above the walls of the maze. They found their way around easily.* 2. to be far superior to someone or a group. (Figurative.) ☐ *The new vice president towers head and shoulders above the old one.* ☐ *The chairman towered head and shoulders above the rest of the committee.*

TOWER ▶ OVER

tower over someone or something to stand much taller than someone or something. ☐ *Tom towers over his older brother, Stan.* ☐ *Tom towered over the little desk he had been assigned to.*

TOY ▶ WITH

toy with someone or something to play with someone or something; to treat someone or something in an insincere manner. ☐ *You are just toying with me!* ☐ *Please don't toy with the stereo controls.*

TRACE ▶ AROUND

trace around something to press something against paper and draw a line around the edges that are in contact with the paper. ☐ *Trace around this pattern and cut out a new one.* ☐ *If you trace around the edges carefully, you will end up with a good drawing of the outline.*

TRACE ▶ BACK

trace someone or something (back) (to someone or something) to trail or track the origin of someone or something back to someone or something. ☐ *We traced her back to the car she had ridden in, but lost her trail at that point.* ☐ *We traced the letter back to her.* ☐ *Ann traced the letter back to the main post office.*

TRACE ▶ OVER

trace over something 1. to draw over something lightly. ☐ *Trace over the drawing to make it a little darker.* ☐ *I had to trace over it twice to make it visible.* 2. to copy something by placing a thin sheet of paper over it and drawing an outline of the thing to be copied. ☐ *Trace over this picture and then photocopy about ten copies for us all.* ☐ *This needs to be traced over again.*

TRACE ▶ TO

trace someone or something (back) (to someone or something) See under *TRACE ▶ BACK.*

TRACK ▸ DOWN

track someone or something down to search out where someone or something is. □ *I don't know where Anne is. I'll try to track her down.* 🅃 *I'll track down Anne for you.* □ *I will try to track the book down for you.*

TRACK ▸ IN(TO)

track something in(to some place) to bring something, such as mud, into a place on the bottom of one's feet. □ *Please don't track mud into the office.* 🅃 *Don't track in any mud!* □ *You tracked it in!*

TRACK ▸ OVER

track something (all) over something to spread something everywhere in a place from the bottom of one's feet. □ *You're tracking mud all over my house!* □ *Who tracked stuff over my carpet?*

TRACK ▸ UP

track something up to mess something up by spreading around something dirty or messy with one's feet. □ *Please don't track the floor up!* 🅃 *Claire tracked up the floor.*

TRADE ▸ AT

trade at some place to buy and sell at some place; to shop at someplace. □ *Do you trade at that store anymore?* □ *We don't trade there because their prices are too high.*

TRADE ▸ FOR

trade someone or something for someone or something to exchange someone or something for someone or something. □ *I will trade you Bill Idaho for Magic Wallace and two additional promising ball players.* □ *I will trade you my secretary for a compact car.* □ *I will trade my Mercedes for your secretary.*

TRADE ▸ IN

trade something in (for something) AND **trade something in (on something)** to return something, such as a car, to a place where cars are sold as partial payment on a new car. □ *I traded my old car in on a new one.* 🅃 *I traded in my old jalopy for a newer car.* □ *This car is old. It's time to trade it in.* 🄽 *How much do you think this car is worth as a trade-in?*

trade something in (on something) See the previous entry.

TRADE ▸ OFF

trade something off **1.** to get rid of something in an exchange. □ *I traded my car off.* 🅃 *I traded off my old car for a new one.* **2.** to sacrifice something in an exchange. □ *You end up trading security off for more money.* 🅃 *Don't trade off your job security.* 🄽 *The trade-off is that you don't have the use of your money during the term of the certificate.*

TRADE ▸ ON

See under *TRADE ▸ (UP)ON.*

TRADE ▸ UP

trade up from something to exchange a specific lower-level product for a higher-level product. □ *I decided to trade up from my little car to a much larger one.* □ *I can't afford what I have, let alone be able to trade up to anything.*

trade up (to something) to exchange a lower-level product for a specific higher-level product. □ *I would like to trade up to a more luxurious model.* □ *I would like to trade up.*

TRADE ▸ (UP)ON

trade (up)on something to exploit a personal characteristic of someone. (*Upon* is formal and less commonly used than *on.*) □ *Gary traded upon his disability in a way that embarrassed people.* □ *The way he traded on his handicap shocked me.*

TRADE ▸ WITH

trade something with someone to exchange something with someone. □ *Would you trade seats with me? I want to sit there.* □ *Can I trade books with you? This one is dull.*

trade with someone to make an exchange with someone. □ *I like the one you have. Please trade with me.* □ *Sorry. I don't want to trade with you.*

trade with someone or something **2.** to do business with someone or something. □ *I don't like the owner of that shop. I* *won't trade with him anymore.* ☐ *Thank your for trading with us all these years.* ☐ *We don't trade with that company because their prices are too high.*

TRAFFIC ▸ IN

traffic in something to deal in something; to trade in something, usually something illegal. ☐ *Max had been trafficking in guns for years before they caught him.* ☐ *The president of the country was trafficking in drugs for years.*

TRAIL ▸ AFTER

See the following entry.

TRAIL ▸ ALONG

trail (along) (after someone or something) **1.** to drag along after someone or something. ☐ *His pants were torn, and a piece of his trouser leg trailed along after him.* ☐ *His trouser leg trailed after him.* **2.** to follow along after someone or something. ☐ *A little dog trailed along after Mary and Karen.* ☐ *Is that your dog trailing along?*

TRAIL ▸ AWAY

trail away See under *TRAIL ▸ OFF.*

TRAIL ▸ BEHIND

trail behind (someone or something) **1.** to follow or drag along behind someone or something. ☐ *A long satin train trailed behind the bride.* ☐ *A long train trailed behind.* **2.** to move along behind someone or a group in a competition. ☐ *Sally trailed behind the rest of the marathon runners.* ☐ *Roger trailed behind Dave during most of the race.*

TRAIL ▸ BY

trail someone or something by something to have a smaller score than someone or something by a specific number of points. ☐ *Our team trails the visiting team by only six points.* ☐ *I trailed her by only a few points.*

TRAIL ▸ OFF

trail off AND **trail away** to fade away, as with speech, words, singing, etc. ☐ *Her voice trailed off as she saw who was waiting at the door.* ☐ *Ken's words trailed away as he passed out.*

TRAIL ▸ OVER

trail over something to lie behind, flowing out over something. ☐ *Her long gown trailed over the marble floor.* ☐ *The flowering vine trailed over the wall, making a lovely little garden area.*

TRAIN ▸ AS

train someone or something as something to educate someone or something to serve as a type of person. ☐ *We trained him as a first-rate mechanic.* ☐ *I trained my cocker spaniel as a moderately effective watchdog.*

TRAIN ▸ FOR

train for something to practice or drill for some task. ☐ *I am training for the marathon.* ☐ *We all have to train for the upcoming football season.*

train someone for something to educate someone or some creature for some purpose. ☐ *His parents trained him for work in the family business.* ☐ *He was trained for factory work.*

TRAIN ▸ IN

train someone in something to drill and practice someone in a particular skill or body of knowledge. ☐ *Her mentor trained her in the art of argumentation.* ☐ *I will try to train you in the skills needed to perform this task.*

TRAIN ▸ ON

train someone on something to educate someone in the use of something. (*Someone* includes *oneself.*) ☐ *We trained him on the high diving board, but he isn't ready for competition yet.* ☐ *She trained herself on the computer so she could write a book.*

train something on someone or something to aim something at someone or something. ☐ *Dave trained the spotlight on Fred, who was just coming out of the building.* ☐ *Train your lens on that bush. There is a deer back there.*

TRAIN ▸ UP

train up to something to practice or drill up to a certain level of proficiency. ☐ *I don't have enough stamina for the marathon now, but I am training up to it.* ☐ *Alice trained up to the long-distance swim for years.*

TRAIPSE ▸ AROUND

traipse around (some place) to walk or travel around some place. □ *I spent all afternoon traipsing around town looking for just the right gift for Roger.* □ *She has been traipsing around all day.*

TRAMP ▸ ACROSS

tramp across something to march or stamp across an area. □ *The kids tramped across the yard and wore a path.* □ *Please don't tramp across my garden.*

TRAMP ▸ THROUGH

tramp through something to march or stamp a passage through something. □ *The kids tramped through every puddle in town on their way to school.* □ *Don't tramp through every mud puddle you see.*

TRAMPLE ▸ DOWN

trample someone or something down to crush down someone or something with the feet. □ *Stay out of crowds at rock concerts. Those kids will trample you down if they get excited.* 🅃 *The cows trampled down the stalks of corn.*

TRAMPLE ▸ ON

See also under *TRAMPLE ▸ (UP)ON.*

trample on something to grind something underfoot. □ *Someone has trampled on my tomato plants.* □ *It's hard to keep people from trampling on the low-growing plants.*

TRAMPLE ▸ OUT

trample something out to create a pathway by marching or stamping the same trail over and over. □ *The mail carriers have trampled a path out through my marigolds!* 🅃 *Jim trampled out a path in my garden.*

TRAMPLE ▸ TO

trample someone or something to something to stomp or crush someone or something underfoot to the point of death or destruction. □ *The elephant trampled the photographer to death.* □ *All the joggers trampled the bushes to pieces.*

TRAMPLE ▸ (UP)ON

trample (up)on someone or something to crush someone or something underfoot. (*Upon* is formal and less commonly used than *on.*) □ *Please don't trample upon the children!* □ *The bulls running through the streets trampled on some of the tourists.*

TRANSCRIBE ▸ FROM

transcribe something from someone or something to write something down from an audible source. □ *We transcribed the folktales from authentic storytellers.* □ *I transcribed the tale from an old phonograph recording.*

TRANSCRIBE ▸ IN

transcribe something in something **1.** to transliterate one alphabet into another. □ *Can you translate these romanized Korean words into the Korean script?* □ *We had to transcribe the entire novel into Cyrillic.* **2.** to represent speech sounds in a phonetic transcription. □ *The editor wanted the glossary transcribed in Webster-style phonetics.* □ *It is much easier to transcribe the material in the International Phonetic Alphabet.*

transcribe something in something to write something down in something. □ *Please transcribe this list of names in your notebook.* □ *I can't read what is transcribed in my book.*

TRANSFER ▸ FROM

transfer someone or something (from some place) (to some place) to move or relocate someone or something from one place to another. □ *Her company transferred her from Houston to Los Angeles.* □ *We transferred the boxes from one place to another.* □ *I transferred the phone call to John's phone from mine.*

transfer something (from someone) (to someone else) to reassign something from one person to another. □ *I have to transfer ownership of this car to my daughter.* □ *The title of the car was transferred from me to someone else.*

TRANSFER ► TO

transfer someone or something (from some place) (to some place) See under *TRANSFER ► FROM.*

transfer someone or something to someone to reassign someone or something to someone. □ *I transferred my secretary to Joel, who can get along with almost anyone.* □ *Ann transferred her car registration to her sister.*

transfer to something to have oneself reassigned to something. □ *I am transferring to the accounting department.* □ *Andy wanted to transfer to a different school.*

TRANSFORM ► FROM

transform someone or something (from someone or something) (in)to someone or something to change someone or something from someone or something into someone or something else. (*Someone* includes *oneself.*) □ *Time had transformed gangly little Rachel into a lovely young woman.* □ *Manners transformed Tom from a pest into a prince.* □ *The hairdresser transformed the actor into an old man.* □ *They transformed themselves from mere boys to well-trained fighting men.*

TRANSGRESS ► AGAINST

transgress against someone or something to make an offense against someone or something. (Stilted and formal.) □ *I did not mean to transgress against you.* □ *We did not transgress against the rules of the college.*

TRANSLATE ► FROM

translate something (from something) ((in)to something) to decode something from something, such as a language, to another. □ *Will you please translate this from Russian into English?* □ *I can translate it into Russian from any language.* □ *Would you translate this from the original language?*

TRANSLATE ► (IN)TO

See the previous entry.

TRANSLITERATE ► FROM

transliterate something (from something) ((in)to something) to decode something from one set of symbols to another. □ *Donald transliterated the tale from Cyrillic script into Roman letters and still couldn't read it aloud.* □ *Can you transliterate this from the original Bengali script into the Roman alphabet?* □ *I will transliterate this into Cyrillic.*

TRANSLITERATE ► (IN)TO

See the previous entry.

TRANSMIT ► FROM

transmit something (from some place) (to some place) to send or dispatch something from one place to another. □ *Can you transmit a fax from your car to your office?* □ *I can transmit it to any place in the world.* □ *You can really transmit this from your car?*

TRANSMIT ► TO

See the previous entry.

transmit something to someone or something to send or dispatch something to someone or something. □ *Please transmit this message to Rachel.* □ *I will transmit the message to my office.*

TRANSMUTE ► FROM

transmute something (from something) ((in)to something) to change something from one thing into another. □ *Do you believe that it is possible to transmute gold into lead?* □ *No, you cannot transmute one metal into another.*

TRANSMUTE ► (IN)TO

See the previous entry.

TRANSPORT ► FROM

transport someone or something (from some place) (to some place) to move or convey someone or something from one place to another. (*Someone* includes *oneself.*) □ *In his car, he transported us from our home to the airport.* □ *Please see that this box gets transported from here to the loading dock.* □ *They quickly transported themselves to town.*

TRANSPORT ► TO

See the previous entry.

TRANSPOSE ► FROM

transpose something (from something) ((in)to something) to change something, usually in music, from one musical key to another. ☐ *Can you transpose this from F# to a higher key?* ☐ *It would be easy to transpose it into a higher key.* ☐ *I will transpose it to the key of A.*

TRANSPOSE ▸ (IN)TO
See the previous entry.

TRAP ▸ IN
trap someone in something to catch someone in an inconsistency or contradiction. (Figurative. *Someone* includes *oneself.*) ☐ *The lawyer trapped the witness in his inconsistencies.* ☐ *She trapped herself in her own argument.*

trap someone or something in something to catch someone or something in a trap. ☐ *Jed accidentally trapped Tex in his bear trap.* ☐ *Jerry trapped a rabbit in his trap.*

TRAP ▸ INTO
trap someone into something to get one into such a position that one has little choice but to do something. ☐ *You'll never trap me into going out with Roger!* ☐ *I was trapped into going there.*

TRAVEL ▸ ACROSS
travel across something to make a journey across something or some place. ☐ *We have to travel across the desert to get there.* ☐ *I do not want to travel across that rickety bridge on the way back.*

TRAVEL ▸ BY
See *travel (from some place) (to some place) (by something)* under *TRAVEL ▸ FROM.*

travel by something **1.** to make a journey, using a particular conveyance. ☐ *I will go by train, since I don't like to travel by plane.* ☐ *We traveled by car, since that is the cheapest.* **2.** to make a journey under particular conditions. ☐ *I don't ever travel by night.* ☐ *We like to travel by day so we can see the scenery.*

TRAVEL ▸ FOR
travel for someone or something to go from place to place selling for someone or a company. ☐ *Walter travels for his uncle, who runs a toy factory.* ☐ *She travels for a company that makes men's clothing.*

TRAVEL ▸ FROM
travel (from some place) (to some place) (by something) to make a journey from one place to another, using a particular conveyance. ☐ *We intend to travel from Manchester to Leeds by train.* ☐ *I traveled by rail to London from Leeds.* ☐ *Do you travel by rail often?* ☐ *How often do you travel to London?* ☐ *It is more convenient to travel from Manchester.*

TRAVEL ▸ ON
travel on something **1.** to make a journey on a particular conveyance. ☐ *Do you like to travel on the train?* ☐ *I do not care to travel on the bus.* **2.** to travel having certain bodily states, such as on an empty stomach, on a full stomach. ☐ *I hate traveling on a full stomach.* ☐ *I can't stand to travel on a full stomach.*

TRAVEL ▸ OVER
travel over something **1.** to go over something as part of a journey. ☐ *We had to travel over an old bridge over the Mississippi to get to my sister's house.* ☐ *We will travel over a long narrow strip of land to get to the marina.* **2.** to travel widely over a great area. ☐ *She spent the summer traveling over Europe.* ☐ *I have traveled over the entire country and never failed to find someone I could talk to.*

TRAVEL ▸ THROUGH
travel through something **1.** to make a journey through some area or country. ☐ *We will have to travel through Germany to get there.* ☐ *Do you want to travel through the desert or through the mountains?* **2.** to make a journey through some kind of weather condition. ☐ *I hate to travel through the rain.* ☐ *I refuse to travel through a snowstorm.*

TRAVEL ▸ TO
travel (from some place) (to some place) (by something) See under *TRAVEL ▸ FROM.*

TRAVEL ▸ WITH

travel with someone to associate with someone; to move about in association with someone. (Also literal senses.) □ *She travels with a sophisticated crowd.* □ *I am afraid that Walter is traveling with the wrong group of friends.*

travel with someone to make a journey with someone. □ *Do you mind if I travel with you?* □ *Who are you going to travel with?*

travel with something to have something with one as one travels. □ *I always travel with extra money.* □ *I hate to travel with three suitcases. That is more than I can handle.*

TREAD ▸ ON

tread on someone's toes See *step on someone's toes* under *STEP ▸ ON.*

TREAD ▸ (UP)ON

tread (up)on someone or something to walk or step on someone or something. (*Upon* is formal and less commonly used than *on*. *Step* is more common than *tread*.) □ *Don't tread on Sam, who is napping under the tree.* □ *Please don't tread on the freshly shampooed carpeting on the stairs.*

TREAT ▸ AS

treat someone or something as something to deal with someone or something as something. □ *Please don't treat me as a guest.* □ *You treat the editorial board as a needless barrier.*

TREAT ▸ FOR

treat someone (for something) (with something) to attempt to cure someone's disease with something. (*Someone* includes *oneself*.) □ *The doctor treated me for the flu with aspirin. It didn't work, but it was cheap.* □ *They treated him for his broken bones.* □ *Ann treated him with the appropriate therapy.* □ *I decided to treat myself with medicine for my cold.*

TREAT ▸ LIKE

treat someone or something like someone or something to deal with someone or something as if the person or thing were really someone, a type of a person, or something. □ *I like him. He treats me like a king.* □ *He treats Jane like Mary—he ignores them both.*

TREAT ▸ TO

treat someone to something to provide and pay for something for someone as a gift or as entertainment. (*Someone* includes *oneself*.) □ *I will be delighted to treat you to dinner.* □ *After the play, they treated themselves to pie and coffee.*

TREAT ▸ WITH

treat someone (for something) (with something) See under *TREAT ▸ FOR.*

TREK ▸ ACROSS

trek across something to hike or march across something. □ *The scouts trekked across the fields of the small farming community.* □ *I don't look forward to trekking across the desert.*

TREK ▸ TO

trek to some place to hike or march to some place. □ *I have to trek all the way to the store because my car is in the shop.* □ *We trekked to the cabin and made that our base camp for the whole two weeks.*

TREMBLE ▸ AT

tremble at something to shake with fear or anticipation at the thought of something. □ *David trembled at the thought of having to go to Russia by himself.* □ *Carl trembled at the idea of winning first place.*

TREMBLE ▸ FROM

tremble from something to shake or vibrate in response to something like an explosion or an earthquake. □ *The house trembled from the blast.* □ *I could feel the bridge trembling from the minor earthquake that I was hearing about on the radio.*

TREMBLE ▸ WITH

tremble with something to tremble because of something. □ *The children trembled with fear during the storm.* □ *David trembled with rage when he saw his slashed tires.*

TREND ▸ TOWARD

trend toward something to move gradually toward something. □ *Fashions are* *trending toward the gaudy and flamboyant.* □ *Attitudes are trending toward the more conservative.*

TRESPASS ▸ (UP)ON

trespass (up)on something to intrude or encroach onto a restricted or private area. (*Upon* is formal and less commonly used than *on*.) □ *You had better not trespass upon Mr. Green's land.* □ *I wouldn't trespass on that old buzzard's land!*

TRICK ▸ INTO

trick someone into something to deceive someone into doing something. □ *She tried to trick him into doing it her way.* □ *I didn't want to do it, but I was tricked into it.*

TRICK ▸ OUT

trick someone out of something AND **trick something out of someone** to get something from someone by trickery. □ *You can't trick me out of my money. I'm not that dumb!* □ *Stay alert so that no one tricks you out of your money.* □ *They tricked the information out of Bob.*

TRICKLE ▸ AWAY

trickle away [for a liquid] to seep or dribble away. □ *All the water trickled away down the drain.* □ *After the last of the spilled milk had trickled away, Timmy began to cry.*

TRICKLE ▸ DOWN

trickle down (to someone or something) **1.** [for a liquid] to seep or dribble downward to reach someone or something. □ *The water trickled down the wall to the floor.* □ *It trickled down very slowly.* **2.** [for something] to be distributed to someone or something in little bits at a time. (Figurative.) □ *The results of the improved economy trickled down to people at lower-income levels.* □ *Information about what happened finally trickled down to me.*

TRICKLE ▸ IN(TO)

trickle in(to something) **1.** [for a liquid] to seep or dribble into something or a place. □ *Some of the rainwater trickled into my car through a leak.* □ *It trickled in during the night.* **2.** [for someone or something] to come into something or a place, a few at a time. (Figurative.) □ *The audience trickled into the hall little by little.* □ *They trickled in over a period of an hour or more.*

TRICKLE ▸ OUT

trickle out (of something) **1.** [for a liquid] to leak or dribble out of something or a place. □ *The oil trickled out of the engine little by little.* □ *It trickled out and made a puddle on the floor.* **2.** [for someone or something] to go out of something or a place, little by little. (Figurative.) □ *The dissatisfied members of the audience trickled out of the theater three and four at a time.* □ *They trickled out as the evening wore on.*

TRICKLE ▸ THROUGH

trickle through (something) **1.** [for a liquid] to seep through something. □ *The water trickled through the cracked windowpane.* □ *They taped the glass, but the water trickled through anyway.* **2.** [for someone or something] to move through something little by little. □ *The people trickled through the door into the store in far smaller numbers than we had expected.* □ *They trickled through very slowly.*

TRIFLE ▸ AWAY

trifle something away (on someone or something) to waste something, such as money, on someone or something, little by little. □ *Don't trifle all your money away on your friends.* 🅃 *Don't trifle away any more money on silly purchases.*

TRIFLE ▸ WITH

trifle with someone to flirt with someone. □ *You are just trifling with me. I don't have time for that.* □ *I hope you are not trifling with me.*

trifle with someone or something to act without seriousness or respect toward someone or something. □ *Don't trifle with me! I am not to be trifled with.* □ *I wish that Ann wouldn't trifle with our efforts at reform.*

TRIGGER ▸ OFF

trigger someone or something off to cause someone or something to go into action. □ *Your rude comments triggered her off.* 🅃 *Your comments triggered off quite an uproar.*

trigger something off to set something off, such as an explosion. □ *We were afraid that the sparks from the engine would trigger an explosion off.* 🅃 *The sparks triggered off an explosion.*

TRIM ► AWAY

trim something away (from something) to cut something away (from something). □ *The butcher trimmed the fat away from the steak.* 🅃 *Please trim away the fat from the meat.* □ *Oh, yes. Trim it away.*

TRIM ► DOWN

trim (oneself) down to take action to become slimmer or lose weight. □ *I need to trim myself down before I go on vacation.* □ *I decided to trim down, but I never got around to it.* □ *You really need to trim down and stay at a lower weight.* □ *I have to go on a diet to trim myself down.*

trim something down to reduce the size of something. □ *You will have to trim the picture down to get it into the frame.* 🅃 *Trim down the picture before you frame it.* 🅃 *The Congress seems unable to trim down the size of the budget.*

TRIM ► FROM

trim something from something to cut something away from something. □ *I trimmed the fat from the steaks.* □ *We had to trim a lot of the fat from the meat after we got it home.*

TRIM ► OFF

trim something off ((of) someone or something) to cut something off something. (The *of*-phrase is paraphrased with a *from*-phrase when the particle is transposed. The *of* is colloquial.) □ *I asked the barber to trim the beard off of Ralph.* 🅃 *The barber trimmed off Ralph's beard.* 🄵 *The seamstress trimmed off the ragged edge from the cloth.* □ *Please trim it off.*

TRIM ► WITH

trim something with something to decorate something with something. □ *She trimmed the dress with lace.* □ *Bobby and Timmy trimmed the tree with colorful ornaments.*

TRIP ► ALONG

trip along to move along happily. □ *The kids tripped along on their way to school.* □ *We were just tripping along, not having any notion of what was about to happen.*

TRIP ► OVER

trip over someone or something to stumble on someone or something. □ *The place was filled with sleeping people. I tripped over perfect strangers on my way to the door.* □ *I tripped over a brick and fell into the wall.*

TRIP ► UP

trip someone up 1. to cause someone to trip; to entangle someone's feet. (*Someone* includes *oneself*.) □ *The rope strewn about the deck tripped him up.* 🅃 *The lines tripped up the crew.* □ *He tripped himself up in the lines.* **2.** to cause someone to falter. (Figurative. *Someone* includes *oneself*.) □ *Mary came in while the speaker was talking and the distraction tripped him up.* 🅃 *The noise in the audience tripped up the speaker.* □ *Take care and do not trip yourself up.*

trip someone up (with something) to impede, thwart, or hinder someone with something. □ *She tripped him up with her knowledge of quantum physics.* 🅃 *She tripped up the speaker with her superior knowledge of the subject.* □ *Ann tripped us up again.*

TRIUMPH ► OVER

triumph over someone or something to achieve victory over someone or something. □ *Our team triumphed over all the others.* □ *Our army triumphed over theirs.*

TROOP ► ACROSS

troop across someone or something [for a mass of creatures] to move across someone or something. □ *The huge herds of wildebeest began to troop across the plain in search of food.* □ *The ants trooped across Karen as she lay in the sand.*

TROOP ▶ IN(TO)

troop in(to something) to flock or march into something or some place in numbers. ☐ *The scouts trooped into the mess hall and sat down.* ☐ *They trooped in and sat down.*

TROT ▶ AFTER

trot after someone to follow along after someone, as done by a small dog. ☐ *The puppy trotted along after the kids wherever they went.* ☐ *My little brother would always come trotting after us, annoying us a lot.*

TROT ▶ ALONG

trot along to step along in a lively fashion. ☐ *The horses trotted along in time with the music.* ☐ *The horses were trotting along, going exactly where we aimed them.*

TROT ▶ OUT

trot someone or something out to bring out and display someone or something. ☐ *The boss trotted the new vice president out for us to meet.* 🅃 *The boss trotted out his daughter and introduced her as a new vice president.* ☐ *Fred trotted out his favorite project for everyone to see.*

TROUBLE ▶ ABOUT

trouble one's head about someone or something to worry about someone or something. ☐ *Please don't trouble your head about me. I'll get along.* ☐ *I wish you wouldn't trouble your head about the problem. We can solve it.*

trouble oneself about someone or something to bother or worry oneself about someone or something. ☐ *Please don't trouble yourself about Walter. I'll take care of him.* ☐ *There is no need to trouble yourself over the cost. I'll take care of it.* ☐ *Now, don't trouble yourself about Sally.* ☐ *Sally shouldn't trouble herself about the bill.*

trouble someone about someone or something to bother someone by asking about someone or something. (*Someone* includes *oneself.*) ☐ *Please don't trouble me about Larry.* ☐ *Can I trouble you about a billing problem?* ☐ *Please don't trouble yourself about me.*

TROUBLE ▶ FOR

trouble someone for something to bother someone by asking for something. ☐ *Could I trouble you for a match?* ☐ *Could I trouble you to help me with the door?* ☐ *I didn't want to trouble you for an answer while you were on the phone.*

TROUBLE ▶ TO

trouble oneself to do something to annoy oneself by taking the time or trouble to do something. ☐ *I didn't know if I should trouble myself to carry the bags in or not.* ☐ *Please don't trouble yourself to bring in the paper. I have already done it.*

TROUBLE ▶ WITH

trouble someone with something to bother someone with something, such as a question or a problem. (*Someone* includes *oneself.*) ☐ *I hate to trouble you with this, but could you help me adjust my binoculars?* ☐ *Don't trouble yourself with this matter.*

TRUDGE ▶ ALONG

trudge along to plod along on foot. ☐ *It seemed as if we trudged along for miles.* ☐ *As we trudged along, we forgot how cold it was.*

TRUDGE ▶ THROUGH

trudge through something to work one's way through something difficult. (Either literally on foot or figuratively.) ☐ *We trudged through the snow all the way to town.* ☐ *I used to have to trudge through snow like this every day to get to school.* ☐ *I hate have to trudge through these reports on the weekend.*

TRUE ▶ UP

true something up to straighten something up; to put something into true plumb. ☐ *Please true this door frame up better before you hang the door.* 🅃 *Can you true up this wall a little?*

TRUMP ▶ UP

trump something up to think something up; to contrive something. ☐ *Do you just sit around trumping charges up against innocent people?* 🅃 *They trumped up the charges in an effort to* *disgrace me.* [A] *This is a trumped-up charge, and I'm innocent.*

TRUSS ▸ UP

truss someone or something up to bind, tie, or bundle someone or something up. ☐ *The attendants trussed Walter up and took him to a padded cell.* [T] *They trussed up Walter tightly.* ☐ *Ann trussed the bundle up and sent it off.* [A] *In the corner, the trussed-up robber waited patiently for the police to come.*

TRUST ▸ FOR

trust someone for something to depend on someone for payment for something. ☐ *I will lend you one hundred dollars. I know I can trust you for it.* ☐ *I loaned Ted a lot of money. It's all right. I can trust him for it.*

TRUST ▸ IN

trust in someone or something to believe in someone or something. ☐ *Trust in me. I know what I am saying.* ☐ *Can I trust in the figures in this report?*

TRUST ▸ TO

trust someone or something to someone to leave someone or something in the possession of someone whom you assume will guard someone or something. ☐ *Can I trust my little Jimmy to you?* ☐ *I am perfectly comfortable trusting this money to you.*

trust someone to do something to believe that someone can be relied on to do something. (*Someone* includes *oneself*.) ☐ *You can trust her to be here on time.* ☐ *I can't trust myself to eat wisely.*

TRUST ▸ WITH

trust someone with someone or something to leave someone in the care of someone or something. (*Someone* includes *oneself*.) ☐ *Can I trust you with my uncle? He needs to have his medicine right on time.* ☐ *I am sure I can trust you with the money.* ☐ *Don't leave that cake with me. I can't trust myself with it.*

TRY ▸ AT

try one's hand at something to give something a try; to take a try at something. ☐ *I would like to try my hand at waterskiing.* ☐ *I would like to try my hand at baking a cake.*

try one's luck at something to take a chance and see if one can succeed at something. ☐ *Do you want to try your luck at dice?* ☐ *I tried my luck at cards and lost badly.*

TRY ▸ BACK

try someone back (again) to try to return someone's call again. (Colloquial.) ☐ *She's not in, so I'll try her back later.* ☐ *Jan will try her back.*

TRY ▸ FOR

try for something to try to win or achieve something. ☐ *I am going to try for the silver trophy in this year's race.* ☐ *Will you try for a place on the team?*

try someone for something to put someone through a court trial for some crime or wrongdoing. ☐ *The prosecutor wanted to try Harry for fraud.* ☐ *Anne was tried for speeding.*

try something (on) (for size) See the following entry.

TRY ▸ ON

try something (on) (for size) **1.** to put on an article of clothing to see if it fits. ☐ *Here, try this on for size and see if it fits any better.* ☐ *I'll try this one for size.* ☐ *Try this one on.* [T] *Please try on this shirt for size.* **2.** to evaluate an idea or proposition. (Figurative colloquial.) ☐ *Now, try this idea on for size.* ☐ *Try this plan for size. I think you'll like it.*

try something on with someone to get someone's opinion about an idea or plan. (Figurative.) ☐ *Let me try this idea on with you.* ☐ *She tried the new idea on with the boss, but the response was not good.*

TRY ▸ OUT

try out (for something) to audition for a part in some performance or other activity requiring skill. ☐ *I intend to try out for the play.* ☐ *I'm going to try out too.* [N] *I went to the tryouts for the play, but I didn't try out.*

try someone or something out to test someone or something for a while; to sample the performance of someone or something. ☐ *We will try her out in the editorial department and see how she does.* Ⓣ *We will try out this employee in another department for a while.* ☐ *Can I try this exercise machine out?*

try something out on someone to see how someone responds to something or some idea. ☐ *Let me try this idea out on you and see what you think.* Ⓣ *Let me try out this new medicine on her.*

TUCK ▸ AROUND

tuck something around someone or something to wrap something snugly around someone or something. ☐ *I tucked crumpled newspapers around the cups in the box to keep them from breaking.* ☐ *Molly-Jo tucked the covers around the baby.*

TUCK ▸ AWAY

tuck something away to eat something. ☐ *The boys tucked away three pizzas and an apple pie.* ☐ *When I was younger, I could tuck away my dinner in no time at all.*

tuck something away to hide or store something away. ☐ *Tuck this away where you can find it later.* Ⓣ *Can you tuck away this money somewhere?*

TUCK ▸ IN

tuck something in((to) something) to fold or stuff something into something. ☐ *Please tuck your shirttail into your pants.* Ⓣ *Tuck in your shirttail.* ☐ *When you make the bed, you have to tuck the sheets in.* ☐ *I tucked a handkerchief into the breast pocket of my jacket.* ☐ *She tucked a note into the box with my present.*

TUCK ▸ INTO

tuck into something to begin eating something vigorously. ☐ *The kids really tucked into the stew.* ☐ *I could see from the way that they tucked into their meal that they were really hungry.*

TUCK ▸ IN(TO)

tuck someone in((to) something) to place someone into something carefully; to wrap someone in blankets or something similar. ☐ *Father tucked Jimmy into bed an hour later than he should have.* Ⓣ *Please tuck in Jimmy.* ☐ *I'll tuck him in.*

TUCK ▸ UP

tuck something up to raise up some part of one's clothing and attach it temporarily. ☐ *She tucked her skirt up and waded through the flooded basement.* Ⓣ *She tucked up her skirt.*

tuck something up (under something) to place or push something, such as cloth, up under something. ☐ *Tuck the sheet up under the mattress when you make the bed.* Ⓣ *Tuck up the sheet under the mattress when you make the bed.* ☐ *Tuck it up tight.*

TUCKER ▸ OUT

tucker someone out to tire someone out. (*Someone* includes *oneself*.) ☐ *All this work has tuckered me out.* Ⓣ *The heavy work tuckered out the staff early in the day.* ☐ *I tuckered myself out trying to clean the whole house in one day.*

TUG ▸ AT

tug at someone or something to pull at someone or something. ☐ *Stop tugging at me! I'll talk to you in a minute.* ☐ *The dog tugged at my pants cuff.* ☐ *The wind tugged at my hat.*

TUG ▸ AWAY

tug away (at something) to pull hard at something; to haul something. ☐ *She tugged away at the rope, but the anchor would not budge.* ☐ *No matter how much she tugged away, it didn't move.*

TUMBLE ▸ ALONG

tumble along to roll or bounce along. ☐ *The ball tumbled along, across the lawn and into the street.* ☐ *As the boulder tumbled along, it crushed everything in its path.*

TUMBLE ▸ DOWN

tumble down to fall down; to topple. ☐ *The old barn was so rickety that it almost tumbled down on its own.* ☐ *The pile of books tumbled down all over the floor.* Ⓐ *The tumbledown shack by the railroad tracks burned last night.*

tumble someone or something down something to tip or push someone or something down something. ☐ *Timmy* *tumbled his brother down the stairs.* □ *Ann tumbled her laundry down the chute.*

TUMBLE ▸ FROM

tumble from something to fall from something. □ *The food tumbled from the tray and fell to the floor.* □ *The books tumbled from the shelf during the earthquake.*

TUMBLE ▸ INTO

tumble into someone or something to fall down and roll into someone or something. (Either accidentally or on purpose.) □ *Liz tripped and tumbled into the table.* □ *She tumbled into Ken.*

tumble into something to fall into something. □ *Liz went home and tumbled into bed.* □ *Jeff tumbled into the room and made his way to a chair.*

TUMBLE ▸ OUT

tumble out of something to fall, topple, or drop out of something. □ *Don't let the baby tumble out of the chair!* □ *The children tumbled out of the car and ran for the school building.*

TUMBLE ▸ OVER

tumble over to fall over. □ *The vase tumbled over and broke.* □ *I held Timmy up to keep him from tumbling over.*

tumble over someone or something to trip or stumble over someone or something and fall down. □ *I tumbled over Fred, who was napping under the tree.* □ *I tumbled over a chair and fell down.*

tumble over (something) to fall over the edge of something. □ *Stay away from the edge. I don't want any of you tumbling over it.* □ *Don't go too close. You'll tumble over.*

TUMBLE ▸ TO

tumble to something to catch onto something; to understand something. (Informal.) □ *They didn't seem to tumble to the seriousness of the situation.* □ *The boys tumbled to the importance of our remarks immediately.*

TUNE ▸ IN

tune in (on someone or something) AND **tune in (to someone or something)** **1.** to adjust a radio or television set to receive a broadcast of someone or something. □ *Let's tune in on Johnny Carson.* □ *I don't want to tune in tonight.* □ *Let's tune in to a different program.* **2.** to pay attention to someone or something. (Slang.) □ *I just can't tune in on these professors.* □ *I listen and I try, but I just can't tune in.* □ *Please tune in to me. You need this information!*

tune in (to someone or something) See the previous entry.

tune something in to adjust a radio or television set so that something can be received. (An old-fashioned expression still used with modern tuners.) □ *Could you tune the newscast in?* 🅃 *Please tune in the station a little better.*

tune something (in) to something See also under *TUNE ▸ TO.*

TUNE ▸ OUT

tune out to cease paying attention to anything at all. □ *I wasn't interested, so I just tuned out.* □ *I think that most of the audience tuned out during the last part of the lecture.*

tune someone or something out to put someone or something out of one's consciousness; to cease paying attention to someone or something. □ *I had to tune the radio out in order to concentrate.* 🅃 *I tuned out what the speaker was saying and daydreamed for a while.*

TUNE ▸ TO

tune something (in) to something to adjust a radio or television set to a particular setting, program, or station. □ *We will tune the radio in to some music.* □ *I'll tune it to the news.*

TUNE ▸ UP

tune something up to adjust an engine to run the best and most efficiently. □ *You need to tune this engine up.* 🅃 *Please tune up this engine so it will run more economically.* 🄽 *Do you know where I can get a tune-up at a reasonable price?*

tune up [for one or more musicians] to bring their instruments into tune. □ *You could hear them behind the curtain,* *tuning up.* □ *We have to tune up before the concert.*

TUNNEL ▶ THROUGH

tunnel through something to make a tunnel or passageway through something or a group of people. □ *Roger had to tunnel through the crowd to get to the rest room.* □ *The workers tunneled through the soft soil to reach the buried cable.*

TUNNEL ▶ UNDER

tunnel under someone or something to dig a tunnel under someone or something. □ *All the time she was standing in the yard talking about the moles, they were tunneling under her.* □ *They are tunneling under the English Channel.*

TURN ▶ ABOUT

turn about See *turn around* under *TURN ▶ AROUND.*

turn something about See *turn something around* under *TURN ▶ AROUND.*

TURN ▶ AGAINST

turn against someone or something to attack, defy, or revolt against someone or something. □ *You wouldn't think that your own family would turn against you!* □ *In the last days, everyone turned against the government.*

turn someone or something against someone or something to cause someone to defy or revolt against someone or something; to make someone antagonistic toward someone or something. □ *He turned the whole board against Molly.* □ *She turned the city council against the proposed law.*

TURN ▶ AROUND

turn around AND **turn about** to reverse; to face the opposite direction; to change direction of motion. □ *The bus turned around and went the other way.* □ *Please turn around so I can see who you are.* □ *The bus turned about and returned to the station.* Ⓝ *The turnabout in profits helps the company's stock a lot.*

turn something around AND **turn something about** to reverse the direction of something; to cause something to face the opposite direction. □ *Turn the car around and head it in the other direction.* □ *If you turn the chair around, we can see one another while we talk.* □ *This company is failing. Do you think we can turn it about?* Ⓣ *Karen is an expert in turning about troubled companies.* Ⓝ *The turnaround in profits was welcomed by the shareholders.*

TURN ▶ ASIDE

turn someone aside to divert someone from the flow of people. □ *The attendant turned the poorly dressed man aside.* Ⓣ *The attendant turned aside all the persons who arrived late.*

turn something aside to evade something. □ *Ann turned the awkward questions aside.* Ⓣ *She turned aside the questions she didn't want to answer.*

TURN ▶ AWAY

turn (away) (from someone or something) to turn oneself to avoid someone or something. □ *She turned away from me as I walked past, pretending not to see me.* □ *She turned from Ken and ran.* □ *Claire turned away as I approached.*

turn someone or something (away) (from something) to cause someone or some creature to avoid moving toward something; to cause someone or some creature to avoid moving toward harm. □ *The police officer turned the pedestrians away from the scene of the accident.* □ *He turned the horses away from the gate.*

TURN ▶ BACK

turn back (from some place) to stop one's journey and return. □ *We turned back from the amusement park so we could go home and get the tickets we had forgotten.* □ *We turned back at the last minute.*

turn someone or something back to cause someone or something to stop and go back; to cause someone or something to retreat. □ *The border guards turned us back because we had no passports.* Ⓣ *They turned back the train because the bridge was down.*

TURN ▸ DOWN

turn someone down to issue a refusal to someone. □ *We had to turn Joan down, even though her proposal was okay.* 🅃 *We turned down Joan, even though her credentials were good.* 🄽 *She was stunned by his turndown.*

turn something down **1.** to bend or fold something down. □ *He turned his coat collar down when he got inside the house.* 🅃 *Timmy had turned down his cuffs and caught one of them in his bicycle chain.* **2.** to decrease the volume of something. □ *Please turn the radio down.* 🅃 *Can't you turn down that stereo?* **3.** to reject something. □ *The board turned our proposal down.* 🅃 *They turned down our proposal.* 🄽 *Tom offered everything, but the lawyer's turndown was rude and haughty.*

turn thumbs down (on someone or something) to reject someone or something; to grow to reject someone or something. □ *The boss turned thumbs down on Tom. They would have to find someone else.* □ *The minute I saw it, I turned thumbs down.*

TURN ▸ FROM

turn (away) (from someone or something) See under *TURN ▸ AWAY.*

turn someone or something (away) (from something) See under *TURN ▸ AWAY.*

TURN ▸ IN

See also under *TURN ▸ IN(TO).*

turn in **1.** to go to bed. (Colloquial.) □ *It's time to turn in. Good night.* □ *I want to turn in early tonight.* **2.** to fold or point inward. □ *Do my toes turn in too much?* □ *The legs of the table turned in at the bottom, giving a quaint appearance to the piece of furniture.*

turn in (up)on oneself to become introverted. □ *Over the years, she had turned in upon herself and was quiet and alone.* □ *The death of his dog caused Jed to turn in on himself.*

turn (over) in one's grave to show enormous disfavor for something that has happened after one's death. (A cliché.) □ *If Jerry heard you say that, he'd turn over in his grave.* □ *Please don't bother me when I'm dead. I do not wish to be turning in my grave all the time.*

turn someone or something in (to someone or something) to submit or refer someone or something to someone or a group. □ *The good citizen turned in his neighbor for watering his lawn during the wrong hours.* 🅃 *I turned in the report to the treasurer.* □ *I turned it in on time.*

TURN ▸ INSIDE

turn someone or something inside out to evert someone or something; to pull the inside of someone or something out to become the outside. (With people, this refers to mutilation.) □ *I felt like the explosion was going to turn me inside out.* □ *Ken turned his pockets inside out.*

TURN ▸ INTO

turn into someone or something to change into someone or something. □ *After work is over, he turns into a fairly nice person.* □ *The room changed into a very pleasant place when the lights were dimmed.*

turn someone or something into someone or something to change someone or something into someone or something else. □ *The magician tried to turn Walter into a robin.* □ *She turned the parrot into a dove.* □ *The magician claimed to have turned Bill into his twin brother.*

TURN ▸ IN(TO)

turn in((to) some place) to walk or steer one's vehicle into a place. □ *Turn into the next service station for some gas.* □ *I'll turn in for gas now.* □ *She walked down the street and turned into the drugstore.*

TURN ▸ OFF

turn off [for something] to go off; to switch off. □ *All the lights turn off automatically.* □ *What time do the street lights turn off?*

turn off something to walk or turn a vehicle one way or another so that one leaves the pathway. □ *You are supposed to turn off the highway at the yellow* *mailbox.* 🄽 *The turnoff was partially hidden by bushes.*

turn off (something) onto something to walk or steer one's vehicle from one route to another. □ *I turned off the main highway onto a side road.* □ *Ann turned off onto the shoulder.*

turn off (something) (some place) to walk or steer one's vehicle off a route at a particular place. □ *Turn off the highway at the first exit after the city.* □ *Let's turn off here.* □ *We turned off the path for a rest.*

turn someone off to make someone lose interest; to disgust someone. (Colloquial.) □ *Your bad breath turns everyone off!* 🅃 *Your manner turned off the audience during the first few minutes.* 🄽 *The book was a real turnoff. Nobody was interested at all.*

turn someone's water off to take someone down to size. (Colloquial.) □ *I guess that will turn his water off!* □ *It took a good scolding from the coach to turn Tom's water off.*

turn something off to switch something off so that it stops running. □ *Please turn the light off.* 🅃 *Turn the lights off as you leave.*

TURN ▸ ON

See also under *TURN ▸ (UP)ON.*

See also under *TURN ▸ ON(TO).*

turn on [for something] to switch on and start running. □ *The lights turned on right at dusk.* □ *At what time do the street lights turn on?*

turn on a dime [for a vehicle] to turn in a very tight turn. (Figurative.) □ *This car can turn on a dime.* □ *I need a vehicle that can turn on a dime.*

turn on the waterworks to begin to cry. (Figurative.) □ *The child turned on the waterworks and had to be taken from the hall.* □ *Sally turned on the waterworks when she got yelled at.*

turn on (to someone or something) to become interested or excited by someone or something. (Colloquial or slang.) □ *He turned on to her and became very friendly and talkative.* □ *He turns on to this kind of music.* □ *Ann will turn on if she hears this song.*

turn one's back on someone or something to reject or deny someone or something; to ignore someone or something. (Both literal and figurative uses.) □ *Please don't turn your back on me. I'm still here.* □ *You should not turn your back on these problems.*

turn someone on to interest or excite someone. (Colloquial.) □ *That music really turns me on.* □ *The audience was turned on by the speaker.*

turn something on to switch on something to make it run. □ *I turned the microwave oven on and cooked dinner.* 🅃 *I turned on the lights when the sun went down.*

turn the tables on someone to reverse things so that the one who caused something receives the action. □ *Gary turned the tables on Tiffany when he refused to come to* her *party.* □ *Lee was looking for a chance to turn the tables on Randy.*

TURN ▸ ONTO

turn onto something to walk or steer one's vehicle onto something. □ *Turn onto the main road and go west about a mile.* □ *As she turned onto the familiar highway, she realized that she had left her purse in the store.*

TURN ▸ OUT

turn out [for something] to aim outward. □ *Her toes turned out just right for a ballet dancer.* □ *The legs of the chair turned out just a little, adding a bit of stability.*

turn out (for something) [for people, especially an audience] to [leave home to] attend some event. □ *A lot of people turned out for our meeting.* 🄽 *We had a very small turnout for the dance.* □ *Almost all the residents turned out for the meeting.* 🄽 *We hoped for a good turnout, but nobody came.*

turn out somehow to end in a particular way, such as well, badly, all right. □ *I hope everything turns out all right.* □ *The party did not turn out well.*

turn out to be someone or something

to develop or become someone or something in the end. □ *In the end, he turned out to be a handsome prince in disguise.* □ *The previous prince turned out to be a frog.*

turn someone or something out (of something) to eject someone or some creature from a place. □ *She turned her own son out of the house.* □ *You wouldn't turn a cat out on a night like this, would you?* □ *How could she turn him out?* 🅃 *I wouldn't turn out my own children, would I?*

turn someone out to train or produce someone with certain skills or talents. □ *The state law school turns lawyers out by the dozen.* □ *A committee accused the state university of turning out too many veterinarians.*

turn something out **1.** to manufacture or produce something in numbers. □ *The factory turns too few cars out.* 🅃 *The factory turns out about seventy-five cars a day.* **2.** to turn off a light. □ *Please turn the hall light out.* 🅃 *Turn out the light.*

TURN ▸ OVER

turn over **1.** to rotate so that the side that was on the bottom is now on top. □ *The turtle turned over and crawled away.* □ *She turned over to get some sun on her back.* □ *The dog turned over and continued its nap on its other side.* **2.** [for an engine] to run, if only briefly. □ *The engine won't even turn over!* □ *It was so cold that the engine would not turn over at all.* **3.** to undergo exchange; to be replaced. □ *The employees turn over pretty regularly in this department.* 🄽 *We have a high turnover of employees in this department.*

turn over a new leaf to begin again, fresh; to reform and begin again. (Idiomatic. The leaf is a page—a fresh, clean page.) □ *I have made a mess of my life. I'll turn over a new leaf and hope to do better.* □ *Why don't you turn over a new leaf and surprise everyone with your good characteristics?*

turn (over) in one's grave See under *TURN ▸ IN.*

turn someone or something over to rotate someone or something so that the side that was on the bottom is now on the top. (*Someone* includes *oneself.*) □ *The nurses turned the patient over so they could give her some medicine.* 🅃 *They turned over the unconscious patient.* 🅃 *Liz turned over a rock, hoping to find something for her snake collection underneath.* □ *The restless dog turned itself over and over in the heat.*

turn someone or something over to someone or something to release or assign someone or something to someone or something; to transfer or deliver someone or something to someone or something. □ *The deputy turned the bank robber over to the sheriff.* 🅃 *I turned over the money I found to the police.* □ *The police officer turned Max over to the court.*

turn something over in one's mind to think about something. (Figurative.) □ *I have to turn your suggestion over in my mind a bit before I decide what to do.* □ *After Alice had turned the matter over in her mind, she gave us her verdict.* 🅃 *Please take some time to turn over this matter in your mind.*

TURN ▸ TO

turn a blind eye to someone or something to refuse to see someone or something; to pretend not to perceive someone or something. □ *Mary greeted everyone else, but turned a blind eye to Kelly, with whom she was very angry.* □ *Ann usually turns a blind eye to problems like this.*

turn a deaf ear to someone to refuse to listen to someone. □ *I tried to talk to him, but he turned a deaf ear to me.* □ *The manager turned a deaf ear to everyone who approached him.*

turn a deaf ear to something to refuse to hear something. □ *Jack turned a deaf ear to our pleading.* □ *Please do not turn a deaf ear to the needs of my people.*

turn one's hand to something to begin to or to be able to do something. □ *I would like to turn my hand to Chinese* *cooking.* □ *He gave up accounting and turned his hand to writing poetry.*

turn someone or something to something to aim someone or something to face something. (*Someone* includes *oneself.*) □ *The nurse turned the old man to the sun so he could get warm.* □ *Ken turned the plant to the light.* □ *She turned herself to the east and waited for sunrise.*

turn something to one's advantage to use something otherwise neutral or bad to one's benefit. □ *Jerry saw immediately how he could turn Larry's failure to his advantage.* □ *I hope I can turn this event to my advantage.*

turn to to start working; to start doing one's job. □ *Get going, you guys! Come on! Turn to!* □ *It's time you all turned to and gave us a hand.*

turn to someone or something (for something) to seek or expect something from someone or something. □ *I turned to Sally for advice.* □ *I turn to my dictionary for help two or three times a day.* □ *I can't spell, so I have to turn to a dictionary frequently.*

TURN ► TOWARD

turn someone or something toward someone or something to turn someone or something to face someone or something. (*Someone* includes *oneself.*) □ *The nurse turned the old man toward his daughter, who had come to visit him.* □ *Ken turned the microphone toward the speaker.* □ *Ann turned the plant toward the light.* □ *She turned herself toward the sunrise.*

TURN ► UNDER

turn something under (something) to fold something underneath something. □ *Please turn the frayed edge of the sheet under so that it does not show.* □ *Please turn the edge under.*

TURN ► UP

turn belly-up to die; to fail. (Figurative. As with a dead goldfish.) □ *The gunfighter twitched a bit and turned belly-up.* □ *The business faltered for a while, then turned belly-up.*

turn one's nose up at someone or something to reject someone or something; to make signs of rejecting someone or something. □ *He turned his nose up at Ken.* □ *Don't turn your nose up at this food. It's all you are going to get.*

turn someone or something up **1.** to increase the volume of a device emitting the sound of someone or something. □ *I can't hear the lecturer. Turn her up.* [T] *Turn up the radio, please.* **2.** to discover or locate someone or something. □ *See if you can turn up any evidence for his presence on the night of January 16.* [T] *Have you been able to turn up a date for Friday night?*

turn something up **1.** to bend or fold something up. □ *Please turn your cuffs up. They are getting muddy.* [T] *He turned up his coat collar to keep the rain off his neck.* **2.** to turn playing cards face up. □ *Please turn all the cards up.* [T] *Sally turned up the cards one at a time.*

turn up **1.** [for part of something] to point upward. □ *The ends of the elf's funny little shoes turned up.* [A] *He had a cute little turned-up nose.* **2.** to happen. □ *Something always turns up to prevent their meeting.* □ *I am sorry I was late. Something turned up at the last minute.*

turn up (somewhere) [for someone or something] to appear in a place. □ *Her name is always appearing in the gossip columns.* □ *He turned up an hour late.* □ *Guess who turned up today?* □ *Tom turned up in my office today.* □ *Someone I did not expect to see turned up.* □ *My glasses turned up in the dishwasher.*

turn up the heat (on someone or something) to put pressure on someone or something; apply additional pressure to someone or something. (Colloquial.) □ *They turned the heat up on the gang.* [T] *The police turned up the heat on the people who park illegally every day.* [T] *The police turned up the heat.*

TURN ► (UP)ON

turn (up)on someone or something to attack someone or something, especially the person or group in charge. (*Upon* is formal and less commonly used than *on.)* □ *I never thought that my own dog would turn on me!* □ *The treasurer turned on the entire board of directors.*

TURN ▸ UPSIDE DOWN

turn someone or something upside down to invert someone or something. □ *The wrestler turned his opponent upside down and dropped him on his head.* □ *I turned the bottle upside down, trying to get the last drop out.*

TURN ▸ UPSIDE

turn something upside down to throw things all about in a thorough search for someone or something. □ *We turned this place upside down, looking for the lost ring.* □ *Please don't turn everything upside down, looking for your book.*

TUSSLE ▸ WITH

tussle with someone or something **1.** to struggle or battle with someone or something. □ *Tim tussled with Roger for a while, and then they made peace.* □ *I tussled with the trunk, trying to get it into the attic.* **2.** to argue or contend with someone, a group, or something. (Figurative.) □ *I tussled with Fred for a while over the policy and finally gave up.* □ *I tussled with my conscience all night.* □ *We tussled with the committee and won our point.*

TWEAK ▸ OFF

tweak something off ((of) someone or something) to flick something off someone or something; to remove something from someone or something by pinching. (The *of*-phrase is paraphrased with a *from*-phrase when the particle is transposed. See the Ⓕ example. The *of* is colloquial.) □ *Sarah tweaked a little beetle off of Fred.* Ⓣ *Sarah tweaked off a little bug.* Ⓕ *She tweaked off a bug from Fred's collar.* □ *Ann tweaked it off.*

TWIDDLE ▸ WITH

twiddle with something to play with something; to play with something, using one's fingers; to fiddle with something. □ *I asked Jason to stop twiddling with the pencils.* □ *Someone is twiddling with the stereo controls.*

TWINE ▸ AROUND

twine around something to weave or coil around something. □ *The snake twined around the branch.* □ *As the vine grew, it twined around the lamppost.*

TWINKLE ▸ WITH

twinkle with something [for someone's eyes] to sparkle because of something. □ *Her eyes twinkled with laughter.* □ *Tom's eyes twinkled with recognition when he saw Gwen again.*

TWIST ▸ AROUND

twist around to turn around part way, remaining twisted. □ *Nancy twisted around to get a better look at who was sitting behind her.* □ *I had to twist around to see who was there.*

twist someone around one's little finger to gain control of someone; to have the ability to manipulate someone to one's advantage. □ *So you think you can twist me around your little finger? No way!* □ *She tried to twist him around her little finger, but he simply refused to see her again.*

twist something around someone or something to wrap something around someone or something. □ *Max twisted the wire around Lefty, and totally immobilized him.* □ *I twisted the rope around the post and tied a knot.*

TWIST ▸ INTO

twist something into something to change or distort something into something else, as if by twisting. □ *Kelly twisted the balloons into the shape of a dog.* □ *Ann twisted the silver wires into an earring.*

TWIST ▸ OFF

twist something off ((of) something) to take something off something by twisting. (The *of*-phrase is paraphrased with a *from*-phrase when the particle is transposed. See the Ⓕ example. The *of* is colloquial.) □ *Fran twisted the top off of the bottle of mineral water and poured it.* Ⓣ *She twisted off the top.* Ⓕ *She twisted off the top from the bottle.* □ *Ann twisted it off.*

TWIST ▸ OUT

twist something out of something to remove something from something by twisting. □ *Flo twisted the cork out of the bottle and smelled the wine.* □ *Roger twisted the bulb out of its socket and replaced it with a good one.*

TWIST ▸ UP

twist up **1.** to move upward in a twisting path. □ *The smoke twisted up into the sky.* □ *As the car twisted up the narrow path, we got a good view of the valley.* **2.** to become twisted. □ *The rope twisted up and had to be unwound.* Ⓐ *Why are you making that twisted-up face?*

TYPE ▸ IN(TO)

type something in(to something) to insert information into a form or a place on a form by typing it. □ *Please type your name and address into this box.* Ⓣ *Please type in your name.* □ *I'll type it in right here.*

TYPE ▸ OUT

type something out to make some information presentable by typing it. □ *Please type this out before you submit it to the board for approval.* Ⓣ *Can you type out this report before quitting time?*

TYPE ▸ OVER

type over something to type one letter over another. □ *Just type over the* o *with an* e. *No one will notice.* Ⓝ *There are at least twelve typeovers on this page!*

TYPE ▸ UP

type something up to type a handwritten document. □ *I will give this to you as soon as I type it up.* Ⓣ *Please type up this paper.*

U

UNACCOUNTED ▸ FOR

unaccounted for See under *ACCOUNT ▸ FOR.*

UNBOSOM ▸ TO

unbosom oneself to someone to reveal one's inner thoughts and secrets to someone. ☐ *He unbosomed himself to his best friend.* ☐ *Todd unbosomed himself to almost everyone he met.*

UNBURDEN ▸ TO

unburden oneself to someone to tell someone about one's trouble or anxiety. ☐ *I didn't mean to unburden myself to you. I'm just so upset.* ☐ *She unburdened herself to her mother.*

UNCALLED ▸ FOR

uncalled for See under *CALL ▸ FOR.*

UNCARED ▸ FOR

uncared for See under *CARE ▸ FOR.*

UNDERTAKE ▸ TO

undertake to do something to try to do something; to take the responsibility of doing something. ☐ *The carpenter undertook to repair the door frame.* ☐ *I will undertake to fix it.*

UNFOLD ▸ INTO

unfold into something **1.** [for something folded up] to unfold into something. ☐ *The greeting card unfolded into a little paper house.* ☐ *It unfolded into a cute scene.* **2.** [for a story] to develop into something. (Figurative.) ☐ *The story unfolded into a real mystery.* ☐ *The tale unfolded into a farce.*

unfold something into something to spread something out into something. ☐ *The child unfolded the page into a model village.* ☐ *I unfolded the brochure into a large colorful sheet of advertising.*

UNFOLD ▸ TO

unfold something to someone to tell a complicated story to someone. ☐ *Let me unfold this tale to you.* ☐ *The storyteller unfolded the story skillfully.*

UNIFY ▸ INTO

unify someone or something into something to combine people or things into a united whole. (*Someone* includes *oneself.*) ☐ *The mayor unified his party into a powerful force.* ☐ *I unified the committee into a strong body.* ☐ *They unified themselves into a strong team.*

UNITE ▸ AGAINST

unite against someone or something to join against someone or something. ☐ *We will unite against the opposing forces.* ☐ *We must unite against the incumbent legislators.*

unite someone against someone or something to cause people to join together against someone or something. (*Someone* includes *oneself.*) ☐ *The mayor united his people against the federal investigators.* ☐ *Ted united us against John.* ☐ *They united themselves against the enemy.*

UNITE ▸ FOR

unite for something to join together for some purpose. ☐ *All the forces united for the attack.* ☐ *We will unite for a great party.*

UNITE ▸ IN

unite in something to come together in something. □ *Let us unite in our efforts.* □ *We will unite in song.*

unite someone in something to join two or more people in something, usually marriage. □ *The preacher united the couple in marriage.* □ *A judge united them in marriage.*

UNITE ▸ INTO

unite someone or something into something to form something by merging people together; to form something by merging things together. (*Someone* includes *oneself.*) □ *Let us unite the party into a powerful political force.* □ *We will unite ourselves into a powerful force.* □ *We united ourselves into a strong voice for good.*

UNITE ▸ TOGETHER

unite someone or something together to join people or groups of people together. (*Someone* includes *oneself.* Also without *together*, but not eligible as an entry.) □ *They united all the workers together for the strike.* 🅃 *The event united together the people who cared about the quality of life.* □ *We united the two committees together to improve efficiency.* □ *They united themselves together and hoped for the best.*

UNITE ▸ WITH

unite someone or something with someone or something to join people or things, in any combination. (*Someone* includes *oneself.*) □ *We united Tom with his brother Arnold during the evening.* □ *We united our committee with the president in an effort to expand our influence.* □ *I was happy to unite Fred with his brother.* □ *He united himself with the organization.*

unite with someone to join with someone; to go or come together with someone. □ *I was pleased to unite with my family for the holidays.* □ *The brothers united with their sister after many years of separation.*

UNLEASH ▸ AGAINST

unleash someone or something against someone or something to turn someone or something loose against someone or something. □ *The army unleashed a horrible attack against the enemy.* □ *Max unleashed his bullies against the helpless merchants.*

UNLEASH ▸ (UP)ON

unleash someone or something (up)on someone or something to turn someone or something loose on someone or something. (*Upon* is formal and less commonly used than *on.*) □ *The air force unleashed a bombing attack upon the enemy.* □ *Max unleashed his tough guys on Lefty.* □ *Jill unleashed her dog on Karen's dog.*

UNLOAD ▸ FROM

unload something from something to take things off of something; to remove the burden from something. □ *Please unload the groceries from the car.* □ *I unloaded the groceries from the bags.*

UNLOAD ▸ ON(TO)

unload someone or something on(to) someone to get rid of a burdensome person or thing on someone else. □ *I unloaded my little cousin onto his aunt.* □ *I didn't mean to unload my problems onto you.* □ *She needed someone to unload her problems on.*

UPBRAID ▸ FOR

upbraid someone for something to scold someone for doing something. □ *The judge upbraided David severely for his crime.* □ *Walter upbraided his son for denting the car.*

UPDATE ▸ ABOUT

update someone about someone or something AND **update someone on someone or something** to tell someone the latest news about someone or something. (*Someone* includes *oneself.*) □ *Please update me about the current situation in France.* □ *Please update me about Tony.* □ *Can you update the group on the state of things?* □ *Susan updated herself about the latest problem.*

UPDATE ▸ ON

update someone on someone or something See the previous entry.

UPGRADE ▸ TO

upgrade someone or something to something to raise someone or something to a higher grade or rank. (*Someone* includes *oneself.*) ☐ *Please upgrade me to first class.* ☐ *They upgraded the crisis to code red.* ☐ *She upgraded herself to a higher rank.*

upgrade to something to move up to a higher grade or rank. ☐ *I would like to upgrade to a first-class seat.* ☐ *Please upgrade me to a better cabin.*

UPROOT ▸ FROM

uproot someone from some place to cause someone to move from a well-established home or setting. (*Someone* includes *oneself.*) ☐ *You should not uproot people from the land in which they were born.* ☐ *I just couldn't uproot myself from my home.*

uproot something from some place to take up a plant or tree, roots and all. ☐ *Wally uprooted the bush from the backyard and replanted it on the other side of the house.* ☐ *Who uprooted a rosebush from my garden?*

URGE ▸ ALONG

urge someone along to encourage someone to continue or go faster. ☐ *We urged them along with much encouragement.* ☐ *They won't do well, but we urged them along anyway.*

URGE ▸ FORWARD

urge someone forward to encourage someone to move forward. ☐ *The generals urged the troops forward.* ☐ *Sally urged Timmy forward into the classroom.*

URGE ▸ ON

See under *URGE ▸ (UP)ON.*

URGE ▸ TO

urge someone to do something to try to get someone to do something. ☐ *I urge you to give it a try.* ☐ *Ken urged Lily to finish her dinner.*

URGE ▸ (UP)ON

urge something (up)on someone to try to get someone to take something. (*Upon* is formal and less commonly used than *on.*) ☐ *Arnold urged the new policy on the employees.* ☐ *He urged restraint upon them.*

USE ▸ AS

use someone or something as an excuse to name someone or something as an excuse for not doing something. ☐ *Don't use me as an excuse.* ☐ *He used his illness as an excuse.*

use someone or something as something to make someone or something function as something. ☐ *You have used me as your tool!* ☐ *I don't like your using my car as your private taxi.*

USE ▸ BEFORE

use something before something **1.** to consume or use something before using something else. ☐ *Use this jar before that one. This one is older.* ☐ *I used the old one before the one you just bought.* **2.** to consume or use something before a specified date. ☐ *I will use this bottle of catsup before May.* ☐ *You should use this one before the date stamped on the bottom.*

USE ▸ BY

use something by something to consume or complete the use of something by a specified time. ☐ *Please use this jar of mayonnaise by the last day of the month.* ☐ *Use this one by next week.*

USE ▸ FOR

use someone or something for something to make use of someone or something for a specific purpose. (*Someone* includes *oneself.*) ☐ *Would you please use Don for your errands?* ☐ *You can use my car for the trip.* ☐ *I used myself for a shield.*

USE ▸ OVER

use something over (again) to reuse something. ☐ *Do I have to use this stuff over again?* ☐ *Yes. Please use it over.*

USE ▸ UP

use someone up to use all the effort or talent a person has. (Figurative. *Someone* includes *oneself.*) ☐ *His career simply used him up.* 🄰 *She is a used-up actress who has nothing left to give.* ☐ *I used myself up. I'm done. I can't function anymore.*

use something up to consume or use all of something. ☐ *Use it up. I have more in the cupboard.* 🅃 *Use up every bit of it. Go ahead.* 🄰 *A used-up jar of peanut butter sat on the counter.*

USE ▸ WITH

use something with something to use something in a particular manner. ☐ *Use this tool with a lot of skill and caution.* ☐ *Use this one with great care.*

USHER ▸ FROM

See under *USHER ▸ OUT.*

USHER ▸ IN(TO)

usher someone or something in(to some place) to escort or lead a person, a group, or something into a place. ☐ *The guard ushered the group into the palace.* 🅃 *They ushered in the visitors.* ☐ *They ushered the children into the theater.*

USHER ▸ OUT

usher someone or something out (of some place) to escort or lead someone or a group out of a place. (The *of*-phrase is paraphrased with a *from*-phrase when the particle is transposed. See the 🄵 example.) ☐ *The woman ushered the guest out.* ☐ *We ushered them from the room.* ☐ *They ushered the birthday party out.* 🄵 *Please usher out the people from the hall where the drama was performed.*

USHER ▸ TO

usher someone to something to escort or lead someone to something, such as a seat, the door, etc. ☐ *The well-dressed gentleman ushered the bride to the altar.* ☐ *Her father ushered her to the altar.*

UTILIZE ▸ FOR

utilize someone or something for something to use someone or something for something or for some purpose. ☐ *Is there any way you can utilize Peter for the project?* ☐ *Can you utilize this contraption for anything?*

V

VACCINATE ► AGAINST

vaccinate someone or something against something to inoculate or immunize someone or some creature against some disease. (*Someone* includes *oneself*.) ☐ *They had to vaccinate us against yellow fever.* ☐ *The vet vaccinated the horse against everything that threatened it.* ☐ *The doctor vaccinated herself against the flu, but she caught it anyway.*

VACCINATE ► WITH

vaccinate someone or something with something to inoculate or immunize someone or some creature with some substance. (*Someone* includes *oneself*.) ☐ *This time the doctor vaccinated Tom with killed virus.* ☐ *The vet vaccinated the cat with something that would prevent rabies.* ☐ *The researcher vaccinated herself with the new discovery.*

VACILLATE ► BETWEEN

vacillate between someone and someone else or something and something else to waver between a choice of people or a choice of things. ☐ *He kept vacillating between Fred and Alice.* ☐ *Wayne vacillated between chocolate and vanilla.*

VACUUM ► OUT

vacuum something out to clean an enclosed area out with a vacuum cleaner. ☐ *Please vacuum this car out now!* 🅃 *Can you vacuum out the car?*

VACUUM ► UP

vacuum something up (from something) to clean something up from something with a vacuum cleaner. ☐ *Fred vacuumed the dirt up from the carpet.* 🅃 *He vacuumed up the birdseed from the kitchen floor.* ☐ *He vacuumed up the dirt.* 🄰 *The vacuumed-up coins were found amidst the dirt and dust in the sweeper bag.*

VALUE ► ABOVE

value someone or something above someone or something to hold someone or something to be more important than someone or something. (*Someone* includes *oneself*.) ☐ *I value her above all things.* ☐ *He values his car above his family!* ☐ *Wally valued himself above every other human in the world.*

VALUE ► AS

value someone or something as something to hold someone or something in esteem as something; to find someone or something to be good as something. (*Someone* includes *oneself*.) ☐ *I value you as a close friend.* ☐ *I value this watch as a keepsake.* ☐ *Tom valued himself as a master of ceremonies.*

VALUE ► AT

value something at something to consider something to be worth a certain amount. ☐ *The museum curator valued the vase at one million dollars.* ☐ *I value this vase at one million dollars.*

VALUE ► FOR

value someone or something for something to hold someone or something in esteem for a particular quality. ☐ *I value him for his skill in negotiation.* ☐ *I value this car for its speed and dependability.*

VANISH ► AWAY

vanish away to disappear. (The *away* is considered redundant.) ☐ *The pizza* *vanished away in no time at all.* □ *The city lights vanished away as dawn broke.*

VANISH ► FROM

vanish from something to disappear from something or some place. □ *The money vanished from the desk drawer.* □ *My glasses have vanished from sight again.*

VANISH ► INTO

vanish into something to disappear by going into something. □ *All the deer vanished into the forest.* □ *Money seems to vanish into a black hole.*

VARY ► BETWEEN

vary between someone and something else or something and something else to fluctuate in choosing between people or things. □ *In choosing a running mate, Sam varied between Tom and Wally.* □ *I varied between chocolate and vanilla.*

vary between something and something to fluctuate between one thing and another. □ *The daytime temperatures vary between 80 and 90 degrees.* □ *She varies between angry and happy.*

VARY ► FROM

vary (from something) (in something) to differ from something. □ *This one varies from that one in many ways.* □ *It varies from the other one a little.* □ *It varies in many ways.*

vary from something to something to fluctuate over the range from something to something. □ *The colors vary from red to orange.* □ *It varies from warm to very hot during the summer.*

VARY ► IN

vary (from something) (in something) See under *VARY ► FROM.*

VARY ► WITH

vary with something **1.** to be at variance with someone's figures or a sum or estimate. □ *My figures vary with yours considerably.* □ *Her estimate varies with yours by a few dollars.* **2.** to change according to something. □ *The rainfall in New York State varies with the season.* □ *His mood varies with the stock market average.*

VAULT ► INTO

vault into something to jump or dive into something. □ *The diver vaulted into the pool.* □ *He vaulted into bed and pulled up the covers.*

VAULT ► OVER

vault over someone or something to jump or leap over someone or something. □ *Molly vaulted over Ted and kept on running.* □ *She vaulted over the trunk.*

VEER ► AWAY

See the following entry.

VEER ► FROM

veer (away) (from someone or something) to swerve away from someone or something; to turn aside to avoid someone or something. □ *The plane veered away from the mountain.* □ *It veered from the children who were in its path.* □ *The plane veered away sharply.*

VEER ► OFF

veer off (from someone or something) to turn or steer sharply away from someone or something. □ *The bird veered off from the cluster of trees.* □ *The bird veered off and missed hitting the post.*

VEER ► TOWARD

veer toward someone or something to turn sharply or swerve toward someone or something. □ *The car suddenly veered toward me.* □ *The horse veered toward the side of the bridle path.*

VEG ► OUT

veg out to become sedentary; to collapse and sleep. (Slang.) □ *I just want to go home and veg out.* 🄰 *This vegged-out bunch of kids lay all over the place.*

VENT ► (UP)ON

vent something (up)on someone or something to release one's emotional tension on someone or something. (*Upon* is formal and less commonly used than *on.*) □ *Henry vented his anger on Carl.* □ *It's no use to vent your hatred on a door. Kicking it won't help.*

VENTURE ► FORTH

venture forth **1.** to set out; to go forward; to go out cautiously. □ *George ventured forth into the night.* □ *I think*

I will venture forth. It looks safe. **2.** to go forth bravely. □ *Let us venture forth and conquer the enemy.* □ *We will arm ourselves and venture forth against our foe.*

VENTURE ▸ ON
See under *VENTURE ▸ (UP)ON.*

VENTURE ▸ OUT
venture out ((of) something) to go out of something cautiously. □ *Peter ventured out of his house for only a minute into the cold.* □ *He ventured out the door for only a moment.*

VENTURE ▸ (UP)ON
venture (up)on someone or something to come upon someone or something by chance. (*Upon* is formal and less commonly used than *on*. The entire expression is formal or stilted.) □ *David ventured upon Fred, who was out looking for mushrooms.* □ *I ventured on a little shop on Maple Street that deals in old model trains.*

VERGE ▸ INTO
verge into something to change gradually into something. □ *The reds verged into a violet color that seemed to glow.* □ *The cool morning verged imperceptibly into a steamy midday.*

VERGE ▸ (UP)ON
verge (up)on something to be almost identical to something; to be similar to and almost the same as something. (*Upon* is formal and less commonly used than *on*.) □ *Your actions verge upon mutiny.* □ *What you said verges on an insult.*

VERIFY ▸ WITH
verify something with someone to check with someone to make sure that something is the truth. □ *I will have to verify your story with the storekeeper.* □ *I verified your story with the storekeeper.*

VEST ▸ IN
vest something in someone or something to grant sole power or control over something to someone or some group. □ *The king vested all the military power in General Talmadge.* □ *The constitution vests the power to tax in the legislature.*

VEST ▸ WITH
vest someone with something to grant power, rights, or ownership to someone. (*Someone* includes *oneself*.) □ *Who vested you with the power to order me around?* □ *The dictator vested himself with the power to make war on almost anyone.*

VIE ▸ FOR
vie (with someone) (for someone or something) See under *VIE ▸ WITH.*

VIE ▸ OVER
vie (with someone) (over someone or something) See under *VIE ▸ WITH.*

VIE ▸ WITH
vie (with someone) (for someone or something) AND **vie (with someone) (over someone or something)** to compete or contend with someone for someone or something. □ *They vied with each other for Mary.* □ *I really don't want to have to vie with Randy for recognition.* □ *Ed and Eric vied with me over first authorship.*

VINDICATE ▸ OF
vindicate someone of something to clear or acquit someone of something. (*Someone* includes *oneself*.) □ *The police sought to vindicate Donald of the charges.* □ *They vindicated themselves of the charges.*

VISIT ▸ (UP)ON
visit something (up)on someone to inflict something upon someone. (Stilted. *Upon* is formal and less commonly used than *on*.) □ *The FBI visited a plague of investigations on the mayor's staff.* □ *The storm visited disaster on the little village.*

VISIT ▸ WITH
visit with someone to pay a social call on someone. □ *I would like to come by and visit with you for a while.* □ *I will enjoy visiting with you.*

VISUALIZE ▸ AS
visualize someone or something as someone or something to imagine or envision someone as someone or some-

thing or something as something. (*Someone* includes *oneself.*) ☐ *I can almost visualize you as the president.* ☐ *I visualize this room as a meeting place for everyone.* ☐ *Can't you just visualize Sally as a bastion for truth and justice?* ☐ *She visualized herself as queen of the Nile.*

VOLUNTEER ▸ AS

volunteer as something to submit oneself as a person ready or willing to do something. ☐ *Would you be willing to volunteer as a marcher?* ☐ *I will volunteer as a helper in the hospital.*

VOLUNTEER ▸ FOR

volunteer for something to submit oneself for some task. ☐ *I volunteered for the job.* ☐ *I didn't volunteer for this.*

VOMIT ▸ OUT

vomit something out [for something] to spill forth a great deal of something. ☐ *The volcano vomited the lava out for days.* 🅃 *It vomited out hot lava for months.*

VOMIT ▸ UP

vomit something up to bring up something from the stomach by vomiting. ☐ *The dog vomited the chocolate cake up.* 🅃 *Fido vomited up the rabbit.*

VOTE ▸ AGAINST

vote against someone or something to cast a ballot against someone or something. ☐ *Are you going to vote against the provision?* ☐ *I plan to vote against David.*

VOTE ▸ DOWN

vote someone or something down to defeat someone or something in an election. ☐ *The community voted the proposal down.* 🅃 *They voted down the proposal.* ☐ *The citizens voted Roger down.* 🄰 *The voted-down proposition was to appear on the next ballot too.*

VOTE ▸ FOR

vote for someone or something to cast a ballot in favor of someone or something. (*Someone* includes *oneself.*) ☐ *Did you vote for Alice?* ☐ *I plan to vote for the tax freeze.* ☐ *Of course, I voted for myself! Wouldn't you?*

VOTE ▸ IN(TO)

vote someone in(to something) to elect someone to office or to membership in a group. ☐ *The other party finally voted a candidate into office.* 🅃 *The people voted in the new officers.* ☐ *They voted them in.*

vote something in(to something) to pass a proposal and make it a law. (Usually *into law.*) ☐ *They voted the proposal into law.* 🅃 *If we vote in this proposal, will that solve everything?* ☐ *If you vote it in, it will only cost you more in taxes.* ☐ *The voters voted the tax increase into being.*

VOTE ▸ ON

See under *VOTE ▸ ON(TO); VOTE ▸ (UP)ON.*

VOTE ▸ ON(TO)

vote someone on(to something) to elect someone to something, such as a board. ☐ *Let's vote Christine onto the board.* ☐ *We voted Dave on last term.*

VOTE ▸ OUT

vote someone out (of something) to remove one from office by defeating one in an election. (The *of*-phrase is paraphrased with a *from*-phrase when the particle is transposed. See the 🄵 example.) ☐ *They voted her out of office.* 🅃 *The electorate voted out a number of incumbents.* 🄵 *They voted out a number of incumbents from office.* ☐ *The voters voted them out.*

VOTE ▸ THROUGH

vote something through to get something through a set of procedures by voting in favor of it. ☐ *They were not able to vote the bill through.* 🅃 *They voted through the bill.*

VOTE ▸ (UP)ON

vote (up)on someone or something to make a decision about someone or something by ballot. (*Upon* is formal and less commonly used than *on.*) ☐ *Let's vote on it.* ☐ *Are we going to vote on this?*

VOTE ▸ WITH

vote with one's feet to show one's displeasure by leaving, especially, but not necessarily, on one's feet. (Figurative.) □ *Robert decided to vote with his feet, so he left.* □ *The older people, dissatisfied with the treatment they got from the government, left the country. They voted with their feet.*

VOUCH ► FOR

vouch for someone or something to support or back someone or something; to endorse someone or something. □ *I can vouch for Tom.* □ *I will vouch for Tom's honesty.*

WADE ► ACROSS

wade across something to walk across something covered by water. □ *Let's wade across the stream at this point.* □ *If I wade across it, I will get wet.*

WADE ► IN(TO)

wade in(to something) **1.** to walk into an area covered by water. □ *The horse waded right into the stream.* □ *It waded right in.* **2.** to get quickly and directly involved in something. □ *Don't just wade into things. Stop and think about what you are doing.* □ *Just wade in and get started.*

WADE ► THROUGH

wade through something **1.** to walk through a substance, such as water, mud, garbage, etc. □ *The soldiers waded through the mud on the way to battle.* □ *They waded through the mess to get to where they were going.* **2.** to struggle through something with difficulty. (Figurative.) □ *You mean I have to wade through all these applications?* □ *I have to wade through forty term papers in the next two days.*

WAFFLE ► ABOUT

waffle about See the following entry.

WAFFLE ► AROUND

waffle around AND **waffle about** to be indecisive; to be wishy-washy about making a decision. □ *Make up your mind. Stop waffling around.* □ *Now, don't waffle about. Make up your mind.*

WAGE ► AGAINST

wage something against someone or something to carry on something against someone or a group. □ *They waged war against the aggressors.* □ *Are you still waging your battle against your father?*

WAGER ► ON

wager on someone or something to bet on someone or something. □ *I wouldn't want to wager on the outcome.* □ *I'll wager on Bill, the fastest runner in town.*

wager something on someone or something to bet a certain amount of money on someone or something. □ *I'll wager twenty bucks on you.* □ *I would never wager anything on that horse!*

WAIT ► AROUND

See under *WAIT ► FOR.*

WAIT ► AT

wait at something (for someone or something) to stay at something or some place until something happens or someone or something arrives. □ *Wait at the door for me.* □ *I waited at the office for your call.* □ *I will wait at the end of the hall.*

WAIT ► FOR

wait (around) (for someone or something) to stay somewhere until something happens or someone or something arrives. □ *I'll wait around for you for an hour or so.* □ *I don't want to wait around.* □ *Do I have to wait for dawn?*

WAIT ► ON

See also under *WAIT ► (UP)ON.*

wait on someone hand and foot to serve someone's every need. (Figurative.) □ *Do I have to wait on you hand and foot?* □ *Juan refused to wait on Ken hand and foot.*

WAIT ▸ OUT

wait something out to wait until something ends. □ *I will wait the summer out, and if nothing happens, I'll write again.* T *I can wait out the storm inside.*

WAIT ▸ UP

wait up (for someone or something) **1.** to slow down and pause for someone or something to catch up. □ *Wait up for me. You are too fast.* □ *Please wait up for the bus.* □ *Wait up, you guys!* **2.** to delay going to bed for someone or something or until someone or something does something. □ *I won't wait up for you.* □ *There is no need to wait up.* □ *We chose to wait up for the coming of the new year.*

wait up (until something) to delay going to bed until a certain time or until something happens or arrives. □ *Are you going to wait up until midnight?* □ *We waited up until we heard him come in the back door.*

WAIT ▸ (UP)ON

wait (up)on someone to pay homage to someone. (Stilted.) □ *Do you expect me to wait upon you like a member of some medieval court?* □ *She waited on her grown children as if they were gods and goddesses.*

wait (up)on someone or something **1.** to stay in one place until someone or something arrives. (*Upon* is formal and less commonly used than *on*.) □ *I will wait upon you for a little while.* □ *I will not wait on the bus much longer.* **2.** to serve someone or something. (*Upon* is formal and less commonly used than *on*.) □ *I'm waiting on this table. You can leave.* □ *Is anyone waiting on you?*

WAKE ▸ FROM

wake someone (up) from something to awaken someone from something, such as a sound sleep, sleep, dreams, etc. □ *Henry woke Fred up from his dreams.* T *He woke up Fred from a deep sleep.* □ *Don't wake her from her slumbers.*

wake (up) from something to awaken from something, such as a sound sleep, sleep, dreams, etc. □ *She woke up from a deep sleep.* □ *Elaine woke from her dreams with a start.*

WAKE ▸ TO

wake (up) to something AND **waken to something** to awaken and face something, such as a problem, sunlight, music, noise, etc. □ *I love to wake up to soft music.* □ *We woke to the smell of freshly brewed coffee.* □ *I love to waken to the song of birds.*

WAKE ▸ UP

See also the entries under *WAKE ▸ FROM; WAKE ▸ TO.*

wake someone or something up to cause someone or some creature to awaken. □ *Please don't wake me up until noon.* T *Wake up your brother at noon.* □ *Don't wake the dog up unless you want to take her for a walk.*

wake someone up (to something) to cause someone to become alert and pay attention. □ *We tried to wake them up to the dangers.* T *Try to wake up the students to their responsibilities.* □ *It's time someone woke them up.*

wake up to awaken; to become alert. □ *Wake up! We have to get on the road.* □ *It's time to wake up!*

WAKEN ▸ TO

waken to something See under *WAKE ▸ TO.*

WALK ▸ ACROSS

walk across something to move across something on foot. □ *We walked across the bridge carefully.* □ *Jerry walked across the field and examined the fence on the other side.*

WALK ▸ AHEAD

walk ahead of someone or something to move on ahead of someone or something on foot. □ *Please walk ahead of me where I can see you.* □ *The road was so bad, I had to walk ahead of the car and look for potholes.*

WALK ▸ ALONG

walk along to move along on foot. □ *I was just walking along when my heel broke off.* □ *I'm in no hurry. I'll just walk along at my own speed.*

walk along something to move beside something on foot. ☐ *Let's not walk along the road. It's too dangerous.* ☐ *Walk along the wall where it's safer.*

WALK ▸ AROUND

walk around to move around walking; to pace around. ☐ *I need to walk around and get some fresh air.* ☐ *Why don't we walk around for a while before we go in?*

walk around someone or something to detour on foot around someone or something. ☐ *We had to walk around the hole in the pavement.* ☐ *You had better walk around him.*

walk around something **1.** to walk in a circle around something. ☐ *The wolf walked around the man a few times and then ran off into the woods.* ☐ *I walked around the tree, looking for a way to climb up.* **2.** to make a partial circle around something, walking. ☐ *Just walk around the corner and you will see what I mean.* ☐ *I walked around the hole, thinking how dangerous it was.* **3.** to tour something or some place on foot. ☐ *I will walk around the park while I am waiting for you.* ☐ *Let me walk around the grounds and see what potential they offer.*

WALK ▸ AWAY

walk away from someone or something **1.** to depart from someone or something on foot. ☐ *Don't walk away from me while I am talking to you.* ☐ *I walked away from the concert by myself.* **2.** to abandon someone or something; to go away and leave someone or something. (Figurative.) ☐ *Todd walked away from the problem.* ☐ *I walked away from him and never saw him again.*

walk away with someone or something to lead, take, or carry someone or some creature away. ☐ *I walked away with Tom.* ☐ *The young man walked away with the heifer.*

walk away with something AND **walk off with something** **1.** to steal something. (Informal.) ☐ *The guy in the trench coat just walked away with one of your typewriters.* ☐ *Someone walked off with my typewriter!* **2.** to win something easily. (Slang. With little more effort than is required to carry off the winning trophy.) ☐ *We really walked away with the tournament.* ☐ *Andrew walked off with first place.*

WALK ▸ BACK

walk back ((to) something) to return to something or some place on foot. ☐ *I walked back to my office alone.* ☐ *She walked back home.* ☐ *Thanks for the offer of a ride. I'll walk back.*

WALK ▸ DOWN

walk down something to go down something on foot. ☐ *She walked down the path and turned to the right.* ☐ *Todd was walking down the road when they caught up with him.*

WALK ▸ IN

See also under *WALK ▸ IN(TO).*

walk in on someone or something to interrupt someone or something by entering a place. ☐ *I didn't mean to walk in on you. I didn't know anyone was in here.* ☐ *Alice walked in on the meeting by accident.*

walk right in to enter something directly on foot. ☐ *He went up to the door, opened it, and walked right in.* ☐ *Please just walk right in!*

WALK ▸ INTO

walk (right) into someone or something to bump into someone or something. ☐ *Fred walked right into the edge of the door and broke his nose.* ☐ *Sam walked into Liz and frightened her.*

walk (right) into something to fall right into a trap or deception. (Figurative.) ☐ *You walked right into my trap. Now I have you right where I want you.* ☐ *The unsuspecting agent walked into the FBI setup.*

WALK ▸ IN(TO)

walk in(to something) to enter something on foot. ☐ *We walked into the parking garage and tried to find our car.* ☐ *He walked in and sat down.* 🄰 *This room has two large walk-in closets.*

WALK ▸ OFF

walk off to walk away; to leave on foot abruptly. ☐ *She didn't even say good-*

bye. She just walked off. ☐ *He walked off and never looked back.*

walk off the job 1. to abandon a job abruptly. ☐ *I was so mad I almost walked off the job.* ☐ *Fred almost walked off the job when he saw how bad things were.* 2. to go on strike and abandon a job. ☐ *The workers walked off the job and refused to negotiate.* ☐ *They walked off the job and called a strike.*

walk off with something See *walk away with something* under *WALK ▶ AWAY.*

walk someone's feet off to walk too much and tire out someone's feet, including one's own. ☐ *I've gone all over town today. I walked my feet off, looking for just the right present for Jill.* ☐ *I need to know where I am going before I leave, so I won't walk my feet off.*

WALK ▶ ON

walk on to continue walking. ☐ *Walk on. Go all the way to the end.* ☐ *I knew I wasn't there yet, so I just walked on.*

walk on air to be elated. (Figurative.) ☐ *I was so happy that I was walking on air.* ☐ *We began walking on air when we heard the good news.*

walk on eggs AND **walk on thin ice** to be in a situation where one must be very cautious. (Figurative.) ☐ *This is a very delicate matter. We are just walking on eggs until we complete the project.* ☐ *I hope you know that you are walking on thin ice when you deal with the boss.*

walk on stage and off again to play a very small role where one goes on stage and leaves again. ☐ *It was a very small part. I walked on stage and right off again.* Ⓐ *I had a small walk-on part in a movie made in the city.* Ⓝ *Once I did a walk-on in a school play.*

walk on thin ice See *walk on eggs.*

WALK ▶ OUT

walk out (of something) 1. to exit something or some place. ☐ *We walked out of the shop when we had made our purchases.* ☐ *She went to the door and walked out.* 2. to exit the workplace on strike. ☐ *The workers walked out because of a jurisdictional dispute.* ☐ *The workers walked out in sympathy with another union.* Ⓝ *The workers staged a walkout, and production came to a halt.*

walk out (on someone or something) to leave or abandon someone or something, in anger, disgust, or aversion. ☐ *Sally walked out on Tom because she was fed up with him.* ☐ *Sally finally walked out.*

walk out with someone to exit something or some place with someone on foot. ☐ *After the play, Jane and I walked out together and had a nice talk.* ☐ *We walked out with Mr. Wilson, who had sat next to us during the show.*

walk someone out to accompany someone out, walking. ☐ *I'll walk you out. The exit is hard to find.* ☐ *Please let me walk you out so you don't get lost.*

WALK ▶ OVER

walk all over someone or something to treat someone or something very badly; to beat someone or something soundly in a competition. (Figurative.) ☐ *The prosecution walked all over the witness.* ☐ *The attorney walked all over my case.* ☐ *We walked all over the other team.* Ⓝ *It was not a sporting contest; it was a walkover.*

walk over (to someone or something) to move to someone or something on foot. ☐ *I walked over to her and asked her what she thought.* ☐ *I just walked over.*

walk someone over to someone or something to accompany someone a short distance on foot to someone or something. (*Someone* includes *oneself.*) ☐ *I'll walk her over to the personnel department and show her what to do.* ☐ *I will walk her over to Richard. I think he's in his office.* ☐ *She walked herself over to the window and looked out.*

WALK ▶ THROUGH

walk someone through something 1. to lead or accompany someone through an opening, arch, doorway, etc. ☐ *Mike walked Mary through the arch into a lovely garden.* ☐ *Todd walked Rita through the doorway, into the ballroom.* 2. to lead someone through a complex problem or thought process. □ *Mary walked Jane through the complex solution to the calculus problem.* □ *Do I have to walk you through this solution?*

walk through something to rehearse something in a casual way; to go through a play or other performed piece, showing where each person is to be located during each speech or musical number. □ *Let's walk through this scene one more time.* [N] *We had a walk-through of the wedding last night, and the groom was late.*

WALK ▸ TOGETHER

walk together [for two or more people] to walk as a group. □ *Let's all walk together so we can talk to one another.* □ *We walked together for a while.*

WALK ▸ UP

walk right up (to someone or something) to move up close to someone or something, on foot; not to hesitate to approach someone or something. □ *Walk right up to him and ask him what you want to know.* □ *Please walk right up to the bench and talk to the judge.* □ *Just walk right up.*

walk up something to move up an incline or stairs on foot. □ *Sally will have to walk up the stairs by herself.* [A] *She had a small walk-up flat in the center of town.* [N] *She had a small apartment in a walk-up on Main Street.*

walk up to someone or something to approach someone or something on foot. □ *I walked up to the manager and told him my problem.* □ *Eric walked up to the door and rang the bell.*

WALK ▸ WITH

walk with someone to walk in the company of someone. □ *Why don't you walk with me for a while?* □ *Can I walk with you?*

walk with something **1.** to walk with the aid of something, such as a cane, crutches. □ *You can recognize her easily. She walks with a cane.* □ *Dan walks with the help of a crutch.* **2.** to walk in a characteristic manner, such as with a limp, halting gait, a sprightly step, etc. □ *Martha's uncle walks with a limp.* □ *I have always walked with a halting gait.*

WALL ▸ IN

wall someone or something in to contain someone or something behind or within a wall. (Implies a constriction of space, but not necessarily an inescapable area. See *wall something up*.) □ *The count walled his visitor in permanently.* [T] *Jane decided to wall in the little garden at the side of the house.* □ *She walled the garden in.*

WALL ▸ OFF

wall someone or something off to separate or segregate someone or something by building a wall. □ *She sat right across from me at her desk, listening to every phone call I made. Finally, the manager walled her off so we now can carry on our business in privacy.* [T] *They walled off the south door to the building.* □ *We walled the door off so no one could get in without paying.*

wall something off (from someone or something) to deny access to an area by building a wall as a barrier. □ *The manager was told to wall the incinerator area off from the machinery area.* [T] *Please wall off the incinerator area.* □ *We walled it off for safety reasons.*

WALL ▸ UP

wall something up **1.** to seal something up behind a wall. □ *We simply walled the old furnace up. It was cheaper than removing it.* [T] *They walled up the old furnace.* **2.** to fill up an opening, such as a window or door, by building a wall. □ *We will have to hire someone to wall the doorway up.* [T] *They walled up the doorway.*

WALLOW ▸ AROUND

See the following entry.

WALLOW ▸ IN

wallow (around) in something to roll around in something. □ *Pigs enjoy wallowing around in mud.* □ *They wallow in mud to keep cool.*

wallow in something to experience an abundance of something. (Figurative.) □ *Roger and Wilma are just wallowing in money.* □ *Claire spent the entire day* *wallowing in self-pity.* □ *The villagers are all wallowing in superstition.*

WALTZ ▸ AROUND

waltz around something to move around or through a place happily or proudly. (See also under *PRANCE ▸ AROUND.*) □ *She waltzed around the room, very pleased with herself.* □ *Who is that person waltzing around, trying to look important?*

WALTZ ▸ IN(TO)

waltz in(to some place) to step or walk into a place briskly and easily. □ *She waltzed into the room and showed off her ring.* □ *Eric waltzed in and said hello.*

WALTZ ▸ OFF

waltz off to depart briskly and easily. □ *They said good-bye and waltzed off.* □ *They waltzed off without even saying that they had had a nice time.*

waltz off with something to take or steal something, easily and casually. (Informal.) □ *She came in and just waltzed off with my computer printer.* □ *Who waltzed off with my letter opener?*

WALTZ ▸ THROUGH

waltz through something to move through something casually; to accomplish something easily with little effort. □ *She did not do it well. She just waltzed through it.* □ *The test was very easy. I just waltzed through it.*

WALTZ ▸ UP

waltz up (to someone) to approach someone boldly. □ *He just waltzed up to her and introduced himself.* □ *He waltzed up and said hello.*

WANDER ▸ ABOUT

wander about AND **wander around** to stroll or amble around without any purpose evident; to roam around. □ *We just wandered about downtown all morning, looking at the shop windows.* □ *It's fun to wander around in a strange town.*

WANDER ▸ AROUND

wander around See the previous entry.

WANDER ▸ AWAY

wander away (from someone or something) AND **wander off (from someone or something)** to roam away from someone or something. □ *The little boy wandered away from his mother.* □ *He wandered off from his sister.* □ *The dog wandered off.* □ *My cat wandered away.*

WANDER ▸ FROM

wander from something to stray from something, such as a path, a set of rules, etc. □ *Please do not wander from the path I have set for you.* □ *If you wander from our guidelines, your finished product may not be acceptable.*

WANDER ▸ IN(TO)

wander in(to something) to stray or roam into something or some place. □ *A deer wandered into the parking lot and frightened some of the shoppers.* □ *Someone wandered in and sat down.*

WANDER ▸ OFF

wander off (from someone or something) See under *WANDER ▸ AWAY.*

WANGLE ▸ FROM

wangle something from someone AND **wangle something out of someone** to obtain, through argument or deception, something from someone. (Informal.) □ *Are you trying to wangle money from me?* □ *You can't wangle any money out of me.*

WANGLE ▸ OUT

wangle out of something to get out of having to do something; to argue or deceive one's way out of a responsibility. □ *Don't try to wangle out of this mess. You must stay and face the problems you made.* □ *Mary managed to wangle out of staying late again.*

wangle something out of someone See *wangle something from someone* under *WANGLE ▸ FROM.*

WANT ▸ BACK

want someone or something back to desire the return of someone or something. □ *Timmy wanted his mother back very badly.* □ *I want my money back!*

WANT ▸ FOR

want for something to lack something; to need something. □ *I certainly don't want for advice. In fact, I have had too much.* □ *We don't want for helpers around here.*

want someone for something to desire someone for some job or purpose. □ *I want Fred for my team.* □ *We all want you for a candidate.*

want someone for something to hunt or seek someone as a criminal suspect. □ *The police want Max for Lefty's murder.* □ *They want him for a number of crimes.*

want something for someone or something to desire to have something for someone or something. □ *I want a gift for my wife. What would you suggest?* □ *I want a button for my shirt.*

WANT ▸ IN

want in((to) something) to want to come into something or some place. □ *It's cold out here! I want into the house.* □ *The dog wants in.*

want someone or something in something to desire that someone or something be in something or some place. □ *I want you in my office immediately.* □ *I want some coffee in this room now!*

WANT ▸ OFF

want off ((of) something) to desire to be off or get off something. (The *of* is colloquial.) □ *I want off of this bus this very minute!* □ *Stop this train! I want off!*

WANT ▸ OUT

want out (of something) **1.** to desire to get out of something or some place. □ *I want out of this stuffy room.* □ *Where's the door? I want out.* **2.** to desire to be relieved of a responsibility. □ *I want out of this responsibility. I don't have the time to do it right.* □ *This job is no good for me. I want out.*

want someone or something out of something to desire that someone or something leave or be removed from something or some place. □ *I want you out of here immediately.* □ *I want this box out of here now!*

WAR ▸ AGAINST

war against someone or something to fight against someone or something; to oppose someone or something. □ *That country is always warring against its neighbors.* □ *Why do you want to war against the city council?*

WAR ▸ OVER

war over someone or something to fight about who is to get someone or something. □ *Stop warring over Tom. He refuses to play on either team.* □ *There is no point in warring over the contract.*

WAR ▸ WITH

war with someone to fight or dispute with someone. □ *Ruth is always warring with someone, usually about something trivial.* □ *Please don't war with me!*

WARD ▸ OFF

ward someone or something off to hold someone or something off; to fight someone or something off. □ *The army was able to ward the attackers off repeatedly.* T *We couldn't ward off the attackers any longer.* T *Fred was able to ward off the dogs.*

WARM ▸ OVER

warm something over **1.** to reheat food to serve it as leftovers. □ *I'll just warm the rest over for lunch tomorrow.* T *Jane warmed over yesterday's turkey.* A *I really don't care for warmed-over turkey again.* **2.** to bring up a matter that was thought to have been settled. □ *Please don't warm that business over again. It is settled and should remain that way.* T *Don't warm over that matter. We have discussed it enough.* A *We don't want to hear any of your warmed-over theories about religion.*

WARM ▸ UP

warm someone or something up to make someone or something warmer; to take the chill off someone or something. (*Someone* includes *oneself.*) □ *I put him by the fire to warm him up a little.* T *We warmed up our feet before the fire.* T *Could you warm up my coffee, please?* □ *Is dinner warmed up yet?* □

I need to get in there and warm myself up.

warm someone up to help someone get physically prepared to perform in an athletic event. (*Someone* includes *oneself.*) ☐ *The referee told the coach to warm his team up so the game could begin.* 🅃 *You have to warm up the team before a game.* ☐ *Be sure to warm yourself up before playing.* 🄰 *The pitcher was wearing a warm-up jacket.*

warm up **1.** [for the weather or a person] to become warmer or hotter. ☐ *I think it is going to warm up next week.* 🄽 *I am looking for a little warm-up this weekend.* **2.** [for someone] to become more friendly. ☐ *Todd began to warm up halfway through the conference.* ☐ *After he had worked there for a while, he began to warm up.*

warm up (for something) to prepare for some kind of performance or competition. ☐ *The team had to warm up before the game.* ☐ *They have to warm up.* 🄽 *You need a warm-up before you sing.*

warm up to someone or something to become more fervent and earnest toward someone, something, or a group; to become more responsive and receptive to someone, a group, or something. ☐ *After we talked, he began to warm up to us a little.* ☐ *I warmed up to the committee as the interview went on.* ☐ *Jane warmed up to the idea, so she may approve it.*

WARN ▶ ABOUT

warn someone about someone or something to advise someone about the dangers associated with someone or something. ☐ *Didn't I warn you about the dangers of going there?* ☐ *I warned you about Alice.*

WARN ▶ AGAINST

warn someone against someone or something to advise someone against someone, something, or doing something. ☐ *We warned them all against going to Turkey at this time.* ☐ *I warned her against Gerald.*

WARN ▶ AWAY

warn someone away from someone or something to advise someone to avoid someone or something. ☐ *We warned her away from the danger, but she did not heed our warning.* ☐ *Why didn't you warn me away from Roger?*

WARN ▶ OF

warn someone of something to advise someone that something bad is likely to happen. ☐ *I wish you had warned us of what was going to happen.* ☐ *Please warn John of what is planned.*

WARN ▶ OFF

warn someone off to advise a person to stay away. ☐ *We placed a guard outside the door to warn people off until the gas leak could be fixed.* 🅃 *The guards warned off everyone in the vicinity.*

WASH ▶ AWAY

wash away to be carried away by water or some other liquid. ☐ *The bridge washed away in the flood.* ☐ *All the soil washed away and left the rocks exposed.*

wash someone or something away [for a flood of water] to carry someone or something away. ☐ *The flood washed the boats away.* 🅃 *The high water washed away the shoreline.* ☐ *The storm washed some people on the shore away.*

wash something away to clean something by scrubbing and flushing away the dirt. ☐ *Fresh water will wash the seawater away.* 🅃 *Let's wash away these muddy footprints.*

WASH ▶ DOWN

wash something down something to get rid of something by flooding it down the sewer, drain, sink, etc. ☐ *Wash all the soap suds down the drain and clean the sink, please.* ☐ *Please wash all that stuff down the drain.*

wash something down (with something) **1.** to use fluid to aid the swallowing of food or medicine. ☐ *Molly washed the pills down with a gulp of coffee.* 🅃 *She washed down the pills with a glass of water.* ☐ *Jane washed them down.* **2.** to clean something by flooding with water, alcohol, etc. ☐ *The doctor washed the* *area down and began to stitch up the wound.* 🅃 *She washed down the area with alcohol to clean it thoroughly.* □ *Todd washed the driveway down with water.*

WASH ▶ OF

wash one's hands of someone or something to rid oneself of someone or something. (Figurative.) □ *I wash my hands of you! I can take no more of you.* □ *Dave washed his hands of the whole matter.*

wash something of something to get something cleaned of something by washing. □ *I washed my hair of the cigarette smoke I was saturated with in the meeting.* □ *I have to get home and wash my trousers of this stain.*

WASH ▶ OFF

wash off ((of) someone or something) to be carried off of or away from something by the action of water or another liquid. (The *of* is colloquial.) □ *The dirt washed off of the floor easily.* □ *The label washed off this can, and now I don't know what's in it.*

wash someone or something off to clean someone or something by washing. (*Someone* includes *oneself.*) □ *She washed the muddy children off with a hose and put their clothes right into the washing machine.* 🅃 *Jane washed off the children.* □ *She washed them off.* □ *She washed herself off and then went down to dinner.*

wash something off ((of) someone or something) to clean something off someone or something. (The *of*-phrase is paraphrased with a *from*-phrase when the particle is transposed. See the 🄵 example. The *of* is colloquial.) □ *I have to wash this tomato sauce off my jacket before it stains it.* 🅃 *I will wash off the tomato stains.* 🄵 *Sarah washed off the tomato sauce from her jacket.* □ *Carl washed the stuff off as soon as he got home.*

WASH ▶ OUT

wash a few things out to launder a few things, typically underwear. □ *Excuse me. I have to go back to my room to wash a few things out.* 🅃 *Mike washed out a few things.*

wash out (of something) to fail and have to leave something; to fail to meet the requirements for continuing in something. (Informal.) □ *Jim washed out of med school in the first year.* □ *I didn't do well in school and I washed out in the second year.*

wash someone out to deplete the strength or vitality of someone. □ *The flu really washed me out.* □ *The disease washed out the whole class.* 🄰 *Have you been ill? You look really washed-out.*

wash someone out (of something) to make it necessary for a person to leave a place or program. □ *That professor just loves to wash students out of the course.* 🅃 *The professor washed out over half the class.* 🄰 *The washed-out students left the night after the exam.*

wash something out **1.** to wash out the inside of something; to wash something made of fabric. □ *I have to wash my socks out tonight.* □ *Wash the pitcher out before you put it away.* 🅃 *I will wash out my socks tomorrow.* **2.** to rain on or flood an event so that it must be canceled. □ *Rain washed the game out.* 🅃 *The storm washed out the picnic.* **3.** to wash or erode something out or away. □ *The flood washed the new bushes out.* 🅃 *The rains washed out the paving stones.*

wash something out of something to clean some kind of dirt from something. (The *of*-phrase is paraphrased with a *from*-phrase when the particle is transposed. See the 🄵 example.) □ *You had better wash all the soap out of the clothing before you put it in the dryer.* 🅃 *You will want to wash out the dirt.* 🄵 *Don't you want to wash out the salt from your swim trunks?*

WASH ▶ OVER

wash over someone [for a powerful feeling] to flood over a person. □ *A feeling of nausea washed over me.* □ *A strong feeling of satisfaction washed over me.*

wash over someone or something [for liquid] to flow or flood over someone or something. □ *The waves washed over me as I sat on the sand, watching the sunset.* □ *The stream washed over the rocks, making them glisten in the moonlight.*

WASH ▸ OVERBOARD

wash overboard [for someone or something] to be carried overboard by water. □ *Our chairs washed overboard in the storm.* □ *I was afraid that the dog would wash overboard, so I took her below.*

wash someone or something overboard [for water] to flood up and carry someone or something on a ship into the sea. □ *The high seas washed two of the sailors overboard.* □ *The storm washed our chairs overboard.*

WASH ▸ UP

wash someone or something up **1.** to clean up someone or something by washing. (*Someone* includes *oneself*.) □ *Please wash the baby up as long as you are changing the diaper.* 🅃 *I'll wash up the baby.* □ *Sam will wash himself up before dinner.* □ *Go wash yourself up before dinner.* 🅃 *He washed up the kitchen floor before she came home.* **2.** [for water or the waves] to bring someone or something up onto the shore or beach. □ *Look what the waves washed up! A bottle with a note in it!* 🅃 *The waves washed up a bottle.* □ *The waves washed a body up.*

wash someone up to terminate someone in something. □ *This error is going to wash you up as an account executive.* □ *That washed me up.* 🄰 *The washed-up counterfeiter held out his hands to be handcuffed.*

wash up (for something) to clean [oneself] up for something, such as a meal. □ *Please wash up for dinner.* □ *Go and wash up!*

WASTE ▸ AWAY

waste away to wither or dwindle away. □ *Our money just seemed to waste away.* □ *As she grew older, she just sort of wasted away.*

waste something away to use something up wastefully; to dissipate something. □ *He wasted all his money away and had to live in poverty.* 🅃 *They wasted away everything and regretted it later.*

WASTE ▸ ON

waste something on someone or something to throw something away on someone or something. □ *Please don't waste any sweet potatoes on me.* □ *I can't waste any more money on this car.*

WATCH ▸ FOR

watch for someone or something to keep looking for someone or something to appear. □ *Watch for me. I'll be wearing a red carnation in my hair.* □ *I will watch for the bus.*

WATCH ▸ OUT

watch out (for someone or something) to keep looking for someone or something. □ *Watch out for Millie. She's mad at you.* □ *You had better watch out!* □ *I'll wait here out of the rain. You watch out for the bus.*

WATCH ▸ OVER

watch over someone or something to keep guard over someone or something; to care for someone or something. □ *Could you please watch over my little girl while I go to the store?* □ *I will watch over the cherry pie while you are away.*

WATER ▸ DOWN

water something down **1.** to dilute something. □ *Who watered the orange juice down?* 🅃 *Jim watered down the orange juice.* 🄰 *I don't like watered-down orange juice.* **2.** to water something thoroughly. □ *Will you water the lawn down tonight?* 🅃 *Water down the lawn this evening so it will grow tomorrow.* **3.** to reduce the effectiveness or force of something. □ *Please don't water my declaration down.* 🅃 *The new laws watered down the power of the president.* 🄰 *The watered-down version of the rule wasn't very effective.*

WAVE ▸ AROUND

wave something around to raise something up and move it around so that everyone can see it. □ *When Ruth found the money, she waved it around so ev-*

eryone could see it. 🅃 *She kept waving around the dollar she found in the street.*

WAVE ► ASIDE

wave someone or something aside to make a signal with the hand for someone or something to move aside. □ *The police officer waved us aside and would not let us turn into our street.* 🅃 *The officer waved aside the spectators.* □ *She waved all the traffic aside.*

WAVE ► AT

wave at someone AND **wave to someone** to move the upraised hand in such a way as to signal recognition to someone. □ *The people in the boat waved at us.* □ *They waved to us after we waved at them.*

WAVE ► AWAY

wave someone or something away (from someone or something) to make a signal with the hand for someone or something to move away from someone or something. □ *The officer waved us away from the intersection where we were about to turn left.* 🅃 *The guard waved away the traffic from the intersection.* □ *He waved everyone away.*

WAVE ► BACK

wave back (at someone) to return someone's hand signal of greeting. □ *I waved back at her, but she didn't see me.* □ *She didn't wave back.*

wave someone back (from something) to motion someone to move back from something. □ *The police officer waved the curious onlookers back from the scene of the crime.* □ *The students started to go onstage, but the teacher waved them back.*

WAVE ► OFF

wave someone or something off to make a signal with the hand for someone or something to remain at a distance. □ *There was someone standing in front of the bridge, waving everyone off. The bridge must have collapsed.* □ *He waved all the traffic off.* 🅃 *The police officer waved off all the pedestrians.*

WAVE ► ON

wave someone or something on to make a signal with the hand for someone or something to keep moving. □ *The traffic cop waved us on.* □ *The cop waved us on.* 🅃 *The cop waved on all the pedestrians.*

WAVE ► TO

wave to someone See under *WAVE ► AT.*

WAVER ► BETWEEN

waver between someone and someone else to vacillate between choosing one person or another. □ *I had to appoint the new manager, and I was wavering between Jane and Janet.* □ *We wavered between Bill and Bob for the position.*

waver between something and something else to vacillate between choosing one thing and another; to linger indecisively between doing one thing or another. □ *The captain was wavering between St. Thomas and St. Croix.* □ *We wavered between chocolate and vanilla.* □ *I wavered between going to town and staying at the cottage.*

WEAN ► AWAY

See the following entry.

WEAN ► FROM

wean someone or something (away) from someone or something **1.** to train a person or other creature to eat food other than mother's breast milk. □ *The farmer weaned the piglets away from their mother too early.* 🅃 *He weaned away the little pigs from their mother.* □ *He weaned the piglets away from their mother.* **2.** to force someone or something to break a habit. □ *It was almost impossible to wean her from her high spending habits.* 🅃 *We couldn't wean away the smoker from her habit.* □ *I tried to wean John away from his daily drinks.* □ *I could not wean our fat little hound away from his daily rabbit.*

WEAR ► AWAY

wear away at someone or something to annoy or diminish someone or something. □ *Facing the same problems year after year was wearing away at the presi-*

dent of the company. □ *The rain wore away at the stone through time.*

wear something away to erode something. □ *The constant rains wore the side of the cathedral away.* [T] *The rains wore away the mountains.* [A] *The severely worn-away stairs will have to be replaced.*

WEAR ► DOWN

wear someone down **1.** to exhaust someone. □ *This hot weather wears me down.* [T] *The weather wore down the tourists.* [A] *One very worn-down young man walked up to the door.* **2.** to reduce someone to submission or agreement by constant badgering. □ *Finally they wore me down and I told them what they wanted to know.* [T] *The agents wore down the suspect.*

wear something down to grind something away; to erode something. □ *The constant rubbing of the door wore the carpet down.* [T] *The rubbing of the door wore down the carpet.*

WEAR ► OFF

wear off [for the effects of something] to dissipate or go away. □ *The effects of the morphine began to wear off and Dave began to feel the pain.* □ *As the drug wore off, she was more alert.*

wear off ((of) something) [for something] to be ground or rubbed away. □ *The paint has worn off the porch steps.* □ *The finish is wearing off.*

wear something off ((of) something) to grind or rub something off something. (The *of*-phrase is paraphrased with a *from*-phrase when the particle is transposed. See the [F] example. The *of* is colloquial.) □ *The grinding of the bottom of the boat on the sandbanks wore the barnacles off the hull.* [T] *The sand wore off the barnacles.* [F] *The sand wore off the barnacles from the bottom of the boat.* □ *The rubbing wore the paint off.*

WEAR ► ON

See also under *WEAR ► (UP)ON.*

wear on (for something) [for an event] to continue for a long period of time. □ *The lecture seemed to wear on for hours.* □ *It wore on until I went to sleep.*

WEAR ► OUT

wear out to become worn from use; to become diminished or useless from use. □ *My car engine is about to wear out.* □ *It takes a lot of driving to wear out an engine.*

wear out one's welcome to visit so often that one is no longer welcome; to stay so long as a guest that one is no longer welcome. □ *I would love to visit you again, but I don't want to wear out my welcome.* □ *You will never wear out your welcome. Stay as long as you like.*

wear someone out to exhaust or annoy someone. (*Someone* includes *oneself.*) □ *All this shopping is wearing me out.* [T] *The shopping trip wore out the tourists.* [A] *A group of worn-out soldiers rested near the door.* □ *They will wear themselves out before the game. They should take it easy.*

wear something out to make something worthless or nonfunctional from use. □ *I wore my shoes out in no time at all.* [T] *I wore out my shoes in less than a month.* [A] *What can I do with a worn-out engine?*

WEAR ► THROUGH

wear through something to grind or rub through something. □ *My heel finally wore through the carpeting beneath the accelerator of my car.* □ *The constant rubbing of hands wore through the paint on the railing.*

WEAR ► (UP)ON

wear something (up)on something to have something on something as clothing or adornment. (*Upon* is formal and less commonly used than *on*.) □ *I wore a lovely diamond pin upon my blouse.* □ *I wore it on my lapel.*

wear (up)on someone to diminish someone's energy and resistance; to bore or annoy someone. (*Upon* is formal and less commonly used than *on*.) □ *You could see that the lecture was beginning to wear upon the audience.* □ *This kind of thing really wears on me.*

wear (up)on something to grind or rub at something. (*Upon* is formal and less commonly used than *on*.) □ *The bot-*

tom of the door is wearing upon the carpet and leaving marks. ☐ *It is wearing on the carpet.*

WEARY ▸ OF

weary of someone or something to become tired of or bored with someone or something. ☐ *I am beginning to weary of you. Isn't it time you were going?* ☐ *We soon wearied of chicken twice a week.*

WEARY ▸ WITH

weary someone with something to tire or bore someone with something. ☐ *He wearied her with his constant requests.* ☐ *Please don't weary me with your complaints.*

WEASEL ▸ OUT

weasel out (of something) **1.** to squeeze one's way out of something. ☐ *Somehow, the child managed to weasel out of the hole she was stuck in.* ☐ *The mouse tried to weasel out.* **2.** to evade or avoid a job or responsibility. ☐ *Don't try to weasel out of your responsibility!* ☐ *You can't weasel out! You have to do it.*

WEAVE ▸ AROUND

weave around to move about, changing directions at random. ☐ *The drunken driver wove around all over the road.* ☐ *He was weaving around everywhere.*

WEAVE ▸ FROM

weave something from something **1.** to make a fabric from some type of fiber. ☐ *They weave this cloth from a fine plant fiber.* ☐ *This cloth is woven from silk threads.* **2.** to make a story or explanation out of a small amount of information. (Figurative.) ☐ *You have woven the entire tale from something you heard me say to Ruth.* ☐ *Your explanation has been woven from supposition.*

WEAVE ▸ IN

weave in and out (of something) to move along, twisting and turning into and out of something. ☐ *We saw quite a few drivers weaving in and out of traffic.* ☐ *They were weaving in and out, making dangerous maneuvers.*

WEAVE ▸ INTO

weave something into something **1.** to form fibers into a fabric. ☐ *They could weave the threads into simple cloth with a primitive loom.* ☐ *We will weave this wool into a rug.* **2.** to turn separate episodes into a story. (Figurative.) ☐ *Skillfully, the writer wove the elements into a clever story.* ☐ *Memories from her childhood were woven into a series of short stories.*

WEAVE ▸ THROUGH

weave through something to move through something by turning and dodging. ☐ *The car wove through traffic, almost hitting a number of other cars.* ☐ *We wove through the jungle vines, trying to avoid touching the poisonous ones.*

WED ▸ TO

wed someone or something to something to join someone or something firmly to something. (Figurative. *Someone* includes *oneself.*) ☐ *Don't try to wed me to your way of doing things. I have my own way.* ☐ *You have wed the edge of the frame to the wall permanently.* ☐ *Don't wed yourself to that idea.*

wed someone to someone to marry someone to someone else. ☐ *Her parents wedded her to a young prince when she was only twelve.* ☐ *They cannot wed her to anyone if she has already married someone of her own choosing.*

WEDGE ▸ BETWEEN

wedge someone or something (in) between people or things to work someone or something into a tiny space between people or things. (*Someone* includes *oneself.*) ☐ *The usher wedged us in between two enormously fat people, and we were all very uncomfortable.* T *They wedged in the package between Jane and the wall.* ☐ *We had to wedge Timmy between Jed and the side of the car.* ☐ *She wedged herself between Tom and Jack.*

WEDGE ▸ IN

See the previous entry.

WEED ▸ OUT

weed someone or something out (of something) to separate out someone or something from something. (The *of*-phrase is paraphrased with a *from*-phrase when the particle is transposed. See the 🄵 example.) ☐ *We are trying to weed the poor workers out of the work force.* 🅃 *Jane weeded out the violets.* 🄵 *Jane weeded out the violets from the rose garden.* ☐ *We weeded them out.* 🄵 *We weeded out these workers from the work force.*

WEEP ▸ ABOUT

weep about someone or something to cry about someone or something; to mourn someone or something. ☐ *She was weeping about her grandfather, who had passed away in the night.* ☐ *There is no use weeping about spilled milk.*

WEEP ▸ FOR

weep for joy to cry out of happiness. ☐ *She was so happy, she wept for joy.* ☐ *We all wept for joy at the safe return of the child.*

weep for someone or something to cry out of sorrow for someone or some creature. ☐ *She wept for her puppy when it was terribly sick.* ☐ *Please don't weep for me after I'm gone.*

WEEP ▸ OVER

weep over someone or something to cry about someone or something. ☐ *No need to weep over me. I'll do all right.* ☐ *There is no point in weeping over something you can't do anything about.*

WEIGH ▸ AGAINST

weigh against someone or something to count against someone or something; [for some fact] to work against someone or something. ☐ *I hope my many absences do not weigh against me on the final grade.* ☐ *This will weigh against you.*

weigh something against something to ponder something by balancing it against something. ☐ *I weighed going to town against staying here and sleeping and I decided to stay here.* ☐ *When I weigh your suggestion against my own ideas, I realize that I must follow my own conscience.*

WEIGH ▸ DOWN

weigh someone or something down to burden someone or something. (*Someone* includes *oneself*.) ☐ *Don't let all these problems weigh you down.* ☐ *The heavy burden weighed the poor donkey down.* ☐ *Don't weigh yourself down with more than you can carry.* 🅃 *The load of bricks weighed down the truck.*

weigh someone or something down (with someone or something) to burden someone or something with someone or something, in any combination. (*Someone* includes *oneself*.) ☐ *You have weighed me down with your problems.* 🅃 *I hate to weigh down everyone with all my problems.* ☐ *You should not weigh the animals down with people.* ☐ *You should not weigh the animals down with too much cargo.* ☐ *You should not weigh the porters down with too much cargo.* ☐ *My burdens weigh me down.* ☐ *He weighed himself down with the troubles of the world.*

WEIGH ▸ IN

weigh in (at something) to present oneself at a certain weight. (Usually said of boxers.) ☐ *The fighter weighed in at over two hundred pounds.* ☐ *The contenders weighed in yesterday.* 🄽 *Were you at the weigh-in?*

WEIGH ▸ ON

See also under *WEIGH ▸ (UP)ON.*

weigh on someone's mind to burden someone's mind. ☐ *All these things are weighing on my mind, and I am very worried.* ☐ *A very serious problem is weighing on my mind.*

WEIGH ▸ OUT

weigh something out to weigh something as it is distributed. ☐ *The merchant weighed the portions of grain out to each of the waiting women.* 🅃 *They weighed out the grain carefully.*

WEIGH ▸ UP

weigh something up to find out the weight of something. ☐ *I can't tell you how much this will cost until I weigh it*

up. 🅃 *Liz weighed up the meat and jotted down the price.*

WEIGH ► (UP)ON

weigh (up)on someone to burden or worry someone. (*Upon* is formal and less commonly used than *on*.) □ *The problems at the office were beginning to weigh upon Mr. Franklin.* □ *My problems began to weigh on me.*

WEIGHT ► AGAINST

weight something against someone or something to bias something against someone or something. □ *The prosecutor tried to weight the evidence against the defendant.* □ *The police weighted the case against the accused company.*

WEIGHT ► DOWN

weight someone or something down (with something) to place a heavy weight in or on someone or something; to press down or hold down someone or something with a heavy weight. □ *The inquisitors weighted Giles Corey down with stones, but he still refused to say what they wanted.* 🅃 *Karen weighted down the papers with an ornamental paperweight.* □ *She weighted them down.* □ *We weighted the barrel down with cement. Then we sank it in the lake.*

WELCH

See entries beginning with *WELSH.*

WELCOME ► BACK

welcome someone or something back to greet the return of someone or something. □ *We are delighted to welcome you back to our house.* 🅃 *The students welcomed back the teacher who had been ill.* □ *They welcomed their lost dog back.*

WELCOME ► IN(TO)

welcome someone in(to something) to greet one as one is ushered into something or some place. □ *The Franklins welcomed us into their home.* 🅃 *Please welcome in our new members.* □ *We welcomed them in.*

WELCOME ► TO

welcome someone to something to greet someone who has come into something or some place. □ *I am very pleased to welcome you to Adamsville!* □ *They welcomed us to the party and showed us where to put our coats and hats.*

WELCOME ► WITH

welcome someone with open arms to welcome someone eagerly. □ *Even though we showed up without any notice, they welcomed us with open arms.* □ *Sam and Julie welcomed us with open arms and helped us off with our coats.*

welcome someone with something to present something to someone as a sign of greeting. □ *The natives welcomed us with garlands of flowers.* □ *I welcomed the visitors with gifts and good wishes.*

WELD ► TOGETHER

weld someone and someone else together to bind people together. (Figurative.) □ *Their experiences in the war welded Tom and Sam together for life.* □ *They were welded together by their common goals.*

weld something and something else together to attach things to one another by welding. □ *The worker welded the ends of the rods together.* □ *See if you can weld these things together.*

WELL ► OUT

well out (of something) to gush out of something. □ *The water welled out of the room when I opened the door.* □ *I opened the door and the water welled out.*

WELL ► OVER

well over [for a liquid] to fill up and spill over. □ *The laundry tub finally welled over as it became too full.* □ *The milk glass began to well over, and Timmy began to cry.*

WELL ► UP

well up (from something) AND **well up (out of something)** [for a liquid] to gush or pour up and away from something. □ *The blood welled up from the wound.* □ *Clear water welled up out of the rocks.* □ *A gusher of muddy water welled up.* □ *Tears welled up out of the baby's eyes.*

well up (inside someone) [for a feeling] to seem to swell and move inside one's body. ☐ *A feeling of revulsion began to well up inside Fred.* ☐ *Burning resentment welled up, and George knew he was going to lose his temper.*

well up with something to fill up or gush with something. ☐ *Her eyes welled up with tears.* ☐ *The basement drain welled up with the floodwaters.*

WELSH ▸ ON

welsh on someone to renege on a bet or an agreement made with someone. (Also spelled *welch.*) ☐ *You had better not welsh on me if you know what is good for you.* ☐ *Max welshed on Lefty and made a lot of trouble for himself.*

welsh on something (with someone) to renege on a bet or agreement made with someone. (Also spelled *welch.*) ☐ *Max welshed on his bet with Lefty. That was not a wise thing to do.* ☐ *It is not wise to welsh on a bet.*

WELTER ▸ IN

welter in something 1. to roll about or wallow in something; to be immersed in or surrounded by something. ☐ *Most breeds of pigs will welter happily in mud.* ☐ *I hate having to welter in the heat.* **2.** to be immersed in something such as activity, work, demands, etc. ☐ *Toward the peak of the season, we welter in orders for our goods.* ☐ *She was weltering in work, eager to take a break.* **3.** [for someone or something] to drip or run with liquid, such as blood, sweat, water, etc. ☐ *Three minutes into the jungle, we were weltering in our own sweat.* ☐ *The wounded man weltered in his blood.*

WET ▸ DOWN

wet someone or something down to put water onto someone or something. (*Someone* includes *oneself.*) ☐ *Mother wet the children down with a hose while she was washing the car.* 🅃 *Karen wet down the children with the hose.* ☐ *We wet the new concrete down to help it cure in all the heat.* ☐ *He wet himself down with water to cool himself off.*

WHACK ▸ OFF

whack something off 1. to complete something easily or quickly. (Slang.) ☐ *If you want a pair of these, I can whack them off for you in a few minutes.* 🅃 *The artisan whacked off a set of the earrings in a few minutes.* **2.** to cut or chop something off. (Slang.) ☐ *A tree branch is rubbing against the house. I guess I'll go out and whack that branch off.* 🅃 *Whack off that other branch while you are at it.*

WHACK ▸ UP

whack someone or something up to beat up or damage someone or something. (Slang.) ☐ *Max whacked Lefty up and nearly killed him.* 🅃 *Then Lefty whacked up Max.* ☐ *Who whacked my coffee table up?* ☐ *This car is whacked up and the engine burns oil. I don't want it anymore.*

whack something up to chop something up. (Informal.) ☐ *In about an hour, he had whacked the tree up into small logs.* ☐ *Have you whacked up the chicken for frying yet?*

WHALE ▸ INTO

whale into someone or something to set to work on someone or some creature in a big way; to attack someone or some creature. ☐ *The angry captain whaled into the lazy sailor.* ☐ *The sailor whaled into the dog.*

WHALE ▸ OUT

whale the tar out of someone to beat someone very badly; to spank someone severely. (Folksy or informal.) ☐ *If you ever do that again, I'll whale the tar out of you!* ☐ *Jed will whale the tar out of you if he catches you.*

WHEEDLE ▸ AWAY

wheedle something away from someone AND **wheedle something out of someone** to get something away from someone by begging or flattery. ☐ *The crooks wheedled the old lady's money away from her.* ☐ *Tim wheedled a few dollars out of his uncle.*

WHEEDLE ▸ INTO

wheedle someone into something to get someone to agree to do something by begging or flattery. ☐ *She is always trying to wheedle us into coming for a visit.* ☐ *You can't wheedle me into doing that!*

WHEEDLE ▸ OUT

wheedle something out of someone See under *WHEEDLE ▸ AWAY.*

WHEEL ▸ AROUND

wheel around to turn around quickly; to change direction quickly. ☐ *She wheeled around quickly to face him.* ☐ *Suddenly, Roger wheeled around and started chasing Wally.*

wheel someone or something around to push or steer around someone or something on wheels. ☐ *I had to wheel my great-uncle around all day when we visited the zoo.* 🅃 *I wheeled around my uncle so he could enjoy the park.* ☐ *I wheeled the heavy shopping cart around the grocery store.*

WHEEL ▸ AWAY

wheel someone or something away to push away someone or something on wheels. ☐ *The nurse wheeled the old man away, into the shelter of the porch.* 🅃 *She wheeled away the old man.* ☐ *The librarian wheeled the book cart away.*

WHEEL ▸ IN(TO)

wheel someone or something in(to something) to bring someone or something into something or some place on wheels. ☐ *The orderly wheeled the man into the operating room.* 🅃 *The orderly wheeled in Jeff.* ☐ *I wheeled the cart into the checkout line.*

WHEEL ▸ OFF

wheel someone or something off to push or steer someone or something on wheels some distance away. ☐ *The nurse wheeled the old man off.* 🅃 *Karen wheeled off the patient.* ☐ *I wheeled the wagon off, out of the way.*

WHEEL ▸ OUT

wheel someone or something out (of something) to push or steer someone or something out of something on wheels. (The *of*-phrase is paraphrased with a *from*-phrase when the particle is transposed. See the 🄵 example.) ☐ *The nurse wheeled the new mother out of the hospital.* 🅃 *Liz wheeled out the new mother.* 🄵 *She wheeled out the new mother from the hospital room.* ☐ *Lee wheeled the cart out.*

WHEEZE ▸ OUT

wheeze something out to say something, while wheezing; to say something, using a wheeze for a voice. (As if one is out of breath.) ☐ *He was out of breath from running and was only able to wheeze a few words out.* 🅃 *Liz wheezed out a friendly hello.*

WHILE ▸ AWAY

while something away (doing something) to spend or waste time doing something. ☐ *I whiled an hour away just staring at the sea.* 🅃 *Liz whiled away the entire afternoon, snoozing.* ☐ *I just love to while away the hours.*

WHINE ▸ ABOUT

whine about someone or something to whimper or complain about someone or something. ☐ *Please don't whine about Sally. She is sorry she couldn't come to your party, but it's not the end of the world.* ☐ *The dog is whining about its hurt paw.*

WHINE ▸ OUT

whine something out to say something in a whine; to say something, using a whine for a voice. ☐ *She whined her complaint out so everyone could hear it.* 🅃 *Jake whined out his usual complaints.*

WHIP ▸ AROUND

whip around **1.** to reverse suddenly. (As with the tip of a whip.) ☐ *The rope suddenly whipped around and struck me in the face.* ☐ *A branch whipped around and tore my shirt.* **2.** to turn around very quickly and suddenly. ☐ *John whipped around when he heard the noise.* ☐ *Claire whipped around to face her opponent.*

whip someone or something around to cause someone or something to reverse direction quickly. ☐ *The roller coaster whipped me around, right and left, until*

I was almost sick. ☐ *The sharp turn whipped me around, but I wasn't hurt.*

WHIP ▸ AWAY

whip something away (from someone) to jerk something away from someone suddenly. ☐ *The mugger whipped Sally's purse away from her and ran.* 🅃 *The thief whipped away the purse.* ☐ *As he whipped it away, she scratched him good.*

WHIP ▸ BACK

whip back (on someone) [for something] to snap back and strike someone. ☐ *The branch whipped back and struck Jill in the leg.* ☐ *It whipped back and slapped my side.*

WHIP ▸ INTO

whip into something to go quickly into something or some place. (Figurative.) ☐ *They whipped into the parking space before I could get there.* ☐ *I whipped into the store to pick up a few things.*

whip someone into something to beat someone into doing something. ☐ *The cruel captain whipped his men into going on with the journey.* ☐ *You can't whip me into betraying my friends.*

whip someone into something to excite, arouse, or foment someone into some state. (Figurative.) ☐ *The governor's speech whipped the audience into a frenzy.* ☐ *The angry cries from the audience whipped the speaker into a rage.*

whip someone or something into shape to cause someone or something to be in a better condition. (*Someone* includes *oneself*.) ☐ *The coach was not able to whip the players into shape before the game.* ☐ *I think I can whip this proposal into shape quickly.* ☐ *Hey, Tom, whip yourself into shape. You look a mess.*

whip something into something to beat one soft ingredient into another. ☐ *Whip the butter into the egg and make a smooth paste.* ☐ *First, you must whip the egg whites into the cream.*

WHIP ▸ OFF

whip something off to do or create something quickly. (Colloquial.) ☐ *If you need another receipt, I can whip one off in a jiffy.* 🅃 *She whipped off another set of earrings for the tourist.*

whip something off to someone to write and send off a letter to someone quickly. ☐ *After I got her letter, I whipped an answer off to her the same afternoon.* 🅃 *Liz whipped off a letter to her grandmother.*

WHIP ▸ ON

whip someone or something on to force someone or something to continue by whipping or beating. ☐ *The rider whipped his horse on, faster and faster.* 🅃 *The slaver whipped on the marching slaves.* ☐ *The slave driver whipped the weary workers on.*

WHIP ▸ OUT

whip something out **1.** to complete making or working on something quickly. ☐ *I think I can whip one out for you very quickly.* 🅃 *The factory whips out twenty of these every minute.* **2.** to jerk something out [of some place]. ☐ *Liz whipped a pencil out of her pocket.* 🅃 *She whipped out a pencil and signed the contract.*

WHIP ▸ OVER

whip something over (to someone) to send or give something to someone with great speed. (Informal.) ☐ *I will whip this letter over to Mr. Franklin right away.* ☐ *Sam whipped the package over to Alice immediately.*

WHIP ▸ THROUGH

whip through something to work through something very fast. (Informal.) ☐ *Do this carefully. Don't just whip through it.* ☐ *She whipped through her homework and went outside to play.*

WHIP ▸ UP

whip something up to create something in a hurry. ☐ *We need a floral centerpiece for the head table right now. Do you think you can whip one up?* 🅃 *I will whip up the most beautiful arrangement you have ever seen.*

WHIRL ▸ AROUND

whirl around to turn around very quickly. ☐ *I tapped him on the shoulder* *and he whirled around to see who it was.* □ *Todd whirled around and grabbed Max by the wrists.*

whirl someone or something around to turn someone or something around quickly. (*Someone* includes *oneself.*) □ *I grabbed him by the shoulder and whirled him around to face me.* □ *I whirled the book display around and found what I wanted.* □ *She whirled herself around and stared straight at him.*

WHISK ▸ AROUND

whisk someone around to move someone around rapidly from place to place. □ *I didn't get much chance to see the city. They just whisked me around.* □ *We whisked the visitor around from place to place.*

WHISK ▸ AWAY

whisk someone or something away to move someone or something out of the way rapidly. □ *The agents came and whisked the students away to a safe place.* 🅃 *The agents whisked away a number of people.* □ *The waitress whisked the crumbs away.*

WHISK ▸ OFF

whisk someone or something off to brush [something] off someone or some creature. □ *The barber quickly whisked him off and collected the fee.* 🅃 *The barber whisked off the customer.* □ *The vet whisked off the dog.*

whisk someone or something off (to something) to move someone or something to something or some place rapidly. □ *The government agents whisked the suspect off to a secret place.* 🅃 *They whisked off the suspect to a cabin in the hills.* □ *Todd whisked the emergency medical supplies off to the airport.*

whisk something off ((of) someone or something) to brush something off someone or something. (The *of*-phrase is paraphrased with a *from*-phrase when the particle is transposed. See the 🄵 example. The *of* is colloquial.) □ *The barber whisked the loose hairs off of the customer.* 🅃 *The barber whisked off the loose hairs.* 🄵 *The barber whisked off the loose hairs from the customer.* □ *The barber whisked the hairs off.*

WHISPER ▸ ABOUT

whisper about someone or something to speak about someone or something in a breathy voice, as if telling secrets. □ *I hope they aren't whispering about me.* □ *Everyone is whispering about the incident in the lunchroom.*

WHISPER ▸ AROUND

whisper something around to spread secrets or gossip around. □ *Now, don't whisper this around, but Sam is going to run away from home.* □ *If you whisper this around, you will spoil the surprise.*

WHISTLE ▸ AT

whistle at someone or something to indicate approval or disapproval of someone or something by whistling. □ *The men whistled at the beautiful woman who walked by.* □ *Everyone whistled at the enormous roast of beef the cook's assistant carried in.*

WHISTLE ▸ FOR

whistle for someone or something to summon someone or something by whistling. □ *I stood on the corner and whistled for a cab, but they all ignored me.* □ *I whistled for the dog, but it did not appear.*

WHITTLE ▸ AT

whittle at something to cut or carve at something. □ *He just sat there, whittling at a chunk of wood.* □ *I am not carving anything, I am just whittling at some wood.*

WHITTLE ▸ AWAY

whittle something away to cut or carve something away. (Sometimes figurative.) □ *The carver whittled the wood away until only a small figure was left.* 🅃 *He whittled away the wood.* □ *Her own debts whittled her fortune away rather quickly.*

WHITTLE ▸ DOWN

whittle someone down (to size) to reduce someone to a more appropriate size or to the proper size. (Figurative.) □ *After a few days at camp, the counselors had whittled young Walter down to size.*

☐ *It took some doing, but they whittled him down.*

whittle something down (to size) to cut or diminish something to a more appropriate size or to the proper size. ☐ *I whittled the peg down to size and it fit in the hole perfectly.* ☐ *I whittled it down so it would fit.* 🅃 *You are going to have to whittle down expenses.*

WHITTLE ▸ OUT

whittle something out of something to carve something out of something. ☐ *The young man whittled a small boat out of wood.* ☐ *Can you whittle an elephant out of this chunk of wood?*

WHIZ ▸ PAST

whiz past someone or something to move or travel past someone or something at a high speed. ☐ *The train whizzed past one little town after another.* ☐ *I whizzed past Chuck because I did not recognize him.*

WHIZ ▸ THROUGH

whiz (right) through something **1.** to speed through a place. ☐ *One car after another whizzed right through the little town.* ☐ *We whizzed through the kitchen, stopping just long enough for a glass of iced tea.* **2.** to work one's way through something quickly. ☐ *She whizzed right through the test with no trouble.* ☐ *Jane whizzed through her interview and got the job.*

WHOOP ▸ UP

whoop it up to celebrate, especially with cheers and whoops. (Slang.) ☐ *It was a very noisy party. Everyone was whooping it up well past midnight.* ☐ *We whooped it up until dawn.*

whoop it up for someone or something to attempt to stir up enthusiasm for someone or something; to make a vocal demonstration in favor of someone or something. ☐ *The campaign workers whooped it up for their candidate.* ☐ *I can't get out there and whoop it up for something I don't believe in.*

WIG ▸ OUT

wig out to become alcohol- or drug-intoxicated. (Slang.) ☐ *One more drink and Wally will wig out.* ☐ *This guy has wigged out. Get him out of here.*

WIGGLE ▸ OUT

wiggle out of something **1.** to get out of something or some place; to squirm out of something or some place. ☐ *The kitten was able to wiggle out of the cage in which it had been put.* ☐ *The squirrel wiggled out of the trap we caught it in.* **2.** to manage to get out of a job, the blame for something, or a responsibility. ☐ *Don't try to wiggle out of your job!* ☐ *You are to blame and don't try to wiggle out of it!*

WILL ▸ AWAY

will something away to give something away in a will. ☐ *The old man simply willed all his money away. He said he wouldn't need it when he was dead.* 🅃 *She had willed away all of her treasures to her grandchildren.*

WILL ▸ TO

will something to someone to give something to someone in a will. ☐ *My uncle willed this chair to me. It's an antique.* ☐ *This watch was willed to me by my grandfather.*

WIMP ▸ OUT

wimp out (of something) to get out of something in a cowardly fashion; to chicken out of something. (Slang.) ☐ *Are you trying to wimp out of your responsibilities?* ☐ *You had better not wimp out.*

WIN ▸ AT

win at something to triumph at some competition. ☐ *Will I ever be able to win at golf?* ☐ *She always wins at solitaire.*

win something at something to win a prize in some sort of competition. ☐ *I won this silly doll at the ring-toss game.* ☐ *Did you win anything at the fair?*

WIN ▸ AWAY

win someone away (from someone or something) to convince someone to dissociate from someone or something. ☐ *We were not able to win Christine away from her strange ideas.* ☐ *We tried to win her away, but failed.*

WIN ▸ BACK

win someone or something back (from someone or something) to regain someone or something from someone or something. (Both literal and figurative.) □ *I hope to win the money I lost back from the other poker players.* □ *We were not able to win Sally back from the cult.* □ *We won everything back.* □ *We won Sally back.*

WIN ▸ OUT

win (out) (over someone or something) to defeat someone or something. □ *I hope our team wins out over you guys.* □ *Good teamwork always wins out.* □ *The Bears won over the Tigers.*

WIN ▸ OVER

win (out) (over someone or something) See under *WIN ▸ OUT.*

win someone over (to something) to succeed in make someone favorable to something. □ *I hope I can win them all over to our side.* 🅃 *I won over the mayor to our side.* □ *We can win the voters over!*

WIN ▸ THROUGH

win through something to succeed by a certain method or procedure. □ *Winning is no good if you have to win through dishonesty.* □ *Sally won through her own hard work.*

WINCE ▸ AT

wince at something to shrink back because of something, such as pain. □ *She winced at the pain but did not cry out.* □ *After he had just winced at the pain for a while, he finally screamed.*

WIND ▸ AROUND

wind around [for something, such as a road] to twist around. □ *The road wound around and ended up at the lake.* □ *The path wound around and came to a stop at the cabin door.*

wind around someone or something to twist or coil around someone or something. □ *The python wound around the rabbit, suffocating it.* □ *The vines wound around the gatepost.*

wind someone around one's little finger to control and manipulate someone. (Figurative.) □ *She can wind him around her little finger. She has him hypnotized.* □ *He wound her around his little finger and kept her to himself.*

wind something around something to twist or coil something around something. □ *Wind this cloth around your hand to stop the bleeding.* □ *Wind the string around this stick so it won't get all tangled up.*

WIND ▸ BACK

wind back [for something, such as a road] to turn so that it heads in the direction from whence it came. □ *The road we got lost on wound back and we were not able to reach the lake on time.* □ *When we were lost, we found a stream in the woods, but it wound back and did not lead us in the direction we wanted.*

wind something back to set a clock back. □ *It is time to wind the clock back again.* 🅃 *I'll wind back the clock.*

WIND ▸ DOWN

wind down to start running or operating slower. □ *Things will begin to wind down at the end of the summer.* □ *As things wind down, life will be a lot easier.* □ *The clock wound down and finally stopped.*

wind something down to slow something down; to make something less hectic. □ *Let's wind this party down and try to get people to go home. It's really late.* 🅃 *We tried to wind down the party, but it kept running.*

WIND ▸ IN

wind something in to reel something in. □ *She wound in the rope that was tied to the anchor.* 🅃 *Liz wound in the cable that raised the awning.*

WIND ▸ INTO

wind into something to coil up into something. □ *The snake wound into a tight coil.* □ *The rubber bands wound into a knot and were worthless.*

wind something (up) (into something) See under *WIND ▸ UP.*

WIND ▸ OFF

wind something off to unreel or unwind something. □ *He wound the rope* *off, little by little, until he had as much as he needed.* 🅃 *Karen wound off as much as she needed.*

WIND ▸ ON(TO)

wind something on(to something) to coil or wrap something onto something. ☐ *Wind this string onto the ball and save it.* 🅃 *If you find the string ball, please wind on this string.* ☐ *Here, wind some more on.*

WIND ▸ THROUGH

wind through something [for a pathway] to twist through an area. ☐ *The trail wound through the jungle, avoiding the densest places.* ☐ *A path wound through the woods, leading us to the main road.*

WIND ▸ UP

wind someone up 1. to get someone excited. (Colloquial.) ☐ *That kind of music really winds me up!* 🄰 *The room was filled with wound-up people.* **2.** to get someone set to do a lot of talking. (Colloquial. As with winding up a clock.) ☐ *The excitement of the day wound Kelly up and she talked almost all night.* ☐ *A good movie tends to wind me up for a while.*

wind something up to tighten the spring in something, such as a watch or a clock. ☐ *Please wind your watch up now—before it runs down.* 🅃 *Wind up your watch before you forget.* 🄰 *All the little windup toys got rusty and stopped running.*

wind something (up) (into something) to coil something up into a ball or similar shape. ☐ *Tony wound all the string up into a ball.* ☐ *Please wind this into a ball.* ☐ *Can you wind this up?* 🅃 *I wound up all the yarn into a ball.*

wind up (as) something to end up as something. ☐ *Roger wound up as a millionaire.* ☐ *He thought he would wind up a pauper.*

wind up (by) doing something to end by doing something [anyway]. ☐ *I wound up by going home early.* ☐ *I wound up eating out.*

wind up some place to end up in a particular place; to land up in some place. ☐ *I don't want to wind up in jail!* ☐ *We wound up right where we thought we would.*

wind up somehow to end up in some fashion. ☐ *I don't want to wind up broke and depressed.* ☐ *You don't want to wind up like Ted, do you?*

wind up with someone or something to end up having someone or something. ☐ *I don't want to wind up with all the kids for the weekend.* ☐ *We wound up with Thanksgiving at our house again.*

WINK ▸ AT

wink at someone to close one eye at a person as a sign of flirtation. ☐ *She winked at him and he was shocked.* ☐ *I hope she winks at me again.*

wink at something to pretend not to see something; to condone something wrong. ☐ *The police officer winked at my failure to make a complete stop.* ☐ *I cannot wink at blatant infractions of the law!*

WINK ▸ AWAY

wink something away to blink the eyes to try to clear them of tears, dirt, etc. ☐ *He looked up at me and tried to wink away his tears, but he was just too upset.* 🅃 *Jane winked away her tears.*

WINTER ▸ OVER

winter over (some place) to spend the winter at some place. ☐ *The bears all winter over in their dens.* ☐ *All the animals are getting ready either to migrate or to winter over.* ☐ *My parents winter over in Florida.*

WIPE ▸ AWAY

wipe something away to clean or mop something away. ☐ *Wipe all this mud away and scrub the floor clean.* 🅃 *Jake wiped away the mud.*

WIPE ▸ DOWN

wipe something down to rub or mop something down. ☐ *Wipe the counter down and keep it clean!* 🅃 *Don will wipe down the counter.*

WIPE ▸ OFF

wipe someone or something off to clean someone or something of something by wiping. (*Someone* includes *one-*

self.) ☐ *She wiped the baby off and put clean clothes on him.* 🅃 *Please wipe off your shoes.* ☐ *John fell in the mud and Sam wiped him off.* ☐ *She wiped herself off, getting all the mud off her shoes, at least.*

wipe someone or something off the face of the earth to demolish someone or something. (Figurative.) ☐ *A great storm will come and wipe all the people off the face of the earth.* ☐ *The wind blew my old barn off the face of the earth! Nothing was left.*

wipe someone or something (off) (with something) See under *WIPE ▸ WITH.*

wipe something off ((of) someone or something) to remove something from someone or something by wiping. (The *of*-phrase is paraphrased with a *from*-phrase when the particle is transposed. See the 🄵 example. The *of* is colloquial.) ☐ *The mother wiped the ice cream off of her child.* 🅃 *She wiped off the ice cream.* 🄵 *She wiped off ice cream and other stuff from the face of her child.* ☐ *Tony wiped the mud off.*

wipe something (off) (on something) to remove something by wiping it on something else. ☐ *Don't wipe your feet off on the carpet.* 🅃 *Don't wipe off your feet on the carpet.* ☐ *Wipe them on the mat.* ☐ *Wipe them off outside.*

wipe something off (one's face) to remove a smile, grin, silly look, etc., from one's face. (Figurative. Usually a command.) ☐ *Wipe that silly grin off your face, private!* ☐ *Wipe that smile off!*

WIPE ▸ ON

See *wipe something (off) (on something)* under *WIPE ▸ OFF.*

WIPE ▸ OUT

wipe out 1. to have a wreck. (Slang.) ☐ *Tommy wiped out on that tight curve.* ☐ *Did you see how fast he was going? No wonder he wiped out.* 🄽 *He was injured in the wipeout.* **2.** to fail badly. (Slang.) ☐ *The test was terrible! I'm sure I wiped out.* ☐ *It was a bad test. I wiped out for sure.* ☐ *The whole test was a wipeout.*

wipe someone or something out to wreck or destroy someone or something. (Slang. *Someone* includes *oneself.*) ☐ *The wreck wiped half the basketball team out.* 🅃 *The wreck wiped out half the basketball team.* 🅃 *The party wiped out our potato chip supply.* ☐ *They wiped themselves out in a wreck.*

wipe someone out 1. to kill someone. (Slang.) ☐ *Max intended to wipe Lefty's gang out.* 🅃 *Lefty wiped out Max's gang.* **2.** to exhaust or debilitate someone. (Slang.) ☐ *The long walk wiped me out.* 🅃 *The trip wiped out the hikers.*

WIPE ▸ UP

wipe something up 1. to clean something up by wiping. ☐ *Please wipe that spilled milk up.* 🅃 *Jim wiped up the spill.* **2.** to clean something by wiping. ☐ *The floor was sticky so I wiped it up.* 🅃 *Please wipe up the countertop.*

wipe the floor up with someone to beat someone to a pulp. (Figurative slang.) ☐ *I'm going to wipe the floor up with you!* 🅃 *Max threatened to wipe up the floor with Lefty, but Lefty just ignored him.*

WIPE ▸ WITH

wipe someone or something (off) (with something) to clean someone or something by wiping with something. (*Someone* includes *oneself.*) ☐ *Tony wiped the baby off with a soft cloth.* 🅃 *Jane wiped off the counter with a rag.* ☐ *Tom fell in the mud and asked Ralph to wipe him off.* ☐ *Todd wiped himself off with a towel.*

WIRE ▸ AHEAD

wire ahead (for something) to send a telegram to one's destination, requesting something to be available upon one's arrival. ☐ *I wired ahead for a room. I hope that they still have one by the time we get to the hotel.* ☐ *We wired ahead for reservations.* ☐ *I told you we should have wired ahead.*

WIRE ▸ BACK

wire something back to someone to send something, such as a reply or money, back to someone. ☐ *Please wire* *your answer back to me by tomorrow.* □ *The reply wasn't wired back in time.*

WIRE ▸ FOR

wire for something to send for something by telegram. □ *I wired for money, but it hasn't come yet.* □ *I will have to wire for further advice.*

wire someone or something for something to send a telegram to someone or something requesting something. □ *I wired my father for some money. I'm sure he'll send it, officer.* □ *Sarah wired the supplier for a replacement part.*

WIRE ▸ IN

wire something in to send something into a central point by telegram. □ *I can't mail my story to my editor in time, so I will have to wire it in.* [T] *I've got to wire in this story.*

WIRE ▸ TOGETHER

wire something together to bind the pieces of something together with wire; to bind things together with wire. □ *I wired the car's exhaust pipe together, hoping to get a few more miles out of it.* □ *I will wire it together to keep it from dragging on the roadway.*

WIRE ▸ UP

wire something up 1. to repair or reattach something with wire, especially something electrical. □ *I will wire this radio up and it will work like new.* [T] *As soon as I wire up this radio again, it will run very well.* [A] *I had to have my old wired-up muffler replaced.* **2.** to attach something to a high place with wire. □ *We wired the television antenna up to the top of the chimney.* [T] *We wired up the antenna to the chimney.*

WISE ▸ UP

wise someone up (about someone or something) to instruct someone about something; to give someone important information. (Slang.) □ *Let me wise you up about the way we do things around here.* □ *I will do what I can to wise her up.*

wise up (to someone or something) to figure out someone or something. (Slang.) □ *It's time you wised up to John and what he has been doing.* □ *You ought to wise up to what's going on.* □ *It's time you wised up.*

WISH ▸ AWAY

wish someone or something away to wish that someone or something would go away. □ *You can't just wish him away. You'll have to ask him to leave!* [T] *Don't wish away the days of your life.* □ *Even if you wish him away, he won't go.*

WISH ▸ FOR

wish for someone or something to wish to have someone or something. □ *She spent most of her life wishing for Prince Charming, who would come along and sweep her off her feet.* □ *She still wishes for escape.* [A] *The wished-for outcome did not occur.*

WISH ▸ OFF

wish someone or something off on someone to foist someone or something off on someone else. □ *I would never wish my uncle off on you, even for an hour.* [T] *I wouldn't wish off my cousin Roger on anyone.* □ *Fred couldn't wish his problem off on anyone.*

WISH ▸ ON

wish someone or something on someone to wish someone or something were someone else's problem. □ *I wouldn't wish the obnoxious Mr. Chunder on you for anything, but someone has to deal with him.* □ *I wouldn't wish this matter on you.*

WITHDRAW ▸ FROM

withdraw from something 1. to pull out of something physically. □ *I withdrew from the smoky room and ran to the open window to get some air.* □ *I withdrew from the unpleasant-looking cafe, and looked for something more to my liking.* **2.** to end one's association with someone or something. □ *I decided to withdraw from all my professional organizations.* □ *I had to withdraw from the association because the dues had become too high.*

withdraw someone from something 1. to pull someone out of something physically. □ *She withdrew the child from the* *water just in time.* □ *I had to withdraw my child from the kindergarten room. He was having such a good time, he wouldn't leave on his own.* **2.** to remove someone from an organization or a nomination. □ *The committee withdrew John from nomination and put up someone else.* □ *I withdrew my son from kindergarten.*

withdraw something from someone or something to pull something out of someone or something. □ *She withdrew the book from the stack.* □ *I withdrew the arrow from Dave carefully.*

WITHDRAW ▸ INTO

withdraw into oneself to become introverted; to concern oneself with one's inner thoughts. □ *After a few years of being ignored, she withdrew into herself.* □ *I have to fight to keep from withdrawing into myself.*

withdraw into something to pull back into something. □ *The turtle withdrew into its shell.* □ *The mouse withdrew into its hole.*

withdraw something into something to pull something back into something. □ *The turtle withdrew its head into its shell.* □ *It then withdrew its feet into the shell also.*

WITHER ▸ AWAY

wither away to shrivel up; to shrink up. □ *Soon, the wart withered away.* □ *Many of our roses withered away in the hot sun.*

WITHER ▸ ON

wither on the vine **1.** [for fruit] to shrivel on the vine, unharvested. (Figurative for a fruit that does not grow on a vine.) □ *If we don't get out there into the field, the grapes will wither on the vine.* □ *The apples will wither on the vine if not picked soon.* **2.** [for someone or something] to be ignored or neglected and thereby be wasted. □ *I hope I get a part in the play. I don't want to just wither on the vine.* □ *Fred thinks he is withering on the vine because no one has chosen him.*

WITHER ▸ UP

wither something up to cause something to shrivel up. □ *Will the sun wither the new plants up?* 🅃 *The hot sun withered up the delicate foliage.*

wither up to shrivel up. □ *It was so hot that the leaves of the trees withered up.* 🄰 *A withered-up old man sat by the gate.*

WITHHOLD ▸ FROM

withhold something from someone or something to hold something back or in reserve from someone or some creature. □ *We withheld some of the food from the guests.* □ *I had to withhold some food from the dog so there would be enough for tomorrow.*

WITNESS ▸ FOR

witness for someone or something to serve as a witness for some person or some deed. □ *They could find no one to witness for the accused person.* □ *The police found someone to witness for the hour of the crime.*

WITNESS ▸ TO

witness to something to serve as a witness to some act or deed. □ *I was witness to the beating.* □ *We were not witness to any of the activities you have described.*

WOBBLE ▸ ABOUT

wobble about AND **wobble around** to rock, quiver, or flounder around. □ *The little baby wobbled about and finally fell.* □ *The vase wobbled around a little and fell over.*

WOBBLE ▸ AROUND

wobble around See the previous entry.

WOLF ▸ DOWN

wolf something down to eat something very rapidly and in very large pieces. (As a wolf might eat.) □ *Don't wolf your food down!* 🅃 *Liz would never wolf down her food.*

WONDER ▸ ABOUT

wonder about someone or something to be curious or in doubt about someone or something. □ *I wonder about Carl and what he is up to.* □ *Sometimes I wonder about life on other planets.* □

Jenny's performance record made me wonder about her chances for success.

WONDER ▸ AT

wonder at someone or something to be amazed at or in awe of someone or something. (Stilted.) □ *We all wondered at Lee and the way he kept his spirits up.* □ *The people wondered at the bright light that lit up the sky.*

WOO ▸ AWAY

woo someone away (from someone or something) to lure someone away from someone or something; to seduce someone away from someone or something. □ *The manager of the new bank wooed all the tellers away from the old bank.* □ *She wooed them away.* 🅃 *They wooed away all the experienced people.*

WORK ▸ AGAINST

work against someone or something **1.** [for someone] to struggle against someone or something. □ *She worked hard against the passage of the law.* □ *Dave worked against Betty.* **2.** [for something] to militate against someone or something. □ *This sort of works against your plan, does it not?* □ *Everything you said works against your client.*

WORK ▸ ALONG

work one's way along something to move or labor alongside something or a route. □ *She worked her way along the ledge and finally came to a wide space where she could relax.* □ *They worked themselves along the jungle path, chopping and cutting as they went.*

WORK ▸ AMONG

work among someone or something to do one's work among some people or things. □ *I wanted to work among the Indians, but I set up my medical practice in the inner city.* □ *I want to get a job in forestry and work among the trees.*

WORK ▸ AROUND

work around someone or something to manage to do one's work while avoiding someone or something. □ *He is being a problem, but he will have to leave pretty soon. You'll just have to work around him.* □ *You have to work around the piano. It is too heavy to move.*

work around to someone or something to get around to dealing with someone or something. □ *You're not next in line. We will have to work around to you.* □ *I can't take care of it now. I'll have to work around to it.*

WORK ▸ AS

work as something to work in the capacity of something. □ *I worked as a waiter for a year when I was in college.* □ *I will work as a stockbroker for a while, and then move on to something else.*

WORK ▸ AT

work at something **1.** to work in a particular trade or craft. □ *He works at carpentry when he has the time.* □ *Julie works at editing for a living.* **2.** to work on a specific task, machine, device. □ *She was working at repairing the cabinet when I came home.* □ *Todd is working at his computer.*

WORK ▸ AWAY

work away (at something) to continue to work industriously at something. □ *All the weavers were working away at their looms.* □ *They just kept working away.*

WORK ▸ DOWN

work down the line to progress along a line of people or things. □ *She took each one of them in turn, working down the line until she got to the end.* □ *I am working down the line and I will get to you when your turn comes.*

work down (the line) (to someone or something) to progress through a series until someone or something is reached. □ *I will work down to the papers on the bottom gradually. You can't hurry this kind of work.* □ *We will work down the line to Katie.* □ *We have to work down to the last one.* □ *They are working down the line as fast as they can, but everyone has to be taken in order.*

work something down to lower or reduce something. □ *Over a few months, they worked the price down, and the house soon was sold.* 🅃 *They worked down the price so much that the house was a steal.*

work something down (into something) to manipulate something downward into something. □ *The crane operator worked the load down into the ship's hold.* □ *The operator worked it down carefully.*

work something down (over something) to manipulate something downward over something. □ *Now, you work this part down over this little tube, and then it won't leak.* □ *Liz worked the lid down and tightened it on.*

WORK ▸ FOR

work for someone **1.** to be employed by someone. □ *She works for Scott Wallace.* □ *Who do you work for?* **2.** to work as a substitute for someone. □ *I will work for you while you are having your baby.* □ *Right now, I am working for Julie, who is out sick.*

work for something **1.** to work for a group, company, etc. □ *Everyone at the picnic works for the same employer.* □ *We work for the telephone company.* **2.** to work for a certain amount of money. □ *She says she works for a very good wage.* □ *I won't work for that kind of pay.* **3.** to work for an intangible benefit, such as satisfaction, glory, honor, etc. □ *The pay isn't very good. I just work for the fun of it.* □ *Sam says he works for the joy of working.*

WORK ▸ IN

work something in with something to mix something in with something. □ *Now, work the butter in with the egg mixture over a very low heat.* 🅃 *Work in the butter with the eggs.*

WORK ▸ INTO

work (one's way) into something **1.** to get into something tight or small gradually and with effort. □ *He worked himself into the cupboard and hid there for a while.* □ *The mouse worked into the crack and got stuck.* **2.** to get more deeply involved in something gradually. □ *I don't quite understand my job. I'll work my way into it gradually.* □ *Fred worked into the daily routine gradually.*

work oneself (up) into a lather (about someone or something) to get very angry or excited about someone or something. □ *You shouldn't work yourself up into a lather about the cost of the hotel.* □ *There's no need to work yourself into a lather about Larry.* □ *He shouldn't work himself into a lather.* □ *Don't work yourself up into a lather!*

WORK ▸ IN(TO)

work someone or something in(to something) **1.** to manage to fit someone or something into something physically. (*Someone* includes *oneself.*) □ *The magician worked the lady into the tiny cabinet from which she was to disappear.* 🅃 *The magician opened the little box and worked in the lady.* □ *The magician worked the lady in.* **2.** to fit someone or something into a sequence or series. □ *I don't have an appointment open this afternoon, but I'll see if I can work you into the sequence.* 🅃 *I can't work in all of you.* □ *I can work Karen in late in the day.*

work something in(to something) to press, mix, or force a substance into something. □ *You should work the butter into the dough carefully.* 🅃 *Work in the butter carefully.* □ *Work it in bit by bit.* □ *Work the lard into the flour with a fork.*

WORK ▸ OFF

work one's butt off AND **work one's tail off** to work very hard. (Figurative slang.) □ *You had better start working your butt off if you want to get anywhere in the world.* □ *I've been working my tail off for weeks now.*

work something off **1.** to get rid of body fat by doing strenuous work. □ *I was able to work a lot of weight off by jogging.* 🅃 *I need to work off some fat.* **2.** to get rid of anger, anxiety, or energy by doing physical activity. □ *I was so mad! I went out and played basketball to work my anger off.* 🅃 *I need to work off some fat.* **3.** to pay off a debt through work rather than by money. □ *I had no money so I had to work the bill off by washing dishes.* 🅃 *I have to work off my debt.*

WORK ▸ ON

See also under *WORK ▸ (UP)ON.*

work on someone **1.** [for a physician] to treat someone; [for a surgeon] to operate on someone. □ *The doctor is still working on your uncle. There is no news yet.* □ *They are still working on the accident victims.* **2.** to try to convince someone of something. □ *I'll work on her, and I am sure she will agree.* □ *They worked on Max for quite a while, but he still didn't speak.* **3.** [for something, such as medication] to have the desired effect on someone. □ *This medicine just doesn't work on me.* □ *Your good advice doesn't seem to work on Sam.*

work wonders on someone or something to accomplish something very good for or with someone or something. (Cliché.) □ *The medicine worked wonders on Betsy.* □ *The training school worked wonders on their German shepherd.*

WORK ▸ OUT

work itself out [for a problem] to solve itself. □ *Eventually, all the problems worked themselves out without any help from us.* □ *This will work itself out. Don't worry.*

work out **1.** [for something] to turn out all right in the end. □ *Don't worry. Everything will work out.* □ *This will work out. Don't worry.* **2.** [for someone] to do a program of exercise. □ *I work out at least twice a week.* □ *I need to work out more often.* Ⓝ *I need a good workout about three times a week.*

work out (as something) to perform satisfactorily in a particular role. □ *We all hope she works out as a security monitor.* □ *I'm sure she will work out.*

work out (at something) **1.** to perform satisfactorily doing something in particular. □ *I hope I work out at my new job.* □ *I'm sure you'll work out.* **2.** to perform satisfactorily working in a particular location. □ *I hope I work out at the factory. I really need that job.* □ *Things will work out at home in time.*

work out for the best [for a bad situation] to turn out all right in the end. (Idiomatic.) □ *Don't worry. Everything will work out for the best.* □ *I think that nothing ever works out for the best.*

work something out (of something) to manipulate something to get it out of something. (The *of*-phrase is paraphrased with a *from*-phrase when the particle is transposed. See the Ⓕ example.) □ *You have to work the bubbles out of the paint before you use it.* Ⓣ *You have to stir it to work out the bubbles.* Ⓕ *You stir it to work out the bubbles from the paint.* □ *Work them all out.*

work something out (with someone) to come to an agreement with someone; to figure out with someone a way to do something. □ *I think we can work this out with you so that all of us are satisfied.* Ⓣ *I will work out something with Karen.* □ *I'm sure we can work it out.*

WORK ▸ OVER

work someone or something over to give someone or something a thorough examination or treatment. □ *The doctor really worked me over but couldn't find anything wrong.* Ⓣ *They worked over the patient but found nothing.* □ *They worked her over thoroughly.*

work someone over to beat someone up. (Slang.) □ *Max and his boys worked Lefty over and left him in the street.* Ⓣ *Then Lefty worked over Max and his boys.* Ⓝ *Lefty gave Max a workover.*

work something over to rework something. □ *He saved the play by working the second act over.* Ⓣ *Would you work over this job and see if you can improve it?*

WORK ▸ THROUGH

work (one's way) through something **1.** to work to earn money to pay the bills while one is in college, medical school, law school, etc. □ *I worked my way through college as a waiter.* □ *I had to work through college and I appreciate it more.* **2.** to progress through something complicated. □ *I spent hours working my way through the tax forms.* □ *I worked through the forms very slowly.* **3.** to struggle through an emotional trauma. □ *When she had finally worked through her grief, she was able* *to function normally again.* ☐ *Larry worked through the pain.*

work something through (something) **1.** to guide or push something through a physical barrier. ☐ *I could hardly work the needle through the tightly woven cloth.* ☐ *I worked the needle through.* **2.** to guide or maneuver a law, proposal, motion, through a governing body. ☐ *The lobbyist was unable to work the law through the legislature.* ☐ *The usual party hacks worked the law through.*

work through channels to operate or progress through the proper offices or procedures. ☐ *You cannot expect special treatment. You have to work through channels.* ☐ *It was hard for me to learn to work through channels when I got my new job.*

WORK ▸ TO

work one's fingers to the bone to work very hard. (Figurative.) ☐ *I worked my fingers to the bone all day to fix this dinner for you!* ☐ *I am tired of working my fingers to the bone for such a low wage.*

work someone or something to someone or something to struggle to manipulate someone or something to someone or something. ☐ *The football player worked the ball to the quarterback so that the opposition didn't know what was going on.* ☐ *The rescuers worked the child to the top of the tunnel.*

WORK ▸ TOGETHER

work together [for people or things] to cooperate or function together. ☐ *Come now! Let's all work together and get this done on time!* ☐ *We will work together on this and enjoy it more.*

WORK ▸ TOWARD

work toward something **1.** to progress toward a goal, such as a promotion. ☐ *He was working toward a position with the new company.* ☐ *She was working toward a law degree when the accident happened.* **2.** to struggle physically to move toward something or some place. ☐ *The turtle worked toward the water despite the hot sun.* ☐ *I worked toward the cabin in the forest, fighting mosquitoes all the way.*

WORK ▸ UNDER

work something under something to manipulate something beneath something. ☐ *She worked the knife blade under the window and tried to pry the window up.* ☐ *Work the envelope under the office door. She will find it when she opens the door in the morning.*

work under someone to have one's work supervised by someone. ☐ *I work under Michael, who is head of the department.* ☐ *Who do you work under?*

work under something to work underneath something. ☐ *I have to work under the car for a while. Please don't start it.* ☐ *The plumber had to work under the house to fix the pipes.*

WORK ▸ UP

work one's way up (to something) See *work oneself up (to something).*

work oneself (up) into a lather (about someone or something) See under *WORK ▸ INTO.*

work oneself up into something **1.** to struggle to raise oneself upwards into something or some place. ☐ *I worked myself up into the top of the tree.* ☐ *I worked myself up into the attic and couldn't get down.* ☐ *The explorers worked themselves up into the upper reaches of the cavity.* ☐ *Fred worked himself up into the rafters and began to look for bats.* **2.** to bring oneself into an extreme emotional state. ☐ *I worked myself up into a state of hysteria.* ☐ *Don't work yourself up into hysteria.* ☐ *Sally worked herself up into a rage.* ☐ *Don't work yourself up into a rage.*

work oneself up (to something) **1.** to prepare oneself with sufficient energy or courage to do something. ☐ *I can't just walk in there and ask for it. I have to work myself up to it.* ☐ *I worked myself up and went into the boss's office.* ☐ *I have to work myself up to undergoing surgery.* **2.** AND **work one's way up (to something)** to progress in one's work to a particular rank or status. ☐ *I worked myself up to sergeant in no time at all.* ☐ *Claude worked his way up to master sergeant.* ☐ *She worked her way up to the top.*

work something up to prepare something, perhaps on short notice. ☐ *There are some special clients coming in this weekend. We need to make a presentation. Do you think you can work something up by then?* 🅃 *I will work up something for this weekend.*

work something up into something to develop something into something. ☐ *I will work this story up into a screenplay in a few months.* 🅃 *I can work up this idea into a good novel.*

work up to something 1. [for something] to build or progress to something. (Usually concerning the weather.) ☐ *The sky is working up to some kind of storm.* ☐ *The weather is working up to something severe.* 2. [for someone] to lead up to something. ☐ *You are working up to telling me something unpleasant, aren't you?* ☐ *I think I am working up to a good cry.*

WORK ▸ (UP)ON

work (up)on something 1. to repair or tinker with something. (*Upon* is formal and less commonly used than *on*.) ☐ *He's out in the kitchen, working upon his tax forms.* ☐ *He's working on his car.* 2. [for something] to have the desired effect on something. (*Upon* is formal and less commonly used than *on*.) ☐ *This medicine should work well upon your cold.* ☐ *I hope it will work on your cold.*

WORK ▸ WITH

work with someone or something to manipulate or work on someone or something. ☐ *Let me work with him for a while. I'll convince him.* ☐ *I want to work with this engine and see if I can get it started.*

work with something to do work with some tool or instrument. ☐ *She is working with a chisel now. In a minute she will switch to a tiny knife.* ☐ *Do you know how to work with a voltmeter?*

work wonders with someone or something to have a very good effect on someone or something. ☐ *I know a hairstylist who could work wonders with you.* ☐ *The medicine will work wonders with your cough.*

WORM ▸ IN(TO)

worm (one's way) in(to something) 1. to wiggle into something or some place. ☐ *The little cat wormed her way into the box and got stuck.* ☐ *The cat wormed into the opening.* ☐ *The cat wormed in and got stuck.* 2. to manipulate one's way into participation in something. ☐ *She tried to worm her way into the play, but the director refused.* ☐ *You can have a part, so don't try to worm in.*

WORM ▸ OUT

worm (one's way) out (of something) 1. to wiggle out of something or some place. ☐ *Somehow she managed to worm her way out of the handcuffs.* ☐ *Frank wormed out of the opening.* ☐ *He struggled and struggled and wormed out.* 2. to manipulate oneself out of a job or responsibility. ☐ *Don't try to worm yourself out of this affair. It is your fault!* ☐ *You can't worm out of this.* ☐ *Don't try to worm out.*

worm something out of someone to draw or manipulate information out of someone. ☐ *I managed to worm the name of the doctor out of her before she ran off.* ☐ *You can't worm the names out of me!*

WORRY ▸ ABOUT

worry about someone or something to fret or be anxious about the welfare of someone or something. ☐ *Please don't worry about me. I'll be all right.* ☐ *Don't worry about the bill. I'll pay it.*

worry oneself about someone or something to allow oneself to fret or become anxious about someone or something. ☐ *Please don't worry yourself about me. I'll be all right.* ☐ *There is no need for Karen to worry herself about this.* ☐ *You shouldn't worry yourself about Todd.*

WORRY ▸ OUT

worry something out of someone to annoy some information out of someone. ☐ *They finally worried the correct number out of me.* ☐ *You can't worry the information out of her. It will require force.*

worry something out of something to pester some creature until it leaves something or some place. □ *The cat finally worried the mouse out of its hole and caught it.* □ *We worried the squirrel out of the attic by making lots of noise.*

WORRY ▸ OVER

worry over someone or something to fret or be anxious about someone or something. □ *She worried over dinner, but it came out all right.* □ *Jerry is worried over his daughter, Alice.*

WORRY ▸ THROUGH

worry through something to think and fret through a problem. □ *I can't talk to you now. I have to worry through this tax problem.* □ *We worried through the financial problem over a three-day period.*

WORSHIP ▸ AS

worship someone as something to revere or honor one as if one were something. □ *He worships her as a goddess.* □ *She worships her father as a god.*

WRANGLE ▸ ABOUT

wrangle (with someone) (about someone or something) See under *WRANGLE ▸ WITH.*

WRANGLE ▸ OVER

wrangle (with someone) (over someone or something) See under *WRANGLE ▸ WITH.*

WRANGLE ▸ WITH

wrangle (with someone) (about someone or something) to bicker or argue with someone about someone or something. □ *Stop wrangling with everyone about Tom. He can take care of himself and does not need any special treatment.* □ *You can wrangle about Fred with everyone!* □ *Stop wrangling with everyone you meet.*

wrangle (with someone) (over someone or something) to bicker or argue with someone over who will end up with someone or something. □ *I don't want to wrangle with Kelly over the contract.* □ *I see no need to wrangle over Dolly.* □ *Dan doesn't want to wrangle with you.*

WRAP ▸ AROUND

wrap around someone or something to enclose or fold about someone or something. □ *The snake wrapped around the helpless man and it was soon all over.* □ *The flames wrapped around the barn and swallowed it up.* Ⓐ *She was wearing a wraparound skirt.* Ⓝ *Her dress was a green wraparound.*

wrap one's car around something to wreck one's car by running into something. (Slang.) □ *She wrapped her car around a telephone pole and hurt herself badly.* □ *Slow down or you will wrap your car around a tree!*

wrap someone or something around something to bend or coil someone or something around something. □ *I'll wrap you around that lamp post unless you cooperate!* □ *Don wrapped his car around an oak tree and was seriously injured.*

wrap something around someone to fold or drape something onto someone. (*Someone* includes *oneself.*) □ *He wrapped a towel around himself and went to answer the telephone.* □ *She wrapped a blanket around her little boy to keep him warm.*

WRAP ▸ IN

wrap someone or something (up) (in something) to enclose or enfold someone or something inside of something. (*Someone* includes *oneself.*) □ *I will have to wrap the baby up in a heavy blanket if we are going out in this cold.* Ⓣ *We wrapped up the children in their warmest clothing.* □ *Please wrap the package up in pretty paper.* □ *Would you wrap this in yellow paper?* Ⓐ *The wrapped-up package sat on the table, waiting.* □ *She wrapped herself up in the towel.*

WRAP ▸ UP

See *be wrapped up (with someone or something)* under *BE ▸ UP.*

wrap someone or something (up) (in something) See under *WRAP ▸ IN.*

wrap someone or something (up) (with something) to enclose or enfold someone or something, using something.

(*Someone* includes *oneself*.) □ *Try to wrap the baby up with something warmer.* 🅃 *We will have to wrap up the baby with extra blankets tonight.* □ *Could you wrap the package up with two or three layers of paper?* □ *Please wrap yourself with something.*

wrap something up to complete work on something; to bring something to an end. □ *I will wrap the job up this morning. I'll call you when I finish.* 🅃 *I can wrap up this little project in a week.*

WRAP ▸ WITH

wrap someone or something (up) (with something) See under *WRAP ▸ UP.*

WREAK ▸ (UP)ON

wreak something (up)on someone or something to cause damage, havoc, destruction to someone or something. (*Upon* is formal and less commonly used than *on*.) □ *The storm wreaked destruction upon the little village.* □ *It wreaked much havoc on us.*

WREATHE ▸ AROUND

wreathe (itself) around someone or something [for something] to form itself into a wreath or circle around someone or something. □ *The smoke wreathed around the smokers' heads, almost obliterating sight of them.* □ *The smoke wreathed around the green tree near the fire.* □ *The cloud wreathed itself around the top of the mountain.*

wreathe something around someone or something to form something into a wreath around someone or something. □ *The smoke wreathed a ring around the old man holding a pipe.* □ *The cloud wreathed a huge halo around the tip of the mountain.*

WREATHE ▸ IN

wreathe someone or something in something to enclose someone or something in a wreath or a wreath-shaped area. □ *The trees wreathed them in a lovely frame. It made a beautiful photograph.* □ *The vines wreathed the campers in a gentle bower.*

WRENCH ▸ FROM

wrench something from someone to grab or twist something out of someone's grasp. □ *Max wrenched the gun from Lefty's hand and called the police.* □ *Max wrenched the wallet from Jed's hand and fled with it.*

WRENCH ▸ OFF

wrench something off ((of) someone or something) to yank or twist something off someone or something. (The *of*-phrase is paraphrased with a *from*-phrase when the particle is transposed. See the 🄵 example. The *of* is colloquial.) □ *He wrenched the shoes off the sleeping man and ran away.* 🅃 *He wrenched off the catsup bottle cap.* 🄵 *He wrenched off the cap from the catsup bottle.* □ *Frank wrenched it off.*

WRENCH ▸ OUT

wrench something out of something to yank or twist something out of something. □ *Max wrenched the gun out of Lefty's hand and told Lefty to put his hands up.* □ *Tom wrenched the bone out of the dog's mouth and threw it away.*

WREST ▸ AWAY

See the following entry.

WREST ▸ FROM

wrest someone or something (away) from someone or something to struggle to get someone or something from the grip of someone or something. □ *The kidnappers wrested the baby from his mother and ran away with him.* □ *Max wrested the gun away from Lefty.*

WREST ▸ OFF

wrest something off ((of) something) to struggle to get something off something. (The *of*-phrase is paraphrased with a *from*-phrase when the particle is transposed. See the 🄵 example. The *of* is colloquial.) □ *Somehow he wrested the hubcap off the wheel.* 🅃 *He wrested off the hubcap.* 🄵 *He wrested off the broken branch from the tree.* □ *With much effort, Wally wrested it off.*

WRESTLE ▸ FROM

wrestle something from someone to get something away from someone after a physical struggle. □ *Wally wrestled the gun away from Max and threw it out* *the window.* ☐ *I could not wrestle my wallet from the thief.*

WRESTLE ▶ INTO

wrestle something into something to struggle with something large to get it into something or some place. ☐ *She wrestled the packages into the backseat of the car.* ☐ *I wrestled the suitcases into the rack over my seat.*

WRESTLE ▶ WITH

wrestle with someone to contend with someone in a physical wrestling match. ☐ *You are too big to wrestle with him!* ☐ *I want to wrestle with someone my own size.*

wrestle with something **1.** to struggle with something large to move it about. ☐ *He wrestled with the piano, and finally got it to move.* ☐ *The two men were wrestling with the heavy trunk for nearly ten minutes, trying to get it up the stairs.* **2.** to grapple or struggle with some large animal. ☐ *The man wrestled with the tiger for a while, but was fatally mauled in a short time.* ☐ *Sam liked to wrestle with the family dog.* **3.** to struggle with a difficult problem; to struggle with a moral decision. (Figurative.) ☐ *We wrestled with the problem and finally decided to go ahead.* ☐ *Let me wrestle with this matter for a while longer.*

WRIGGLE ▶ IN(TO)

wriggle in(to something) to wiggle and squeeze into something or some place. ☐ *You will never be able to wriggle into that swimming suit.* ☐ *I can just wriggle in!*

WRIGGLE ▶ OUT

wriggle out (of something) **1.** to wiggle and squeeze out of something or some place. ☐ *She wriggled out of her tight skirt and changed into something more comfortable.* ☐ *The skirt was so tight, she had to wriggle out. She couldn't pull it off.* **2.** to get out of having to do something; to get out of a responsibility. ☐ *Don't try to wriggle out of this.* ☐ *I won't let you wriggle out this time.*

WRING ▶ FROM

wring something from something AND **wring something out of something** to remove liquid from something by squeezing or twisting. ☐ *She wrung the water from the cloth and wiped up the rest of the spill.* ☐ *Alice wrung the water out of the washcloth.*

WRING ▶ OUT

wring something out to squeeze something dry of liquid. ☐ *He wrung the rag out and wiped up more of the spilled milk.* 🅃 *Liz wrung out the rag and wiped up more of the spilled milk.*

wring something out of someone to pressure someone into telling something. (Figurative.) ☐ *The police will wring the truth out of her.* ☐ *After a lot of questioning, they wrung the information out of Max.*

wring something out of something See under *WRING ▶ FROM.*

WRINKLE ▶ UP

wrinkle something up to make something get wrinkles and creases. ☐ *I love the way you wrinkle your nose up.* 🅃 *Don't wrinkle up your jacket.* 🄰 *The child's wrinkled-up nose revealed something about the way the air smelled.*

wrinkle up [for something] to draw up in wrinkles; [for something] to become wrinkled. ☐ *His nose wrinkled up as he smelled the burning pie.* ☐ *The cloth wrinkled up in the intense heat.*

WRITE ▶ ABOUT

write about someone or something to write a narrative or description of someone or something. ☐ *I wanted to write about wild canaries, but there is not much to say.* ☐ *Sally writes about famous people.*

write someone or something about something to send an inquiry or statement to someone about someone or something. ☐ *I will write her about what you just told me.* ☐ *Sarah wrote the company about the faulty merchandise.*

WRITE ▶ AGAINST

write against someone or something to oppose someone or something in writing. □ *John writes against the current administration too much.* □ *Almost everyone enjoys writing against the vice president.*

write something against someone or something to write something in opposition to someone or something. □ *I wrote an article against her proposal, but they refused to print it.* □ *Sarah wrote an essay against the president.*

WRITE ▸ AWAY

write away to write a lot; to continue writing. □ *There he was, writing away, not paying attention to anything else.* □ *I spent the entire afternoon writing away, having a fine, productive time.*

write away for something to send for something in writing, from a distant place. □ *I wrote away for a book on the rivers of the world.* □ *You will have to write away for another copy of the instruction manual.*

WRITE ▸ BACK

write back to someone to write a letter to someone in return for a letter received from someone. □ *I wrote back to her at once, but I have heard no more from her.* □ *Please write back to me when you have a chance.*

write something back to someone to write a letter answering someone. □ *I wrote an answer back to her the same day that I received the letter.* □ *Will you please write something back to Julie? She complains that you are ignoring her.* □ *I wrote a letter back to Harry, explaining what had happened.*

WRITE ▸ DOWN

write down to someone to write to someone condescendingly. □ *You should never write down to your audience, if you want to be convincing.* □ *I have to write down to them, because they are very young.*

write someone down as something to list someone's name, noting something. □ *I'll write you down as a contributor.* □ *Can I write you down as a charter member?*

write something down to make a note of something; to record something on paper in writing. □ *Please write this down.* 🅃 *Please write down what I tell you.*

WRITE ▸ FOR

write for something **1.** to write and request something. □ *I wrote for clarification but received none.* □ *Julie wrote for another copy of the instruction book.* **2.** to produce writing in order to get money. □ *I write for the money I earn from my stories.* □ *I write for about twenty dollars an hour.* **3.** to produce writing for a particular kind of publication. □ *I write for science magazines.* □ *Sam writes for the local newspaper.*

write in(to something) (for something) See under *WRITE ▸ IN(TO).*

write someone for something to send a request to someone for something. □ *Henry wrote Harry for a firm quote, but Harry never responded.* □ *Did you write me for permission?*

WRITE ▸ IN

write someone in (on something) to write the name of someone in a special place on a ballot, indicating a vote for the person. □ *Please write my name in on the ballot.* 🅃 *I wrote in your name on the ballot.* □ *I wrote you in.* 🄰 *How many write-in ballots were there?* 🄽 *You can't run for mayor as a write-in!*

WRITE ▸ IN(TO)

write in(to something) (for something) to send a request to something, such as a radio station, for something. □ *Please write in for a schedule of next month's music.* □ *I am going to write in for a clarification.* □ *I will write in and find out.*

write something in(to something) **1.** to write information into something. □ *I wrote her telephone number into my notebook.* 🅃 *I wrote in her number.* □ *I took out my notebook and wrote it in.* **2.** to include a specific statement or provision in a document, such as a contract or agreement. □ *I want you to write a stronger security clause into my contract.* 🅃 *I will write in a stronger clause.*

☐ *There is no security clause, so I will write one in.*

WRITE ▶ OF

write of someone or something to write about the general topic of someone or something. ☐ *He wrote of the beauty of nature and the way we are destroying it.* ☐ *She wrote of Henry, her ancient house cat.*

WRITE ▶ OFF

write off (to someone) (for something) to send a request for something away to someone. ☐ *I wrote off to my parents for some money, but I think they are ignoring me.* ☐ *I wrote off for money.* ☐ *I need money so I wrote off to my parents.*

write someone or something off (as a something) **1.** to give up on turning someone or something into something. (*Someone* includes *oneself.*) ☐ *I had to write Jill off as a future dancer.* 🅃 *The inventor almost wrote off the automobile as a dependable means of transportation.* ☐ *He would never work out. We wrote him off.* ☐ *Don't write yourself off just yet.* **2.** to give up on someone or something as a dead loss, waste of time, hopeless case, etc. (*Someone* includes *oneself.*) ☐ *Don't write me off as a has-been.* 🅃 *We almost wrote off the investment as a dead loss.* ☐ *We wrote the cash loss off.* ☐ *They wrote themselves off as a loss.* **3.** to take a charge against one's taxes. ☐ *Can I write this off as a deduction, or is it a dead loss?* 🅃 *Can I write off this expense as a tax deduction?* ☐ *Write it off and see what happens.* 🄽 *Your contribution can be used as a tax write-off.*

write something off (on something) to deduct something from one's federal income taxes. ☐ *Can I write this off on my income taxes?* 🅃 *I'll write off this trip on my taxes.* ☐ *Oh, yes! Write it off!*

WRITE ▶ ON

write on and on to write too much; to write endlessly. ☐ *You tend to write on and on. Try to focus on one point and leave it at that.* ☐ *I think you write on and on just to fill up space.*

WRITE ▶ OUT

write something out to put thoughts into writing, rather than keeping it in memory. ☐ *Let me write it out. Then I won't forget it.* 🅃 *Karen wrote out her objections.*

WRITE ▶ TO

write something to someone **1.** to send specific information to someone in a letter. ☐ *I wrote the facts to John, and he thanked me for the information.* ☐ *They wrote all the details to me, and I filed them.* **2.** to compose a letter and send it to someone. ☐ *Sam wrote a letter to his father.* ☐ *Did you write that memo to Mark yet?*

write something to something to write something that is supplementary to something else. ☐ *Molly wrote the end to the symphony overnight.* ☐ *I will write the introduction to the book this afternoon.*

write to someone to compose a letter and send it to someone. ☐ *I will write to her again, but I don't expect to hear anything.* ☐ *Please write to me as soon as you can.*

WRITE ▶ UP

write someone or something up to write a narrative or description of someone or something. ☐ *The reporter wanted to write me up, but I think I am just too dull.* 🅃 *The reporter wrote up the charity ball.* ☐ *The reporter wrote Sam and June up.* 🄽 *The write-up was rejected by the editor.*

WRITE ▶ (UP)ON

write (up)on someone or something **1.** to write about someone or something. (*Upon* is very formal here and much less commonly used than *on.*) ☐ *I had to write an essay, so I wrote on my uncle.* ☐ *What are you going to write upon?* **2.** to write on someone's skin or some thing. (*Upon* is formal and much less commonly used than *on.*) ☐ *Don't write on Billy. After all, he's your brother.* ☐ *Who wrote on this page of the book?* **3.** to use someone [someone's back] or something as a flat base to support something that is being written upon. ☐ *I have to sign this check. Here, let me* *write on you.* □ *Do you mind if I write on your desk? I just need to sign this.*

WRITHE ▸ IN

writhe in something See under *WRITHE ▸ WITH.*

WRITHE ▸ UNDER

writhe under something **1.** to squirm with pain from being beaten with something. (Stilted.) □ *The sailor writhed under the sting of the lash.* □ *The child writhed under the pain of his spanking.* **2.** to suffer under a mental burden. (Figurative.) □ *I writhed under her constant verbal assault and finally left the room.* □ *Why do I have to writhe under her insults?*

WRITHE ▸ WITH

writhe with something **1.** AND **writhe in something** to squirm because of something, such as pain. □ *Carl writhed with pain and began to cry.* □ *He was writhing in pain when the paramedics arrived.* **2.** [for something] to support or contain something that is writhing. □ *The pit was writhing with snakes and other horrid things.* □ *The floor of the basement was writhing in spiders and crawly things.*

WROUGHT ▸ UP

See *be wrought up* under *BE ▸ UP.*

X

X ▸ OUT

x someone or something out to mark out something printed or in writing, with *x's*. (*Someone* includes *oneself*.) □ *Sally* x'*d the incorrect information out.* [T] *Sally* x'*d out the incorrect information.* □ *You should* x *Tom out. He's not coming.* □ *Please* x *out this line of print.* [A] *The* x'*d-out words could still be read.* □ *He* x'*d himself out with a pen.*

Y

YACK ▸ OFF

yack one's head off to talk a great deal. (Figurative slang.) ☐ *Jane yacked her head off and ended up with a sore throat.* ☐ *Don't yack your head off!*

YACK ▸ UP

yack something up to talk a great deal [about someone or something]. (Slang. The *something* is often *it*.) ☐ *She yacked the concert up endlessly.* 🅃 *Sally yacked up the concert, trying to get people to attend.* ☐ *Yack it up and see if you can get people to attend.*

YAMMER ▸ ABOUT

yammer (away) about someone or something to talk endlessly about someone or something. ☐ *What are you yammering about?* ☐ *They were yammering away about the state of the economy.*

YAMMER ▸ AWAY

See the previous entry.

YANK ▸ APART

yank someone or something apart **1.** to pull, tear, or rip someone or something to pieces. ☐ *Please don't yank the book apart!* 🅃 *He yanked apart the book!* ☐ *He threatened to yank his opponent apart.* **2.** to separate people or things. ☐ *The teacher yanked them apart.* 🅃 *The teacher yanked apart the fighting boys.* 🅃 *Liz yanked apart the freshly glued boards before they were permanently stuck together.*

YANK ▸ AROUND

yank someone around to give someone a hard time about something. (Figurative slang.) ☐ *Yank him around a bit and see if he decides to cooperate.* ☐ *We yanked Sam around for a while and he decided to cooperate.*

YANK ▸ AT

yank at someone or something to pull or tug at someone or something. ☐ *Please don't yank at the drapery cord.* ☐ *Stop yanking at me!*

YANK ▸ AWAY

yank someone or something away (from someone or something) to jerk someone or something away from someone or something. ☐ *He yanked his hand away from the fire.* ☐ *Please yank that rug away from the fire before it gets burned.* ☐ *She yanked the child away from the nurse and ran out.*

YANK ▸ IN(TO)

yank someone or something in(to something) to jerk or pull someone or something into something. (Slang.) ☐ *Mary yanked Sally into the car and sped off.* 🅃 *She yanked in the anchor rope and we rowed away.*

YANK ▸ OFF

yank someone or something off ((of) something) to jerk someone or something off something. (The *of*-phrase is paraphrased with a *from*-phrase when the particle is transposed. See the 🄵 example. The *of* is colloquial.) ☐ *She yanked the coffeepot off the counter and ran upstairs.* 🅃 *She yanked off the box lid.* 🄵 *She yanked off the lid from the box.* ☐ *Sam yanked Jill off the crumbling pavement just in time.* ☐ *He yanked her off in time.*

yank something off to pull or jerk off a piece of clothing. ☐ *She yanked her* *jacket off.* 🅃 *She yanked off her jacket and threw it on the chair.*

YANK ▸ ON

yank on something to pull or tug on something. ☐ *Don't yank on my hair!* ☐ *Yank on this rope to send a signal to the worker on the surface.*

YANK ▸ OUT

yank someone or something out (of something) to pull or jerk someone or something out of something. (The *of*-phrase is paraphrased with a *from*-phrase when the particle is transposed. See the 🄵 example.) ☐ *Sam yanked the turnips out of the ground one by one.* 🅃 *He yanked out the best of the young carrots from the rich soil.* ☐ *Karen yanked the child out of the car.* 🅃 *Sarah opened the car door and yanked out the child.* 🄰 *Yanked-out hair marked the scene of the fight.*

YANK ▸ UP

yank something up to pull or jerk something up. ☐ *He yanked his pants up.* 🅃 *He yanked up his pants and threw on his shirt.*

YAP ▸ ABOUT

yap about someone or something to talk casually about someone or something; to gossip about someone or something. (Slang.) ☐ *Stop yapping about Molly.* ☐ *Claire is always yapping about her salary.*

YAP ▸ AT

yap at someone **1.** [for a small dog] to bark at someone or something. ☐ *The dog yapped at the cat in great frustration.* ☐ *I am tired of that dog yapping at me all the time!* **2.** [for someone] to scold or bark at someone shrilly. ☐ *Don't yap at me. I didn't do it.* ☐ *Bob yapped at Bill for something he didn't do.*

YEARN ▸ FOR

yearn for someone or something to long for someone or something; to desire someone or something strongly. ☐ *Sam sat alone in his room, yearning for Mary.* ☐ *Mary yearned for a big bowl of high-butterfat ice cream.*

YELL ▸ AT

yell at someone or something to shout at someone or something, usually in anger. ☐ *Please don't yell at me.* ☐ *There is no point in yelling at a cat.*

yell something at someone or something to shout something at someone or something, usually in anger. ☐ *Please don't yell those things at me.* ☐ *He stood on the porch, yelling curses at a dog on his lawn.*

YELL ▸ OUT

yell one's guts out to yell or shout a great amount or with great volume. (Figurative slang.) ☐ *Tom yelled his guts out at the game.* ☐ *I wish you wouldn't yell your guts out.*

yell out to cry out; to shout loudly. ☐ *The pain caused the child to yell out.* ☐ *I yelled out, but no one heard me.*

yell something out (at someone or something) to shout something loudly at someone or something. ☐ *The dictator yelled curses out at the troops.* 🅃 *The director yelled out his disgust at the cast of the play.* ☐ *Richard yelled his hatred out at the cat.* 🅃 *Finally, Jim yelled out the password so everyone could hear it.*

YEN ▸ FOR

yen for someone or something to long for someone or something. ☐ *I yen for a great big bowl of highly fattening ice cream.* ☐ *Frank yenned for Sally.*

YIELD ▸ OVER

yield someone or something (over) (to someone or something) to give up someone or something to someone or something. (*Someone* includes *oneself.* The *over* is typically used where the phrase is synonymous with *hand over.*) ☐ *You must yield Tom over to his mother.* ☐ *Will you yield the right-of-way over to the other driver, or not?* ☐ *Please yield the right-of-way to me.* ☐ *You must yield Tom to his mom.* ☐ *He yielded himself over to the federal agents.* 🅃 *She yielded over the baby to the nurse.*

YIELD ▸ TO

See the previous entry.

yield something to someone 1. to give the right-of-way to someone. □ *You must yield the right-of-way to pedestrians.* □ *You failed to yield the right-of-way to the oncoming car.* **2.** to give up something to someone. □ *The army yielded the territory to the invading army.* □ *We yielded the territory to the government.*

yield to someone 1. to let someone go ahead; to give someone the right-of-way. □ *Please yield to the next speaker.* □ *She yielded to the next speaker.* **2.** to give in to someone. □ *She found it hard to yield to her husband in an argument.* □ *I will yield to no one.*

YIELD ▸ UP

yield someone or something up (to someone) to give someone or something up to someone. (*Someone* includes *oneself.*) □ *He had to yield his daughter up to Claire.* 🅃 *The judge required that Tom yield up his daughter to his ex-wife.* □ *Finally, he yielded up the money.* □ *He yielded himself up to the police officer.*

YOKE ▸ TOGETHER

yoke people or things together to connect two people together with a yoke; to connect two things or creatures together with a yoke. □ *Todd yoked the oxen together for the parade.* □ *Sam yoked Fred and Tom together so they could pull the load.*

Z

ZERO ► IN

zero in (on someone or something) to aim directly at someone or something. ☐ *The television camera zeroed in on the little boy scratching his head.* ☐ *It zeroed in on the glass of cola.* ☐ *Zero in when I tell you.* ☐ *Let's zero in on the important points in this discussion.*

ZIP ► ALONG

zip along to move along very fast. (Slang.) ☐ *The motorcycle zipped along nicely.* ☐ *Let's zip along and get there on time.*

ZIP ► ON

zip something on to put on a piece of clothing and zip it up. ☐ *She zipped her jumper on and headed toward the door.* 🅃 *Zip on your jacket and let's go.*

ZIP ► PAST

zip past someone or something to run or move past someone or something very rapidly. ☐ *The deer zipped past the hunter, who stood there, startled.* ☐ *The cars zipped past the intersection.*

ZIP ► UP

zip something up **1.** to close a zipper. ☐ *You should zip that zipper up.* 🅃 *You should zip up that zipper.* **2.** to close a garment by zipping a zipper closed. ☐ *You had better zip your jacket up.* 🅃 *You had better zip up your jacket.* 🄰 *The zipped-up jacket was warmer than one might expect.* **3.** to close one's mouth. (Usually a command: **Zip it up!**) ☐ *Zip your mouth up, Fred!* 🅃 *Zip up your mouth, Fred.*

ZONE ► AS

zone something as something to create a particular legally defined area within a governmental or other local area. ☐ *They zoned this area as a shopping district.* ☐ *The city council zoned the vacant lot as a park.*

ZONE ► FOR

zone something for something to specify what can be built or what can be done within a particular legally defined area within a governmental area. ☐ *Did the council zone this area for business?* ☐ *They zoned this area for residences.*

ZONE ► OFF

zone something off to create a special regulatory zone in an area. ☐ *The council zoned part of the land off for a park.* 🅃 *They zoned off land for a park.*

ZONK ► OUT

zonk someone out **1.** to make someone tired or exhausted. (Slang. *Someone* includes *oneself*.) ☐ *All the work zonked him out.* 🄰 *The zonked-out kid just lay there.* ☐ *She zonked herself out with all that exertion.* **2.** to cause someone to become drug-intoxicated. (Slang. *Someone* includes *oneself*.) ☐ *The drug zonked Max out totally.* 🅃 *It zonked out Max.* 🄰 *This street is filled with zonked-out tourists.* ☐ *She zonked herself out with a couple of belts of rum.*

ZOOM ► ACROSS

zoom across (something) to run or move across something very fast. ☐ *The missile zoomed across the sky.* ☐ *We looked at the sky just as a comet zoomed across.*

ZOOM ▸ ALONG

zoom along to move along very rapidly. ☐ *The bus zoomed along rapidly all night long.* ☐ *Let's zoom along while the road is clear.*

ZOOM ▸ IN

zoom in (on someone or something) AND **pan in (on someone or something)** **1.** to move in to a close-up picture of someone or something, using a zoom lens or a similar lens. ☐ *The camera zoomed in on the love scene.* ☐ *The camera operator panned in slowly.* **2.** to focus sharply on a matter related to someone or a problem. ☐ *Let's zoom in on this matter of debt.* ☐ *She zoomed in and dealt quickly with the problem at hand.* ☐ *Sally zoomed in on Tom and demanded an explanation.*

ZOOM ▸ OFF

zoom off to leave in a hurry. ☐ *Sorry, I have to zoom off.* ☐ *We will zoom off soon.*

ZOOM ▸ OUT

See *pan out* under *PAN ▸ OUT.*

ZOOM ▸ OVER

zoom over someone or something to fly over someone or something at high speed. ☐ *The plane zoomed over the treetops.* ☐ *A small bird zoomed over the hikers, shrieking wildly.*

zoom someone or something (over) to something See under *ZOOM ▸ TO.*

ZOOM ▸ PAST

zoom past someone or something to run or move past someone or something very rapidly. ☐ *The runners zoomed past the spectators.* ☐ *Our train zoomed past town after town.*

ZOOM ▸ THROUGH

zoom through (something) **1.** to pass through a town or some other location very fast. ☐ *Don't just zoom through these little towns. Stop and explore one or two.* ☐ *We didn't stop. We just zoomed through.* **2.** to work one's way through something very rapidly. ☐ *She zoomed through the reading assignment and went on to something else.* ☐ *Jeff can open a book and zoom through in record time.*

ZOOM ▸ TO

zoom someone or something (over) to something to send something to someone very fast. ☐ *Please use my car to zoom Molly over to the bank.* ☐ *Would you zoom this package to the downtown office?*

ZOOM ▸ UP

zoom up to pull up some place in a vehicle rapidly. ☐ *The car zoomed up and came to a stop.* ☐ *The bus zoomed up and let a few people off.*